tools that are accessible on sı
studying any time anywhere!

MW00651930

LearningCurve Adaptive Quizzing
macmillan learning

LearningCurve is a cutting-edge study tool designed to build your understanding and memory of the core concepts in every chapter. Based on insights from learning and memory research, the LearningCurve system uses multiple-choice questions to identify how well you understand key material. The system then adapts to your level of understanding and shows you more questions targeted at areas where you need improvement. LearningCurve makes your study time more efficient by focusing more on the material you still need to learn. A game-like interface and instant feedback make it fun and easy for you to track your improvement!

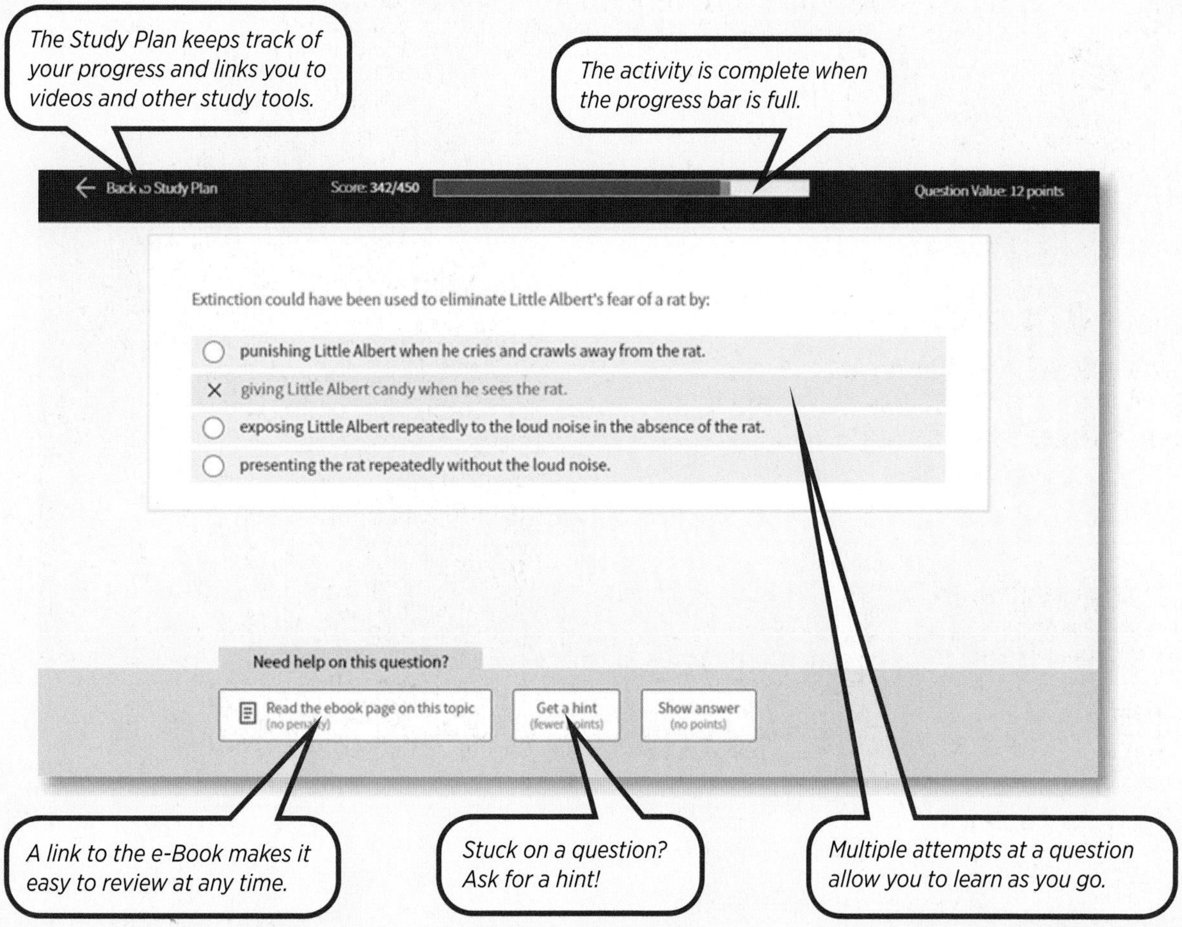

These features and the complete e-Book of *My Psychology* are available as part of LaunchPad for *My Psychology*.
To learn more, to register an access code, or to purchase access, go to launchpadworks.com. LaunchPad macmillan learning

My Psychology

ANDREW M. POMERANTZ

Southern Illinois University Edwardsville

worth publishers
Macmillan Learning
NEW YORK

Vice President, Social Sciences: Charles Linsmeier
Director of Content and Assessment, Social Sciences: Shani Fisher
Executive Program Manager: Daniel DeBonis
Development Editor: Michael Kimball
Assistant Editor: Katie Pachnos
Senior Marketing Manager: Lindsay Johnson
Marketing Assistant: Morgan Ratner
Market Development Manager: Stephanie Ellis
Executive Media Editor: Noel Hohnstine
Media Editor: Lisa Dotson
Assistant Media Editor: Nik Toner
Director, Content Management Enhancement: Tracey Kuehn
Managing Editor: Lisa Kinne
Content Project Manager: Won McIntosh
Media Project Manager: Elizabeth Dougherty
Senior Photo Editor: Robin Fadool
Photo Researcher: Rona Tuccillo
Senior Workflow Project Manager: Paul Rohloff
Director of Design, Content Management: Diana Blume
Senior Design Manager: Blake Logan
Interior Design: Tom Carling, Carling Design Inc.
Cover Design: Blake Logan and Evelyn Pence
Art Manager: Matthew McAdams
Illustrations: Eli Ensor
Composition: codeMantra
Printing and Binding: LSC Communications

Cover and Table of Contents Photos: Main cover photo: mavo/Shutterstock; Photos from right to left: serts/Getty Images; jeffbergen/Getty Images; Aldo Murillo/Getty Images; visualspace/Getty Images; visualspace/Getty Images; mimagephotography/Shutterstock; Kerkez/Getty Images; Eugenio Marongiu/Getty Images; PeopleImages/Getty Images; xavierarnau/Getty Images; Jose Luis Pelaez Inc/Getty Images; michaeljung/Getty Images; PeopleImages/Getty Images; hadynyah/Getty Images; Dragon Images/Shutterstock; bowdenimages/Getty Images

Library of Congress Control Number: 2017935764

ISBN-13: 978-1-4292-6018-3
ISBN-10: 1-4292-6018-1

Printed in the United States of America
First printing

Worth Publishers
One New York Plaza
Suite 4500
New York, NY 10004-1562
www.macmillanlearning.com

In My Psychology, *numerous examples describe clients with whom the author has personally worked in his clinical practice. In those cases, any identifying information has been changed, disguised, or omitted to maintain client confidentiality.*

To my kids, Benjamin and Daniel.
I love you and I'm proud of you every day!

About the Author

Photo by Felise Waxman

Andrew M. Pomerantz is Professor of Psychology and Director of the Clinical Psychology Graduate Program at Southern Illinois University Edwardsville (SIUE). For over two decades, he has taught Introduction to Psychology as well as undergraduate and graduate courses related to clinical psychology. His research on teaching in psychology has been published in *Teaching of Psychology, Scholarship of Teaching and Learning in Psychology,* and *Training and Education in Professional Psychology,* and been presented at conferences of the American Psychological Association and the National Institute on the Teaching of Psychology. At SIUE, Pomerantz has received the Paul Simon Outstanding Teacher-Scholar Award and was an invited member of the Peer Consultant Team of the Excellence in Learning and Teaching Initiative. He is also the author of the textbook *Clinical Psychology: Science, Practice, and Culture,* winner of a 2017 Textbook Excellence Award ("Texty") from the Textbook & Academic Authors Association.

His research focuses on various topics within clinical psychology, especially those related to ethical and professional issues in psychotherapy. He has served on the editorial boards of *Journal of Clinical Psychology, Ethics & Behavior,* and *Journal of Contemporary Psychotherapy.* He maintains a part-time private practice of psychotherapy in St. Louis, Missouri, where he sees adults and children with a wide range of issues and disorders. He also served two terms as president of Psychotherapy Saint Louis, a multidisciplinary therapist organization.

He earned his B.A. degree in psychology from Washington University in St. Louis and his M.A. and Ph.D. in clinical psychology from Saint Louis University. He completed his predoctoral internship at the Indiana University School of Medicine Psychology Training Consortium.

When Andy isn't doing psychology things, he does fun things, like hanging out with his two wonderful kids and his amazing wife. He enjoys discovering new music, either online or in record stores (while they still exist). He likes watching, coaching, and playing basketball, but he'll settle for running or riding his bike too. He also watches some high-quality TV shows and perhaps even more low-quality TV shows.

Brief Contents

Contents

1 The Science of Psychology 1

2 Brain and Behavior 34

3 Sensation and Perception 66

4 Consciousness 102

5 Memory 140

6 Learning 176

7 Cognition: Thinking, Language, and Intelligence 212

8 Motivation and Emotion 248

9 Development Across the Life Span 286

10 Diversity in Psychology: Multiculturalism, Gender, and Sexuality 332

11 Stress and Health 364

12 Personality 398

13 Social Psychology 434

14 Psychological Disorders 472

14 Psychological Disorders *(continued)*

15 Therapy 518

Instructor's Preface

Recent research shows students are eager to make personal connections between their personal lives and the major topics in psychology. Hero Images/Getty Images

Why *My Psychology?*

Psychology is unique among academic disciplines—uniquely *personal*. Its concepts, theories, and research overlap with so much of our daily lives: how we perceive, remember, and learn about the world around us; how we experience and express thoughts and feelings; how our personalities and development shape our experience; how we relate to others; and how we experience hardship and healing, among others. College students may identify with elements of introductory courses in many disciplines, but more than any other course, Intro Psych is Intro *Me*. For that reason, *My Psychology* distinguishes itself from competing texts by inviting students to make a personal connection to the science of psychology.

Every time I teach Intro Psych, my students are eager to make that personal connection. Recent research illustrates that many other students share that eagerness. One study found that almost every major topic in the field—memory, learning, personality, social psychology, disorders, development, stress and health, and more—was rated by current Intro Psych students as "important" or "quite important" to their lives (McCann et al., 2016). Another study asked Intro Psych students the extent to which they agreed with statements about what they expect to learn from the course. The statements were all adapted from the first version of the American Psychological Association's *Guidelines for the Undergraduate Psychology Major* (American Psychological Association, 2007). Students agreed most enthusiastically with the statements that connected psychology to their personal lives: "I will be more insightful about my own behavior, and use some of the concepts studied during the course in my own life." "I will have improved my critical thinking skills when examining my own behavior and the behavior of others." "I will understand people better, especially regarding cultural differences and diverse viewpoints" (Landrum & Gurung, 2013).

My Psychology connects the science of psychology with the personal experience of students by engaging with them on their level. Indeed, student engagement is a primary theme of the text. From the students' point of view, one key to engagement is accessibility—a sense that the book is written in a way they can grasp, not at a level that outstrips their reading level and causes them to lose interest. *My Psychology* deliberately strikes this level of accessibility, using language that students at all levels find approachable and intelligible, not intimidating or bewildering. Another key to engagement in any educational endeavor is a sense of immediacy. Teachers create immediacy through "behaviors that promote students feeling heard, included, valued, and known" (Rogers, 2015, p. 20; see also McCroskey & Richmond, 1992). When teachers have high levels of immediacy, students tend to like them, and feel motivated to engage more fully and willingly in the material being taught (Mazer, 2015; Allen et al., 2006; Witt et al., 2004). Immediacy is a quality typically measured in teachers, but textbooks should deliver it, too. For your students and mine, I strove to maximize the level of engagement in *My Psychology* in four pioneering ways: technology (including smartphones); applications; diversity coverage; and pedagogy.

My Psychology includes a variety of mobile-friendly tools, including Chapter Apps, My Take videos, Show Me More links, and a full e-Book. Alejandro Rivera/E+/Getty Images

Technology That Brings Psychology to Students' Lives

Our Intro Psych students live on their smartphones and computers. *My Psychology* meets them there.

My Psychology addresses the need for a contemporary textbook that recognizes not only what students experience in their daily lives, but also the mode of those

experiences. Students can access this entire suite of technological features on their smartphones and computers. These features can also be assigned and assessed via LaunchPad, Macmillan's online learning environment.

Chapter Apps are real free apps that students can download onto smartphones, or use on computers. Each app demonstrates a real-life *app*lication of an important psychology concept to students' daily lives. Students read a brief description of the app and then consider applied and critical thinking questions. For example, a Chapter App in the Social Psychology chapter is *Waze*, a popular app that many drivers prefer to Google Maps and other navigation apps because it lets drivers share information

TABLE 1: Chapter Apps

	CONCEPT	CHAPTER APP
CHAPTER 1	College Success	MyHomework, p. 21
CHAPTER 2	Localization Plasticity	3D Brain, p. 47 GlassesOff, p. 53
CHAPTER 3	Vision Visual Illusions Audition	Biodigital Human 3D Anatomy, p. 81 300 Optical Illusions, p. 84 Illusions of the Brain, p. 84 Mimi Hearing Test, p. 89 Test Your Hearing, p. 89
CHAPTER 4	REM Sleep Depressants	Sleep Cycle Alarm Clock, p. 111 Sleep Time Smart Alarm Clock, p. 111 IntelliDrink Lite, p. 128 AlcDroid Alcohol Tester, p. 128
CHAPTER 5	Retrieval Efforts to Improve Memory	Quizlet, p. 152 Elevate, p. 164
CHAPTER 6	Classical Conditioning Reinforcement Punishment	Aqualert Water Reminder, p. 186 ChoreMonster, p. 190 stickK, p. 195
CHAPTER 7	Intelligence Tests	Mr. IQ, p. 243 Intelligence Test, p. 243
CHAPTER 8	Motivation Set Point Promoting Healthy Eating	Checky - Phone Habit Tracker, p. 257 Lose It! p. 260 HealthyOut, p. 267
CHAPTER 9	Prenatal Development Imaginary Audience	What to Expect, p. 292 Twitter, p. 311
CHAPTER 10	Multiculturalism Cultural Intelligence Transgender	Culture Compass, p. 343 Vent, p. 347 Refugee Restrooms, p. 352
CHAPTER 11	Appraisal Social Support Decreasing Stress with Exercise	Serenita, p. 368 ReachOut, p. 389 Runkeeper, p. 394
CHAPTER 12	Five-Factor Model of Personality	Your Five Basic Personality Traits, p. 422
CHAPTER 13	Social Facilitation Prosocial Behavior/Altruism	CoachMe Habit Tracker, p. 449 Waze, p. 467
CHAPTER 14	Anxiety Disorders Depressive and Bipolar Disorders	MindShift, p. 487 Moodtrack Diary, p. 492
CHAPTER 15	Cognitive Therapy Cybertherapy	SAM: Self-Help for Anxiety Management, p. 532 Doctor on Demand, p. 548

CHAPTER APP 13.2

Prosocial Behavior/Altruism

Waze

Preview one of the links and consider the following questions.

WEBSITE: http://tiny.cc/1vi7jy

ANDROID: http://tiny.cc/fe92iy

IPHONE: http://tiny.cc/3682iy

VIDEO DEMO: http://tiny.cc/chapterapps

There are lots of apps to help you drive from Point A to Point B, but Waze is unique among them. As its Web site describes, Waze is "community-based," which means that drivers share info about the roads with each other. For example, Waze users can alert each other to the specific locations of police cars, accidents, traffic jams, cars on the shoulder, and even cheap gas stations they encounter. The Web site explains that Waze users are "outsmarting traffic, together" by getting a "heads-up from a few million of your friends on the road."

How does it APPly to your daily life?
Would you use an app like Waze? If so, would you share road information with other drivers, or only use the road information they shared with you?

How does it APPly to your understanding of psychology?
Which explanation of *prosocial behavior* (or *altruism*) best explains the decision by a Waze user to voluntarily give a heads-up to other drivers without any external reward (money, etc.)?

Chapter Apps are free apps that students can download onto smartphones or use on computers. They appear in every chapter, and they demonstrate applications of key psychological concepts to students' daily lives.

MY TAKE VIDEO 4.2

Circadian Rhythm

"The last job I worked, I worked overnight, and so that kind of messed up my circadian rhythm..."

YOUTUBE: http://tiny.cc/mytake
LAUNCHPAD: launchpadworks.com

My Take videos are brief interviews with real Intro Psych students about their personal connection with important psychological concepts. They occur in every chapter of the text.

about the roads (e.g., accidents, traffic jams, cheap gas stations) with each other as a "community" of drivers. Whether they use the app or simply read the brief description in the textbook, students then consider questions about which theory of prosocial behavior (or altruism) best explains the behavior of contributing road information for the benefit of other Waze users. In the Learning chapter, one Chapter App (ChoreMonster) illustrates the use of reinforcement for doing household chores, and another (stickK) illustrates the use of punishment for failing to uphold commitments to change undesired behavior. The Chapter Apps are proven to engage students. In an extensive class test campaign with more than 500 students, more than 95% reported enjoying the Chapter App activities.

My Take Videos are brief, professionally produced interviews in which real Intro Psych students provide their own takes on, or personal connections with, important concepts from the chapter. For example, the Social Psychology chapter features "My Take on the Fundamental Attribution Error," in which several students recount personal stories about this concept in their own lives. One student tells the tale of attributing a fellow driver's decision to steal her parking space to unflattering personality traits until she later discovered that the driver was in an emergency situation. As with Chapter Apps, students can use smartphones to access these videos in multiple ways. The videos are a reminder of the diverse experiences students bring to the study of psychology and emphasize the power of connecting experience to the course concepts.

Show Me More links provide students with bonus material illustrating key concepts in the chapter. These links take students to brief videos (e.g., news clips, documentary YouTube videos) or interactive Web sites where they can delve more deeply into important, often personally relevant material. For example, in the Cognition chapter, one Show Me More link takes students to a brief video interview of Daniel Kahneman (author of *Thinking, Fast and Slow*) describing how dual process theory can affect their decision making. In the Diversity in Psychology chapter, a Show Me More link

TABLE 2: My Take Videos

	CONCEPT
CHAPTER 1	Belief Perseverance, p. 22 Correlation-Causation Fallacy, p. 24
CHAPTER 2	Parts of the Brain, p. 42
CHAPTER 3	Difference Threshold, p. 70 Sensory Adaptation, p. 71
CHAPTER 4	Sleep Deprivation, p. 106 Circadian Rhythm, p. 107
CHAPTER 5	Recall versus Recognition, p. 153 Flashbulb Memory, p. 161 Memory Mistakes, p. 168
CHAPTER 6	Classical Conditioning, p. 180 Reinforcement Schedules, p. 191
CHAPTER 7	Affective Forecasting, p. 221 Intelligence, p. 236
CHAPTER 8	Intrinsic and Extrinsic Motivation, p. 250 Emotion Regulation, p. 277
CHAPTER 9	Parenting Styles, p. 306 Emerging Adulthood, p. 319
CHAPTER 10	Culture, p. 336 Microaggressions, p. 349 Gender and Sex, p. 350
CHAPTER 11	Appraisal, p. 369 Coping, p. 385
CHAPTER 12	Locus of Control, p. 416 Five-Factor Model of Personality, p. 419
CHAPTER 13	Fundamental Attribution Error, p. 438 Conformity, p. 444 Social Comparison, p. 454
CHAPTER 14	Abnormal vs. Normal, p. 475 Categorical vs. Dimensional Models of Psychopathology, p. 481
CHAPTER 15	Exposure Therapy, p. 529 Cognitive Distortions, p. 534 Understanding Psychotherapy, p. 540

SHOW ME MORE

6.1 Classical Conditioning

launchpadworks.com LaunchPad macmillan learning

This video offers some good examples and explanations of classical conditioning.

The Show Me More links at the end of each chapter provide students with interesting bonus material for important psychological concepts.

takes students to a video in which Derald Wing Sue narrates several examples of microaggressions.

Applications That Make Psychology Personally Meaningful

Our Intro Psych students learn best when they see how psychology relates to their lives. *My Psychology* helps them understand how core concepts are personally meaningful.

These features recur in every chapter, highlighting the applicability of psychology concepts to students' own lives. They point out the parallels between students' own experiences and the science of psychology. They complement the coverage within each chapter by providing students with distinct, novel ways of understanding and personalizing important psychology concepts.

From Research to Real Life features directly connect psychological research to an aspect of the students' daily activities. In the Science of Psychology chapter, the From

TABLE 3: From Research to Real Life Topics

CHAPTER 1:	Psychologists' Research on College Success, p. 20
CHAPTER 2:	The Murderer's Mind, p. 60
CHAPTER 3:	Variety, the Key to Happiness? p. 73
CHAPTER 4:	Do Your Realize What Sleep Deprivation Does to You? p. 107
CHAPTER 5:	Is Forgetting Good?/Improving Your Memory, pp. 149, 162
CHAPTER 6:	Classical Conditioning in Advertising, p. 181
CHAPTER 7:	Intelligence Correlates with..., p. 238
CHAPTER 8:	Does Money Buy Happiness? p. 280
CHAPTER 9:	A Well-Running Brain, p. 296
CHAPTER 10:	Does Gaydar Work? p. 355
CHAPTER 11:	Don't Stress Out about Stress, p. 387
CHAPTER 12:	What's Happening to Our Locus of Control? p. 417
CHAPTER 13:	Milgram, Obedience, and the NFL's Bounty Scandal, p. 448
CHAPTER 14:	How Powerful Are Magazines in the Development of Eating Disorders? p. 497
CHAPTER 15:	Psychotherapy Changes the Brain, p. 539

Research to Real Life application focuses on college student success, including studies that examine sleep patterns, extracurricular engagement, academic self-efficacy, study schedules, and class attendance. In the Motivation and Emotion chapter, the feature focuses on the relationship between financial success and happiness.

LIFE HACK 8.3

If you want to feel happier, do something kind for someone else, or think about acts of kindness you've already done.

(Otake et al., 2006; Pressman et al., 2015; Lyubomirsky & Layous, 2013)

Life Hacks offer suggestions to students for how to improve their lives according to psychological research. They can be found in every chapter of the text.

Life Hack minifeatures offer direct suggestions to students for how to improve their lives according to the findings of psychological research. These one- or two-sentence tips steer students toward higher levels of well-being, productivity, and other desirable outcomes. For example, in the Consciousness chapter, students come across a Life Hack that instructs them to get a good night's sleep before a big test, because sleep enhances memory.

TABLE 4: A Selection of Life Hacks

CHAPTER 1:	How to boost your grades in college courses, p. 21
CHAPTER 2:	How physical exercise can provide an endorphin boost and elevate your mood, p. 40
CHAPTER 3:	How eating healthier foods consistently can change your taste preferences, p. 94
CHAPTER 4:	How limiting screen time right before bed can improve your sleep, p. 119
CHAPTER 5:	How good sleep enhances your memory, p. 163
CHAPTER 6:	How suggesting a replacement behavior can increase the effectiveness of punishment, p. 196
CHAPTER 7:	How awareness of the durability bias can influence happiness, p. 222
CHAPTER 8:	How doing kind things for others can increase your happiness, p. 280
CHAPTER 9:	How exercising can maximize your brain's level of functioning, p. 296
CHAPTER 10:	How reading, training, and interacting with others can boost your cultural intelligence, p. 348
CHAPTER 11:	How viewing stress as an opportunity rather than a threat can enhance coping, p. 379
CHAPTER 12:	How difficult it can be to change another person's personality, p. 400
CHAPTER 13:	How spending time and developing relationships with people different from yourself can reduce your prejudices, p. 456
CHAPTER 14:	How avoiding rumination can protect you against depression, p. 494
CHAPTER 15:	How a strong therapeutic alliance can benefit your psychotherapy results, p. 543

It's Like... features use the power of analogy to help students understand concepts that may be unfamiliar but share important similarities with concepts they already know well. For example, in the Development chapter, the concepts of assimilation and accommodation are likened to the process of sorting a basket of clean laundry into folded piles. In the Sensation and Perception chapter, top-down processing is likened to the autocomplete feature in texting apps and Google searches.

TABLE 5: "It's Like..." Text Features

CHAPTER 2	Plasticity Is Like an Athlete Switching Positions, p. 52
CHAPTER 3	Top-Down Processing Is Like Autocomplete, p. 75
CHAPTER 4	Consciousness Is Like a Light Controlled by a Dimmer, p. 104
CHAPTER 5	Your Smartphone Is Like a Flash Drive for Your Brain, p. 151

TABLE 5: "It's Like…" Text Features (CONTINUED)

CHAPTER 6	Dogs Discriminating Between Similar Shapes Are Like You Discriminating Between Similar Logos, p. 183
CHAPTER 7	The Hierarchical Model of Intelligence is Like the National U.S. Weather Report, p. 241
CHAPTER 8	The Thrifty Gene Hypothesis Is Like Buying Gas for a Nickel a Gallon, p. 261
CHAPTER 9	Assimilation and Accommodation Are Like Sorting Laundry, p. 297
CHAPTER 10	Dynamic Sizing Is Like Appreciating Brittney Griner's Height, p. 337
CHAPTER 11	Stifling Your Fight-or-Flight Response Is Like Stepping on the Gas and Brake at the Same Time, p. 367
CHAPTER 12	Self-Reports on Personality Questionnaires Are Like Self-Reports in Real Life, p. 428
CHAPTER 13	Fighting Prejudice Is Like Treating Phobias, p. 455
CHAPTER 14	The Categorical Model Is Like an HIV Test, and the Dimensional Model Is like a Blood Pressure Test, p. 482
CHAPTER 15	Eclectic Therapy Is Like Fruit Salad, and Integrative Therapy Is like a Smoothie, p. 536 Common Factors in Therapy Are Like the Common Active Ingredient in Toothpaste, p. 542
APPENDIX A	Standard Deviation Is Like the Variation in Daily High Temperature, p. A-3

Watching Psychology features use popular TV shows and movies to illustrate key concepts. For example, in the Social Psychology chapter, the feature focuses on *The Voice* (in which judges often hear singers without seeing them) and the impact of physical attractiveness on impression formation. In the Cognition chapter, Watching Psychology focuses on *Family Feud* and its demand for both convergent thinking (to get the top answers on the board) and divergent thinking (to get the lower or remaining answers).

TABLE 6: Watching Psychology Text Features

CHAPTER 1:	Survey Says? *Family Feud* and Random Sampling, p. 27
CHAPTER 2:	The Hippocampus in Hollywood, p. 45
CHAPTER 3:	More Touch, More Wins? p. 96
CHAPTER 4:	What (Body Clock) Time Is Kickoff? p. 108
CHAPTER 5:	The Serial Position Effect on *American Idol*? p. 160
CHAPTER 6:	Home Runs and Schedules of Reinforcement, p. 194
CHAPTER 7:	Convergent and Divergent Thinking on *Family Feud*, p. 223
CHAPTER 8:	This Show Is Scary: The Effect on Children of Frightening TV and Movies, p. 281
CHAPTER 9:	Screen Time and Kids' Development, p. 303
CHAPTER 10:	TV, Sexual Attitudes, and Sexual Behaviors, p. 352
CHAPTER 11:	Sudden Death? The Stress-Related Health Risks of Watching Sports on TV, p. 371
CHAPTER 12:	Personality and Preferences in Movies and TV, p. 421
CHAPTER 13:	*The Voice*, *American Idol*, and Attractiveness, p. 462
CHAPTER 14:	*A Beautiful Mind*, p. 501
CHAPTER 15:	Psychotherapists in Movies and on TV, p. 544

Current Controversy features encourage critical thinking and an appreciation of the scientific process by introducing students to ongoing debates and disagreements within personally relevant areas of psychology. For example, in the Consciousness chapter,

TABLE 7: Current Controversy Topics

Current Controversy focuses on whether high schools should start later in the morning to accommodate teens' circadian rhythms. In the Psychological Disorders chapter, Current Controversy focuses on whether premenstrual dysphoric disorder (PMDD) should qualify as a disorder.

New Ways of Emphasizing Diversity

Our Intro Psych students are increasingly diverse, as is the world in which they live. *My Psychology* emphasizes and embraces diversity in many forms.

Diversity is an essential element of psychology. It is also an essential element of students' lives, so, fittingly, diversity-related coverage is included in every chapter of the book, including a full chapter devoted to culture, sex, and gender

Diversity Matters flags call attention to the role that diversity and culture play in many important psychology concepts. These Diversity Matters flags show that diversity is woven throughout the entire text rather than compartmentalized. Diversity is appreciated in broad terms—not just ethnicity or race, but other areas of individual difference as well, including age, gender, sexual orientation, socioeconomic status, religion, and more. As an example, a Diversity Matters flag in the Social Psychology chapter highlights coverage of the impact of individualism and collectivism on conformity.

***My Psychology* dedicates a full chapter to diversity.** The title of Chapter 10—Diversity in Psychology: Multiculturalism, Gender, and Sexuality—indicates that its focus (relative to comparable chapters in other textbooks) is uniquely inclusive and focused on social awareness. Expert advice and feedback from widely recognized scholars of diversity in psychology—Rachel Farr of the University of Kentucky, Stephen Forssell of The George Washington University, and Debra Roberts of Howard University—ensure the quality of this important material. The chapter begins by recognizing many forms of diversity in the way students live, including race, ethnicity, language, religion, age, sexual orientation, education, income, and big city versus small town. It then educates students about a variety of other broad-based concepts, including how cultures can be defined, diversity *within* groups (dynamic sizing), acculturation, cultural intelligence, and microaggressions. Of course, the chapter also delivers complete coverage of the topics of gender and sexuality, including discussion of the concepts of cisgender, transgender, and transition.

TABLE 8: Diversity Coverage

CHAPTER 1: THE SCIENCE OF PSYCHOLOGY
Influential African Americans in the history of psychology, p. 11
Influential women in the history of psychology, p. 12
Differences across cultures in acceptance of Freud's ideas, p. 14
Differences across cultures in acceptance of behaviorism around the world, p. 15
How multiculturalism challenged assumptions held by some older schools of psychology, p. 16

CHAPTER 2: THE BRAIN AND BEHAVIOR
How poverty can influence brain development, p. 53

CHAPTER 3: SENSATION AND PERCEPTION
How culture can influence vision, p. 85
How culture can influence audition, p. 90
How gender and ethnicity can influence olfactory abilities, p. 92
Why people from different cultures enjoy different foods, p. 94

CHAPTER 4: CONSCIOUSNESS
How culture can influence circadian rhythms, p. 109
How gender, ethnicity, and age can influence sleep, pp. 112–115

CHAPTER 5: MEMORY
How ethnicity can influence what we remember, p. 163

CHAPTER 6: LEARNING
How ethnicity can influence perceptions of reinforcements, pp. 190–191

CHAPTER 7: COGNITION: THINKING, LANGUAGE, AND INTELLIGENCE
How culture interacts with expertise, pp. 216–217
How culture can influence concept formation, p. 217
How multiple cultural backgrounds and languages can influence creativity, p. 224
How ethnicity and socioeconomic status can create test bias in measures of intelligence, p. 243
How culture-fair intelligence tests aim to minimize bias, pp. 243–244

CHAPTER 8: MOTIVATION AND EMOTION
How ethnicity can influence Maslow's hierarchy of needs, p. 257
How gender can influence motivation, pp. 257–258
How age can influence motivation, pp. 258
How sex, stress, and economic factors can influence eating behaviors, pp. 262–264
How age, ethnicity, and gender can interact with emotion, pp. 281–283

CHAPTER 9: DEVELOPMENT ACROSS THE LIFE SPAN
How culture can influence the development of mathematical abilities, p. 290
How culture can influence the likelihood of co-sleeping, p. 290
How television watching can foster stereotypes regarding ethnicity and gender, p. 303
How culture can influence the evaluation of various parenting styles, p. 306
How culture can interact with goodness-of-fit between kids and parenting styles, p. 307
How ethnicity can influence the development of childhood friendships, p. 308
How ethnicity can influence the moral sense of what is right, p. 312
How ethnicity can influence dating patterns in teens, p. 318
How ethnicity can influence perceptions of emerging adulthood, p. 320
How ethnicity can influence the experience of empty nest syndrome, p. 325

CHAPTER 10: DIVERSITY IN PSYCHOLOGY: MULTICULTURALISM, GENDER, AND SEXUALITY
This whole chapter focuses on diversity!
How race, ethnicity, language, religion, age, and other culture variables vary within the United States, pp. 334–335
What dynamic sizing is, and how it relates to understanding people from diverse cultures, pp. 336–337
How the definition of culture has changed over the years, pp. 338–339
How multiculturalism has come to play an important role in psychology, pp. 338–340
What acculturation is, and how acculturation strategies differ, pp. 340–341
What acculturative stress is, pp. 341–342
Which specific variables differ between cultural groups, pp. 342–344
How cultural differences can translate into differences in daily life, pp. 344–347
What cultural intelligence is, pp. 347–348
What microaggressions are, pp. 348–349
How gender and sex are defined, pp. 350
What influences gender development, pp. 350–354
What cisgender, transgender, and transition mean, pp. 352–354
How sexual orientation is defined, pp. 354–358
How cultural variables can influence attitudes toward sexual minorities, pp. 357–358
How gender differences translate into differences in daily life, pp. 358–361

CHAPTER 11: STRESS AND HEALTH
How culture can influence the appraisal of stressors, p. 368
How culture can influence the experience of stress, pp. 381–383
How ethnicity and gender can influence coping strategies, pp. 385–386

Diversity is an essential part of psychology. *My Psychology* features unique coverage of diversity throughout the text as well as a full chapter (Chapter 10) dedicated to diversity.
(Top to bottom) Peathegee Inc/Blend Images/Getty Images; commerceandculturestock/Getty Images; zhang bo/Getty Images

TABLE 8: Diversity Coverage (CONTINUED)
CHAPTER 12: PERSONALITY How culture can influence the evaluation of humanistic theory, p. 414 How research has confirmed the Big Five personality traits in countries around the world, pp. 420–423 How cultural competence plays an important role in personality assessment, p. 425
CHAPTER 13: SOCIAL PSYCHOLOGY How ethnicity can influence the likelihood of the fundamental attribution error, p. 437 How culture can influence the likelihood of conformity, p. 446 How ethnicity and gender can influence bodily attractiveness, pp. 452, 461–463 How ethnicity and gender can influence aggressive behavior, p. 460
CHAPTER 14: PSYCHOLOGICAL DISORDERS How culture can influence perceptions of normality and abnormality, p. 475 How ethnicity can influence the experience of anxiety disorders, p. 488 How ethnicity can influence the experience of major depressive disorder, p. 494 How ethnicity can influence the experience of eating disorders, p. 497–498 How urban or rural lifestyle can influence the experience of schizophrenia, p. 503
CHAPTER 15: THERAPY How cultural variables can influence determinations of logical and illogical cognitions in cognitive therapy, p. 534 How the lack of diversity in efficacy studies limits their generalizability, p. 540 How ethnicity, age, socioeconomic status, relations, sexual orientation, and other cultural variables are relevant to evidence-based psychotherapy, pp. 540–541 How essential cultural competence is to therapists, p. 543 How essential cultural self-awareness is to therapists, p. 543 Narrow versus broad definitions of what constitutes a culture, p. 543

Pedagogy That Enriches the Learning Experience

Our Intro Psych students benefit from effective learning tools integrated into their reading experience. *My Psychology* provides a full, multifaceted program of these tools.

My Psychology is packed with pedagogical tools that maximize students' engagement with and understanding of the science of psychology. These tools aim to include students from all educational backgrounds, and many leverage personal connections to the material to boost memory and comprehension.

YOU WILL LEARN:

1.1 what psychology is.

1.2 what psychology is *not*.

CHECK YOUR LEARNING:

1.1 What is psychology?

1.2 What are the primary differences between psychology and psychiatry?

Each major section of each chapter starts with learning objectives ("You Will Learn") and ends with a corresponding question about each learning objective ("Check Your Learning"). The Chapter Summary then answers each question at the end of the chapter. The synchronized numbering system for the preview–question–answer process helps students to learn the core knowledge in every chapter.

CHAPTER SUMMARY

What Is Psychology?

1.1 Psychology is the scientific study of behavior and mental processes, which means that psychology focuses on *both* our outer actions *and* our inner experiences.

1.2 Psychology is not just therapy, not exclusively about people with mental disorders, not all about Sigmund Freud, not psychiatry, and not just a bunch of ideas with no research to back them up.

Three-step synced pedagogical system. Each major section of each chapter starts with learning objectives ("You Will Learn") and ends with a question about each one ("Check Your Learning"). The Chapter Summary then provides the answers to each of those questions. A simple, synchronized numbering system makes it easy for students to follow any particular concept through these three stages. This preview–question–answer process provides students with the core knowledge delivered in each chapter.

What's Your Take? Critical thinking questions invite the students to connect their own experiences to important psychological concepts. For example, in the Learning chapter, a What's Your Take? question prompts students to think about how their own pets have been classically conditioned. In the Development chapter, another question prompts students to think about how the college environment might represent a "strange situation" (often used in infant attachment research) for themselves or other students.

An example-rich approach. An Intro Psych textbook is only as good as its examples, and *My Psychology* stands out in both the quantity and quality of examples it offers. Every major concept is explained with at least one example, and minor concepts frequently receive the same treatment. These examples resonate with students by providing a real-world (*students'* real world) context to help them appreciate the material. For example, in the Motivation and Emotion chapter, when describing the theories of emotion, textbooks typically use the example of a dog or a wolf attacking a person as an event that evokes strong emotion. *My Psychology* instead uses the example of water spilling on a smartphone—something far more common and immediate to today's Intro Psych student. Collectively, the examples in *My Psychology* strike an ideal balance between accessibility and rigor. (Numerous examples describe clients with whom the author has personally worked in his clinical practice. In those cases, any identifying information has been changed, disguised, or omitted to maintain client confidentiality.)

TABLE 9: Selected Real-World Examples for Psychological Concepts

CHAPTER	PSYCHOLOGY CONCEPT	EXAMPLE
1 The Science of Psychology	Conditions of worth (Carl Rogers)	Dashon, a 10-year-old boy who loves ballet but whose parents push him to play football
	Biopsychosocial theory	Leo, a college student who has panic attacks attributable to multiple factors
	Confirmation bias	Selectively reading Yelp restaurant reviews that agree with the opinion you already hold
2 Brain and Behavior	Sensory and motor neurons	Searching for your smartphone in a dark room by reaching through a crowded backpack
	Parts of the brain working together	The many simultaneous microbehaviors involved in the simple act of drinking a can of soda
	Frontal lobe	The steps involved in shopping for a car (gathering information, determining pros and cons, choosing a way to purchase and pay, etc.)
3 Sensation and Perception	Sensation and perception	The Boston Marathon bombing and the sights, sounds, and smells of its aftermath
	Difference threshold	A gradually dimming flashlight due to a declining battery
	Sensory adaptation	Getting used to the smell of fresh-baked bread while working an 8-hour shift at a bakery
	Perceptual constancy	A gradually closing laptop computer
	Gestalt	A college basketball team walking together through an airport
4 Consciousness	Mindfulness	Brushing your teeth as an opportunity for mindfulness
	Unihemispheric sleep	Mallard ducks sleeping with one eye open
	Insomnia	An excerpt from the autobiography of English professor Gayle Green
	Addiction	An excerpt from the autobiography of actor Rob Lowe
	Lesser-known risks of nicotine use	Third-hand smoke

TABLE 9: Selected Real-World Examples for Psychological Concepts (CONTINUED)

CHAPTER	PSYCHOLOGY CONCEPT	EXAMPLE
5 Memory	Fallibility of memory	Jean Piaget's false autobiographical memory of a near-kidnapping incident during his childhood
	Chunking	A condensed list of TV networks—NBCHBOCNNMTVTNTCBS
	Encoding specificity	Two new coworkers meeting on an elevator and later finding it easiest to remember each other's names on the same elevator
	Priming	A personal story involving snow shoveling on a frigid day and the words chilly and chili
	Misinformation effect	A personal story about a young boy being asked where in a Target store he took his gift card out of this pocket, when he actually had no pockets at all
6 Learning	Classical conditioning	The pffst sound of an opening soda can as a conditioned stimulus
	Discrimination and generalization	Logos that feature similar M's (Monster energy drink, M & M's candy, and McDonalds)
	Variable-ratio and fixed-ratio schedules of reinforcement	Slot machines and soda machines
	Variable-interval and fixed-interval schedules of reinforcement	Email and mail
	Shaping	A basketball coach teaches a young player to shoot a lay-up by reinforcing each small action along the way—jumping off the correct foot, shooting with the correct hand, hitting the right spot on the backboard, etc.
7 Cognition: Thinking, Language, and Intelligence	Concept formation, fuzzy boundaries	Chili as a soup
	Superordinate, basic, and subordinate concepts	Vehicles, bicycles, and mountain bikes
	Framing	Different ways the issue of fracking can be presented
	Creativity	The popcorn hoodie
	Convergent and divergent thinking	Guessing the answers at the top and bottom of the list on Family Feud
	Test bias	Gap year and kale as vocabulary items on an intelligence test
8 Motivation and Emotion	Intrinsic and extrinsic motivation	Playing basketball for the love of the game or to earn a scholarship; teaching for the fulfillment of student learning or the paycheck it brings
	Achievement goal theory	Two students in a Spanish class, one motivated to get a good grade and the other motivated to learn the language
	Theories of emotion	The emotional responses to seeing water spill on your smartphone
	Recognition of emotion	A 7-year-old child falls during a soccer game and uses coach's facial expression as an indication of how bad the injury is
	Emotion and gender	Male and female coworkers are both laid off from their jobs but respond in different ways.
9 Development Across the Lifespan	Cross-sectional vs. longitudinal design	Designing a study on how digital literacy changes from childhood to older adulthood
	Cultural influence on development	Co-sleeping frequency around the world
	Egocentrism	A 3-year-old child brings a Band-Aid and a teddy bear to his elderly relative who has fallen and broken a hip
	Ethnicity and friendship	Why two classmates, one with strong grades and one with weak grades, would befriend each other in Western vs. Eastern cultures
	Personal fable	Teens who think "I won't crash if I text while driving"
	Moral decision making	The true story of a record shop owner who stumbled across a valuable record collection left behind by a legendary hip hop producer

CHAPTER	PSYCHOLOGY CONCEPT	EXAMPLE
10 Diversity in Psychology: Multiculturalism, Gender, and Sexuality	Defining culture	Variables including ethnicity, race, gender, age, religion, education level, socioeconomic status, sexual orientation, urban vs. rural setting, and more
	Subcultures	Military subculture, college student subculture, young parent subculture, and more
	Microaggressions	Sophia, a fourth-grade girl standing by her science project, is asked by a judge, "How did you get so good at science?"
	Gender differences in communication	Move-in day for first-year college students when the two roommates are male vs. when the two roommates are female
	Dynamic sizing	The height of basketball star Brittney Griner, illustrating tremendous variability within a group
11 Stress and Health	Primary and secondary appraisal	Tyler and Chelsea, two single 20-somethings with the same job, get transferred to the same place but have different appraisals of the situation.
	Appraisal and diversity	College entrance exams as experienced by members of different ethnicities; the flu as experienced by members of different age groups
	Benefit finding	A soldier who loses a leg to a roadside bomb gains a more appreciative outlook on life and closer relationships
	Collectivism, individualism, and stress	People from two different cultural backgrounds, one more collectivistic and the other more individualistic, approach medical school applications in different ways
	Social support	Molly, a young adult stressed out about doing her own taxes for the first time, seeks out help from friends and family
	Proactive coping	Hannah discovers she is pregnant and takes immediate steps to prepare for all the changes that will come with the baby's arrival
12 Personality	Psychic determinism	Jason, a sales rep who leaves his computer bag on the ground as he drives away to do a big presentation saved on his laptop
	Defense mechanisms	Rick uses projection when he repeatedly accuses his partner of wanting to cheat on him when Rick is truly the one who wants to cheat.
	Conditions of worth	Parents' positive regard for their children depending on the grades they get, the sports they play, or the friends they choose
	Behavioral view of personality	Josh, a 7-year old boy, whines a lot not because he has a whiny disposition but because his dad reinforces the whining behavior
	Locus of control	Isabella and Eve are passed over for a promotion at the company where they work, but each has a different explanation for the decision
	Cultural competence in personality assessment	Murjanah's psychologist knows what is normal and expected on a personality measure for people of Murjanah's ethnicity, gender, and age
13 Social Psychology	Fundamental attribution error	Speeding versus watching another driver speed
	Foot-in-the-door technique	Asking to borrow a friend's car for a 2-mile trip before asking to borrow it for a much longer trip
	Deindividuation	An audience member heckles a comedian when shrouded by darkness but not when the lights are turned on
	Groupthink	City council members discuss whether to budget for new playground equipment, a new police cruiser, improvements to highway signs, or other expenses
	Common group identity	Various religious organizations in Joplin, Missouri, worked together to help victims of their devastating 2011 tornado
	Mere exposure effect	The Intel logo and the sound that accompanies it during TV commercials

TABLE 9: Selected Real-World Examples for Psychological Concepts (CONTINUED)

CHAPTER	PSYCHOLOGY CONCEPT	EXAMPLE
14 Psychological Disorders	Categorical model of psychopathology	Diseases that have positive-or-negative tests, like cancer or the flu
	Dimensional model of psychopathology	Medical conditions that exist on a continuum, like blood pressure
	Social anxiety disorder	An excerpt from the autobiography of Emily Ford, a high school English teacher with the disorder
	Obsessive-compulsive disorder	An excerpt from the autobiography of Jenny Traig, who suffered with the disorder as a teen
	Neuroticism	A baseball fan on the way to a game seeing rain and thinking "We could get hit by lightning! We could slip and fall as we walk to our seats! The roads could flood, and we could end up stranded at the stadium!"
	Hallucinations	Janet, a psychiatric inpatient who argues with a voice only she can hear
15 Therapy	Resistance	Ana, a therapy client, abruptly changes the subject and no-shows the next appointment when faced with an especially emotionally threatening question
	Transference	Juan, a therapy client who mistakenly presumed that his therapist was bored and felt resentful toward him, just as his father had reacted toward Juan throughout his childhood
	Participant modeling	Terrence, a client with a fear of elevators, observes others successfully ride elevators
	Group therapy	Steven and Monique, group therapy clients who gain insight on their own psychological problems through feedback from group members about their interaction during group
	Cultural competence of therapists	Dr. Martels, a Christian psychologist, appropriately accommodates the schedule of Saalim, a Muslim client, during Ramadan

- **Addressing the student directly.** As appropriate, *My Psychology* speaks straight to the student. The text does not shy away from using words like *you*, *your*, and *yours* to explain concepts to students. Such use of second-person language furthers the students' sense of engagement and interaction with the material. The second-person approach is used judiciously, woven tactfully in and out of more standard didactic language—enough to hook the student into persisting through the assigned reading, but not so much that more typical presentation of material is compromised.
- **Big, bold print**. Rather than simply using bold print to identify key terms, the book features two levels of identification: **bold print** and **big, bold print**. Big, bold print is reserved for the most essential of key terms. This two-tier system of identifying key terms eliminates the problems created by too many Intro Psych textbooks, in which too many key terms are identified within a single chapter, leaving students confused as to which key concepts are most essential and which are secondary. It is a tremendous asset to the student to distinguish which of the key terms are most essential and which are not quite as crucial.
- **Student dialogue questions**. In my own experience teaching Intro Psych, I have noticed common questions that arise from my students when we cover particular topics. In *My Psychology*, those questions (and others) are embedded as student dialogue questions. Distinguished by a colorful font and an icon of a student with a raised hand, student dialogue questions anticipate students' confusion or difficulties and provide clear-cut answers. For example, in the Learning chapter, the distinction between negative reinforcement and punishment is notorious for tripping up students. A student dialogue question inserted at that very point in the text—"Wait, what's the difference between negative reinforcement and punishment?"—gives voice to the student's puzzlement and sets the stage for the clarifying answer that immediately follows.

Wait, what's the difference between negative reinforcement and punishment?

These student dialogue questions are common questions that students have asked in Intro Psych courses. They give voice to the student's potential puzzlement and set the stage for clarifying answers.

Correspondence to the APA Guidelines for the Undergraduate Psychology Major 2.0 and MCAT Categories

Our Intro Psych students deserve a textbook with content that matches the guidelines set forth by the leading psychological organization. *My Psychology* delivers that content.

In 2013, the American Psychological Association offered its second version of its Guidelines for the Undergraduate Psychology Major (APA, 2013). For those Introductory Psychology students who will go on to major in psychology (as well as those who will never take another psychology course), *My Psychology* corresponds to the learning goals identified in APA's guidelines in many important ways.

TABLE 10: APA Guidelines for Pomerantz, *My Psychology*

Goal 1: Knowledge Base in Psychology

1.1 Describe key concepts, principles, and overarching themes in psychology

1.2 Develop a working knowledge of psychology's content domains

1.3 Describe applications of psychology

TEXT CONTENT

Chapter 1: 1.1–1.15
Chapter 2: 2.1–2.34
Chapter 3: 3.1–3.31
Chapter 4: 4.1–4.26
Chapter 5: 5.1–5.26
Chapter 6: 6.1–6.31
Chapter 7: 7.1–7.34
Chapter 8: 8.1–8.17
Chapter 9: 9.1–9.26
Chapter 10: 10.1–10.21
Chapter 11: 11.1–11.24
Chapter 12: 12.1–12.29
Chapter 13: 13.1–13.20
Chapter 14: 14.1–14.49
Chapter 15: 15.1–15.31
Appendix A: A.1–A.4
1.6–1.7; Psychology's Many Subfields, pp. 5–8
4.8; Treating and Preventing Sleep Problems, pp. 118–119
4.23–4.24; Meditation and Mindfulness, pp. 132–134
5.22; Efforts to Improve Memory, pp. 161–163
Applying Classical Conditioning to Your Life, pp. 186–187
Applying Operant Conditioning to Your Life, pp. 198–199
8.11; Promoting Healthy Eating, pp. 267–268
8.15; Emotion Regulation, pp. 277–278
8.16; Why Emotion Regulation Matters, pp. 278–280
10.8–10.9; Acculturation: Managing Multiple Cultures, pp. 340–342
11.16–11.21; Coping with Stress: Psychological Strategies and Social Strategies, pp. 385–391
13.4; Attitude Persuasion Strategies, pp. 439–440
13.15; Toward Fairness and Cooperation: Fighting Prejudice, pp. 454–456

FEATURE CONTENT

The knowledge base and major topics of psychology are further reinforced by all Chapter Apps, My Take videos, From Research to Real Life text features, Watching Psychology text features, Current Controversy text features, It's Like... text features, Diversity Matters flags, Life Hack text features, Show Me More links, student dialogue questions, the study guide, LaunchPad resources, the LearningCurve quizzing system, and the Instructor's Resource Manual.

Goal 2: Scientific Inquiry and Critical Thinking

2.1 Use scientific reasoning to interpret psychological phenomena

2.2 Demonstrate psychology information literacy

2.3 Engage in innovative and integrative thinking and problem solving

2.4 Interpret, design, and conduct basic psychological research

2.5 Incorporate sociocultural factors in scientific inquiry

TEXT CONTENT

1.10; Multiculturalism, p. 16
1.10; Biopsychosocial Theory, p. 18
1.11–1.15; The Science of Psychology, pp. 19–29
2.30–2.34; How We Know All of This: Viewing the Brain, pp. 58–62
3.15; How Culture Influences Vision, pp. 85–86
3.21; How Culture Influences Hearing, pp. 89–90
4.5–4.6; Diversity in Normal Sleep, pp. 112–115
Culture and Memory, pp. 163–164
Reinforcement and Diversity, pp. 190–191
Expertise, Culture, and Concepts, pp. 216–217
7.5–7.8; Problem Solving and Decision Making, pp. 217–220
7.14; Creativity and Culture, p. 224
7.32; Test Bias, pp. 243–244
7.33; Stereotype Threat, p. 244
7.34; Group Differences, pp. 244–245
8.6; Motivation and Diversity, pp. 257–258
8.10; Environmental and Social Cultural Factors in Hunger and Eating, pp. 264–267
8.17; Emotion and Diversity, pp. 281–283
9.12–9.14; Psychosocial Development in Infancy and Childhood, pp. 304–306
9.19–9.23; Psychosocial Development in Adolescence, pp. 313–320
9.26; Psychosocial Development in Adulthood, pp. 323–328
10.1–10.21; Chapter 10, Diversity in Psychology: Multiculturalism, Gender, and Sexuality, pp. 334–363
11.12–11.15; Stress and Culture, pp. 380–384
11.17; Culture and Coping, pp. 385–386
13.13–13.15; Prejudice: Us Versus. Them, pp. 452–454
14.6; The Sociocultural Theory of Abnormality, pp. 477–478
14.7; The Biopsychosocial Theory of Abnormality, p. 478
15.16–15.18; The Importance of Culture in Psychotherapy, pp. 543–544
A.1–A.4; Appendix A: An Introduction to Statistics in Psychological Research

FEATURE CONTENT

Chapter 1: Current Controversy: Should Psychologists Prescribe Medication?; From Research to Real Life: Psychologists' Research on College Success; Life Hack 1.1; Chapter App 1.1: College Success;

TABLE 10: APA Guidelines for Pomerantz, *My Psychology* (CONTINUED)

My Take Video 1.1: Belief Perseverance; Life Hack 1.2; My Take Video 1.2: Correlation-Causation Fallacy; Life Hack 1.3; Watching Psychology: Survey Says? *Family Feud* and Random Sampling; Show Me More 1.1: Nature Versus Nurture; Show Me More 1.2: Wilhelm Wundt and William James; Show Me More 1.3: The Placebo Effect

Chapter 2: Life Hack 2.1; My Take Video 2.1: Parts of the Brain; Watching Psychology: The Hippocampus in Hollywood; Chapter App 2.1: Localization; It's Like ...: Plasticity Is Like An Athlete Switching Positions; My Take Video 2.2: Plasticity; Chapter App 2.2: Plasticity; Life Hack 2.2; From Research to Real Life: The Murderer's Mind; Current Controversy: Neuroeverything?; My Take Video 2.3: Sympathetic and Parasympathetic Divisions of the Autonomic Nervous System; Life Hack 2.3; Show Me More 2.1: A Split-Brain Patient; Show Me More 2.2: Your Brain on Politics?

Chapter 3: My Take Video 3.1: Difference Threshold; My Take Video 3.2: Sensory Adaptation; From Research to Real Life: Variety, the Key to Happiness?; It's Like ...: Top-Down Processing Is Like Autocomplete; Life Hack 3.1; Current Controversy: Can Your Retina or Iris Unlock Your Smartphone?; Chapter App 3.1: Vision; Chapter App 3.2: Visual Illusions; Life Hack 3.2; Chapter App 3.3: Audition; Life Hack 3.3; Watching Psychology: More Touch, More Wins?; Show Me More 3.1: The McGurk Effect; Show Me More 3.2: Mudsplashes, Gorillas, and Change Blindness; Show Me More 3.3: Breakfast Around the World

Chapter 4: It's Like ...: Consciousness Is Like a Light Controlled by a Dimmer; Life Hack 4.1; My Take Video 4.1: Sleep Deprivation; From Research to Real Life: Do You Realize What Sleep Deprivation Does to You; My Take Video 4.2: Circadian Rhythm; Watching Psychology: What (Body Clock) Time Is Kickoff?; Chapter App 4.1: REM Sleep; Current Controversy: Should High School Start Later in the Day?; Life Hack 4.2; Chapter App 4.2: Depressants; Life Hack 4.3; Show Me More 4.1: Natural Light and Circadian Rhythms; Show Me More 4.2: Sleepwalking with a Comedian

Chapter 5: From Research to Real Life: Is Forgetting Good?; It's Like ...: Your Smartphone Is Like a Flash Drive for Your Brain; Chapter App 5.1: Retrieval; My Take Video 5.1: Recall versus Recognition; Life Hack 5.1; Watching Psychology: The Serial Position Effect on *American Idol*; My Take Video 5.2: Flashbulb Memory; Life Hack 5.2; From Research to Real Life: Improving Your Memory; Life Hack 5.3; Chapter App 5.2: Efforts to Improve Memory; Current Controversy: Do Sports Head Injuries Cause Memory Loss?; My Take Video 5.3: The Fallibility of Memory; Show Me More 5.1: Moonwalking with Einstein; Show Me More 5.2: Retrograde Amnesia; Show Me More 5.3: Sports Head Injuries and Memory Loss

Chapter 6: My Take Video 6.1: Classical Conditioning; From Research to Real Life: Classical Conditioning in Advertising; It's Like ...: Dogs Discriminating Between Similar Shapes Are Like You Discriminating Between Similar Logos; Chapter App 6.1: Classical Conditioning; Chapter App 6.2: Reinforcement; My Take Video 6.2: Reinforcement Schedules; Watching Psychology: Home Runs and Schedules of Reinforcement; Chapter App 6.3: Punishment; Life Hack 6.1; Current Controversy: Does Violence in the Media Cause Violence in Real Life?; My Take Video 6.3: Observational Learning; Life Hack 6.2; Show Me More 6.1: Classical Conditioning

Chapter 7: My Take Video 7.1: Affective Forecasting; Life Hack 7.1; Watching Psychology: Convergent and Divergent Thinking on *Family Feud*; Life Hack 7.2; Current Controversy: What Is Texting Doing to Language?; My Take Video 7.2: Intelligence; From Research to Real Life: Intelligence Correlates with ...; It's Like ...: The Hierarchical Model of Intelligence Is Like the National U.S. Weather Report; Chapter App 7.1: Intelligence Tests; Show Me More 7.1: Daniel Kahneman Discusses Dual-Process Theory; Show Me More 7.2: Nicaraguan Sign Language

Chapter 8: My Take Video 8.1: Intrinsic and Extrinsic Motivation; My Take Video 8.2: Maslow's Hierarchy of Needs; Chapter App 8.1: Motivation; Chapter App 8.2: Set Point; It's Like ...: The Thrifty Gene Hypothesis Is Like Buying Gas for a Nickel a Gallon; Current Controversy: Advertising Unhealthy Food to Kids; Life Hack 8.1; Chapter App 8.3: Promoting Healthy Eating; My Take Video 8.3: Emotion Regulation; Life Hack 8.2; From Research to Real Life: Does Money Buy Happiness?; Life Hack 8.3; Watching Psychology: This Show Is Scary; Show Me More 8.1: Derek Redmond and His Father Cross the Finish Line; Show Me More 8.2: Serving Size Versus What You Really Eat

Chapter 9: From Research to Real Life: A Well-Running Brain; Life Hack 9.1; Watching Psychology: Screen Time and Kids' Development; It's Like ...: Assimilation and Accommodation Are Like Sorting Laundry; Chapter App 9.1: Prenatal Development; My Take Video 9.1: Parenting Styles; Chapter App 9.2: Imaginary Audience; Current Controversy: Social Networking and Computer Gaming; My Take Video 9.2: Emerging Adulthood; Life Hack 9.2; Show Me More 9.1: Piaget's Conservation Task; Show Me More 9.2: Attachment and Harlow's Monkeys; Show Me More 9.3: Moral Decision Making and a Legendary Producer's Records

Chapter 10: My Take Video 10.1: What Constitutes a Culture?; Life Hack 10.1; Chapter App 10.1: Multiculturalism; Chapter App 10.2: Cultural Intelligence; My Take Video 10.2: Microaggressions; It's Like ...: Dynamic Sizing Is Like Appreciating Brittney Griner's Height; Life Hack 10.2; My Take Video 10.3: Gender Versus Sex; Watching Psychology: TV, Sexual Attitudes, and Sexual Behaviors; Chapter App 10.3: Transgender; Current Controversy: How Does Facebook Affect Body Image?; From Research to Real Life: Does Gaydar Work?; Show Me More 10.1: Microaggressions; Show Me More 10.2: Cultural Characteristics of Countries Around the World

Chapter 11: It's Like ...: Stifling Your Fight-or-Flight Response Is Like Stepping on the Gas and Brake at the Same Time; My Take Video 11.1: Appraisal; Chapter App 11.1: Appraisal; Watching Psychology: Sudden Death? The Stress-Related Health Risks of Watching Sports on TV; Current Controversy: What Counts as a Trauma?; Life Hack 11.1; My Take Video 11.2: Types of Coping; Life Hack 11.2; From Research to Real Life: Don't Stress Out about Stress; Chapter App 11.2: Social Support; Life Hack 11.3; Chapter App 11.3: Decreasing Stress with Exercise; Show Me More 11.1: Human vs. Animal Experience of Stress; Show Me More 11.2: Type A Personality Explained

Chapter 12: My Take Video 12.1: Internal vs. External Locus of Control; From Research to Real Life: What's Happening to Our Locus of Control?; Current Controversy: Is There an Upside to Neuroticism?; Life Hack 12.1; My Take Video 12.2: Five-Factor Model of Personality; Watching Psychology: Personality and Preferences in Movies and TV; Chapter App 12.1: Five-Factor Model of Personality; It's Like ...: Self-Reports on Personality Questionnaires Are Like Self-Reports in Real Life; Show Me More 12.1: Locus of Control and Academic Potential; Show Me More 12.2: The Big Five and the Personality of College Majors

Chapter 13: My Take Video 13.1: The Fundamental Attribution Error; Life Hack 13.1; My Take Video 13.2: Conformity; From Research to Real Life: Milgram, Obedience, and the NFL's Bounty Scandal; Chapter App 13.1: Social Facilitation; Life Hack 13.2; My Take Video 13.3: Social Comparison; It's Like ...: Fighting Prejudice and Phobia Treatment; Life Hack 13.3; Current Controversy: Cyberbullying and Social Psychology; Watching Psychology: *The Voice*, *American Idol*, and Attractiveness; Chapter App 13.2: Prosocial Behavior/Altruism; Show Me More 13.1: Social Roles in the Stanford Prison Experiment; Show Me More 13.2: The Give and Take of the Reciprocity Norm; Show Me More 13.3: An Act of Kindness

Chapter 14: My Take Video 14.1: Abnormal Versus Normal; My Take Video 14.2: The Biopsychosocial Theory of Abnormality; My Take Video 14.3: Categorical vs. Dimensional Models of Psychopathology;

Current Controversy: Premenstrual Dysphoric Disorder; It's Like ...: The Categorical Model Is Like an HIV Test, and the Dimensional Model Is Like a Blood Pressure Test; Life Hack 14.1; Chapter App 14.1: Anxiety Disorders; Chapter App 14.2: Depressive and Bipolar Disorders; Life Hack 14.2; From Research to Real Life: How Powerful Are Magazines in the Development of Eating Disorders; Watching Psychology: *A Beautiful Mind*; Show Me More 14.1: Eating Disorders in Fiji; Show Me More 14.2: Hannah Upp's Dissociative Amnesia and Dissociative Fugue

Chapter 15: My Take Video 15.1: Exposure Therapy; Chapter App 15.1: Cognitive Therapy; My Take Video 15.2: Cognitive Distortions; It's Like ...: Eclectic Therapy Is Like Fruit Salad and Integrative Therapy Is Like a Smoothie; My Take Video 15.3: How Well Does Psychotherapy Work?; From Research to Real Life: Psychotherapy Changes the Brain; Current Controversy: Therapies That Work ... for Whom?; It's Like ...: Common Factors in Therapy Are Like the Common Active Ingredient in Toothpaste; Life Hack 15.1; Watching Psychology: Psychotherapists in Movies and TV; Life Hack 15.2; Chapter App 15.2: Cybertherapy; Show Me More 15.1: Judith Beck and Cognitive Therapy; Show Me More 15.2: Cultural Competence; Show Me More 15.3: Virtual Reality Exposure Therapy for Phobias

Scientific inquiry and critical thinking in psychology are reinforced with the three-step synched pedagogical system (You Will Learn, Check Your Learning, and Chapter Summary), the Self-Assessment quiz, What's Your Take? critical thinking questions, the study guide, LaunchPad, LearningCurve, and the Instructor's Resource Manual.

Goal 3: Ethical and Social Responsibility in a Diverse World

3.1 Apply ethical standards to evaluate psychological science and practice

3.2 Build and enhance interpersonal relationships

3.3 Adopt values that build community at local, national, and global levels

TEXT CONTENT

1.15; Ethics in Psychological Studies, p. 29
7.15–7.21; Language, pp. 225–235
8.5; One Motivation after Another: Maslow's Hierarchy, pp. 254–256
9.12–9.13; Psychosocial Development, pp. 304–308
9.14; Friend Relationships, pp. 307–308
9.22; Relationships with Parents, pp. 316–317
9.22; Relationships with Peers, pp. 317–319
10.1–10.21; Diversity in Psychology: Multiculturalism, Gender, and Sexuality, pp. 334–363
11.20; Decreasing Stress by Improving Relationships, pp. 388–389
11.21; Decreasing Stress by Behaving Differently, pp. 390–391
13.1–13.5; Social Cognition, pp. 436–443
13.6–13.11; Social Influence, pp. 443–451
13.12–13.17; Social Relations, pp. 451–464
13.18–13.20; Prosocial Behavior, pp. 465–468
15.15; What Makes Therapy Work, pp. 541–543
15.16–15.18; The Importance of Culture in Psychotherapy, pp. 543–544
15.19–15.22; Ethics in Psychotherapy, pp. 545–546

FEATURE CONTENT

Chapter 2: Show Me More 2.2: Your Brain on Politics?

Chapter 3: Watching Psychology: More Touch, More Wins?; Show Me More 3.3: Breakfast Around the World

Chapter 7: Show Me More 7.2: Nicaraguan Sign Language

Chapter 8: My Take Video 8.2: Maslow's Hierarchy of Needs

Chapter 9: Show Me More 9.3: Moral Decision Making and a Legendary Producer's Records

Chapter 10: My Take Video 10.1: What Constitutes a Culture?; Life Hack 10.1; Chapter App 10.1: Multiculturalism; Chapter App 10.2: Cultural Intelligence; My Take Video 10.2: Microaggressions; It's Like ...: Dynamic Sizing Is Like Appreciating Brittney Griner's Height; Life Hack 10.2; Watching Psychology: TV, Sexual Attitudes, and Sexual Behaviors; Chapter App 10.3: Transgender; From Research to Real Life: Does Gaydar Work?; Show Me More 10.1: Microaggressions; Show Me More 10.2: Cultural Characteristics of Countries Around the World

Chapter 11: Chapter App 11.2: Social Support; Life Hack 11.3

Chapter 12: Life Hack 12.1

Chapter 13: My Take Video 13.1: The Fundamental Attribution Error; Life Hack 13.1; My Take Video 13.2: Conformity; From Research to Real Life: Milgram, Obedience, and the NFL's Bounty Scandal; Chapter App 13.1: Social Facilitation; Life Hack 13.2; My Take Video 13.3: Social Comparison; It's Like ...: Fighting Prejudice and Phobia Treatment; Life Hack 13.3; Chapter App 13.2: Prosocial Behavior/Altruism; Show Me More 13.1: Social Roles in the Stanford Prison Experiment; Show Me More 13.2: The Give and Take of the Reciprocity Norm; Show Me More 13.3: An Act of Kindness

Chapter 14: From Research to Real Life: How Powerful Are Magazines in the Development of Eating Disorders; Show Me More 14.1: Eating Disorders in Fiji

Chapter 15: Chapter App 15.2: Cybertherapy; 15.2: Cultural Competence

Ethical responsibility and social responsibility in a diverse world are reinforced by dozens of Diversity Matters flags throughout the entire text.

Goal 4: Communication

4.1 Demonstrate effective writing for different purposes

4.2 Exhibit effective presentation skills for different purposes

4.3 Interact effectively with others

TEXT CONTENT

1.14; How Psychologists Share Their Results, pp. 28–29
7.15–7.21; Language pp. 225–235
8.14; Communicating Emotions, pp. 273–277
9.14; Friend Relationships, pp. 307–308
9.22; Relationships with Parents, pp. 316–317
9.22; Relationships with Peers, pp. 317–319
10.1–10.21; Chapter 10, Diversity in Psychology: Multiculturalism, Gender, and Sexuality, pp. 334–363
13.12–13.17, Social Relations, pp. 451–464
13.18–13.20, Prosocial Behavior, 465–468
15.16–15.18; The Importance of Culture in Psychotherapy, pp. 543–544

FEATURE CONTENT

Chapter 3: Watching Psychology: More Touch, More Wins?; Show Me More 3.2: Mudsplashes, Gorillas, and Change Blindness

Chapter 7: Current Controversy: What Is Texting Doing to Language?; Show Me More 7.2: Nicaraguan Sign Language

Chapter 10: My Take Video 10.1: What Constitutes a Culture?; Life Hack 10.1; Chapter App 10.1: Multiculturalism; Chapter App 10.2: Cultural Intelligence; My Take Video 10.2: Microaggressions; It's Like ...: Dynamic Sizing Is Like Appreciating Brittney Griner's Height; Life Hack 10.2; My Take Video 10.3: Gender Versus Sex; Watching Psychology: TV, Sexual Attitudes, and Sexual Behaviors; Chapter App 10.3: Transgender; Current Controversy: How Does Facebook Affect Body Image?; From Research to Real Life: Does Gaydar Work?; Show Me More 10.1: Microaggressions; Show Me More 10.2: Cultural Characteristics of Countries Around the World

TABLE 10: APA Guidelines for Pomerantz, *My Psychology* (CONTINUED)

Chapter 11: Chapter App 11.2: Social Support

Chapter 13: My Take Video 13.1: The Fundamental Attribution Error; Life Hack 13.1; My Take Video 13.2: Conformity; From Research to Real Life: Milgram, Obedience, and the NFL's Bounty Scandal; Chapter App 13.1: Social Facilitation; Life Hack 13.2; My Take Video 13.3: Social Comparison; It's Like ...: Fighting Prejudice and Phobia Treatment; Life Hack 13.3; Current Controversy: Cyberbullying and Social Psychology; Chapter App 13.2: Prosocial Behavior/Altruism; Show Me More 13.1: Social Roles in the Stanford Prison Experiment; Show Me More 13.2: The Give and Take of the Reciprocity Norm; Show Me More 13.3: An Act of Kindness

Chapter 15: Chapter App 15.2: Cybertherapy; Show Me More 15.2: Cultural Competence

Communication skills are reinforced through What's Your Take? critical thinking questions and essay questions in the Test Bank, as well as LaunchPad, LearningCurve, and the Instructor's Resource Manuel.

Goal 5: Professional Development

5.1 Apply psychological content and skills to career goals

5.2 Exhibit self-efficacy and self-regulation

5.3 Refine project-management skills

5.4 Enhance teamwork capacity

5.5 Develop meaningful professional direction for life after graduation

TEXT CONTENT

1.2; What Psychology Is *Not*, pp. 2–4
1.6–1.7; Psychology's Many Subfields, pp. 5–8
5.7; Effortful Processing, pp. 146–148
7.5–7.8; Problem Solving and Decision Making, pp. 217–220
8.1–8.6; Motivation, pp. 250–258
8.15; Emotion Regulation, pp. 277–278
8.16; Why Emotion Regulation Matters, pp. 278–280
11.8; How Stress and Your Body Affect Each Other, pp. 370–373
11.9–11.11; How Stress and Your Mind Affect Each Other, pp. 373–379
11.20; Decreasing Stress by Improving Relationships, pp. 388–389
11.21; Decreasing Stress by Behaving Differently, pp. 390–391
12.10–12.14; Humanistic Theory of Personality, pp. 411–414
12.18; Albert Bandura, Reciprocal Determinism, and Self-Efficacy, pp. 415–416
13.1–13.5; Social Cognition, pp. 436–443
13.13–13.15; Prejudice: Us Versus Them, pp. 452–454
13.20; Why Don't People Help, pp. 467–468
15.12–15; How Well Does Psychotherapy Work?, pp. 539–543
15.26; Biomedical Therapies, pp. 547–552

FEATURE CONTENT

Chapter 1: Current Controversy: Should Psychologists Prescribe Medication?; My Take Video 1.1: Belief Perseverance; Life Hack 1.2; My Take Video 1.2: Correlation-Causation Fallacy; Show Me More 1.3: The Placebo Effect

Chapter 2: It's Like ...: Plasticity Is Like An Athlete Switching Positions; My Take Video 2.2: Plasticity; Chapter App 2.2: Plasticity; Life Hack 2.2

Chapter 3: From Research to Real Life: Variety, the Key to Happiness?; Life Hack 3.1; Chapter App 3.1: Vision; Life Hack 3.2; Chapter App 3.3: Audition; Life Hack 3.3; Watching Psychology: More Touch, More Wins?

Chapter 4: Life Hack 4.1; My Take Video 4.1: Sleep Deprivation; From Research to Real Life: Do You Realize What Sleep Deprivation Does to You; My Take Video 4.2: Circadian Rhythm; Chapter App 4.1: REM Sleep; Life Hack 4.2; Life Hack 4.3

Chapter 5: From Research to Real Life: Is Forgetting Good?; Life Hack 5.1; Life Hack 5.2; From Research to Real Life: Improving Your Memory; Life Hack 5.3; Chapter App 5.2: Efforts to Improve Memory; Current Controversy: Do Sports Head Injuries Cause Memory Loss?; My Take Video 5.3: The Fallibility of Memory; Show Me More 5.1: Moonwalking with Einstein; Show Me More 5.3: Sports Head Injuries and Memory Loss

Chapter 6: Life Hack 6.1; Life Hack 6.2

Chapter 7: My Take Video 7.1: Affective Forecasting; Life Hack 7.1; Watching Psychology: Convergent and Divergent Thinking on *Family Feud*; Life Hack 7.2; Current Controversy: What Is Texting Doing to Language?; My Take Video 7.2: Intelligence; From Research to Real Life: Intelligence Correlates with ...; Chapter App 7.1: Intelligence Tests

Chapter 8: My Take Video 8.1: Intrinsic and Extrinsic Motivation; My Take Video 8.2: Maslow's Hierarchy of Needs; Chapter App 8.1: Motivation; Chapter App 8.2: Set Point; Life Hack 8.1; My Take Video 8.3: Emotion Regulation; Life Hack 8.2; From Research to Real Life: Does Money Buy Happiness?; Life Hack 8.3

Chapter 9: From Research to Real Life: A Well-Running Brain; Life Hack 9.1; Watching Psychology: Screen Time and Kids' Development; My Take Video 9.1: Parenting Styles; Current Controversy: Social Networking and Computer Gaming; My Take Video 9.2: Emerging Adulthood; Life Hack 9.2

Chapter 10: Life Hack 10.1; Chapter App 10.1: Multiculturalism; Chapter App 10.2: Cultural Intelligence; My Take Video 10.2: Microaggressions; It's Like ...: Dynamic Sizing Is Like Appreciating Brittney Griner's Height; Life Hack 10.2; Chapter App 10.3: Transgender; Show Me More 10.1: Microaggressions

Chapter 11: My Take Video 11.1: Appraisal; Chapter App 11.1: Appraisal; Current Controversy: What Counts as a Trauma?; Life Hack 11.1; My Take Video 11.2: Types of Coping; Life Hack 11.2; From Research to Real Life: Don't Stress Out about Stress; Chapter App 11.2: Social Support; Life Hack 11.3; Chapter App 11.3: Decreasing Stress with Exercise

Chapter 12: My Take Video 12.1: Internal vs. External Locus of Control; From Research to Real Life: What's Happening to Our Locus of Control?; Current Controversy: Is There an Upside to Neuroticism?; Life Hack 12.1; My Take Video 12.2: Five-Factor Model of Personality; Chapter App 12.1: Five-Factor Model of Personality; Show Me More 12.1: Locus of Control and Academic Potential; Show Me More 12.2: The Big Five and the Personality of College Majors

Chapter 13: My Take Video 13.1: The Fundamental Attribution Error; Life Hack 13.1; My Take Video 13.2: Conformity; From Research to Real Life: Milgram, Obedience, and the NFL's Bounty Scandal; Chapter App 13.1: Social Facilitation; Life Hack 13.2; My Take Video 13.3: Social Comparison; It's Like ...: Fighting Prejudice and Phobia Treatment; Life Hack 13.3; Current Controversy: Cyberbullying and Social Psychology; Chapter App 13.2: Prosocial Behavior/Altruism; Show Me More 13.1: Social Roles in the Stanford Prison Experiment; Show Me More 13.2: The Give and Take of the Reciprocity Norm; Show Me More 13.3: An Act of Kindness

Chapter 14: Life Hack 14.1; Life Hack 14.2

Chapter 15: My Take Video 15.2: Cognitive Distortions; From Research to Real Life: Psychotherapy Changes the Brain; Current Controversy: Therapies That Work ... for Whom?; Life Hack 15.1; Life Hack 15.2; Chapter App 15.2: Cybertherapy; Show Me More 15.2: Cultural Competence

Professional development is further reinforced by LaunchPad, LearningCurve, and the Instructor's Resource Manual.

The Medical College Admission Test (MCAT) started including psychology topics on its exam in recent years. Coverage within *My Psychology* matches with many MCAT categories, as outlined in the sample in Table 11. A full correspondence document is available in LaunchPad at www.launchpadworks.com.

TABLE 11: Sample Correspondence to MCAT Categories

MCAT 2015: CATEGORIES IN SENSATION AND PERCEPTION	*MY PSYCHOLOGY*, FIRST EDITION
CONTENT CATEGORY 6A: SENSING THE ENVIRONMENT	**SECTION TITLE AND PAGE NUMBERS**
SENSORY PROCESSING	**SENSATION AND PERCEPTION, pp. 66–101**
Sensation	The Difference Between Sensation and Perception, pp. 68–69
Thresholds	Thresholds: What Your Senses Can and Cannot Do, pp. 69–71 Absolute Threshold, pp. 69–70 Difference Threshold, pp. 70–71
Weber's Law	Difference Threshold, p. 71
Sensory adaptation	Sensory Adaptation, pp. 71, 73 (From Research to Real Life feature)
Sensory receptors	Rods & cones (vision receptor cells), pp. 78–79 Olfactory receptor cells, p. 91 Taste buds, pp. 93–94 Somatosensory receptor cells (touch, temperature), pp. 94–97
Types of sensory receptors	Rods, cones (vision receptor cells), pp. 78–79 Olfactory receptor cells, p. 91 Taste buds, pp. 93–94 Somatosensory receptor cells (touch, temperature), pp. 94–97
Vision	Vision, pp. 77–86
Structure and function of the eye	Your Eye: Its Parts and Their Functions, pp. 77–79
Visual Processing	How You See: Eye Movements, Depth Perception, Color Perception, and More, pp. 79–84
Hearing	Hearing, pp. 86–90
Auditory Processing	Your Ear: Its Parts and Their Functions, pp. 87–88
Other Senses	Smell and Taste, pp. 90–94 Other Senses, pp. 94–98
Somatosensation	Skin Deep: Your Somatosense, pp. 94–98
Pain perception	Pain, pp. 95–97
Taste	Detectable as Delectable: Your Sense of Taste, pp. 93–94
Taste buds, chemoreceptors that detect specific chemicals	Taste Buds: The Gustation Receptor Cells, pp. 93–94
Smell	The Nose Knows: Your Sense of Smell, pp. 91–92
Olfactory cells/ chemoreceptors that detect specific chemicals	How Olfaction Receptor Cells Work, p. 91
Pheromones	Olfaction and Sex, pp. 91–92
Olfactory pathways in the brain	How Olfaction Receptor Cells Work, p. 91
Kinesthetic sense	On the Move and in Balance: Your Kinesthetic Sense and Vestibular Sense, pp. 97–98
Vestibular sense	On the Move and in Balance: Your Kinesthetic Sense and Vestibular Sense, pp. 97–98

TABLE 11: Sample Correspondence to MCAT Categories (CONTINUED)

Perception	The Fundamentals of Sensation and Perception, pp. 68–76 Vision, pp. 77–86 Hearing, pp. 86–90 Smell and Taste, pp. 90–94 Other Senses, pp. 94–98
Perception	The Difference Between Sensation and Perception, pp. 68-69
Bottom-up/Top-down processing	Bottom-Up and Top-Down Processing, pp. 74-75
Perceptual organization (e.g., depth, form, motion, constancy)	Perceptual Constancy, p. 71 Perceptual Set, p. 75 Depth Perception, pp. 80–81 Separating and Grouping Objects, pp. 83–84
Gestalt principles	Separating and Grouping Objects, pp. 83–84

Through its many features and everything else it offers, *My Psychology* helps you teach the science of psychology by helping your students connect the material to their own lives. It invites students into our rich field and welcomes them by demonstrating how personally relatable, applicable, and accessible psychology can be.

Media and Supplements

LaunchPad Featuring LearningCurve Quizzing

A comprehensive Web resource for teaching and learning psychology, LaunchPad combines Macmillan's award-winning media with an innovative platform for easy navigation. For students, it is the ultimate online study guide, with rich interactive tutorials and videos, as well as an e-Book and the LearningCurve adaptive quizzing system. For instructors, LaunchPad is a full-course space where class docu-

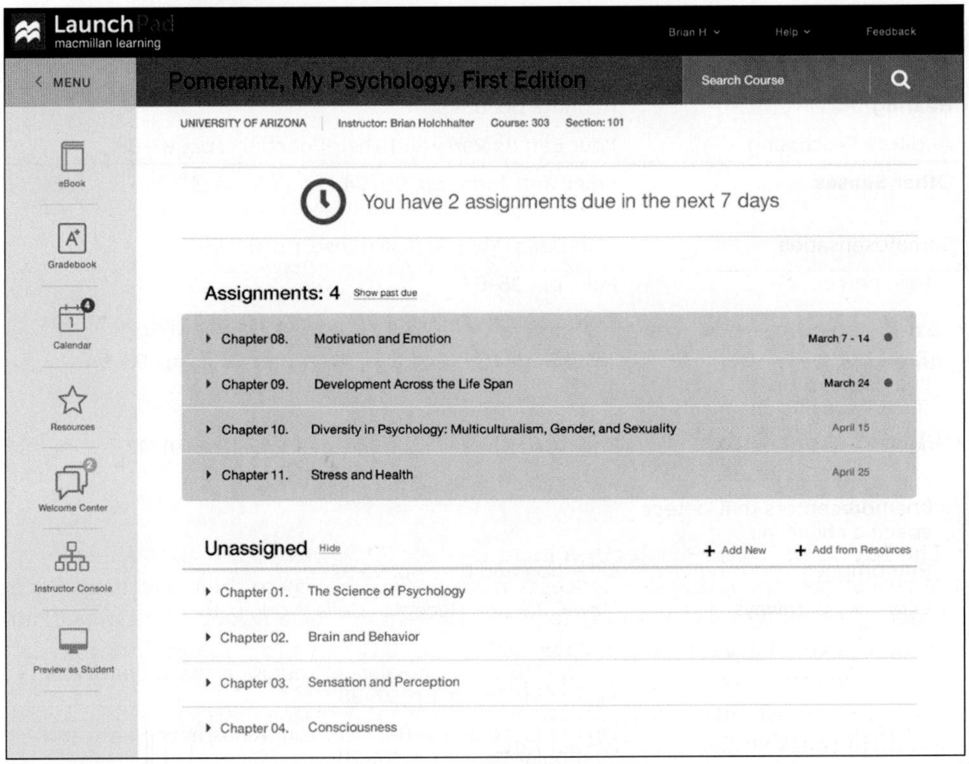

ments can be posted, quizzes easily assigned and graded, and students' progress assessed and recorded. Whether you are looking for the most effective study tools or a robust platform for an online course, LaunchPad is a powerful way to enhance your class.

LaunchPad to Accompany *My Psychology* can be previewed and purchased at launchpadworks.com.

My Psychology and LaunchPad can be ordered together with ISBN-10: 1-319-17041-2 / ISBN-13: 978-1-319-17041-7.

LaunchPad for *My Psychology* includes all the following resources:

- The design of the **LearningCurve** quizzing system is based on the latest findings from learning and memory research. It combines adaptive question selection, immediate and valuable feedback, and a gamelike interface to engage students in a learning experience that is unique to them. Each LearningCurve quiz is fully integrated with other resources in LaunchPad through the Personalized Study Plan, so students will be able to review using Macmillan's extensive library of videos and activities. And state-of-the-art question analysis reports allow instructors to track the progress of individual students as well as their class as a whole.

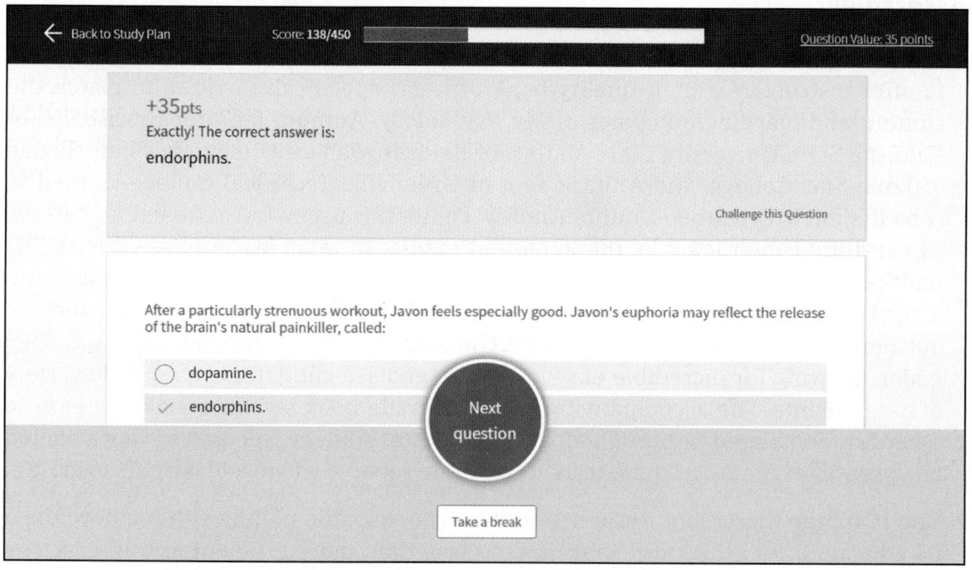

- **An interactive e-Book** allows students to highlight, bookmark, and add their own notes on the e-Book page, just as they would in a printed textbook. Google-style searching and in-text glossary definitions make the text ready for the digital age.
- **Chapter Apps Quizzes** combine the popular Chapter Apps features in every chapter with a quiz to assess students' understanding of how each app relates to important concepts.
- The **My Take Video Collection** includes over 30 professionally produced videos of real students relating key concepts from *My Psychology* to their own lives. Each video is accompanied by a quiz for easy assessment. In addition, the LaunchPad includes over 100 **Video Activities** that instructors can easily assign. Videos cover classic experiments, current news footage, and cutting-edge research, all of which are sure to spark discussion and encourage critical thinking. Each activity includes a quiz to check students' understanding.

- The newly revised series of **Concept Practice** activities by Tom Ludwig (Hope College) allow students to practice their understanding of more than 100 important concepts in less than 5 minutes each. All the activities feature new art and assessment tools to deepen students' interaction with the material.
- The award-winning tutorials in **PsychSim 6.0** by Tom Ludwig (Hope College) and John Krantz (Hanover College) give students an engaging, interactive introduction to psychological phenomena, integrating demonstrations and experimental tasks. In addition, each activity includes integrated formative and summative assessment questions.
- **The *Scientific American* Newsfeed** delivers weekly articles, podcasts, and news briefs on the very latest developments in psychology from the first name in popular-science journalism.
- **Deep integration** is available between LaunchPad products and most learning management systems, including Blackboard, Brightspace by D2L, Canvas, and Moodle. These deep integrations offer educators single sign-on and grade-book sync, now with auto refresh. These best-in-class integrations offer deep linking to all Macmillan digital content at the chapter and asset levels, giving professors maximum flexibility within their LMS.

Assessment

- The **Computerized Test Bank**, powered by Diploma, is built from the ground up to offer instructors a high-quality bank of items specifically written to match the content and learning outcomes of *My Psychology*. Authors Jennifer Branscome of Valdosta State University, Clare Mathes of Baldwin Wallace University, Cindy Sledge of Lone Star College, and Anita P. Tam of Greenville Technical College worked in consultation with textbook author Andrew Pomerantz to craft an assessment package as carefully constructed as the book and media. In total, it comprises over 2,500 multiple-choice and essay items written at several levels of Bloom's taxonomy and tagged to the text's learning outcomes, the book page, the chapter section, and the outcomes recommended in the 2013 APA Guidelines for the undergraduate psychology major, allowing for incredible ease in finding and selecting items for a wide variety of assessments. The accompanying Diploma grade book software makes it easy to record students' grades throughout a course, to sort students' records, to view detailed analyses of test items, to curve tests, to generate reports, and to add weights to grades.
- The **iClicker** Classroom Response System is a versatile polling system, developed by educators for educators, that makes class time more efficient and interactive. iClicker allows you to ask questions and instantly record your students' responses, take attendance, and gauge students' understanding and opinions. iClicker is available at a 10% discount when packaged with *My Psychology*. For more information, visit www1.iclicker.com.

Presentation

- The **Instructor's Resource Manual** features a variety of materials that are valuable to new and veteran teachers alike. Driven by research and content from the scholarship of teaching and learning, and authored by Debra Roberts of Howard University and Charity Peak in consultation with textbook author Andrew Pomerantz, this manual serves as a concise introduction to how the science of teaching can enrich the classroom. In addition to background on the chapter reading and suggestions for in-class lectures, the manual is rich with ideas and activities to engage students. The Instructor's Resources are available to download in LaunchPad at launchpadworks.com.

- **Lecture Slides** are provided complimentary to adopters of *My Psychology* and are perfect for technology novices and experts alike. They include images from the text, concise presentation of the major points from the book, and in-class discussion prompts. The presentation slides are available for download in LaunchPad at launchpadworks.com
- **The Video Collection for Introductory Psychology** includes over 150 unique video clips to bring lectures to life. Provided complimentary to adopters of *My Psychology*, this rich collection includes clinical footage, interviews, animations, and news segments that vividly illustrate topics across the psychology curriculum. Request a copy from your local Macmillan representative.

Macmillan Learning Curriculum Solutions

Macmillan Learning Curriculum Solutions can help transform your Introductory Psychology course by delivering unique course solutions. Visit macmillanlearning.com/curriculumsolutions for more information on how to tailor print and digital solutions to your course.

ForeWords Custom Publishing Library

The ForeWords Library contains special chapters and other print content to supplement *My Psychology*. ForeWords content is authored by recognized experts and can be added to a custom book at little or no cost. Current offerings include:

- Psychology and Sustainability by Susan Clayton of The College of Wooster
- A Practical Guide to Study Skills by Amy Himsel of El Camino College
- Industrial/Organizational Psychology and Human Factors by Paul Levy of The University of Akron and Karen Marando of Argosy University
- The Basics of Scientific Writing in APA Style by Pam Marek of Kennesaw State University
- And many others!

For more information, visit macmillanlearning.com/curriculumsolutions.

Acknowledgements

In Chapter 15, in the coverage of psychotherapy, you'll find the *therapeutic alliance*. Defined as a trusting and collaborative relationship in which therapist and client work toward shared goals, the alliance is the cornerstone of success for therapy of all kinds. In the psychotherapy field, the alliance has earned its place as a key active ingredient in the realization of goals that require tremendous, sustained, and concerted effort.

What's true about alliances between clients and their therapists is also true for alliances between authors and their publishing team. I have been exceedingly fortunate to feel a tremendous alliance with so many people who have supported, championed, and contributed to this book. At the top of the list is Michael Kimball, development editor. For all aspects of this project, from the biggest picture to the smallest detail, Michael has delivered exactly what I needed (even though I often didn't realize I needed it until after I received it). Somehow, Michael brings to our shared work the ideal combination of reliability, expertise, wisdom, constructive criticism, support, respect, advice, and camaraderie. His dedication to the success of this project improved both my writing and my thinking, and his touch is evident in all of the best parts of this book.

Dan DeBonis, senior acquisitions editor, has also been a vitally important and valued ally throughout this publishing process. Every textbook author should be fortunate enough to work with someone like Dan, who blends the professional talents of broad editorial expertise and astuteness with the personal assets of cooperativeness, openness, and thoughtfulness. I am continually impressed by Dan's ability to keep the ship steered toward what's best for the book. I am also appreciative of Katie Pachnos, assistant editor, for all of her support throughout the review process and her help moving chapters into production.

Chuck Linsmeier was actually my senior acquisitions editor for a short time at the beginning of this project, before he was promoted to his current position of Vice President, Social Sciences. Chuck's willingness to take a chance on me in the first place, to have faith in my ability as an author for a project of this scope, is something I will always deeply appreciate. I similarly appreciate the perspective he now offers through his continued involvement and dedication to the project.

Speaking of vice presidents, I am extremely grateful for the many contributions of Kevin Feyen (Vice President, Digital Product Development) and Catherine Woods (Vice President, Content Management). I am also indebted to video producer Kate Super and her team, whose video-making talents and cooperative spirit were the key ingredients in the My Take videos throughout the book.

For the look of the book, I owe tremendous gratitude to many people for their talents: Eli Ensor for the consistently outstanding illustrations; Matthew McAdams for the diligent management of the art program; Blake Logan, Tom Carling, and Diana Blume for the excellent design work; and Rona Tuccillo and Robin Fadool for their conscientious help with photo selection. Thanks for working so collaboratively with me.

Many thanks also go to those who, in various ways, expertly converted the words on my computer screen into the fully produced pages of this textbook: content project manager Won McIntosh; managing editor Lisa Kinne; senior workflow project manager Paul Rohloff; copyeditor Kate Daly; and proofreader Jean Erler.

Additional thanks to those who helped with media and print supplements, including executive media editor Noel Hohnstine and media editor Lisa Dotson.

To those whose efforts involved publicizing and promoting the book, I am tremendously grateful: senior marketing manager Lindsay Johnson; director of advertising Todd Elder; and market development manager Stephanie Ellis.

Of course, there are many people outside of the Worth family toward whom I also feel great appreciation. That list begins with my own family. To my wife, Melissa Lynn Pomerantz: Your love, support, confidence, understanding, belief, and patience made this book (and most of what I do) possible. To my kids, Benjamin and Daniel Pomerantz: I love you and I'm proud of you every day. To my parents, Carol and Bill Pomerantz: Thank you for a lifetime of love and support.

The SIUE Department of Psychology has been a wonderful place to work for over two decades. Thanks for the opportunity and collegiality you have always provided. My undergrad professors at Washington University in St. Louis sparked my interests in both psychology and academic writing. My graduate professors at Saint Louis University fostered and nurtured those interests. Thanks to all of you.

Long before I reached college, I had teachers cultivating my writing skills. At Parkway Central High School and Parkway Central Middle School, at Green Trails Elementary, and even at Lucky Lane Preschool, you were encouraging and shaping my ability to express myself through the written word. Your time, effort, and care played a significant role in the skill and confidence I needed to create this book. I sincerely thank you.

Another important advance in my writing skills, particularly for textbook authorship, came from Mary Ellen Lepionka, whose book about writing and developing college textbooks I found invaluable. Thanks for sharing your expertise with me.

To my own students, especially those in my Intro Psych courses, thanks for everything you have taught me. I extend the same thanks to all of the clients with whom I have had the privilege to work.

Thanks to the staff at my various library hangouts, who provided a variety of resources: SIUE, WUSTL, St. Louis County Library, and University City Public Library, among others.

Thanks to the musicians who inhabit my iPod and online music libraries, many of whom were my frequent companions throughout my work on this project.

Special thanks to all of the professors, instructors, and experts who offered their feedback on various drafts and components of this textbook. Your time, effort, and expertise provided tremendously valuable guidance in reviews, focus groups, surveys, and class testing.

Joe Adamo, *Cazenovia College*
Judi Addelston, *Valencia College*
Mary Beth Ahlum, *Nebraska Wesleyan University*
Matthew Alcala, *Santa Ana College*
Omar Alhassoon, *San Diego Mesa College*
Patrick Allen, *College of Southern Maryland*
Maya Aloni, *Western Connecticut State University*
William Altman, *SUNY Broome Community College*
Karen Amesbury, *Luzerne County Community College*
Abby Ridge Anderson, *The Catholic University of America*
Cheryl Armstrong, *Fitchburg State College*
Sherry Ash, *San Jacinto College*
Sheryl Attig, *Tri-County Technical College*
Adam Austin, *Columbia Basin College*
Renee Babcock, *Central Michigan University*
Stacy Bacigalupi, *Mt. San Antonio College*
Kevin Ball, *Bloomsburg University of Pennsylvania*
Padmini Banarjee, *Delaware State University*
Alicia Barr, *South Plains College*
Deanna Barthlow-Potkanowicz, *Bluffton University*
Wendy Bartkus, *Albright College*
Dave Baskind, *Delta College*
Stacey Baugh, *Trinity Washington University*
Kiersten Baughman, *Ball State University*
Barbara Beaver, *University of Wisconsin-Whitewater*
Richard Bernstein, *Broward College-South Campus*
John Bickford, *University of Massachusetts Amherst*
Christopher Bishop, *Trinity Washington University*
Andrew Blair, *Palm Beach State College*
Michele Bogue, *College of Southern Nevada*
Rebecca Boncoddo, *Central Connecticut State University*
Kristin Bonnie, *Beloit College*
Christi Boren, *San Jacinto College*
Gerald Braasch, *McHenry County College*
Christopher Brady, *John Tyler Community College*
Nicole Brandt, *Columbus State Community College*
Jennifer Branscome, *Valdosta State University*
Deborah Briihl, *Valdosta State University*
Christopher Brill, *Old Dominion University*
Michael Britt, *Marist College*
Dava Brock, *Arkansas State University-Beebe*
Coral Bruni, *Palomar College*
Carrie Bulger, *Quinnipiac University*
Ann Bullis, *College of Southern Nevada*
Myra Bundy, *Eastern Kentucky University*
Krisanne Bursik, *Suffolk University*

Allison Burton-Chase, *Albany College of Pharmacy and Health Sciences*
Jennifer Butler, *Case Western Reserve University*
Sarah Butler, *College of DuPage*
Gary Capstick, *University of Ottawa*
Kristen Capuozzo, *University of Houston*
Anthony Carboni, *St. Johns River State College*
Jenel Cavazos, *University of Oklahoma*
Nivia Cavic, *Mohawk Valley Community College*
Shawn Charlton, *University of Central Arkansas*
Shao-Ying Cheng, *Austin Community College*
Carl Chica, *Corban College*
Chrisanne Christensen, *Worcester Polytechnic Institute*
Diana Ciesko, *Valencia College*
Benjamin Clark, *Florida State College at Jacksonville*
Judy Colson, *Quinsigamond Community College*
Deborah Conway, *Community College of Allegheny County*
Kristi Cordell-McNulty, *Angelo State University*
Barry Corenblum, *Brandon University*
Cheryl Cotten, *Wor-Wic Community College*
Lauren Coursey, *The University of Texas at Arlington*
Myra Cox, *City Colleges of Chicago-Harold Washington*
Emily Coyle, *Saint Martin's University*
Carmen Culotta, *Wright State University*
Gregory Cutler, *Bay de Noc Community College*
Scott Debb, *Norfolk State University*
Lesli Deichman, *Northeastern Oklahoma A&M College*
Meliksah Demir, *Northern Arizona University*
Van Dempsey, *Rowan-Cabarrus Community College*
Ben Denkinger, *Augsburg College*
Dianne DeSousa, *Prairie State College*
George Diekhoff, *Midwestern State University*
Matthew Diggs, *Collin College*
Rachel Dinero, *Cazenovia College*
Mary Dolan, *University of Redlands*
Julian Dooley, *Cleveland State University*
Stefanie Dorough, *Ave Maria University*
Joanne Dufilho, *Brevard College*
April Dye, *Carson-Newman University*
Traci Elliot, *Alvin Community College*
Mark Evans, *Tarrant County Community College*
Marte Fallshore, *Central Washington University*
Karen Farley, *Cuyahoga Community College*
Rachel Farr, *University of Kentucky*
Adriana Faur Krogstad, *Cleveland State University*
Christine Feeley, *Suffolk County Community College*
Kristin Flora, *Franklin College of Indiana*
Deborah Flynn, *Luzerne County Community College*
Stephanie Foley, *Long Beach City College*
Jonathan Forbey, *Ball State University*
Kenneth Foster, *Texas Woman's University*
Stephen Fox, *University of Hawaii–Maui College*
Lisa Fozio-Thielk, *University of Hawaii–Maui College*
Stacey Frank, *Tri-County Technical College*
Natasha Fratello, *American River College*
Ahni Fritton, *Lesley University*
Perry Fuchs, *The University of Texas at Arlington*
Tamatha Gager, *Collin College*
David Gersh, *Houston Community College*
Bryan Gibson, *Central Michigan University*
Sherry Ginn, *Rowan-Cabarrus Community College*
Jennifer Gonder, *Farmingdale State College*
Leamarie Gordon, *Assumption College*
Sissy Gray, *Black River Technical College*
Jeffery Gray, *Charleston Southern University*
Joe Green, *The Ohio State University at Lima*
Jerry Green, *Tarrant County Community College*
Christine Grela, *McHenry County College*
Monique Guishard, *Bronx Community College*
Nancy Gup, *Perimeter College at Georgia State University*
Justin Hackett, *California University of Pennsylvania*
Kelly Hagan, *Bluegrass Community and Technical College*
Gordon Hammerle, *Adrian College*
Michelle Haney, *Berry College*
Moira Hanna, *Greenville Technical College*
Stephen Hard, *Central Connecticut State University*
Gregory Harris, *Polk State College*
John Haworth, *Chattanooga State Community College*
Katie Heaton, *El Camino College*
Carol Hetzel, *Cardinal Stritch University*
Jennifer Higa-King, *Honolulu Community College*
Larry Hilgert, *Valdosta State University*
Alan Ho, *Ambrose University College*
Brian Hock, *Austin Peay State University*
Gay Holcomb, *Asbury University*
Alex Holdaway, *Ohio University*
Jennifer Holmes, *Lone Star College*
Robin Howse, *Asheville-Buncombe Technical Community College*
Lisa Hoyman, *De Anza College*
Vivian Hsu, *Pennsylvania State University Abington*
Amber Hughes, *University of Southern Indiana*
Thomas Hutcheon, *Bard College*
Robert Ichihana, *Mohawk Valley Community College*
Benetha Jackson, *Angelina College*
Sabra Jacobs, *Big Sandy Community and Technical College*
Catherine Jockell, *University of Houston*
Wendi Johnson, *Texas Woman's University*
Joyce Bateman Jones, *Central Texas College*
Samuel Jones, *Jefferson State Community College*
Kristin Juarez, *Cochise College*
Hillary Kalagher, *Drew University*
Katrina Kardiasmenos, *Bowie State University*
Courtney Kelley, *Cuyahoga Community College*
Yuthika Kim, *Oklahoma City Community College*
Franz Klutschkowski, *North Central Texas College*
Kristie Knows His Gun, *George Fox University*
Robyn Kondrad, *Appalachian State University*
Holly Korta, *Caldwell Community College and Technical Institute*
Nicole Korzetz, *Lee College*
Crystal Kreitler, *Angelo State University*
John Krueger, *San Jacinto College*
Dana Kuehn, *Florida State College at Jacksonville*
Michelle LaBrie, *College of the Canyons*
Rachel Laimon, *Mott Community College*
Terese Landry, *Houston Community College*
Caitlin Lapine, *Nassau Community College*
Elizabeth Laurer, *Owens Community College*
Robert Lawyer, *Delgado Community College*
Melissa Lea, *Millsaps College*
Kristen Leraas, *Columbus State Community College*

Kirsten Li-Barber, *High Point University*
Irv Lichtman, *Houston Community College*
Stephen Lippi, *George Mason University*
Dan Lipscomb, *Collin College*
Brian Littleton, *Mott Community College*
Jacquelyn Loupis, *Rowan-Cabarrus Community College*
Jeff Love, *Pennsylvania State University*
Tammy Mahan, *College of the Canyons*
Eric Mania, *Quinsigamond Community College*
George Martinez, *Eastern Kentucky University*
Robert Martinez, *Northwest Vista College*
Toby Marx, *Union County College*
Bernadette McCarthy, *Kean University*
Kristin McCombs, *Zane State College*
Jason McCoy, *Cape Fear Community College*
Tammy McKenzie, *Brandon University*
Emalinda McSpadden, *Bronx Community College*
Ticily Medley, *Tarrant County Community College*
Helen Meldrum, *Bentley University*
Kathleen Mentink, *Chippewa Valley Technical College*
Mitchell Metzger, *Ashland University*
Kenneth Michniewicz, *Muhlenberg College*
Felix Mireles, *Madison Area Technical College*
Susan Moerschbacher, *Polk State College*
Evelyn Montfort, *College of Central Florida*
Sharon Moore, *University of Louisville*
Robin Morgan, *Indiana University Southeast*
Kim Morris, *Athens Technical College*
Kristie Morris, *Rockland Community College*
Elizabeth Moseley, *Cleveland State Community College*
Darlene Mosley, *Pensacola State College*
Courtney Mozo, *Old Dominion University*
Maria A. Murphy, *Florida Community College at Jacksonville*
Lisa Murphy, *York County Community College*
Robin Musselman, *Lehigh Carbon Community College*
Ronnie Naramore, *Angelina College*
Jeffrey Nicholas, *Bridgewater State University*
Gerald Nissley, *East Texas Baptist University*
Dennis Norman, *Owens Community College*
Nezhat Olia, *Community College of Baltimore County*
Don Osborn, *Bellarmine University*
Krista Paduchowski, *University of Massachusetts Lowell*
Jennifer Pemberton, *Community College of Baltimore County—Catonsville*
Debbie Podwika, *Kankakee Community College*
Sara Powers, *The College of Saint Rose*
Kasey Powers, *College of Staten Island*
Neelam Rattan, *San Jose State University*
Evette Reagan, *Coastline Community College*
Bridget Reigstad, *Normandale Community College*
Joseph Reish, *Tidewater Community College*
Danielle Richards, *College of Southern Nevada*
Brandi Rima, *Bronx Community College*
Mark Rittman, *Cuyahoga Community College*
Vicki Ritts, *St. Louis Community College*
Debra Roberts, *Howard University*
Kelly Rodgers, *Borough of Manhattan Community College*
Jaclyn Ronquillo-Adachi, *Cerritos College*
John Roop, *Columbus State University*
Armida Rosiles, *South Plains College*
Traci Sachteleben, *Southwestern Illinois College*
Brian Saltsman, *Allegheny College*
David Sangster, *Champlain College Lennoxville*
Julie Schatz-Stevens, *Aquinas College*
Laura Schwab-Reese, *Clinton Community College*
Marc Sebrechts, *The Catholic University of America*
Janis Seeley, *Luzerne County Community College*
Jillene Seiver, *Bellevue College*
Aya Shigeto, *Nova Southeastern University*
Mark Sibicky, *Marietta College*
Aisha Siddiqui, *Midwestern State University*
Stacy Simmelink-Johnson, *Walla Walla Community College*
Patty Slaughter, *Anderson University*
Cindy Sledge, *Lone Star College-CyFair*
Morgan Slusher, *Community College of Baltimore County*
Wallace Smith, *Union County College*
Joseph Sonsalla, *Chippewa Valley Technical College*
Jonathan Sparks, *Vance-Granville Community College*
Jason Spiegelman, *Community College of Baltimore County*
Steven St. John, *Rollins College*
Betty Stack, *Rowan-Cabarrus Community College*
Caroline Stanley, *Bridgewater State University*
Emily Stark, *Minnesota State University, Mankato*
Brent Steffens, *Grand Valley State University*
Stephen Stelzner, *College of Saint Benedict*
Cari Stevenson, *Kankakee Community College*
Jutta Street, *Campbell University*
Eva Szeli, *Arizona State University*
Anita P. Tam, *Greenville Technical College*
Gary Taylor, *Campbell University*
Lisa Taylor, *Palomar College*
Kristi Teed Thoreson, *Nicolet Area Technical College*
Brian Thomas, *Baldwin Wallace University*
Geneene Thompson, *Greenville Technical College*
Maura Tighe-Stickles, *Quinsigamond Community College*
Stacey Todaro, *Adrian College*
David Tom, *Columbus State Community College*
Sarah Trost, *Cardinal Stritch University*
Sharmin Tunguz, *DePauw University*
Margot Underwood, *Joliet Junior College*
Glen Valdez, *Grand Valley State University*
Michael Vandehey, *Midwestern State University*
Donald Varakin, *Eastern Kentucky University*
Joseph Vielbig, *Arizona Western College*
Kevin Volkan, *California State University, Channel Islands*
T. Joel Wade, *Bucknell University*
Benjamin Wallace, *Cleveland State University*
Shawn Ward, *Le Moyne College*
David Wasieleski, *Valdosta State University*
Diane Webber, *Curry College*
Dessiree Weeks, *Central Carolina Technical College*
Eric Weiser, *Curry College*
Mark Whatley, *Valdosta State University*
Chris Whelan, *College of Southern Nevada*
Lawrence White, *Beloit College*
Brian Wiley, *Florida State College at Jacksonville*
Khara Williams, *University of Southern Indiana*
Jessica Williams, *Barstow College*
Marc Wolpoff, *Riverside College*
Larolyn Zylicz, *Cape Fear Community College*

Student Preface

Welcome to psychology! More accurately, welcome to your psychology!

To help you succeed in this course, you'll find lots of tools and strategies throughout the pages of *My Psychology*. Here are a few specific suggestions for success in this course (and perhaps other courses as well) to keep in mind from the beginning. All of these are based on research that is explained and referenced in Chapter 1 or 5:

- Show up to class. Students who attend class, even when attendance is not mandatory, get better grades.
- When studying for a test, it is better to start early and space your study sessions with some time between them than it is to study by cramming.
- Get plenty of sleep and exercise, and eat healthy. These healthy habits set the stage for academic success.
- Believe in your ability to succeed in this class. Self-efficacy of this kind, specifically applied to this class, makes it more likely that you will actually achieve that success.
- Set a specific goal for yourself from the outset. Aiming for a specific letter grade or percentage often produces better results than a less-focused effort toward success.
- Minimize multitasking. Even among people who think they are good at it, doing multiple things at once usually results in lower levels of performance on each thing.
- Make the material as personally meaningful as you can. If it's relevant to your life, it's easier to remember.

That last point—making the material as personally meaningful as you can—is something that *My Psychology* prioritizes. Since I taught my first Intro Psych class over 20 years ago, I have always tried to make connections between the textbook's presentation of psychology and my students' experience of psychology in their own personal lives. After all, psychology is already woven into your life. Its concepts are the ideas and behaviors that explain what you do and why you do it (perhaps more than any other class you'll take in college). That's why I wrote a textbook that maximizes your personal connection to the science of psychology: *My Psychology*.

As you'll see, this book includes lots of features to maximize that connection, to engage you with the material in a way that recognizes the experiences you've had and the way you live your life. Here's a preview of those features—categorized as technology (including smartphones); applications; diversity coverage; and learning tools—that can serve as a guide for how to get the most out of the book:

Technology

My Psychology meets you where you live—on your smartphones and computers. As a textbook for the contemporary college student, *My Psychology* recognizes not only what you experience in your daily lives, but also how you experience those things. You can access all of these technological features on your smartphone or computer, as well as via LaunchPad at launchpadworks.com

Chapter Apps Most of you have smartphones, and if you do, you probably use apps all the time. I do, and along the way I have noticed that quite a few apps do a great job illustrating important psychology concepts. So, in each chapter, I provide two or three Chapter Apps, each placed near the psychological concept it illustrates. You can download each app—for free—on your smartphone. (You can also access each app on your computer and through LaunchPad.)

CHAPTER APP 13.2

Prosocial Behavior/Altruism

Waze

Preview one of the links and consider the following questions.

WEBSITE: http://tiny.cc/1vi7jy

ANDROID: http://tiny.cc/fe92iy

IPHONE: http://tiny.cc/3682iy

VIDEO DEMO: http://tiny.cc/chapterapps

There are lots of apps to help you drive from Point A to Point B, but Waze is unique among them. As its Web site describes, Waze is "community-based," which means that drivers share info about the roads with each other. For example, Waze users can alert each other to the specific locations of police cars, accidents, traffic jams, cars on the shoulder, and even cheap gas stations they encounter. The Web site explains that Waze users are "outsmarting traffic, together" by getting a "heads-up from a few million of your friends on the road."

How does it APPly to your daily life?
Would you use an app like Waze? If so, would you share road information with other drivers, or only use the road information they shared with you?

How does it APPly to your understanding of psychology?
Which explanation of *prosocial behavior* (or *altruism*) best explains the decision by a Waze user to voluntarily give a heads-up to other drivers without any external reward (money, etc.)?

My Take Videos In my own classes, students' own personal stories are among the most memorable moments, especially when those stories are on-target examples of a key concept. My Take Videos, which you'll see two or three times per chapter, are exactly that—real Intro Psych students sharing their own stories, or takes, regarding a psychology concept. These are brief, professionally made videos, created exclusively for this textbook in which students like you reveal their own connections to psychology, which may resemble your own quite closely.

MY TAKE VIDEO 4.2

Circadian Rhythm

"The last job I worked, I worked overnight, and so that kind of messed up my circadian rhythm..."

YOUTUBE: http://tiny.cc/mytake
LAUNCHPAD: launchpadworks.com

Show Me More links The Internet is full of wonderful videos, articles, and Web sites that give you the chance to delve deeper and learn even more about many important psychology concepts. Show Me More links appear at the end of each chapter to guide you toward them. This bonus material includes news clips and articles, TED Talks, documentary footage, Web sites that invite interaction, and more. Like Chapter Apps and My Take Videos, Show Me More links are accessible with your smartphone or on your computer through LaunchPad.

SHOW ME MORE

6.1 Classical Conditioning

launchpadworks.com LaunchPad macmillan learning

This video offers some good examples and explanations of classical conditioning.

Applications

The applications in every chapter highlight the parallels between your experiences and the science of psychology. These applied features complement the coverage within each chapter by providing you with distinct, fresh ways of understanding psychological concepts and making them personally relevant.

From Research to Real Life We zoom in on a particular area within psychology and explain how research on that topic directly applies to your real life.

FROM RESEARCH TO REAL LIFE

Does Money Buy Happiness?

Many college students list earning potential as one of the primary reasons they are seeking a college degree. But does money necessarily equal happiness? This question produces mixed results (Lucas & Diener, 2008; Diener & Biswas-Diener, 2002). People from wealthier countries tend to be happier than people from poorer countries. However, when a country becomes richer, those happiness ratings don't increase much. Also, there is a lot of individual variability surrounding the connection between wealth and well-being. Trends suggest that people in rich countries are happier than people in poor countries, but there are plenty of unhappy rich people and plenty of happy poor people around the world.

Perhaps the most interesting finding is that the connection between money and happiness is strongest for people on the border of meeting their basic needs (Biswas-Diener & Diener, 2001; Diener et al., 1993). If more money means the difference between food and hunger, or between home and homelessness, or between medical care and sickness, having it produces much more happiness. But if your basic needs like food, shelter, safety, and medical care are met, getting more money won't produce the same increase in happiness. Actually, if you are well-off, a rise in income won't produce any increase in your happiness if your material desires rise even faster (Diener & Biswas-Diener, 2002). In that way, happiness is less about your money and more about the comparison between your money and the stuff you want to buy with it. It is also important to point out that even when money does affect happiness, it is just one of many factors. Good relationships with family and friends, a good marriage, and a healthy spiritual life are among many other factors that play a role (Suh et al., 1998; Diener & Diener, 2009; Diener et al., 1993; Ellison, 1991; Lucas et al., 2003).

Life Hacks Life hacks are quick hits—just a sentence or two to offer a recommendation for how to live your life according to psychology research. They appear as brightly colored little boxes on the page, and they draw a direct line between the conclusions of psychological studies and your own attempts to live happier, more productive lives.

LIFE HACK 8.3

If you want to feel happier, do something kind for someone else, or think about acts of kindness you've already done.

(Otake et al., 2006; Pressman et al., 2015; Lyubomirsky & Layous, 2013)

It's Like... You already have a wealth of knowledge and understanding of the world around you. Sometimes, a psychology concept runs parallel to something you already know. It's Like..., which appears once per chapter, points out those parallels.

IT'S LIKE...

Top-Down Processing Is Like Autocomplete

When you type the first few letters of a text into your phone, the phone's autocomplete (or autofill) feature offers to complete the word for you. The same thing happens when you google something—your computer guesses the rest of the word or phrase you might be typing. It is as if it knows what to expect, based on what you have typed in the past. Your brain uses top-down processing much like your devices use this autocomplete feature. Your brain knows what you might be sensing, based on what you have sensed in the past.

Of course, neither autocomplete nor top-down processing can function alone. Your phone or computer combines its top-down expectations with the bottom-up processing of the first few letters you actually type in, and your brain combines its top-down expectations with the first few milliseconds of a sound sent to your ear (Carlson, 2010). The main point here is that it is not bottom-up processing alone that creates your sensation (or completes the line you type into your device), but a combination of that bottom-up processing with the top-down processing that it triggers.

There is one important distinction between the way your devices and your brain do top-down processing: your phone gives you the *option* to autocomplete your words and phrases, but your brain doesn't always do that. Sometimes, your brain acts like an autocomplete feature with too much power, jumping to a conclusion about what you're sensing before you've had a chance to fully sense it. For example, if you're expecting a delivery from UPS, your brain might use "autocomplete" to convert a quick glance out the front window at a person in a brown shirt to the conclusion that your delivery is here. But that might just be someone who happens to be wearing a brown shirt walking by, not the UPS delivery person. That is the double-edged sword of top-down processing—it offers shortcuts that can be helpful when accurate, but problematic when premature. ●

Watching Psychology Lots of TV shows and movies directly relate to psychology concepts. Watching Psychology explores these on-screen experiences.

WATCHING PSYCHOLOGY

Convergent and Divergent Thinking on *Family Feud*

The beginning of each round on *Family Feud*, when a member of each family walks up front and puts a hand on the buzzer, is all about convergent thinking. The goal, after all, is to guess the most common answer provided in a survey of 100 people.

After one contestant wins that face-off, the host moves down the line of that family, posing the same question to each one. Eventually, most of the answers on the board have been uncovered, but it is difficult to get those last few. That is when the contestants need to get creative and use divergent thinking. They need to think past the first several answers that come to mind, and come up with that less obvious answer hiding near the bottom of the board. That is what the other family is doing as they huddle up, hoping for a chance to steal—brainstorming possible answers beyond the ones already on the board.

For example, consider this *Family Feud* question: Name a food that goes well with peanut butter. Convergent thinking leads you right away to the obvious #1 answer: jelly. Then it starts getting tougher, especially if the list of top answers on the board is long. You may have to think a bit more divergently to come up with bread or crackers, then even more divergently to come up with honey or chocolate, and then very divergently to come up with celery or apples. That divergent thinking—moving past the first and most obvious answer to other answers that may work—is what creativity is all about. ●

Current Controversy In many areas of psychology, the experts (and their research results) don't agree. In Current Controversy, we examine these areas, with special emphasis on how the controversy might affect your life or the lives of people you know.

CURRENT CONTROVERSY

Should High School Start Later in the Day?

Everybody knows that teenagers like to stay up later and wake up later than they did when they were younger. You probably remember that shift happening yourself, perhaps in middle school but almost certainly by high school. It is not just a trend or a U.S. thing. Teens show this pattern around the world: South America, Europe, Australia, Asia, and Africa (Yang et al., 2005; Andrade & Menna-Baretto, 2002; Gibson et al., 2006; Saarenpaa-Heikkila et al., 1995; Thorleifsdottir et al., 2002; Dorofaeff & Denny, 2006; Reid et al., 2002). There is even some evidence that other mammals, including monkeys, rats, and mice, exhibit the same circadian shift around the same point in their life span (Hagenauer et al., 2009). The reasons for this shift are not entirely clear, but puberty has a lot to do with it (Wolfson & O'Malley, 2012). Research on sixth-grade girls found that those who started puberty earlier had a stronger preference for later bedtimes and wake-up times (Carskadon et al., 1993, 2004).

Whatever the cause of this push toward later bedtimes in teens, it's a terrible match for early-morning start times in high school (Carskadon & Tarokh, 2013). According to researchers, high schoolers are simply "expected to function at school at a time when their bodies were meant to sleep" (Wolfson & Richards, 2011, p. 269). School performance isn't the only undesirable outcome from this situation. So are car crashes. One study compared accident rates in two similar neighboring high schools in Virginia—one in Virginia Beach and the other in Chesapeake. Over a 2-year stretch, the accident rate for teen drivers in Virginia Beach, where school starts 75–80 minutes earlier, was about 35% higher than in Chesapeake (Vorona et al., 2011). Another study found that teen accident rates dropped 16% in the year after a school district pushed back its high school start times an hour (Danner & Phillips, 2008).

Delayed start times have produced other positive results too, including better attendance, grades, and graduation rates (Wahlstrom, 2002a; Wolfson et al., 2007). But districts typically run into strong opposition when they suggest a shift to a later high school day. Arguments against the later start include complications with the scheduling of buses, interference with after-school sports, lack of child care for younger kids if they arrive home before their high school–age siblings, and the mistaken parental belief that teens would go to sleep an hour later if they had a later start time (Kirby et al., 2011; Wolfson et al., 2007; Owens et al., 2010; Wahlstrom, 2002b; Wolfson & Carskadon, 2005). Hopefully, as awareness of the sleep and safety issue continues to grow, more districts will reconsider their schedules. ●

Diversity Coverage

Diversity is an important part of psychology and all of its subfields. Diversity is also an important part of your life and all its aspects.

Diversity Matters Dozens of times throughout the book, diversity takes center stage. (Actually, it takes center stage most prominently in the Diversity in Psychology chapter, which is dedicated entirely to the topic.) When it does take the stage, a Diversity Matters flag calls your attention to it. Often, diversity is characterized by ethnicity or race, but it takes many other forms too, including age, gender, sexual orientation, socioeconomic status, religion, and more. As an example, a Diversity Matters flag in the Social Psychology chapter highlights the ways that individualism and collectivism can influence conformity to social norms. Diversity Matters flags in the Motivation and Emotion chapter highlight coverage of the influence that gender and age can have on motivation.

A full chapter dedicated to diversity. The title of Chapter 10—Diversity in Psychology: Multiculturalism, Gender and Sexuality—indicates its inclusive focus. The chapter was developed in consultation with experts in the field and begins by recognizing many forms of diversity with which you live, including race, ethnicity, language, religion, age, sexual orientation, education, income, and big cities versus small towns. It then covers a variety of concepts to help you appreciate diversity in a broad sense, including how cultures can be defined, diversity within groups (dynamic sizing), acculturation, cultural intelligence, and microaggressions. The chapter also offers detailed coverage of the topics of gender and sexuality, including discussion of the concepts of cisgender, transgender, and transition.

Learning Tools

My Psychology is packed with learning tools that will maximize your engagement with and understanding of the science of psychology. These learning tools make use of personal connections to the material to boost memory and comprehension.

Three-step synced pedagogical system. As a learning strategy designed to boost your understanding of the material, the sections of each chapter feature a three-step method for previewing, questioning, and confirming what you learn. Each section starts with a "You Will Learn" list—essentially a preview of major points the section will cover. At the end of that section, you'll see a corresponding list of questions, one for each item on the list ("Check Your Learning"). At the end of the chapter, in the Chapter Summary, all of those questions are answered. In all three places, a synchronized numbering system keeps you organized, so you know which preview points go with which question and which answers. Of course, this system doesn't cover every detail—there's no shortcut for a thorough reading the full chapter—but it does highlight the core knowledge.

YOU WILL LEARN:

1.1 what psychology is.

1.2 what psychology is *not*.

CHECK YOUR LEARNING:

1.1 What is psychology?

1.2 What are the primary differences between psychology and psychiatry?

CHAPTER SUMMARY

What Is Psychology?

1.1 Psychology is the scientific study of behavior and mental processes, which means that psychology focuses on *both* our outer actions *and* our inner experiences.

1.2 Psychology is not just therapy, not exclusively about people with mental disorders, not all about Sigmund Freud, not psychiatry, and not just a bunch of ideas with no research to back them up.

What's Your Take? At the end of each chapter, you'll encounter questions that invite you to offer your perspective or your experience with a particular concept. For example, you'll be asked if your pets have ever demonstrated the kinds of conditioning that you'll read about when we cover learning. You'll be asked if your experience as a new college student parallels the experience that some psychologists have used with babies to test their attachment to their parents and their reaction to new situations.

WHAT'S YOUR TAKE?

1. When you think about your own culture, your first thought may be your ethnicity or your race. But there may be many other cultural variables that are at least as important. As a clinical psychologist, I have learned from some of my own clients that certain cultural characteristics other than ethnicity or race were at the core of their identities. For one woman, it was her religion (she was a Modern Orthodox Jew); for another, it was his sexual orientation (he was gay); for another, it was her geographical

2. I have noticed a strong positive correlation in my own life: when I do more laundry, I'm in a better mood. I first noticed this correlation in college, when I tended to feel a bit more upbeat during weeks when I found myself in the laundry room more than once and a bit more down on weeks when the pile of dirty laundry didn't grow so fast. What's up with that? Could it be that washing, drying, and folding *caused* my good mood? Or that my good mood *caused* me to do more laundry? Neither of those made much sense. Eventually,

An example-rich approach. Simply put, the book has *lots* of examples designed to relate to your day-to-day life. The goal is for these examples to resonate with you by connecting to your real world.

Big, bold print. You've seen many textbooks in which the key terms are printed in bold. The problem in many Intro Psych textbooks is that each chapter can have a long list of key terms—long enough to make it difficult for you to know which of them are most important. *My Psychology* solves this problem by breaking key terms into two tiers, signified by **bold print** and **big, bold print**. Big, bold print signifies the key terms that are the most crucial to your learning.

Student dialogue questions. I teach Intro Psych, so I know what kinds of questions students often ask. I embedded many of them into the book itself. You'll see them—they feature an icon of a student with a raised hand, speaking in a different, colored font—and some of them may accurately anticipate questions that occurred to you as you were reading. Each of these questions is followed by a direct answer, enabling you to understand confusing or challenging concepts more clearly by means of a greater level of interaction with the material.

> I know some very shy people, and this social anxiety disorder diagnosis sounds like it would fit them pretty well. What's the difference between social anxiety disorder and extreme shyness?

With the help of these many features focusing technology, application, diversity, and learning tools, *My Psychology* helps you learn the science of psychology by helping you connect the material to your own life. It invites you into our rich field and makes you feel welcome by demonstrating how personally relatable, applicable, and comprehensible psychology can be.

1 The Science of Psychology

visualspace/Getty Images

This may be your first psychology course,

but you've been a student of psychology—what people do and why they do it—since the day you were born.

As a baby, you focused your psychological research on the effects of crying. Specifically, you wondered, if I cry when I'm hungry, will someone feed me? Every day, you ran experiments on this question, keeping track of the results in your head, until eventually you had enough data to draw a conclusion about the connection between crying and food. You then moved on to more sophisticated experiments in which you explored what happened when you cried around certain people, at certain times, and in certain places.

As a toddler, your research interests shifted toward toys. Specifically, you questioned, what happens when one kid yanks a toy out of another kid's hands? The scene played out before your eyes at your second birthday party, and the outcome was clear: the victim shrieks and the toy bandit gets a scolding from a parent. You took note of this result, but wondered, Is that the outcome every time? Might the result change under different circumstances—another toy, another kid, another place, another parent?

In middle school and high school, your research focus expanded to academic performance. You asked, what's the relationship between the time I spend on Twitter the night before a test and the grade I get? You manipulated Twitter time—some nights you stayed away from it completely, some nights you tweeted for hours—and noticed a strong pattern: more Twitter time usually meant lower grades. But you wondered, did time spent tweeting actually *cause* the lower grades, or were there other factors? For example, could it be that tweeting time takes away from sleeping time, and lack of sleep is what really caused the lower test scores?

As a college student, your psychology research continues. With this course, you take an important step toward becoming an expert in the field. Beginning with this chapter, you will learn the vocabulary of psychology. You will learn what psychologists specialize in, how they conduct research, and how they apply their knowledge to help real people.

You will learn how the field of psychology got its start, how it evolved, and where it is now. Together with the later chapters, this information will equip you to continue your work as a psychologist, whether amateur or professional, through the course of your life.

CHAPTER OUTLINE

What Is Psychology?

YOU WILL LEARN:

1.1 what psychology is.

1.2 what psychology is *not*.

1.3 what big questions underlie much of the field of psychology.

As we embark on this journey into the vast world of psychology, we'll explore its big questions and clear up some common misunderstandings about the field. Let's start with a clear definition of the word.

Defining Psychology

Psychology is the scientific study of behavior and mental processes. The *and* in that definition is important: it means that psychology focuses on *both* our outer actions and our inner experiences. Our behavior—what we do outwardly—tends to be observable and easy to measure. Our mental processes—the thoughts, feelings, and other experiences that occur inside our mind—tend not to be so observable or easy to measure. For psychologists, both topics deserve attention.

As an example, consider Jessica, a young woman who struggled with but is now overcoming *bulimia nervosa*, an eating disorder we'll cover more in the chapter on disorders. Whether psychologists are treating Jessica or studying her disorder, they are interested in both her behavior and her mental processes. Psychologists want to know about Jessica's observable behaviors as she improves: for example, the increased frequency of healthy meals and snacks and the decreased frequency of binges and purges. Psychologists also want to know what mental processes might trigger those behaviors: positive feelings Jessica has about her body, reasonable thoughts about the influence of her weight on her self-worth, and so on. Considering only her behavior or only her mental processes would produce an incomplete understanding of Jessica.

Another important word in the definition of psychology is *scientific*. Psychologists don't just speculate about behavior and mental processes, accepting guesses and gut feelings as the truth. Instead, we measure the merit of those ideas by applying the *scientific method*. Psychologists put their ideas to the test, share the results, and—together with all the other psychologists doing similar work—accumulate knowledge about behavior and mental processes. There is much more on the scientific method in psychology coming up later in this chapter.

Psychology, as the scientific study of behavior *and* mental processes, focuses on both what we do and why we do it. Consider bulimia, an eating disorder with which many people, including comedian Margaret Cho and actor Russell Brand, have struggled. In the treatment of bulimia, psychologists are interested in improvements in eating behavior *and* improvements in the thoughts that underlie those behaviors. (top) Frederick M. Brown/Getty Images; (bottom) Mark Cuthbert/Getty Images

What Psychology Is *Not*

To accurately understand what psychology *is*, it's essential to understand what psychology is *not*. The portrayal of psychology in the media—in movies, on TV shows, in the news—can actually be quite misleading. So let's correct some misconceptions that you may have about psychology.

Psychology is *not* just therapy. Check the table of contents of this psychology textbook: 15 chapters but just one on therapy. Of course, many psychologists do therapy, but many do not. In fact, about one-third of psychologists have specializations that have nothing to do with therapy or any other kind of helping services. Of the two-thirds who become experts in therapy, some teach, supervise, or study it rather than practice it (Norcross et al., 2005; Norcross & Karpiak, 2012). We'll look at specializations in psychology later in this chapter, but for now, the point is that psychology covers much more than just therapy.

On a related note, psychology is *not* exclusively about people with mental disorders. Most of the research that psychologists do focuses on normal processes that occur in all of us: how we think, learn, develop, remember, speak, and interact, among other everyday activities. Again, check this textbook's table of contents: just a single chapter on psychological disorders. So despite the fact that almost every time a psychologist appears in a television show or movie, he or she is working with a mentally ill person—often helping the police track down a crazed killer or doing therapy with

severely disturbed people—that portrayal of psychologists is more Hollywood than reality (Young, 2012; Gharaibeh, 2005; Gabbard, 2001).

Psychology is also *not* all about Sigmund Freud. Freud may be the first name that pops up for many people when they think about psychology, but that's way out of date. Yes, there was a time when Freud's ideas dominated the field, but that time—the early 1900s, basically—is long gone (Wegenek et al., 2010). Today, only a small minority of psychologists—fewer than 10%—practice what Freud preached (Stanovich, 2013). Of course, it would be an overstatement to call Freud irrelevant. He was, after all, *the* central figure of psychology for decades, and his therapy has influenced many newer treatments that are still practiced today. But psychology today is much more varied, and Freud's voice is now just one of many.

Psychology is also *not* **psychiatry**, the medical specialization focusing on the brain and its disorders. The two words sound the same, and many people mistakenly lump the two professions together, but there are important distinctions (Balon et al., 2004; Jorm et al., 1997). Psych*iatrists* are medical doctors. They go to medical school and earn MD degrees to become physicians. In fact, they do much of their medical training alongside med students on their way to becoming other kinds of physicians—pediatricians, obstetrician–gynecologists, dermatologists, cardiologists—before they specialize in psychiatry. Like the rest of these physicians, psychiatrists prescribe medication.

Psych*ologists* are different kinds of doctors. They are not medical doctors. Their graduate training is focused on behavior and mental processes, not on the physical and biological systems emphasized in medical school. Psychologists earn PhD or PsyD degrees, not MDs. Psychologists generally don't prescribe medication (Current Controversy box). Instead, psychologists use talk therapies and other forms of behavioral intervention to help clients (DeLeon et al., 2011; Harris, 2011; Burns et al., 2008). The training of psychologists includes more emphasis on research methods than does

psychology
The scientific study of behavior and mental processes.

psychiatry
The medical specialization that focuses on the brain and its disorders.

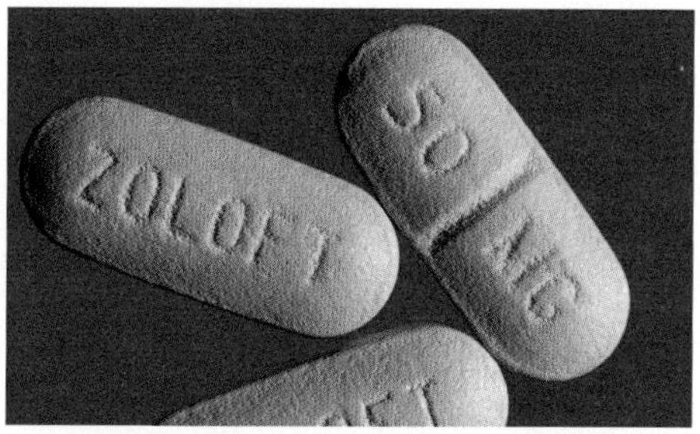

Many people confuse psychologists with psychiatrists. Psychiatrists, because of their medical training, prescribe drugs such as Zoloft. Psychologists rely instead on talk therapy and other nondrug strategies to help their clients. Some people with disorders received help from both psychiatrists and psychologists. Lessin Leonard/Science Source/Getty Images

CURRENT CONTROVERSY

Should Psychologists Prescribe Medication?

Traditionally, a primary distinction between psychiatrists and psychologists was that psychiatrists prescribed medication but psychologists did not (Balon et al., 2004). However, a movement within psychology has blurred that distinction a bit, and it may get blurrier in the near future.

The movement started in the 1980s, when a handful of practicing psychologists argued that with extra training they should be allowed to prescribe medications to their clients. Their movement has gained momentum over the past few decades, and many states considered legislation that specify exactly what a psychologist would have to do to earn the right to prescribe. So far, just a few states, including New Mexico, Louisiana, and Illinois, have approved such legislation. Some states have rejected similar legislation, and the debate continues in others (Sammons, 2011).

Those who argue that psychologists *should* be allowed to prescribe medication focus on a few key points:

- In many states, particularly in rural areas, there's a shortage of psychiatrists (Long, 2005).
- Most psychiatric medications (e.g., Prozac, Xanax, and Zoloft) are prescribed not by psychiatrists but by primary care doctors and pediatricians (Cummings, 2007). Those kinds of physicians actually don't receive much specialized training in mental health issues. Psychologists could gain more training than those physicians and provide more effective prescriptions.
- There are already other professions whose members are not physicians but who can prescribe medication, including dentists, podiatrists, optometrists, and advance practice nurses.
- Seeing a psychologist for both therapy and medication is more convenient for clients than seeing a psychologist for therapy and a medical doctor for medication.

Those who say that psychologists *should not* be allowed to prescribe medication focus their arguments on a few key points:

- It isn't clear how much extra training psychologists would need to be qualified to prescribe. Some argue that it's necessary to go all the way through medical school—in addition to getting a doctoral degree in psychology (Griffiths, 2001; Robiner et al., 2002). Others say that less training is enough (Resnick & Norcross, 2002). Even a compromise would be a time-consuming and expensive undertaking for psychologists.
- It isn't clear that all psychologists would become prescribers. If it's optional, then the general public might get confused about what psychologists do.
- There is a concern that prescriptions could phase out talk therapy if psychologists could prescribe. Psychologists would be able to see more clients per hour for med checks than for therapy, thereby making more money. If so, that might be a disservice to some clients (McGrath, 2004).

The controversy about prescription privileges for psychologists continues today. ⬢

"The title of my science project is 'My Little Brother: Nature or Nurture.'"

The New Yorker Collection, Michael Shaw from cartoonbank.com.

the training of psychiatrists, which results in a higher percentage of psychologists than psychiatrists pursuing careers in research (Abrams et al., 2003).

Perhaps most important, psychology is *not* just a bunch of ideas with nothing to back them up. Too often, psychology is wrongly associated with unsupported guesswork and unproven opinions—from psychics who claim to know people's innermost thoughts and feelings via extrasensory perception (ESP) to the Dr. Phils of the world, who claim to understand people based on a 3-minute TV interview in front of a live studio audience. Instead, the enduring ideas in psychology are backed up by science. In fact, the scientific method is the cornerstone of psychology, and it transforms ideas from speculation to scholarship.

Psychology's Big Questions

Psychology is a huge field of study, with researchers taking it in many directions. There is no single overarching question that captures psychology, but a few big questions underlie the topics psychologists explore most.

Nature or Nurture? Were you born that way, or were there factors in your upbringing that made you the person you are? Is your behavior genetic, stemming from the DNA you inherited from your biological parents, or is it environmental, stemming from the experiences you've had over the years? These questions drive research in many areas of psychology.

For example, psychologists who study language have long asked whether our ability to speak is inborn or learned through observation and reinforcement (Saxton, 2010; Oliver & Plomin, 2007; Plomin & Dale, 2000). Similarly, psychologists who study psychological disorders have conducted thousands of studies to determine the extent to which genes or environment contribute to schizophrenia, depression, borderline personality disorder, and almost every other kind of mental illness (Sullivan et al., 2012; McClellan & King, 2010; Keller & Miller, 2006). These studies often involve adopted children or twins separated at birth, whose unique childhood circumstances allow us to untangle nature from nurture. Of course, the answer always involves an interaction of both nature and nurture—a phenomenon we will explore in more detail in a later chapter (Rutter, 2006; Wermter et al., 2010).

Change or Stability? To what extent do you change over time? To what extent do you remain the same? When you change, how does it happen—slowly and surely or in abrupt spurts? Many specializations in psychology focus on questions like these. For example, developmental psychologists explore how we change from birth through old age in many ways: how we reason, how we interact, and how our morals influence our decisions at every age (Piaget, 1954, 1983; Kesselring, 2009; Kohlberg, 1984; Moshman, 2009; Erikson, 1950, 1959). Personality psychologists, who study the traits that define us, also focus on change versus stability—examining the extent to which our personality changes over time or stays the same (Caspi et al., 2003; Nave et al., 2010).

Universal or Unique? When psychological researchers come to a conclusion, for whom is it true? Do some psychological truths apply universally? Or are such truths unique to certain people in certain places at certain times? Consider emotions. When psychologists study them, one of their primary questions has been whether there are basic emotions—and basic facial expressions to go along with them—that are similar around the globe, as opposed to specific emotions that occur only in certain cultures (Ekman, 2003; Ekman & Cordaro, 2011; Kayyal & Russell, 2013; Russell, 1994). Similarly, questions of culture occur when researchers evaluate how beneficial a particular form of psychotherapy is. Most often, the people included in such studies are Americans who are not members of a minority. So the question is, if it works for some people, will it also work for U.S. minorities or people in other countries (Bernal et al., 2009; Castro et al., 2010; Griner & Smith, 2006)?

DIVERSITY MATTERS

CHECK YOUR LEARNING:

1.1 What is psychology?

1.2 What are the primary differences between psychology and psychiatry?

1.3 What are the three big questions that underlie the field of psychology?

Psychology's Many Subfields

YOU WILL LEARN:

1.4 about the size and breadth of the field of psychology.

1.5 how applied and basic research specializations differ.

1.6 about specific applied specializations within psychology, such as clinical psychology, counseling psychology, and industrial/organizational psychology.

1.7 about specific basic research specializations within psychology, such as personality psychology, developmental psychology, and social psychology.

As a profession, psychology is immense and diverse (Norcross, Kohout, & Wicherski, 2005). In 2010, over 5100 people earned a doctoral degree in psychology. About 75% were female, and about 25% were members of an ethnic minority group—both big increases from just a decade before (Kohout & Pate, 2013). Tens of thousands of people belong to the American Psychological Association (APA), the country's largest organization of psychologists (American Psychological Association, 2014). APA includes 54 divisions, each of which focuses on a particular topic within psychology. That large number of divisions shows you the tremendous breadth of topics contained within psychology—from child and adolescent psychology to media psychology, from the psychology of women to the psychology of religion and spirituality, from exercise and sport psychology to military psychology, and so many more.

The major specializations in psychology can be divided into two big categories: *applied* specializations and *basic research* specializations. Let's consider both, along with specific examples of each.

Applied Specializations

Applied psychology specializations are areas in which psychologists apply their expertise to real-world problems. These are the psychologists who *practice*. In other words, they use their knowledge of mind and behavior to enhance some important aspect of their clients' lives. They work in hospitals, clinics, schools, companies, agencies, private practices, and other organizations.

Before we consider specific types of applied psychologists, it is important to note that not *all* of them practice, at least not full time. A few teach or conduct research *about* practicing, often as professors in university psychology departments (Prinstein et al., 2013). After all, someone has to train the next generation of applied psychologists and do research on the techniques they will use. Take me, for example: I'm a psychologist with an applied specialization (clinical). I practice (I see clients in private practice), and I also work as a professor teaching and doing research related to clinical psychology.

Clinical Psychology. **Clinical psychology** is an applied specialization in which psychologists focus on psychological disorders. Clinical psychologists do many professional activities, but psychotherapy is at the top of the list. About three-quarters of this therapy is done with individual clients and the rest with groups, families, or couples. Clinical psychologists also do psychological assessment, including intelligence tests and personality tests, often to diagnose people with psychological disorders. Clinical psychologists work in lots of settings, including hospitals, clinics, and mental health agencies, but private practice is the most common (Norcross, Karpiak, & Santoro, 2005). As illustrated in **Figure 1.1**, clinical psychology is by far the most popular specialization in psychology.

Counseling Psychology. **Counseling psychology** is an applied specialization in which psychologists focus on improving the functioning of people who are struggling through difficult times in their lives.

applied psychology specializations
Areas in which psychologists apply their expertise to real-world problems, using their knowledge of mind and behavior to enhance some important aspect of their clients' lives.

clinical psychology
An applied specialization in which psychologists focus on psychological disorders.

counseling psychology
An applied specialization in which psychologists focus on improving the functioning of people who are struggling through difficult times in their lives.

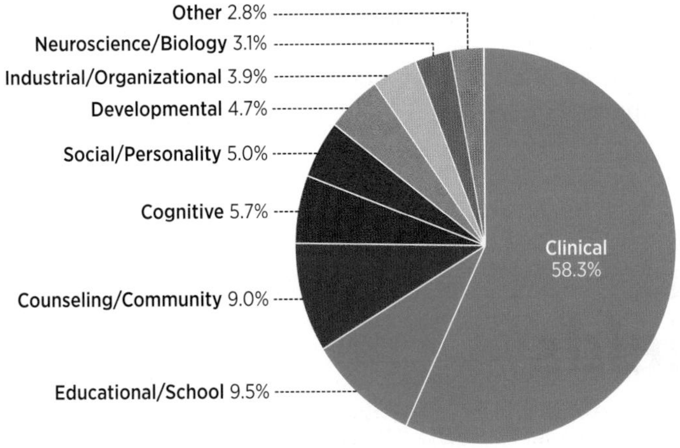

FIGURE 1.1 Doctoral Degrees in Psychology. Psychology contains many specializations. Basic research specializations focus on conducting investigations, while applied specializations like clinical psychology (the largest specialization) apply their expertise to real-world problems.

Counseling psychology sounds a lot like clinical psychology. What's the difference?

You're right about the overlap: counseling psychologists are similar to clinical psychologists. They both do psychotherapy, often in private practice settings, with individuals, groups, families, and couples (Norcross, 2000). Decades ago, there was a noticeable difference between counseling psychologists and clinical psychologists. Clinical psychologists saw people with more serious, diagnosable problems, while counseling psychologists saw people who generally functioned quite well but were going through a rough patch in their lives. To help you remember: *clinical* comes from the same root as *recline*, as in a patient so impaired that he or she needs bedside care; *counseling* comes from the same root as *consult*, as in a person who just needs guidance or advice (Roger & Stone, 2014).

That distinction is still true to some extent, but the two specializations have drifted toward each other and now share quite a bit of professional territory (Gaddy et al., 1995). In many agencies—university counseling centers and mental health clinics, for example—counseling psychologists and clinical psychologists work side by side, serving the same clients. So the old distinction, in which clinical psychologists focused on more severe problems and counseling psychologists focused on milder problems, is not quite as true as it once was. Counseling psychologists are still less likely to seek jobs in places like inpatient psychiatric units, where the clients are likely to have relatively debilitating problems. Another distinction is that counseling psychologists tend to do more career counseling and vocational (job) counseling than clinical psychologists (Norcross & Sayette, 2012).

Industrial/Organizational Psychology. **Industrial/organizational (I/O) psychology** is an applied specialization focused on the workplace. Some I/O psychologists concentrate on issues of personnel—helping companies hire the right people, place them in jobs that fit their abilities, and train them to maximize their performance. Other I/O psychologists focus on the organization as a whole—its management structure, leadership style, work environment (including minimization of stress, harassment, and discrimination), and development over time. I/O psychologists typically work as consultants, sharing their expertise with businesses, school districts, governmental agencies, or other organizations who seek their services (Blanton, 2007; Pass, 2007). For example, they might help a Fortune 500 corporation develop a training program for new employees hired straight out of college, or they might meet with the managers in a small business to advise them about how they can interact with their employees in a way that increases morale and production.

Industrial/organizational psychologists apply their expertise in a variety of workplaces, including professional office settings like this one. Konstantin Chagin/Shutterstock

Community Psychology. **Community psychology** is an applied specialization in which psychologists focus on the wellness of entire communities. Rather than helping individuals with a problem one by one as they experience it, community psychologists try to address community-wide problems that make its members vulnerable to that problem in the first place. As a result, community psychologists often participate in large-scale efforts to empower people and enhance their lives through prevention (Society for Community Research and Action, 2016; American Psychological Association, 2007). For example, the community psychologists' approach to the problem of teen suicide emphasizes educating large groups of people within the community (high school students, teacher groups, parent groups) about risk factors, warning signs, and resources, as opposed to waiting until a teen becomes suicidal and then (hopefully) intervening to save that one person.

Forensic Psychology. **Forensic psychology** is an applied specialization in which psychologists focus on legal and criminal justice issues. Forensic psychologists—whose

degrees are often actually in clinical psychology, with a concentration in forensic issues—often do psychological assessment (DeMatteo et al., 2009; Otto & Heilbrun, 2002; Otto et al., 2003). For example, they may give psychological tests to children and parents in a custody dispute or to a defendant whose competence to stand trial is in question or to a prisoner who is eligible for parole. Forensic psychologists do psychotherapy too, for victims, offenders, and law enforcement officers. They also serve as expert witnesses in trials, as well as consultants to lawyers and companies or individuals in court cases (Sullivan & Pomerantz, 2013).

Educational Psychology. **Educational psychology** is an applied specialization in which psychologists focus on learning and teaching. Together with the members of the closely related (and more applied) specialization *school psychology*, they improve students' performance by examining how students organize their materials, study, motivate themselves, and deal with challenges. There is significant overlap between educational psychologists and school psychologists, but there is one major difference. Educational psychologists tend to do more research and focus on the big picture of how people generally learn. School psychologists tend to work more directly with kids, parents, and teachers, and they focus in a more targeted way on how a particular kid learns. Many educational psychologists and school psychologists work in schools, often providing services like testing for learning styles or learning problems. They also coordinate efforts between parents, teachers, and administrators to meet a student's special needs, such as coping with specific learning disorders (Helms & Rogers, 2015; Barringer & Saenz, 2007).

Basic Research Specializations

Basic research psychology specializations are areas in which psychologists conduct research for the sake of enhancing the understanding of behavior and mental processes. These are the psychologists who *run studies*. They don't do therapy or assessment or consult with organizations or necessarily apply their expertise in any other way. Psychology is not something they practice, it's something they investigate. They conduct research that collectively builds psychology's knowledge base. Interestingly, basic research specializations existed long before applied specializations—that is, in the earliest days of the field, psychology was a topic of study, not a human service industry (Matthews & Matthews, 2012; Jakobsen, 2012; Smith & Davis, 2003).

Most basic research psychologists have academic jobs in universities, typically in psychology departments but occasionally in medical schools, business schools, or other parts of the university (Roediger, 2007; Calfee, 2007; Vroom, 2007; Grigorenko, 2007). Let's examine the specific academic subjects in which they work.

Developmental Psychology. **Developmental psychology** is a basic research specialization in which psychologists focus on how people change throughout the life span. In the early days, developmental psychologists focused exclusively on childhood and adolescence, but in recent decades, they have also focused on development during the adult years. Developmental psychologists conduct research on how our reasoning, thinking, relationships, emotions, and other aspects of our lives evolve as we age. They are interested in discovering how these processes normally take place, how they may differ across cultures, and how they can be influenced by such factors as parenting, peers, media, and technology (Kuther & Morgan, 2013).

Personality Psychology. **Personality psychology** is a basic research specialization in which psychologists focus on people's traits. Personality psychologists try to determine what personality is made of—its basic ingredients, essentially. They also explore factors that influence personality, including genes and family environment, in an attempt to understand how those traits develop. Additionally, they study the ways that personality may interact with culture (does it have the same basic ingredients

industrial/organizational (I/O) psychology
An applied specialization in which psychologists focus on the workplace.

community psychology
An applied specialization in which psychologists focus on the wellness of entire communities.

forensic psychology
An applied specialization in which psychologists focus on legal and criminal justice issues.

educational psychology
An applied specialization in which psychologists focus on learning and teaching.

basic research psychology specializations
Areas in which psychologists conduct research for the sake of enhancing the understanding of behavior and mental processes.

developmental psychology
A basic research specialization in which psychologists focus on how people change throughout the lifespan.

personality psychology
A basic research specialization in which psychologists focus on people's personality traits.

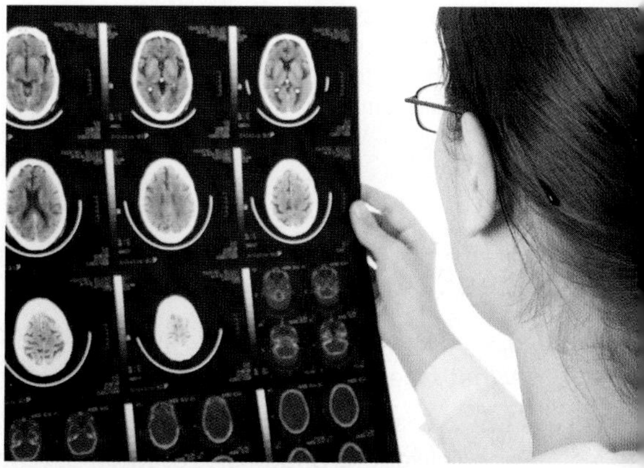

Physiological psychologists study the parts of the brain and their connections to mental processes and behavior. Jose Elias/iStock/Getty Images

around the world?) and with age (does personality change in predictable ways as we get older?) (Barenbaum & Winter, 2008).

Health psychologists study the relationship between physical and mental wellness, including the connection between exercise and mood. Tom Merton/OJO Images/Getty Images

Physiological Psychology. **Physiological psychology** is a basic research specialization in which psychologists focus on the neural basis of behavior. It goes by many names: biological psychology, psychobiology, behavioral neuroscience, and neuropsychology, among others. Physiological psychologists conduct studies to determine the roles of various parts or processes within the brain in various behaviors, from hearing and sight to memory and sleep. They also explore how the various parts of the brain communicate with each other and how the brain communicates with the rest of the body. Additionally, they study the biological underpinnings of psychological disorders like schizophrenia, depression, and bipolar disorder (Garrett, 2009).

Social Psychology. **Social psychology** is a basic research specialization in which psychologists focus on how people think about, influence, and relate to each other. Social psychologists explore our attitudes toward others, including prejudices and stereotypes, and how they relate to our interpersonal actions. They compare the way we explain the behavior of others to the way we explain the behavior of ourselves. They examine how other people—their mere presence, the actions they take, or the orders they give—can affect our behavior. They also try to understand what attracts us to each other as friends and romantic partners (Aronson et al., 2013; American Psychological Association, 2007).

Health Psychology. **Health psychology** is a basic research specialization in which psychologists focus on the relationship between mind and body. Most health psychologists are researchers, but some work in other specialization areas (like clinical and counseling), directly with clients on health-related issues. They study eating, exercise, and other topics related to weight; smoking, drinking, and other topics related to harmful substances; and sexual behavior and sexually transmitted diseases. They also examine the relationship between mental health and physical health, especially the immune system and stress-related conditions like heart disease (Brownell & Salovey, 2007; Wegenek et al., 2010; Gurung, 2014).

Comparative Psychology. **Comparative psychology** is a basic research specialization in which psychologists focus on the behavior of species other than humans. They conduct experiments on a wide variety of species, from bees to birds to baboons. And the range of topics they study mirrors the topics studied in humans: social interactions, development through the life-span, personality characteristics, cognitive processing, and even psychological disorders (Leighty et al., 2013; Pepperberg et al., 2013; Ferdowsian et al., 2013; Tu & Hampton, 2013; Manson & Perry, 2013). Comparative psychology research carries the dual purpose of understanding the behavior of the animals being studied and applying that understanding, as appropriate, to people as well.

physiological psychology
A basic research specialization in which psychologists focus on the neural basis of behavior.

social psychology
A basic research specialization in which psychologists focus on how people think about, influence, and relate to each other.

health psychology
A basic research specialization in which psychologists focus on the relationship between mind and body.

comparative psychology
A basic research specialization in which psychologists focus on the behavior of species other than humans.

CHECK YOUR LEARNING:

1.4 The largest psychological association has 54 divisions. What does that suggest about the field of psychology?

1.5 What's the main difference between applied psychology specializations and basic research psychology specializations?

1.6 What is the main focus of each of these applied psychology specializations: clinical psychology, forensic psychology, and industrial/organizational psychology?

1.7 What is the main focus of each of each of these basic research psychology specializations: developmental psychology, physiological psychology, and social psychology?

Psychology Then and Now

Psychology is relatively new, but its roots go way, way back.

YOU WILL LEARN:

1.8 How the older fields of philosophy and physiology influenced the creation of psychology.

1.9 What the early schools of psychology—structuralism, functionalism, psychoanalysis, behaviorism, and humanism—emphasized.

1.10 What the more contemporary schools of psychology—multiculturalism, evolutionary psychology, cognitive psychology, neuroscience, and biopsychosocial theory—emphasize.

Relatively new? Weren't there psychologists all the way back in the late 1800s?

Yes, there were. However, the late 1800s is not so long ago in the broad scope of history. For an academic field, being only a century and a half old is like being a toddler (Benjafield, 2012).

The *really* old academic fields, the ones that originated in ancient times, include the two from which psychology emerged: *philosophy* and *physiology* (Goodwin, 2003; Fuchs, 2002; Robinson, 1997; Green & Groff, 2003; Wertheimer, 2012). Philosophy, of course, is the seeking of wisdom about the world in which we live, the attempt to discover the truths that govern our lives. It has been around about as long as people have, with notable contributions from Greek, Roman, Chinese, Judaic, Hindu, and other cultures (Stagner, 1988). (Those black-and-white photos of old-time psychologists start to look pretty modern when you compare them to the stone carvings and hand-made drawings of philosophers like Aristotle, Plato, and Confucius.)

Among the questions that the philosophers pondered, many touch on the inner workings of the mind and the reasons for our behavior. For example, in France in the 1600s, René Descartes famously pondered how our reflexes might work—what exactly happens within your brain and body when you touch a burning hot object and involuntarily yank your hand away. Their answers to those questions traditionally came from opinion and insight, not from scientific experiment. In fact, the questions themselves—for example, is human nature good or bad, how much free will do people really have, what's the best moral path—don't really lend themselves to testing. So philosophers' wisdom, as perceptive as it may be, had no science to back it up. That's the niche that psychology filled: the study of the human mind and behavior grounded in science rather than speculation (Malone, 2009; Watson & Evans, 1991).

Any study of the human mind would be incomplete without study of the human brain as well. After all, mental activity is a bodily function like any other. Physiology—another field with a history stretching back more than two millenia—focuses on these brain–body functions. (Today, we would probably use the term *biology* to describe much of what was traditionally called *physiology*.) As early as the Middle Ages, physiologists were making important discoveries about the human body, like how blood circulates, how the bones of the skeleton are arranged, and how diseases damage organs. But even by the late 1800s, physiology still had relatively little to say about the inner workings of the human brain. Of course, technological limitations made it difficult to see what happens in the brain. Imaging technologies, like MRIs, CAT scans, and even x-rays were a long way away. Yet the desire to understand how the brain works was certainly there, and that desire, along with the scientific methods used by physiologists, inspired many of the earliest experiments in psychology.

Old-School Psychology

There are a few notes to keep in mind as we explore the history of psychology. First, the way that history is organized in this chapter—old-school versus new-school—may be a bit oversimplified. There is no clear-cut boundary or landmark event to separate the two. But as time has passed, some of the original *schools of thought* in psychology have faded and newer ones have taken their places. That's not to say that the older

schools of thought aren't still influential—most of them are, in updated forms—but they don't dominate the field as they once did.

Second, although the history of psychology tends to highlight events and people from Europe and the United States, it's important to remember that psychology is a global science with a global history (Brock, 2006; Danziger, 2006; Blowers, 2006). The American Psychological Association may be the largest and the oldest (founded in 1892), but about 100 other countries including many outside of the Western world, have national psychological associations of their own. Some have been thriving for almost a century, like the Indian Psychological Association (founded in 1925), the Japanese Psychological Association (1927), and the Argentine Psychological Society (1930). Even the Association of Icelandic Psychologists has been around since the 1950s. **Figure 1.2** illustrates the many other national associations, which cover every continent except Antarctica and show just how worldwide psychology and its history are (Baker & Benjamin, 2012; Benjamin & Baker, 2012; Dodgen et al., 2013).

Third, the history of psychology in the United States includes contributions from diverse populations (Leong, 2009). For example, Black psychologists have made many notable historical achievements. In 1920, Francis C. Sumner became the first Black man to earn a PhD in psychology in the United States, and in 1937, Alberta Banner Turner became the first Black woman to do so. In the 1950s, psychologists Kenneth Clark and Mamie Phipps Clark, a married couple, provided expert testimony about their own research on racial issues during the historic U.S. Supreme Court case *Brown v. Board of Education*, which led to public school desegregation. The Clarks also opened a child guidance clinic in Harlem, which Mamie Phipps Clark directed for over 30 years and which is still in operation today. In 1971, Kenneth Clark became the first Black president of the American Psychological Association (Holliday, 2009; Benjamin & Crouse, 2002).

FIGURE 1.2 **Psychology Worldwide.** With national psychological associations around the globe, some of which have been around for nearly a century, it is clear that psychology is a global science with a global history.

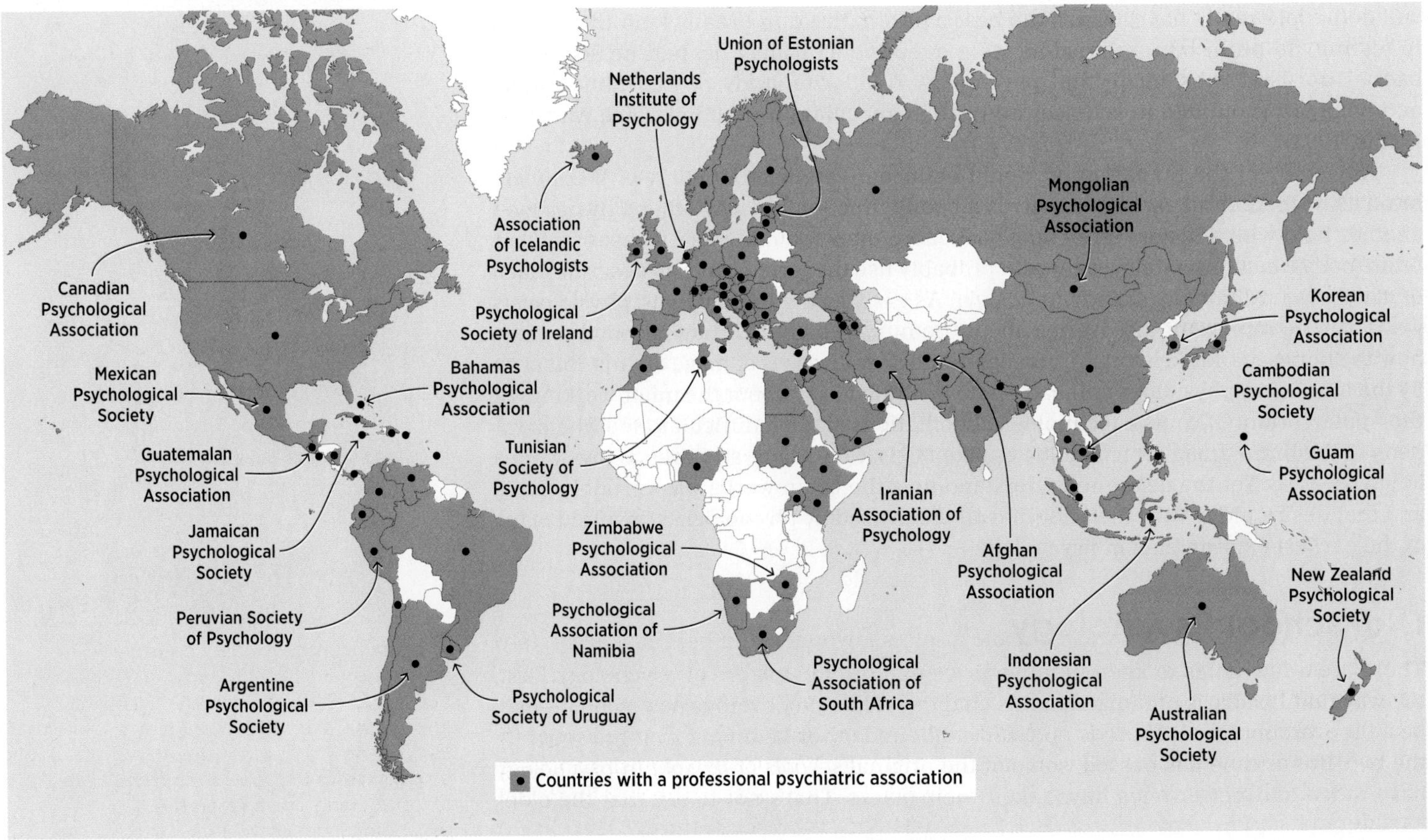

In the late 1960s, Robert L. Williams helped to found the Association of Black Psychologists. In the 1970s, he pioneered the study of (and coined the term) *ebonics*, legitimizing the African American vernacular of the English language. Williams also developed the Black Intelligence Test of Cultural Homogeneity (BITCH), designed to illustrate how linguistic and cultural bias in intelligence tests placed minority groups at a disadvantage (Belgrave & Allison, 2014; Williams, 1972).

The history of psychology in the United States has been significantly influenced by the work of members of other ethnic groups as well (Sue, 2009). Carolyn Lewis Attneave founded the Society of Indian Psychologists in the 1970s and devoted her career to studying mental health needs and treatment among Native Americans (Trimble & Clearing-Sky, 2009). Also in the 1970s, Derald Sue was among the founders of the Asian American Psychological Association and served several years as its first president (Leong & Okazaki, 2009). George I. Sanchez was the first Latino psychologist, earning his doctoral degree in 1934. He went on to conduct pioneering research on cultural issues regarding intelligence tests and other psychological assessment tools (Padilla & Olmedo, 2009).

Psychologists Kenneth Clark and Mamie Phipps Clark were a husband-and-wife team who made significant contributions to the history of psychology. Their research and expert testimony played a key role in the historic United States Supreme Court case *Brown v. Board of Education*, which made it unconstitutional for states to establish separate public schools for black students and white students.

Structuralism and Functionalism. Wilhelm Wundt (pronounced *Vilhelm Voont*) lived in Germany from 1832 to 1920. He is considered by many to be the father of psychology, but before he focused on the mind at all, he focused on the body. He earned a medical degree in 1856 and worked as a research assistant for a famous medical researcher, Hermann Helmholtz, for years after. He even wrote a textbook on physiology during that time. But his interests steadily drifted into areas that physiology and medicine had not yet explored: the inner workings of the mind. Of course, philosophers had long been speculating about the inner workings of the mind, but with his background in physiology and medicine, Wundt approached it differently than the philosophers did: *as a science*. Wundt insisted that his new science—to which he gave the name *psychology*—should be conducted like any other science, emphasizing highly controlled methods of data collection. Wundt taught the first course in the new science of psychology in 1862 at the University of Heidelberg, wrote its first textbook (*Principles of Physiological Psychology*) in 1874, and established the first psychology research laboratory at the University of Leipzig in 1879 (Capaldi & Proctor, 2003; Stewart, 2008; Hunt, 2007; Blumenthal, 1997).

In that research laboratory, Wundt's experiments resembled experiments in physiology and medicine. They typically focused on such mental processes as reaction time, attention, and the way we perceive things around us through sight, hearing, touch, and other senses (Danziger & Ballyntyne, 1997; Bringmann et al., 1997; Popplestone & McPherson, 1998). Wundt used an approach similar to the way physiologists studied the human body: trying to determine its structure, what it was made of, what organs and bones it contained, and how everything connected to each other. But while physiologists could open the body to take a peek at the structure of the body (in surgeries or autopsies), Wundt lacked such a direct way to investigate the structure of mental processes like reaction time, perception, and attention. Instead, he relied on his psychology research participants to *introspect*, or look inside themselves, and describe what was going on inside their own mind (Goodwin, 2003). Wundt asked participants to narrate exactly what mental activities took place when they felt a particular sensation or reacted to a particular stimulus.

Wait a minute—Wundt asked his participants to describe in detail the processes going on inside their own head? Were they any good at it?

No. In fact, participants were terrible at it, as anyone would be. (How accurately, specifically, and completely could you use words to explain the processes that take place in your brain when you think, feel, see, hear, or react?) For this reason, introspection has long been discredited and abandoned as a scientific method in psychology. In spite of the shortcomings of his introspective methods, Wundt's accomplishments are still recognized as groundbreaking for psychology as a scientific field, and he is still considered its original pioneer (Blumenthal, 2002; Pickren & Rutherford, 2010).

Wilhelm Wundt is widely considered to be the father of psychology. In Germany in the late 1800s, he was the first to approach the inner workings of the mind as a science. He taught the first psychology course, wrote the first psychology textbook, and established the first psychology research lab.

Edward Titchener worked in Wilhelm Wundt's research lab in Germany and later moved to the United States, bringing the science of psychology with him.

Structuralism. As an undergraduate student in the 1880s in England, Edward B. Titchener read Wilhelm Wundt's writings and became fascinated with Wundt's research. After graduating, he moved to Germany to become a graduate student in Wundt's lab. Titchener's own research continued to be guided by what he learned under Wundt. He tried to break down the structures of mental processes "in much the same way as a chemist breaks down chemicals into their component parts—water into hydrogen and oxygen, for example" (Stewart, 2008, p. 273). This approach evolved into **structuralism**: a perspective from the early history of psychology that focused on breaking down mental processes into their structure or basic parts.

After Titchener earned his doctoral degree, he moved to the United States in 1892 and became a professor at Cornell University in Ithaca, New York. So more than any other single person, it was Titchener who brought Wundt's new science of psychology from Europe to the United States (Stagner, 1988; Watson & Evans, 1991; Tweney, 1997).

One more note about Titchener—his attitude toward female collaborators illustrates how the sexist attitudes common in his time made it difficult for talented women to fully participate in the early development of psychology (Stewart, 2008). In the early 1900s, Titchener established and led psychological organizations that deliberately kept women out. One woman, Christine Ladd-Franklin, fought back. Ladd-Franklin had fulfilled all requirements for a PhD at Johns Hopkins but was denied the degree until 44 years later. The university, like many others at the time, would not formally enroll her in the program.

Ladd-Franklin went on to conduct research and publish papers on such topics as the psychological processes of color vision. In 1912, Titchener excluded Ladd-Franklin from a conference for psychological researchers and she responded: "I am shocked to know that you are still—at this year—excluding women from your meeting of experimental psychologists. It is such a very old-fashioned standpoint!" Two years later, Titchener again excluded Ladd-Franklin from a psychological conference, a move she called "so immoral—worse than that, so unscientific!" Titchener grumbled to a male colleague: "I have been pestered by abuse by Mrs. Ladd-Franklin for not having women at the meetings... Possibly she will succeed in breaking us up, and forcing us to meet—like rabbits—in some dark place underground..." (all quotations from Benjamin, 2006, pp. 131–133).

Titchener was certainly not the only male psychologist at the time with chauvinist attitudes—he actually became more open-minded later in his career—nor was Ladd-Franklin the only woman whose career was stifled by them. In spite of this, many women made significant contributions to the field of psychology. In 1905, Mary Whiton Calkins became the first female president of the American Psychological Association. The same year, Margaret Floy Washburn became the first U.S. woman to officially earn a PhD in psychology, and she was named president of the American Psychological Association in 1921. The trailblazing of Ladd-Franklin, Calkins, and Washburn is a primary reason that the majority of today's doctoral degrees in psychology are earned by women (Furumoto & Scarborough, 2002; Kohout & Pate, 2013; Carpenter, 1997; Stewart, 2008).

Christine Ladd-Franklin (left) was among the first women to complete psychology PhD coursework and to conduct psychological research. Mary Whiton Calkins (middle) became the first woman to be named president of the American Psychological Association. Margaret Floy Washburn (right) became the first U.S. woman to officially earn a PhD in psychology. All three overcame biases against women in the field to become pioneers of psychology.

Functionalism. Structuralism faded rather quickly as psychology expanded in the United States. The approach that took its place was **functionalism**: a perspective from the early history of psychology that focused on the function of our mental processes and behaviors. Unlike structuralism, which tried to determine what the mental processes *are*, functionalism tried to determine what the mental processes are *for*—their purpose, or their value to the person performing them (Goodwin, 2012; Angell, 1907). Of course, functionalism was strongly influenced by Charles Darwin's theory of evolution, which was rapidly gaining acceptance at the time and which focused heavily on the function of various behaviors and physical attributes for survival and reproduction (Fitzpatrick & Bringmann, 1997; Darwin, 1877).

Functionalism was also promoted by William James, whom many consider to be the father of U.S. psychology. James was born in New York City in 1842, the son of a wealthy and prominent family. He earned a degree in medicine at Harvard and landed a job there as a professor, a position he kept for 25 years. Beginning in 1874, he taught courses in psychology and ran a psychology lab, widely acknowledged as the first in the United States. Because psychology was such a new discipline, James himself had never taken a course in it himself. As he put it, "The first lecture in psychology that I ever heard was the first I ever gave" (quoted in Hunt, 2007, p. 150). But soon, psychology was being taught and studied around the country. There were about 20 psychology labs in the United States by 1892 and about 40 by 1900—due in large part to James's popularization of the new field (Benjamin, 2007; Sokal, 2002).

James promoted psychology through teaching and publishing research studies, many of which expanded the range of psychological research to new topics like children, animals, intelligence, and learning. But James's most significant single contribution was the landmark *Principles of Psychology*, a textbook he published in 1890 that gave this up-and-coming field its first authoritative source. The text remained popular and influential for many decades (James, 1890; Simon, 1998; Hunt, 2007; Leary, 2002, 2003; Bruder, 1997; Nordby & Hall, 1974).

William James is widely considered to be the father of psychology in the United States. His psychology research lab at Harvard was the first in the United States.

Sigmund Freud popularized psychology in the United States and around the world in the late 1800s. His psychoanalytic theory emphasized unconscious mental activity and the impact of childhood experiences on adult life.

Psychoanalysis. By the early 1900s, Wundt, Titchener, and James had put psychology on the map. But it was another pioneer—Sigmund Freud—who made psychology a household term. His ideas are collectively known as **psychoanalysis**: a perspective in psychology created by Sigmund Freud that emphasizes unconscious mental activity and the long-lasting influence of childhood experiences.

Freud was born in Austria, in an area now part of the Czech Republic, in 1856. By his early 20s, he had earned an MD in neurology. Early in his career, he began to specialize in what he called nervous disorders—basically, aches and pains for which doctors could find no biological basis. With the help of another physician, Joseph Breuer, Freud started to recognize that when people with nervous disorders discussed their symptoms, especially when they revealed thoughts and feelings that had previously been hidden (often stemming from painful childhood experiences), those symptoms improved. The discovery of this "talking cure" (as it was called by Anna O., a patient whose treatment was famously described by Breuer) led Freud to two historic ideas.

The first historic idea was the existence of the *unconscious*, thoughts and feelings of which the person is unaware that yet have the power to strongly affect the person's life. The second historic idea was *psychoanalytic psychotherapy*, a form of psychotherapy designed to make the unconscious conscious. (Both of these ideas are discussed in more detail in Chapter 12.) The term *psychoanalysis* was eventually used to capture all of Freud's ideas, whether they related to psychotherapy techniques or simply his theories of the inner workings of the mind (Fancher & Rutherford, 2012; Keen, 2001; Federn, 1997).

Psychoanalysis drew tremendous attention, not only from professors who studied it and physicians who used it but from the general public as well. This attention elevated Freud to a level of fame that was way beyond that of any psychology figure before (and perhaps since). In the process, it elevated psychology to a level of acceptance as a discipline way beyond that which it had previously reached. Freud

structuralism
A perspective from the early history of psychology that focused on breaking down mental processes into their structure or basic parts.

functionalism
A perspective from the early history of psychology that focused on the function of our mental processes and behaviors.

psychoanalysis
A psychological perspective created by Sigmund Freud that emphasizes unconscious mental activity and the long-lasting influence of childhood experiences.

came to the United States in 1909 to deliver a series of lectures, which were very influential in spreading psychoanalysis beyond Europe (as were his many books). In the 1910s, articles on psychoanalysis increasingly appeared in journals, and by the 1920s, psychoanalytic training institutes and psychoanalytic professional associations were multiplying (Goodwin, 2012). Freud's popularity and influence, based largely on the notion of the unconscious and how it could be uncovered, continued to grow even after his death in 1939 (Stewart, 2008; Hothersall, 2004). Current interest in psychoanalysis is far below its peak levels—in fact, it is heavily criticized by some—but it retains some influence in certain pockets of the field (Gabbard, 2009).

DIVERSITY MATTERS

It is worth noting that while the United States embraced Freud's ideas, other countries resisted them. For example, Freud's ideas did not take hold in Argentina, Turkey, or China at anywhere near the level they did in the United States and other places (Hsueh & Guo, 2012; Taiana, 2006; Gulerce, 2006).

All that Freud stuff—the unconscious, psychoanalysis—seems really unscientific. Did anybody point that out?

B. F. Skinner (top) and John Watson (bottom) were pioneers of behaviorism, which emphasizes observable behavior over internal mental processes.

Behaviorism. Yes—the behaviorists pointed out that problem, and quite a few others, regarding psychoanalysis. **Behaviorism** is a perspective in psychology that emphasizes observable behavior over internal mental processes. The rationale behind behaviorism is simple: behavior can be seen and measured, but mental processes like feelings and thoughts cannot. Behaviorists believed psychology could be a science if it focused on behavior rather than mental processes—a point that Wundt, Titchener, James, and other pioneers of psychology had already highlighted.

Freud's theories, of course, delved much more deeply into mental processes than observable behavior. So you can understand how some people—behaviorists, specifically—would cringe when they saw Freud's theories stealing the spotlight in the early 1900s. Freud's primary method was to look inside the mind and try to explain its inner workings. Perhaps he was good at it, and perhaps his ideas were attention-grabbing, but this was just another form of introspection—a method that had already been rejected as unscientific.

John Watson led the behaviorists' charge. Watson was born in 1878 in South Carolina. He grew up on a farm, which may explain why he became interested in research on animal behavior as a graduate student and continued that work during his career as a professor at the University of Chicago and Johns Hopkins (Stewart, 2008; Wozniak, 1997). He wrote an influential behaviorist "manifesto" in which he declared that for psychology, the "goal is the prediction and control of behavior [not mental processes]. Introspection forms no essential part of its methods..." (Watson, 1913, p. 158).

By the 1920s and 1930s, behaviorism was picking up steam through Watson's continued promotion. Also, the research of the Russian Ivan Pavlov on conditioning in dogs was published in English for the first time. Pavlov's research focused on animals' behavior with strong implications for humans, a mode of study that U.S. behaviorists eagerly adopted (Goodwin, 2012). Behaviorism continued to flourish through the mid-1900s thanks to the work of B. F. Skinner, who became the new face of the movement. Skinner was both a researcher—he focused primarily on the relationship of reinforcement and behavior in rats, pigeons, and other animals—and a spokesperson—in the 1960s and 1970s, he was a bestselling author, TV talk show regular, and overall academic celebrity (Coleman, 1997; Rutherford, 2009; Smith, 1996; Mills, 1998).

The heyday of behaviorism has passed, but it remains a force in psychology. This is true particularly for those interested in behavior change in animals (as in the training of service dogs) or people whose ability to identify and communicate their own thoughts is limited, as in treatment of unwanted behaviors in children at the severe end of the autism spectrum. Like psychoanalysis, behaviorism gained much more

popularity in the United States than in some other countries. In fact, in much of Europe, behaviorism never had more than a minor influence. In India, it never overtook or even blended with the spiritual and mystical emphasis so prominent in that country's approach to psychology (Brock, 2006; Paranjpe, 2006).

DIVERSITY MATTERS

Carl Rogers was a pioneer of humanism, which emphasizes the notion that human nature is generally good and people are naturally motivated to grow toward their own potential.

Humanism. By the mid-1900s, psychology had two prominent schools of thought: psychoanalysis and behaviorism. Neither of them painted a favorable picture of human nature. The *unconscious* was the centerpiece of the psychoanalytic point of view, and it depended on the idea of destructive animalistic impulses in each of us. Behaviorists' portrayal was not quite so negative, but it certainly wasn't positive either. The behaviorists believed human nature was neutral, if it existed at all, since we are no more than products of the environment around us. Psychology was ripe for a third approach that shined a light on what is good in all of us, and *humanism* became that approach (Cain, 2010). **Humanism** is a perspective in psychology that emphasizes the notion that human nature is generally good and people are naturally motivated to grow toward their own potential.

Carl Rogers led the humanistic movement. When Rogers went to graduate school in psychology, he was actually trained to do Freud's psychoanalysis, like most other graduate students of his time. Early in his therapy career, however, his experiences with his clients didn't match his Freudian training. To Rogers, people who experienced psychological problems weren't struggling with unconscious drives toward unrestrained aggression or indulgent gratification. Rogers thought people were just stifled in their quest to grow. In other words, people just want to blossom and bloom into their true selves—to *self-actualize*, as Rogers put it—but sometimes obstacles got in the way of that natural process (Rogers, 1959, 1961; Bohart & Tallman, 1999).

What got in the way, according to Rogers, were *conditions of worth* imposed by others, which forced people to choose between being their true selves and being someone whom their loved ones would accept. For example, consider Dashon, a 10-year old boy. Dashon loves ballet, but his parents feel that he should pursue more traditionally male hobbies, like football. In fact, they make it clear to Dashon that their acceptance of him as a son depends on which of these activities he pursues. Understandably, Dashon goes with football, but he doesn't enjoy it, and he feels a nagging unhappiness about his inability to pursue the dance that he feels is an essential part of his identity. Ongoing experiences like this—having to sacrifice aspects of his true self to gain acceptance from important people in his life—will make Dashon vulnerable to depression, anxiety, and other psychological problems. The point here is that Dashon's original motivation was nothing evil or nasty—just the need to be true to himself. According to Rogers and the humanists who followed him, that's the fundamental need for all of us.

Another leading figure in the humanistic movement, Abraham Maslow, pointed out that the need to be true to yourself can emerge only after more basic needs are met. Maslow created a *hierarchy of needs* in which he listed these prerequisites, like hunger, thirst, safety, and feeling connected to other people (Maslow, 1968).

Humanism rose to prominence in the 1960s and 1970s. In fact, during that time it was often called third force psychology (Stagner, 1988; Murray, 1988), a nickname that showed how it had come to rival the psychoanalytic (first force) and behavioral (second force) approaches. The influence of humanism has faded since that time, particularly after Rogers's death in 1987. However, the basic ideas of humanism remain vital, especially among many psychologists who practice psychotherapy and who hold fundamentally positive views about human nature.

behaviorism
A psychological perspective that emphasizes observable behavior over internal mental processes.

humanism
A psychological perspective that emphasizes the notion that human nature is generally good and people are naturally motivated to grow toward their own potential.

New-School Psychology

The past few decades have seen the rise of entirely new schools of thought in psychology. That doesn't mean that the older schools are long gone. In fact, all of them remain in one form or another, and among some groups of psychologists, the old schools of thought remain quite influential. But the new schools—most notably, *multiculturalism*,

Multicultural psychology is an approach that emphasizes the impact of culture on our thoughts, feelings, and actions. Culture can be defined by many variables, including race, ethnicity, gender, age, religion, spirituality, socioeconomic status, sexual orientation, geography, region, and ability or disability status. (From top) Peathegee Inc/Blend Images/Getty Images; Commerceandculturestock/Getty Images; Zhang bo/Getty Images

evolutionary psychology, *cognitive psychology*, *neuroscience*, and *biopsychosocial theory*—more accurately capture the movements that characterize psychology's present and immediate future.

Multiculturalism. **Multiculturalism** is a perspective in psychology that emphasizes the influence of culture on behavior and mental processes. Multiculturalism challenges an assumption held by the older schools of psychology (almost all of which were founded by White men from the United States and Europe) that an explanation of human behavior was equally true for *all* humans. That's simply not true. Increasingly, psychologists are recognizing that cultural variables have a powerful impact on what we think, feel, and do (Van de Vijver & Matsumoto, 2011; Matsumoto, 2003).

DIVERSITY MATTERS

What, exactly, do psychologists mean when they say culture?

Psychologists think of a *culture* as a shared lifestyle with its own unique norms, expectations, and values. There are actually lots of characteristics on which a culture can center. For many of us, race or ethnicity comes to mind first (Mio et al., 2009). But many other characteristics can be culturally important, including gender, religion and spirituality, age, socioeconomic status, sexual orientation, geographic region, and disability or ability status (Artman & Daniels, 2010; Lyons et al., 2010; McGoldrick et al., 2005; McKitrick & Li, 2008; Robinson-Wood, 2009; Sewell, 2009). This broader understanding of culture means that each of us has quite a few cultural characteristics. In fact, when you consider all of your cultural variables together, your combination may be rather unique. A research psychologist who develops theories to explain your behavior, or a practicing psychologist who conducts therapy with you when you are struggling, should consider your unique combination of cultural variables rather than applying a one-size-fits-all approach (Leong & Kalibatseva, 2013; Johnson et al., 2011).

Evidence of the rise of multiculturalism is all over the field of psychology. Dozens of professional psychological journals that focus on multicultural issues (such as *Cultural Diversity & Ethnic Minority Psychology*, *Culture & Psychology*, and *Psychology of Sexual Orientation and Gender Diversity*) have sprung up in recent decades, rapidly earning respect and popularity among professionals. New divisions of the American Psychological Association, such as Division 44: Society for the Psychological Study of Lesbian, Gay, and Bisexual Issues, and Division 45: Society for the Study of Ethnic Minority Issues, have been established. Our profession's ethical code has added new standards that require psychologists to consider a wide range of cultural variables when they conduct therapy, assessment, or research (American Psychological Association, 2002). The requirements for graduate programs in psychology to be accredited (that is, approved) by APA also include more emphasis on cultural diversity than ever before (American Psychological Association, 2005).

For psychologists in the United States, the importance of multiculturalism is highlighted by the increasing diversity within the population. According to the U.S. Census Bureau, Hispanic Americans, who constitute 16% of the population, will constitute 30% of the population by 2050. In the same time frame, the Asian American population will jump from 4.5% to 7.6%. And the White European population will drop from 64.7% to 46.3%, meaning that no single ethnicity will represent a majority of the population (Leong & Kalibetseva, 2013). With these population trends ahead, the importance of multiculturalism within psychology is likely to increase even more.

Evolutionary Psychology. **Evolutionary psychology** is a perspective in psychology that emphasizes Charles Darwin's theory of evolution as an influence on behavior. Evolutionary theory is well over 100 years old, and its influence on psychology can be traced back as far as William James's functionalism, but its impact on psychology continues to grow. Contemporary psychologists increasingly turn to evolutionary theory to explain and predict all kinds of human behavior.

For example, psychologists use evolution to explain *altruism*, feeling concern for other people and helping them in a completely unselfish way. Why would you help when it brings you no benefit? According to evolutionary theory, it may be that among our ancestors, people who helped were more likely to receive help later—perhaps even life-saving help. So helpers had a better chance at survival because of the goodwill they had accumulated among friends and family (de Waal, 2008; Neuberg et al., 2010). Or if Darwin's assumption that getting our genes into the next generation is what drives us, then altruism toward those who share at least some of our genes makes a lot more sense. According to this evolutionary theory, helping a relative is like helping part of yourself (Van Vugt & Van Lange, 2006; Neyer & Lang, 2003).

Evolutionary psychology also offers explanations of psychological disorders. For example, the most common phobias—heights, snakes, insects, small animals, the dark, enclosed spaces—are actually not the biggest threats to our survival today. But they *were* the biggest threats to the survival of our ancestors. Ancestors who feared those things were more likely than the fearless to live long enough to have kids of their own. Those kids inherited their parents' fearful disposition and passed it on to their own kids. Fast-forward many generations to today, and many of us have phobias of things that actually aren't so threatening anymore (Öhman & Mineka, 2001; Debiec & LeDoux, 2009; Bracha & Maser, 2008).

Evolutionary psychology emphasizes Charles Darwin's theory of evolution as an influence on behavior. For instance, evolutionary psychology might explain helping behavior (altruism) by emphasizing that people who provide help are likely to receive help later, or that helping a biological relative improves the odds of shared genes carrying on the next generation. Thinkstock/Stockbyte/Getty Images

Cognitive Psychology. **Cognitive psychology** is a perspective in psychology that emphasizes processes such as thinking, language, attention, memory, and intelligence. These are the processes of acquiring and using information. Some cognitive psychologists do research to determine how these functions take place normally; others focus on how they can go awry or how they can be enhanced (Sternberg & Sternberg, 2010).

The cognitive perspective arose largely as a reaction against the behavioral perspective, which came before it. In particular, psychologists associated with the cognitive perspective argue against the behavioral emphasis on issues *outside* of the mind, like observable behavior and external conditions. Instead, cognitive psychologists highlight the fact that what happens *inside* the mind is essential to understanding humans. Cognitive psychologists study a wide range of inside-the-mind questions, like how we solve problems and make decisions, how we learn languages, what stimulates creative thinking, and what influences intelligence.

Neuroscience. **Neuroscience** is a perspective in psychology that emphasizes the link between behavior and the biological functioning of the brain. This link has always been an important part of psychology, but technological advances in recent decades that allow researchers access to the inner workings of the brain—including functional magnetic resonance imaging, computed tomography, and positron emission tomography (fMRI, CT, and PET, respectively)—have enabled this perspective to explode in popularity and influence (Gerber & Gonzalez, 2013). (By the way, neuroscience often goes by other names, such as *neuropsychology* and *biopsychology*.)

Neuroscience provides explanations for all kinds of behavior. For example, particular parts of the brain respond to addictive drugs (like morphine, crack, or meth), as well as addictive behaviors (like gambling and compulsive eating) (Kelley & Berridge, 2002; Everitt & Robbins, 2005; Reuter et al., 2005; Potenza, 2006). The hallucinations common to people with schizophrenia activate the same visual and auditory areas of the brain that are activated by normal sights and sounds (Allen et al., 2008; Silbersweig et al., 1995; Shergill et al., 2000; McGuire et al., 1993). People with out-of-control aggression, including some murderers, have unusually high activity of certain brain regions (Raine et al., 1998; Miczek et al., 2007). Certain kinds of intelligence seem to stem from certain brain areas. For example, your ability to do math depends on the activity of certain brain regions, while your ability to use language depends more on other brain regions (Dehaene, 2011; Dehaene et al., 1999).

Neuroscience has become so hot in recent years that some experts have started a backlash. Some critics of neuroscience point out that PET scans and fMRIs give us previously unimaginable images of the inner workings of the brain, but those images

multiculturalism
A psychological perspective that emphasizes the influences of culture on behavior and mental processes.

evolutionary psychology
A psychological perspective that emphasizes Charles Darwin's theory of evolution as an influence on behavior.

cognitive psychology
A psychological perspective that emphasizes cognitive processes such as thinking, language, attention, memory, and intelligence.

neuroscience
A psychological perspective that emphasizes the link between behavior and the biological functioning of the brain.

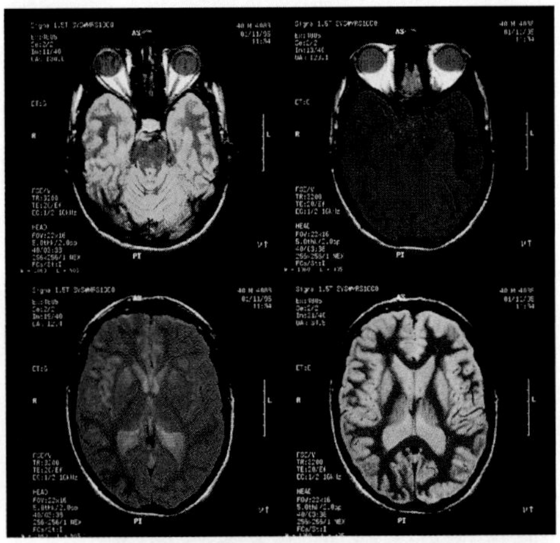

Neuroscience (also known as neuropsychology or biopsychology) emphasizes the link between behavior and the biological functioning of the brain. Great advances in brain imaging technology have enabled great advances in neuroscience.
Laurence Dutton/The Image Bank/Getty Images

can make the link between brain and behavior seem simple when it is remarkably complex. The same critics also point out that it doesn't mean that the brain activity *causes* the behavior just because a certain brain activity goes along with a certain behavior (Satel & Lilienfeld, 2013; Shulman, 2013; Burton, 2013). That is, certain brain activity can only be said to be associated with certain behavior.

Positive Psychology. **Positive psychology** is a perspective in psychology that emphasizes people's strengths and successes. When positive psychology rose to popularity in the 1990s and 2000s, it contrasted with the dominant focus within much of psychology: people's *problems*, in the forms of disorders, weaknesses, and failings. Much of mainstream psychology still maintains that focus, but those associated with the positive psychology movement promote a very different message. They conduct research and offer services designed to help people maximize their psychological assets and virtues. Positive psychologists see psychology as more than a tool for helping people overcome misery and impairment. They see it as an opportunity to help people flourish and be happy (Seligman et al., 2005; Seligman & Czikszentmihalyi, 2000; Snyder et al., 2011; Gable & Haidt, 2005).

For example, positive psychologists have extensively studied positive emotions like happiness. They have explored such questions as how to bring more authentic happiness into your life, the health-related benefits of happiness, and the connection between happiness and parts of everyday life like job performance, relationship quality, and self-esteem (Lyubomirsky et al., 2005; Seligman, 2004; Frederickson, 2001).

Biopsychosocial Theory. **Biopsychosocial theory** is a uniquely comprehensive popular perspective in psychology that emphasizes biological, psychological, and social factors as influences on behavior. Biopsychosocial theory is as inclusive as it gets among the schools of psychology. Unlike other old and new approaches, biopsychosocial theory does not claim that one factor alone explains your behavior. Instead, it recognizes that your brain and genetic inheritance (biological factors) *and* your thoughts and feelings (psychological factors) *and* your family and culture (social factors) all interact (Melchert, 2011; Campbell & Rohrbaugh, 2006).

Consider Leo, a college student who has panic attacks. What causes them? Biopsychosocial theory allows us to consider a wide range of factors. Regarding his biology, Leo may have inherited a tendency toward panic from his parents, who are quite panicky themselves. This inheritance may take the form of unique brain activity, such as overactivity in an area called the *amygdala* (Forsyth et al., 2009; Liverant et al., 2007; Faravelli et al., 2009; Debiec & LeDoux, 2009). Regarding his psychology, Leo may have a tendency to *catastrophize*, or make a mountain out of a molehill, especially when he notices minor changes in his own body. He may notice his heart rate going up a bit after climbing a few flights of stairs, mistakenly believe that he's about to have a heart attack, and bring a panic attack on himself (Clark & Beck, 2010). Regarding his social environment, the fact that Leo has watched not only his parents but his older brother, older sister, and grandfather have panic attacks means that panic was modeled for him throughout his childhood (Ehlers, 1993; Mineka & Cook, 1993). Biopsychosocial theory does not require that all three of these factors be given equal weight. After all, in a specific case (like Leo's), one factor may outweigh the others. But biopsychosocial theory does enable psychologists to consider multiple factors rather than just one, which can produce a more accurate and complete explanation of what's really going on.

positive psychology
A perspective in psychology that emphasizes people's strengths and successes.

biopsychosocial theory
A uniquely comprehensive psychological perspective that emphasizes biological, psychological, and social factors as influences on behavior.

CHECK YOUR LEARNING:

1.8 Which two older fields influenced the development of psychology?

1.9 What was the emphasis of each of the original schools of psychology—structuralism, functionalism, psychoanalysis, behaviorism, and humanism?

1.10 What is the emphasis of each of the more contemporary schools of psychology—multiculturalism, evolutionary psychology, cognitive psychology, neuroscience, positive psychology, and biopsychosocial theory?

The Science of Psychology

YOU WILL LEARN:

1.11 why psychology requires a scientific approach.

1.12 about the three primary types of research that psychologists do: descriptive, correlational, and experimental research.

1.13 the steps of the scientific method.

1.14 how psychologists share results.

1.15 what ethical obligations psychology researchers have.

Remember how we defined psychology at the beginning of this chapter: the scientific study of behavior and mental processes. The *scientific* part of that definition is crucial. It means that psychologists don't settle for answers that are just speculation, guesswork, or common sense. Instead, psychologists *test* any possible answer to determine how legitimate that answer actually is. So when clinical psychologists wonder, do genes cause bipolar disorder? they don't just throw out a yes or no based on a hunch or their personal experience with a family that has both a parent and a kid with bipolar disorder. They measure the rate of bipolar disorder in identical twins raised apart or in adopted kids whose biological parents are bipolar but whose adoptive parents are not. In other words, these clinical psychologists produce an answer based on data that they have carefully and purposefully collected (Lichtenstein et al., 2009; Craddock & Jones, 1999).

When developmental psychologists wonder, do kids who play violent video games behave more violently in real life than kids who don't? They don't just argue yes or no based on intuition or the kid next door who plays *Call of Duty* and throws rocks at the dog. They meticulously measure video game playing and violent behavior in hundreds of kids and calculate how strongly the two go together (Bushman & Huesmann, 2010; Polman et al., 2008; Carnagey et al., 2007).

As a psychology researcher myself, I have seen firsthand how a question can evolve past speculation into science. Once, during my undergrad clinical psychology class, my students and I were discussing how well psychotherapy works. The emphasis was on the beneficial effects of psychotherapy: how often it works, what kinds of positive changes it can bring, and how those positive changes can be measured. But soon the class discussion veered in a new and interesting direction: possible effects of therapy on the client's *partner*. Specifically, we started to ponder the ways that psychotherapy could—unintentionally, of course—cause distress in the person who was dating or married to the client. I asked my students, what would make *you* feel uncomfortable about your own partner's therapy? Luke spoke up first: "If my girlfriend kept me in the dark about it—if she wouldn't even tell me why she was going to therapy or what she was talking about there—I would hate that!" Taylor responded, "I wouldn't even need to know exactly why my boyfriend's in therapy, but I definitely don't want him seeing some hot female therapist!" Then Nathan chimed in, "If my partner was in therapy for just a few sessions, no problem. But if he's going for months and months, I'd start getting nervous." The spirited discussion continued for a while, with lots of other students agreeing, disagreeing, and offering new ideas of their own.

Then class ended, and everyone left—except Elizabeth. She stayed after and asked me some questions that advanced the conversation past speculation and into science: "Has anyone actually *investigated* that question? I mean, have any psychologists ever actually *run a study* to see what makes people feel uncomfortable about their partners' therapy? And if not, can *we* do that study?" Elizabeth was not satisfied with the conjecture that her classmates had offered. She was intrigued by it, as the rest of us were, but she wanted to test possible answers rather than just accepting the ones that seemed most believable on the surface. So we did exactly that.

Over the next few months, Elizabeth and I read other articles on the topic, designed an original study, and ran it with over 400 participants. We found some interesting results, too: our participants were especially uncomfortable with the idea of their partner keeping the reasons for therapy secret; refusing to talk about therapy sessions with them; being in therapy for more than 6 months; and seeing an attractive therapist. Other factors, like how much the client talked about the partner in therapy and the therapist's age and marital status didn't make such a big difference. When our study was complete, Elizabeth and I wrote it up, submitted it to a journal, and got it published (Pomerantz & Seely, 2000). We also presented the results at a professional conference. In these ways,

Psychologists take a scientific approach to important questions. For example, psychologists research questions about the possible connection between violent video games and violent behavior in kids. Srdjan Srdjanov/E+/Getty Images

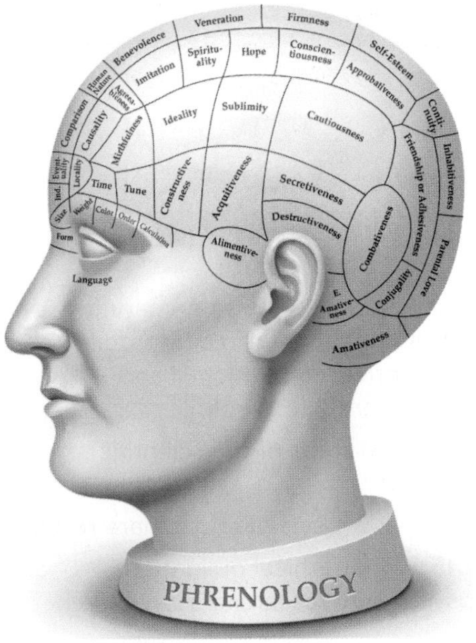

FIGURE 1.3 Pseudopsychology and Phrenology. In the late 1800s, many members of the public believed in phrenology, or the idea that bumps in the skull revealed personality characteristics and mental abilities. Disproving this kind of unsupported pseudopsychology is a major reason it is important for psychology to be a science.

pseudopsychology
Psychological information that is not supported by science but may appear to be.

critical thinking
An inquisitive, challenging approach to ideas and assumptions.

we shared our findings with other psychologists in the hope that they might advance the science of psychology.

The Need for Science in Psychology

When psychology got its start in the late 1800s, it was swimming in a sea of nonscientific thought (Cattell, 1895). That's why pioneers like Wundt, Titchener, and James had to work so hard to distinguish their new field *as a science*. These early psychologists worked to separate their new scientific field from nonscientific fields like philosophy, which emphasized the theories of John Locke, David Hume, and John Stuart Mill. These philosophers covered important topics—how people learn, what knowledge and abilities we are born with, and how we are shaped by experience—but they covered it through debate, rather than testing (Benjamin, 2007).

Pseudopsychology.

But an even bigger foe to the science of psychology was the popular psychology of the day. These were ideas the general public believed in but that had no basis in science—like we have astrology, horoscopes, and the vaccines-cause-autism theory today. In the late 1800s, popular psychology included phrenology, physiognomy, mesmerism, and spiritualism (Benjamin, 2007).

Phrenology. According to phrenology, bumps in the skull revealed personality characteristics and mental abilities (**Figure 1.3**). Phrenologists would travel from town to town, run their hands over the heads of the townspeople, and inform them that a bump over their right ear meant they were selfish; a bump on the top of their head meant they were kind; and a bump on the back of their head meant they were friendly and loving.

Physiognomy. Physiognomy was like phrenology but about the face rather than the skull. Supposedly your eyelids indicated how sympathetic you were, and the area around your lips told how patriotic you were.

Mesmerism. Mesmerism (named after its inventor, Franz Anton Mesmer) was a practice in which a healer moved magnets or in some cases just empty hands over your body to adjust your balance of fluids or to induce a hypnotic trance.

Spiritualism. Spiritualism took many forms, typically including communicating with spirits or the deceased. Clairvoyants, fortunetellers, palm readers, and séance

FROM RESEARCH TO REAL LIFE

Psychologists' Research on College Success

Among the many, many topics that psychologists study, one should be of particular interest to you: what predicts academic success in college students? Such a topic could interest many kinds of psychologists, from health psychologists to educational psychologists to developmental psychologists to cognitive psychologists to clinical psychologists. Here are some of their findings:

- Students who stay up later and wake up later get lower GPAs. In one study, GPA dropped 0.13 points (on a standard 0–4.0 scale) for each hour the sleep cycle was pushed back (Trockel et al., 2000).
- Students who are more engaged in college life—involved in more curricular and extracurricular activities for longer periods—get higher GPAs (Kuh et al., 2008; Wolf-Wendel et al., 2009).
- Students who have higher academic self-efficacy—in other words, those who believe that with effort they can succeed—earn higher GPAs (Robbins et al., 2004).
- Students who use performance goals—specifically setting out, from the beginning of the semester, to achieve a high standard in a course—earn higher GPAs than those who don't (Harackiewicz et al., 2002).
- Students who spend more time on Facebook get lower GPAs than students who don't, particularly when their Facebook time involves socializing rather than collecting and sharing information (Junco, 2012).
- Students who cram for tests get lower GPAs than those whose study sessions are spaced out and consistent (Roediger & Karpicke, 2011; Landauer, 2011).
- Just showing up makes a big difference. Students who attend class regularly, especially when attendance is not mandatory, earn higher GPAs than those who don't. In fact, one study concluded that attendance was a better predictor of college students' grade in a course than their SAT or ACT score, high school GPA, study habits, or study skills (Credé et al., 2010).

conductors could tell you all about your past, present, and future, according to these techniques.

These unsupported techniques were popular for some time, but they were bogus and have since been discredited. Perhaps more important, they were unscientific. So early psychologists fought hard to make sure that psychology was scientific, which made its claims more valid and respectable than those of all the nonscientific techniques.

Today, we call unsupported theories and practices in popular psychology **pseudopsychology**: psychological information that is not supported by science but may appear to be. (*Pseudo-* is Greek for false.) Unfortunately, pseudopsychology is still around and still persuades lots of people. Some believe that psychics can predict their future. Some have faith in horoscopes or numerology. Some are sure that their dreams can be accurately analyzed or the TV ads they see contain subliminal messages that force them to buy products. Fortunately, real psychology—that is, scientific psychology—is now well established, producing thousands of empirical studies every year and disproving the myths of pseudopsychology loudly and often (e.g., Lilienfeld, 2010; Lilienfeld et al., 2015; Lawson, 2007).

Critical Thinking. Perhaps the biggest enemy to pseudopsychology and the greatest friend to real psychology is **critical thinking**: an inquisitive, challenging approach to ideas and assumptions. Critical thinking is essential to advancement in any kind of science. After all, somebody had to say, "wait, maybe the earth isn't flat," or "hey, maybe there's a way we can connect all our computers together in some kind of web." In psychology, critical thinking is vital. Without it, psychologists would never generate new ideas about how your personality was formed, how your memory works, what the various regions of your brain do, how your mood and your health affect each other, and what helps people with psychological disorders.

With critical thinking, we become less dependent upon "common sense" (or "folk wisdom," or the proverbs that everybody "knows" to be true), which is especially helpful when common sense contradicts itself. That actually happens quite a bit. Which is true: "there's no place like home," or "the grass is always greener on the other side"? "Better safe than sorry," or "nothing ventured, nothing gained"? "You can't judge a book by its cover," or "the clothes make the man"? "Birds of a feather flock together," or "opposites attract"? Common sense certainly has its place, but science, fueled by critical thinking, can help us confirm or disconfirm the common sense explanations that occur to us.

Confirmation Bias. Critical thinking also helps us avoid some of the common errors in thinking that can lead us to conclusions that feel true but are actually false. One such error is the **confirmation bias**: a tendency to prefer information that confirms what you thought in the first place. You've experienced the confirmation bias in real life many times. For example, maybe you try a new restaurant and hate it. Later, you come across that restaurant on Yelp and notice that it has 100 reviews. You scroll quickly past the (many) glowing five-star reviews but spend plenty of time on the (few) one-star reviews, agreeing enthusiastically with all of them. By the time you click away from that page, you're more convinced than ever that it is indeed a terrible restaurant despite the reality that the restaurant's average rating was 4.5 stars. In other words, thanks to the confirmation bias, you looked for and found information that confirmed what you originally thought.

As scientists, psychologists dedicate themselves to overcoming confirmation bias. That is, we have to be open to ideas different from our own, even if that means we have to admit those ideas weren't perfect. For example, for a while in the late 1960s and 1970s, many clinical psychologists respected flooding as a form of therapy for people with anxiety disorders like phobias and posttraumatic stress disorder (Levis & Carrera, 1967; Willis & Edwards, 1969; Boulougouris et al., 1971; Emmelkamp & Wessels, 1975). Flooding involves exposing people to what they're afraid of—not little by little but all at once. A client who is afraid of dogs gets put into a room full of dogs, a client afraid of flying gets put on a plane, and so on.

confirmation bias
A tendency to prefer information that confirms what a person thought in the first place.

LIFE HACK 1.1

To boost your grades in college courses, study consistently instead of cramming; go to sleep and get up early; attend class regularly; get involved in extracurricular activities; and limit your time on social media.

(Credé, et al., 2010; Junco, 2012; Roediger & Karpicke, 2011; Landauer, 2011; Trockel et al., 2000; Kuh et al., 2008; Wolf-Wendel et al., 2009)

CHAPTER APP 1.1

College Success

MyHomework

Preview one of the links and consider the following questions.

WEBSITE:
http://tiny.cc/36g7jy

ANDROID:
http://tiny.cc/3vjyiy

IPHONE:
http://tiny.cc/tpjyiy

VIDEO DEMO:
http://tiny.cc/chapterapps

The MyHomework app allows you to schedule and track any school-related responsibilities, like classes, homework, long-term assignments, papers, and exams. It also sends reminders for classes, study sessions, and meetings.

How does it APPly to your daily life?
How could an app like this one help you be successful as a college student? In particular, how could it help you schedule consistently spaced study sessions rather than cramming?

How does it APPly to your understanding of psychology?
How does following consistently spaced study schedules and other advice supported by psychologists' research help you appreciate the need for science (as opposed to pseudoscience) in psychology?

Which is true: "the clothes make the man" or "you can't judge a book by its cover"? Critical thinking, which fuels science, decreases our reliance on these often contradictory proverbs. Kiselev Andrey Valerevich/ Shutterstock

As the decade went by, the number of studies supporting flooding declined, but they didn't disappear altogether. Occasionally, into the 1980s and even in recent years, studies would pop up with some kind of claim that flooding worked for particular clients (Keane et al., 1989; Marshall, 1985; Rychtarik et al., 1984; Levis, 2008; Zoellner et al., 2008). The point is this: a clinical psychologist who was pro-flooding from the beginning could fall victim to confirmation bias and with tunnel vision seek out those few studies that continued to support flooding as a treatment. In doing so, that clinical psychologist would ignore the many studies that found flooding to be ineffective or harmful. That clinical psychologist would also have to ignore the many studies finding that other therapies worked much better—especially systematic desensitization, in which the exposure is more gradual and humane (Pitman et al., 1991; Morganstern, 1973; Barlow et al., 2007; Head & Gross, 2009; Gamble et al., 2010).

Belief Perseverance. Another error that critical thinking helps us overcome is **belief perseverance**: a tendency to maintain a belief even when evidence suggests it is incorrect. Belief perseverance happens when you can't avoid beliefs that prove yours wrong but you cling to yours anyway. Going back to that restaurant example, if several of your friends tell you that restaurant was their all-time favorite, you might think, "What do they know about good food? It was awful." If it wins awards from local restaurant critics, you dig your heels in even more: "Restaurant critics are such idiots."

Psychologists don't like to admit they are wrong either. They will sometimes stand by a belief that is crumbling under the weight of evidence to the contrary. But ultimately it's their responsibility to overcome any belief perseverance and let critical thinking reign. This process happened with the old idea of the "schizophrenogenic mother"—the notion, put forth in the mid-1900s, that a certain style of mothering could cause schizophrenia, a serious mental disorder, in children (Fromm-Reichmann, 1948; Zuckerman et al., 1958; Jackson, 1960; Lidz et al., 1965). Some psychologists stuck with that idea even as evidence came forth that schizophrenia was not caused by a certain kind of mothering but was in fact caused by a combination of factors, with genes at the top of the list. In other words, some psychologists who originally agreed with the schizophrenogenic mother theory stayed with it even when there was plenty of evidence that it was wrong and another theory was right (Hartwell, 1996; Cardno & Gottesman, 2000; Kendler & Diehl, 1993). Ultimately, critical thinking overcame belief perseverance: the schizophrenogenic mother theory has been discredited and abandoned (Neill, 1990; Seeman, 2009).

Besides confirmation bias and belief perseverance, there are plenty of errors in thinking that psychologists, as scientists, use critical thinking to overcome. **Table 1.1** explains some of them.

The Goals of Psychological Studies

When psychologists conduct scientific studies, they have one of three aims: (1) to *describe* people in terms of a particular variable, (2) to see how two variables *correlate* with each other, or (3) to *experiment* by manipulating one variable and measuring how another variable responds. Let's consider each of these goals separately.

Descriptive Research. Descriptive research is research in which the goal is simply to describe a characteristic of the population. The psychologist specifies a group of people and then measures some quality, behavior, or other feature within that group. Imagine yourself as a psychologist with a strong interest in social media usage among U.S. college students. Descriptive research on that topic might simply measure how many hours per day college students spend on social media—nothing more, nothing less.

You'd report your findings of this descriptive study in the form of a *measure of central tendency*, like the *mean*, *median*, or *mode*. You'd also report the scatter, or *variance*, around those measures of central tendency, such as the *standard deviation*. Find more information about these concepts in Appendix A1.

TABLE 1.1: Thinking Errors

THINKING ERROR	DEFINITION	EXAMPLE
Confirmation bias	You prefer information that confirms what you already believe.	While shopping for a car, you start with a favorite model, and you seek out positive reviews of that car on the Internet.
Belief perseverance	You maintain a belief even when evidence suggests it is incorrect.	It has been raining hard for hours, but you believe that your softball game tonight will not get rained out.
Bandwagon fallacy	You believe something because lots of other people believe it.	Every house on the street has a yard sign endorsing the same candidate, so you think she must be worth voting for.
Emotional reasoning	You believe something because of how it makes you feel rather than how logical it is.	You believe your friend is a peaceful and well-behaved person even though he's been in several fistfights this semester.
Authority fallacy	You believe something because an authority figure believes it.	You change your beliefs about raising the minimum wage after hearing the opinion of an expert on the subject.
Antiquity fallacy	You believe something because people have believed it for a long time.	You believe that the roads in your overcrowded city don't need to be expanded because they were good enough for generations before you.
Black-or-white fallacy	You take an absolute or extreme belief when a more moderate belief would be more accurate.	You believe that your weight gain was entirely caused by a side effect of your medication, when in fact it was due to many factors.

Information from Lepper et al., 1986; Wason & Johnson-Laird, 1972; Tindale, 2007.

Correlational Research. Correlational research is research in which the goal is to determine the relationship between two variables. Descriptive research focuses on variables in isolation, but correlational research focuses on variables in tandem: how changes in one variable are linked to changes in the other variable, or how *predictive* one variable is for another. In other words, if you know how someone scores on one variable, how confidently can you predict how he or she scores on the other variable?

As an example, let's say you have finished your descriptive research on social media usage by college students. Now you are interested in doing a correlational study on college students' social media usage *and* their self-esteem (basically, how positively they think and feel about themselves). In other words, you want to find an answer to this question: if you know either the number of hours per day someone spends on social media *or* how much self-esteem that person has (as measured by a numeric questionnaire), how accurately can you predict the other variable?

To measure correlations, psychologists use the **correlation coefficient**: a statistic that shows the relationship between two variables, ranging from highly positive (+1) to highly negative (–1) (**Figure 1.4**). A *positive correlation coefficient* means that as one variable goes up, the other variable goes up with it. In your study, a positive correlation would mean that the more time a student spent on social media, the higher his or her self-esteem. The stronger the positive correlation is—the closer it falls to +1—the more confidence you can have in the prediction. So if you had a correlation coefficient around +.9 (quite rare in psychology), you could conclude that the two variables move together very closely, but if you got a correlation coefficient around +.4 (more common in psychology), you could conclude that the two variables were connected but more loosely.

A *negative correlation coefficient* means that as one variable goes up, the other variable goes down and vice versa. In your study, a negative correlation coefficient would mean that the more time a student spends on social media, the lower his or her self-esteem. The stronger the negative correlation is—the closer it falls to –1—the more confidence you can have in the prediction. So if you have a correlation coefficient around –.9 (quite rare in psychology), you could conclude that the two variables were very much opposites. However, if you have a correlation coefficient around –.4 (more common in psychology), you could conclude that the two variables had a looser inverse relationship.

Between the positive and the negative, there's the *zero correlation coefficient*, also known as no correlation, or the absence of a correlation. In your study, a zero

LIFE HACK 1.2

To make your own thinking as scientifically sound as possible, make a deliberate effort to overcome confirmation bias and belief perseverance, even if it means admitting you were wrong.

(Tindale, 2007; Wason & Johnson-Laird, 1972)

belief perseverance
A tendency to maintain a belief even when evidence suggests it is incorrect.

descriptive research
A type of research in which the goal is simply to describe a characteristic of the population.

correlational research
A type of research in which the goal is to determine the relationship between two variables.

correlation coefficient
A statistic that shows the relationship between two variables, ranging from highly positive (+1) to highly negative (–1).

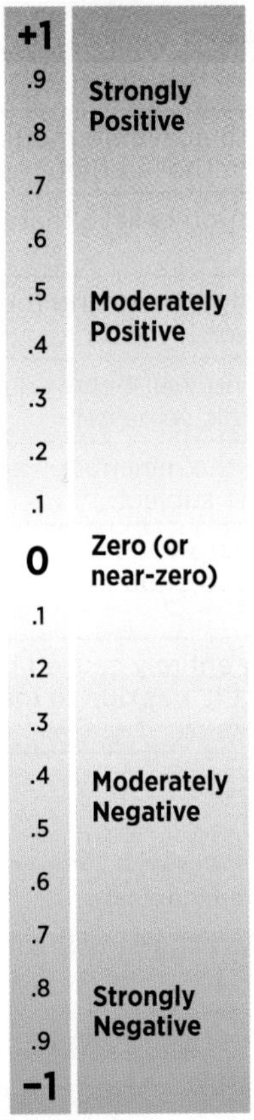

FIGURE 1.4 Correlation Coefficients. Correlation coefficients, which show how two variables relate to each other, range from +1.0 to −1.0. The closer they are to those extremes, the stronger they are. The closer they are to the middle (zero), the weaker they are.

MY TAKE VIDEO 1.2

Correlation-Causation Fallacy

"I would chew gum a lot and think that it would help me with my tests..."

YOUTUBE: http://tiny.cc/mytake
LAUNCHPAD: launchpadworks.com

correlation coefficient would mean that the time a student spent on social media told you absolutely nothing about his or her self-esteem and vice-versa. The two variables would have nothing—or zero—to do with each other. Correlation coefficients that fall very close to zero, like +.1 or −.1, are often interpreted by psychologists as being essentially the same as a zero correlation coefficient. Even though such coefficients may lean in either a positive or negative direction, they lean so slightly that they have no real predictive value.

When a correlation is strong (in either a positive or negative direction), there's a temptation to think that one variable *made* the other variable change (Thompson, 2013; Dickter, 2006). But that would be an error that psychologists call the **correlation–causation fallacy**: the mistaken belief that when two variables correlate strongly with each other, one must cause the other (see My Take Video 1.2). Simply put, *correlation does not necessarily mean causation*. Let's say you have a strong positive correlation coefficient in your study: as social media hours increase, so does self-esteem. Does that mean that spending more time on social media *causes* self-esteem to rise? Not necessarily. What about causation the other way around: does high self-esteem *cause* people to spend more time on social media? Again, not necessarily. You simply can't tell from a correlation coefficient. That statistic tells what *varies with* what, but not what *causes* what. In the case of a strong positive correlation, it could be the case that the first variable causes the second or that the second variable causes the first or both or neither (perhaps a third variable outside of the focus of the study causes both). To determine the causal relationship between variables, you'd have to upgrade from a correlational study to *experimental research*, which we turn to now.

Experimental Research. Experimental research is research in which the goal is to determine the cause-and-effect relationship between two variables by manipulating one and observing changes in the other. In your work on social media and self-esteem, you'd be running experimental research if you controlled one of the two variables—that is, if you determined how much or how little of it your participants have—rather than simply measuring what was already there. In this case, neither variable is easy to manipulate, but your best bet would be to manipulate social media time. Changing a person's self-esteem is too much of a challenge, both practically and ethically. (Could you effectively lower your participants' self-esteem? Could you live with yourself if you did?) Also, you may have reason to believe that social media time influences self-esteem more than self-esteem influences social media time, based on experts' theory or the results of similar studies on this topic. The difficulty of completely manipulating one of these variables highlights a common problem for psychologists: it's difficult to experiment on people. Unlike chemists experimenting on chemicals or physicists experimenting on objects, psychologists have to consider both what's realistically doable and what's morally permissible for those whom they study (Hock, 2013; Wampold, 2006).

With a research design based on the idea that changes in social media time cause changes in self-esteem, social media time would be your **independent variable (IV)**: in experimental research, a variable that is manipulated by the researcher. By contrast, self-esteem would be your **dependent variable (DV)**: in experimental research, a variable that is expected to depend upon the independent variable. In your study, you might initially measure both social media time and self-esteem in your participants and then double their social media time for a week, with the expectation that such an increase would cause changes in self-esteem. (Did you know there are apps that can limit time on social media sites?)

Actually, you would only double social media time for half of your participants, and leave social media time unchanged for the other half. The group whose social media time you doubled would be your **experimental group**: in experimental research, the group of participants who receive the treatment that is the focus of the study. The group whose social media time remained the same would be your **control group**: in experimental research, the group of participants who do not receive the treatment that is the focus of the study.

Of course, you'd want to put participants into those two groups via **random assignment**: a procedure in experimental research by which the assignment of participants into either the experimental or control group happens entirely by chance. If you used some factor (gender, for example) other than chance to assign participants to the experimental group or the control group, that factor rather than the variable you are manipulating could be the reason the groups differ, which would confound the results (Meltzoff, 1998). Assuming you did assign participants randomly, at the end of the study you'd measure whether your experimental group showed changes that your control group didn't. In other words, did those whose social media time got doubled demonstrate changes in their self-esteem, while those whose social media time remained the same stayed at the same level of self-esteem?

When possible, psychologists like to run their experiments using a **double-blind procedure**: a way of conducting experimental research in which neither the participants nor the researchers are aware of which participants are in each group. The purpose of keeping both the participants and the researchers "blind" is to minimize the **placebo effect**: the effect of expectations rather than the experimental manipulations. The double-blind procedure might not be possible for your study of social media and self-esteem, since your participants will notice any changes to their social media time. But in other studies, particularly those in which the placebo effect is a real risk, the double-blind procedure is both possible and desirable. For example, consider a clinical psychologist overseeing an experiment on a new type of therapy for depression. She might give half of her participants (the experimental group) the new therapy and the other half (the control group), a therapy already proven to work. However, she would not tell any of the participants which group they were in. She might also ask other clinicians to conduct the interviews to assess clients' depression levels at the end of the study and keep those clinicians in the dark about which clients got which kind of therapy.

The Scientific Method

The **scientific method** is a way of asking and answering questions that follows a predetermined series of steps: posing a question, conducting a literature review, developing a hypothesis, testing the hypothesis by collecting data, and analyzing the data and drawing conclusions (**Figure 1.5**). Psychologists, like scientists in other disciplines, follow the scientific method as a primary way of learning more about the topic they study (Hershey et al., 1996, 2006). Let's consider each step of the scientific method as it might apply to your study on social media time and self-esteem.

Posing a Question. The question on which the study focuses depends on the kind of research you conduct (Leong et al., 2012). If the research is descriptive, the question might simply be, "how many hours per day do students spend on social media?" If the research involves self-esteem and is correlational, the question could be, "to what extent are social media time and self-esteem linked?" If it involves self-esteem and is experimental, the question could be, "to what extent does time on social media influence self-esteem?"

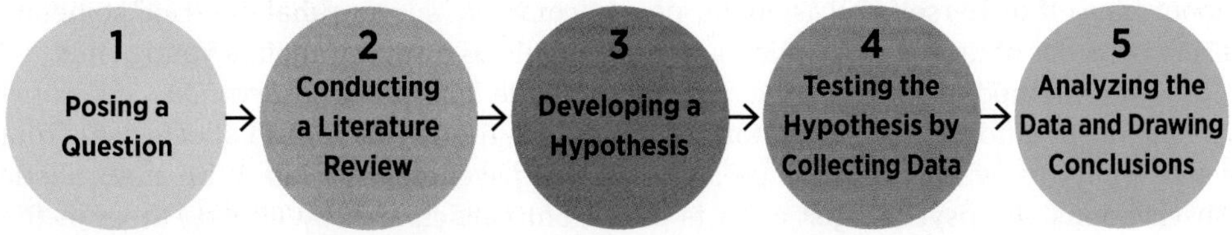

FIGURE 1.5 The Steps of the Scientific Method. When psychologists conduct scientific research, they move through certain steps in a certain order: posing a question, conducting a literature review, developing a hypothesis, testing the hypothesis by collecting data, and analyzing the data and drawing conclusions.

LIFE HACK 1.3

When you notice a correlation between two things in your own life, don't automatically assume that one causes the other. You might have the cause and effect reversed, or they could both be caused by something else, or the connection could be coincidental rather than causal.

(Thompson, 2013; Dickter, 2006)

correlation–causation fallacy
A mistaken belief that when two variables correlate strongly with each other, one must cause the other.

experimental research
A type of research in which the goal is to determine the cause-and-effect relationship between two variables by manipulating one and observing changes in the other.

independent variable (IV)
A variable in experimental research that is manipulated by the researcher.

dependent variable (DV)
A variable in experimental research that is expected to depend upon the independent variable.

experimental group
The group of participants in experimental research who receive the treatment that is the focus of the study.

control group
The group of participants in experimental research who do not receive the treatment that is the focus of the study.

random assignment
A procedure in experimental research by which the assignment of participants into either the experimental or control group happens entirely by chance.

double-blind procedure
A way of conducting experimental research in which neither the participants nor the researchers are aware of which participants are in the experimental group and which are in the control group.

placebo effect
The effect of expectations in experimental research rather than the effect of experimental manipulations.

scientific method
A way of asking and answering questions that follows a predetermined series of steps: posing a question, conducting a literature review, developing a hypothesis, testing the hypothesis by collecting data, and analyzing the data and drawing conclusions.

FIGURE 1.6 The Importance of Random Sampling. If you want to know what Skittles taste like, just eating the small bag on the right wouldn't give you the full experience. You'd know what green Skittles taste like, but not the other colors. A more random sample—like the small bag on the left—would give you a much better sense, since it was obviously selected at random so its mix matches the mix in the big bag. The same logic holds true for psychologists trying to measure some quality of a population: the more random their sample, the better their data will correspond to all of the people in that population.

Conducting a Literature Review. Of course, the question a researcher poses should be informed by what other researchers have found before. So you will need to do a **literature review**: a step in scientific research during which a researcher learns what previous research on the topic already exists. You may not be the first researcher to study social media time and self-esteem. In fact, there may be a whole body of research on the topic, and if so, your best contribution would be to add to what's already there rather than repeat the research (Baumeister, 2013; Rothstein, 2012; Marczyk et al., 2005). (For the emerging body of literature on social media and self-esteem-related topics, see Junco, 2013a, 2013b, 2012; Gonzalez & Hancock, 2011; Kalpidou et al., 2011; and Chou & Edge, 2012, among others.)

Developing a Hypothesis. Psychological research is typically based on a **theory**: a proposed explanation for observed events. For example, your experimental research on social media time and self-esteem might be based on the theory that as social media time goes up, self-esteem goes down. Ideally, this theory is influenced by previous research on the topic (Gelso, 2006). To see how strong your theory is, that theory must be translated into a **hypothesis**: a prediction, typically based on a theory, that can be tested.

An important part of translating a theory into a hypothesis is to make the concepts in the theory more specific and easier to measure, often in numbers. In other words, for each concept you need an **operational definition**: a specific, measurable definition of a variable for the purpose of a scientific study. *social media time* might be operationally defined as participants' response to the question, how many hours per day do you use social media? Or if they allow you to track their social media use directly by monitoring their devices, it might be the number of hours revealed by that method. *Self-esteem* might be operationally defined as participants' total score on a 10-item self-esteem questionnaire.

Testing the Hypothesis by Collecting Data. When you collect data for your study of social media and self-esteem, you'll have to decide whose social media time and self-esteem you are most interested in. In other words, you have to identify the study's **population**: the whole range of people on whom the research is focused. In this case, as we have already discussed, your population is U.S. college students. But you certainly won't be able to include all of them in your study; there are way too many, and you couldn't get to them all.

That means you'll have to settle for a **sample**: the subset of the population who actually participate in the research. It's important for the sample to match the population (**Figure 1.6**). If the sample differs in a significant way from the population, your results may be true only for your sample, not more generally across your whole population. For example, if you recruited your sample only from a college that had a high proportion of students of a particular religion, race, gender, or major, then the data those students provide might be specific to their sample but not generalizable to all college students. Your best bet in terms of matching your sample to the population is to obtain a *random sample*, a subset of the population recruited randomly to participate in the research—a strategy that isn't always possible but that psychologists strive for nonetheless.

This social media study would be conducted as a *survey*, or a set of questions addressed to a group of people about their behavior or attitudes. Surveys are usually done in a *self-report* format, which means that the person completing the survey answers questions about himself or herself. Occasionally, people complete surveys that describe someone else's behavior or attitudes, as when a parent completes a survey about a young child.

Other methods for descriptive research include *laboratory observations* and naturalistic observations. With laboratory observations, the psychologist collects data from participants by watching their behavior in the psychologist's lab. With naturalistic observations, the psychologist collects data from participants by visiting them in the real-world location where their behavior happens naturally. Neither laboratory observations nor naturalistic observations would be ideal for a social media study, since it wouldn't be practical to keep participants in the lab or follow them around in their personal lives for days at a time.

literature review
A step in scientific research during which a researcher learns what previous research on the topic already exists.

theory
A proposed explanation for observed events.

hypothesis
A prediction, typically based on a theory, that can be tested.

operational definition
A specific, measurable definition of a variable for the purpose of a scientific study.

population
The whole range of people on whom a study's research is focused.

sample
The subset of the population who actually participate in the research.

replication
Conducting a study again to confirm or disconfirm the results.

WATCHING PSYCHOLOGY

Survey Says? *Family Feud* and Random Sampling

You've probably heard the *Family Feud* host say it many times: "100 people surveyed, top answers on the board." But which 100 people? Are those 100 people a random sample of the U.S. population? Or are certain people more likely to be sampled and others less likely to be sampled, based on how *Family Feud* recruits them? If they call random phone numbers, the 100 people could be reasonably close to a random sample, although it would be tilted toward those who are willing to pick up the phone from an unknown number and spend time answering a stranger's questions. But if *Family Feud* surveys its own studio audience, the 100 people would all be those who live in or visit Hollywood, who probably don't represent the country at large in terms of likes, dislikes, experiences, and other factors that could influence their answers.

Think about how different the top answers to these *Family Feud* questions could be depending on where the 100 people surveyed came from:

- *Name a movie you enjoy watching over and over again.* Think you'd get different top answers from 20-somethings and 60-somethings?
- *Name a place kids go after school.* Think you'd get different top answers in rich and poor neighborhoods?
- *Name a food you have on special occasions.* Think you'd get different top answers in Hawaii and Maine?
- *Name a feature of a car that would make you want to buy it.* Think you'd get different top answers from men and women?

When psychologists conduct research, they sample as randomly as possible to make sure that the data they collect is representative of the population they are studying. And when random sampling isn't entirely possible, they explain this fact, being careful not to overestimate the range of people for whom their results might be true.

For other studies, however, laboratory observations or natural observations can be excellent strategies for data collection. For example, imagine a group of psychologists conducting a study to determine gender differences in physically aggressive behavior in kids. They could do a laboratory observation study in which the psychologists invite small groups of kids to their lab and monitor them while they interact. Or they could do a naturalistic observation study in which the psychologists visit elementary schools and monitor the kids at recess, at lunch, and in the classroom. A particular advantage of naturalistic observation is that it sidesteps any differences between how people might behave in the unique environment of a psychology lab and how they actually behave in their own environment.

A small number of psychologists conduct research in which the sample consists of just one person (or a very small group) studied in great depth. This type of research is called a *case study* (Davison & Lazarus, 2007; Kazdin, 2011). Often, case studies read more like stories than scientific research, with words rather than numbers used to detail what happened. Sigmund Freud, for example, was known for writing lengthy, captivating case studies about his clients (Gay, 1995). Other times, case studies are empirical. For instance, a clinical psychologist might count a particular behavior of a client—say, a disruptive child's verbal outbursts during class—when that client is alternately on and off a particular form of therapy (Gallo et al., 2013; Freeman & Eagle, 2011; Photos et al., 2008).

Analyzing the Data and Drawing Conclusions. Once the data is collected, it's time to make sense of it. Most often, that process begins by entering numbers into a data file in a statistics computer program and conducting a *data analysis* with the appropriate statistical tests. The best statistical tests are the ones that directly address the hypothesis. For example, if you ran a correlational study on social media time and self-esteem, a correlation coefficient would tell you exactly what you want to know. With the statistics in hand, the next step is to interpret them, or explain in a way that is understandable to others what it all means and why it matters.

Often, this final step in analyzing the data includes suggestions for **replication**: conducting a study again, for the purpose of confirming or disconfirming the results. A single study means something, but a bunch of studies conducted in a similar way that reach the same conclusions means much more. If your experimental study led to the conclusion that more time on social media caused self-esteem to drop, that's a conclusion with some impact. But if you or other researchers replicate your study—perhaps with different or larger samples—and got the same results again and again, the impact of your conclusion grows, as does the confidence you can have that it is true across time and place.

One important step of the scientific method is data analysis, which usually involves running statistical tests on numbers entered into a computer program. Jacob Ammentorp Lund/iStock/Getty Images

How Psychologists Share Their Results

So do psychologists just post their research results on a Web site or a blog when they're done?

No! Psychologists who have conducted research are certainly eager to share their results, but they do so in a way that ensures higher quality than simply putting those results out there without any oversight or scrutiny. Psychologists make their research known to others via the **peer review process**: the appraisal of research by people who are as expert as (or more so) on the subject than the researcher. The peers involved in the peer review process take an evaluative role: they receive submissions from researchers and decide whether they are worthy to be shared with the professional community (Kazdin, 2013).

There are two main outlets for psychologists (and their students) to share their research—presentations at professional conferences and articles in professional journals. The peer review process is a big part of both outlets. If you wanted to give a talk or present a poster about your study on social media and self-esteem at a professional conference, you can't just show up and claim a time slot—it doesn't work that way. You would anonymously submit a proposal to the conferences' *reviewers*, other psychologists who know a lot about this particular subject and have probably done similar research themselves (Cohen et al., 2013; Beins & Beins, 2008). If you wanted to publish an article about your study, you couldn't just post it on a journal's site as easily if you were posting a product review on amazon.com. You'd have to submit your manuscript to the editor of a particular journal, who passes it along to reviewers to be read and evaluated (Drotar et al., 2013; Tesser & Martin, 2005). The reviewers at the conference or the journal would then provide you with feedback: a rejection, an acceptance, or often (for journals) something in between that researchers call a revise-and-resubmit (Nagata & Trierweiler, 2006; Osipow, 2006; Peterson, 2006).

The main point about the peer review process is this: for psychologists to share their research results with others in the field, that research has to be reviewed by professional peers with expertise in the same area. Those peers have to judge it as soundly designed and conducted and as providing something new and important to the field. This peer review system motivates researchers to produce high-quality studies and allows those who read or hear a presentation about the research to trust that the research is first-rate.

Before psychologists can share their results at professional conferences (top) or in professional journals (bottom), they first have it evaluated through peer review. (top) Fuse/Getty Images; (bottom) Roman Sigaev/Hemera/Getty Images

To illustrate the peer review process, consider what happened with a study I did with a graduate student and a couple of my professor colleagues (Wozenilek et al., 2012). Our study focused on what therapists did when clients missed appointments without letting the psychologists know (a "no-show"). We contacted hundreds of therapists and asked them to read brief descriptions of different no-show situations and then answer questions about how they would handle them. We found that almost all therapists try to contact the client, but how soon and how often depended significantly on the client. For example, when the client was depressed and had a history of suicide attempts, the therapists would call sooner and more frequently than if the client had anxiety problems.

We believed our study was of high quality, answered a question that previous studies had not, and produced results that other psychologists would find informative and meaningful. So we tried to share our findings. Our first attempt was a proposal to the APA convention, attended by thousands of psychologists every year. Through the APA convention Web site, we submitted a summary of our study to be read by reviewers who knew the topic well. After waiting a few months, an email from the main reviewer brought good news: our proposal was accepted! Later that year, we were off to a huge convention center in Washington, DC, to present our study at the conference.

Later, after we analyzed our data a bit more, we wanted to share our results in the form of a published article. We found a professional journal that seemed like a good fit (*Journal of Contemporary Psychotherapy*), polished up our manuscript, and submitted it through the journal's Web site. The editor forwarded it to several members of

the journal's editorial board (a couple of dozen researchers with highly specialized expertise) to be read and critiqued. After a few months, they told the editor what they thought of it, and the editor shared those thoughts with us. In this case, those thoughts were mixed—some positive, some negative. The editor invited us to address the negative comments and then send it back for reconsideration. We did exactly that, and after waiting a bit longer for a second review by the same reviewers, good news: it was accepted for publication! Our study appeared as an article in the journal soon after that.

peer review process
The appraisal of research by people who are at least as expert on the subject as the researcher.

informed consent to research
An ethical requirement for psychologists by which they must inform people about the research and obtain their consent before participation can occur.

Ethics in Psychological Studies

When psychologists conduct research, they are required to do so ethically (Fisher & Vacanti-Shova, 2012; Fried, 2012; Koocher, 2013). This requirement comes from multiple sources, including an *Institutional Review Board* (IRB) and the American Psychological Association (APA). The IRB at each university or research center makes sure that psychologists' studies don't put any participants at risk (Dell et al., 2006; Miller, 2003). (Early in the history of psychology, before IRBs were common, some studies with questionable ethics were conducted.) The APA publishes a code of ethics that offers guidelines about conducting ethical psychological research (American Psychological Association, 2002).

In the 2002 APA Code of Ethics, the standards on research are essentially a list of important dos and don'ts. Namely, psychologists conducting research ethically *do*:

- Get approval from their own IRB, which requires proof that participants won't be harmed, before beginning any study.
- Tell any possible participant enough about the study beforehand to enable him or her to make an educated decision about whether to participate (Fischman, 2000). Researchers call this obtaining **informed consent to research**: an ethical requirement for psychologists by which they must inform people about the research and obtain their consent before participation can occur.
- Allow participants to withdraw without penalty if they feel uncomfortable.
- Keep confidential the information they collect from participants.
- When the study is over, offer the participant an explanation, or *debriefing*, of the study's purpose and the opportunity to learn about its results and conclusions (Eyde, 2000).
- If animals are used as subjects, treat them humanely.
- Include as authors those who made significant research contributions, with the order of authors reflecting the size of the contribution; the one who made the biggest contribution is the first author.

And psychologists conducting research ethically *don't*:

- Force people to participate against their will.
- Deceive possible participants about the research unless doing so won't cause them pain or distress, is essential to the study, is disclosed after participation, and is the only option (no undeceptive alternative is available).
- Fabricate, or make up, data.
- Plagiarize, or claim as their own, ideas or words that belong to someone else.

CHECK YOUR LEARNING:

1.11 Why does psychology require a scientific approach?

1.12 How do the three main types of psychology research—descriptive, correlational, and experimental—differ?

1.13 What are the five steps of the scientific method?

1.14 In what ways do psychologists share their research results?

1.15 What ethical obligations do psychology researchers have?

CHAPTER SUMMARY

What Is Psychology?

1.1 Psychology is the scientific study of behavior and mental processes, which means that psychology focuses on *both* our outer actions *and* our inner experiences.

1.2 Psychology is not just therapy, not exclusively about people with mental disorders, not all about Sigmund Freud, not psychiatry, and not just a bunch of ideas with no research to back them up.

1.3 Three big questions underlie the field of psychology: Nature or nurture? Change or stability? Universal or unique?

Psychology's Many Subfields

1.4 The field of psychology is large and diverse. Tens of thousands of people belong to the American Psychological Association, which has 54 divisions focusing on a wide variety of topic areas.

1.5 Applied psychology specializations are areas in which psychologists apply their expertise to real-world problems. Basic research psychology specializations are areas in which psychologists conduct research to further the understanding of behavior and mental processes.

1.6 Areas of applied psychology include clinical psychology, counseling psychology, community psychology, forensic psychology, educational psychology, and industrial/organizational psychology.

1.7 Areas of basic research in psychology include developmental psychology, personality psychology, physiological psychology, comparative psychology, social psychology, and health psychology.

Psychology Then and Now

1.8 Psychology evolved from two much older fields of study: philosophy, which focuses on questions about the inner workings of the mind, and physiology, which focuses on the biological functioning of brain and body.

1.9 Structuralism was a perspective in psychology that focused on breaking down mental processes in terms of their structure or basic parts. Functionalism was a perspective in psychology that emphasized the function of mental processes and behaviors. Psychoanalysis is a perspective in psychology that focuses on unconscious mental activity and the long-lasting influence of childhood experiences. Behaviorism is a perspective in psychology that insists on studying observable behavior instead of internal mental processes. Humanism is a perspective in psychology that concentrates on the notion that human nature is generally good and people are naturally motivated to grow toward their own potential.

1.10 Multiculturalism is a perspective in psychology that highlights the influence of culture on behavior and mental processes. Evolutionary psychology is a perspective in psychology that emphasizes Charles Darwin's theory of evolution as an influence on behavior. Cognitive psychology is a perspective in psychology that emphasizes cognitive processes such as thinking, language, attention, memory, and intelligence. Neuroscience is a perspective in psychology that studies the link between behavior and the biological functioning of the brain. Positive psychology is a perspective in psychology that emphasizes people's strengths and successes. Biopsychosocial theory is a popular and comprehensive perspective in psychology that acknowledges biological factors, psychological factors, and social factors as influences on behavior.

The Science of Psychology

1.11 Psychology requires a scientific approach to make its claims more valid and respectable than all the nonscientific techniques of pseudopsychology.

1.12 In descriptive research, the goal is simply to describe a characteristic of the population. In correlational research, the goal is to determine the relationship between two variables. In experimental research, the goal is to determine the cause-and-effect relationship between two variables by manipulating one and observing changes in the other.

1.13 The five steps of the scientific method are (1) posing a question, (2) conducting a literature review, (3) developing a hypothesis, (4) testing the hypothesis by collecting data, and (5) analyzing the data and drawing conclusions.

1.14 Psychologists share results through a peer review process, the two main outlets of which are presentations at professional conferences and articles in professional journals.

1.15 Psychology researchers are ethically obligated to not harm participants, to obtain informed consent from them, to allow participants to withdraw, to keep their information confidential, and to debrief participants.

KEY TERMS

psychology, p. 3
psychiatry, p. 3
applied psychology specializations, p. 5
clinical psychology, p. 5
counseling psychology, p. 5
industrial/organizational (I/O) psychology, p. 7
community psychology, p. 7
forensic psychology, p. 7
educational psychology, p. 7
basic research psychology specializations, p. 7
developmental psychology, p. 7
personality psychology, p. 7
physiological psychology, p. 8
social psychology, p. 8
health psychology, p. 8
comparative psychology, p. 8
structuralism, p. 13
functionalism, p. 13
psychoanalysis, p. 13
behaviorism, p. 15
humanism, p. 15
multiculturalism, p. 17
evolutionary psychology, p. 17
cognitive psychology, p. 17
neuroscience, p. 17
positive psychology, p. 18
biopsychosocial theory, p. 18
pseudopsychology, p. 20
critical thinking, p. 20
confirmation bias, p. 21
belief perseverance, p. 23
descriptive research, p. 23
correlational research, p. 23
correlation coefficient, p. 23
correlation-causation fallacy, p. 25
experimental research, p. 25
independent variable (IV), p. 25
dependent variable (DV), p. 25
experimental group, p. 25
control group, p. 25
random assignment, p. 25
double-blind procedure, p. 25
placebo effect, p. 25
scientific method, p. 25
literature review, p. 26
theory, p. 26
hypothesis, p. 26
operational definition, p. 26
population, p. 26
sample, p. 26
replication, p. 26
peer review process, p. 29
informed consent to research, p. 29

SELF-ASSESSMENT

1. Psychology is defined as the scientific study of ______ and ______ ______.

2. Dr. Hernandez is a psychologist conducting research on shyness. Specifically, she compares the shyness of adopted children to the shyness of their adoptive parents and biological parents. Which of the big questions of psychology is most closely connected to Dr. Hernandez's study?
   a. Nature or nurture
   b. Change or stability
   c. Universal or unique
   d. All of the answers are correct.

3. Dr. Jenkins is a psychologist who works with corporations and organizations to help them with hiring decisions and provide advice about the best ways for managers to supervise employees. Dr. Jenkins is most likely a(n) ______ psychologist.
   a. forensic
   b. counseling
   c. clinical
   d. industrial/organizational

4. The two academic fields from which psychology emerged are ______ and ______.

5. The contemporary, or "new," schools of psychology include ______, ______, and ______.
   a. psychoanalysis, multiculturalism, neuroscience
   b. multiculturalism, neuroscience, evolutionary psychology
   c. humanism, multiculturalism, evolutionary psychology
   d. behaviorism, multiculturalism, neuroscience

6. According to the biopsychosocial theory, the three types of factors that influence behavior are ______ factors, ______ factors, and ______ factors.

7. Psychology is a ______, which means that psychologists test every theory that attempts to explain behavior and mental processes.

8. A group of psychologists conduct a research study to determine the connection between the number of hours of sleep teenagers get per night and their grade point average. This study is best described as ______ research.
   a. correlational
   b. experimental
   c. descriptive
   d. psychiatric

9. Dr. Matsumi is a psychologist who conducts research on how people make group decisions. Specifically, she's interested in learning more about how important it is to members of groups to avoid conflict with others even when they disagree. Which of the following psychology specializations does Dr. Matsumi's research best represent?
   a. comparative psychology
   b. clinical psychology
   c. physiological psychology
   d. social psychology

10. The goal of ______ research is to determine the cause-and-effect relationship between two variables by manipulating one variable and observing changes in the second variable.

Self-Assessment Answers

1. behavior, mental processes 2. a, 3. d, 4. philosophy, physiology, 5. b, 6. biological, psychological, social, 7. science, 8. a, 9. d, 10. experimental

WHAT'S YOUR TAKE?

1. When you think about your own culture, your first thought may be your ethnicity or your race. But there may be many other cultural variables that are at least as important. As a clinical psychologist, I have learned from some of my own clients that certain cultural characteristics other than ethnicity or race were at the core of their identities. For one woman, it was her religion (she was a Modern Orthodox Jew); for another, it was his sexual orientation (he was gay); for another, it was her geographical upbringing (she grew up and still lived in a tiny rural town). One teenage client even proudly told me that he was from "skater culture"—not just that he skateboarded, but he had adopted the entire lifestyle that encompasses skateboarding—and that if I didn't get skater culture, I couldn't get him.

If you saw a psychologist, which of your cultural characteristic(s) would the psychologist have to get in order to get you? Are you a typical member of that culture, or do you differ from most others in some way?

2. I have noticed a strong positive correlation in my own life: when I do more laundry, I'm in a better mood. I first noticed this correlation in college, when I tended to feel a bit more upbeat during weeks when I found myself in the laundry room more than once and a bit more down on weeks when the pile of dirty laundry didn't grow so fast. What's up with that? Could it be that washing, drying, and folding *caused* my good mood? Or that my good mood *caused* me to do more laundry? Neither of those made much sense. Eventually, I settled on a more likely interpretation: there was a third factor—exercising—that caused both. In weeks when I ran or played basketball more often, the exercise improved my mood, *and* it increased the amount of sweaty clothes in the hamper, which meant I needed to do laundry more often.

How about you? Have you ever noticed two things correlating in your own life—increasing together, decreasing together, or one increasing when the other decreased in a predictable way—but without a causal relationship between them? If so, what were they, and how do you explain their correlation?

SHOW ME MORE

1.1 Nature Versus Nurture

launchpadworks.com LaunchPad

This video offers interesting ideas regarding the interacting roles of nature and nurture as influences on behavior.

Courtesy HealthCentral Network

1.2 Wilhelm Wundt and William James

http://tiny.cc/showmemore

This animated video provides a quick overview of the contributions of Wilhelm Wundt and William James to the history of psychology.

© Macmillan

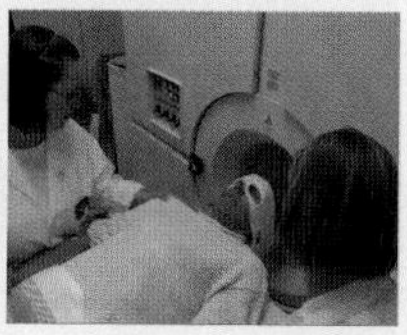

1.3 The Placebo Effect

launchpadworks.com LaunchPad

This video presents a study of the placebo effect on levels of dopamine in the brain and other treatment outcomes.

© Worth Publishers

2 Brain and Behavior

serts/Getty Images

We live in an exciting time for studying the brain. Rapid advances in technology allow psychologists and other researchers to view the brain and its inner workings more vividly than ever before. These researchers make eye-popping discoveries that pinpoint specific brain structures or brain activities associated with specific behaviors or experiences. Their research is often accompanied by astonishingly brilliant images of the brain at work. Yet the finding that I have found most amazing is not one of these brain discoveries or brain images. It is a simple story that a team of brain researchers shared about a stray sick kitten that wandered into their lives.

The researchers named the four-week-old kitten Diesel, who unfortunately lost both eyes to feline herpes. But Diesel doesn't behave like a blind cat. In fact, Diesel rapidly developed a mental map of the lab that allows him to run and jump with remarkable speed. This is due, in part, to the "rapid processing of information from his whiskers, which are always a step in front of him when he is in motion" (Yeshurun et al., 2009, p. 321). But Diesel's most amazing ability is catching flies. This blind cat can hear a fly buzzing through the lab, and then he seems to track it even though he can't actually see it. Then, at the exact instant, Diesel springs up into "the air, catching the fly between his clapped paws."

How does Diesel do all of that? More specifically, how does Diesel's *brain* help him to do all of that? Without sight, how does his brain capitalize so keenly on his remaining senses, like hearing and touch? Without sight, how does his brain create a mental map of the room? Without sight, how does his brain maneuver his legs to steer him around furniture straight to the fly, and then coordinate his two front paws to rise and smack together at exactly the right moment in exactly the right spot to catch the fly? Come to think of it, even *with* sight, the ability of Diesel's brain to do any of those things is pretty remarkable. And that's just a cat catching a fly. When you take the time to appreciate the additional things that the human brain empowers you to do—talking, planning, reasoning, creating, and computing, among many others—the abilities of your brain are absolutely mind- (or brain-) boggling.

In this chapter, we will examine what psychologists have learned about the brain. We'll learn how the brain interacts with the rest of the body, what various parts of the brain are responsible for, and how microscopic activities within the brain translate into thoughts and actions. We'll also learn about the tools and technologies that researchers use to uncover all of this knowledge about the brain.

CHAPTER OUTLINE

Brain and Behavior Connections: An Introduction

YOU WILL LEARN:

2.1 how a head injury and an autopsy discovery in the 1800s led to better understanding of brain and behavior connections.

2.2 how our approach to understanding the brain will start with microscopic activity within the brain, then expand to the parts of the brain, and then expand more to how the brain interacts with the whole body.

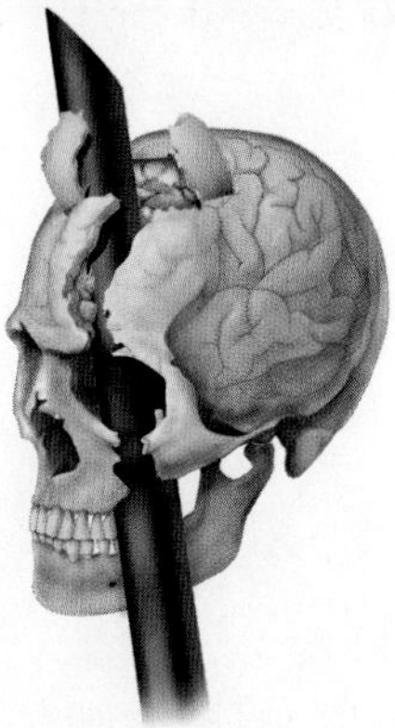

In 1848, a railroad worker named Phineas Gage experienced a horrible injury: An accidental explosion sent an iron rod up through the roof of his mouth, through his brain, and out the top of his skull. He survived the accident, and he retained many abilities, like walking, talking, and remembering. However, his personality changed drastically. The case of Phineas Gage provided early evidence that certain parts of the brain influence certain traits or abilities. Warren Anatomical Museum in the Francis A. Countway Library of Medicine. Gift of Jack and Beverly Wilgus

Today, we take for granted the fact that the brain and behavior are closely connected. A couple of centuries ago, however, that connection wasn't so obvious. Let's examine some historic events that advanced the understanding of how the brain connects to behavior.

Phineas Gage's Accident and Paul Broca's Discovery

It's September 13, 1848, and a railroad crew lays new tracks across a small town in Vermont. Tools of the trade surround the railroad, including blasting powder (to blast through hills and mountains) and iron rods used to tightly pack that blasting powder into compact spaces. Suddenly, there's an unexpected explosion, followed by the anguished screams of the 25-year-old crew leader, Phineas Gage. The railroad crew rushes to Phineas and discovers that an accidental explosion of blasting powder had shot one of those iron rods—over an inch thick and over three feet long—up through the roof of Phineas' mouth, *through his brain,* and out the top of his skull. Somehow, after just a momentary loss of consciousness, Phineas comes to his senses. He even talks, stands up, and walks with the support of his crew members.

When this accident took place—and yes, it really happened like that—people were fascinated that Phineas Gage survived at all (Macmillan, 2000a, b). But as the months and years went by, a different fascination emerged, one that focused on the way Phineas' brain injury impacted him as a person. In some ways, he remained the same. He retained his basic abilities (moving, walking, talking, etc.), and his intelligence and memory seemed intact, too. But in other ways, he was quite different. Specifically, his personality had changed. Before the accident, Phineas was a reliable, calm, kind man, but now he was irresponsible, hot-headed, and mean. He notably lacked the self-control he once had, which meant that he had a hard time keeping a job and living independently. Sadly, by the time of his death in 1860, Phineas had become a heavy drinker without a stable home (Wilgus & Wilgus, 2009).

No autopsy was performed when Phineas Gage died, but many years later his skull was exhumed and reexamined with more modern technology. Researchers found that the damaged regions of his brain were largely limited to those that heavily impact decision making and managing emotions. This was no surprise, considering what changed and what stayed the same about Phineas Gage in the aftermath of his accident (Damasio et al., 1994). The idea that certain parts of the brain are related to certain functions or abilities is the lasting impact of Phineas Gage's accident (and the reason that his name has become legendary in the field of psychology). After all, it is rare that a real-world event produces a situation in which a healthy person loses a specific part of his brain, and that loss corresponds to a specific change in behavior. Of course, the phrenologists (whom we discussed in Chapter 1) made claims about such links, but their claims were unfounded speculations about how certain bumps on the skull might match certain characteristics and tendencies. Phineas Gage's accident focused the exploration not on the skull, but on the brain inside of it.

A year after Phineas Gage died, a French doctor named Paul Broca did an autopsy on a man who lost the ability to speak after he had a stroke. Broca found damage to only one small part near the front of the left side of the man's brain (LaPointe, 2013). The identification of that part—still called *Broca's area* today—was

another early step in determining connections between particular brain regions and particular behaviors. By the early 1900s, even the eminent Sigmund Freud recognized that psychology was on a path toward discovering all kinds of brain and behavior connections: "We must recollect that all of our provisional ideas in psychology will presumably one day be based on an organic substructure" (Freud, 1914/1989, p. 549).

Fast-forward about a century to today, and we have traveled far down that path of understanding brain and behavior connections (Kandel & Hudspeth, 2013). In fact, the people who marveled at Phineas Gage's survival and subsequent transformation in the mid-1800s couldn't have imagined the modern technologies that now allow us to see the inner workings of the brain. Nor could they have predicted the surge of brain research happening today. Articles and books on brain and behavior connections, both in professional journals and the popular press, have become exceedingly widespread (Aminoff et al., 2009).

neurons
The cells that facilitate communication within the nervous system.

interneurons
The neurons that serve only to connect to other nearby neurons, rather than reaching farther out into the body.

Learning the Brain: A Three-Step Strategy

There is a lot to learn about brain and behavior connections. In this chapter, we'll follow an easy, three-step organizational structure for understanding the brain:

First, we'll start with the microscopic activity *within* the brain that allows for communication throughout the brain and to other parts of the body.

Second, we'll zoom out to the whole brain and its parts, examining their connections to various behaviors.

Third, we'll zoom out even more to see the big picture: whole body systems including the *nervous system* and the *endocrine system*, which both interact directly and continually with the brain.

CHECK YOUR LEARNING:

2.1 What is the story of Phineas Gage, and why is his story important to the relationship between brain and behavior?

2.2 In this chapter, our approach to understanding the brain is to start small and zoom out: What are the three levels of understanding?

Activity Within the Brain

On a microscopic level, your brain is bustling with activity. Let's take a close look. Specifically, let's examine how information travels deep within your brain.

YOU WILL LEARN:

2.3 about the brain's network of neurons.

2.4 what neurons do.

2.5 why the myelin sheath is important for axons.

2.6 what dendrites do.

2.7 what synapses are.

2.8 what neurotransmitters are.

2.9 what the process of reuptake is.

2.10 about action potentials.

Neurons

The building blocks of brain activity are **neurons**: the cells that facilitate communication within the nervous system. The neurons in your brain connect with parts of your body outside your brain—receiving sensory input from your hands, sending motor output to your feet, and so on. But your neurons actually do a tremendous amount of communicating *among each other* (Schwartz et al., 2013). In fact, most of the neurons in your brain are **interneurons**: neurons that serve only to connect to other nearby neurons, rather than reaching farther out into the body. Interneurons are also known as *connector neurons* or *relay neurons*, names that reveal their function, like kids in the

FIGURE 2.1 Neurons and Their Connections. The cell body (or soma) is the centerpiece of each neuron and keeps it functioning. Farther from the center, axons carry information away from the neuron and toward the next neuron in the chain. (In this illustration, as the arrow indicates, the movement is from left to right.). Toward the end of each axon, it splits into axon terminals, the small branches that form connections with the next neuron. In that next neuron, the dendrites are the receiving branches that accept what the axon terminals deliver.

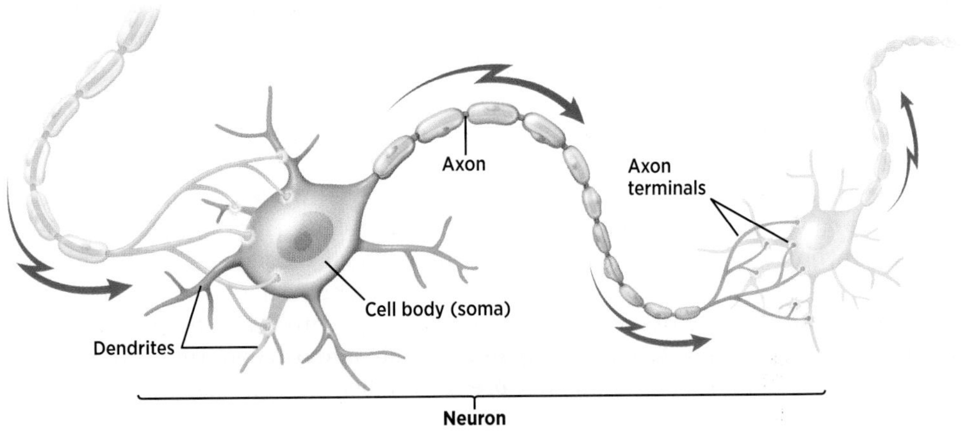

middle of a classroom passing along a note that was sent from a kid in the front to a kid in the back (Kandel, Barres, & Hudspeth, 2013).

The sheer number of neurons in your brain—nearly 100 *billion*—is staggering (Azevedo et al., 2009; Nolte, 2008; Post & Weiss, 1997; Pakkenberg & Gundersen, 1997). It is even more staggering to realize that these billions of neurons are interconnected, forming an astoundingly efficient and intricate web through which information travels. Picture a map of the United States that features its 100 biggest cities and all of the highway connections between each of them. That number of criss-crossing roads would certainly look complex, but now imagine how complex that network gets if the map included 1000 or 10,000 cities—still tiny numbers compared to the number of neurons your brain contains. Even if a map connected every *house* in the United States to each other, it would connect only 100 million houses—still a thousand times fewer than the number of neurons interconnected in your 3-pound, 6.5-inch-long brain.

Sensory Neurons and Motor Neurons. Many of the neurons that extend beyond your brain fall into two categories: neurons that deliver messages *to* your brain, and neurons that deliver messages *from* your brain (Kandel et al., 2013; Schwartz et al., 2013). Specifically, **sensory neurons** carry information to your brain from your senses (sight, hearing, smell, taste, touch). And **motor neurons** carry messages from your brain to your muscles. (Sensory neurons are sometimes called *afferent* neurons, and motor neurons are sometimes called *efferent* neurons.) For example, if you accidentally touch a hot stove, you'll witness how quickly both sensory neurons and motor neurons can convey their messages. Your sensory neurons carry the message "This is hot!" to your brain, and your motor neurons carry the message "Move away!" to the muscles controlling your hand—all within a fraction of a second (Pearson & Gordon, 2013). That kind of instant, no-thinking-required response is a **reflex**: an automatic motor response to sensory input.

Of course, most of the exchanges between your sensory neurons and your motor neurons are not so reflexive. Instead, the interaction involves a bit more control on your part. For example, imagine that you're trying to find your phone, which is in your backpack, while you're in a dark movie theater. Because you can't see, you put your hand in and start feeling around. As your hand feels various things—a pen, your phone's power cord, a pack of gum—it's sending messages through sensory neurons to your brain about the shape, size, texture, and other tactile features of those items. Each time your hand does that, your brain sends back a message through your motor neurons to your hand that says, "Keep feeling around." Then, when your hand runs across the smooth glass rectangular surface of your phone screen, that sensation (communicated through your sensory neurons) causes your brain to respond (through your motor neurons), "Grab it!"

The Parts of a Neuron. As **Figure 2.1** illustrates, the center of each neuron is the **cell body** (or **soma**): the large central region of a neuron that performs the

sensory neurons
The cells that carry information to the brain from the senses (sight, hearing, smell, taste, touch).

motor neurons
The cells that carry messages from the brain to the muscles.

reflex
An automatic motor response to sensory input.

cell body (soma)
The large central region of a neuron that performs the basic activities, including the production of energy, to keep the neuron functional.

axon
The part of the neuron that carries information toward other neurons.

axon terminals
The small branches at the end of an axon that form connections with the next neuron.

dendrites
The branches at the end of neurons that receive signals from other neurons.

myelin sheath
A protective sleeve of fatty material that surrounds the axon.

glial cells
The cells that support and protect neurons throughout the brain.

synapse
The gap between two connecting neurons.

neurotransmitters
The chemical messengers that travel across synapses from one neuron to the next.

endorphins
The neurotransmitters involved in reducing pain and increasing pleasure.

synaptic vesicles
The tiny, sacklike containers for neurotransmitters.

receptor sites
The openings in dendrites that match specific neurotransmitters like a lock fits a specific key.

basic activities, including the production of energy, to keep the neuron functional. The passageway extending from each neuron is the **axon**: the part of the neuron that carries information toward other neurons. At the end of the axon, the axon splits into **axon terminals**: small branches at the end of an axon that form connections with the next neuron. (The word *terminal* lets you know that it is the end of the first neuron.) On the receiving end of that next neuron, smaller passageways take in what the axon terminals deliver. Those smaller passageways are **dendrites**: branches at the end of neurons that receive signals from other neurons. So, the signal shoots through the axon, into an axon terminal, and travels to a dendrite on the next neuron.

In many neurons, the axon is covered with a layer of insulation called the **myelin sheath**: a protective sleeve of fatty material that surrounds the axon (**Figure 2.2**). Myelin is just one of many substances manufactured by **glial cells**: cells that support and protect neurons throughout the brain (Jessell & Sanes, 2013). The myelin sheath has an important role in neuronal communication: it makes sure that messages travel across axons, which can be quite long in some cases, at maximum speed and with minimal loss (Filley, 2013; Bauman & Pham-Dinh, 2001). One problem that arises from deterioration of the myelin sheath is *multiple sclerosis* (*MS*), a disease that can affect both movement and sensation. Specifically, in people suffering from MS, the signals sent via motor neurons don't arrive as intended at the body part that is supposed to move, or the information sent via sensory neurons doesn't arrive as intended in the brain (Hurley et al., 1999).

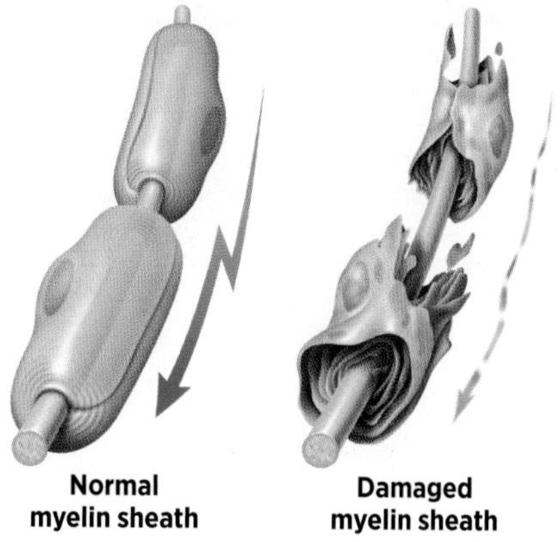

FIGURE 2.2 Myelin Sheath. The myelin sheath is a protective sleeve of fatty material that surrounds the axon. The myelin sheath makes sure that communication between neurons happens at maximum speed and with minimal loss. Deterioration of the myelin sheath is one feature of multiple sclerosis, a disease in which motion is impaired because of slowed signals from the body to the brain.

Communication Between Neurons

When a signal from a neuron makes it successfully through the axon, the message travels from an axon terminal of one neuron to a dendrite of the next neuron. That trip is a vital part of neuronal communication (Siegelbaum & Kandel, 2013a; Siegelbaum et al., 2013b). Between the axon terminal and the dendrite—the space that needs to be crossed—is the **synapse**: a gap between two connecting neurons (**Figure 2.3**).

Neurotransmitters. The substances that actually travel across the synapse are **neurotransmitters**: chemical messengers that travel across synapses from one neuron to the next. You are probably familiar with quite a few specific neurotransmitters. For example, **endorphins** are neurotransmitters involved in reducing pain and increasing pleasure. They occur naturally in our brains, in response to feel-good stuff like food, fun, sex, and exercise. (Our natural endorphins are mimicked closely by such pain-killing drugs as morphine and codeine.) Other neurotransmitters include *dopamine* (involved in the reward system and in movement), *serotonin* (involved in mood, and possibly sleep and appetite), *epinephrine* (involved in the fight-or-flight response), and *histamine* (involved in the immune system) (Schwartz & Javitch, 2013). See **Table 2.1** for a list of these and other important neurotransmitters.

Some drugs enhance the impact of a neurotransmitter. Those drugs are called *agonists*, and they include the morphine example mentioned previously. Other drugs interfere with the impact of a neurotransmitter. Those drugs are called *antagonists* (a word you may remember from an English class as a character that puts up opposition or stands in the way). Examples of antagonists include common antihistamines (which literally means "against the histamine neurotransmitter") like Benadryl, Claritin, and Zyrtec.

Until they reach the synapse, neurotransmitters travel in **synaptic vesicles**: tiny, sacklike containers for neurotransmitters (Siegelbaum et al., 2013a). To complete their journey across the synapse, the neurotransmitters emerge from the synaptic vesicles and find their way to **receptor sites**: openings in dendrites that match specific neurotransmitters like a lock fits a specific key. That lock-and-key relationship means that not every neurotransmitter

FIGURE 2.3 The Synapse. The synapse is the gap between two connecting neurons. Neurotransmitters cross the synapse and land in receptor sites, or openings in dendrites that match specific neurotransmitters as a lock fits a specific key. Neurotransmitters that don't find a receptor site may return to the sending neuron in a process called reuptake.

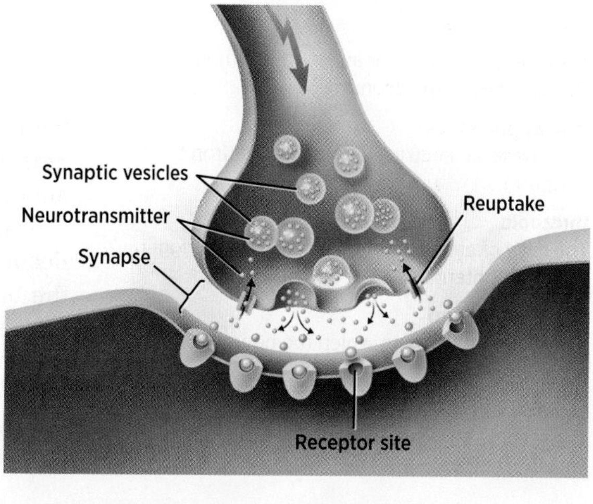

TABLE 2.1: Some Important Neurotransmitters

NEUROTRANSMITTER	HOW IT AFFECTS YOUR DAILY LIFE
Endorphins	Reduce pain, increase pleasure
Dopamine	Influences brain's reward system and body's movement
Serotonin	Influences mood, and perhaps sleep and appetite
Epinephrine	Helps the fight-or-flight response
Histamine	Influences the immune system
Acetylcholine	Helps to activate muscles
GABA (gamma-aminobutyric acid)	Helps to control anxiety

will find a home as it passes from the axon terminal of one neuron to the dendrite of the next neuron. Actually, even if the neurotransmitter could fit a lock, sometimes there are not enough receptor sites to accept them all.

LIFE HACK 2.1

When you are feeling sad or anxious, physical exercise can provide an endorphin boost and an improved state of mind.

(Stathopoulou et al., 2006; Daley, 2008; Salmon, 2001)

So what happens to neurotransmitters that don't successfully cross the synapse and find a receptor site in the next neuron?

To handle some of these excess neurotransmitters, the first neuron carries out **reuptake**: the process when a neurotransmitter is taken back up by the sending neuron after failing to land in a receptor site in the receiving neuron. This tiny chemical interaction in which some neurotransmitters successfully reach the receiving neuron while others get taken back up into the sending neuron can have a significant impact on your day-to-day life experience. For example, consider the neurotransmitter serotonin, which (as mentioned previously) plays a powerful role in mood, and possibly sleep and appetite as well. In some cases, low serotonin levels correlate with feelings of depression. One class of drugs commonly prescribed for depression are SSRIs, or selective serotonin reuptake inhibitors. (This class of drugs includes familiar brands like Paxil, Celexa, Zoloft, and Lexapro.) As their name indicates, SSRIs inhibit the reuptake of serotonin that didn't make it across the synapse. By doing so, they can affect the amount of serotonin flowing through your brain, ultimately improving your mood.

Action Potentials. Another important part of communication between neurons is how a neuron initiates the transmission of a signal. This start is called an **action potential**: the release, or *firing*, of an electrical impulse that travels through the axon. Action potentials either happen completely or don't happen at all, a phenomenon known as the *all-or-none response*. Most of the time, a neuron is not firing, but is at rest (Kandel et al., 2013). In those moments, the neuron is in a state of **resting potential**: the low-level electrical charge in a neuron that is not firing (Koester & Siegelbaum, 2013a). The neuron shifts from rest into action when the electrical charge reaches a certain **threshold**: the level of electrical charge required to trigger an action potential (Koester & Siegelbaum, 2013b). Each action potential is followed by a **refractory period**: a waiting time before another action potential can begin, during which the neuron is reset.

Here is a final point about the way neurons connect. In humans, those connections depend heavily on experience, especially early in life. In other species, the brain is largely "hard-wired" at birth, meaning that certain axon terminals are connected to certain dendrites across synapses from day one. That enables those animals to "hit the ground running" more than humans can. For example, a newborn horse can walk within hours. The human brain is relatively underdeveloped at birth, but this means it can be shaped to adapt to unique circumstances. That adaptability allows each of our brains to customize the synaptic connections we need *as* we

reuptake
The process when a neurotransmitter is taken back up by the sending neuron after failing to land in a receptor site in the receiving neuron.

action potential
The release, or *firing*, of an electrical impulse that travels through the axon.

resting potential
The low-level electrical charge in a neuron that is not firing.

threshold
The level of electrical charge required to trigger an action potential.

refractory period
A waiting time, during which the neuron is reset before another action potential can begin.

localization
The idea that specific parts of the brain do specific things.

determine that we need them, and our brains make that determination while we grow up (Sanes & Jessell, 2013a, b, c). It is like the difference between a computer with lots of preloaded software that fills almost its entire hard drive before it leaves the factory, and a computer with plenty of gigs available to use the software it needs for particular purposes that may arise.

CHECK YOUR LEARNING:

2.3 What are neurons, and approximately how many of them does your brain contain?

2.4 How do sensory neurons and motor neurons differ?

2.5 What is the myelin sheath and what function does it serve?

2.6 What is the function of dendrites?

2.7 What is the synapse and how is it involved in communication between neurons?

2.8 What are neurotransmitters and what do they do?

2.9 How does the process of reuptake work?

2.10 What is the role of an action potential in communication between neurons?

The Brain and Its Parts

Now we broaden our focus from the microscopic activity of neurons deep within the brain to the whole brain and its parts. As we do, let's keep two major ideas in mind. The first involves **localization**: the idea that specific parts of the brain do specific things. In this section, we will discuss examples of localization, but let's remember not to oversimplify. When identifying what various parts of the brain do, it is important to remember that no part of the brain does anything entirely *by itself*.

In fact, the brain is perhaps the most awesome display of cooperation and coordination that human beings have ever encountered. The brain's components interact in such a way that certain parts may play a significant role in a certain behavior, but that behavior still depends on other parts for its successful execution. Don't be fooled by media reports that dumb down this complexity of the brain, with headlines like "Scientists discover the part of the brain that controls [some behavior]..."—the brain's parts are far too densely interconnected to be reduced to such isolated, one-to-one connections (Satel & Lilienfeld, 2013; Rose & Abi-Rached, 2013).

As an example, consider the simple act of drinking a can of soda. To make that happen, different parts of your brain have to do many things: experience thirst, recall where the refrigerator is, command your legs to walk there, command your hand to open the refrigerator, see the can of soda, move your hand toward the can, grip the can, pull the tab on top of the can, lift the can to your mouth at the proper angle, enjoy the taste, and experience the quenching of thirst. That's *a lot* of microbehaviors, each of which relies on different combinations of brain parts, required to do a common and easy action (Amaral & Strick, 2013; Rizzolatti & Kalaska, 2013). (And we're not even counting the behind-the-scenes stuff your brain takes care of automatically while you're busy with the soda, like keeping your heart beating and your lungs pumping.) Even if the behavior is mental rather than physical (like *remembering* the soda you drank), multiple parts of the brain are almost always involved (Schacter & Wagner, 2013; Siegelbaum & Kandel, 2013b).

The second major idea to keep in mind as we consider the brain and its parts involves a comparison between our brains—*human* brains—and the brains of other animal species. Look at the shape of our heads and the shapes of their heads. What you'll notice is that our heads are bigger on top and up front. (As **Figure 2.4** shows,

YOU WILL LEARN:

2.11 what localization is.

2.12 how the human brain compares to the brains of other animals.

2.13 where the brainstem is located and what it does.

2.14 where the cerebellum is located and what its function is.

2.15 about the main function of the thalamus.

2.16 what the limbic system is and what its primary function is.

2.17 about the parts of the brain involved in the limbic system.

2.18 why the cerebrum and cerebral cortex are important parts of the human brain.

2.19 what the corpus callosum is.

2.20 why the corpus callosum is cut in split-brain surgery.

2.21 about the cerebrum's four lobes.

2.22 what association areas are and what they do.

2.23 what plasticity is and when it takes place.

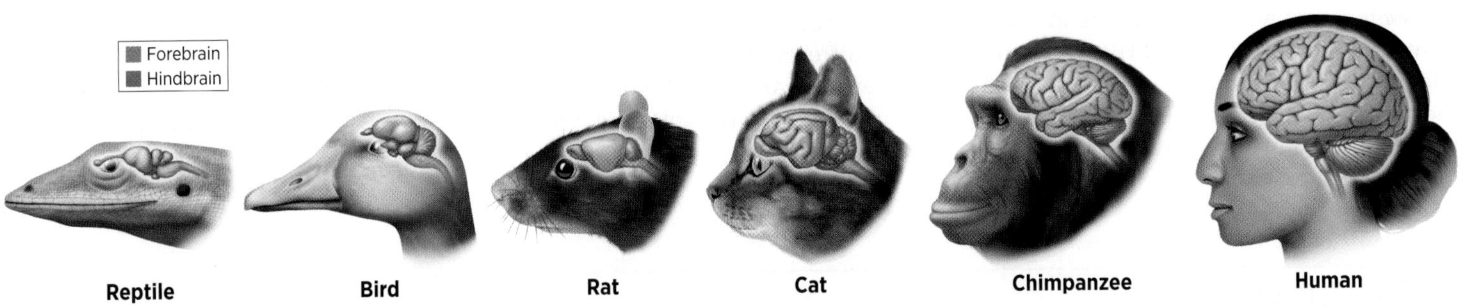

FIGURE 2.4 Comparing Heads and Brains Across Species. Compared to the heads of other species, the heads of humans are bigger on top and up front. That reflects the fact that our *brains* are bigger on top and up front. Generally, the parts on top and up front are involved in our uniquely human abilities, like planning, decision making, and complex cognitive tasks. By contrast, the parts near the back and the bottom of the brain—which all species have—are involved in the abilities common to both humans and other types of animals, like breathing, balancing, hunger, sleeping, and heartbeat.

MY TAKE VIDEO 2.1

Parts of the Brain

"I use the frontal lobe of my brain by..."

YOUTUBE: http://tiny.cc/mytake
LAUNCHPAD: launchpadworks.com

that difference is evident with our close primate relatives, and even more obvious in reptiles and birds.) That means that our *brains* are bigger on top and up front. That provides a big hint about specific regions within the brain where certain functions are controlled (Preuss, 2009).

As a rule of thumb, the parts of our brains that are closest to the back and the bottom (near the connection to the spine) control the basic functions that we share with other species, especially stuff like heartbeat, hunger, arousal, breathing, and balancing. After all, other animals have those brain parts, just like we do (Saper et al., 2013). The farther we move up and out (especially toward the front of the brain), the more we encounter parts of the brain that control functions more unique to humans, like decision making, planning, speech, and complex tasks involving emotions and learning. After all, we have much more of those parts of the brain than other animals do. (That difference is largely due to evolution, specifically the fact that our species emerged more recently than other species [Schneider, 2014].)

Following this rule of thumb can often help you figure out which parts of the brain are responsible for which kinds of behaviors. For example, if the question is what part of the brain is in charge of making you feel sleepy and waking you up, the fact that all animals do those things tells you that it is a part near the back and bottom of the brain, which all animals have. If the question is what part of the brain allows you to develop a strategy for a complex, long-term behavior (like creating an exercise plan for the next 6 months), the fact that nonhuman animals don't do that tells you that it's a part near the front or top of your brain, which only humans have. Combine this rule of thumb with the fact that many brain parts have names that indicate their location, like *brainstem* (at the bottom and back, near the spine) or *frontal lobe* (at the front of your brain, right behind your forehead), and you've got some helpful clues for learning which brain parts go with which functions.

As we now consider specific parts of the brain, let's start at the bottom and the back, and work our way up and toward the front.

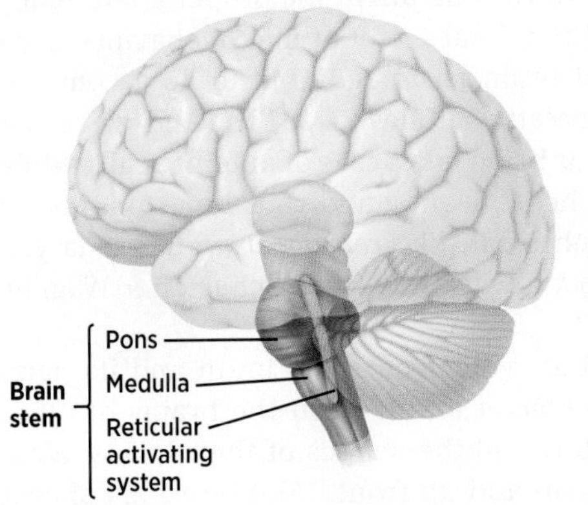

FIGURE 2.5 The Brainstem. The brainstem is the part of the brain that connects to the spine and controls the functions most essential to staying alive, like breathing, heartbeat, sexual reproduction, and swallowing. The brainstem includes the reticular activating system, pons, and medulla.

The Brainstem

The **brainstem** is the part of the brain that connects to the spine and controls the functions most essential to staying alive (**Figure 2.5**). These functions include not only 24/7 behaviors like breathing and a heartbeat, but also other bodily functions that take place only at certain times, like sexual reproduction, swallowing, sneezing, and even vomiting (Anderson et al., 2013; Hurley et al., 2010). The *-stem* in the word

brainstem accurately depicts how it fits into the larger structure of the brain—like a stem, with the rest of the brain blossoming up and around it like a flower.

The brainstem contains a few important brain structures within it. One of these is the **reticular activating system**: a collection of neurons in the brainstem involved in arousal. (*Reticular* means netlike, which is the shape this collection of neurons takes.) The *activating system* part of this key term refers to the activation of waking and sleeping, but the reticular activating system is also involved in related functions like alertness and attention (Saper et al., 2013). The brainstem also contains the **pons**: a part of the brainstem involved in transmitting information, sleep, breathing, and equilibrium. Because of its position near the top of the brainstem, the pons conveys messages between the brainstem and higher regions of the brain. Near the bottom of the brainstem is the **medulla**: the part of the brainstem most specifically involved in heartbeat and breathing. Together, the pons and medulla also control swallowing.

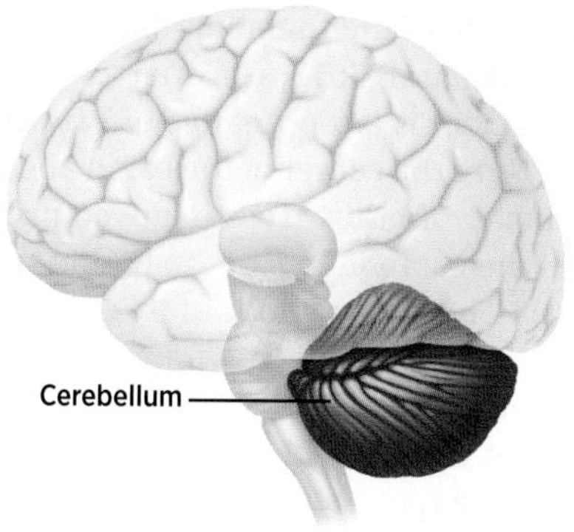

FIGURE 2.6 The Cerebellum. The cerebellum is near the bottom and back part of the brain. It is primarily involved in balance and the coordination of movement. Your cerebellum occupies only about 10% of the space in your brain but contains over half of its neurons.

The Cerebellum

Adjacent to the brainstem is the **cerebellum**: the part of the brain near the bottom and the back primarily involved in balance and the coordination of movement (**Figure 2.6**). The main role of the cerebellum involves motion, though it may also be involved in other functions, including attention and memory (Graybiel & Mink, 2009; Dum & Strick, 2009). Your cerebellum does not initiate movement, but it regulates it. For example, imagine that you need to slow down your car to about half its current speed. Your cerebellum would not send the message "Step softly on the brake," but it would make sure that you step on the brake with just the right amount of force and consistency. Without your cerebellum, a simple act like stepping on the brake could go wrong in many ways: You could tap it so weakly that the car doesn't slow down; you could slam on it so hard that the car comes to a jolting stop; or you could step on it in an inconsistent, herky-jerky way that makes the car lurch back and forth.

The cerebellum, which is about the size of a small fist, is only about 10% of your brain but contains over 50% of its neurons. This fact still puzzles researchers, but it may represent the important role of the cerebellum within the brain (Lisberger & Thach, 2013). Damage to the cerebellum creates serious problems across a wide range of everyday movement-related tasks, from tremors and spastic movements to severely impaired walking and talking (Manto, 2010).

brainstem
The part of the brain that connects to the spine and controls the functions most essential to staying alive.

reticular activating system
The collection of neurons in the brainstem involved in arousal.

pons
The part of the brainstem involved in transmitting information, sleep, breathing, swallowing, and equilibrium.

medulla
The part of the brainstem most specifically involved in heartbeat and breathing.

cerebellum
The part of the brain near the bottom and the back, primarily involved in balance and the coordination of movement.

thalamus
The brain's main sensory processing center, located near the center of the brain.

The Thalamus and the Limbic System

At this point we move up a level, from the "ground floor" of the brain (containing the brainstem and cerebellum) to its "middle floor." A centerpiece of this middle level is the **thalamus**: the brain's main sensory processing center, located near the center of the brain (**Figure 2.7**). The thalamus, which is shaped like a small egg, receives the information you take in through your eyes, ears, mouth, and skin, then directs this information to the parts of your brain that need to process it. Passing along sensory information is the

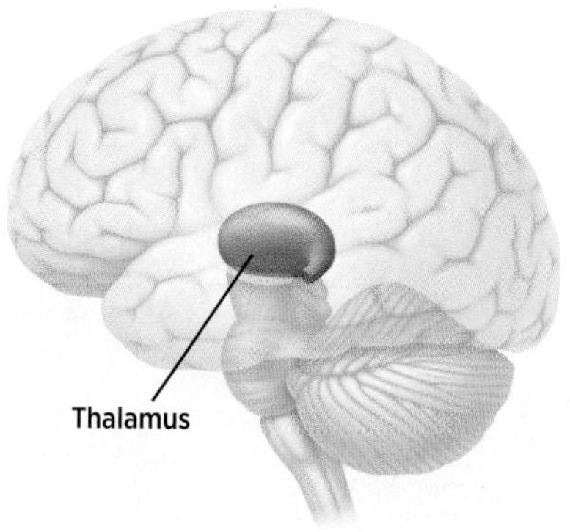

FIGURE 2.7 The Thalamus. The thalamus is the brain's main sensory processing center, located near the center of the brain. It directs the information you take in through your eyes, ears, mouth, and skin to other parts of your brain for further processing.

main role of the thalamus, but it is also involved in arousal and movement in a limited way (Amaral, 2013; Gardner & Johnson, 2013; Taber et al., 2004). Its involvement in movement is a cooperative effort with a nearby brain structure, the *basal ganglia*.

Near the center of the brain and surrounding the thalamus is the **limbic system**: a cluster of brain areas involved primarily in emotion. (The word *limbic* means border, and the components of the limbic system do appear to form a border around the thalamus.) There is an old (but true) joke among people who study the brain that the limbic system is all about the "four f's": fleeing, fighting, feeding, and, um, sexual intercourse (Pinel, 2011; Pribam, 1960). Those four f's are all considered primary motivations of human beings. When you recognize that the words *emotion* and *motivation* come from the same root—*mot-*, which is Latin for move—it is easy to see that the limbic system is the part of the brain most responsible for initiating the impulses and feelings designed to move you.

As **Figure 2.8** illustrates, the limbic system includes several distinct parts: the *hypothalamus*, the *hippocampus*, and the *amygdala*.

The Hypothalamus. The **hypothalamus** is the part of the limbic system involved in maintaining steadiness in bodily functions. One way the hypothalamus achieves this steadiness is by exerting control over the *pituitary gland*, which (as described in more detail later in this chapter) is the master gland of the endocrine system and therefore has tremendous influence on the release of hormones. The hypothalamus also has significant influence over the *autonomic nervous system*, which means that it affects your heartbeat, breathing, and other involuntary functions (Horn & Swanson, 2013). The hypothalamus also influences the triggers you feel to eat or drink. In this way, your hypothalamus helps you maintain *homeostasis*, or a relatively constant internal environment (Shizgal & Hyman, 2013; Richerson et al., 2013). For example, homeostasis ensures that your heartbeat increases while you work out on the elliptical machine, and makes sure your heartbeat returns to normal soon after your workout. Homeostasis also means that your body temperature stays about the same, even when Mother Nature (or the air conditioning or heating) causes great fluctuations in the temperature around you.

The Hippocampus. The **hippocampus** is the part of the limbic system involved in memory, especially spatial memory and long-term memory. Spatial memory is your memory for physical spaces, such as the layout of the house you grew up in, or the hallways of your high school. Those mental maps, including the emotional connections to those spaces, become long-term memories thanks to your hippocampus (Siegelbaum & Kandel, 2013b). Long-term memory takes place when things that you focus on temporarily (that is, things that are in short-term memory) become stored in such a way that they endure indefinitely. Your hippocampus is the part of your brain most responsible for that conversion, and your awareness of that conversion (Shrager & Squire, 2009; Suzuki, 2009; Squire, 1992; Kandel & Siegelbaum, 2013).

Damage to the hippocampus impairs the ability to convert short-term memories to long-term memories—that is, to stop memories from simply fading away. In severe cases, it causes *anterograde amnesia*, a complete inability to form new long-term memories after a certain point in time (Winocur et al., 2001). We'll cover anterograde amnesia and other memory problems in more detail in Chapter 5. For now, just know that anterograde amnesia is fascinating to observe but devastating to live through. People who experience it can recall their long-term memories from before the onset of anterograde amnesia, but they can't create any new long-term memories. So,

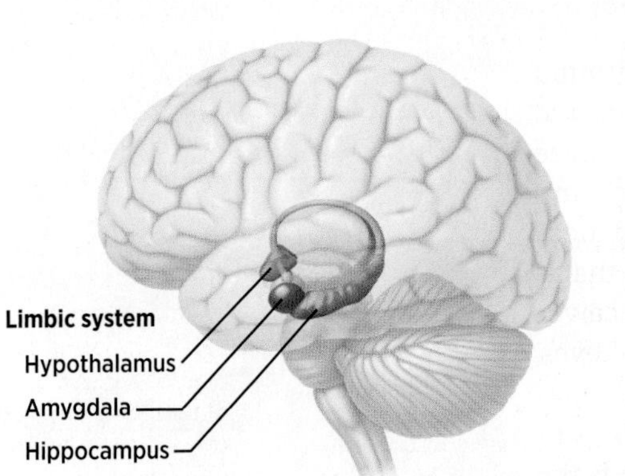

FIGURE 2.8 The Limbic System. The limbic system, located near the center of the brain, is a cluster of brain areas involved primarily in emotion. The limbic system includes the hypothalamus, the hippocampus, and the amygdala.

if a 55-year-old woman experiences this kind of damage to her hippocampus, she'll have no problem recognizing the person she married or recalling the wedding they had 30 years ago, but she won't be able to form a new memory of her grandchild being born next week.

Henry Molaison is one of the people most responsible for our knowledge about the connection between the hippocampus and anterograde amnesia. Henry wasn't a researcher, but a man who suffered from severe epilepsy. In 1953, Henry was 27 years old and desperate for improvement in his symptoms. He underwent an experimental brain surgery in which the hippocampus was removed. That surgery improved his epilepsy, but it had another unexpected effect: for the 55 remaining years of his life, Henry could not form new memories. After the surgery, he couldn't learn people's names or remember new information he heard. He repeatedly completed the same puzzles without getting bored, because they were new to him every time he did them. Henry (and his family) allowed researchers to conduct hundreds of studies on him while he was alive, and donated his brain to science after his death. His contributions have greatly increased our understanding of the function of the hippocampus (Scoville & Milner, 1957; Corkin, 2013; Ogden, 2012).

One way the hippocampus can become damaged is through stress. In particular, high levels of stress that last for a long time can damage the hippocampus and, in turn, the ability to form new spatial and long-term memories (McEwen, 1999). One study of older adults found strong positive correlations between three things: levels of cortisol (the "stress hormone," as we will discuss later in this chapter), damage to the hippocampus, and impairment in simple memory tasks (Lupien et al., 1998). Other studies have found that people who have lived through childhood abuse or active combat during war—both undeniably high-stress experiences—show physical damage to the hippocampus and deficits in the ability to form new memories (Bremner, 1999). Another way the hippocampus can become damaged is through Korsakoff's syndrome, a condition that happens to some long-term alcoholics in which the hippocampus actually shrinks in size (Stavro et al., 2013; Sullivan & Marsh, 2003).

limbic system
The cluster of brain areas involved primarily in emotion, located near the center of the brain and surrounding the thalamus.

hypothalamus
The part of the limbic system involved in maintaining a steadiness in bodily functions.

hippocampus
The part of the limbic system involved in memory, especially spatial memory and long-term memory.

WATCHING PSYCHOLOGY

The Hippocampus in Hollywood

There are plenty of movies about memory loss (*The Vow*, *The Bourne Identity*, and *Eternal Sunshine of the Spotless Mind*, among others), but most stray quite a bit from the scientific facts, creating symptoms that simply don't match real-world experiences of memory loss patients. For example, some characters only lose memories of an isolated part of their past (like certain people they've known or experiences they've had). Other characters experience significant memory loss, but without any accompanying distress or personality change. And some characters "magically" regain their memories thanks to some futuristic high-tech device or a (second) bump on the head. But there are at least a couple of movies—*50 First Dates* and *Memento*—that get a lot about memory loss right.

In the 2004 comedy *50 First Dates*, Drew Barrymore stars as Lucy, a young woman who begins to date Henry (played by Adam Sandler). When she shows up for her second date with no recollection of the first date, Henry realizes there is a problem. That problem is *anterograde amnesia*, which Lucy has experienced ever since she injured her head—presumably, her hippocampus—in a car accident. (Anterograde amnesia is the inability to create new memories after an event such as a head injury, even though memories made before the event stay intact.) The result is one first date after another, at least from Lucy's perspective, due to her inability to form new memories. *50 First Dates* does make some mistakes regarding how the hippocampus (and other parts of the brain) function, but its portrayal of anterograde amnesia is at least somewhat accurate.

Memento is even more accurate. In the 2001 thriller, Leonard Shelby (played by Guy Pearce) also can't form new memories due to anterograde amnesia. In his case, the brain injury (that presumably damaged his hippocampus) happens when he steps in to protect his wife from an attacker. The attacker kills his wife, and Leonard subsequently devotes his life to tracking him down. His inability to form new memories in the aftermath of the attack makes that task incredibly difficult, so he tries to compensate by writing notes to himself, taking Polaroids (this was before smartphones), and even tattooing important reminders on his body. The backward-in-time plot line of this film illustrates Leonard's memory limitations in a creative and fascinating way.

Both *50 First Dates* and *Memento* include some features of memory loss that are uncommon. For example, it is rare for a head injury to injure only the hippocampus; usually, other brain regions are also affected, so the symptoms are more complex than just anterograde amnesia. Also, the cause of injury to the hippocampus is not always a blow to the head; instead, it is often activity within the head, such as a series of strokes or recurrent epileptic seizures (Pendick, 2002; Kälviäinen et al., 1998). Nonetheless, these two films (*Memento* especially) do a respectable job of representing some of the most life-altering effects of damage to the hippocampus (Baxendale, 2004). ●

The Amygdala. The **amygdala** is the part of the limbic system involved most directly in emotion, especially fear. (*Amygdala* comes from the Latin word for almond, which is the shape of this part of the brain as it was originally defined.) There are certainly other parts of the brain involved in emotion, but recent research has clearly identified the amygdala as an especially important part of the brain, perhaps the *most* important part of all, in terms of emotion (LeDoux & Damasio, 2013; Phelps & LeDoux, 2005; Phelps, 2006). For example, other parts of the brain may influence how the fight-or-flight response plays out (whether you fight, or fly, or do something else), but the amygdala sounds the fight-or-flight alarm in the first place (LeDoux et al., 2009; Schafe & LeDoux, 2004).

Damage to the amygdala causes all kinds of problems with emotional processes, especially the experience of fear. For example, one case study found that a person with a damaged amygdala could recognize the faces of people she knew, but failed to identify whether those faces showed fear (Adolphs et al., 1994). Another study of nine people with amygdala damage found that they struggled to recognize fear in the facial expressions of others, but had no problems recognizing happiness in those faces (Adolphs et al., 1999). In another study, researchers used sudden, randomly timed, loud blasts of noise to startle a man with a damaged amygdala (and eight control subjects as well). The researchers found that his startle reflex—his involuntary, immediate fear response—was weaker than the startle reflexes of the control subjects (Angrilli et al., 1996).

Other researchers stumbled upon a different kind of finding about the amygdala by studying altruists, people who commit acts of kindness for others that provide no payoff for themselves. Specifically, these researchers examined the brains of 19 people whom they called "extraordinary altruists"—people who had donated kidneys to strangers. (Can you think of a more altruistic act?) Compared to the average member of a control group, the average extraordinary altruist had an amygdala that was not only larger, but also more responsive to fearful facial expressions in other people. These results suggest that an extraordinary altruist is motivated to act by an amygdala that enhances the ability to recognize the fear of others (like medical patients needing kidneys) and to respond with compassion (Marsh et al., 2014).

amygdala
The part of the limbic system involved most directly in emotion, especially fear.

cerebrum (forebrain)
The front and upper part of the brain, consisting of two hemispheres and involved in sophisticated, often uniquely human, abilities.

cerebral cortex
The outer layer of the cerebrum, where sensory information is processed.

association areas
Brain material that is devoted to synthesizing and interpreting information rather than merely taking information in.

cerebral hemispheres
The left and right halves of the cerebrum.

corpus callosum
The bundle of neurons that connects and allows communication between the two cerebral hemispheres.

split-brain surgery
A surgical procedure in which the corpus callosum is cut, typically to reduce epileptic seizures.

The Cerebrum and Cerebral Cortex

If the brainstem and cerebellum represent the brain's ground floor, and the thalamus and limbic system represent its middle floor, it is now time to move up to the top floor. The **cerebrum** (also known as the **forebrain**) is the upper front part of the brain, which consists of two hemispheres and is involved in sophisticated, often uniquely human, abilities. The cerebrum fits over the parts of the brain that we have already discussed (brainstem, cerebellum, thalamus, limbic system) like a thick helmet covering a relatively small head. So, when you see photos of the brain, looking wrinkled and resembling a walnut, what you're actually seeing is the cerebrum—the same way you see a football player's helmet, but you know the player's head is underneath (**Figure 2.9**). More specifically, you're seeing the **cerebral cortex**: the outer layer of the cerebrum, where sensory information is processed. *Cortex* comes from a Latin word that means bark of a tree, which describes its position on the outer layer of the brain. (Brain experts often use the terms *cerebrum* and *cerebral cortex* interchangeably.)

More than any other part of the brain, the cerebrum (especially its cerebral cortex) is what makes humans human. Compared to other animals, we simply have much more cerebrum than they do: ten times more than a macaque monkey, and a thousand times more than a rat (Rakic et al., 2004). The cerebrum occupies most of our brains, but only a small fraction of the brains of many animals. That big cerebrum

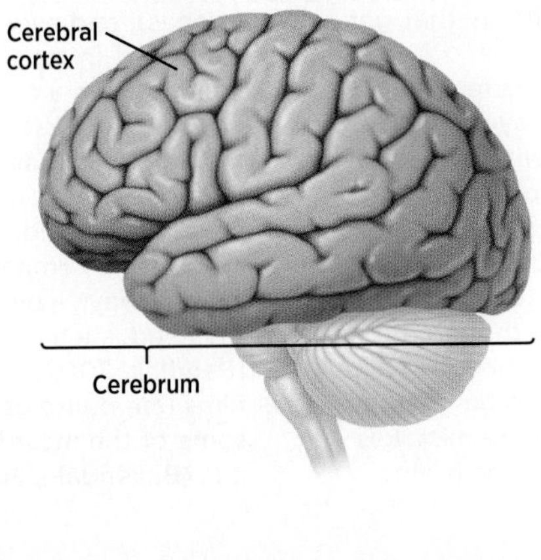

FIGURE 2.9 The Cerebrum and Cerebral Cortex. The cerebrum (also known as the forebrain) is the upper front part of the brain. It consists of two hemispheres and is involved in sophisticated, often uniquely human, abilities. The cerebrum contains lots of association areas, which are brain regions devoted to synthesizing and interpreting information rather than merely taking in information. The cerebral cortex is the outer layer of the cerebrum, where sensory information is processed.

is what makes humans so, well, cerebral. The cerebrum gives us many distinctly human abilities, including thinking, reasoning, planning, creating, communicating, computing, multitasking, and so much more (Rakic et al., 2009; Premack, 2010).

The cerebrum contains lots of **association areas**: brain material that is devoted to synthesizing and interpreting information rather than merely taking in information. To understand what happens in association areas, imagine that an ambulance approaches your car from behind. There are specialized parts of your brain that process the sight of the flashing lights in your rearview mirror and the sound of the blaring siren that grows louder as it gets closer. But somewhere in your brain, that information has to be integrated to make sense. That is what the association areas do. They associate, or combine, these various bits of information so they have meaning: There's an ambulance behind me, which means there's an emergency nearby, so I need to pull over to let the ambulance get to the person who needs help. Without the synthesis that the association areas provide, you would be limited simply to processing and reacting to isolated bits of information rather than understanding what they collectively mean.

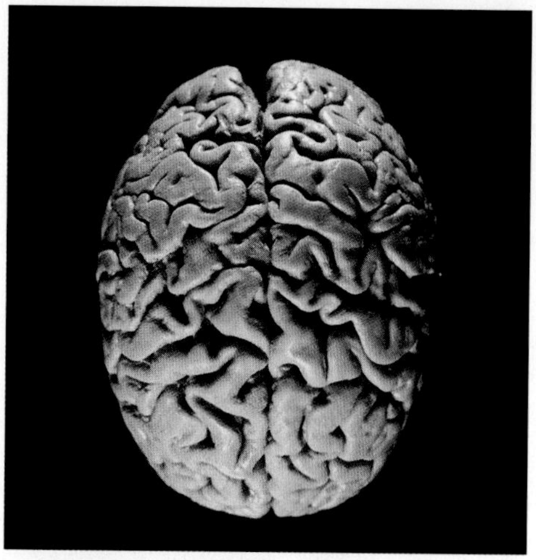

The cerebrum, which gives the outer brain its wrinkled appearance, is involved in sophisticated, often uniquely human abilities. The Image Bank/Getty Images

The Cerebral Hemispheres and the Corpus Callosum

Just as the globe can be divided into Western and Eastern hemispheres, the cerebrum can be divided into two halves, or **cerebral hemispheres**: the left and right halves of the cerebrum. (Actually, lower parts of the brain are similarly divided in half, but the hemispheres are particularly relevant in the cerebrum.) The link between the two hemispheres is the **corpus callosum**: the bundle of neurons that connects and allows communication between the two cerebral hemispheres.

The corpus callosum enables an interesting relationship to occur between the two halves of your brain and the two halves of your body: each is matched with its opposite. Your left cerebral hemisphere is paired with the right half of your body, and your right cerebral hemisphere is paired with the left half of your body. So, if you drop a bowling ball on your left foot, it is your right hemisphere that receives the pain message. Or, if you want to give someone a high-five with your right hand, it's your left hemisphere that sends the message to raise that hand. This cross-relationship between brain and body also explains why an illness or injury to one side of the brain, such as a stroke, affects only the opposite side of the body. Tedy Bruschi, former Pro Bowl linebacker for the New England Patriots, suffered a mild stroke at the unusually young age of 31. The stroke was caused by a blood clot in his brain's right hemisphere, which caused damage to his body's entire left side. The day of the stroke, "there was total numbness in my left arm and leg… My 5-year-old son came in from my left, and I couldn't see him." After a trip to the ER, Bruschi had surgery to fix the cause of the blood clot, "and the rest of my recovery was learning how to … use the left side of my body again" (Bruschi, 2014).

On rare occasions, serious problems can emerge from faulty communication between the hemispheres. In such cases, one treatment option is a serious and infrequent operation called **split-brain surgery**: a surgical procedure in which the corpus callosum is cut, typically to reduce epileptic seizures (**Figure 2.10**). Epileptic seizures typically start in

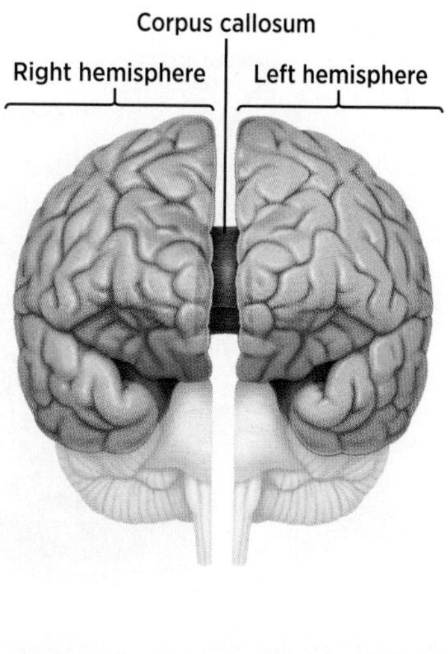

FIGURE 2.10 Split-Brain Surgery. The cerebrum consists of two halves, or hemispheres. The left and right hemispheres communicate through a bundle of neurons known as the corpus callosum. Each hemisphere controls the movement in the opposite half of the body. On rare occasions (typically as a last-resort effort to reduce severe epileptic seizures), split-brain surgery is performed by cutting the corpus callosum.

CHAPTER APP 2.1

Localization

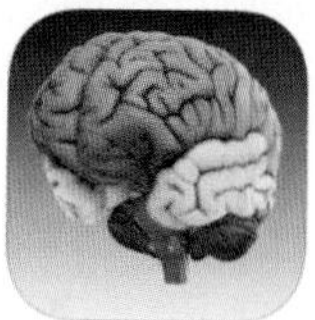

3D Brain

Preview one of the links and consider the following questions.

WEBSITE:
http://tiny.cc/ndh7jy

ANDROID:
http://tiny.cc/5vjyiy

IPHONE:
http://tiny.cc/bqjyiy

VIDEO DEMO:
http://tiny.cc/chapterapps

This app shows great 3D images of the brain—better than what is possible on textbook pages because they rotate on-screen and make outer parts of the brain transparent so you can see inner parts directly.

How does it APPly to your daily life?
How does such a high-tech, vivid, rotatable, 3D view of the brain affect your appreciation of your own brain? Will it increase the odds that you will do things to take care of it, like wearing a seat belt in the car, wearing a helmet on your bike, or eating or drinking healthy?

How does it APPly to your understanding of psychology?
How do these images improve your understanding of the brain, its parts, and their functions?

Tedy Bruschi, a three-time Super Bowl champion with the New England Patriots, experienced a mild stroke in the right hemisphere of his brain that impacted the left side of his body. Getty Images Sport/Getty Images

one hemisphere and then gain power as they bounce back and forth, across the corpus callosum, between both hemispheres. If the corpus callosum is severed, the seizures are restricted to one hemisphere, making them much less severe. (The vast majority of people with epilepsy improve with antiseizure medications. Split-brain surgery is a last resort, considered only if such medications prove ineffective over long periods of time.)

As you might imagine, some of the side effects of split-brain surgery have proven fascinating. People who have the operation typically retain most of their personality characteristics and intelligence. However, they demonstrate some peculiar abilities and inabilities based on the fact that the two sides of their brain have lost communication with each other. In some cases, for example, each side of the body does its own thing, with no apparent awareness of what the other side is doing. Because the two hemispheres can't coordinate with each other, the right hemisphere tells the left side what to do, while the left hemisphere tells the right side what to do. Literally, the right hand doesn't know what the left hand is doing. In one particular case, a woman who had undergone a split-brain surgery found her hands competing with each other in the supermarket aisles—her right hand would reach for a box of cereal, but her left hand would stop her from putting it in her cart (Wolman, 2012).

The effects of split-brain surgery are evident not only in the hands, but in many other parts of the body as well. In some experiments, researchers asked split-brain patients to look at a dot on a screen and then flashed words to either the right or left of that dot, so the word was in the field of vision of only one eye. Let's imagine that the word was *banana* (**Figure 2.11**). When asked what word they saw, the patients were good at saying "banana" when the word was on the right (and processed by the left hemisphere). However, if the same word was on the left (and processed by the right hemisphere), the patients could not *say* "banana," but could *draw* a banana with their left hand. This curious finding helped researchers understand that each hemisphere may dominate certain tasks. As this example shows, the left hemisphere is dominant for language tasks, such as word reading. The right hemisphere, by contrast, is dominant for the recognition of objects and faces (Gazzaniga et al., 1962; Gazzaniga, 1998, 2005).

Indeed, the brain's two hemispheres may look like mirror images of each other, but **Table 2.2** shows some important differences in how they function (Gazzaniga, 1995). The left hemisphere tends to emphasize tasks that are more logical and detail-oriented, while the right hemisphere tends to emphasize tasks that are more emotional and big-picture-oriented (McGilchrist, 2010; Carter, 2010; Navon, 1977). For example, when listening to music, your left hemisphere is more involved in identifying individual notes or lyrics, but your right hemisphere is more involved in appreciating and *feeling* the song as a whole (Ohnishi et al., 2001; Gaser & Schlaug, 2003). When you're driving, your left hemisphere is more involved in noticing what each individual car does, while your right hemisphere is more involved in picking up the broader traffic patterns (**Figure 2.12**).

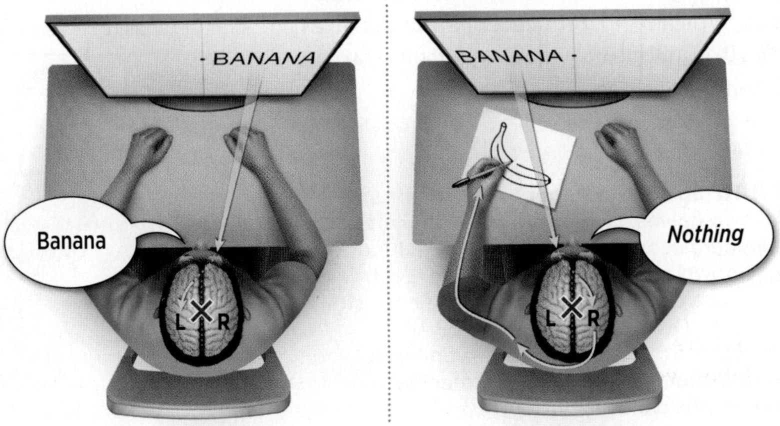

FIGURE 2.11 The Aftermath of Split-Brain Surgery. In patients who have undergone split-brain surgery, communication between the two hemispheres of the brain is impaired, resulting in some unusual effects. Numerous research studies support findings like the one illustrated here. If the word *banana* appears in the right side of their field of vision (and is processed by their left hemisphere), patients could correctly say the word *banana*. If the word *banana* appears in the left side of their field of vision (and is processed by their right hemisphere), patients could not say *banana*, but could draw a banana with their left hand. These results indicate not only the importance of communication between the hemispheres of the brain, but also that certain tasks are dominated by particular hemispheres. For example, the left hemisphere is dominant for language tasks, like word reading, while the right hemisphere is dominant for the recognition of objects (Gazzaniga et al., 1962; Gazzaniga, 1998, 2005).

TABLE 2.2: The Specialties of Each Hemisphere

THE LEFT HEMISPHERE EXCELS AT...	THE RIGHT HEMISPHERE EXCELS AT...
thinking logically.	feeling intuitively.
appreciating the small details.	appreciating the big picture.
picking up the literal meaning of language.	picking up the emotional tone of language.
understanding things in isolation.	understanding things in context.
all-or-nothing, decisive thinking.	nuanced, shades-of-gray thinking.
focusing on *what* happens.	focusing on *how* things happen.

Information from McGilchrist, 2009.

FIGURE 2.12 Not Seeing the Forest for the Trees. The unique emphasis of each cerebral hemisphere is clear in the way that people with right-hemisphere damage view this figure: They see the details (the little Ds), but they don't see the big picture that those Ds collectively make (a B). (McGilchrist, 2009).

The Lobes

Figure 2.13 illustrates how the cerebrum consists of four distinct regions, or *lobes*, each of which has a right half and a left half. (As with your ear*lobe*, here the word *lobe* simply means rounded or curved part.)

Occipital Lobe.

If we begin at the back of the brain and move forward, we start with the **occipital lobe**: the lower back part of the brain involved in vision. Your occipital lobe connects (through the thalamus) with your eyes, taking in the raw images you see and beginning to process (or extract meaning from) them. Damage to the occipital lobe can cause a range of sight-related problems, including difficulty seeing certain parts of the visual field, difficulty seeing certain movements or colors, visual hallucinations (seeing things that aren't really there), or complete blindness (Werth, 2006; Beniczky et al., 2002; Anderson & Rizzo, 1994; Ferber & Karnath, 1999).

Temporal Lobe.

As we take a step toward the front of the brain (but remain in the bottom half), we reach the **temporal lobe**: the lower middle part of the brain, involved in hearing and speech production. The location of the temporal lobe is roughly between your ears, which makes sense considering how vital it is to the perception of sound. The temporal lobe is the first place sound goes after it moves through your ear, and also where the brain starts to make sense of those sounds.

The temporal lobe contains **Wernicke's area**: part of the temporal lobe specifically involved in understanding speech. Researchers know that Wernicke's area exists because they have seen people with damage to that specific area demonstrate **Wernicke's aphasia**: dysfunction in understanding or creating coherent speech caused by damage to Wernicke's area. People with Wernicke's aphasia fail to understand even simple statements by others. They can produce words, but those words are often made up, and they can produce sentences, but the sentences are often gibberish or irrelevant to the conversation. In addition to its auditory emphasis, the temporal lobe appears to play some role in visual processing, including the identification of objects, as well as long-term memory for verbal material (Albright, 2013; Kandel & Siegelbaum, 2013; Schacter & Wagner, 2013; Wagner et al., 1998).

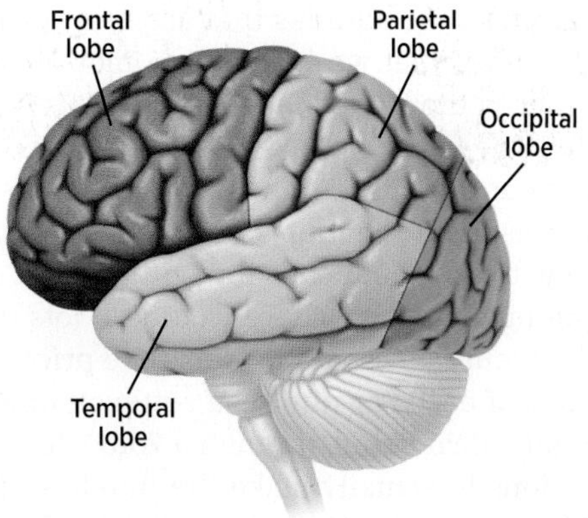

FIGURE 2.13 The Lobes. The cerebrum consists of four lobes. The occipital lobe is involved in vision. The temporal lobe is involved in hearing and speech production. The parietal lobe is involved in touch and perception. The frontal lobe is involved in complex thinking tasks, planning, and other advanced functions, most of which are unique to humans.

Parietal Lobe.

Above the occipital and temporal lobes we find the **parietal lobe**: the part of the brain near the top and back

occipital lobe
The lower back part of the brain, involved in vision.

temporal lobe
The lower middle part of the brain, involved in hearing and speech production.

Wernicke's area
The part of the temporal lobe specifically involved in understanding speech.

Wernicke's aphasia
The dysfunction in understanding or creating coherent speech caused by damage to Wernicke's area.

parietal lobe
The part of the brain near the top and back of the head, involved in touch and perception.

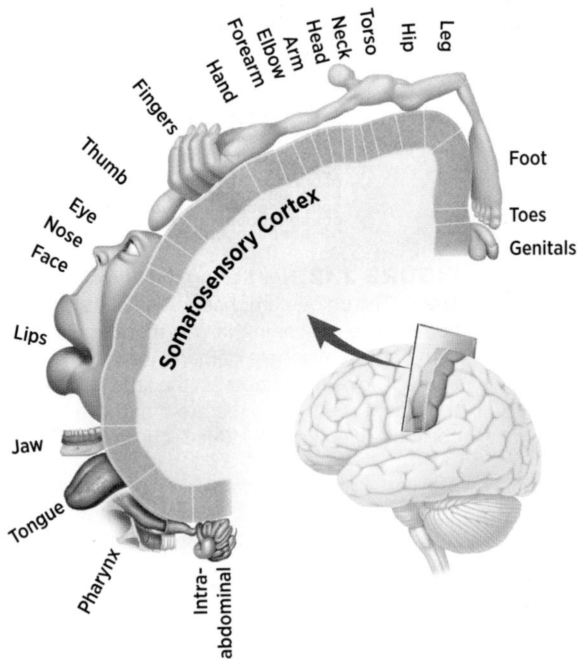

FIGURE 2.15 The Somatosensory Cortex. Within the parietal lobe is a strip of brain matter called the somatosensory cortex, which is involved in receiving information from the senses. The amount of space in the somatosensory cortex devoted to a particular body part is determined not by the size of that body part, but by its sensitivity. For example, your lips get more space than your torso, despite the fact that the lips are much smaller, because your lips are much more sensitive to touch.
BSIP/Science Source

of the head involved in touch and perception. A particularly important part of the parietal lobe is the **somatosensory cortex**: a strip of brain matter near the front of the parietal lobe involved in receiving information from the senses. The somatosensory cortex takes in visual information that has been relayed from the occipital lobe, as well as auditory information that has been relayed from the temporal lobe. But one of the main functions of the somatosensory cortex is to directly monitor the sensation of touch (including contact, pressure, pain, temperature, and itch) everywhere on your body (Amaral, 2013). In fact, specific spots on the somatosensory cortex correspond to specific parts of your body.

Does the size of the body part match the amount of space it takes up on the somatosensory cortex?

Interestingly, no. The size of each spot doesn't correspond to the size of the corresponding part of your body. Instead, the size of each spot corresponds to the *sensitivity* of that part of your body (Gardner & Johnson, 2013; Nakamura et al., 1998).

Take a look at **Figure 2.15**, which illustrates how much space on the somatosensory cortex is devoted to various body parts. The first thing you'll notice is how out of proportion those body parts seem. For example, why would the somatosensory space for your lips—a tiny part of your body—be bigger than the space for your whole torso—a huge part? The answer is that the lips are far more sensitive—for good reason, Darwin would tell us, since what touches (and passes) the lips could affect human survival much more than what touches the abdomen or the back. Think about it this way—if a fly lands on your back, you might notice it, but you might not. But if the same fly lands on your lips, you'll instantly sense it. In other species, the somatosensory cortex reveals the evolutionary importance of their body parts too. For example, in rats, the somatosensory cortex devotes a huge amount of space to the whiskers, with each individual whisker having its own oversized corresponding spot (Pinto et al., 2000).

Frontal Lobe. The remaining lobe, and the one located in the front of the brain, is appropriately named the **frontal lobe**: the part of the cerebral cortex right behind the forehead, which is involved in complex thinking tasks, planning, purposeful actions, and other advanced functions. Remember one of the major points from earlier in this chapter—the abilities that are most uniquely human tend to be located in the part of the brain that we have much more of than other species. That part, more than any other, is the frontal lobe.

The frontal lobe does lots of things, some of which are still being discovered, but it is clear that most of those things are distinctively human, such as integrating multiple pieces of information, deciding what to do in response to that information, figuring out how to do it, and carrying out the task. For example, imagine that you were considering buying a car. There would be lots of steps involved: gathering information about different makes and models (like price, mileage, safety ratings); weighing the pros and cons of each car until you settle on one; determining exactly how you're going to buy it (at a dealership, through a Web site, with a loan, etc.); and then taking the necessary actions to actually make the purchase (going to the dealership, negotiating the price, filling out the paperwork, etc.). Every one of those steps relies on your uniquely human frontal lobe.

There is one part of the frontal lobe—the *prefrontal* region, located all the way up front—that is especially devoted to these kinds of uniquely human behaviors. The prefrontal region accounts for 29% of the human cerebral cortex, which makes it twice as big as it is in our closest primate relatives (Schoenemann et al., 2005; Schoenemann, 2006; Rilling, 2006; Semendeferi et al., 2001). The prefrontal region is often described as being important in *executive control* (Olson & Colby, 2013).

somatosensory cortex
The strip of brain matter near the front of the parietal lobe, involved in receiving information from the senses.

frontal lobe
The part of the cerebral cortex right behind the forehead, involved in complex thinking tasks, planning, purposeful actions, and other advanced functions.

motor cortex
The strip of brain matter near the back of the frontal lobe, involved in voluntary movement.

Broca's area
The part of the left side of the frontal lobe heavily involved in speaking.

Broca's aphasia
The speech dysfunction caused by damage to Broca's area.

To understand what executive control means, think about what an executive at a company does. The executive does *not* do routine, automatic tasks—that is what the lower-level employees do. Instead, the executive oversees those routine, automatic tasks, and handles any unusual issues that come up during the process. The executive's job might involve identifying and defining problems, considering multiple solutions, making tough decisions, forming strategies, and instructing others on how to implement those strategies.

The prefrontal region of the frontal lobe performs tasks similar to those of an executive (Arciniegas, 2013; Banich, 2009). It oversees the routine and automatic tasks that the other parts of the brain are doing, evaluates and integrates unusual situations on a case-by-case basis, and decides what to do about them. For example, if you hit a traffic jam on your way to an important doctor's appointment, many parts of your brain do their routine, automatic tasks: Your occipital lobe sees the cars lined up bumper to bumper; your temporal lobe hears the traffic report on the radio; and your amygdala feels the fear of missing the exam and even sends out the initial fight-or-flight response. But it is your frontal lobe, particularly your prefrontal region, that integrates all of those sources of information, ponders them, generates options (take another route? call to reschedule?), chooses one, and acts on that decision.

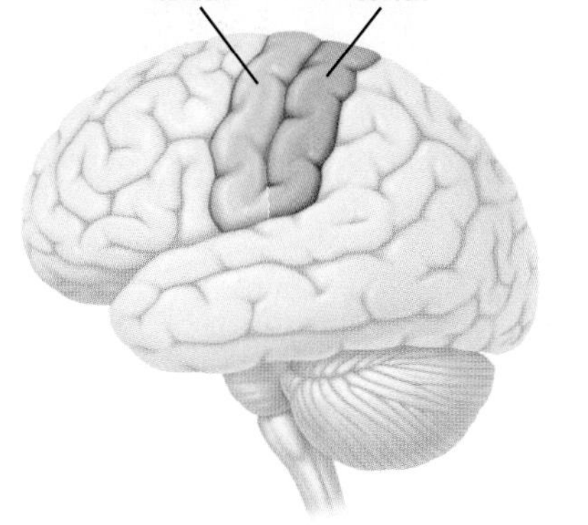

FIGURE 2.16 The Somatosensory Cortex and the Motor Cortex. Within the frontal lobe, and adjacent to the somatosensory cortex, is the motor cortex. The motor cortex is a strip of brain matter involved in voluntary movement.

Another important part of the frontal lobe is the **motor cortex**: the strip of brain matter near the back of the frontal lobe involved in voluntary movement. The motor cortex lies just in front of the somatosensory cortex (**Figure 2.16**). Like the somatosensory cortex, it connects to parts throughout the body, but rather than taking information *from* them (in the form of sensations), the motor cortex sends information *to* specific parts of the body (in the form of motor instructions) (Rizzolatti & Strick, 2013; Wolpert et al., 2013). It is your motor cortex, with the help of your somatic nervous system, that tells your thumbs to move when you text and your feet to move when you dance.

Like the somatosensory cortex, the motor cortex allocates its space according to need rather than size, as shown in **Figure 2.17**. The parts of your body that need more motor control get more representation on the motor cortex, regardless of their size. That is why body parts like your fingers, thumb, and tongue—all of which are small but have tremendous dexterity—occupy lots of space on the motor cortex. That is also why your hips and thighs—which have a much more limited range of motion, but are much bigger—occupy very little space on the motor cortex. In nonhuman animals, the motor cortex reflects the movements typical for that species (Brown et al., 2013). In monkeys, for example, the space on the motor cortex for feet is much larger than the corresponding space for human feet, which makes sense when you realize that monkeys use their feet to grasp objects and swing from branches, while we don't use ours for much more than walking and wiggling our toes (Kalaska & Rizzolatti, 2013).

The frontal lobe also contains **Broca's area**: a part of the left side of the frontal lobe heavily involved in speaking. As described earlier, this area of the brain was discovered by French surgeon Paul Broca in the mid-1800s, when he conducted an autopsy on a person who had severely limited speech after a stroke. Broca found that this particular part of the frontal lobe, located near but not within the motor cortex, was the only part of the brain that had experienced any damage. **Broca's aphasia** is the speech dysfunction caused by damage to Broca's area. People with Broca's aphasia have no problem comprehending speech (assuming Wernicke's area remains intact), but have a difficult time producing speech (Kuhl & Damasio, 2013). There are very long pauses between their words, and when they put together a sentence, it often includes just the most essential words: "Need...bread..." rather than "We need to go to the store to buy more bread." Broca's aphasia is often called an *expressive* aphasia, since the problems primarily involve getting language out. By contrast, Wernicke's aphasia is often called a *receptive* aphasia, since the problems primarily involve taking language in.

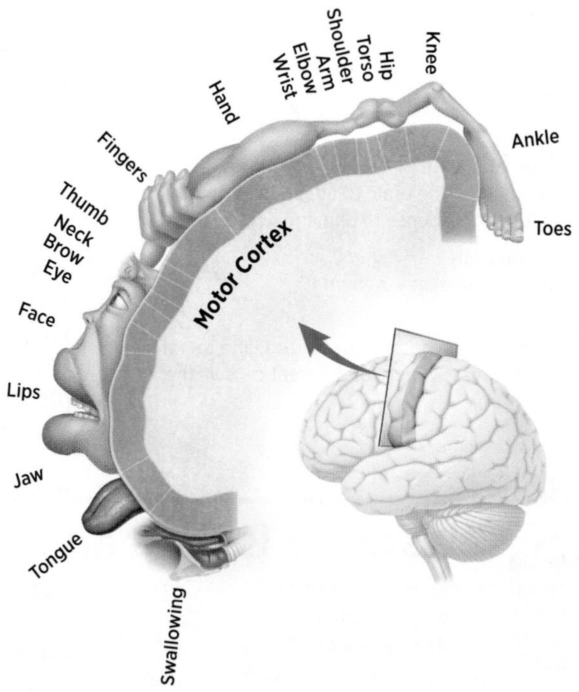

FIGURE 2.17 The Motor Cortex. Like space in your somatosensory cortex, space in your motor cortex depends not on the size of the body part but on its need for motor control. For example, your fingers, thumbs, and tongue are all small body parts but all require great motor control, so they have disproportionately large amounts of space in your motor cortex.
BSIP/Science Source

Brain Plasticity

Remember the example earlier in this chapter about Tedy Bruschi, the NFL player who experienced a stroke? When he said that his recovery required "learning how to…use the left side of my body again," it is important to note that in a matter of months, he achieved that goal. And it wasn't just his body that changed—his brain changed too. A comparison of images of Tedy Bruschi's brain before and after his treatment would show that certain parts of his brain actually modified their size, shape, or capabilities to help him regain what the stroke took from him (Liepert et al., 2000). In other words, his brain demonstrated **plasticity**: the ability of the brain to adapt its structure or function in response to damage or experience. The word *plasticity* makes sense when you think of how versatile and adaptable plastic can be. We mold plastic into many different forms for many different purposes, from soda bottles to trash bags to video game consoles to prosthetic limbs. Amazingly, your brain shows some of the same versatility and adaptability (Neville & Sur, 2009; McEwen, 2004; Bavelier et al., 2009).

In terms of brain plasticity after his stroke, Tedy Bruschi had the advantage of his youth. (Strokes actually happen much more often to senior citizens than to 31-year-olds.) The younger you are, the more plasticity your brain has (Kolb & Gibb, 2011; Kolb & Whishaw, 1998; Van Horn, 2004). Young children's brains are especially plastic. That doesn't mean kids will fully recover from a brain injury, but they typically recover better than adults with similar brain injuries. Kids' brains are more plastic because they are less fully developed. Specifically, the various parts of the brain haven't finished specializing yet, which means that sometimes they can switch to a different function (that a damaged part of the brain can no longer do), at least to some extent.

Neurogenesis. Another advantage that young brains have over old brains is the capacity for **neurogenesis**: the creation of new neurons. Neurogenesis is an especially beneficial strategy for dealing with damage to a part of the brain. Rather than taking existing neurons and overhauling the way they work, neurogenesis involves the manufacture of neurons that didn't exist before. For many years, experts believed that children were the only ones capable of neurogenesis, but now it is clear that adults are too, although in a much more limited way and only in certain parts of the brain (such as the hippocampus) (Ming & Song, 2011; van Praag et al., 2002, 2004; Eriksson et al., 1998). This discovery is encouraging to researchers who seek answers to common brain malfunctions in adults (especially older adults), including certain memory impairments and psychological disorders (Deng et al., 2010).

Within the brain (and also found in other parts of the body), perhaps the most plastic elements of all are **stem cells**: cells that have not yet specialized, and therefore

plasticity
The ability of the brain to adapt its structure or function in response to damage or experience.

neurogenesis
The creation of new neurons.

stem cells
Cells that have not yet specialized, and therefore can become a variety of different cells as the need arises.

IT'S LIKE...

Plasticity Is Like an Athlete Switching Positions

Imagine asking a talented 7-year-old softball player who has only played first base to switch positions. That probably won't be much of a problem. As a beginner, that girl probably can take her general athletic skills to shortstop, centerfield, or any other position on the diamond because she hasn't specialized too much yet. By contrast, imagine asking a 30-year-old Major League veteran first baseman to become a shortstop, a centerfielder, or play any other position. He would find it challenging, maybe even impossible. For years, he has spent every game and practice, day after day, exclusively at first base. His skills have become so highly specialized to the first base position that he might not be able to play another position well. Of course, there is a chance that it *could* work, at least to a limited extent—sometimes you can teach an old dog new tricks. But all of that time spent playing just one position makes a change much tougher than it would be for a player with less experience.

Brain plasticity works the same way. In very young brains, many parts of the brain haven't specialized much yet. So if there is a need to cover for a damaged brain region (an injured teammate, so to speak), those parts of the brain have the flexibility necessary to make the switch. In older brains, however, the brain parts have specialized more, which means that their ability to adapt and change is more limited. Thankfully, even in adults, there is often some plasticity among brain parts, just like some baseball players can take on a new position when pressured to do so later in their careers. ●

can become a variety of different cells as the need arises. As the word *stem* implies, stem cells have begun to grow but have not finished. They are sensitive to demands within the brain to serve a certain purpose, perhaps based on specific parts of the brain that need help (Woodbury & Black, 2004). In this way, stem cells can repair damage and help brain regions recover functions they might otherwise lose (Gage, 2000; do Nascimento & Ulrich, 2015; Zhao, 2015).

Plasticity after Brain Damage. Sometimes, as in the case of a stroke, the brain shows its plasticity in response to damage (Sanes & Jessell, 2013d). In one study, researchers simulated the amputation of fingers by using anesthetic (the same stuff your dentist injects to make your mouth numb) on two fingers of their research participants—specifically, their ring fingers and index fingers. They discovered that in the participants' somatosensory cortex, the amount of space dedicated to those two fingers decreased, and the amount of space dedicated to the pinky finger, middle finger and thumb increased. The brain physically adapted to help functional parts to take over for nonfunctional parts (Rossini et al., 1994).

In a study with rats, researchers cut the facial neurons that carry movement commands to the whiskers. They soon observed some interesting reactions in the motor cortex of each rat: a decrease in the space dedicated to the whiskers, and a corresponding increase in the space dedicated to the front legs (Sanes & Donoghue, 2000; Sanes et al., 1990, 1992; Donoghue et al., 1990). It is as if the brain adopted the strategy that if it could no longer move the whiskers around, it would try the next best thing—increasing the dexterity of the front legs instead. That is a vital adaptation for rats, who constantly move their whiskers around to feel what is around them (as a blind person might use a cane). In this situation, the plasticity in a rat's motor cortex might make the difference between living (by finding food and avoiding danger) and dying.

Plasticity after Life Experience. In addition to showing its plasticity in response to damage, the brain shows its plasticity in response to everyday experience (Sanes & Jessell, 2013c). One study examined the brains of people who read Braille, the writing system in which letters are represented by patterns of small dots or bumps, across which the visually impaired person moves his or her finger (Pascual-Leone & Torres, 1993). They discovered that in the somatosensory cortex of these individuals, the space dedicated to the "reading finger" (the right index finger) had become significantly larger than the space dedicated to the left index finger. That space was also larger than the space for either index finger in the somatosensory cortex of someone who doesn't read Braille at all.

Poverty is another experience that, over time, may change the brain. Specifically, in the brains of people who spend long stretches of their lives in poverty, the average size of the hippocampus, occipital lobe, prefrontal cortex, and other brain regions is smaller than in people who live in wealthier conditions. In addition to those size differences, there are functional differences—those parts of the brain don't work as fast or as well for people in poor conditions (Hanson & Hackman, 2012). These findings are consistent across several different measurements of poverty, including socioeconomic status, family income, and education level. The specific reasons for this connection between poverty and the brain are still under investigation, but could include higher stress levels, lack of environmental stimulation, or other factors (Hanson et al., 2012).

DIVERSITY MATTERS

The experience of living in a specific cultural group may change the brain too (Dominguez et al., 2009; Rule et al., 2013; Freeman et al., 2009b). Several studies have found specific brain differences between members of Western cultures, who tend to be more individualistic (such as in the United States and many European countries) and members of Eastern cultures, who tend to be more collectivistic (such as in many Asian countries) (Tang & Liu, 2009). For example, one group of researchers found that parts of the brain linked to the feeling of reward, including a part of the prefrontal cortex (the medial prefrontal cortex, to be specific), respond in different ways to contrasting body

CHAPTER APP 2.2

Plasticity

GlassesOff

Preview one of the links and consider the following questions.

WEBSITE: http://tiny.cc/qfh7jy

ANDROID: http://tiny.cc/iwjyiy

IPHONE: http://tiny.cc/oqjyiy

VIDEO DEMO: http://tiny.cc/chapterapps

This app offers a series of vision exercises that with repetition, according to the app's description, increase your brain's ability to process visual information, a great example of plasticity based on experience.

How does it APPly to your daily life?
The makers of this app claim that these vision exercises can improve vision and decrease the need for reading glasses, which suggests plasticity of the brain based on experience. To what extent do you believe such innovations can replace reading glasses, or Lasik, or other eye surgeries?

How does it APPly to your understanding of psychology?
How do vision exercises like the ones in this app illustrate *plasticity*? At what age would these exercises be most effective?

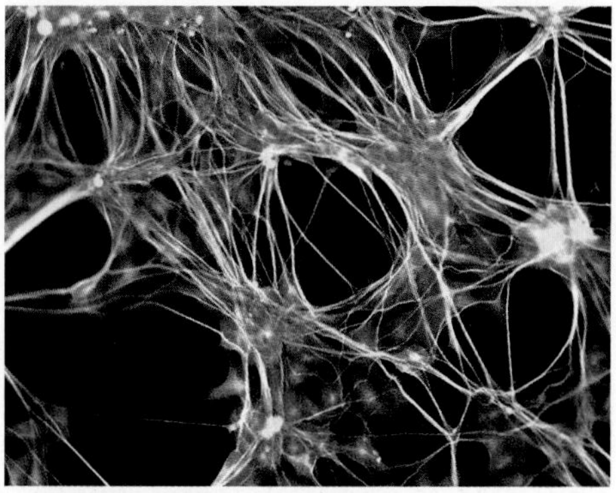

These are stem cells, which have not yet specialized and can become a variety of different cells as the need arises. In the brain, stem cells can help to repair damage and enable recovery of function that might otherwise be lost. Science Photo Library/Getty Images

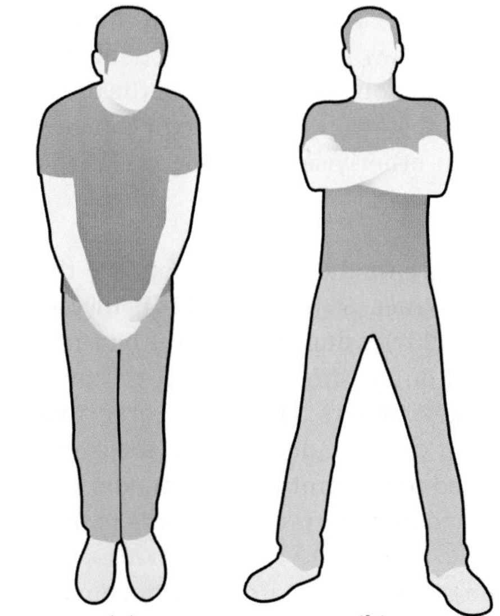

FIGURE 2.18 Culturally Distinct Brain Responses to Dominant and Submissive Body Language. Cultural experiences can influence brain activity. In one study, participants saw drawings of human figures displaying either submission (generally viewed more favorably in collectivistic cultures) or dominance (generally viewed more favorably in individualistic cultures). The parts of the brain linked to the feeling of reward (including parts in the prefrontal cortex) were more active in Japanese participants when they saw the submissive figure, but more active in American participants when they saw the dominant figure (Freeman et al., 2009a).

language. Specifically, researchers showed two kinds of drawings to both Japanese and American participants—some drawings of a person showing submission (more favored in collectivistic cultures), and some drawings of a person showing dominance (more favored in individualistic cultures). The reward systems in the brains of the Japanese participants were more active when they saw the submissive figure, but the reward systems in the brains of the American participants were more active when they saw the dominant figure (Freeman et al., 2009a) (**Figure 2.18**).

Even languages may affect the brain differently (Chen et al., 2009; Bolger et al., 2005; Gandour, 2005). For example, one study found that different parts of the occipital lobe are activated by English words (formed by a string of letters) versus Chinese characters (formed by holistic visual stimuli) (Tan et al., 2000). Other studies found that in English, verbs and nouns are each processed in specific parts of the brain, but in Chinese, a language that does not make distinctions between verbs and nouns like English does, a single word can be processed in many different parts of the brain depending on the context in which it is used (Li et al., 2004).

Plasticity after Psychotherapy. Another experience that changes the brain is psychotherapy. It probably comes as no surprise that the treatment of psychological problems with medication changes the brain. After all, that is what drugs like Xanax, Zoloft, and Concerta are designed to do. But studies show that psychotherapy—talk therapy, with no medication involved—changes the brain too, often in ways that mimic medication (Cozolino, 2010; Linden, 2012). For example, clients with phobias (an anxiety disorder covered in more detail in Chapter 14) showed similar changes in the activity of the limbic system and other parts of the brain whether they were treated with medication or cognitive-behavioral psychotherapy (Linden, 2006; Paquette et al., 2003; Johanson et al., 2006; Straube et al., 2006). Similar findings—that therapy and medication change the same parts of the brain in the same ways—have also been found in clients with obsessive-compulsive disorder, panic disorder, depression, and other disorders (DeRubeis et al., 2008; Baxter et al., 1992; Nakatani et al., 2003; Furmark et al., 2002; Sakai et al., 2006; Goldapple et al., 2004; Brody et al., 2001; Penades et al., 2002; Wykes et al., 2002).

LIFE HACK 2.2

When you practice a behavior extensively, you change your brain in ways that enhance your ability to do that behavior well.

(Sanes & Jessell, 2013c; Pascual-Leone & Torres, 1993)

CHECK YOUR LEARNING:

2.11 To what extent can specific brain functions be localized exclusively to specific parts of the brain?

2.12 In general, how do the parts near the base of the human brain differ from the parts near the outer regions of the human brain?

2.13 Where is the brain stem located and what does it do?

2.14 Where is the cerebellum located and what is its primary function?

2.15 What is the main function of the thalamus?

2.16 What is the limbic system and what is its primary function?

2.17 What parts of the brain are contained in the limbic system, and what is the main function of each part?

2.18 What are the primary functions of the cerebrum and cerebral cortex?

2.19 What is the corpus callosum and what is its primary function?

2.20 Why is the corpus callosum cut in split-brain surgery?

2.21 What are the four lobes of the cerebrum, and what is the focus of each lobe?

2.22 What are the association areas and what do they do?

2.23 What is plasticity and when is it most likely to occur?

The Nervous System and the Endocrine System

Your body features two fine-tuned communication systems, each designed to send and receive different kinds of information: the *nervous system* and the *endocrine system*.

YOU WILL LEARN:

2.24 how the nervous system connects the brain to the rest of the body.

2.25 the difference between the central nervous system and the peripheral nervous system.

2.26 the two parts of the peripheral nervous system.

2.27 the two divisions that make up the autonomic nervous system.

2.28 what the endocrine system is.

2.29 which gland is the "master gland."

The Nervous System

The **nervous system** is the full set of nerves that connect your brain with all the other parts of your body. The nervous system is what enables your brain to act as a command center, sending and receiving messages from all over your body. As described earlier in the chapter, the building blocks of your nervous system are *neurons*, the cells that facilitate communication within the nervous system.

The Central Nervous System and the Peripheral Nervous System.

The core of the nervous system is known as the **central nervous system**: the brain and the spinal cord. All communication with the brain must move through the central nervous system, but often—as the example of searching for a smartphone in the dark illustrates—the communication moves beyond the brain and spinal cord to other body parts, like your hands or feet (Brodal, 2010). That kind of communication requires not only your central nervous system, but also your **peripheral nervous system**: the neurons that connect the central nervous system to other parts of the body. You've heard the word *peripheral* before in the term *peripheral vision*—not what's in the center, but what's off to the side. Peripheral means the same thing here—the neuronal connections that extend from your center (your brain and spine) to all other parts of your body.

The Somatic Nervous System and the Autonomic Nervous System.

The peripheral nervous system has two parts: the *somatic nervous system* and the *autonomic nervous system*. Your **somatic nervous system** is the part of the peripheral nervous system that connects the central nervous system to the parts of the body you control voluntarily. The example in which you move your hand around inside your backpack to find your phone illustrates the somatic nervous system. In fact, any sensation or action that you are aware of moves through your somatic nervous system.

By contrast, your **autonomic nervous system** is the part of the peripheral nervous system that connects the central nervous system to the parts of your body you control involuntarily. Your autonomic nervous system regulates the bodily functions that you never have to think about, like the beating of your heart and the digestion of your food. Unlike your somatic nervous system, which spreads throughout your entire body, your autonomic nervous system covers only your core, where most of your organs are (Amaral & Strick, 2013; Horn & Swanson, 2013).

As **Figure 2.19** illustrates, your autonomic nervous system has two parts of its own: one that helps you "turn up," and another that helps you "turn down" (Garrett, 2015). Specifically, the **sympathetic division** is the part of your autonomic nervous system that revs your body up in response to stressors. By contrast, the **parasympathetic division** is the part of your autonomic nervous system that calms your body down when stressors decrease. In Chapter 11, when we discuss stress in more detail, we'll delve into the *fight-or-flight response*, which is an autonomic emotional and physical reaction to a perceived threat that prepares us to either attack it or run away from it. For now, it is important to know that the sympathetic division cranks up your fight-or-flight response, and your parasympathetic division winds it down.

You've probably noticed that your body's response to stressors, especially sudden stressors, is largely outside of your control (or *autonomic*). For example, if you're

nervous system
The full set of nerves that connect the brain with all other parts of the body.

central nervous system
The brain and the spinal cord.

peripheral nervous system
The neurons that connect the central nervous system to other parts of the body.

somatic nervous system
The part of the peripheral nervous system that connects the central nervous system to the parts of the body controlled voluntarily.

autonomic nervous system
The part of the peripheral nervous system that connects the central nervous system to the parts of the body controlled involuntarily.

sympathetic division
The part of the autonomic nervous system that revs the body up in response to stressors.

parasympathetic division
The part of the autonomic nervous system that calms the body down when stressors decrease.

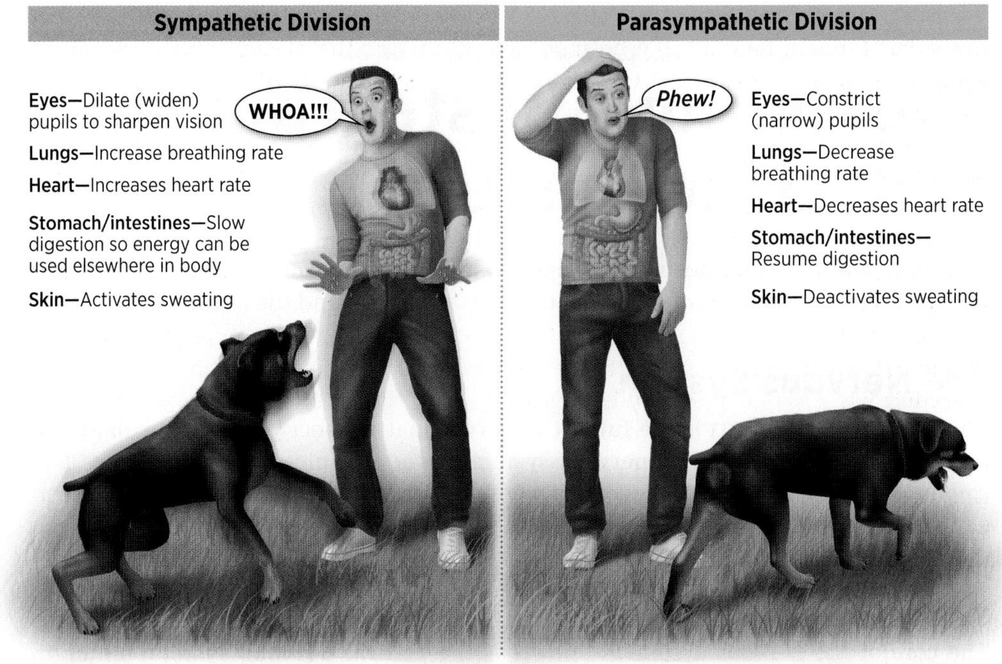

FIGURE 2.19 The Sympathetic and Parasympathetic Divisions. Within your autonomic nervous system, the sympathetic division helps your body "turn up" in response to stressors by widening your pupils, increasing your heart rate, and increasing your breathing rate. The parasympathetic division helps your body "turn down" when the stressors decrease by returning all of your body parts to their resting state.

walking alone through a neighborhood and without warning you see a huge, growling, unleashed dog sprinting toward you, your sympathetic division triggers a set of bodily changes: Your heart races and beats more strongly, you breathe more heavily and quickly, and you start to sweat. (Actually, the changes include others that are less noticeable too: your pupils dilate (enlarge), your stomach slows digestion, and your liver and kidney produce more of certain substances as well.) All of these changes are designed to help you do what the term *fight or flight* suggests: either fight the threat or fly away from it as fast as possible. Very soon, however, the dog comes to a sudden stop, just a few feet away from you. You notice in the dog's yard a sign indicating that it is enclosed by an invisible electric fence. Within a few seconds, you're past that house, past that dog, past that threat.

That is when your parasympathetic division activates, undoing all of the bodily changes that the sympathetic division revved up. It brings your heart, lungs, stomach, and everything else back to normal. But it doesn't happen instantly. Even though your mind knows the threat is no longer there, it may take your body many minutes to return to normal. In fact, you may notice that the sweating, heart-pounding, and heavy breathing are still with you even when you've gotten several blocks away from that dog. As **Figure 2.20** shows, that is the nature of the autonomic nervous system and its sympathetic and parasympathetic divisions: They automatically control your reactions to stressors (and their absence) to maximize your chances of survival, but you don't have much voluntary control over the process.

The Endocrine System

Unlike the nervous system, which sends messages between the brain and the rest of the body via neurons, the **endocrine system** is the set of glands that send hormones throughout the body via the bloodstream. **Hormones**, chemicals made by the glands of the endocrine system, affect certain tissues throughout the body. Hormones influence virtually every important function within your body, including your appetite, mood, energy level, sleep schedule, sex drive, metabolism, digestion, and more.

Does the endocrine system operate at the same speed as the nervous system?

No. The endocrine system operates much more slowly than the nervous system. Messages dart through neurons, but hormones ooze through the bloodstream, often taking a long time to get started, build up, and ultimately stop. Consider the familiar hormones most closely tied to sexual development (puberty): *testosterone* and *estrogen*. If you recall your middle school years, you'll remember that those hormones kicked in over months, not seconds. Your male classmates did not grow beards, and your female classmates did not develop breasts, instantly. Instead, in a gradually increasing way, the boys' endocrine systems released testosterone and the girls' endocrine systems released estrogen. Little by little, those hormones had the expected effect on the appropriate body parts, and eventually (in some cases, quite a few years after they started), the messages slowed and stopped.

The endocrine system features many glands, but the most important is the **pituitary gland**: the "master gland" in the brain, which produces human growth hormone and also controls all of the other glands in the body. Although it is no bigger than the eraser on the end of a pencil, your pituitary gland is in charge, either directly or via control of other glands, of some remarkably important stuff: how tall you grow, your metabolism rate, the ratio of muscle to fat in your body, when puberty kicks in, your blood pressure, your body temperature, the production of breast milk after childbirth, and much more.

Figure 2.21 includes the pituitary gland among a list of important glands in the endocrine system. Also on that list are the **adrenal glands**: glands located on top of the kidneys that produce hormones to arouse the body in response to stress. One of those hormones, named after the gland itself, you know well: *adrenaline*. When you notice that your "adrenaline is pumping"—when you're gearing up for a big game, or walking through a haunted house, or mountain-biking down a steep incline—that is actually your adrenal glands working overtime. Adrenaline is also known as *epinephrine*. An EpiPen is injectable epinephrine, which can be life-saving if an allergic reaction causes impaired breathing. That extra boost of epinephrine, when combined with the epinephrine already produced by the adrenal gland, helps to activate the body's natural stress responses—especially opening the airways and increasing the heartbeat—sufficiently to get through the crisis. Epinephrine injections have also been used to save heart attack patients.

Another hormone produced by the adrenal gland is *cortisol*, which is nicknamed the stress hormone (Cozolino, 2008). Psychologists who study stress often use cortisol levels as an objective way of measuring stress—not only because cortisol levels are good stress indicators, but because cortisol is easy to measure. It doesn't require a blood test (although that works too): All it takes is an analysis of someone's hair or saliva. For example, one study found that the hair of women in the third trimester of pregnancy—a time notorious for high stress levels—has double the cortisol content of women who were not pregnant (Kirschbaum et al., 2009). Studies of infants have found that their saliva contains more cortisol in the immediate aftermath of things

endocrine system
The set of glands that send hormones throughout the body via the bloodstream.

hormones
The chemicals made by the glands of the endocrine system that affect certain tissues throughout the body.

pituitary gland
The "master gland" in the brain that produces human growth hormone and controls all of the other glands in the body.

adrenal glands
The glands located on top of the kidneys that produce hormones to arouse the body in response to stress.

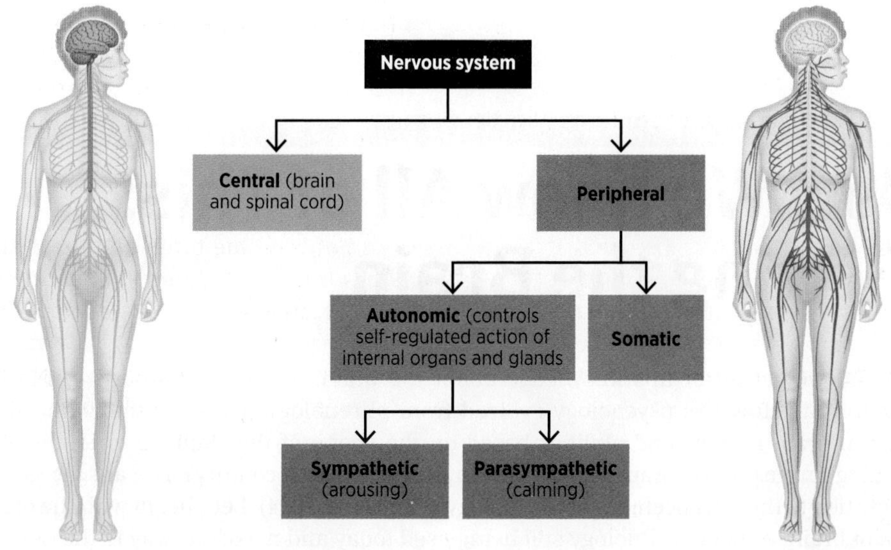

FIGURE 2.20 The Organization of the Nervous System. The most basic division of the human nervous system is between the central and peripheral nervous systems. The peripheral nervous system is further divided between the somatic and autonomic nervous systems. The autonomic nervous system is even further divided into the sympathetic and parasympathetic divisions.

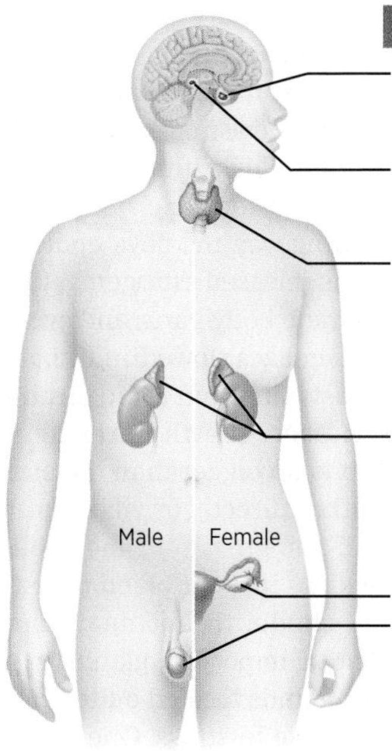

Gland	Location	Function
Pituitary	Brain	"Master" gland; controls other glands and produces human growth hormone
Pineal	Brain	Produces melatonin, a hormone related to serotonin that influences sleep and wake cycles
Thyroid	Throat	Produces hormones that influence metabolism, body temperature, and blood pressure
Adrenal	Kidneys	Produce adrenaline and other hormones to respond to stress
Ovary (female) Testes (male)	Reproductive system	Produce testosterone and estrogen, which influence sexual development and drive

FIGURE 2.21 Selected Glands of the Endocrine System. The endocrine system includes a variety of glands. Some are located in the brain, and others are located in other parts of the body. The pituitary gland, or "master gland," controls all of the other glands.

that they find stressful, including separation from mom and unexpected physical pain (Kirschbaum & Hellhammer, 1994; Lewis & Thomas, 1990; Larson et al., 1991). Recently, researchers have even developed a smartphone app (currently awaiting FDA approval) on which people can test their own saliva for cortisol content, bypassing the time and expense of sending the sample to a lab (Choi et al., 2014).

CHECK YOUR LEARNING:

2.24 How does the nervous system connect the brain with all other parts of your body?

2.25 What is the difference between the central nervous system and the peripheral nervous system?

2.26 What are the two parts of the peripheral nervous system, and what does each part do?

2.27 What are the two divisions of the autonomic nervous system, and what does each division do?

2.28 What is the endocrine system?

2.29 Which gland called the master gland, and why does it deserve that label?

How We Know All of This: Viewing the Brain

How did we get all of this knowledge about the brain, including the parts and activity within it? How has psychology evolved from phrenology (guessing the connections between brain regions and abilities based on the shape of the skull) to vivid, detailed, stunning images of the brain's inner workings in just over a century? The answer is intimately tied to the advancement of technology (Van Horn, 2004). Let's begin with the oldest form of brain-viewing technology still being used today and make our way to the newest.

Electroencephalography (EEG)

Electroencephalography (EEG) is a technique in which electrodes are placed on the scalp to record electrical activity in the brain. EEGs, which were first used in the 1920s, don't produce pictures of the brain, but graphs that illustrate the activity between any two points in the brain (Millett, 2001). Specifically, EEGs measure the difference in electrical voltage between any two points in the brain, which indicates the activity of neurons between them (Frey & Spitz, 2013; Olejniczak, 2006; Coburn et al., 2006). Psychologists and other professionals who use EEGs know what normal graphs between particular points look like, and they use that knowledge as a comparison when examining patients' EEGs for abnormalities. If that comparison indicates excessive electrical activity in certain neuronal connections, that activity could indicate the likelihood of seizures. For that reason, EEGs are well suited for the assessment of seizure-based disorders like epilepsy (Westbrook, 2013).

YOU WILL LEARN:

2.30 how electroencephalography (EEG) works.

2.31 how computed tomography (CT) works.

2.32 how magnetic resonance imaging (MRI) works.

2.33 how positron emission tomography (PET) works.

2.34 how functional magnetic resonance imaging (fMRI) works.

Computed Tomography (CT)

Psychologists' abilities to see brain activity, especially to locate it in specific parts of the brain, took a big step forward from EEGs with the introduction in the 1970s of **computed tomography (CT)**: a technique in which multiple x-rays are combined to make a 3D image of the brain. Each x-ray (which can also be viewed alone) provides a 2D image of a "slice" of the brain; when computers combine these 2D images, they can make the image 3D. (That process is actually similar to the way 3D printers work—combining 2D slices of an object to make a 3D whole.) CT scans produce images of the brain in shades of gray. These images allow psychologists to distinguish brain matter (which is dense and appears close to white) from ventricles or space in the brain (which appears black). This distinction is important when assessing whether a patient has a disease that features enlarged ventricles, like Alzheimer's disease or schizophrenia (Hurley et al., 2013). Subtle differences in the shades of gray also allowed psychologists to detect the specific location of a **lesion**: damage or destruction of brain tissue. The ability to detect lesions in CT scans is actually rather crude compared to the more sophisticated forms of technology that followed.

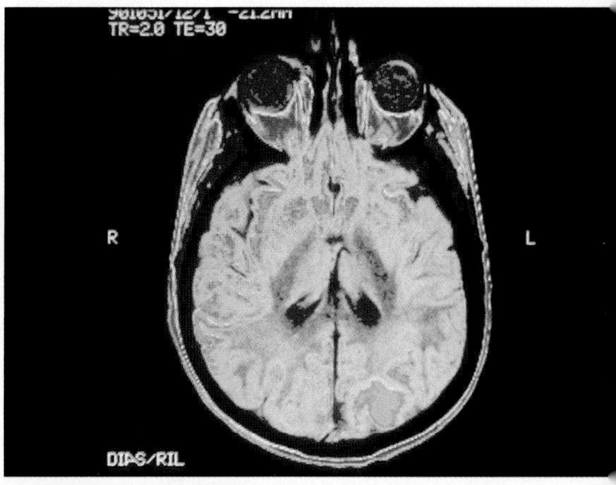

Magnetic resonance imaging (MRI) is a technique in which magnetic fields and radio waves are used to make images of brain structure. MRIs offer much more detail than computed tomography (CT) scans.
Universal Images Group/Getty Images

Magnetic Resonance Imaging (MRI)

The next step forward in brain imaging, which came along in the 1980s, was **magnetic resonance imaging (MRI)**: a technique in which magnetic fields and radio waves are used to make images of brain structure. MRIs offer much more detail than CT scans. The *magnetic* in its name indicates that MRIs work by putting a strong magnetic field around the brain to measure the radio waves that naturally come from hydrogen atoms (remember, like the rest of the body, the brain is H_2O). This magnetic field is contained in a large tube in which the patient lies down (or in some newer machines, stands or sits up)—a procedure that can cause problems for people who are too big for the tube or too fidgety to stay still. Like CT scans, MRIs are good for finding lesions as well as tumors and other abnormalities in brain structures. Although MRIs can take longer (30–60 minutes, typically) and cost more than CT scans, the higher resolution provides psychologists with a better view of the brain (Erhart et al., 2005; Symms et al., 2004; Gupta et al., 2004).

Positron Emission Tomography (PET)

The definition of MRI ends with *brain structure*, meaning that it (along with CT scans) shows the brain's parts, but not the activity within those parts—like seeing the architectural blueprint of a building but not the movement patterns of the people within it. The two most recent innovations in brain imaging make the jump from brain structure to brain *function*, which means they are able to illustrate activity within the brain. One recent innovation is **positron emission tomography (PET)**: a technique in which

electroencephalography (EEG)
A technique in which electrodes are placed on the scalp to record electrical activity in the brain.

computed tomography (CT)
A technique in which multiple x-rays are combined to make a 3D image of the brain.

lesion
The damage or destruction of brain tissue.

magnetic resonance imaging (MRI)
A technique in which magnetic fields and radio waves are used to make images of brain structure.

positron emission tomography (PET)
A technique in which activity in various brain structures is illustrated by a radioactive sugar injected into the body.

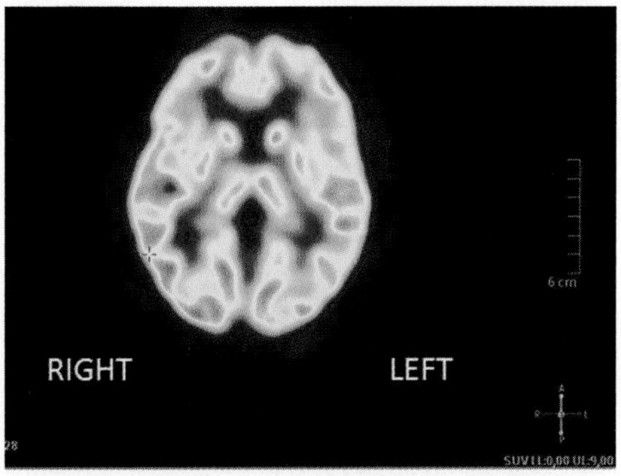

Positron emission tomography (PET) is a technique in which activity in various brain structures is illustrated by a radioactive sugar injected into the body. Unlike MRIs and CT scans, PET scans show brain function, not just brain structure. iStock/Getty Images

activity in various brain structures is illustrated by a radioactive sugar injected into the body. That radioactive sugar is typically injected into a vein near the elbow, but can also be inhaled as a gas if necessary. Once in your bloodstream, the radioactive sugar travels throughout your body, including your brain. In your brain, blood rushes to each part according to how heavily that part is being used—when a part of the brain is being used a lot, it pulls a lot of blood.

When the blood is carrying a radioactive sugar, PET scanners can detect it. So, PET scans are good for making connections between particular activities and particular parts of the brain (Miletich, 2009; Little et al., 2013). For example, certain parts of the brain will light up on a PET scan when you are watching an exciting basketball game on TV, others when you are feeling hungry, and others when you are recalling a childhood memory. One study found that PET scans of the brains of people listening to their favorite music featured very high levels of activity in parts of the brain involved in reward and emotion, including the prefrontal cortex and amygdala (Blood & Zatorre, 2001). In another study, PET scans of the brains of ten long-distance runners after running a half-marathon showed that the euphoric feeling of the runner's high is based in heightened activity in certain parts of the brain, including the prefrontal cortex and the limbic system (Boecker et al., 2008).

Functional Magnetic Resonance Imaging (fMRI)

Similar to PET in its ability to illustrate brain function rather than just brain structure is **functional magnetic resonance imaging (fMRI)**: a technique in which magnetic fields are used to make images of brain activity.

How are fMRIs different from MRIs?

fMRIs use the same kind of magnet-based technology as regular MRIs, but they can detect metabolism (energy use) in particular parts of the brain at particular times (Small & Heeger, 2013; Dickerson, 2007). That metabolism is indicated by oxygen in the

FROM RESEARCH TO REAL LIFE

The Murderer's Mind

The new generation of brain imaging, including PET scans, illuminates not just the parts of the brain, but what is going on inside of them. So what is going on inside the brain of a killer?

Psychologist Adrian Raine has dedicated his career to that question. He describes the method that he and his team used to study convicted killers in one study:

> *...complete with shackles and chains, and flanked by guards, our forty-one murderers trooped into the brain-scanning facility... The technique we used to scan their brains was positron-emission tomography—PET for short... We used the continuous performance task to activate or "challenge" the prefrontal cortex. The subject had to press a response button every time they saw the figure "o" flashed on a computer screen. This went on for thirty-two minutes.*
>
> —*Raine, 2013, p. 66*

What they found was that the PET scans of these murderers looked just like PET scans of nonmurderers in some ways, such as activation of the occipital lobe. But the PET scans showed a couple of important differences: an overactive limbic system and an underactive prefrontal cortex (Raine et al., 1997; Amen et al., 2007). Think about that combination. The limbic system is all about emotion and impulse—it is the part of the brain that says, "Let's do this!" (Barrash et al., 2000). The prefrontal cortex is all about executive control and decision making—it is the part of the brain that says, "Wait a minute—is this a good idea?" (Bechara et al., 1997; Blair, 2007; Bechara & Demasio, 2005). When the balance between those two is off, the result could be behavior that satisfies a momentary urge but lacks judgment and forethought. In the terrible cases of these murderers, that behavior is homicide.

Studies have found that this balance of the limbic system versus prefrontal cortex is often a key factor not just in murderous behavior, but in other kinds of aggressive behavior such as assault, domestic abuse, and even social insensitivity (Raine, 2013; Damasio, 1994; Haycock, 2014). Current research points to an underactive prefrontal cortex as the single strongest correlate of antisocial and violent behavior (Yang & Raine, 2009). Assuming this finding is confirmed by further research, it suggests that among murderers, the brain's inability to keep impulses in check is as dangerous as the brain's ability to produce those impulses in the first place.

blood, which has unique magnetic properties that respond to the magnetic field used in fMRI. As such, fMRIs can identify which parts of the brain are most active when we talk, think, or perform other activities (Bandettini, 2012). In one fMRI study, participants were excluded from playing a game with others, and researchers found that the pain of social rejection activates the same parts of the brain (including parts of the cerebral cortex and prefrontal cortex) as physical pain (Eisenberger et al., 2003). Another study found that when heterosexual men and women were looking at sexually explicit photos, their fMRIs were similar in some ways (high activation of parts of the occipital, parietal, and temporal lobes), but different in others (men had much more amygdala and hypothalamus activation than women) (Hamann et al., 2004).

functional magnetic resonance imaging (fMRI)
A technique in which magnetic fields are used to make images of brain activity.

Although fMRIs provide perhaps the most breathtaking images yet of the inner workings of the brain, the technology is relatively new and has limitations. For example, fMRIs may not be entirely reliable across time (Caceres et al., 2009). One study conducted fMRIs on participants viewing fearful faces at three different points in time (the initial session, 2 weeks later, and 8 weeks later) and got significantly different results at each point (Johnstone et al., 2005). Also, some researchers have conducted exploratory fMRI studies. ***Exploratory*** here means that the researchers have participants perform a particular behavior and simply see what lights up (instead of forming a hypothesis ahead of time about specific parts of the brain that should light up). This kind of research can produce connections that appear strong in a single study but are not replicated because they were due to chance rather than actual relationships between variables (Yarkoni, 2009).

Adding to the problem is the fact that researchers sometimes divide the 3D fMRI image of the brain into a huge number of tiny cubic regions—often 40,000 to 500,000 of them—each of which might be as small as a cubic millimeter. (They call these regions ***voxels***, which is the 3D or volume-based version of pixels, like your TV or computer screen has.) When researchers then try to see if brain activity in any of those many voxels correlates with a particular behavior, they are bound to find something, even if it is just a fluke (Vul et al., 2009). This is like the way that your odds of having a winning lottery ticket increase if you have thousands and thousands of tickets rather than just a few.

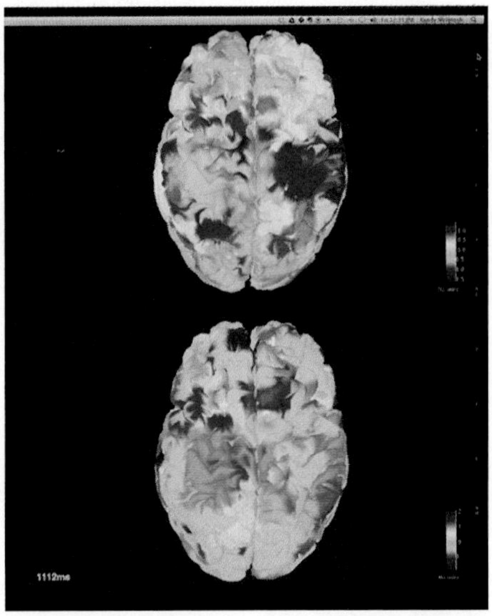

Functional magnetic resonance imaging (fMRI) is a technique in which magnetic fields are used to make images of brain activity. Like PET scans, fMRIs show brain function, not just brain structure. Toronto Star/Getty Images

CURRENT CONTROVERSY

Neuroeverything?

One by-product of the newest brain imaging technology, including PET scans and fMRIs, is that those images appear all over the popular media. New psychological findings—whether presented in a TV news story, news or magazine article, or blog post—are often accompanied by a high-tech picture of a human brain with certain parts glowing bright red, orange, yellow, or blue. Often, the words that accompany these pictures include *neuropsychology* (or *neuropsychiatry*, *neuroscience*, or another *neuro-* term) along with an explanation of how these pictures explain all kinds of human experiences. As stated by Sally Satel and Scott O. Lilienfeld in their book *Brainwashed: The Seductive Appeal of Mindless Neuroscience*:

> *You've seen the headlines: This is your brain on love. Or God. Or envy. Or happiness. And they're reliably accompanied by articles boasting pictures of color-drenched brains—scans capturing Buddhist monks meditating, addicts craving cocaine, and college sophomores choosing Coke over Pepsi. The media—and even some neuroscientists, it seems—love to invoke the neural foundations of human behavior to explain everything from the Bernie Madoff financial fiasco to slavish devotion to our iPhones, the sexual indiscretions of politicians, conservatives' dismissal of global warming, and even an obsession with self-tanning.*
>
> —*Satel & Lilienfeld, 2013, p. ix*

The problem is that those brain pictures can be quite misleading (Illes et al., 2009; Rose & Abi-Rached, 2013). To be more accurate, the people explaining the brain imaging can overreach and oversimplify. Too often, they make the leap from what the pictures actually show—for example, certain brain regions working harder than others—to very specific conclusions about exactly what thoughts or feelings are taking place (Racine et al., 2010). (It is one thing to see that it is raining in Michigan, but another thing to claim that your cousin in Kalamazoo is getting wet.) Too often they also reduce a feeling or behavior down to activity in a solitary part of the brain, glossing over the fact that almost everything we do involves a complex web of brain regions, even if one plays the biggest role (Racine et al., 2005).

One study found that participants considered brain-related scientific findings more credible if they saw a version of the story with fMRI images than participants who saw the same story with either bar graphs or no visuals (McCabe & Castel, 2008). Another study found that just adding neuropsychology explanations, even without the images, powerfully influenced many readers to believe the results (Weisberg et al., 2008). In other words, the words and images of neuropsychology are remarkably persuasive. However, before fully believing the neuro-news you encounter in the popular media, think critically about the limitations of this technology and how findings should be responsibly interpreted.

CHECK YOUR LEARNING:

2.30 How does an electroencephalography (EEG) work?

2.31 How does computed tomography (CT) work?

2.32 How does magnetic resonance imaging (MRI) work?

2.33 How does positron emission tomography (PET) work?

2.34 How does functional magnetic resonance imaging (fMRI) work?

CHAPTER SUMMARY

Brain and Behavior Connections: An Introduction

2.1 Phineas Gage's tragic brain injury changed his personality and behavior, and Paul Broca's autopsy of a stroke victim found damage to just one part of the man's brain. These two findings helped researchers understand that certain parts of the brain are related to certain functions or abilities.

2.2 A good way to understand the brain is to start small and then zoom out. In this chapter, we begin with microscopic activity within the brain. Then, we focus on the brain itself, its parts, and how different parts are connected to different behaviors. Finally, we cover the whole body and how it interacts with the brain.

Activity Within the Brain

2.3 Your brain contains a network of about 100 billion neurons, the building blocks of brain activity.

2.4 Sensory neurons carry information from the senses to the brain, while motor neurons carry information from the brain to the muscles. Neurons send messages through their axons, which end with axon terminals.

2.5 Axons are often covered with a myelin sheath, a sleeve of fatty material that protects the message from getting lost as it travels.

2.6 Dendrites receive messages from the axon terminals of the previous neuron.

2.7 Between the axon terminal of one axon and the dendrites of the next axon, there is a small space called a synapse that must be crossed.

2.8 The substances that cross the synapse are neurotransmitters, which travel from synaptic vesicles to specific receptor sites within the dendrites.

2.9 When neurotransmitters don't successfully cross the synapse, they return to the sending neuron through a process called reuptake.

2.10 The process of sending a message between neurons starts with an action potential, which happens when the electrical charge within the neuron exceeds a certain threshold.

The Brain and Its Parts

2.11 Certain brain functions can be localized to certain parts of the brain, but no part of the brain does anything entirely by itself.

2.12 As a rule of thumb, the parts of the human brain that control functions most other animals can do are located near the base of the brain. The parts of the human brain that control uniquely human functions are closer to the outer regions, especially the front, of the brain.

2.13 The brainstem connects to the spine and controls the functions most essential to staying alive.

2.14 The cerebellum is located near the base of the brain and primarily controls balance and coordination of movement.

2.15 The thalamus is the brain's main sensory processing center.

2.16 The limbic system is a cluster of brain areas surrounding the thalamus and involved primarily in emotion.

2.17 The limbic system contains the hypothalamus, which maintains a steadiness in bodily functions; the hippocampus, which is involved in memory; and the amygdala, which controls fear and other emotions.

2.18 The cerebrum and cerebral cortex are involved in sophisticated, often uniquely human abilities.

2.19 The corpus callosum is the bundle of neurons that connects and allows communication between the right and left halves, or hemispheres, of the cerebrum.

2.20 On rare occasions, the corpus callosum is cut in a surgery called split-brain surgery, which can alleviate seizures but often results in decreased communication between the two hemispheres.

2.21 The cerebrum consists of four lobes: (1) the occipital lobe, which focuses on vision; (2) the temporal lobe, which focuses on hearing and speech production; (3) the parietal lobe, which focuses on touch and perception; and (4) the frontal lobe, which focuses on complex thinking tasks and other advanced functions.

2.22 The cerebrum and its lobes contain high concentrations of association areas, which synthesize and interpret information taken in by other parts of the brain.

2.23 Plasticity refers to the ability of the brain to adapt its structure or function. It can take place after injury or life experience, including psychotherapy or cultural experiences. Plasticity is greater in younger brains than older brains, due in part to younger brains' greater ability for neurogenesis, or creation of new neurons.

The Nervous System and the Endocrine System

2.24 The nervous system connects your brain with all other parts of your body through neurons.

2.25 The central nervous system consists of the brain and spinal cord, and the peripheral nervous system consists of the neurons that connect the central nervous system to other parts of the body.

2.26 The peripheral nervous system has two parts: (1) the somatic nervous system, which oversees voluntary movement, and (2) the autonomic nervous system, which oversees involuntary movement.

2.27 The autonomic nervous system consists of two divisions: (1) the sympathetic division, which revs your body up, and (2) the parasympathetic division, which calms your body down.

2.28 The endocrine system is the set of glands that uses hormones to communicate through the bloodstream to various tissues throughout the body.

2.29 Among the glands, the pituitary gland is the "master gland," which controls many systems in your body.

How We Know All of This: Viewing the Brain

2.30 Electroencephalography (EEG) is a technique that involves electrodes placed on the scalp to record electrical activity within the brain.

2.31 Computed tomography (CT) is a technique in which multiple x-rays are combined to make a 3D image of the brain.

2.32 Magnetic resonance imaging (MRI) is a technique in which magnetic fields and radio waves are used to make images of brain structures.

2.33 Positron emission tomography (PET) is a technique in which activity within various brain structures is visible after a radioactive sugar is injected into the body.

2.34 Functional magnetic resonance imaging (fMRI) is a technique in which magnetic fields are used to make images of brain activity.

KEY TERMS

SELF-ASSESSMENT

1. The cells that facilitate communication within your nervous system are called ______.

2. What's the main function of the parasympathetic division of your autonomic nervous system?
   a. to rev up your body in response to stressors
   b. to calm down your body when stressors decrease
   c. to control your sense of vision
   d. to help you comprehend human speech

3. The ______ is the part of your limbic system most directly involved in emotion, especially fear.
   a. cerebellum
   b. corpus callosum
   c. amygdala
   d. pons

4. Compared to the brains of other species, human brains have a high proportion of ______, which are devoted to synthesizing and interpreting information rather than just taking information in.
   a. association areas
   b. dendrites
   c. myelin sheaths
   d. synaptic vesicles

5. In split-brain surgery, what gets cut?
   a. the parietal lobe
   b. Wernicke's area
   c. the medulla
   d. the corpus callosum

6. Ashley experienced a brain injury in a car accident. Since the injury, her ability to see is impaired. Damage to which lobe of Ashley's brain is most likely to be responsible for the sight impairment?
   a. occipital
   b. temporal
   c. parietal
   d. adrenal

7. Which of the following is true about your frontal lobe?
   a. It is located at the back and base of your brain, near the spinal cord.
   b. It is involved in complex thinking tasks, planning, and other advanced functions that many nonhuman animal species cannot perform.
   c. It controls breathing and heartbeat.
   d. It controls patterns of waking and sleeping.

8. Jayla experienced a brain injury as a young child. Fortunately, her brain demonstrated an ability to adapt its structure or function in response to the injury. That ability is called ______.

9. When information passes from one neuron to the next, it specifically moves through the ______ ______ of the first neuron into the ______ of the second neuron.
   a. interneurons; myelin sheath
   b. receptor sites; stem cells
   c. axon terminals; dendrites
   d. dendrites; glial cells

10. What's the main difference between magnetic resonance imaging (MRI) and functional magnetic resonance imaging (fMRI)?
   a. An MRI shows the brain's structure, but an fMRI shows the brain's activity.
   b. An MRI can be conducted on the brain of any species, but an fMRI can be conducted only on human brains.
   c. An MRI can only provide images of microscopic parts of the brain, but an fMRI can only provide images of the whole brain.
   d. An MRI involves electrodes being placed on the head, but an fMRI does not.

Self-Assessment Answers

1. neurons, 2. b, 3. c, 4. a, 5. d, 6. a, 7. b,
8. plasticity, 9. c, 10. a

WHAT'S YOUR TAKE?

1. If you saw a psychotherapist, you'd probably measure your improvement by describing changes in your behaviors, thoughts, or feelings. However, those ways of assessing improvement can be difficult to quantify and vulnerable to subjectivity. Would measuring changes in your brain be better? There are plenty of research studies that show how psychotherapy changes the brain, but in the "real world" of outpatient psychotherapy—counseling centers, clinics, private practice offices—measuring progress with brain imaging technology is still rare (Etkin et al., 2005; Barsaglini et al., 2014; Weingarten & Strauman, 2015). As the years go by, however, it may become more common, especially if scanning equipment becomes more convenient and less expensive. If you were the client, how would you want your therapy progress to be measured—by changes that a scanner notices in your brain, or by changes that you notice in your day-to-day life? What are the pros and cons of each?

2. Increasingly, lawyers use brain images to defend their clients in court (Meixner, 2015; Teitcher, 2011; Bonnie & Scott, 2013; Farah, 2010). In three recent court cases, juries deciding whether a convicted killer should receive the death penalty were provided (by the defendant's attorneys) PET scans, MRIs, and fMRIs of the killer's brain. In each case, experts explained that those images illustrated a variety of abnormalities involving parts of the brain such as the frontal lobe, amygdala, cerebellum, and corpus callosum, among others. In two cases, the jury decided against the death penalty. In one, the jury decided for the death penalty (Miller, 2013). If you were on the jury, how much impact would brain scan evidence have on you? Would it matter if the crime was murder or something less serious? Would it matter if you were determining guilt or sentencing someone who had already been found guilty?

SHOW ME MORE

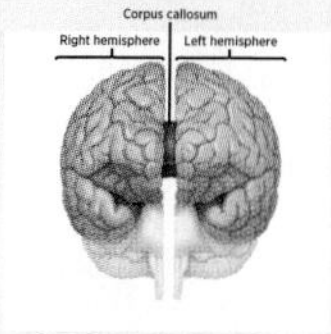

2.1 A Split-Brain Patient

http://tiny.cc/showmemore

In this video, a patient who underwent split-brain surgery explains and illustrates the effect of the surgery on his functioning.

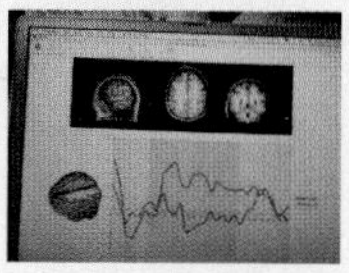

2.2 Your Brain on Politics?

http://tiny.cc/km9mjy

What happens inside the brains of undecided voters when they see and hear various candidates? This *New York Times* article describes fMRI images when such voters considered 2008 presidential candidates, including Barack Obama, John McCain, Hillary Clinton, and Mitt Romney.

AP Photo/Reed Saxon

3 Sensation and Perception

PeopleImages/Getty Images

On April 15, 2013, bombs exploded near the finish line of the Boston Marathon, killing three and injuring hundreds. The horrific event dominated the news for months, along with the hunt for the terrorists who planted the bombs and the trial of the one who was captured alive. The terrible attack left painful scars, both emotional and physical, for everyone who experienced it.

Many subfields within psychology can help us understand the horrors of the Boston Marathon bombing and its aftermath. For example, the focus of Chapter 5 is memory. Anyone who experienced the bombings firsthand will remember unforgettable images, sounds, and feelings for the rest of their lives. Chapter 11 describes stress and ts impact on physical and mental health—experiences all too familiar to survivors and their loved ones. Chapters 14 and 15 cover psychological disorders and the treatments available, both of which are more likely to become part of life for those who experience tragedies like this one.

Before the Boston Marathon bombing could become a memory, cause stress, or contribute to psychological disorders, it had to be *sensed* and *perceived* by the people who experienced it. More generally, people's sensory organs have to pick up the sights, sounds, smells, and other stimuli in the world around them, and transmit that information to their brain. Once there, the brain quickly translates those aw sensations into something meaningful that they can understand. Many eyewitness accounts of the Boston Marathon bombing highlight he processes of sensation and perception. Most described what they aw and heard. Jeff Bauman, who lost both legs in the explosion, "saw a flash, heard three or four pops;" he "was on the ground... looked down, and ...could see [his] legs, and it was just complete carnage" (Valencia, 2015). A few described what they smelled. William Richard, whose 8-year-old son, Martin, was killed in the bombing and whose daughter and wife were injured, testified that the bombing scene "smelled like gunpowder, sulfur, burned hair...It smelled vile" (Gessen, 2015).

In this chapter, we will examine how your sensory organs (eyes, ears, nose, tongue, and skin) cooperate with your brain to sense and perceive the world around you in moments of terror, moments of joy, and every moment in between. We will explore your ability to notice new sensations and stop noticing old ones. We will explore the way your senses interact with each other, as well as the impact your expectations and previous experiences can have on what you perceive. And we'll take an in-depth look at the specific senses of vision, hearing, smell, taste, and touch.

CHAPTER OUTLINE

The Fundamentals of Sensation and Perception

YOU WILL LEARN:

3.1 the difference between sensation and perception.

3.2 how evolution has influenced sensation and perception.

3.3 about the thresholds that mark the limits of sensory abilities.

3.4 how your senses adapt to unchanging stimuli.

3.5 how your perception deals with changing stimuli.

3.6 how simultaneous input from multiple senses can result in competition or integration.

3.7 how expectations and experiences can affect what you sense and perceive.

Sensation and perception determine how we take in and make sense of the world around us. Let's begin our discussion of them by defining and distinguishing between the two concepts.

The Difference Between Sensation and Perception

Sensation is the ability of your sensory organs to pick up energy in the environment around you and transmit it to your brain. It is the way you absorb the information your surroundings have to offer. Because sensation happens so quickly and so automatically, you might take it for granted. To better appreciate how your body and brain do it, think about the ways your phone constantly "senses" its surroundings. It senses whether an Internet signal (Wi-Fi, LTE, etc.) is present, and if so, how strong it is. It senses whether a cellular signal (for phone calls and texts) is present, and if so, how strong it is. It senses whether a Bluetooth device is in range to connect. It even senses whether a power cord is plugged into its charging port. (Your phone shows you what it senses with those little symbols on the edge of your screen.) Your body's senses work in very much the same way. Your eyes, ears, nose, tongue, and skin are constantly monitoring the environment, sending simultaneous messages to your brain about what they detect around you.

An essential step in sensation is **transduction**: the conversion of energy outside your body, like light or sound, into neural energy, like brain activity. Transduction explains how that yellow banana on the table becomes a yellow banana-shaped *image* in your brain. Transduction explains how the blaring horn of an oncoming truck becomes a blaring horn-like *sound* in your brain. This is much like when a digital camera uses transduction to make a photo from an object, or when voicemail uses transduction to make a recording of a human voice. In a similar way, your senses and brain use transduction to make mental representations of what happens around you (Levine, 2001; Eatock, 2010; Gegenfurtner, 2010).

Sensation, for both your phone and your body, involves only the detection of available information—nothing more. What happens to that information next is **perception**: the ability of your brain to interpret the raw sensations it has taken in. Perception is your brain's ability to translate the sights, sounds, and smells into something meaningful or understandable. For example, on the Fourth of July, you may see colorful explosions in the sky and hear thunderous booms going along with them. Those sights and sounds are initially taken in through your eyes and ears as simple sensations—sheer brightness and loudness.

Those sensations become perceptions when you start comprehending what they are. Rather than isolated or unfamiliar sights and sounds, perceptions are things you recognize and put into context. You might see one firework send streams of light cascading down in a circle of curves and say, "Ooh, that one looks like a willow tree!" You might see a bunch of quick flashes light up one spot in the sky in rapid succession, each producing a single blast of light and sound, and say, "Cool—like a strobe light!" Toward the end, you might see dozens of fireworks exploding together, and say, "This is the grand finale!" Each of those statements requires that you perceive what those lights and sounds are, and what they mean. That is the difference between sensation and perception. Sensation is more passive, simply detecting information from the environment and making it available to your brain. Perception is more active, transforming that sensory information into something meaningful you can use.

Just as a smartphone senses Wi-Fi, a cellular signal, or Bluetooth, your body senses your surroundings to pick up sights, sounds, smells, touches, and tastes.
Georgejmclittle/Shutterstock

The Evolution of Sensation and Perception. Sensation and perception *evolved*. Throughout human history, survival of the fittest often meant survival for those whose abilities to sense and perceive the world were most advanced. As a result, your brain devotes a lot of space and energy to sensation and perception. (Recall from Chapter 2 how many parts of the brain are involved in seeing, hearing, smell, taste, and touch.) So sensation and perception must serve an important purpose (Huber & Wilkinson, 2010). Many psychologists have argued that people devote all that brain power to sensation and perception so we can take action. By accurately sensing and perceiving the world around us, our ancestors could take actions that increased their chances of survival (Zanker, 2010). Remember that example about the banana? Once you sense it and perceive it, you can reach for it, peel it, and eat it. Remember that example about the blaring horn of an oncoming truck? Once you sense it and perceive it, you can swerve out of its path. Both of those actions help to keep you alive.

Interestingly, the sensation and perception abilities of various species in the animal kingdom match perfectly with the kinds of sights, sounds, and other sensory stimuli that increase their survival chances. For example, elephants' ears are perfectly suited for picking up low-frequency sounds, like the rumble of a rival pack of elephants a long distance away. Insects' ears, by contrast, are perfectly suited for picking up higher-frequency sounds, such as the rapidly flapping wings of another insect just a centimeter away (McBurney, 2010a). Frogs have specialized cells within their eyes that serve as bug detectors—their only function is to spot small, quick-moving objects within range of the frog's jutting tongue and send a message straight to the part of the frog's brain that controls prey catching (Goodale & Humphrey, 2001; Ewert, 1987). Our own human ancestors developed color vision capabilities that may have enabled them to better detect ripe fruits in trees, as well as slight changes in other people's skin color (e.g., getting red in the face) that could indicate anger (Jacobs, 2009; Changizi et al., 2006; Regan et al., 2001; Dominy & Lucas, 2001).

sensation
The ability of the sensory organs to pick up energy in the environment around the body and transmit it to the brain.

transduction
The conversion of energy outside the body, like light or sound, into neural energy, like brain activity.

perception
The ability of the brain to interpret the raw sensations it has taken in.

extrasensory perception (ESP)
The debatable notion of perception without sensation.

parapsychology
The study of topics that fall outside the range of mainstream psychology.

absolute threshold
The minimum level of a stimulus necessary for a person to detect its presence at least half of the time.

Extrasensory Perception (ESP) and Parapsychology. As you repeatedly read the words *sensation* and *perception*, you may be reminded of the term **extrasensory perception (ESP)**: the debatable notion of perception without sensation. As scientists, psychologists don't debate ESP with each other. Psychologists largely reject the notion of ESP, which can supposedly take a number of forms: "mental telepathy," in which a person supposedly knows another person's thoughts through mind reading; "clairvoyance," in which a person can know what will happen in the future by merely imagining it; and a special ability to perceive ghosts that can't be seen, heard, or otherwise sensed by other people. The debate about ESP therefore pits psychologists against people who deal in **parapsychology**: the study of topics that fall outside the range of mainstream psychology. Parapsychology overlaps a lot with *pseudopsychology*, psychological information that is not supported by science but may appear to be. Believers may call ESP a sixth sense, but scientists, including psychologists, who have studied it almost uniformly conclude that ESP is not a sense (McBurney, 2010b).

The sensations that your eyes and ears take in, including the brightness and loudness of fireworks, become perceptions when you begin to make sense of what they are.
Moment/Getty Images

Thresholds: What Your Senses Can and Cannot Do

Even though your sensation and perception abilities are highly evolved, they do have limits.

Absolute Threshold. For example, for one of your senses to notice something, there has to be enough of that something to detect. In other words, the amount has to exceed the **absolute threshold**: the minimum level of a stimulus necessary for you to detect its presence at least half of the time (**Figure 3.1**). In a silent room you would hear a dog barking, but could you hear it breathing? On a pitch-black night, you would see the brake lights of a car 100 feet ahead of yours, but could you see them if they were a mile ahead? If you were drinking water, you'd certainly notice if

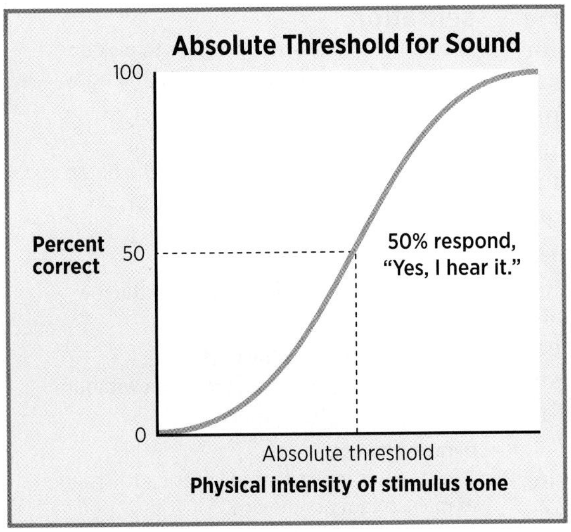

FIGURE 3.1 Absolute Threshold. Absolute threshold is the point at which the intensity of the stimulus (for example, the brightness of the light or the loudness of the sound) is strong enough to be detected at least 50% of the time.

someone had dropped a spoonful of salt into it, but would you notice a single granule? All of these are questions of absolute threshold.

So what *is* the absolute threshold for each human sense?

You might expect psychologists to have determined the specific measures of absolute threshold for each of our senses. However, these numbers vary so broadly from person to person, and even from situation to situation for the same person, that pinpointing any particular amount would be an oversimplification. For example, a common estimate of the absolute threshold of frequency for hearing is around 20 hertz with a maximum around 20,000 hertz (Moller & Pedersen, 2004; Krumbholz et al., 2000; Pressnitzer et al., 2001). But it depends on a few factors: (1) Females generally hear better than men (although males may hear better at the lowest frequencies). (2) Young adults generally hear better than older adults. (3) Hearing loss happens at a higher rate in White Americans than Black Americans. (4) Hearing tends to be worse in people who use firearms, smoke heavily, or have diabetes (Agrawal et al., 2008, 2009; Helzner et al., 2005; Morrell et al., 1996; Pearson et al., 1995).

Absolute threshold for smell also depends on a few factors: (1) Younger adults have more sensitive noses than older adults. (2) Females have more sensitive noses than males (even as newborns). (3) Women's sense of smell is most sensitive during ovulation (Pause et al., 1996; Doty et al., 1985; Doty & Kamath, 2014). Further, absolute threshold for all senses depends on a person's motivations and expectations in the moment: You're more likely to notice a sound, sight, or smell when you are instructed to seek it out ("What's that noise?" "Can you smell that?"), but more likely to miss it if no one calls your attention to it (Pagliano, 2012).

MY TAKE VIDEO 3.1

Difference Threshold

"Because I do art, I really notice the differences in changes in colors..."

YOUTUBE: http://tiny.cc/mytake
LAUNCHPAD: launchpadworks.com

Difference threshold. Absolute threshold revolves around a common question regarding sensation: Is it there? Another common question occurs when you know it's there, but you wonder, Is it different? That question involves the **difference threshold** (or **just noticeable difference**): the smallest change in a stimulus necessary for you to detect it at least half of the time. When differences are well above this threshold—like the difference between high-definition and standard-definition TV—they are easy to notice. And when the differences are well below this threshold—like the microscopic difference in softness between two Kleenexes from the same box—you don't have a chance.

The most interesting difference threshold questions are the ones very close to the threshold itself. For example, imagine that your flashlight is gradually getting dimmer over the course of several hours as its batteries run down. How much brightness will the flashlight have to lose before your eyes notice? Or maybe your old freezer has started to wear out. How many degrees will the temperature have to rise before you notice a difference in the coldness of your ice cream on your tongue?

Like absolute threshold, difference threshold for various senses depends on a number of factors, often including age and gender (Kidd, 2010). Another important variable is experience. Specifically, we are much better at detecting differences in things with which we have plenty of experience (Green & Bavelier, 2007; Li et al., 2006). For example, if you drink a lot of cola, you may have a strong preference for a certain brand (Coke vs. Pepsi), type (diet vs. caffeine-free vs. regular), or even container (aluminum can vs. plastic bottle vs. glass bottle vs. fountain drink). A prerequisite for that preference is a low difference threshold, which comes from a lifetime of cola drinking. If you rarely drink cola, your difference threshold is much higher—essentially, they all taste the same to you.

The difference threshold for a particular stimulus is somewhat predictable according to the *Weber–Fechner law*, which is named after Ernst Heinrich Weber and Gustav Theodor Fechner, two researchers who studied the topic in the 1800s (Hoagland, 1930; Sobkowicz et al., 2013). The Weber-Fechner law states that the difference threshold is proportional to the amount of the stimulus present in the first

difference threshold (just noticeable difference)
The smallest change in a stimulus necessary for a person to detect it at least half of the time.

sensory adaptation
The tendency of a person's sensation of a stimulus to decrease when the stimulus remains constant.

perceptual constancy
The brain's ability to maintain the same perception of an object even when conditions around it cause it to produce different sensations.

place. The bigger the original amount, the bigger the difference will have to be for you to notice. For example, if you frequently order a quarter-pound hamburger in a restaurant, it will probably only take an extra ounce for you to notice that it seems heavy when you lift it. But if you frequently bench-press 100 pounds, it will take much more than an ounce of extra weight—at least a couple of pounds, probably—for you to notice the extra weight.

Difference threshold depends on experience. The more coffee you drink, the better your ability to notice the difference between coffee beans sourced from different regions
Tomwang112/Getty Images

Sensory Adaptation. Difference thresholds are important when sensory stimuli change, but what about when they stay the same? In those situations, you experience **sensory adaptation**: the tendency of your sensation of a stimulus to decrease when the stimulus remains constant. When you see, hear, or feel the same unchanging thing for a long time, you get used to it and eventually stop noticing it (He, 2010; Webster, 2010). (Sensory adaptation often goes hand in hand with *habituation*—when you decrease or stop *responding* to a stimulus that repeats or stays constant.) As an example of sensory adaptation, think about what you hear as you start to drive on a highway. When you accelerate on the entrance ramp, you hear the engine rev louder until you reach, say, 60 miles per hour. But if you turn on cruise control and stay at 60 mph for a long time, you will stop noticing the sound of the engine. Of course, the engine is still making the same amount of noise as when you first reached 60 mph, but you have become accustomed to the constant hum. Another example: You walk into a bakery and immediately smell the strong, wonderful fragrance of fresh-baked bread. But if you work in that bakery, by the time your 8-hour shift is over, you don't smell bread at all, even though every new customer does. See the From Research to Real Life box on page 73 for more about sensory adaptation and variety as a key to happiness.

Perceptual Constancy. Sometimes, sensory stimulation appears to change even when the object you're sensing stays the same. You have a remarkable ability to recognize that the object remains unchanged even though it may look, sound, or otherwise seem different (Goldstein, 2010a). This is **perceptual constancy**: your brain's ability to maintain the same perception of an object even when conditions around it cause it to produce different sensations (**Figure 3.2**). For example, imagine you're playing kickball and you're deep in the outfield. A powerful kicker sends a high pop-up your way. When it first leaves the kicker's foot, that red rubber ball looks minuscule from your spot in the field. As it soars toward you, however, the ball seems to get bigger and bigger until your whole field of vision is nearly filled with the red ball when it reaches you. According to your eye, that ball actually got bigger, but your brain converts that changing *sensation* into a constant *perception*. Your brain knows that red rubber ball is the same size whether it is far away or in your arms.

As an auditory example, consider the sound of your friend's voice as you walk from one campus building to another. Specifically, imagine that the two of you start in a small classroom with a low ceiling, then walk outside into the open air, and then enter a large atrium with high ceilings. The sound of your friend's voice strikes your ear differently in each of these three settings because of the different acoustics—louder in the small room, quieter in the open air, and with more echo in the atrium. But it never crosses your mind that your friend's voice changes. You perceive it as constant even though the conditions cause the sensations your friend's voice creates to change (Watkins et al., 2011; Watkins & Makin, 2007).

MY TAKE VIDEO 3.2

Sensory Adaptation

"At first I'm like "Ah! I feel like I'm freezing to death," but then..."

YOUTUBE: http://tiny.cc/mytake
LAUNCHPAD: launchpadworks.com

Sensory Overload: When Senses Compete for Your Attention

Your senses don't take turns. They work simultaneously, which means they send competing messages to your brain. Somehow, your brain has to decide how to prioritize or blend all of this sensory input.

FIGURE 3.2 Perceptual Constancy. As this laptop closes, the image its screen casts on your eye changes. It becomes an increasingly narrow rectangle until it is eventually just a horizontal line. Thanks to perceptual constancy, however, you know that the laptop actually retains the same shape no matter how open or closed it is (Goldstein, 2010a).

Selective Attention. With so much sensory information steadily arriving from your eyes, ears, nose, tongue, and skin, your brain constantly makes decisions about which sense to focus on (Dosher & Lu, 2010). Your brain often meets this challenge through **selective attention**: paying more attention to one sensory channel than others. Selective attention is necessary in most situations, especially those that engage all of your senses simultaneously. Consider a carnival. Your eyes take in the sights of rides, games, animals, clowns, and crowds. Your nose takes in the smells of cotton candy and popcorn. Your tongue takes in the tastes of funnel cake and fresh-squeezed lemonade. Your skin takes in the heat of the warm sun. But your friend is trying to ask you something, so just for the moment, your brain uses selective attention to "turn down" the inputs from your eyes, nose, tongue, and skin and "turn up" the input from your ears. All of those sensations are still coming through, of course, but they aren't registering as strongly as before. As soon as you hear your friend say, "Ferris wheel next?" and you start walking together in that direction, your brain stops selectively attending to your hearing and attends to all of your senses. (By the way, sometimes you boost your brain's selective attention ability by blocking off one of your senses, as when you choose to close your eyes to concentrate on a phone call or music.)

Sometimes, the competition for your brain's attention comes from the same sense. Like at the carnival—your friend's voice would not be the only sound you'd hear when she speaks. At the same moment, your ears take in the shouts of kids on nearby rides, the music drifting out of the carousel, the chirps of birds flying above, and many other noises. The power to hear your friend in spite of all of this auditory competition is the **cocktail party effect**: the ability to attend to certain stimuli within one sense (such as hearing) over other stimuli within the same sense.

The cocktail party effect got its name from the common experience of being in a crowded party, surrounded by loud conversations in all directions but focusing your attention only on the person in front of you (Cherry, 1953). An interesting thing often happens in such situations—you catch something meaningful, often personal, in a conversation you thought you were tuning out (Wood & Cowan, 1995; Loebach et al., 2010; Yost, 2001). For example, you're at a party talking to a small group of friends and you hear someone in a nearby group mention your name (or your friend or family member's name, your hometown, or anything else personally relevant to you). In fact, your name seems to jump out of that conversation even though none of the words before it even registered. But it is obvious that the sounds register at least at some shallow level, because you process them enough to determine if they are personally meaningful to you.

Humans are the only species who go to cocktail parties, but we're not the only ones who demonstrate the cocktail party effect. Researchers have identified many animals, including insects, birds, and more, who display a remarkable ability to pay attention to one sound while ignoring others (Bee & Micheyl, 2008; Brumm & Slabbekoorn, 2005). In a swamp full of dozens of different frog species, females have an uncanny ability to pick out the mating calls from their own species (Hulse, 2002; Gerhardt & Bee, 2006). Bats, who rely on the echo of their own voice to determine exactly where to fly, somehow distinguish their own voice from the racket created by hundreds of nearby bat voices in the same cave (Moss & Surlykke, 2001). And in a crowded colony with hundreds of penguins, baby penguins have a remarkable ability to zoom in on the call of a parent above the constant call of all the other penguins, even when the parent is far away and relatively quiet compared to nearby voices (Aubin & Jouventin, 1998, 2002).

The cocktail party effect is your ability to attend to certain stimuli within one sense (such as hearing) over other stimuli within the same sense. Other species have this ability, too, including baby penguins, who can pick out the voices of their parents in a loud crowd (Aubin & Jouventin, 1998, 2002).
AWL Images/Masterfile

Sensory Interaction. Sometimes it is not about choosing one sensation over others—as illustrated by selective attention and the cocktail party effect—but about blending sensations. When that blending happens, sensations can affect each other in interesting ways. **Sensory interaction** is the idea that your senses can influence each other. One obvious example of sensory interaction is ventriloquism—when a performer (usually a comedian) gives voice to a dummy. We hear words that coordinate with the timing of the dummy's mouth moving (rather than the ventriloquist's mouth),

FROM RESEARCH TO REAL LIFE

Variety, the Key to Happiness?

We're rooting for sensory adaptation to kick in when we can't escape the rattle of a noisy air conditioner or the stench of a nearby trashcan. After a while, you get used to it and don't notice how bad it is. But we're rooting against sensory adaptation when we do things we enjoy. We don't want the tenth bite of cake or the tenth show in our Netflix binge to feel any less pleasurable than the first.

A team of psychologists offers a theory of happiness—the hedonic adaptation prevention model—that tackles this problem head on (Sheldon et al., 2012). According to this model, variety keeps us happy. Repeatedly experiencing *different* enjoyable things prevents sensory adaptation from kicking in. (Check the name of the theory closely—it's all about "adaptation prevention.") Too often, researchers say, we strive for happiness by seeking out the things that provided it in the past. The downside to "more of the same" is that sensory adaptation may have diminished our sensitivity to it; at the same time, our expectations for happiness from it have gone up. The solution might be variety.

These researchers asked undergraduate participants to list acts of kindness they could perform (Sheldon et al., 2012). They came up with a varied list, including doing chores for roommates, lending books to classmates, cooking dinner for friends, and allowing cars to merge in front of them on the highway. The researchers then told them to do these kind acts for the next 10 weeks, but with a catch: half were told they had to stick with the same single kind act each week, while the other half were told to vary their kind acts each week so the acts wouldn't be repeated. At the end of 10 weeks, the high-variety group reported much higher levels of happiness than the low-variety group. In fact, the low-variety group was less happy than when the study began (a finding that could also partially reflect other factors, like the stress of an ongoing semester). The take-home message is this: In your own day-to-day life, it may be the *variety* of enjoyable activities, rather than repeatedly doing the same few over and over, that underlies your happiness.

According to the hedonic adaptation prevention model, variety increases happiness by limiting sensory adaptation to the things you like (Sheldon et al., 2012).
Melpomene/Shutterstock

and we perceive that the dummy is talking, at least until we remind ourselves that dummies can't talk. What we see influences what (we think) we hear. A similar thing happens when you watch a movie in a theater with speakers positioned on the sides of the room—you perceive the dialogue as coming from the mouths of the actors on the screen directly in front of you, when in reality they are coming from your left and right (Shams, 2010).

When sensory inputs don't match—as when overdubs in a foreign language movie don't match the mouth movements of the actors—we often experience the *McGurk effect*, in which the words we perceive others saying are influenced by our vision as well as our hearing (Soto-Faraco & Alsius, 2009; Summerfield, 1992; Moore, 2012). In the classic study that identified the McGurk effect, researchers created a brief video in which participants *heard* a person saying "ma ma" but simultaneously *saw* that person's lips form the sound "ta ta." In this particular case, many participants reported hearing "na na"—a curious and distinct blend of what they saw and what they heard (McGurk & MacDonald, 1976). In other cases, what goes in your eyes actually overrides what goes in your ears, and you report "hearing" what you see, even though the sound clearly differs from the sight.

The power that vision has over our other senses is illustrated not only by the McGurk effect but by many other situations as well (Zellner, 2013). For example, researchers have found that vision can influence and even trump taste. In a study about candy, participants who ate lemon drops that had been colored purple frequently reported that the candy had a grape taste (Zellner et al., 1991; Doty, 2010). In a study of beverages, participants who drank a cherry-flavored drink that was colored orange often mistakenly labeled the flavor of the drink as orange (Zellner, 2010). (An interesting side note to highlight how important the sight of food and drinks can be, and how aware food and drink manufacturers are of

selective attention
When the brain pays more attention to one sensory channel than others.

cocktail party effect
The ability to attend to certain stimuli within one sense (such as hearing) over other stimuli within the same sense.

sensory interaction
The idea that the senses can influence each other.

When multiple senses interact, vision has an especially strong impact. The color of a food or drink can strongly influence the way you perceive its taste. Chuck Wagner/Shutterstock

this: At Gatorade.com, the response to the FAQ "Why are there artificial colors in Gatorade?" begins with this sentence, "The colors in Gatorade provide visual appeal and help reinforce the flavor perception.")

Some researchers have theorized that sensory interaction can, under certain circumstances, lead to feelings of queasiness and nausea. This idea is **sensory conflict theory**: a theory that states that motion sickness is a byproduct of sensory interaction. Sensory conflict theory is certainly not the only explanation of motion sickness, and there is research both supporting and disputing it (Oman, 1990; Stoffregen & Riccio, 1991; Yardley, 1992; Warwick-Evans et al., 1998). Basically, sensory conflict theory suggests that you feel sick when you are moving and what you see doesn't match what you otherwise sense, especially within your body in terms of balance, position, and touch (Bos et al., 2008). That is why you're at greater risk for motion sickness when you read, watch a screen, or close your eyes as a passenger in a car. Your eyes tell your brain you're sitting still, but your bodily senses tell your brain you're zooming ahead, slowing down, turning left, turning right, or speeding up as your body leans due to the car's movements.

Bottom-Up and Top-Down Processing

When you were a newborn baby, every sight, sound, smell, taste, and touch was new. You experienced the world purely through **bottom-up processing**: a way of processing information in which what you sense becomes a perception with no influence of expectations or previous experiences. With each passing day, however, you gained life experience, which you stored away as memories. Soon your mind was no longer a blank slate but full of expectations for what you might sense in any given situation. Those expectations then began to *shape* what you perceived in much the same way that you can guess the ends of your best friend's sentences because your previous conversations have taught you what he or she tends to say. This is **top-down processing**: a way of processing information in which your expectations or previous experiences influence what you perceive.

Your current day-to-day experience involves a combination of bottom-up and top-down processing (Lewkowicz, 2010; Chun & Wolfe, 2001). In less familiar situations—like when you visit a new restaurant that features tastes, smells, sights, and sounds from a part of the world you've never seen—it is more bottom-up processing. In more familiar situations—like when you sit at "your" table in your favorite old restaurant and order the usual from the server who knows you by name—it is more top-down processing.

Sometimes, both types of processing are easy to identify. Imagine that your friend Ayana leaves your house to drive home, a 15-minute trip. The weather is terrible, so as you say goodbye, you tell Ayana, "Text me when you get there." About 15 minutes later, a text comes through. Instantly, some bottom-up processing happens—you feel your phone vibrate against your skin or your ear picks up the sound of the text alert. These are sensations you would experience even if you had no expectation of an incoming text around that time. But you do have expectations, so almost as instantly, some top-down processing happens too. Even before you can bring the phone to your eyes to read the text, speculations flash into your mind: "It's probably Ayana letting me know she made it home." The point is that your top-down processing uses expectations and experience to predict what you might see even before you actually see it, and sometimes those predictions can influence what you see (or think you see).

Top-down processing comes into play when you listen to digital music or a voice in a phone call too. In both cases, the sounds you hear are actually tiny bits of sound alternating with tiny bits of silence. Your top-down processing allows you to fill in the blanks, since the surrounding sounds tell you what to expect (Moore, 2010). The same thing happens in a more obvious way when you're on a phone call in which the other person's voice cuts in and out for a full second or more at a time. You use top-down

sensory conflict theory
The theory that explains motion sickness as a byproduct of sensory interaction.

bottom-up processing
A way of processing information in which what a person senses becomes a perception with no influence of expectations or previous experiences.

top-down processing
A way of processing information in which expectations or previous experiences influence what a person perceives.

perceptual set
The tendency to perceive things in a certain way because of a person's previous experiences or attention strategy.

change blindness
The failure to notice changes in the visual field simply because a person expects otherwise.

inattentional blindness
The failure to notice something in your visual field simply because your attention was focused elsewhere.

IT'S LIKE...

Top-Down Processing Is Like Autocomplete

When you type the first few letters of a text into your phone, the phone's autocomplete (or autofill) feature offers to complete the word for you. The same thing happens when you google something—your computer guesses the rest of the word or phrase you might be typing. It is as if it knows what to expect, based on what you have typed in the past. Your brain uses top-down processing much like your devices use this autocomplete feature. Your brain knows what you might be sensing, based on what you have sensed in the past.

Of course, neither autocomplete nor top-down processing can function alone. Your phone or computer combines its top-down expectations with the bottom-up processing of the first few letters you actually type in, and your brain combines its top-down expectations with the first few milliseconds of a sound sent to your ear (Carlson, 2010). The main point here is that it is not bottom-up processing alone that creates your sensation (or completes the line you type into your device), but a combination of that bottom-up processing with the top-down processing that it triggers.

There is one important distinction between the way your devices and your brain do top-down processing: your phone gives you the *option* to autocomplete your words and phrases, but your brain doesn't always do that. Sometimes, your brain acts like an autocomplete feature with too much power, jumping to a conclusion about what you're sensing before you've had a chance to fully sense it. For example, if you're expecting a delivery from UPS, your brain might use "autocomplete" to convert a quick glance out the front window at a person in a brown shirt to the conclusion that your delivery is here. But that might just be someone who happens to be wearing a brown shirt walking by, not the UPS delivery person. That is the double-edged sword of top-down processing—it offers shortcuts that can be helpful when accurate, but problematic when premature. ●

processing to guess, often with impressive accuracy, what words filled the moments you couldn't catch (Loebach et al., 2010).

Perceptual Set. Top-down processing is a major contributor to your **perceptual set**: your tendency to perceive things in a certain way because of your previous experiences or your attention strategy (**Figure 3.3**). Your perceptual set helps you know what to expect, to quickly assess a situation, especially the parts of it that are most important to you, rather than slowly and methodically examining every detail as if it were unlike anything you'd ever encountered before. For example, consider how the perceptual set influenced the reaction of Hillary Anderson, a witness to the Boston Marathon bombing, when she heard the first explosion: "I remember looking up, looking for planes. I remember exactly where I was during 9/11, and my first instinct was to look up and see what was coming" (*New York Times*, 2013).

Change Blindness and Inattentional Blindness. Often, your perceptual set offers shortcuts that are beneficial, allowing you to extract the information you need more quickly and accurately than you could if you didn't have any particular expectations or goals in that moment. But sometimes, your perceptual set can be quite misleading. For example, consider **change blindness**: a failure to notice changes in your visual field simply because you expect otherwise. Some of the first instances of change blindness happened in Hollywood movies made back in the 1930s, when scenes were spliced together by literally cutting and pasting clips of film reels. Sometimes, two pasted-together clips would include blatant mistakes, like an actor delivering the first few words of a line with one shirt button open and the last few words of the same line with two shirt buttons open, because the two takes were recorded on different days. The interesting thing is not that these editing mistakes happened, but that almost none of the filmmakers or audience members noticed them (Rensink, 2010). The same kinds of continuity errors still happen today, and although most of us are blind to these changes, with bigger audiences and the ever-present Internet, they eventually get seen.

Closely related to change blindness is **inattentional blindness**: a failure to notice something in your visual field simply because your attention was focused elsewhere. With change blindness, you fail to see an item change, but with inattentional blindness, you fail to see the item *at all* (Rensink, 2000, 2013; Mack, 2003). For example, a distracted driver whose full attention is devoted to reading a text from a friend might completely fail to see a stop sign, even though that stop sign falls within the driver's field of vision.

FIGURE 3.3 Top-Down Processing and Perceptual Set. Is the number in the middle eleven or two? If you read across, so that the numerals are Hindu-Arabic, it looks like eleven. But if you read down, so that the numerals are Roman, it looks like two. This illustrates how the context around a stimulus influences your top-down processing and your perceptual set.

LIFE HACK 3.1

When you are driving, minimize any potential distractions (like glancing at a phone) that might cause change blindness or inattentional blindness like mudsplashes do. In a very short time, you could fail to see something important and potentially dangerous.

(Simons & Ambinder, 2005; O'Regan et al., 1999)

Change blindness and inattentional blindness have been the focus of much psychological research (Simons & Rensink, 2005; Simons & Levin, 1997). They also have serious implications for some real-world issues. For example, change blindness or inattentional blindness can undermine the validity of eyewitness testimony in a courtroom trial (Davies & Hine, 2007). They can influence what police officers or security guards see and don't see when they monitor situations (Durlach, 2004). They can also affect what players and officials see during sporting events (Werner & Thies, 2000).

Some of the research on change blindness and inattentional blindness focuses on the role of distraction. Specifically, when your eye is drawn toward one part of a scene, how likely are you to miss something—even something big—in another part of the scene? One influential study used a "mudsplash" technique to illustrate how surprisingly strong change blindness and inattentional blindness can be. They showed participants a photo for three seconds and then "splashed" the photos for a fraction of a second with several small splotches at random places on the screen (to simulate a mudsplash on a car windshield). At the same time as the mudsplash, the experimenters also changed something else in the photo, and that new photo remained on the screen for 3 more seconds. When the change from photo 1 to photo 2 was blatantly obvious, most participants noticed it in spite of the mudsplashes. But when the change was moderate (completely noticeable without mudsplashes), most participants had to watch the sequence two or more times before they saw it. In about a quarter of these moderate cases, the changes were not seen at all, even after many repetitions (O'Regan et al., 1999). These findings have implications for numerous real-world activities, including drivers who miss something important on the road in front of them when something hits their windshield or their attention is otherwise drawn to just one part of their field of vision (Simons & Ambinder, 2005).

In another study of change blindness and inattentional blindness, researchers showed a video of two groups of people, some in white shirts and some in black shirts, passing basketballs back and forth within their groups. As the two groups weaved in and out of each other's paths, participants were told to count the number of passes made by the group in white shirts. A few seconds in, a person in a gorilla suit wandered into the scene, stopped in the middle of the players, did some chest-thumping, and then walked off. At the end of the 20-second scene, most participants accurately reported the number of passes made by the group in white shirts, but about half (!) failed to notice the person in the gorilla suit. Their concentration on the passes made them oblivious to other things happening in the scene that they weren't looking for (Simon & Chabris, 1999). The take-home message from these change blindness and inattentional blindness studies is this: When you allocate your attention to certain sensations (like using your phone while driving), you are surprisingly vulnerable to missing other sensations completely, no matter how obvious they might be.

CHECK YOUR LEARNING:

3.1 What is the difference between sensation and perception?

3.2 What role have sensation and perception played in evolution?

3.3 What is the difference between absolute threshold and difference threshold?

3.4 What is sensory adaptation?

3.5 How does perceptual constancy help you to perceive stimuli that produce changing sensations?

3.6 What is the difference between selective attention and sensory interaction?

3.7 What is the difference between bottom-up processing and top-down processing?

Vision

Vision—your sense of sight—dominates the human senses (Goodale & Milner, 2013). All of the senses are important, of course, but we are influenced by what we see more often and more powerfully than by what we hear, smell, taste, or touch. This dominance shows in many ways. For instance, vision occupies more brain space than any other sense (Medina, 2014). In an online poll asking, "If you had to give up a sense, which would it be?", vision ranked last among the 4000+ respondents (only 4% chose it) (quibblo.com). Even our language reflects how our visual sense permeates the way we think. We use visual terms as metaphors for brain activities that actually have nothing to do with vision. For example, when we understand something, we "see what you mean." When we ignore something, we "turn a blind eye." When we expect something to happen, we "see the writing on the wall." And when we concentrate exclusively on one goal, we have "tunnel vision."

Earlier in the chapter, we mentioned that sensation and perception evolved, which implies that they provide some advantage in terms of survival. In terms of vision, some researchers have argued that the advantages of vision involve two distinct functions: identification and action (Milner & Goodale, 2008; Goodale & Westwood, 2004). The idea is that the identification of an object allows you to recognize it, categorize it, and think about it. Action, of course, means doing something in response to that object—moving toward it, running away from it, holding it, hitting it, talking to it, etc.

Interestingly, neurological research has found that human and primate brains have two distinct pathways, or streams, of visual information within the brain that reflect these two distinct functions (Goodale & Milner, 2013; Goodale, 2011; Goodale & Milner, 1992). One stream, the *ventral* stream, controls identification of an object—determining *what* it is. A second stream, the *dorsal* stream, controls action toward the object—determining *where* it is. If the ventral stream is damaged, the person cannot recognize an object but can pick it up; if the dorsal stream is damaged, the person can recognize an object but cannot pick it up (Goodale & Humphrey, 2001). So when you see a dozen glazed circles in a cardboard box, it is your ventral stream that allows you to identify those objects as donuts and your dorsal stream that allows you to grab one and bring it to your mouth. Obviously, both streams are crucial to your ability to eat that donut.

YOU WILL LEARN:

3.8 how vision dominates the senses.

3.9 the functions of various parts of the eye, including the cornea, iris, lens, retina, rods, cones, fovea, and blind spot.

3.10 how eye movements facilitate vision.

3.11 how depth perception works.

3.12 how color perception works.

3.13 how to determine whether objects that are seen together belong to a group.

3.14 how certain objects, including faces and bodies, are visually processed in a special way.

3.15 how culture influences vision.

Your Eye: Its Parts and Their Functions

The hardware of your eye is an engineering marvel. Let's go through your eye as a ray of light does—starting on the outer surface and moving toward the back, where the pathway to the brain begins.

Cornea. First, the light hits your **cornea**: a thin transparent cover for the whole eye (**Figure 3.4**). The cornea refracts (or bends) images to improve vision, but it cannot change its own shape to do so. (The purpose of refractive surgery, which helps with nearsightedness and farsightedness, is to alter the shape of the cornea.) The cornea also serves as a protective cover and tends to recover quickly from minor scratches that might do serious damage to inner parts of the eye if they were unprotected. However, a serious scratch can leave a scar on the cornea that obstructs vision. In many ways, the cornea functions as a built-in contact lens—in fact, the original contact lenses developed in the mid-1900s were called "corneal lenses" (Barr, 2005).

Iris. Just behind the cornea is the **iris**: a colored circular muscle situated in the center of the eye. The iris gives your eyes their unique shade; when someone says that Taylor

vision
The sense of sight.

cornea
The thin transparent cover for the whole eye.

iris
The colored, circular muscle situated in the center of the eye.

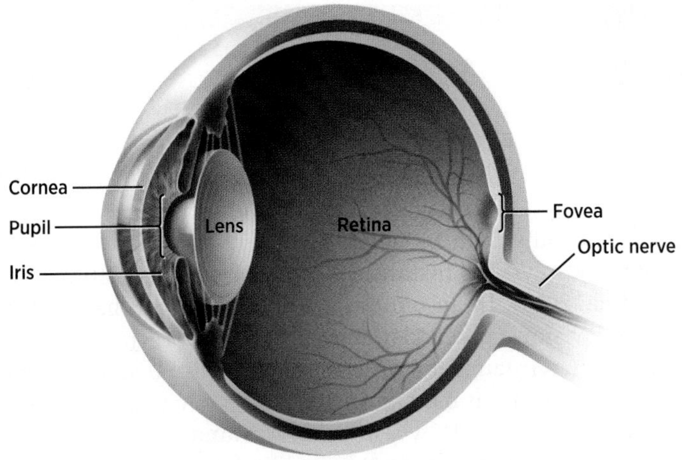

FIGURE 3.4 The Parts of the Human Eye. The human eye includes the cornea, a thin transparent cover; the iris, the circular muscle that gives the eye its unique color; the pupil, the opening inside the iris; the lens, which varies its shape to maintain focus; the retina, the rear part that receives visual stimulation; the fovea, an area in the center of the retina containing many cones but no rods; and the optic nerve, which delivers visual information from the retina to the brain.

Swift or Jake Gyllenhaal has blue eyes, they really mean that they have blue irises. The iris acts as a diaphragm that opens and closes, and the **pupil** is the opening in the middle. The size of the pupil determines how much light the eye allows through. In the dark, the pupil expands to about 8 mm to let in as much scarce light as possible. In bright light, the pupil contracts to about 2 mm to keep the amount of light manageable. The pupil also expands in moments of arousal, either sexual or intellectual (Fong, 2012).

Lens. After the light travels through the pupil, it moves on to the **lens**: a clear layer beneath the surface of your eye that maintains focus on an object by varying its own shape. Specifically, the lens changes its own curvature (the degree and shape of curve) to maximize focus. This is quite similar to the lenses you might choose for your glasses or your camera: You want the curve to be just right to produce the clearest, most focused image. Unlike the immobile lenses in your glasses or camera, your eye's lens can adjust its shape as necessary, shifting focus between near and far. This is called **visual accommodation**: the process by which the lens changes shape to focus on objects at varying distances from your eyes. As you age, the lens loses some of its elasticity, which is one reason contacts, glasses, or surgery is likely to become more of a necessity. Also with age come *cataracts*: cloudy spots on the lens that can hamper vision like cloudy spots on your car's windshield (Artal et al., 2006).

Taylor Swift's eye color is actually the color of her iris: the circular muscle situated in the center of the eye. Jon Kopaloff/FilmMagic/Getty Images

Retina. Once past the lens, light reaches the **retina**: the rear part of the eyeball that receives visual stimulation and sends it to the brain via the optic nerve. The retina is basically a screen at the back of your eye. The collective goal of all these parts of your eye is to cast a focused, clear image on that screen. That image includes miniature versions of all of the items in your field of vision. For example, a single letter in a newspaper headline held at arm's length makes an image about 1.5 mm high on your retina (Mather, 2011).

The retina is where visual *transduction* starts to happen, which means that outside stimuli (light) get converted into internal brain signals (neural activity) (Gegenfurtner, 2010). The passageway from the retina to your brain is the *optic nerve*. Visual information carried by your optic nerve makes its first stop at your thalamus and then moves farther back, to the occipital lobe (Goldstein, 2010b; Lee, 2010).

Rods and Cones. The retina contains receptor cells called *rods* and *cones* that are specially designed to detect certain kinds of visual stimuli under certain conditions (Gordon & Abramov, 2001). **Rods** are receptor cells in the retina that detect shades of gray and allow us to see in low light. **Cones** are receptor cells in the retina that detect

CURRENT CONTROVERSY

Can Your Retina or Iris Unlock Your Smartphone?

To unlock your smartphone, you might use a passcode. You might use a visual pattern, moving your finger from one point to another in a specific sequence. You might even use your fingerprint. One day soon, will you use your eye?

New technologies enable a scanner in your smartphone to use the individuality of your retina or iris—eye components as unique to you as your fingerprints—to unlock your phone. Just as your eye would see your phone, your phone would see your eye. These eye-based recognition technologies have been around for a while (*retinal scanning* is a bit older; *iris recognition* is more recent), and are used in limited capacity by military, security, and police forces for identification purposes (Bodade & Talbar, 2014; Burke & Bowyer, 2013; Newman, 2010). It has also been fictionally portrayed in TV shows like *NCIS* and movies like *The Avengers*.

There are many pros and cons to retinal scanning and iris recognition (Li & Ma, 2012; Rankin et al., 2012; Bhattacharyya et al., 2009). Advantages, especially as they apply to your smartphone, include convenience and the facts that criminals can't steal your eyes and that you would never have to remember another passcode. Disadvantages include expense, the fact that criminals might create high-quality images that mimic your eyes, and scanning complications involving contact lenses or eye injuries. Time will tell whether retinal scanning or iris recognition technology become common methods of unlocking smartphones or providing identification at airport security checkpoints or voting booths. ●

color when light is plentiful. (Try to remember the *C* connection: cones = *c*olor). In the human eye, there are a staggering number of both types of receptor cells in the retina, but far more rods (about 100 million) than cones (about 6 million) (Frishman, 2001).

Fovea. Occupying a small part of the retina is the **fovea**: an area in the center of the retina that contains many cones but no rods. The fovea (which comes from a Latin root meaning *small pit*) is where cones are most densely packed, so that's where the other parts of the eye send as much visual information as possible, especially information containing color and detailed features (Artal, 2010). The fovea in the eye of an eagle is even more densely packed than that of humans, which allows eagles to spot prey more than a mile away (Livingstone, 2014).

Blind Spot. Also within the retina is the **blind spot**: the part of the retina that contains no rods or cones, which means it can't sense light. The blind spot is basically the part of the retina where the optic nerve connects. Fortunately, with two eyes focusing on an object from slightly different angles, what strikes the blind spot in one of your eyes will probably be seen normally by your other eye. Check **Figure 3.5** for a demonstration of the blind spot in each of your eyes.

FIGURE 3.5 Blind Spot Demonstration. Cover one of your eyes and then focus your open eye on one of the letters. If your right eye is open, focus on the "R." If your left eye is open, focus on the "L." If you move your face toward or away from the image, you'll find a spot where the other letter disappears. That's the blind spot in that eye.

How You See: Eye Movements, Depth Perception, Color Perception, and More

We've covered the parts of the eye. Now, let's focus on how those parts work together to enable you to see.

pupil
The opening in the middle of the iris.

lens
The clear layer beneath the surface of the eye that maintains focus on an object by varying its own shape.

visual accommodation
The process by which the lens changes shape to focus on objects at varying distances from the eyes.

retina
The rear part of the eyeball, which receives visual stimulation and sends it to the brain via the optic nerve.

rods
Receptor cells in the retina that detect shades of gray and allow a person to see in low light.

cones
Receptor cells in the retina that detect color when light is plentiful.

fovea
The area in the center of the retina that contains many cones but no rods.

blind spot
The part of the retina that contains no rods or cones and is therefore unable to sense light.

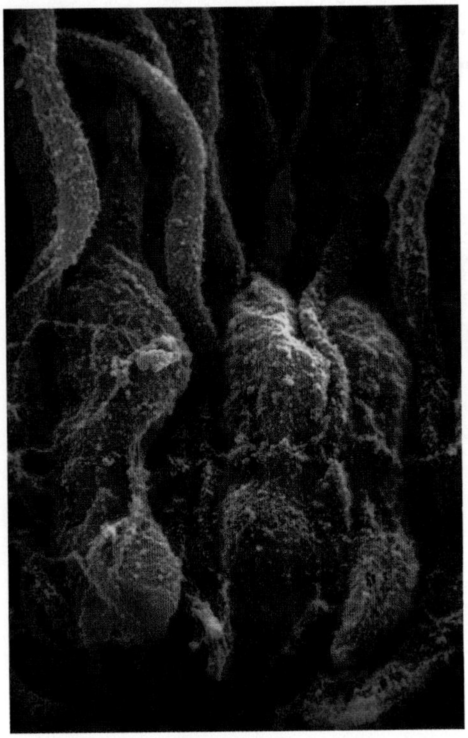

Rods (red in this photo) are receptor cells in the retina that detect shades of gray and allow us to see in low light. Cones (purple in this photo) are receptor cells in the retina that detect color when light is plentiful. Science Source/Getty Images

Eye Movements. In order to see something, first it has to catch your eye—or more precisely, first your eyes have to catch it. Thankfully, your eyes feature a sophisticated, coordinated system of movement that enables you to focus and refocus your gaze as necessary. You never notice it because it happens so automatically, but the movement within your eye is continual and impressive.

Vision researchers have identified many kinds of eye movements, but they place most of them in three categories: (1) *saccadic*, (2) *compensatory*, and (3) *vergence* (Kowler & Collewijn, 2010). Saccadic eye movements are "jumps" that take your gaze from one particular point to another. Between these jumps (actually called *saccades*) are pauses, known as *fixations*. Picture yourself at the airport gate, waiting for your flight to take off. Within just a few seconds, your eyes may jump through many sights, from the kid eating a bag of chips to the woman talking on her phone to the man reading a book to your hands holding your boarding pass. Between each of those saccades is a fixation, whether a fraction of a second or many seconds long.

But some visual movements, like reading words across the page, are smooth rather than jumpy, right?

Not exactly. Even though reading seems like a smooth visual glide from one side of the page to the other, it actually involves lots of little saccades (about 20–30 milliseconds long) and fixations (about 200–300 milliseconds long). Fixations are a bit longer for unfamiliar or difficult words and a bit shorter for expected words. Your eyes actually suppress vision during the saccades and then restart it during the fixations. This eliminates the blur that you would see during those jumps (picture the moments in an amateur video in which the camera operator yanks the camera from one scene to the next). In English, each fixation includes the target word plus about 3 or 4 letters to the left and 14 or 15 letters to the right (about three to four words total). The left–right pattern is reversed in Hebrew, a language that reads right to left. In Chinese, in which each written character is denser than a typical English letter, the fixation is narrower, including the target word plus just one character to the left and 2 or 3 to the right (Rayner & Pollatsek, 2010; Rayner, 1998; Snowling & Hume, 2005).

The second type of eye movements is *compensatory* eye movements, or movements that compensate for the movement of your head. Right now, as you focus on these words, shake your head no. Now shake it yes. Notice how effortless it is to maintain your focus on a particular word, even a particular letter, while your head moves up and down or side to side. (If you were wearing a GoPro camera mounted on your head, especially if it didn't feature image stabilization, just think about how jumpy the video would be from that simple head shake.) That is what compensatory eye movements do: They keep your eyes focused on a chosen image even though your head containing your eyes moves around continuously.

The third type of eye movements is *vergence* eye movements, which move your two eyes in unison to focus on a single chosen image. Vergence comes from the same root as *converge*, as in *come together*. Imagine holding a flashlight in each hand and then adjusting them to converge upon various objects in front of you, some near, some far, some up, some down, some slightly to the left, some slightly to the right. Those adjustments you would make to your wrists and hands to converge the lights on any particular object are the equivalent of vergence eye movements.

Depth Perception. **Depth perception** is your ability to judge the distance and depth of objects. Depth perception tells you whether you can reach the remote at the other end of the couch without getting up. It allows you to know whether the extra-large pizza box that just arrived will fit on the narrow countertop in your kitchen. It helps you decide whether you have time to stop before you get to the intersection with the yellow light or you need to drive through.

depth perception
The ability to judge the distance and depth of objects.

monocular depth cues
The qualities of visual stimuli that indicate depth when using only one eye.

binocular depth cues
The qualities of visual stimuli that indicate depth when using both eyes.

retinal disparity (stereopsis)
The brain's measurement of the difference between the images of a single object sent by each of the two eyes.

hue
The color of light, as determined by its wavelength.

Monocular and Binocular Depth Cues. Depth perception depends on many features of visual information (Peterson, 2001). Some of these features are **monocular depth cues**: qualities of visual stimuli that indicate depth when you use only one eye. Monocular depth cues are the kinds of things you notice in a two-dimensional painting or photograph. For example, relative size, which is how big two things are in comparison to each other, can suggest depth.

Consider a photo taken at a baseball game at which the photographer is in the front row behind home plate, and the camera faces directly forward. The batter looks much bigger than the pitcher, who looks much bigger than the center fielder. Of course, those players are all probably of somewhat similar heights and weights, which means the different-sized images they cast on your retina are indicators of their distance from you, not actual size. Other monocular cues include linear perspective (as when you look at a road leading off into the distance), surface texture (the way a close-up of a face shows wrinkles and pores, but a more distant photo doesn't), and shading (how the sides of a cardboard box appear slightly different shades of brown because light from one direction hits them at different angles) (Timney, 2010).

Claude Monet was a master of using monocular cues to convey depth. In this painting, *Springtime through the Branches*, notice how he uses differences in relative size (among other features) to show that the branches are in front and the buildings are behind. The Banks of the Seine or, Spring through the Trees, 1878 (oil on canvas)/Monet, Claude (1840-1926)/ MUSEE MARMOTTAN MONET, PARIS/Musee Marmottan Monet, Paris, France/Bridgeman Images

Monocular depth cues are good for depth perception, but even better are **binocular depth cues**: qualities of visual stimuli that indicate depth when you use both eyes. Binocular depth cues help us when we look at things in three dimensions—consider the difference between watching a regular movie and a movie with 3D glasses. Binocular depth cues depend on **retinal disparity** (or **stereopsis**): your brain's measurement of the difference between the images of a single object sent by each of your two eyes. Retinal disparity is greater for objects that are close up than for objects that are far away. Your brain assesses that retinal disparity and then follows the logical rule that the more retinal disparity there is, the closer the object must be.

You can see retinal disparity by taking pairs of photos with your phone. First, take two photos of your doorknob just a few inches in front of your face—one with the phone in front of your right eye and the other with the phone in front of your left eye. Then repeat the process from across the room. You'll see that the difference between the left and right perspectives—the disparity—is greater when the doorknob is close than when it is far away. Researchers have found that the human ability to perceive depth using retinal disparity is quite impressive. For example, most people can tell that one coffee cup is closer than another (assuming they are at about arm's length) even if the disparity of the distance is equivalent to the thickness of a fingernail (Wilcox & Allison, 2010).

Depth perception comes in handy for nonhuman species too—birds trying to land on a window ledge, giraffes extending their necks toward leaves on a tree branch, and dogs jumping down from the back of a pickup truck onto the ground, to name a few. Only some animals, however, can use binocular depth cues—the animals with overlap in the fields of vision in each eye (Timney, 2010; Fox et al., 1977). Cats, dogs, and primates have it. Horses do too, but only a little—think about how their eyes face different, but not completely opposite, directions (Timney & Keil, 1999). Animals whose eyes do face opposite directions, like many fish, have entirely distinct inputs coming from each eye and therefore lack binocular depth cues (Sedgwick, 2001).

Color Vision. Your ability to tell a red light from a green light or pick your favorite flavor of Skittles from the pack is basically your ability to detect **hue**: the color of light, as determined by its wavelength.

The wavelengths that your eyes can detect represent just a small fraction of the full range of wavelengths. As **Figure 3.6** shows, your eyes can sense wavelengths ranging from 400 to 750 nanometers in length. The waves just outside our visible range have names that connect them to their neighboring colors: ultraviolet rays at the low end of the spectrum (just below the waves you perceive as violet) and infrared rays at the high end (just above the waves you perceive as red).

CHAPTER APP 3.1

Vision

BioDigital Human

Preview one of the links and consider the following questions.

WEBSITE:
http://tiny.cc/cih7jy

ANDROID:
http://tiny.cc/pwjyiy

IPHONE:
http://tiny.cc/rqjyiy

VIDEO DEMO:
http://tiny.cc/chapterapps

This app enables you to see the human eye even better than the photos on these pages. The images are 3D and can be rotated to view all parts of the eye from all angles.

How does it APPly to your daily life?
How do these 3D rotatable images of the human eye help you appreciate what your eyes do for you all the time? How could you take better care of your eyes to protect your vision for the long term?

How does it APPly to your understanding of psychology?
How do these images enhance your understanding of *depth perception* and *retinal disparity*?

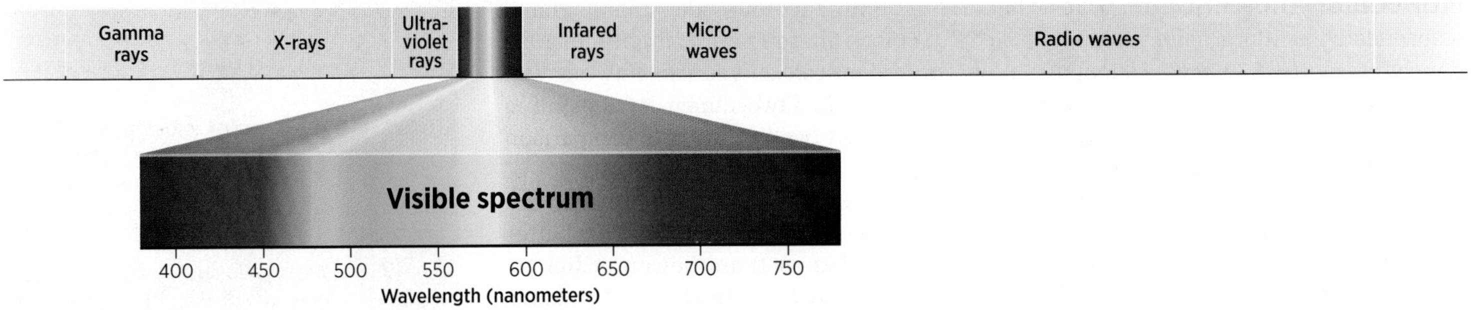

FIGURE 3.6 Visual Light and the Wavelength Spectrum. The rainbow of colors that your eyes can sense come from just a small fraction of all wavelengths in the environment.

It may seem that hue is completely objective—purple is purple, yellow is yellow, etc.—but hue actually depends on context. For example, the colors surrounding an object—known as the surround—can affect the way you perceive that object's color (Webster, 2010). Check **Figure 3.7** to see how a square of the same color looks different depending on the color of the circle surrounding it. You've probably noticed subtle real-life versions of this surround effect too, especially if you've ever tried the same picture or photo in different-colored frames or even tried on different-colored shirts to see which ones bring out the color of your eyes.

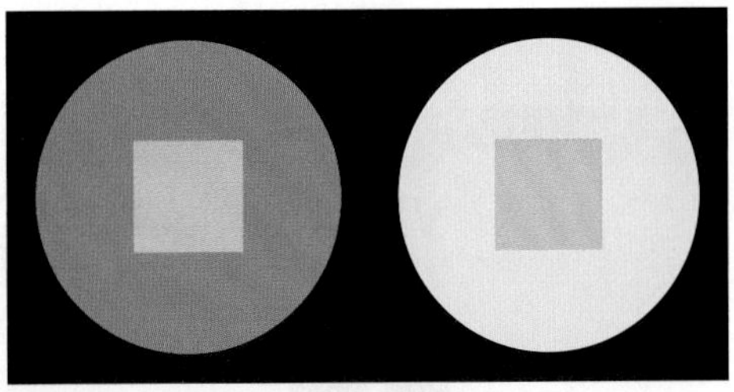

FIGURE 3.7 The Effect of the Surround. The squares inside the circles are exactly the same color, but the circles around them make them seem slightly different. That's the effect of the surround.

Another type of context that can influence your perception of color is the amount of time you spend looking at it. Remember *sensory adaptation* from earlier in this chapter? Just as your ears get used to the sound of an air conditioner and your nose gets used to the smell of coffee when you're around either for a long time, your eyes get used to certain colors if you stare at them long enough. For example, stare at the green circle in the red square in **Figure 3.8** for 30–60 seconds, then move your eyes to the white square. When you do this, the white will look like a red circle in a green square, because red is the opposite of green and your sensors for each get worn out by continuous use (Gordon & Abramov, 2001; Livingstone, 2014).

Trichromatic Theory of Color Vision.

Earlier, we discussed the fact that cones are the specialized receptor cells in your retina that detect color. There are actually three types of cones, each capable of sensing only a certain range of colors: (1) *short-wavelength–sensitive* (*S*) cones, which pick up bluish colors; (2) *middle-wavelength–sensitive* (*M*) cones, which pick up greenish colors; and (3) *long-wavelength–sensitive* (*L*) cones, which pick up reddish colors (Lee, 2010; Gegenfurtner, 2010). (Recall the well-known Roy G. Biv mnemonic for the colors of the rainbow you learned as a child, and keep in mind that the sequence of colors in that acronym represents decreasing wavelengths.) The presence of these three distinct types of cones is the basis of the **trichromatic theory of color vision**: an explanation of color vision based on the idea that your cones are specialized to sense either red, green, or blue. In fact, many TV screens and computer monitors work the same way—portraying a full range of colors by mixing just a few (Stockman, 2010).

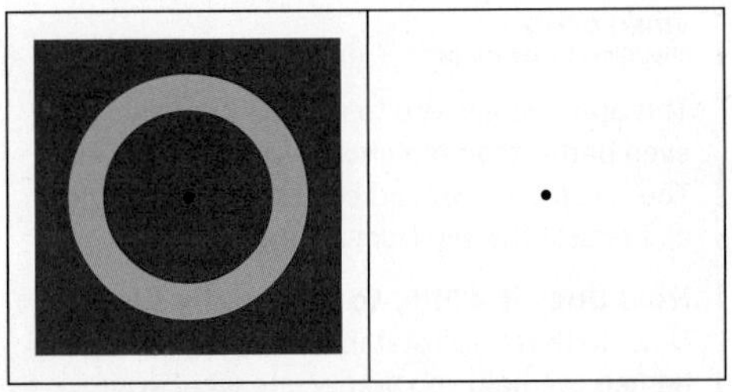

FIGURE 3.8 Sensory Adaptation in Vision. Stare continuously at the red and green figure for 30–60 seconds, then shift to the white square. The aftereffect you see, in which white appears either red or green (the opposite of what it had been before), happens because the cones that sense particular colors get temporarily exhausted, allowing the opposite color to emerge. Information from Zanker, 2010.

Deficiencies can occur in any one of the three kinds of cones, resulting in distinct kinds of colorblindness (including some that involve more than one deficiency). The most common form of colorblindness is red–green colorblindness, which happens when either the M cones or L cones (but not both) are deficient. This is relatively common (7%–10%) in males of Western European descent. If the S cones are deficient, that's blue–green (or tritan) colorblindness, which occurs much more rarely (in just 1 of 10,000 people). Complete colorblindness (achromatopsia), in which none of the cones work properly and the person sees the world in shades of gray, is even rarer (1 in 30,000 people) (Tait & Carroll, 2010; Mollon et al., 2003).

Opponent-Process Theory of Color Vision.

Trichromatic theory is not the only theory to explain color vision. Another is the **opponent-process theory of**

color vision: an explanation of color vision based on the idea that your visual system is specialized to sense specific opposite pairs of colors (like red–green, blue–yellow). Among researchers of color vision, these two theories of color vision have a long history of rivalry dating back to the 1800s (Helmholtz, 1852; Young, 1802; Hering, 1878, 1964; Goldstein, 2001a). Supporters of the opponent-process theory emphasize that while certain pairs of colors can complement each other, other pairs can't. There is such a thing as bluish purple or reddish orange, but no such thing as reddish green or bluish yellow. (It is similar to the way we can combine certain directions on a map, like northeast or southwest, but not others, like northsouth or eastwest.) So according to opponent-process theory, the pairs that don't blend may be *opponents*. That means the process by which we see colors may depend heavily on specific *processes* within our eyes in response to the red–green or blue–yellow components of what we see.

Experts in color vision recognize that trichromatic theory and opponent-process theory both play roles in color vision. So the question is not which theory is correct, but how the two work together. Research indicates that they operate at different levels of the vision process. Trichromatic theory applies near the beginning of the color vision process, when the visual stimulus reaches the cones, while opponent-process theory kicks in later in the color vision process, after the stimulus passes cones and heads through the optic nerve toward the brain (Gegenfurtner & Kiper, 2003; Buchsbaum & Gottschalk, 1983).

Separating and Grouping Objects. When your eyes take in a scene, how do you know which items have nothing to do with each other and which are part of a group? One key is your capability for **figure–ground organization**: your tendency to visually distinguish between an object and its background. Usually, distinguishing the *figure* (the item in front) and the *ground* (what's behind it) is easy—you see your car in front of the brick wall, or your sandwich on top of your plate. But sometimes it can be tough, as in **Figure 3.9**. Researchers have found that when it's not obvious, we tend to rely on several rules of thumb. More often than not, the figure is smaller than the ground, the figure is more symmetrical than the ground, the figure appears closer than the ground, the figure is more likely to be convex (with outward curves or bulges) than the ground, and if there's anything moving, it's more likely to be the figure than the ground (Pomerantz & Portillo, 2010; Goldstein, 2001b; Vecera & Lee, 2010).

The figure–ground challenge involves separating items, but what about grouping them together? Again, it's often easy to know whether individual items belong together as a group. For example, once I was at the airport to pick up a friend. As I watched the passengers heading toward baggage claim, I saw about a dozen young men walk by. All were wearing warm-up suits that were blue with white trim and carrying matching blue and white duffel bags over their shoulders. All appeared to be about 20 years old, give or take a couple of years. All were tall and athletically built. All were walking near each other in the same direction at the same time. I certainly did not think to myself, "What a coincidence! All of these tall athletes decided on their own to dress in blue and white warm-up suits, and now they all happen to be at the same place at the same time heading the same direction!" Instead, I thought to myself, "I bet that's a college basketball team." When they got close enough for me to read the logo on their warm-ups, I saw that I was right. When you group items together like that, you form a **gestalt**: an organized whole that you perceive as different from just the sum of its parts.

What features cause us to make a gestalt out of a collection of things we see?

Researchers who study visual organization have identified several characteristics of groups of objects that increase the odds that we will see them as a gestalt, or a whole rather than a collection of parts (Schirillo, 2010; Pomerantz & Portillo, 2010; Goldstein, 2010b):

trichromatic theory of color vision
An explanation of color vision based on the idea that the cones are specialized to sense either red, green, or blue.

opponent-process theory of color vision
An explanation of color vision based on the idea that the cones are specialized to sense specific opposite pairs of colors (like red–green and blue–yellow).

figure–ground organization
The tendency to visually distinguish between an object and its background.

gestalt
An organized whole that is perceived as different than just the sum of its parts.

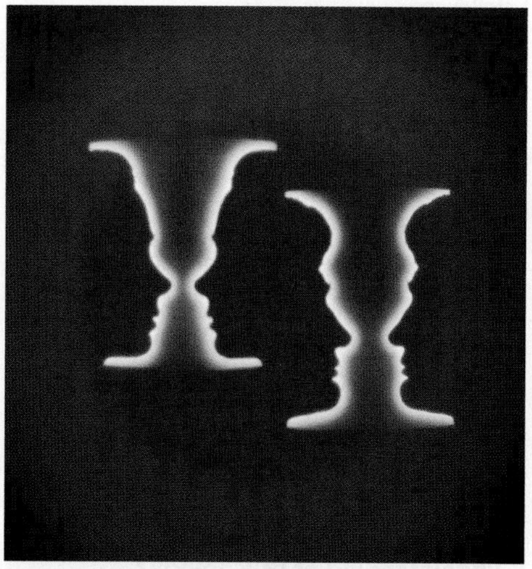

FIGURE 3.9 Distinguishing Figure from Ground. Sometimes it's not easy to tell the figure (the focal item) from the background. Do you see faces or vases? BILL LONGCORE/ Getty Images

A gestalt is an organized whole that you perceive as different from just the sum of its parts. For example, when your eyes see these patterns of black on a white background, you form a gestalt of a soccer ball.

- **Proximity.** The closer objects are to each other, the more likely they belong together. Lots of space, especially if other things occupy that space, decreases the odds that you'll form a gestalt. Think about a tightly packed herd of sheep as opposed to the same sheep spread out across miles of land with lots of other animals in between them.

- **Similarity.** If objects share the same color, size, orientation (facing the same direction), or distance from you, they're probably a group rather than a collection of individuals. Think about uniformed soldiers marching in formation.

- **Common fate.** If objects change together rather than each changing on its own, they are likely to go together. Think about a group of birds flying: If their takeoffs, turns, and landings are all synchronized, we see them as a flock.

- **Connectedness.** If objects are touching, they probably go together. Two people sitting next to each other at a concert could be strangers, but if they're holding hands, they're a couple.

- **Closure.** If one part is missing in an otherwise complete shape, you're likely to overlook what's missing and assume the parts make a whole. Check the figure in the margin: It's just a series of black pentagons, but your eyes fill in what's missing to make it a soccer ball.

CHAPTER APP 3.2

Visual Illusions

Illusions of the Brain
300 Optical Illusions

Preview one of the links and consider the following questions.

WEBSITE:
http://tiny.cc/2jh7jy

ANDROID:
http://tiny.cc/1wjyiy

IPHONE:
http://tiny.cc/vqjyiy

VIDEO DEMO:
http://tiny.cc/chapterapps

These apps show examples of visual illusions, including some described in the chapter.

How does it APPly to your daily life?
What other visual illusions like these have you encountered in your daily life? If you worked in the marketing or advertising field, how might you use visual illusions like these to sell products?

How does it APPly to your understanding of psychology?
How do the illusions in this app demonstrate the difference between *sensation* and *perception*?

Special Modes of Vision? In recent years, psychologists have increasingly discovered we perceive certain visual objects—namely, faces, bodies, and maybe words—in specialized ways (Gauthier, 2010; Goldstein, 2010b). You have mechanisms in your brain specially designed to process faces, much like your smartphone (with the right apps) has mechanisms specially designed to process QR codes, bar codes, business cards, and other special kinds of visual stimuli. One source of evidence for this finding—known as *modular* perception, or perception in a particular mode—is the fact that some people have visual inabilities that reflect these very specific tasks. For example, among people who have otherwise intact perception, a few can't perceive or recognize faces (prosopagnosia), and a few others can't perceive or recognize words (alexia) (Humphreys & Riddoch, 2001).

Some of the strongest evidence of modular vision involves faces (Kanwisher et al., 1997; Morton & Johnson, 1991). Some researchers even claim that your brain has a *face processor*, a small spot in your temporal lobe called the *fusiform face area* that receives images of the faces you see (Sinha et al., 2010; Nakayama, 2001). The Margaret Thatcher photo (on page 85) illustrates the difference in perception your face processor makes. It is the same pair of photos—one right side up and the other upside down. The upside down pair seems only slightly different from each other. But the right side up pair seems extremely different from each other, with one appearing grotesque because the eyes, nose, and mouth are inverted. Because of modular vision for faces, you notice that violation of expectation (those inverted features) much more strongly when your face processor is activated (when the photos are right side up) than when it isn't. Because the first photos demonstrating this effect featured a photo of the former British prime minister, it's called the *Margaret Thatcher effect* (Thompson, 1980).

Similarly, other studies have used upside down photos to illustrate that human bodies and specific body parts (arms, legs, etc.) are also perceived in a modular way. Specifically, these studies found that the time it takes to compare two bodies (or two arms or two legs) is significantly shorter when those bodies are shown right side up rather than upside down. The same difference does not appear for other stimuli, such as houses (or parts of houses). This implies that our brains have a special way of fast-tracking the perception of human bodies as well as faces (Reed, 2010; Reed et al., 2003, 2006).

How Culture Influences Vision

DIVERSITY MATTERS

Increasingly, psychologists are recognizing that your cultural background influences how, and even what, you perceive (Nisbett & Miyamoto, 2005). This is especially evident in cross-cultural studies of vision (Masuda, 2010).

Color Naming Across Cultures. One example involves color vision. In some ways, cultures around the world tend to name colors similarly. The same set of 11 colors appears in almost all languages: black, white, red, yellow, green, blue, gray, orange, brown, pink, and purple (Berlin & Kay, 1969; Lindsey & Brown, 2006; Regier et al., 2005; Kay & Regier, 2007). Interestingly, those colors actually appear in young children's vocabularies in that order too—black and white first, pink and purple last (Hansen, 2010).

In other ways, there are some differences in color naming from one culture to the next (Roberson et al., 2000; Caskey-Sirmons & Hickerson, 1977). For example, one group of English-speaking researchers found that a small culture in Papua New Guinea used only five names to cover the whole spectrum of colors. Similarly, a tribal group in southern Africa had a list of color categories that didn't match with common English categories at all (Roberson et al., 2004, 2005a,b). Another study has found that in Italian, Russian, and Polish, the colors that English speakers call light blue and dark blue are entirely distinct—basic colors rather than variations on a single color (blue), as they are in English (Winawer et al., 2007). Yet another study noticed that some languages fail to make a distinction between blue and green (using a combined term the researchers call *grue*). Researchers discovered that those languages are typically spoken in very sunny parts of the world—in particular, regions where people are exposed to high levels of short-wavelength ultraviolet (UV) rays, which tend to wear out the cones involved in the perception of colors in the part of the spectrum around blue and green (Lindsey & Brown, 2002).

The point here is not just that diverse cultures have unique ways of naming colors, but that their ways of naming colors may influence how they see their world (Roberson, 2005; Roberson & Hanley, 2010; Kay & Regier, 2006). For instance, if you spoke a language that used the name *grue* for what you call blue and what you call green, you might be more likely to see a blue shirt and a green shirt as being the same color. On the other hand, if you were wearing a sky blue shirt and navy blue pants, whether you'd think, "I'm wearing all the same color," depends on whether you speak English or one of the languages (Italian, Russian, or Polish) that labels those hues as entirely distinct.

Collectivism, Individualism, and Vision. Other cultural differences in vision relate to cultural differences in individualism versus collectivism, or the extent to which the culture tends to emphasize the well-being of the individual person versus the well-being of the family or larger group. In collectivistic cultures, connections or relationships between people or objects—generally called *context*—are prioritized over independence of each person or object. Some researchers have found that that visual perception of the members of individualistic and collectivistic cultures often reflect these priorities (Chiao & Harada, 2008).

Consider the studies that use the rod and frame test, as illustrated in **Figure 3.10**. Participants in these studies receive a simple instruction: make the rod vertical. Sometimes the frame is at a right angle with the rod, but other times the frame is slightly tilted. Asian participants make more mistakes than U.S. participants on this task. The mistakes tend to be in the direction of making the rod line up with the frame—parallel to the sides of the frame and perpendicular to the frame's top and bottom—even when the frame leans to one side. Researchers in these studies offer the interpretation that Asian participants, who come from more collectivistic cultures, have more difficulty separating the rod from its context (the frame) than U.S.

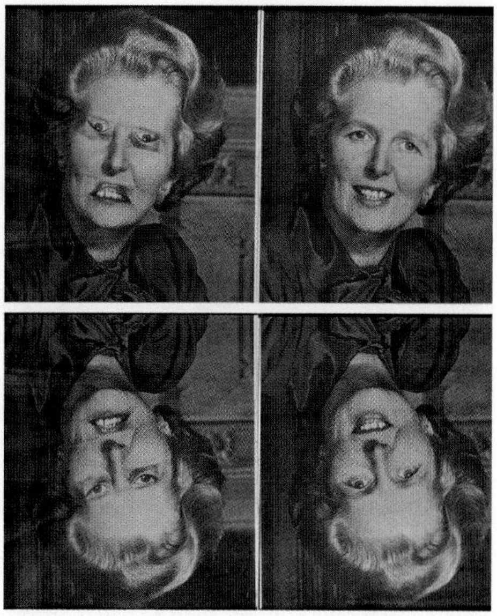

The irregularities in Margaret Thatcher's face are much more obvious when looking at her face right side up as opposed to upside down. That difference suggests specialized modular processing of faces in the brain.
Courtesy of Peter Thompson, from Thompson, P. (1980) Margaret Thatcher: a new Illusion *Perception* 9 383-4

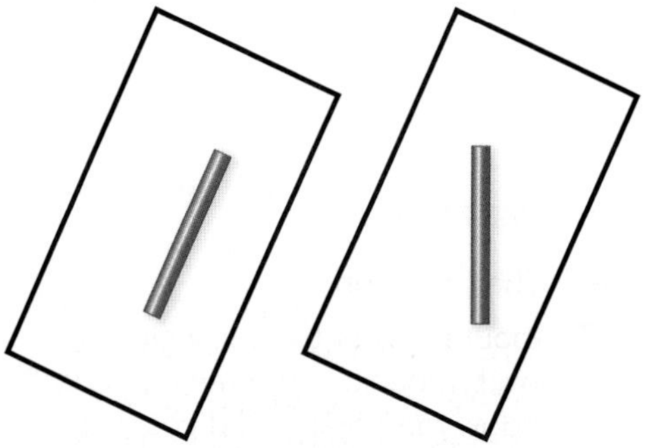

FIGURE 3.10 The Rod and Frame Test. In the rod and frame test, the task is to make the rod completely vertical, regardless of the orientation of the frame. People from more collectivistic cultures, where appreciation of context and relationships is emphasized, struggle with this task more than people from more individualistic cultures, where independence is emphasized (Kitayama et al., 2003; Ji et al., 2000).

FIGURE 3.11 Cultural Differences in Vision: Focal Items Versus Background. When viewing images like this one, people from collectivistic cultures tend to pay more attention to items in the background, while people from individualistic cultures tend to pay more attention to the big fish up front. Takahiko Masuda and Richard E. Nisbett

participants, who come from a more individualistic culture (Kitayama et al., 2003; Ji et al., 2000).

More studies produce results that also demonstrate how people from collectivistic cultures (compared to people from individualistic cultures) tend to see the context more and the featured item within the context less (Nisbett & Masuda, 2003). For example, in one study, participants in Japan and the United States watched short video clips of underwater scenes or wildlife scenes before being quizzed about them. U.S. participants did better on questions regarding the items up front, like the big fish in **Figure 3.11**, but Japanese participants did better on questions regarding items in the background (Masuda & Nisbett, 2001). Similarly, East Asian participants did better at noticing changes in the background of rapidly flashing pictures, but participants from Western countries did better at noticing changes in the main objects in the front (Masuda & Nisbett, 2006). Studies of eye tracking show that when Westerners and East Asians look at the same photo, Westerners' eyes spend more time focused on the focal objects, while East Asians' eyes spend more time focused on objects in the background (Chua et al., 2005; Rayner et al., 2007). Collectively, these studies suggest that people from collectivistic cultures tend to focus their vision more on contextual features or relationship-based features of the visual field than people from individualistic cultures.

CHECK YOUR LEARNING:

3.8 For most people, which of the five senses dominates?

3.9 What are the functions of the various parts of the eye, including the cornea, iris, lens, retina, and fovea?

3.10 What is the difference between these three kinds of eye movement: saccadic, compensatory, and vergence?

3.11 What is depth perception, and on what features in the stimulus does it depend?

3.12 What is hue, and what are the two competing theories of color vision?

3.13 What factors determine help people to determine if objects that are seen together belong to the same group?

3.14 What kinds of objects are processed in special ways?

3.15 How does culture influence vision?

Hearing

YOU WILL LEARN:

3.16 what audition is.

3.17 about parts of the ear, including the pinna, tympanic membrane, ossicles, oval window membrane, and cochlea.

3.18 how you hear pitch.

3.19 how you determine the location from which a sound is coming.

3.20 how the perception of speech may be different from the perception of other sounds.

3.21 how culture influences hearing.

Audition is your sense of hearing. When you think about the benefits of audition, you may first think about the pleasures that it brings. After all, your ears bring in the sounds of babies' laughter, ocean waves, your cat's purr, and your favorite music booming through your headphones. But the sense of hearing is important for the necessities of life too. In fact, over the course of human history, hearing has been vital to survival, just like vision. It is interesting that you can easily turn off vision (close your eyes), but unless you stick your fingers in your ears, you can't turn off hearing. Similarly, you can see only what's in front of you, but you can hear what's in every direction. In these ways, the sense of hearing has always alerted humans, as well as other species, to predators and other dangers that may be nearby. Those auditory alerts enable us to turn toward what we hear so we can see it too, further increasing the chances of our survival (Moore, 2001a, 2010). Remember that time you were walking through the neighborhood, heard a menacing growl behind you, and turned to see a dog baring its teeth? Or that time the screeching of tires made you turn to the left, see the skidding car, and swerve out of its way at the last second? If so, you know the survival value of an intact sense of hearing.

Your Ear: Its Parts and Their Functions

Now let's go through the parts of your ear as a sound would (**Figure 3.12**). We'll start on the outer surface and move toward the inner regions, where the ear ultimately connects to the brain. But first, let's consider exactly what sound is. Essentially, sound is vibration. Sometimes, you can actually see the vibration sending sound your way, like a single guitar string quivering after you pluck it. This vibration—or sound wave, as it is often called—travels through the air and reaches the edge of the ear. Your outer ear steers it toward the inner part, where the vibrations that started outside of your ear start a chain reaction of vibration of tiny parts inside your ear (the details of which we will describe shortly). The vibration of those tiny parts gets translated, through *transduction*, into neural activity that your brain can process (Eatock, 2010). So in short, you hear because your ears convert a vibration made around you into a vibration happening within you.

Some of those vibrations sound a lot louder than others. Loudness is measured in units called *decibels* (abbreviated *dB*). Exposing your ears to too many decibels, especially for too long a period of time, can damage your hearing. That is true whether the noise is something you can't control, like a thunderstorm, or something you can control, like the volume on your headphones. By the way, hearing loss due to wearing loud headphones for a long time is a real risk, happening to a sizable number of people even at young ages (Sulaiman et al., 2013, 2014; Breinbauer et al., 2012). Check **Figure 3.13** for examples of sounds across the range of decibels.

Audition is your sense of hearing. Your ears have some distinct advantages over your eyes. For example, your ears don't close, and they pick up sensation from every direction (rather than just in front of you, as with your eyes). These advantages of our ears increased the chances of survival for our ancestors. Blue Jean Images/Alamy

Outer Ear. When sound moves toward your ears, it first reaches your **pinna**, or outer ear. Your pinna basically consists of the parts of your ear that you can easily touch with your fingers. Your pinna functions as a funnel that guides sound toward the inner ear, where the real work of hearing is done. When you cup your hand around your ear to strengthen a sound, you're enhancing the job your pinna always does automatically. In some animals, the pinna is relatively huge. For example, consider bats and foxes. Both are nocturnal animals that move around in the dark and therefore rely disproportionately on hearing rather than sight, and with both animals, the pinna is oversized. In other animals, like horses and cats, the pinna moves toward sound to better enhance it (Wallace, 2010).

Middle Ear. The pinna leads to the **tympanic membrane**: a surface stretched taut across the ear canal to form the boundary between the outer ear and the middle ear. Your tympanic membrane is commonly called your eardrum (which is easy to remember if you learned in high school band about the *timpani*, a large percussion

LIFE HACK 3.2

Be smart about the volume of your headphones, especially if you wear them for long periods. If it is too loud for too long, it can damage your hearing.

(Sulaiman et al., 2013, 2014; Breinbauer et al., 2012)

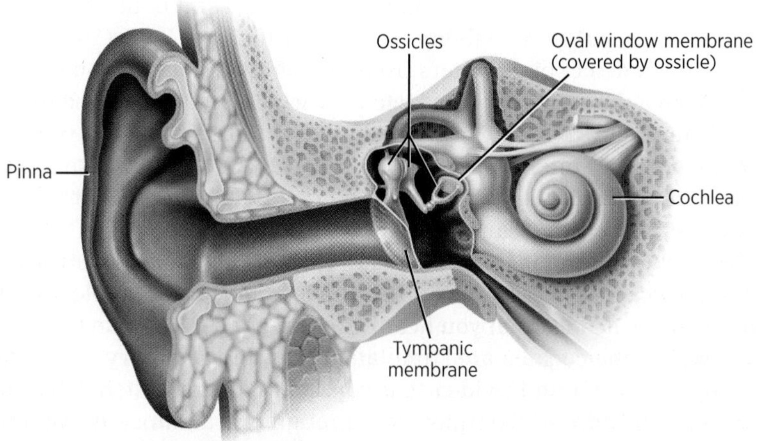

FIGURE 3.12 The Parts of the Human Ear. The parts of the human ear include the pinna, tympanic membrane, ossicles, oval window membrane, and cochlea.

audition
The sense of hearing.

pinna
The outer ear.

tympanic membrane
A surface stretched taut across the ear canal to form the boundary between the outer ear and the middle ear.

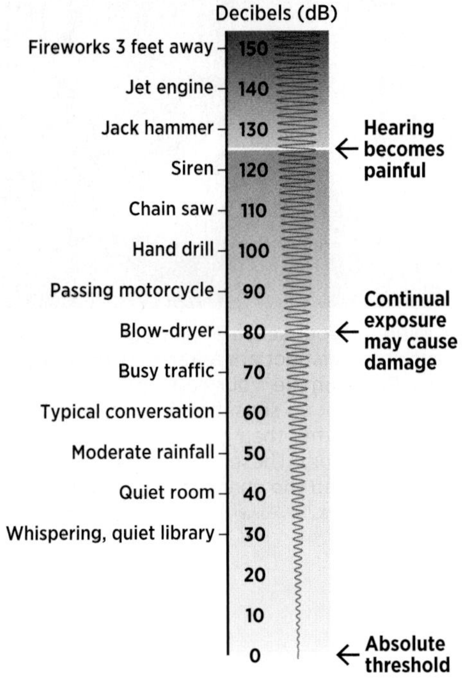

FIGURE 3.13 The Loudness of Common Sounds. As the decibel level goes up, the risk for hearing damage does too, especially if the loudness is chronic. Source: http://www.asha.org/public/hearing/Noise/

instrument). On the inner side of the tympanic membrane is a chain of very small bones called **ossicles** connected in ball-and-socket fashion. On the other side of the ossicles, there's a second membrane between the middle ear and the inner ear called the **oval window membrane**. In between those two membranes, your ossicles amplify sound to about 17 times its entry level (Hackney, 2010).

Inner Ear. Once the sound makes its way through the middle ear, it enters the inner ear. Your inner ear consists primarily of your **cochlea**, a spiral fluid-filled structure in the inner ear that sends sound waves to the brain via the auditory nerve. Vibrations of cochlear fluid are the final step of hearing within the ear. Everything else happens in the brain, beginning with the arrival of auditory information at the main auditory nucleus in the midbrain.

Disorders of the cochlea, which can be inborn or acquired via exposure to excessive noise, are a common source of hearing loss (Gomersall & Baguley, 2010). Such disorders can be treated with *cochlear implants*, a small prosthetic device that includes parts both inside and outside of the ear. Specifically, cochlear implants consist of a microphone behind the ear that looks like a common hearing aid. The microphone picks up auditory information and sends it to a processor that is either attached to it or carried separately, typically in a pocket. That processor sends the information to a receiver surgically implanted under the skin on the skull near the ear. That receiver is connected by electrodes to the cochlea and auditory nerve, which ultimately receive the auditory information with more strength than it could on its own. Over 100,000 people have received cochlear implants, including about 6000 with one in each ear (Houston et al., 2010).

How You Hear: Pitch, Location, and More

We've discussed the parts of your ear. Now, let's consider how they work together to help you hear.

Pitch. **Pitch** is the description of how "high" or "low" a sound is. Pitch is produced by the frequency of vibrations: The more frequent the vibrations, the higher the pitch. (Pitch is measured in hertz, which means vibrations per second.) Consider the guitar string we mentioned earlier. If you pluck that string with no fingers on the fret, it will produce a certain pitch. But if you pluck it again with a finger pressing it down onto the fret—essentially shortening the vibrating part of the string—the pitch goes up because it doesn't take as much time for the shorter string to complete each full vibration. The same principle explains why violins and ukuleles are higher-pitch instruments than cellos and upright basses—it's all about how long it takes for the strings to vibrate.

If you couldn't perceive pitch, all music would sound like beats on the same drum and all speech would sound like a monotone drone. You'd still notice the loudness and length of each sound, but no variability in terms of highs or lows (Yost, 2010; Moore, 2012). Your ability to detect pitch differs from that of other species. You've noticed this if you've ever seen a dog respond to dog whistles, which produce a pitch they can hear but we can't. Your ability to detect pitch might also differ from that of your parents or grandparents, since high-pitch hearing is the first to decline with age. That is why some clever entrepreneurs in the tech field have marketed high-pitch ringtones to teens, with the idea that mom or dad can't hear them (Kidd, 2010).

There are two prominent theories about exactly how you perceive pitch: *place theory* and *frequency theory* (Moore, 2001b). **Place theory** is an explanation of pitch perception based on the idea that you hear different pitches because tiny hairs in different places within the cochlea are stimulated. **Frequency theory** is an explanation of pitch perception based on the idea that you hear different pitches because nerve impulses travel with different frequencies through the auditory nerve. The names of these theories are good indicators of the difference between them: Place theory emphasizes the specific *place* where the sound stimulates the cochlea, and frequency theory emphasizes the speed or *frequency* at which the sound makes a nerve impulse travel from the cochlea through the auditory nerve.

ossicles
A chain of very small bones connected in ball-and-socket fashion on the inner side of the tympanic membrane.

oval window membrane
A membrane between the ossicles of the middle ear and the inner ear.

cochlea
The spiral fluid-filled structure in the inner ear that sends sound waves to the brain via the auditory nerve.

pitch
The description of how "high" or "low" a sound is.

place theory
The explanation of pitch perception based on the idea that a person hears different pitches because tiny hairs in different places within the cochlea are stimulated.

frequency theory
The explanation of pitch perception based on the idea that a person hears different pitches because nerve impulses travel with different frequencies through the auditory nerve.

sound localization
The ability to perceive the location from which a sound originates.

A big difference between the two theories about pitch is the location at which the sound is processed. According to place theory, the sound is processed in the inner ear and then sent to the brain. According to frequency theory, however, the sound moves unprocessed through the inner ear and the auditory nerve and then is processed in the brain. There is evidence that both place theory and frequency theory explain pitch perception, but in different ways: At low frequencies, frequency theory is most supported; at high frequencies, place theory is more supported; and in the middle, they both play important roles (Moore, 2012; Horowitz, 2012; Pickles, 2013; Schnupp et al., 2012).

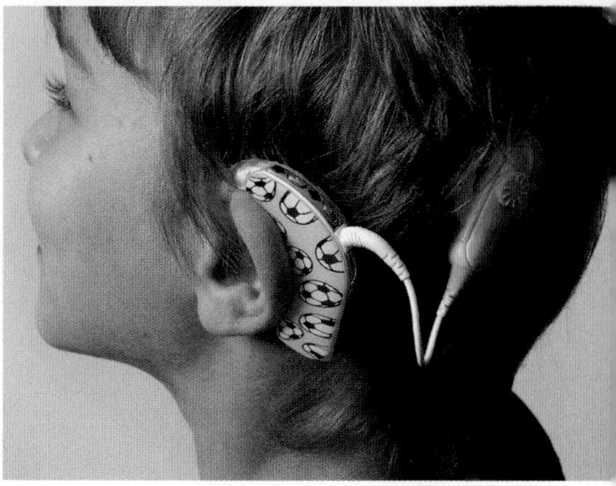

A disorder of the cochlea can cause hearing loss but can be treated with a cochlear implant, a small prosthetic device featuring parts both inside and outside of the ear. John Robertson / Barcroft Media / Getty Images

Sound Localization. **Sound localization** is your ability to perceive the location from which a sound originates. Imagine talking on the phone with a friend about a half-mile away as a thunderstorm develops. Lightning strikes, and you hear a loud boom of thunder immediately. You start to say, "Whoa, did you hear that?" but as soon as you get to "Whoa," your friend hears the same thunder at her house and interrupts you with her own, "Whoa, did you hear that?" That brief delay between the thunder reaching your ears and the thunder reaching her ears tells you a lot about the location of that lightning strike: it hit closer to you than to your friend, since it got to you sooner.

Your brain uses the same method to determine sound location, but your left ear and right ear take the place of you and your friend. Your brain measures the discrepancy between the sound's arrival times at each of your ears. Your ears are only inches apart, so thankfully your brain can detect microseconds (millionths of a second) of difference between your two ears receiving the same sound. Of course, if the sound comes from directly in front or in back of you, the discrepancy will be zero. However, if the sound is even slightly to your right or left, your brain will register the difference and use that to determine where to look for the sound (Yost, 2001; Brand et al., 2002).

A sound coming from your left side would not only hit your left ear sooner than your right ear, but be louder as well. Your brain also uses this discrepancy in volume to aid in sound localization. Your brain is highly sensitive to this difference in loudness, needing only a fraction of a decibel of extra volume to determine that the sound is louder in, and therefore closer to, one ear than the other (McAlpine, 2010).

Speech Perception. In recent decades, an increasing amount of research has focused on whether human speech is perceived in a different way than all other sounds. Some evidence suggests that the way people hear speech may be a specialized process (somewhat similar to the modular kinds of visual perception we discussed earlier with regard to how you see faces, bodies, and perhaps words). However, the extent of this specialization is still unclear (Bowers & Davis, 2004; Fowler & Magnuson, 2012; Hickock & Poeppel, 2007).

One interesting line of evidence for specialized perception of speech comes from studies in which participants wear earphones that present a different audio stream into each ear. When those streams contain music, participants tend to listen to what they hear in their left ear, but when those streams contain speech, participants tend to listen to what they hear in their right ear. This suggests that, at least in comparison to music, different regions in different hemispheres of the brain may be dedicated to speech perception (Moore, 2012; Kimura, 1967; Broadbent & Gregory, 1964). There is even some fMRI evidence that 3-month-old babies, who have not yet begun to speak, use certain parts of their brains more than other parts when they hear speech, which suggests that some specialized speech perception mechanisms may be present from birth (Dehaene-Lambertz et al., 2002).

How Culture Influences Hearing

DIVERSITY MATTERS

Earlier, we examined how cultural variables influenced the way people see. The same question has been examined for hearing as well. The number of hearing studies is not as great, but the evidence is similar: At least in some ways, culture shapes how and what you hear.

CHAPTER APP 3.3

Audition

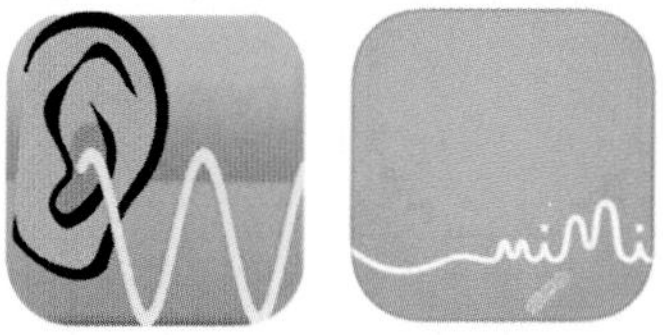

Test Your Hearing
Mimi Hearing Test

Preview one of the links and consider the following questions.

WEBSITE: http://tiny.cc/qkh7jy

ANDROID: http://tiny.cc/9wjyiy

IPHONE: http://tiny.cc/arjyiy

VIDEO DEMO: http://tiny.cc/chapterapps

Apps like these play tones at a variety of frequencies. You respond by indicating whether you heard the tone or not—much like a traditional hearing test. It tells you your hearing range and your "hearing age."

How does it APPly to your daily life?
What range of frequencies can you hear? What's your "hearing age"? Apps like this one could replace what some highly trained professionals do (for example, hearing tests by those who sell hearing aids)—what do you think of that possibility?

How does it APPly to your understanding of psychology?
How does this relate to the material in the textbook about high-frequency phone ring tones?

Exposure to certain sounds within a culture, especially at an early age, seems to shape hearing. Numerous studies have used music to demonstrate this finding (Morrison & Demorest, 2009; Hannon & Trainor, 2007; Dowling, 2001; Lynch et al., 1990, 1991). Across cultures, there are certain similarities in how musical sounds are organized. For instance, the most pleasing combinations of tones are separated by exactly one octave, which means they are multiples of each other's frequency (Levitin & Tirovolas, 2010). (In the Western musical system, an A tone can have a frequency of 110, 220, 440, or 880 hertz, depending on the octave in which it falls.)

Within that octave, however, different cultures divide the pitch range into a different number of distinct tones, usually between 5 and 15 (Levitin & Tirovolas, 2010). Those distinct tones are collectively known as the scale, and—here's the impact of culture—listening to music in your culture's scale makes you more sensitive to that scale but less sensitive to other scales. One study found that both adults and 10- to 13-year-old kids from Western cultures were much better at noticing out-of-tune notes in familiar Western scales than in unfamiliar Indonesian scales (Lynch & Eilers, 1991). A follow-up study found the same results for children as young as a year old, but dissimilar results for 6-month-old babies, suggesting that it takes at least half a year of exposure to a certain musical scale for a child's pitch sensitivity to shift in that direction (Lynch & Eilers, 1992).

The findings are similar for rhythms too: Kids from Western cultures, as long as they are at least a year old, are better at noticing rhythmic mistakes (music that is "off beat) in familiar Western music than in unfamiliar Balkan music (Hannon & Trehub, 2005a). When they listened to the Balkan music over and over again, 1-year-olds gained an equal sensitivity to those formerly unfamiliar rhythms, but adults did not (Hannon & Trehub, 2005b).

Gender is another factor that seems to influence hearing. Around the world, men are more likely than women to experience hearing impairment, but that finding can largely be attributed to men more often working at high-decibel jobs (construction, for example) likely to damage hearing (Nelson et al., 2005; Mathers et al., 2000). However, there's evidence that even among newborn babies, females hear better than males—a finding that can't be explained by experience in the workplace or anywhere else (Popple, 2010).

CHECK YOUR LEARNING:

3.16 What is audition?

3.17 What are the functions of the various parts of the ear, including the pinna, middle ear, and inner ear?

3.18 What is pitch, and what are the two competing theories that explain it?

3.19 How do you determine the location from which a sound is coming?

3.20 How does the perception of speech differ from the perception of other sounds?

3.21 How does culture influence hearing?

Smell and Taste

As crucial as vision and hearing are to humans, they are not the most universal senses among all the species. Smell and taste are. Even organisms as tiny and simple as the single-celled amoeba have them. They may not have recognizable noses or mouths, but they definitely have a way of sensing the chemicals around them (smell) and the substances they might consume (taste) (Sell, 2014). Let's examine your sense of smell and then your sense of taste.

The Nose Knows: Your Sense of Smell

Olfaction is your sense of smell. It is well known that other species (dogs, for example) have better olfaction than humans, but don't underestimate the sophistication of your sense of smell. Remember our discussion of receptor cells in your eyes? There were four kinds: rods and three types of cones. There are at least *350–450* kinds of receptor cells in your nose, and a total of about 6 million to 10 million receptor cells, the most for any sense other than vision (Munger, 2010; Doty, 2010). Equipped with so many receptor cells of so many different types, your nose can detect about a *trillion* different scents (Bushdid et al., 2014).

YOU WILL LEARN:

3.22 what olfaction is.

3.23 how olfaction receptor cells work.

3.24 how olfaction relates to sex.

3.25 how olfaction abilities vary across people.

3.26 what gustation is.

3.27 how gustation receptor cells, or taste buds, work.

3.28 how experience can influence taste.

How Olfaction Receptor Cells Work. The presence of so many different kinds of receptor cells means that even a simple smell is actually a complex combination. It is like the three types of cones in your retina blending red, green, and blue to make other colors. With olfaction, however, hundreds of different kinds of receptor cells do the blending. So even a smell as basic as cinnamon or chocolate is the product of many different kinds of receptor cells combining their inputs. Speaking of chocolate, one study found that humans can use olfaction to track chocolate like animals who hunt by scent. Participants in this study wore blindfolds and earplugs and were asked to trail a path of chocolate (chocolate essential oil, actually) through an open field. Results showed not only that they could do it, but that their zig-zag pattern was similar to the zig-zag pattern used by hunting dogs tracking pheasants (Porter et al., 2005).

These researchers (and others) also found that people use *internostril comparison* to determine the location of a source of a smell. Remember how your brain localizes sound by noticing the discrepancy in the time and the volume in each ear? Your brain does the same thing with the scents coming through each nostril, even though they are right next to each other. Your brain can tell which nostril is picking up a scent sooner and more strongly, then use that information to deduce what direction it's coming from (Porter et al., 2005; Arzi & Sobel, 2010). Humans are not the only ones to use internostril comparison—there's evidence some sharks do it too in their search for smaller fish to eat. That led some researchers to speculate that the hammerhead shark, with its nostrils on either side of its unusually wide head, might represent an extreme evolutionary adaptation based on this ability (Gardiner & Atema, 2010).

Olfaction is your sense of smell. With 350–450 kinds of receptor cells, your nose can detect about a trillion different scents.
-101PHOTO-/iStock/Getty Images

Each of the millions of olfactory receptor cells deep in your nose extends about 20 **cilia**: tiny scent-seeking threads through the mucus. Those cilia essentially sweep the nose for scent-carrying chemicals, then carry them through the receptor cells and onto the two **olfactory bulbs**: brain structures located on the underside of your brain (behind the bridge of your nose) that receive scent information from cilia. The olfactory bulbs then send the olfactory information to the **olfactory cortex**: a collection of brain regions involved in smell, which includes the amygdala and parts of the cerebral cortex (Shah et al., 2010; Doty, 2010; Cowart & Rawson, 2001). Remember how we learned that the amygdala plays a prominent role in emotion, especially fear (Chapter 2)? With olfaction, the amygdala determines the emotional meaning of smells. It responds strongly when a smell is associated with a feeling, especially a feeling of fear or anxiety, but it responds weakly when a smell has no emotional importance (Winston et al., 2005; Zald, 2003). So when the smell of grandma's oatmeal cookies brings back the joy of Sunday afternoons playing at her house or when the smell of cut grass brings back the exhaustion of that summer you spent mowing lawns, you have your amygdala to thank.

Olfaction and Sex. Sometimes the emotion associated with a smell is sexual excitement. For many species, olfaction plays a significant role in sexual attraction. (Ever seen dogs sniffing each other?) There is even evidence that in some species, like lizards, voles, spiders, and bees, the male can use olfaction to determine whether the

olfaction
The sense of smell.

cilia
Tiny scent-seeking threads that extend from olfactory receptor cells through the mucus of your nose.

olfactory bulbs
Brain structures located on the underside of your brain (behind the bridge of your nose) that receive scent information from cilia.

olfactory cortex
A collection of brain regions involved in smell, including the amygdala and parts of the cerebral cortex.

female is a virgin, and if not, how many times she has mated. And in other species, such as moths, females who have just mated stop producing the scent that attracts males and start producing a scent that repels them (Thomas, 2011).

Humans rely on olfaction during the mating, or dating, process too. Two types of olfactory information can play a role. The first is *odors*, which are smells of which you are aware. If it's an odor, you realize you're smelling it, and you also realize the effect it has on you. A person you meet at a party is more likely to become more than just a person you meet at a party if they smell fresh rather than filthy. The second type of olfactory information is *pheromones*, chemical signals detected by your nose without your awareness. You don't *smell* pheromones, exactly, at least not in the same way you smell odors. You are not conscious of them, but they can influence your behavior, especially in terms of attraction to others.

People use internostril comparison, or the discrepancy in the times that a scent reaches each nostril, to determine the location of a smell. Other species do, too. Some researchers argue that the hammerhead shark, with its nostrils set very far apart, might be especially advanced in this ability (Gardiner & Atema, 2010). Moment/Getty Images

Of course, for humans, pheromones are just one of many attraction factors (many of which are visual and verbal), but for other species, pheromones are the dominant attraction factor. For example, a male silk moth needs to smell just eight molecules of a particular pheromone from the female to set into motion a full sequence of mating behavior (Brennan, 2010). Research continues on particular human pheromones and their effects, but at the moment one of the most widely recognized is androstadienone, which is found in male sweat and which increases positive mood and sexual arousal in heterosexual females (Wyart et al., 2007; Lundström et al., 2003). Another study on androstadienone found that it evoked similar responses in homosexual men as in heterosexual women (Zhou et al., 2014).

In recent years, some researchers have proposed that there may be a third category of olfactory signals, somewhere between odors and pheromones, called *vasanas*. Vasanas are largely unconscious, but they affect mood, attention, arousal, and other characteristics (McClintock, 2010).

Variations in Olfactory Ability. About 1–2% of the U.S. population experiences either hyposmia (limited ability to smell) or anosmia (no ability to smell), which is usually temporary and caused by the flu or a sinus infection (Gilbert, 2008). Rates of hyposmia and anosmia increase with age, as does the danger: Among older adults a declining sense of smell can be an early sign of more serious diseases, like Alzheimer's or Parkinson's (Velayudhan et al., 2013; Amrutkar et al., 2015; Picillo et al., 2015; Doty, 2010, 2012. One study tested the olfactory abilities of over 1600 adults over age 60. Five years later, 21.8% of those with olfactory impairment had died, compared to fewer than 10% of those with an intact sense of smell (Gopinath et al., 2012). The good news is that regular exercise maintains and in some cases improves olfactory abilities (among many other abilities) in older adults (Schubert et al., 2013).

Pheromones are chemical signals detected by your nose without your awareness. In many species, pheromones have a powerful impact on sexual attraction. In humans, a pheromone found in male sweat (androstadienone) has been found to increase arousal in those attracted to men (Wyart et al., 2007; Lundström et al., 2003; Zhou et al., 2014). Stockbyte/Getty Images

Age is not the only predictor of a relatively weak sense of smell. Another predictor is gender: Men are worse than women at noticing and identifying scents (Ferdenzi et al., 2013). One study asked men and women to predict which smells each gender would be better at identifying. The participants guessed that men would be better at identifying stereotypical "man stuff" like motor oil, beer, and cigars, while women would be better at identifying stereotypical "woman stuff" like nail polish remover, baby powder, and Ivory soap, as well as foods like potato chips, grape juice, and Juicy Fruit gum. The results? Women were better at identifying all the smells, even the man stuff (Cain, 1982).

Another study gave smell identification tests to hundreds of men and women from four cultural groups: Black Americans, White Americans, Korean Americans, and native Japanese. Across all four groups, women outperformed men to almost exactly the same extent (Doty et al., 1985). There may be an ethnic component to olfactory abilities too. One study found that among 3000 older adults in the United States, African Americans and Hispanics had significantly worse senses of smell than Whites. Other relevant variables, like socioeconomic status, education level, and overall physical health accounted for only some of these differences for Hispanics and none for African Americans (Pinto et al., 2014).

DIVERSITY MATTERS

Detectable as Delectable: Your Sense of Taste

Gustation is your sense of taste. *Gust*ation comes from the same root as dis*gust*ing, and the Spanish verb *gust*ar (as in "*me gustan las enchiladas*"), all of which generally refer to how pleasing something is (or tastes) to you. How good it tastes is important not just for enjoyment but for health too. Gustation allows you to sense, and spit out, toxins and other substances that would cause you disease or discomfort if you ate them. For example, if you have ever taken a swig of spoiled milk, you understand this reaction. Gustation also encourages you to take in what you need to maintain homeostasis, or a good balance of essential elements in your body. That is why sports drinks like Powerade and Gatorade taste so good after you work out—your body loses a lot of salt when you sweat, and those high-sodium sports drinks put it right back (Di Lorenzo & Rosen, 2010).

Taste Buds: The Gustation Receptor Cells. The taste buds on your tongue, which regenerate about every 10 days, are your receptor cells for taste. As **Figure 3.14** and **Table 3.1** show, our taste buds can detect at least four basic qualities, and maybe a fifth, that combine to create the characteristic tastes of the foods and drinks you consume. The four definite taste qualities are sweet, sour, salty, and bitter. The fifth is *umami*, a Japanese word for *delicious taste* or *yummy* (Mather, 2011). In the gustatory world, there's a controversy about umami and whether it is a basic taste quality of its own or a combination of others (Lawless, 2001). Umami is a savory protein-rich flavor that you taste when you eat foods with MSG (monosodium glutamate). MSG occurs naturally in a few foods (some potatoes, mushrooms, tomatoes, and cheeses, among others), but it has also been manufactured and used as a flavor enhancer in many foods (Di Lorenzo & Rosen, 2010). The manufactured version originally earned a reputation as an addition to dishes in some Chinese restaurants, but MSG also appears commonly in U.S. fast-food restaurants, in many processed foods, and as a flavor enhancer that people often sprinkle onto their meats and vegetables at home (for example, as Accent flavor enhancer in the United States).

We may all share the same kinds of taste buds, but our taste buds don't share the same levels of sensitivity. Indeed, there are supertasters among us. Supertasters are people with unusually sensitive palates. Supertasters were first identified by researchers examining high sensitivity to bitterness, but it soon became clear that the same people are highly sensitive to other taste sensations too (Duffy & Bartoshuk, 2000). Supertasters are more likely to be female than male, a fact that's not surprising when you consider that women have more taste buds than men do (Bartoshuk et al., 1994). In experiments, supertasters can detect smaller changes in a food's ingredients ("this batch of cookies has a little more brown sugar than that one"), and are also better at determining whether a particular ingredient is present or absent within a mixture ("there's a dash of cayenne pepper in this chili") (Dinehart et al., 2006).

There are both advantages and disadvantages to being a supertaster. On the upside, the bitterness of beer or "burn" of whiskey and other hard drinks is more intense, which decreases the likelihood of alcohol consumption and its negative consequences. Also, scrumptious foods taste extra-scrumptious. Actually, that could be a

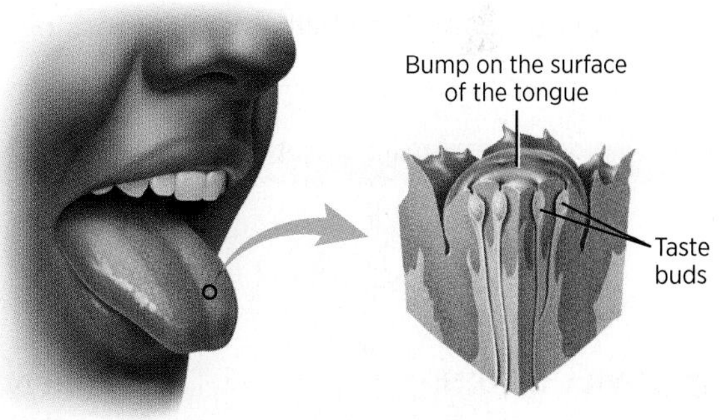

FIGURE 3.14 Taste Buds. Taste buds are the receptor cells of gustation. They are located on the edges of each papilla, or little bump, on the surface of your tongue.

TABLE 3.1: Taste Receptor Cells and the Foods That Activate Them

TASTE RECEPTOR CELLS	TASTES DETECTED	EXAMPLES AT YOUR GROCERY STORE
Sweetness	Sugars	Sugary cereals, cookies, cakes, flavored yogurts
Saltiness	Salts	Chips, crackers, macaroni & cheese
Sourness	Acids	Lemons, limes, sour candies
Bitterness	Plant alkaloids	Coffee, dark chocolate, arugula
Umami (?)	Savory proteins (MSG)	Beef, chicken, mushrooms, soy

gustation
The sense of taste.

LIFE HACK 3.3

If you eat healthier foods consistently for a long time, your taste preferences will eventually change too. You will like the healthier foods more and like the unhealthy foods less.

(Tuorila, 2010; Mattes, 1997; Sullivan & Birch, 1990).

downside too: if chocolate chip cookies taste not just good, but irresistible, there's a chance that supertasters will eat more than they should. Another downside has to do with green leafy vegetables like spinach and kale—their characteristic bitter tastes comes across to supertasters as extra-bitter, which means supertasters are less likely to eat them and enjoy their health benefits (Prescott, 2010).

The Influence of Experience on Taste. Just as experience can shape how you see, hear, and smell, experience can shape how you taste as well (Wardle et al., 2003; Prescott et al., 1997). It is no secret that people from different cultures enjoy different foods. The reason people come to prefer certain foods is largely exposure: what they ate as kids. Exposure, or lack thereof, may explain why certain tastes that typically come along later in life, like coffee, alcohol, and fancy chocolates and cheeses, often take a while to become acquired tastes. Check Show Me More 3.3 for a global sampling, including photos, of what kids around the world eat for breakfast. It's not all Cheerios or bacon and eggs.

DIVERSITY MATTERS

If your diet is less than perfect, the good news is that changing what you eat, and maintaining those changes over time can actually change your preferences. If you lay off the Lay's potato chips for a while, you'll eventually find them less appetizing—too salty or too heavy for your new taste (Tuorila, 2010; Mattes, 1997). In one study, 4- and 5-year-old kids were given only one kind of tofu—sweetened, salty, or plain—15 times over several weeks. By the end of the study, kids had developed a greater preference for the kind they were exposed to, but not the others—an important lesson for how you feed your kids and yourself (Sullivan & Birch, 1990).

CHECK YOUR LEARNING:

3.22 What is olfaction?

3.23 How do olfaction receptor cells work?

3.24 How does olfaction relate to sex?

3.25 How do olfaction abilities vary across people?

3.26 What is gustation?

3.27 What are the four basic qualities that taste buds can detect and what is the fifth possible quality?

3.28 How can experience influence taste?

Other Senses

YOU WILL LEARN:

3.29 what your somatosenses are.

3.30 what your kinesthetic sense is.

3.31 what your vestibular sense is.

It is not just the holes in your head that draw in important sensory information. Your entire body does. Let's start our exploration of these bodily senses with a focus on what your skin takes in.

Skin Deep: Your Somatosenses

Your **somatosenses** are the senses you experience through your skin, primarily touch, temperature, and pain. Other senses, like itch, tickle, and tingle, are somatosenses too, but because they are so sparsely researched by psychologists, we won't cover them in detail (Carstens, 2010).

somatosenses
The senses experienced through the skin, primarily touch, temperature, and pain.

Touch. Your skin consists of two primary layers: the epidermis, visible on the outside, and the dermis below it (Linden, 2015; Weisenberger, 2001). Your skin has separate receptor cells for touch (mechanoreceptors), temperature (thermoreceptors), and pain (nociceptors) (Klatzky & Lederman, 2010). So if something makes you feel all three sensations—like a snowball in the face—it is because all three kinds of receptor cells were activated. You use those receptor cells to very quickly detect a

lot of information about the objects you touch, including their size, shape, weight, texture, and more. Because of that, you're good at recognizing objects by touch when you can't see them. In fact, research shows that common household objects are typically recognized within 3 seconds with an accuracy rate of about 95% (Hsiao, 2010). For those who rely more on touch than other senses—like a person who is blind feeling the contours of the face of a loved one—recognition by touch is undoubtedly even more impressive.

Your touch (or tactile) receptors detect not only whether you are being touched, but how much pressure is being applied and whether the touch is accompanied by movement (Cholewiak & Cholewiak, 2010). People who study touch consider lots of variables about the way things feel against your skin, including how rough or smooth it is (sandpaper vs. satin sheets), how hard or soft it is (granite countertops vs. sofa cushions), and how sticky or slippery it is (chewed gum vs. a stick of butter). They also consider how the surface goes up and down in ridges, bumps, and other patterns (Hollins, 2010).

A snowball in the face will activate all three types of receptor cells in your skin: touch (mechanoreceptors), temperature (thermoreceptors), and pain (nociceptors). Cultura RM/Alamy

One measure of the strength of your sense of touch is called the grating orientation discrimination test. If you took this test, you'd be blindfolded and then touch objects that feature a pattern of ridges and grooves. The challenge is to say what direction the ridges and groove run. If the object is a George Foreman grill, it's easy, because those ridges and grooves are big enough for your fingers to ride over like a roller coaster. But as they get smaller (picture the ridges in corduroy pants), the challenge gets tougher. Generally, the limit is around the point when the grooves are narrower than 1 mm (Bensmaia, 2010).

Another measure of tactile sensory ability is the two-point threshold test. This is a simple test in which a device with two points—a lot like the compass you may have used in your geometry class—is placed on your skin. The question is how far apart the points need to be in order for you to perceive them as two points rather than one. Different parts of your body produce different results. Parts that are extremely sensitive to touch, like the fingers, lips, and cheeks, require a distance of just a few millimeters. Parts that are less sensitive, like the back, calf, and upper arm, require multiple centimeters (Bensmaia, 2010; Mather, 2011). Check **Figure 3.15** for more. And see the Watching Psychology box on sports and the benefits of touching.

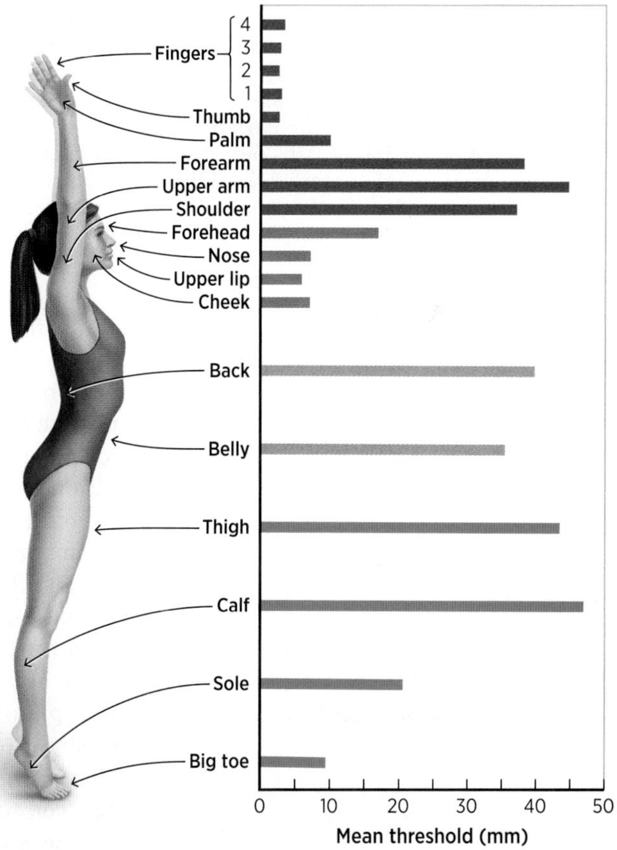

FIGURE 3.15 Touch Sensitivity of Different Skin Regions. How far apart do two simultaneous touches have to be for you to detect that they are two rather than one? On more sensitive areas of your skin, like your fingers and face, just a few millimeters. On less sensitive areas of your skin, like your legs and back, a lot more. Sources: Mather, 2011; Bensmaia, 2010.

Temperature. Your skin senses temperature through two types of thermoreceptors, each of which is specially designed to detect either hot or cold (but not both). A cluster of these on a particular area of your skin is known as a cold spot or a hot spot. Overall, your skin has more cold spots than hot spots, and certain areas on your body, including some on your forearm, likely have postage-stamp-sized regions where hot spots are completely absent (Green, 2004). Your cold thermoreceptors get their input to your brain about 10 times faster than your hot thermoreceptors do. Your face, especially your lips and cheeks, are among the most sensitive to temperature changes in either direction; your extremities, especially your feet, are least sensitive (Jones, 2010).

Pain. Unlike touch and temperature, pain is difficult to measure, which poses a significant challenge to researchers who try to study it (Turk & Melzack, 2011; Cervero, 2013). There is no such thing as an objective, accurate "pain meter," no equivalent to pounds of pressure for touch or degrees for temperature. Instead, the experience of pain is highly subjective.

Sometimes, the same injury causes one person excruciating pain and another person none, such as two same-age children who receive the same shot from their pediatrician. Sometimes, an injury causes pain well after it occurs, when the person

WATCHING PSYCHOLOGY

More Touch, More Wins?

When you watch basketball on TV, you see lots of touching—not just players committing fouls, setting screens, or boxing out for rebounds, which are all part of the game—but extra, intentional touching. To congratulate, console, or celebrate, teammates touch in all kinds of ways: high fives, chest bumps, flying shoulder bumps, head slaps, and bear hugs. A team of psychological researchers wondered, Do teams that touch more win more? (Kraus et al., 2010).

To answer this question, these researchers watched TV broadcasts of a game featuring each of the 30 NBA teams early in the 2008–2009 season. Every time two teammates touched, they counted it. Then they compared touchy-feely teams to non-touchy-feely teams in a couple of ways. First, they looked at just the five games immediately following the one they watched. They found that teams with winning records in that five-game span touched about 50% more than teams with losing records. Next they waited until the season ended and correlated the amount of touch with the total number of wins. That correlation was strongly positive (.42), indicating that the extent to which teammates touched each other during that early season game predicted the number of wins that team would earn throughout the season. (When they calculated that correlation, they took into account the team's success so far as a way to eliminate the explanation that playing well comes first and touching follows.)

Of course, it's important to keep in mind that a strong correlation does not necessarily indicate cause. To assume that touch *causes* success on the basketball court, based only on the results of this study, would be flawed scientific logic. It could be that success on the basketball court causes more touching or that both variables are influenced by a third variable outside the scope of this study. However, the finding that NBA teammates who touch each other more also succeed more does raise some interesting questions. For example, could the same correlation be true for other teams as well, including not only sports teams, but teams or groups who work together in any activity?

Touch is important even among professional sports teams. Research indicates that successful NBA teams, like the Golden State Warriors, tend to high-five, hug, and otherwise touch each other more than less successful teams (Kraus et al., 2010). Getty Images Sport/Getty Images

can shift attention away from the task at hand, such as when a soldier gets injured on the battlefield but only feels pain after reaching safety. Sometimes, the experience of pain can depend upon expectation, such as the difference between soreness that comes the day after a grueling workout and similar soreness that arises for no apparent reason. It is clear that pain serves an adaptive purpose in the evolutionary sense, steering us away from things and situations that could harm or kill us, but it is unclear why we experience it in such idiosyncratic ways (Eccleston & Crombez, 1999).

Psychologists and other researchers have offered many theories to explain pain. None is perfect, but one that has powerfully influenced our understanding of pain for decades is the *gate control theory of pain* (Melzack & Wall, 1967; Nathan, 1976; Moayedi & Davis, 2013). The basic idea of the gate control theory of pain is that pain has three dimensions (Rollman, 2010; Melzack & Wall, 2008; Melzack & Casey, 1968):

1. The sensory–discriminative system identifies where pain is and how bad it is (how the pain feels).
2. The motivational–affective system produces the emotions you have about pain (how having the pain makes you feel).
3. The cognitive–evaluative system determines your interpretation and response to pain (how you think about and what you do about the pain).

The presence of these three dimensions of pain can at least partially explain why pain can be so subjective. It is not just about what happened to your body, such as the severity of the ankle sprain, the number of stitches, or the size of the bruise.

It is also about the thoughts and feelings you have about the pain ("Oh no—this is a catastrophe!" vs. "This will be a minor hassle for a couple of days"). Additionally, it is about your response ("I'm helpless—there's nothing I can do about it" vs. "I'll get medical attention, get educated about it, and do what I can to minimize it"). Although gate control theory has needed some updates since its introduction in the 1960s, and improvements in technology have allowed for more details about the neurological basis of pain, it remains a strong guide to our understanding of pain (Mendell, 2014).

One particularly vexing question about pain that gate control theory (or any other theory) cannot fully explain is *phantom limb pain*. Phantom limb pain is felt in a part of the body that no longer exists, such as an amputee feeling pain in the arm or leg that was amputated. Amputees feel other sensations in their phantom limbs as well, but pain, unfortunately, is relatively common and at times excruciating. Similar experiences are often described in people whose limbs are still there but do not function because of paralysis from a brain or spinal cord injury (Brugger, 2010; Lackner, 2010a).

What little research has been done on phantom limb pain suggests that perhaps the pain has something to do with brain plasticity (as described in Chapter 2), or the brain's attempt to reorganize after the loss of the limb (Flor et al., 2006; Ramachandran & Hirstein, 1998). It also seems to relate to pain in that limb before it was lost—the more pain was present when the limb was there, the more phantom pain is likely after it's lost (Flor, 2002). Functional prostheses, or replacement body parts that keep the corresponding part of the brain active, can be helpful in some cases (Brugger, 2010; Lotze et al., 1999; Foell & Flor, 2013).

Tightrope walkers depend heavily on their kinesthetic sense to know precisely the location and movement of each body part and on their vestibular sense to maintain balance. Photolibrary/Getty Images

On the Move and in Balance: Your Kinesthetic Sense and Vestibular Sense

Your **kinesthetic sense** is your sense of the position and movement of your body parts. Your kinesthetic sense comes from sensors in the muscles, tendons, and joints throughout your body (Reed, 2010; Lackner, 2010b). Closely related is your **vestibular sense**: your sense of balance. Your vestibular system is largely located in your inner ear (Lackner, 2010c). Together, your kinesthetic sense and vestibular sense provide you with constant feedback about the position of your body and each of its parts, including the direction each is moving and the speed with which that movement is happening.

You typically take kinesthetic sense and vestibular sense for granted, but you notice them from time to time. For example, if you are sitting in an adjustable desk chair and it suddenly drops from one height to another, you notice yourself sinking, even if your eyes are closed. If your alarm beeps but you don't want to get up, you can reach your hand toward it to hit the snooze without even opening your eyes because you know where your hand is in space. If an earthquake rattles your room, even without any of the sights or sounds you'd experience at the time, your body would tell you that you're being shaken.

Even when you're taking in visual information, your kinesthetic and vestibular senses provide additional information about where you are, especially related to landmarks you come across (Chance et al., 1998). In one study, researchers led participants along an unfamiliar pathway on a college campus, passing landmarks like a water fountain, a courtyard, a fence, a restroom, and a set of stairs. These participants wore a video recording device over both eyes that included a screen, so they saw only what was on the screen rather than seeing the environment directly. Later, a different group of participants sat in the lab and watched the videos that the first group made. Both groups were later tested on their knowledge of the route. The first group—those who actually walked the route—did much better. They made fewer mistakes when asked to point from one landmark to another, and also when they drew a map of the route. Both groups *saw* the route in the same way, but only the first group *felt* it with their bodily senses—kinesthetic and vestibular (Waller et al., 2004).

kinesthetic sense
The sense of the position and movement of the body parts.

vestibular sense
The sense of balance.

Researchers have found that certain experiences can affect your kinesthetic or vestibular senses. On the downside, multiple injuries can inhibit your kinesthetic sense. One study focused on participants who had sprained one ankle, but not the other, between 2 and 20 times. These participants sat in a chair in which their vision of their lower bodies was blocked. The experimenter made slight turns of each ankle and found that it took much more of a turn for participants to notice a change in the position of their often-injured ankle than in their never-injured ankle. The injuries had reduced their kinesthetic sensitivity in their bad ankles (Garn & Newton, 1988). On the upside, certain training experiences can boost your kinesthetic or vestibular senses. For example, practicing the martial art of tai chi can improve your kinesthetic sense and balance (Wu, 2002; Jacobson et al., 1997).

CHECK YOUR LEARNING:

3.29 What are your somatosenses?

3.30 What is your kinesthetic sense?

3.31 What is your vestibular sense and where is it located?

CHAPTER SUMMARY

The Fundamentals of Sensation and Perception

3.1 Sensation is the ability of your sensory organs to pick up energy in the environment around you and transmit it to your brain. Perception is the ability of your brain to interpret the raw sensations it has taken in.

3.2 Human sensation and perception evolved in ways that have been critical for survival.

3.3 Absolute threshold is the minimum level of a stimulus necessary for you to detect its presence at least half of the time. Difference threshold (or just noticeable difference) is the smallest change in a stimulus necessary for you to detect that change at least half of the time.

3.4 Sensory adaptation is the tendency of your sensation of a stimulus to decrease when the stimulus remains constant.

3.5 Perceptual constancy is your brain's ability to maintain the same perception of an object even when conditions around it cause it to produce different sensations.

3.6 Selective attention is paying more attention to one sensory channel than others. Sensory interaction is the idea that your senses can affect each other in often interesting ways.

3.7 In bottom-up processing, what you sense becomes a perception with no influence from expectations or previous experiences. In top-down processing, your expectations or previous experiences influence what you perceive.

Vision

3.8 Each sense is important, but people are influenced by what they see more than by what they hear, smell, taste, or touch.

3.9 The cornea is a thin, transparent cover for the eye that bends images to improve vision. Just behind the cornea is the iris, a colored circular muscle in the center of the eye. The iris opens and closes the pupil in the middle of the eye. The lens is a clear layer beneath the surface of the eye that helps to maintain focus by varying its shape. The retina is the rear part of the eyeball, which receives visual stimuli and sends them to the brain via the optic nerve. The retina contains receptor cells called rods and cones, which helps to see visual stimuli under varying conditions. The fovea is a part of the retina that contains many cones but no rods, and the blind spot is a part of the retina that contains no rods or cones. There are three types of eye movements that help people to see: (1) saccadic, (2) compensatory, and (3) vergence.

3.11 Depth perception is the ability to judge the distance and depth of objects. It depends on monocular and binocular depth cues, as well as retinal disparity.

3.12 Hue is the color of light, as determined by its wavelength. The two competing theories of color vision are trichromatic theory, which is based on the idea that cones are specialized to sense either red, green, or blue, and opponent-process theory, which is based on the idea that cones are specialized to sense specific opposite pairs of colors (like red–green and blue–yellow).

3.13 Factors such as proximity, similarity, common fate, connectedness, and closure help people to determine whether objects are separate or part of a group.

3.14 People view certain objects in specialized ways, particularly faces, bodies, and maybe words.

3.15 Cultural influences how and what people perceive, including color vision and focus on isolated objects versus objects in relation to each other.

Hearing

3.16 Audition is your sense of hearing.

3.17 The outer ear, called the pinna, consists of the parts of the ear that you can easily touch. The middle ear is made up of the tympanic membrane, the ossicles, and the oval window membrane. The inner ear primarily consists of the cochlea, which sends sound waves to the brain by way of the auditory nerve

3.18 Pitch is the description of how "high" or "low" a sound is. There are two competing theories that explain how we perceive pitch: place theory and frequency theory.

3.19 To determine sound location, or where a sound originates, your brain measures the discrepancy between the sound's arrival times at your left ear and right ear.

3.20 Research suggests that speech perception is a specialized human ability.

3.21 Many variables influence hearing, including gender and exposure to specific cultural sounds.

Smell and Taste

3.22 Olfaction is your sense of smell.

3.23 Hundreds of types of olfaction receptor cells blend input to create each smell sensation.

3.24 Olfaction plays a significant role in sexual attraction and mating in many species, including humans.

3.25 Age and gender are variables that influence sense of smell.

3.26 Gustation is your sense of taste.

3.27 Your tongue's taste buds can detect at least four basic qualities (sweet, sour, salty, and bitter) and possibly a fifth (umami).

3.28 Experience shapes how people taste. People from different cultures enjoy different foods, which is largely due to exposure.

Other Senses

3.29 Somatosenses are the senses you experience through your skin, primarily touch, temperature, and pain.

3.30 Kinesthetic sense is your sense of the position and movement of body parts, which comes from sensors in the muscles, tendons, and joints.

3.31 Vestibular sense is your sense of balance. The vestibular system is largely located in the inner ear.

KEY TERMS

sensation, p. 69
transduction, p. 69
perception, p. 69
extrasensory perception (ESP), p. 69
parapsychology, p. 69
absolute threshold, p. 69
difference threshold (just noticeable difference), p. 70
sensory adaptation, p. 70
perceptual constancy, p. 70
selective attention, p. 73
cocktail party effect, p. 73
sensory interaction, p. 73
sensory conflict theory, p. 74
bottom-up processing, p. 74
top-down processing, p. 74
perceptual set, p. 74
change blindness, p. 74
inattentional blindness, p. 74
vision, p. 77
cornea, p. 77
iris, p. 77
pupil, p. 79
lens, p. 79
visual accommodation, p. 79
retina, p. 79
rods, p. 79
cones, p. 79
fovea, p. 79
blind spot, p. 79
depth perception, p. 80
monocular depth cues, p. 80
binocular depth cues, p. 80
retinal disparity (stereopsis), p. 80
hue, p. 80
trichromatic theory of color vision, p. 83
opponent-process theory of color vision, p. 83
figure-ground organization, p. 83
gestalt, p. 83
audition, p. 87
pinna, p. 87
tympanic membrane, p. 87
ossicles, p. 88
oval window membrane, p. 88
cochlea, p. 88
pitch, p. 88
place theory, p. 88
frequency theory, p. 88
sound localization, p. 88
olfaction, p. 91
cilia, p. 91
olfactory bulbs, p. 91
olfactory cortex, p. 91
gustation, p. 93
somatosenses, p. 94
kinesthetic sense, p. 97
vestibular sense, p. 97

SELF-ASSESSMENT

1. ______ is the ability of your sensory organs to pick up energy in the environment around the body and transmit it to your brain.

2. Your ability to determine whether the amount of salt varies between two potato chips indicates your ______. Your ability to determine whether salt is present at all on a potato chip indicates your ______.
   a. difference threshold; absolute threshold
   b. absolute threshold; difference threshold
   c. perceptual constancy; extrasensory perception (ESP)
   d. cocktail party effect; top-down processing

3. When you are in a noisy crowd of people, you have the ability to tune out other conversations to concentrate on yours, yet you may also notice your name if it is mentioned in another conversation. This experience describes
   a. sensory conflict theory.
   b. perceptual constancy.
   c. the cocktail party effect.
   d. change blindness.

4. When you tell someone your eye color, you're really telling them the color of your ______, the circular muscle in the center of your eye.
   a. retina
   b. lens
   c. cornea
   d. iris

5. Cones are receptor cells
   a. in your nose.
   b. in your ear.
   c. in your eye that detect shades of gray.
   d. in your eye that detect color.

6. ______ is an organized whole that is perceived as different from just the sum of its parts.

7. What's the function of your pinna?
   a. to enhance the ability of your taste buds
   b. to guide sound in the environment toward your inner ear
   c. to enlarge or shrink the opening in your iris to adjust the amount of light your eye takes in
   d. to form tiny scent-seeking threads that extend from olfactory receptors through the mucus of your nose

8. The ______ is the spiral fluid-filled structure in your inner ear that sends sound waves to the brain via the auditory nerve.

9. ______ is your sense of smell.

10. A person experiencing problems with the vestibular sense is most likely to have
    a. a very high difference threshold when tasting food.
    b. a tendence to fall down because of an inability to stay balanced.
    c. extreme sensitivity to temperature.
    d. an inability to detect scents.

Self-Assessment Answers

1. Sensation, 2. a, 3. c, 4. d, 5. d, 6. Gestalt, 7. b, 8. cochlea, 9. Olfaction, 10. b

WHAT'S YOUR TAKE?

1. Experience shapes your difference thresholds. What do you have a lot of experience with? Do you have a difference threshold to match? Do you have areas of expertise in which you can notice subtle differences where other people wouldn't? Perhaps you drink lots of bottled water and can detect big differences between brands that your friends don't notice. Maybe you've used many different types of headphones, and you have developed a sensitivity to each pair's ability to deliver bass and treble while your friends think they're all the same. Maybe you're a barbecue expert who tastes the difference between sauces, even if they claim to be the same flavor.

2. Young babies all respond similarly to various kinds of music, but they soon become accustomed to music from their own culture. Do you know from your parents or other caretakers how this worked in your life? Did your earliest months and years make you more familiar with certain scales, rhythms, or styles of music? If you were surrounded by rap, pop, country, classical, or jazz, how does that shape the way you respond to those kinds of music now?

SHOW ME MORE

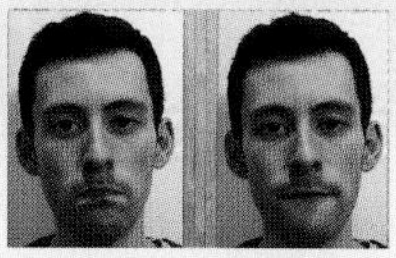

3.1 The McGurk Effect: Does Lipreading Override Hearing?

launchpadworks.com LaunchPad macmillan learning

This brief video illustrates the McGurk effect.

Timothy Revell

3.2 Mudsplashes, Gorillas, and Change Blindness

http://tiny.cc/showmemore

This video gives you a chance to experience change blindness for yourself.

Visual Generation/Shutterstock

3.3 Breakfast Around the World

http://tiny.cc/0n5njy

This article illustrates the wide range of food preferences around the world with photos and descriptions of kids' breakfast foods in various countries.

Zurijeta/Shutterstock

4 Consciousness

Dragon Images/Shutterstock

You will find Mammoth Cave National Park in southern Kentucky, about halfway between Louisville and Nashville. The cave attracts thousands of visitors every year to explore its 400-mile maze of pitch-black pathways. For over a hundred years, out-of-town visitors to the cave have stayed at the Mammoth Cave Hotel, where the rooms feature a mini-fridge, a coffee maker, and satellite TV.

In June 1938, Nathaniel Kleitman and Bruce Richardson visited Mammoth Cave, but they didn't stay in Mammoth Cave Hotel. They stayed in the cave itself. In the dark. For over a month.

Kleitman was a professor at the University of Chicago and a pioneer of sleep research. Kleitman and Richardson, his student, lived in Mammoth Cave as an early attempt to understand why we sleep when we do. They wondered: If we stay in a chamber deep inside a cave for weeks, with no sunlight or stars to indicate day or night, will we still sleep and awaken on the same 24-hour schedule? Could we shift to a different schedule—for example, one that lasts 28 hours—and, if so, what would be the consequences of such a shift? The study produced mixed results, as the younger Richardson had more flexibility in his sleep-wake pattern, while the older Kleitman was more closely tied to he standard 24-hour schedule. More important, though, the study was a major early step into the largely unexplored science of sleep. In his later experiments, Kleitman took more adventurous steps in the study of leep: Keeping himself awake for a week straight, spending two weeks in a submarine, and taking his family to a town in Norway above the Arctic Circle to live for two months in constant sunlight (Gottesmann, 2013; Wolf-Meyer, 2013; Kleitman & Kleitman, 1953; Kleitman, 1963).

Research on sleep has progressed significantly since the Mammoth Cave experiment. Of course, research on sleep is just one type of research on *consciousness*, the focus of this chapter. Consciousness is basically awareness—of what's happening around you and inside of you. And sleep is just one state of consciousness. In this chapter, we'll cover many varieties of consciousness. We'll examine what contemporary researchers have learned about sleep and the biological rhythms that ffect it. We'll explore insomnia and other sleep-related problems, including why they happen and how they can be treated. We'll consider drugs, both legal and illegal, that influence consciousness. And we'll onsider other topics related to consciousness too, including hypnosis, meditation, mindfulness, déjà vu, and near-death experiences.

CHAPTER OUTLINE

Consciousness is your awareness of yourself and your surroundings. That definition may make the concept seem simple, but many different experts offer many different definitions of consciousness (Velmans, 2009; Vimal, 2009). Some experts say that the main ingredients of consciousness are the ability to monitor and control what's going on both inside and outside your mind (Kihlstrom, 2007). Other experts say the ability to think about thinking (yours and others') is at the heart of consciousness (Corballis, 2007). Still others say that what makes you conscious is your ability to pick up on intention: what you intend to do and what others intend to do (Bering & Bjorklund, 2007). The common thread across the many definitions of consciousness is awareness, or an ability to recognize and be responsive to what's happening in and around you.

Let's take a more detailed look at the state of consciousness that has been most extensively studied by psychologists and other researchers: sleep.

Sleep

YOU WILL LEARN:

4.1 why you sleep.

4.2 how sleep deprivation affects you.

4.3 what your circadian rhythm is and what influences it.

4.4 what the stages of normal sleep are.

4.5 how sleep differs across various groups of people.

4.6 what co-sleeping is and how common it is.

4.7 what various sleep abnormalities are.

4.8 how to prevent and treat sleep problems.

Everybody sleeps. And not just people—other mammals, birds, and reptiles sleep too. There is some evidence that amphibians and fish also sleep or at least do something similar (Lesku et al., 2006; Rattenborg et al., 2009; Rattenborg, 2007). Even insects have daily patterns of high activity followed by less activity or rest. In fact, sleep "appears to provide restoration for all living organisms. Even plants have a time-keeping … mechanism allowing them to 'anticipate' daily changes in light and temperature" (Espie & Morin, 2012, p. 1).

Some animals, including certain species of birds, whales, dolphins, and porpoises, can actually sleep with one eye open (Peigneux et al., 2012; Lyamin et al., 2008; Siegel, 2005). For example, consider mallard ducks. When they gather together to sleep, the mallards on the left edge of the pack sleep with their left eye open and the mallards on the right side sleep with the right eye open, all for the purpose of looking out for predators approaching from that side. Sleeping with one eye open is called *unihemispheric sleep*, a practice that allows the half of the brain opposite the closed eye to rest while the half opposite the open eye remains alert. By the way, the mallards in the middle sleep with both eyes shut (*bihemispheric sleep*), confident that their partners on the edges are protecting them (Rattenborg et al., 1999; Lima et al., 2005).

In humans, there have been some significant changes in sleep throughout our long history. For Neanderthals (70,000–40,000 B.C.), sleep was probably similar to the way nonhuman primates still sleep now—lots of little sleeps, including many during

IT'S LIKE...

Consciousness Is Like a Light Controlled by a Dimmer

It is easy to think of consciousness like a light switch, something that is on when you're awake and off when you are asleep. But it would be more accurate to think of consciousness as a dimmer, something that can be adjusted to any level. Of course, sleep and wakefulness are common levels of consciousness, but they are not the only ones. There are lower levels of consciousness than sleep. Remember, even when you sleep, you are conscious enough to respond if the fire alarm blares in your ear or your phone's vibrations shake the bed or the bright sunlight streams through a crack in the blinds onto your closed eyes. That is not true for a person in a coma or under anesthesia for a medical operation.

There are also levels of consciousness between sleep and wakefulness—that gray area of brief experiences like daydreaming, half-sleeping before you actually drift off, and half-awakening as sleep comes to an end (LaBerge, 2007; Gurstelle & De Oliveira, 2004; Gillespie, 1997). And in some cultures, there are higher levels of consciousness than merely being awake. For example, Buddhists describe higher states of consciousness that stem from transcending the material world and that can break the chains that bind us to suffering (Patel, 2012).

daytime hours. (Ever go to the zoo and find the chimpanzees or baboons dozing through a sunny afternoon?) By the Neolithic period (around 10,000 B.C.), humans were increasingly getting all of their z's in one big nighttime session and staying awake through most, if not all, of the day (Espie & Morin, 2012). That was true until a recent development on the human timeline: the invention of the electric light bulb. Artificial light meant that the setting of the sun did not require the end of a day's activity. So more than humans could before, we stayed up well into the night—working, reading, attending baseball games under the lights—and slept well into the morning (Thorpy, 2010).

consciousness
A person's awareness of his or her self and surroundings.

Why Do We Sleep?

We spend one-third of our lives sleeping, but researchers don't have a clear-cut explanation for why (Frank, 2006a). There is no shortage of sleep theories, but so far, none of these theories can fully explain the function of sleep. An obvious answer is that we sleep to rest, to give the body and brain some time off from the heavy use they get during our busy days. But sleep is much more than rest. (If you're doubtful, spend tonight just resting—awake—rather than sleeping, then see how refreshed you feel and how well you function the next day.)

Sleep Theories and Evolution. Many sleep theories emphasize evolution. After all, this widespread behavior must have provided some adaptive advantage to our species. But what, exactly, could that advantage be?

Staying Still. *Inactivity theory* suggests that the main advantage of sleep is simply staying still during the dark hours of night, which kept our ancestors out of danger. In the dark of night, early humans couldn't do much good in terms of hunting or gathering, but they could do a lot of harm in terms of injury, getting lost, or falling prey to animals that see well at night (Siegel, 2009). However, inactivity theory doesn't explain why sleep, which makes us mostly unaware of our surroundings, is better than merely resting while awake.

Saving Energy. *Energy conservation theory* highlights the fact that we spend far fewer calories when asleep than when awake. This was a crucial difference for our ancestors, who didn't have a refrigerator full of food or a 24-hour grocery store down the street (Schmidt, 2014; Penev, 2007). Energy conservation theory considers sleep a type of nightly mini-hibernation.

Recharging the Body. *Restorative theory* suggests that sleep allows the body to recharge and strengthen itself, an idea supported by the fact that good sleep boosts the immune system, speeds recovery from injury and illness, and activates human growth hormone (Siegel, 2005; Bryant et al., 2004).

Developing the Brain. *Brain plasticity theory* emphasizes the fact that sleep allows the brain to change, grow, and reorganize itself, which makes sense when you notice how much babies sleep during those early months when the brain is growing so quickly (Frank, 2006b).

Enhancing Memory. *Evolutionary theory* points out that sleep is essential for consolidating memories and for resting our vision system (Walker, 2012; Kavanau, 2004, 2005, 2006, 2008; Diekelmann & Born, 2010). It is noteworthy that vision is the only sense that shuts off entirely when you sleep: Hearing, smell, taste, and touch stay on, at least to a limited extent. By shutting off vision when you sleep, your brain gets time to process all of the visual images you've taken in during the day. It is like filling the memory of your phone with video all day, and then giving your phone a break from recording at night while all of that video gets downloaded to your computer's hard drive. Interestingly, researchers who studied a particular species of fish found that those who live near the surface of the water, where light allows them to see, sleep far more than those who live in caves, where darkness prevents sight (Duboué et al., 2011). Other researchers have refuted this idea, pointing out that some animals rely heavily on the visual system yet don't sleep as much as might be expected (Harrison, 2012; Capellini et al., 2008).

All humans sleep. So do mammals, birds, reptiles, and many other forms of life.
(From top) Image Source/Getty Images; iStock/Getty Images; PhotoAlto Agency RF Collections/Getty Images

MY TAKE VIDEO 4.1

Sleep Deprivation

"I don't get enough sleep because..."

YOUTUBE: http://tiny.cc/mytake
LAUNCHPAD: launchpadworks.com

Sleep Deprivation. All of these sleep theories make sense, and each is supported by some scientific evidence. However, no one sleep theory eclipses the others, so the puzzle of sleep remains unsolved. Most likely, the full answer involves a combination of these advantages, as well as others still to be identified by researchers (Frank, 2010). But there's one thing we know for sure: When you don't get enough sleep, you feel it. **Sleep deprivation** is the failure to get enough sleep, regardless of the reason.

Sleep deprivation is remarkably common in the United States, with about 50 million to 70 million of us getting too little sleep on a regular basis (Committee on Sleep Medicine and Research, 2006). That number cuts across all of us in terms of gender, age, and culture, but the rates for women and older adults are especially high (Lichstein et al., 2004). Unfortunately, the consequences of sleep deprivation are far-reaching in terms of how you feel and how you perform. For example, sleep deprivation causes irritability and moodiness (Hall et al., 2012). In one study of 750 teenagers, the day after a bad night's sleep featured significantly higher levels of anxiety than the day after a good night's sleep (Fuligni & Hardway, 2006). Similar results were found in studies of college students and medical residents (Zohar et al., 2005; Galambos et al., 2009).

Sleep deprivation wrecks not just your feelings but your performance too. Your brain is simply not as sharp and not as quick when it operates on too little sleep. There are four reasons why (Monk, 2012):

1. **Cognitive slowing.** Your neurons and the connections between them just don't function as fast when you are sleep deprived. You notice this when you play Tetris or any other game that involves repetitive fast responding. Poor sleep the night before rarely results in good gaming.
2. **Cognitive rigidity.** Lack of sleep kills your creativity. You are less likely to create an original masterpiece or even offer witty comments when talking with your friends if you haven't slept well.
3. **Decreased motivation.** It is not just that you can't perform well when you're sleepy; it is also that you don't *care* that much about your poor performance when you're sleepy. As a result, your decreased effort compounds your poor performance.
4. **Likelihood of unintended sleep.** The day after a sleepless night, there's a greater chance that you'll doze off—or at least daydream or space out a lot—which interferes with performance.

LIFE HACK 4.1

Avoid sleep deprivation, which causes real impairment in memory, attention, reasoning, and mood. It happens not only if you pull an all-nighter but also if you string together consecutive nights of insufficient sleep.

(Von Dongen et al., 2003; Lim & Dinges, 2010; Monk, 2012; Hall et al., 2012)

Aside from the occasional all-nighter, complete sleep deprivation is, thankfully, a relatively uncommon occurrence for most of us. What is far more common is partial sleep deprivation, caused by a night when you hit the sack too late, get up too early, or sleep fitfully throughout the night. String together a series of nights with partial sleep deprivation, and the negative effects accumulate (Lim & Dinges, 2010). One study tracked people who were limited to 5 hours of sleep per night for a week straight and found that their alertness, memory, attention, and reasoning all worsened throughout the week (Dinges et al., 1997). Another study extended the partial sleep deprivation to 2 weeks, and the effects were even worse. Those who slept 6 hours per night during the second week performed as poorly as someone who had just pulled an all-nighter, and those who slept only 4 hours per night during the second week performed as poorly as someone who had just pulled two consecutive all-nighters (Van Dongen et al., 2003).

As the From Research to Real Life box shows, what is especially scary about these sleep deprivation studies is that sleep-deprived people often don't recognize how impaired they are (Van Dongen et al., 2003; Pilcher & Walters, 1997). When a sleep-deprived person drives a car, that lack of recognition gets dangerous (Horne & Reyner, 1999; Howard et al., 2004). One study of more than 5000 drivers found that the most sleep-deprived were the most likely to crash, whether the driver was a professional (truck or bus operator) or an ordinary car driver (Carter et al., 2003). One study estimates that in the United States, fatigue among truck drivers causes about 2700(!) highway fatalities every year (Bonnet & Arand, 1995).

FROM RESEARCH TO REAL LIFE

Do You Realize What Sleep Deprivation Does to You?

Research shows that sleep deprivation leads to crabby moods, slowed thinking, and decreased motivation. People who are sleep-deprived don't always recognize that they are sleep-deprived and that their sleep deprivation might impair them significantly (Van Dongen et al., 2003). What about college students in particular? How well do they recognize their own sleep deprivation?

One study used an overnight method to answer this question (Pilcher & Walters, 1997). The study, which involved psychology students as participants, lasted from 10 P.M. on a Friday night to 11 A.M. on Saturday morning. On Friday night, after everyone arrived at the sleep lab, they randomly sent half of the students home with the instruction to sleep a full 8 hours and then come the next day. The other half of the students stayed at the sleep lab—and stayed up—all night. They hung out, talked with each other, played video games, watched movies, or did homework, but they were not allowed go to sleep.

On Saturday morning, the students who slept at home came back, and all of the students took the same tests. These tests measured their cognitive abilities (reasoning, reading comprehension, evaluating written arguments, and logic). The students also estimated their own level of performance on the tests. The results are no surprise: The students who stayed up all night in the sleep lab performed worse on the tests. The big surprise was in the students' estimates of their own performance: Those who stayed up all night thought they did *better* than the participants who got a good night's sleep. The sleep-deprived students performed worse than their peers who got 8 hours of sleep but believed they performed better. These findings suggest sleep deprivation impairs a person's ability to recognize the effects of their own sleep deprivation. ●

Circadian Rhythm: Your Biological Clock

A good understanding of sleep requires a broader understanding of the daily pattern in which sleep is included. That pattern is controlled by your **circadian rhythm**: the 24-hour cycle on which your brain and body function. (Knowledge of Spanish can help your memory with this term: *circadian* breaks down to *circa-*, which means about, and *-dia*, which means day, so *circadian* means *about a day*.) Your circadian rhythm is what makes you predictably sleepy at certain times of the day and predictably alert at others. Most of us have circadian rhythms that fall into step with each other, and with the rhythm of the sun as well, but there is some variability. For instance, you probably know a few night owls and a few morning people.

As **Figure 4.1** shows, our alertness tends to start at around midlevel when we wake up, then rise throughout the morning, peak sometime around noon, decline through the afternoon, and drop to its lowest levels through the evening until we're back in bed. This common circadian rhythm matches the timing of car accidents: Drivers are more likely to crash late at night or early in the morning than at midday, partly because of lowered alertness at those times (Mitler et al., 1988).

MY TAKE VIDEO 4.2

Circadian Rhythm

"The last job I worked, I worked overnight, and so that kind of messed up my circadian rhythm..."

YOUTUBE: http://tiny.cc/mytake
LAUNCHPAD: launchpadworks.com

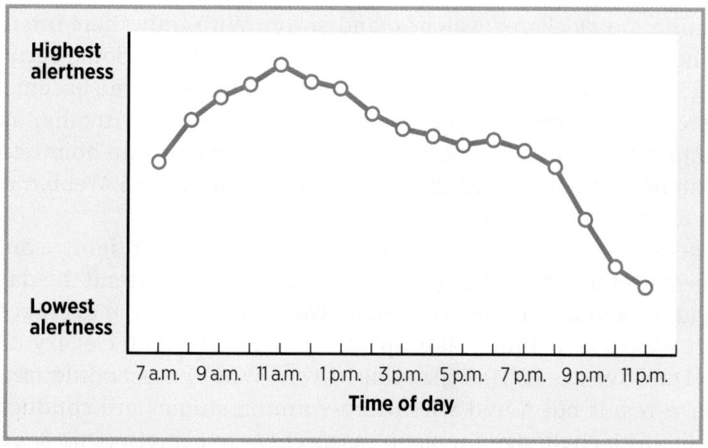

FIGURE 4.1 Alertness Through the Day and Night. During the waking hours of 7 A.M. to 11 P.M., alertness climbs through the morning, peaks around 11 A.M. or noon, fades slightly through the afternoon, and drops to its lowest levels before bedtime. Data from Monk 2012; Monk et al., 1994.

sleep deprivation
The failure to get enough sleep, regardless of the reason.

circadian rhythm
The 24-hour cycle on which the brain and body function.

WATCHING PSYCHOLOGY

What (Body Clock) Time Is Kickoff?

Imagine that you had to play an intramural flag football game at 3 A.M. And imagine that the other team had already recalibrated their body clocks to be wide awake at that time of day. Would that seem fair?

To a lesser extent, the same kind of thing happens when NFL teams from across the country play each other: Because of time zone differences, one of the teams is playing later on their own internal body clocks than the other team. That difference can be substantial, especially considering how our circadian rhythm begins to drop in the afternoon and then drops rapidly at night. One study examined 25 seasons' worth of *Monday Night Football* games, with special attention to games in which teams from the Pacific time zone (San Francisco 49ers, Seattle Seahawks, San Diego Chargers, etc.) played against teams from the Eastern time zone (New York Giants, Philadelphia Eagles, New England Patriots, etc.) (Smith et al., 1997). After taking into account other influences (the point spread, home field advantage, etc.), the researchers found that West Coast teams won more often and by more points than expected. In fact, they beat the spread about 68% of the time.

The researchers explained their findings in circadian terms. Specifically, by kickoff at 9 P.M. Eastern time, the East Coast players' circadian rhythms have dropped much lower than those of their West Coast opponents. So if the San Francisco 49ers play the New England Patriots, the 49ers are playing at 6 P.M. on their body clocks, while the Patriots are playing at 9 P.M. on their body clocks. This 3-hour difference could translate into a lapse by the Patriots—a missed field goal or a missed tackle, for example—that makes the difference in the game.

A study of Major League Baseball also found that circadian rhythms can influence who wins and who loses in that sport (Winter et al., 2009). Over 10 years and 24,000 games, teams that had a *circadian advantage*—playing a game in which their circadian rhythm has been less disrupted in the past 24 hours than their opponent's—won significantly more often than expected. This effect is slightly stronger than home field advantage. In fact, home teams tend to *lose* games when they have just returned home from another time zone if they play a visiting team that has already adjusted to that time zone. For example, if the Chicago Cubs return home to Wrigley Field (in the Central Time Zone) from a West Coast trip to play the St. Louis Cardinals, the Cubs are actually at a slight *disadvantage* if the Cardinals have played their most recent games in St. Louis, Milwaukee, or any other Central time zone location. So, the next time you watch sports on TV, don't forget about the body clock factor as you decide who to root for. ●

Research on professional football and baseball games shows that circadian rhythm can play a role in the outcome of sporting events in which one team travels across time zones to play another (Winter et al., 2009; Smith et al., 1997). Getty Images Sport/Getty Images

Sleep Studies. Since the early days of sleep research, scientists have tried to learn about circadian rhythm by conducting *free-running* sleep studies (Lack & Wright, 2012; Duffy & Dijk, 2002). In these sleep studies, people spend days or weeks in an environment devoid of time cues—no windows to reveal sunlight or darkness, no changes in internal lighting, no clocks or watches, and so on. With only their internal clock to guide them, how would these participants schedule their time? Some early attempts at free-running sleep studies, which were done in caves, bunkers, and basements, showed varied results. In some, people stuck closely to a 24-hour clock. In other sleep studies, people fell into a 25-hour rhythm, essentially waking up about an hour later every day, with a few extending the day even more than that (Aschoff, 1965; Webb & Agnew, 1974; Wever, 1984; Kleitman, 1963; Czeisler & Dijk, 2001).

More recent studies, done in professional sleep labs under tightly controlled conditions, suggest that people in free-running studies tend to extend the day, but not by much. Instead, these participants sleep and wake on a cycle that averages about 24.2 hours, which means that they wake up about 12 minutes later every day (Czeisler et al., 1999; Duffy et al., 2001; Dijk et al., 1999). Why the schedule strays from 24 hours at all—a result not found when free-running studies are conducted on mice and rats—remains a challenge for sleep researchers to explain (Dijk & Lazar, 2012).

Circadian Rhythm and Internal Forces. Your circadian rhythm is determined by two things: (1) internal forces and (2) external cues (Borbély, 1982; Saper et al., 2005).

The internal forces are driven by a very particular part of your brain: the *suprachiasmatic nucleus* (*SCN*), which is within the hypothalamus (**Figure 4.2**). This tiny structure is a mighty timekeeper. If you've ever set a daily timer for an air conditioner—programming it to be cooler at certain hours of the day and warmer at others—then you have some idea of how the SCN turns up and turns down your brain and body. The SCN actually controls a whole system of clock-like mechanisms throughout your body (known as the *peripheral* body clocks), including your digestive tract, liver, muscles, and fat tissue (Froy, 2010). In rare cases when the SCN is damaged or disrupted, major sleep-related problems occur (Menaker et al., 2013).

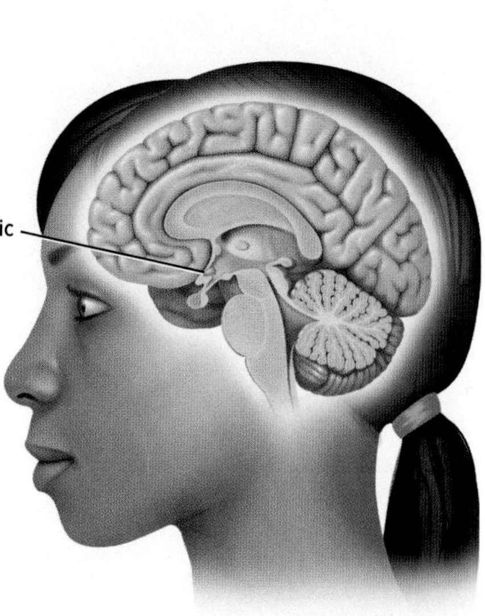

FIGURE 4.2 Suprachiasmatic Nucleus. The suprachiasmatic nucleus, a tiny structure within the hypothalamus, is the main timekeeper within your body.

Circadian Rhythm and External Cues. Your SCN is sensitive to its surroundings, which makes it more sophisticated than the 24-hour timer on an air conditioner (Asher & Sassone-Corsi, 2015). Your SCN picks up external cues such as light that might call for changes in your pattern of sleep or wakefulness (Dijk & Lazar, 2012). If your eyes take in lots of light during nighttime (or to a lesser extent, lots of darkness during daytime), your circadian rhythm adjusts slightly, as if they are pulled toward staying awake when light is available and sleeping when it's not (Duffy & Wright, 2005).

This adaptation to light and dark is probably a leftover from the evolution-based human tendency to stay awake when the sun shines and stay asleep when it doesn't. Interestingly, people who live in rural areas have circadian rhythms that match with natural sunrise–sunset patterns more than people who live in big cities, where artificial light is more inescapable (Roenneberg et al., 2007). One group of researchers took participants camping for a week, where their eyes saw no light other than the sun (and a nighttime campfire). The campers' circadian rhythms shifted noticeably during that week to synchronize with the rise and fall of the sun, which meant that they became early birds, going to sleep closer to nightfall and getting up closer to the crack of dawn than they typically did at home (Wright et al., 2013).

For you, the most important consequence of this circadian responsiveness to light might be the brightness with which you surround yourself in your day-to-day life. This light includes not just overhead lights and lamps, but the TVs, computers, and smartphones that you might stare at before bed. To your suprachiasmatic nucleus, that bright light means it is still daytime, so it tries to keep your brain and body awake. Interestingly, treatment of circadian rhythm disorders often includes bright light therapy, in which people are simply exposed to bright lights—at the right times of day—to reset their body clocks (Lack & Wright, 2012).

Another external cue that can affect your circadian rhythm is food. The time at which you eat can determine how sleepy or alert you feel throughout the day. This effect may not be evident after a single oddly timed meal—like eating a sandwich at an all-night diner at 3 A.M. However, making a consistent shift to different eating times can disrupt your circadian rhythm. In a study of rats, researchers shifted mealtime for 1 week and found that the rats' circadian rhythm was disrupted, affecting not only activity levels but also blood sugar levels and metabolism (Yoon et al., 2012).

Of course, it is harder to manipulate mealtimes in humans than in rats, but one group of researchers used an innovative method to get around that inconvenience. They followed people observing Ramadan, the month on the Islamic calendar in which Muslims don't eat or drink between sunrise and sunset. Researchers found that several signs of circadian rhythm, including the timing and amount of certain hormones, were different during Ramadan than at other times of the year (Bogdan et al., 2001). Some researchers have suggested that persistently poor "chrono-nutrition," in which the eating schedule mismatches the natural highs and lows in energy levels (and which is, unfortunately, common to many Western lifestyles) can contribute to obesity, diabetes, and cardiovascular disease (Froy, 2010; Huang et al., 2011; Maury et al., 2010; Portaluppi et al., 2012).

DIVERSITY MATTERS

Circadian rhythms are sensitive to external cues such as the rise and fall of the sun.
Iconica/Getty Images

One activity that can throw off your circadian rhythms significantly is *shift work*, particularly working the overnight shift (Richardson, 2006). Shift work reschedules when you can eat, sleep, and do almost everything else. The number of shift workers who suffer from significant problems related to sleep and wakefulness is noteworthy: 14–32% of people who consistently work overnight and 8–26% of people whose shift rotates between overnight and other times (Drake et al., 2004). The obvious reason is that the human body can only adjust so much to a schedule that strays from the sleep-when-it's-dark strategy that evolution selected for us. However, there are other reasons for this disruption too. For example, shift work often causes strain on important relationships (Vallières & Bastille-Denis, 2012; Newey & Hood, 2004). (How long could you maintain a dating relationship or a marriage if one of you worked nights and the other worked days?)

Sleeping during the day comes with practical problems too: neighbors making noise, kids demanding attention, and sunlight seeping through the windows. A variety of serious health problems, including obesity, heart problems, strokes, ulcers, and possibly cancer, happen at a high rate among shift workers (Haus & Smolensky, 2013; Manenschijn et al., 2011; Vyas et al., 2012; Newey & Hood, 2004; Reid & Zee, 2004). For women, even more health-related problems have been associated with shift work: increased menstrual pain and bleeding, irregular timing of the menstrual cycle, premature birth, and spontaneous abortion (Mahoney, 2010; Knutsson, 2003; Nurminen, 1998; Labyak et al., 2002; Chung et al., 2005; Cone et al., 1998). When shift work throws off circadian rhythms, the consequences can be much worse than just a little daytime sleepiness.

Normal Sleep

We've already mentioned sleep problems, and soon we will be covering them in even more detail. Let's focus here on what happens during normal sleep.

Stages of Sleep. At its most basic, your sleep can be divided into two types, *REM sleep* and *non-REM sleep*. **REM** is rapid eye movement, or the flitting of the eyeballs behind the eyelids during sleep. **REM sleep** is the stage of sleep in which intense brain activity and vivid dreams are most likely to occur. By contrast, **non-REM sleep** is any sleep other than REM sleep, when rapid eye movement, intense brain activity, and dreams are unlikely to occur.

As **Figure 4.3** shows, non-REM sleep can be further divided into stages (Silber et al., 2007; Rama et al., 2006; Moore, 2006). *Stage 1 sleep* is the lightest sleep, which happens right when you fall asleep and for a short time afterward (Carskadon & Dement, 1996; Ohayon et al., 2004). When you're in stage 1 sleep, you've just drifted off. You stop responding when people call your name, but if you do wake up, you may say you hadn't even been sleeping yet. *Stage 2 sleep* is a bit deeper. Your body temperature drops, your heart rate slows, and it takes more to wake you up.

Stage 3 and *stage 4* are the deepest stages of sleep and together are often called *slow-wave sleep*. In slow-wave sleep, an EEG shows that brain activity produces big, slow waves that are markedly different from any other stage of sleep or wakefulness. In slow-wave sleep, you are difficult to wake up. If you do arise from slow-wave sleep, you are likely to be confused and disoriented for a short time, a condition sleep researchers sometimes call *sleep inertia*, or being "sleep drunk" (Silva & Duffy, 2008; Wertz et al., 2006; Jewett et al., 1999).

Following stages 3 and 4 sleep is REM sleep. Following REM sleep, the whole cycle repeats again. In a typical night of high-quality sleep, the cycle lasts about 90 minutes and repeats about 5 times. The cycle differs slightly throughout the night, such that early cycles are heavier on stages 3 and 4 sleep, but later cycles are heavier on REM sleep (Peigneux et al., 2012; Feinberg & Floyd, 1979).

The discovery of REM sleep in the mid-1900s was a landmark of early sleep research, revealing a universal state of consciousness into which we all fall every night (Aserinsky & Kleitman, 1953). REM sleep features a fascinating combination of characteristics: The brain is very active (producing EEG waves that resemble those

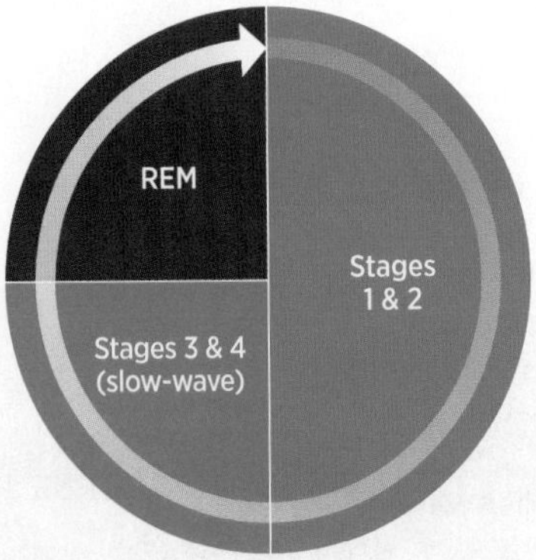

FIGURE 4.3 Type of Sleep Each Night. A typical 8-hour night of sleep consists of about 5 sleep cycles, each of which lasts about 90 minutes. As illustrated here, each cycle consists of about half stage 1 and stage 2 sleep. About a quarter is stage 3 and stage 4 sleep, and about a quarter is REM sleep.

during waking hours), but the body is completely inactive (**Figure 4.4**). That is due to **REM paralysis**: temporary immobility during REM sleep. This discrepancy between the high level of activity of your brain and the complete inactivity of your body is the reason early sleep researchers also called REM sleep *paradoxical sleep*. There is a paradox, or contradiction, between the amount of action in brain and body (Jouvet et al., 1959).

That action in your brain during REM sleep is most likely a dream (Kramer, 2006). If sleep researchers wake up somebody during REM sleep, there is about an 80% chance of the sleeper recalling a dream, a much higher chance than if the sleeper woke up during non-REM sleep (Nielsen, 1995, 2000, 2004; Vogel, 1991). You probably have experienced this. Certain mornings, the alarm wakes you up from the most vivid dream imaginable. Other mornings, the alarm catches you at a non-REM point in your sleep cycle, and you wake up empty-minded, as if you haven't dreamt all night. Early sleep researchers argued that dreams happened exclusively during REM sleep, but more recent research suggests that at least some kind of dreamlike activity also happens during other stages (Dement, 1960; De Koninck, 2012).

REM Rebound. When you don't get enough dream time one night, the next night you experience **REM rebound**: an increase in REM sleep after a period of REM sleep deprivation. REM rebound is part of the more general experience of *sleep rebound*—catching up on hours in the sack after a night (or more) in which sleep was scarce. When your body responds to a sleep debt in this way, it adds hours to your sleep total and fills those hours with a higher percentage of REM sleep than usual (Endo et al., 1998; Ocampo-Garcés et al., 2000). When this happens, your body rushes past the non-REM sleep stage more quickly than usual to get to REM sleep sooner.

In terms of more general sleep rebound, you never fully recover the lost hours of sleep. If you typically sleep 8 hours per night but pull an all-nighter on Sunday night, you won't sleep 16 hours on Monday, or somehow squeeze in all 8 of those missing hours during the rest of the week. One study found that people who were kept awake one night and were then given 24 hours straight in bed recouped only about 5–6 hours of extra sleep—far short of the full 8 hours that they lost (Rosenthal et al., 1991).

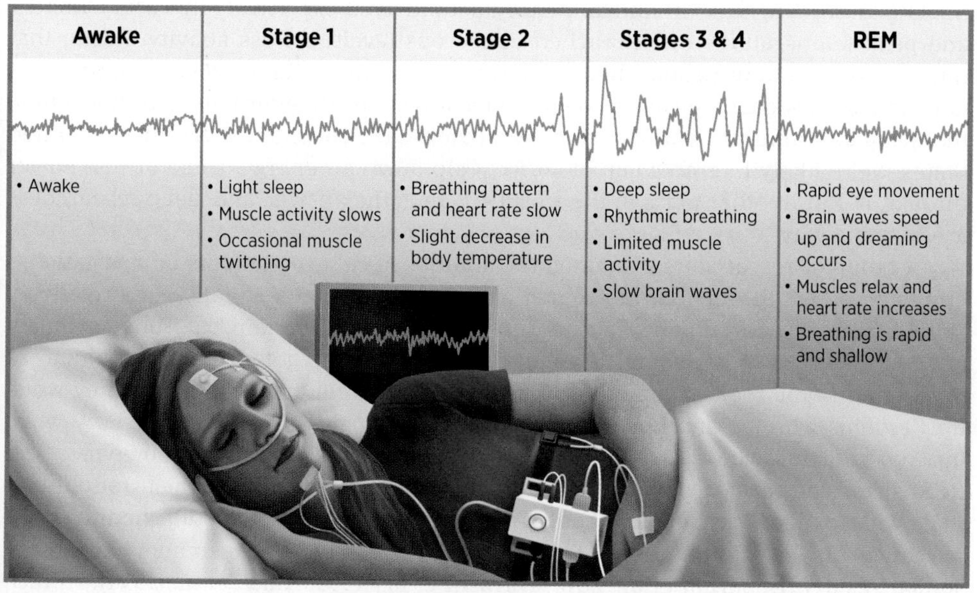

FIGURE 4.4 Sleep Waves. Stage 3 and stage 4 sleep earned the nickname slow-wave sleep because of the slower, bigger patterns they produce on EEG readings. Notice also the similarities between the waves of wakefulness and REM sleep.

CHAPTER APP 4.1

REM Sleep

Sleep Time Smart Alarm Clock
Sleep Cycle Alarm Clock

Preview one of the links and consider the following questions.

WEBSITE:
http://tiny.cc/j1h7jy
http://tiny.cc/hqh7jy

ANDROID:
http://tiny.cc/mxjyiy

IPHONE:
http://tiny.cc/frjyiy

VIDEO DEMO:
http://tiny.cc/chapterapps

These kinds of apps monitor your sleep. Specifically, they track your stages of sleep and provide you with feedback regarding how much time you spent in each stage. They also wake you up in an ideal (lighter, rather than deeper) stage of sleep.

How does it APPly to your daily life?
How could this kind of app improve your sleep, and more broadly, your life?

How does it APPly to your understanding of psychology?
How does this kind of app enhance your understanding of the various stages of sleep, including REM?

REM
Rapid eye movement, or the flitting of the eyeballs behind the eyelids during sleep.

REM sleep
The stage of sleep in which intense brain activity and vivid dreams are most likely to occur.

non-REM sleep
Any sleep other than REM sleep, when rapid eye movement, intense brain activity, and dreams are unlikely to occur.

REM paralysis
Temporary immobility during REM sleep.

REM rebound
An increase in REM sleep after a period of REM sleep deprivation.

Diversity in Normal Sleep

DIVERSITY MATTERS

We all progress through the stages of non-REM and REM sleep in the same way. However, many aspects of our sleep vary across different groups of people.

Gender and Sleep. Consider gender and sleep. Women's sleep typically contains more slow-wave sleep than men's (Dijk & Lazar, 2012). Women generally sleep for slightly longer periods than men do, but they also experience more sleep problems than men (Morgan, 2012; Groeger et al., 2004; Ursin et al., 2005; Yager, 2010). Women also experience more disruptive patterns of sleep when they are pregnant, nursing, experiencing PMS, or going through menopause, including difficulty falling asleep and staying asleep (Driver, 2012; Baker & Driver, 2004, 2007; Moline et al., 2003; Manber & Bootzin, 1997).

Ethnicity and Sleep. Let's consider how sleep differs among people of various ethnicities. In certain groups of people around the world, sleep is almost exclusively limited to a single long nighttime slumber. That is called *monophasic* sleep, and it's most common in the United States and other Western countries. In other regions, sleep is more typically *biphasic*, meaning that it happens two times per day—overnight plus a nap in the afternoon. Spain and many Spanish-speaking countries, including Mexico, are good examples of this "siesta" culture. Lots of other places around the world are neither monophasic nor biphasic but *polyphasic*, which means that they sleep not only at night and at siesta time but at various other times, often more than once during daylight hours for brief catnaps. Cultures in which polyphasic sleep is common include Japan, China, and a variety of other places around the world (Arber et al., 2012; Steger & Brunt, 2003; Steger, 2003; Richter, 2003; Brunt, 2008).

Sounds like naps are common in lots of cultures. Are naps beneficial?

Most of the research says yes (Milner & Cote, 2009). Napping enables you to catch up on (at least some) of last night's lost sleep and maintain alertness through the afternoon and evening. Another less obvious benefit of naps may be avoidance of activity in the late afternoon. Early in human history, people lived exclusively in warm climates, and peak temperatures often reached dangerous levels, so less activity during that time could have kept people safe and alive (Takahashi & Kaida, 2006). That time of day—late afternoon, or siesta time—is the most popular time for naps, and it is a time that people around the world start to drag (Dinges & Broughton, 1989). In the United States, we're likely to grab a cup of coffee, gulp down an energy drink, or just power through it. But in other parts of the world, a nap is the answer, and sleep researchers are learning why.

A group of researchers examined the abilities of college students on a visual discrimination task throughout the course of the day and night. The task was relatively simple: basically, participants had to determine whether certain bars on a complex grid were vertical or horizontal. Students who took no nap got worse as the day went on. Students who took a half-hour nap at 2 P.M. didn't get any worse after they woke up. Students who took an hour-long nap at 2 P.M. actually got better after they woke up. And students who took a 90-minute nap—which contained both slow-wave and REM sleep—performed best of all (Mednick et al., 2002, 2003). Another study found that even a quick 10-minute nap had significant positive effects on both cognitive performance and feelings of fatigue (Tietzel & Lack, 2002). Other researchers have found similar results (Debarnot et al., 2011; Hayashi et al., 1999; Karni et al., 1994). In fact, some researchers have suggested that strategic napping should become part of the daily regimen for such professionals as pilots and emergency room doctors (Hartzler, 2014; Cheng et al., 2014).

In many parts of the world, daytime naps are common. E+/Getty Images

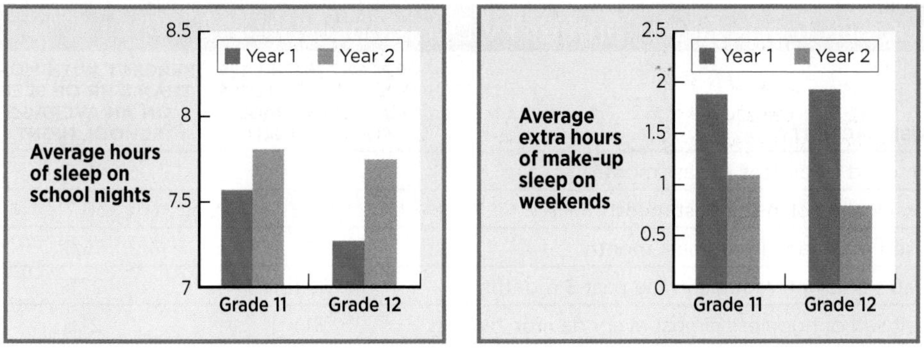

(a) (b)

FIGURE 4.5 Benefits of Later Start Times for High School. In one study of a school district in Kentucky, high school start times were moved back from 7:30 A.M. (Year 1) to 8:30 A.M. (Year 2). That change resulted in high schoolers getting 12–30 minutes more sleep per weekday and needing about an hour less makeup sleep on weekends. Students also reported significantly lower levels of sleepiness and were involved in fewer car accidents after the start time change. Data from Danner & Phillips, 2008.

Age and Sleep. In addition to gender and culture, age is another factor that can determine what normal sleep patterns look like. Of course, kids sleep more, especially when they're very young. In the first few weeks after birth, babies are zonked out about 16 hours per day. Those 16 hours, to the chagrin of new parents, are evenly distributed through the 24-hour day, which means they awaken frequently during the night. By about 4 months, however, most of babies' sleep happens at night, and by about 6 months, most babies are giving their parents a solid 6-hour block of overnight sleep (Rivkees, 2003; Lee & Rosen, 2012). Two naps a day are the norm for most kids into the second year of life, with the first nap usually around 10 A.M. and the second usually around 3 P.M. Two-year-olds typically drop that morning nap, and between ages 3 and 5, most kids no longer need daytime naps to function well (Sadeh et al., 2009).

When kids hit puberty, an important shift happens. They don't seem to need more sleep, but they do seem to shift their sleep time to a later hour of the day (Wolfson & O'Malley, 2012; Carskadon & Tarokh, 2013; Feinberg & Campbell, 2010). As the preteen years begin, kids strongly prefer a later bedtime and a later wake-up call. This preference clashes with most high school schedules, which demand early wake-up times. As **Figure 4.5** suggests, this clash has led to significant debate regarding policies about high school start times (Au et al., 2013). Check the Current Controversy box for more.

CURRENT CONTROVERSY

Should High School Start Later in the Day?

Everybody knows that teenagers like to stay up later and wake up later than they did when they were younger. You probably remember that shift happening yourself, perhaps in middle school but almost certainly by high school. It is not just a trend or a U.S. thing. Teens show this pattern around the world: South America, Europe, Australia, Asia, and Africa (Yang et al., 2005; Andrade & Menna-Baretto, 2002; Gibson et al., 2006; Saarenpaa-Heikkila et al., 1995; Thorleifsdottir et al., 2002; Dorofaeff & Denny, 2006; Reid et al., 2002). There is even some evidence that other mammals, including monkeys, rats, and mice, exhibit the same circadian shift around the same point in their life span (Hagenauer et al., 2009). The reasons for this shift are not entirely clear, but puberty has a lot to do with it (Wolfson & O'Malley, 2012). Research on sixth-grade girls found that those who started puberty earlier had a stronger preference for later bedtimes and wake-up times (Carskadon et al., 1993, 2004).

Whatever the cause of this push toward later bedtimes in teens, it's a terrible match for early-morning start times in high school (Carskadon & Tarokh, 2013). According to researchers, high schoolers are simply "expected to function at school at a time when their bodies were meant to sleep" (Wolfson & Richards, 2011, p. 269). School performance isn't the only undesirable outcome from this situation. So are car crashes. One study compared accident rates in two similar neighboring high schools in Virginia—one in Virginia Beach and the other in Chesapeake. Over a 2-year stretch, the accident rate for teen drivers in Virginia Beach, where school starts 75–80 minutes earlier, was about 35% higher than in Chesapeake (Vorona et al., 2011). Another study found that teen accident rates dropped 16% in the year after a school district pushed back its high school start times an hour (Danner & Phillips, 2008).

Delayed start times have produced other positive results too, including better attendance, grades, and graduation rates (Wahlstrom, 2002a; Wolfson et al., 2007). But districts typically run into strong opposition when they suggest a shift to a later high school day. Arguments against the later start include complications with the scheduling of buses, interference with after-school sports, lack of child care for younger kids if they arrive home before their high school–age siblings, and the mistaken parental belief that teens would go to sleep an hour later if they had a later start time (Kirby et al., 2011; Wolfson et al., 2007; Owens et al., 2010; Wahlstrom, 2002b; Wolfson & Carskadon, 2005). Hopefully, as awareness of the sleep and safety issue continues to grow, more districts will reconsider their schedules. ●

This large-scale survey illustrates the connection between insufficient sleep and risky decisions about drugs, sex, and self-harm. Whether that connection is causal—whether sleepiness causes teens to make different decisions—remains unclear.

TABLE 4.1: Teens, Sleep, and Risky Decisions

RISKY ACTIVITY	PERCENT WITH LESS THAN 8 HR OF SLEEP ON AN AVERAGE SCHOOL NIGHT	PERCENT WITH MORE THAN 8 HR OF SLEEP ON AN AVERAGE SCHOOL NIGHT
Smoked cigarettes in past month	24.0	15.0
Drank alcohol in the past month	50.3	36.7
Used marijuana in the past month	23.3	15.6
Had sexual intercourse in the past 3 months	39.1	27.8
Felt sad or hopeless almost every day for 2 weeks	31.1	21.6
Seriously considered suicide in past 12 months	16.8	9.8

Data from McKnight-Eily et al., 2011.

Whether caused by early start times or any other reason, insufficient sleep in teens correlates with all kinds of questionable, even dangerous decision making (Hershner, 2013). A study of over 12,000 high school students throughout the United States found that kids who sleep less than 8 hours a night are much more likely to smoke, drink, use drugs, and consider suicide (McKnight-Eily et al., 2011). Check **Table 4.1** for more details. Of course, this data is correlational, which means that we can't be sure that the lack of sleep causes the poor decision making. The explanation could be that these risky behaviors cause insufficient sleep (too busy partying to sleep), or that a third factor (stress, depression, etc.) causes both the risky behaviors and the insufficient sleep.

For healthy older adults, the amount of sleep is typically the same as when they were younger. The key word there is *healthy*, though. The increased frequency of injury and illness in older adults often produces less sleep and lower sleep quality, including more frequent awakenings at night and sleepiness during the day (Dijk et al., 2010; Foley et al., 2004).

Solitary Sleeping and Co-Sleeping. We've discussed a lot about the differences in *how much* and *when* people sleep, but what about *with whom* they sleep? For many who grew up in mainstream U.S. culture, the childhood norm is **solitary sleeping**: sleep in which you are the only person in your bed or in your room. By contrast, in many cultures the childhood norm is **co-sleeping**: sleeping in the same room or same bed with another person (usually a caregiver).

Co-sleeping can take many forms (Worthman, 2011; Ball et al., 1999). The most common, especially with very young children, is the *family bed*, in which the child and parent(s) sleep together. Other arrangements include separate beds within reaching distance or separate beds on opposite sides of the same room. Worldwide, co-sleeping is actually more common than solitary sleeping (Burnham & Gaylor, 2011; Shweder et al., 1995). In fact, sleep researchers believe that the emphasis on solitary sleep so prevalent in the United States and other Western cultures is a relatively recent development in the course of human history. Human children typically haven't slept by themselves in their own rooms (Super & Harkness, 2013).

TABLE 4.2: Co-Sleeping Around the World

COUNTRY	PERCENT OF 3-MONTH-OLD BABIES SLEEPING IN THE SAME BED AS THEIR PARENT(S)
China	88
Sweden	65
Chile	64
United States	34
Germany	23
Canada	23
Argentina	15
Turkey	2

Data from Hauck et al., 2008; Nelson et al., 2001.

As **Table 4.2** shows, co-sleeping rates vary around the world, but it tends to be especially common in Asian cultures (Sourander, 2001). One study found that among kids between 6 months and 6 years old, 59% of Japanese kids regularly co-slept with parents (and most of those fell asleep while physically touching a parent), but only 15% of U.S. kids did (Latz et al., 1999). Some researchers believe that sleeping collectively rather than individually is an effect (and perhaps also a cause) of the collectivistic mind-set so common in Asian cultures. However, plenty of other factors, including the money to afford a home with separate bedrooms for each family member, influence the likelihood of family members sleeping together in Asian and other cultures (Giannotti et al., 2008; Brenner et al., 2003; Weimer et al., 2002; Willinger et al., 2003). Perhaps because of this variety of factors, co-sleeping rates within the United States vary by

ethnic group. For example, the rate for African American young children is at least double the rate for their White peers (Wolf et al., 1996; Landrine & Klonoff, 1996).

Some U.S. parents believe that co-sleeping will foster too much dependence in children. When it is bedtime, these parents want kids to get to sleep on their own rather than relying on mommy or daddy for comfort. This belief supports the parental decision to gradually require babies to self-soothe, or "cry it out," at bedtime—an approach that 61% of Western parenting books endorse (Jenni & O'Connor, 2005; Ramos & Youngclarke, 2006). But sleep research doesn't support that belief (Burnham, 2013). For example, one study found that preschoolers who were co-sleepers from birth were actually better at making friends by themselves and getting dressed by themselves than their solitary-sleeping peers (Keller & Goldberg, 2004). Another longitudinal study that followed kids from birth through high school found that kids who co-slept when they were young had no more emotional, behavioral, relationship, criminal, drug-related, or sexual problems than their peers who slept in their own rooms (Okami et al., 2002).

Other U.S. parents believe that co-sleeping could increase the risk of injury or even sudden death (for example, by suffocation) to the baby. Research suggests this too is an assumption without strong support (McKenna & McDade, 2005; Nelson et al., 2001).

solitary sleeping
Sleep in which only one person is in the bed or in the room.

co-sleeping
Sleeping in the same room or same bed with another person (usually a caregiver).

insomnia
A sleep disorder featuring consistent difficulty falling asleep, staying asleep, or achieving high-quality sleep.

Sleep Abnormalities

You know from firsthand experience what it means to have a bad night's sleep. You may have had the occasional scary dream after a slasher movie marathon or difficulty dozing off because you thought that coffee was decaf. But some people have persistent sleep problems that interfere with their daily functioning. Let's explore what they are and why they happen.

Insomnia. Insomnia is a sleep disorder featuring consistent difficulty falling asleep, staying asleep, or achieving high-quality sleep. People with insomnia just can't sleep. No matter how much advice they get from friends and family, how many self-help books they read, or which kind of pills they take, they can't string together a few consecutive nights—or in some cases, even a few consecutive hours—of decent sleep. The consequences are awful, not just during the night staring at the ceiling, but also during the subsequent day.

Consider Gayle Greene, an English professor at Scripps College, who wrote a book about the anguish that severe bouts of insomnia caused her (Greene, 2008):

> I look at the clock and it's 6:05 A.M. The last time I looked it was 4:30, which, considering that I went to bed at 3:00, is not good. Must have been that cup of tea I had before class—no, one cup of tea doesn't do this. Maybe it was the wine I had with dinner—no, that was hours ago. It could be anything I did, it could be nothing I did, I have no idea—classes went fine, dinner with a friend, nothing on my mind ...I give up and get up, and it is bad, bad as the worst hangover... Head aches, eyes sting...back aches...I stare out the window at the blank, dead day...I tell myself, it will look better in the morning—tomorrow morning, that is, this day's a dead loss... They call this a "sleep disorder," but it's actually an all-day disorder. Insomnia is not just something that happens to the night; it happens to the day... (pp 26–28)

Insomnia is, unfortunately, common. About one-third of us experience at least some symptoms of insomnia, and 10% have full-blown cases (Ohayon et al., 2002). Many factors contribute to insomnia (Gehrman et al., 2012 Perlis et al., 1997). As **Figure 4.6** illustrates, disorders of mind and body are common sources of sleeplessness, as you know if you've ever spent the night with a sore back, a queasy stomach, or relentless worry. Work can be a source of that worry. Studies have demonstrated that worrying about your job—or losing your job altogether—increases your odds for insomnia (Åkerstedt & Kecklund, 2012). Money (or a lack of it) can also be a source of that worry. People of low socioeconomic status have higher rates of insomnia than the rich—not just because they worry about how to pay the rent but also because they live

In the latter part of his life, Michael Jackson suffered from severe insomnia. According to news reports, his death in 2009 was related to questionable types and amounts of prescription medication intended to help him sleep. Michael Ochs Archives/Getty Images

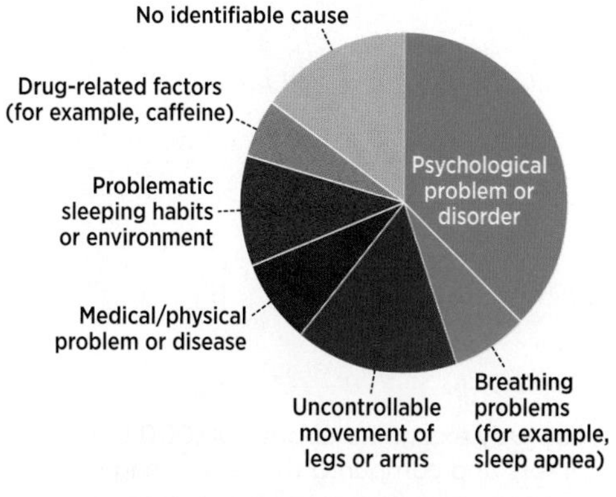

FIGURE 4.6 Sources of Insomnia. There are many sources of insomnia, with psychological disorders being the most common. Information from Ohayon & Guilleminault, 2006.

in more crowded, noisy homes and often lack education about things that can disrupt sleep (like caffeine and cigarettes) (Arber et al., 2009; Paine et al., 2004; Friedman et al., 2007).

The cost of insomnia is tremendous, not just the personal aftereffects of a sleepless night, but also in dollars and cents (Leger, 2012). Sleep problems become workplace problems, such as higher absenteeism, higher accident rates, and lower productivity (**Table 4.3**). In total, insomnia-related work problems cost the United States tens of billions of dollars per year (Kleinman et al., 2009; Leger, 1994; Stoller, 1994). Additionally, the annual cost of U.S. health care for insomnia, including medications and hospital care, is about $14 billion (Walsh & Engelhardt, 1999).

Sleepwalking. **Sleepwalking (somnambulism)** is walking while asleep. Sleepwalkers usually can't be woken up easily. When sleepwalkers do wake up, they are often confused about what just happened (how they got to the living room, the basement, or the backyard). Occasional sleepwalking happens to only about 3% of us, and sleepwalking at least once a week is even rarer (less than 0.5%) (Hublin et al., 1997). But when sleepwalking does happen, it is a bizarre experience for the sleepwalker and anyone watching. Stand-up comedian Mike Birbiglia made a movie and wrote a book about his own struggles with sleepwalking (called *Sleepwalk with Me*) that led to him sleeping in a zipped-up sleeping bag with mittens on his hands to prevent him from unzipping it (Birbiglia, 2011). He even sleepwalked through a closed second-story hotel window (as he dreamed that a missile was heading for his room), waking up on the lawn below, and then walking in the front entrance covered with blood to explain to the front desk clerk what he had just done.

The cause of sleepwalking is still being researched, but it's clear that heredity is a factor (Cartwright, 2006). A study that examined almost 3000 pairs of twins found much higher correspondence rates of sleepwalking between identical twins than nonidentical twins, which means the odds of sleepwalking are higher when all of the genes, rather than just half of them, are shared with a sleepwalker (Hublin et al., 1997; Hublin & Kaprio, 2003). More generally, about 80% of sleepwalkers have at least one biological relative who also sleepwalks (Zadra & Pilon, 2012). Stress and psychological problems also seem to contribute to sleepwalking, with high overlap between sleepwalking and anxiety, depression, and other mental disorders (Gau & Soong, 1999; Ohayon et al., 1999; Lam et al., 2008).

More recently, a couple of variations of sleepwalking have been more widely recognized. In *sleep-related eating behaviors*, the sleeper eats while staying asleep. This typically takes place during the first few hours of the night and is most common in young women (Howell et al., 2009; Auger & Morgenthaler, 2006; Schenck & Mahowald, 1994). People who sleep-eat have relatively high rates of other sleeping, eating, and psychological disorders (Auger, 2006; Schenck et al., 1993; Winkelman, 1998).

In *sleep-related sexual behaviors*, the sleeper gropes another person, tries to have intercourse, masturbates, or performs other sexual behaviors while staying asleep. Typically, these behaviors are more unrestrained and inconsiderate than the sexual

TABLE 4.3: Lost Sleep, Lost Money

TYPE OF EXPENSE	EMPLOYER'S ANNUAL INCREASED COST TO COVER AN EMPLOYEE WITH INSOMNIA
Medical care	$751
Prescription drugs	735
Sick leave	208
Short- and long-term disability	189
Worker's compensation	170
Total	**$2053**

Data from Kleinman et al., 2009.

This study examined about 300,000 U.S. workers and compared those who had been diagnosed with or treated for insomnia with those who had not. Over the course of a year, those with insomnia missed 3 more days of work and cost their employers about $2000 more in medical and other expenses.

behaviors the person does while awake (Andersen et al., 2007; Schenck et al., 2007; Shapiro et al., 2003). When they realize what they have done, sleepers with sleep-related sexual behaviors often feel ashamed and embarrassed, and their intimate relationships often suffer (Guilleminault et al., 2002; Mangan, 2004).

sleepwalking
Walking while asleep, or *somnambulism*.

narcolepsy
A disorder of "sleep attacks" characterized by immediate and unexpected shifts from wakefulness to REM sleep.

sleep terrors
Brief, sudden awakenings in which the person feels frightened and confused.

sleep apnea
A sleep disorder caused by interruptions of breathing that cause repeated waking.

Narcolepsy. **Narcolepsy** is a disorder of "sleep attacks" characterized by immediate and unexpected shifts from wakefulness to REM sleep. (The *–lepsy* part of the word is the same as in *epilepsy*—it suggests a "seizure" of sleep.) Narcolepsy is rare, occurring in fewer than one-fourth of one percent of the population (Dauvilliers et al., 2007; Ohayon et al., 2002). When it happens, it typically begins in the teenage or early adult years and tends to continue through the life span (Dauvilliers et al., 2001).

Narcolepsy is an obvious disorder: The person goes from completely alert to completely asleep almost immediately, much like an MMA fighter getting knocked out. Muscle tone typically goes limp in these sleep attacks, which causes the person to sag in their seat or flop down on the ground. Sometimes, the sleep attacks are triggered by certain strong emotional reactions, such as laughter or surprise. The sleep attacks are usually brief—just 15–20 minutes—followed by a normal state of wakefulness (Pelayo & Lopes, 2006). The cause of narcolepsy is not known, and no cures are yet available. Some medications seem to bring minor reductions in the frequency of sleep attacks, however, as do good sleep habits and the avoidance of situations that trigger narcoleptic attacks (Dauvilliers & Bayard, 2012).

Sleep Terrors. **Sleep terrors** are brief sudden awakenings in which the person feels frightened and confused. Sleep terrors are often called *night terrors*, but many researchers prefer the term *sleep terrors* because the experience can happen during daytime sleep as well (Zadra & Pilon, 2012). Sleep terrors are distinct from *nightmares*—the scary dreams that wake us up. Nightmares are quite common in the general population (Germain, 2012; Robert & Zadra, 2008). About 80% of college students in one survey experienced at least one nightmare in the previous year, and about 15% experience about one per month (Belicki & Belicki, 1982; Belicki, 1992a, 1992b). By contrast, sleep terrors have happened to only about 2% of adults (Zadra & Pilon, 2012). About three-quarters of children have nightmares, but only 1–6% have sleep terrors (Mindell & Owens, 2015; Ivanenko & Larson, 2013). Another distinction: Nightmares happen during REM sleep, but sleep terrors happen during non-REM sleep.

A person experiencing a sleep terror is essentially having a panic attack while sleeping. It features intense fear, screaming, sweating, rapid breathing, and a pounding heart. It typically happens within the first 90 minutes of sleep and lasts just a few minutes. When it is over, the sleeper usually returns to normal sleep rather than waking up and often can't remember the sleep terror when the morning rolls around. The cause of sleep terrors is not entirely known, but genetics appears to play a substantial role (Abe et al., 1993; Nguyen et al., 2008). Children with parents who have sleep terrors are twice as likely to have sleep terrors as their peers whose parents don't have sleep terrors (Abe et al., 1984). Sleep terrors also tend to overlap with psychological problems like anxiety and depression. Sleep terrors tend to begin in childhood and go away without treatment during adolescence or early adulthood (Petit et al., 2015; Thiedke, 2001; LaBerge, 2000).

Sleep terrors are brief sudden awakenings during non-REM sleep in which the person feels frightened and confused. Creatas Images/ Thinkstock

Sleep Apnea. **Sleep apnea** is a sleep disorder caused by interruptions of breathing that cause repeated waking. Sleep apnea happens to about 3% of middle-aged adults, about twice as often in men as in women, and more often in obese people than people of normal weight (Young et al., 1993, 1996; Young & Peppard, 2005; Weaver & Ye, 2012). Sleep apnea is obvious (and often disturbing) to anyone who can see or hear the sleeper, with symptoms like loud snoring, snorting, gasping, choking, and breathless pauses (Sanders & Givelber, 2006). But sleep apnea is not always obvious to the sleepers themselves, because they are usually not awake enough to be fully aware of their surroundings. People suffering from sleep apnea feel sleepy the next day, but

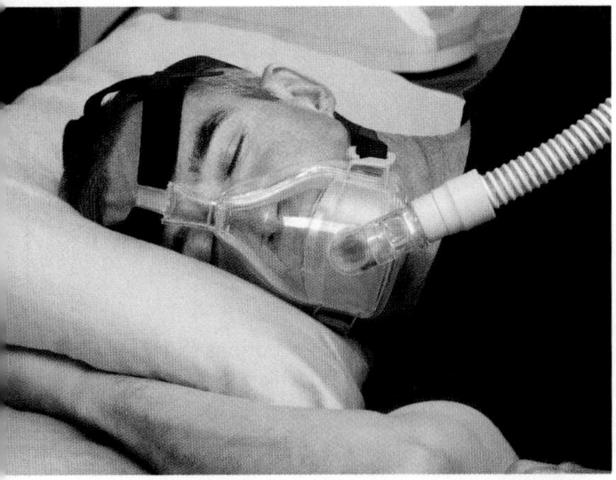

A CPAP (continuous positive air pressure) machine often helps people with sleep apnea, a sleep disorder caused by interruptions of breathing that cause repeated wakening. iStock/Getty Images

the sleepiness starts to seem normal because sleep apnea happens every night. The biggest risk factor for sleep apnea is obesity, as the excessive mass around the upper airway narrows or blocks the flow of breath in and out of the lungs (Young et al., 2004; Eckert et al., 2009).

The most common and effective treatment for sleep apnea is a *continuous positive air pressure*, or *CPAP*, machine (Ferguson et al., 2006; Gay et al., 2006; Hirshkowitz & Lee-Chiong, 2006). The CPAP typically sits on the sleeper's bedside table and pumps out a continuous flow of air, which is delivered through a tube connected to a mask that the sleeper wears all night. The mask completely covers the nose and mouth, delivering a steady stream of air that prevents the airway from closing. CPAP treatment can be life-changing for someone whose nights and days are ravaged by sleep apnea. One man who was probably "sleep deprived for 15 years" started using a CPAP machine. He describes waking up in the lab as "amazing": "I felt like a 10-year-old who had polished off a pot of coffee. I couldn't believe how completely refreshed I felt!" (American Sleep Apnea Association, 2015).

Other treatments for sleep apnea include oral appliances (devices similar to mouth guards) designed to keep the airway open, surgery, and weight loss to reduce obesity levels (Chan & Cistulli, 2009; Kapen, 2006; Sher, 2006; Bailey, 2006).

Treating and Preventing Sleep Problems. The best way to deal with sleep problems is to engage in good **sleep hygiene**: routine behaviors that promote healthy sleep. For good sleep hygiene, experts generally include both behaviors you should do and those you shouldn't do (Lichstein et al., 2012; Gradisar & Short, 2013).

Do:

- Wake up and go to sleep at the same time every day.
- Exercise during daytime hours.
- Allow yourself no more than a light bedtime snack.
- Create a sleep environment that is comfortable, quiet, dark, and a comfortable temperature.

Don't:

- Drink caffeine after noon.
- Take a nap in the late afternoon or evening.
- Smoke cigarettes, drink alcohol, eat a heavy meal, or exercise close to bedtime.
- Use any device with a bright screen (TV, computer, smartphone, etc.) close to bedtime.

The last of these tips—avoiding screens before bed—is increasingly problematic for many of us, especially teens and children. Decades ago, the brightest thing anyone saw in their bedroom at night was a nightlight. Then came the TVs. Only 6% of sixth-graders had a TV in their bedroom in 1970, but that number jumped to 77% in 1999 and remained at 76% in 2010 (Roberts et al., 1999; Rideout et al., 2010). By 2009, even 17% of *toddlers* had a TV in their bedroom (Mindell et al., 2009). Studies have found that the presence of a TV in the bedroom correlates with fewer hours of sleep and higher levels of daytime sleepiness, along with higher rates of other sleep-related problems (Van den Bulck, 2004; Shochat et al., 2010).

Today, many of us share our bedroom not only with our TV but also with our smartphone. A 2011 study found that 72% of teenagers used a phone as they tried to fall asleep—a number that has probably increased in the years since (National Sleep Foundation, 2011). The same study found that 28% of those teens leave their phone's ringer (or vibrate function) on all night, and 18% woke up at least a few nights a week to respond to a call, text, or other alert.

Looking at a bright screen around bedtime can disrupt sleep. AnaBGD/Thinkstock

There are many ways that smartphones at bedtime can interfere with your sleep: (1) Time you spend doing smartphone activities (texts, social media, videos, etc.) can push back your sleep to the wee hours of the night. (2) The content of what you see on

your smartphone (exciting gossip from a friend, a funny video, etc.) can make it difficult to wind down and drift off. (3) The bright light in your eyes can confuse your circadian rhythm. (4) Waking up in the middle of the night to respond to an alert on your phone reduces your overall sleep time (Gradisar & Short, 2013). Certainly, the increasing presence of tablets and other screened devices multiply the problems caused by TVs and smartphones.

If prevention hasn't worked, there are plenty of popular treatments for sleep problems (Lee-Chiong & Sateia, 2006). Many treatments are pharmaceutical, including prescription drugs like Ambien and Lunesta, as well as over-the-counter drugs like Unisom and ZzzQuil. These drugs can be helpful short-term for certain people, but they don't work for everyone, and they are generally not considered long-term solutions to long-term sleep problems. Plus, the side effects can be awful, including grogginess the next day, a need for ever-increasing dosages, and potential for misusing or getting hooked on the drug (Riemann & Nissen, 2012).

Another popular drugstore option is melatonin tablets, which deliver extra amounts of the natural bodily hormone related to sleep and arousal. However, the data for melatonin is weak. One meta-analysis covering hundreds of sleepers found that on average, melatonin enabled people to fall asleep just 4 minutes sooner and sleep a total of just 13 minutes longer (Brzezinski et al., 2005). Other studies show similar outcomes for the use of melatonin, although it is worth mentioning that the side effects are generally less risky than for many medications (Ferracioli-Oda et al., 2014).

Many people have turned to herbal substances to help them sleep, such as chamomile, kava, and valerian, but again scientific data on their helpfulness is lacking. A meta-analysis covering over 1600 sleepers found no differences between those who used herbal sleep aids and those who didn't (Leach & Page, 2015). The bottom line appears to be that better sleep can't be found in a pill bottle, at least not for the long haul.

As a result, many sleepy people have searched for nonmedical solutions. A first step is to improve upon any shortcomings in sleep hygiene, as listed previously. Beyond that, more deliberate techniques for improving sleep can include counseling or psychotherapy focused on reducing worry, especially worry that happens at bedtime or worry about sleep itself (Sivertsen et al., 2006, Jacobs et al., 2004; Bélanger et al., 2007).

Sleep-improving techniques can also include *stimulus control* and *sleep restriction* (Means & Edinger, 2006; Spielman et al., 1987; Lacks et al., 1983; Kaplan & Harvey, 2013). With stimulus control, the bed is used exclusively for sleeping (not for watching TV or talking on the phone or doing homework or lying awake through the night). With sleep restriction, the sleeper condenses sleep into a small number of hours (as if the bed is only "open" for a strictly controlled and consistent period each night) and then gradually expands the open hours as needed. Research indicates that in general, nonpharmacological treatments for sleeping problems are as effective as pharmacological treatments (and may be significantly more effective and longer-lasting) and lack any of the unwanted side effects (Smith et al., 2002; Jacobs et al., 2004; Murtagh & Greenwood, 1995).

LIFE HACK 4.2

Limit the amount of time you spend looking at screens, like TVs and smartphones, right before bed. Too much exposure to bright lights at bedtime can interfere with sleep.

(Gradisar & Short, 2013)

sleep hygiene
Routine behaviors that promote healthy sleep.

CHECK YOUR LEARNING:

4.1 Why do we sleep?

4.2 How does sleep deprivation affect people?

4.3 What is your circadian rhythm and what influences it?

4.4 What are the stages of normal sleep?

4.5 Different sleep patterns have been found between which groups of people?

4.6 What is co-sleeping and how common is it?

4.7 How are the sleep abnormalities of insomnia, sleepwalking, narcolepsy, sleep terrors, and sleep apnea different from one another?

4.8 What strategies can you use to prevent and treat sleep problems?

Dreams

YOU WILL LEARN:

4.9 what theories of dreams have been proposed.

4.10 how dreams can affect daily functioning through such techniques as imagery rehearsal therapy and lucid dreaming.

Dreams have been a focus of psychologists since early in the history of the field—even before 1900, when Sigmund Freud's famous book *The Interpretation of Dreams* was published. Besides sleeping, breathing, eating, and drinking, dreaming is one of the few experiences you share with every other human being from every culture at all points in history. And dreaming is frequent too: You do it every single night. You'd think, then, that psychologists would know a lot about dreaming. The truth is, they don't.

Theories of Dreams

Dreaming has been studied extensively by sleep researchers, but much of that study has been theoretical. Many sleep experts have offered opinions about why we dream and what dreams mean, but the scientific study of dreams is relatively recent.

Historically, many different tribes and cultures around the world have offered their own theories of dreaming. Many of these are "folk theories," supported by belief and tradition more than scientific evidence, but they are still powerful influences on the lives of those who accept them. Among these folk dream theories (Lohmann, 2007) are:

- **Nonsense theory.** Dreams are just imaginary nonsense, random images and stories to be enjoyed for what they're worth and then forgotten.
- **Message theory.** Dreams contain important messages, perhaps from others (family members, ancestors, etc.) or from parts of yourself that need to be heard.
- **Generative theory.** Dreams not only predict the future but generate or determine it.
- **Soul travel theory.** Dreams are the experience of your soul wandering outside of your body.
- **Visitation theory.** Dreams are visits by supernatural spirits to the dreamer.

"I dreamed I got eight hours of sleep."

William Haefeli, The New Yorker Collection/The Cartoon Bank

Freud's theory of dreaming arrived in the early 1900s and had a tremendous impact on society that continues to a lesser extent today. Freud argued that dreams revealed the unconscious mind, particularly deep-down wishes of which you are largely unaware while awake. According to Freud, the wishes don't show themselves directly but get converted into stories that utilize lots of symbolism. In Freud's terms, the *latent content* of the dream (the unconscious wish) gets translated into the *manifest content* of the dream, which is the actual story you see acted out in your mind. He called that translation process *dream work*, and in therapy, Freud and his clients would try to undo that dream work to figure out what the dream meant (Freud, 1900; Cabaniss et al., 2011). Unfortunately, in terms of science, Freud's theory of dreaming lacks testability and therefore lacks empirical support.

The Scientific Study of Dreaming

The scientific study of dreaming began in the post-Freud era with the observation in the late 1950s that dreaming usually happened during REM sleep. This connection was established by researchers watching sleepers' eyes and then waking them when their eyes moved rapidly beneath their eyelids. Those awakened during that rapid eye movement were far more likely to report that they had been dreaming than those in other sleep stages (Dement & Kleitman, 1957; Dement, 1960; Nielsen, 1995, 2000, 2004; Vogel, 1991).

This link between eye movement and dreaming led some researchers to take a more neuropsychological approach to dreaming, attempting to determine how the

various parts of the brain function during REM sleep. This neuropsychological research led to the influential *activation–synthesis hypothesis* in the 1970s, which states that dreams are initiated by the pons, a structure in the brainstem (Hobson & McCarley, 1977). The occipital lobe then becomes involved, adding random visual elements to give the dream some structure. Those random visual elements are meaningless until the sleeper wakes up and assigns some meaning to them.

In more recent years, with great advances in technology, neuropsychological theories of dreaming have expanded from the activation–synthesis hypothesis. In fact, one researcher suggested that dreams during REM sleep represent a different level of consciousness from other types of sleep. His theory is that dreaming provides a virtual reality model of the world so the dreamer has an expanded library of images, concepts, and emotions with which to respond to daily life (Hobson, 2009). Another neurological finding regarding dreams is the fact that the amygdala and hypothalamus are quite active during dreams, suggesting that emotions (especially negative emotions such as fear) are especially relevant to dreaming (Maquet et al., 1996). Other neuropsychological researchers have pointed out that those parts of the brain are involved in memory formation, which suggests dreaming may function to create and solidify memories, especially memories that involve emotions (Wagner et al., 2001; Nishida et al., 2009).

The Effect of Dreams on Daily Functioning

Other dream research has focused on how dreams help a person function after waking up. Several studies suggest that your nighttime dreams help you function better in the morning, especially in terms of mood regulation. (The old saying that everything will look better in the morning actually has some science behind it.) In a study of people with depression, the themes of their dreams were more negative in the first half of the night and more positive in the second half. When participants rated their moods, they were much more positive in the morning than the night before. This finding suggests that dreams perform a fresh start function (Cartwright et al., 1998a; Cartwright, 2005).

Some research suggests that dreams can improve mental health (Cartwright et al., 1998b). Some people suffering from posttraumatic stress disorder (PTSD), including many military veterans who have recurring nightmares, have benefited from *imagery rehearsal therapy*. Imagery rehearsal therapy is a simple technique in which the nightmare sufferer retells the nightmare to a therapist or counselor—but with a better ending. The veteran goes through an exercise during waking hours in which he or she takes control of the dream. It may start the same way as the nightmare usually starts, but the veteran gives it a happy finish. The veteran then reviews, or *rehearses*, the new and improved version of the dream several times a day, including right before bedtime. For example, one patient used imagery rehearsal therapy to change a nightmare about being chased by a bad guy to a cheery, playful story about being chased by his brothers as a child. Results of imagery rehearsal therapy are encouraging, with many veterans eliminating or drastically reducing the occurrence of PTSD nightmares (Krakow et al., 2001; Krakow & Zadra, 2006; Moore & Krakow, 2007).

It's interesting that you can influence your dreams by controlling aspects of your waking hours. But can you control your dreams *while* you're dreaming?

Lucid Dreaming

Some sleep experts believe that some people can control their dreams while they are dreaming, though it requires training and practice (LaBerge, 1985). They call this **lucid dreaming**: a dreaming experience in which you have some control over the dream while you remain asleep. Lucid dreaming happens most often during REM sleep but

lucid dreaming
A dreaming experience in which a person has some control over the dream while remaining asleep.

occasionally in stage 1 or stage 2 sleep as well (LaBerge, 1988). It is most likely when the person returns to sleep after being awakened during the first hour of sleep. Even then, lucid dreaming still often requires lots of training and practice and might remain impossible for many people (LaBerge, 1985).

The key element of lucid dreaming is the knowledge that you are dreaming. The decision to control it is optional (LaBerge, 2007). It is a bit like watching a movie on TV with the remote in your hand. You know you're watching the movie, so you can decide to pause, fast-forward, or rewind. But with lucid dreaming, you also can control the content, as if you are the director of the movie. You can decide what happens as well as what the characters in the dream do or say. Like imagery rehearsal therapy, lucid dreaming has been used as a therapeutic tool to help people overcome recurring nightmares. Lucid dreaming has also been used by athletes such as tennis players, high divers, and long-distance runners to "practice" their sports (Erlacher, 2012; Spoormaker & Lancee, 2012). However, both applications of lucid dreaming are new and have little evidence of success at this point.

CHECK YOUR LEARNING:

4.9 How have various theories attempted to explain dreams?

4.10 How do the themes of dreams tend to differ between bedtime and wake-up time, and how can dreams affect mental health?

Hypnosis

YOU WILL LEARN:

4.11 what hypnosis is and how it works.

4.12 what purposes hypnotism has been used for.

4.13 who can be hypnotized.

4.14 whether hypnotism is actually nothing more than people simply complying with the social and situational role they feel pressured to fill at that moment.

Hypnosis is an altered state of consciousness in which one person, the participant, becomes very suggestible to another person, the hypnotist. Many people new to psychology assume that hypnosis is a big part of what psychologists do, perhaps because Freud is widely known to have used it with his clients (Tinterow, 1970). Actually, it's not. Few researchers study it, and few practitioners use it with their clients. But hypnosis has been a part of psychology's history since the field began. For those who do study and apply it, hypnosis is a powerful technique.

The roots of hypnosis go back hundreds of years, all the way to the idea of animal magnetism (put forth by Franz Mesmer, of *mesmerism* fame in the late 1700s and early 1800s) and even the exorcism procedures of Johann Gassner decades earlier (Peter, 2005; Pattie, 1994). But hypnotism today bears little resemblance to either of those outdated practices or to the myths that most people believe about it. Hypnosis does not involve a suspicious or sinister character passing his hands across a helpless victim or instantly "putting under" anyone. Hypnosis does not require the hypnotist to have a special gift or personality. Hypnotized people are not weak, gullible, or faking, either (Barnier & Nash, 2008; Kihlstrom, 2008). Instead, hypnotism is simply a technique in which one person alters the consciousness of another. Then the hypnotist suggests new behaviors (usually for the purpose of helping the client) that can be tried under hypnosis or after the client comes out of hypnosis (Kihlstrom, 2005; Kirsch & Braffman, 2001).

The Procedure of Hypnotism

hypnosis
An altered state of consciousness in which one person, the participant, becomes very suggestible to another person, the hypnotist.

The procedure of hypnotism begins with an *induction*, an attempt to change the consciousness of the person receiving the technique. The hypnotist typically conducts induction by reading or reciting a script that instructs the person to unwind and calm

themselves to a point that approaches sleep (but does not drift into sleep). During induction, the client either focuses their eyes on a target or feels their muscles relax. Here's an example of an induction focusing on the eyes:

> Now I would like you to find a spot or an object on the wall. … Eyes comfortable and heavy…Just concentrate on the target and listen to my words, allowing yourself to relax more and more…you find that your eyelids are beginning to get heavier and heavier…Soon your eyes will close themselves and when they do, you can really allow yourself to relax completely…your eyes are closed now and they will remain closed for the duration of our work together…In a moment I'm going to touch the very top of your head with my hand and, when I do, I would like you to notice these warm waves of relaxation that begin to emanate from the very top of your head and pass through your entire body…the muscles of your forehead, your eyes, your face become limp and relaxed…your breathing is becoming more and more slow and regular…it is so comfortable, so pleasurable to be so deeply hypnotized and relaxed…" (Nash, 2008, pp. 490–491)

Savage Chickens

Once the induction is complete, the next step in the hypnosis procedure is a *suggestion*, in which the hypnotist tells the person to perform a certain behavior. For example, the hypnotist may tell the person to extend his arm forward and imagine it being lifted by helium-filled balloons. The hypnotist can tell that the person is hypnotized not just because his arm goes up, but because his arm goes up in a way that feels involuntary. The person believes that rather than choosing to move his arm up, it simply moved up on its own (Kihlstrom, 2008; Barnier & Nash, 2008). Once the suggestions are complete, the hypnotist terminates the hypnosis. This often happens by simply telling the person that at the count of 1 (after counting backward from 10), they will come out of hypnosis and be fully conscious (Nash, 2008).

Often, the first suggestion (like the arm levitation) is just a test to make sure that the induction has worked and the person is in a suggestible state. Once that test is passed, the hypnotist can offer all kinds of suggestions to improve all kinds of problems. For example, hypnosis can be used to help people with a phobia (Bryant, 2008). Consider a person with a phobia of airplanes. The hypnotist can suggest that she picture, while she's hypnotized, going through the motions of getting on an airplane, beginning with walking through the airport, arriving at the gate, walking onto the plane, taking her seat, taking off, and so on. The hypnotist can also suggest that after she comes out of hypnosis, she will complete these actions for her upcoming real flight. (That's a *posthypnotic* suggestion.)

If it sounds a bit like an exercise in imagination, it is—but with the extra power that comes from a change in consciousness. Other problems to which hypnosis has been applied include depression, chronic pain, smoking, drinking, and overeating (Yapko, 2008; Jensen & Patterson, 2008; Elkins & Perfect, 2008). Hypnosis can also be used to enhance performance in other areas, like sports (Morgan & Stegner, 2008). The evidence for these hypnosis-based treatments is generally limited, however (Moore & Tasso, 2008). The best evidence is for the treatment of pain (Montgomery et al., 2000) and stopping smoking (Green & Lynn, 2000).

Who Can Be Hypnotized?

There are wide differences in whether a person can become hypnotized (Friedlander & Sarbin, 1938; Piccione et al., 1989; Laurence et al., 2008). A person who is not willing to be hypnotized or who strongly doubts that hypnosis will work generally can't be hypnotized. People who are more likely to be hypnotized have a more general open-mindedness and are high in absorption, or the tendency to get wrapped up in immediate sensory experiences (Glisky et al., 1991; Roche & McConkey, 1990). Men and women are equally likely to be hypnotized (Kihlstrom et al., 1980).

What's the most extreme suggestion that a hypnotized person can follow?

A few studies have tested the limits of hypnosis (McConkey, 2008). In one study, hypnotists suggested a sex change to participants (Noble & McConkey, 1995). For example, they told hypnotized male participants: "In a moment you will no longer be a man, you will be female in every way....[after 30 seconds passed] Tell me about yourself? What is your name?" (pp. 70–71). The majority of participants did not follow that suggestion, but some who were among the most likely to be hypnotized did, even going so far as to change their name to one more typical of the opposite sex. (By the way, there were no posthypnotic suggestions in this study—any effects ended when the person came out of hypnosis!)

Another study did involve posthypnotic suggestion (Barnier & McConkey, 1998). In this one, the researchers gave 120 postcards to each participant and told them to send one per week to the researchers. Half of the participants received this instruction as a posthypnotic suggestion. The other half were not hypnotized at all and received this instruction essentially as a request for a favor. The nonhypnotized participants sent in more postcards, but they described their attitude toward doing so as work, like a chore they had to make themselves complete. The hypnotized participants said they sent the postcards effortlessly, as if it was happening automatically.

One last note about hypnotism: It is not just role playing by the person being hypnotized (Barabasz & Barabasz, 2008; Oakley, 2008). That explanation was put forth by the **social-cognitive theory of hypnosis**: a theory of hypnosis that emphasizes pressure to play the role assigned to a person being hypnotized. The social-cognitive theory suggests that a "hypnotized" person is really just a person conforming to the social pressure (from the hypnotist or others watching) to act hypnotized, but brain studies say otherwise. In fact, neuropsychological evidence shows that hypnosis affects many parts of the brain, including the regions that control arousal and attention (Rainville & Price, 2003; Speigel, 2003). In one study, half of the participants underwent hypnosis in which they received the suggestion that their left leg was paralyzed. The other half underwent the same hypnosis, but were told ahead of time to fake being hypnotized and fake the leg paralysis. PET scans revealed that completely different parts of the brain were activated by the two groups, which suggests that those who were truly hypnotized were engaged in something quite different from merely playing along with the social role of a person under hypnosis (Ward et al., 2003).

CHECK YOUR LEARNING:

4.11 What is hypnosis and how does it work?

4.12 What types of issues has hypnosis been used to treat?

4.13 What characteristics are associated with greater hypnotizability?

4.14 What is the social-cognitive theory of hypnosis and how strongly is it supported by neuropsychological studies?

Psychoactive Drugs and Consciousness

YOU WILL LEARN:

4.15 what psychoactive drugs are.

4.16 how psychoactive drugs work.

Psychoactive drugs are substances that alter mental functioning. When you take psychoactive drugs, they alter not only your consciousness but other brain activities like thinking, mood, memory, and perception. Some psychoactive drugs are illegal, while others are legal. Some of the legal drugs require a prescription, while others are sold over the counter. Some are remarkably common, while others are obscure. Before

we consider specific categories of psychoactive drugs, let's consider how those drugs work within your body.

YOU WILL LEARN: (*Continued*)

4.17 what tolerance and withdrawal are.

4.18 what addiction is.

4.19 what depressants do.

4.20 what stimulants do.

4.21 what opiates do.

4.22 what hallucinogens do.

How Psychoactive Drugs Work

If we zoom in to the level of the neuron, we see that all psychoactive drugs do their work on neurotransmitters. Recall from Chapter 2 that neurotransmitters are the chemical messengers (like endorphins, serotonin, and dopamine) that travel across the synapses between neurons. A psychoactive drug can affect neurotransmitters in one of four ways (Brick & Erickson, 2013):

1. Increase the release of a neurotransmitter from the sending neuron
2. Block or activate the receptors of neurotransmitters in the receiving neuron
3. Inhibit the reuptake of neurotransmitters that didn't complete the trip across the synapse back into the sending neuron
4. Inhibit enzymes in or near the neuron that would break down the neurotransmitter.

There is one thing shared by all four of these particular effects on neurotransmitters: a change in the amount of neurotransmitter that successfully makes the trip from one neuron to the next. Regardless of whether that change is an increase or a decrease, it alters brain functioning.

Tolerance and Withdrawal. Many psychoactive drugs, when taken repeatedly over time, cause the user to build up a **tolerance**: decreased effectiveness of a particular amount of a drug. A tolerance requires a user to seek out more and more of the drug to match the same effect that a smaller amount had earlier. This can become dangerous when the amount grows to levels that the body can't handle in a healthy way.

Another possible outcome of repeated use of certain drugs over time is **withdrawal**: stressful and uncomfortable symptoms caused by discontinuing a drug that had become habitual. Withdrawal symptoms vary from one drug to another, but they often include jumpiness, trembling, headaches, nausea, insomnia, anxiety, irritability, and fatigue. Depending on the drug, withdrawal symptoms can last hours, days, weeks, or longer.

Withdrawal is often a by-product of *dependence* on a drug, which can take two forms, physical and psychological. **Physical dependence** is a bodily need for a particular drug in order to function normally. **Psychological dependence** is a mental need for a particular drug in order to function normally. For people who have never experienced dependence before, it can be difficult to imagine or even understand. It is easy to think, "What do you mean you absolutely *need* a drink? Just use some will power and quit!" To understand dependence, try to imagine life without something that's an important part of your day-to-day functioning, something that would make you panic if you lost it. Your smartphone? The Internet? Your TV or your car? Playing video games or gambling? Like most psychoactive drugs, these things and activities are not necessities. Babies are not born with an inherent need for them. In fact, many people around the world live full and happy lives without ever doing them. But for some of us, these activities become so deeply ingrained in our lives that they seem like requirements. That is what physical or psychological dependence feels like for people who continuously use certain psychoactive drugs. The drugs become a need and the people using them establish a new, chemically enhanced normal for their brains and bodies.

Addiction. Physical and psychological dependence are major contributors to **addiction**: problematic drug use that persists in spite of serious negative consequences. A person becomes an addict by prioritizing the continued use of a psychoactive drug above just about everything else—work, relationships, family, even their own life. Their actions make no sense to the people around them, who often intervene or plead with them to stop. Unfortunately, addiction gives people a sort of tunnel vision that limits their focus to the next hit, the next high, the next buzz.

social-cognitive theory of hypnosis
A theory of hypnosis that emphasizes pressure to play the role assigned to a person being hypnotized.

psychoactive drugs
Substances that alter mental functioning.

tolerance
Decreased effectiveness of a particular amount of a drug.

withdrawal
Stressful and uncomfortable symptoms caused by discontinuing a drug that had become habitual.

physical dependence
A bodily need for a particular drug in order to function normally.

psychological dependence
A mental need for a particular drug in order to function normally.

addiction
Problematic drug use that persists in spite of serious negative consequences.

When Rob Lowe was in his 20s, he was gaining fame as an actor, but his personal life was harmed by his addiction to alcohol. WireImage/Getty Images

Consider the story of Rob Lowe, the actor you've probably seen on TV (*The Grinder*, *Parks and Recreation*, *The West Wing*) and who also appeared in hit movies in the 1980s and 1990s. In 1990, he was 26 years old and a rising Hollywood star. But he was addicted to alcohol—a fact that hit him hard when he saw his drinking threaten his relationships with his girlfriend and his family on the same night:

> It takes less than twenty-four hours back in L.A. for me to destroy this relationship…I'd found the right person, Sheryl…But back in my bachelor pad in the Hollywood Hills, this vision is immediately fogged by fear and force of habit… As usual, a night out with the boys leads to tequila and a party…I look for the cutest girl I can find…I'm drunk and back at my place with a total stranger…At about midnight [my girlfriend] Sheryl calls to check in on me…She hears a girl's laugh in the background. I try to play it off, but she knows what's going on… "I can't be your girlfriend…Good-bye, Rob."…
>
> …It's a few hours later and I'm standing over my answering machine with its seventy-three unanswered messages. "Rob, please. Are you there?" begs my mother, clearly in a panic. But I am too f***ed-up to pick up the phone… "Your grandfather is in the hospital. He's had a massive heart attack."… I stare at the answering machine, frozen, until my mother hangs up. As shame and guilt begin to penetrate my altered state, I begin to hatch a plan of attack. *I need to chug the last of the tequila,* I tell myself. *So I can get to sleep, so I can wake up ASAP and deal with this.* This insane logic holds right up until I catch a glance of myself in the bathroom mirror… The girl I love has just left me… My grandfather is dying. My mother is in crisis, desperate for help and comfort, and I am cowering and hiding in shameful avoidance. I have arrived at the bottom. (Lowe, 2011, pp. 249–251, italics in original)

Rob Lowe responded to hitting bottom by entering rehab, as many addicts do. For some people, addiction has to do even more serious damage to their lives before they are motivated to take action.

Types of Psychoactive Drugs

Lots of substances affect the brain. Let's consider the four best-understood categories: *depressants*, *stimulants*, *opiates*, and *hallucinogens*.

Depressants. **Depressants** are drugs that slow bodily functions. One subset of depressants, *benzodiazepines,* reduce nervousness and are often prescribed for problems relating to anxiety or insomnia. Another subset of depressants, *barbiturates,* are depressant drugs that have a calming effect. Barbiturates were used for many years as prescription medications for sleep and anxiety (and often sold on the street as downers), but their popularity has decreased in recent decades because the more recent generation of sleep and anxiety medications are more effective and have fewer side effects.

By far, the most commonly used depressant, both in the United States and around the world, is alcohol.

Alcohol is the most commonly used depressant drug. Vetta/Getty Images

Wait—alcohol is a depressant? When I see people drinking alcohol, they don't look depressed to me.

The effects of alcohol can seem to bring a relaxed, pleasant feeling (or buzz), but that is usually at low doses. At higher doses, the depressant effects of alcohol are much more obvious: speech, movement, coordination, reasoning, and reaction time all slow down. Alcohol also delays the drinker's inhibitions to the point where they can't keep up with the drinker's impulses. This often leads to behaviors that the drinker would have decided against if sober. Sometimes, these behaviors are

FIGURE 4.7 Crash Likelihood and Blood Alcohol Concentration. Just a few drinks multiply the odds of a car crash. Many more raise the odds exponentially. Data from Ingraham, 2015; Compton & Berning, 2015.

depressants
Drugs that slow bodily functions.

aggressive or sexual acts that later bring regret, legal trouble, or even more traumatic consequences.

As an example, consider the connection between alcohol and sexual assault. Alcohol is a factor in half of all sexual assaults (Abbey et al., 1996, 2004). Multiple studies have found that college men who drink more alcohol are more likely to commit sexual assaults (Abbey et al., 1998, 2001, 2014; Abbey & McAuslan, 2004). In fact, one such study found that, for college men who had committed sexual assault, their most common justification for doing so was that the woman had been drinking (Wegner et al., 2015).

Unfortunately, the dangers of alcohol extend beyond sexual assault. Continued use of alcohol is toxic to many essential body parts, including the liver, pancreas, heart, stomach, and brain. It is well established as a contributor to birth defects in the babies of women who drink while pregnant. (See the section on *fetal alcohol syndrome* in Chapter 9.) Alcohol interacts dangerously with dozens of commonly taken medications, including aspirin, antihistamines, antidepressants, antianxiety medications, and more. An overdose of alcohol (also known as alcohol poisoning) kills hundreds of people in the United States every year. (Brick & Erickson, 2013; Room et al., 2005). As **Figure 4.7** illustrates, drunk driving kills thousands.

Because alcohol comes in so many different forms, it is important to understand how those forms compare to each other in terms of alcohol content. Generally speaking, the amount of alcohol is the same in a 12-ounce beer, a 5-ounce glass of wine, and a 1.5-ounce shot of hard liquor. However, the impact of these drinks can differ because of the different rates at which they can be consumed. It typically takes longer to drink a whole bottle of beer or sip a whole glass of wine than it does to down a shot in a single gulp. That difference, multiplied by several (or many) drinks, leads to a different rate of absorption of alcohol by the body. The faster the alcohol gets into the body, the higher the peak level of blood alcohol concentration (BAC).

BAC also depends on the size of the person. Smaller people feel the effects of alcohol more quickly than bigger people. Remember when you were young and took children's medication in liquid form? The bottle had a chart based on weight (or age, which correlates with weight in kids) because the appropriate dosage depends on how big the kid is. The same is true with alcohol—bigger people need more of it to feel the same effects as smaller people. That's one reason why alcohol affects men and women differently, at least if they match average gender size, in which men are bigger than women.

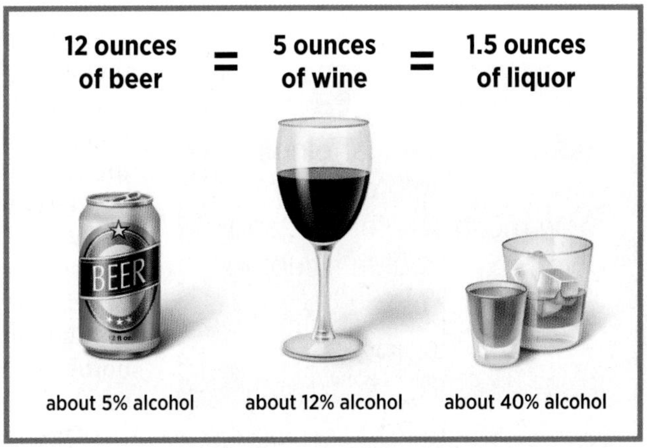

FIGURE 4.8 Alcohol Content of Various Drinks. A 12-ounce can of beer, a 5-ounce glass of wine, and a 1.5 ounce shot of liquor contain approximately the same amount of alcohol.

CHAPTER APP 4.2

Depressants

AlcDroid Alcohol Tester
IntelliDrink Lite

Preview one of the links and consider the following questions.

WEBSITE:
http://tiny.cc/73h7jy
http://tiny.cc/y2h7jy

ANDROID:
http://tiny.cc/sxjyiy

IPHONE:
http://tiny.cc/nrjyiy

VIDEO DEMO:
http://tiny.cc/chapterapps

These apps and others like them allow drinkers to estimate their own blood alcohol content by entering the specific alcoholic beverages they drink. These apps also indicate how long it will take for their blood alcohol content to drop to safer levels.

How does it APPly to your daily life?
What kind of impact could apps like these have on the frequency of drunk driving? How could drinkers be encouraged to use them?

How does it APPly to your understanding of psychology?
How do these apps enhance your understanding of the effects of alcohol?

Stimulants. **Stimulants** are drugs that speed up bodily functions. One of the best-known, and perhaps the most addictive, is cocaine, which is typically taken in powder or solid forms ("crack"). The stimulant category also includes amphetamines, which are most commonly found in prescription drugs for ADHD (like Adderall, Ritalin, Concerta, and Vyvanse), as well as in methamphetamine (or "meth"). Caffeine—found in coffee, tea, energy drinks, many sodas, and even chocolate—is also a low-grade stimulant. In low to moderate doses, stimulants make people feel more energetic. They quicken heart rate and breathing rate, as well as help to fight fatigue.

These benefits explain why caffeine is so ever-present in our society (and many others around the world). They also explain why the abuse of prescription ADHD drugs, especially on college campuses, has become so rampant in recent years. A recent meta-analysis of over 30 studies on the subject, covering thousands of students across a wide range of colleges, found that 17% of college students misused or abused stimulant medications (Benson et al., 2015). To clarify—this is not the rate of students diagnosed with ADHD taking the drugs as prescribed by a physician, but the rate of students getting their hands on the drugs in other ways for other reasons.

Studies that delve into those reasons for the misuse or abuse of stimulants find that academic performance is among the leading reasons. These drugs help students stay awake and alert when studying, writing papers, and taking tests (White et al., 2006; DeSantis et al., 2008). College students asked to estimate the percentage of their classmates who misuse or abuse ADHD stimulant medications generally overestimate the actual rate, and the amount by which they overestimate it correlates with their own odds of doing it (Kilmer et al., 2015). When students think everybody's doing it, it's easier for them to decide to try it for themselves.

Trying it for yourself can be dangerous, however. Remember: ADHD medications are stimulants, chemically similar to cocaine. Taking any prescription stimulant without the supervision of a physician can lead to health problems, including irregular heartbeat, muscle tremors and twitching, paranoia, hallucinations, excessive sweating, hypertension, and insomnia. Even overuse of caffeine can bring on similar symptoms. Further, the addictive quality of stimulants means that withdrawal can be a nightmare—everything from headaches and fatigue to depression, pain, and vomiting.

So how much caffeine is too much?

Researchers are still working on this question, but there is growing evidence that keeping caffeine intake below 400 mg per day seems to be best for your health. Studies indicate that the adverse effects of caffeine don't kick in until intake gets higher than that (Nawrot et al., 2003; de Mejia & Ramirez-Mares, 2014). Of course, that amount is based on an average-sized adult. For smaller adults, children, and pregnant women, the healthy amount of caffeine has a lower limit. If you're trying to convert that 400 mg total into a particular number of caffeinated drinks, the key is to know how much caffeine *your* drinks contain. Check **Table 4.4**—it lists common caffeine sources like sodas, energy drinks, tea, and more. When you do, pay attention not only to the amount of caffeine, but the serving size as well. If you drink big bottles of soda, venti cups of coffee, or tall cans of Red Bull, you might have to do some multiplying.

One last note about stimulants—nicotine, the key ingredient in tobacco, is also considered a stimulant. Surely, you've already been bombarded with knowledge of the health dangers of smoking and chewing tobacco. For example, nicotine is highly addictive, and many people who quit smoking end up starting again. It is the leading preventable cause of death in the United States: It kills hundreds of thousands of

LIFE HACK 4.3

Remember that caffeine is a stimulant drug. Keep track of how much you take in, and if you have trouble sleeping, consider cutting down.

(Nawrot et al., 2003; de Mejia & Ramirez-Mares, 2014)

stimulants
Drugs that speed up bodily functions.

TABLE 4.4: How Much Caffeine?

PRODUCT		SERVING SIZE	AMOUNT OF CAFFEINE (MG)
Coke, Pepsi, Diet Coke, Diet Pepsi		12 ounces	23–47
Mountain Dew, Diet Mountain Dew		12 ounces	42–55
Red Bull, Rockstar, Amp		8 ounces	70–80
Black tea		8 ounces	14–70
Coffee		8 ounces	100–200
Espresso		1 ounce	50–75
5-hour energy shot		2 ounces	200

How much caffeine do you consume per day? Remember, many experts suggest that the closer you get to 400 mg per day, the closer you get to health risks. Also, remember to compare these serving sizes to your actual drink sizes. Data from Mayo Clinic Staff, 2014. (Photos) Costi Iosif; Ian Dagnall/Alamy; Steve Stock/Alamy; Pakhnyushchy/Shutterstock; Everything/Shutterstock; B and E Dudzinscy/Shutterstock; Spencer Platt/Getty Images.

people every year in the United States and millions around the world. (For about half of the people who smoke continuously throughout their lives, the habit will kill them.) A pregnant woman who smokes does serious damage to her fetus, and secondhand smoke damages the people who inhale it.

Do you know about *thirdhand smoke*? Thirdhand smoke is not smoke itself, but the cancer-causing residue that smoke leaves behind. That residue embeds itself in almost everything the smoke touches—clothes, carpets, drapes, sofas, car seats, even human hair. And that residue remains there long after the smoke itself has cleared (Sleiman et al., 2010; Dreyfuss, 2010). So, if you smell cigarettes—on someone's jacket, in their car, in their apartment, anywhere at all—you're exposed to thirdhand smoke, even if there is no longer any smoke to be seen.

Unfortunately, far fewer people recognize the dangers of thirdhand smoke than secondhand smoke (Winickoff et al., 2009). Perhaps that is because the evidence, and the public awareness, regarding the dangers of thirdhand smoke are just starting to grow (Tuma, 2010). But consider what researchers have already learned. For example,

"Say when."
Harry Bliss, The New Yorker Collection/The Cartoon Bank

Smoking is dangerous not only for the smoker but also for other people who breathe in the smoke or the residue it leaves behind. Matthias Ritzmann/Corbis

in one study, nonsmokers who moved into apartments that had previously been occupied by smokers showed significant jumps in their own nicotine levels, even if the apartment had been cleaned between residents and had stayed vacant for as long as 2 months (Matt et al., 2010). Another study measured thirdhand smoke in people who had stayed in two different kinds of "nonsmoking" hotel rooms: rooms in completely nonsmoking hotels and nonsmoking rooms in hotels that also contain some smoking rooms. People who stayed in the nonsmoking rooms in hotels that also contain some smoking rooms had higher levels of nicotine, presumably from breathing in thirdhand smoke from the other rooms and hallways of the hotel, than people who stayed in the completely nonsmoking hotel (Matt et al., 2014).

Opiates. **Opiates** are pain-relieving drugs made from the poppy plant. *Opioids* are synthetic versions of opiates, but they are so similar that the two terms are often used interchangeably. (Both opiates and opioids are also sometimes called *narcotics*. Here, for simplicity, we'll use the term *opiates* to cover them all.) Opiates include some street drugs, like heroin and opium, and also some prescription painkillers like morphine, codeine, hydrocodone (Vicodin), and oxycodone (OxyContin, Percocet, Percodan). Opiates activate the same receptors in our brains as *endorphins*. As we learned in Chapter 2, endorphins are neurotransmitters in the brain that occur naturally when we increase pleasure or reduce pain. So, using an opiate is like getting a straight shot of the pleasure that comes naturally from good sex, good food, good exercise, or a good laugh.

That is the primary reason why opiates are so addictive. People who take opiates experience such an intense rush of pleasure (or relief from pain) that the previous state of mind seems undesirable, perhaps unbearable. They often focus exclusively on finding another dose of opiates (another hit) to return them to the euphoric, often semiconscious state they were in when they had taken the opiate. Decades ago, opiate addiction typically took the form of people hooked on illegal drugs like heroin or morphine. In recent decades, however, prescription opiate addiction has become much more common (Popova et al., 2009; Fischer et al., 2014). According to one estimate, in 2013 (National Institute on Drug Abuse, 2014):

- There were 2 million people in the United States with a substance use disorder involving opiates.
- There were 207 million prescriptions written for opiate-based pain-killers.
- The number of deaths from overdoses of opiate-based pain-killers had quadrupled in the previous 15 years and exceeded the number of deaths from all illegal drugs.

Celebrities whose deaths have been linked to painkiller addiction or overdose include Prince, Heath Ledger, Philip Seymour Hoffman, and Anna Nicole Smith. Other celebrities who have publicly described their problems with painkillers include rappers Eminem and Macklemore, actor Matthew Perry, radio host Rush Limbaugh, and football players Brett Favre and Walter Payton.

In some cases of opiate addiction, the person becomes addicted after taking the opiates for a prescribed reason, such as severe back pain or postsurgical pain. One study found that about a quarter of the people who received a prescription for opiates for back pain took the medication in a way that didn't match instructions (Martell et al., 2007). In other cases, the person becomes addicted with no history of legitimate opiate use. They obtain the pills from a friend, family member, unethical medical professional, or on the street. In fact, among physicians who treat patients with chronic pain, a significant challenge is distinguishing true pain sufferers from opiate addicts scamming for meds (Haller & Acosta, 2010; Fields, 2011). Increasing numbers who become addicted to the pain pills later turn to heroin or other street forms of opiates (Jones, 2013).

There is no surefire treatment for addiction to painkillers. A common treatment is methadone, a substance that is itself an opiate. It is safer than the drugs it typically

opiates
Drugs made from the poppy plant that relieve pain.

hallucinogens
Drugs that produce unrealistic sensations such as hallucinations.

treats, but it is not entirely safe, and its misuse can cause further problems or even death. Nonetheless, many people have recovered from addiction to painkillers with the help of methadone, other substances, or non-medical therapies.

Hallucinogens. **Hallucinogens** are drugs that produce unrealistic sensations such as hallucinations. Hallucinogens were known as "psychedelic" drugs in past generations, when the most common examples were LSD (lysergic acid diethylamide, or "acid"), PCP, and certain psychoactive varieties of mushrooms. Currently, a more common hallucinogen is MDMA ("ecstasy"), which also has some stimulant qualities. Some other drugs that may or may not chemically qualify as hallucinogens but often have hallucinogenic effects include "bath salts," cannabis (marijuana, "weed," or "pot"), and synthetic cannabis ("K2" or "spice").

Hallucinogens cause people to see, hear, and feel things that are not really there. During "trips" on these drugs, some people claim to experience unusual cross-sensory distortions, like seeing smells or hearing colors. Hallucinogens also cause a strong detachment from reality (often described as a dreamlike state) and impair people's judgment and reasoning, which causes them to do blatantly dangerous things that they would never otherwise do. For example, people tripping on hallucinogens might try to fly from a high story of a building or try to drive a car through a wall. Sometimes, people experience these hallucinations as "bad trips" in which the hallucinations feel scary and the person fears that they may be losing their mind.

Marijuana is included in this category, but it is different from the more "hard-core" hallucinogens in many ways. First, it is not always hallucinogenic. Many people do not report any drastically different sensations when on marijuana than when off it. Instead, the primary effect is often described as a pleasantly relaxed feeling, with any sensory changes secondary if present at all. Second, marijuana is much less toxic. A single overdose of MDMA, LSD, or another hallucinogen can cause serious damage or death, but there is little evidence of such risks for marijuana. In fact, some experts describe marijuana use as safer than such legal drugs as alcohol and nicotine (Brick & Erickson, 2013). Third, marijuana is prescribed by doctors for a number of conditions, including glaucoma (a disease involving excessive pressure in the eye) and nausea from chemotherapy. Fourth, marijuana is legal for recreational use in an increasing number of states. Marijuana is not without risk, however. It can become addictive. In higher doses or after long-term use, it often causes memory loss, impairs driving ability, and decreases overall motivation. Long-term smoking of marijuana can also lead to lung cancer.

One final note about psychoactive drugs: The drugs used to treat psychological disorders are psychoactive drugs too. That is what they are designed to do. They include *antipsychotic* drugs to help with hallucinations and other bizarre experiences; *antianxiety* drugs to help with fear and nervousness; *antidepressant* drugs to help with sadness and hopelessness (and anxiety as well); and *mood-stabilizing* drugs to help reduce the intensity of extreme emotional highs and lows. All of these drugs are described in Chapter 15 as treatments for psychological disorders. **Table 4.5** summarizes the effects of the various types of psychoactive drugs.

TABLE 4.5: Types of Psychoactive Drugs

TYPE	EXAMPLES	COMMON EFFECTS
Depressants	Alcohol, benzodiazepines, barbiturates	Slow bodily functions; enhance relaxation
Stimulants	Cocaine, amphetamines (including many ADHD medications), methamphetamines, caffeine, nicotine	Speed up bodily functions; enhance energy and overcome fatigue
Opiates	Heroin, opium, morphine, codeine, hydrocodone, oxycodone	Relieve pain; enhance pleasure
Hallucinogens	LSD ("acid"), PCP, selected mushrooms, MDMA ("ecstasy"), "bath salts," cannabis, synthetic cannabis	Produce hallucinations or dreamlike "trips"

CHECK YOUR LEARNING:

4.15 What are psychoactive drugs?

4.16 How do psychoactive drugs work?

4.17 What is the difference between tolerance and withdrawal?

4.18 What is addiction?

4.19 What do depressants do, and what are some common examples?

4.20 What do stimulants do, and what are some common examples?

4.21 What do opiates do, and what are some common examples?

4.22 What do hallucinogens do, and what are some common examples?

Other Altered States of Consciousness

YOU WILL LEARN:

4.23 what meditation is.

4.24 what mindfulness is.

4.25 what déjà vu is.

4.26 what a near-death experience is.

Beyond sleep and wakefulness, even beyond hypnosis and psychoactive drugs, are other states of consciousness. For some people, certain occurrences temporarily put the mind in a different mode—including trances, out-of-body experiences, seizures, fasting- or fever-induced stupors, mystical revelations, and spiritual or religious visions (Barušs, 2003). Generally, these types of altered states have not received much serious study by mainstream psychologists. Let's consider a few that have been studied at least somewhat: *meditation* and *mindfulness*; *déjà vu*; and *near-death experiences*.

Meditation and Mindfulness

Meditation is an activity designed to increase focused attention with the ultimate purpose of improving your mental state. Historically, that improvement of mental state emphasized a more direct connection with a higher being or spirit, such as Buddha or God. More recently, especially as practiced in the United States and other Western cultures, that emphasis on spiritual connection is accompanied by an emphasis on personal or psychological gain (Das, 2014). These gains are usually psychological such as lowered stress levels or improvement in symptoms of anxiety or depression, often with an eye toward improvement in physical health too (Eberth & Sedlmeier, 2012; Shapiro & Walsh, 2003).

Meditation has been around for thousands of years in cultures all around the world, often tied to religious or spiritual practices (Harrington, 2008; West, 1987). During that long history, meditation has taken many different forms, but most have one of two primary goals. In the first type of meditation, the goal is to empty the mind of all thoughts. The person meditating tries to achieve an entirely clear mind, a mind not occupied by thoughts or feelings. This clear mind then allows the person to experience the sensations of life as they arrive. The person meditating loses sense of time or space, and the world around the person begins to feel like a single, connected entity.

In the second type of meditation, the goal is to focus the mind wholly on a specifically chosen stimulus. This stimulus can be a word, phrase, or sound that the person says over and over again (a mantra, like "Om, om, om..."), a visual object that the person sees or imagines, or a concept that the person holds in mind. The idea is that the person reaches a transcendent, transformative state by becoming completely absorbed with this stimulus. By continuously contemplating this stimulus, all other thoughts and impulses fall away, leaving the mind to focus on inner experience (Gunaratana, 2014; Simpkins & Simpkins, 2009; Newberg, 2010; van Vugt, 2015).

Meditation often lowers stress levels and improves mental and physical health.
George Rudy/Getty Images

Meditation has grown in popularity in recent decades, and there are plenty of how-to books available, each providing its own methods for practicing meditation. One of those books is written by the Dalai Lama, the spiritual leader of all Tibetan Buddhism, a religion closely associated with meditation practices both currently and historically. Here are some of the Dalai Lama's insights and suggestions for beginning mediation (His Holiness the Dalai Lama, 2011):

- Meditation can be challenging when it is new, and it requires extensive practice.
- At first, aim for 10–15 minutes of meditation per day. Even a few minutes of successful meditation is a big accomplishment in the early stages.
- Meditate in the early morning hours, if possible, when the mind tends to be clearest and most unaffected by the events of the day.
- Meditation can be practiced anywhere, but it is better at first to find a quiet place free of visual and auditory distractions.
- Any comfortable position is fine, but sitting cross-legged is preferred because it is both comfortable and upright, decreasing the odds of drifting off to sleep.
- Start meditation by noticing your breath, deliberately concentrating on how it passes in and then out through your nostrils.

The goal of meditation is to achieve a neutral or blank state of mind, one that directly experiences the immediate inner sensations to such an extent that it can't get caught up in distracting thoughts about day-to-day life. Of course, those thoughts will at least occasionally occur, even if you don't want them to, but you can let go of them and gently remind yourself to refocus exclusively on your breathing. The Dalai Lama describes that process of letting mental events run their course rather than fighting them, as well as the benefits of doing so (His Holiness the Dalai Lama, 2011, pp. 169–170):

> When you initially engage in this meditation, inevitably you will find that your mind wanders off, thoughts and images float through your conscious awareness, or a memory pops up for no apparent reason. When this happens, do not get caught up in the energy of these thoughts and images by trying to suppress or reinforce them. Simply observe them and let them go, as if they are clouds appearing in the sky and fading from view … every now and then you will come to experience short intervals of what feels like an absence or a vacuum, when your mind has no particular content. Your first successes in this will only be fleeting. But with persistence … you can start to understand that the mind is like a mirror, or clear water, in which images appear and disappear ... Like a detached onlooker watching a spectacle, you will learn how to see your thoughts for what they are, namely constructs of your mind. So many of our problems arise because, in our naïve untrained state, we confuse our thoughts with actual reality. …. In so doing, we tie ourselves ever tighter into a world that is essentially our own creation and become trapped in it, like a length of rope entangled in its own knots.

Several parts of this description by the Dalai Lama illustrate that meditation leans heavily on the concept of **mindfulness**: awareness of your moment-to-moment experiences fully, deliberately, and without distraction. There is some discrepancy between the original Eastern definition of mindfulness and the way the term is used more recently in Western countries, but the essence remains largely the same (Grossman, 2011; Grossman & Van Dam, 2011; Quaglia et al, 2015; Gethin, 2015; Davis & Thompson, 2015; Carmody, 2015). That essence of mindfulness is all about experiencing what is happening in the present moment. This also means a mindful person does not focus on what happened in the past (even a minute or a day ago), and does not worry about what the future may bring. Experience of the present moment is without judgment or wishful thinking either. There is no approval or disapproval, no desire that what is happening will change or remain, just accepting it no matter how it makes you feel (Germer,

meditation
An activity designed to increase focused attention with the ultimate purpose of improving a person's mental state.

mindfulness
Awareness of one's moment-to-moment experiences fully, deliberately, and without distraction.

2005; Hick, 2008; Roemer & Orsillo, 2009; Kabat-Zinn, 1994; Bishop et al., 2004; Brown & Ryan, 2004).

As an example of an opportunity for mindfulness, consider brushing your teeth. Without mindfulness, you'd do it mindlessly: like a robot, zoned out, going through the motions, not noticing anything about the process at all. With mindfulness, there is a lot to notice: the colors on the toothpaste tube, the firmness of the toothbrush bristles against your teeth, the minty sting of the toothpaste on your tongue, the way the water swirls around the sink before it goes down the drain. Without mindfulness, you might distract yourself by listening to the radio or peeking at your smartphone as you brush your teeth. With mindfulness, brushing your teeth gets your full attention. Without mindfulness, your mind might wander to the past or the future ("Did my friend understand that text I sent last night?" "Am I ready for that exam later today?"). With mindfulness, your mind stays zoomed in on today, on this moment, on the sensations of brushing your teeth.

The underlying idea of mindfulness has risen dramatically in terms of popularity in the United States since the 1990s (Brown et al., 2015). Psychologists and other kinds of therapists have used mindfulness as the basis of treatments for various problems, and have woven it into forms of treatment too (Irving et al., 2015; Hayes-Skelton & Wadsworth, 2015; Segal et al., 2012; Shapiro, 2009). And those treatments have shown impressive results. In terms of biology, mindfulness changes the brain (Zeidan, 2015). In one particular study, participants were shown photos designed to evoke negative emotions, including funerals, people crying, burn victims, and dead animals. The fMRI images of participants showed that those higher in mindfulness had greater activation of the prefrontal cortex and lower activation of the amygdala as they viewed the pictures (Modinos et al., 2010). These results (and similar results from other studies) suggest that mindfulness helps the parts of the brain that interpret events to calm the part of the brain that produces anxiety (Creswell et al., 2007; Brown et al., 2012; Vago & Silbersweig, 2012; Zeidan et al., 2011). Brain differences like these can be obtained after a minimal amount of mindfulness training: just 20 minutes a day for 4 days (Zeidan et al., 2013).

The evidence of the power of mindfulness is not limited to brain scans. Many studies show that incorporating mindfulness into your life can make you significantly happier and healthier (Khoury et al., 2013; Chiesa & Serretti, 2011; Gu et al., 2015; Arch & Landy, 2015). Specifically, there is evidence that mindfulness-based psychotherapies provide great benefits to people with anxiety, depression, eating disorders, personality disorders, addiction, and many other psychological diagnoses (Piet & Hougaard, 2011; Vøllestad et al., 2012: Sedlmeier et al., 2012; Baer, 2006; Hofmann et al., 2010; Bowen et al., 2015).

Mindfulness brings psychological benefits to people without psychological disorders as well (Brown, 2015; Shapiro & Jazaieri, 2015). Higher levels of mindfulness in couples correlates with lower levels of hostility (even right after an argument) and higher levels of relationship satisfaction (Barnes et al., 2007; Carson et al., 2004). College students who underwent an 8-week mindfulness training program had significantly lower rates of daily hassles, stress, and medical symptoms 3 months after it ended (Williams et al., 2001). Middle-aged adults without psychological disorders who underwent a similar 8-week mindfulness training program reported significant gains in positive emotions and overall quality of life (Nyklíček & Kuijpers, 2008). It is also noteworthy that mindfulness aids in the treatment of many physical and medical problems, including cancer, chronic pain, diabetes, hypertension, heart disease, and HIV/AIDS (Carlson, 2015; Keng et al., 2011; Grossman et al., 2004).

Mindfulness is awareness of your moment-to-moment experiences, fully, deliberately, and without distraction. PathDoc/Shutterstock

Déjà Vu

Déjà vu is an experience that feels vaguely like it has already happened even though it has not. It is that odd, otherworldly sense you might get when you walk into a new movie theater but feel like you have been there before. As it is happening, you think

to yourself (and maybe say to your friend), "This is so weird, but I feel like I've already been here," even though you know it is impossible. You double-check your memory to make sure you've never been to that theater, and you're right, you haven't. Still, there is a lingering familiarity about not just the place but the whole experience—buying the ticket, walking through the lobby, and finding your seat all seem like they are repeats of another experience that you just can't quite place.

déjà vu
An experience that feels vaguely like it has already happened even though it has not.

near-death experience
An altered state of consciousness caused by the belief that death is about to happen.

Scientific research on déjà vu reveals some interesting findings (Brown, 2003, 2004):

- About two-thirds of people have experienced déjà vu, typically between once a month and once a year.
- The most common trigger is a physical setting, like a room or a building, but other triggers include spoken words ("Seems like I've heard this story before...").
- Stress and fatigue increase the odds that déjà vu will happen.
- A déjà vu episode typically lasts about 30 seconds, although they may seem longer because time often seems to slow down (and feel somewhat surreal) during the episode.
- People experiencing déjà vu typically find it surprising or confusing.
- Déjà vu is more common among people with high education, high income, liberal beliefs, and younger age.
- There is no link between déjà vu experiences and psychological disorders.

You've probably heard of, and perhaps experienced, déjà vu yourself. But do you know about *jamais vu*? Jamais vu is the opposite of déjà vu—an inappropriate unfamiliarity with a situation that should be familiar. For example, if you step into the shower in your bathroom, where you've taken hundreds of showers before, but it feels as strange as your first shower in a new hotel room, that's jamais vu. (In French, *déjà vu* means already seen; *jamais vu* means never seen.) One survey of 2500 people found that jamais vu was significantly less common than déjà vu (Ardila et al., 1993).

The causes of déjà vu, jamais vu, and similar experiences have not been studied extensively and are not known. Some experts believe that it involves minor abnormalities in neurological, memory, or cognitive processes (Brown, 2003; Wild, 2005; Cleary, 2008).

Near-Death Experiences

A **near-death experience** is an altered state of consciousness caused by the belief that death is about to happen. Near-death experiences are reported by about 10–20% of people who are declared clinically dead but survive (Greyson, 2012). It also happens to a sizable number of people who are approaching death due to illness or who fear they will soon die, even if they do not have reason for that belief (Owens et al., 1990).

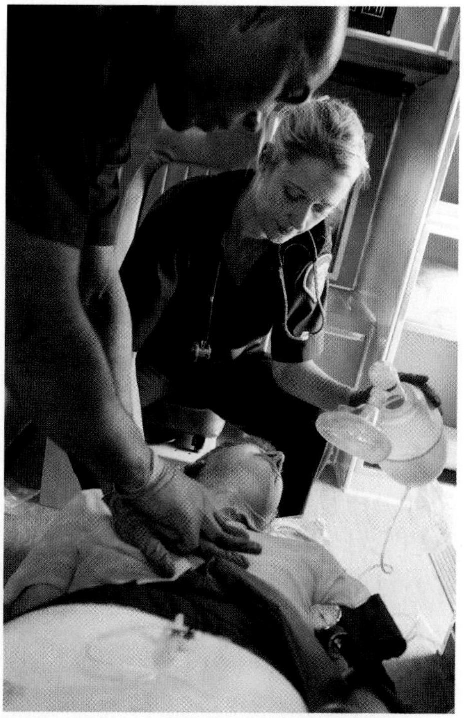

People who have near-death experiences often describe life flashing before their eyes, movement toward a bright light, and revelations about the meaning of life (Greyson, 1985). Afterward, they often become much more spiritual and more compassionate toward other people (Sutherland, 1990; Musgrave, 1997). Cathy Yeulet/Thinkstock

Near-death experiences happen around the world, with remarkably similar features (McClenon, 1994). People who have near-death experiences frequently describe being outside of their own bodies ("I was above my hospital bed, watching what was happening to me"); a review of their life's experiences ("my life flashed before my eyes"); a slowed sense of time; a vision of a bright light to which they were moving closer and closer; a sense of being in another dimension; visions of spirits or deceased relatives; a tremendous revelation or insight about the meaning of life; and an overwhelming feeling of peace, joy, and unity with everything and everyone (Greyson, 1985). Consider this example, shared by a cardiologist who quit practicing medicine and started studying near-death experiences after hearing his patients' stories, such as this one (van Lommel, 2010, pp. 34–35):

> In the distance I saw a light that I had never seen on earth. So pure, so intense, so perfect. I knew it was a being I had to go to. .... It's the pinnacle of everything there is. Of energy, of love especially, of warmth, of beauty. I was immersed in a feeling of total love. .... That very same moment, in a split second, I gained access to a wealth of knowledge, a complete knowing and understanding. All knowledge. Universal knowledge. I understood the origins of the cosmos, how the universe works, and why people do what they do...I realized that this grand scheme not only includes me, but everything and everybody, every human being, every soul, every animal, every cell, the earth and every other planet, the universe, the cosmos, the Light. Everything is connected and everything is one.

There is not yet an explanation for the cause of near-death experiences. Experts have suggested theories that focus on the poor physical health of the dying, including low oxygen levels, abnormal neurotransmitter levels, and side effects of heavy medication (Greyson, 2012). Interestingly, expectations appear to have nothing to do with it. People who have near-death experiences are not just going through the motions of something they expected to happen because of religious or cultural beliefs. Kids who are too young to know those expectations have near-death experiences that match those of adults (Bush, 1983; Herzog & Herrin, 1985; Morse et al., 1986). People who know nothing about near-death experiences, people who hold very different beliefs about the dying process, and people of different religious backgrounds all have very similar near-death experiences (Athappilly et al., 2006; Greyson, 1991; Greyson & Stevenson, 1980; McLaughlin & Malony, 1984).

Near-death experiences change people's spirituality in a major way. One researcher interviewed 50 people who had near-death experiences and found that the number who described themselves as spiritual jumped from 16% before to 76% after the experience. Interestingly, the number who described themselves as religious actually dropped, as did their involvement in organized religion (Sutherland, 1990).

Near-death experiences change people's behavior in a major way too. In another study in which people with near-death experiences were interviewed, the majority agreed that they had become more helpful and compassionate toward others, more appreciative of life, emotionally stronger, more purposeful, and less fearful of death (Musgrave, 1997). Near-death experiences can also have powerful secondhand effects on the friends and family of those who have them. Friends and family often acquire a greater appreciation of life and a greater sense of fearlessness and emotional strength (Flynn, 1986; Ring & Valarino, 2006; Ring, 1984, 1996).

CHECK YOUR LEARNING:

4.23 What is meditation and what purpose does it serve?

4.24 What is mindfulness and what effects can it have?

4.25 What is déjà vu?

4.26 What is a near-death experience?

CHAPTER SUMMARY

Sleep

4.1 The function of sleep is not entirely clear, but many theories emphasize evolutionary benefits like staying still to avoid harm, saving energy, recharging the body, developing the brain, and enhancing memory.

4.2 Partial sleep deprivation is quite common, and it has strong (but often unrecognized) negative consequences in terms of emotion and performance.

4.3 Your circadian rhythm is your internal body clock, which affects alertness and sleepiness throughout each day. It is primarily controlled by your suprachiasmatic nucleus, but it can be influenced by external cues like schedules of light exposure, eating, work shifts, and jet lag.

4.4 Normal sleep can be divided into rapid eye movement (REM) sleep and non-REM sleep. REM sleep involves intense brain activity and dreaming. Non-REM sleep involves stage 1, stage 2, and stages 3 and 4 (slow-wave sleep), which occur in increasing depth.

4.5 People of different genders, ethnicities, and ages exhibit different kinds of sleep patterns.

4.6 Co-sleeping involves family members sleeping in the same room or same bed (usually a child with an adult). For young children, co-sleeping is much more common in Asia and some other parts of the world than it is in most of the United States.

4.7 Sleep abnormalities include insomnia (difficulty sleeping), sleepwalking, narcolepsy (sleep attacks), sleep terrors (brief awakenings marked by fright and confusion), and sleep apnea (sleep interruptions caused by breathing difficulties). Physical illness often goes hand in hand with these sleep abnormalities.

4.8 To treat or prevent sleep problems, maintain a consistent sleep–wake schedule, exercise daily, don't each much at night, and sleep in a comfortable, dark, quiet room. Also, close to bedtime avoid caffeine, naps, cigarettes, alcohol, exercise, and bright light.

Dreams

4.9 There are many theories of dreaming, including folk theories, Sigmund Freud's theory that dreams reveal unconscious wishes, and theories that focus on neuropsychological functioning.

4.10 Themes of dreams tend to be more positive closer to wakeup time than bedtime. In some cases, dreams can improve mental health through imagery rehearsal therapy and lucid dreaming.

Hypnosis

4.11 Hypnosis is an altered state of consciousness in which one person, the participant, becomes very suggestible to another person, the hypnotist. The procedure of hypnotism includes induction, suggestions (some of which can be posthypnotic), and termination.

4.12 Hypnosis has been used to treat various behavioral problems and mental disorders and to improve performance in other areas, including sports, but the evidence for its effectiveness is limited.

4.13 Some people are much more hypnotizable than others, especially those who are more open-minded and have a tendency to get engrossed in sensory experiences.

4.14 The social-cognitive theory of hypnosis, which states that a hypnotized person is really just conforming to social pressure to act hypnotized, is disconfirmed by neuropsychological studies showing that parts of the brain are actually affected by hypnosis.

Psychoactive Drugs and Consciousness

4.15 Psychoactive drugs are substances that alter mental functioning.

4.16 Psychoactive drugs work by changing the amount of neurotransmitter that travels between neurons.

4.17 Tolerance is the decreased effectiveness of a particular amount of a drug caused by repeated use of that drug. Withdrawal involves stressful and uncomfortable symptoms caused by discontinuing a drug that has become habitual, often after a person has become physically or psychologically dependent on that drug.

4.18 Addiction is problematic drug use that persists in spite of serious negative consequences.

4.19 Depressants are drugs that slow bodily functions, and include alcohol, benzodiazepines, and barbiturates. Alcohol has been linked to a variety of negative outcomes, including drunk driving, sexual assault, overdose, dangerous interaction with common medications, birth defects, and damage to vital organs.

4.20 Stimulants are drugs that speed up bodily functions. Stimulants include cocaine, amphetamines (such as those found in ADHD prescription medications), methamphetamine ("meth"), nicotine, and caffeine.

4.21 Opiates (a term that often overlaps with *opioids* and *narcotics*) are drugs made from opium that relieve pain by activating the endorphin receptors in the brain. They are highly addictive and include heroin, morphine, codeine, hydrocodone, and oxycodone.

4.22 Hallucinogens, formerly known as psychedelics, are drugs that produce unrealistic sensations, or "trips," such as hallucinations. They include LSD ("acid"), PCP, certain varieties of mushrooms, and MDMA ("ecstasy"). Other drugs that may have hallucinogenic effects include "bath salts" and cannabis.

Other Altered States of Consciousness

4.23 Meditation is an activity designed to increase focused attention with the ultimate purpose of improving your mental state, often for spiritual or psychological gain.

4.24 Mindfulness is an awareness of your moment-to-moment experiences, fully, deliberately, and without distraction. Mindfulness has been used to improve the mental health of people with and without mental disorders; neuropsychological studies show that it produces changes in the brain.

4.25 Déjà vu is an experience that feels vaguely like it has already happened even though it has not.

4.26 A near-death experience is an altered state of consciousness caused by the belief that death is about to happen.

KEY TERMS

consciousness, p. 105
sleep deprivation, p. 107
circadian rhythm, p. 107
REM, p. 111
REM sleep, p. 111
non-REM sleep, p. 111
REM paralysis, p. 111
REM rebound, p. 111
solitary sleeping, p. 115
co-sleeping, p. 115
insomnia, p. 115
sleepwalking (somnambulism), p. 117
narcolepsy, p. 117
sleep terrors, p. 117
sleep apnea, p. 117
sleep hygiene, p. 119
lucid dreaming, p. 121
hypnosis, p. 122
social-cognitive theory of hypnosis, p. 125
psychoactive drugs, p. 125
tolerance, p. 125
withdrawal, p. 125
physical dependence, p. 125
psychological dependence, p. 125
addiction, p. 125
depressants, p. 127
stimulants, p. 128
opiates, p. 130
hallucinogens, p. 130
meditation, p. 133
mindfulness, p. 133
déjà vu, p. 135
near-death experience, p. 135

SELF-ASSESSMENT

1. ______ is your awareness of yourself and your surroundings.
   a. REM sleep
   b. Consciousness
   c. Insomnia
   d. Circadian rhythm

2. Lanesha is dreaming. Lanesha is most likely to be in which stage of sleep?
   a. REM sleep
   b. stage 1 sleep
   c. stage 2 sleep
   d. stage 3 sleep

3. Anthony experiences ______, which involves sleep "attacks" happening at any time of day.
   a. sleep terrors
   b. sleep apnea
   c. insomnia
   d. narcolepsy

4. Research on the dreams of people with depression shows that:
   a. people with depression don't dream.
   b. people with depression dream about five times as much as people without depression.
   c. dreams that occur in the first half of the night tend to be more negative than dreams that occur in the second half, and dreamers report more positive moods when they wake up than when they went to bed.
   d. depression is caused by nightmares.

5. ______ is an altered state of consciousness in which one person, the participant, becomes very suggestible to another person, the hypnotist.
   a. Hypnosis
   b. Sleep apnea
   c. Sleepwalking
   d. Déjà vu

6. Which of the following is true about psychoactive drugs?
   a. All psychoactive drugs are illegal.
   b. No psychoactive drugs cause tolerance or withdrawal.
   c. Psychoactive drugs are substances that alter mental functioning.
   d. All of the statements are correct.

7. Sean starts using a drug on a regular basis. Eventually, he needs higher doses of the drug to achieve the same effect that a lower dose had earlier. Sean is exhibiting a(n) ______ to this drug.

8. ______ is problematic drug use that persists in spite of serious negative consequences.

9. Barbiturates, benzodiazepines, and alcohol are all examples of ______.
   a. stimulants
   b. hallucinogens
   c. opiates
   d. depressants

10. ______ is awareness of your moment-to-moment experiences, fully, deliberately, and without distraction.

Self-Assessment Answers

1. b 2. a 3. d 4. c 5. a 6. c 7. tolerance 8. Addiction 9. d 10. Mindfulness

WHAT'S YOUR TAKE?

1. Many undergraduate students have worked the night shift, either part-time or full-time. Some of you may be doing so now. Others may have a friend or family member who has worked night shifts. What effect did it have on you? Did it disrupt your sleep? Did it negatively influence your health or happiness? If so, how long did it take to notice these effects?

2. Consider the number of brightly lit screens to which you expose your eyes and your suprachiasmatic nucleus every night: TVs, computers, tablets, smartphones, and perhaps even more. How much time do you spend on these screens? How close to bedtime? Do you look at any screens while you're *in* bed? How have you noticed your sleep being influenced by screen time near bedtime? Will you (or do you) allow your kids to use screens when their bedtime approaches?

SHOW ME MORE

4.1 Natural Light and Circadian Rhythms

http://tiny.cc/sq5njy

Here's a video summary of a study on the effect of natural light (as experienced in a week-long camping trip in the Rocky Mountains) versus electrical light on circadian rhythms.

Iconica/Getty Images

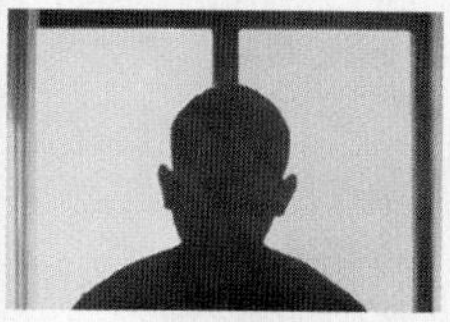

4.2 Sleepwalking with a Comedian

http://tiny.cc/nr5njy

In this clip from the radio show *This American Life*, stand-up comedian Mike Birbiglia finds humor in his own experience with sleepwalking (which involves walking through a closed second-story hotel window).

sfam_photo/Shutterstock

5 Memory

xavierarnau/Getty Images

Imagine that one of your earliest

childhood memories involves nearly getting kidnapped. This is what you remember: You are 2 years old, in a stroller pushed by your babysitter, heading down a crowded street. Suddenly, a would-be kidnapper appears. You see him try to unfasten the buckles of your stroller so he can snatch you and run. Your babysitter does her best to stop him, receiving scratches on her face from her struggle. More people gather around your stroller, and a police officer shows up. The bad guy takes off, and the officer chases him. Even today, the whole scene remains vivid in your mind.

But none of it actually happened. Thirteen years later, your babysitter confessed that she fabricated the whole story. By that time, you were a teenager. You had heard (and told) the story many times—o often, in fact, that you had created a vibrant memory of living through the story even though it was entirely fictional.

It may seem far-fetched that a false memory could seem so real, but this entire episode—the fabricated kidnapping story by the babysitter, the formation of a seemingly real first-hand memory caused by repetition of the story over many years, and the confession by the babysitter thirteen years later—happened to a real person. That real erson was Jean Piaget, one of the most influential and renowned sychologists of all time (Haggbloom et al., 2002; Loftus, 1979; see lso Piaget, 1962 and Macknik & Martinez-Conde, 2010). Piaget was he father of developmental psychology whose work still forms its oundation (as we will learn in Chapter 9), but his memory was as mperfect as yours and mine.

Piaget's experience—and any similar experiences you may have had n which a seemingly accurate memory turned out to be inaccurate—aises many important questions about memory. How do you create memories? How are they stored, and how do you retrieve them? Why o some memories endure, while others fade away? What enhances memory, and what disrupts it? In this chapter, we explore all of these uestions about memory and more.

CHAPTER OUTLINE

Defining Memory

YOU WILL LEARN:

5.1 how psychologists define memory.

5.2 about the role that memory can play in personal identity.

5.3 about the extremes in memory achievement.

Memory is the process of taking in information, saving it over time, and calling it to mind later. Memory is so essential that it would be difficult to imagine human life without it. Try to imagine just the first 2 minutes of your day without a well-functioning memory. You wake up in your bed, but you have no recollection of where you are. The room seems completely unfamiliar. Disoriented, you wander to the next room, stand at the sink and see a face in the mirror, but you don't recognize it. Looking down, you see a small plastic stick with bristles on the end of it next to a tube that says Crest, but you can't remember what those items are or how to use them. You hear something vibrate and ring on your bedside table. Bewildered, you track down the sound. It is some kind of glass-screened small rectangle connected by a cord to the power outlet on the wall, and it's lighting up. "What is this rectangle, and what should I do with it," you wonder. You catch another glimpse of yourself in the bedroom mirror, but again, that face is completely unfamiliar, as if you hadn't just stared at it a minute ago.

Memory and Identity

Memory is indispensable, not just to our functioning but to our identities. Your memories define you as a unique person. No one else knows exactly what you know, has experienced exactly what you have, and knows how to do exactly what you do. In this way, there's an overlap between your memory and your personality. What you remember from your past shapes the way you think, feel, and behave today.

Nelson Dellis has one of the most impressive memories ever documented, having won numerous national memory contests and memorized an endless number of long lists of names and numbers along the way. However, even Dellis knows that memory is about much more than filing away facts:

> What's scary to me ... about potentially losing memories is not forgetting all the stuff I learned ... it's more those small moments with people we love and care about that make us who we are, and if you lose those memories ... then who are you, and how can you enjoy life? —Dellis, 2012.

This link between memory and identity became clear to me as my family watched Alzheimer's disease increasingly overtake my grandma in the last years of her life. Toward the end, she struggled to recognize even her own children and recall even her own name. It was painful and saddening to watch. As we discussed her condition and tried to comfort each other, some of my relatives lamented, "Her memory is really slipping now." Others used slightly different wording: "Grandma is really slipping now." We all meant the same thing, of course, but I noticed that we were using *her memory* and *Grandma* interchangeably. Without realizing it, we highlighted the fact that her lifetime of memories—who her family and friends were, what ingredients went into her chicken soup, the words to her favorite songs—is what made Grandma who she was.

The Extremes of Memory Achievement

When psychologists study memory, sometimes they focus on impairment like my grandma's. Such impairments can come not only from Alzheimer's but from other brain diseases, disorders, or injuries. Sometimes, researchers focus on the other extreme—memory excellence—including those rare people who have the ability to remember nearly everything (Lockhart, 2000). In rare cases, they are born with this ability. For example, Kim Peek (the real person on whom Dustin Hoffman's *Rain Man* character was based) had a memory for facts that was nearly perfect and boundless. He could answer the most obscure trivia questions regarding history, music, sports, movies,

memory
The process of taking in information, saving it over time, and calling it to mind later.

information processing model
A model of memory that involves the three steps of *encoding*, *storage*, and *retrieval*.

religion, and many other subjects. He memorized, word for word, over 9000 books—more than some Kindles can hold! He not only knew the exact location of every zip code and every area code in the United States; he knew the TV stations in every one of them. He memorized calendars going back decades, to the point that if you told him your date of birth, he could flawlessly and instantly tell you the day of the week on which it fell. He had memorized the exact wording of so many of Shakespeare's plays that his family stopped taking him to see them, because he would stand up and correct the actors when they missed a word (Weber, 2009; Treffert & Christensen, 2009).

If (like all the rest of us) you're not born with a mind like Kim Peek's, you can train your mind to excel in memory. *Moonwalking with Einstein* (Foer, 2011) describes the USA Memory Championship, an annual event in New York City where mental athletes from around the world gather to see who can most quickly and successfully memorize all kinds of information. They commit to memory astonishingly long lists of random numbers or words, 50-line poems they have never seen or heard before, and extensive sequences of photos of strangers' faces and names. Particularly impressive is Ben Pridmore, a competitor who can memorize a list of over *1500* random numbers in order, recite the first 50,000 digits of pi, and learn the order of a newly shuffled deck of cards in just over half a minute. Pridmore was not born with these abilities but learned them through training in memory enhancement techniques that any of us could use. The author of *Moonwalking with Einstein*, Joshua Foer, became so intrigued and inspired by these mental athletes that he entered the competition the next year—and won.

But much of the research that psychologists conduct on memory falls between the two extremes, where most of us spend our day-to-day lives (Bower, 2000; Kahana, 2000). Memory researchers strive to understand how memories form, how we access memories, how different kinds of memory work, and ways to help or hurt our ability to remember. Although many questions remain, psychologists have learned a lot about memory. Much of what we now know centers on the fundamental fact that memory generally involves a three-step process of getting information into our minds (*encoding*), holding onto it (*storage*), and taking it back out later (*retrieval*)—a process that we will now examine in detail.

Dustin Hoffman's character in *Rain Man* was based on a real person, Kim Peek (pictured here), whose feats of memory were astounding. He memorized thousands of books, the locations of all U.S. zip codes, and many of Shakespeare's plays, among other things. TV/REX/Newscom

CHECK YOUR LEARNING:

5.1 How do psychologists define memory?

5.2 What role does memory play in personal identity?

5.3 Is an extremely strong memory something you can train yourself to have, or does it depend entirely on inborn ability?

The Three Steps of Memory

Much of what we now understand about memory centers on the **information processing model**: a model of memory that involves the three steps of *encoding*, *storage*, and *retrieval* (**Figure 5.1**). We will examine these three steps in detail, but essentially, they refer to getting information into our minds (*encoding*), holding onto information (*storage*), and taking information back out later (*retrieval*) (Brown & Craik, 2000; Baddeley, 2002; Cowan, 1988). This way of understanding human memory is similar to the way we understand computer memory. First, information enters your computer— for example, a photo transferred from your camera or a document attached to an email. Then the computer saves that information somewhere among its many gigs of available memory. And of course, that information then remains available to be pulled up later when needed.

YOU WILL LEARN:

5.4 what the three steps of memory are according to the information processing model.

5.5 what encoding is and how it involves sensory memory.

5.6 what echoic memory and iconic memory are.

YOU WILL LEARN: (*Continued*)

5.7 how encoding depends on level of processing and how level of processing can be enhanced.

5.8 how encoding involves the physiological changes of long-term potentiation.

5.9 what storage is and where it occurs.

5.10 what retrieval is and how it happens through recall or recognition.

5.11 how retrieval can be affected by retrieval cues.

5.12 how encoding specificity and priming can enhance retrieval.

It can be tempting to take this metaphor between human memory and computer memory too far, but they are not exactly the same (Draaisma, 2000; Randall, 2007). The three steps (encoding, storage, retrieval) are definitely involved in our memory process, but the human mind is far more complex than any computer. So it is best to understand this computer metaphor as an oversimplified version of what goes on in your own memory—a good place to start but not a comprehensive explanation. That's why psychologists call it the information processing *model*, rather than the information processing *fact*. It's an approximation of how our memory works, but not a perfect description.

FIGURE 5.1 The Three Steps of Memory. The three big steps in the memory process are encoding (taking information in), storage (holding information), and retrieval (pulling information out).

Encoding

Encoding is entering information into memory. Without encoding, there's nothing to store and nothing to retrieve later (Brown & Craik, 2000). What you encode, of course, depends on what your senses detect. For that reason, encoding is closely related to **sensory memory**: the earliest part of the memory process, in which the senses take in and very briefly hold information. To explain, let's return to the computer metaphor for a moment. The exterior of your computer has numerous ports through which the computer can "sense," or take in, information from other devices. They allow your computer to "see" an image from a scanner plugged into a USB port or "hear" a voice through a microphone plugged into the minijack port.

Your head also has ports that take in information from around you—your eyes, ears, nose, and mouth. These sense organs are constantly monitoring all of the sights, sounds, smells, and tastes that surround you. The vast majority of this incoming data gets discarded. For example, many of the sounds around you seem to go in one ear and out the other. In a crowded movie theater, your ears pick up lots of little sounds—the air conditioner blowing, chairs creaking, popcorn bags crinkling, other people coughing—but because you're focused on the sounds of the movie, those sounds get filtered out. More specifically, these sounds last only as long as sensory memory can hold them—about 3 or 4 seconds for sounds, about half a second for sights—and then disappear (Turkington & Harris, 2001). The sounds of the movie, however, progress past sensory memory and get fully encoded, entering your mind in such a way that it helps you make sense of the rest of the film and perhaps persisting for some time after.

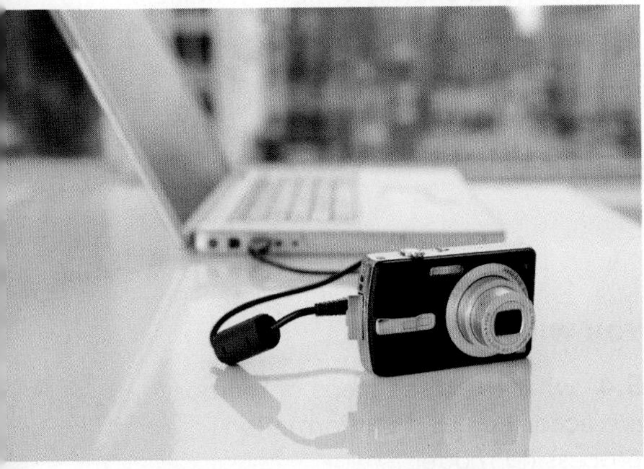

In some ways, human memory works like computer memory, by taking in information (like this computer is taking in photos from the camera), storing them, and retrieving them. In other ways, however, the model of computer memory doesn't match the way human memory actually works. Allison Michael Orenstein/The Image Bank/Getty Images

Echoic Memory. That brief sensory memory for the ambient sounds of the movie theater is an example of **echoic memory**: auditory sensory memory, or all the information your ears took in during the past few seconds. Echoic memory is what allows you to cover for yourself when you momentarily space out, or get distracted, while listening to someone speak. I've taken advantage of it many times, including a few when I was practicing therapy.

Once, a client of mine was tearfully telling me about the moment she caught her boyfriend cheating on her with his ex-girlfriend. "So I walk into the restaurant, and he's actually holding hands with her across the table! I couldn't believe it! I didn't know what to do at first, but then I decided to..." Suddenly I heard a dog bark. A dog? In my therapy office? What was going on? It took me a few seconds, but finally I figured out that the dog bark sound was coming from my client's purse, where she kept her phone. (Later, she explained to me that she loved dogs so much that she made barking her ringtone.) During those few seconds, she was still telling her story, but I was certainly not paying attention. Somehow, within a split second, the last few seconds of her story echoed in my mind. Without missing a beat, I said, "So you decided

to march right over there and throw water in his face. How did he react?" Thank you, echoic memory.

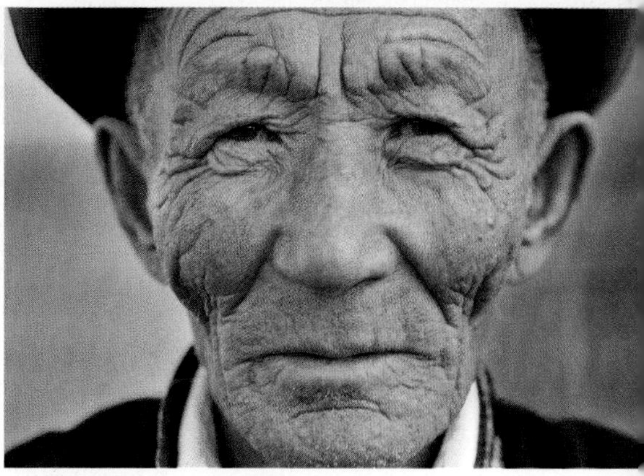

Encoding is entering information into memory. This happens through sensory memory, in which your eyes, ears, nose, and mouth take in information much as ports on your computer do. Matthieu Paley/Photonica/Getty Images

Iconic Memory. Your eyes' version of this very temporary holding area for incoming information is **iconic memory**: visual sensory memory, or all the information your eyes took in during the last fraction of a second (Jiang et al., 2009; Hollingworth, 2009; Long, 1980; Coltheart, 1980).

In a classic study, George Sperling (1960; see also Irwin & Thomas, 2008) demonstrated that the amount of information we hold in iconic memory is much greater than researchers had previously believed (**Figure 5.2**). He flashed a 3 × 4 matrix (a tic-tac-toe board with an extra column, basically) with a different letter in each of the 12 boxes in front of participants for a very brief period—just one-twentieth of a second. He then asked them to list all the letters they remembered. In this free-recall situation, participants typically remembered only about half of the letters. However, Sperling had a hunch that many more than half of the letters were present in iconic memory. He guessed that the memory of certain letters faded away during those seconds in which participants were recalling the ones that first occurred to them. Sperling tested this hunch by sounding a tone immediately after the flash, which indicated a specific row (top, middle, or bottom) that participants should recall. Their recall went up to 76% of the target row, supporting Sperling's hypothesis. A follow-up study (Averbach & Sperling, 1961) with larger grids found similar results with the use of a visual cue (a bar next to a particular row) rather than a tone.

Level of Processing. The likelihood that information progresses past sensory memory and becomes encoded, stored long-term, and retrieved depends upon its **level of processing**: how deeply information is processed. Also known as *depth of processing*, the idea here is that we tend to forget information quickly when we think about it in shallow ways, but we tend to remember information well when we think about it in deep ways (Craik, 2002, 2007; Craik & Tulving, 1975; Craik & Lockhart, 1972). In this context, *shallow* means superficial, and *deep* means meaningful. So the more meaning we attach to information—the more we relate it to other information or connect it to emotion, for example—the more it becomes embedded in our memory.

For example, imagine shopping for wedding invitations. As you look through the dozens of samples, you pay attention to many features of the words—the font, the size, the color of the ink, the capitalization—but you don't pay attention to their meaning. In other words, even if every one of these invitation samples contains the same information—the same bride's and groom's names, the same wedding date, the same wedding location—odds are you'll quickly forget it because you were focusing on shallow characteristics of the words rather than deep ones.

Contrast this shopping memory to a memory for an actual wedding invitation you receive from a friend, which causes you to think about what their wedding means to you. You will buy an airline ticket and a wedding gift, take a day off of work, and see old friends at the wedding. All of these meaningful thoughts enhance your memory for the

L	G	Q	W
D	T	N	R
P	M	Z	K

FIGURE 5.2 Sperling's Iconic Memory Task. When asked to recall all of these letters after seeing them for a fraction of a second, most participants could recall no more than half. But when participants were asked to remember a particular row, their recall rates improved significantly, illustrating the capacity of iconic memory. Research from Sperling, 1960.

encoding
The entering of information into memory.

sensory memory
The earliest part of the memory process, in which the senses take in and very briefly hold information.

echoic memory
The auditory sensory memory, or all the information the ears took in during the previous few seconds.

iconic memory
The visual sensory memory, or all the information the eyes took in during the previous fraction of a second.

level of processing
How deeply information is processed.

TABLE 5.1: Shallow Processing versus Deep Processing of Written Text

Shallow processing happens when you consider questions about superficial characteristics of the material, like these:	*Deep processing* happens when you consider questions about the significance of the material, like these:
• What type and size is the font?	• What does it mean?
• What color are the letters?	• What are its most important points?
• Are the letters in upper case or lower case?	• How does it relate to information I already know?
• How many words does it contain?	• How does it affect my life?

information on the invitation. **Table 5.1** further explains the differences between shallow and deep processing.

Let's consider another real-world application of the impact of level of processing. Ted is an English-speaking American who is taking his first trip to Mexico. Ted knows no Spanish but is trying to memorize a few phrases he might need. One phrase is, *¿Tiene agua?* (which means, Do you have water?). If Ted tries to memorize this Spanish phrase as a series of meaningless syllables—*Ti. En. E. A. Gua.*—his processing is shallow, and he will probably struggle to remember the phrase.

Deeper processing about the underlying meanings of the words and how they connect to English words would help Ted. For example, Ted could recognize that the verb *tiene* comes from the same Latin root (*tain-*) as lots of English words that mean something similar to *have*, like con*tain*, main*tain*, or ob*tain*. Ted could also recognize that the noun *agua* comes from the same Latin root (*aqua*) as lots of English words that refer to water, like *aqua*tic, *aqua*rium, and *aque*duct. Appreciating what these words mean rather than just what they sound like would move Ted from shallow processing to deep processing, which in turn would help him secure them in his memory.

Research involving PET (positron emission tomography) scans has found that different levels of processing take place in different areas of the brain. Researchers presented words to participants, half of whom were asked whether the word contained the letter *A* (shallow processing), and half of whom were asked whether the word was a living or nonliving thing (deep processing). As expected, the deep processors remembered more of the words, but this study also discovered something new: the deep processors utilized their left prefrontal cortex much more extensively than the shallow processors (Kapur et al., 1994). The finding that shallow processing and deep processing rely on different parts of the brain suggests that they are distinct functions.

Effortful Processing. To some extent, we can deliberately control the level of processing that we apply to incoming information, which is known as *effortful processing* (Hasher & Zacks, 1979, 1984). One effective type of effortful processing is **chunking**: grouping pieces of information together in a meaningful way to enhance memory. For example, you might find it impossible to remember a string of letters this long: NBCHBOCNNMTVTNTCBS. However, if you chunk it into three-letter codes—which are meaningful because they are TV networks—the task becomes much easier: NBC, HBO, CNN, MTV, TNT, CBS. Similarly, if you think of any choreographed dance—the Whip, the Nae Nae, the Dougie—as a series of individual steps, you'll have a harder time remembering them all than if you see them as groups, or chunks, of steps. See **Table 5.2** for an example about chunking and grocery shopping.

We often chunk deliberately to boost our memories, but chunking happens automatically and outside of our awareness too (Gobet et al., 2001). This happens often in our memory for faces, in which we chunk numerous facial features into a package rather than viewing eyes, nose, mouth, hair, skin color, and so on as isolated features to be remembered separately (Thornton & Conway, 2013). Chunking may also happen automatically when experts in particular fields view and remember complex patterns. For example, chess champions chunk. They see the board not as a collection of isolated pieces (the way a novice would), but as a meaningful pattern—a whole rather than a

chunking
Grouping pieces of information together in a meaningful way to enhance memory.

rehearsal
Deliberately repeating information to enhance memory.

maintenance rehearsal
Information repeated in exactly the same form as it was originally encoded.

elaborative rehearsal
Adding meaning or associations to information to enhance memory.

TABLE 5.2: Chunking at the Supermarket

WHAT YOU NEED TO REMEMBER IF YOU DON'T CHUNK	WHAT YOU NEED TO REMEMBER IF YOU CHUNK
Lettuce	Salad ingredients
Dressing	
Croutons	
Carrots	
Tomatoes	
Pizza crust	Pizza ingredients
Tomato sauce	
Shredded cheese	
Oregano	
Pepperoni	
Mushrooms	
Detergent	Laundry items
Fabric softener	
Dryer sheets	
Bleach	

collection of parts (Gobet & Simon, 1998; Chase & Simon, 1973). Chunking has also been identified in the way experienced football, basketball, soccer, and hockey players perceive and remember plays in their respective sports (Garland & Barry, 1990, 1991; Allard & Burnett, 1985; Williams et al., 1993).

Another type of effortful processing is **rehearsal**: deliberately repeating information to enhance memory. Rehearsal commonly takes the form of saying verbal material over and over, either aloud or silently, to yourself. For example, let's say you get a phone call from your roommate while grocery shopping and she asks you to pick up peanut butter, bananas, and bread. You might recite that short list to yourself again and again—"Peanut butter, bananas, and bread. Peanut butter, bananas, and bread. Peanut butter, bananas, and bread"—until you have those items in your cart. But rehearsal can involve nonverbal sounds as well as words, as when a guitarist mentally replays a riff again and again. Rehearsal can be visual too, such as when a wide receiver repeatedly envisions a pass route or a cheerleader repeatedly envisions a routine in an attempt to memorize it (Awh et al., 1998, 1999; Godijn & Theeuwes, 2012).

Psychologists who study memory make a distinction between two kinds of rehearsal, *maintenance rehearsal* and *elaborative rehearsal* (Craik & Watkins 1973). In **maintenance rehearsal**, information is repeated in exactly the same form it was originally encoded. By contrast, **elaborative rehearsal** involves adding meaning or associations to information, which enhances memory. Maintenance rehearsal (as exemplified by the grocery store example) can help a little, but elaborative rehearsal can help a lot more (Greene, 1987; Gardiner et al., 1994; Naveh-Benjamin & Jonides, 1984). The reason centers on *level of processing*: maintenance rehearsal is shallow, but elaborative rehearsal is deep (Craik & Tulving, 1975).

To illustrate the difference between the two types of rehearsal, imagine that you move to the Nob Hill area in Portland, Oregon, and you want to learn the streets. One strategy is to repeat the names of the streets over and over again (maintenance rehearsal), in order as you move north: start with Alder Street, then move north to Burnside Street, then Couch Street. Slowly you may get through the whole map, but your retention may not be as sharp as you like. If you realize, however, that in Nob Hill, the streets go in alphabetical order: Alder, Burnside, Couch, Davis, Everett, Flanders, Gilsan, Hoyt…all the way to York Street on the far north side, your rehearsal becomes connected to the alphabet you've known since childhood (elaborative rehearsal), and the memorizing gets much more effective.

Chunking involves grouping pieces of information together in a meaningful way. Chunking strengthens memory, and it also enables experts in chess (and other fields) to grasp complex patterns among a variety of parts. Cristian Zamfir/Shutterstock

Exercise enhances long-term potentiation, the improvement in the connectivity of neurons in the brain that forms the biological basis of memory. Mark Bowden/iStock/Getty Images

As another example of elaborative rehearsal, consider two high school students, Molly and Ellie, learning about the 2008 presidential election in their history class. Molly approaches it as nothing more than a list of unrelated bits of information to be committed to memory: Barack Obama was the Democratic nominee and John McCain, the Republican nominee. Obama's running mate was Joe Biden. McCain's running mate was Sarah Palin. The election took place on November 4. And so on. Ellie, on the other hand, uses a different strategy. She seeks out the context for these facts and what they meant to voters at the time: attitudes toward the outgoing president, George W. Bush; controversies over health care, the Iraq war, and the economic recession; the significance of an African American candidate, and so on. Ellie reads about these issues in books and Web sites and sees the same facts reported in different ways. Even if Molly spends an equivalent amount of time doing rote memorization, her maintenance rehearsal will never be as deep or as effective as Ellie's elaborative rehearsal.

Long-Term Potentiation. When encoding takes place, the memory-based physiological changes of the brain have begun. One physiological change is **long-term potentiation**: the increased connectivity between simultaneously stimulated neurons that forms the biological basis of memory. Long-term potentiation is what memory looks like up close, at the neuron level, in the brain (Malenka & Nicoll, 1999; Bliss & Collingridge, 1993). Think back to the metaphor we used in Chapter 2, in which cell bodies are like cities and axons (with their terminal branches, dendrites, and synapses) are like highways between them. Long-term potentiation is basically an improvement to those highways that enhances the flow of traffic. The improvement takes place because it is frequently traveled—like a single-lane country road that gets upgraded to a highway because of an increase in traffic.

Interestingly, physical exercise helps long-term potentiation. In one study, some rats were given the chance to run on exercise wheels, while others were not. Not only did the running rats learn a maze more quickly than the others; their brains showed much more evidence of long-term potentiation—in particular the hippocampus, where much of memory is centered (van Praag et al., 1999). A later study found the same effect to be especially strong for rats whose mother was given alcohol during pregnancy, a finding with hopeful implications for children whose mothers drank during their pregnancies and who now suffer with fetal alcohol syndrome (covered in Chapter 9). These children often struggle with cognitive impairments such as limited memory capacity (Christie et al., 2005).

More recently, researchers have discovered the process of *long-term depression*. (Although the word *depression* suggests a sadness that may last many months, that's not what it means in this discussion of the biological basis of memory.) Long-term depression is the opposite of long-term potentiation, which means it is a decrease in the connectivity between neurons in the brain that correlates with memory fading (Malenka & Bear, 2004; Linden, 1994; Linden & Connor, 1995; Bear & Abraham, 1996). Long-term depression may be the basis of forgetting (the box From Research to Real Life), which is actually quite functional when applied to unimportant information (Nicholls et al., 2008; Malleret et al., 2010).

Wait—forgetting is functional? Isn't it bad to forget stuff?

Actually, forgetting stuff that is no longer important is beneficial. It makes more room in the neurons for the important stuff, which enhances memory overall. In our cities and roads metaphor, long-term depression is like a once-popular road being abandoned and becoming overgrown with weeds. Its demise allows the department of transportation to devote more time and energy to building new roads or improving the roads that drivers actually use (Bjork, 2011; Smith, 2011; Bluck et al., 2010).

Storage

Storage is retaining information in memory. It's the second of the three fundamental memory steps, or what happens to information between its intake (*encoding*) and its

long-term potentiation
The increased connectivity between simultaneously stimulated neurons that forms the biological basis of memory.

storage
Retaining information in memory.

short-term memory
A limited amount of new information being held briefly until it is either discarded or encoded into long-term memory.

long-term memory
A seemingly limitless amount of information being held for extensive periods of time.

FROM RESEARCH TO REAL LIFE

Is Forgetting Good?

We hate to forget. As one author describes it: "To most people, forgetting is a terrible thing. To students taking exams, forgetting can mean poor grades. ....To the elderly, forgetting can mean imminent cognitive decline. The downside of forgetting is quite clear to everyone." (Smith, 2011, p. 153).

But if forgetting has a downside, does that mean it has an upside too? One memory scholar strongly argues that there is (Bjork, 1972, 1978, 1989; Bjork et al., 1998). His argument is supported by this fact about human memory: our storage capacity (especially in long-term memory) is essentially limitless, but our retrieval capacity is severely limited. Our ability to retain information outpaces our ability to recall it. This may be a good thing, though: "We do not *want* everything in our memories to be accessible...We need to remember our current phone number, not our prior phone number; we need to remember where we parked the car today, not yesterday or a week ago..." (Bjork, 2011, p. 2)

He goes on to argue that forgetting actually helps remembering. Specifically, when you forget old stuff that is no longer important in your day-to-day life, it lets you remember new stuff that is important (Bjork, 2011). He emphasizes that with the help of retrieval cues, what is forgotten one day can be remembered the next. For example, if you forget how to drive a stick shift car because you have driven an automatic for years, you will probably remember at least some of your stick-shift skills when you find yourself in the driver's seat of a stick-shift car, with your hand on the gear shift and your foot on the clutch.

I've noticed that when I enter the first letter of a search term into Google, the autofill function on my computer "remembers" a few of my most recent search terms and fills them in. That's helpful. But it would be distinctly unhelpful if autofill remembered *all* of the search terms I'd *ever* used. They would instantly fill the screen with so many options that I'd be overwhelmed. In other words, I'm glad autofill "forgets" some of the search terms that I used infrequently and long ago. This keeps things simple and keeps the focus on the most likely terms. When our brain forgets, it serves the same function. Suppressing information we don't need makes room to take in or highlight new information we do need. ⬢

output (*retrieval*). It's a lot like saving files on your computer's hard drive—a process by which you hold onto information you've taken in until you need to open it later.

Traditionally, psychologists have divided the storage of memory into two basic types based on how long it lasts. (Actually, some researchers consider the previously discussed *sensory memory*, the extremely brief lingering of all information that enters our senses, a third type of storage, but here we'll just focus on the two that everyone agrees upon.) The first type of storage is **short-term memory**: a limited amount of new information being held briefly until it is either discarded or kept long-term. The second type of storage is **long-term memory**: a seemingly limitless amount of information being held for extensive periods of time.

Short-Term Memory. Information in short-term memory is like a customer who has just entered the waiting area of a crowded restaurant. Imagine that customer is you. You've entered the restaurant, but you're not necessarily staying. What happens next could go either of two ways. After a short wait, you might progress past the waiting area and be seated in the main dining room, where you'll stay for a long time. Or you might quickly turn around and leave (perhaps because the restaurant is too crowded or the host loses you in the shuffle of other customers or the host is too busy doing other things to pay attention to you). Either way, your stay in the waiting area won't last long.

Information in short-term memory doesn't last long either (Baddeley, 2000). Researchers have found that short-term memory is very brief. In a matter of seconds, short-term memory either fades or, if it is processed sufficiently, enters long-term memory (Atkinson & Shiffrin, 1968; Brown, 1958; Peterson, 1966; Baddeley et al., 2009). A classic study established this finding by giving participants a random three-letter code to remember (like PQC) and then immediately requiring them to perform an unrelated distracter task. In this case, the distracter task was counting backward by either threes or fours from a three-digit number (e.g., 309) spoken by the experimenter until told to recall the three-letter code. If the experimenters kept the participants counting for 15 seconds, almost none of them remembered the code (**Figure 5.3**). Even if the delay was only 3 seconds, recall was only about 50% (Peterson & Peterson, 1959).

Even without a distracter task, information fades from memory quickly. A classic study by Ebbinghaus (1885) found that people who learned three-letter codes forgot

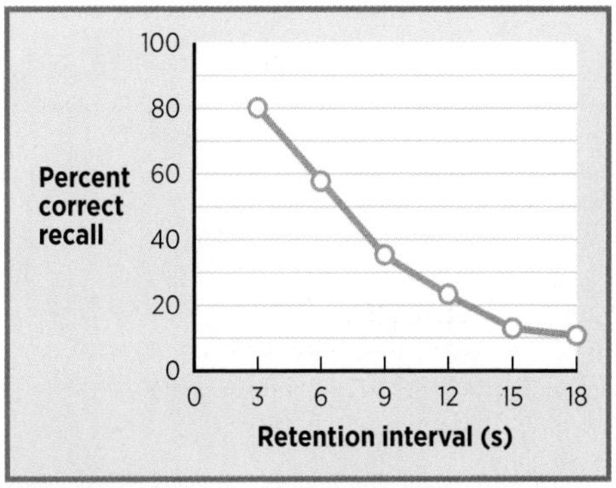

FIGURE 5.3 The Short Life of Short-Term Memory. This graph shows how quickly short-term memory fades. Participants trying to remember a three-letter code while counting backward from a random number started to falter significantly after just 3 seconds and had almost no success after just 15 seconds (Peterson & Peterson, 1959).

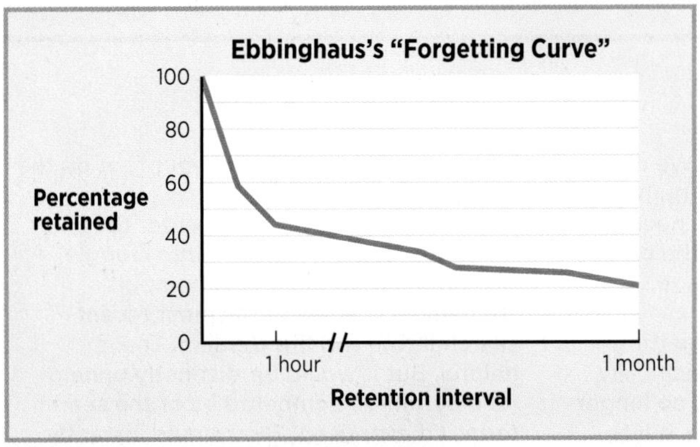

FIGURE 5.4 How Quickly We Forget. A classic memory study found that people who memorized a set of three-letter codes forgot half within an hour, three-quarters within a day, and more over the next month (Ebbinghaus, 1885).

over half of the items within an hour and about three-quarters of the items within a day. For the next month, the rate of recall continued to drop, but never down to zero. See **Figure 5.4** for more on this "forgetting curve."

In addition to this limited duration, short-term memory features a limited capacity (just as the restaurant waiting area has only enough space for a limited number of people). In a review of some early memory studies, Miller (1956) consistently found that the capacity for short-term memory is seven items, plus or minus two. In other words, Miller concluded that most of us can hold about seven items at a time in short-term memory, with a range of five to nine. Miller referred to this finding of seven plus or minus two as the "magic number" of memory capacity. Some more recent researchers question just how magical this number is, however. Some studies have found that our limit is actually a bit higher—and even more have found that our limit is a bit lower—than Miller estimated (Baddeley, 1994, 2000; Gobet & Clarkson, 2004; Shiffrin & Nosofsky, 1994; Schweickert & Boruff, 1986). For example, Cowan (Cowan, 2001, 2005, 2010) has proposed that if there's a magic number of short-term memory capacity, research evidence points to three or four much more strongly than seven.

An important determination in this debate over the magic number of memory capacity is how we define *item*—in other words, how the information to be remembered is *chunked* (Mathy & Feldman, 2012). As we discussed earlier, chunking allows us to take multiple bits of information and group them into a single unit. By chunking, you can multiply the amount of information you remember. Phone numbers are a great example—if you consider each digit to be an item, as in 3-1-4-5-5-5-9-7-4-2, that's 10 items to remember. But if you chunk them together as 314-555-9742, that's only three items. If you can consider the whole series of digits to be a single meaningful piece of information, then that's just one item. That's why companies who want you to remember their phone number get a phone number that translates nicely to words (ideally, one word). Consider 1-800-FLOWERS. It's a lot easier to remember than 1-800-356-9377, because the word *flowers* is a single meaningful chunk, while that random series of seven numbers is, well, a random series of seven numbers **(Table 5.3)**.

But I don't have to memorize phone numbers. My phone does that for me.

Yes, it does, and that's a big change in the way many of us use our memories. We have phones—not to mention computers, tablets, external drives, and other ways to store information digitally—doing the jobs that our brain used to do. This may be old news for your generation, but it's unprecedented in the larger time frame of human history. Check the box It's Like ... for a discussion of the impact of this change.

TABLE 5.3: Why Companies Chunk Phone Numbers

What's easier for you to remember?		
1-800 FLOWERS	or	1-800-356-9377
1-800 CONTACTS	or	1-800-266-8228
1-800 WALGREENS	or	1-800-925-4733
1-800 RITE AID	or	1-800-748-3243
1-800 GO UHAUL	or	1-800-468-4285
1-888 BESTBUY	or	1-888-237-8289
1-800 PETMEDS	or	1-800-738-6337

IT'S LIKE...

Your Smartphone Is Like a Flash Drive for Your Brain

Years ago, if you had asked me for my best friend's phone number, I'd point to my head and say "I've got it up here." Now, I point to my phone and say "I've got it in here."

That's true for lots of us, and for lots of information besides phone numbers too. Our smartphones (not to mention our computers, tablets, and other devices) are like flash drives for our brains—external storage devices that now hold information that we once carried within ourselves.

Numerous authors have debated the pros and cons of this "outsourcing" of human memory (e.g., Carr, 2008). One author laments the fact that "a third of people under 30 can't remember their own phone number. Their smartphones are smart, so they don't need to be. Today's young people are forgoing memory before they even have a chance to lose it" (Brooks, 2007). Another writer admits the shortcomings of his own memory for big events in the lives of his close friends. Here he explains why he never deletes the text messages he receives from friends announcing the birth of their children:

> ...I know why I've kept them [on my phone]: *without referring to them, I have no idea of the names or the birthdays of most of my close friends' firstborn children.* I've replied to these texts, sometimes sent a card or gift as well, ... and then put the entire event out of mind.
>
> —Chatfield, 2012 (italics added)

Flash drives and other external memory devices can improve the memory capacity of our computers tremendously. They allow us to store more information than our computers' built-in hard drives ever could. But when we use those devices, we run the risk of them malfunctioning or information getting lost. And they can actually become inconvenient if we rely on them for frequently needed information. Perhaps the same can be said for our smartphones: they greatly increase our brains' memory capacity, but overreliance on them can be an inconvenience if it becomes necessary too often. It also puts us in jeopardy of major problems if they get lost or damaged (or the battery runs down). ⬢

Increasingly, our smartphones hold information that we once carried within our brains.
Alejandro Rivera/E+/Getty Images

Working Memory. More recent research into short-term memory has offered a different way of understanding it. Specifically, new research suggests that in many cases short-term memory is not merely a holding cell where information passively waits to be either processed or forgotten. Instead, short-term memory often bustles with activity. That is, the information short-term memory contains is often manipulated, operated upon, and otherwise used during its short stay (Baddeley, 2000, 2003, 2007; Baddeley & Hitch, 1974; Cowan, 2008; Gathercole, 2007; Alloway & Alloway, 2013). This now widely accepted idea is known as **working memory**: a type of memory in which processing, or work, is done on briefly held information.

Your working memory is operating almost all of your waking hours. For example, consider watching a TV show. As you take in all the images and words, they don't just sit there—you *do* something with them. You figure out what they mean; connect that meaning to other events that have already happened in the show; speculate about upcoming plot twists they might predict; evaluate the quality of the acting and writing; and much more. In other words, even if the words of a particular scene will occupy your memory for only a very short time, you work on them while they're there.

Working memory is crucial to learning and academic performance (Alloway & Gathercole, 2005; Alloway et al., 2005; Gathercole et al., 2004; Dehn, 2008; Swanson & Berninger, 1996). First, consider the ability to follow a teacher's directions. One researcher found that most kids' working memories enable them to follow verbal instructions with about five specific pieces of information, but kids with learning disabilities can only handle three pieces of information (Henry, 2001). Next, consider the activities that those instructions might contain: hearing a spelling word aloud, thinking about its correct spelling, and writing those letters in order; hearing a phrase in English, thinking about its proper translation, and saying it in French; reading a long paragraph, comprehending it, and answering a question about it. All of these tasks and many more during a school day require the student not just to take new information into short-term memory but to do something with it while it is there (Levin et al., 2010; Gathercole & Alloway, 2008).

working memory
A type of memory in which processing, or work, is done on briefly held information.

The ability to read music and play it on the piano depends on working memory, which is the processing, or work, done on information you take in. Huntstock/Getty Images

Researchers have linked working memory to a variety of complex tasks, including verbal comprehension, reasoning, decision making, and problem solving (Hambrick et al., 2005; Engle, 2002). As a specific example, researchers have found that working memory capacity predicts sight-reading ability among both novice and expert pianists (Meinz & Hambrick, 2010; Hambrick & Meinz, 2011). The task of playing written music is complex. The pianist must read the notes on the page; translate them into specific movements of fingers, hands, arms, and feet; and then execute those movements in the right order, time, and volume. So it makes sense that people who have greater ability to cognitively work on the musical notes they read would sight-read more successfully.

As the research on piano playing suggests, working memory is also closely related to multitasking. Consider watching that TV show again: could you follow it while also reading email and texting? Or while talking on the phone? Or while studying? Researchers have found that multitasking ability, as measured by speed and accuracy of responses, depends heavily on working memory capacity (Hambrick et al., 2010; Bühner et al., 2006). One study focused on multitasking among applicants for air traffic controller training courses and found that working memory, even more than overall intelligence, predicts how successfully they could multitask (Colom et al., 2010).

Long-Term Memory. Beyond short-term memory and working memory lies *long-term memory* (Bahrick, 2000). There isn't much research on the capacity of long-term memory, largely because most experts assume that it is limitless. It may well be. This is one aspect of the memory-as-computer metaphor that does not fit. Every type of computer memory storage device, from old floppy disks to new external hard drives, has a finite limit that cannot be exceeded. Human long-term memory simply does not appear to have such a limit (Dudai, 1997; Voss, 2009).

The typical path to long-term memory involves a passage through short-term memory assisted by processing of some kind. If information doesn't get focused on, thought about, or used in some way, then it usually fails to enter long-term memory. But sometimes information takes a shortcut to long-term memory (Hasher & Zacks, 1979, 1984). Psychologists call this shortcut **automatic processing (automatic encoding):** the entrance of some information into long-term memory without any conscious processing. Comparing automatic processing to the effortful processing that we discussed earlier (which can take such forms as chunking and rehearsal) is like comparing a feeding tube to eating. The contents of a feeding tube bypass the processing that typically takes place in the mouth (chewing and swallowing). Likewise, automatically processed information bypasses the processing that typically takes place in short-term memory. For example, researchers have found that we automatically process the frequency with which events occur (Zacks et al., 1982; Zacks & Hasher, 2002). In other words, you don't deliberately count how often you do particular things—eat peach pie, ride a roller coaster, swim in an ocean, attend a rodeo—but unconsciously, you're keeping track, at least well enough to provide an approximation.

CHAPTER APP 5.1

Retrieval

Quizlet

Preview one of the links and consider the following questions.

WEBSITE:
http://tiny.cc/hmh7jy

ANDROID:
http://tiny.cc/eyjyiy

IPHONE:
http://tiny.cc/3rjyiy

VIDEO DEMO:
http://tiny.cc/chapterapps

Quizlet is an app on which you make flashcards (or use a previously saved set) to help you learn terms and definitions. After you study, Quizlet can test you with multiple choice questions, true/false questions, or questions that require you to fill in the answer

How does it APPly to your daily life?
How could Quizlet benefit your study habits? For which classes could it be most helpful—foreign languages, history, biology, psychology, or others?

How does it APPly to your understanding of psychology?
Of the different types of test questions that Quizlet could ask you (multiple choice, true/false, fill-in), which would you find easiest and most difficult? What does your answer tell you about recognition and recall as different types of retrieval?

Retrieval

Retrieval is pulling information out of memory. It is the third and final step among the three basic steps of memory (Brown & Craik, 2000; Spear, 2007; Gardiner, 2007). When you consider the vastness of your long-term memory, your ability to retrieve memories quickly and accurately is truly astonishing. Imagine that you come across an old photo of you on Halloween when you were 6 years old. So much related information, tucked away for over a decade, suddenly comes back: the costumes of the friends you trick-or-treated with, "The Monster Mash" playing at your next-door neighbors' house, the joy you felt as you dumped out your plastic pumpkin full of candy on the kitchen table, the taste of the Reese's Peanut Butter Cup you ate, and so much more. All in a split second, and all without much effort at all, these details pour forth. Even the fastest and most user-friendly computer can't begin to compete with that kind of retrieval of stored information.

Psychologists make an important distinction between two kinds of retrieval, *recall* and *recognition* (Foster, 2009; Lockhart, 2000; Tulving, 1976; Mandler, 1980). **Recall** is a

type of retrieval in which you access stored information without any comparison to external information. **Recognition** is a type of retrieval in which you determine whether stored information matches external information.

When I answer different kinds of exam questions, do I use those different kinds of retrieval?

Yes! In fact, the best way to understand the difference between recall and recognition is to think about your experiences with short-answer essay exams versus multiple-choice exams. Let's consider a specific exam question from a U.S. history test: Who was president during the Civil War? If this was a short-answer question—if it was followed by just a blank, with no options to choose from—you would have to rely on recall. You'd be entirely on your own, scanning your memory for the answer, without the luxury of a list of possibilities to remind you of the right answer. That list of possibilities is exactly what a multiple-choice version of that question would provide. So with a multiple-choice question, you could rely on recognition rather than recall. In other words, if the same question was followed by choices—(a) George Washington, (b) Thomas Jefferson, (c) Abraham Lincoln, and (d) Theodore Roosevelt—you wouldn't have to generate the right answer entirely on your own but could merely spot the choice that matches what's stored in your memory (which, of course, is Lincoln).

Exam questions are certainly not the only real-life situations that illustrate the difference between recall and recognition. Once I attended a wedding and saw a familiar face among the groomsmen. "I know that guy," I said to myself, but I just could not come up with his name. Then it occurred to me that the entire bridal party was listed in the program I was given when I walked in. I scanned the list, and there were the names of all five groomsmen: no, no, no, no, yes! Tommy Green! Even though I couldn't recall it, when his name was right there in front of my eyes, I recognized Tommy's name instantly.

Another time a friend of mine called with this question: "You know that restaurant you found when you stopped in Effingham, Illinois, on your way to Chicago? The one that you said was so fantastic? We're on the road right now, and we're just a few minutes away from Effingham—what's the name of that place?" To my surprise, I drew a blank. "Um, uh, let me call you right back," I said. I immediately Googled "Effingham restaurants" and scrolled through the links that popped up: not Ruby Tuesday, not El Rancherito, not TGI Fridays—yes, Firefly Grill! My recall may have failed me, but my recognition came through just in time to call my friend back before he passed the exit.

Retrieval Cues. Whether it takes the form of recall or recognition, retrieval depends upon a number of factors. One such factor is **retrieval cues**: reminders that facilitate retrieval of information from memory. Retrieval cues are things that prompt you to remember. They make stored information pop into your mind when it otherwise might not (Thomson & Tulving, 1970; Tulving & Osler, 1968; Bower, 2000).

Let's consider that example about my favorite restaurant in Effingham, Firefly Grill. Many months passed before I had another chance to drive through Effingham and stop there again. By that time, I remembered liking the restaurant a lot, but I couldn't remember exactly what I had ordered there. As I entered the parking lot, things started looking familiar. Retrieval cues were all over, and they were jogging my memory: the restaurant's logo on the front door, the big open kitchen, the high ceiling, the distinctive tables and chairs, the oversized photos on the walls, the unique uniforms of the servers. Suddenly, effortlessly, my first meal appeared in my mind with as much detail as if I had pulled up a digital photo: a grilled chicken sandwich with caramelized onions on a pretzel bun, a mound of thin-cut French fries with homemade ketchup, and a spinach salad with almonds and apple slices to start. When the restaurant was many miles away, I couldn't retrieve what I had ordered the first time I went there for. However, when I saw all the sights I had associated with it, they served as powerful retrieval cues. In fact, they enabled me to retrieve that information with such confidence that I didn't even have to open the menu to know what I wanted to order on my return visit.

When you recall events such as a Halloween from your childhood, you're using retrieval, the stage of memory in which you pull stored information out. monkeybusinessimages/Getty Images

MY TAKE VIDEO 5.1

Recall versus Recognition

"When somebody has to point out the perpetrator..."

YOUTUBE: http://tiny.cc/mytake
LAUNCHPAD: launchpadworks.com

automatic processing
The entrance of some information into long-term memory without any conscious processing.

retrieval
Pulling information out of memory.

recall
A type of retrieval in which stored information is accessed without any comparison to external information.

recognition
A type of retrieval in which stored information is compared to external information to determine if it matches.

retrieval cues
Reminders that facilitate retrieval of information from memory.

Multiple-choice questions depend on recognition, a type of retrieval in which you determine whether your stored information matches any of the choices. By contrast, fill-in-the-blank or essay questions depend on recall, a type of retrieval in which you can't compare your stored information with any external information. gece33/iStock/Getty Images

Sometimes, as I did in Firefly Grill, you encounter retrieval cues by chance. But you can bring up retrieval cues on purpose as well. For example, picture yourself at a party where you see a woman across the room. You know you've met her before, but you can't remember her name or how you crossed paths with her. Asking yourself general questions like "Who is she?" or "Where do I know her from?" may not be enough to spark your memory. But more specific questions might. In other words, thinking of specific places or situations may provide the retrieval cues you need. "Is she in my chemistry class? Does she live in my building? Did I meet her at that concert in the park? Did I play sports with her? Yes, that's it—she was on the team that beat us in intramural softball last week. She made that great catch when I smashed a long fly ball into left-center field, and then I caught her line drive when I was playing third base the next inning. After the game, we briefly joked about how we robbed each other. Her name is Tamisha." If you hadn't brought softball to mind as a retrieval cue, Tamisha and everything you know about her might have remained buried in the storage of your mind.

Encoding Specificity. Related to retrieval cues is the idea of **encoding specificity**: the effect of contextual information present when memory was encoded, such as physical surroundings, on retrieval. Encoding specificity (also known as *context-dependent memory*) means that where you are when you are trying to remember something can make a difference. Specifically, if you're in the same place where you learned the information, you have a better chance of recalling it (Koriat, 2000; Fisher & Craik, 1977; Tulving & Thomson, 1973; Brown & Craik, 2000). For example, picture a new employee, Kirsten, who shows up for her first day at work and meets her coworker, Drew, in the elevator on the way up to their office. She is more likely to remember Drew's name later that day if she bumps into him in the elevator again rather than in the conference room, in the parking lot, or in a grocery store that evening.

Studies have found that encoding specificity works in all kinds of situations. In one early study, half of the participants memorized a list of words underwater, while the other half learned the same list on dry land. When they were quizzed, each group remembered more when they were in the same place where they learned it (Godden & Baddeley, 1975). Other studies have found similar results based on the odor in the room (flowers, peppermint, or fresh pine), the type of music being played (jazz or classical), whether the participant was riding an exercise bike, whether the participant was smoking, and even whether the participant was chewing a particular kind of gum (Balch & Lewis, 1996; Balch et al., 1992; Herz, 1997; Baker et al., 2004; Peters & McGee, 1982; Miles & Hardman, 1998). For your own academic purposes, the take-home message is clear: study in an environment as similar as possible to the classroom where you will take the test (Smith & Vela, 2001). Along the same lines, attending class and paying attention in class can only help your memory (assuming it's in the same room as the exams).

Just as being in the same location can help retrieval, so can being in the same state of mind, which psychologists call *state-dependent learning*. Studies have found that when you put yourself in the same mood you were in when you learned new information, you are more likely to remember it (Eich, 1995a, b, 2007; Ucros, 1989; Bower, 1981). For example, one study put participants in either a good mood or bad mood by having them make statements about themselves that were either flattering or insulting. While in those moods, they memorized lists of words. Two days later, they were asked to recall their lists. Their recall performance depended on their mood when they were tested. Those in the same mood at both points in time, regardless of whether that mood was good or bad, remembered significantly more than those in one mood when they learned and in a different mood when they recalled (Beck & McBee, 1995).

Encoding specificity (or context-dependent memory) means that you are more likely to remember something if you're in the same context as when you learned it. For example, if you meet someone on an elevator, you're more likely to remember that person's name on the same elevator than in a different location. Odilon Dimier/PhotoAlto/Getty Images

Priming. A final type of influence on retrieval is **priming**: recent experiences cause an increased likelihood of recalling certain memories. For example, spending time on any beach is likely to increase your recollection of all of your memories related to beaches. Priming can even influence the way that individual words enter our mind (Lukatela & Turvey, 1994a,b). For example, if you ask people to spell the word *marry/merry*, you're more likely to get the first spelling from a wedding planner, and you're

more likely to get the second spelling from a Santa Claus impersonator (especially in December). Their different day-to-day experiences—most important, the words and concepts that occupy their minds on a regular basis—predispose them toward different recollections of the spelling of that homonym.

When researchers study priming, they often show participants a list of words and then distract them for a few minutes. After the distraction, the researchers provide word stems—that is, the first few letters of a word—and then ask the participants to complete the word. So if the word stem is *tel-*, participants could come up with the word *tell*, *teller*, *television*, or *telephone*, among others. However, if the original list included the word *telescope*, participants are especially likely to choose that word. They would also be primed to choose *telescope* if the original word list contained words semantically related to telescopes (but not the word *telescope* itself), like *star*, *moon*, *planet*, and *constellation* (Turkington & Harris, 2001).

In a twist on this methodology, one group of researchers showed participants photos of celebrities whose names happened to sound exactly like ordinary words. For example, they used a photo of Brad Pitt, whose last name is a homophone for *pit* (**Figure 5.5**). The likelihood that participants correctly identified the celebrity depended upon whether they had been primed with a fill-in-the-blank task in which the homophone was the right answer. In other words, participants were more likely to correctly say "That's Brad Pitt" if they had previously been asked what the name of the hard inner part of a cherry or plum is rather than another unrelated question (Burke et al., 2004).

Here is a personal example of priming. I once spent several hours shoveling foot-high snow from my driveway in single-digit temperatures. The whole time, all I could think about was how far below freezing it was and the increasing chances of frostbite. As I finally finished shoveling, I heard my phone ring. By the time I managed to pull off a snow-caked glove and move my frozen fingers into my pocket, I had missed the call and had a new voicemail. It was from my next door neighbor, and it consisted of just one word: "Chilly?" Was she joking? Or mocking me from her toasty living room? She knew it was way past chilly—it was absolutely frigid. I disgustedly shoved the phone back in my pocket and trudged toward my door when I heard her knock on her kitchen window. I looked up and saw her holding a steaming bowl with a spoon in it, and she mouthed the word to me again: "Chili?" Oh, *chili*, not *chilly*. She wasn't mocking me—she was offering me lunch. I had been so focused on the cold that I was primed to bring to mind *chilly* when I heard that word. On any other day, without such priming, I would have been more likely to consider what she actually meant.

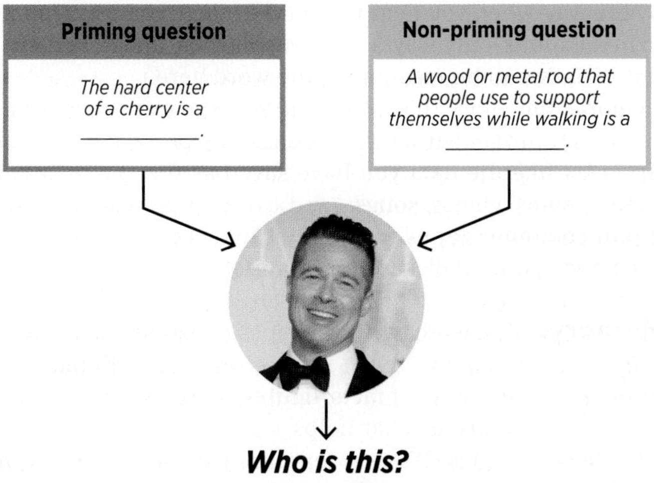

FIGURE 5.5 Brad Pitt and Cherry Pits. Researchers found that the likelihood of correctly recognizing Brad Pitt increased if participants had been asked a question about pits (as in cherries) as opposed to a question about something unrelated to his name (like a cane). The sound of the word pit *primed* participants to remember similar-sounding words (Burke et al., 2004). Jason Merritt/Getty Images

LIFE HACK 5.1

Take advantage of context-dependent memory and state-dependent learning. If you're struggling to remember something, try to put yourself back in the same situation or the same mood you were in when you first learned it.

(Eich, 2007; Koriat, 2000; Fisher & Craik, 1977; Tulving & Thomson, 1973)

encoding specificity
The effect that contextual information that was present when memory was encoded, such as physical surroundings, has on retrieval.

priming
When recent experiences cause an increased likelihood of recalling certain memories.

CHECK YOUR LEARNING:

5.4 What are the three steps of memory according to the information processing model?

5.5 What is encoding, and how does it involve sensory memory?

5.6 What is the difference between echoic memory and iconic memory?

5.7 How does encoding depend on the level of processing?

5.8 What is long-term potentiation, and how does it relate to encoding?

5.9 What is storage, and where in the brain does it occur?

5.10 What is retrieval, and what are the two ways it happens?

5.11 What are retrieval cues, and how do they affect retrieval?

5.12 What are encoding specificity and priming, and how does each enhance retrieval?

Types of Memory

YOU WILL LEARN:

5.13 what explicit memory is.

5.14 about two types of explicit memory: semantic memory and episodic memory.

5.15 what implicit memory is.

5.16 about a type of implicit memory known as procedural memory.

Psychologists have identified many types of memory. One legendary memory researcher made a note of every type of memory he ever saw defined in any article or book. His final list included 256 types of memory, including such peculiar labels as particular *political memory*, *chemical memory*, and even the oxymoronic *forgotten memory* (Tulving, 2007). Since there's no way we can explore all of the types of memory, let's zoom in on the types that are most widely studied by memory experts.

One way of categorizing memory focuses on conscious awareness of memories. In other words, there are memories that we *know* we know (and can describe well), and there are other memories that we *don't know* we know (and can't describe well). In this section, we consider the two labels that capture these different kinds of memory—*explicit memory* and *implicit memory*—as well as some related concepts.

Explicit Memory

Explicit memory is memory of which you are consciously aware. It is also known as *declarative memory*, which refers to the fact that it is memory that you can declare (or more simply, tell) to another person (Lockhart, 2000; Baddeley et al., 2009; Squire & Zola, 1996). (By the way, when you hear the word *explicit*, you may initially think that it means graphic in an adults-only way, as in some movies, music, and video games with "explicit content." That's not the meaning of the word here.)

Explicit memory is memory that you *know* you know. It consists of all the factual knowledge you have accumulated, as well as all of the personal experiences you have tucked away. It's a bit like the data you have saved as files on your computer's hard drive—documents, photos, videos, songs—and can pull up whenever the need arises. (Don't include your computer's apps or programs in this grouping—those are more like *procedural memory*, which we'll discuss in a minute.)

Semantic memory is a kind of explicit memory that consists of facts, figures, and other general information—the kind of knowledge that makes *Jeopardy!* contestants successful. Everett Collection

Semantic Memory. There are two basic types of explicit memory: *semantic memory* and *episodic memory* (Tulving, 1983; Ryan et al., 2008). **Semantic memory** is a type of explicit memory consisting of facts, figures, word meanings, and other general information. Semantic memory is what helps *Jeopardy!* contestants answer all those questions on all those subjects. It's the depository of available information—trivia, basically—that you have in mental storage: stuff you learned in school, like the seven continents; stuff you learned from friends and family, like what kind of car your Uncle Tim bought last year; stuff you learned through media, like the fact that the NHL team with the most Stanley Cup championships is the Montreal Canadiens; and much, much more.

Episodic Memory. By contrast, **episodic memory** is a type of explicit memory consisting of personal firsthand experiences. Episodic memory is your internal autobiography, a record of the episodes of your life (Tulving, 1972, 1983, 1998; Neisser & Libby, 2000; Wheeler, 2000; Mace, 2010). It's your recollection of what happened to you rather than what facts you happened to pick up along the way. Your episodic memory contains your replay of minor events in your life, like last night's dinner and last week's trip to the dentist. It also contains major events in your life, like your high school graduation and your last conversation with a dying relative. The small stuff often fades rather quickly from episodic memory, being replaced by more recent events, but the big stuff tends to endure (Conway, 2008).

Research suggests that different regions of the brain may be responsible for semantic memory and episodic memory. One study describes three children who experienced brain injuries with hippocampus damage. All three had severely limited episodic memory. They couldn't remember what took place in their own lives, but they still succeeded in mainstream schools and reached an average or slightly below average level of achievement in areas like language competence, literacy, and factual knowledge. Their experiences indicate that the hippocampus is much more involved in episodic memory than semantic memory (Vargha-Khadem et al., 1997). Other studies have suggested that semantic memory relies more heavily on the prefrontal cortex, which makes sense, since that part of the brain is also heavily involved with the kind of deliberate thought often used to form semantic memories (but not as often used to form episodic memories) (Martin & Chao, 2001; Gabrieli et al., 1998).

Procedural memory is implicit memory for tasks you do automatically. Those tasks, like following particular dance steps, often enter your procedural memory through repetition.
Dario Lo Presti/iStock/Getty Images

Implicit Memory

Implicit memory is memory of which you are not consciously aware. It is also called *nondeclarative memory*, because you cannot easily declare (or tell) it to another person. Implicit memory is memory that you *don't know* you know. You can't explicitly state it, but you can *imply* its presence by your actions, which is why it is called *implicit* (Lockhart, 2000; Baddeley et al., 2009; Squire & Zola, 1996). For example, if you are an experienced driver, you might not be able to describe the exact steps involved in starting the car (e.g., turning the key in the ignition, putting on your seatbelt, stepping on the brake, putting it in gear, stepping on the gas, steering). However, the fact that your car goes from parked to moving down the road within seconds of you sitting in the driver's seat implies that you know how to drive.

Procedural Memory. Much of implicit memory is **procedural memory**: a type of implicit memory consisting of how to perform tasks that you do automatically. The key word in that definition is *how*. Procedural memory is your recollection of how to do things (Schacter et al., 2000). For example, you rely on your procedural memory to know how to ride a bike, how to brush your teeth, how to buckle a belt, how to use a fork and knife, and lots of other behaviors that you can do on autopilot. This emphasis on *how*, on procedures rather than facts, is what makes procedural memory more like apps or computer programs than like data files. Procedural memory is remembering an action rather than a thing or remembering a verb rather than a noun.

It is important to remember that actions don't enter procedural memory the first time we do them. It takes many, many repetitions for them to become so ingrained that we no longer need to make a deliberate effort to complete them (Ofen-Noy et al., 2003; Gupta & Cohen, 2002). For example, a new ballroom dancer trying to learn the cha-cha will definitely have to hear (from an instructor, a partner, or himself) the "one, two, cha cha cha" count and work with purpose to make his feet take the correct steps on every beat. But after a little experience, his need to hear the count fades. After a lot of experience, he does the cha-cha without thinking, as if what was once entirely foreign has become entirely intuitive.

explicit memory
Memory of which one is consciously aware.

semantic memory
A type of explicit memory consisting of facts, figures, word meanings, and other general information.

episodic memory
A type of explicit memory consisting of personal firsthand experiences.

implicit memory
Memory of which one is not consciously aware.

procedural memory
A type of implicit memory consisting of how to perform tasks that are done automatically.

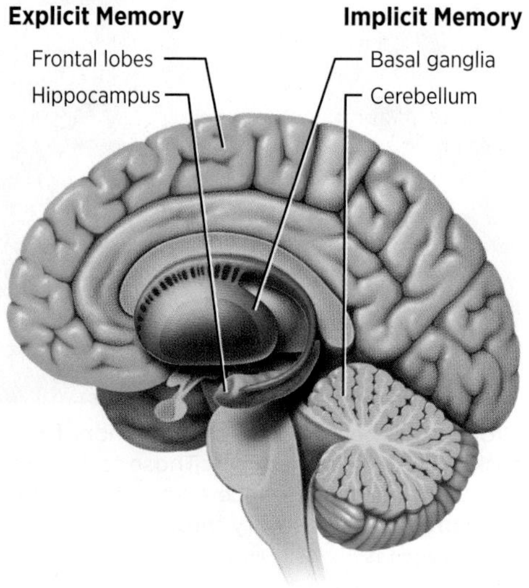

FIGURE 5.6 Localizing Implicit Memory and Explicit Memory. Implicit memory relies on the cerebellum and basal ganglia, but explicit memory relies on the frontal lobes and hippocampus.

Sometimes we don't realize that our procedural memories are so deeply ingrained until we need to teach another person how to do the same procedure. (If a 4-year-old asked you how to tie shoes, could you explain all the steps?) I was once filling my car with gas when a father and his 15-year-old son, with a brand-new driver's permit, pulled up to the opposite side of the pump. Dad handed his son a credit card and said, "Go ahead—fill it up." The son looked completely bewildered, and the dad seemed equally bewildered about the fact that his son was so bewildered. The son said, "How?" The dad said, "What do you mean, how? You just fill it up. It's so easy." Eventually, the dad realized that he had filled the tank so many times that he could do it without thinking. It was embedded in his procedural memory. But he was going to have to take his inexperienced son step by step through this process: open the fuel door, unscrew the gas cap, insert the credit card in the reader, select a particular grade of gas, lift the nozzle, insert it in the tank, squeeze the handle to start the flow, and so on. By the time he was finished, Dad realized that you don't just "fill it up." You learn a series of steps that is initially complex but eventually becomes a procedure committed to memory.

Research indicates that implicit memory and explicit memory are very distinct processes in the brain. In fact, they utilize different brain regions (**Figure 5.6**). Explicit memory relies primarily on the frontal lobes and hippocampus. Specifically, verbal information (like your Facebook password) is stored in the left side of the frontal lobes and hippocampus, but visual information (like what your backpack looks like) is stored on the right side of these brain structures. Implicit memory, on the other hand, relies primarily on the cerebellum and (at least for implicit memories involving motion) basal ganglia (Squire, 2004; Eichenbaum, 2010).

CHECK YOUR LEARNING:

5.13 What is explicit memory?

5.14 What are the two basic types of explicit memory, and how do they differ?

5.15 What is implicit memory?

5.16 What is procedural memory?

What Affects Memory?

YOU WILL LEARN:

5.17 how memory can be affected by decay over time.

5.18 how memory can be affected by context, or "other" information around it.

5.19 what retroactive interference and proactive interference are.

5.20 what the primacy effect and recency effect are.

5.21 how feelings can influence memory, such as the flashbulb memory of an especially emotional event.

5.22 how to improve memory, including mnemonics, study frequency, and sleep habits.

Sometimes your memory is amazing, pulling up an unimportant fact or trivial experience you buried deep many years ago and haven't thought about since. ("Wow, I can't believe I remember my kindergarten room number.") Other times, your memory lets you down, leaving you fumbling for important facts ("What's the passcode for my phone?") or information you've used recently and regularly ("What's my lab partner's name again?"). Psychologists can't entirely explain why memory can be so fickle, but they have identified certain factors that affect it in predictable ways.

Time and Memory

Time is generally the enemy of memory. Psychologists call the process by which time erodes memory **decay**: the dwindling or loss of information from memory due to the passing of time. Decay happens most often when information is not used. For instance, if it is not used, information that enters sensory memory will decay before it enters short-term memory. Similarly, unused information that enters short-term memory will decay before it enters long-term memory.

Once information is in long-term memory, its recall still depends on use. If you bring it out once in a while (rather than leaving it untouched for long periods), the information is more likely to be there when you need it later (Brown et al., 2007; Barrouillet et al., 2009; Carrier & Pashler, 1992). For example, consider a family reunion at which

you bump into a cousin whom you haven't seen in 5 years. If you haven't heard or thought his name in all that time, there's a decent chance his name has decayed from your long-term memory and you'll need to peek at his nametag. However, if you occasionally talk about him with other family members or you've seen his Facebook posts once in a while, those experiences have refreshed your memory enough to lessen the chances of decay.

decay
The dwindling or loss of information from memory due to the passing of time.

retroactive interference
Problems remembering older information caused by newer information.

proactive interference
Problems remembering newer information caused by older information.

serial position effect
The tendency to remember the first and last items in a series better than the items in the middle.

primacy effect
The tendency to remember the first items in a series particularly well.

recency effect
The tendency to remember the last items in a series particularly well.

Context and Memory: "Other" Information

Your ability to remember a particular piece of information depends on its context—that is, what other information surrounds it (Roediger et al., 2010; Dewar et al., 2010; Wixted, 2010). In general, other information interferes with the memory of the target information, much as a pocketful of coins makes it difficult to find the one dime you need.

One particular form of this interference is **retroactive interference**: problems remembering older information caused by newer information. Retroactive interference is what happens when you watch two movies in a row and have difficulty recalling the details of the first one. The second movie sort of bumps the first one (or at least parts of it) out of your mind. The opposite form of interference is **proactive interference**: problems remembering newer information caused by older information. Proactive interference is what happens when you watch two movies in a row and have difficulty recalling the *second* one. In this case, the first movie refuses to make room for the second one, so parts of it don't get processed into memory (Underwood, 1957; Keppel & Underwood, 1962; Bäuml, 1996).

"I shop to forget what I bought last year."

Position Effects. Related to both types of interference is the **serial position effect**: the tendency to remember the first and last items in a series better than the items in the middle. Psychologists actually have terms for the specific effects at either end. The **primacy effect** is the tendency to remember the first items in a series particularly well. The **recency effect** is the tendency to remember the last items in a series particularly well. For the first items in the list, there's no chance of proactive interference, because nothing came before. For the last items, there's no chance of retroactive interference, because nothing came after—unless there's a delay before recall, in which case retroactive interference does take place and the recency effect is not so strong (Postman & Phillips, 1965). However, the items in the middle are susceptible to both types of interference, so they tend to be forgotten more often (Greene, 1986; Murdock, 1962; Feigenbaum & Simon, 1962; Raffel, 1936; Tzeng, 1973).

The serial position effect, primacy effect, and recency effect were described early in the history of psychology by Hermann Ebbinghaus (1885). For over a century, his findings about these effects have been replicated again and again (Craik & Watkins, 1973; Bower, 2000; Crowder & Greene, 2000). In a free recall situation immediately after hearing a list of about a dozen items ("Name all the words you can remember…"), participants typically begin with the last items, correctly naming the last three items about 80–90% of the time. Next, participants name the first couple of items on the list, correctly naming them about 60–70% of the time. Then, if they can, participants name items from the middle of the list, but only about 30–40% of them (**Figure 5.7**).

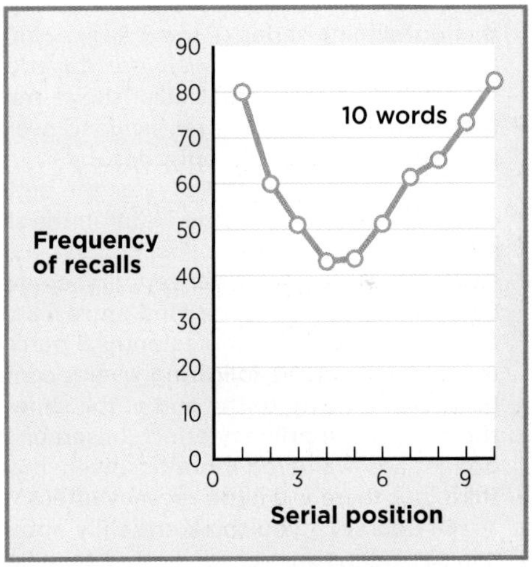

FIGURE 5.7 Serial Position Effect. When you recall a series right after it ends, you are much more likely to remember the first and last items than the items in the middle (Postman & Phillips, 1965).

Researchers often study the serial position effect by presenting a list of spoken or written words and then asking participants to recall all they can (Crowder & Greene, 2000). But serial position makes a difference in all kinds of situations in which there is a series of stimuli. For example, if you meet 10 people at a party, you are more likely to remember the names of the first few people and the last few people than the people in the middle. If you go to a concert and hear 20 songs, you are most likely to remember what the band opened with or what it did as an encore than what it did halfway through.

More recent research has explored these kinds of real-world applications of the serial position, primacy effect, and recency effect. As an example of the primacy effect, one study found that wine tasters who tried five wines tended to prefer the first wine

A flashbulb memory is an unusually clear, vivid memory of an event that was out of the ordinary and emotionally charged. In some cases, many people share the same flashbulb memory, such as the Boston Marathon bombing in April 2013. David L. Ryan/ The Boston Globe via Getty Images

they tasted, no matter which one that was—perhaps because their memory for the first one was stronger than for the others (Mantonakis et al., 2009). A meta-analysis of 11 studies on food preferences found the same result. The first food tasted is disproportionately chosen as the favorite, even when the order was randomly determined (Dean, 1980). By contrast, the recency effect was demonstrated in a study of figure skating results. Skaters who went last received the best ratings from the judges, even when their order was randomized according to their previous scores (Bruine de Bruin, 2005, 2006).

Relearning. Sometimes your memory depends not so much on the presence of "other" information, but on the fact that you have already remembered and forgotten that particular information. Psychologists call this process relearning: the process of committing information to memory for a second time after it has been forgotten. A few paragraphs ago, we imagined a family reunion in which you forgot your cousin's name. If he reintroduces himself ("Johnny, of course! How have you been?"), you are more likely to remember his name than you are to remember the name of Johnny's new wife whom you are meeting for the first time. You are learning Johnny's wife's name but *relearning* Johnny's name, so his is more likely to stick (Nelson, 1985; MacLeod, 1988).

Flashbulb Memory. Other times, your memory depends upon the emotional context of the information you learn. Specifically, information and events that arouse powerful feelings are especially likely to be recalled, often as if they happened yesterday (Fivush et al., 2009; Schooler & Eich, 2000; Schmidt, 2007). A memory of this type is a **flashbulb memory**: a distinctively clear and vivid memory of an emotionally charged and novel event (Luminet & Curci, 2009; Curci & Luminet, 2009; Brown & Kulik, 1977).

WATCHING PSYCHOLOGY

The Serial Position Effect on *American Idol*?

In many competitions contestants take turns showcasing their talents: beauty contests, gymnastics, political debates, speed dating, and job interviews, among many others. Does it matter whether you go first, last, or somewhere in the middle?

A team of researchers explored this question in the results of the *Idol* singing series (Page & Page, 2010). They examined not just *American Idol* but *Australian Idol, Canadian Idol, Indian Idol, X-Factor* (England), and similar shows from Brazil, the Netherlands, and Germany. Their dataset included over 1500 singing performances from 165 episodes.

Their basic finding? The later, the better. That is, *Idol* contestants who performed later in the show were most likely to survive to the next week. *Idol* contestants who performed earlier (with the exception of the very first contestant) were most likely to be voted off (as illustrated in Figure 5.8). Specifically, the researchers calculated that a contestant is 5 percentage points more likely to advance into the following week's competition for each position he or she is closer to the end of the show. The authors found that there is a small primacy effect, based on the fact that singers who go first are evaluated more positively than those who go second or third, but there is a huge recency effect.

Of course, if you think critically about these results, you can see numerous reasons other than serial position effects to explain them. The authors themselves point out many of them: the show's producers may save the best for last rather than presenting the singers in random order. Also, more viewers may watch the latter part of the show than the earlier part of the show. Further, later singers have the advantage of hearing earlier singers, as well as the judge's feedback, so they can make adjustments accordingly.

Even with these alternative explanations, these researchers argue that the order of appearance makes a major difference for each contestant. Other studies have offered similar results and conclusions (Li & Epley, 2009).

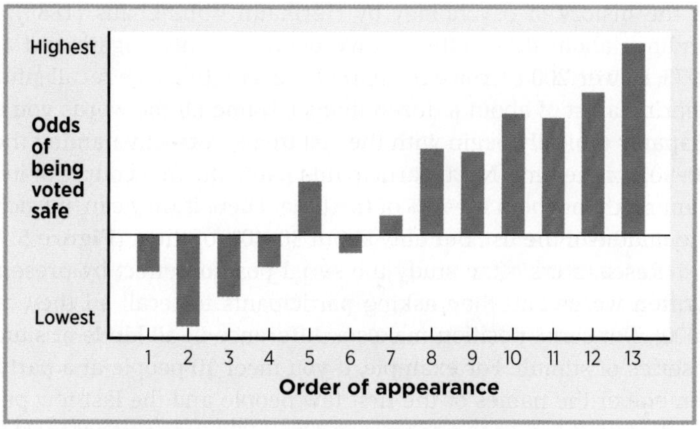

FIGURE 5.8 American Idol and the Serial Position Effect. On *American Idol*, singers who perform later in the show have better odds of receiving enough votes to survive to the next week. This finding may reflect the recency effect (among other factors). Data from Page & Page, 2010.

Flashbulb memories are often shared by those who experienced or witnessed them: the terrorist attacks of 9/11; the school shooting at Sandy Hook Elementary in Newtown, Connecticut; Hurricane Katrina; the Boston Marathon bombing; the election or inauguration of a president; even a championship victory by a favorite sports team. These major events contain so much emotional power that many of us not only remember them with detail and feeling but can also recall exactly where we were and what we were doing when they took place.

flashbulb memory
A distinctively clear and vivid memory of an emotionally charged and novel event.

mnemonic
A specific technique or strategy deliberately used to enhance memory.

Does something have to be a society-wide event to be a flashbulb memory?

Not at all. Many of your flashbulb memories are personal: things that happened not to everyone but just to you. Bad things, like car accidents, robberies, or deaths of loved ones can produce flashbulb memories. But good things, like first kisses, graduations, or surprise parties also produce flashbulb memories if we are sufficiently moved by them (Davidson, 2008).

Flashbulb memories are more vivid than regular memories, but they are not any more accurate than regular memories (Talarico & Rubin, 2009). One important factor about the reliability of flashbulb memories is how direct the experience is. If you experience the event firsthand, you are less likely to forget or distort the memory than if you see or hear it on the news (Pillemer, 2009; Er, 2003). In one study, researchers asked people to recall the earthquake that rocked the San Francisco area in October 1989, which killed over 60 and injured over 3000. (Coincidentally, the World Series was taking place in the area at the time, featuring both Bay Area teams, the San Francisco Giants and the Oakland A's. For this reason, the earthquake was witnessed live by millions on TV and radio.) People from California, who were more likely to have felt the earth move under their own feet, recalled their own experiences of the earthquake and the news reports about it with a high degree of accuracy. People from a faraway city such as Atlanta, who could only learn about the earthquake second-hand, showed much lower rates of recall about the event (Neisser et al., 1996).

Efforts to Improve Memory

So far, our discussion of what affects memory has focused on factors over which you have no control, like the passage of time and the context that surrounds the information you hope to remember. But memory also depends on some factors we can control, including deliberate efforts to enhance our memory of certain facts or events.

Mnemonics. A **mnemonic** is a specific technique or strategy deliberately used to enhance memory. Mnemonics are the mental devices, or tricks, commonly used by memory champions, such as the USA Memory Championship competitors described earlier in this chapter (Worthen & Hunt, 2011). You've used them too. For example, in a science class, you may have memorized the colors of the rainbow in order as Roy G. Biv (rather than directly remembering the sequence red, orange, yellow, green, blue, indigo, violet). If so, you were using an *acronym* as a mnemonic (Stalder, 2005). In a math class, you may have used a variation of an acronym to learn the order of operations by memorizing the sentence Please excuse my dear Aunt Sally, the first letters of which correspond to parentheses, exponents, multiplication, division, addition, and subtraction.

In addition to mnemonics that rely on letters and words, many mnemonics rely on rhythm and rhyme, such as making a song out of the 50 states and their capitals. Others rely on visual imagery—in particular, associating new information with distinct visual stimuli. Ben Pridmore, who won the USA Memory Championship, describes a mnemonic based on this kind of visualization called the *method of loci* (Moe & DeBeni,

MY TAKE VIDEO 5.2

Flashbulb Memory

"I just remember, pinpoint, every single detail..."

YOUTUBE: http://tiny.cc/mytake
LAUNCHPAD: launchpadworks.com

LIFE HACK 5.2

Use the spacing effect to your advantage. Rather than cramming for tests, study the material in multiple, spaced-apart sessions.

(Roediger & Karpicke, 2011; Landauer, 2011)

2004, 2005). He uses it to memorize the order of cards in a deck in a matter of seconds. In his mind, he converts the cards "into a mental image of an object or person, and [I] visualize them at different points [locations, or loci] along a journey—in this case, around the rooms of my grandma's old house" (https://www.youtube.com/watch?v=Yp9qF-SjJZk). For example, if Ben's first card is the king of hearts, he might picture a king with a visibly pounding heart opening the front door and welcoming him into his grandma's entryway. If his next card is the three of diamonds, he might imagine a stack of three oversized glistening diamonds on the coffee table in grandma's living room.

Similar to the method of loci is the *peg word method*, in which you pair images of the items you need to remember with a series you already have committed to memory, like *run, blue, bee, door, drive*, which rhyme with 1, 2, 3, 4, 5 (Elliott & Gentile, 1986; Wang & Thomas, 2000; Massen & Vaterrodt-Plunnecke, 2006). Imagine that while jogging, you think of five people you need to send party invitations to when you finish running. Simply picture each of them interacting with the items on the previously memorized list: Tina running, Greg painted blue, Devonte being stung by a bee, Darren slamming a door, and Deya driving. Later, when your run is over, you are likely to recall those images of your five friends as you recite your memorized list.

spacing effect
The tendency to have better long-term memory for information when attempts to study it are spaced apart rather than crammed together.

Spacing Effect. Another memory enhancement effort is studying. In your academic career, you have undoubtedly tried a variety of study strategies. Researchers have found that some strategies work better than others. Specifically, they have identified the **spacing effect**: the tendency to have better long-term memory for

FROM RESEARCH TO REAL LIFE

Improving Your Memory

Much of the research on memory applies directly to your life during college and beyond. To maximize your ability to remember everything from the information that will be on tomorrow's exam to the names of the people you met at last night's party, follow these evidence-based memory tips:

- **Make it meaningful.** Think about what the information *means* to you—how you feel about it, what opinion you have about it. For example, if you're trying to remember the names of your friend's three dogs, think about your previous interactions with each of them (Princess startled you with her loud bark; Bailey grossed you out with his bad breath; Bandit amazed you with his Frisbee-catching abilities). Such deep processing helps memories sink in better than shallow, superficial processing.
- **Use mnemonics.** Mnemonics—like acronyms, or the method of loci—are great, as long as your goal is mere memorization, not comprehension. For example, HOMES is a great way to remember the names of the Great Lakes (Huron, Ontario, Michigan, Erie, and Superior), but it doesn't help with any meaningful information about them, like where they are in relation to each other.
- **Organize ideas.** Organize ideas into some kind of structure or hierarchy, rather than just a random assortment. For example, to remember everyone on your softball team, categorize them by position: infielders, outfielders, pitchers, and catchers.
- **Visualize information.** Visualize information rather than just thinking about the word or repeating it verbally. This can even include drawing objects if you have the chance. For example, visualizing the things you still need to put in your suitcase when you get back from class—running shoes, toothbrush, phone charger, and jacket—will give you a better chance of remembering them than simply saying the list over and over to yourself.
- **Use context cues.** Go back to the same place you learned something to help you remember it now. Going back to the same mood (or at least imagining it) can help too.
- **Imagine teaching the information.** Imagine yourself teaching the information to someone else. By doing that, you'll think about (or process) the information especially deeply. You can even anticipate questions you might get from your students and answer those too.
- **Don't multitask.** Memory suffers significantly when you do more than one thing at once. You may see your friends "studying" with their eyes darting between their textbook and their phone (and a TV on in the background), but don't follow their lead—turn off all unnecessary screens.
- **Keep your mind healthy.** Keep your mind—and your memory capacity—healthy by getting enough sleep, eating right, and exercising. Some particularly memory-enhancing foods include fish (especially wild salmon), pomegranates and blueberries, green tea and coffee (in moderation), tree nuts (especially walnuts and almonds), and dark chocolate (with at least 70% cacao content). Exercise helps memory most when it is aerobic and happens outside in fresh air.
- **Exercise your mind.** Whether old-school, like crossword puzzles, or new-school, like memory-enhancing apps, brain activities keep your brain in shape and ready to form, store, and recall memories.

Sources: Alloway & Alloway, 2013; Alloway, 2011; Baddeley, 2004.

information when your attempts to study it are spaced apart rather than crammed together. The spacing effect (also known as the advantage of *distributed practice* over *massed practice*) basically boils down to one important point for you as a test taker: cramming does not work as well as consistent, repeated studying. Cramming can certainly be effective to a limited extent. However, information learned through repeated exposures on multiple days becomes more deeply embedded in long-term memory, making it more likely to be recalled on test day and more likely to be retained long after the test (Roediger & Karpicke, 2011; Landauer, 2011; Landauer & Bjork, 1978; Bahrick, 2000).

The inferiority of cramming to spaced studying is a particularly important finding when you consider that it isn't obvious to people. When given a choice, many people choose cramming, even when they have the time for more spaced study and even though cramming produces lesser results (Son, 2004, 2005; Son & Kornell, 2008). In one study, the participants' task was to memorize random patterns on the number pad of a computer keyboard. They learned these patterns in one of two ways: massed practice (many repetitions at once, similar to cramming), or distributed practice (repetitions spread out over time). Participants who learned via massed practice *predicted* higher levels of performance but *delivered* lower levels of performance than those who learned via distributed practice (Simon & Bjork, 2001).

One mnemonic that can boost memory for a list of items is the method of loci, in which you picture the items in particular locations you already have memorized. If you had the specific locations within this kitchen memorized, you could remember the countertop to your left first, then the sink, stove, and fridge. Then, if you needed to call four friends in a particular order, you could visualize each friend at a specific spot in the kitchen: Jasmine at the countertop, Ella washing her hands in the sink, Caleb turning on the stove, and Diego opening the fridge.

Joseph Calev/iStock/Getty Images

Culture and Memory

DIVERSITY MATTERS

The basics of memory, especially the encoding–storage–retrieval process, are the same around the world. But *what* you remember depends quite a bit on your specific cultural background. A growing body of recent research has found interesting differences between the memories of people of European descent (often Americans), who tend to approach life with a more individualistic, self-focused orientation, and people of Asian descent, who tend to approach life with a more collectivistic, other-focused orientation (Wang, 2013; Ross & Wang, 2010; Wang & Aydin, 2009).

For example, one group of researchers asked participants from China and the United States to freely recall any 20 specific memories from their own lives. The memories provided by the U.S. participants included twice as many memories in which they were the only person mentioned, while the memories provided by the Chinese participants included twice as many mentions of social interactions or group activities (Wang & Conway, 2004; Conway et al., 2005). In another study, Asian Americans were asked to describe themselves as either Asian or American. Then, they were instructed to remember events from their own past. Those who had described themselves as American were much more likely to remember events that were self-focused and much less likely to remember events that involved social interaction (Wang, 2008). Similar cultural differences have been found in very young children. When asked to share their memories for things that had happened to them, European American preschoolers include far more of their own personal feelings, preferences, and opinions, while Asian preschoolers include far more discussion of other people (especially authority figures) and social correctness (Wang, 2004; Wang et al., 2000).

Even the language you speak can influence what you remember. In a pair of studies, people who spoke both Russian and English were interviewed in one language or the other and asked to share some of their personal memories. It was no surprise that those who were interviewed in Russian remembered more events from the time in their lives when they primarily spoke Russian, while those who were interviewed in English remembered more events from the time in their lives when they primarily spoke English. More striking, however, was the difference in content of their memories: those interviewed in English provided memories that were much more about themselves, while those interviewed in Russian provided memories that were much more about other people and relationships (Marian & Neisser, 2000; Marian & Kaushanskaya, 2004).

LIFE HACK 5.3

Get a good night's sleep before a big test, because sleep enhances memory and sleeplessness impairs it.

(Brown & Lewandowsky, 2010; LeDoux, 2007; Gais et al., 2006; Whitney & Rosen, 2013)

CHAPTER APP 5.2

Efforts to Improve Memory

Elevate

Preview one of the links and consider the following questions.

WEBSITE:
http://tiny.cc/qnh7jy

ANDROID:
http://tiny.cc/0yjyiy

IPHONE:
http://tiny.cc/csjyiy

VIDEO DEMO:
http://tiny.cc/chapterapps

The Elevate app offers memory activities designed to keep your mind sharp and either maintain or enhance your memory if played on a regular basis. It includes a variety of personalized activities designed to enhance memory and other cognitive functions.

How does it APPly to your daily life?
Apps like Elevate often claim to improve users' memory capabilities. In your opinion, could it improve your memory? If so, which activities would be most effective, and how much time would you have to spend using them? As you consider apps like Elevate, how important is it to you to know that well-done scientific studies support their claims about memory?

How does it APPly to your understanding of psychology?
Of all of the various types of memory described in this chapter, which do you think would be most and least improvable by apps like Elevate?

In addition to affecting which events you remember, culture can affect *how* you remember events. Specifically, researchers have found that when people of European descent recall an event, they tend to tell the story from their own point of view. By contrast, people of Asian descent are more likely they tell the story from the point of view of other people (Cohen & Gunz, 2002; Leung & Cohen, 2007). For example, if they were remembering the day their city's team won a basketball championship, the person of European background would be more likely to describe what it was like for him or her as an individual: "I saw that shot go in at the last second, and I was ecstatic! I jumped and screamed and felt such a rush of happiness." The person of Asian background might incorporate a more collective point of view for a memory of the same event: "When we saw that shot go in at the last second, everyone in the gym cheered! The fans in the stands celebrated while the players and coaches ran to hug each other on the court."

Sleep and Memory

An important but often overlooked factor that affects memory is sleep. One interesting aspect of the relationship between sleep and memory is that memories are typically stronger if the time interval between encoding and retrieval includes sleep than if it doesn't (Brown & Lewandowsky, 2010). In other words, sleeping on it helps memory. Researchers believe that sleep serves two important functions related to memory: (1) sleep allows for *consolidation* of memories, strengthening memory formation (LeDoux, 2007), and (2) sleep prevents any kind of interference from taking place (MacLeod & Hulbert, 2011; Born et al., 2006; Ellenbogen et al., 2006). This effect is strongest if the sleep takes place closer to the time of encoding than the point of retrieval. Sleeping right after you study helps your mind form strong memories of the material (Ekstrand, 1972). The flip side of sleep helping memory is that the *lack* of sleep hurts memory (Gais et al., 2006; Marshall & Born, 2007; Whitney & Rosen, 2013; Mu et al., 2005). You probably know this firsthand. The day after pulling an all-nighter studying for a test, your memory sputters. Your absent-mindedness extends even to things you typically remember with ease—where you put your keys, why you went into the kitchen, what time your friend said she'd pick you up. On these drowsy days, these kinds of memories are lost in a fog. However, on days when you are well rested, this stuff is practically written on the back of your hand. Interestingly, research has found that even after two consecutive nights of good sleep, information learned right before a sleepless night is frequently forgotten (Peigneux et al., 2010). If you don't sleep the night you learn something, you're likely to forget it—and sleeping well the next couple of nights won't bring it back.

In kids, the link between sleep and memory has prompted some researchers to recommend taking a second look at kids with learning problems before diagnosing them with learning-related disorders. The thinking is that it might actually be a sleep-related problem that underlies their struggles at school (Steenari et al., 2003; Taras & Potts-Datema, 2005; Curcio, 2006). This link has also fueled the debate about school start times, with some arguing that pushing back the opening bell to later in the morning would facilitate numerous benefits, including increased memory for what students learn during the school day (Wahlstrom, 2002; Wolfson & Carskadon, 2003).

CHECK YOUR LEARNING:

5.17 What is decay?

5.18 How is memory affected by context?

5.19 What's the difference between retroactive interference and proactive interference?

5.20 What's the difference between the primacy effect and the recency effect?

5.21 How can emotion influence memory, especially in relation to flashbulb memory?

5.22 How can mnemonics, the spacing effect, and sleep each improve memory?

Memory Problems

In this section, we consider some of the ways that memory can go wrong. Each of us knows all too well about such memory problems. They take many forms, from distorted memories to intrusive memories to memory failure. Thankfully, these problems typically limit themselves to certain times and places, even among older adults showing the normal age-related reduction in memory capacity (Anderson & Craik, 2000). In severe cases, however, these memory problems can be disruptive to people's lives for extended periods of time (Mayes, 2000; Hodges, 2000).

YOU WILL LEARN:

5.23 how psychologists define amnesia.

5.24 what the difference between retrograde amnesia and anterograde amnesia is.

5.25 about the misinformation effect and the types of memory mistakes it can produce.

5.26 how certain psychological disorders have a negative impact on memory.

Amnesia

Amnesia is the inability to remember some or all information, either temporarily or permanently. Most cases of amnesia have a definitive cause in the form of a brain injury or disease, but amnesia occasionally takes place without a physical cause (O'Connor & Verfaellie, 2002). In cases without physical cause, known as *dissociative* amnesia, the incidents often occur in the aftermath of psychological trauma, severe abuse, or overwhelming stress (Brand & Markowitsch, 2010; Brand et al., 2009). Sometimes, amnesia is global, meaning that the person's entire memory is wiped out. Other times, amnesia is situation-specific, meaning that the lost memories are limited to a certain part of the person's life. For example, people suffering from psychogenic amnesia may not recall anything related to the trauma or abuse that preceded it, but their memories for unrelated material remain intact (Kopelman, 2002).

It is worth noting that people with amnesia often retain their implicit memory despite an obvious loss of explicit memory. In computer terms, they lose their data files, but their apps still work. In 1911, a Swiss psychiatrist named Edouard Claparède illustrated this point about implicit memory by shaking hands with an amnesia patient while holding a tack that pricked the patient's hand. On previous days, the patient had no recollection of Claparède when he shook her hand. But the day after he held a tack, the patient refused to shake Claparède's hand. She did not recognize him and had no conscious recollection of the tack, but her implicit memory of the pain held her back (Claparède, 1911).

Retrograde Amnesia. Psychologists have identified specific types of amnesia. **Retrograde amnesia** is the inability to retrieve information that took place before a certain point in time. When you hear a survivor of a car accident say, "I can't remember anything from before the accident," he or she is describing retrograde amnesia. For example, Scott Bolzan hit his head after slipping in the bathroom and lost all memory for what came before—his wife, his kids, his career as an NFL player, pilot, and business owner.

In his memoir (titled *My Life, Deleted,* coauthored by his wife and another writer), Bolzan explains the experience: "I'd lost my life as I'd known it—my knowledge, my experiences, and even my identity—when my skull hit that tile floor...on the way to the hospital, I could almost feel the information draining away, leaving me in a foggy, disoriented haze. From that point on, my life was forever changed..." (Bolzan et al., 2011, p. 4). Speaking of his wife, he added, "She was the woman I'd fallen in love with, married, and fathered three children with, and yet I had forgotten everything there was to know about her and our life together. But one question was nagging me even more: Who the hell was *I*?" (p. 9). Although Bolzan's retrograde amnesia appears long-lasting, other cases last just a matter of minutes, hours, or days (Papagno, 1998). This is commonly seen in athletes who get their bell rung, incurring mild head injuries and temporarily struggling to remember simple facts about themselves; usually, these athletes soon return to full memory function (Kapur et al., 1998; Kopelman, 2002). See the Current Controversy box about sports head injuries and memory loss.

amnesia
The inability to remember some or all information, either temporarily or permanently.

retrograde amnesia
The inability to retrieve information that took place before a certain point in time.

According to many studies, memory loss can come not only from concussions but also from repeated contact to the head (including headers in soccer) that doesn't cause concussions. John Patriquin/Portland Press Herald via Getty Images

Anterograde Amnesia. In contrast to retrograde amnesia, **anterograde amnesia** is the inability to form new memories after a certain point in time. In this case, the memory for what took place before the life-changing event remains intact. These people can remember their childhood, family, job, and so on, but they can't create new memories. They don't remember what has happened since the onset of the amnesia, which means they don't remember what they just said or did or what others just said or did to them. This results in lots of repeating from people with anterograde amnesia—the same questions, the same stories, the same actions—because there's no recollection that they've already been done (Mayes, 2002). In one well-known case of anterograde amnesia, Clive Wearing, a music producer and conductor from England, suffered brain damage from a virus. In 1985, Wearing found himself waking up over and over, unable to remember that he had already woken up. His condition required hospitalization and ruined his career, although he has shown some memory improvement over the years (Wearing, 2005).

Source Amnesia. Sometimes people have no problem remembering information, but they can't recall how they learned it (Mitchell & Johnson, 2000). This is **source amnesia**: the inability to remember the source, or how you obtained, a particular memory (but not the memory itself). Full-fledged cases of source amnesia involve a complete inability to remember the sources of memories, but you may have experienced fleeting moments of source amnesia. There might have been times when you were completely confident about a memory, but you couldn't identify how you came to know the information when pressed by others to explain it. For example, picture yourself in a car with friends trying to find a party to which you are all invited. No one else quite remembers the address, but you do: 7476 Gannon Avenue. "How do you know that?" they ask. "I don't know—I just do," you reply. When you arrive, it's clear that your memory was correct, but you still can't remember how you knew. Did the host tell you or text you? Did you hear another friend mention it?

The existence of source amnesia indicates that when our memory is working correctly, we engage in *source monitoring*. We pay attention not only to information but to where it comes from (Ranganath et al., 2012; Johnson et al., 1993).

CURRENT CONTROVERSY

Do Sports Head Injuries Cause Memory Loss?

Sydney was a ninth-grader in Nebraska playing on her high school soccer team. After one header, she had intense headaches and nausea that lasted for months. She also had significant memory loss: she not only can't remember the play on which the head injury occurred, she can't remember *that entire soccer season*.

Was Sydney's experience a fluke, or do head injuries from sports cause memory loss? This question is at the center of a major debate involving amateur and professional athletes and those who treat and care about them. In recent years, Major League Baseball has required first-base and third-base coaches to wear helmets at all times while on the field. The National Football League has introduced new rules to outlaw blows to the head and neck, as well as leading with one's own helmet while tackling or carrying the ball. The National Hockey League has similarly made new rules to penalize hits to the head. The rationale for all of these moves was to reduce the aftereffects of head injuries, one of which is memory loss.

Numerous studies support this rationale. For example, multiple studies have found a negative correlation between the number of headers by professional soccer players and memory ability. The more headers, the worse the memory ability, (Lipton et al., 2013; Matser et al., 2001). Another study found that college football players who had accumulated at least three concussions had significantly lower working memory capacity than those with two, one, or none (Theriault et al., 2011). A study on high school and college athletes found that the aftereffects of a concussion depend strongly on how many concussions the athlete had before it: those with multiple prior concussions were over seven times more likely to show a significant drop in memory ability than those with no prior concussions (Iverson et al., 2004).

Other studies reach different conclusions, however. In one, researchers found no cumulative effects on memory after two concussions (Iverson et al., 2006). Another study of over 1000 college athletes found that those who had previous concussions demonstrated no impairment in memory as long as no concussion had taken place in the last 6 months (Bruce & Echemendia, 2009). A meta-analysis showed mixed results: no general memory loss due to multiple mild head injuries, but some possible effects on particular kinds of memory (Belanger et al., 2010).

The bottom line is that despite extensive study, it is difficult to draw specific conclusions about the way head injuries affect memory, whether they involve concussions or not. Given the inconclusive research, perhaps the most important part of Sydney's story is her (eventual) honesty about her symptoms and the involvement of professional health care providers in her assessment and treatment.

Misinformation Effect

The **misinformation effect** is the tendency of false or misleading information presented after the fact to become mistakenly incorporated into memory. In other words, memories often become distorted when new information enters our minds, as if the new information somehow seeps into our original version of the memory (Pickrell et al., 2004). This is not an error of omission, in which memories are lost, but an error of commission, in which memories are twisted, revised, or supplemented with information that is not true (Roediger & McDermott, 2000).

One summer day, I took my 4-year-old son to Target. He had just received a gift card and was eager to spend it. But in the checkout line, with dinosaur Legos in his little hands, he looked up at me and burst into tears: "I lost my gift card!" The cashier tried to help by saying, "This happened to a little girl yesterday too, but she remembered where she was when she took it out of her pocket, and then she went back to that part of the store and found it. Where were you when you took the gift card out of your pocket?" He sniffed, thought for a few seconds, and said, "The toy part, by the Legos." Back to the toy section we went, retracing his steps, looking on every shelf, but no gift card. After a long search, we headed back to the car sad and empty-handed. But as he climbed into the car, my son's misery turned to delight—"Daddy, here's my gift card! On the back seat!" As I watched him run excitedly back into the store with the gift card clutched tightly in his little hand, I happened to notice that his shorts and t-shirt actually had no pockets at all. He couldn't have taken the gift card out of his pocket anywhere in the store. Yet the cashier's question *suggested* that he did, and that suggestion was powerful enough to create a misinformed, false memory.

To some, it may seem surprising or disturbing to recognize the misinformation effect, the very idea that our memories are so imperfect. But they are. A leading memory researcher, Daniel Schacter, describes it this way:

> ...we now know that we do not record our experiences the way a camera records them. Our memories work differently. We extract key elements from our experiences and store them. We then recreate or reconstruct our experiences rather than retrieve copies of them. Sometimes, in the process of reconstructing we add on feelings, beliefs, or even knowledge we obtained after the experience. In other words, we bias our memories of the past by attributing to them emotions or knowledge we acquired after the event.
>
> —Schacter, 2001, p. 9.

The misinformation effect can be especially important if the memory was a crucial element of a courtroom trial. Indeed, the misinformation effect is particularly relevant—and threatening—to the validity of eyewitness testimony. Elizabeth Loftus, a leading researcher on this topic, and a colleague describe the limitations of eyewitness testimony:

> ...[an] honest and sincere witness cannot be presumed to be entirely accurate. Human information processors are simply overwhelmed by the magnitude of incoming information and efforts to process and remember it accurately, leaving us vulnerable to error. Some information is necessarily lost, and other information may be confused or distorted.
>
> —Davis & Loftus, 2007, pp. 223–224.

The story of the wrongful conviction and imprisonment of Clarence Elkins illustrates how unreliable eyewitness testimony can be (Neuschatz et al., 2007). Elkins was convicted of killing his mother-in-law and raping and beating his 6-year-old niece in 1998. There was no physical evidence to connect Elkins to the crime. His conviction was based on the testimony of the niece, who supposedly witnessed Elkins murdering his mother-in-law and of course experienced her own traumatic events firsthand. After his sentencing, Elkins continued to claim his innocence. As a jail inmate, Elkins got a hold of a cigarette butt discarded by a fellow inmate, Earl Mann. At the time of the attack, Mann had been living next door to Elkins, and Mann

Source amnesia is the inability to remember the source of a particular memory. Unless source amnesia occurs, as a person forms a memory of the words or images they see on a smartphone screen, they will also form a memory of where they learned that information. Roberto Westbrook/Getty Images

anterograde amnesia
The inability to form new memories after a certain point in time.

source amnesia
The inability to remember the source of a particular memory (but not the memory itself) or how it was obtained.

misinformation effect
The tendency of false or misleading information presented after the fact to be mistakenly incorporated into memory.

MY TAKE VIDEO 5.3

Memory Mistakes

"It wasn't until a lot later, where we were watching family videos, when I looked at it and saw..."

YOUTUBE: http://tiny.cc/mytake
LAUNCHPAD: launchpadworks.com

was a convicted sex offender. DNA evidence from the cigarette butt matched evidence from the crime scene. Mann, not Elkins, was the murderer. Elkins was exonerated, but not before he spent 7 years in prison, largely because of eyewitness testimony tainted with misinformation.

Research suggests that young children, especially preschoolers (like my son, from the example a few paragraphs ago), are particularly suggestible to new information as they recall their memories of events (Melnyk et al., 2007). At the other end of the age spectrum, elderly adults are particularly prone to making memory errors when they serve as eyewitnesses (LaVoie et al., 2007), which can cause concern when they offer their version of events during a courtroom trial. People with psychological disorders such as schizophrenia, posttraumatic stress disorder, and alcohol abuse are also especially prone to memory inaccuracies (Soraci et al., 2007). Also, emotional arousal matters: people in a highly emotional state tend to get the central feature of the memory right but often forget or distort the peripheral details (Reisberg & Heuer, 2004, 2007). For example, a witness to an assault may accurately describe the type of weapon used (gun, knife, etc.), but inaccurately describe the clothing or eye color of the attacker.

Types of Memory Mistakes. Psychologists have identified a number of specific kinds of memory mistakes based on the misinformation effect. For example, the *Moses illusion* is named after this famous question: how many animals of each kind did Moses take on the ark? Most people recall that Moses took two of each animal, but that's wrong—not the number, but the person. It was Noah, not Moses, who took animals on the ark, but the incorrect information embedded in the question convinces you otherwise (Park & Reder, 2004).

The *orientation illusion* occurs when you remember the orientation or other physical attributes of an item incorrectly (**Figure 5.9**). For example, when asked to remember what common coins look like, people often remember the heads facing the wrong direction or other features on the wrong part of the coin (Jones & Martin, 2004).

The *association illusion* works this way: you remember things associated with what you saw or heard, even though you did not actually see or hear those particular things. In studies of the association illusion, researchers typically present a list of words that all relate to a target word, but the target word is intentionally left out. For example, the list of words may include *cola, drink, pop, bubbles, bottle, can, cup, machine, beverage*—all words that relate to *soda*, but *soda* is not on the list. When the participants did a free recall of the list—just remembering any words they could, in any order—they recalled the target word 55% of the time. When they did a recognition task—saw words one by one and replied yes or no about whether they were on the list—they said yes to the target word 57% of the time (Roediger & Gallo, 2004). These are remarkably high recall rates when you consider that the word being remembered was not actually on the list. The lesson of the association illusion: your memory may have a hard time distinguishing between what you actually witnessed and closely associated things that you didn't witness. These and other common memory mistakes are summarized in **Table 5.4**.

Such memory distortion can be small and simple, like falsely remembering a word that was not actually presented among a list of related words, but it can also be much bigger and more elaborate—a memory mistake called *rich false memory* (Loftus, 2005). In the 1990s, research by Elizabeth Loftus and others focused on news stories featuring court cases in which people claimed to have been abused or otherwise victimized by family members or friends. In some cases, their stories were lengthy and detailed but either highly unlikely or impossible based on the available evidence (Loftus & Cahill, 2007).

For example, some people claimed to have been abused for long periods of time by large numbers of people who were Satanic cult members and murdered hundreds of young children. However, no evidence of these Satanic cults was found, nor was there any evidence of murdered children (let alone hundreds) to corroborate their stories.

The imperfections of human memory are at times illustrated through eyewitness testimony. Clarence Elkins was convicted of murder and rape based on eyewitness testimony that was overturned by DNA evidence after Elkins spent 7 years in prison.

Many of these accusers later retracted their stories. In many cases, they were found to have "recovered" these formerly "repressed memories" when in therapy with clinicians who convinced the clients that they were true by strongly suggesting that the events took place. In other words, these false memories were aided by input from others who were attempting to shape the client's thinking (Goodman et al., 2007; Bottoms et al., 1996).

In one study related to this false memory phenomenon, Loftus gave participants descriptions of events that actually happened to them as children (as collected from participants' family members), but she mixed in one false story too. The false story went something like this: "One time, when you were 5 or 6 years old, you got lost in a shopping mall. You got very upset, but an elderly woman stopped to help you, and she brought you back to us." A quarter of the participants "remembered" (completely or partially) this story happening to them, even though it never did (Loftus & Pickrell, 1995)! Similar studies followed, with similar percentages of people "remembering" being attacked by animals or being pulled out of the water by a lifeguard despite the fact that these events never took place (Porter et al., 1999; Heaps & Nash, 2001).

Other researchers have used altered photos for the same effect. After confirming with participants' family members that they had never been on a hot air balloon as a child, the researchers essentially Photoshopped a childhood image of the participant onto a hot air balloon background. They then interviewed the participants, on three occasions, about the experience. Most participants couldn't remember the hot air balloon ride at first, but about half "remembered" it either fully or partially by the third interview. A few participants even included details in their false recollections: "basically for $10 or something you could go up in a hot air balloon and go up about 20 odd meters..." (Wade et al., 2002, p. 600). It is noteworthy that the researchers in these studies were actively encouraging the participants to remember all they could about the event, which illustrates that false memories can be the product of people's suggestible memory and the suggestions they receive from other people.

Research on false and recovered or repressed memory, like the kind Elizabeth Loftus conducted, has slowed in recent years. However, there continues to be at least some interest in the related topic of *motivated forgetting*, or the notion that some experiences may be so unpleasant or traumatic that people choose, perhaps unconsciously, to forget them. One study found that people who cheated at a game had "forgotten" the rules they broke—a convenient slip, considering that if they remembered the rules, they'd feel more guilty (Shu et al., 2011). Some researchers have speculated that motivated

FIGURE 5.9 Orientation Illusion. Lincoln faces right on the U.S. penny, but most students mistakenly remember him facing left (perhaps because the faces on most U.S. coins do)—an example of the orientation illusion (Rubin & Kontis, 1983). A schema for common cents, David C. Rubin and Theda C. Kontis, *Memory & Cognition* 1983, 11 (4), 335–341, The Psychonomic Society, Springer

TABLE 5.4: Common Memory Mistakes

MEMORY MISTAKE	DESCRIPTION	EXAMPLE
Moses illusion	Allowing mistaken information in the question or prompt to influence the memory	When asked, "What kind of tree did Lincoln chop down?" you "remember" that Lincoln chopped down a cherry tree, but (according to myth, at least) Washington actually did.
Orientation illusion	Remembering aspects of spatial orientation, such as what direction something faces	When asked what side the face on a penny or nickel looks toward, you mistakenly say left for penny and right for nickel.
Associative illusion	Remembering things that you never actually saw or heard because you saw or heard similar things	After hearing a word list containing sandals, sneakers, high heels, clogs, cleats, pumps, and boots, you also "remember" hearing the word *shoe*.
Labeling effects	Remembering things differently because of the labels others use for them	After watching a video of a car accident, you are likely to report higher speeds if asked, "How fast were they going when they *smashed into* each other?" rather than "How fast were they going when they *hit* each other?"
Hindsight bias	Remembering your predictions incorrectly after the outcome is determined	After the basketball season ends, you remember correctly predicting the team that won the championship, when you really predicted another team to win it.

Information from Park & Reder, 2004; Jones & Martin, 2004; Roediger & Gallo, 2004; Pohl, 2004a, b; Loftus & Palmer, 1974.

One study illustrated how false memories can be created by showing participants a Photoshopped image of the participant as a child on a hot air balloon ride. (The participants did not know that their family members had told the researchers no such event ever happened.) About half of the participants "remembered" this hot air balloon ride—that never happened—after being interviewed about it several times. Some even recalled specific details (Wade et al., 2002). A picture is worth a thousand lies: Using false photographs to create false childhood memories, Kimberly A. Wade, Maryanne Garry, J. Don Read, and D. Stephen Lindsay. *Psychonomic Bulletin & Review* 2002, 9 (3), 597–603, Springer

forgetting makes evolutionary sense, particularly if the forgotten event is a major betrayal by a loved one, like a child who has been abused by a parent. In such a situation, an accurate memory of the abuse could prompt the child to confront or run away from the parent, either of which could threaten the child's well-being or survival. Wiping the abuse from memory, although it leaves the child with an unrealistic view of the parent, might actually serve the child's best interests (DePrince et al., 2012).

Memory and Psychological Disorders

Some psychological disorders are largely defined by memory problems. *Dissociative amnesia* is essentially the clinical name for the amnesia that we have already discussed, with an emphasis on the loss of autobiographical information. *Major neurocognitive disorder* and *mild neurocognitive disorder*, which can stem from Alzheimer's disease, brain injury, excessive substance use, and various medical illnesses, are also characterized by serious memory problems (American Psychological Association, 2013; Becker & Overman, 2002). Although often overlooked, these memory-based disorders can contribute to other psychological problems as well. Imagine how your life might be affected if your memory became significantly impaired. You might experience bouts of sadness about your memory difficulties or nervousness about your ability to function academically, professionally, or socially. Your self-image might worsen as you begin to see yourself as incompetent. Indeed, the frequency of depression and anxiety disorders increases when people experience significant memory disorders (Tate, 2002).

Anxiety, Depression, and Memory. But memory can also play an important role in more common psychological problems in which memory problems are not the primary symptoms (Burt et al., 1995). For example, many studies have linked anxiety to memory problems. Specifically, they find that working memory capacity in people high in anxiety is often quite low. This is true especially when the material to be remembered is verbal (as opposed to visual) and they feel pressure to respond quickly (Crowe et al., 2007; Hayes et al., 2008; Ikeda et al., 1996; Leigh & Hirsch, 2011; Visu-Petra et al., 2011). The attention that the anxiety demands is attention that the person can't devote to working memory, so distraction takes place (Visu-Petra et al., 2013; Rapee, 1993). This finding is particularly important for anxious kids, because working memory is crucial to learning and school performance (Alloway & Gathercole, 2005; Alloway et al., 2005; Gathercole et al., 2004; Dehn, 2008; Swanson & Berninger, 1996).

Memory can play an important role in psychological disorders. For instance, people who are depressed tend to ruminate about their most unfortunate past moments. Image Source/Getty Images

Interestingly, people with anxiety disorders (generalized anxiety disorder and phobias, among others) tend to remember the events of their lives rather accurately. Their memories do not center on anxiety, even though their current feelings might (MacLeod & Mathews, 2004). The story is different for people with depression, however. Numerous studies indicate that people in depressed moods remember depressing things (Hertel, 2004; Dalgleish & Cox, 2002). For example, when presented with a long list of words that includes some that suggest positive feelings (*happy, smile, delighted,* etc.) and some that suggest negative feelings (*miserable, cry, gloomy,* etc.), people in depressed moods recalled significantly more negative than positive words, including some negative words that weren't even on the list (Bower, 1981; Watkins et al., 1996; Howe & Malone, 2011). People suffering from depression tend to recall their unfortunate experiences and emotions frequently but fail to recall the good stuff (Hertel, 2004; Watkins et al., 1992; Wenzlaff et al., 2002). Psychologists call this tendency *rumination*, and it can be a difficult habit to

break, keeping some people locked into a melancholy mindset for extended periods (Nolen-Hoeksema, 2000).

A meta-analysis of this relationship between memory and depression confirms that clinically depressed people remember depressing things disproportionately—and, as a side note, that people who are not depressed tend to disproportionately remember uplifting things (Matt et al., 1992). Some researchers have even suggested that therapy for depression should include deliberate attempts to recall more positive memories (Josephson, 1996; Rusting & DeHart, 2000), but others have found that this is an especially difficult task for people whose personality predisposes them to depression in the first place (Joormann & Siemer, 2004).

involuntary memory
The spontaneous retrieval of information in the absence of any intention to retrieve it.

PTSD and Memory. Posttraumatic stress disorder (PTSD) is another psychological disorder in which memory plays a prominent role. Of course, in some cases, traumatic events can impair memory (Levin & Hanten, 2002). But more typically, people with PTSD remember too much, too often. In other words, they are tormented by **involuntary memory**: spontaneous retrieval of information in the absence of any intention to retrieve it. For example, a person who weeks ago witnessed a murder re-hears the bang of the gun or a survivor of a serious traffic accident re-sees the oncoming car months afterward, even though neither person has any desire to relive these events. Sometimes these involuntary memories are triggered by external cues like sights or sounds or internal cues like thoughts or feelings, but other times they just pop into the sufferer's head (Bernsten, 1996, 2001; Mace, 2004; Williams & Moulds, 2010; Kvavilashvili & Mandler, 2004; Helstrup et al., 2007). In PTSD, these memories are often experienced as flashbacks, as they take the person, at least in their mind, right back to the traumatic event even though they have no desire to go there. It's one thing to experience an assault, robbery, accident, or other trauma in the first place, but to relive it again and again through such vivid memory can turn a one-time event into an extended nightmare. People suffering from PTSD have little control over when the memory interrupts their daily life (Krans et al., 2010; Grey & Holmes, 2008; Holmes et al., 2005).

PTSD may also predispose people to experience involuntary memories of additional negative events they live through after the original trauma. One study measured the reactions to the 9/11 terrorist attacks by people who had PTSD before the event. For the first month or so, their memories of the attacks were very similar to the memories of those without PTSD. However, at the 10-month point, people with PTSD experienced more involuntary memories of the attacks, and those memories included fewer objective facts and more fearful emotions. Over time, people who had previously been traumatized remembered the 9/11 attacks in a less controlled, less accurate, more upsetting way than those who had no previous traumatization (Qin et al., 2003; Budson & Gold, 2009).

One final note regarding PTSD: it is worth emphasizing that most people who experience a trauma don't experience PTSD. One study found that 90% of adults in Detroit have experienced an event that could be categorized as a trauma, but only about 10% of them developed PTSD (Breslau et al., 1998). So even if involuntary memories occur in the days or weeks after the event (which is relatively common), they typically fade with time (Verwoerd & Wessel, 2010).

These people are walking through the debris of the explosions in New York City on 9/11, an event that left many people suffering from posttraumatic stress disorder (PTSD). Some people who have PTSD experience memory loss, but others experience involuntary memory, in which they spontaneously remember the scary sights and sounds without intending to do so. Mario Tama/Getty Images

Schizophrenia and Memory. Research has also found significant memory impairment in people with schizophrenia, a debilitating disorder featuring hallucinations, delusions, and other symptoms that indicate a detachment from reality (Danion et al., 2004; Aleman et al., 1999). Specifically, people with schizophrenia show remarkably low levels of episodic memory and long-term memory and somewhat low levels of short-term memory. However, procedural memory and implicit memory typically remain at normal levels (Aleman et al., 1999; McKenna et al., 2000; Brebion et al., 1997; Bazin & Perruchet, 1996). So a person with schizophrenia is more likely to remember *how* to do things (like button up his jacket), but less likely to remember *what* he did (like where he left his jacket). These kinds of memory deficits can cause significant

day-to-day problems for these individuals. In one study, caregivers of schizophrenics completed a questionnaire that asked about forgetfulness and daily functioning, with questions like "Did he/she forget where things are normally kept or look for things in the wrong places?" These caregivers reported rates much higher than those found in people without schizophrenia and similar to those found in people with brain damage due to strokes (McKenna et al., 2002).

CHECK YOUR LEARNING:

5.23 What is amnesia?

5.24 What is the difference between retrograde amnesia and anterograde amnesia?

5.25 What is the misinformation effect, and what kinds of memory mistakes can it produce?

5.26 How do anxiety, depression, PTSD, and schizophrenia each involve memory?

CHAPTER SUMMARY

Defining Memory

5.1 Memory is the process of taking in information, saving it over time, and retrieving it later.

5.2 Memories define each individual as a unique person.

5.3 Research on memory excellence shows that some people are born with the ability to remember nearly everything and that other people can train their mind to do amazing memory tasks as well.

The Three Steps of Memory

5.4 The information processing model of memory involves three steps: encoding, storage, and retrieval.

5.5 Encoding is entering information into memory. It depends on sensory memory, in which the senses take in and very briefly hold information.

5.6 Echoic memory is auditory sensory memory, and iconic memory is visual sensory memory.

5.7 The likelihood that information gets encoded depends upon how deep the level of processing is. That depth can be enhanced by effortful processing such as chunking and rehearsal.

5.8 When encoding takes place, long-term potentiation occurs, which is an increase in connectivity between neurons that form the biological basis of memory.

5.9 Storage is retaining information in memory. It occurs in short-term (or working) memory and long-term memory.

5.10 Retrieval is pulling information out of memory. It happens in two ways: recognition, in which there is comparison to external information, and recall, in which there is not.

5.11 Retrieval cues are reminders that facilitate retrieval of information from memory.

5.12 Due to encoding specificity, memories are easier to retrieve when there is similar contextual information present. Because of priming, recent experiences create an increased likelihood of recalling particular memories.

Types of Memory

5.13 Explicit memory is memory of which one is consciously aware.

5.14 There are two basic types of explicit memory: semantic memory and episodic memory. Semantic memory consists of facts, figures, word meanings, and other general information, while episodic memory consists of personal firsthand experiences.

5.15 Implicit memory is memory of which one is not consciously aware.

5.16 Procedural memory is a type of implicit memory consisting of how to perform tasks that one does automatically.

What Affects Memory?

5.17 Decay is the dwindling or loss of information from memory due to the passing of time.

5.18 The ability to remember a particular piece of information depends on its context. Surrounding information can interfere with remembering the target information.

5.19 Retroactive interference is the difficulty remembering older information that is caused by newer information. Proactive interference is the difficulty remembering newer information that is caused by older information.

5.20 The primacy effect is the tendency to remember the first items in a series particularly well, while the recency effect is the tendency to remember the last items in a series particularly well.

5.21 A memory that arouses powerful feelings is especially likely to be recalled and is known as a flashbulb memory.

5.22 Three ways to improve one's memory are mnemonics, spacing apart study sessions, and getting enough sleep.

Memory Problems

5.23 Psychologists define amnesia as the inability to remember some or all information, either temporarily or permanently.

5.24 Retrograde amnesia is the inability to recall information acquired before a certain point in time, while anterograde amnesia is the inability to form new memories after a certain point in time.

5.25 The misinformation effect is the tendency of false or misleading information presented after the fact to become mistakenly incorporated into memory. The different types of memory mistakes based on the misinformation effect include the orientation illusion, the association illusion, and rich false memory.

5.26 Anxiety, depression, PTSD, and schizophrenia each impair memory in ways that are particular to the specific psychological disorder.

KEY TERMS

memory, p. 142
information processing model, p. 142
encoding, p. 145
sensory memory, p. 145
echoic memory, p. 145
iconic memory, p. 145
level of processing, p. 145
chunking, p. 146
rehearsal, p. 146
maintenance rehearsal, p. 146
elaborative rehearsal, p. 146
long-term potentiation, p. 148
storage, p. 148
short-term memory, p. 148
long-term memory, p. 148
working memory, p. 151
automatic processing, p. 153
retrieval, p. 153
recall, p. 153
recognition, p. 153
retrieval cues, p. 153
encoding specificity, p. 155
priming, p. 155
explicit memory, p. 157
semantic memory, p. 157
episodic memory, p. 157
implicit memory, p. 157
procedural memory, p. 157
decay, p. 159
retroactive interference, p. 159
proactive interference, p. 159
serial position effect, p. 159
primacy effect, p. 159
recency effect, p. 159
flashbulb memory, p. 161
mnemonic, p. 161
spacing effect, p. 162
amnesia, p. 165
retrograde amnesia, p. 165
anterograde amnesia, p. 167
source amnesia, p. 167
misinformation effect, p. 167
involuntary memory, p. 171

SELF-ASSESSMENT

1. According to the information processing model, the three steps of memory are ________.
   a. encoding, processing, and storage
   b. encoding, storage, and retrieval
   c. processing, retrieval, and forgetting
   d. chunking, short-term memory, and recall

2. ________ ________ is an early part of the memory process in which the senses take in and very briefly hold information.

3. Level of processing refers to ________.
   a. how severe a case of amnesia is
   b. how strongly certain contextual stimuli may prime recall of a memory
   c. how many numbers a person can recall in a particular order
   d. how deeply and meaningfully information is thought about

4. ________ ________ is the increased connectivity between simultaneously stimulated neurons that form the biological basis of memory.

5. ________ is grouping pieces of information together in a meaningful way to enhance memory.
   a. Priming
   b. Recognition
   c. Recall
   d. Chunking

6. A group of students take an exam in the same room where they studied for it. The match between where they learned the information and where they remember it is called ________ ________.
   a. semantic memory
   b. episodic memory
   c. encoding specificity
   d. implicit memory

7. Jamia, a server at a restaurant, has a problem remembering older information that is caused by receiving newer information. Specifically, when a customer asks her for something, it causes her to forget what the previous customer asked for. Jamia is experiencing ________ ________.
   a. proactive interference
   b. retroactive interference
   c. the spacing effect
   d. the misinformation effect

8. A ________ ________ is a distinctively clear and vivid memory of an emotionally charged and novel event.

9. After he injured his head in a car accident, Tony could remember events from before the accident but couldn't create memories of events after the accident. Tony suffered from ________ ________, the inability to form new memories after a certain point in time.
   a. retrograde amnesia
   b. anterograde amnesia
   c. source amnesia
   d. encoding specificity

10. ________ ________ is the spontaneous retrieval of information without any intention to retrieve it.
    a. Involuntary memory
    b. Semantic memory
    c. Proactive interference
    d. Long-term memory

Self-Assessment Answers

1. b 2. Sensory memory, 3. d, 4. Long-term potentiation, 5. d, 6. c, 7. b, 8. flashbulb memory, 9. b, 10. a

WHAT'S YOUR TAKE?

1. Different kinds of exams rely on different kinds of memory. On a multiple-choice exam, you have to recognize the right answer, but on a short-answer or essay exam, you have to generate it yourself. Which do you prefer? Do you study differently for one versus the other? What about *none of the above* options on multiple-choice exams—do they change your task from pure recognition to something involving recall? Do you think standardized testing should rely less on multiple-choice questions (based on recognition) and more on short-answer and essay questions (which rely more on recall)?
2. I was cleaning out the basement when I came across an old photo: my basketball team from kindergarten. I hadn't seen that photo, or thought about that team, in decades. But that photo served as a retrieval cue, and memories came flooding back. I remembered how itchy the uniforms were. I remembered how impossibly high the basket seemed, and how big and heavy the ball felt in my little 6-year-old arms. I remembered the sound of parents erupting with cheers on the rare occasion one of us kids made a basket during a game. I even remembered the taste of the basketball-shaped cake we got at our end-of-the-season party.

   How about you? Has a particular retrieval cue—a particular sight, sound, smell, or taste from your past—ever opened a door to a world of memories you had otherwise tucked away?

SHOW ME MORE

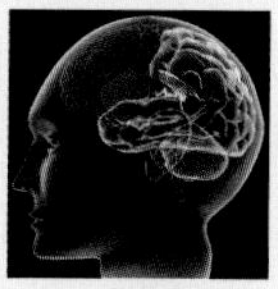

5.1 Moonwalking with Einstein

http://tiny.cc/showmemore

In this video, author Joshua Foer explains how he wrote a book about memory championship competitions and ultimately learned their techniques to become a memory champion himself.

Yakobchuk Vasyl/Shutterstock

5.2 Retrograde Amnesia: A Head Injury Wipes Out a 46-Year-Old Man's Memory

launchpadworks.com LaunchPad macmillan learning

In this video, see how former NFL player Scott Bolzan's life was affected by retrograde amnesia. A head injury left him unable to remember his wife, kids, career, and anything else that happened before the injury.

© ABC News

5.3 Sports Head Injuries and Memory Loss

launchpadworks.com LaunchPad macmillan learning

This video illustrates the potential dangers of sports head injuries by telling the story of high school soccer player Sydney Urzendowski.

John Patriquin/Portland Press Herald via Getty Images

6 Learning

As you enter the Mexican restaurant, he host greets you with a smile. You return the smile and hold up two ingers. He escorts you and your friend to an open booth and offers ou glasses of ice water along with chips and salsa.

Soon, your server sees you close your menus. This brings her over o your table to take your order—fajitas for two. As you dive into the hips and salsa, you finish your water. You make eye contact with your erver and point to your empty glass. A minute later, she brings the itcher and refills it for you.

Ten minutes later, your server approaches your table carrying a ouble order of fajitas fresh from the kitchen. The sizzle makes your nouth water immediately, well before you take a bite.

As ordinary as they may seem, your behaviors in this Mexican estaurant display the remarkable ability each of us has to learn rom experience. Think about it: how did you know that entering he restaurant and gesturing for a table for two would get you a omfortable seat along with ice water, chips, and salsa? How did you now that pointing to your glass would deliver more water? And why lid your mouth water when you heard the sizzle of fajitas?

The answer to all of these questions is *learning*. When sychologists use this term, we don't necessarily mean the kind f deliberate learning that happens in schools, through reading extbooks or attending lectures. (You certainly didn't learn what o do in a Mexican restaurant by reading a manual about Mexican estaurants.) We use *learning* to refer to the process by which the vents of everyday life influence future behavior. This kind of learning an happen when we notice that certain things always happen around he same time, so we associate them with each other, like the sizzle of he fajitas and their delicious taste. Or it can happen when we notice hat certain actions bring about certain consequences—like pointing t your glass brought about more water. These are behaviors you idn't know from birth (a baby at the next table wouldn't display any f them), but that you acquired over the course of your life.

Humans aren't the only species with the capacity to learn. In fact, ll animals learn from their experiences. The same general rules that overn the way animals learn govern the way humans learn, too. This imilarity enables psychologists to conduct research on animals, as well s humans, to better understand the learning process. That learning esearch forms the foundation of this chapter.

CHAPTER OUTLINE

What Is Learning?

YOU WILL LEARN:

6.1 how psychologists define learning.

6.2 how learning fits into the nature-nurture debate.

6.3 that learning occurs universally across species.

All species learn. Even the California sea slug, a biologically small, simple animal found in the Pacific Ocean, shows the ability to learn to avoid electric shock by behaving in particular ways in response to particular conditions. Darren J. Bradley/Shutterstock

Learning is the process by which life experience causes change in the behavior or thinking of an organism. You adjust your behavior accordingly as consequences happen to you, especially those that result from your own actions. Consider Jenny, a 9-year-old girl with two uncles. Uncle Joe always takes Jenny out for ice cream in his red sports car. Now, whenever Jenny sees a red sports car coming down her street, she gets excited. Her Uncle Carl doesn't take Jenny out for ice cream when he comes over, but Jenny has noticed something else—whenever she asks to play basketball with Uncle Carl, he's out in the driveway shooting hoops with her within a minute. Now she asks him to shoot hoops as soon as he arrives.

In both of these situations, Jenny has learned what goes with what. Through her own experience, she has learned to *associate* certain pairs of events. And Jenny remembers what she has learned about each uncle. What you've learned tends to endure unless new experiences come along to change it. Consider your own relatives, including those you might not see for months at a time. What are the chances that you'll completely forget what you've learned about them and react as if they are complete strangers the next time you see them?

Learning is the essence of the nurture side of the nature–nurture debate that surrounds all of human behavior. On the nature side of the argument is *maturation*, which causes some behaviors to take place because the animal's biological clock says it is time for them. For example, potty training works with most kids at age 2 or 3 (but not earlier) because younger children simply don't have the mental or physical capabilities to learn this behavior, no matter the efforts of their parents. Dating follows a similar pattern—the main reason it emerges in the teenage years (and not, say, around kindergarten) is puberty. Of course, maturation and learning (that is, nature and nurture) often work in tandem. For example, when the toddler starts potty training or when the teenager starts to date, positive experiences will accelerate the process and negative experiences will delay it.

So far, all of the examples have featured people, but don't let that mislead you: learning isn't unique to humans. All species learn. Consider the California sea slug (*Aplysia californica*), which is found in the ocean off the west coast of the United States and Mexico. Researchers study this little animal—only about 6 to 8 inches long and weighing far less than a pound—because it learns through life experience, as larger, more complex animals (including humans) do. For example, when researchers poked one part of its body and then immediately delivered electric shock to another part, it soon learned to withdraw the second body part as soon as it sensed another poke in the first body part (Carew et al., 1983, 1981). In a separate study, researchers delivered the electric shock only if the sea slug allowed its gill to fall below a certain height. In these cases, the sea slug kept its gill raised high much longer than normal, which it apparently learned to do in order to avoid the shock (Hawkins et al., 2006).

As implied by the studies of the California sea slug, researchers who study learning make few distinctions between species. Some biological factors are unique to certain species (we will consider them later), but the processes by which one type of animal learns are basically the same as the processes by which any other type of animal learns. For this reason, a lot of learning studies use animals as participants—from pigeons to rats, from dogs to cats—with the assumption that the findings can be applied to the way humans learn (Ator, 1991; Delgado et al., 2006; Barad, 2005). Some of the earliest and most important learning research was stumbled upon by Ivan Pavlov in his work with dogs. Let's consider Pavlov's pioneering work next.

CHECK YOUR LEARNING:

6.1 How do psychologists define learning?

6.2 How does learning fit into the nature-nurture debate?

6.3 Is learning unique to humans?

Classical Conditioning

Ivan Pavlov, one of the most prominent figures in the history of psychology, was not a psychologist at all. He was a Russian medical researcher (a physiologist, to be specific) who in the late 1800s devoted his professional life to the study of the digestive system (Windholz, 1997; Babkin, 1949). Pavlov examined secretions made by various parts of the digestive tract, including saliva, which is produced in the mouth to start the digestive process. Pavlov was measuring the amount of saliva that dogs produced when food entered their mouths when he made an accidental discovery.

YOU WILL LEARN:

6.4 who Ivan Pavlov was and why his research with dogs was important.

6.5 what classical conditioning is and how it occurs in your life.

6.6 the components of classical conditioning.

6.7 how we generalize or discriminate what we learn.

6.8 how learned associations can be acquired and extinguished.

6.9 how multiple learned associations can be linked to produce higher-order conditioning.

6.10 how we learn vicariously through others' life experiences.

Pavlov's Accidental Discovery

Initially, everything in Pavlov's digestive research was going well. Pavlov had the dogs in their harnesses. His assistant would bring the food to the dogs, and they would measure how much the dogs' mouths watered with the help of specialized equipment.

But a problem arose. The dogs started salivating too soon. They weren't salivating *when* the food arrived, but *before* the food arrived. At first, this problem frustrated and perplexed Pavlov. The dogs had picked up on cues that the food was on the way—perhaps the sight of the assistant who brought the food or the sound of the door opening as the assistant entered the room—and were salivating in *anticipation* of the food (Mook, 2004). Pavlov realized that the dogs' expectant mouth-watering was a problem for his digestive research, but he also realized this "problem" was actually a fascinating phenomenon that happened to the dogs, to humans, and to other species as well. By the early 1900s, Pavlov decided to shift the direction of his research entirely to the study of what he called *conditioned reflexes*—a bold move for a researcher who had won the Nobel Prize for his studies of digestion (Fancher & Rutherford, 2012). These learning studies Pavlov conducted shaped the field of psychology.

In his research, Pavlov focused on **classical conditioning:** a form of learning in which animals or people make a connection between two stimuli that have occurred together such that one predicts the other. Essentially, Pavlov designed studies that intentionally created the kind of anticipatory salivation in dogs that originally happened by accident (Pavlov, 1927, 1928). His first step was to identify a **neutral simulus**: a stimulus that causes no response at all. He used sounds such as a bell for the neutral stimulus because its sound produced no salivation (or any other reaction) in the dog (**Figure 6.1**). Next, he identified food as the **unconditioned stimulus**: a stimulus

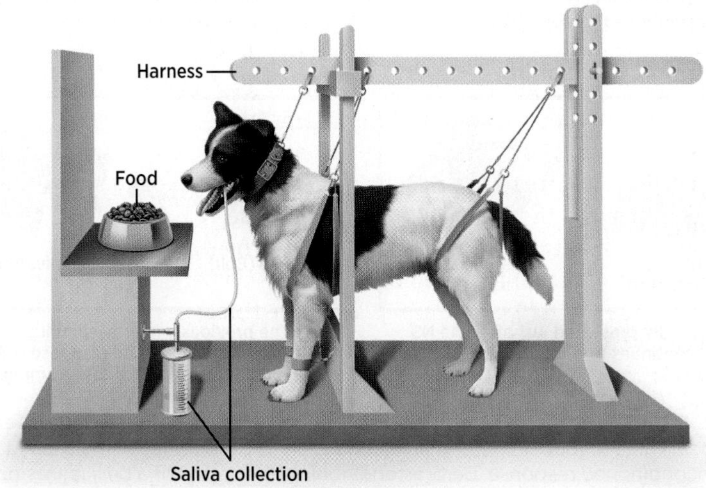

FIGURE 6.1 Pavlov's Classical Conditioning For his research on classical conditioning, Pavlov placed dogs in an apparatus that allowed him to measure their salivation. At first, dogs salivated only when food was placed in front of them, but after Pavlov repeatedly paired the food with the sound of a bell, dogs eventually salivated to the sound of the bell by itself.

learning
The process by which life experience causes change in the behavior or thinking of an organism.

classical conditioning
A form of learning in which animals or people make a connection between two stimuli that have occurred together, such that one predicts the other.

neutral stimulus
A stimulus that causes no response at all.

unconditioned stimulus
A stimulus that causes a response automatically, without any need for learning.

Ivan Pavlov and his colleagues were conducting research on the digestive system in the late 1800s in Russia when they shifted their focus to learning and more specifically classical conditioning. Sovfoto/UIG via Getty Images

that causes a response automatically, without any need for learning. Food certainly fits the bill, since a dog instinctively salivates to food as a natural biological reflex. That salivation in response to the food is the dog's **unconditioned response**: the automatic response to a stimulus that occurs naturally, without any need for learning.

Next, the conditioning happens. In other words, Pavlov paired the neutral stimulus and the unconditioned stimulus by ringing the bell, then immediately putting food in the dog's mouth (**Figure 6.2**). The dog eventually notices the repetition of this sequence—*bell–food, bell–food, bell–food*. Soon enough the dog salivates to the sound of the bell *even if there is no food*. By this process, the bell transforms from a neutral stimulus to a **conditioned stimulus**: a formerly neutral stimulus that now causes a response because of its link to an unconditioned stimulus. This salivation—specifically, salivation in response to the bell rather than the food—is called the **conditioned response**: the response to a conditioned stimulus acquired through learning.

So Pavlov made dogs' mouths water in response to the sound of a bell that had absolutely no effect on them just hours before. This happened because the bell sounded before the food, which naturally caused the salivation before any conditioning took place. Once the dogs learned that the bell predicted food, they salivated to the bell just as automatically and involuntarily as they always had to food itself (Pavlov, 1927, 1928; Kehoe & Macrae, 1998).

That may happen to dogs in a lab study, but does it happen to people in the real world too?

Ever notice your mouth water when you hear the *pffst* of a soda can opening? It's the same phenomenon. Soda automatically makes your mouth water. It is an unlearned biological response to good-tasting liquids entering your mouth. In this case, soda is the unconditioned stimulus, and your salivation to soda is the unconditioned response.

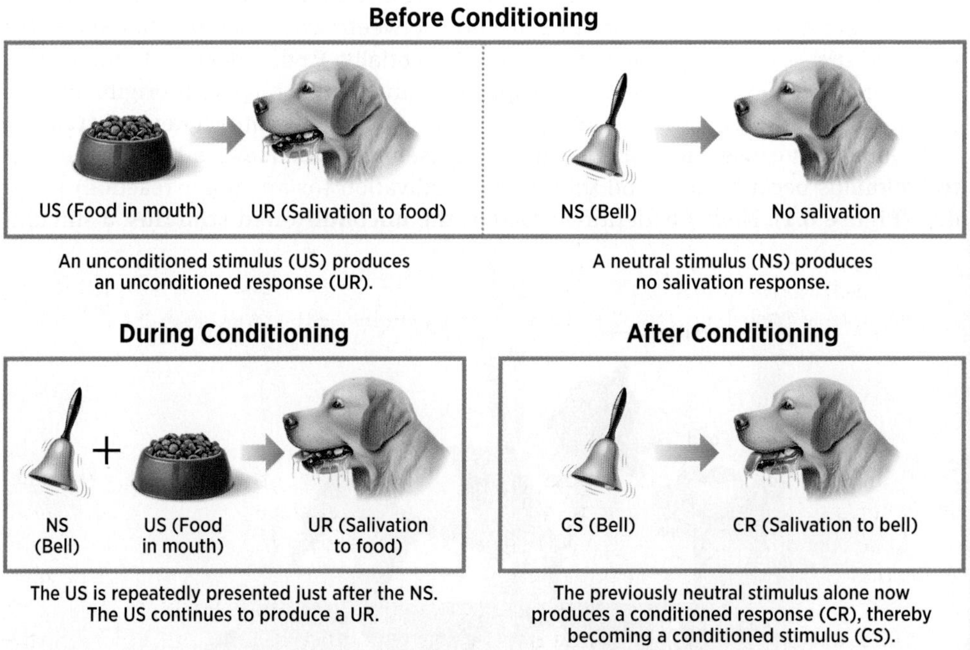

FIGURE 6.2 Pavlov's Classical Conditioning Experiment *Before* a dog undergoes any conditioning, it salivates to food. In other words, food is an unconditioned stimulus, and salivating to food is an unconditioned response. Before conditioning, the sound of a bell causes no response in the dog at all. *During* conditioning, the food and bell are presented at the same time over and over again (*bell–food*; *bell–food*; *bell,–food*...). *After* conditioning, because of what the dog has learned by the repeated pairing of the bell and the food, the dog salivates to the bell. The bell, which used to be a neutral stimulus, is now a conditioned stimulus. And salivating to the bell is now a conditioned response.

FROM RESEARCH TO REAL LIFE

Classical Conditioning in Advertising

If Pavlov's dogs had money, they might have spent it on bells. That's quite odd, given that dogs are usually indifferent to bells. But Pavlov did such a good job pairing bells with food, which the dogs inherently liked, that he transformed bells from irrelevant to exciting. It's as if some of the thrill dogs naturally feel toward food rubbed off on the bell.

Advertisers do the same thing to us every day. They don't call it classical conditioning, though. They call it branding. Just as Pavlov did, they pair their product (which is originally irrelevant to us) with something we inherently like or find exciting. With repetition, the product begins to take on the qualities of the well-liked, exciting person or thing with which it has been paired (Schachtman et al., 2011; Till & Priluck, 2000; De Houwer et al., 2001).

Why does Nike pay millions of dollars to athletes like LeBron James and Maria Sharapova? It's simple: classical conditioning. Nike knows that if it pairs its swoosh with exciting, successful athletes frequently enough, you'll learn to respond to the swoosh as exciting and successful too. This happens in much the same way that Pavlov's dogs learned to salivate to a bell that was originally neutral to them.

ChinaFotoPress/Getty Images; Mike Stobe/Getty Images

Let's consider Nike, with its iconic swoosh logo, as an example. This may be difficult to imagine, given how much Nike advertises, but there was a time early in your life when that swoosh meant absolutely nothing to you. It was just a random, meaningless shape, much as the bell was a random, meaningless sound to a dog entering Pavlov's lab for the first time. Over time, though, you saw the swoosh again and again. And Nike was very selective about who you saw it paired with: Michael Jordan, Pete Sampras, Michelle Wie, LeBron James, Roger Federer, Serena Williams, Carli Lloyd, Kevin Durant, Rory McIlroy, Maria Sharapova, Cristiano Ronaldo, and Russell Westbrook. In short, you saw the Nike swoosh paired with exciting and wildly successful athletes. In time, some of that excitement and success rubbed off on to the swoosh, so that the swoosh itself carried those qualities.

If Pavlov had worked for Nike, he would have explained it this way: the athlete is the unconditioned stimulus, and your positive reaction to the athlete is the unconditioned response. Nike knows that you already have that reaction built in. Nike's strategy is to pair its swoosh with the athlete, so the swoosh eventually becomes the conditioned response. Your positive response to the swoosh is the conditioned response—the advertising equivalent of a dog salivating to a bell.

But I don't salivate when I see a Nike swoosh. I don't have any reaction at all.

Your response may not be as obvious as the dogs' response to the bell, but if you find yourself responding more positively to Nike shoes and clothes than you would to the same items without the swoosh, you've been conditioned. Of course, the Nike swoosh is just one example. You may also have immediate reactions to shirts with the Polo Ralph Lauren logo, purses with the Chanel logo, or coats with The North Face logo.

Over time, you have learned that the *pffst* sound is consistently followed by the cold, sweet sensation of the soda on your tongue. Just as Pavlov's dog's experienced *bell–food, bell–food, bell–food,* you experienced *pffst–soda, pffst–soda, pffst–soda*. As a result, the *pffst* sound has transformed from a neutral stimulus (*pffst*) to a conditioned stimulus, and your salivation in response to the *pffst* sound is the conditioned response.

Other examples of classical conditioning are all around us. Many examples, like the soda, involve associations with food or drink; think about your conditioned responses to the sight of a Snicker's candy bar wrapper or to the sound of ice cubes landing in a glass.

Many others involve associations to sex. For example, consider high heels. Many people find high heels sexy, but high heels are not naturally sexy. In fact, without classical conditioning, high heels are just another pair of shoes. With classical conditioning, however, after high heels are repeatedly paired with sexy people, high heels

unconditioned response
The automatic response to a stimulus that occurs naturally, without any need for learning.

conditioned stimulus
A formerly neutral stimulus that now causes a response because of its link to an unconditioned stimulus.

conditioned response
The response to a conditioned stimulus acquired through learning.

become a conditioned stimulus rather than a neutral stimulus. The same can be true for any number of sights (certain kinds or brands of clothes), sounds (certain music), or smells (certain colognes or perfumes). If these things get paired with sex, they become a little bit sexy themselves, and in some cases can become fetishes (Darcangelo, 2012; Hoffman et al., 2004; Lalumiere & Quinsey, 1998). One study found that heterosexual men can even get turned on by the sight of a jar of pennies after it has been paired with photos of attractive nude women (Plaud & Martini, 1999). Another study found that simple black-and-white cartoon drawings that were initially rated as neutral became sexually stimulating to women after they repeatedly viewed the drawings while sexually aroused (Both et al., 2011).

Processes Related to Classical Conditioning

Once Pavlov established the basics of classical conditioning, he examined a variety of processes related to it so he could better understand exactly how it works (Fancher & Rutherford, 2012; Windholz, 1997; Babkin, 1949).

Generalization and Discrimination. For example, Pavlov noticed that a dog conditioned to salivate to a particular bell might also salivate to another bell as long as the sound of the second bell was close enough to the sound of the first one. In other words, the dog might exhibit **generalization**: the process by which stimuli that are similar to the conditioned stimulus cause the same conditioned response. On the other hand, if the dog detected that the second bell's sound was quite different from the first bell's sound, the dog would not salivate to the second bell at all. This illustrates **discrimination**: the process by which stimuli that are different from the conditioned stimulus fail to cause the same conditioned response.

Generalization and discrimination are complementary processes. When generalization stops, discrimination begins (Wyrwicka, 2000; Brown, 1965). A classic study (Shenger-Krestovnikova, 1921, as described in Gray, 1979, 1987) illustrates the extent to which animals can learn to discriminate between stimuli even when they are remarkably similar (**Figure 6.3**). First, dogs were shown a circle immediately before receiving food. As a result, the dogs began salivating to the sight of the circle. They were

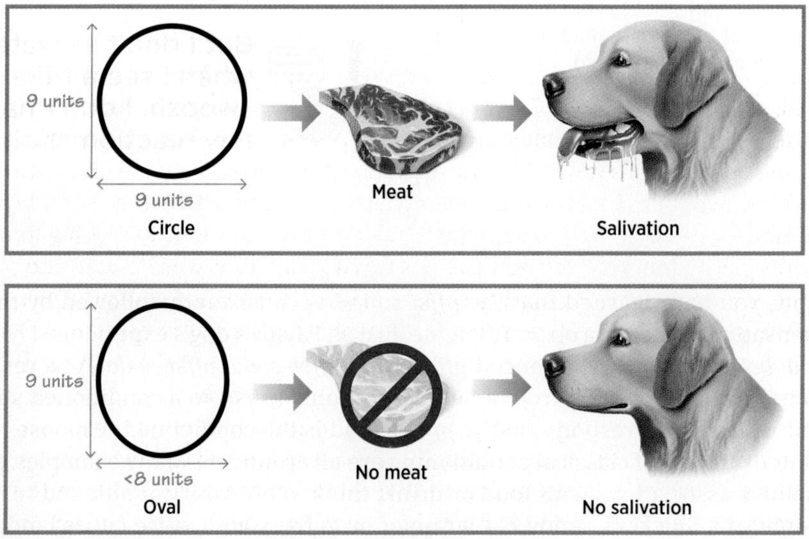

FIGURE 6.3 Generalization and Discrimination In a classic study of generalization and discrimination, dogs learned to respond differently to very similar shapes (a circle and a nearly circular oval). Those two shapes served as meaningful predictors to the dogs: the circle meant that food was coming, but the oval did not (Shenger-Krestovnikova, 1921, as described in Gray, 1979, 1987).

generalization
The learning process by which stimuli that are similar to the conditioned stimulus cause the same conditioned response.

discrimination
The learning process by which stimuli that are different from the conditioned stimulus fail to cause the same conditioned response.

IT'S LIKE ...

Dogs Discriminating Between Similar Shapes Are Like You Discriminating Between Similar Logos

Dogs viewing the circles and nearly circular ovals learned to discriminate between those two shapes only when the difference between the two stimuli became *meaningful* to them (Shenger-Krestovnikova, 1921, as described in Gray, 1979, 1987). At first, the dogs generalized. They salivated to both circles and ovals, presuming that since circles predicted food, ovals would too. Only when their experience taught them that circles predicted food but ovals did not did discrimination become important.

Our own discrimination behaviors are a lot like those of the dogs in that study. We discriminate more when the difference between items means a lot to us. Think for a minute about the number of times in a typical day that you make important distinctions between things that appear alike but have different meanings to you. In the parking lot, your blue Ford Focus looks just like the other three blue Ford Focuses, but a quick check of the cars' details (trim color, dings, license plate) makes it obvious which is yours. Your phone, your laptop, your wallet—they probably look a lot like many others', but you zoom in on the particulars of your items because they mean so much to you. When the difference between the items doesn't mean that much—two nearly identical empty carts at the grocery store, for example—you might not discriminate between them at all.

We often generalize what we've learned, but when slight differences between stimuli suggest big differences in terms of their meaning, we often discriminate instead. McDonald's, Monster, and M&Ms all share M logos, but those M's mean very different things—french fries versus energy drink versus candy—so discriminating between them happens easily. (Left to right) JOKER/Erich Haefele/ullstein bild via Getty Images; Karen Bleier/AFP/Getty Images; © Ekaterina Minaeva/Alamy

The same rules of discrimination apply to your responses to the many logos you see every day. You associate each of them with a distinct product or place (at least you should, if the advertisers have done their jobs well). Some are similar to each other, but you will discriminate between them and react in different ways if they represent things that hold some meaning in your life. Consider the three logos shown all consist of nothing but the letter M, but you probably find yourself reacting differently to each. One M means fries, one M means candy, and one M means energy drink. At one point, none of them meant anything to you. Only when each logo was paired with the product it represents did you begin to discriminate it from the other M's of the world.

then shown an oval (taller than it was wide) immediately before receiving food, and as expected, salivated to that too. The dogs generalized what they learned about the circle to another figure that resembled a circle. The researchers then presented the circle and the oval many more times, but with an important difference: the circle was always followed by food, but the oval was never followed by food. The dogs soon learned to discriminate: they continued to salivate to the circle but stopped salivating to the oval. Finally, the experimenters showed the dogs new ovals that were closer and closer to the shape of a circle. The dogs only began to salivate to the oval when the oval's height became very close to its width—specifically, when the height-to-width ratio was 9 to 8—but not any sooner.

One of the most famous—and controversial—studies in the history of psychology attempted to explore the generalization and discrimination processes in classical conditioning. It was conducted by John B. Watson, a U.S. psychologist who promoted the results of Pavlov's studies in the United States in the early 1900s in the form of *behaviorism* (Watson, 1913, 1914; Buckley, 1989; Benjafield, 2015). In his 1920 Little Albert study, Watson and his student, Rosalie Rayner, worked with an 11-month-old baby boy. Sitting on the floor with him, they presented Albert with a variety of things to see and touch. Among them was a white rat, to which Albert showed no fear at all. In fact, he seemed rather curious about it, reaching his hand out to touch it. However, the next time they presented the white rat to Albert, Watson made a sudden, loud noise

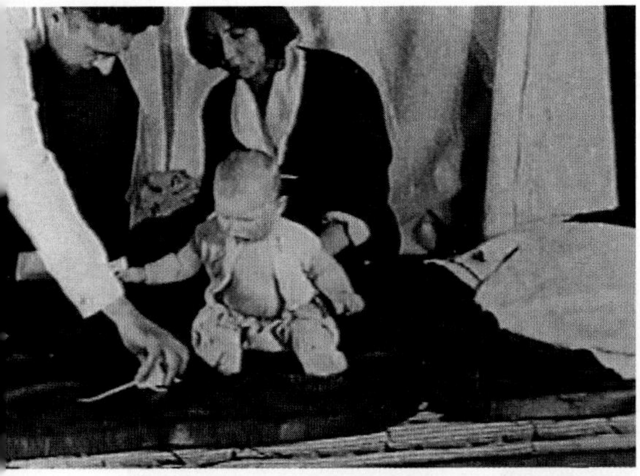

In the Little Albert study (which would not be allowed by today's ethical standards), a baby boy was classically conditioned to fear one white fuzzy thing (a rat), and then he generalized his fear to other white fuzzy things. He discriminated, or did not feel fear of, things that were not white and fuzzy. The Drs. Nicholas and Dorothy Cummings Center for the History of Psychology, The University of Akron

right behind Albert's head by whacking a steel bar with a hammer. Of course, Albert's natural reaction to the loud noise was fear, illustrated by his immediate startle response and crying. Watson then repeated the pairing—*rat–noise, rat–noise, rat–noise*—until he eventually presented the rat by itself. As you might expect, Albert began to cry and show fear of the rat—the same one he had earlier not feared at all, thanks to the association it now had with the scary noise.

This was a vivid early example of classical conditioning, but the part most relevant to the idea of generalization and discrimination was that Albert began to fear objects similar to the white rat. Almost anything that Watson or Rayner presented that was white and furry like the rat made Albert cry, including a rabbit, a dog, a fur coat, and even (to some extent) Watson's own hair. However, items that did not resemble the white rat, such as toy blocks, caused no negative reaction in Albert at all. He reacted positively to them, just as he had before any conditioning took place. In other words, Albert showed generalization by fearing things that were furry and white (like the rat), and he showed discrimination by *not* fearing things that were *not* furry and white.

It is important to emphasize that the methods Watson and Rayner used would never be approved by ethics boards today. Their treatment of Little Albert caused far too much harm to the participant to justify its use. In fact, this methodology has been the subject of significant controversy, not only for the way Watson and Rayner conditioned this infant but also for the fact that they did nothing afterward to try to reduce the fears they had created (Fridlund et al., 2012). Indeed, studies of this type sparked the movement toward institutional review boards put in place to examine and possibly prohibit potentially risky or unethical studies before they can be conducted (Rosnow et al., 1993; Ceci et al., 1985).

Acquisition. In addition to generalization and discrimination, Pavlov identified particular components of the classical conditioning process. For example, he recognized that there is a particular moment when the animal initially makes the link between the two stimuli (Gleeson, 1991). We call this **acquisition**: the point in the learning process at which the neutral stimulus becomes a conditioned stimulus because it causes the conditioned response. An important point regarding acquisition is that it is based on the ability of one stimulus to *predict* the other. Specifically, the conditioned stimulus (formerly the neutral stimulus) predicts the unconditioned stimulus. For Pavlov's dogs, the bell predicts the food. For Jenny, a red sports car predicts ice cream. As with any prediction, it makes sense only if the order of events is correct. If the sequence were reversed—if the dogs heard the bell *after* they received food or if Jenny saw a red sports car *after* she ate ice cream—then the neutral stimulus would not serve as a predictor, and conditioning would be far less likely to occur (Rescorla, 1988a,b).

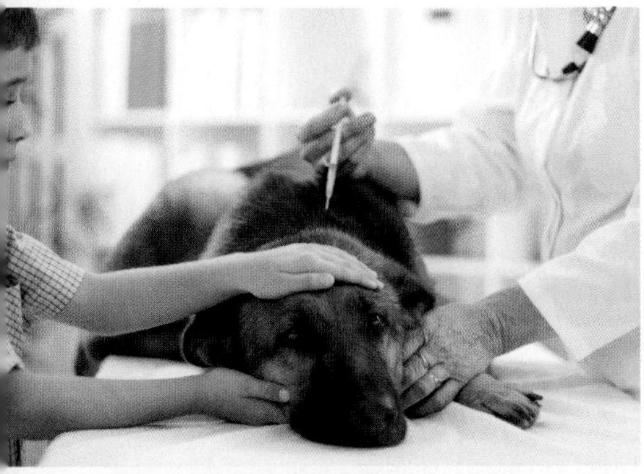

Acquisition happens when a neutral stimulus becomes a conditioned stimulus because it is paired with a conditioned response. For example, if you give your dog a new food shortly before it gets a painful shot, it may acquire a learned connection between that food and the feeling of pain. VP Photo Studio/Shutterstock

For acquisition to take place, it is also important that the two stimuli happen within a very brief time of each other. If a long delay separates the neutral stimulus from the unconditioned stimulus, the two may never become associated with each other, so learning may never take place. Remember the study in which men became sexually turned on by a jar of pennies after it was paired with photos of attractive naked women? The researchers got those results by presenting the photos *immediately* after the pennies (Plaud & Martini, 1999). If they had allowed significant time to pass between the pennies and the photos, the link between the two might not have been made, and the pennies would not have caused arousal. Similarly, imagine that you give your dog a new kind of food before the dog gets a painful shot at the vet's office. The dog is much more likely to associate the taste of the food with the pain of the shot if only 5 seconds, rather than 5 hours, separate the two events.

Extinction. At the other end of the classical conditioning timeline is **extinction**: the point in the learning process at which the conditioned stimulus no longer causes the conditioned response because it is no longer linked to the unconditioned stimulus. To study extinction, Pavlov took dogs that had been conditioned

to salivate to the bell, then repeatedly presented the bell without food. Eventually, the bell no longer predicted food. In fact, the bell predicted the absence of food. As a result, the dogs stopped salivating to the bell, and the conditioned response was extinguished.

As an example of extinction in humans, consider David, an 8-year-old boy who loves Hershey bars. In fact, just as Pavlov's dogs learned to salivate to the sound of a bell, David learned to get excited at the mention of the word *Hershey*. However, David's response to the word *Hershey* changed when his family moved to the town of Hershey, Pennsylvania. In his new town, David saw and heard the word *Hershey* every day in ways that were decidedly *not* exciting: the Hershey bus station, Hershey High School, Hershey Medical Center, and Hotel Hershey. With all of these new experiences, the word *Hershey* no longer predicted the excitement of a chocolate treat for David. Over time, David's response of excitement to the word *Hershey* became extinct.

***Extinct* sounds so permanent. Once extinction happens, is that learning gone forever?**

Spontaneous Recovery. Not exactly. The learned association between the two stimuli seems to be hidden rather than deleted entirely. We know this because of Pavlov's discovery of **spontaneous recovery**: after a temporary period of inactivity, the return of a conditioned response that had become extinct. After he extinguished the dog's conditioned response of salivating to the bell, Pavlov waited awhile (several hours at least) and then presented the bell again. The dog salivated—not as much as it had when the bell–food connection was at its strongest but certainly more than it had before the bell was ever paired with food. This response suggests that the dog, after the pause, is unsure whether the bell predicts food, as it once did, or the absence of food, as it did more recently. As a result, the dog's response falls somewhere between those two extremes (Falls, 1998; Pavlov, 1927, 1928; Rescorla, 1997).

Spontaneous recovery happens to people too. Consider Ron, a 55-year-old man who just helped his elderly mother move into Autumn View, an assisted living facility. Ron programs his phone with customized rings, and he chose the old-fashioned *brrrringgg* of analog phones for Debbie, the director of Autumn View. The first few times Debbie called Ron, the news was alarming: his mother had fallen and injured her arm; his mother was having trouble breathing; his mother was experiencing chest pain. Soon, via classical conditioning, Ron was responding to Debbie's *brrrringgg* with panic before he even answered the phone. However, the next several calls from Debbie were not alarming at all. In fact, they were quite mundane: a call to let Ron know he had left his jacket there when he last visited, a reminder about an upcoming Mother's Day party at the facility, a minor question about the bill. Soon, the *brrrringgg* that had predicted panic was predicting, well, not much at all. At that point, Ron's panic response to the *brrrringgg* became extinct. He reacted to that ring no differently than to any other ring. He then received no calls from Debbie for a quite a while, until one morning he heard the *brrrringgg* for the first time in weeks. Ron reacted with mild anxiety—not the full-fledged panic he had felt after the first few calls from Debbie, but certainly more anxiety than he would have felt if he had never associated her ring with alarming news.

Higher-Order Conditioning. Pavlov also found that sometimes during classical conditioning, the number of associated stimuli is not limited to two. The stimuli can be linked in a chain of three or more. This is called **higher-order conditioning**: classical conditioning that involves three or more stimuli. (Higher-order conditioning is also known as *second-order conditioning* [Holland & Rescorla, 1975; Nairne & Rescorla, 1981; Rescorla, 1976, 1980].) Specifically, a learning process in which a conditioned stimulus from a previous learning process serves as an unconditioned stimulus, producing a new conditioned stimulus that causes the same conditioned response.

acquisition
The point in the learning process at which the neutral stimulus becomes a conditioned stimulus because of its link to the conditioned response.

extinction
The point in the learning process at which the conditioned stimulus no longer causes the conditioned response because it is no longer linked to the unconditioned stimulus.

spontaneous recovery
After a temporary period of inactivity, the return of a conditioned response that had become extinct.

higher-order conditioning
Classical conditioning that involves three or more stimuli.

CHAPTER APP 6.1

Classical Conditioning

Aqualert Water Reminder

Preview one of the links and consider the following questions.

WEBSITE:
http://tiny.cc/t9g7jy

ANDROID:
http://tiny.cc/3igyiy

IPHONE:
http://tiny.cc/vigyiy

VIDEO DEMO:
http://tiny.cc/chapterapps

This app is designed to help you drink sufficient amounts of water throughout the day. You input your personal information (weight, sex, activity level) and the app helps you develop a schedule for how much water you should drink. At scheduled times, you hear alerts sent by the app that remind you to drink water. It also gives you feedback on your water consumption, allowing you to track your progress.

How does it APPly to your daily life?
Think about the way Pavlov's dogs learned through *classical conditioning* to salivate to the sound of a bell when it was followed by food. What do you think will happen if *you* use this app in which the sound of the alert is followed by water? Does some version of this classical conditioning already happen in your day-to-day life? Have certain sounds (or sights or other stimuli) become predictors of certain foods or drinks?

How does it APPly to your understanding of psychology?
There are four essential parts of classical conditioning for the Pavlov bell-food studies: the *unconditioned stimulus*, the *unconditioned response*, the *conditioned stimulus*, and the *conditioned response*. Can you identify those four parts of classical conditioning from your experience with this app?

Let's think again about the way the *pffst* of opening a soda causes you to salivate. As a reminder, this response is caused by the fact that you have repeatedly heard the sound right before you taste the soda. That's a two-step process (*pffst–soda*), but could it be extended to three steps? In other words, is there another stimulus that repeatedly happens right before (predicts) the *pffst* sound? If you typically get your soda from a vending machine, the thud sound that the can makes as it falls to the machine's opening could be that third stimulus. In this three-step sequence—*thud–pffst–soda*—the thud predicts the *pffst*, and the *pffst* predicts the soda. With enough repetition, the thud produces a salivation response. The sequence could even be extended to four steps if we consider the sound of the coins dropping into the slot at the beginning of the process, such that the sound of the coins dropping causes salivation through a *coins–thud–pffst–soda* connection.

Vicarious Conditioning. A final note on classical conditioning: it can happen to you because of what you see happening to the people around you in addition to what happens directly to you. We call this **vicarious conditioning**: conditioning that takes place via observation of others' life experiences rather than one's own. Jenny—whose Uncle Joe takes her out for ice cream in his red sports car—has a close friend named Seiko. Jenny has told Seiko stories about how Uncle Joe takes her for ice cream in his red sports car, and in fact, once Seiko was at the ice cream shop herself when she saw Jenny and Uncle Joe pull up. On several occasions, Seiko has been playing with Jenny in her front yard when a red sports car drives by, and she has noticed Jenny's excitement when she sees it. Now, if Seiko happens to see a red sports car before Jenny does, she gets excited too—even though she's never actually ridden in a red sports car.

Applying Classical Conditioning to Your Life

Classical conditioning is often an important part of efforts to improve people's lives. For example, psychologists use principles of classical conditioning to help clients overcome *phobias*. Phobias are strong, irrational fears of a particular thing or situation. Most psychologists believe that a phobia is produced by a learned pairing of a specific thing with an extremely unpleasant feeling, so the best way to overcome a phobia is to break that pairing (Hazlett-Stevens & Craske, 2008; Spiegler & Guevremont, 2010). For example, consider Teresa, a young woman with a phobia of buses, which developed after she was robbed on a bus. She learned to avoid buses through her experience of the bus–robbery pairing, which is problematic because she needs to take a bus to her job. Her psychologist, Dr. Sumule, helps Teresa overcome her phobia by encouraging her to gradually expose herself to buses—getting near them, then getting on them briefly, then staying on for longer periods. As she does, she repeatedly finds that the learned pairing of the bus with the robbery doesn't occur. In other words, Teresa experiences the bus without the fear of robbery. As she spends more time on buses *without* being robbed, Teresa's phobia diminishes and gradually becomes extinct. (We'll discuss phobias and their treatment in much more detail in the chapters on disorders and treatment.)

Classical conditioning can be used in the treatment of physical disorders too. The basic idea is that if a drug improves a disorder, what's paired with that drug can bring about similar improvement. It's just like Pavlov's dogs, which learned to salivate to a bell because the bell had been paired with food, but for human beings, the reaction can take other physical forms (Ader & Cohen, 1982; Cohen et al., 1994; Longo et al., 1999; Exton et al., 2000).

For example, in studies of patients with serious airborne allergies, patients took an effective allergy drug and then immediately drank a very unusual drink—let's imagine it is pineapple soda. After this pairing of effective drug with pineapple soda was repeated a number of times, the researchers gave the patients the pineapple soda by itself. The patients' reactions to the pineapple soda by itself was similar to their reactions to the effective allergy drug with which it had been paired. Not only did the

vicarious conditioning
Conditioning that takes place via observation of others' life experiences rather than one's own.

operant conditioning
A form of learning in which the consequences of a voluntary behavior affect the likelihood that the behavior will recur.

patients describe similar improvements in their allergy symptoms, their bodies had similar physiological reactions in terms of producing antibodies, as well. The formerly neutral stimulus of pineapple soda had come to have a medical effect in these patients because of its learned association with a drug that did have a medical effect (Gauci et al., 1994; Goebel et al., 2008).

This research raises the question of the power of *placebos*, medically inactive substances that somehow have a positive effect on patients (Vits et al., 2011). In one study, researchers treated patients with psoriasis, a common skin disease in which the elbows, knees, or other areas become very red and itchy. At first, all patients were treated repeatedly with an ointment that had a unique smell and color. The ointment contained a steroid as its active ingredient. Then the patients were divided into two groups. (They did not know which group they were in.) Group 1 continued to get the exact same ointment they had been using, including the steroid. Group 2 got the same ointment too, but theirs only contained the active ingredient 25% to 50% of the time. As you would expect, Group 1 got better. Specifically, 78% of them were cured of their psoriasis. The second group—whose ointment *lacked the medicine* most of the time—got better at almost the same rate (73%). Through classical conditioning, the patients in Group 2 had learned the pairing of the steroid with the unique smell and color of the ointment. The pairing was so strong that the smell and the color of the ointment caused the patients' skin to react as if it were actually receiving the medicine (Ader et al., 2010).

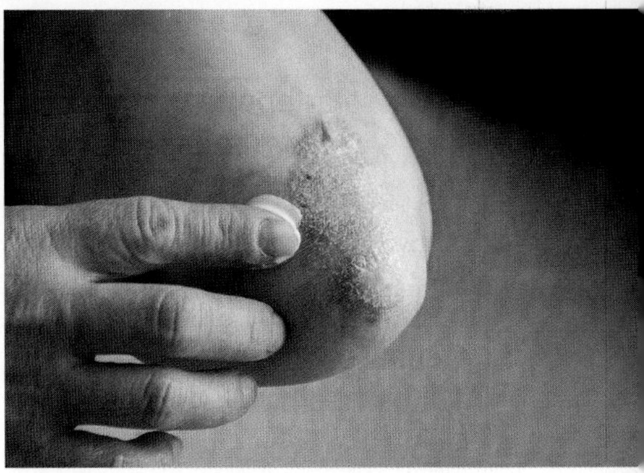

In one study, ointment for a skin disease continued to work even after the active ingredient (a steroid) was removed (Vits et al., 2011). This result illustrates the power of classical conditioning: The other features of the ointment—smell, color, and so on—were paired with the active ingredient closely enough to produce a medicinal effect by themselves. Suze777/iStock/Getty Images

CHECK YOUR LEARNING:

6.4 Who was Ivan Pavlov, and why is his research with dogs important?

6.5 What is classical conditioning, and how commonly does it occur in your life?

6.6 What are the five main components of classical conditioning?

6.7 With regard to classical conditioning, what do generalization and discrimination mean?

6.8 With regard to classical conditioning, what do acquisition and extinction mean?

6.9 What is higher-order conditioning?.

6.10 How does learning take place through vicarious conditioning?

Operant Conditioning

YOU WILL LEARN:

6.11 what operant conditioning is.

6.12 how operant conditioning relates to the law of effect.

6.13 who B. F. Skinner was and why his research on operant conditioning was important.

6.14 how psychologists define reinforcement.

6.15 the differences between various types of reinforcement.

6.16 the differences between various schedules of reinforcement.

You may have noticed that learning via classical conditioning is quite passive. In Pavlov's classic studies, the dogs weren't really *doing* anything voluntarily. Things were being done *to* them. Food was placed near their mouths and bells were rung in their ears, but the dogs' role was simply to stand there and demonstrate any natural involuntary reflexes that might occur (salivation).

Often, learning is a more active process. In these moments, we learn by connecting what we do with what happens to us as a result. Psychologists call this **operant conditioning**: a form of learning in which the consequences of a voluntary behavior affect the likelihood that the behavior will recur. The word *operant* shares its root with the word *operate*, so *operant conditioning* refers to what you learn when operating on the environment around you (Flora, 2004). As you operate on your environment, you develop your own personal if–then statements that explain past behavior and govern future behavior. These if–then statements are called *contingencies*. Here are a few examples of contingencies: (1) If I run outside without shoes, then I get a cut on my foot. (2) If I answer the phone when my friend Steve calls, then I laugh at his jokes. (3) If I blow off my math homework, then I bomb the test.

YOU WILL LEARN: *(Continued)*

6.17 how psychologists define punishment.

6.18 how discriminative stimuli affect operant conditioning.

6.19 how shaping takes place.

6.20 the relevance of some classical conditioning concepts to operant conditioning.

If one of Pavlov's dogs had whimpered and then received a treat or scratched at the door and then received a smack, perhaps Pavlov would have focused on operant conditioning rather than classical conditioning. As it happens, though, operant conditioning has a different pioneer: Edward L. Thorndike. Thorndike was a U.S. psychologist who conducted many studies on animal behavior in the late 1800s and early 1900s (Thorndike, 1898, 1900). In the best known of these studies, he placed cats inside a small box he called a puzzle box. As **Figure 6.4** illustrates, the cat could open the door to the puzzle box by performing a particular behavior, such as stepping on a button on the box's floor or pulling on a weight hanging from the box's ceiling, much like the pulls on overhead ceiling fans. Thorndike gave the cats food when they escaped, and he timed how long it took them to do so. He found that the first escape took quite a while as the cats moved randomly around the box, but each additional escape took a shorter and shorter time. Through trial and error, the cat seemed to be learning: if I step on this button, then the door opens and I get to exit and eat.

Thorndike said that the cats were demonstrating the **law of effect**: the observation that a behavior is more likely to be repeated if its effects are desirable but less likely to be repeated if its effects are undesirable (1911, 1927). It's a simple but powerful rule by which we all (animals and people) live: we pay attention to the outcome of each of our actions. If we like the outcome, we will probably repeat that action; if we don't like the outcome, we probably won't repeat the behavior.

B. F. Skinner: Operant Conditioning for Everyone

B. F. Skinner was a psychology professor at the University of Minnesota, Indiana University, and Harvard. Inspired by Thorndike, Skinner spent his career conducting extensive studies on animal behavior, trying to expand what we know about the law of effect and operant conditioning (Mills, 1998; Richelle, 1993). While Thorndike's work remained relatively unknown to most people outside of academia, Skinner's work made him a household name. By the 1960s and 1970s, Skinner was as much of a rock star as a psychology professor could be: he frequently appeared on TV talk shows, wrote two books that sold millions of copies and made the *New York Times* bestseller list, was on *Esquire* magazine's 1970 list of the 100 most important people, and was the subject of a cover story in *Time* magazine in September 1971 (Rutherford, 2009; Smith, 1996; Mills, 1998). Most of Skinner's fame stemmed from his ability to apply his findings about animal behavior to human behavior. Perhaps the most controversial of these was that *all* behavior is determined by its consequences, so we have no free will to act as we want. This claim—which may be easier to accept for other animals than for humans—remains controversial today (Altus & Morris, 2009; Baer et al., 2008).

FIGURE 6.4 Thorndike's Puzzle Box When Edward Thorndike placed hungry cats inside puzzle boxes, they learned which behaviors caused the door to open and allowed them to eat the food outside. Thorndike explained that the cats' learning process illustrated the law of effect, or the idea that a behavior is likely to be repeated if its outcome is desirable but unlikely to be repeated if its outcome is undesirable (Thorndike, 1911, 1927).

FIGURE 6.5 Skinner Box B. F. Skinner's Skinner boxes (or operant chambers) were new and improved versions of Edward Thorndike's puzzle boxes. They allowed animals to bring food or water into the box by pressing a lever or button. Also, because the boxes were wired for electricity, they could automatically record the frequency of animals' behavior and control lights that indicated whether a reward was available at a particular time.

Skinner's first step as a researcher was to improve Thorndike's puzzle box. The **Skinner box** (originally called an *operant chamber*) is a container into which animals such as pigeons or rats could be placed for the purpose of observing and recording their behavior in response to consequences (**Figure 6.5**). Many of the advantages of the Skinner box had to do with automation and the use of electricity. For example, it automatically dispensed food or water when the animal pressed the right lever or button. The Skinner box recorded the animal's lever-pressing behavior automatically (through an electrical device), which meant there was no need for a person to observe continuously. And it could use a light to indicate that a reward was available if a behavior was performed. It also kept the animal in the box, so the experimenter didn't have to catch the escaped animal and wrestle it back into the box for another trial (as was required by Thorndike's cats) (Toates, 2009; Ator, 1991).

Reinforcement. With his new boxes, Skinner ran a multitude of studies on how consequences shape actions. The type of consequence upon which he focused most was **reinforcement**: any consequence of a behavior that makes that behavior more likely to recur. In general, reinforcement can be described as anything that helps the animal experience pleasure or avoid pain (Flora, 2004; Donahoe, 1998). Usually, what's reinforcing to one member of a species is reinforcing to all members of that species. But sometimes, what we expect to be reinforcing to a person or animal is not. In other words, reinforcement, like beauty, is in the eye of the beholder. For example, Jodi, a summer camp counselor, offers two 13-year-old girls—Abby and Bianca—peanut butter cookies for cleaning their cabins. Abby finds cookies reinforcing and cleans her area quickly. Bianca, on the other hand, is allergic to peanuts, so she does not find the cookies reinforcing at all and the offer does not motivate her to clean up.

Reinforcement can be categorized in many ways. For example, it can be labeled as either *positive* or *negative*. **Positive reinforcement** involves getting something desirable. **Negative reinforcement** involves removing something undesirable. Keep in mind that both of these are reinforcement, which means that they both increase the likelihood of the behavior happening again in the future. Positive reinforcement comes in many forms—for example, a restaurant server receiving a tip for providing good service, a 5-year-old child getting a hug for a successfully tying her shoes, or a college football team being awarded a trophy for winning a bowl game. Negative reinforcement also takes many forms—for example, a homeowner getting rid of bugs by calling an exterminator, a woman stopping harassing phone calls by obtaining a restraining order, or a child overcoming strep throat by taking an antibiotic. Remember that in this context, *positive* and *negative* don't mean good and bad. In terms of reinforcement,

Reinforcement is an essential part of animal training. Dogs learn to fetch, shake hands, roll over, or jump over a bar by associating those behaviors with the reinforcements, such as treats, that come after them. iztok noc/E+/Getty Images

law of effect
The observation that a behavior is more likely to be repeated if its effects are desirable but less likely to be repeated if its effects are undesirable.

Skinner box
(originally called an *operant chamber*) a container into which animals such as pigeons or rats could be placed for the purpose of observing and recording their behavior in response to consequences.

reinforcement
Any consequence of a behavior that makes that behavior more likely to recur.

positive reinforcement
A type of reinforcement that involves getting something desirable.

negative reinforcement
A type of reinforcement that involves removing something undesirable.

positive means plus (plus something desirable, to be specific) and negative means minus (minus something undesirable, to be specific).

Primary and Secondary Reinforcers. Reinforcement can also be categorized as either *primary* or *secondary*. A **primary reinforcer** is an innate reinforcer that requires no learning to have a reinforcing effect because it satisfies a biological need. A few basic things serve as primary reinforcers, not only to humans, but to most species, because they have value to keep us alive and healthy: food, water, physical touch, sex, reduction in pain or discomfort. Through your life experience (and classical conditioning), you come to associate other stimuli with those core primary reinforcers.

We call a stimulus that has been paired with a primary reinforcer a **secondary reinforcer**: a reinforcer that requires a learned link to a primary reinforcer to have a reinforcing effect. Money is the ultimate secondary reinforcer (Delgado et al., 2006). Any value that a rectangular green piece of paper or a small silver circle may have to you is something that you had to learn. You weren't born with an appreciation for dollar bills and coins. For example, picture two children, a 1-year-old and a 12-year-old. Grandma gives them identical Amazon.com gift cards. The 12-year-old reacts with excitement. She has learned, through her experience, that the gift card can be exchanged for books, music, toys, and lots of other cool stuff online. The 1-year-old tries to eat the gift card for a minute and then discards it with great indifference. To him, a gift card is not yet linked to the fun things it can bring, so it hasn't become a secondary reinforcer. Plenty of other powerful reinforcers in your day-to-day life are secondary rather than primary reinforcers—from applause to grades to plaques.

Another example of secondary reinforcement is the use of clickers by dog trainers. Specifically, a dog trainer teaches a dog to perform a behavior (heel, sit, and so on) by following the behavior with not only a treat (primary reinforcer), but also with a click (secondary reinforcer). Soon enough, the dog forms such a strong association between the treat and the click that the click alone becomes a powerful reinforcer (Pryor, 2009). (In fact, a click can be more powerful than typical secondary reinforcers like the praise words *good* or *yes* because dogs overhear people use those words in many contexts, which can confuse them.)

Immediate and Delayed Reinforcement. It is also possible to describe reinforcement as *immediate* or *delayed*. This is an important distinction, as a single behavior can have very different short-term effects and long-term effects. For example, eating a whole pizza can feel like a wonderful indulgence at the time but can cause weight gain (not to mention a stomachache) later on. The second consequence (weight gain and stomachache) should probably outrank the first consequence (good taste of pizza). However, the immediacy of the first consequence paired with the delay of the second consequence can cause you to behave in ways that you later regret. Just imagine if the order of the immediate and delayed reinforcers were somehow reversed. Your behavior would likely change if the weight gain and stomachache came immediately but the good taste of the pizza came days later.

Reinforcement and Diversity What is reinforcing to people from one culture might not be reinforcing to people from a different culture (Spiegler, 2016; Pantalone et al., 2010; Gelfand et al., 2007). For example, consider money. Money is a powerful reinforcer, but different types of money mean different things to different people. Imagine that an American brother and sister shoveled snow from their neighbor's driveway. If the neighbor handed each of them an American $10 bill when they finished, they would probably feel reinforced, and likely would repeat the behavior the next time it snowed. However, if the neighbor handed each of them $10 worth of Japanese yen, Indian rupees, or Swiss francs, they would probably not feel reinforced (unless they could somehow exchange the foreign money for American dollars).

DIVERSITY MATTERS

Individualism and collectivism can also play a role in the way reinforcements are perceived in various cultures. Specifically, awards for individual achievements

CHAPTER APP 6.2

Reinforcement

ChoreMonster

Preview one of the links and consider the following questions.

WEBSITE: http://tiny.cc/obh7jy

ANDROID: http://tiny.cc/ejgyiy

IPHONE: http://tiny.cc/9igyiy

VIDEO DEMO: http://tiny.cc/chapterapps

There are dozens of apps designed to help you use operant conditioning—and reinforcement in particular—to make changes to your (or your kids') behavior. For example, ChoreMonster is an app that helps parents reinforce their kids for specifically chosen behaviors. The parent lists the particular behavior for each kid: taking out the trash, doing the dishes, walking the dog, brushing teeth, etc. The parent also decides how many points the kid earns for completing the behavior, and what those points can be exchanged for: TV time, computer time, dessert, allowance, etc. Kids can even check chores off the list themselves with their own version of the app.

How does it APPly to your daily life?
What are the most important decisions for the parent using this kind of operant conditioning app: the number of points each chore is worth, the specific reinforcements that the kid is working toward, the exchange rate between points and reinforcements, or something else? If you were the kid, which of these factors would have the most powerful influence on your behavior?

How does it APPly to your understanding of psychology?
Consider what you've learned about shaping, or the way people can gradually learn a complex behavior by reinforcing each of its small steps. If your parents had used an app like ChoreMonster when you were a kid, would it have helped them shape your behavior? If you are a parent yourself, how effectively could you use an app like this to shape your own kids' behaviors?

are often more well-received in cultures that emphasize individualism—such as the United States, Australia, and some European countries—than in cultures that emphasize collectivism—such as many Asian, Hispanic, and Native American groups (Nelson, 1995; Baruth & Manning, 1992; Kallam et al., 1994). In fact, among more collectivistic cultures, a person who is singled out for an individual award might be teased or belittled by his or her peers for standing out from the crowd. For teachers, coaches, employers, or anyone else who might use reinforcements to influence the behavior of people from diverse backgrounds, this is an important point to keep in mind (Moran et al., 2014; Pierangelo & Giuliani, 2008).

Speaking of employers and reinforcements, one study asked undergraduate business students in three countries (United States, Australia, and Mexico) what they would find most reinforcing about a job offer. There were some common preferences, including good pay and recognition for high levels of performance. But there were some differences between the groups too. In particular, Mexican students expressed stronger preferences for the opportunity to get jobs for their relatives and the opportunity to contribute to society and the well-being of others. These preferences may reflect the fact that Mexico is generally more collectivistic and less individualistic than either the United States or Australia (McGaughey et al., 1997). Another study of undergraduate students from different countries (this time, the United States and Chile) found differences between cultures and differences between genders. Specifically, compared to men, women from both countries placed more reinforcement value on good working conditions and convenient working hours (Corney & Richards, 2005).

A study of high school students' perceptions of reinforcements covered an even broader range of cultures (Homan et al., 2012). The researchers asked 750 teenagers from 7 countries (United States, Australia, Tanzania, Denmark, Honduras, Korea, and Spain) to rate dozens of activities, including sports, social activities, Internet use, games, and sleep on a scale of 1 to 5. Higher scores meant that they found the activity more rewarding. There were some consistencies across cultures, but the results showed plenty of cultural differences. For example, in Tanzania, shopping received the highest rating of all but shopping didn't rate higher than 8th in any other country. In Honduras, visiting relatives was the second-highest rated activity, but its rating was nowhere near as high in any other country. In Denmark, downhill skiing was the highest-rated sport, but it didn't crack the top 5 sports of any other country. In the United States, the top five sports included two (American football and fishing) that didn't appear in the top five of any other country. Soccer, on the other hand, did not make the American top 5, but it made the top 5 in most other countries. The lesson here is that the reinforcement value of any particular item or activity can depend on the cultural background of the person who receives it.

Schedules of Reinforcement

When it comes to reinforcement, timing is everything. The simple distinction between immediate and delayed reinforcement is just the beginning (Lattal, 1991). Indeed, Skinner identified a variety of specific **reinforcement schedules**: patterns by which reinforcements occur in response to a particular behavior. The basic distinction is between *continuous* and *partial* reinforcement. **Continuous reinforcement** is a pattern by which a behavior is reinforced every time it occurs. By contrast, **partial reinforcement** (also known as *intermittent* reinforcement) is a pattern by which a behavior is reinforced only some of the time. For example, let's say a father (Alex) wants his teenage son (Zach) to take over the chore of cutting the grass. If Alex takes Zach out to his favorite restaurant for dinner every day Zach cuts the grass, that's continuous reinforcement. If Alex takes Zach out to his favorite restaurant only on some of the days Zach cuts the grass, that's partial reinforcement.

The distinction between continuous and partial reinforcement is important in terms of *acquisition* and *extinction*, which we mentioned earlier. (Those terms appeared in the section on classical conditioning, but they apply to operant conditioning as well.)

MY TAKE VIDEO 6.2

Reinforcement Schedules

"I would personally check social media less if..."

YOUTUBE: http://tiny.cc/mytake
LAUNCHPAD: launchpadworks.com

People from one culture may value a reinforcement more or less than people from another culture. In one study, high school students indicated how reinforcing they found various activities, including sports. In many countries, soccer was near the top of the list. In the U.S., however, soccer ranked much lower. Some countries featured a sport (or two) high on their list that didn't appear on other countries' lists at all (Homan et al., 2012). Christian Bertrand/Shutterstock

primary reinforcer
An innate reinforcer that requires no learning to have a reinforcing effect because it satisfies a biological need.

secondary reinforcer
A reinforcer that requires a learned link to a primary reinforcer to have a reinforcing effect

reinforcement schedule
A pattern by which reinforcements occur in response to a particular behavior.

continuous reinforcement
A pattern by which a behavior is reinforced every time it occurs.

partial reinforcement
(*intermittent* reinforcement) a pattern by which a behavior is reinforced only some of the times it occurs.

Acquisition happens more quickly with continuous reinforcement—after just a couple of times cutting the grass, Zach will have learned that "If I cut the grass, I get to go to my favorite restaurant" is a hard-and-fast rule. But continuous reinforcement results in faster extinction too—if Alex forgets to reinforce Zach just once or twice, Zach will realize quickly that the deal is off.

With partial reinforcement, acquisition happens more slowly if at all, because it can be difficult to detect a connection between the behavior and the outcome. But once the connection has been acquired, behaviors on a partial reinforcement schedule are quite resistant to extinction. If Zach has learned that grass cutting leads to eating at his favorite restaurant only some of the time, he won't necessarily quit if he doesn't get rewarded with the restaurant the next time he cuts the grass. He might not even quit after two or perhaps even ten grass cuttings don't bring about the reward. This is because the next grass cutting might still bring the reward. The bottom line is that continuous reinforcement is best for making acquisition happen initially, but partial reinforcement is best for maintaining that behavior over time.

Within the broad category of partial reinforcement, Skinner (1961) identified four more specific reinforcement schedules: *fixed-ratio*, *variable-ratio*, *fixed-interval*, and *variable-interval* (**Table 6.1**). They differ from each other in two important ways—whether the reinforcement is predictable (*fixed*) or unpredictable (*variable*); and whether it is based on the number of repetitions of the behavior (*ratio*) or the passage of time (*interval*)—but these differences can powerfully influence behavior.

Ratio Schedules. A **fixed-ratio schedule** is a reinforcement schedule in which a behavior is reinforced after a consistent, predictable number of occurrences. By contrast, a **variable-ratio schedule** is a reinforcement schedule in which a behavior is reinforced after an inconsistent, unpredictable number of occurrences. Consider soda machines versus slot machines. With a soda machine, you know with great confidence that if you put the money in once and press the button once, you'll get your reinforcement. There's no mystery, no uncertainty—this is an example of a fixed-ratio schedule. With a slot machine, you *don't* know what will happen after you put your money in and press the button (or pull the arm). There *is* mystery and uncertainty—you could get nothing or a little something or a lot. The difference between *fixed ratio* and *variable ratio* is important, particularly in terms of extinction, which is essentially giving up on the possibility that your behavior will bring about the reward. With the soda machine, if you put in your money, press the button, and get nothing, you are extremely unlikely to insert money even once more. But with the slot machine, if you put in your money, press the button (or pull the arm), and get nothing, you may insert money again and again, because you know you might hit the jackpot on the next try (Horsley et al., 2012).

Interval Schedules. A **fixed-interval schedule** is a reinforcement schedule in which a behavior can be reinforced after a time interval that is consistent and predictable. By contrast, a **variable-interval schedule** is a reinforcement schedule in which a behavior can be reinforced after a time interval that is inconsistent and

TABLE 6.1: Summary of Reinforcement Schedules

	FIXED	VARIABLE
RATIO	Reinforcement comes when you perform the behavior a predictable number of times. *Example: soda machine*	Reinforcement comes when you perform the behavior an unpredictable number of times. *Example: slot machine*
INTERVAL	Reinforcement comes when you perform the behavior after a predictable amount of time has passed. *Example: mail*	Reinforcement comes when you perform the behavior after an unpredictable amount of time has passed. *Example: email*

fixed-ratio schedule
A reinforcement schedule in which a behavior is reinforced after a consistent, predictable number of occurrences.

variable-ratio schedule
A reinforcement schedule in which a behavior is reinforced after an inconsistent, unpredictable number of occurrences.

fixed-interval schedule
A reinforcement schedule in which a behavior can be reinforced after a time interval that is consistent and predictable.

variable-interval schedule
A reinforcement schedule in which a behavior can be reinforced after a time interval that is inconsistent and unpredictable.

punishment
Any consequence of a behavior that makes that behavior less likely to recur.

unpredictable. Consider mail versus email. (For the sake of this discussion, let's assume that you find your mail and your email to be equally reinforcing in terms of the amount of pleasure each gives you.) With mail, you know to check your mailbox at a certain time—say, after 2:00 P.M. every day but Sunday. In other words, mail is delivered on a fixed-interval schedule. If you receive your mail at 2:30 P.M. on Monday, will you check the mailbox again at 2:45 P.M.? At 7:00 P.M.? At 9:00 A.M. on Tuesday? Of course not—you know that you can't possibly receive the next batch of mail until Tuesday after 2:00 P.M., so you'll wait until then to check again. (As 2:00 P.M. approaches, you may check quite often, only to stop completely once it arrives.)

Email, on the other hand, doesn't arrive at predictable times. It is on a variable-interval schedule. If you receive your email at 2:30 P.M. on Monday, will you check it again at 2:45 P.M.? You very well might—after all, there's no need to wait until 2:30 P.M. Tuesday, or any other predetermined time, to check. Because you never know when the next reinforcing email might arrive, you are likely to check email far more frequently than you check your snail mail.

Fixed-Ratio Schedule

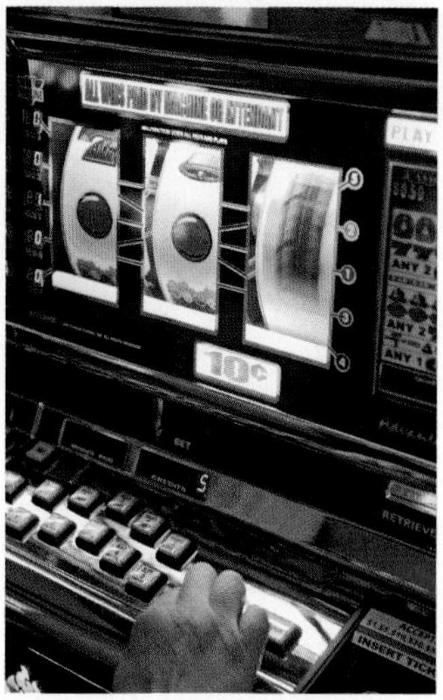

Variable-Ratio Schedule

Fixed-ratio schedules of reinforcement are like soda machines—what you get after you perform the behavior (in this case, inserting money) is predictable. Variable-ratio schedules of reinforcement are like slot machines—what you get after you perform the behavior (again, inserting money) is unpredictable. The degree of predictability makes a big difference when you decide whether to give up on a behavior (or let it become extinct) when you get nothing. (Left) © Graham Oliver/Alamy; (right) Folio Images/Alamy

Punishment

So far, our discussion of operant conditioning has focused on behaviors followed by reinforcements, but of course, many behaviors are not followed by reinforcement. Many behaviors are followed by **punishment**: any consequence of a behavior that makes that behavior less likely to recur.

Wait, I'm confused. What's the difference between punishment and negative reinforcement?

Many students find the terminology confusing. But there's a simple rule to clarify it: if the term includes the word *reinforcement*, it makes the behavior happen *more* often; if the term includes *punishment*, it makes the behavior happen *less* often, whether it is positive or negative (**Table 6.2**). Like reinforcement, punishment can be positive (getting something undesirable) or negative (removing something desirable). For example, a parent who spanks a child for cursing is using positive punishment. But a parent who takes away a child's handheld video game system is using negative punishment. Of course, both punishments are intended to reduce the cursing behavior.

Some consequences that are meant to be punishments can actually be experienced as insignificant (having no effect on the frequency of the behavior) or even reinforcing (increasing its frequency). A parent who "punishes" a teenager for lying by sending him to his room may not see a reduction in lying behavior if the child's room

Fixed-Interval Schedule

Variable-Interval Schedule

Mail arrives on a fixed-interval schedule—you know exactly how long to wait until its next arrival. Email arrives on a variable-interval schedule—you never know when the next one might arrive. That difference between fixed (predictable) and variable (unpredictable) schedules of reinforcement has powerful influences on the frequency of your behavior. Specifically, it explains why you are likely to check your email more often than your mail. Imagine how the frequency of your email-checking behavior would change if your email were only delivered once per day, like mail. (Left) Huntstock/DisabilityImages/Getty Images; (right) m-imagephotography/iStock/Getty Images Plus

TABLE 6.2: Responses to a Behavior that Influence Its Frequency

	REINFORCEMENT	PUNISHMENT
POSITIVE	*Increase* frequency of behavior by getting something good	*Decrease* frequency of behavior by getting something bad
NEGATIVE	*Increase* frequency of behavior by removing something bad	*Decrease* frequency of behavior by removing something good

includes a TV and computer. A kindergarten teacher who "punishes" a child for hitting a classmate by scolding her in the hallway is also giving the girl plenty of one-on-one attention. The girl may actually find this attention to be a reinforcement rather than punishment.

Drawbacks of Punishment. Skinner and other researchers who have studied operant conditioning warn that the use of punishment to change behavior has quite a few drawbacks that the use of reinforcement doesn't. For example, punishment teaches people (and animals) what behavior to avoid, but not what behavior to choose instead (Lerman & Toole, 2011). Punishment also provides a model of aggressiveness (and in some cases violence) that individuals (especially children) might follow when it is their turn to influence others' behavior. In fact, children who were physically disciplined are particularly likely to become physically aggressive (Gershoff, 2002, 2008, 2010; Gershoff & Bitensky, 2007). And punishment can encourage lying and other kinds of deceptiveness—hiding the punished behavior rather than eliminating it ("I didn't do it!") (Rotenberg et al., 2012).

Punishment can create high levels of anxiety and fear, which can interfere with the desired behavior change. For example, a child punished harshly for failing to take out the trash might withdraw altogether rather than complete the chore. In families where harsh physical punishment is common, children are at greater risk for developing anxiety disorders and other kinds of mental disorders as adults, as illustrated in **Figure 6.6** (Afifi et al., 2012). ("Harsh physical punishment" goes way beyond spanking;

WATCHING PSYCHOLOGY

Home Runs and Schedules of Reinforcement

One of the joys of tuning in to a baseball game on TV is the thrill of the home run. Some sluggers deliver the long ball at an amazing rate—a feat measured by the statistic at-bats per home run. This number reflects the average number of plate appearances you'd have to wait to see a particular batter send one over the fence.

Babe Ruth, Mark McGwire, and Barry Bonds are at the top of the all-time list for at-bats per home run. Among more current players, one of the best is Mike Trout. Throughout his career, Trout has earned a ratio of about 17:1. So as a fan, you have a 1 in 17 chance of seeing a homer when Trout steps to the plate.

Now think about how important the schedule of reinforcement is to baseball-viewing habits. You can't predict when Mike Trout will hit his next homer. His home runs reinforce you on a *variable-ratio* schedule. You have a general idea that he hits one about once every 17 at-bats (or one every 3 or 4 games), but you can't know which at-bats specifically will produce a home run. Let's imagine that you are a huge fan of Mike Trout and his home runs. In fact, they're the main reason you watch the game. If he hits a homer in the first inning, will you continue to watch the game? Of course! He might hit another in a later inning. If he hasn't hit one in a week, will you watch? Of course! He could smash a home run (or even 2 or 3 of them) tonight. Because the schedule of reinforcement is variable, you keep watching.

Now imagine if Mike Trout's home runs were delivered on a *fixed-ratio* schedule instead of a variable-ratio schedule. He still hits them at the same rate—1 home run every 17 at-bats—but now they're predictable. Tonight, if he hits one in the first inning, will you continue to watch the game? Of course not! He's going to go homerless in his next 16 at-bats, so he definitely won't hit another one out of the park tonight. You'll only regain interest 17 at-bats from now, which is days away. Imagine the massive changes in TV ratings, attendance at games, and advertisement revenue if home runs in baseball somehow switched from a variable-ratio schedule to a fixed-ratio schedule—not because the number of home runs would decrease, but because their predictability would increase.

Thank goodness, such a switch is entirely unrealistic. The excitement of sports (and many other activities) lies not just in the thrill of the next big moment but in the fact that you never know when that thrill might come. ●

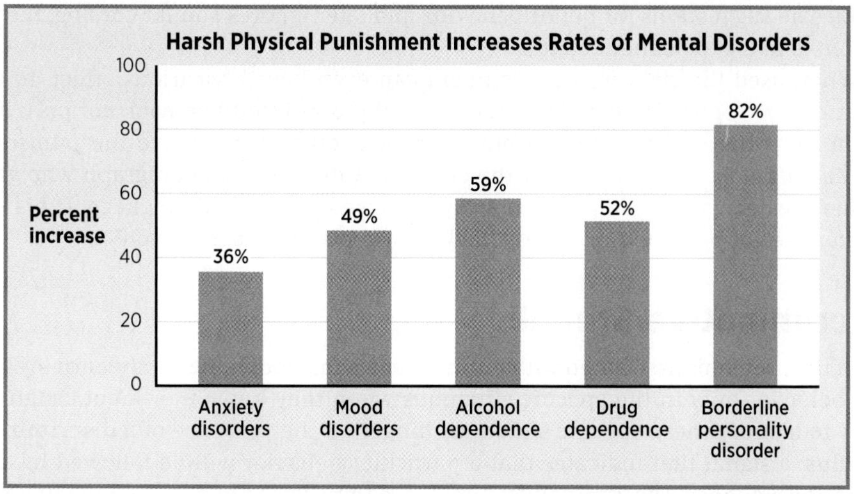

FIGURE 6.6 Harsh Physical Punishment Increases Rates of Mental Disorders Adults who experienced harsh physical punishment as children are at significantly greater risk for many mental disorders than adults who did not. They have an approximately 36% greater chance of anxiety disorders, 49% greater chance of mood disorders, and an 82% greater chance of borderline personality disorder. Data from Afifi et al., 2012

it includes pushing, shoving, grabbing, and slapping. Spanking is not associated with such negative effects on children, especially when parents use it in moderation and only after other punishments, like time-outs, have failed [Ferguson, 2013; Larzelere & Kuhn, 2005; Oas, 2010].)

The message accompanying the punishment must be very clear. Otherwise, there can be confusion about which behavior brought it on (Wacker et al., 2009; Johnston, 1972). For example, consider a teenager who spends an evening on his family's home computer checking social media, watching YouTube videos, listening to music, and shopping for clothes. He then gets grounded by his parents "for what you did on the computer last night." Would he know exactly how to change his behavior? Perhaps it was one particular online activity, or just a couple of them, or the total amount of time he spent doing all of them. His parents' vague explanation does not offer enough information for him to determine specifically what he did wrong.

For all of these reasons, experts in operant conditioning tend to recommend the use of reinforcement of wanted behaviors over punishment of unwanted behaviors. For example, reinforcement has been successfully applied to increase desired behaviors in children with autism (Kern & Kokina, 2008), as well as corporate workers' compliance with computer security procedures (Villamarin-Salomon & Brustoloni, 2010).

Effective Use of Punishment. Punishment can certainly be effective if used wisely. For example, when punishing a behavior, recommend a better behavior, and then strongly reinforce the better behavior when it occurs (Mayhew & Harris, 1979; Murphey et al., 1979; Petscher et al., 2009; Hanley et al., 2005). Make sure the punishment happens immediately after the bad behavior, and explain specifically what the punishment is for (Tanimoto et al., 2004; Walters & Demkow, 1963). This increases the odds that the individual will make the right connection between the behavior and the consequence. If you threatened a punishment, make sure you deliver it as promised, or the individual learns that the threats are meaningless.

Finally, punish the same bad behavior consistently each time it happens. For example, consider the parent who takes away the child's handheld video game system as a punishment for cursing. If the parent does so within seconds of the offensive word; explains, "This is for cursing"; suggests "Say 'darn' instead"; and handles future incidents similarly, the punishment is likely to be effective. If the parent waits hours or days to take away the video game system, offers no explanation why it is happening,

CHAPTER APP 6.3

Punishment

StickK

Preview one of the links and consider the following questions.

WEBSITE:
http://tiny.cc/uch7jy

ANDROID:
http://tiny.cc/sjgyiy

IPHONE:
http://tiny.cc/ljgyiy

VIDEO DEMO:
http://tiny.cc/chapterapps

The app stickK helps individuals change their own behavior, and it relies on punishment rather than reinforcement. Specifically, stickK allows you to set a behavioral goal—exercising 4 times a week, losing 10 pounds, studying 2 hours a day, etc.—and then "bet" your own money that you will succeed. You can specify where the money goes if you fail, including an "anti-charity" (a cause that you personally oppose) of your choosing. This arrangement increases your commitment to complete your chosen behavior so you can avoid the punishment of contributing to a political party, a social movement, or some other organization that disgusts you.

How does it APPly to your daily life?
Consider what you've learned about *punishment*. If you used an app like stickK, would the threat of punishment motivate you to change your behavior? How would the specifics of the punishment (how much money, who receives it, etc.) influence the power of the punishment? stickK also has a searchable list of users, including their behavioral goals and their track record of success and failure. For you, how would the punishment of people knowing you failed compare to the punishment of losing money?

How does it APPly to your understanding of psychology?
Unlike many apps (like ChoreMonster) that utilize reinforcement to change behavior, stickK utilizes *punishment*. Which strategy would you expect to be more effective? Why? What do your answers tell you about the difference between the concepts of reinforcement and punishment? What do your answers tell you more generally about wise use of *operant conditioning?*

provides no suggestions for better behavior, and later ignores similar cursing, the punishment is likely to be ineffective.

When used the right way, punishment can even have a vicarious effect. In other words, effective punishment often decreases the unwanted behavior not only in the person receiving the punishment but in other people who observe the punishment too (Malouff et al., 2009). Consider the child from the previous paragraph who got his handheld video game system taken away because he used bad language. If his sister sees how he got punished, she's less likely to use bad language herself.

This Krispy Kreme *Hot Doughnuts Now* sign is a discriminative stimulus, letting doughnut lovers know that a new batch is fresh out of the oven. © Allen Creative/Steve Allen/Alamy

Discriminative Stimuli

One of the problems associated with punishment is that individuals may learn to change their behavior only in the specific situations when they know they'll get caught. The ability to identify these specific situations hinges on the presence of a **discriminative stimulus**: a signal that indicates that a particular behavior will be followed by a particular consequence. Discriminative stimuli are important not only to punishment but to any kind of learning.

Recognizing a discriminative stimulus allows us to act when the chances of obtaining reinforcement are greatest and the chances of getting punished are least. For example, Jeff is a professional drummer who lives in a small apartment building with a policy against loud noise. The landlord has fined Jeff for drumming in the past, but Jeff has learned to look in the parking lot for the landlord's yellow Ford Mustang. If it is there, he doesn't drum for fear of the fine. If it's gone, he pounds away. That Mustang serves as a discriminative stimulus for Jeff. Its presence signals that drumming brings financial loss, but its absence signals that the same behavior brings enjoyment.

Discriminative stimuli need not be visual, as in Jeff's case. Animals and people can also learn that certain sounds, smells, tastes, and touches signal certain kinds of feedback. For example, you know you'll get a new text message if you check your phone right after you feel it vibrate in your pocket. One fascinating experimental study found that rats could learn to use music as discriminative stimuli. First, they placed rats in a Skinner box and provided food whenever the rats pressed a lever. Then, they added a new rule. Lever pressing brought about food when the Beatles' "Yesterday" was playing but not when Mozart's *Die Zauberflöt* was playing. Sure enough, with enough experience, the rats became music connoisseurs and pressed the lever when they heard the Beatles but not Mozart (Okaichi & Okaichi, 2001).

Shaping

Sometimes, the behavior to be learned isn't as simple as pressing a lever or pecking at a button. In these cases, the behavior isn't learned all at once, but *shaped*, little by little (Skinner, 1938, 1974; Krueger & Dayan, 2009.). **Shaping** is the process of gradually learning a complex behavior through the reinforcement of each of its small steps. Animal trainers are experts in shaping, especially those who work in a circus or zoo where the animals perform. For example, if the trick calls for a dolphin to circle the pool and then jump out of the water through a hoop, the trainer begins by reinforcing the first step in that behavior—say, swimming halfway around the pool. Then the trainer ups the ante, offering reinforcement only when dolphin circles three-quarters of the pool, then the whole pool. Next, to earn the reinforcement the dolphin must peek its beak out of the water after circling the pool, then its fins, then its whole body, then touch the hoop, then go through the hoop. Through the reinforcement of each baby step, the dolphin learns to do the full trick.

Does shaping happen with people as well as animals?

LIFE HACK 6.1

When you use punishment to change someone else's behavior, provide a specific suggestion for a better behavior they can do instead.

(Mayhew & Harris, 1979; Murphey et al., 1979; Petscher et al., 2009; Hanley et al., 2005)

Yes, human behavior is often shaped as well. Consider DeAndre, a youth basketball coach trying to teach his first-grade player, Derrick, to shoot a layup. A layup may look easy, but it's actually a complex behavior, particularly for a young child. Consider the parts: jump off the proper foot, shoot with the correct hand, and bounce the ball off the backboard. If DeAndre's plan is to wait for Derrick to spontaneously shoot a perfect layup and then reinforce him for it, he may be waiting forever. Derrick may never do it on his own. Instead, DeAndre teaches the first part in isolation—jumping off the proper foot as he approaches the basket. Every time Derrick gets it right, he gets a heartfelt "Good job!" from his coach. After some repetition and success with the feet, DeAndre adds the next step, shooting with the correct hand, praising Derrick only when he does both well. Once Derrick masters this, DeAndre shows Derrick the spot to hit on the backboard and praises him only when he puts it all together—good foot, good hand, and good backboard. (The swish of the net doesn't hurt either—it's a bonus reinforcement when Derrick does every part of the layup right!)

To get an animal (or a person) to learn a complex behavior, it is most effective to use shaping, or reinforcing each of the small steps of the behavior. Konstantin Kirillov/iStock/ Getty Images Plus

Operant Conditioning Versions of Some Classical Conditioning Concepts

Many of the terms we introduced earlier in this chapter under the classical conditioning heading apply to operant conditioning too. For example, ***generalization*** and ***discrimination*** happen in operant conditioning. Let's consider Derrick, the first-grade basketball player, one more time. When he receives praise for successfully performing the layup and all of its parts, he's receiving it from a particular coach in a particular gym. Let's imagine that Derrick's next opportunity for a layup takes place in a different gym and with a different coach. Would Derrick expect to receive similar praise in this new setting? To the extent he does, he's generalizing what he learned from DeAndre. To the extent he doesn't, he's discriminating between the original situation and the new one.

Acquisition and *extinction* are also important concepts in operant conditioning. In this context, acquisition refers to the point when the learner makes the connection between a particular behavior and its consequence. Extinction refers to the point when the learner realizes that that connection no longer applies. Remember our discussion of the operant conditioning involved with soda machines? Acquisition occurs when we learn that "If I insert money and press a button, then I get soda." Extinction occurs when we later learn—from a broken soda machine—that "If I insert money and press a button, then I *don't* get a soda."

When extinction occurs in operant conditioning, it follows a predictable pattern—the behavior actually *increases* first and dies out later, as shown in **Figure 6.7**. Psychologists call the first part of this pattern, when the behavior gets more intense or

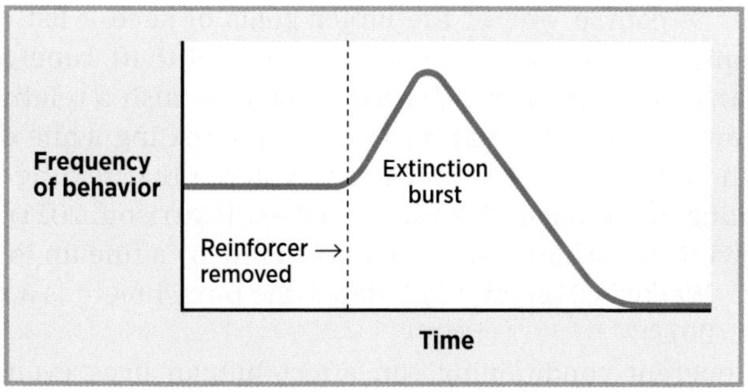

FIGURE 6.7 Extinction Here's how extinction works: When you've learned that a behavior that used to bring you reinforcement no longer brings any reinforcement, you'll eventually decrease that behavior. However, before that decrease starts, your first reaction will be an *increase* in the frequency or intensity of the behavior—that increase is the extinction burst. As long as that increase doesn't result in the return of the reinforcement, extinction will follow.

discriminative stimulus
A signal indicating that a particular behavior will be followed by a particular consequence.

shaping
The process of gradually learning a complex behavior through the reinforcement of each small step that is a part of the complex behavior.

Sometimes you're in control of the reinforcement that another person gets. If so, you have the power to influence his or her future behavior. If you were caring for this child, your response to the tantrum would influence whether the child decided to throw another tantrum the next time a similar situation came up. Joel Sartore/National Geographic/Getty Images

frequent, an *extinction burst*. Picture yourself at that broken soda machine. When you insert the money, press the button, and get nothing, you press the button again and again, try the other buttons, and even shake the machine. Only after all of these efforts fail do your efforts to get a soda extinguish.

Imagine for a minute that intensifying your behavior made the soda come out. You would learn that when you don't get the reinforcer you expect, you should just try harder and you'll get it. This is a powerful lesson to keep in mind when you *are* the soda machine—that is, when you are the source of reinforcement for someone else. For example, let's say you have a regular babysitting gig for a 6-year-old boy. He has learned from experience that if he says, "I'm not tired," after you tuck him in, you let him get out of bed and watch TV. If his parents instruct you to be stricter, what should you expect the boy to do the first time you don't let him watch TV? He certainly won't go down without a fight. He'll ask repeatedly, scream, cry, throw a fit—anything he can think of to get his reinforcer (watching TV). If you stand firm, he'll eventually give up, having learned that there's a new rule in place. If you give in, however, he'll simply learn that he has to redouble his efforts to get what he wants, and that's what he'll do in the future.

Applying Operant Conditioning to Your Life

Anywhere you find a person receiving a consequence for an action, operant conditioning is at work. Many psychologists use operant conditioning to help people reduce unwanted behaviors. (This approach, known as *contingency management*, is discussed in more detail in the therapy chapter.) The logic goes like this: the client is behaving a certain way because of the consequences that follow the behavior, so if the consequences change, then the behavior will change too (Drossel et al., 2008; Kearney & Vecchio, 2002; Villamar et al., 2008).

For example, consider Braden, a 7-year-old boy who refuses to go to school. When his parents try to get him out of bed in the morning, he screams, "I don't want to go!" and pulls the covers over his head. His mother responds to Braden's screams by cuddling with him in his bed for 30 minutes, while his father brings him breakfast in bed. Whether they realize it or not, Braden's parents' behaviors are positive reinforcement for Braden's school refusal behavior. The family's psychologist, Dr. Abrams, suggests that they stop providing such reinforcers and possibly replace them with reasonable punishments (like losing TV time) when Braden refuses to go to school. Dr. Abrams also suggests that Braden's parents shape Braden's behavior by reinforcing small steps in the right direction, like getting out of bed, getting dressed, getting his backpack on, and so on. After a short adjustment period, Braden learns the new consequences and his behavior changes—refusing school far less often and attending school far more often.

Operant conditioning also forms the basis of our legal system. Our laws are really no more than a long list of contingencies: if you commit this crime, you get this punishment. Of course, one of the larger goals of such a list of contingencies is to protect people who might otherwise be victims of theft, rape, murder, or other harmful acts. Many states are grappling with how to punish a relatively new behavior with the potential to cause great harm to others: texting while driving (Ibrahim et al., 2011). Although college students strongly agree that texting while driving is unsafe, an alarming percentage (91%) have done it (Harrison, 2011). In some states, texting while driving is a criminal offense punishable by a fine up to $2500 and up to 12 months in jail (Walker, 2012). In other states, the punishment is a mere $20 infraction (Gershowitz, 2012).

Operant conditioning has been applied in many creative ways. For example, animal trainers have used operant conditioning to teach giant African rats to respond in a particular way to the scent of TNT, an explosive found in landmines. By doing so, they help people locate them so they can be deactivated or removed. Taylor Weidman/Getty Images

Sometimes, operant conditioning can affect human lives even though it's not humans who are being conditioned. For example, dogs can be trained through operant conditioning to help people with a variety of physical disabilities, such as impairments of sight, hearing, or mobility. The dog's training consists of reinforcements and punishments for particular behaviors that correspond with the needs of the person with a disability. For example, trainers reward these dogs for heeling (staying alongside the

leg or wheelchair of their owner) through the use of reinforcements. Similar training underlies bomb-sniffing and drug-sniffing dogs, which are reinforced for barking or otherwise notifying their owners when they smell a particular scent.

Researchers have even trained giant African rats to find landmines! The rats' excellent sense of smell helps them to pick up the scent of TNT, the explosive used in most landmines. The researchers reinforce the rats by offering food when the rats hold their noses over a landmine for a five-second period. The rats are then motivated to scurry across a field and pause over any landmines they find, allowing their owners to deactivate or remove them. This is a vital application of operant conditioning, especially considering that landmines are found in over 70 countries and cause a great deal of injury and death (Poling et al., 2010, 2011).

CHECK YOUR LEARNING:

6.11 What is operant conditioning?

6.12 How does operant conditioning relate to the law of effect?

6.13 Who is B. F. Skinner, and why was his research on operant conditioning important?

6.14 How do psychologists define reinforcement?

6.15 What are the differences between the positive and negative reinforcement?

6.16 What are the differences between these pairs of schedules of reinforcement: continuous versus partial; fixed-ratio versus variable-ratio; and fixed-interval versus variable-interval?

6.17 How do psychologists define punishment?

6.18 What role do discriminative stimuli play in operant conditioning?

6.19 With regard to operant conditioning, what is shaping?

6.20 Which classical conditioning concepts also occur in operant conditioning?

Observational Learning

So far, our discussion of learning in this chapter has focused on the individual's direct experiences—in other words, how you learn from what happens to *you*. But the truth is that you also learn a lot from what you see happening to other people. We call this **observational learning**: learning that occurs as a result of observing others' behavior and consequences rather than your own. For example, if your close friend has a frustrating experience with her new phone—short battery life, dropped calls, and so on—you'll avoid that model when it's time for you to get a new one. If your older brother has a great experience working for a particular company—he's treated fairly, paid well, and so on—you'll apply there as well. Other people's experience counts for you as well.

YOU WILL LEARN:

6.21 what observational learning is.

6.22 how Albert Bandura studied observational learning.

6.23 the relationship between observational learning and brain cells called mirror neurons.

The Bobo Doll Studies

A classic series of studies by Albert Bandura and his colleagues, known as the Bobo doll studies, illustrates the power of observational learning (Bandura et al., 1961, 1963). Here's the scene: a preschool-aged child playing with toys watches an adult (the *model*) interact with a Bobo doll, a large standup inflatable punching bag figure with a clown painted on it. Half of the children saw the model ignore the Bobo doll; the other half saw the model be physically aggressive toward it. The aggressive models kicked the doll, yelled at it, punched it, and hit it with a hammer. All of the children then had their own toys unexpectedly taken away in an attempt to frustrate them and were placed alone in the room with the Bobo doll. How did the children deal with their frustration? It depended on what they had observed in the model. The children who saw the model act

observational learning
A type of learning that occurs as a result of observing others' behavior and consequences rather than our own.

CURRENT CONTROVERSY

Does Violence in the Media Cause Violence in Real Life?

Very few topics in psychology have created as much public controversy as the impact of violence in the media (Kirsh, 2012; Huesmann, 2010; Ferguson & Kilburn, 2010). We are certainly exposed to a lot of media violence:

- Of video games rated T (for Teen), 98% involve intentional violence, 90% reinforce the player for causing injury, and 69% reinforce the player for killing (Haninger & Thompson, 2004).
- On U.S. TV, 61% of shows contain acts of violence, and 54% contain lethal violence. In shows containing violence, 45% of the offenders went unpunished (Federman, 1998).
- Between 1998 and 2006, the amount of violence in PG-13 movies—which children can see without a parent—increased so dramatically that a researcher who conducted the study said that "today's PG-13 movie was yesterday's R movie" (Leone & Barowski, 2011; Leone quoted in "http://www.newswise.com/articles/new-research-reveals-pg-13-movies-are-becoming-more-violent").
- By the age of 12, U.S. kids spend more time in front of screens (TV, movies, computers, video games, and so on) than they do at school (Bushman & Huesmann, 2010).

Hundreds of studies have been conducted to explore the effects of media violence, with widely mixed results (Bushman & Anderson, 2001). Even *meta-analyses*, which statistically combine the results of many studies, come to very different conclusions. Most find that media violence has a definitive link to violent behavior (Anderson et al., 2010; Anderson & Bushman, 2001). Other meta-analyses find just as definitively that no such link exists between media violence and violent behavior (Ferguson & Kilburn, 2009).

One of the significant challenges in determining the impact of media violence is figuring out how to study it (Ferguson & Savage, 2012). Some researchers have used an *experimental* method, in which they manipulate people's exposure to media violence and then observe their reactions, all within a single session. One study, for example, used a procedure very much like Albert Bandura's classic Bobo doll study, but with a more contemporary twist (Shutte et al., 1988). The researchers had children age 5 to 7 play either a violent or nonviolent video game and then gave them free time in a play room. Kids who played violent video games were more likely than kids who played nonviolent video games to hit and kick—not only the large doll in the room but the other kids in the room as well. In another study, participants played either a violent or nonviolent video game and then watched a video of real-life violence. For the participants who played a nonviolent video game, heart rates went up when they watched the real-life violence. However, for the participants who played a violent video game, heart rates actually went down, suggesting that the video game violence had desensitized them (Carnagey et al., 2007).

Other researchers have taken a *longitudinal* approach to studying the impact of media violence. They followed participants over a period of years, rather than testing them in just one sitting, to see how video game violence affected them. One group of researchers studied teens over a three-year period and found that those who played violent video games more often were no more likely to behave aggressively than those who played them less often. Other variables, such as violence in their family home and the extent to which they were depressed, were much better predictors of aggressive behavior (Ferguson et al., 2012). Another longitudinal study tracked participants for a much longer time, from childhood into young adulthood. It found that those who watched more violent TV when they were 6 to 10 years old were more likely to behave violently 15 years later (Huesmann et al., 2003).

With regard to the studies that do find that media violence and violent behavior go together, it is important to remember from Chapter 1 that a correlation does not necessarily mean cause. In other words, if media violence and violent behavior go together, it could be true that media violence causes violent behavior. Or it could be true that other factors—perhaps parenting styles, poverty, or cultural norms—cause people to prefer violent media and to behave violently. It could even be true that a life involving lots of real-world violence influences people to seek out violent TV, movies, and video games. ●

aggressively toward the Bobo doll were more likely to act aggressively themselves than the children who saw the model ignore the Bobo doll. They kicked it, yelled at it, punched it, and hit it with a hammer—just as they had seen the model do moments earlier.

Did the models in those studies get anything—a reinforcement or a punishment—after they acted aggressively toward the Bobo doll?

In these early Bobo doll studies, the model's aggressive behavior did not bring about any consequences. But what if it did? What if the children saw the model receive either reinforcement or punishment after beating up the Bobo doll? Would *vicarious learning* take place? Bandura examined this question and found that the observed consequences do make a difference: children who saw the model get rewarded for aggressive behavior acted more aggressively themselves than did children who saw the model get punished. However, Bandura then offered sticker booklets and juice to the children who saw the model get punished—but only if they

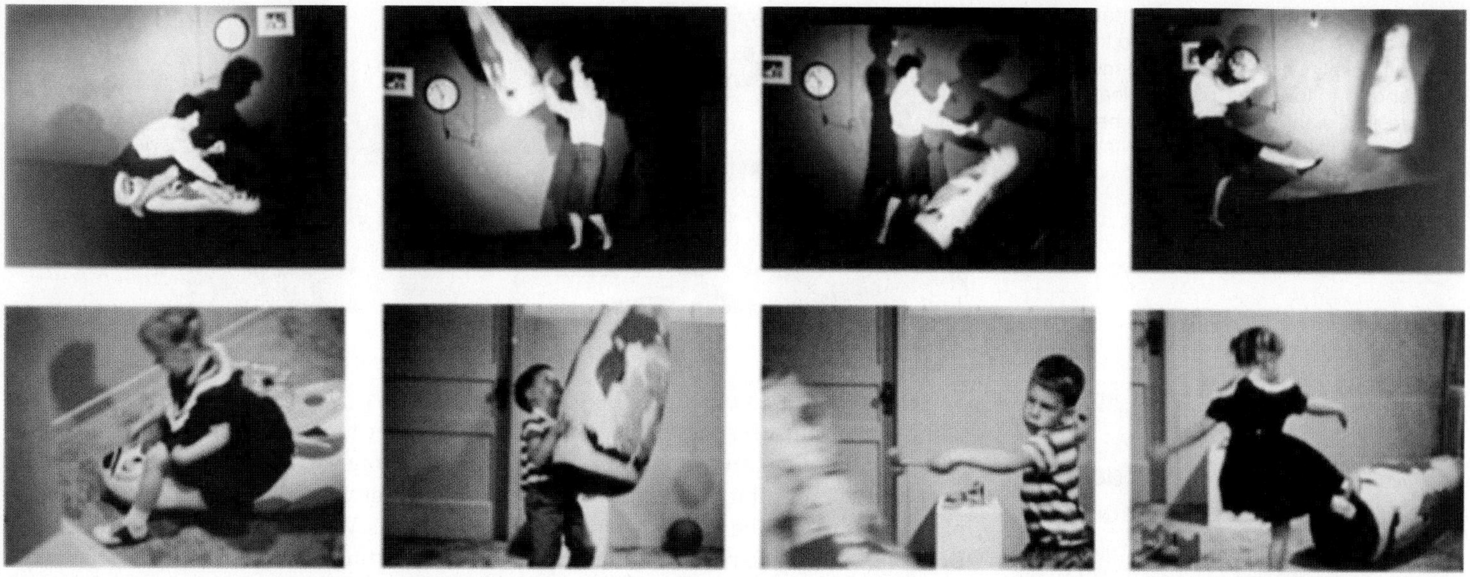

The classic Bobo doll studies by Albert Bandura illustrated that the way kids interact with a doll was strongly influenced by what they learned when they observed adults interacting with the same doll. In each of these pairs of photos, the upper photo shows an adult doing something to the Bobo doll and the lower photo shows a child doing the same thing. Courtesy of Albert Bandura

repeated the aggressive behavior that they saw the model get punished for. They had no problem doing so. This suggests that these children had added the model's aggressive behavior to their own behavioral repertoire even if they had chosen not to display it at first (Bandura, 1965).

The Bobo doll studies demonstrate the often-overlooked power of *modeling*, or imitation of observed behavior. The behavior we watch can strongly influence the behavior we exhibit. And we watch a lot, not only in person but on screens of various kinds: TV, movies, YouTube, video games, and so on. For instance, exposure of children to movies depicting smoking has been shown to significantly predict established smoking patterns when the children reach their late teens (Dalton et al., 2009; Heatherton & Sargent, 2009). In addition, an alarming amount of what we watch in these various media forms is violent, and violent crime statistics are equally alarming. Does the observation of violence in the media contribute to violent behavior? The Current Controversies box examines this issue in detail.

It is important to consider observational learning not only from the perspective of the learner, but from the perspective of the model as well. What behaviors do you model, and who's watching? If you are a parent (or an aunt, uncle, or older sibling, say), this is a particularly relevant question. You may not identify yourself as a model for the children around you, and you may not have invited them to follow your lead, but they are likely to do so anyway. For example, parents who overeat are more likely to have children who overeat; parents who smoke are more likely to have children who will smoke; and parents who use verbal or physical aggression are more likely to have children who do so (Francis et al., 2007; Gilman et al., 2009; Pagani et al., 2004, 2009).

On the other hand, parents who read are more likely to have children who read; parents who do charity work are more likely to have children who do charity work; and parents who eat healthy are more likely to have children who eat healthy (Bus et al., 1995; Bekkers, 2007; Anzman et al., 2010; Skibbe et al., 2008). Simply put, observational learning can lead to behavior that is good or bad, productive or wasteful, prosocial or antisocial. Note that it's not the parents' instruction that we're talking about but the parents' behavior. (It's not parents who tell their kids to read but parents who actually read who are most likely to have kids who read.) Of course, parents' instructions are powerful messages too, but often not as powerful as the example they set.

The power of modeling, or the imitation of observed behavior, is important to keep in mind especially when you are the model. Kids tend to follow their parents' lead with both desirable and undesirable behaviors. (a)Peter Cade/The Image Bank/Getty Images (b) Tetra Images/Getty Images

LIFE HACK 6.2

Remember the Bobo doll studies when kids are around. Kids are learning and making decisions about their own behavior by observing your behavior and the consequences it brings.

(Bandura et al., 1961, 1963; Francis et al., 2007; Gilman et al., 2009; Pagani et al., 2004, 2009)

From the series of studies he conducted, Bandura (1986) identified four particular abilities that must be present in the observer in order to learn from a model: *attention*, *memory*, *imitation*, and *motivation*. Absence of any one of these four abilities in the observer will prohibit observational learning no matter what the model does. For example, consider Danielle, a 3-year-old whose mother knits. Will Danielle learn to knit? First, Danielle will have to pay attention to her mother's knitting behavior. If she's asleep when it happens or is always watching TV instead, she may not pick up on it. Second, Danielle will have to remember what she needed to imitate the behavior—what materials are necessary to knit, where they are, and so on Third, Danielle will require the ability to imitate the behavior. As a three-year old, she may lack the dexterity or the patience that she sees in her mother. Fourth, Danielle will have to be motivated to knit. This is most likely to happen if she sees her mother experience rewards from knitting, either by her mother showing pride in her work or from others rewarding her with money or praise.

Mirror Neurons

In recent years, researchers who focus on the biology of the brain have discovered particular cells that relate directly to observational learning. These brain cells, known as **mirror neurons**, are thought to underlie empathy and imitation and activate when a person performs *or* observes a particular behavior (**Figure 6.8**). The key phrase in that definition is *performs or observes*. In other words, the same neuron in your brain fires whether you perform the behavior yourself or watch someone else do it. If a bowling ball drops on your toe, you cringe. If you see a bowling ball fall on the toe of a stranger a few lanes away, you cringe too. Of course, you don't feel his pain to the same extent that he does, but you feel it a little bit, thanks to your mirror neurons (Iacoboni, 2009; Rizzolatti & Craighero, 2004; Heyes, 2010).

Mirror neurons were actually discovered in monkeys, and our understanding of them in monkey brains is far more advanced than our understanding of them in

FIGURE 6.8 Mirror Neurons in the Brain The discovery of mirror neurons revealed that behavior causes very similar activation of neurons whether you perform the behavior yourself or watch the behavior performed by someone else. Mirror neurons are a relatively recent discovery, but researchers believe that they may play a significant role in observational learning, empathy, and imitation.

human brains (Fabbri-Destro & Rizzolatti, 2008). In these studies, wires are connected directly to the motor cortex in the frontal lobe of monkeys. This allows researchers to identify particular mirror neurons that fire in monkey A when it sees monkey B perform particular behaviors, such as breaking a peanut shell open or grasping a ball. Researchers have identified mirror neurons and located them within the brain, but they still have a lot left to learn. However, researchers are closer to understanding the biological mechanism by which what we observe becomes what we do. Perhaps the old saying, "Monkey see, monkey do," skipped a step. "Monkey see, monkey mirror neurons fire, monkey do" is less catchy but probably more accurate.

mirror neurons
Neurons that are thought to underlie empathy and imitation and that activate when a person performs or observes a particular behavior.

biological preparedness
An animal's evolutionary predisposition to learn that which is most relevant to the survival of that species.

CHECK YOUR LEARNING:

6.21 What is observational learning?

6.22 Who conducted the Bobo doll studies, and what concept did those studies most clearly demonstrate?

6.23 What role do mirror neurons play in observational learning?

Biological Influences on Learning

The impressive findings of Pavlov, Skinner, and others during the early days of learning research led some experts to believe that any animal could be conditioned to learn any behavior (Kimble, 1981). At the time, researchers assumed that animals (and people too) enter the world as blank slates, available to be conditioned (classical or operant conditioning) by any life experience that they might encounter. It turns out to not be entirely true. We actually enter the world with an inborn head start toward certain learning experiences—especially those that increase the chances that we will stay healthy and safe. (Seligman, 1970; Seligman & Hager, 1972; Logue, 1979). The word psychologists use to describe this head start is **biological preparedness**: an animal's evolutionary predisposition to learn what is most relevant to the survival of that species. It's as if we have been primed by our ancestors to have *almost* learned certain connections before we have any experience at all. Then, just a little conditioning is enough to complete the connection.

YOU WILL LEARN:

6.24 what biological preparedness is and how it affects learning.

6.25 how John Garcia and others have studied biological preparedness.

6.26 how learning can be limited by instinctive drift.

Taste Aversion

Consider how easy it is to learn a connection between what you eat and how your stomach feels. Remember the last time you had food poisoning? There's a good chance you developed an immediate strong dislike, or *taste aversion*, to what you ate (say, blueberry yogurt) before you got sick. But there's a poor chance that you developed an immediate strong dislike to what you saw (the tables and chairs, the people you were with) or what you heard (the topic of conversation, the music) as you were eating. You were much more likely to learn that the blueberry yogurt made you sick (rather than the sights and sounds in the room). The reason is that evolution primed—or biologically prepared—you to do so. Your ancestors had a predisposition toward making this taste–sickness connection. Just as they passed on other survival-of-the-fittest characteristics, they passed that predisposition to future generations, including you.

John Garcia and his colleagues conducted classic studies with rats that parallel this taste aversion experience. Their research illustrated that certain learning connections are more likely than others because of biological preparedness (e.g., Garcia et al., 1966,

When doctors know that chemotherapy will cause nausea, they will often give patients a very unusual food—perhaps cucumber popsicles—as a scapegoat food. The intention is to allow patients to develop a taste aversion to something they may never eat again rather than a food they commonly eat. © Larissa Veronesi/Westend61/Agefotostock

1989). They began by giving rats either "sweet water" (water with a sugary substance mixed in) or "bright noisy water" (water that tasted plain but was accompanied by a bright light and a loud sound). Soon after drinking, the rats received one of two consequences: nausea (caused by radiation), or mildly painful electric shock. Rats who drank the sweet water and then experienced nausea avoided the sweet water when it was offered again. However, rats who drank the sweet water and then received an electric shock didn't hesitate to drink the sweet water when it was offered again. It seems they were predisposed to link the water's sweet taste to nausea but not to physical pain.

On the other hand, rats that drank the bright noisy water and then experienced nausea were eager to drink bright noisy water again, but rats who drank the bright noisy water and then experienced electric shock avoided bright noisy water from that point on. They were more likely to connect sights and sounds to physical pain than to nausea (Garcia & Koelling, 1966). Both of these findings are consistent with the evolution of rats (and most other animals). In other words, Garcia's rats seem to have been born, thanks to their genetic inheritance, with a head start toward connecting food with nausea and sights or sounds with physical pain, which would enhance their ability to survive in the wild.

Garcia and other researchers have put their research on taste aversion to practical use (Garcia & Gustavson, 1997; Gustavson et al., 1974, 1976). The real-world problem was that sheep farmers were losing large parts of their flocks to nearby packs of wolves. To stop the wolves from attacking the sheep, the researchers offered the wolves a sheep carcass tainted with a substance that made them very ill. Of course, the wolves devoured the carcass, but they developed a taste aversion to sheep in the process. They very quickly stopped preying on the sheep at all, to the farmers' delight. Similar taste aversion strategies have also been applied to keep raccoons from preying on chickens and to keep blackbirds from plundering sunflower crops (Nicolaus et al., 1982; Gustavson et al., 1982).

For another real-world illustration of the biological preparedness that underlies the learning of food aversions, consider cancer patients going through chemotherapy. Chemotherapy causes nausea, among other side effects. Many patients develop an aversion to food they ate immediately before chemotherapy treatments. They may realize intellectually that the treatment caused the nausea, but the biological predisposition to link food rather than other stimuli with stomach problems is so strong that it's hard *not* to make the connection (Bernstein, 1978; Bernstein & Webster, 1985; Hong et al., 2009). Fortunately, physicians have developed a technique to make sure that chemotherapy patients don't develop aversions to their favorite foods: they give patients a "scapegoat food"—often an unusual kind of ice cream, candy, or fruit juice that the patients have never had before—with the intention that the patient will develop an aversion to that new food instead of an old favorite (Scalera & Bavieri, 2008; Broberg & Bernstein, 1987; Bernstein, 1999).

The most common phobias involve objects that no longer pose threats to our daily lives, like spiders, snakes, and heights. The fact that humans are still predisposed to develop these specific phobias, rather than phobias toward things that actually pose greater contemporary danger, illustrates the biological (and evolutionary) influence on learning. Cathy Keifer/Shutterstock

Are food aversions the only way biology influences learning?

Food aversions are not the only evidence of biological preparedness. Consider phobias (see Chapter 14), especially the things people are most commonly afraid of: spiders, snakes, heights, enclosed spaces, the dark, dogs, and other animals. We remain quick to learn to fear these objects because evolution has biologically predisposed us to do so. For thousands of years they were life-threatening, and we inherited the same readiness to steer clear of them that kept our ancestors alive and well. The fact that these things and situations aren't usually life-threatening anymore or that other things and situations have taken their place in the most recent generations, hasn't had time to register in our collective DNA, so we remain very likely to develop these highly unnecessary phobias. Even though objects like guns, knives, and speeding cars are much greater threats in our modern lives, phobias to these objects are rare (Cook et al., 1986; Gerdes et al., 2009; McNally, 1987; Gamble et al., 2010; Scher et al., 2006; Seligman, 1971).

Instinctive Drift

As a final example of the influence of biology on learning, consider **instinctive drift**: the tendency of animals' behavior to return to innate, genetically programmed patterns. If you offer an animal reinforcement in a way that is inconsistent with its instinct, the reinforcement may work temporarily, but the animal gravitates back toward the behaviors that come naturally. In a classic paper, two former students of Skinner, who had gone on to become animal trainers in a zoo, describe how they were occasionally unable to train animals to perform the desired behavior (Breland & Breland, 1961). The problems always involved the animals doing what instinct rather than reinforcement told them to do. For example, when the trainers tried to teach a raccoon to pick up coins and drop them into a piggy bank, the raccoon couldn't stop rubbing the coins together and dipping them in and out of the piggy bank rather than simply dropping them in—just as the raccoons would with food before eating. Similarly, when they tried to train pigs to do the same drop-the-coin-in-the-bank trick, the pigs too often rooted the coins—that is, dropped them and pushed them around on the ground with their snout—as they would naturally in a search for food.

Anyone who has failed to stick to a weight loss program might appreciate the phenomenon of instinctive drift. You receive reinforcement for healthy eating and exercise behaviors—prizes you promise yourself such as new clothes or kind words from others about your new look. But your instinct is to eat fattening foods—thanks to an evolutionary history in which food was rarely as plentiful as it is today. So you may find yourself drifting back to the same unhealthy eating and exercise habits that led to your excess weight in the first place. The lesson here is that any attempt to use operant conditioning to influence the behavior of an animal or person may have to overcome some strong inborn biological tendencies. Instinctive drift suggests that there may be at least a little bit of truth to the old saying that a tiger—or raccoon or pig or person—doesn't change its stripes.

Instinctive drift is the tendency of an animal's behavior to return to innate, genetically programmed patterns. Researchers who tried to train raccoons to drop coins into a slot ran into difficulties because the raccoons couldn't stop rubbing the coins together and dipping them in and out of the slot, as they naturally do with food in water. © tbkmedia.de/Alamy

instinctive drift
The tendency of animals' behavior to return to innate, genetically programmed patterns.

CHECK YOUR LEARNING:

6.24 What is biological preparedness, and how is it relevant to learning?

6.25 How have John Garcia and others studied biological preparedness?

6.26 What is instinctive drift, and how is it relevant to learning?

Cognitive Influences on Learning

The pioneers of learning research overlooked not only the importance of biology but also the importance of cognition—or *thinking*—on learning. Early researchers seemed to believe that we learned mechanically, automatically, without thought—whether associating stimuli in classical conditioning or associating a behavior with its outcome in operant conditioning. If we reconsider a few of the examples from earlier in this chapter, it's easy to see how some kind of cognition actually plays an important role in learning. Remember Jenny, whose Uncle Joe drives a red sports car and takes her out for ice cream? It's not a stretch to imagine that—between Jenny's sight of a red sports car and her feeling of excitement—there's a quick thought about what a red sports car means to her. Remember Zach, whose father, Alex, reinforced him by taking him to his favorite restaurant when he cut the grass? The contingency Zach learns ("If I cut the grass, then I get to go to my favorite restaurant") is actually a thought, an interpretation that explains the connection between his actions and their consequences. Even when

YOU WILL LEARN:

6.27 that cognition, or thought, influences learning.

6.28 how cognitive maps help us learn.

6.29 that what we learn can remain latent until given the chance to emerge.

6.30 that we sometimes use insight to enhance trial-and-error learning.

6.31 that experiences in which we perceive no control over unpleasant events can lead to learned helplessness.

Developing a cognitive map, or mental diagram, of the physical environment can facilitate learning. Specifically, it can be easier to retrieve a reinforcement if you know the lay of the land that you need to travel to get to it. Rubberball/Mike Kemp/Getty Image

we discuss the way animals learn, we use verbs like *associate* and *expect* and *predict*—all of which suggest that there's some kind of cognitive activity going on in their mind that affects the process.

Cognitive Maps

Edward Tolman conducted some important early studies that provide evidence of cognition during learning (Tolman, 1932, 1948; Tolman & Honzik, 1930). Tolman put rat A in a maze and offered it no reinforcement. Rat A explored the various alleys and corners of the maze. Tolman later replaced rat A with rat B and placed food at the exit. With time, rat B eventually learned to make its way through the maze to reach the food. Finally, Tolman removed rat B, put rat A back in the maze, and placed the food at the exit. That's when Tolman observed the key result of this study: rat A reached the food for the first time *much more quickly* than rat B did. It was as if rat A had been taking mental notes about the maze as it wandered around earlier. Rat A seemed to have developed a **cognitive map**—a mental diagram of the physical environment—while it initially explored when no reinforcement was available.

Rat A's cognitive map clearly improved its ability to navigate the maze to reach the food. Comparing the abilities of rat A and rat B to reach the food for the first time is like comparing two people trying to find a newly opened food court in an airport: an out-of-towner in the terminal for the first time (rat B), and a hometowner who knows the terminal like the back of his hand (rat A). Tolman's conclusion was that rat A—and all other rats, animals, and humans—have the ability to use cognition to speed up the learning process.

Rat A seemed to be mentally stockpiling what it had learned as it explored the maze: where the dead ends were, what sequence of rights and lefts led to a particular spot, and so on Only after the food was offered did rat A have the opportunity to demonstrate what it knew. Rat A's quick solving of the maze once food was offered showed evidence that it was engaged in *latent learning* during its initial time in the maze. **Latent learning** is learning that has taken place but cannot be directly observed.

Here's an example that shows both the cognitive map and latent learning: a teenage girl driving a car for the first time. She has never been behind the wheel before, but for more than 15 years she has been a passenger and learned quite a bit—the layout of the local streets, the functions of various controls around the steering wheel, and what the pedals do. When her nervous mother starts the lesson by saying, "Let's just take a short trip to the park," the girl has at least a rough idea what to do: turn the key in the ignition, put the car in drive, move her right foot from the brake to the gas, make a left and then two rights to arrive at the park. Her mother is there to talk her through the details, but thanks to all of the latent learning she has done over the years, the girl learns to drive in a much shorter period of time than another 15-year-old who has never been in a car before. And the cognitive map is there too: she knows to take a left and two rights to get to the park not because she's getting directions from Google Maps, but because she has her own internal GPS from her years driving the neighborhood streets with her mother.

cognitive map
A mental diagram of the physical environment as it is initially explored when no reinforcement is available.

latent learning
A type of learning that has taken place but cannot be directly observed.

insight
The perception of a solution to a problem that results from cognitive understanding rather than from trial and error.

learned helplessness
The absence of any attempt to help oneself that results from previously learning that such attempts are useless.

Insight

Another type of cognitive activity that can influence learning is **insight**: the perception of a solution to a problem that results from cognitive understanding rather than from trial and error. Simply put, sometimes you just plain figure things out because you use your intelligence to deduce the solution. Picture yourself in a crowded coffee shop receiving an important phone call from your doctor. As your doctor is telling you your medical test results, your phone battery runs out. Your charger is lost, and the doctor's office closes in 10 minutes. What to do?

If cognition had nothing to do with learning, you would have no choice but to operate on your environment in a random, hit-and-miss way until one of your actions brings more power to your phone by chance. You might tap your fingers on the café table, or say hi to another customer, or order a grande latte, hoping that one of those behaviors recharges your phone. Of course, you don't do that because you

have cognition on your side. You *think* about a solution. After a minute, you remember that the coffee shop is in a strip mall. You exit the coffee shop and discover that right next door is an electronics store that sells your charger. You rush in, buy one, plug in your phone, call back your doctor, and finish your call. That experience of suddenly coming up with a solution is called an *aha moment* (as in, "Aha! I figured it out!"). Neuropsychological studies using fMRI (functional magnetic resonance imaging) show that aha moments rely more heavily on activity in certain parts of the brain, including parts of the frontal lobe like the prefrontal cortex and the anterior cingulate, than other kinds of learning (Aziz-Zadeh et al., 2009; Kounios & Beeman, 2009; Topolinski & Reber, 2010).

In the 1920s in Berlin, Wolfgang Kohler studied chimps who seemed to use their own cognitions to solve problems in a similar way. When Kohler placed a banana outside the chimp's cage, just farther away than its arm could reach, it used a stick inside the cage to pull the banana closer. When Kohler placed another banana a bit farther out, beyond the reach of the first stick, the chimp fastened two sticks together to form a double-length stick, which enabled it to retrieve the banana. When Kohler hung a banana from the ceiling, the chimp stacked crates to form a tower that it could climb to grab the banana. In each of these cases, the chimp's action was preceded by a period of frustration that simpler efforts did not bring about the reward, as well as a period of inactivity in which the chimp appeared to be thinking about the situation. There were also failed attempts at each of the strategies that eventually proved successful (Kohler, 1924; Gould & Gould, 1994). The point is that Kohler's chimps didn't perform random acts and wait for the bananas to land in their laps. The chimps used cognition, or thought, to supplement what they learned from the consequences of their actions.

Latent learning is learning that has taken place but has not yet been demonstrated. For example, a teenager who takes the wheel for the first time may show that she has picked up some knowledge of driving but hasn't had a chance to show it yet.
Shannon Fagan/The Image Bank/Getty Images

Learned Helplessness

A lot of animal research illustrates the influence of cognition on learning, but the studies by Martin Seligman and his colleagues are the most relevant to human suffering and wellness (Overmier & Seligman, 1967; Seligman & Maier, 1967; Seligman, 1975; Overmier & LoLordo, 1998). Seligman used dogs in his studies, and he placed them in an apparatus known as a shuttle box, as shown in **Figure 6.9**. The shuttle boxes were divided into two halves by a short wall (no taller than the dogs' legs) that the dogs could easily jump over. One side of the shuttle box (the shock side) contained an electrified floor through which Seligman could shock the dogs' feet; the other side (the safe side) did not.

In one of their best-known studies (Maier et al., 1969), Seligman and his colleagues divided the dogs into three groups, and each group went through two phases of the study. In the first phase, group 1 received controllable shock: they were placed on the shock side but were free to jump to the safe side, which they quickly learned to do upon the first sign of the shock. Group 2 received uncontrollable shock: they were restrained on the shock side in harnesses that prevented them from crossing to the safe side when shock was delivered. Group 3 received no shock at all.

In the second phase, every dog received controllable shock. As you might expect, group 1 quickly learned to jump to the safe side during the second phase, just as they had in the first. Group 3 also learned to jump to the safe side. But group 2—the dogs who were powerless to do anything to avoid the shock in the first phase—never learned to avoid the shock in the second phase at all. They just stayed there and took it. Sometimes they whimpered and cried, but they never made any effort to alleviate their pain, despite the fact that all they needed to do was make a quick jump over a short nearby wall.

Seligman (1975) later explained that even after he tried to lure the dogs to the safe side—by removing the short wall altogether, by calling to the dogs from the safe side, even by putting salami on the safe side—the dogs did nothing to help themselves. Seligman called the dogs' reaction to this situation **learned helplessness**: the absence of any attempt to help oneself that results from previously learning that such attempts are useless. Seligman explained that the dogs had apparently learned, through their

When you solve a problem by figuring it out rather than by random trial and error, that's insight. Animals show some degree of insight, too. For example, this chimp, which recognized that it could reach the food by stacking the boxes into a kind of ladder (Kohler, 1924; Gould & Gould, 1994).
American Philosophical Society/Science Photo Library/Science Source

FIGURE 6.9 Learned Helplessness In a series of classic studies, dogs that were free to avoid shock when they saw a warning light learned to do so. But dogs that were prevented from avoiding shock stopped trying, even when they were no longer being prevented. That failure to try to avoid the shock was labeled *learned helplessness*. Some psychologists believe that learned helplessness explains depression in people who have learned that they can't control the negative experiences in their lives (Maier et al., 1969; Seligman, 1975).

experience in the first phase that their pain was entirely outside of their control. This lesson was so strong that even when the situation changed and they could, in fact, exert some control, they didn't realize or accept this fact. In other words, they continued to *believe* they were helpless, and that cognition had a powerful influence on their learning (or lack thereof).

What do these learned helplessness studies with dogs have to do with people?

Seligman and others applied the findings of their learned helplessness studies to human depression. They suggested that people who are depressed resemble the dogs from group 2: they have experienced pain (often emotional rather than physical) that they perceived as uncontrollable. Through that process, they learn they are helpless. As a result, they stop trying to help themselves—despite encouragement from friends and family and even new life circumstances—and resign themselves to endless days of sadness and apathy. As we will discuss in Chapter 14, many factors can contribute to depression, but learned helplessness may be one of those factors for many people.

A final note: later in his career, Seligman shifted his focus to the flip side of learned helplessness, *learned optimism*, in which people can, via their own cognitions, emphasize positive interpretations of life experiences to enhance happiness and ward off depression (Seligman, 1991, 2011). As an example, consider the ways a factory worker can interpret a job layoff. She can blame herself and consider it a permanent setback, which could lead to depression based on the belief that there is nothing she can do to help herself. Or she can blame external circumstances (the company, the economy) rather than herself and consider the layoff a temporary problem. This explanation suggests that things may work out and that she can play an active role in making that happen. Seligman (1991) argues that even if the "helpless" interpretation is the first one that occurs to her, she can train herself to reject it and replace it with the more optimistic way of thinking. This will not only increase the odds that she works to solve her own problem but that she's happy while doing so.

CHECK YOUR LEARNING:

6.27 How much does cognition influence learning?

6.28 What are cognitive maps, and how are they relevant to learning?

6.29 What is latent learning?

6.30 What is insight, and how is it relevant to both cognition and trial-and-error learning?

6.31 What is learned helplessness, and what experiences are likely to produce it?

CHAPTER SUMMARY

What Is Learning?

6.1 Psychologists define learning as the process by which life experience causes change in the behavior or thinking of an organism.

6.2 Learning is the essence of the nurture side of the nature-nurture debate that surrounds all of human behavior. (Maturation is the nature side of the debate.)

6.3 Learning isn't unique to humans. It occurs across all species.

Classical Conditioning

6.4 Ivan Pavlov was a Russian medical researcher studying the digestive system of dogs. Pavlov's accidental discovery of the learning process led to studies that shaped the field of psychology.

6.5 Classical conditioning is a form of learning in which animals or people make a connection between two stimuli that have occurred together, such that one predicts the other. Classical conditioning occurs in everyday life. People have all sorts of conditioned responses to things they see and hear.

6.6 The components of classical conditioning include a neutral stimulus, unconditioned stimulus, unconditioned response, conditioned stimulus, and conditioned response.

6.7 Generalization is the process by which stimuli that are similar to the conditioned stimulus cause the same conditioned response. Discrimination is the process by which stimuli that are different from the conditioned stimulus fail to cause the same conditioned response.

6.8 Acquisition happens when the neutral stimulus becomes a conditioned stimulus by its link to the conditioned response. Extinction happens when the conditioned stimulus no longer causes the conditioned response because it is no longer linked to the unconditioned stimulus.

6.9 Higher-order conditioning is a learning process in which a conditioned stimulus from a previous learning process serves as an unconditioned stimulus, producing a new conditioned stimulus that causes the same conditioned response.

6.10 Vicarious conditioning is conditioning that takes place by way of observation of others' life experiences rather than one's own.

Operant Conditioning

6.11 Operant conditioning is a form of learning in which the consequences of a voluntary behavior affect the likelihood that the behavior will recur.

6.12 The law of effect suggests that the likelihood of repeating a behavior depends on the effects of that behavior.

6.13 B. F. Skinner was a U.S. psychologist who conducted extensive operant conditioning studies on animal behavior. Skinner's research on operant conditioning made him a household name, in part because he applied his findings about animal behavior to human behavior.

6.14 Reinforcement is any consequence of a behavior that makes that behavior more likely to recur.

6.15 Positive reinforcement involves getting something desirable, while negative reinforcement involves removing something undesirable.

6.16 A reinforcement schedule is a pattern by which reinforcement occurs in response to a particular behavior. Continuous reinforcement is a pattern by which a behavior is reinforced every time it occurs, while partial reinforcement is a pattern by which a behavior is reinforced only some of the times it occurs. A fixed-ratio schedule is a reinforcement schedule in which a behavior is reinforced after a consistent, predictable number of occurrences. By contrast, a variable-ratio schedule is a reinforcement schedule in which a behavior is reinforced after an inconsistent, unpredictable number of occurrences. A fixed-interval schedule is a reinforcement schedule in which a behavior can be reinforced after a time interval that is consistent and predictable. By contrast, a variable-interval schedule is a reinforcement schedule in which a behavior can be reinforced after a time interval that is inconsistent and unpredictable.

6.17 Punishment is any consequence of a behavior that makes that behavior less likely to recur.

6.18 Recognizing a discriminative stimulus allows a person to act when the chances of obtaining reinforcement are greatest and the chances of getting punished are least.

6.19 Shaping is the process of gradually learning a complex behavior through the reinforcement of each of its small steps.

6.20 Generalization, discrimination, acquisition, and extinction are all concepts that occur in both classical conditioning and operant conditioning.

Observational Learning

6.21 Observational learning is learning that occurs as a result of observing others' behavior and consequences rather than our own.

6.22 Albert Bandura's Bobo doll studies demonstrated the power of modeling, imitation of observed behavior.

6.23 Mirror neurons are thought to underlie empathy and imitation and to activate when a person performs or observes a particular behavior.

Biological Influences on Learning

6.24 Biological preparedness is an animal's evolutionary predisposition to learn what is most relevant to the survival of that species.

6.25 John Garcia's research on taste aversion provided solid evidence for biological preparedness.

6.26 Instinctive drift is the tendency of animals' behavior to return to genetically programmed patterns, making it difficult to teach animals behavior that is inconsistent with instinct.

Cognitive Influences on Learning

6.27 Cognition, or thought, influences learning more than the original learning researchers believed it did.

6.28 A cognitive map is a mental diagram of a physical environment that can speed up the learning process.

6.29 Latent learning is learning that has taken place but cannot be directly observed until it is given a chance to be performed.

6.30 Insight is the perception of a solution to a problem that results from cognitive understanding and that allows one to skip some of the steps of trial-and-error learning.

6.31 Learned helplessness is the absence of any attempt to help oneself, resulting from previously learning that the situation is outside of one's control.

KEY TERMS

learning, p. 179
classical conditioning, p. 179
neutral stimulus, p. 179
unconditioned stimulus, p. 179
unconditioned response, p. 181
conditioned stimulus, p. 181
conditioned response, p. 181
generalization, p. 182
discrimination, p. 182
acquisition, p. 185
extinction, p. 185
spontaneous recovery, p. 185
higher-order conditioning, p. 185
vicarious conditioning, p. 186
operant conditioning, p. 186
law of effect, p. 189
Skinner box, p. 189
reinforcement, p. 189
positive reinforcement, p. 189
negative reinforcement, p. 189
primary reinforcer, p. 191
secondary reinforcer, p. 191
reinforcement schedule, p. 191
continuous reinforcement, p. 191
partial reinforcement, p. 191
fixed-ratio schedule, p. 192
variable-ratio schedule, p. 192
fixed-interval schedule, p. 192
variable-interval schedule, p. 192
punishment, p. 192
discriminative stimulus, p. 197
shaping, p. 197
observational learning, p. 199
mirror neurons, p. 203
biological preparedness, p. 203
instinctive drift, p. 205
cognitive map, p. 206
latent learning, p. 206
insight, p. 206
learned helplessness, p. 206

SELF-ASSESSMENT

1. When a person salivates to the sight of a logo on a pizza box, that salivation is a(n) _____ _____.
   a. unconditioned response
   b. conditioned response
   c. unconditioned stimulus
   d. conditioned stimulus

2. A child has learned through experience that a certain bell sound means that the ice cream truck is nearby, and she responds to that bell with excitement. When that child reacts with similar excitement to a similar-sounding bell, she's exemplifying _____.
   a. extinction
   b. generalization
   c. biological preparedness
   d. shaping

3. Conditioning that takes places through observation of others' life experiences rather than one's own is known as _____ _____.
   a. vicarious conditioning
   b. higher-order conditioning
   c. operant conditioning
   d. classical conditioning

4. _____ is any consequence of a behavior that makes that behavior more likely to recur.
   a. Reinforcement
   b. Acquisition
   c. Generalization
   d. Punishment

5. A ______ ______ schedule is a reinforcement schedule in which a behavior is reinforced after an unpredictable number of occurrences—like winning money by buying lottery tickets.
   a. fixed-ratio
   b. variable-ratio
   c. fixed-interval
   d. variable-interval

6. A ______ ______ is a signal indicating that a particular behavior will be followed by a particular consequence.

7. When an animal trainer teaches a dolphin to jump out of the water and through a hoop by reinforcing each of the smaller behaviors required to do that action, the learning process is known as ______.

8. ______ ______ is an animal's evolutionary predisposition to learn what is most relevant to the survival of that species.

9. If a teenager—who has never driven a car before but has watched others driving many times—can drive well on her first attempt, then she is probably exhibiting ______ ______.
   a. biological preparedness
   b. classical conditioning
   c. latent learning
   d. spontaneous recovery

10. ______ ______ is the absence of any attempt to help oneself after learning through experience that the situation is outside of one's control.

Research shows quizzing is a highly effective learning tool. Continue quizzing yourself using LearningCurve, the system that adapts to *your* learning.

LaunchPad macmillan learning — LearningCurve macmillan learning

GO TO: launchpadworks.com

Self-Assessment Answers

1. b 2. b 3. a 4. a 5. b 6. discriminative stimulus 7. shaping
8. Biological preparedness 9. c 10. Learned helplessness

WHAT'S YOUR TAKE?

1. Before Pavlov intentionally conditioned his dogs to salivate to previously neutral stimuli (like the bell), they were classically conditioned by accident. The dogs picked up on sights and sounds that regularly occurred before they were given food in the lab, and soon those sights and sounds triggered anticipatory mouth-watering. Our own pets get classically conditioned by accident too. My childhood dog came running and jumped with excitement whenever she heard the crinkle of her bag of treats. We never intended for her to make this association, but over time, she learned that the sound of that particular bag meant that a treat would soon follow.

How have your own pets demonstrated this kind of accidental classical conditioning? What kinds of previously neutral stimuli—the sight of the leash, the sound of the electric can opener, and so on—have they identified as precursors to food? What kinds of conditioned reactions do your pets show to those stimuli now? Are there other unconditioned stimuli besides food that your dog has been conditioned to anticipate? If so, what are they, and what conditioned responses have they developed?

2. Texting while driving is dangerous. In fact, some studies have found that texting drivers were more likely to miss the brake lights of the car in front of them, swerve out of their lane, and take their eyes off the road than were drivers talking on phones or drivers who were drunk (Crisler et al., 2008; Libby & Chaparro, 2009; Hosking et al., 2009; Drews et al., 2009). Any one of these mistakes could result in injury or death to the driver or someone else.

Based on the risk of texting while driving and what you know about operant conditioning, how would you change this behavior? What punishment would you enforce? What form would it take—a fine, jail time, a suspended driver's license, or something else? How severe should the punishments be? Would reinforcement (for *not* texting) be part of your contingency system?

SHOW ME MORE

6.1 Classical Conditioning

launchpadworks.com LaunchPad macmillan learning

This video offers some good examples and explanations of classical conditioning.

© Worth Publishers

7 Cognition: Thinking, Language, and Intelligence

michaeljung/Getty Images

Imagine that you accidentally leave your jacket in a classroom. Even worse, your wallet is in the pocket. Later that night, when you realize this, you hurry back to retrieve your jacket. The building is open, but the classroom door is locked. You peek through the narrow window in the classroom door, and see your jacket right where you left it—so close, but yet so far.

You have a problem. Thankfully, you also have *cognitive* abilities—*thinking*, *intelligence*, and *language*—to solve that problem. To start, you need to generate possible solutions. Is there another entrance to the classroom? Is there someone working in the building who might let you in the classroom? You have to be creative enough to think of many possible solutions and intelligent enough to narrow the list to the best ones.

Throughout your problem-solving and decision-making process, you need to communicate clearly with anyone else involved. If you text a friend for help, you need to explain the situation thoroughly and accurately enough so they understand it. If you find someone working in the building, you need to describe the problem persuasively enough to convince them to unlock the classroom door.

You think about your problem for a few minutes and settle on a strategy: calling campus police. As clearly as you can, you explain your dilemma (and your location) to the dispatcher, who agrees to send an officer to meet you by the classroom door. When the officer arrives, you explain again, and even list some of the contents of the wallet, including the student ID with a photo that the officer can compare to your face. The officer understands, unlocks the door, checks your ID, and hands you the jacket and wallet—problem solved.

The successful resolution of this dilemma illustrates the value of *cognition*—your ability to use information productively. Exactly how we use information, especially our capacities to think and use language in intelligent ways, is the focus of many psychology researchers. It will be our focus in this chapter as well.

CHAPTER OUTLINE

Cognition is what your brain does with information, including understanding it, organizing it, analyzing it, and communicating it. Simply put, cognition is all about *knowledge* and what you do with it. In fact, the root of the word—*cogn-*—means *to know* in Latin. You're already familiar with other words that come from the same root, like re*cogn*ize (to reknow something), *cogn*izant (being knowledgeable of something), and in*cogn*ito (unknowable because of a disguise).

Cognition is something we do so continuously and so automatically that it's easy to take it for granted. Perhaps the best way to appreciate cognition is to notice what happens when people experience cognitive problems. Sometimes, these cognitive problems are fleeting. For example, you may have noticed that a friend or family member wasn't "thinking straight" in the hours after an operation, before the anesthesia had worn off. Other times, cognitive problems can last longer, as when an older person develops Alzheimer's disease or another form of dementia. During interactions with people experiencing cognitive problems, the striking thing is their limited ability to use knowledge. They just don't seem to understand it, communicate it, or reason intelligently about it at an expected level.

Psychologists who study cognition focus on three main areas: thinking, language, and intelligence. (Actually, psychologists who study cognition focus on memory too, but that topic had its own chapter earlier in this book.) We'll consider all three topics in this chapter, beginning with thinking.

Thinking

YOU WILL LEARN:

7.1 how psychologists define and research cognition.

7.2 how psychologists define the term *concept*.

7.3 about the three main types of concepts.

7.4 the three levels psychologists use to organize concepts.

7.5 the difference between problem solving and decision making.

7.6 the difference between an algorithm and a heuristic.

7.7 the different ways people stray from reason when solving problems.

7.8 about the different types of heuristics.

7.9 about the two types of thinking involved in dual-process theory.

7.10 whether people are good at affective forecasting.

7.11 how psychologists define creativity.

7.12 the difference between divergent thinking and convergent thinking.

7.13 about functional fixedness.

7.14 about other factors that are linked to creativity.

Any discussion of thinking has to start with an explanation of the term **concept**: a mental representation of a category of similar things, actions, or people. Concepts are the most basic building blocks of thinking, the pieces that you use to string together thoughts. For example, to have even the simple thought such as, "My cousin borrowed my hoodie," first you'd need to understand the concept of *cousin*, the concept of *borrow*, and the concept of *hoodie*. Concepts like these have been in your repertoire so long that you probably can't remember not having them, but there are probably other concepts that you can remember picking up more recently. Did you always understand the concept of *live-tweeting*? *Binge-watching*? *E-cigarette*? *Catfish* (the fake online profile, not the actual fish)?

Concepts facilitate thinking in important ways. First, they allow us to apply what we already know to something new (Markman & Rein, 2013). Let's go back to the concept of "hoodie." Once you have that concept, you have a pretty good idea about what it means for an item to belong to it: that item is clothing, it covers the top half of your body, it has a hood, and so on. So when you get a new hoodie as a gift, you don't find yourself bewildered or perplexed. You recognize it as a hoodie, and you know exactly what it's for and what to do with it. (Imagine how differently you might react if you opened the gift and found a completely unfamiliar piece of clothing, perhaps from another part of the world, for which you had no concept.) Second, concepts facilitate communication (Rips et al., 2012). Imagine a phone call in which you tell your friend about the gift you received. Without the concept of "hoodie," you'd struggle through a lengthy description that might or might not be effective: "It's a piece of clothing that covers my chest and arms, and it's got this part that covers my head..." With both of you grasping the concept of "hoodie," that single word precisely conveys to your friend the gift you received.

Concepts: What Holds Them Together?

Each concept must have some kind of "glue" that holds it together, some similarity among the things that concept contains. What exactly is that glue? Psychologists have studied this question extensively. The answer that has received the most attention has been *features*, characteristics that the items have in common. However, other answers include the *goals* shared by the items and the *relationships* between the items

(Markman & Rein, 2013). Let's consider all three of these similarities within concepts (**Table 7.1**).

Feature-Based Concepts. Originally, psychologists believed that concepts were defined by a list of characteristic features. This was an all-or-nothing way of understanding concept membership: if an item had all the features, it was in, but if it was missing any of those features, it was out (Smith & Medin, 1981). Logically, this understanding of concepts made a lot of sense, but it didn't work well practically. As an example, let's consider the concept of a "ball." If you were going to make a list of the required features for something to belong to this concept, it might include these: it's round, it bounces, and it's used in sports. That would certainly capture most balls: soccer balls, basketballs, baseballs, volleyballs, tennis balls, kickballs. But it doesn't capture all of them. Footballs aren't round. Neither are rugby balls. Bowling balls and medicine balls don't bounce. And plenty of balls, such as wrecking balls, cotton balls, meatballs, and matzah balls, aren't used in sports.

So psychologists started looking for other ways to understand how people form concepts. In the 1970s, a researcher named Eleanor Rosch proposed that the object only needs the *most representative* features rather than *all* of the features to become a member of a concept (Rosch, 1975; Rosch & Mervis, 1975; Rosch et al., 1976; Hampton, 1995). Rosch argued that our minds form a **prototype**: the most typical or best example within a concept. The prototypes we form are averages, or abstract blends, of the best members of the category. This means that a prototype is something we imagine, rather than some specific thing we have actually encountered (Reed, 1972; Posner & Keele, 1970). So we don't choose any specific ball—a basketball, a tennis ball, a soccer ball, and so on—to serve as the prototype of a *ball*. Instead, we morph together these good examples of balls into a new mental creation that falls right in the middle of all of them. Then we compare any new ball-like items to that prototype to see if it belongs in the concept of a *ball*.

Other researchers disagreed with Rosch's prototype theory, especially the "imagined" or "morphed together" quality of prototypes (Medin & Schaffer, 1978; Brooks, 1978; Smith & Minda, 1998, 2000; Nosofsky et al., 1989; Nosofsky & Johansen, 2000; Murphy, 2002; Kruschke, 2005; Murphy & Hoffman, 2012). These other researchers argued that you choose a real "textbook example" of the definition of the concept—the best example you have actually seen, heard, or touched, rather than morphing several of them together into an imaginary prototype. They call this "best example" an *exemplar* to distinguish it from a prototype. This exemplar theory states that one type of real ball you have encountered—let's say a soccer ball—serves as the exemplar in your mind for the concept of *ball*. Whether you include a new ball-like object in that concept—let's say a golf ball or a racquetball—depends on how closely that new object resembles a soccer ball.

Concept formation has proven to be a complex and challenging area of research for psychologists. As a result, the debate about how we form concepts is far from over. A couple of conclusions are certain, however. One is that concepts often have fuzzy boundaries, with some items definitely in, some items definitely out, and some items in between (**Figure 7.1**). This means that some items are simply better or more typical members of concepts than others (Hampton, 1995). For example, consider the concept of *soup*. Tomato

TABLE 7.1: Types of Concepts

TYPE OF CONCEPT	WHAT HOLDS THE CONCEPT TOGETHER	FOR EXAMPLE...
Feature-based	Similar features or characteristics	Beagles, bulldogs, Great Danes, Chihuahuas, and huskies are all *dogs*.
Goal-based	The same goal or purpose	Cash, checks, credit cards, debit cards, gift cards, and Paypal are all *methods of payment*.
Relationship-based	The same relationship or connection between people or things	Hungry Hungry Hippos, checkers, dodge ball, Clue, and volleyball are all *games*.

Information from Markman & Rein, 2013.

A prototype is the most typical or best example within a concept. You form a prototype by imagining an average member of the category, rather than choosing an actual example. So, your prototype for a "ball" is not necessarily a basketball, football, or any other specific kind of ball. Instead, it is a blend that falls somewhere between all of them. Kim Reinick/Shutterstock

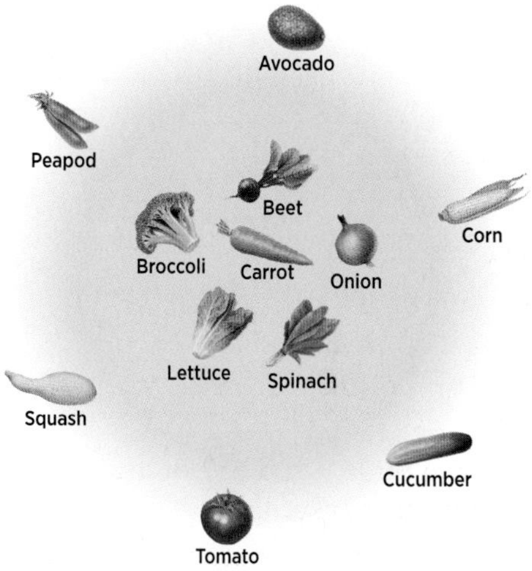

FIGURE 7.1 Fuzzy Boundaries: Is It a Vegetable? Some foods are just more vegetable-ish than others. In other words, the vegetable concept has fuzzy boundaries, with some items definitely in and others possibly in and possibly out. The foods near the edge here are sometimes considered fruits rather than vegetables.

cognition
What the brain does with information, including understanding it, organizing it, analyzing it, and communicating it.

concept
A mental representation of a category of similar things, actions, or people.

prototype
The most typical or best example within a concept.

soup definitely fits within that concept. Hamburgers definitely don't. But what about chili? Maybe it belongs to the concept of *soup*, but if it does, it's not the most typical member.

Goal-Based Concepts. It is possible that the most distinctive thing shared by members of a concept is not a feature but the goal that those members point toward. Objects may be tied together not by how they look or what they individually do but by what larger purpose they collectively serve (Barsalou, 1983, 1985, 2003, 2012; Chrysikou, 2006). As an example, two researchers discuss the concept of exercise equipment (Markman & Rein, 2013). The items within this category span a wide range of examples, and can even possess contrasting characteristics. Some exercise equipment, like treadmills and elliptical machines, are big things that you stand on and pay a lot of money for. Other exercise equipment, like dumbbells and jump ropes, are small things that you hold in your hand and pay little money for. Things like stationary bikes and rowing machines you sit on; things like activity trackers (FitBit, etc.) and running shoes you wear. But all of these items belong to the concept of exercise equipment because they all share the goal of promoting exercise and physical fitness.

Relationship-Based Concepts. Sometimes, a concept hangs together because the items in it all describe similar kinds of relationships between things or people (Markman, 1999; Gentner & Kurtz, 2005; Goldwater et al., 2011; Kurtz et al., 2013). For example, the concept of "teaching" evokes a certain type of relationship: one person who is more knowledgeable in a particular subject area sharing that knowledge with another person who is less knowledgeable. The concept includes a wide assortment of examples—a kindergarten teacher, a high school hockey coach, an ACT tutor, a law school professor—but in every case, the concept is based on the same kind of relationship.

Expertise, Culture, and Concepts

Psychologists often organize concepts into three levels: *superordinate*, *basic*, and *subordinate* (Neisser, 1987; Johnson, 2013). As **Figure 7.2** shows, the basic idea here is that the "middle-sized" concepts we use most often in our thinking (*basic*) fall within much broader concepts (*superordinate*) and also contain many more specific concepts (*subordinate*). As an example, consider the basic concept of a "bicycle." *Bicycle* falls within the superordinate concept of "vehicle," along with cars, trucks, motorcycles, boats, and spaceships. Bicycle also contains many subordinate concepts, such as "mountain bikes," "road bikes," "racing bikes," "BMX bikes," and "cruiser bikes."

But what you consider basic—in other words, the conceptual level at which you typically think—depends on your level of expertise and your cultural background. If you're an expert on a topic, you tend to zoom in on concepts in such a way that what's subordinate to most people is basic to you (Medin et al., 2002; Johnson & Mervis, 1997; Tanaka & Taylor, 1991). Let's consider bicycles again, but from the perspective of Tim, who owns a bike shop specializing in mountain bikes. For Tim, who spends hours every day reading about, discussing, repairing, and riding mountain bikes, "mountain bike" isn't a subordinate concept, it is a basic concept. Tim is so immersed in mountain bikes, rather than bikes in general, that mountain bikes represent his typical level of thinking. (He may not have even ridden another type of bike for years.) If so, Tim's subordinate concepts would be specific subtypes of mountain bikes, like cross-country, downhill, trail, or dirt-jumping styles.

DIVERSITY MATTERS

Culture works much the same way as expertise, providing knowledge that focuses your thinking to an extent that people outside of the culture simply can't do. For example, consider someone who has no Indian heritage and who only rarely eats Indian food. For this person, "Indian food" may be a subordinate concept, under the basic concept "Asian food" (along with "Chinese food" and "Japanese food"). But for someone of Indian heritage, who eats or cooks Indian food every day, "Indian food" could be basic, or even superordinate. It could contain the more specific concepts "North Indian cuisine" and "South Indian cuisine" (the latter of which is typically more spicy), and either of those concepts could include concepts based on more specific regions or states within India, such as "Hyderabadi cuisine,"

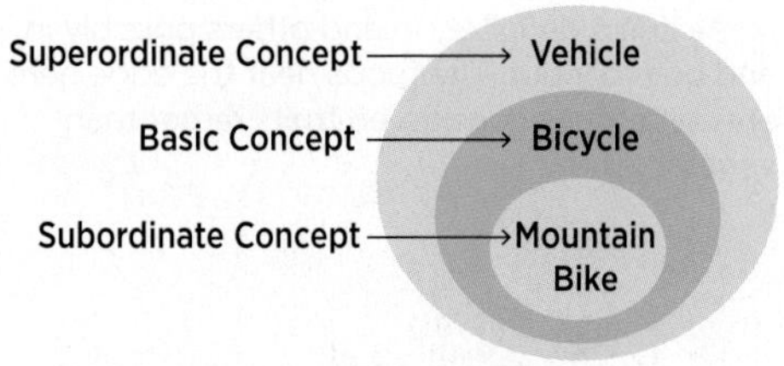

FIGURE 7.2 Superordinate, Basic, and Subordinate Concepts. We tend to focus our thinking on basic concepts (bicycle) rather than zooming out to superordinate concepts (vehicle) or zooming in to subordinate concepts (mountain bike). But for a person with specific expertise in mountain bikes, mountain bike could become the basic concept, with specific kinds of mountain bikes occupying the subordinate level.

"Bihari cuisine," "Maharashtrian cuisine," and "Goa cuisine." The point here is that culture, because of the expertise it brings, can powerfully influence whether a particular concept is superordinate, basic, or subordinate for you.

Culture can influence concept formation in other ways as well. Researchers have found that people of Asian descent and people of European descent often show differences in how they organize items into concepts. Generally, when organizing objects into concepts, people of Asian descent tend to take a more relationship-based approach, while people of European descent tend to take a more feature-based approach (Nisbett, 2003; Chiu, 1972). Some have speculated that this distinction stems from the greater emphasis on collectivism in Asian cultures than European cultures (Miyamoto & Wilken, 2013).

In one particular study, Chinese and U.S. college students were given lists of three items and asked to group a pair of the items together conceptually (Ji et al., 2004). The lists were constructed such that some pairs of items related to each other in some relationship-based way, but other pairs of items were similar in terms of features. Chinese students tended to put items together because they related to or interacted with each other. U.S. students tended to put items together because they had similar features. For example, one list contained the words *monkey*, *panda*, and *banana* (**Figure 7.3**). Chinese students were more likely to group together *monkey* and *banana* (the relationship being that monkeys eat bananas). U.S. students were more likely to group together *monkey* and *panda* (the shared feature being that both are animals).

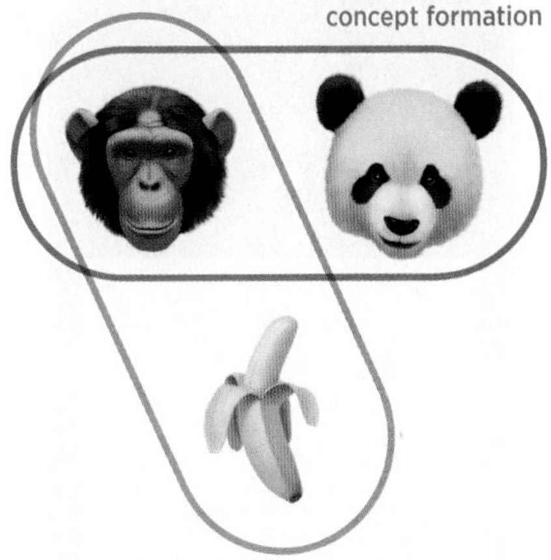

FIGURE 7.3 Cultural Influence on Concept Formation. In one study, Chinese students were more likely to group monkeys and bananas together conceptually, while U.S. students were more likely to group monkeys and pandas together conceptually. That difference in concept formation may indicate a tendency toward relationship-based concepts (monkeys eat bananas) versus feature-based concepts (monkeys and pandas are both animals). Research from Ji et al., 2004.

Problem Solving and Decision Making

Problem solving is using cognition to find a way to achieve a goal. Problem solving is closely related to **decision making**, which is using cognition to choose between available options. To help distinguish between problem solving and decision making, keep this in mind: When you solve problems, you often have to create the answers from scratch, but when you make decisions, the possible answers are usually already presented.

Another distinction between problem solving and decision making is how badly the right answer is *needed*. For problem solving, the need is pressing, but for decision making, the need may be less urgent or even absent (Mayer, 2013; Bassok & Novick, 2012). For example, if your car gets a flat tire but you need to get to a job interview, you're in problem-solving mode, trying to generate possible solutions and then choose the right one. (Fix the flat? Call a friend or roadside assistance? Take the bus? Ride your bike? Reschedule?) But if you're driving to that job interview and trying to decide which of your radio preset buttons to press, you're in decision-making mode. (A pop station? Hip-hop? Country? Metal? Talk radio?)

Algorithms. A key question in the study of both problem solving and decision making is the extent to which they are based on reason. In recent decades, psychologists have acknowledged that decision making involves more than just reason. Whether you are choosing a candy bar or a college, your values and preferences mix with your reasoning to determine your response (Oaksford et al., 2012; Chater et al., 2005). But for a long time, psychologists assumed that when it comes to problem solving, we are all about reason (Evans, 2012). In fact, they believed that we solve problems like machines, using an **algorithm**, or a formula-like method of problem solving. Algorithms are what Google Maps uses to give you directions from point A to point B—an entirely logic-based set of rules based on essential data (distance, roads, traffic) that produces the most rational, sensible, practical route. But psychologists soon recognized that people are not entirely algorithmic as problem solvers (Speekenbrink & Shanks, 2013; Evans, 2013; McKenzie, 2005; Arkes, 1991). Sometimes, we're not even close.

Problems with Problem Solving. A number of different factors can cause us to stray from reason when solving problems. One such factor is your **mental set**, or the limits you place on your approach to problem solving based on what has worked in the past. Let's go back to the flat tire example. If you've always dealt with flat tires

problem solving
Using cognition to find a way to achieve a goal.

decision making
Using cognition to choose between available options.

algorithm
A formula-like method of problem solving.

mental set
The limits a person places on an approach to problem solving based on what has worked in the past.

To give you directions from point A to point B, Google Maps uses an algorithm, a method of problem solving based entirely on logic and rationality. Humans, however, often combine algorithms with other factors, like preferences and values, to solve problems. That is why you may choose to take the scenic route rather than the most efficient one. Alexey Boldin/Shutterstock

in the past by putting on the spare yourself, then it may be the only possibility within your mental set. But in this particular situation, in which you need to get to your job interview quickly (and without sweat or stains on your clothes), it isn't the best option.

Another factor that overrides reason in many problem-solving situations is **confirmation bias**: a tendency to prefer information that confirms what you thought in the first place. For example, if you're looking to buy a new phone, your first thought might be to get the kind that your brother has, since he raves about it constantly. You do a little research online, and you find that there are plenty of positive reviews of your brother's phone model, but plenty of negative ones too. You also notice other phones that have plenty of positive reviews with far fewer negative reviews. But you find yourself playing down the good reviews of competing phones (and the bad reviews of your brother's phone), and playing up the good reviews of your brother's phone (and the bad reviews of competing phones). In the end, you convince yourself of what you half-believed when you started, even if reason suggests otherwise—your brother's phone is the one to get.

Your reasoning can also be swayed by **framing**: the particular way a question or problem is presented, which can influence how you respond to it. You can see the importance of framing in the way people on either side of an argument try to define the argument itself. For example, in the debate over fracking, those in favor of fracking frame it as an exploration of new homegrown oil resources that can create jobs and stimulate the economy, while those opposed to fracking frame it as a threat to natural resources that can damage water quality and human health (Mercado et al., 2014; Thompson, 2013).

Numerous studies have found that the way a problem is framed can indeed have a powerful influence on the way people solve it (Tversky & Kahneman, 1981, 1986; Slovic, 1975; LeBoeuf & Shafir, 2012). One study found that more people are willing to undergo a medical procedure when they hear about how successful it is (for example, "this operation has an 85% success rate") than its chance of failure (for example, "this operation fails 15% of the time") (Levin et al., 1988). Another study found that a package of ground beef is viewed more positively when it is labeled as "75% lean" than as "25% fat" (Levin, 1987).

Heuristics. Our reasoning can be affected by such contextual factors as what we've done before (mental set), what we thought in the first place (confirmation bias), and how the problem is presented (framing). Even when reasoning isn't affected by these contextual factors, we still tend to use shortcuts when we solve problems. Although we're generally unaware of it, our minds commonly return to quick, logically flawed thought processes rather than grinding out more time-consuming answers that might be more accurate. Instead of relying on an algorithm when we solve problems, we more often rely on a **heuristic**: an educated guess or rule-of-thumb method of problem solving. Pioneering researchers Daniel Kahneman and Amos Tversky in the early 1970s were the first to identify the role of heuristics. Since that time, their many studies offer compelling and often disconcerting evidence of just how illogical we can be, usually without even realizing it (Kahneman & Tversky, 1972, 1973, 1979, 1996, 2000; Tversky & Kahneman, 1971, 1974, 1986; Griffin et al., 2012). Let's examine the four heuristics that have received the most attention from Kahneman, Tversky, and other researchers: the *representativeness heuristic*, the *availability heuristic*, the *affect heuristic*, and the *anchoring heuristic*.

The **representativeness heuristic** is an educated guess based on similarity to a prototype. According to the representativeness heuristic, we tend to draw conclusions about people or things based on how closely they resemble a "textbook case" of a certain category, even if those conclusions might be premature or illogical (Tversky & Kahneman, 1982; Gilovich & Savitsky, 2002). It is basically a more scholarly version of the old "duck test": "If it looks like a duck, swims like a duck, and quacks like a duck, then it's probably a duck." The key word in that expression is *probably*—it's often an appropriate leap to make, but not always. For example, most sports cars have small trunks, so if your friend shows up to take you to the airport in his new sports car, you may assume that there won't be room for all your luggage. But when he pops the trunk, you find that it actually has plenty of room for your luggage. In fact, this trunk is as roomy as those in most other cars you've seen, sports car or otherwise. The leap your mind made about the size of the trunk in your friend's car,

"Of course, this could also be confirmation bias from me wanting you to get sick."

The New Yorker Collection, Paul Noth from cartoonbank.com. All Rights Reserved.

based on how representative that car was of the sports car category in your mind, proved inaccurate.

The **availability heuristic** is an educated guess based on the information that most quickly and easily comes to mind. Just because an answer pops into your head first doesn't necessarily make it more accurate than another answer that would require a little more digging. In one study of the availability heuristic, Kahneman and Tversky (1973) asked participants if there were more words that started with the letter R or words that have R as their third letter. Most participants quickly responded that there were more words that start with R, but the truth is that there are three times as many words that have R as the third letter. The explanation is that the words that start with R were more *available*, or easy to bring to mind.

As another illustration, Tversky & Kahneman (1973) read aloud a list of names that included more female names than male names. If the study were done today, the list might look like this: Linda Jennings, Tonya Brown, Lakisha Smith, Gabriela Rodriguez, Barack Obama, Teresa McKee, Catherine Meyer, David Templeton, Michelle Goldman, Matt Damon. They then asked the participants if the list included more men's names or women's names. Participants were likely to answer incorrectly when the gender with fewer names included more famous names. (The seven female names in this list don't include any famous women, but the three male names include one U.S. president and one movie star.) This mistake happens because the famous names are more available, or easy to recall, than the unfamiliar names.

The **anchoring heuristic** is an educated guess in which the starting point has a strong influence on the conclusion you ultimately reach. When you're not sure what to think, but someone else provides a suggestion (an *anchor*), it is unlikely that your suggestion will stray too far from theirs. Tversky and Kahneman (1974) illustrated the anchoring heuristic by asking U.S. participants what percentage of African nations were in the United Nations—a fact that most of them did not know. Before letting the participants answer, they spun a roulette-style wheel to give the participants a random percentage to consider (the anchor). When the anchor was 10%, the median guess by participants was 25%. When the anchor was 65%, the median guess by participants was 45%. The participants' guesses didn't stray far from the anchor they were provided, even though they knew that anchor was randomly determined. In another study, half of the participants were asked if Mahatma Gandhi died before or after the age of 140, and the other half were also asked if he died before or after the age of 9. Both anchors were extremely inaccurate, but they nonetheless pulled participants' responses in their respective directions: the anchor of 140 yielded an average guess of 67, while the anchor of 9 yielded an average guess of 50 (Strack & Mussweiler, 1997).

The anchoring heuristic even has a powerful effect on how much you might be willing to pay for an item at the store. One study asked students to use the last two digits in their social security numbers—a completely random number between 00 and 99—as the anchor. They were then shown a variety of retail products, from a wireless computer keyboard to a fancy box of chocolates (**Table 7.2**). First, they were asked if they would pay their anchor (in dollars) for them and then they were asked the maximum they would pay for them. Their responses to the second question were most fascinating:

confirmation bias
A tendency to prefer information that confirms what a person thought in the first place.

framing
The particular way a question or problem is presented, which can influence how a person responds to it.

heuristic
An educated guess or rule-of-thumb method of problem solving.

representativeness heuristic
An educated guess based on similarity to a prototype.

availability heuristic
An educated guess based on the information that most quickly and easily comes to mind.

anchoring heuristic
An educated guess in which the starting point has a strong influence on the conclusion that is ultimately reached.

If you thought this was a duck, you were misled by the representativeness heuristic, the tendency to take an educated guess based on similarity to a prototype. This animal may look like a duck, but it is actually a loon.
Jim Cumming/Moment/Getty Images

TABLE 7.2: Anchored

LAST TWO DIGITS OF SOCIAL SECURITY NUMBER	WHAT THEY'D PAY FOR A CORDLESS KEYBOARD	WHAT THEY'D PAY FOR A BOX OF FANCY CHOCOLATES
00–19	$16.09	$9.55
20–39	26.82	10.64
40–59	29.27	12.45
60–79	34.55	13.27
80–99	55.64	20.64

Data from Ariely et al., 2003.

Imagine that you were asked if you would spend a dollar amount equivalent to the last two digits of your social security number on a product. Then, with that two-digit number still fresh in your mind, you were asked the maximum you would pay for that product. In one study, that maximum was anchored remarkably closely to a random two-digit number. In fact, people using the highest last two digits of their social security numbers would pay two or three times the amount of money as people with the lowest two-digit numbers for the same item.

affect heuristic
An educated guess in which the worth of something is strongly influenced by how a person feels toward it.

dual-process theory
The notion that every person possesses two separate types of thinking, one automatic and one deliberate.

affective forecasting
Predicting how a person will feel about the outcomes of his or her decisions.

people with high anchors were willing to pay significantly more—sometimes even double or triple the price—than people with low anchors. For example, participants with anchors below 20 were willing to pay only $16.09 for the wireless keyboard and $9.55 for the chocolates, while participants with anchors above 80 were willing to pay $55.64 for the wireless keyboard and $20.64 for the chocolates (Ariely et al., 2003).

The **affect heuristic** is an educated guess in which the worth of something is strongly influenced by how you feel toward it. (In this context, "affect" means feelings.) So if you like something a lot, you tend to conclude that it is worthwhile and good, but if you dislike it a lot, you tend to conclude that it is worthless and bad (Kahneman & Fredrick, 2002). In one study, researchers described nuclear power to participants as very risky, which elicited fear, or as very beneficial, which elicited more positive feelings. When they then asked participants to evaluate nuclear power as an option for their own communities, their evaluations closely mirrored their emotions (Finucane et al., 2000). The affect heuristic undoubtedly plays a role in your judgment of things of which you are a fan. Your passion for any particular thing makes you more likely to judge it in a positive way. You expect your favorite sports team to win even when a purely objective, logical analysis (your favorite sports team hasn't won a game all season) would lead to a more negative, and more accurate, conclusion.

Cognition and Emotion

The affect heuristic is just one attempt to explain the impact that emotions can have on thinking. The contemporary theory that best captures this combination of emotion with reason is **dual-process theory**: the notion that each of us possesses two separate types of thinking, one automatic and one deliberate. As indicated by the title of Daniel Kahneman's best-selling book *Thinking, Fast and Slow* (2011), dual-process theory states that when you face a problem or a decision, you can respond in two distinct ways: one based on fast thinking and the other based on slow thinking (Evans & Over, 1996; Sloman, 1996; Stanovich, 2011).

Type 1 and Type 2 Thinking. Type 1 thinking is thinking fast. It happens instantly, effortlessly, and often without your full awareness. It is your impulse, your gut response, your intuition. It produces quick responses that can be fueled primarily by emotion (**Table 7.3**). It may, in fact, often activate the heuristics that we just discussed. Type 2 thinking is thinking slowly. It happens more deliberately and purposefully. It is your ability to analyze, evaluate, and think things through. Type 2 thinking takes longer and requires more effort than Type 1 thinking, but it does a much better job of emphasizing reason over emotion (Evans & Stanovich, 2013; Laird-Johnson, 2012).

When you're trying to solve problems or make decisions, both types of thinking can be beneficial. Type 1 thinking happens first, and it can be persuasive. Type 2 thinking sometimes comes up with a better solution, but you may have started to follow Type 1 thinking's instructions by the time it does (Kahneman & Fredrick, 2005). As an example, imagine that a friend offers you a business opportunity: to open a cupcake shop near your college campus. Your immediate reaction to that idea is your Type 1 thinking. Perhaps your Type 1 thinking leans in a positive direction: opening a cupcake shop with your friend would be a good idea. Why does your Type 1 thinking produce this response? Perhaps because of reasons (the money you could make, the student loans you would no longer need), but perhaps because of emotion (the excitement of starting a new business, the ego boost of being an entrepreneur with a successful business). If your Type 1 thinking is more negative, that too would be based on both reason (the money you could lose, the debt you'd take on) and emotion (the aggravations of starting a new business, the embarrassment of a failure).

If you give yourself a little time, however, Type 2 thinking will have a chance to kick in. Like Type 1 thinking, Type 2 thinking may come down either in favor of or against the cupcake shop idea. Whatever your Type 2 thinking decides, that decision will be based more on reason, and

TABLE 7.3: Dual-Process Theory: Type 1 Versus Type 2 Thinking

TYPE 1 THINKING IS...	TYPE 2 THINKING IS...
Fast	Slow
Automatic	Effortful
Outside your awareness	Under your control
More emotional	More logical
Your immediate impulse	Your careful analysis

Information from Evans, 2013; Evans & Stanovich, 2013.

feelings will be disentangled from the process. Type 2 thinking may prompt you to consider questions like these: How much money would I have to invest, and what rate can we get on a small business loan? How many cupcakes would we have to sell to make a profit? How many other local cupcake shops would we compete against, and what advantages would our shop have over theirs? How would we advertise, and how much would that cost? With such a thorough analysis, based on data rather than emotion, Type 2 thinking is likely to arrive at a better, more rational, and perhaps a better, decision—if you can wait for it.

Type 1 thinking can be quite valuable in terms of producing rapid responses to situations in which overthinking can be detrimental, such as reacting to loud noises to avoid danger or responding to a greeting from another person in a quick and appropriate way. However, lots of studies indicate how Type 1 thinking, with its emotional influence, can take over the reasoning process, even when Type 2 thinking could generate a more logical answer. For example, one study asked participants to imagine that they were playing Russian roulette and could pay to have one bullet removed (Kahneman & Tversky, 1979). Then they asked, Would you pay as much to reduce the number of bullets from 4 to 3 as you would to reduce the number from 1 to 0? The vast majority said no. Type 1 thinking tells them that it is worth more to reduce the number of bullets from 1 to 0. But according to Type 2 thinking, that is inaccurate. Each reduction increases the odds of survival by the same amount. (If the gun holds five bullets, for example, each removal of a bullet means a 20% greater chance of survival.) But the relief associated with the drop to zero bullets overrides the mathematical logic (Wu & Gonzalez, 1996).

In another study, participants see two jars of jellybeans of various colors (Epstein, 1991; Denes-Raj & Epstein, 1994). The smaller jar contains 10 jellybeans, 1 of which is green (**Figure 7.4**). The larger jar contains 100 jellybeans, 9 of which are green. The researchers explain these numbers to the participants and then allow them to reach their hand into one jar, with their eyes closed, to try to select a green jellybean. Type 2 thinking says go for the smaller jar, since the odds are greater than for the larger jar (10% vs. 9%). But 61% of participants chose the larger jar, presumably because they couldn't resist the temptation of nine chances of winning (versus just one chance). The researchers then reduced the number of green jellybeans in the larger jar to 5 out of 100. Even in this situation, in which odds of pulling a green jellybean from the smaller jar were double the odds of pulling one from the larger jar (10% vs. 5%), about a quarter of the participants still chose the larger jar. A few of them even said out loud that they knew their decision didn't make mathematical sense, but the feeling of having more chances to win was too strong to override.

FIGURE 7.4 I'll Get a Green One; I Can *Feel* It. In one study where the goal was to pick out a green jellybean without looking, participants could choose their odds: 1 in 10 in the small jar, or 9 in 100 in the big jar. According to logic, this should be a no-brainer: go for the small jar, where your chances are 10%, rather than the big jar, where your chances are only 9%. But 61% of participants went for the big jar, presumably because they felt like it gave them more chances to win. Even when the experimenters dropped the number of green jellybeans in the big jar to 5, many still chose it rather than the small jar. Research from Epstein, 1991; Denes-Raj & Epstein, 1994.

Affective Forecasting. One more note regarding the role of emotion in cognition: When trying to solve a problem or make a decision, you're not just hoping that the situation will turn out well. You're also hoping that *your feelings* about the situation will turn out well. The question isn't just "What will happen if I...?" but also "How will I feel if I...?" (Schwartz & Sommers, 2013). Imagine that you are babysitting for a neighbor's toddler when he tells you that his tummy hurts. What should you do—call his parent, give him medicine, call an ambulance, ignore him? Of course, your main goal is to ensure that the boy feels OK. But *your* feelings are in the mix too. How would you feel if you did nothing and it turned out the boy had a serious illness? How would you feel if you rushed him to the hospital and it turned out the boy just had a mosquito bite near his bellybutton? Psychologists call this emphasis on the subjective results of decisions, rather than the objective results, **affective forecasting**: predicting how you will feel about the outcomes of your decisions.

Research on affective forecasting suggests that we are not very good at it (Kahneman, 1999, 2000; Kahneman et al., 1993; Redelmeier et al., 2003). In one study, researchers texted college students repeatedly during spring break in South Florida to get moment-to-moment ratings of how much fun they were having (Wirtz et al., 2003). According to those ratings, most of their moments were pretty blah, with ratings in the middle of the fun scale. But when the students came back to school, their memories of the trip included lots of the highs and lows but almost none of the middle. Here's the key point regarding affective forecasting: when asked whether they would go back to the same place next

MY TAKE VIDEO 7.1

Affective Forecasting

"I thought I was going to be so much happier when..."

YOUTUBE: http://tiny.cc/mytake

LAUNCHPAD: launchpadworks.com

When you overestimate the expected length of a feeling, you are experiencing the durability bias. In one study, college students expected the feelings related to a win or loss by their school's team to last well into the next week, but by Monday, those feelings had faded (Dunn et al., 2003). Michael Shroyer/Getty Images

LIFE HACK 7.1

Keep the durability bias in mind the next time you consider spending lots of money on something to make yourself happy. There is a good chance that the happiness it brings will not last as long as you expect.

(Gilbert & Wilson, 2000, 2007; Gilbert, 2006; Gilbert et al., 1998)

Creativity is the capacity to come up with original ideas or approaches to a problem. In some cases, creative solutions change the world. In other cases, creative solutions just give you a convenient place to hold your popcorn. Anjali Prasertong

spring, their answers depended not on their average ratings (most of which fell in the middle range), but on whether they had more highs or lows. Students didn't consider all of the available data when they predicted how they would feel on the same trip next year. In fact, they ignored most of it, concentrating only on the extremely good and bad moments.

Affective forecasting is also misled by the **durability bias**: the overestimation of the expected length of the feeling produced by the outcome of a decision. When looking ahead to a big decision, you expect that the outcome will influence your emotions for a long time, but it typically doesn't. You get used to whatever happens, and the feeling passes (Gilbert & Wilson, 2000, 2007; Gilbert, 2006; Gilbert et al., 1998). Think of how great you thought your life would be after you got that new hairstyle, that new big-screen TV, that new job, or that new romantic partner. You may have imagined "happily ever after," but "happily" probably didn't last that long. What was new became routine, and eventually didn't bring as much excitement as you expected it to.

In one study of the durability bias, researchers asked students from the University of Virginia and Virginia Tech how the outcome of a big Saturday football game between the two schools would make them feel, and how long they would feel that way (Wilson et al., 2000). Most expected the outcome to have a major impact on their happiness well into the next week. It didn't. Win or lose, by Monday, most students' happiness was no longer affected.

In another study (also involving students from the University of Virginia), first-year students took a survey about the impact of a housing lottery that would determine the buildings in which they would live for their remaining years on campus (Dunn et al., 2003). The lottery did not determine roommates, just location. Before the lottery, students predicted that its outcome would have a huge impact on their happiness for years to come. They were wrong. Follow-up questionnaires 1 year and 2 years after the housing lottery found that the students' level of happiness at that time had nothing to do with where the housing lottery had placed them.

Cognition and Creativity

Creativity is the capacity to come up with original ideas or approaches to a problem. Creative acts can be something as small and personal as the invention of the Internet-famous "popcorn hoodie"—a hoodie worn backward with the hood full of popcorn—or as big and globally transformative as the development of Facebook (Kaufman & Beghetto, 2009). Either way, creativity goes beyond selecting among preexisting solutions to a problem—it is the invention of a completely new solution.

As an example of a creative solution, consider this real-world problem: when first responders (police officers, firefighters, search-and-rescue workers) arrive at a building, how can they get a good look at what's inside? The obvious solution is to enter themselves, but sometimes that's too risky. (Is there a shooter inside? A fire? A bomb?) Other times, entering is simply impractical, such as when a building has been damaged so badly that debris blocks access to survivors. Another solution might involve sending in a trained dog or a robot, but dogs' ability to communicate is limited, and robots can be expensive and clunky. A team of inventors has created a device—the Bounce Imaging Explorer—as a solution for this problem. The Bounce Imaging Explorer is a small ball—no bigger than a softball—equipped with 6 digital cameras, a thermometer, an oxygen sensor, and flashing LED lights. First responders can toss it into any space—a burning building, a hostage situation, the rubble caused by a natural disaster—and it automatically transmits panoramic photos and information about the environment to any linked device, such as a smartphone or tablet in a first responder's hands. The creation was inspired by rescue efforts after the massive earthquake in Haiti in 2010, when rescuers had difficulty determining from the outside whether partially collapsed buildings contained survivors or were structurally sound enough to enter. The inventors demonstrated some genuine outside-the-box creativity when they conceived of this relatively inexpensive and potentially life-saving device.

Divergent Thinking and Convergent Thinking. When the creators of the Bounce Imaging Explorer saw a need for a better way to see inside hazardous situations,

they probably generated a variety of ideas before settling on that particular solution. They engaged in **divergent thinking**: a problem-solving strategy in which you come up with lots of different possible solutions. Divergent thinking is essentially brainstorming, even if you do it alone. It's most evident in that early part of the creative process when the goal is to think open-mindedly and generate many ideas, even if you know that many will be discarded in the process of choosing the best one (Sternberg, 2006; Sternberg & Lubart, 1991). The opposite of divergent thinking is **convergent thinking**: a problem-solving strategy in which you use logic to deduce the single best solution.

As you might expect, creative people tend to be divergent thinkers rather than convergent thinkers (Smith & Ward, 2012). To assess creativity, psychologists sometimes use the "brick test," in which people think of as many uses for a brick as they can (Silvia et al., 2009; Carson et al., 2005). (The same kind of test can focus on any common object—a chair, a paper clip, etc.) Convergent thinkers tend to think that bricks are for building houses. That is appropriate, certainly, but not creative. Divergent thinkers would imagine many other uses for a brick: some innovative (a doorstop, a bookend, a paperweight), some imaginative (a hammer, a garden stepping stone, a weight for arm exercises), and some way out there (a weapon, a canvas on which to paint, an alternative to chalk for writing on the sidewalk).

durability bias
The overestimation of the expected length of the feeling produced by the outcome of a decision.

creativity
The capacity to come up with original ideas or approaches to a problem.

divergent thinking
A problem-solving strategy in which a person comes up with lots of different possible solutions.

convergent thinking
A problem-solving strategy in which a person uses logic to deduce the single best solution.

functional fixedness
Thinking about something in only the way it is most typically used rather than other possible uses.

Functional Fixedness. To engage in such divergent thinking (about bricks or anything else), it is important to overcome the tendency toward **functional fixedness**: thinking about something in only the way it is most typically used, rather than other possible uses. Thinking of an object's most typical use (like bricks for houses) doesn't thwart creativity, but *stopping* there does (Simonton & Damian, 2013; Maier, 1931; Glucksberg & Weisberg, 1966). If you've ever seen magazines or Web sites with those lists of creative uses (or "hacks") for household items and thought "wow, that really is a good idea," then you appreciate the creativity that can flow when people get past functional fixedness. Examples of getting past functional fixedness include using a drinking straw as a protective covering for a necklace to keep it from tangling or kinking, using uncooked rice (or kitty litter) to dry out a wet phone, using a piece of spaghetti as a long match for tough-to-reach candle wicks, and using a comb to hold a nail in place so you don't smash your fingers. All of these ideas originally popped into the head of someone who thought past the most obvious use of an object and was not restrained by functional fixedness.

Getting past functional fixedness can lead to exciting artistic developments too. Consider the turntable. For decades, it was used solely for its intended function: playing music. But in the late 1970s, a few pioneering DJs—Kool Herc and Grandmaster Flash, most notably—forged a new function for turntables: *making* music (Hill, 2013; Piskor, 2013). Grandmaster Flash had noticed that at his parties, dancers' favorite parts of the songs he played were the brief stretches when the vocals and often some of the instruments dropped out, leaving just the groove from the rhythm section. He lamented that

WATCHING PSYCHOLOGY

Convergent and Divergent Thinking on *Family Feud*

The beginning of each round on *Family Feud*, when a member of each family walks up front and puts a hand on the buzzer, is all about convergent thinking. The goal, after all, is to guess the most common answer provided in a survey of 100 people.

After one contestant wins that face-off, the host moves down the line of that family, posing the same question to each one. Eventually, most of the answers on the board have been uncovered, but it is difficult to get those last few. That is when the contestants need to get creative and use divergent thinking. They need to think past the first several answers that come to mind, and come up with that less obvious answer hiding near the bottom of the board. That is what the other family is doing as they huddle up, hoping for a chance to steal—brainstorming possible answers beyond the ones already on the board.

For example, consider this *Family Feud* question: Name a food that goes well with peanut butter. Convergent thinking leads you right away to the obvious #1 answer: jelly. Then it starts getting tougher, especially if the list of top answers on the board is long. You may have to think a bit more divergently to come up with bread or crackers, then even more divergently to come up with honey or chocolate, and then very divergently to come up with celery or apples. That divergent thinking—moving past the first and most obvious answer to other answers that may work—is what creativity is all about.

A key to creativity is overcoming functional fixedness, or thinking about something in only the way it is most typically used. In the 1970s, Grandmaster Flash (shown here) and a few other DJs overcame functional fixedness with regard to turntables and treated them as devices for making music rather than only devices for playing music. Rick Diamond/WireImage/Getty Images

those stretches—the breaks, as he called them—lasted just a few seconds. He wondered if he could somehow use two turntables to fuse these breaks into a long-lasting beat. As he describes it:

> I knew I wanted a continuous groove.... I need to stop the record on the left and start the record on the right at a precise moment in time so that you, the listener, can't tell where one stops and the next one starts.... Finally, I found a way to start the first record with my hand physically on the vinyl itself. The platter would turn but the music wouldn't play because the needle wouldn't be traveling through the groove. However, when I took my hand off the record...BAM! The music started right where I wanted it.... What if I could do this with two turntables at once? It wasn't easy, but I kept winding the second record back and forward until I got it just right and ... BAM!... The break played twice without missing a beat.... I'd gone from breaking a song apart in my head to breaking it apart on the turntable. The possibilities were endless" (Flash & Ritz, 2008, pp. 74–79).

Those possibilities include looping, in which the same break is juggled between two turntables for as long as the DJ wants (and often used by rappers to rhyme over), and blending, in which different breaks are strung together into an overlapping syncopated mix. These innovations with turntables as musical instruments paved the way for the sample-based method of music making (now used by music makers in every genre), in which computer programs are used to combine segments from different songs (Schloss, 2004; McLeod & DiCola, 2011).

Creativity and Culture. Another factor linked to creativity is culture (Lubart, 1999). People who experience multiple cultures or speak multiple languages are relatively high in creativity, presumably because their diverse experiences help them think in multiple ways (Ricciardelli, 1992; Simonton, 2008; Leung et al., 2008). Also, people from Western cultures tend to think more divergently than people from Eastern cultures, which leads to a higher level of creativity (Kharkhurin & Motalleebi, 2008; Niu & Sternberg, 2001). In fact, the number of patents per capita—an interesting way to measure how many new ideas a culture creates—is higher in cultures with high individualism, which is generally more prominent in Western than Eastern cultures (Shane, 1992, 1993).

DIVERSITY MATTERS

While individualism may facilitate creative ideas, it doesn't necessarily facilitate implementation of those ideas (Hofstede, 2001). So if genius is 1% inspiration and 99% perspiration (as the old saying goes), pure individualism may be good for the start but not necessarily the follow-through. Often, what produces the best results is a partnership of "idea people," who come up with creative plans, and "worker bees," who translate those plans into reality. Consider the work of Dale Chihuly, who is recognized as one of the premier glass sculptors in U.S. history. He is the designer of many enormous and intricate works, many of which contain hundreds of specially made pieces of glass arranged in a particular way. As an artist, Chihuly is the main creative force behind his glass sculptures, but the execution of his art—the conversion of the idea in Chihuly's mind into actual sculpted glass—requires a team of coworkers (Chihuly, 2007). The shaping of even a single piece of glass often involves the coordinated efforts of dozens of people to blow, hold, and turn the glass in its liquefied state. The assembly of his finished works in museums, which involves painstakingly arranging hundreds of smaller glass pieces to form the large work of art, is another major group effort. Without all of these teammates, Chihuly's creations would remain uncreated.

The magnificent glass sculptures of artist Dale Chihuly are a product of creativity that depends on both individualism and collectivism. Individualism tends to promote the kind of divergent thinking that leads to creative ideas. Collectivism tends to promote the kind of teamwork necessary to carry out those ideas. Chihuly's sculptures require a large team of people to blow, hold, turn, and assemble the many separate pieces of glass. Insights/Contributor/Universal Images Group Editorial/Getty Images

CHECK YOUR LEARNING:

7.1 How do psychologists define cognition and what are the three main areas of research?

7.2 How do psychologists define the term *concept*?

7.3 What are the three main types of concepts?

7.4 What three levels do psychologists use to organize concepts?

7.5 What is the difference between problem solving and decision making?

7.6 What is the difference between an algorithm and a heuristic?

7.7 What are three ways in which people stray from reason when solving problems?

7.8 What are the four main types of heuristic?

7.9 According to dual process theory, what are the two types of thinking and how do they differ?

7.10 What is affective forecasting, and, in general, how good are people at it?

7.11 How do psychologists define creativity?

7.12 What is the difference between divergent thinking and convergent thinking?

7.13 What is functional fixedness?

7.14 What types of factors contribute to creativity?

Language

Language is your ability to communicate with others using words or other symbols combined and arranged according to rules. Language, if you stop and think about it, is absolutely amazing. Just think about the word-related things you could *not* do at all when you were born—say them, write them, read them, or understand them. Somehow, just a few years later, you were doing all of those things fluently. By this point in your life, your brain uses language as easily and automatically as your lungs use air. One expert illustrates the often-overlooked marvels of linguistic ability by detailing, in slow motion, what happens in just a brief snippet of conversation:

> Without any real effort, we identify over a dozen speech sounds...per second, recognize the words they constitute, almost immediately understand the message generated by the sentences they form, and often elaborate appropriate verbal and nonverbal responses before the utterance ends (Mattys, 2013, p. 391).

Let's examine many aspects of language, such as how it evolved in our species, how it develops during childhood, how it is structured by grammatical rules, and how it interacts with thinking.

YOU WILL LEARN:

7.15 how psychologists define language.

7.16 how researchers speculate that language evolved.

7.17 about different theories of language development.

7.18 about the various stages of a child's language development.

7.19 about the four levels of grammar.

7.20 how extralinguistic information can influence communication.

7.21 whether language influences thinking.

The Evolution of Language

How did humans get so good at language? Other animals communicate, of course, but how did our use of language become so sophisticated? The truth is that we don't know for sure. In fact, we may never know for sure, since the evolution of language took place so many thousands of years ago (Bickerton & Szathmáry, 2009; Gibson & Tallerman, 2012; Christiansen & Kirby, 2003; Carstairs-McCarthy, 2001; Aitchison, 1996). But that hasn't stopped speculation.

Some experts believe that early in human history, there was a kind of "protolanguage"—a primitive way of communicating that was just a step or two beyond grunting (Bickerton, 1992, 2009). This protolanguage may have been made up of isolated sounds, each of which carried a complete message that was fundamentally important to survival at that time. For example, one sound may have declared "LookOutAPredatorIsBehindYou!" while another sound may have communicated "Don'tEatThatItWillMakeYouSick!" (Bickerton, 2013). These sounds might have been similar to the language of car horns now—isolated blasts of communication that lack detail but quickly convey crucial information that makes sense in context. Over long periods of time, humans may have broken down these single sounds into smaller parts—rudimentary words—that could be combined in new ways (Wray, 1998, 2000). But again, this protolanguage theory is an educated guess rather than a proven fact, and not all experts agree with it (Arbib, 2008).

language
The ability to communicate with others using words or other symbols combined and arranged according to rules.

But how did language grow to include so many words?

That is a good observation: the languages we use today are far more expansive than the isolated single sounds of our ancestors. The average U.S. adult has a vocabulary of between 60,000 and 100,000 English words (Pinker, 1994), and that's just a fraction of the complete English language. The English language adds new words all the time—see **Table 7.4** for some new dictionary entries. That gives us many options for saying what our ancestors said with their single sounds.

Why would our language produce so many ways to convey the same basic message? Some experts have speculated that a more sophisticated use of language is socially impressive, attracting both friends and potential mates. If you use a rich vocabulary when you speak, including words often used by highly educated people, then listeners will understand your message and admire the manner in which you communicated it (Lange et al., 2013; Rosenberg & Tunney, 2008). Think of it this way: you're exchanging messages with a person on a dating app, and this person offers an opinion about a new movie: "Yeah, I seen that movie. I hated it. I don't know what them people was thinking when they was talking about how good it was." Would you get a different impression if your date wrote this instead? "Yes, I have seen that film. To be honest, I didn't care for it. I'm aware of the glowing praise it has received from critics, yet I fail to see how they could have come to such a conclusion." Both messages carry the same content, but the *way* that content is carried differs greatly. That difference, in turn, tells you something about the speaker. In this way, complex language functions for humans like decorative feathers function for a peacock or elaborate songs for a songbird—a way of displaying attractiveness and status to others (Locke, 2012).

Linguistic complexity can certainly benefit individuals, but it can benefit groups too. Some theories state that language may have evolved beyond single sounds so information could be shared with family members about food, tools, and other basic elements of survival (Gibson, 2012). A single sound couldn't explain how best to use a small hand axe or how best to connect an arrowhead to a shaft when those primitive tools were first used. A single sound can't communicate "There is no fresh water past those hills" or "There are plenty of animals to hunt and berries to pick on the other side of that lake"—crucial information for finding food and water early in human history. So, in the same way we use the Yelp app to share our news about the quality of food and drink at various places where we forage now, early humans may have expanded their linguistic skills to yelp similar information to their kin to help them survive.

TABLE 7.4: What's the Word? Terms Added to the Dictionary in Recent Years

1. Crowdfunding	a. Accessing oil and natural gas by injecting fluid into shale beds deep underground
2. Fracking	b. Inhaling and exhaling from an electronic cigarette
3. Freegan	c. Adding game-like elements to a task to increase participation
4. Gamification	d. A person who lives in the upper peninsula of Michigan
5. Tweep	e. Asking for monetary contributions from a large online community
6. Yooper	f. Fear of being without a working phone
7. Nomophobia	g. A Twitter user
8. Vape	h. A person who scavenges for free food, often in trash cans, as a way to reduce consumption of resources

Can you match these recent additions to the dictionary with their meanings?
(Answers: 1-e, 2-a, 3-h, 4-c, 5-g, 6-d, 7-f, 8-b)

Information from http://www.merriam-webster.com/new-words/2014-update.htm; http://www.oxforddictionaries.com/; http://time.com/4299634/merriam-webster-fomo-mx-dox-update/.

The Development of Language

We've discussed the way language might have evolved over the course of human history. Now let's discuss the way language develops over the course of *each* human's history. When you enter the world, your language skills are practically nonexistent. Crying doesn't count. Within months, however, you understand many words and sentences. By your first birthday, you're chiming in with a few words of your own. In just the next couple of years, you become fluent both as a listener and a speaker, with an extensive vocabulary and the ability to form all kinds of sentences. How is that possible? How can such a young child master the incredibly complex task of language acquisition so quickly?

Babies understand language within their first few months, and use words themselves by the time they reach their first birthday. Within the next couple of years, their linguistic abilities expand greatly. Marlon Lopez MMG1 Design/Shutterstock

Nativist Theory of Language Development. Maybe you're simply born with the ability to acquire language. Maybe there is something built in to human beings, similar to the abilities to see and to breathe, that enables you to acquire language. This is the basic idea behind **nativist theory**: a theory of language development that says the ability to use language is inborn. Nativist theory, which overlaps with the more recent theories of *universal grammar* or *linguistic universalism*, has been at the center of a long-lasting debate in psychology. Renowned linguist Noam Chomsky (1959, 1995) has been among the most vocal champions of nativist theory for many decades. On the other side of the debate, other experts say that learning language is about nurture just as much as it is about nature. From their point of view, language is not an inborn ability but learnable, just like anything else (Elman et al., 1996; Bybee & McClelland, 2005). This debate illustrates how language, like many other topics within psychology, is a hotspot for the nature–nurture issue.

Those who support nativist theory typically believe that every person is born with a **language acquisition device**: a specific capacity within the brain that provides the ability to use language. Like software that comes preloaded on a new computer, the language acquisition device would empower you to learn language quickly from day one. The word *device* makes it sound like the language acquisition device is literally a small piece of equipment implanted in your brain, but, as we learned back in Chapter 2, such a device would actually be a circuit of numerous brain regions that interact to produce language.

Nativist theory (or at least the general idea that there is an inborn component to language acquisition) gets some support from observations of children who are deaf. One observation involves the way children who are deaf often interact with their parents. When these parents do not use standard sign language, the families often develop an idiosyncratic "home sign" language of their own. Typically, these languages feature many of the same properties as any human language (signed or spoken), such as the ways words are combined and the structures of sentences. Moreover, they are quite complex and enable expression of a wide range of thoughts and feelings—way beyond anything found in any nonhuman species. It is also notable that the child is typically better at this home sign language than his or her parents, suggesting that it was the kid who primarily created it (Goldin-Meadow, 2005). All of this suggests that language emerges naturally, even in an environment in which it might not have otherwise existed.

In the 1980s, Nicaragua introduced its first schools for deaf children. These children had never used standard sign language. When they were brought together, they quickly developed their own sign language. That occurrence supports nativist theory, the idea that the ability to use language is inborn rather than learned. © Susan Meiselas/Magnum Photos

Another observation involves children who were deaf and living in Nicaragua in the 1980s, when schools for the deaf were first created in that country. None of the children who entered the school had ever been exposed to standard sign language. Quickly and spontaneously, these kids formed their own sign language. At first, teachers dismissed it as simplistic and limited, so they tried (unsuccessfully) to teach the students standard sign language. However, further research indicated that the kids' indigenous sign language featured a wide vocabulary and a complex structure that resembled many other languages (Kegl et al., 1999; Senghas et al., 2004). Today, that indigenous sign language is recognized as Nicaraguan Sign Language and is widely considered a legitimate version of sign language. Again, it seems that in the absence of a shared language, a new one emerged naturally. Such stories suggest that, at least to some extent, we humans have an innate disposition to develop and use our linguistic abilities (Jackendoff, 2012).

nativist theory
A theory of language development that says the ability to use language is inborn.

language acquisition device
A specific capacity within a person's brain that provides the ability to use language.

Nonnativist Theories of Language Development. Just because our linguistic abilities are strongly influenced by nature doesn't mean that nurture is uninvolved

Social-pragmatic theory suggests that a child's use of language develops from a desire to interact socially. Reading books with young children, especially in a way that encourages lots of questions and commentary about the book (rather than just sticking to the script) has been found to improve language use in children (Whitehurst et al., 1988). Roberto Westbrook/Blend Images/Getty Images

(Fitch, 2012; Baldwin & Meyer, 2007). Numerous studies show that rewarding kids for language-related behaviors leads to an increase in those behaviors. In one such study, 2- to 4-year-old kids with serious language delays heard a parent make a particular sound. The kids then immediately received something from that parent that made them happy—such as tickling, clapping, or saying "Yay!" With repetition of this sequence, each of the children began to make that particular sound themselves (Sundberg et al., 1996). Studies like this support the *formalist theory* of language development, which suggests that kids learn language through the process of hearing others speak it (Bruner, 1975, 1981).

More recently, another nonnativist theory of language development has received more attention from researchers. **Social-pragmatic theory** suggests that a child's use of language develops from a desire to interact socially. Beginning with their earliest nonverbal communications, kids want to be part of the conversation that their parents, grandparents, and older siblings are having. Improving their language abilities by emulating the language they hear helps them accomplish that (Gopnik & Meltzoff, 1997; Brooks & Meltzoff, 2005; Ramirez-Esparza et al., 2014; Tomasello, 2004).

In a study that illustrates this process, one group of parents read picture books to their young kids for a month at home in their typical way. The second group of parents was instructed to read picture books to their young kids in a way that was specifically designed to get kids talking: ask lots of open-ended questions about the book, frequently stop to discuss with the child what happened on a particular page (rather than strictly sticking to the text), and avoid questions that the child could answer by pointing rather than speaking. Afterward, kids from the second group outperformed kids from the first group on a number of linguistic tasks. They used language more expressively, spoke in longer utterances, and more frequently used phrases than single words to get their points across (Whitehurst et al., 1988).

Parentese. Collectively, the evidence suggests that language development, like so many other human activities, is undeniably influenced by both nature and nurture. Regardless of which one is actually more prominent, the process starts in the earliest days of life. Around that time, parents speak to babies in that special way: sing-songy, high-pitched, with elongated vowel sounds and lots of repetition. Many people call this baby talk, but psychologists prefer the terms *infant-directed speech*, *motherese*, or the more gender-neutral *parentese* (Mithen, 2012; Fernald, 1994). As the first form of verbal communication, parentese strengthens bonds between infants and their caretakers. It is often accompanied by physical touch, such as hugging, caressing, and kissing. It may have originally evolved as a way for human babies, who unlike our primate relatives, can't cling to their mothers, to get mom's attention when mom wasn't holding them (Falk, 2012).

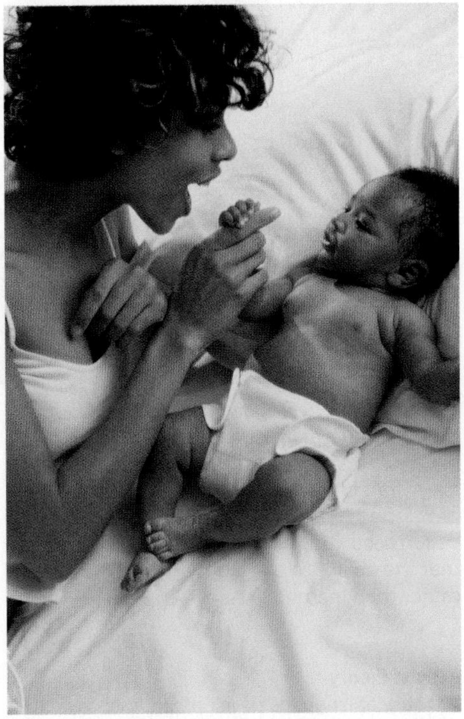

Parentese (commonly known as "baby talk") is a sing-songy, high-pitched, repetitive way of speaking that strengthens bonds between babies and caretakers. Purestock/Getty Images

Babbling. The baby's role in responding to parentese is **babbling**: an early stage of speech development during which the baby vocalizes a wide variety of nonword sounds. Babbling begins just a few months after birth, with single-syllable sounds like *ba*. A few months later, babies' babbling becomes *reduplicated*, which is a fancy way of saying a single syllable sound gets repeated over and over: "*ba*" becomes "*ba-ba-ba-ba*." A few months after that, babies string together a variety of different single syllable sounds (*variegated babbling*) to make longer babbles like "*ba-ga-mi-nu*" or "*pa-go-ki-ba*" (Fenson et al., 1994; Oller, 2000; Levey, 2013). The babbles themselves may be meaningless, but the process of babbling is important to the baby's development of spoken language. Babbling elicits verbal responses from caregivers, which babies then hear and mimic. This is how babies learn how to shape their babbles into the words, phrases, and sentences that they will ultimately use (Goldstein & West, 1999; Goldstein et al., 2003; Gros-Louis et al., 2006).

The best learning happens when caregivers reply immediately and responsively to the babies' babbles. Language develops much better when babies genuinely *interact* with adults (as in a face-to-face exchange with mom or dad) than when they merely hear random adult voices (as in overhearing parental conversations or the chatter on TV or radio) (Goldstein & Schwade, 2008). When babies do have those direct, back-and-forth interactions with adults, they are doing some pretty intense listening.

Wait, how can you tell how intensely a baby is listening? Obviously, they can't just tell you.

social-pragmatic theory
Suggests that a child's use of language develops from a desire to interact socially.

babbling
An early stage of speech development during which the baby vocalizes a wide variety of nonword sounds.

one-word stage
A stage of speech development during which the young child uses a single word as a full sentence.

We can tell how intensely babies listen to language from some creative studies in which babies hear a certain kind of babble many times in a row—enough to get used to it—and then hear either a similar type of babble or a different type. At that moment, they spend much more time looking in the direction of the different type of babble—their nonverbal way of saying "Huh?" when they hear something unfamiliar (Gerken, 2007; Saffran & Thiessen, 2003; Gómez & Gerken, 2000). It is a similar reaction to the one you would have if you were with a group of friends speaking one language and then someone started speaking a completely foreign language. You'd turn your head toward that person, taking some time to understand what was going on.

In one such study, some babies heard a 2-minute recording containing only babbles that followed an A-B-A syllable pattern, like *ga-ti-ga*, or *li-na-li*. Other babies heard a 2-minute recording containing only babbles that followed an A-B-B syllable pattern, like *ga-ti-ti* or *li-na-na*. Next, each group of babies heard new babbles that were either consistent or inconsistent with the patterns of the babbles they had just heard for 2 minutes. The babies whose new babbles were inconsistent stared much longer at the speaker that those babbles came from—as if intrigued or puzzled by the different sound—than the babies whose new babbles were consistent (Marcus et al., 1999). Studies like this one indicate that babies pick up speech patterns more quickly than we might realize, which helps them learn what kinds of sounds are common in their native languages (Koenig & Cole, 2013).

LIFE HACK 7.2

When you care for a baby, talk with him or her. The baby will learn more from conversing with you, even if the conversation contains lots of baby talk, than from hearing voices on TV or hearing nothing at all.

(Goldstein & West, 1999; Goldstein & Schwade, 2008; Gros-Louis et al., 2006)

One-Word Stage. After the babbling stage, usually around the first birthday, comes the **one-word stage**: a stage of speech development during which the young child uses a single word as a full sentence. If you've ever spent time around a 1-year old, you know that you have to rely on context to understand these one-word exclamations. Babies' imperfect pronunciation can make it even tougher (MacWhinney, 2001). For example, consider 1-year-old Megan saying, "Ca!" She could be referring to *cat*, and if she is, she could mean, "I want to pet the cat" or "I'm afraid of the cat." Or, she could be referring to her big sister, Catherine, and if she is, she could mean, "Yay, Catherine just walked into the room!" or "That's Catherine's toy." Or, she could be doing her best to say *clap*, which could be her recognition of someone clapping or her request to play a patty-cake clapping game. Your knowledge of what might be going on inside little Megan's mind—what's going on around her at the moment, what she's been learning about recently, what she's looking or pointing at—can be essential in deciphering what her one-word utterances mean.

There is remarkable similarity in the first words spoken by babies around the world. One study asked caregivers of hundreds of babies around a year old from three cultures that speak three different languages (Hong Kong, Beijing, and the United States) to report the first 10 words the babies said (Tardif et al., 2008). As **Table 7.5** illustrates, 6 words (listed here in their English forms) appeared in the top 20 for all three cultures: *mommy*, *daddy*, *hi/hello*, *bye*, *uh-oh*, and *woof-woof*. *Mommy* and *daddy* were actually in the top three in all three cultures. Also, babies in all three cultures produced far more nouns (words for things, people, etc.) among their first words than verbs, adjectives, or other kinds of words. The differences between the lists show interesting cultural trends: babies in the more collectivistic cultures of Beijing and Hong Kong produce more family-related words, like sister, brother, grandma, grandpa, auntie, and uncle, than babies in the more individualistic United States. Babies in the United States are also the only ones for whom the word *no* makes the top 20.

"Butterflies in your stomach" is an example of figurative language, in which metaphors, idioms, and proverbs are used to mean something different from what they literally say.

Expanding Language Use. Within months, those one-word utterances become two- and three-word utterances until kids form full sentences by age 3. Of course, kids' mastery of language is far from complete at that early age. Their vocabulary expands greatly during childhood, with a base of about 10,000 words by kindergarten (Anglin, 1993). Their ability to use language effectively—forming complex sentences accurately,

Babies in various cultures, speaking various languages, share some of the same first words. Here's a rank-ordered list of the words (translated into English from the Cantonese of Hong Kong and the Putonghua of Beijing) that appear most commonly among babies' first 10 words in three of those cultures. The words in bold print appear in all three lists.

TABLE 7.5: First Words Around the World

UNITED STATES	HONG KONG	BEIJING
Daddy	**Daddy**	**Mommy**
Mommy	Aah	**Daddy**
Baa baa	**Mommy**	Grandma-paternal
Bye	Yum yum	Grandpa-paternal
Hi	Sister-older	**Hello**
Uh oh	**Uh oh**	Hit
Grr	Hit	Uncle-paternal
Bottle	**Hello**	Grab
Yum yum	Milk	Auntie-maternal
Dog	Naughty	**Bye**
No	Brother-older	**Uh oh**
Woof woof	Grandma-maternal	Wow
Vroom	Grandma-paternal	Sister-older
Kitty	**Bye**	**Woof woof**
Ball	Bread	Brother-older
Baby	Auntie-maternal	Hug/hold
Duck	Ball	Light
Cat	Grandpa-paternal	Grandma-maternal
Ouch	Car	Egg
Banana	**Woof woof**	Vroom

Information from Tardif et al., 2008.

mastering irregular verbs (*went* rather than "*goed*"), even pronouncing tough words correctly (*spaghetti* rather than "*psgetti*")—continues to develop throughout childhood.

Figurative Language. From around age 9 through the teenage years, kids even master the challenges of *figurative language*—the metaphors, idioms, and proverbs that mean something different from what they literally say (Cacciari & Padovani, 2012; Nippold & Duthie, 2003; Levorato & Cacciari, 2002; Levorato et al., 2004). Our language is full of these figures of speech—about six of them per minute of conversation, according to one estimate—so wrapping your head around them (hey, "wrapping your head around"—there's one right there) is essential to fully understanding language (Glucksberg, 1989; Gibbs et al., 2012).

For example, if you say, "Break a leg!" to a 6-year-old before the kindergarten songfest, he might burst into tears, thinking that you hope he gets injured. But 10 years later, that same kid will know exactly what you mean when you use the same figurative language before the high school musical. Similarly, older kids are much better than younger kids at recognizing that having "butterflies in your stomach" does not mean that insects have flown into your open mouth, and that "we're all in the same boat" does not mean that anyone needs to put on a lifejacket. By the end of high school, kids have not only picked up hundreds of examples of figurative language, they have also expanded their vocabulary to about 50,000 words and growing (Gabig, 2014). As a result, they have mastered the basics of language.

Indirect Language. Of course, there is much more to language than the basics, so certain kinds of language development continue past the teenage years. For example, the use of *indirect language*—language that relies on implications and inferences rather than direct statements—develops well into adulthood (Coolidge & Wynn, 2012). To understand indirect language requires reading between the lines—understanding what is meant when the speaker hints at something rather than saying it outright. For

grammar
The set of rules within a language.

phoneme
The smallest distinct unit of speech.

example, if you meet someone at a party who says, "It's so loud in here—do you want to go to my place so we can talk?" that person may be just as interested in romance as conversation. If your next-door neighbor, who has complained several times about your loud music, asks, "Is that your new car? It's beautiful. I sure hope no one scratches it," that's a way of posing the threat, "If you don't turn that music down, I will scratch your car," without actually saying it.

Indirect language can serve many strategic purposes (Lee & Pinker, 2010; Pinker, 2007, 2011; Terkourafi, 2011). It enables people to get their messages across while still being able to deny they ever actually *said* it. That's quite valuable when the message is unacceptable in some way—illegal, immoral, or just impolite. Indirect language can also be a way to gauge the mind-set of the listener—to know if he or she is thinking along the same lines as the speaker. Once that feeling-out process is complete, the speaker knows whether the listener will be cooperative in the future. For example, if you did in fact keep your music quiet after your neighbor made that comment about scratches on your new car, your neighbor would know that you understood the unspoken message and might be more likely to use such messages in the future.

The Rules of Language: Grammar

Grammar is the set of rules within a language. If you're fluent in any language, you know its grammar by heart. Though grammar rulebooks may have helped, it is likely that you learned it primarily through immersion, lots of experience listening to and speaking your language. Grammar is so woven into language that it's easy to take it for granted. In fact, the best reminders that grammar governs language take place when we hear someone break grammatical rules. For example, when native Spanish speakers begin to learn English, their speech often contains some minor differences from the speech of native English speakers. English words that start with the letters "st-" are pronounced as if they start with "est-," so "study" sounds like "estudy." The wording of questions can also seem out of order to native English speakers, "You are hungry?" rather than "Are you hungry?" Both of these distinctions, of course, stem from Spanish grammar, but the fact that they sound unusual to English speakers highlights the fact that there are some powerful underlying rules to the way each language operates (Wasow, 2001).

Phonemes. Language includes everything from the formation of words to the formation of sentences, so it makes sense that grammar can be broken down into rules for each level. At the smallest level, *phonology* is how sounds are combined to form words (Owens, 2014). Each one of those sounds is a **phoneme**: the smallest distinct unit of speech. You might automatically equate phonemes with the letters of the alphabet, but phonemes are the *sounds* the letters make, not the letters themselves. In English, the same phoneme can be produced by multiple letters, such as the *k* sound in these words: *c*ar, *k*angaroo, *ch*orus, plu*ck*, Ira*q*. Or the same letter can produce different phonemes, such as the way *j* is used in these words: *j*ump, *j*alapeño, hallelu*j*ah. Or multiple letters can combine to form a single phoneme, as in *sh* (*sh*op), *ph* (*ph*one), and *ch* (*ch*ill). That is why *Wheel of Fortune* can be so tough when only a few letters are showing—you can't always be sure what phonemes those letters represent.

When words are short and simple, combining phonemes is easy. For example, the three phonemes represented by the letters *c*, *u*, and *p* combine to form the word *cup*. Longer and more complex words are more challenging, but the rules of phonemes help you sound them out (Cohn, 2001). Words borrowed from other languages containing phonemes that English doesn't feature can also be difficult. For example, the first sound in the French-derived word *genre* (softer than the *g* in *giant*) or the last sound in the Vietnamese soup *pho* (shorter than the *o* in *go*) can be tough for some English speakers to say. Words from other languages can also present phonemic challenges when the letters appear out of order, at least according to the grammar of your first language. For example, former NFL quarterback Brett Favre's name contains the unusual (in English) "vr" sequence, but most fans (and Favre himself, for that matter), have taken the liberty of flipping those two letters so they can go with the more familiar "rv" sound and pronounce the name as if it rhymes with *carve*.

A phoneme is the smallest distinct unit of speech. In English, when a word or name borrows a phoneme from another language, speakers often convert it to a more familiar phoneme. That explains why the last name of Hall of Fame NFL quarterback Brett Favre is typically pronounced as if it contains the sequence "rv," when in fact the sequence is "vr." Al Bello/Getty Images

Morphemes. The next level of grammar is *morphology*, which involves combining bits of language—not just phonemes, but bits with specific meanings (Spencer, 2001). Each one of these little bits of language is a **morpheme**: the smallest meaningful unit of a language. Morphemes can be full words (like *play*), but they can also be parts of words, like the prefix *re-* to signify something happening again (*re*play) or the suffix *-ed* to signify that something happened in the past (play*ed*). More morphemes can be linked together to form more complex words. For example, *antidisestablishmentarianism* has quite a few morphemes!

People new to a language often have a difficult time learning when *not* to use certain morphemes (Levey, 2013). For example, in English we usually add the morpheme *-s* at the end of a word to make it plural, but there are some cases when we change the letter before the *-s* as well (*knife* becomes *knives*, not *knifes*), and other cases in which we abandon that grammatical rule altogether (*child* becomes *children*, not *childs*).

"What can I say? I was an English major."

Syntax. The next level of grammar is **syntax**: the rules by which words are put together to make phrases and sentences. Syntax helps you put together your statements in ways that others will understand, especially regarding the order of the nouns, verbs, adjectives, and other types of speech (Garnham, 2005; Baker, 2001). For example, if you said, "Your shoe is untied," your syntax would be perfectly understandable. Slight bendings of syntax rules are typically easy enough to understand. For example, Yoda from *Star Wars* might say, "Untied your shoe is." However, if you said, "Shoe your untied is," you'd be breaking the rules of syntax so badly that it would confuse others. Syntax rules typically involve at least a noun and verb in each statement, but the order may vary from one language to another. For example, a Spanish speaker might introduce himself by saying, *"Me llamo Esteban"* ("Myself I call Esteban"), but in English he might say, "I call myself Steven."

Semantics. A final level of grammar involves the comprehension of language rather than the production of it. **Semantics** is the rules by which you extract meaning from words and sentences. Semantics is at work when you automatically translate the words and sentences that you've heard other people say into the meaning they are trying to convey (Lappin, 2001). For example, if your friend Kara utters the words, "I might dye my hair," you instantly know five things: (1) "I" is Kara. (2) "Might" indicates the following action is a possibility rather than a sure thing. (3) "Dye" means color (as opposed to "die," meaning the ending of life). (4) "My" refers to something belonging to Kara. And (5) "hair" refers to what's growing out of Kara's head. You also can synthesize those five individual meanings into the single idea that she is trying to convey: she's considering a change to her look, and she's apparently interested in your opinion. If you think of Kara's statement as a package she delivered to you, semantics is what allows you to unpack it. She had that idea in her mind, translated it into language, sent that language aloud to you. Then, you used semantics to decode the language so that you could hold her idea in your mind. This is pretty impressive considering that whole semantic process takes just a fraction of a second.

FIGURE 7.5 How It Feels to Go Home. Extralinguistic information like tone of voice and nonverbal cues is crucial to human speech. When we text, we often include emojis to communicate exactly how we mean what we say. These texts provide very different information about how this person feels about going home, even though the words remain exactly the same.

Extralinguistic Information. Even more impressive, when listening to Kara, you appreciate not only *what* she said but also *how* she said it. That is because in addition to paying attention to her language, you're paying attention to her **extralinguistic information**: components of language other than the literal meaning of the words. Extralinguistic information can include the volume, pitch, or speed of spoken words. Often, it communicates a speaker's emotions or intentions just as powerfully as the words themselves. (Of course, if you can see the speaker, extralinguistic information can also include facial expressions, gestures, and other visual cues.)

Extralinguistic information is the difference between reading a screenplay and seeing it acted out. The way the speakers say the lines can bring meaning to them that the written page simply can't provide. That is why you have to add emojis to your words sometimes when you text (**Figure 7.5**)—without those hints about how you mean the words you're texting, the recipient might understand the message incompletely or incorrectly. That is also why, in some cases, you feel the need to call rather than text—when you want the other person to hear *how* your words come out. In

Kara's case, if she exclaims, "I might dye my hair!" with excitement and quickness in her voice, she's letting you know that she's leaning toward doing it and she's expecting you to support her. If she mutters, "I *miiiight* dye my hair...," emphasizing "might" and trailing off at the end, she's letting you know that she's considering it, but she's definitely not sold on it.

Research has found that extralinguistic information can have a powerful influence on communication. One study played brief audio clips of politicians speaking on C-SPAN. These clips were specifically edited to omit any meaningful political comments, but to include just enough words to give the participant a chance to rate the attractiveness of the politician's voice. Politicians with more attractive voices were rated as more competent and trustworthy than politicians with less attractive voices, even when both voices were paired with identical photos (Surawski & Ossoff, 2006).

Another study adjusted the pitch of recordings of former U.S. presidents' speeches and then asked participants to rate those presidents' personality characteristics. Participants rated the lower-pitched versions as more honest and intelligent and less likely to be involved in a scandal than the higher-pitched versions (Tigue et al., 2012). Another study found that participants listening to 2-second clips of phone calls between two other people—just the question "How are you?"—could reliably guess whether the speaker was addressing a friend or a romantic partner based on vocal qualities like tone and pitch (Farley et al., 2013).

morpheme
The smallest meaningful unit of a language.

syntax
The rules by which words are put together to make phrases and sentences.

semantics
The rules by which a person extracts meaning from words and sentences.

extralinguistic information
Components of language other than the literal meaning of the words.

dialect
A group's particular version of a language with its own unique characteristics.

Dialect. Another illustration of the importance of *how* language is spoken comes from **dialect**: a group's particular version of a language with its own unique characteristics. Dialect includes accent, but it is much more than that. Dialect can influence the way we shape our sentences, the way we conjugate verbs, the expressions we use, and the words we choose as well. U.S. English is full of dialects. Many are based on region, but dialects can also center around ethnicity, age, social class, or other variables (Labov et al., 2006; Akmajian et al., 2010).

Imagine that you're standing on a street corner and you notice that across both streets, there is a boy wearing sleeping clothes. If you were raised in the northern United States, you're likely to say, "Look *kitty-corner, you guys*! He's wearing pa-*jah*-mas!" But if you were raised in the South, you're likely to say, "Look *catty-corner, y'all*! He's wearing pa-*ja*-mas!" (Vaux, 2003). Dialects of English are often even more distinct when we compare the United States to other countries that speak the language, such as Australia, Canada, and England (where gasoline is petrol, an apartment is a flat, and an elevator is a lift). **Figure 7.6** illustrates one of the linguistic questions that divides the U.S. dialects most clearly: what do you call carbonated soft drinks?

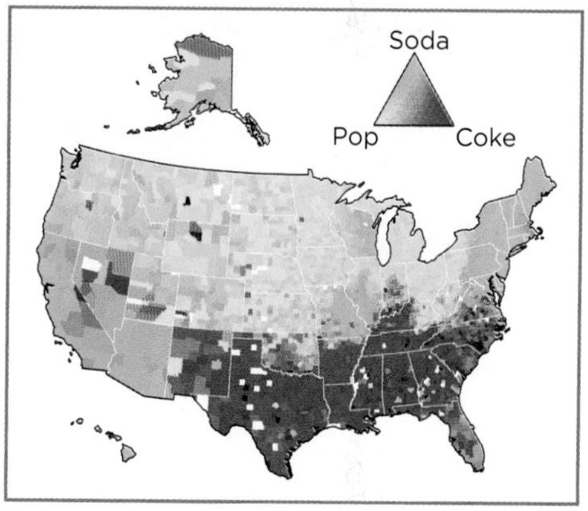

FIGURE 7.6 Soda, Pop, or Coke? What word do you use for *soft drink*? Throughout the United States, it depends on dialect. It's *soda* in Maine, *pop* in Montana, and *Coke* in Mississippi. Information from popvssoda.com.

CURRENT CONTROVERSY

What Is Texting Doing to Language?

"Texting is bleak, bald, sad shorthand, which masks dyslexia, poor spelling and mental laziness." This statement comes from a prominent professor in England (Crystal, 2008), but you may have heard your parents, high school teachers, or college professors say that texting is the demise of language, reducing young people's literacy.

Texting is so new that research on its effects has only begun, but most of the available evidence suggests that the negative claims are false. Some studies have found that reading textisms (words spelled the way they are in texts, like "2nite" and "gr8") have no negative effects on the ability to spell properly (Powell & Dixon, 2011; Plester et al., 2008). In one study, 9- and 10-year-old kids who hadn't yet gotten their first phone were given one for a 10-week period. Their spelling actually improved, and they continued to develop their reading and writing skills as their classmates without phones did (Wood et al., 2011). Other studies found that among college students, larger numbers of texts correlated with better reading accuracy and fluency (Drouin, 2011; Kemp, 2010).

Language expert John McWhorter makes the argument that texting is not the destruction of standard language, but is the development of an entirely new language with a grammar all its own (McWhorter, 2013a). In a widely viewed TED Talk, McWhorter calls texting "fingered speech," and claims that it actually comes closer to speech—the original form of language, and the only one that humans had throughout most of their history—than any other kind of writing does. He also claims that people who text are becoming bilingual, and their fluency in texting language will enhance their overall cognitive abilities. He even describes texting as a "linguistic miracle happening right under our noses" (McWhorter, 2013b).

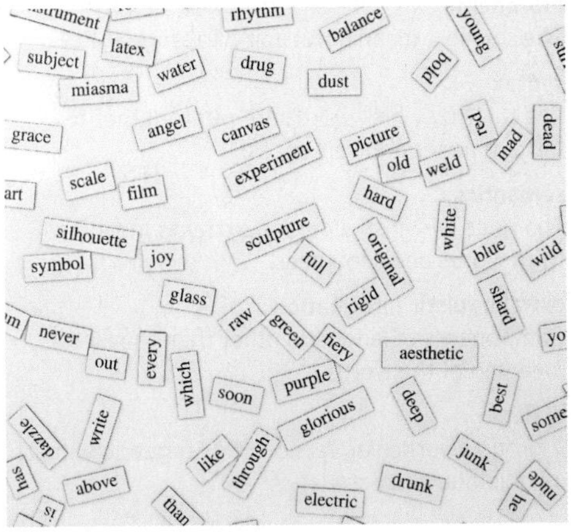

The theory of linguistic relativity states that language influences thought. To the extent this theory is correct, the size of your vocabulary affects the breadth of your thinking. matabum/Shutterstock

Does Language Influence Thinking?

Think of your vocabulary as a box of those magnet words that you have probably seen scattered on a refrigerator. The number and type of words contained in the box would certainly affect the sentences you could create. But would they also affect the thoughts you could think? Would a huge box of words enable you to think more broadly? Would lots of words in a particular category—for example, dozens of words for colors, rather than just the primary ones—make you more likely to be an expert in that area? These are the questions surrounding **linguistic relativity**: the theory that language influences thought.

A well-known early study of linguistic relativity strongly claimed that language did in fact influence, and often limit, thinking (Whorf, 1956). But current experts continue to debate the issue (Gleitman & Papafragou, 2013; Reiger et al., 2010; Pederson et al., 1998). Those who oppose linguistic relativity point out that your language could never keep up with your thoughts, no matter what kind of vocabulary you possess. Even if you are an eloquent speaker, your words are just a rough sketch of the full range of thoughts rapidly running through your mind (Gleitman & Papafragou, 2013; Papafragou, 2007; Bloom, 2002; Clark, 1992). For example, if you send a text that says "Home at 7," that language is really an abbreviation of the full-length thought you had: "I'm leaving my current location now, and I estimate travel between my current location and home to require 25 minutes. It's 6:35 now, so according to the laws of mathematics, I should arrive home at 7 P.M."

Other opponents of linguistic relativity point out that the mere fact that languages differ does not necessarily mean that its speakers think differently. In fact, when you consider the great diversity of languages around the world, our thinking seems remarkably similar (McWhorter, 2014). For example, consider the people who speak North Saami. They live near the Arctic Circle in Sweden, Finland, and Norway, where they herd reindeer across wide swaths of land. Ice and snow are major parts of their daily lives. To get by, they need to know whether ice on a lake is thick enough to walk on without cracking, or thin enough for their reindeer to break through to graze. They need to know whether snow has fallen evenly or in random drifts, and whether snow has a path from previous travelers or remains untouched. It should come as no surprise, then, that North Saami features dozens of words for what we simply call "ice," and dozens more for what we simply call "snow." For example, *rovda* is ice too thin to support the weight of a reindeer; *čođđi* is ice over stones or trees; *oppas* is snow that has not yet been walked across; and *čahki* is snow in hard lumps (Magga, 2006). But regarding linguistic relativity, the key question is this: does that linguistic difference mean that they think differently about ice and snow than we do?

Those who support the theory of linguistic relativity would say yes to that question, and they offer some fascinating examples of the relationship between language and thought (Boroditsky, 2011). For example, in a language (Kuuk Thaayorre) spoken by an Australian aboriginal tribe, there are no words for left or right. Instead, speakers of this language rely much more on the directions—north, south, east, and west—to orient themselves. One researcher asked a group of Kuuk Thaayorre–speaking 5-year-olds to point southeast, and they did it instantly and correctly. Later at a professional conference, she asked a room full of English-speaking adults to point southeast, and they hesitated, struggled, and mostly got it wrong. She didn't ask Kuuk Thaayorre–speaking adults to point southeast because she didn't want to insult their intelligence: It would be like testing your ability to point to the left (Boroditsky, 2012)!

In another study, the same researcher gave participants a sequence of cards that depicted an action (like frames of a cartoon) and asked participants to put them in order from start to finish. For example, a set of five cards may have shown a person picking up a banana, peeling it, holding the banana with one bite missing, holding the banana with several bites missing, and then holding the empty peel (**Figure 7.7**). When English speakers put the cards in order, they automatically arranged them left to right. When Kuuk Thaayorre speakers put the cards in order, they automatically arranged them east to west—corresponding to the way the sun moves as time progresses—no matter what direction they happened to be facing at that moment (Boroditsky & Gaby, 2006).

Another study of linguistic relativity focused on German and Spanish, two languages that are *gendered*, which means some nouns are feminine and some are masculine

linguistic relativity
The theory that language influences thought.

intelligence
The ability to gain knowledge and learn from experience.

general intelligence (*g*)
Overall intelligence that applies across all tasks and situations.

specific intelligences (*s*)
Intelligences that apply to only a particular area.

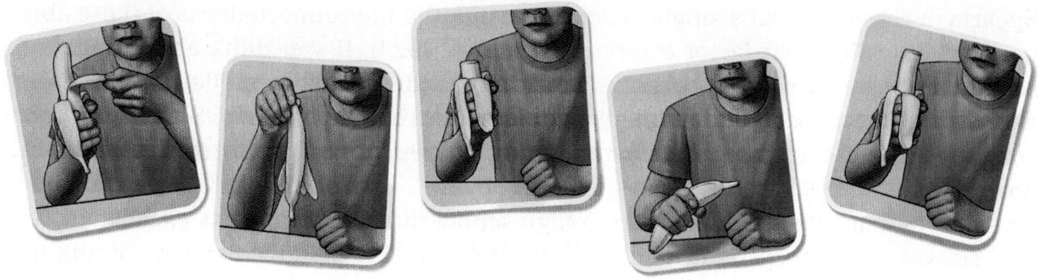

FIGURE 7.7 Left to Right or East to West? When given sets of cards like these, English speakers had no problem arranging them in sequential order. Neither did Kuuk Thaayhorre speakers. But while English speakers automatically arranged them left to right, Kuuk Thaayorre speakers arranged them east to west, no matter what direction they were facing when they did it. Kuuk Thaayorre has no words for left or right, so they rely on the movement of the sun (east to west) to orient themselves, suggesting some degree of linguistic relativity. Information from Boroditsky & Gaby, 2006.

(Boroditsky et al., 2003). The researchers found a few nouns that are masculine in one language and feminine in the other, and then asked native speakers of each language to describe those objects. The word for *key* is masculine in German, and German speakers described keys with words like hard, heavy, jagged, and useful—a masculine-sounding set of adjectives. The word for *key* is feminine in Spanish, and Spanish speakers described keys with feminine-sounding adjectives like lovely, little, golden, shiny, and intricate. Then the researchers tried *bridge*, which is feminine in German and masculine in Spanish. German speakers described bridges as beautiful, elegant, pretty, and fragile. Spanish speakers described bridges as big, strong, sturdy, and dangerous. Collectively, these studies suggest that language may influence thought in some meaningful ways, though it is an overstatement to say that "language is a straitjacket for thought" (Boroditsky, 2012, p. 628).

CHECK YOUR LEARNING:

7.15 How do psychologists define language?

7.16 How do researchers think language may have evolved?

7.17 What is the difference between the nativist theory and nonnativist theories of language development?

7.18 What are the stages of a child's language development?

7.19 What is grammar and what are its four levels?

7.20 What forms of extralinguistic information can influence communication?

7.21 What is linguistic relativity, and how widely is it accepted among experts in the field?

Intelligence

YOU WILL LEARN:

7.22 how psychologists define intelligence.

7.23 about the difference between general intelligence and specific intelligences and how they fit into a hierarchical model of intelligence.

7.24 about multiple intelligences.

7.25 what emotional intelligence is.

7.26 how the nature–nurture debate applies to intelligence.

7.27 how psychologists measure intelligence.

7.28 about different types of intelligence tests.

Intelligence is the ability to gain knowledge and learn from experience. Actually, the word *ability* in that definition is controversial. Since the early days of psychology, there has been quite a debate about whether the singular word *ability* in that definition should be replaced with the plural word *abilities* (Sternberg, 2000; Wasserman & Tulsky, 2005) In other words, is intelligence one thing or many separate things?

One Intelligence or Many?

Those who argue that intelligence is one thing support the notion of **general intelligence** (or simply ***g***): overall intelligence that applies across all tasks and situations. Those on the other side of the argument support the notion of **specific intelligences** (or simply ***s***): intelligences that apply to only a particular area. The first champion of general intelligence was Charles Spearman, a prominent figure in psychology in the early 1900s. Spearman was among the first to measure mental abilities (like reading, writing, math ability, and sensory abilities) scientifically. He observed that there were strong positive correlations among those various abilities for most of his participants. If the person was good at one of the mental abilities, that person was probably good at all of them.

YOU WILL LEARN: *(Continued)*

7.29 about the difference between intelligence tests and achievement tests.

7.30 about the extremes of intelligence.

7.31 how psychologists evaluate measures of intelligence.

7.32 what test bias is and why intelligence tests should avoid it.

7.33 how stereotype threat can negatively influence test-taking.

7.34 about group differences on intelligence tests and the controversy that surrounds them.

Spearman reasoned that a single factor must underlie the connectedness of these abilities, and he called that factor *g* (Spearman, 1904, 1923). If you think about your high school classmates, you may remember that many of the kids who excelled in one subject excelled in others too. If so, you might come to a conclusion similar to Spearman's: how smart you are, in the most fundamental sense, influences your performance across the board.

But you may also remember from high school that some students excelled in certain classes while they struggled mightily in others. Those kids' patterns of abilities support the viewpoint of Louis Thurstone, Spearman's primary opponent in the intelligence debates. Thurstone relied on a statistical process called *factor analysis*, which determines which variables in a long list tend to cluster together. If intelligence is in fact a single thing, a factor analysis of different cognitive tasks would reveal only one big cluster. But if intelligence is made up of different things, a factor analysis would reveal several different clusters (like verbal ability, math ability, and memory), and that is what Thurstone found. Thurstone's findings led him to claim that there isn't a single underlying intelligence that determines how well you perform across the board. Instead, there are different specific intelligences, some of which may be stronger than others, that cause your abilities to potentially differ (Thurstone, 1938; Brody, 2000; Mackintosh, 2011).

MY TAKE VIDEO 7.2

Intelligence

"I think it definitely plays a part in everything..."

YOUTUBE: http://tiny.cc/mytake
LAUNCHPAD: launchpadworks.com

Both Spearman and Thurstone eventually acknowledged that the other one had a point. There is no denying either general intelligence or specific intelligences, they reasoned, so a *hierarchical model of intelligence* seems ideal: one that contains numerous specific intelligences, each of which is considered a part of a single general intelligence (**Figure 7.8**).

In the years since the intelligence debates between Spearman and Thurstone, other experts have offered specific versions of the hierarchical model (Willis et al., 2011; Davidson & Kemp, 2011). In the 1960s and 1970s, James Cattell argued that general intelligence is made up of two primary specific intelligences: *fluid intelligence*, or the ability to solve new problems, and *crystallized intelligence*, or stored knowledge (Cattell, 1971; Horn & Cattell, 1966).

In the 1990s, John Carroll developed a *three-stratum theory* of intelligence, in which a singular general intelligence contains a handful of broad specific intelligences, and then each of those broad specific intelligences contains several much more specific intelligences (Carroll, 1993). (*Stratum* means layer, and Carrol's theory says that intelligence contains three of them: *g*, big *s*, and little *s*.) For example, you may have a certain overall intelligence (*g*), a certain memory ability (big *s*) within that, and a more particular short-term memory ability (little *s*) within that.

More recently, Carroll's work has been integrated with that of others into the *Cattell–Horn–Carroll (CHC) theory of intelligence*, which proposes a single general intelligence, 10 broad abilities, and over 70 more narrow abilities (Kaufman et al., 2013; Horn & Noll, 1997; Flanagan et al., 2000, 2013). The main point here is that these various hierarchical models of intelligence all include a general or overall intelligence, as well as one or two levels of more specific intelligences contained within it.

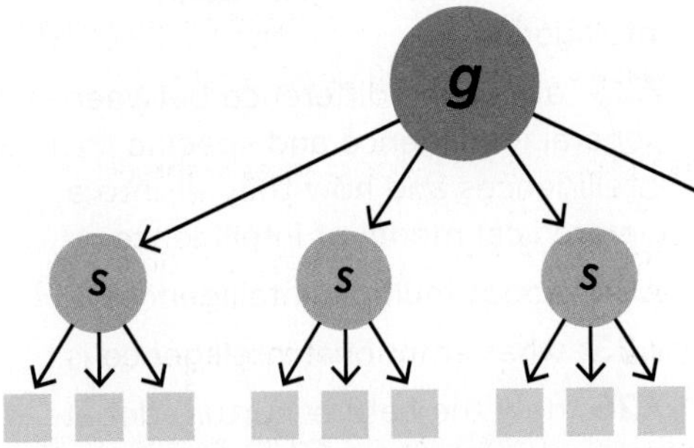

FIGURE 7.8 Hierarchical Model of Intelligence. According to the hierarchical model of intelligence, you have a general intelligence (*g*) that is made up of several specific intelligences (*s*), each of which can be further broken down into more particular abilities.

Multiple Intelligences

According to the hierarchical theories of intelligence described previously, your overall intelligence is essentially a combination of your separate intelligences. Some experts disagree with the notion that those separate intelligences should be combined (Davis et al., 2011). These experts believe that our separate intelligences are as distinct as apples and oranges. This belief is known as the *multiple intelligences* approach, and its most widely respected proponent is Howard Gardner (Gardner, 1985, 1995, 1999). In the 1980s, Gardner identified and defined eight distinct intelligences (he added a ninth more recently) that each of us possess to one degree or another. Gardner required an ability to have certain characteristics to count as an intelligence. For example, it must correspond to specific locations in the brain (as indicated by the connections between

certain kinds of brain damage and certain kinds of impairment), and it must be something in which at least a few people (savants) have naturally exceptional capabilities.

Gardner's multiple intelligences are described in **Table 7.6**. They include the kinds of intelligences that relate to success in school or standardized tests—such as *linguistic* intelligence and *logico-mathematical* intelligence, but also nonacademic intelligences—such as *bodily–kinesthetic* intelligence (at which athletes and dancers would excel) and *naturalistic* intelligence (at which farmers, hikers, and other outdoorsy types would excel) (Gardner, 2006).

Some intelligence experts have argued that even Gardner's broad view of multiple intelligences is too limited. They assert that other abilities—some of which matter little at school, but a lot outside of school—deserve to be recognized as parts of the intelligence puzzle (Austin & Saklofske, 2005). For example, some have pointed out that the ability to maintain harmonious relationships with friends and family is a core element of intelligence as defined in many parts of the non-Western world (Niu & Brass, 2011). Other researchers have proposed *cultural* intelligence (how well you respond to situations of cultural diversity) and even *mating* intelligence (how good you are at dating and forming romantic relationships) (Ang et al., 2011; Ang & Van Dyne, 2008; Earley & Ang, 2003; Geher & Kaufman, 2011).

Still other intelligence experts argue for the acknowledgment of more real-world kinds of intelligence, often called *practical* intelligence or *successful* intelligence—the kind of street smarts that help you get by in your day-to-day lives just as much as book smarts do (Wagner, 2011; Wagner & Sternberg, 1985; Sternberg, 1999). One study illustrated the distinctiveness of real-world intelligence by asking child street vendors in Brazil to make change—something they do many times every day when their customers pay for goods with large bills (Carraher et al., 1985). When they were given the change-making task as a pencil-and-paper arithmetic problem (for example, 500 – 50 = ?), only 37% got it right. But when they were actually handed a 500-cruzeiros bill to pay for a 50-cruzeiros item, 98% of them correctly handed back 450 cruzeiros in change. (Cruzeiros were the currency in Brazil at the time of the study.) These street vendors struggled to do an abstract written problem but had little problem calculating a meaningful real-world task.

emotional intelligence
A person's ability to sense and manage his or her own emotions as well as the emotions of others.

Practical intelligence is the street smarts needed to successfully complete the tasks necessary in daily life. For street vendors, practical intelligence involves making change correctly, whether or not they can do a corresponding math problem with pencil and paper. Alex Treadway/National Geographic/Getty Images

Emotional Intelligence

Of all of the nontraditional types of intelligence proposed by researchers, the most prominent is **emotional intelligence**: the ability to sense and manage emotions in yourself and others. Emotional intelligence is a relatively recent development in psychology—the first articles and books on the topic came out in the 1990s—but it has received lots of attention since that time (Salovey & Mayer, 1989; Goleman, 1998, 2006; Mayer & Salovey, 1997; Salovey, 2005). Emotional intelligence has four branches (Mayer et al., 2008):

- **Accurately perceiving emotions in yourself and others.** How well can you read your mom's facial expressions or tone of voice? How sensitive are you to your own stress level?
- **Using emotions to facilitate thinking.** If you sense that your mom is sad, will you rethink your plan to ask her for a big favor, and instead give her a chance to talk about her own problems? If you sense that you are stressed out, will you make it a priority to figure out how to reduce your stress?
- **Understanding emotions.** If your mom is indeed sad, what might this mean—problems with her job, her friends or family, her health, or something else? If you are indeed stressed out, what could this signify about the lifestyle you've been living?
- **Managing emotions.** What actions can you intentionally take to help lift your mom's sadness? What behaviors can you deliberately do to reduce your own stress levels?

TABLE 7.6: Gardner's Theory of Multiple Intelligences

INTELLIGENCE	PEOPLE WITH HIGH LEVELS EXCEL AT...
Linguistic	Writing, speaking, and understanding language.
Logico-mathematical	Math, science, logic, and problem solving.
Spatial	Reasoning about physical objects in three-dimensional space.
Musical	Playing instruments, singing, and creating and appreciating music.
Bodily-kinesthetic	Dancing, sports, and movement-related tasks.
Interpersonal	Interacting with others, as well as understanding others' thoughts and feelings.
Intrapersonal	Self-awareness.
Naturalistic	Understanding and appreciating plants, animals, weather, and other aspects of the environment.
Existential	Contemplating the meaning of life and other deep philosophical topics.

FROM RESEARCH TO REAL LIFE

Intelligence Correlates with...

Experts may debate the definition of intelligence, but there is little debate about how powerfully it correlates with a number of real-world outcomes. It is probably no surprise that intelligence is linked to how well students do in school and how many adults do in their careers (Deary et al., 2007; Kaufman et al., 2012; Naglieri & Bornstein, 2003; Rohde & Thompson, 2007; Schmidt & Hunter, 2004). But intelligence also correlates with many other things. (Keep in mind that a correlation does not necessarily mean causation.) Specifically, higher intelligence correlates with:

- higher socioeconomic status (SES) (Neisser et al., 1996; Strenze, 2007)
- higher income (several hundred dollars annually per IQ point increase) (Zagorsky, 2007)
- higher levels of extraversion and lower levels of neuroticism and psychoticism (Ackerman & Heggestad, 1997)
- longer life span (Batty et al., 2007)
- better physical health (Gottfredson & Deary, 2004)
- higher likelihood of having an opinion about politics and higher likelihood of that opinion being near the center of the political spectrum rather than at an extreme (Rindermann et al., 2012)

Advocates of emotional intelligence claim that it is a vital and often underrated factor across most areas of your life, from school to work to health to relationships (Schulze et al., 2005; Neubauer & Freudenthaler, 2005). As an example, consider the importance of emotional intelligence in one important situation: a job interview. Robert's education, experience, and résumé all suggest to the interviewer that he is smart enough to handle the job—that's how he landed the interview in the first place. During the interview, however, he shows some signs of low *emotional* intelligence. At one point, Robert misreads the interviewer's facial expressions, mistakenly thinking she disapproves of his answer when she's just giving it serious thought. He becomes overly concerned about this perceived disapproval, so he decides to tell a joke, which backfires and confuses the interviewer. The interview still might be salvageable at this point, but Robert gets so angry at himself that he pounds the desk and shouts, "I'm so stupid!" At that point, he begins to cry while begging the interviewer for another chance. No matter how impressive his credentials might be, these mistakes in terms of reading emotions, using emotions as cues for behavior, and controlling emotions made it clear that Robert might not be the best person for the job.

Research suggests that emotional intelligence correlates with job performance (Abraham, 2005; O'Boyle et al., 2011; Van Rooy & Viswesvaran, 2004). Employees who are high in emotional intelligence are more likely to emerge as leaders among their coworkers, and leaders high in emotional intelligence are more effective in managing their workers than leaders low in emotional intelligence (Côté et al., 2010; Mandell & Pherwani, 2003; George, 2000; Rosete & Ciarrochi, 2005). Emotional intelligence correlates with other desirable outcomes too, including physical health, mental health, high-quality relationships with friends and family, academic achievement, and avoidance of alcohol and tobacco by teens (Mayer et al., 2008; Trinidad & Johnson, 2002; Schutte et al., 2007). The value of emotional intelligence has become so widely recognized that many schools now teach lessons in emotional intelligence (Goetz et al., 2005). Some researchers have quibbled that emotional intelligence is perhaps more of a personality trait than an intelligence, but there is little doubt of its significance or its impact on day-to-day functioning (Perez et al., 2005; Austin & Saklofske, 2005).

Emotional intelligence is the ability to sense and manage emotions in yourself and others. Your emotional intelligence can influence the success of many of your interactions, including job interviews.
ONOKY - Eric Audras/Brand X Pictures/Getty Images

Nature, Nurture, and Intelligence

The nature–nurture debate that runs through psychology applies to intelligence as much as any other variable. What determines your intelligence—your genes or your environment? The short answer is both. There is simply no way to dismiss either the genes with which you are born or the surroundings in which you live as influences on your intelligence (**Table 7.7**).

A better question, then, is how much influence does each factor have? This question has been answered primarily through twin studies and adoption studies. In twin studies, researchers can compare identical (monozygotic) twins to non-identical

TABLE 7.7: Gene-ius

TYPE OF SIBLINGS	CORRELATION BETWEEN SIBLINGS' INTELLIGENCE LEVELS
Monozygotic (identical) twins raised together	.86
Monozygotic (identical) twins raised apart	.72
Dizygotic (non-identical) twins raised together	.60
Nontwin siblings raised together	.47
Nontwin siblings raised apart	.24

Data from Bouchard & McGue, 1981; Deary et al., 2006.

As the amount of shared genes increases, the correlations between siblings' IQ increases. That correlation gets very high for identical twins, but it doesn't reach 1.00, suggesting that the environment has some influence. The fact that pairs raised together have higher correlations than the same type of pairs raised apart also points to the importance of the environment.

(dizygotic) twins. Identical twins share all of their genes, but non-identical twins share only half. If identical twins' intelligence levels match more often than non-identical twins' intelligence levels match, that would suggest that genes play a powerful role. In adoption studies, researchers can compare the intelligence levels of adopted kids with their adoptive parents and biological parents. To the extent that kids' intelligence levels are similar to their adoptive parents, environment matters; to the extent that kids' intelligence levels are similar to their biological parents, genes matter. These studies have produced a number of key findings (Nisbett et al., 2012; Rizzi & Posthuma, 2013; Mandelman & Grigorenko, 2011; Neisser et al., 1996; Bouchard, 2013; Bouchard et al., 1990; Bouchard & McGue, 1981, 2003; Bartels et al., 2002; Deary et al., 2006):

- **Overall, genes have a substantial influence on intelligence.** Estimates of the heritability of intelligence vary across studies but tend to hover in the 50–75% range. This suggests that to a significant extent, when it comes to intelligence, you're born with it. However, it also leaves plenty of room for impact by the environment.
- **Heritability rates depend on when intelligence is measured.** Compared to a young child's intelligence, an adult's intelligence is much more likely to follow predictions based on genetic inheritance. It is not uncommon to find a 4-year-old whose intelligence doesn't match his or her biological parents' intelligence, but it is quite uncommon to find a 40-year-old who shows such a mismatch with his or her parents.
- **There are many important environmental variables.** The way you were raised, the schools you attend, the jobs you get, the food you eat, the socioeconomic level at which you live, and the people with whom you interact all have the power to affect your intelligence.
- **Genes and environment interact in complex ways**. Consider Sean, a child with bright parents who, because of his genetic inheritance of intelligence, is one of the smartest kids in his elementary school. His parents notice his intelligence and foster it with after-school activities and brain-training computer games. His teachers also notice his intelligence and challenge him with customized class work and advanced educational opportunities. These new environmental influences further boost Sean's intelligence. As a young adult, Sean enrolls in an academically rigorous college and surrounds himself with classmates and professors who keep his mind sharp. Sean's genes not only affect his intelligence directly, they also influence the kinds of environments in which he lives, and those environments further influence his intelligence.

An intelligence test is an assessment technique used by psychologists to numerically measure intelligence. BSIP/UIG Via Getty Images

As we've seen in the previous sections, there are plenty of psychologists who study intelligence, but there are even more who measure it. In fact, among clinical psychologists (like me), measuring intelligence is among the most common professional activities besides conducting interviews and therapy (Watkins et al., 1995; Camara et al., 2000; Cashel, 2002; Archer & Newsom, 2000). We do this by administering an **intelligence test**: an assessment technique used by psychologists to numerically measure intelligence.

intelligence test
An assessment technique used by psychologists to numerically measure intelligence.

When you picture a psychologist giving a client an intelligence test, do not picture the psychologist handing the client a question booklet, an answer sheet, and a #2

"I'm sorry—his I.Q. is actually on the charts."

pencil. Also, do not picture the client taking the intelligence test on a computer. Many of the so-called "intelligence tests" floating around on the Internet make psychologists cringe. They're more about making money from Web site ads than giving you a legitimate measure of your intelligence (Burnett, 2013).

Intelligence tests are face-to-face interactions. To learn to give them, the psychologist takes one course (or more) in graduate school in which the focus is learning to administer, score, and interpret these tests (Raiford et al., 2010). Typically, the psychologist and the client sit on opposite sides of a table or desk. The psychologist's setup generally includes a test manual to guide him or her through all parts, or *subtests*, of the test in a standardized way; a blank form on which to write down the client's responses; and often a small collection of items such as pictures, objects, and brief written activities that the psychologist will share with the client at various points in the test. Most subtests involve the psychologist asking questions out loud, the client responding out loud, and the psychologist writing down what the client says. The intelligence test typically lasts between 30 minutes and 3 hours. When it is over, the psychologist assigns points to the client's responses, calculates the appropriate scores, and writes up the results in the form of a report.

Intelligence Quotient (IQ). The primary result of the intelligence test is the **intelligence quotient (IQ)**: a single number used to represent a person's overall intelligence. Keep in mind that before the publishers of an intelligence test make it available to psychologists, they administer it to hundreds or thousands of people of various ages. That way, they can collect data on how many points were earned by people at every age. This process establishes age-based *normative data* (or *norms*) for the test. When a psychologist later buys the test, the manual that comes with it includes this normative data.

IQ has a median of 100. As scores move up from 100, they indicate above-average intelligence. As scores move down from 100, they indicate below-average intelligence. Those scores have to move up or down a sizable amount to make a meaningful difference. A person whose IQ is just a couple of points above or below 100 is still in the average range.

As Figure 7.9 indicates, over two-thirds of people have IQs that fall within 15 points of 100. (The *standard deviation*, which we covered back in Chapter 1, of IQ tests is 15.) About 95% fall within 30 points of the mean and about 99%, within 45 points of the mean. The illustration of this finding, as featured in **Figure 7.9**, is known as the **normal curve**: a graph showing that the frequency of scores on a test is greatest in the middle and decreases toward the extremes. The normal curve has also been called a *bell curve*, since it is shaped like a bell. The main idea communicated by the normal curve of intelligence is that we, as a population, tend to cluster around the middle of the IQ range. IQ is a lot like height in that way: most of us are within a couple of inches of average height, and most of us are within a small number of points of average IQ.

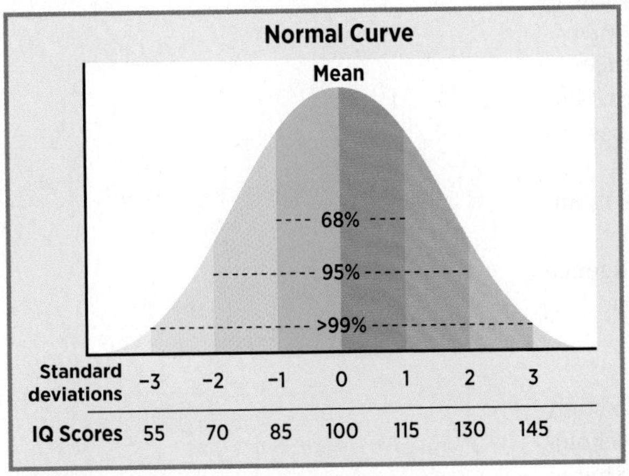

FIGURE 7.9 The Normal Curve. When they are graphed, intelligence scores of the population create a normal curve, in which scores near the mean are most common. The farther from the mean in either direction, the more uncommon the score is. Data from Urbina, 2011.

Wechsler Intelligence Tests. Among the specific intelligence tests that psychologists use, most prominent are the **Wechsler Intelligence Tests**: a widely used and highly respected set of intelligence tests originally developed by David Wechsler (Lichtenberger & Kaufman, 2009; Goldstein, 2008). When Wechsler created his first IQ test in the early 1900s, it was designed for adults only, but now, there are three separate versions to cover nearly the entire life span:

- The *Wechsler Adult Intelligence Scale* (*WAIS*), appropriate for people age 16–90
- The *Wechsler Intelligence Scale for Children* (*WISC*), appropriate for people age 6–16
- The *Wechsler Preschool and Primary Scale of Intelligence* (*WPPSI*), appropriate for people age 2.5–7

The Wechsler intelligence tests each include about a dozen subtests, many of which are shared by all three tests. These subtests are grouped into four or five categories. In the adult version of the test, those categories are

- **Verbal comprehension.** Subtests that assess how well you understand and use words and sentences
- **Perceptual reasoning.** Subtests that assess your ability to solve visual problems, often including designs and puzzles
- **Working memory.** Subtests that assess your ability to hold, manipulate, and retrieve information from short-term memory
- **Processing speed.** Subtests that assess how quickly and accurately you can scan and make decisions about simple visual information

For each of these four groups of subtests, the client receives an *index score*, which is on the same scale as the IQ score we discussed earlier (median score of 100, etc.). These four index scores are then combined to determine the overall (or full-scale) IQ score. By comparing the four index scores to each other, the psychologist can go a step beyond the clients' general level of intelligence (what Spearman called *g*) and consider some of the client's more specific areas of intelligence (what Thurstone called *s*) (Groth-Marnat, 2009; Weiss et al., 2010). For example, I once gave a WAIS to Ellie, a 30-year-old woman. Her full-scale IQ was 102—near the middle of the average range. But her index scores were scattered pretty widely: 120 in Verbal Comprehension, 81 in Perceptual Reasoning, 108 in Working Memory, and 99 in Processing Speed. In the report I wrote, I discussed not only Ellie's full-scale IQ, but her index scores too, which helped her understand her strengths and weaknesses. (The way the Wechsler tests are organized—with a single full-scale IQ score, a handful of index scores, and about a dozen subtest scores—shows that they follow the hierarchical model of intelligence discussed earlier in the chapter.)

Stanford-Binet Intelligence Test. An alternative to the Wechsler tests is the **Stanford-Binet Intelligence Test**: a widely used and highly respected intelligence test originally developed by Alfred Binet and then revised by Lewis Terman and appropriate across the life span. In terms of structure, the Stanford-Binet is similar to the Wechsler tests, with many subtests grouped into a smaller number of categories, which are then pulled together to form the full-scale IQ score. One big difference is that the Stanford-Binet is a single test for clients age 2 to 85 rather than three tests for various age groups, as with the Wechsler. Another difference is that the hardest items are harder and the easiest items are easier on the Stanford-Binet (compared to the Wechsler tests). That's an advantage for a psychologist testing a client at the very high end or the very low end of the range of intelligence (Kamphaus & Kroncke, 2004).

intelligence quotient (IQ)
A single number used to represent a person's overall intelligence.

normal curve
A graph showing that the frequency of scores on a test is greatest in the middle and decreases toward the extremes.

Wechsler Intelligence Tests
A widely used and highly respected set of intelligence tests originally developed by David Wechsler.

Stanford-Binet Intelligence Test
A widely used and highly respected intelligence test originally developed by Alfred Binet and Lewis Terman and appropriate across the life span.

IT'S LIKE...

The Hierarchical Model of Intelligence Is Like the National U.S. Weather Report

When you watch a weather report on TV, especially on a national network (rather than local), you often get a big, broad overview first, "It's hot all around the country or "A cold front is moving across the United States." Next, the weathercaster might zoom in on a big part of the U.S. map, and provide some information about that region, "Up in the Northwest, there's a lot of precipitation" or "Down in the Southeast, it's dry with high winds." Then, the weathercaster might zoom in even closer within one of those regions, focusing on specific states, "There's plenty of rain in Oregon" or "It's sunny and warm in Florida."

Just as the weathercaster offers multiple levels of description—country, region, and state—the hierarchical model of intelligence offers multiple levels of description as well. Especially in such forms as the three-stratum theory of intelligence, it offers an overall summary of intelligence (*g*), a few specific areas of intelligence (*s*), and a larger number of very specific areas of intelligence. Most of the intelligence tests that psychologists use produce numbers that reflect this nested, one-within-the-other approach to intelligence. This allows psychologists to take all the views on a person's intelligence that a U.S. weathercaster might take on the weather: zoomed all the way out on the whole country (general intelligence), zoomed in somewhat on one region (specific intelligence), or zoomed in further on a more specific ability.

achievement test
An assessment technique used by psychologists to numerically measure the level of learning a person has attained.

giftedness
Significantly above-average intelligence.

specific learning disorder
A mental disorder in which achievement in reading, writing, or math is significantly below age expectations.

intellectual disability
A mental disorder based on significantly below-average intelligence and impaired day-to-day functioning.

reliability
The extent to which an assessment technique provides consistent, repeatable results.

validity
The extent to which an assessment technique measures what it claims to measure.

test bias
The tendency of a test to produce scores in a consistently inaccurate way for members of particular groups.

Achievement Tests. Often, when a client takes an intelligence test, the client also takes an **achievement test**: an assessment technique used by psychologists to numerically measure the level of learning a person has attained.

Achievement tests sound pretty similar to intelligence tests. What's the difference?

The main difference is that intelligence tests measure what a person *can* accomplish, but achievement tests measure what a person *has* accomplished, particularly in school-related areas like reading, writing, and math (Mayer, 2011). Generally, these two scores match pretty closely: smart people are usually high achievers, and not-so-smart people are usually low achievers. Occasionally, a person's achievement falls significantly below their intelligence level, which typically comes to light when that person struggles in school ("Alyssa's so bright—I wonder why she's having such a hard time learning long division.").

The comparison between intelligence tests and achievement tests is similar to the comparison between athletic ability and achievement in sports. As a rule, people who have good basic athletic ability—they can run fast, jump high, and have good hand–eye coordination—do pretty well when they apply that ability in basketball, soccer, or another sport. But exceptions do exist, in both athletics and intelligence—both overachievers and underachievers. Psychologists who conduct intelligence tests and achievement tests focus on helping those whose achievement lags behind their intelligence. They measure the gap between intelligence and achievement, and then figure out ways to close it.

Extremes of Intelligence. There is a wide range of reasons why psychologists give intelligence tests. One is to test for **giftedness**: significantly above-average intelligence. The official definition "significantly above-average" differs between states or school districts, but a common definition is two standard deviations above the mean on an intelligence test. On a Wechsler test or the Stanford-Binet, that would mean a score of at least 130, which is obtained by only the top 2–3% of students. (Often, there are other factors besides a single IQ score that affect whether a student receives the giftedness designation.) Kids who are labeled as gifted often participate in school activities and classes that are designed to provide them with cognitive challenges that they might not otherwise experience (Reis & Renzulli, 2011). Many gifted students attain high levels of achievement at school and eventually as professionals, but some do not, especially when they find school unchallenging or when they have trouble applying their intelligence to the kinds of tasks demanded of them (Reis & McCoach, 2000; Renzulli & Park, 2002).

Another reason why psychologists use intelligence tests is to determine whether a client has a **specific learning disorder**: a mental disorder in which achievement in reading, writing, or math is significantly below age expectations. The term *dyslexia* is often used to refer to a specific learning disorder that focuses on reading. As with giftedness, the official cutoff for "significantly below age expectations" varies across states and districts. The diagnosis of a specific learning disorder often gives a kid access to educational resources that might not have been available otherwise—specially designed teaching or tutoring sessions, an individualized educational plan for teachers to follow, and other accommodations intended to help maximize the student's achievement. Children with specific learning disorders have an increased likelihood of other diagnoses, including attention-deficit/hyperactivity disorder (ADHD), anxiety, and depression (Tannock, 2013; Willcutt & Pennington, 2000). However, a diagnosis of a specific learning disability does not necessarily predict long-term hardship: Many people, including actors Keira Knightley and Will Smith, have overcome learning disabilities to reach high levels of success.

Both Keira Knightly and Will Smith have overcome specific learning disorders to achieve remarkably successful careers. (a) Jim Spellman/WireImage/Getty Images (b) Jon Kopaloff/FilmMagic/Getty Images

A third reason why psychologists give intelligence tests is to test for **intellectual disability**: a mental disorder based on significantly below-average intelligence and impaired day-to-day functioning. Prior to 2013, intellectual disability was called *mental retardation*, a term that is now considered by many to be disrespectful. The diagnosis is based not just on an IQ score approximately two standard deviations below the mean (around a 70), but also on significant problems doing basic tasks independently—like getting dressed, communicating, exhibiting appropriate social skills, and other adaptive behaviors. Intellectual disability can only be diagnosed when it arises in childhood (American Psychiatric Association, 2013). Down syndrome, which occurs once per every 800–1000 births, is the most common genetic problem leading to intellectual disability (Hodapp et al., 1999, 2011).

Evaluating Measures of Intelligence. When psychologists measure intelligence (or anything else, for that matter), they use only tests that meet their high professional standards. Specifically, they seek tests that are high in *reliability* and *validity*.

An intelligence test should be high in **reliability**: the extent to which an assessment technique provides consistent, repeatable results. A reliable intelligence test doesn't depend on who administers it, where it was administered, or when it was administered. You might remember that when psychologists give IQ tests, they keep a manual in front of them. That manual tells them exactly what to do at every step, which increases reliability, since differences in the way the test is given could lead to differences in scores.

An intelligence test should also be high in **validity**: the extent to which an assessment technique measures what it claims to measure. A valid intelligence test provides results that are similar to what other well-established intelligence tests measure, and results that are different from what tests of other abilities measure. You've taken enough tests in school to know about valid and (unfortunately) invalid tests. It's the difference between "That math test covered exactly the material we were told it would cover" and "That math test didn't even have problems like the ones we were told to study!"

DIVERSITY MATTERS

Test Bias. In addition to having high levels of reliability and validity, the best intelligence tests have *low* levels of **test bias**: the tendency of a test to produce scores in a consistently inaccurate way for members of particular groups. Unfortunately, the history of intelligence testing has featured controversies about test bias. In particular, critics of intelligence tests have accused the test makers of including items that give certain groups an advantage (typically middle- to upper-class Whites, which also describes most of the test *makers*, historically), while giving other groups a disadvantage (typically ethnic and racial minorities and poorer people).

This type of bias happens when intelligence tests tap into aspects of life that some groups have more access to and familiarity with than others (Helms, 2006). For example, imagine that a 17-year-old boy is asked to define *kale* as a vocabulary question on an intelligence test. If that boy is from an upper-middle class family, he's more likely to have eaten, or at least heard of, kale, than if he's from a family that struggles to make ends meet. Imagine that later, the same boy faces this question: "What are some advantages and disadvantages to taking a gap year?" Again, if the boy is from an upper-middle class family, he has a decent chance of knowing that "gap year" refers to a year between high school and college when young people often seek additional experiences or education. But if his family is of a lower socioeconomic status, a *gap year*, or any other term related to college, is less likely to be familiar to him. A higher proportion of ethnic and racial minorities fall into a lower socioeconomic category, so intelligence tests can be unfair to entire cultural groups when they are loaded with items that reflect higher socioeconomic categories (Suzuki et al., 2011; Bornstein & Bradley, 2003).

Culture-fair intelligence tests use tasks that do not depend heavily on language, such as mazes, puzzles, and visual memory games, to assess intelligence without the influence of cultural factors. Marijus Auruskevicius/Shutterstock

In the 1970s, one researcher decided to make a statement about how test bias disadvantages some cultural groups. A pioneer in the field of African-American psychology named Robert Williams turned the tables by creating an intelligence test based entirely

CHAPTER APP 7.1

Intelligence Tests

Intelligence Test
Mr. IQ

Preview one of the links and consider the following questions.

WEBSITE:
http://tiny.cc/ror9jy

ANDROID:
http://tiny.cc/vw77iy

IPHONE:
http://tiny.cc/yv77iy

VIDEO DEMO:
http://tiny.cc/chapterapps

These apps offer "IQ tests" that are entirely nonverbal. Their items include no words, only symbols and other visual stimuli.

How does it APPly to your daily life?
In your daily life, how much of your intelligence depends on your verbal ability—reading, writing, speaking, or comprehending words? In your opinion, to what extent should intelligence be defined by those verbal tasks?

How does it APPly to your understanding of psychology?
How does this kind of app influence your opinion of *culture-fair intelligence tests*? How does it illustrate the difference between *general intelligence* and *specific intelligences*?

on knowledge familiar to people who grew up in the Black community, not the White. He called it the Black Intelligence Test of Cultural Homogeneity, or the BITCH. Not surprisingly, Whites found the test much more difficult than Blacks did and scored much lower on it. One question asked what *Jet* is (a news and gossip magazine); another asked what Juneteenth commemorates (the freeing of the slaves in Texas); another asked what deuce-and-a-quarter means (a Buick Electra 225). The BITCH has not been widely used in more recent years, but its impact has endured. Specifically, the test enabled one minority group to show the majority group what it feels like to be evaluated by a test that values others' social and cultural experiences over their own (Williams, 1972; Wingate, 2011; Thaler et al., 2015).

Thankfully, today's widely used intelligence tests are far less biased than the intelligence tests from decades ago. Their authors have repeatedly revised them, making special efforts to reduce test bias. These authors strive to create **culture-fair intelligence tests**: intelligence tests that aim to reduce or remove any cultural factors leading to bias. A few more recently created tests adopt the strategy of minimizing the use of words at all, since words are the primary source of test bias. For example, the Universal Nonverbal Intelligence Test (UNIT) is an intelligence test published in 1996 that is completely language-free (Bracken & McCallum, 2009; McCallum & Bracken, 2005). All of the instructions are given with hand gestures, and clients respond by pointing to answers or arranging items in a particular way. None of the items involve words at all. Its subtests involve mazes, puzzles, visual memory games, and similar tasks. As with other tests of this type, the UNIT is not (yet) widely used, it is only appropriate for clients in a limited age range (school-aged children), and data on its reliability and validity are limited (Ortiz & Dynda, 2005). But the existence of the UNIT and other tests like it indicate that psychologists are increasing their efforts to minimize test bias and maximize cultural fairness.

Stereotype Threat. In addition to test bias, minority groups often face the obstacle of **stereotype threat**: the expectation that others may judge you according to stereotypes about a group to which you belong. When you sense that others are stereotyping you in a negative way—they think people like you are stupid, for example—your awareness of their stereotype can detract from your ability to prove them wrong (Steele & Aronson, 2004; Steele, 1997). You could become so preoccupied with the stereotype, and so worried that anything you say or do might be misinterpreted to confirm it, that your intelligence can't shine through (Schmader & Johns, 2003; Schmader et al., 2008). It is a self-fulfilling prophecy of sorts. They prejudge you as unintelligent, and your mindfulness of that prejudice actually makes you seem less intelligent than you really are. Since stereotype threat was originally identified in the 1990s, a growing body of research has demonstrated how real it is. Separate studies have found that when people feel judged by others who hold stereotypical expectations, test-takers who are Black, Latino/a, female, poor, or older adults all earn significantly lower scores on intelligence-related tests than they otherwise would (Spencer et al., 1999; Cadinu et al., 2005; Taylor & Walton, 2011; Gonzales et al., 2002; Croizet & Claire, 1998; Hess et al., 2003).

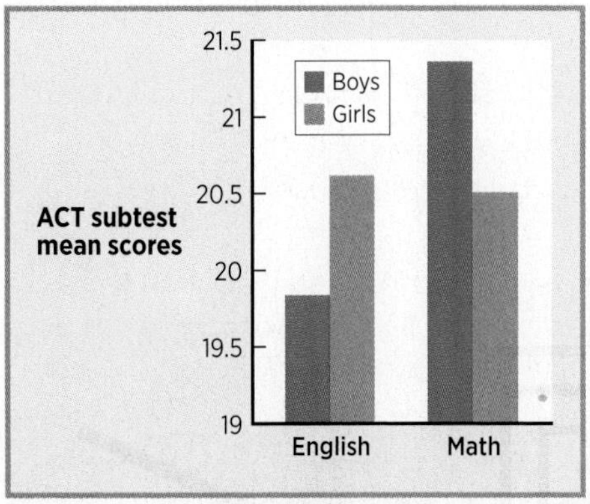

FIGURE 7.10 English, Math, and Gender: Average Scores on the ACT Subtests. Although overall intelligence does not differ between genders, men and boys as a group tend to perform slightly better on mathematical tasks, and women and girls as a group tend to perform slightly better on verbal tasks (Halpern, 2012; Halpern et al., 2011). That group difference is reflected in these ACT subtest means for English and Math, which are for 2013 but are typical of other years as well. Research from Buddin, 2014.

Group Differences. With such factors as test bias and stereotype threat in the mix, many findings about intelligence differences between groups—especially racial groups—have been the subject of great controversy. In particular, the finding in the 1990s that African Americans tend to score lower than Whites on intelligence tests—and the claim that these lower scores were due in part to genetics rather than environment—was met with swift and effective criticism (Herrnstein & Murray, 1994; Gardner, 1995; Lind, 1995; Nisbett, 1995; Daley & Onwuegbuzie, 2011; Fraser, 1995).

Nonetheless, researchers have explored questions of intelligence differences between groups of various kinds. One particularly well-studied question focuses on the differences in intelligence between males and females. In terms of general intelligence, there is no difference: the average overall intelligence (or IQ, or g) score is the same in both sexes. Male and female averages are remarkably similar in many particular areas of intelligence too. However, there are a few particular areas of intelligence in which one sex slightly, but consistently, outperforms the other across many countries and cultures (**Figure 7.10**). Females tend to have a slight advantage in most verbal abilities, including

reading and writing, while males tend to have a slight advantage in math and most tasks that involve visual or spatial orientation (Halpern, 2012; Halpern et al., 2011; Hedges & Nowell, 1995; Torres et al., 2006; Schultheis & Carlson, 2013; Hegarty & Waller, 2005).

It is important to keep in mind that just because a group of people tend to score a certain way on intelligence tests, a particular person from that group won't necessarily follow that trend. In other words, the differences *within* a group can be as large and as important as the differences *between* groups. Men tend to be taller than women, but it is entirely possible that the next man you meet will be shorter than most women (like comedian Kevin Hart—he is 5′2″) or that the next woman you meet will be taller than most men (like Malia Obama, who was seeing eye to eye with her 6′1″ father, President Barack Obama, before he left office in 2017). In much the same way, any particular female could excel at math or visual–spatial abilities, and any particular male could excel at verbal abilities.

culture-fair intelligence tests
Intelligence tests that aim to reduce or remove any cultural factors that could lead to bias.

stereotype threat
The expectation that others may judge you according to stereotypes about a group to which you belong.

CHECK YOUR LEARNING:

7.22 How do psychologists define intelligence?

7.23 What is the difference between general intelligence (*g*) and specific intelligences (*s*), and how do they fit into the hierarchical model of intelligence?

7.24 What is the theory of multiple intelligences?

7.25 What is emotional intelligence?

7.26 How does the nature–nurture debate apply to intelligence?

7.27 How do psychologists measure intelligence?

7.28 What are the two main intelligence tests that psychologists use?

7.29 What is the difference between intelligence tests and achievement tests?

7.30 What are the two extremes of intelligence?

7.31 What is the role of reliability and validity in measures of intelligence?

7.32 What is test bias and why is it detrimental to intelligence tests?

7.33 How can stereotype threat negatively influence test-taking?

7.34 Are there group differences between males and females in terms of intelligence?

CHAPTER SUMMARY

Thinking

7.1 Psychologists define cognition as what your brain does with information, including understanding it, organizing it, analyzing it, and communicating it. Psychologists study cognition by focusing on three main areas: thinking, language, and intelligence.

7.2 Psychologists define the term *concept* as a mental representation of a category of similar things, actions, or people.

7.3 The three main types of concepts are feature-based concepts, goal-based concepts, and relationship-based concepts.

7.4 Psychologists often organize concepts into three levels: superordinate, basic, and subordinate.

7.5 Problem solving is using cognition to find a way to achieve a goal (when the options are unknown), while decision making is using cognition to choose between available options.

7.6 An algorithm is a formula-like method of problem solving, while a heuristic is an educated guess, or rule-of-thumb, method of problem solving.

7.7 People stray from reason in a variety of ways when solving problems, including mental set, confirmation bias, and framing.

7.8 Four main types of heuristic are the representative heuristic, the availability heuristic, the affect heuristic, and the anchoring heuristic.

7.9 Dual-process theory is the idea that people possess two separate types of thinking, one automatic (Type 1 thinking) and one deliberate (Type 2 thinking).

7.10 People are not good at affective forecasting, which is predicting how we will feel about the outcomes of our decisions.

7.11 Psychologists define creativity as the capacity to come up with original ideas or approaches to a problem.

7.12 Divergent thinking is a problem-solving strategy in which you come up with lots of different possible solutions, while convergent thinking is a problem-solving strategy in which you use logic to deduce the single best solution.

7.13 Functional fixedness is thinking about something in the one way it is most typically used, rather than other possible uses.

7.14 A number of factors contribute to creativity, including culture.

Language

7.15 Psychologists define language as the ability to communicate with others using words or other symbols combined and arranged according to rules.

7.16 Some experts believe a "protolanguage" of isolated sounds evolved into rudimentary words that could then be combined in new ways.

7.17 The nativist theory of language development argues that the ability to use language is inborn, while nonnativist theories suggest that nurture has a strong influence in language development.

7.18 The stages of a child's language development include babbling, one-word stage, expanding language use, and use of figurative language.

7.19 Grammar is the set of rules within a language, and it has four levels: phonemes, morphemes, syntax, and semantics.

7.20 Extralinguistic information such as facial expressions, gestures, and how the language is spoken can influence communication.

7.21 Current experts continue to debate linguistic relativity, which is the theory that language influences thought.

Intelligence

7.22 Psychologists define intelligence as the ability to gain knowledge from experience.

7.23 General intelligence (*g*) is overall intelligence that applies across all tasks and situations, while specific intelligences (*s*) are intelligences that apply to only a particular area. The hierarchical model of intelligence suggests that people contain numerous specific intelligences, each of which is considered a part of a single general intelligence.

7.24 The theory of multiple intelligences, put forth primarily by Gardner, states that every person has many distinct intelligences, including some that contribute to traditional success in school and others that focus on nonacademic parts of life.

7.25 Emotional intelligence is the ability to sense and manage emotions in yourself and others.

7.26 Overall, genes have a substantial influence on intelligence, but there are many important environmental variables. Genes and environment interact in complex ways to influence intelligence.

7.27 An intelligence test is an assessment technique used by psychologists to numerically measure intelligence.

7.28 Psychologists mostly use the Wechsler Intelligence Tests to measure intelligence, while a respected alternative is the Stanford-Binet Intelligence Test.

7.29 Intelligence tests measure what a person *can* accomplish, while achievement tests measure what a person *has* accomplished.

7.30 One extreme of intelligence is giftedness, significantly above-average intelligence, while the other extreme is intellectual disability, a mental disorder based on significantly below-average intelligence and impaired day-to-day functioning.

7.31 For psychologists, measures of intelligence must be high in reliability and validity.

7.32 Test bias is the tendency of a test to produce scores in a consistently inaccurate way for members of particular groups. Unfortunately, the history of intelligence testing has featured controversies about test bias.

7.33 When people sense others are stereotyping them in a negative way, it can detract from their ability to perform well on tests.

7.34 In terms of general intelligence, there is no difference between males and females. However, there are a few particular areas of intelligence in which one sex slightly, but consistently, outperforms the other.

KEY TERMS

cognition, p. 215
concept, p. 215
prototype, p. 215
problem solving, p. 217
decision making, p. 217
algorithm, p. 217
mental set, p. 217
confirmation bias, p. 219
framing, p. 219
heuristic, p. 219
representativeness heuristic, p. 219
availability heuristic, p. 219
anchoring heuristic, p. 219
affect heuristic, p. 220
dual-process theory, p. 220
affective forecasting, p. 220
durability bias, p. 223
creativity, p. 223
divergent thinking, p. 223
convergent thinking, p. 223
functional fixedness, p. 223
language, p. 225
nativist theory, p. 227
language acquisition device, p. 227
social-pragmatic theory, p. 229
babbling, p. 229
one-word stage, p. 229
grammar, p. 230
phoneme, p. 230
morpheme, p. 233
syntax, p. 233
semantics, p. 233
extralinguistic information, p. 233
dialect, p. 233
linguistic relativity, p. 234
intelligence, p. 234
general intelligence (*g*), p. 234
specific intelligences (*s*), p. 234
emotional intelligence, p. 237
intelligence test, p. 239
intelligence quotient (IQ), p. 241
normal curve, p. 241
Wechsler Intelligence Tests, p. 241
Stanford-Binet Intelligence Test, p. 241
achievement test, p. 242
giftedness, p. 242
specific learning disorder, p. 242
intellectual disability, p. 242
reliability, p. 242
validity, p. 242
test bias, p. 242
culture-fair intelligence tests, p. 245
stereotype threat, p. 245

SELF-ASSESSMENT

1. Psychologists define the term _____ as a mental representation of a category of similar things, actions, or people.

2. ______ ______ is using cognition to find a way to achieve a goal.
   a. Decision making b. Concept creation
   c. Problem solving d. Affective forecasting

3. A(n) ______ is a formula-like method of problem solving.
   a. algorithm b. heuristic
   c. frame d. semantic

4. The ______ heuristic is an educated guess based on the information that most quickly and easily comes to mind.
   a. availability b. representative
   c. anchoring d. affect

5. Rachel was searching for a new apartment. She found one she liked, and expected that after she moved in, she would be happy for a long time. However, the happiness didn't last long. Within a week, the new apartment was just a place to live. Rachel's misjudgment of how she'd feel after an event in her life is an example of which of the following?
   a. affective forecasting b. durability bias
   c. functional fixedness d. confirmation bias

6. ______ is the capacity to come up with original ideas or approaches to a problem.

7. ______ is the set of rules within a language.
   a. Grammar b. Syntax
   c. Semantics d. Phonemes

8. A ______ is the smallest distinct unit of speech.

9. _____is the tendency of a test to produce scores in a consistently inaccurate way for members of particular groups.
   a. Test bias b. Validity
   c. Divergent thinking d. Syntax

10. ______ ______ is the expectation that others may judge you according to stereotypes about a group to which you belong.

Research shows quizzing is a highly effective learning tool. Continue quizzing yourself using LearningCurve, the system that adapts to *your* learning.

LaunchPad macmillan learning LearningCurve macmillan learning

GO TO: launchpadworks.com

Self-Assessment Answers

1. concept, 2. c, 3. a, 4. a, 5. b, 6. Creativity, 7. a, 8. phoneme, 9. a, 10. Stereotype threat

WHAT'S YOUR TAKE?

1. Are we getting smarter? James Flynn and other researchers found that average IQ scores in the United States continue to get higher (Flynn, 1984, 1987). The average score on Wechsler tests in 1947 was 100, but without adjustments, the average would have increased to 107.5 in 1972, 111.7 in 1989, and 115.1 in 2001 (Flynn, 2011). We're smarter than the generations that came before us, at least as measured by standard IQ tests. Some interesting theories have emerged as to why this increase, known as the Flynn effect, has taken place, including better diet, better medical care, better technology, more education, more familiarity with IQ tests, and other lifestyle changes that have taken place over the decades (Urbina, 2011). Why do you think your generation performs better on IQ tests than your parents' or your grandparents' generation?

SHOW ME MORE

7.1 Daniel Kahneman Discusses Dual-Process Theory

http://tiny.cc/722ojy

In this video, Daniel Kahneman explains dual-process theory and how the difference between thinking fast and thinking slow can influence decision making.

Sean Gallup/Getty Images

7.2 Nicaraguan Sign Language

launchpadworks.com LaunchPad macmillan learning

This documentary clip explains and illustrates the development of Nicaraguan Sign Language.

BBC Worldwide Learning

8 Motivation and Emotion

jeffbergen/Getty Images

Imagine that you are Derek Redmond.

You are a track champion and a record-holding sprinter in your own country. Now, you are going for the gold at the Olympics.

When the real Derek Redmond bolted out of the starting blocks for the 400-meter semifinals representing Britain in the 1992 Olympics, he felt great. But in the middle of the race, it happened: a torn hamstring. Redmond grabbed the back of his leg and limped along, but after a few steps he dropped to the ground. Olympic officials ran over to help as Redmond knelt on the track, his head hanging. But within seconds, he stood up and continued the race. He was essentially hopping on his left leg, given that his right leg was so injured he couldn't place much weight on it. Redmond was determined to cross the finish line, even though his dreams of an Olympic medal were shattered. As he hobbled forward, another runner approached him from behind—not a competitor, but Derek's father, who had witnessed his son's injury from the stands. Jim Redmond caught up to his son, put his arm around him, and joined him as he continued around the track. As Derek wept, father and son finished the race (Redmond, 2012; Weinberg, 2004). See Show Me More 8.1 at the end of the chapter for more on Derek Redmond.

Derek Redmond's story is considered one of the most memorable and inspirational moments in Olympic history, largely because it is so rich with *motivation* and *emotion*, the two primary topics of this chapter. Consider the motivations that fueled the sprinter: to train for years to become a world-class athlete, and to fight through severe injury to finish the race. Consider the motivations of his father: to comfort his son and help him reach his goal in spite of devastating circumstances. Consider the emotions of the sprinter: excitement and nervousness before the race, which transformed into heartbreak and anguish at the worst moment. Consider the emotions of his father: alarmed at seeing his son motionless on the track, pride when his son rises up to continue the race, and compassion when his son cries in his arms.

You may not be an Olympic sprinter, but you have undoubtedly experienced your own extraordinary moments of motivation and emotion. In this chapter, we will cover classic and contemporary explanations for what motivates us to behave the way we do. We will also consider how different motivations interact with one another, and explore one motivation of hunger and eating that drives us all. We will also discuss many aspects of emotions: how they arise, how we communicate them, how we regulate them, and how they interact with ethnicity, gender, and age.

CHAPTER OUTLINE

Derek Redmond displayed intense motivation and emotion when he experienced an injury as an Olympic athlete.
PASCAL PAVANI/Getty Images

Motivation

YOU WILL LEARN:

8.1 what motivation is.

8.2 the difference between intrinsic motivation and extrinsic motivation.

8.3 about classic theories of motivation.

8.4 about contemporary theories of motivation.

8.5 about Abraham Maslow's hierarchy of needs.

8.6 how motivation is experienced by people of diverse backgrounds.

Motivation is a desire that stimulates and steers behavior. Your motivation is what stirs you to take action. In some cases, the goal behind a motivation is something specific and short-term. For example, your energy level is dragging, so you are motivated to find something caffeinated. That motivation translates into the behavior of getting in line at a nearby coffee shop or grabbing a soda out of the fridge. In other cases, the goal behind a motivation is more abstract and long-term. For example, you experience an ongoing sense of loneliness, so you are motivated to find a romantic partner. That motivation translates into the behavior of downloading a dating app to find a match. Of course, motivation does more than simply prompt you to act: It prompts you to act *with purpose* toward a goal (Ryan, 2012; Fiske, 2008).

Sometimes, a behavior is its own motivation. You do it because you enjoy it. That is **intrinsic motivation**: the desire to perform a behavior because the behavior itself is rewarding. Other times, a behavior is a means to an end. You do it not because you enjoy it, but because you enjoy what it delivers. That is **extrinsic motivation**: the desire to perform a behavior to obtain an external reward (Ryan et al., 1990; Ryan & Deci, 2000a,b). That external reward is an **incentive**: an object or situation outside yourself that you are motivated to acquire.

Let's consider some examples, beginning with intrinsic motivation. Danielle, a tenth-grader, is intrinsically motivated to play on the JV basketball team because of her love for the game. Javier, a college senior majoring in education, is intrinsically motivated to do his student teaching at a local elementary school because of the thrill he gets from educating young kids. In both cases, the behavior begins because the behavior itself brings pleasure. There is a chance that the behavior will continue because of intrinsic motivation. However, there is also a chance that the same behavior could become extrinsically motivated. For example, maybe Danielle continues to play basketball because of the social status it gives her among her peers and for the chance of earning a college scholarship. Maybe Javier continues teaching because the job provides him with a salary, health insurance, and 3 months off every summer.

Does it really matter whether the motivation for a behavior is intrinsic or extrinsic?

It really does. Research shows that intrinsic motivation and extrinsic motivation produce different patterns of behavior. Specifically, extrinsic motivation often undermines intrinsic motivation. Your behavior on an intrinsically motivated task is likely to decrease if that behavior becomes extrinsically motivated. That decrease can take the form of less frequent behavior, lower quality performance, or diminished interest in the behavior (Deci et al., 1999). When the extrinsic motivation is financial, such as a paycheck, the effect tends to be more powerful than when the extrinsic motivation is verbal reinforcement or positive feedback—such as when a parent, boss, or teacher says, "Good job!" (Deci, 1971). The lesson here is this: Don't lose sight of why you chose a behavior in the first place—what intrigued you about your partner, your major, your job, your hobby, or your pet. That is intrinsic motivation, and that—more than any extrinsic motivation that may come along—has the best chance of maintaining that behavior long term. In addition, behaving according to intrinsic motivation, as opposed to extrinsic motivation, is linked to higher self-esteem and well-being, less depression, and less anxiety over time (Twenge, et al., 2010; Niemiec et al., 2009; Williams et al., 2000; Kasser & Ryan, 1993, 1996).

Of course, extrinsic motivation is important too. It fuels behaviors that might be boring or unpleasant (like a kid earning an allowance for taking out the trash, or an adult earning a living for driving a garbage truck). And under the best circumstances,

MY TAKE VIDEO 8.1

Intrinsic and Extrinsic Motivation

"Something that motivated me intrinsically is..."

YOUTUBE: http://tiny.cc/mytake
LAUNCHPAD: launchpadworks.com

the incentives you might earn through extrinsic motivation—whether payment, praise, or prizes—can complement rather than undermine your own intrinsic motivation (Cerasoli et al., 2014; Henderlong & Lepper, 2002).

"I'll quit when it stops being fun."

Mike Twohy The New Yorker Collection/The Cartoon Bank

Classic Theories of Motivation

Early psychologists who studied motivation offered a number of theories that have stood the test of time and remain relevant today. A more recent generation has also produced intriguing theories of motivation. Let's consider the old-school theories first, and then move on to the new-school theories in the next section.

Instinct Theory. An **instinct** is a motivation that is biologically innate. Some instincts, like eating and reproducing, are common across species. Others are more particular to a type of animal, like a newborn kangaroo climbing into its mother's pouch the moment it is born, or birds building nests for their eggs (Keeping, 2006). As these examples illustrate, instincts are not limited to simple, short behaviors. Sometimes, they take the form of elaborate routines or patterns that play out over hours or days.

Instincts are at the core of **instinct theory**: a theory of motivation stating that humans, like all other animals, are motivated primarily by instinct. Instinct theory was one of the first motivation theories, and it was held in high regard through the early and mid-1900s (Tolman, 1923; Gillespie, 1971; Moltz, 1965; Wells, 1923). Today, however, instinct theory is widely acknowledged as incomplete. That does not mean it is wrong. After all, humans are an animal species, and all animals have instincts. But we've come to understand that instinct can't explain everything about a person's behavior. For example, we have an instinct to make homes for ourselves, much like birds have an instinct to nest. However, the ways we behave to achieve that outcome are far more adaptable than the rigid behavior of many bird species, whose nest building seems to happen on autopilot. People aren't limited to gathering building materials and assembling them in a safe location, as birds do when they build nests. People can drive down streets looking for "for rent" signs on apartment buildings, search the Internet for listings of houses and condos for sale, hire a contractor to remodel a kitchen or bathroom, and shop in a furniture store for sofas, tables, and chairs. Instinct is certainly in the mix, but there are other motivations influencing us too.

Drive Reduction Theory. **Drive reduction theory** is a theory of motivation stating that unmet biological drives cause unpleasant sensations that motivate you to meet those needs. You have a handful of basic biological drives—including hunger, thirst, sex, and physical comfort. According to drive reduction theory, satisfying these drives is what motivates your behavior. The bad feelings your body experiences when those needs get neglected, like hunger, thirst, and pain, are increasingly loud alerts to satisfy these drives. After you satisfy them, you have regained **homeostasis**: steadiness or balance in your bodily state.

Like instinct theory, drive reduction theory was most prominent in the early and mid-1900s (Hull, 1943, 1952). Also like instinct theory, drive reduction theory has been criticized for reducing human motivation to something too simplistic and too biologically based to account for all human behavior (Ryan, 2012). For example, drive reduction theory can't account for *curiosity*. Curiosity fuels all kinds of behavior, from stalking a friend of a friend's social media pages to wandering into the grand opening of a shoe store even though you don't really need any shoes. Curiosity isn't a drive and doesn't stem from a biological need. But curiosity (and the related concept of *interest*) does motivate people to gather information and learn about otherwise new situations and things (Silvia, 2008, 2012; Renninger & Hidi, 2011; Renninger & Su, 2012; Loewenstein, 1994).

Arousal Theory. **Arousal theory** is a theory of motivation stating that you are motivated to obtain and maintain an optimal level of arousal. The term *arousal* is often used in a sexual context, but here it refers to a more general excitement or attentiveness.

motivation
A desire that stimulates and steers behavior.

intrinsic motivation
A desire to perform a behavior because the behavior itself is rewarding.

extrinsic motivation
A desire to perform a behavior to obtain an external reward.

incentive
An object or situation outside the person that the person is motivated to acquire.

instinct
A motivation that is biologically innate.

instinct theory
A theory of motivation stating that humans, like all other animals, are motivated primarily by instinct.

drive reduction theory
A theory of motivation stating that unmet biological drives cause unpleasant sensations that motivate the person to meet those needs.

homeostasis
Steadiness or balance in the person's bodily state.

arousal theory
A theory of motivation stating that the person is motivated to obtain and maintain an optimal level of arousal.

An instinct is a motivation that is biologically innate, such as a bird's motivation to build a nest. Humans are motivated by instincts too, but ours are typically more flexible than those of other species. JHVEPhoto/Getty Images

Actually, arousal is how some people explain the curiosity motivations we just discussed. Specifically, they say that curiosity allows you to stay at least mildly aroused in situations in which you might otherwise become completely bored.

The ideal level of arousal differs across people and across situations, but it is clear that the ideal falls somewhere in the middle rather than at either extreme. Your best performance happens when you are mildly or moderately aroused, not when you are minimally or maximally aroused (Berlyne, 1960; Fiske & Maddi, 1961; Hunt, 1965). This finding is described by the **Yerkes–Dodson law**: the finding that moderate levels of arousal are linked to higher levels of performance than high or low levels of arousal. Yerkes and Dodson actually performed their research in 1908, long before arousal theory appeared, but they did find that a moderate level of electric shock was more beneficial than high or low levels of shock when teaching rats to behave in particular ways, so arousal theorists adopted it (Yerkes & Dodson, 1908; Teigen, 1994; Winton, 1987).

As an example of the Yerkes–Dodson law, consider Josh, a teenager taking his driver's license test. He has already passed the written exam, and now he is behind the wheel about to start the driving portion with the examiner. If you're rooting for Josh, you don't want him to be overly aroused—so nervous that he freaks out and loses his focus. You also don't want him to be underaroused—so uninterested that he hardly tries. You want him to be optimally aroused—enough to keep him alert and help him make a genuine effort, but not so much that he panics. Many of the things you do on a regular basis—studying for and taking exams, meeting new people, playing computer games, competing in intramural sports, completing your work at your job—similarly benefit from just the right level of arousal.

Contemporary Theories of Motivation

Now, let's consider some of the contemporary theories of motivation that have had the greatest impact.

Self-Determination Theory. **Self-determination theory** is a theory of motivation stating that the strongest and healthiest motivations are those that come from within yourself. According to self-determination theory, it is best to be *autonomous*—to do what you do because you find it naturally rewarding, rather than behaving in ways that bring external rewards. If that sounds a lot like an endorsement of intrinsic motivation, it should: Self-determined and autonomous motivations are almost equivalent to intrinsic motivation. There is one important difference, though: Sometimes, extrinsic motivations can become autonomous too. The key is how *controlling* those extrinsic motivations feel to you. If they feel very controlling, they will never become integrated into yourself, never become part of what fundamentally fuels you. But if they do not feel controlling, they can become integrated into yourself, and you can find yourself motivated autonomously by them (Deci & Ryan, 2012; Ryan & Deci, 2003; Ryan et al., 1990).

As an example, consider Antonio, an eleventh-grader who becomes a member of his school's chapter of the National Honor Society (NHS). To maintain his NHS membership, he needs to participate in community service. Specifically, he needs to spend every Wednesday afternoon tutoring second-graders who struggle with basic math skills. At first, he sees the tutoring as a meaningless chore. He drags himself to the first tutoring session at the elementary school, and rolls his eyes when he finds out that he has been assigned to a small group of students who need help with simple addition and subtraction. Soon enough, however, Antonio starts to enjoy the tutoring. The progress the kids make, and the connections Antonio makes with them, generate an unexpected sense of satisfaction. Now he tutors every Wednesday not because he *has* to, but because he *wants* to. An extrinsic motivation that initially made Antonio feel like he was being controlled has now become integrated into Antonio's own autonomous, self-determined motivation.

Research on self-determination theory shows that *autonomous motivation* produces superior behavior in terms of both quality and quantity. For example, compared

to students who study just to get good grades, students who are autonomously motivated actually learn the material in a deeper and longer-lasting way (Wang, 2008; Ryan et al., 1990; Benware & Deci, 1984). Similar results have been found for healthy eating, increasing exercise, and quitting smoking too. People who make the changes because they want to, rather than making changes to impress friends or follow doctor's orders, make more significant improvements that last longer (Williams et al., 1996, 1998, 2006a,b). In fact, in the broadest sense, people who allow autonomous motivation to guide their lives have higher levels of psychological wellness than people who feel controlled by outside forces (Sheldon et al., 2004).

Yerkes–Dodson law
The finding that moderate levels of arousal are linked to higher levels of performance than high or low levels of arousal.

self-determination theory
A theory of motivation stating that the strongest and healthiest motivations are those that come from within the person.

regulatory focus theory
A theory of motivation stating that there are two primary motivation systems—promotion and prevention—that affect different people in different ways.

achievement goal theory
A theory of motivation stating that when the person is motivated to achieve a goal, certain goals (mastery goals) produce better outcomes than other goals (performance goals).

Regulatory Focus Theory. **Regulatory focus theory** is a theory of motivation stating that there are two primary motivation systems—*promotion* and *prevention*—that affect different people in different ways. *Promotion motivation* is all about getting more good stuff: advancing, accomplishing, acquiring, and maximizing. *Prevention motivation* is all about holding on to what you have: staying vigilant, avoiding risk, and preventing loss (Scholer & Higgins, 2012; Higgins, 1997, 2000, 2002, 2011; Crowe & Higgins, 1997). The key is living a life that matches your balance of promotion and prevention motivation, achieving *regulatory fit* (Higgins, 2008).

To better understand promotion and prevention motivations, imagine two friends, Owen and Evan, planning a camping trip. Owen is motivated more by promotion and Evan is motivated more by prevention. As they drive out to the campsite, Owen is eager: "I can't wait to get out there! Maybe we'll see some wild animals up close! And food always tastes better when cooked over an open fire." By contrast, Evan is cautious: "I just hope neither one of us gets hurt—camping can be dangerous. Let's make sure we extinguish the campfire completely. The last thing we want is a forest fire. And if we do see any animals, I hope it's from a safe distance." For Owen, camping (and everything else) is an opportunity, an experience full of delight and exhilaration if they have any luck. For Evan, camping (and everything else) is a responsibility, an experience full of disappointment and pain if they're not careful.

Promotion motivation focuses on getting something good. Prevention motivation focuses on not losing what you already have. We all have some of both, but not necessarily in equal amounts. The dominating type of motivation can influence the way you experience many things, such as a camping trip: It can be an opportunity for new adventures or a challenge to avoid pain. Buena Vista Images/Getty Images

Most of us have a nice balance between promotion and prevention motivations, but some lean one way or the other pretty strongly. As you might expect, Evan and other prevention-oriented people are vulnerable to worry and anxiety disorders (Klenk et al., 2011; Scott & O'Hara, 1993; Strauman, 1989). On the other hand, Owen and other promotion-oriented people are vulnerable to depression and even suicidal thoughts when their hopes fall flat or their efforts fail (Strauman, 2002; Cornette et al., 2009). These two types of people also respond differently to common situations. In one study, researchers interviewed 52 employees of businesses that were switching to entirely new computer systems. Promotion-oriented employees were much more accepting of the big switch than their more prevention-oriented coworkers (Stam & Stanton, 2010).

In another study, researchers presented two kinds of antismoking ads: one ad emphasized obtaining positive outcomes, like better breath, whiter teeth, and improved physical endurance; a second ad emphasized avoiding negative results, like lung cancer, bad breath, and yellow teeth. (Notice that some of those outcomes are the same things phrased in alternative ways.) Each type of ad had its most powerful effect when there was good fit between the ad's approach and whether the particular participant was promotion-oriented or prevention-oriented (Kim, 2006).

Achievement Goal Theory. **Achievement goal theory** is a theory of motivation stating that when you are motivated to achieve a goal, certain goals (*mastery goals*) produce better outcomes than other goals (*performance goals*). Achievement goal theory is actually the most recent version of an achievement-based motivation theory that has been around since the mid-1900s (Atkinson, 1964; McClelland, 1961). In those early days, the basic idea was simply that the achievement of goals was a primary human motivation. Today, that idea is accepted as a given, and the focus of the theory has shifted to two different kinds of goals (mastery vs. performance) and the different results they yield (Ames, 1992; Dweck & Leggett, 1988). Mastery goals involve doing something well, or *mastering* it. By contrast, performance goals involve *demonstrating* that you can do

something well, or *performing* for others (Murayama et al., 2012; Ames & Archer, 1987, 1988).

That distinction between mastery and performance has proven to be important in terms of its influence on behavior. There is a big difference in what you'll do when you're motivated to *actually* achieve something versus *showing* that you have achieved it (Senko et al., 2008). For example, consider Patrick and Matthew, two seventh-graders in the same introductory Spanish class. Patrick is motivated to do what he needs to do to get a good grade in the class—attend class, memorize vocabulary words, cram before the exams, and so on. Those are performance goals. Matthew, on the other hand, is motivated to actually learn Spanish—speak it meaningfully with others and appreciate the language and the culture surrounding it (whether or not an exam is coming up). Those are mastery goals.

Studies show that students motivated by mastery goals like Matthew are much more likely to sustain motivation for a longer time, remain persistently interested in the material, and understand the material more deeply than students like Patrick (Maehr & Midgley, 1991; Harackiewicz et al., 2002b; Heyman & Dweck, 1992; Pintrich & De Groot, 1990; Kaplan & Midgley, 1997; Elliott & Dweck, 1988; Elliot et al., 1999; Wolters, 2004). However, students motivated by performance goals like Patrick are more likely to learn the material only superficially through rote memorization, and to cheat to get good grades (Anderman et al., 1998; Harackiewicz et al., 2000; Meece & Holt, 1993). Even so, performance goals like Patrick's often produce exam scores that are as good as, or even better than, mastery goals like Matthew's (Harackiewicz et al., 2002a; Senko et al., 2008; Koestner et al., 1987; Miller & Hom, 1990). This sets up a dilemma for educators. They want students to be motivated by mastery goals, but exams and other evaluations of students often encourage more of a performance goal motivation.

The consequences of mastery versus performance goals extend beyond just achievement in the classroom. They influence self-esteem too. People motivated by mastery goals tend to view their abilities (for example, intelligence) and personality characteristics (for example, shyness) as changeable. They believe they can actually improve themselves. As a result, over time, their self-esteem tends to rise (Dweck & Grant, 2008). People motivated by performance goals tend to view their abilities as unchangeable. They believe they can't learn more to improve themselves, and that their only hope is to better demonstrate their ability on tests. As a result, over time, self-esteem tends to drop for people motivated by performance goals (Robins & Pals, 2002).

In some studies, researchers have actually trained students to have more of a mastery mindset than a performance mindset. The researchers teach participants to see their own abilities as changeable (or *incremental*) as opposed to seeing their abilities as fixed (or an *entity*). The results are remarkably positive (Cury et al., 2008; DaFonseca et al., 2008). For example, in one study, researchers taught a group of middle school students about the incremental improvements their own brains can make—including how their brains form new connections every time they learn, how challenging themselves with new material could improve their brain power, and so on. Compared to another group of students who received no such training, this mastery mindset–trained group showed improved scores on math tests, and their teachers noticed that they had become more motivated to actually learn the material (Blackwell et al., 2007).

One Motivation after Another: Maslow's Hierarchy

With so many possible motivations fueling our behaviors, it wouldn't be surprising if someone offered a meta-theory of motivation, one that focuses on not just a single motivation but on many motivations working in a particular order. In fact, there is such a meta-theory, and it has remained influential since its introduction in the mid-1900s. The **hierarchy of needs** is an explanation of motivation created by Abraham Maslow based on the idea that certain needs must be satisfied before others (**Figure 8.1**). Maslow argued that some basic needs demand more of your focus and attention than others at first. Only when those needs are met will you move on to

others (Maslow, 1943, 1954, 1967, 1968; Fiske, 2008). You don't need to deliberately think about this sequence, according to Maslow. It happens to all of us automatically. It is like prerequisites in college. You have to pass the 100-level class before you can register for the 200-level class. Then you have to pass the 200-level class before you can register for the 300-level class, and so on. Maslow's theory originally included five needs, but he later added a sixth. Let's consider them in order, starting with the most basic.

Physiological Needs. *Physiological needs* include food, water, sleep, and sex. They focus on your body, keeping it alive and healthy. So, it makes sense that these are the most primary needs, the ones that must be met before any others. Without a well-functioning body, nothing else matters. People who are unfortunate enough to live on the brink of starvation are driven entirely by physiological needs—for example, figuring out where their next meal is coming from. If you've ever been temporarily desperate for food or water, you know the feeling too. You might also know the feeling if you've ever really, *really* had to go to the bathroom. As the need becomes more pressing, it is difficult to even think about anything else but getting that physiological need met right now.

Safety Needs. *Safety needs* include security and stability in your daily life. People who are unfortunate enough to live in war zones or in neighborhoods where gun violence is a constant threat feel the press of safety needs—securing a life in which they can feel protected and free of danger. If you've ever found yourself in a threatening situation, like an assault or even behind the wheel of a car skidding on icy roads, you know the feeling too. You might also know the feeling if you've suddenly heard fire alarms or tornado sirens. You drop everything else and refocus entirely on getting yourself to a safe place.

Safety needs include security and stability in daily life. Unfortunately, meeting safety needs remains a struggle for many people.
Anadolu Agency/Getty Images

Belongingness and Love Needs. *Belongingness and love needs* involve connections with other people, making connections and keeping them. These needs push people toward togetherness, as opposed to living in isolation and solitude. The need to connect with other people is remarkably strong and universal. In every culture around the world, people tend to congregate and share their lives with small groups of friends and family. Throughout the course of evolution, belonging to a cooperative group made any individual more fit to survive (Barash, 1982).

Once those social bonds form, we work hard to keep them and feel pain and sadness if they break. And if broken social bonds ever reconnect, the reunion is usually considered cause for celebration (Richman & Leary, 2009; Baumeister & Leary, 1995; Leary et al., 2001). If you've ever experienced periods of genuine loneliness, had a falling-out with a close friend, or broken up with a romantic partner, you know how strong the drive to belong can be. Prolonged periods in which the need for belonging and love go unmet often produce stress, depression, and physical illness (Leary & Cox, 2008). That is something that even prisoners, who typically fear solitary confinement even more than living among a community of criminals, understand.

Esteem Needs. *Esteem needs* involve feeling positive about yourself—having a good sense of self-worth and the confidence that you can live your life competently and effectively. This is the need that drives you to do things that make you feel proud. For young children, that might mean behaving well enough to get approval or praise from parents. For teens, that might mean getting good grades or excelling on a sports team, a school club, or a part-time job. For adults, that might mean making a living or a meaningful contribution to society. Any activity that enhances your sense of self satisfies your esteem needs: This enhancement can come from others in the form of popularity and acceptance, or it can come from within yourself in the form of self-respect and honor.

Self-Actualization Needs. *Self-actualization needs* involve living a life that matches who you truly are. These needs are based, of course, on **self-actualization**: fully becoming the person you have the potential to become. As the term suggests, self-actualization means

hierarchy of needs
An explanation of motivation created by Abraham Maslow based on the idea that certain needs must be satisfied before others.

self-actualization
Fully becoming the person one has the potential to become.

making *actual*, or real, your unique capabilities. You don't meet your self-actualization needs by becoming what *other* people want you to become. You meet your self-actualization needs by becoming what *you*, deep down, want to become. If you've ever had a job or been in a relationship in which you spent too much time meeting other people's demands, you know how it feels to have your self-actualization needs go unmet. But if you've ever had a job, a relationship, or any experience in which you felt yourself truly being yourself, you know how it feels to have your self-actualization needs met.

Sometimes, you're lucky enough to have a **peak experience**: a moment of self-actualization that produces strong, often mystical, feelings of personal fulfillment. In these blissful moments, you typically lose track of time and space, as well as any problems or concerns that were troubling you (Maslow, 1970). Peak experiences often take place during periods of **flow**: performing a behavior with complete immersion and enjoyment, or feeling like you're "in the zone." Flow involves total absorption in an activity, usually one in which you are quite skilled and also optimally challenged, as opposed to overwhelmed or bored (Jackson, 2012; Csikszentmihalyi, 1975; Seligman & Csikszentmihalyi, 2000). Any activity can produce flow or a peak experience as long as it is intrinsically motivated, but some activities that do so frequently include playing sports, creating art (music, visual art, writing, etc.), and even certain uses of the Internet (Chen, 2006; Chen et al., 1999, 2000; Csikszentmihalyi, 1990; Jackson & Csikszentmihalyi, 1999; Jackson, 1995).

Self-Transcendence Needs. *Self-transcendence needs* were added to Maslow's hierarchy of needs long after it was originally proposed (Maslow, 1969, 1971). They involve needs beyond the self, often involving religious or mystical transformation or a connection to something larger than the self. Positioned at the highest end of the hierarchy, self-transcendence needs arise only when all of the other needs are met. They focus on a feeling of unity with all other people, but not in the same way as the need for belonging. Instead of a connection between you and one other person, or even a group of people, self-transcendence involves connection with the universe and all beings (not just people) in it (Koltko-Rivera, 1998). People can meet self-transcendence needs in a variety of ways. For example, they might dedicate their lives to spiritual activity in which they feel a connection to a higher power, to a social or political cause in which they deeply believe, or to selflessly serving others in need (Koltko-Rivera, 2006).

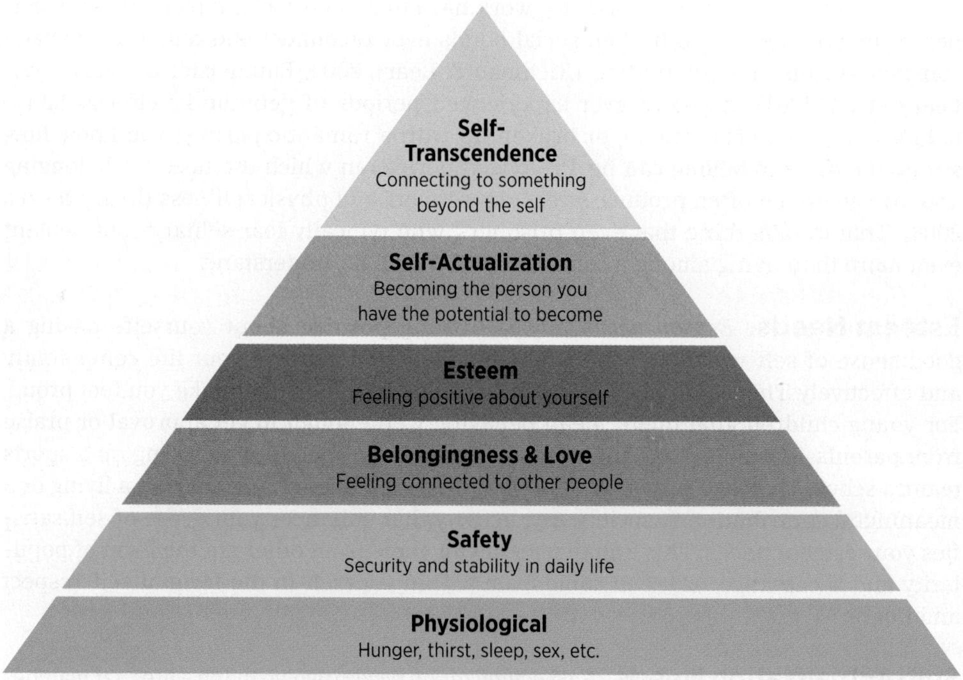

FIGURE 8.1 Maslow's Hierarchy of Needs. According to Abraham Maslow's hierarchy of needs, you must satisfy your basic needs (toward the bottom of the hierarchy) before moving on to others.

peak experience
A moment of self-actualization that produces strong, often mystical, feelings of personal fulfillment.

flow
Performing a behavior with complete immersion and enjoyment, or feeling like one is "in the zone."

Motivation and Diversity

Many theories of motivation are limited because they assume that the same motivations drive everyone. That is simply not true. Different groups of people, as defined by ethnicity, gender, age, and other factors, are motivated by different forces. Thankfully, that fact is increasingly recognized and researched by psychologists.

Motivation and Ethnicity. A cornerstone of Maslow's hierarchy of needs is the need for esteem. In the United States and other individualistic societies, the quest for self-esteem is hardly questioned. We assume everyone wants it and suffers if they don't have it. However, there is growing evidence that the need for self-esteem does not apply equally around the world. Specifically, in East Asian countries and other collectivist cultures, the need for an accurate view of the self, even if it is unflattering or critical, often outweighs the need for a positive view of the self (Crocker & Park, 2004; Heine et al., 1999).

DIVERSITY MATTERS

In studies in which Western and Eastern participants are asked to predict the future events of their lives, Western participants are much more likely to look ahead with unrealistic optimism (for example, to expect an exceptionally high salary), while Eastern participants are much more likely to predict an ordinary future filled with events that are more likely and common (Ohashi & Yamaguchi, 2004; Heine & Lehman, 1995). When researchers ask participants about their views of their *relationships* (with close friends, family members, and romantic partners) rather than their views of themselves, Eastern participants' views are as positive as Western participants' views (Endo et al., 2000). This finding is consistent with the collectivistic value of connectedness with others rather than the individualistic value of independence and self-promotion.

These differences in the need for individual self-esteem also show up in the way people from different cultures respond to challenges. Generally, people from individualistic cultures tend to work harder on tasks they know they can do well, but people from collectivistic cultures tend to work harder on tasks they know they *can't* do well (Morling & Kitayama, 2008). In one study, participants worked on a series of word games (for example, coming up with one word that connects to three others, such as *sleep*, *fantasy*, and *day* all connecting to *dream*). The key question was what participants did when they got feedback that they failed. Participants from the United States and Canada didn't persist much. Instead, they gave up rather quickly. By contrast, participants from Japan persisted much longer, and they also assigned more importance to the task than the U.S. and Canadian participants did. The researchers interpreted these results as consistent with a self-enhancing strategy by the Western participants (consistent with the need to maintain self-esteem), but a self-improving strategy by the Eastern participants, which is easier to do when the need for self-esteem is not so strong (Heine et al., 2001).

Motivation and Gender. The idea that some groups are more motivated by goals focusing on relationships than by goals focusing on the self may apply to gender as well. Specifically, women appear to be more motivated by goals that emphasize working together and helping others, than men. However, men appear to be more motivated by goals that emphasize personal power over other people and things, than women (Diekman & Eagly, 2008). These differences probably stem from gender-based roles that society has historically promoted, in which women are encouraged to become caretakers and men are encouraged to become authority figures (Eagly, 1987; Eagly et al., 2000; Eagly & Crowley, 1986). In recent decades, as women have increasingly taken on jobs formerly dominated by men (especially leadership positions), women's personal power goals have increased somewhat, but the change in the opposite direction for men working together and helping others has not been as strong (Eagly & Diekman, 2003).

DIVERSITY MATTERS

This discrepancy between these goals may play a significant role in the decisions of girls and women regarding STEM (science, technology, engineering, and mathematics) careers. In one study, researchers asked hundreds of college students how well they believed they would meet both types of goals if they chose a STEM career. The helping

CHAPTER APP 8.1

Motivation

Checky - Phone Habit Tracker

Preview one of the links and consider the following questions.

WEBSITE: http://tiny.cc/mai7jy

ANDROID: http://tiny.cc/ia92iy

IPHONE: http://tiny.cc/w382iy

VIDEO DEMO: http://tiny.cc/chapterapps

This app performs one simple function: It tracks the number of times you check your phone per day.

How does it APPly to your daily life?
How many times a day do you check your phone? How does that number compare to the number of times a day you'd like to check your phone? If those numbers are far apart, what can you do to make them closer?

How does it APPly to your understanding of psychology?
Which theory of motivation discussed in this chapter (the classic theories of motivation, the contemporary theories of motivation, or the motivations included in Maslow's hierarchy of needs) best explains your phone-checking behavior?

goals included things like helping others, serving humanity, serving community, caring for others, and connection with others. The personal power goals included things like power, recognition, achievement, status, focus on the self, and financial rewards. The difference was drastic: participants believed that with a STEM career, they would be significantly more likely to fulfill personal power goals than helping goals. The researchers concluded that even though interest in STEM careers has risen among females, the perception that such careers may impede helping goals may prevent some women from sticking with that interest long-term (Diekman et al., 2010).

Motivation and Age. Adults at different stages of their lives are likely to experience different motivations. Younger adults tend to be more motivated to gain, while older adults tend to be more motivated to avoid loss (Freund et al., 2012; Freund & Ebner, 2005; Ebner et al., 2006; Heckhausen, 2006). Consider Adriana, a 20-year-old woman, and her 70-year-old grandmother, Mary. Adriana is looking to build a life, so her primary motivations are to get new things, like job skills, a romantic relationship, financial independence, and material possessions. Mary already has those things, so her primary motivations are to hold on to them (along with her health), especially as she notices her same-age peers losing some of theirs.

DIVERSITY MATTERS

Even when younger and older adults engage in the same behavior, they might be driven by different motivations. Younger adults tend to value the outcome more, while older adults tend to value the process more. In one study, among adults who were starting a new exercise program, younger adults reported that they were exercising because of the results that the exercise provided (like sexual attractiveness, muscle tone, and weight loss), but older adults reported that they were exercising because of the process of exercise itself (like the fun of the workouts and the interaction with other people at the gym) (Freund et al., 2010).

CHECK YOUR LEARNING:

8.1 What is motivation?

8.2 What is the difference between intrinsic motivation and extrinsic motivation?

8.3 What are the basic ideas of the classic theories of motivation: instinct theory, drive reduction theory, and arousal theory?

8.4 What are the basic ideas of the contemporary theories of motivation: self-determination theory, regulatory focus theory, and achievement goal theory?

8.5 What is the sequence of levels in Abraham Maslow's hierarchy of needs?

8.6 What are some forms of diversity that can influence motivation?

A Primary Motivation: Hunger and Eating

YOU WILL LEARN:

8.7 what body mass index (BMI) is, and how it is used to define being overweight or obese.

8.8 consequences of being overweight or obese.

8.9 biological factors that can contribute to being overweight or obese.

There are many competing theories of motivation, and many diversity-related factors that might influence how any of those theories apply to any particular person. But there is one fundamental motivation that we all share: to eat. Let's explore the many reasons why we eat, with special emphasis on why we might eat too much at times.

Obesity and Overweight

Words like *obese* and *overweight* are thrown around a lot, so let's begin by defining them clearly. Both definitions will be based on **body mass index (BMI)**: a number calculated from a person's height and weight that indicates body fat and overall fitness level. Your

BMI is calculated by dividing your body weight (in kilograms) by the square of your height (in meters) (Centers for Disease Control and Prevention, 2015). Of course, your BMI depends on your ratio of food intake (especially fats and added sugars) to physical activity—in other words, the number of calories you consume versus the number of calories you burn (Must et al., 2006). If you're interested to learn your own BMI, there are plenty of simple BMI tables and calculators available online, including http://www.nhlbi.nih.gov/health/educational/lose_wt/BMI/bmi_tbl.htm.

BMIs are placed into four categories (Must & Evans, 2011). *Normal/healthy weight* is defined as a BMI between 18.5 and 24.9. A BMI below 18.5 is considered *underweight*. **Overweight** is a BMI between 25 and 29.9. **Obesity** is a BMI of 30 or higher. As an example, consider Dylan, who stands 5'8". If he weighs 145 pounds, his BMI is 22, which puts him in the normal/healthy category. If he weighs 180 pounds, his BMI is 27.4, which puts him in the overweight category.

Consequences of Overweight and Obesity. As we consider the consequences that often happen to people who are overweight or obese, remember again that the causal relationship is not always definite. The research discussed in this section presents a convincing case that these are indeed *consequences* of overweight and obesity, but some of these consequences could be causes too.

Perhaps the most firmly established and widely known consequence of being overweight or obese is disease. People who carry excess weight are at heightened risk for a long list of medical problems, including diabetes, cardiovascular disease, cancer, hypertension, arthritis, stroke, gallbladder disease, and high cholesterol (Calle et al., 2003; Bray, 2004; Anderson et al., 2007; Adams et al., 2006; Lavie et al., 2009; Must et al., 1999). Diabetes has an especially close link to being overweight and obesity, and given the rise in overweight and obesity rates in recent decades, the rate of diabetes is correspondingly expected to double between 2000 and 2030 (Wild et al., 2004; Schwartz & Porte, 2005; Hartz et al., 1983). In addition to the diseases themselves, there are financial costs: People who are overweight or obese have far more doctor's office visits, overnight stays in hospitals, and prescription medications than people of healthy weight, costing significantly more in medical costs (Finkelstein & Yang, 2011; Quesenberry et al., 1998; Thompson et al., 2001; Sturm, 2002). In total, obesity-related illnesses account for more than 10% of medical spending in the United States, with an annual cost well over $100 billion (Finkelstein et al., 2009).

In addition to physical health problems, people who are overweight or obese suffer with mental health problems at high rates too (Simon et al., 2006). Several longitudinal studies show that obesity is often followed by depression, especially in women (Roberts et al., 2003; Bjerkeset et al., 2008). In one review of longitudinal studies of obesity and depression, researchers found far more evidence for an obesity-to-depression sequence than a depression-to-obesity sequence (Faith et al., 2011). Even when excess weight does not result in diagnosable depression, it often lowers self-esteem, which impedes happiness (Wardle & Cook, 2005). Anxiety is also relatively common in overweight and obese adults, especially among women and the very obese (Scott et al., 2008). Obesity has even been linked to dementia later in life. One longitudinal study explored the medical records of over 10,000 people over a 30-year span—in particular, their weight when they were in their 40s, and whether they had been diagnosed with dementia by their 70s. They found that those who were overweight or obese in middle age had significantly higher rates of dementia as older adults. Specifically, compared to people who were of normal weight in their 40s, overweight people had a 35% greater risk of developing dementia, and obese people had a 74% greater chance (Whitmer et al., 2005).

The increased risk of depression, anxiety, and other mental disorders among overweight and obese people is probably connected to the stigma and discrimination that they face on a regular basis (Moskovich et al., 2011; O'Brien et al., 2013). By any name—"fat shaming," "sizism," or any other—disapproving or hateful attitudes toward overweight and obese people cause significant damage (McHugh & Kasardo, 2012). But those attitudes are often present. For example, these attitudes are present among

YOU WILL LEARN: (*Continued*)

8.10 environmental and sociocultural factors that can contribute to being overweight or obese.

8.11 tips for eating healthy.

body mass index (BMI)
A number calculated from a person's height and weight that indicates body fat and overall fitness level.

overweight
A BMI between 25 and 29.9.

obesity
A BMI of 30 or higher.

children: One study of 5- to 10-year old children found that they were much more likely to not want to be friends with a kid who was overweight (or even a normal-weight girl standing next to other girls who were overweight) (Penny & Haddock, 2007). These attitudes are present among doctors: Over one-third of physicians view obese patients as lazy, sloppy, weak-willed, and unattractive (Foster et al., 2003; Wear et al., 2006). These attitudes are present in job interviews as well: In one study, over 300 college students watched job interviews in which applicants appeared either as their normal-weight selves or with prosthetics (a "fat suit") to make them look obese. The students were much less likely to recommend hiring the "fat" applicant than the normal-weight applicant (Pingitore et al., 1994). In their actual jobs, overweight or obese workers are much more likely to be viewed as potentially weak workers, and to receive negative performance evaluations from their supervisors (Rudolph et al., 2009; Polinko & Popovich, 2001).

Biological Factors in Hunger and Eating

Within your body, there are numerous factors that cause you to feel hungry, eat, and, under certain circumstances, overeat. Let's consider the primary factors.

Hormones. Your body contains hunger-related hormones that respond to your need for food at any particular time. One pair of these hormones, *leptin* and *ghrelin*, is especially important. **Leptin** is a hormone that signals feelings of fullness. **Ghrelin** is a hormone that signals feelings of hunger. These two hormones essentially monitor the amount of food in your stomach and send messages to your brain about what action to take next. Leptin's message, which happens after you eat a big meal, is "Stop eating—your stomach is full." Ghrelin's message, which happens when many hours have passed since that big meal, is "Start eating—your stomach is empty" (Berk, 2008a; Wren et al., 2001). Researchers are still determining exactly how leptin and ghrelin work (they were just discovered in the 1990s), but it is clear that these two hormones greatly impact your appetite at any given moment (Ernsberger, 2008). In lab experiments, injecting extra leptin into mice caused them to eat less, but this finding does not translate directly to humans (Stein, 2008; Margetic et al., 2002).

Set Point/Settling Point. Another biological factor that influences your eating behavior is your **set point**: a particular weight to which your body tends to return after increases or decreases. Your set point is like the temperature to which a thermostat is set. If the room gets a little too hot, cold air blows, and if the room gets a little too cold, hot air blows, with the goal of returning to the predetermined temperature without ever straying far from it. In much the same way, your body (especially through its use of leptin and ghrelin) returns your body to its set point of weight by increasing or decreasing appetite as necessary.

Wait—if there's a set point, how do people ever gain or lose weight?

Actually, set point is one reason why losing a significant amount of weight—and more importantly, *keeping* it off—is so difficult. But there are some people who manage to lose weight and keep it off. There are also people who gain significant weight and keep it on. To explain these drastic and long-lasting weight changes, some experts argue that the set point may better be described as a *settling point*, a term intended to sound more flexible and more responsive to external factors than *set point*. Set point, as it was originally conceived, focused exclusively on what happens inside your body, but ignored external factors. So, according to set point, your body is "hard-wired" to retain roughly the same weight whether you live where food is sparse or plentiful. But that's not how it actually works. People tend to gain weight when the environment enables them to do so. *Settling point* suggests that those environmental influences do

CHAPTER APP 8.2

Set Point

Lose It!

Preview one of the links and consider the following questions.

WEBSITE:
http://tiny.cc/fbi7jy

ANDROID:
http://tiny.cc/ta92iy

IPHONE:
http://tiny.cc/d482iy

VIDEO DEMO:
http://tiny.cc/chapterapps

This app can help you manage your weight by tracking how many calories you take in and how many you burn. You tell it how much you eat and how much you exercise, and it tells you how much weight you'll lose (or gain, as the case may be).

How does it APPly to your daily life?
How would the feedback you get from this app affect your response to hunger? How would it affect how much you eat?

How does it APPly to your understanding of psychology?
If you saw someone lose lots of weight with this app (or any similar app or program), what would you think about the concepts of *set point* and *settling point*? What would you think if you see those people gain the weight back?

matter, especially in terms of weight gain (Speakman et al., 2011; Egger & Swinburn, 1997; Pinel et al., 2000).

If you live in a developed country like the United States, your environmental influences are probably quite different from the way they were thousands of years ago. For most of human history, food was scarce. It was especially difficult to find foods rich in calories, fats, and salts. (Vegetables and fruits were easier to come by.) So, our ancestors stuffed themselves when they found rich foods, intentionally trying to build up fat that might enable them to survive the next period of food deprivation. They would feast now to survive famine later.

You are a descendant of those opportunistic overeaters, which means that your body and brain use the same strategy: When you find rich foods, eat as much as possible and accumulate fat, since food may not be available later. But in your daily lifestyle, food *is* available later. In fact, you probably spend most of your life with quick and easy access to fast food restaurants, 24-hour convenience stores, all-you-can-eat buffets, or pizza delivery. So instead of *occasional* overeating, as your ancestors did, you have the opportunity for *continual* overeating. You'll probably never encounter the famine that would burn off the fat resulting from such eating habits, so that fat stays with you, creating all kinds of health risks. This phenomenon is known as the *thrifty gene hypothesis*: You inherited genes that promote an eating strategy to build up fat whenever possible. This strategy may have kept your ancestors alive, but it can backfire and contribute to your death if left unchecked (Neel, 1962, 1999; Myles et al., 2011; Chakravarthy & Booth, 2004; Berk, 2008b).

The problems related to the thrifty gene hypothesis are made worse by the fact that your daily lifestyle requires far less exercise than your ancestors' lifestyles. Sure, you can *choose* to work out, but there was no choice for your ancestors. They got their workouts every day while foraging for and running after food. In some less developed societies today, people still live a lifestyle similar to that of our shared human ancestors, spending much of their day in pursuit of food and eating a relatively low-fat, low-salt, low-calorie diet. Obesity, and the many health problems that come with it, are extremely rare in those societies.

Genetics. The thrifty gene hypothesis applies broadly to all humans, but the specific genes you inherit from your parents also play a significant role in your eating behavior and your weight (Bell et al., 2005). The heritability of being overweight is 40–70%, meaning that roughly half (or more) of the variability in your BMI is due to your genes rather than your environment (Samaras, 2008; Flier, 2004). Adoption studies find that

leptin
A hormone that signals feelings of fullness.

ghrelin
A hormone that signals feelings of hunger.

set point
A particular weight to which the person's body tends to return after increases or decreases.

Bruce Eric Kaplan The New Yorker Collection/
The Cartoon Bank

IT'S LIKE...

The Thrifty Gene Hypothesis Is Like Buying Gas for a Nickel a Gallon

After a lifetime of high gas prices, imagine how you'd feel if you saw a gas station selling gas for a nickel a gallon. You'd grab that deal, assuming that you won't soon find it again. You'd fill your tank, and you might also fill up so many gas cans that they'd fill the trunk, the back seat, the roof rack, and maybe even a trailer. You could make your car fat with gas.

But what if you went around the corner and saw another gas station also selling gas for a nickel a gallon? And what if that price remained consistent for the rest of your life, available at gas stations everywhere you go? If you maintained the same mentality—stock up as much as you can every chance you get—your car would soon become seriously obese with gas. No matter how much you drove, there's no way your car could burn gas at the same rate you acquire it.

Thankfully, your logic would take over and prevent this stockpiling of gas. But when it comes to food intake, your logic is up against thousands of years of evolution. As the thrifty gene hypothesis states, your genes drive you to stock up on high-calorie, high-fat foods because they have been hard to find safeguards against famine over the course of human history. But if your lifestyle is like that of most Americans, your world is not like that anymore. All kinds of food is inexpensive and readily available at many nearby restaurants, supermarkets, convenience stores, and vending machines. Thanks to your evolutionary inheritance, you feel the urge to stock up on calories even if you don't need them. That is a big reason why obesity has become such a problem in countries like the United States. It is an inherited challenge to resist the temptation of a supersized fast food meal or a king-size candy bar even when you know you don't need those calories.

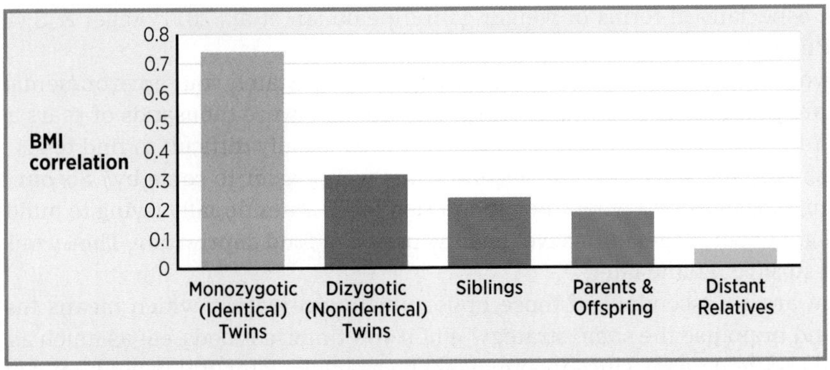

FIGURE 8.2 Genes and BMI. Genes play a significant role in BMI. The correlation between BMIs of people who share a larger percentage of their genes is substantially higher than the correlation between BMIs of people who share a smaller percentage of their genes. Information from Maes et al., 1997.

when adopted kids grow up, their BMIs correlate positively with the weights of their biological parents, but don't correlate at all with the weights of their adoptive parents (Stunkard et al., 1986b; Vogler et al., 1995). Twin studies reach similar results: identical (monozygotic) twins have a much higher BMI correlation than fraternal (dizygotic) twins (Stunkard et al., 1986a; Bouchard et al., 1994). In fact, the more genes you share with someone, the higher the correlation between their weight and yours (Maes et al., 1997). Check **Figure 8.2** for details.

By the way, in spite of oversimplified reports you may hear in news stories about a single "fat gene" or "obesity gene," the genetic influence on weight comes from a collection of many genes (Marti et al., 2004; Alfredo Martínez et al., 2007). Those genes influence many things related to your BMI, including how you experience hunger, how you experience fullness, and how your body stores nutrients (Stein, 2008).

Metabolic Rate. Additionally, those genes influence your **metabolic rate** (or **metabolism**): the rate at which your body burns energy. Of course, your metabolic rate varies. It is lower when you rest, higher when you exercise, and tends to vary across the life span. But it also differs between you and other people. Your metabolic rate is simply faster or slower than the metabolism of some other people. You probably have a friend who can eat constantly without ever gaining a pound, and another friend who can exercise and diet constantly without losing a pound. Difference in metabolic rate is a likely explanation.

Sex. Another biological factor that influences your eating behavior is your sex. Men eat more than women (Davy et al., 2007; Laessle et al., 2007). Of course, men (on average) are bigger than women, but the difference in food intake goes beyond that: One study found that men were 16% heavier, but ate 33% more than women (Bates et al., 1999). Men also have slightly faster resting metabolism than women on average, which demands slightly more refueling (Herman & Polivy, 2010).

DIVERSITY MATTERS

Of course, there is also the impression that eating makes in social situations. Women tend to be much more concerned not only about gaining weight as a result of eating, but about looking gluttonous while they're eating (Vartanian et al., 2007). Both men and women change their eating habits depending upon who they're eating with, but the most significant changes are the decreases in food intake by women when they eat with an eligible, attractive, unfamiliar man—perhaps to convey an image of femininity (Salvy et al., 2007; Mori et al., 1987; Pliner & Chaiken, 1990). Generally, women eat more fruits and vegetables than men, which is a by-product of women generally caring more about eating healthy (Beer-Borst et al., 2000; Serdula et al., 1995). In a study of over 19,000 young adults from 23 countries, women were 50% more likely than men to report avoiding high-fat foods, 25% more likely to report eating fruit daily, and 6% less likely to report adding salt to their food (Wardle et al., 2004).

Psychological Factors

Eating may be driven by biology, but it is affected by many psychological factors as well, including stress and psychological disorders (Moskovich et al., 2011).

Stress and Eating. There is little doubt that stress affects eating (Greeno & Wing, 1994). You may assume that stress increases eating, especially if you've seen scenes in movies where emotionally distraught people scarf down a whole container of ice cream or a big bag of chips. However, that increase in eating isn't automatic (Steere & Cooper, 1993). In fact, some research has found that among people experiencing stress, an increase in eating is actually less common than a decrease in eating. But the same research finds that gender and the amount of stress make big differences too. If the stress levels are only moderate, both men and women tend to eat less, but if the stress levels are high, women tend to eat more while men still tend to eat less (Stone & Brownell, 1994). Stress-related changes in eating amounts also depend on dieting, with dieters much more likely to respond to stress by overeating than nondieters (Zellner et al., 2006).

DIVERSITY MATTERS

In addition to influencing *how much* you eat, stress can influence *what* you eat. Generally, stress causes less healthy food choices (Oliver & Wardle, 1999). One study that asked teachers and nurses to keep a personal food and stress journal for 8 weeks found that they ate at fast-food restaurants more often when they were highly stressed (Steptoe et al., 1998). A survey of over 4000 adolescents found that when they were highly stressed, they ate more fatty foods, fewer fruits and vegetables, and skipped breakfast more often (Cartwright et al., 2003).

There are significant differences in how and what women and men eat, especially when they eat in front of each other. Hero Images/Getty Images

What about the "freshman 15"? Is that an example of how stress can affect eating?

The first year of college can be stressful, but research on the well-known freshman 15 (gaining 15 pounds during the first year of college) suggests that it is not so common after all (Vadeboncoeur et al., 2015). A meta-analysis that combined the results of over 20 studies (covering thousands of students) on the freshman 15 found that the average weight gain during the first year of college was only 3–4 pounds (Vella-Zarb & Elgar, 2009).

Students most likely to gain the full freshman 15 (or more) are those with a combination of high BMI before entering college and high stress levels (Boyce & Kuijer, 2015). As **Figure 8.3** illustrates, studies that follow students through college find that weight gain gradually continues across all 4 years, with an average total gain of 9 pounds in men and 7 pounds in women (Girz et al., 2013). So, the freshman 15 is not inevitable,

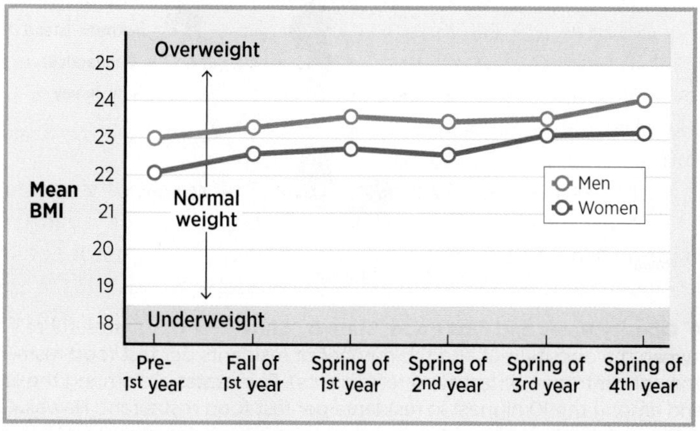

FIGURE 8.3 Weight Gain During College. The freshman 15 is more of a myth than a fact. According to research on weight gain during college (including this study of nearly 500 students at six colleges followed from before their first day through their fourth year), both men and women show a pattern of more gradual weight gain that continues through all 4 years. Data from Girz et al., 2013.

metabolic rate (or **metabolism**) The rate at which one's body burns energy.

but gradual weight gain throughout the college years is quite common and could lead to health concerns if it continues through adulthood.

Environmental and Sociocultural Factors

Besides the biological and psychological factors *within* you, factors *outside* of you influence your eating and your weight. Let's consider some of the most important.

Economic and Shopping-Related Factors. What you eat depends on how much money you have (cost) and where you can spend it (access).

DIVERSITY MATTERS

Cost and access make it especially difficult for people of low SES to eat healthy. First, consider cost. While the overall price of food (adjusted for inflation) has decreased since the 1970s, the price of *healthy* food (such as vegetables and fruit) has risen (Cawley, 2011; Auld & Powell, 2009). A meta-analysis of the difference between healthy diets (vegetables, fruits, nuts, fish, etc.) and unhealthy diets (processed foods, junk food, sugary sodas, etc.) found that the healthy diet costs about $1.50 more per day per person—a negligible amount to some, but a real obstacle to others (Rao et al., 2013; Shaw, 2014). Higher prices of healthy foods correlate with higher BMI in children, primarily because the kids and their parents buy cheaper, more fattening foods instead (Sturm & Datar, 2005; Powell & Bao, 2009).

Those cheaper, more fattening foods often come from fast food restaurants. Where fast food restaurants are prevalent, BMIs tend to increase. (Niemeier et al., 2006). Specifically, in the United States, there is a strong correlation between a state's obesity rate and its concentration of fast food restaurants (**Figure 8.4**). In states where it is easier to find a McDonalds, Wendy's, Burger King, or Taco Bell, it is also easier to find obese people (Maddock, 2004). On the other hand, if the prices of fast food and healthy food are closer together, healthy eating slightly increases: Specifically, when fast food prices go up 10% (approaching the prices of healthier foods), the likelihood of teenagers frequently eating fruits and vegetables increases 3% and the likelihood of teenagers being overweight drops 6% (Powell et al., 2007).

Even if you can afford healthy food, you have to get to stores that sell it. That is not easy in a *food desert*, an area with few if any stores and restaurants offering healthy options. If you're affluent, you probably live near supermarkets (or even high-end food

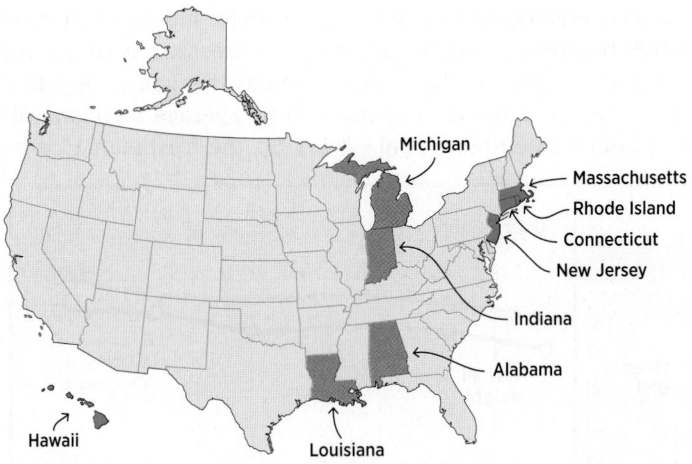

FIGURE 8.4 Obesity Rates and Fast Food, State by State. For U.S. states, there's a strong correlation between the obesity rate and the number of residents per fast food restaurant (one way of measuring the concentration of fast food restaurants). Five states are among the 10 lowest in obesity rates and among the 10 highest in residents per fast food restaurant: Hawaii, Connecticut, Massachusetts, Rhode Island, and New Jersey. Four states are among the 10 highest in obesity rates and among the 10 lowest in residents per fast food restaurant: Alabama, Louisiana, Michigan, and Indiana. In some cases, a state from one category has twice as many residents per fast food restaurant as the other. For example, in Louisiana, there are fewer than 8000 people for every fast food restaurant, but in Hawaii, there are over 16,000. Information from Maddock, 2004.

stores specializing in wholesome, nutritious foods) and restaurants where healthy food is sold. You also probably have a car, or at least bus fare, to get to those kinds of places. But if you're poor, your best (or only) nearby options may be convenience stores and fast food restaurants, and you may not have access to transportation to get you to another part of town (Smith & Cummins, 2011). As a result, people who live in food deserts tend to have higher BMIs (Morland et al., 2006; Fiechtner et al., 2013).

Lifestyle Factors. Many aspects of day-to-day life can affect how an individual or a family eats. Researchers have paid special attention to the amount of time spent watching TV.

As the amount of time watching TV (or computers, or any other screens) expands, so do waistlines (Vandewater & Wartella, 2011). Not only is TV watching sedentary (you're a couch potato while you do it), but it is often accompanied by snacking on unhealthy foods (Matheson et al., 2004; Crespo et al., 2001). To make matters worse, the ads during those shows often promote even more unhealthy foods. (Ever see a commercial for exactly what you're eating at that moment?) Shows marketed to children and Black viewers have especially high rates of ads for fast food, candy, soda, and similarly unhealthy foods (Tirodkar & Jain, 2003; Vandewater & Wartella, 2011; Henderson & Kelly, 2005). For kids, sugary cereals are another commonly advertised product. As **Table 8.1** indicates, many of the *least* nutritious cereals marketed to kids are the *most* frequently advertised during kids' shows. When the cereals are actually named after candies and other sweets—*Cookie Crisp, Reese's Puffs, Count Chocula*—it is probably a safe bet that nutritional content is not the top priority.

The constant barrage of ads for unhealthy foods on kids' shows probably contributes to obesity in kids (World Health Organization, 2003). In fact, the relationship is so strong, and has received so much attention, that some children's advocacy groups have called for limitations (or a complete ban) on advertising for unhealthy food on kids' shows, like there is for cigarettes and alcohol during adult programming (Institute of Medicine, 2006). Check the Current Controversy box for more this issue.

Opportunities for Exercise. The flip side to consuming calories is burning them off through exercise. Unfortunately, some people simply don't have as much opportunity for exercise as others. Of course, some of the obstacles involve time and money. Some people just don't have enough of either to join a gym or dedicate themselves to a regular exercise program. But another factor is the *built environment*, or the exercise opportunities built into the physical surroundings and day-to-day life in a particular neighborhood. Ideally, the built environment facilitates exercise by containing a number of features: a good quality and quantity of parks; streets that are walkable (well-lit, low traffic, with well-maintained sidewalks and traffic lights designed for pedestrians as well as cars); shops and restaurants within walking distance; and low levels of crime. These features

TABLE 8.1: Kids' Cereals, Nutrition, and Advertising

ADVERTISED CEREALS WITH THE POOREST NUTRITION RANKINGS	MOST FREQUENTLY MARKETED TO CHILDREN ON TELEVISION
1. Reese's Puffs	1. Cinnamon Toast Crunch
2. Corn Pops	2. Honey Nut Cheerios
3. Lucky Charms	3. Lucky Charms
4. Cinnamon Toast Crunch	4. Cocoa Puffs
5. Cap'n Crunch	5. Trix
6. Trix	6. Frosted Flakes
7. Froot Loops	7. Fruity and Cocoa Pebbles
8. Fruity and Cocoa Pebbles	8. Reese's Puffs
9. Cocoa Puffs	9. Corn Pops
10. Cookie Crisp	10. Froot Loops

Information from http://cerealfacts.org/media/Cereal_FACTS_Report_Summary_2009.pdf.

Notice the overlap between the 10 least nutritious cereals and the 10 cereals most frequently marketed to children: 8 cereals appear on both lists. Information like this motivates some people to consider limitations on advertising of unhealthy foods, especially during children's programming.

CURRENT CONTROVERSY

Advertising Unhealthy Food to Kids

Through much of her husband's presidency, Michelle Obama campaigned for healthier lifestyles for kids. Part of that campaign focused on advertising—the TV commercials, Internet ads, billboards, and signs (including many at schools) that promote junk food to children. As she stated in a speech to food manufacturers:

As a mom, I know it is my responsibility—and no one else's—to raise my kids. But what does it mean when so many parents are finding that their best efforts are undermined by an avalanche of advertisements aimed at their kids? And what are these ads teaching kids about food and nutrition? That it's good to have salty, sugary food and snacks every day—breakfast, lunch, and dinner? —White House, 2010

Michelle Obama dedicated much effort during her husband's presidency to promoting healthier lifestyles for children, including a reduction in advertising of unhealthy foods. Andrew Burton/Getty Images

Michelle Obama was not alone in her efforts. Numerous organizations have called for limits or even an outright ban on such advertising targeted toward children (Institute of Medicine, 2006). And one group of researchers estimates that a ban would make a significant impact—a drop of approximately 14-33%—on obesity rates in U.S. kids (Veerman et al., 2009).

Both food companies and researchers agree that advertising foods to kids works. It has a powerful impact on their preferences and actual eating behaviors (Boyland & Whalen, 2015; Harris et al., 2009). But banning the ads works too. When Australia did it, the mean BMI for both boys and girls dropped quickly (Magnus et al., 2009). The opposition to efforts to ban or limit advertising of unhealthy foods to children comes from numerous sources. For example, the food and beverage companies whose profits depend heavily on sales to children don't like the ban. The recipients of those advertising dollars, such as television networks, Internet sites, and even some schools, don't like the bans either. In the meantime, the controversy over how much to allow this kind of advertising continues. ⬢

promote walking, jogging, bike riding, and other nonmotorized ways of getting around that burn calories and combat obesity. Sadly, less affluent neighborhoods (the same ones less likely to have supermarkets and healthy restaurants) tend not to have such picturesque built environments (Morland et al., 2002a,b; Burke et al., 2009). As a result, weight problems are even more difficult to overcome in these areas (Sallis et al., 2011).

Portion Size. How much food there is influences how much you eat. In terms of portion size, we tend to eat whatever we receive (Wansink, 2011). That tendency becomes an obesity risk when what we receive is much more than what we need. In recent decades, we receive much more than what we need from fast food restaurants (Young & Nestle, 2002). Consider McDonalds, for example. Picture your grandparent ordering a burger, fries, and soda in the late 1950s. Now picture yourself walking into McDonalds today and ordering your own burger, fries, and soda, all supersized to the largest on the menu. Your burger is 5 *times* as big, your order of fries is 2.5 *times* as big, and your soda is 4.5 *times* as big (Young & Nestle, 2007)! It is no wonder why your generation has much more of an obesity problem than your grandparents'. That is especially true when you consider that eating out—where portion sizes are controlled by someone other than yourself—has also become much more common in recent decades. In fact, in recent years the amount of money that Americans spend eating out has risen to double its level in the 1950s, matching the amount we spend eating at home (United States Department of Agriculture, 2014).

The built environment, or the exercise opportunities built into a neighborhood, include parks, sidewalks, trails, and nearby shops and restaurants. Such features promote walking, jogging, biking, and other activities that reduce obesity. Cultura RM Exclusive/Edwin Jimenez/Getty Images

Food size matters at home too, but often it is the size of the package or container (rather than the size of the portion) that matters. In one study, participants were given a box of uncooked spaghetti and asked to take out enough for dinner for two. If the box was small (1 pound), they took out an average of 234 strands. But if the box was large (2 pounds), they took out an average of 302 strands—an increase of almost 30% (Wansink, 2006). Another study found that when participants poured juice into glasses, they poured 88% more into short, wide glasses than tall, narrow glasses, presumably because of differences in how "tall" the amount appeared (Wansink & van Ittersum, 2003). (The same study found that even bartenders are susceptible—they poured 26% more hard liquor into tumbler glasses than highball glasses.)

Does the portion size determine how much people actually eat?

Yes, it does. Whether the reason is the need to "clean our plates," eating out of boredom, or just accepting that the size we received is "normal," larger portions lead people to eat larger amounts (Wansink, 2011). One study examined the amount of Chex Mix eaten by football fans at a Super Bowl party, and found that fans eating out of bigger containers ate 53% more than fans eating out of smaller containers (Wansink & Cheney, 2005). Similar results were found with popcorn at a movie theater: whether the popcorn was fresh or stale, people eating out of larger containers ate significantly more (Wansink & Park, 2001; Wansink & Kim, 2005).

What is especially scary about how portion size affects eating is that people generally don't realize it. After that Super Bowl study, the researchers told the participants eating out of bigger containers that their group ate much more than the other group, but 63% of them responded by claiming that they did not actually eat more (Wansink & Cheney, 2005).

LIFE HACK 8.1

To limit how much you eat, limit your portion size. Don't eat directly out of the family-size bag of chips, the tub of ice cream, or the giant pizza box. Instead, put a reasonable-sized serving on a plate or in a bowl.

(Wansink, 2011; Wansink & Park, 2001; Wansink & Kim, 2005)

Promoting Healthy Eating

With so many factors influencing how and what you eat—and so many of those influences leading to people being overweight and obese—what is the best strategy for healthy eating? Experts and researchers offer lots of suggestions, ranging from how you can manage your own eating to how organizations, including the government, can make large-scale social changes (Roberto et al., 2015).

Individual Strategies. There are quite a few individual strategies for promoting healthy eating—including shopping smart, lifestyle changes, and professional help.

Shop smart. The grocery store is just as important as the kitchen table in terms of healthy food choices. Filling your fridge and cupboard with healthy stuff will prevent you from potentially making unwise choices when you get that late night craving for double fudge brownies. And take advantage of your knowledge about portion size: If you must eat too much once in a while, eat too much of something healthy. One study found that when kids were served double portions of vegetables with their meals, they ate much more of them (Mathias et al., 2012).

Think lifestyle change, not quick fix. Crash diets and short-term exercise programs don't work, at least not long-term. A better approach involves bigger changes in how you live your life. These changes can include not only what you eat, but also the social support you get from friends and family regarding weight loss and how much you prioritize exercise and integrate it into your regular schedule (Wadden, 1995; Wadden et al., 2007; Jeffrey et al., 2003; Perri & Corsica, 2002).

Consider professional help. If you continue to have serious struggles with weight, numerous options are available. For example, there are therapies based on behavioral change, like keeping a record of your eating and exercise behavior and rewarding yourself for meeting specific goals (Jones-Corneille et al., 2011). There are also therapies based on changing irrational thoughts about weight, like "I'll never get in shape" or "I'm such a loser for letting myself get to this point" (Brownell, 2004). Of course, there are also pills and surgeries to consider as weight loss strategies. Unfortunately, those pills often have unwanted side effects and questionable effectiveness (especially long-term), and the surgeries are often expensive and produce other medical complications (Encinosa et al., 2009, 2011).

Social Strategies. There are also many social strategies for promoting healthy eating—including better food labeling, limiting advertising of unhealthy foods, taxing unhealthy foods, and increasing community interventions.

Require more prominent and realistic food labeling. Packaged food already includes food labels, but often the serving sizes are unrealistically small. (*Seven* Tostitos chips is one serving? Really? [FritoLay, 2016].) Also, the nutrition information on restaurant menus could be more easily available and complete (Kersh & Morone, 2011).

CHAPTER APP 8.3

Promoting Healthy Eating

HealthyOut

Preview one of the links and consider the following questions.

WEBSITE: http://tiny.cc/ubi7jy

ANDROID: http://tiny.cc/i2mkjy

IPHONE: http://tiny.cc/51mkjy

VIDEO DEMO: http://tiny.cc/chapterapps

With this app, you enter an address and it gives you directions to nearby restaurants that serve healthy meals. Click on a restaurant, and the app lists specific healthy dishes available there, complete with detailed nutrition information (total calories, fat grams, protein, etc.) and modifications you can request to make the dish even healthier (skip the sour cream, choose grilled chicken instead of fried, etc.). You can even filter results for particular nutritional preferences, including vegetarian, gluten-sensitive, low carb, or heart healthy.

How does it APPly to your daily life?
What would be the greatest benefits and drawbacks of having this app on your phone? What would happen to the frequency with which you eat healthy food, rather than unhealthy or fast food, when you eat out?

How does it APPly to your understanding of psychology?
How do apps like this one compare to the other individual strategies and social strategies designed to promote healthy eating?

Healthy school lunches are one of many social strategies to promote healthy eating.
XiXinXing/Thinkstock

Limit advertising of unhealthy foods. Numerous experts and advocacy groups have called for limitations on the advertising of unhealthy foods, especially on kids' shows (Ippolito, 2011). Similar efforts were part of the plan that worked well in changing behaviors regarding tobacco, seat belt use, and recycling, which has prompted some experts to suggest using them against unhealthy foods as well (Chaloupka, 2011; Economos et al., 2001).

Tax unhealthy food. In some states, there are already taxes on some unhealthy foods, like soda, potato chips, and candy, but these policies could be expanded and improved (Powell & Chaloupka, 2009). Speaking of taxes, the government could provide tax incentives to supermarket chains (and any other seller of healthy foods) for opening stores in food deserts, and for existing stores in those neighborhoods to get the equipment and inventory necessary to supply healthier food to their customers (Roberto & Brownell, 2011).

Increase community-wide interventions. These efforts could include more offerings from the parks & recreation department (such as exercise and recreation classes), community classes on healthy food and cooking, and health education campaigns (Economos & Sliwa, 2011).

Promote healthy eating at schools and workplaces. Schools could place more emphasis on food and nutrition education, offer more opportunity for physical education and after-school sports, and offer healthier options in the cafeteria and vending machines (Brown, 2011). Employers could offer educational programs, create workplaces that promote physical activity (make gyms available, encourage stairs over elevators, limit sedentary activity), financially reward employees who participate in fitness programs, offer inexpensive healthy snacks at meetings, meals, and in vending machines, install bike racks, and create walking trails nearby (Goetzel et al., 2011).

CHECK YOUR LEARNING:

8.7 What is body mass index (BMI) and how does it define being overweight or obese?

8.8 What are the negative consequences of being overweight or obese?

8.9 What biological factors contribute to being overweight or obese?

8.10 What environmental and sociocultural factors contribute to being overweight or obese?

8.11 Do healthy eating strategies occur at the individual level, the social level, or both?

Emotion

YOU WILL LEARN:

8.12 what emotion is.

8.13 about a variety of theories that explain the connection between the physical and mental aspects of emotion.

8.14 how people communicate emotions, and whether certain emotions are communicated by all people.

8.15 what emotion regulation is, and how different strategies of emotion regulation compare to each other.

8.16 why emotion regulation is important, especially in relation to positive emotions.

8.17 how emotion interacts with age, ethnicity, and gender.

Emotion is all aspects of feeling, including changes to the body, behavior, and consciousness. Notice that the letters *mot* in the word e*mot*ion also appear in the word *mot*ivation. Both words come from the same root, which means *to move*. The purpose of emotion is to move you, to stir you into action (Solomon, 2008; Frijda, 2008). That action may be obvious, like when joy makes a child run and hug a parent returning from a military deployment. Or it may be subtle, like when anger makes you glare at a friend or family member. Throughout human history (and still today), those actions often produced survival advantages. People who ran away from something that made them feel scared or who avoided food that made them feel disgust were more likely to live (Plutchik, 2001, 2003). You are a descendant of those people whose emotions moved them to survive, and many of the genes that predisposed them to behave emotionally have been passed along to you.

Theories of Emotion

Emotions are both mental and physical experiences. Consider sadness, for example. One of my psychotherapy clients, Cody, had an appointment with me the day after the death of his dog, who had provided 12 years of loving companionship. Cody tried to

describe what was going through his mind: He was enduring pure despair, thinking about how much he would miss her, and remembering great times they shared. But he also communicated his sadness through tears, a headache, and physical exhaustion that made him look like he was dragging himself around. His sadness saturated not just his mind, but his body as well.

As psychologists have studied emotions over the years, some of their main questions have focused on this combination of mind and body experiences that emotions produce. Specifically, the question of *which comes first*—the sequence in which emotions affect the mind and the body—has prompted a variety of theories, each backed by its own research. Let's explore the main ones by examining how each of them would explain what happens to you in a very specific situation: a bottle of water spills on your smartphone, and you feel fear (**Figure 8.5**).

James–Lange Theory. **James–Lange theory** is a theory of emotion stating that you experience emotion by noticing bodily changes first and then interpreting them as particular feelings. The *James* in James–Lange theory is William James, whom you remember from Chapter 1 as the father of U.S. psychology. Back in 1884, James wrote one of the earliest psychology papers about emotion, which argued that the physical sensation comes first and that the sensation is followed by the feeling (James, 1884).

How does James–Lange theory explain the fear you feel when water spills on your smartphone? It says that first, your heart starts pounding, your breathing quickens, and your muscles tense up. *After* that bodily reaction, you become consciously aware of the emotion, and your mind feels fear. The key here is that your physical reaction, and your awareness of it, trigger the mental reaction.

There is research supporting the notion that certain emotions are characterized by certain patterns of biological reactions. For example, most participants in a study who saw unpleasant pictures involuntarily flexed their "frown" muscle (in their eyebrows) and also revealed subtle differences in the amount of electric energy contained within the skin. However, not all participants reacted this way. In fact, a sizable number did not (Lang et al., 1993; Lang, 1994). Also working against the James–Lange theory is the fact that often, the physical reaction simply can't happen as quickly as the mental reaction because the human body doesn't respond that quickly. (Think about it—if you saw a water bottle tip over and splash water onto your phone, would your heart, breathing, and muscles even have a chance to react in that first instant before your mind registered fear?) So, the James–Lange theory has garnered significant support in the many years since its introduction, but it also received significant criticism—much of which led to the theories of emotion we consider next.

Cannon–Bard Theory. The first prominent alternative to James–Lange theory was developed by Walter Cannon and Philip Bard in the early 1900s. **Cannon–Bard theory** is a theory of emotion stating that you experience emotion by simultaneously becoming aware of bodily changes and feelings. So, rather than the physical part of emotion hitting you first and the mental part hitting you next, they hit at the same time.

In our example, seeing water spill onto your smartphone would simultaneously produce the conscious experience of fear in your mind and produce the heart rate, breathing, and muscle changes in your body. Cannon and Bard, who were physiologists and tested their theory by experimenting on the brains of cats, explained that their theory reflected the important role of the thalamus within the brain (Bard, 1934). Specifically, the thalamus is where the processing of the image of the stimulus—in this case, water spilling onto your phone—divides into two separate and simultaneous streams, one that heads toward the cerebral cortex to produce the conscious experience of fear and another that heads toward the hypothalamus to produce the bodily changes (LeDoux, 1996).

Like the James–Lange theory before it, the Cannon–Bard theory received some support from research (Dror, 2014; Cannon, 1931; Bard, 1928). For example, in their own studies, Cannon and Bard found that a cat with its sensory cortex and motor cortex removed could still have emotional reactions. This experience should not be possible,

emotion
All aspects of feeling, including changes to the body, behavior, and consciousness.

James–Lange theory
A theory of emotion stating that the person experiences emotion by noticing bodily changes first and then interpreting them as particular feelings.

Cannon–Bard theory
A theory of emotion stating that the person experiences emotion by simultaneously becoming aware of bodily changes and feelings.

according to the James–Lange theory, since it depends on the perception of bodily change (Bard & Rioch, 1937; Cannon, 1927; Dalgleish, 2004).

The Cannon–Bard theory also received criticism, including the fact that it didn't allow for thought to influence the emotion process. According to Cannon–Bard theory (and James–Lange theory too, for that matter), emotions happened automatically. That may be true for most animals, but not for humans: We think too much. That is why the theories of emotion that came next historically focus on how thinking might influence the experience of emotion.

Schachter–Singer Theory. **Schachter–Singer theory** is a theory of emotion stating that the label you assign to your bodily reaction determines your mental reaction. (Schachter–Singer theory is also known as *two-factor theory*, with the two factors being your bodily reaction and your label for it.) When Stanley Schachter and Jerome Singer created their theory in the mid-1900s, they pointed out that the physical component of many emotions is quite similar. For example, consider the physical reactions

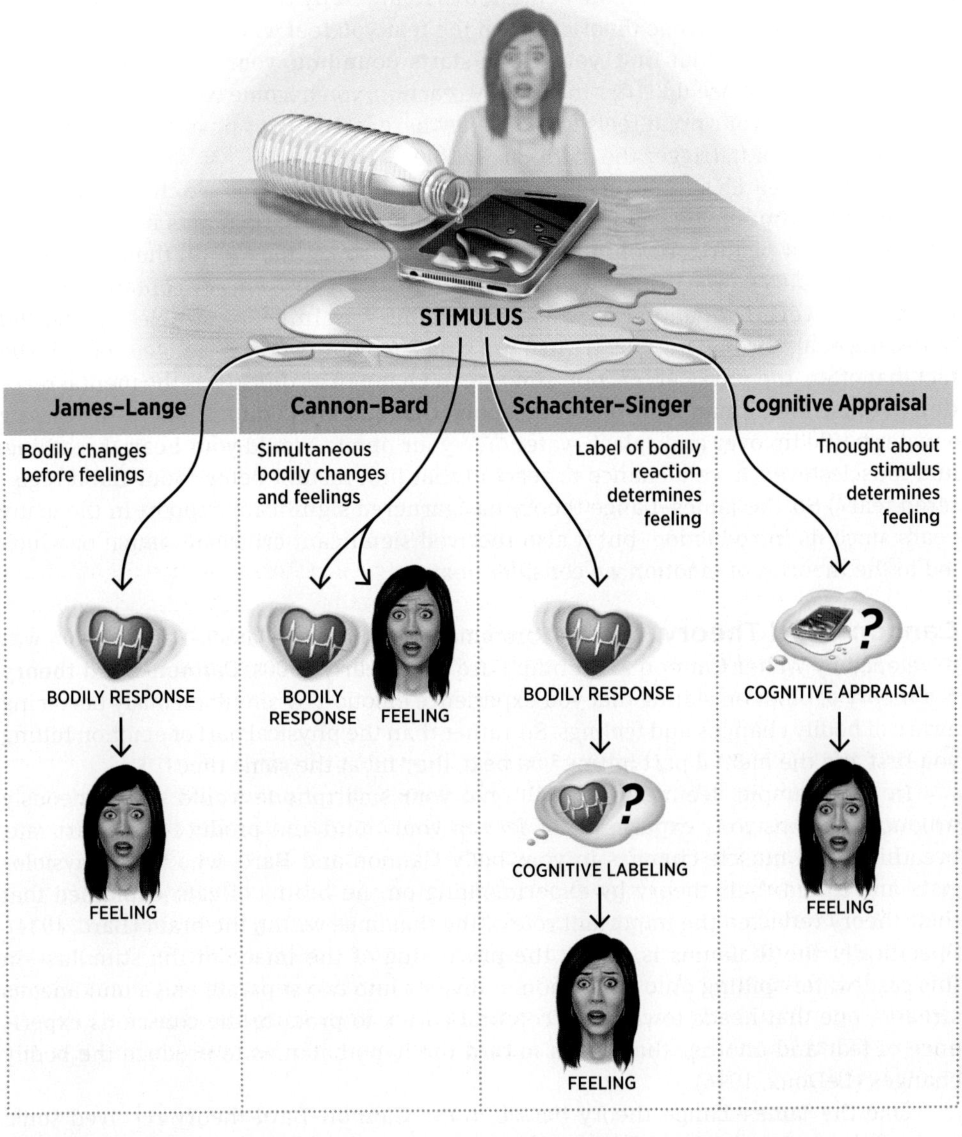

FIGURE 8.5 Theories of Emotion. If a bottle of water spilled on your smartphone, you'd feel fear. But how exactly would that emotion arise? Four major theories of emotion offer different explanations, especially in terms of the role of bodily arousal and the sequence of events.

we've been discussing in our example about water spilling on your phone: increased heart rate, rapid breathing, and tensed muscles. So far, we've tied those physical reactions to fear, but they are actually so generic that they could signal any number of emotions: excitement, anger, surprise, and more.

As an alternative example, consider Ronnie, a high school basketball player taking the court for a big game immediately after finding out that a scout from a local college team is in the crowd to check him out for a potential scholarship. Ronnie notices that his heart is pounding, and (unconsciously and instantly) wonders why. The options are many: shock (from just learning about the scout), nervousness (about the stakes of his performance in this particular game), exhilaration (about the opportunity to earn a college scholarship), or irritation (that he didn't get any advance notice about the scout). It is not the physical reaction itself, but the label that Ronnie places on it after he notices it, that determines how he experiences it mentally.

In a classic study, Schachter and Singer told participants that they were going to inject them with a vitamin solution and measure how it affected their visual abilities. But that wasn't what the study was really about. In truth, participants received an injection of epinephrine, which (as you recall from Chapter 2) is essentially adrenaline and is used in EpiPens to increase breathing rate and heart rate for people having allergic reactions. Some participants were told that the "vitamins" would have "side effects" (the actual effects of epinephrine), but others received no such information. Then, the participants waited in a room with another person, supposedly another participant who had received the same injection, but actually an actor pretending to be either euphoric (playing games and acting excited and happy) or angry (complaining and refusing to do what the researchers had requested).

Twenty minutes later, participants were asked how they felt. Those who had received the accurate "side effect" information attributed any physical sensations to the injection they had received. But those who had received no "side effect" information described feelings that matched those of the actor with whom they shared the room. If the injection made the "other participant" euphoric, the real participant was likely to report feeling euphoric, and if the injection made the "other participant" angry, the real participant was likely to report feeling angry (Schachter & Singer, 1962; also see Cotton, 1981). The main point here is that when physical sensations are ambiguous, they are open to interpretation. That interpretation can lead to a wide range of labels and subsequent mental experiences of emotion.

Schachter–Singer theory has been quite influential, but it has been criticized as well (Sinclair et al., 1994; Reisenzein, 1983). Some researchers who tried to replicate the classic Schachter–Singer study got different results (Maslach, 1979; Marshall & Zimbardo, 1979). Also, emotions don't necessarily require labels to be felt: When you were a baby and lacked vocabulary, this happened all the time, and it still might once in a while today when you have a feeling that you can't quite describe in words.

Cognitive Appraisal Theory. **Cognitive appraisal theory** is a theory of emotion stating that what you think about a stimulus causes the emotion. The key difference between this theory (developed largely by Richard Lazarus) and other theories of emotion is that it deemphasizes physical reactions. Unlike the other three theories we have considered, the definition of cognitive appraisal theory doesn't mention bodily or physical reactions. According to cognitive appraisal theory, you experience an emotion because of your interpretation of the event that brought it on (Lazarus, 1964, 1982, 1984; Lazarus & Alfert, 1964; Folkman et al., 1986). In our example of water spilling on your smartphone, cognitive appraisal theory explains that your reaction of fear happens simply because you interpret what you see—a spill that could ruin your phone (not because you interpret any bodily reaction).

Cognitive appraisal theory leaves lots of room for interpretation of events, which could differ between one person and another, or even differ for one person under different circumstances. For example, imagine that water spilled on your smartphone while you were at the store buying a new one. Would your emotional reaction differ

Schachter–Singer theory
A theory of emotion stating that the label one assigns to one's bodily reaction determines your mental reaction.

cognitive appraisal theory
A theory of emotion stating that what the person thinks about a stimulus causes the emotion.

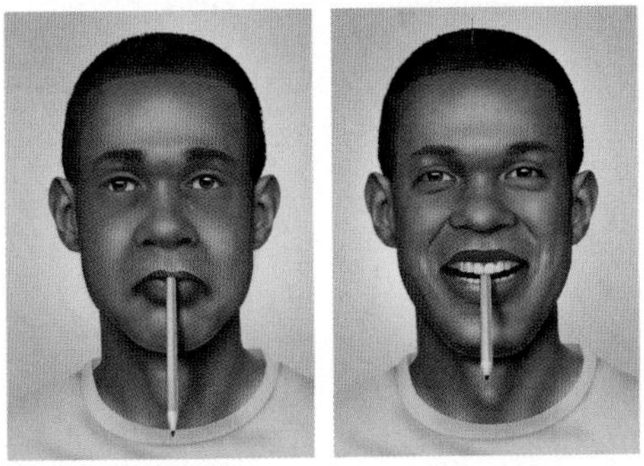

Facial feedback theory states that your brain can influence your emotions by monitoring your facial expressions. Researchers have tested this theory by having participants hold a pencil in their mouths in such a way that it forces either a pout or a smile and then asking them to rate the funniness of cartoons. Smilers rated the same cartoons as funnier than pouters, presumably because their facial expressions influenced their mood (Soussignan, 2002).

if the water spilled on the one you were finished with or the one you just bought? Or, imagine that water spilled on your smartphone, but it was in a waterproof case. Would your emotional reaction differ from the same spill on your phone in a regular case?

A criticism of the cognitive appraisal approach centers on the notion that thought must take place before emotion. Instead, in some cases, emotion may actually come first (Zajonc, 1980, 1984). The reason for this may be that in some situations, the mind generates emotions more automatically and easily than it generates thoughts. For example, you may occasionally hear a sound (perhaps the voice of an old friend) or smell a scent (perhaps a food you ate often as a young child) and for a brief moment have an emotional reaction to it *before* you can identify it ("I like that! What is it?"). Here is another example:

> We may completely fail to notice a person's hair color or may hardly remember what it was shortly after meeting the person. But we can seldom escape the reaction that the person impressed us as pleasant or unpleasant, agreeable or disagreeable, as someone to whom we were drawn or someone by whom we were repelled. And these affective reactions—and, more important, the retrieval of affect—occur without effort. In contrast, some cognitive judgments require substantial effort. —Zajonc, 1980, p. 156

Facial Feedback Theory. **Facial feedback theory** is a theory of emotion stating that your brain can influence your emotions by monitoring your facial expressions. Facial feedback theory is the most recent theory of emotion we'll discuss, having been developed in the 1970s and 1980s and researched heavily in the 1990s and 2000s (Buck, 1980; Davis et al., 2009). The logic goes like this: Your face sensitively responds to situations around you in all kinds of ways—smiles, frowns, winces, squints, raised eyebrows, flared nostrils, and more. Those expressions don't *result* from emotion, however. They *cause* emotion.

Wait, my face makes an expression *before* I feel the emotion?

According to the facial feedback hypothesis, yes. Consider again our example of water spilling on your smartphone. The facial feedback hypothesis states that *first*, your face shows fear: Your eyes widen, your eyebrows slant upward, and your mouth opens. Soon *after*, your brain notices that your face has made these adjustments, and comes to the conclusion that you must be feeling fear. It is like catching a glimpse of the bags under your eyes in the mirror and realizing "Wow, I must be tired," but instead of a mirror, your brain monitors your facial expressions. In a way, the facial feedback theory resembles the James–Lange theory, but emphasizes the face, rather than the entire body, as what determines emotion (McIntosh, 1996).

When researchers study facial feedback theory, they come across an unusual challenge: How do they get participants to make particular facial expressions and then measure how those expressions influence the participants' emotions? In some studies, researchers simply tell participants to smile, frown, or hold their faces in a particular position. For example, in one study researchers told participants to lower their eyebrows and participants reported a worsening of mood (Lewis, 2012). Other researchers attach devices to the face, such as one study that taped golf tees to participants' foreheads and asked them to touch the tees together. To do so, they had to make a face that mimicked a sad expression, and they reported increased sadness when they did it (Larsen et al., 1992).

Many emotion researchers use a remarkably simple method to get participants to make facial expressions: putting a pen in their mouths (Soussignan, 2002). The trick is in *how* the pen is held by the mouth. Holding the pen with your teeth only (no lips) forces your face into a smiling position, but holding it with your lips only (no teeth) forces your face into a pouting position and prevents it from smiling. In one study,

participants rated the funniness of cartoons while holding the pen in one of those ways. Those whose mouths were forced into a smile rated the cartoons as significantly funnier than those whose mouths were prevented from smiling, presumably because smiling put them in a happier mood. Similar results have been found in studies in which participants' facial expressions were controlled by having them repeat the same vowel sound over and over again. Participants who repeated the *ee* sound (which produces a smile, like when a photographer tells you to say *cheese*) reported more pleasant emotional experiences than those who repeated other vowel sounds that don't produce smiles (Zajonc et al., 1989; McIntosh et al., 1997).

facial feedback theory
A theory of emotion stating that one's brain can influence one's emotions by monitoring one's facial expressions.

Other studies have explored whether the effects of "putting on a happy face" might extend to other parts of the body as well. Researchers have tested whether putting your body into positions that mimic nonverbal emotional expressions influences the likelihood that you will feel those emotions (Stepper & Strack, 1993). The answer appears to be yes. In one study, researchers gave participants specific instructions about how to sit in their chair, to mimic either fear, sadness, or anger. For fear, they sat on the edge of the chair with their feet together under the chair and their hands together near their mouths. For sadness, they leaned back, let their legs fall loosely, dropped their head, and let their body go limp. For anger, they put their feet flat on the floor, kept their forearms and elbows on the arm of the chair, leaned slightly forward, and clenched their fists. In each posture, participants rated how fearful, sad, and angry they felt. As predicted, the feeling that matched the posture got the highest rating every time, as if each posture prompted the participants to feel that way (Duclos et al., 1989).

In another study, participants read a brief story about a man named Donald whose behavior was vaguely aggressive (he demanded his money back from a cashier after buying something, and he got into a conflict with his landlord, among other things). Some participants read the story with their index finger extended; others read it with their middle finger extended (yes, "flipping the bird"). Those with their middle finger extended not only rated Donald as more hostile, they also rated themselves as feeling less happy—again, presumably because that hand gesture indicating anger and displeasure prompted them toward negative emotions (Chandler & Schwarz, 2009; Srull & Wyer, 1979).

Communicating Emotions

It is almost impossible to experience emotions without communicating them. When your friend whispers something funny to you during class, it is hard to hold in that laugh. When you accidentally bite the inside of your mouth at a fancy dinner, it is hard to mask that pain from the others at the table. Communicating emotion is so automatic that even when you talk on the phone, you gesture as much as you would if the person were in the room with you. You even add emojis to your texts because the words alone can't capture the feelings behind what you write. Poker players wear sunglasses and hoods in an attempt to hide the any facial reactions to the hand they've been dealt (and their toughest opponents can read through even the straightest poker face and notice even the slightest "tell.")

Nonverbal communication of emotions is so powerful that card players have to make great effort to maintain a "poker face" that reveals no emotion about the hand they hold. Ethan Miller/Getty Images

Many psychologists believe that sharing emotions has an evolutionary social function (Shiota, 2014). In particular, the communication of emotions strengthens the bonds that you have with the people around you (Fischer & Manstead, 2008). Let's go back to that example about water spilling on your smartphone. The fearful look on your face serves as a warning to the others around you. In general, that fearful look says, "Something dangerous is happening, so watch out!" In this particular case, it says, "If your phone is on the table too, pick it up!" If you discovered that your phone was indeed ruined by the water, your fear might turn to sadness. Expressing that sadness is likely to draw helpful responses from those around you, such as compassion for your loss, offers to use their phones, or help obtaining a new one (Bonanno et al., 2008; Keltner & Kring, 1998; Eisesnberg et al., 1989; Batson & Shaw, 1991).

Can emotions be contagious? If someone near you feels something, do you feel a little bit of it yourself?

That happens, and psychologists call it *empathy*—the tendency to identify with and to some extent experience the emotions of others. Empathy varies from one person to the next. Bullies, child abusers, and violent criminals typically experience little empathy for the feelings of others (Jolliffe & Farrington, 2006; Schaffer et al., 2009; Miller & Eisenberg, 1988; Perez-Albeniz & de Paul, 2003). Those at the other end of the scale can be so empathic that they can't help but mirror the facial expressions of those around them. One study found that high-empathy people smiled slightly when they saw photos of happy faces and frowned slightly when they saw photos of angry faces, while low-empathy people kept a straight face no matter which photo they saw. The high-empathy people also rated the faces they saw as more emotional than the low-empathy people did. The happy faces struck them as very happy and the angry faces struck them as very angry, as if the emotions were coming through at a higher intensity (Dimberg et al., 2011). Other studies have found that this facial mimicry by high-empathy people happens automatically, unconsciously, and accurately within just a fraction of a second (Sonnby-Borgström, 2002; Dimberg & Thunberg, 2012).

Let's take a closer look at the two specific components of communicating emotions: expressing them and recognizing them.

Expressing Emotions. From day one, human beings express emotions. If you've ever held a baby for even a few minutes, you've seen their faces show a wide range of feelings, from miserable to happy, and from attentive to sleepy. By the age of 2 or 3, young children typically show the full range of adult emotions, differentiated to a greater extent than in their first months (Lewis, 2008). What may come across as a more general "sad" in a baby is a bit more distinguishable as a particular kind of sad in a toddler: heartbroken because mommy or daddy just left the house, gloomy because a rainy day is keeping them from going to the park, or dejected because they can't find the last piece to their puzzle.

Not only do babies express emotion, they express the *same* basic emotions around the world (Hess & Thibault, 2009). This is true even in blind babies, who obviously can't be imitating faces they've seen, which leads many experts to conclude that all humans are born with the capacity to experience and express certain feelings (Eibl-Eibesfelt, 1973; Camras et al., 1991). The research on babies' emotional expression is just a small part of the research on how people of all ages express emotion. In general, the conclusion is the same: human beings around the world express the same basic set of emotions (Matsumoto et al., 2008a).

A leading researcher on emotional expression, Paul Ekman, conducted classic studies in the early 1970s that examined whether people from a wide range of countries and cultures showed the same facial expressions. In one, he showed U.S. and Japanese participants the same films and (without their knowledge, initially) recorded their facial reactions. He found that participants from both cultures showed basically the same facial reactions at the same moments in each film. Ekman also categorized the emotional expressions of the participants into six basic categories, each thought to be a basic human emotion: anger, disgust, fear, happiness, sadness, and surprise (Ekman, 1972).

Many more recent studies support Ekman's early findings that there are a small number of basic emotions that people express around the world (Ekman, 1974, 1993, 2003; Harris & Alvarado, 2005; Mauss et al., 2005; Ruch, 1995). In one such study, researchers took advantage of a situation in which people from around the world come together and are likely to experience similar emotions: the Olympics. Researchers analyzed the facial expressions of athletes immediately after winning a medal in judo in the 2004 Olympics in Athens. Using the same facial coding system that Ekman used, they examined the facial expressions of 85 athletes from 35 countries at three points in

People around the world show the same six basic facial expressions: anger, sadness, fear, happiness, disgust, and surprise. (a) BONNINSTUDIO/Getty Images (b) master1305/Getty Images (c) Gogosvm/Getty Images (d) Blend Images/Getty Images (e) E+/Getty Images (f) Paul Burns/Getty Images

time: when they won their medal match, when they received their medal, and when they posed on the podium. The main finding was that these athletes' facial expressions were so similar to each other that they must represent basic universal human emotions (Matsumoto & Willingham, 2006).

Is it possible that people have such similar expressions of emotion because they see other people displaying them?

That possibility—that people's facial expressions are shaped by the facial expressions they see in the people around them—also occurred to those researchers who studied the Olympic athletes. So, they also visited the 2004 Paralympic Games in Athens and did the same study with blind athletes. In this case, there were 59 blind judo competitors from around the world, about half of whom had been blind their entire lives. The results were essentially the same: The spontaneous emotions expressed on the faces of these blind athletes when they won their matches, received their medals, and stood on the podium were the same as each other, and the same as the sighted athletes from the Olympic study (Matsumoto & Willingham, 2009). These findings provide even stronger support for the idea that basic human emotions are universal and innate.

Recognition of Emotion. To successfully communicate emotions, you must not only express them, but also recognize them. Earlier, in the example of water spilling on your smartphone, we mentioned that your friends around the table might benefit from your facial expression and realize they need to move their phones before theirs get wet too. Now let's reverse the roles. You're one of the friends, and water is spilled on someone else's phone. You can see how important it is to recognize another person's emotions, which prompts you to get your phone off the table before yours gets wet too. Their fear is your forewarning.

Research indicates that the emotion you recognize in the facial expressions of others can powerfully influence your own behavior. In one study, 12-month-old

babies were placed on a *visual cliff* (**Figure 8.6**), a large glass surface that has a shallow end (where wallpaper is right under the glass) and a deep end (where wallpaper is many inches below the glass). The researchers adjusted the deep end to be deep enough to make the babies hesitate crawling across it, but not necessarily refuse. To start the experiment, the baby is placed on the shallow side, and mom stands by the edge of the deep side. The question is, Will the baby crawl across the deep end to mom, or will the baby stay on the shallow side? According to the results of this study, it all depends on mom's facial expression. When mom made a happy or interested facial expression, most of the babies crawled across the deep end, but few of them did when mom made an angry or sad facial expression. And when mom looked fearful, *none* of the babies crawled across (Sorce et al., 1985). The main point of these findings is that babies—and perhaps the rest of us—look to other people's facial expressions to help us decide what actions we should take, especially when the right answer is unclear.

In real life, you may have seen this influence of others' facial expressions play out when a child sees an adult express emotion about the child's injury. For example, picture a 7-year-old child at soccer practice falling and scraping his knee. In that brief moment immediately after the fall, the kid is silent, but scans eagerly for his coach. If he sees a look of panic come over the coach's face, the child will probably panic too, complete with screaming and crying. But if the coach's face stays calm and cool, communicating that the injury is no big deal, odds are that the child will gather himself after a minute and resume playing, without any of the screaming and crying, even though it is the same injury. It is as if the boy is unsure how badly he is hurt, so he waits for the cue of the coach's facial expression to decide on his own emotional reaction.

Just as researchers have explored whether the expression of emotion is universal, they have also explored whether recognition of those emotions is universal. Again, the answer seems to be yes. In another classic study by Paul Ekman and his colleagues, over 500 participants from 10 countries in Europe, Asia, and North America were shown 18 photos of the faces of White people expressing a basic emotion (anger, disgust, fear, happiness, sadness, or surprise). When asked what emotion was being expressed, they made few mistakes. The percentage of participants from a particular country who correctly identified the target emotion never fell below 60%, and about

FIGURE 8.6 The Power of Facial Expression. The emotions expressed in the faces of those around you can have a powerful influence on your behavior. In one study, most babies crawled across the deep end of a glass-topped visual cliff (which made them at least somewhat unsure about their safety) if mom's face looked happy or interested. Few of them crossed if mom's face looked angry or sad, and none crossed if mom looked fearful. Information from Sorce et al., 1985.

a third of the time it was above 90%. As **Table 8.2** indicates, participants were especially good at identifying happiness. In most countries, over 90% of participants got it right. The participants also agreed with each other quite strongly about how intense the emotion was in each photo. Overall, the results of this study suggest that people around the world recognize facial expressions in largely the same way (Ekman et al., 1987).

Other studies have also supported the recognition of emotions as universal (Ekman & Friesen, 1971; Matsumoto et al., 2002). Remember that 2004 Olympic study we discussed earlier? Those authors also showed those photos to participants from around the world to see how accurately they could recognize the emotion in the athletes' faces. Overall, they were quite good at it, with the majority of participants making the correct choice the majority of the time (Matsumoto & Willingham, 2009). Kids make the correct choices too: They have roughly the same accuracy rates as adults for sad and angry expressions, and lag only slightly behind in the other emotions (Lawrence et al., 2015). A meta-analysis of many studies confirms that recognition of emotion through facial expressions is universal, but also points out that people from the same country or ethnic group were slightly better at recognizing the emotions of people within their group than people outside that group (Elfenbein & Ambady, 2002). Only rare exceptions to the universality of emotion recognition have been found, including people with autism spectrum disorder, schizophrenia, or antisocial personality disorder (Marsh & Blair, 2008; McCleery et al., 2015; Philip et al., 2012).

TABLE 8.2: A Smile Is a Smile Around the World

COUNTRY	PERCENT OF PARTICIPANTS WHO CORRECTLY IDENTIFIED HAPPINESS IN THE SAME TARGET PHOTO
Estonia	90
Germany	93
Greece	93
Hong Kong	92
Italy	97
Japan	90
Scotland	98
Sumatra	69
Turkey	87
United States	95

When participants from countries around the world were shown a photo of the same face expressing happiness, the vast majority from every country identified the emotion correctly. They identified other basic emotions, such as surprise, sadness, fear, disgust, and anger, with only slightly less accuracy. Data from Ekman et al., 1987.

Emotion Regulation

Emotion regulation is your ability to manage the type, intensity, length, and expression of your own emotions. Of course, you're never in *complete* control of your emotions. For example, you can't force yourself to be happy when you hear about the death of a relative, or force yourself to be calm when a tornado siren shrieks. But you can have *some* control over your emotions. For example, you might try to hold back your sadness about your relative's death when other family members need you for support, or you might try to avoid panicking when you hear the tornado siren so you can calmly find safety. That ability to not let your emotions get the best of you is emotion regulation (Gross, 1998a,b).

MY TAKE VIDEO 8.2

Emotion Regulation

"A time when I used an emotion regulation strategy was..."

YOUTUBE: http://tiny.cc/mytake
LAUNCHPAD: launchpadworks.com

Methods of Regulating Emotions.

James Gross, a leading researcher on emotion regulation, describes five strategies for emotion regulation (Gross, 2008, 2014). The strategies occur at different points in time, beginning before the emotion has a chance to occur and ending when you're already starting to feel it. Let's walk through them with one particular example in mind: Your cousin Bryan, whom you find annoying but to whom you owe a favor, has left you a voicemail asking you to have lunch with him next Saturday.

- *Situation selection.* If you use situation selection to regulate emotion, you will say no to Bryan. Or you might not even return his call. Situation selection means that you deliberately put yourself in situations where you are likely to experience positive emotions and avoid negative emotions (like the annoyance you feel around Bryan). This is a strategy that involves lots of planning and anticipating. It can, if taken to the extreme, cause you to make significant modifications to your daily schedule.
- *Situation modification.* If you use situation modification to regulate emotion, you will see Bryan on Saturday, but you will structure your time together in such a way that it minimizes your feelings of annoyance. For example, you might tell Bryan that you'd rather see a movie than get lunch, because at the movie you won't have to interact with him as much. Situation modification is not quite as proactive as situation selection, but it can still involve some planning.

emotion regulation
The ability to manage the type, intensity, length, and expression of one's own emotions.

- *Attentional deployment.* If you use attentional deployment to regulate emotion, you will have lunch with Bryan, but you will distract yourself. You will draw your attention to other things besides Bryan's annoying personality. Perhaps you will concentrate hard on the food you order and the Yelp review you plan to post about it, or perhaps you will daydream about how you will be spending Sunday doing more enjoyable things, or perhaps you will sneak peeks at your phone during lunch. Any of these behaviors would draw your attention away from the annoyance you would otherwise feel.

- *Cognitive change.* If you use cognitive change to regulate emotion, you will have lunch with Bryan. If you start to feel annoyed, then you will rethink the situation or your capacity to deal with it. For example, instead of thinking about how annoying he is, you might think it is nice to keep the family ties close. And if you start to think you can't stand it, you might remind yourself that it's only for a couple of hours. If you can't escape or reshape your situation, rethinking it in this way can take the edge off of negative emotions, and perhaps even flip them into positive emotions.

- *Response modulation.* If you use response modulation, you will go to lunch with Bryan, and feel annoyed, but you will try to suppress it (or "hold it in"). You might take deep breaths, put a fake smile on your face, or just suffer through it. Response modulation is a strategy for dealing with the emotion after it happens. You're just trying to control how intensely you feel it.

LIFE HACK 8.2

To minimize negative emotions in your life, it is better to prevent them by rethinking, changing, or avoiding the situations that cause them than to suppress the negative emotions after you start to feel them.

(Demaree et al., 2006; Gross & Levenson, 1993, 1997; Webb et al., 2012)

Research indicates that some of these five emotion regulation strategies work better than others—a key point to keep in mind for managing your own emotions in your daily life. One clear finding is that response modulation doesn't work well, especially the kind that involves suppression of negative feelings. Suppression isn't particularly effective in reducing negative emotions, and in some cases it actually compounds (or worsens) them (Demaree et al., 2006; Gross & Levenson, 1993, 1997). Suppression also interferes with memory, as if your brain's effort to suppress the feeling subtracts from its ability to form memories of what actually happened (Richards & Gross, 2000, 2006). Suppression has bad social consequences too—the people around you often notice you doing it, and when they do they are likely to feel stressed, like you less, and distance themselves from you (Butler et al., 2003; English et al., 2013; Srivastava et al., 2009).

On the other hand, the emotion regulation strategies that take place earlier than suppression—that is, before you begin to feel the feeling—tend to work better. In particular, cognitive change tends to produce more desirable results, especially when it involves rethinking the situation and your capacity to deal with it (Gross, 1998a; Hayes et al., 2010; Koole, 2009). In fact, a meta-analysis of almost 200 studies that compared the results of the five different strategies for regulating emotion found that cognitive change or rethinking proved much more effective overall than the other available strategies (Webb et al., 2012).

Why Emotion Regulation Matters

It is easy to see why emotion regulation matters in your everyday life—it maximizes your positive feelings, such as happiness, contentment, enthusiasm, pride, amusement, and awe. Beyond those fleeting emotional moments, however, there are more enduring reasons why emotion regulation matters too: Positive emotions improve the long-term quality of your life.

For example, consider your physical health. As **Figure 8.7** shows, experiencing happiness and other positive feelings improves your physical wellness and decreases your susceptibility to both serious diseases and the common cold (Moskowitz & Saslow, 2014; Fredrickson & Cohn, 2008; Cohen & Pressman, 2006; Ong & Allaire, 2005; Cohen et al., 2003). The more positive emotions a person has, the lower the odds of stroke or heart disease (Ostir et al., 2001; Davidson et al., 2010). Among people with chronic

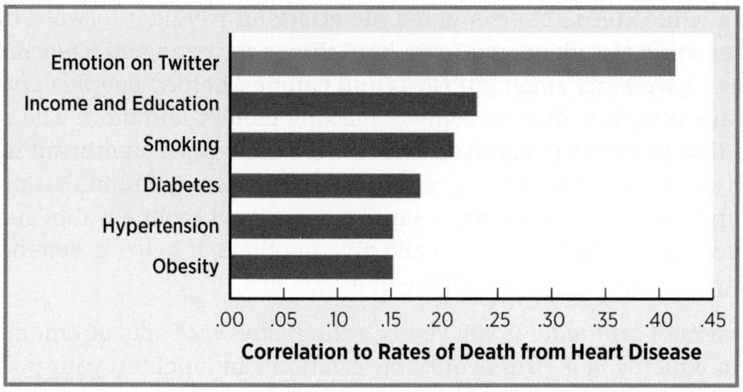

FIGURE 8.7 Twitter, Happiness, and Heart Disease. Researchers explored the connection between the emotional language used in 148 million tweets (collected over a 10-month period) to the rates of death from heart disease. Those death rates were highest in U.S. counties where the tweets contained lots of words expressing negative emotions like hostility and tension (*hate*, *grrr*, *despise*, *jealousy*, *stupid*, and plenty of curse words). Those rates were lowest in counties where the tweets contained lots of words expressing positive emotions like optimism and happiness (*wonderful*, *great*, *hope*, *fantastic*, *enjoyed*, etc.). The emotional tone of the tweets correlated with a county's rate of death by heart disease better than smoking, diabetes, obesity, and other variables. Bottom line: negative emotions seem to go hand in hand with disease, while positive emotions seem to go hand in hand with wellness. Data from Eichstaedt et al., 2015.

diseases, those who experience more positive emotions experience lower levels of pain and disability (Gil et al., 2004).

In a unique study concerning the connection between positive emotions and health, researchers found that baseball players who were smiling in their 1952 baseball cards were half as likely to die in any specific year within the next five decades as those who were not smiling (Abel & Kruger, 2010). More generally, reviews of studies on positive emotions and mortality consistently find a strong positive correlation between positive emotions and age of death: Simply put, happier people live longer (Chida & Steptoe, 2008; Diener & Chan, 2011).

In addition to improving your long-term physical health, positive emotions promote an open-minded approach to life that makes people better at solving problems and interacting with other people. Recent research supports the *broaden-and-build theory of positive emotions*, which states that from an evolutionary standpoint, positive emotions mean safety, and safety allows you to expand your thinking beyond mere survival or avoidance of harm. So, when you're happy, you explore new ways of thinking and new ways of interacting with others. This leads to more creative solutions to problems and more helpful connections to the people around you (Tugade et al., 2014; Fredrickson & Branigan, 2005; Johnson & Fredrickson, 2005; Isen, 2008).

Positive emotions correlate with longer lives. A study of baseball cards from the mid-1900s supports this finding, showing that smiling players tended to live longer than nonsmiling players (Abel & Kruger, 2010). For example, Roger Maris (top) died at 51, while Stan Musial (bottom) lived to 92. (a) Focus On Sport/Getty Images (b) Focus On Sport/Getty Images

Wow, the benefits of positive emotions are impressive. How can I maximize positive emotions in my own life?

You know yourself better than anyone, so you probably know plenty of ways to boost your own happiness. But psychologists have conducted research on a number of specific ways to increase positive emotions, and they have found a few techniques that work for most people (Nelson & Lyubomirsky, 2014; Seligman et al., 2006):

- *Perform acts of kindness.* People who do nice things for others feel happier themselves (Lyubormirsky et al., 2005; Weinstein & Ryan, 2010; Lyubomirsky & Layous, 2013). Ever hear of "paying it forward"? It happens when people do random acts of kindness for strangers, like paying for the coffee of the stranger behind you in line or sending an uplifting text to a friend or relative you haven't

seen in a while. Researchers studied the effects of paying it forward by sending dozens of college students out to do kind things for strangers. They did all kinds of things—gave away small gift cards and candies, helped people carry heavy items, gave compliments, put coins in parking meters, and more. The results showed that the people who paid it forward experienced significant increases in positive emotions (Pressman et al., 2015). Another study found that people can feel happier just by deliberately counting the acts of kindness they have already performed for others. When you can't give to others, it helps to remind yourself of what you've already given (Otake et al., 2006).

LIFE HACK 8.3

If you want to feel happier, do something kind for someone else, or think about acts of kindness you've already done.

(Otake et al., 2006; Pressman et al., 2015; Lyubomirsky & Layous, 2013)

- *Write letters of gratitude.* If you've been the *recipient* of acts of kindness, writing letters in which you express your appreciation can heighten your positive emotions (Seligman et al., 2005; Toepfer et al., 2012; Rash et al., 2011; Wood et al., 2010). One 8-month longitudinal study found that people who spent 15 minutes a week writing letters to people in their lives who had done things that made them feel grateful (but not sending the letters) experienced more positive emotions than a control group who did not (Lyubomirsky et al., 2011). Another study of kids from third to twelfth grade found that those who generally experienced few positive emotions experienced a significant increase in positive emotions when they wrote and sent gratitude letters (Froh et al., 2009).
- *Count your blessings.* People who make an effort to count their blessings, or appreciate what they have, as opposed to focusing on what they don't have, generally experience more positive emotions (Emmons & McCullogh, 2003; Lyubomirsky et al., 2005; Froh et al., 2008). One study of college students found that those who counted their blessings were significantly more likely to remember positive events from their lives, which are likely to boost happiness (Watkins et al., 2004). Another study found that the more people count their blessings, the fewer symptoms of depression they experience (Lambert et al., 2012).
- *Visualize a bright future.* People who picture the future as a happy time tend to experience happiness in the present (Sin & Lyubomirsky, 2009; Boehm et al., 2011). One study found that college students who wrote essays once a week about the best version of themselves they could imagine in the future felt happier than those who did not (Layous et al., 2013). Another found that students who wrote similar essays every day for just 4 days experienced a similar increase in happiness even 3 weeks later (King, 2001).

FROM RESEARCH TO REAL LIFE

Does Money Buy Happiness?

Many college students list earning potential as one of the primary reasons they are seeking a college degree. But does money necessarily equal happiness? This question produces mixed results (Lucas & Diener, 2008; Diener & Biswas-Diener, 2002). People from wealthier countries tend to be happier than people from poorer countries. However, when a country becomes richer, those happiness ratings don't increase much. Also, there is a lot of individual variability surrounding the connection between wealth and well-being. Trends suggest that people in rich countries are happier than people in poor countries, but there are plenty of unhappy rich people and plenty of happy poor people around the world.

Perhaps the most interesting finding is that the connection between money and happiness is strongest for people on the border of meeting their basic needs (Biswas-Diener & Diener, 2001; Diener et al., 1993). If more money means the difference between food and hunger, or between home and homelessness, or between medical care and sickness, having it produces much more happiness. But if your basic needs like food, shelter, safety, and medical care are met, getting more money won't produce the same increase in happiness. Actually, if you are well-off, a rise in income won't produce any increase in your happiness if your material desires rise even faster (Diener & Biswas-Diener, 2002). In that way, happiness is less about your money and more about the comparison between your money and the stuff you want to buy with it. It is also important to point out that even when money does affect happiness, it is just one of many factors. Good relationships with family and friends, a good marriage, and a healthy spiritual life are among many other factors that play a role (Suh et al., 1998; Diener & Diener, 2009; Diener et al., 1993; Ellison, 1991; Lucas et al., 2003). ●

Emotion and Diversity

display rules
Norms within a group about the acceptable verbal and nonverbal expression of emotion.

We all experience emotion, but we all experience it differently. Let's explore differences in emotion according to age, ethnicity, and gender. As we get into each of those differences, it is important to keep in mind the idea of **display rules**: norms within a group about the acceptable verbal and nonverbal expression of emotion. Many different kinds of groups have their own sets of display rules, including ethnic groups, age groups, and gender-based groups (Brody, 2000; Matsumoto, 1990; Safdar et al., 2009). We begin to pick up on display rules during infancy and continue to incorporate these rules throughout our lives (Malatesta & Haviland, 1982; Misailidi, 2006). You've noticed the effects of these different display rules if you've ever seen a large, diverse group of people experience the same event at the same time. For example, imagine an audience in a crowded movie theater. If a sad scene happens, some people openly weep, some quietly shed a single tear, some show a slightly sorrowful facial expression, and others may reveal no emotion at all. How you respond depends not only on the amount of sadness you actually feel, but also on the display rules that tell you how, or whether, you are allowed to display it.

One large-scale study of over 5000 people from 32 countries asked participants what they should do if they feel a particular emotion in front of other people. Results indicated that participants from more individualistic cultures (such as the United States, Canada, and Australia) were much more likely to approve of expressing happiness and surprise (but not sadness) than people from more collectivistic cultures (such as Indonesia and Hong Kong) (Matsumoto et al., 2008b). A review of literature on gender-based display rules found that throughout childhood, girls are likely to show more happiness, sadness, anxiety, and sympathy than boys, while boys are likely to show more anger than girls (Chaplin & Aldao, 2013). Another study illustrated that display rules can depend on who is watching: elementary school–aged kids reported a much lower likelihood of expressing anger, sadness, or pain in front of peers than when they were alone or with a parent (Zeman & Garber, 1996).

Other than those who are very near death, older adults tend to experience more positive emotions than younger adults (Carstensen et al., 2000, 2011; Riedeger et al., 2009; Gerstof et al., 2010; Magai, 2001, 2008). diego_cervo/Getty Images

Emotion and age. Many people assume that older adults feel less positive emotion. In fact, several studies have found that some facial features common in older adults, like wrinkles and sagging skin, often give younger adults the impression that the older adults are unhappy (Hess et al., 2012; Hummert, 2014; Ebner, 2008). However, the opposite appears to be true: Other than those who are very near death, older adults experience more positive emotions than younger adults (Carstensen et al., 2000, 2011; Riedeger et al., 2009; Gerstorf et al., 2010; Magai, 2001, 2008). Older adults also tend to experience less emotional variability

DIVERSITY MATTERS

WATCHING PSYCHOLOGY

This Show Is Scary: The Effect on Children of Frightening TV and Movies

Between R-rated movies, 24-hour news stations, and even network programming (like any of the *CSI* shows), there is plenty on TV that could produce fear in children. What's the effect of watching scary stuff on TV?

Some research suggests that the long-term effects could be quite strong in terms of anxiety and fear (Cantor, 2011; Hoekstra et al., 1999). In one study of college students, about 25% of them reported that they still felt significant emotional impact of a scary show or movie they watched when they were much younger (Harrison & Cantor, 1999). Another study found that among college students who had seen either *Jaws* or *Poltergeist* before age 12, 37% said the fright or other emotions caused by that movie was still negatively affecting some aspect of their waking life (Cantor, 2004). A survey of elementary school-aged kids found that over 75% had been scared by something they had seen on TV or other media. Of these, 38% of them had such significant fear that immediately afterward they couldn't perform a behavior they had previously performed (like being alone in a bedroom), and almost 25% said the effects were still at least somewhat with them at the time of the study even though months or years had gone by (Cantor et al., 2010).

There is other research that reports different findings—that any effects of scary media on kids is fleeting and largely inconsequential, especially in kids over 10 years old (Pearce & Field, 2016). Other researchers have emphasized that the emotional vulnerability of the particular child may play a key role. One study of kids from New Orleans found that those who experienced Hurricane Katrina in 2005 had a more fearful reaction to the media coverage of Hurricane Gustav in 2008 than those kids who had not experienced Katrina (Weems et al., 2012). Of course, the way parents handle scary images on TV makes a difference too. Kids who discuss scary shows with their parents generally respond better than kids whose parents take a more passive approach (Buijzen et al., 2007; Browne & Hamilton-Giachritsis, 2005).

than younger adults, staying more "even-keeled" and less reactive to life events (Riediger & Rauers, 2014; Brose et al., 2013; Steptoe et al., 2011; Röcke et al., 2009).

There are several possible explanations for these emotional tendencies in older adults. Compared to younger adults, they may have learned through life experience to "choose their battles," which enables them to stay happy when daily hassles happen rather than blowing them out of proportion (Mikels et al., 2014). Especially if they are retired and have grown, independent children, they may experience fewer obligations than younger adults who are being pulled in multiple directions by work and family (Riedeger & Freund, 2008; Charles et al., 2010). The explanation most supported by research relates to the five strategies of emotion regulation we discussed earlier: older adults have learned to improve their emotion regulation, particularly by dealing with emotions before they occur rather than after (Riffin et al., 2014; John & Gross, 2004; Gross & John, 2003). Remember that example about your annoying cousin Bryan asking you to have lunch with him next Saturday? Because of their extensive life experience, older adults are more likely to use the emotion regulation techniques that fall earlier in the sequence, like situation selection or situation modification, rather than one that falls later in the sequence, like response modulation (Morgan & Scheibe, 2014). Older adults have been there and done that with Bryan, and they know right away how annoying he can be, so they're wise enough to avoid him.

Emotion and Ethnicity. What makes people in one culture happy does not necessarily make people in another culture happy (Mitamura et al., 2014). For example, in one study, researchers asked U.S. and Japanese preschoolers to perform a task in which they had to match colored stickers to animal pictures (put the correct color of sticker by each animal). When they were successful, U.S. kids were more likely to express pride, but Japanese kids were more likely to express embarrassment. When they were unsuccessful, U.S. kids were more likely to express sadness and shame (Lewis et al., 2010). Also among preschoolers, U.S. kids prefer more excited smiles, while Taiwanese kids prefer calmer smiles (Tsai et al., 2007).

DIVERSITY MATTERS

In individualistic cultures like the United States, people typically attribute their happiness to personal achievements, like doing well on an exam or getting a raise at work. By contrast, in collectivistic cultures, people typically attribute their happiness to interpersonal harmony, like getting along well with family members or improving the quality of a friendship (Uchida et al., 2004; Diener & Suh, 2003). In the United States, maximizing happiness is often seen as the goal, but in Asian countries, such a one-sided emphasis on positive emotions is often discouraged, especially since it can lead to jealousy and interpersonal conflict (Uchida & Kitayama, 2009). The correlation between positive emotions and physical wellness is stronger in the United States than Japan, but the correlation between balanced positive/negative emotions and physical wellness is stronger in Japan than the United States (Miyamoto & Ryff, 2011).

Regarding emotion regulation, research shows that suppression (which is common to the fifth strategy of emotion regulation, response modulation) is viewed quite differently in collectivistic cultures (primarily Asian) versus individualistic cultures (primarily the United States). Specifically, suppression has fewer negative consequences in collectivistic cultures (Butler et al., 2003; Matsumoto et al., 2008b, c). In one study, researchers had pairs of participants—both Asian American women, or both European American women—watch and discuss a disturbing, graphic documentary about bombings during World War II. When European American women expressed emotion about what they saw, their blood pressure went down, but when Asian American women expressed emotion about what they saw, their blood pressure went up (Butler et al., 2003). Overall, suppression seems more acceptable, and perhaps even beneficial, in collectivistic cultures than in individualistic cultures.

Emotion and Gender. In general, emotion plays different roles in the lives of men and women. Women describe their emotional experiences as more intense, express their emotions more freely, and pick up on others' emotions more accurately (Brody & Hall, 2008; Robinson & Johnson,

DIVERSITY MATTERS

1997; Briton & Hall, 1995; Timmers et al., 2003). This gender difference appears to be rather universal. In a study involving participants from 37 countries, women had more intense, longer-lasting, more openly expressed feelings than men in every country (Fischer & Manstead, 2000).

Women also have a wider range of people with whom they will discuss their emotions (Rimé et al., 1991). For example, let's say James and Cassandra are both laid off from their jobs at the same time and feel sad about it. James is more likely to limit his discussion of his sadness to his romantic partner or his closest friends (or to keep it entirely to himself), while Cassandra is more likely to share her sadness with a larger number of friends and family. To some extent, the decision about whom to share feelings with depends on the emotion of the recipient too: Both men and women report greater comfort sharing their emotions with women than with men (Timmers et al., 1998). Women also report a greater likelihood of "emotional contagion," or experiencing the same emotions as the people around them (Doherty, 1997; Dimberg & Lundquist, 1990).

Around the world, women tend to express emotion more openly than men (Fischer & Manstead, 2000). (a) Hero Images/Getty Images (b) Guolker/Getty Images

CHECK YOUR LEARNING:

8.12 What is emotion?

8.13 Compare and contrast the five theories that explain the connection between the physical and mental aspects of emotion (James-Lange theory, Cannon-Bard theory, Schachter-Singer theory, cognitive appraisal theory, and facial feedback theory).

8.14 What is a probable evolutionary benefit of communicating emotions? To what extent are the communication and recognition of facial expressions universal?

8.15 What is emotion regulation and what are the best strategies of emotion regulation?

8.16 Why is emotion regulation important, especially in relation to positive emotion?

8.17 How does emotion interact with age, ethnicity, and gender?

CHAPTER SUMMARY

Motivation

8.1 Motivation is a desire that stimulates and steers your behavior.

8.2 Intrinsic motivation is the desire to perform a behavior because the behavior itself is rewarding. Extrinsic motivation is the desire to perform a behavior to obtain an external reward.

8.3 Classic theories of motivation include instinct theory (behaving according to innate instincts), drive reduction theory (reducing unpleasant biological sensations), and arousal theory (maintaining an optimum level of arousal).

8.4 Contemporary theories of motivation include self-determination theory (behaving autonomously), regulatory focus theory (achieving regulatory fit between promotion and prevention motivations), and achievement goal theory (pursuit of mastery goals versus performance goals).

8.5 Abraham Maslow's hierarchy of needs states that certain needs must be met before others. Specifically, needs must be met in this sequence: physiological needs, safety, belongingness and love, esteem, self-actualization, and self-transcendence.

8.6 People of diverse ethnicities, genders, and ages experience different motivations.

A Primary Motivation: Hunger and Eating

8.7 Body mass index (BMI) is a number calculated from a person's height and weight that indicates overall fitness level. Overweight people have BMIs between 25 and 29.9. Obese people have BMIs at or above 30.

8.8 Being overweight or obese increases the odds of many medical problems, mental health problems, and stigma.

8.9 Biological factors contributing to being overweight or obese include hormones, set point or settling point, genetics, and metabolic rate.

8.10 Environmental and sociocultural factors contributing to being overweight or obese include economic and shopping-related

factors, lifestyle factors, opportunities for exercise, portion size, and food presentation.

8.11 Healthy eating can incorporate strategies at the individual level and the social level.

Emotion

8.12 Emotion is all aspects of feeling, including changes to the body, behavior, and consciousness.

8.13 James–Lange theory states that you experience emotion by noticing bodily changes first and then interpreting them as particular feelings. Cannon–Bard theory states that you notice the bodily changes and feelings simultaneously. Schachter–Singer theory states that the label you assign to your bodily reaction determines your mental reaction. Cognitive appraisal theory states that what you think about a stimulus causes the emotion. Facial feedback theory states that your brain determines your emotions by monitoring your facial expressions.

8.14 Communicating emotions happens automatically and probably had the evolutionary benefit of social bonding. People around the world use facial expressions to show the same basic emotions from the day they are born. People around the world also recognize the same basic emotions in the faces of others.

8.15 Emotion regulation is your ability to manage the type, intensity, and expression of your own emotions. The best emotion regulation strategies are those that enable you to avoid, change, or rethink situations that cause negative emotions before you actually feel them, rather than suppressing them after the feeling has begun.

8.16 Emotion regulation is important because it maximizes positive emotion, which improves physical health, problem solving, and social interactions.

8.17 Older adults generally tend to experience more positive emotions than younger adults. People from different ethnicities often experience different patterns of emotion, even in response to the same situations. Women tend to express emotions more freely and recognize emotions more accurately than men.

KEY TERMS

motivation, p. 251
intrinsic motivation, p. 251
extrinsic motivation, p. 251
incentive, p. 251
instinct, p. 251
instinct theory, p. 251
drive reduction theory, p. 251
homeostasis, p. 251
arousal theory, p. 251
Yerkes–Dodson law, p. 253
self-determination theory, p. 253
regulatory focus theory, p. 253
achievement goal theory, p. 253
hierarchy of needs, p. 255
self-actualization, p. 255
peak experience, p. 256
flow, p. 256
body mass index (BMI), p. 259
overweight, p. 259
obesity, p. 259
leptin, p. 261
ghrelin, p. 261
set point, p. 261
metabolic rate (metabolism), p. 263
emotion, p. 269
James–Lange theory, p. 269
Cannon–Bard theory, p. 269
Schachter–Singer theory, p. 271
cognitive appraisal theory, p. 271
facial feedback theory, p. 273
emotion regulation, p. 277
display rules, p. 281

SELF-ASSESSMENT

1. A 7-year-old basketball player plays for the love of the game. A veteran professional basketball player plays for the money it brings. The 7-year old is motivated by _____. The pro is motivated by _____.
   a. intrinsic motivation; intrinsic motivation.
   b. extrinsic motivation; extrinsic motivation.
   c. intrinsic motivation; extrinsic motivation.
   d. extrinsic motivation; intrinsic motivation.

2. _____ is a theory of motivation stating that the strongest and healthiest motivations are those that are autonomous, or come from within yourself.
   a. Self-determination theory
   b. Achievement goal theory
   c. Arousal theory
   d. Drive reduction theory

3. Kianna's primary motivation in life is to find a close group of friends and a dating partner to whom she feels truly connected. According to Maslow's hierarchy of needs, Kianna is focused on _____ needs.
   a. physiological
   b. self-actualization
   c. self-transcendence
   d. belongingness and love

4. Body mass index indicates overall fitness level and amount of body fat. To determine body mass index, which of the following pieces of information is necessary?
   a. weight only
   b. height and weight
   c. height, weight, and ethnicity
   d. height, weight, ethnicity, and age

5. Jonathan is a middle-aged adult who is obese. As Jonathan gets older, if he remains obese he will be at high risk for
   a. physical problems, including diabetes.
   b. psychological problems, including anxiety and dementia.
   c. both a and b.
   d. neither a nor b.

6. Which of the following is true about the hormones leptin and ghrelin?
   a. They signal feelings related to fullness and hunger.
   b. They signal feelings related to fear and relaxation.
   c. They control sleep and wakefulness.
   d. Leptin triggers self-actualization; ghrelin triggers self-transcendence.

7. Hannah has a difficult time losing weight no matter how little she eats. Tianna has a difficult time gaining weight no matter how much she eats. In terms of biology, it is likely that Hannah and Tianna have different ______.

8. According to research on the "freshman 15,"
   a. the freshman 15 happens to most men, but not most women.
   b. the freshman 15 happens to most women, but not most men.
   c. the freshman 15 happens to most college students.
   d. the freshman 15 does not happen to most college students.

9. ______ theory is a theory of emotion stating that you experience emotion by simultaneously becoming aware of bodily changes and feelings.

10. Which of the following is true regarding research on emotion?
   a. The facial expressions of people around the world show the same basic emotions.
   b. People around the world accurately recognize facial expressions showing the basic emotions.
   c. Both a & b are true
   d. Neither a nor b is true.

Research shows quizzing is a highly effective learning tool. Continue quizzing yourself using LearningCurve, the system that adapts to *your* learning.

LaunchPad macmillan learning LearningCurve macmillan learning

GO TO: launchpadworks.com

Self-Assessment Answers

1. c, 2. a, 3. d, 4. b, 5. a, 6. a, 7. metabolic rates, 8. d, 9. Cannon-Bard, 10. c

WHAT'S YOUR TAKE?

1. When have you had peak experiences? When have you experienced flow? What kinds of activities facilitate these experiences for you? Are they planned or spontaneous? Do they involve other people, or just you? How can you experience more peak experiences and flow in the future?

2. The research indicates that although the freshman 15 is more fiction than fact, it is true that college students consistently gain slight amounts of weight over the 4-year period. So far, does that appear true for yourself and your friends? When weight gain does happen to college students, why does it happen? What factors contribute most to it, and what can you do about them?

SHOW ME MORE

8.1 Derek Redmond and His Father Cross the Finish Line

http://tiny.cc/showmemore

This video shows what the opening page of this chapter describes: sprinter Derek Redmond's famous moment from the 1992 Olympics, including his father's efforts to help his injured son reach the finish line.

Pascal Pavani/Getty Images

8.2 Serving Size Versus What You Really Eat

http://tiny.cc/showmemore

In this video, see the difference between the serving size listed on the packages of popular foods and the amount that many people actually eat.

Pamela D. Maxwell/Shutterstock

9 Development Across the Life Span

hadynyah/Getty Images

Psychologists have written hundreds of books about development, but none capture it better than the classic children's book *The Giving Tree*, by Shel Silverstein (1964). The story starts with a young boy, eager and full of energy. For the first few pages, the boy plays and climbs and swings on his beloved tree, content and happy.

"But time went by. And the boy grew older." With these lines, we begin to see the boy *develop*. He develops physically: taller and stronger through his teen years and young adulthood, then a gradual decline through middle and old age. He develops socially: As a child he establishes friendships with peers, and as an adult he ventures out to support himself. He develops psychologically: His primary needs shift from play to work to raising a family of his own. By the end of this brief book, the bounding boy who frolicked in the tree's branches has become an old man just looking for a nice tree stump on which to rest.

Developmental psychologists focus on the issues so poignantly illustrated in *The Giving Tree*: how people change over the course of their lives. In this chapter, we explore the theories and research that developmental psychologists use to explain how our bodies, brains, and social lives transform as we move through life. First, we'll consider some of the big issues relevant to development at any age, like the impact of nature and nurture on development, whether development happens gradually or in big spurts, and whether anything about us stays the same throughout all of these developmental changes. Then we'll move chronologically through the life span and examine what happens along the way, from the prenatal months through infancy, childhood, and adolescence. We'll look at the phases of adulthood too, from its emergence to the end of the life cycle.

CHAPTER OUTLINE

Big Questions About Developmental Psychology

YOU WILL LEARN:

9.1 what developmental psychology is.

9.2 the difference between cross-sectional and longitudinal research designs.

9.3 what developmental psychology's three big questions are.

Developmental psychology is the study of the changes to body, mind, and interpersonal interaction that people experience across the life span. The phrase "across the life span" means that development happens at every age. Early in the history of the field, developmental psychologists focused almost exclusively on children, with the assumption that once people reached adulthood, development was done. In fact, in 1890, psychology pioneer William James said that "for most of us, by age 30, the character has set like plaster and will never soften again" (James, 1890, p. 124). The focus of developmental psychology has changed drastically in recent decades (Cairns & Cairns, 2006; Bennett, 1999). Kids still receive lots of attention from developmental psychologists, but adults—from twenty-somethings to ninety-somethings—now do as well (Overton, 2006, 2010; Lerner, 2006).

Developmental psychologists focus on how people change over time. To examine these changes, they design their studies in two distinct ways, each with its own benefits. A **cross-sectional design** is a research design in which people of different ages are compared to each other at the same point in time. By contrast, a **longitudinal design** is a research design in which the same group of people is compared to itself at different points in time (**Table 9.1**). As an example, consider Dr. Kirk, a developmental psychologist who is interested in how digital literacy—basically, how tech-savvy a person is—changes as people get older. The quickest way to answer that question would be for Dr. Kirk to design a cross-sectional study in which she measures the digital literacy of people who are 10, 30, 50, and 70 years old *right now*. The quickness of the study is the main upside of the cross-sectional design. It provides an immediate answer to the research question without having to wait until people actually get older.

Of course, the longitudinal design has an upside too: higher validity, or a better chance of measuring what the study actually intends to measure (Little et al., 2009). If Dr. Kirk designed a longitudinal study, she would measure the digital literacy of people who are 10 years old right now, and then measure digital literacy of *the same people* again when they are 30, 50, and 70 years old. Your childhood was full of computers, tablets, and cell phones, but your grandparents' childhood wasn't. Computers were something they tried to get used to in midlife. Each generation moves through history at a unique point in time, and its members form a *cohort* whose experiences are unlike those of any other generation. A cross-sectional study might make it look like digital literacy drops drastically across the life span, but that drop may be a *cohort effect* rather than true development. A longitudinal study, even though it takes many years, could eliminate the cohort effect (Cavanaugh & Whitbourne, 2003).

Developmental psychologists conduct lots of cross-sectional studies *and* longitudinal studies (Card & Little, 2007). However, they also use other research methods, from observing babies and making educated guesses about their thoughts and feelings

Developmental psychology is the study of the changes to body, mind, and interpersonal interaction that people experience across the life span. (a) Plume Creative/Stone/Getty Images (b) Alex Treadway/National Geographic/Getty Images (c) Kajetan Kandler/Stone/Getty Images

TABLE 9.1: Cross-Sectional versus Longitudinal Design

	CROSS-SECTIONAL DESIGNS	LONGITUDINAL DESIGNS
Advantages	• Can be done quickly • Since data is collected only once from each participant, no concerns about dropout	• Not vulnerable to cohort effects negatively affecting validity
Disadvantages	• Vulnerable to cohort effects negatively affecting validity	• Takes a long time • Some original participants drop out • Often expensive

to using MRIs to see how the brain changes over time (Paus, 2009; Perrin et al., 2008; Bornstein, 1999). Regardless of how research is conducted, developmental psychologists often focus on a few big questions: *stability versus change*, *stage development versus continuous development*, and *nature versus nurture* (Lerner et al., 2005).

Stability Versus Change

As we get older, how much do we change, and how much do we stay the same? We do plenty of both, of course (Magnusson & Stattin, 2006; Roberts et al., 2003). Think of relatives you see only once in a while. You probably notice new developments as they get older—how they look but also how they think, feel, and interact with others—and you probably notice qualities that stay the same year after year. For example, a 4-year-old girl who sings and dances in her own homemade talent shows at every family get-together becomes a 14-year-old girl who would be mortified at such immature behavior. However, her attention seeking is still a core characteristic, as illustrated by her frequent fights with friends and other adolescent drama. Her continuing desire for attention illustrates stability, but her new ways of seeking attention illustrate change.

Stage Development Versus Continuous Development

When we do change, do we change suddenly or gradually? The way a caterpillar changes into a butterfly provides a good example of sudden—*stage*—development (**Figure 9.1**). The caterpillar stays a caterpillar for quite a while, then abruptly transforms into a butterfly, staying in that form for the rest of its life. Developmental psychologists point to certain changes—the bodily changes of puberty, for example—as being stage developments. Boys and girls have child bodies for the first 11–13 years or so, then enter the brief cocoon of adolescence in which the body rapidly transforms into its adult version. However, many of the changes that people go through are less rushed and less noticeable than puberty. For example, our decline in intelligence (as discussed in Chapter 7) doesn't happen overnight, but little by little during the latter half of adulthood. This is an example of *continuous* development.

Nature Versus Nurture

The nature versus nurture question, which is central to the entire field of psychology, holds a prominent place in developmental psychology (Beauchaine et al., 2008). What determines how we change over time: an inborn blueprint that unfolds inevitably (nature), or the influences of the world around us (nurture)? Of course, an interaction of nature and nurture underlies most of the changes we experience (Ehrlich & Feldman, 2003; Marcus, 2004). We are born with certain personality characteristics (nature), but

One of the big questions that developmental psychologists explore is the extent to which people change or remain stable over the course of their lifetimes. (a) Inti St Clair/Blend/Getty Images (b) diego cervo/iStock/Getty Images

FIGURE 9.1 Stage Development Versus Continuous Development. One of the major questions for developmental psychologists is whether people develop in stages or continuously. Stage development is like running your hand up a staircase—it stays level for a while, then suddenly jumps up to a new level, then stays at that level for a while. Continuous development is like running your hand up a ramp—steady, slow movement upward.

developmental psychology
The study of the changes to body, mind, and interpersonal interaction that people experience across the life span.

cross-sectional design
A research design in which people of different ages are compared to each other at the same point in time.

longitudinal design
A research design in which the same group of people is compared to itself at different points in time.

Development is influenced by culture. For example, the age at which children begin to sleep in their own bed (as opposed to co-sleeping with parents) often depends on norms that differ in various parts of the world. Volt Collection/Shutterstock

those characteristics are affected by powerful experiences (nurture), especially those that affect us continuously for a long time. For example, people whose long-term jobs and relationships bring satisfaction show increases in emotional stability, while the opposite is true of people whose long-term jobs and marriages bring them aggravation (Roberts et al., 2003; Robins et al., 2002; Roberts, 1997).

The influence of nurture on our development often depends greatly on the cultural circumstances in which we live (Fung, 2011; Quintana, 2011; Schlegel, 2009; Cole, 2005). For example, the ability to do math problems develops, to some extent, according to the type of math that our culture demands of us. Brazilian kids working as street vendors are experts in the type of math that job requires—on-the-fly, in-your-head addition, subtraction, and multiplication. They have trouble, however, doing written math problems that tap into the same types of calculations (Sternberg, 2011; Carraher et al., 1985).

DIVERSITY MATTERS

As another example of cultural influence on development, consider this question: At what age do children begin to sleep in their own bed rather than the same bed as their parents? For many in the United States, the answer may seem obvious: immediately. Babies have their own cribs in their own rooms when they come home from the hospital. In fact, babies even sleep in a separate crib for those first few days *in* the hospital. In many other parts of the world (and for some in the United States), however, the "family bed" is the norm (Shweder et al., 1995, 2006). Specifically, young kids and parents co-sleeping is common in many parts of Asia, Africa, and Central America. Members of these families often prefer this even when there are other beds available in other rooms. At least one longitudinal study found that young kids who co-sleep with their parents are just as well-adjusted at age 6 and age 18 as their separate-sleeping peers (Okami et al., 2002). Other studies, especially those citing risk of injury or death (via suffocation) of infants in bed with adults, offer mixed results and recommendations (Goldberg & Keller, 2007).

CHECK YOUR LEARNING:

9.1 What is developmental psychology?

9.2 What is the difference between cross-sectional and longitudinal research designs?

9.3 What are the three big questions for developmental psychologists?

Development Before Birth

YOU WILL LEARN:

9.4 about the sequence of prenatal development.

9.5 what teratogens are.

9.6 what fetal alcohol syndrome is.

zygote
The prenatal human organism from the moment the egg is fertilized by sperm to about 2 weeks.

embryo
The prenatal human organism from about 2 weeks to about 2 months after conception.

fetus
The prenatal human organism from about 2 months after conception to birth.

As we start our exploration of development across the life span, we start well before the baby makes his or her grand entrance. Lots of important developmental events take place during pregnancy.

Conception

You probably don't need your psychology textbook to tell you how conception happens, but here's a quick refresher: About midway through a woman's menstrual cycle, her body ovulates, or releases an ovum (egg) capable of being fertilized. If she has sexual intercourse with a man during that time, the sperm contained in his ejaculation—hundreds of millions of them—race toward the egg. As the leading sperm (it only takes one) reaches the egg, it passes through the egg's outer layer, and within hours, the nucleus of the sperm joins with the nucleus of the egg to form a new single cell. At this point, conception has occurred, and this new cell will double many millions of times over the next 9 months to develop a human baby.

From the moment the sperm and egg merge into a new single cell, that cell typically contains 46 chromosomes, 23 from the egg and 23 from the sperm. As the cells multiply, every cell contains the same set of chromosomes. Each chromosome contains deoxyribonucleic acid, or *DNA*. The DNA contains the *genes*, which drive every aspect of development through the life span.

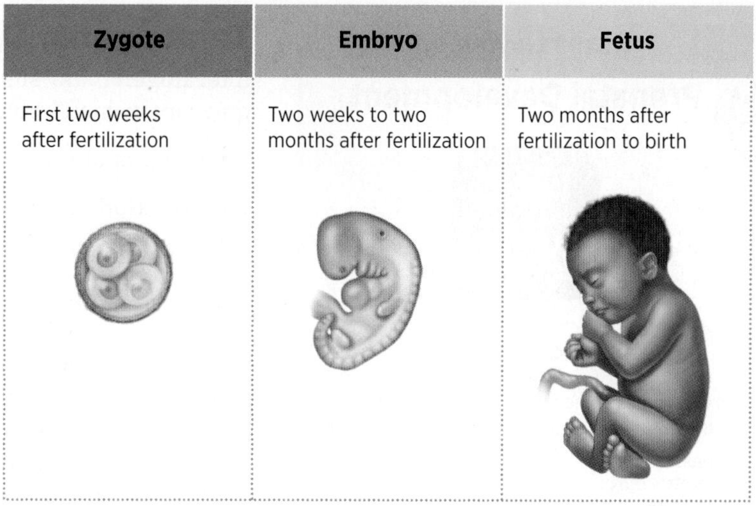

FIGURE 9.2 Stages of Prenatal Development. The stages of prenatal development progress from zygote to embryo to fetus.

Prenatal Development

We use different terms to describe the organism at various points during prenatal development (**Figure 9.2**). The first term is **zygote**: the prenatal human organism from the moment the egg is fertilized by sperm to about 2 weeks. Around that point, we begin to use the term **embryo**: the prenatal human organism from about 2 weeks to about 2 months after conception. For the remainder of the pregnancy, we say **fetus**: the prenatal human organism from about 2 months after conception to birth.

Zygotes don't always reach the embryo stage. (In many of these cases, the woman will not know she conceived.) Among the zygotes that do survive, a few divide into two (for reasons we don't completely understand). Each of these new zygotes develops into a separate embryo, fetus, and eventually, baby. You know these pairs as identical twins, but the more scientific name is *monozygotic twins*, with *mono-* referring to the fact that they started as one zygote. In contrast, the fraternal (or nonidentical) twins you know are *dizygotic twins*, with *di-* referring to the fact that they started as two separate zygotes—that is, two eggs fertilized by two sperm.

During the embryonic period, the cells specialize more than they had during the zygotic period. Each cell is devoted to a specific body part, beginning with the most essential, such as the spinal cord, heart, and brain. Facial features and arms and legs start to develop too. Assuming that no complications arise, the formation of a fully functioning human body is well under way.

During the fetal period—the last 7 months or so of pregnancy—the sheer increase in size is extraordinary. Around the end of the embryonic period (about 2 months into pregnancy), the embryo has a length of just 1 inch and a weight of just 1 ounce. The size of a newborn baby carried to a full 9-month term is typically 20 inches long and 7–8 pounds! During this exponential growth, the fetus' internal organs begin to function more independently. The fetus starts moving around too, with the mother (and anyone with a hand on her belly) feeling an increasing number of friendly kicks (Hepper, 2003). The ratios of the various body parts also change (as **Figure 9.3** illustrates): the legs and torso stretch out quite a bit, making the head seem less oversized in comparison to the rest of the body (Adolph & Berger, 2005).

Another fascinating finding about fetuses: They pay attention. We know this because researchers have studied fetuses' *habituation*, the tendency to ignore stimuli that repeat or stay constant (as discussed in Chapter 3). How do researchers study this? They played specific sounds through small speakers placed on the pregnant mom's belly near the fetus' head. Using the same ultrasound technology that allows parents-to-be to know whether to expect a boy or a girl, they observed the fetuses' reactions. At first, the fetuses responded noticeably, by blinking or by moving their arms or legs. But eventually, after hearing the sounds repeatedly, they no longer responded—the same way you might learn to disregard a false car alarm (Bellieni et al., 2005; Hepper et al., 2012; Joy et al., 2012). Fetuses even showed a memory for the sound to which they had habituated by not responding as strongly when they were reintroduced to it after a delay of several weeks (Dirix et al., 2009)!

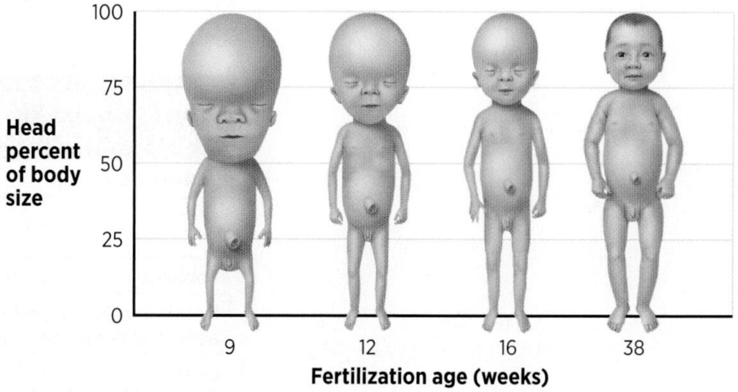

FIGURE 9.3 The Fetus Takes Shape. At the beginning of the fetal period of prenatal development, the head comprises about 50% of the fetus' length. As the weeks go by, that percentage decreases to about 25%.

CHAPTER APP 9.1

Prenatal Development

What to Expect

Preview one of the links and consider the following questions.

WEBSITE:
http://tiny.cc/idi7jy

ANDROID:
http://tiny.cc/oy77iy

IPHONE:
http://tiny.cc/2x77iy

VIDEO DEMO:
http://tiny.cc/chapterapps

This app is connected to the popular *What to Expect When You're Expecting* franchise, which also offers books and online information about pregnancy, babies, and toddlers. The app tells parents what's typical at each week and month of pregnancy, such as how the fetus is developing, as well as what's typical at each month throughout the first couple years of life, such as how much babies should be eating and when they should be sitting up, crawling, and so on.

How does it APPly to your daily life?
If you (or someone close to you) were expecting or were parenting a baby, would this app help you? If so, what specific benefits would it provide?

How does it APPly to your understanding of psychology?
How could the information provided by this app help you appreciate development before birth (including teratogens and fetal alcohol syndrome) and during infancy?

Teratogens: Dangers in the Womb

A **teratogen** is any substance that harms the embryo or fetus. Teratogens can enter the pregnant woman's body in many forms (Fryer et al., 2008):

- Drugs of abuse, like alcohol, nicotine, tobacco, or cocaine
- Prescription drugs, like the acne drug Accutane and many others
- Environmental pollution, like pesticides, mercury, and lead
- Diseases, like chickenpox, rubella, Zika, and some other viruses

Because some women are unaware of their pregnancy until well into the embryonic stage, they may expose themselves to teratogens without realizing it. This is true particularly in unplanned pregnancies, which constitute more than half of the pregnancies in the United States (Finer & Zolna, 2011). **Table 9.2** links some common teratogens to their possible effects on the embryo or fetus.

By far, the most studied teratogen is alcohol (Jones & Streissguth, 2010). It is common knowledge that pregnant women should avoid alcohol, but the specific consequences are not as well known. The most hazardous consequence is **fetal alcohol syndrome**: a pattern of physical and behavioral abnormalities common in people whose mothers drank alcohol excessively during pregnancy. Fetal alcohol syndrome affects about 1 per 1000 children, but *fetal alcohol effects*—basically a less extreme version of fetal alcohol syndrome—affect another 9 per 1000. Fetal alcohol syndrome involves a number of physical abnormalities that include small size, both before and well after birth. There is also a distinct set of facial features, including small eyes, a thin upper lip, and a near absence of the groove between the bottom of the nose and the upper lip.

But the psychological and behavioral abnormalities of fetal alcohol syndrome are often far more problematic than the physical abnormalities (Riley & McGee, 2005). One study found that 87% of children with fetal alcohol syndrome were diagnosable with a mental disorder (O'Connor et al., 2002). The most common disorders are attention-deficit/hyperactivity disorder (ADHD), oppositional-defiant disorder, conduct disorder, anxiety, and depression (Fryer et al., 2007). Many of these disorders are associated with disruptive or illegal behavior, so it may come as no surprise that among juvenile delinquents, 23% have fetal alcohol syndrome or fetal alcohol effects. Among the general population, only 1% have either of these (Fast et al., 1999; Fast & Conry, 2004). In addition to psychological disorders, kids with fetal alcohol syndrome also show many school-related impairments, including difficulties with attention, memory, mathematical abilities, and language development (Mattson & Riley, 1998; Fast & Conry, 2009; Meintjes et al., 2010).

TABLE 9.2: Common Teratogens and Possible Consequences for the Embryo or Fetus

TERATOGEN	POSSIBLE CONSEQUENCES
Alcohol	Psychological disorders, cognitive impairment, facial abnormalities, physical underdevelopment
Tobacco	Premature birth, physical deformities, physical underdevelopment
Retinoic acid (found in acne medicine Accutane)	Cognitive impairment, various deformities, psychological problems
Lead	Cognitive impairment, various physical illnesses
Mercury	Cognitive impairment, problems with movement
Rubella virus	Cognitive impairment; heart, eye, and ear abnormalities
Chickenpox virus	Cognitive impairment, low birthweight, vision problems
Zika virus	Undersized skull and brain, developmental delays

What happens to kids with fetal alcohol syndrome? Do they grow out of it?

Kids with fetal alcohol syndrome typically don't outgrow their psychological or behavioral problems. Research has found that 92% of adults with fetal alcohol syndrome were diagnosable with a mental illness, most often drug problems, alcohol problems, or depression (Famy et al., 1998; Barr et al., 2006). The impairments that made schoolwork especially challenging in childhood also tend to persist and cause problems in adulthood.

More recently, researchers have turned their attention to another teratogen on the rise: methamphetamines, or "meth." Results of their studies indicate that meth may do as much damage as alcohol, possibly more. Kids whose moms used meth during pregnancy have at least double the risk for behavior problems by the time they are just 5 years old, including ADHD, disruptive or rule-breaking behavior, and social withdrawal (LaGasse et al., 2012; Twomey et al., 2013). These kids also show significant shortcomings in controlling their emotions and actions, paying attention, solving problems, and using short-term memory (Abar et al., 2013).

A final note about teratogens: Education is the key. Teaching women who are pregnant (or could become pregnant) about the substances that could cause serious, lifelong problems for their children is essential to reducing the teratogen risk (Shahin & Einarson, 2011; Conover & Polifka, 2011). Along the same lines, doing healthy things to combat the effects of teratogens helps women who are pregnant (or could become pregnant). For example, folic acid (which is contained in many green vegetables, like spinach and broccoli, and can also be taken as a supplement) has been shown to reduce the risk of birth abnormalities (Hernández-Díaz et al., 2000).

teratogen
Any substance that harms the embryo or fetus.

fetal alcohol syndrome
A pattern of physical and behavioral abnormalities common in people whose mothers drank alcohol excessively during pregnancy.

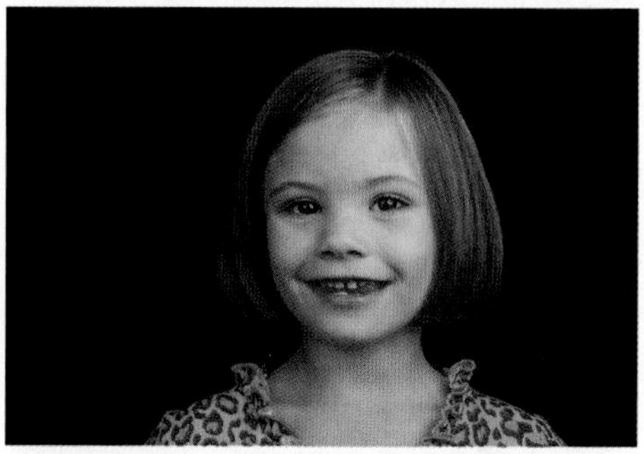

People whose mothers drank alcohol during pregnancy can develop fetal alcohol syndrome, which involves not only psychological and behavioral problems but physical abnormalities too, including facial features like small eyes, a thin upper lip, and a nearly absent groove between nose and upper lip. Rick's Photography/Shutterstock

CHECK YOUR LEARNING:

9.4 What is the sequence of prenatal development?

9.5 What are teratogens?

9.6 What is fetal alcohol syndrome?

Infancy and Childhood

For developmental psychologists, a new bundle of joy is a new bundle of research opportunities. To learn about what infants think and feel, developmental psychologists often rely on *inferences*, educated guesses based on what babies *can* communicate (Bornstein, 1999; Cohen & Cashon, 2006). Developmental psychologists infer that a particular behavior by a baby—how long it stares at something, its facial expressions and actions, or whether it cries—tells us something about the workings of its mind. As we consider studies that rely on inference, keep in mind that this approach requires researchers to take some logical leaps, so it is far from perfect. With babies, however, it is the best we can do.

YOU WILL LEARN:

9.7 what abilities newborns have.

9.8 how physical development proceeds through predictable stages.

9.9 how, according to Piaget, children develop schemas (or mental categories) and either assimilate new information into them or accommodate the schemas to account for the new information.

9.10 how, according to Piaget, children develop through cognitive stages.

9.11 about the ways researchers have challenged some of Piaget's conclusions.

The Abilities of Newborns

Brand-new babies seem so helpless. What *can* they do?

Brand-new babies can do a lot. For starters, all five senses work remarkably well from day one (Bornstein et al., 2005). A baby's ability to smell is particularly impressive. When researchers placed foods that people generally like (such as butter or

YOU WILL LEARN: (*Continued*)

9.12 about the three distinct types of attachment and why secure attachment to others is so important.

9.13 about different types of parenting styles.

9.14 what temperament is and how it can affect parent–child relationships.

Newborn babies have strong sensory abilities. For example, at just 2 weeks of age, a baby can distinguish the smell of his or her own mother from the smell of other women (Cernoch & Porter, 1985). SelectStock/Vetta/Getty Images

bananas) near the noses of newborns, the babies gave them a smile. However, when the researchers presented rotten eggs, the babies gave them a "yucky" face (Steiner, 1977).

In another study, researchers had the mothers of 2-week-old babies, as well as other women, sleep with gauze pads under their arms. The next day, they gave each baby a "smell test" by placing the mother's gauze pad and the other woman's gauze pad near the baby's head. Then, researchers measured how long the baby turned its head toward each gauze pad. Consistently, the babies pointed themselves toward the mother's gauze pad, which contained mother's odor, for much longer than the non-mother's gauze pad. Researchers interpreted this finding as an ability to distinguish odors and show a preference for one smell over the other (Cernoch & Porter, 1985).

Newborn babies' vision isn't as sharp as their sense of smell, but it is good enough for the important (to them) stuff. Babies can't focus at every distance, but they can focus quite well at objects about 8–12 inches away—the very distance between baby's face and mom's face during breastfeeding (Slater & Johnson, 1998). Within a few days of birth, babies prefer their mother's face to the faces of other women—a finding that researchers inferred from the fact that they stare longer at mom's face (Bushnell et al., 1989; Pascalis et al., 1995; Bushnell, 2001). Actually, newborn babies prefer looking at faces of any kind over looking at other types of images, even within the first few hours of their lives (Opfer & Gelman, 2011; Legerstee, 1992). Specifically, their eyes follow a moving face-like image for a longer period of time than they follow an image resembling a scrambled or blank face (**Figure 9.4**). This finding was discovered in babies as young as 9 *minutes* old (Goren et al., 1975; Johnson et al., 1991; Valenza et al., 1996; Nelson et al., 2006; Fantz et al., 1975; Rakison & Poulin-Dubois, 2001; Mondloch et al., 1999).

With hearing, newborns are born with limited but essential abilities. They can tell the difference between their mother's voice and the voices of other women. Researchers came to this conclusion by measuring the rate at which babies suck on a pacifier-like device when hearing different voices. They suck faster when hearing the voice of their mom than for a stranger's voice (DeCasper & Fifer, 1980; DeCasper & Spence, 1986).

Beyond their sensory abilities, babies can do lots of other things. They exhibit a variety of reflexes, as shown in **Figure 9.5**. Babies *suck* when a nipple (or fingertip, or almost anything) is placed inside their mouths. They *grasp* when a finger is placed in their palms and *step* with their legs when they are held upright with their feet touching the ground. Babies *root* (turn their heads and open their mouths) when an object brushes one of their cheeks. They also fling their arms out in response to a sudden surprise, a reaction called the *Moro reflex* (Adolph & Berger, 2005; von Hofsten, 2003; Kisilevsky et al., 1991). And of course, we're all very familiar with babies' ability to cry to make their needs known. Clearly, babies' brains function at an impressive level as soon as they arrive.

FIGURE 9.4 What Newborn Babies See. Just minutes after birth, babies stare longer at the figure on the left than the figure on the right, which suggests that they can tell the difference between face-like images and other images.

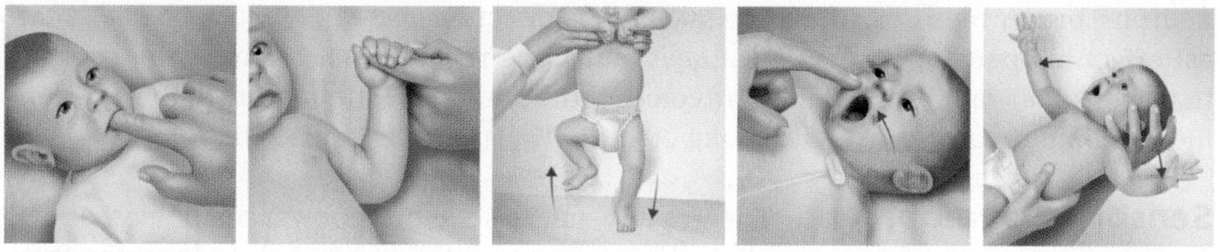

FIGURE 9.5 The Reflexes of Newborns. Newborn babies exhibit many reflexes, including sucking, grasping, stepping, rooting (turning their heads and opening their mouths when an object touches the cheek), and the Moro reflex (flinging arms outward when startled).

Physical Development

At some point in your life, someone has probably said, "Wow, I can't believe how much you've grown!" The physical development that takes place during infancy and childhood is remarkable. Let's consider three facets of that physical development: brain development, sensory development, and motor development.

Brain Development. In the first 3 years of life, a child's brain triples in weight. It continues growing at a slower pace until about age 10. Between a child's first and second birthday, the number of synapses (connections between neurons) increases by 40,000 *per second*, for a total of about 1 quadrillion through early childhood (Zelazo & Lee, 2010).

This exuberant formation and connection of neurons occurs in a predictable order. The first surge takes place in the visual cortex, followed by the areas of the brain that help with hearing and language. Eventually, the prefrontal cortex develops, which enables thought, planning, and problem solving (Huttenlocher & Dabholkar, 1997). The neurons in the frontal lobe that shape the memory system take a while longer to fully develop, which explains *infantile amnesia*, our inability to remember what happened to us before ages 2–4 (Schneider, 2011; Bauer et al., 2011).

Nature may drive the development of the young brain, but nurture steers it. The experiences a child has during these early years affect the way a child's brain grows (Cole, 2006; Le Grand et al., 2001; Maurer et al., 2005). For example, researchers examined the visual abilities of people who, as very young children, were successfully treated for serious vision problems, including severe cataracts (Le Grand et al., 2004). Their ability to see human faces accurately later in life still fell far below normal. The reason is that *prior* to their treatment, their lack of visual stimulation caused the vision-related areas of the brain to be underdeveloped, and those brain areas never entirely caught up.

Similarly, babies' babbling contains the basic sounds of every human language, but within the first years of life, babies typically hear only one language. As a result, the wiring in their brain for that one language gets strengthened while the unused parts fall away. The neurons and synapses go through a natural *pruning* process, in much the same way that a gardener might prune certain branches of a bush but allow others to grow larger and more complex (Nelson et al., 2006; Kuhl, 2004). That is also why young children are so much better at picking up new languages than adults—their pruning process isn't complete yet, so they still have the "wires" to enable the new connections in their brains.

A series of classic experiments highlight the impact of environment on brain development (e.g., Rosenzweig et al., 1962; Diamond et al., 1966, 1975; Krech et al., 1966; Globus et al., 1973; Renner & Rosenzweig, 1987). In the 1960s and 1970s, a group of researchers placed young rats in either an *enriched environment* or an *impoverished environment*. The enriched environment featured a wide array of things to see, hear, and do, along with some other rats with whom to interact. The impoverished environment featured nothing besides food and water—no sights, no sounds, no activities, and no rat buddies. The researchers examined the brains of these rats and found that rats from the enriched environments showed enriched brain wiring—including more

LIFE HACK 9.1

To maximize the functioning of your brain, exercise your body.

(Voss et al., 2011; Smith et al., 2010)

neurons, bigger neurons, and more synaptic connections between neurons. The greatest effect happens at the youngest ages, but more recent studies have demonstrated that even older rats' brains can be affected by the amount of stimulation in the environment (Kempermann et al., 1997; Song et al., 2005; van Praag et al., 2000).

Sensory Development. The rapidly increasing brainpower in babies allows them to improve their sensory skills. In the first months of life, babies increase their ability to perceive facial expressions in the people around them. In fact, some research has found that babies of depressed moms show a preference for different intensities of smiles and frowns—presumably to match the downcast faces they often see in their moms—than did babies of non-depressed moms (Kellman & Arterberry, 2006). Newborns' visual preference for faces over non-faces becomes even more obvious as the months go by. At 2 months, newborns smile and coo more at people than at toy monkeys (Legerstee et al., 1987). At 3 months, they gaze longer at (and have more rapid heartbeats when viewing) a real person than at a mannequin or a doll (Klein & Jennings, 1979; Brazelton et al., 1974; Field, 1979). In terms of hearing, babies also develop a strong preference for speech over non-speech sounds in their first few months of life (Vouloumanos et al., 2001, 2010; Vouloumanos & Werker, 2004, 2007).

Motor Development. Many parents can attest to the fact that the immobile infant becomes a scampering toddler seemingly overnight. Many parents can also describe the sequence of motor skills the child develops in the process. Once they develop the ability to prop themselves up on their hands or elbows (to lift their head and torso), babies use these movements to get around (in this order): rolling, sitting up, crawling, standing, cruising (getting around on two feet while holding on to still objects like chairs or low tables), and finally, walking (Adolph & Berger, 2005, 2006). Children around the world follow the same sequence, at around the same points in time, with only minimal influences by family or culture. This suggests that motor development is determined more by biology than environment, more by nature than by nurture.

FROM RESEARCH TO REAL LIFE

A Well-Running Brain

Research on enriched environments versus impoverished environments provides clear evidence that activity—especially exercise—physically enhances the brains of rats. What about the brains of people? Do our brains respond the same way when we keep ourselves active?

A growing body of research suggests that physical exercise increases the physical condition of the human brain (Voss et al., 2011). One study randomly assigned 120 older adults to one of two groups: 60 walked at a moderate pace 3 days a week for up to 40 minutes, and the other 60 simply stretched instead. Researchers found that the hippocampus, which is closely linked to memory and which shrinks with age, actually *increased* in size by 2% in the walkers but not in the stretchers (Erickson et al., 2011). Other studies have found that the volume of the whole brain increases in older adults who participate in moderate aerobic exercise walking—again, a finding that runs counter to the typical course of brain development (Colcombe et al., 2006; Erickson & Kramer, 2009). In addition to a sheer increase in brain size, older adults also show increased connections between different regions of their brains after a year of walking exercise (Voss et al., 2010).

These physical improvements in the brain translate into improvements in day-to-day life as well. For example, 6 months of a regular exercise regimen (4 days a week, 45–60 minutes a day on a treadmill, bike, or elliptical machine) boosted the memory, attention, and processing speed of older adults. A control group who participated in stretching classes for the same amount of time showed no such gains (Baker et al., 2010). This result is typical. A meta-analysis that combined the results of 29 studies and over 2000 participants, age 18 and over, found that memory, attention, and processing speed all improve with aerobic exercise (Smith et al., 2010).

Researchers suggest that the positive effects could be maximized by linking physical exercise to cognitive activity (Fabel & Kempermann, 2008). Rather than mindless time on a treadmill (like a mouse on a running wheel), exercise accompanied by social interaction (like walking while talking with friends) or a cognitive challenge (like reading a thought-provoking article while riding a stationary bike) is likely to be most beneficial to the brain. ●

Physical exercise enhances brain functioning at any age. Jose Luis Pelaez Inc/Blend/Getty Images

The motor development of babies follows the same sequence around the world. Three of the major milestones are (in order) sitting up, crawling, and walking. (a) David A Land/Blend Images/Getty Images (b) khoa vu/Moment/Getty Images (c) Miodrag Gajic/E+/Getty Images

Cognitive Development

Our understanding of children's cognitive development—the changes in the way children think about and understand the world around them—is dominated by the ideas of Jean Piaget (Beins, 2012; Messerly, 2009; Smith, 2009). Piaget, who lived in Switzerland from 1896 to 1980, developed a comprehensive theory of childhood development in more than 100 books and more than 600 published papers (e.g., Piaget, 1924, 1926, 1929, 1936/1952; 1983). His theories have inspired empirical research by generations of developmental psychologists. Whether this research supports his ideas (as much of it has) or refutes them (as some has), Piaget founded the study of how kids' minds work. Let's consider some of Piaget's most important ideas, including *schemas* and *stages of cognitive development*. Then, let's consider an alternative to Piaget's theories, as well as more recent research that tests Piaget's theories.

Schemas. One of Piaget's most fundamental observations was that a primary task for each of us is to sort the vast range of things in the world into categories, or mental "boxes" (Birney et al., 2005; P. H. Miller, 2011; Halford & Andrews, 2006). Each category, or box, according to Piaget, is a **schema**: a concept or mental representation that guides the way you make sense of new information. Once the schema is in place, it can be reused indefinitely for new things you encounter. That classification process is **assimilation**: making sense of new information by sorting it into already existing schemas. Of course, sometimes an item doesn't fit into an existing schema, or a schema needs to be subdivided or redefined (Gelman & Kalish, 2006). We deal with these situations by using **accommodation**: making sense of new information by revising or creating new schemas.

To illustrate schemas, assimilation, and accommodation, let's consider Eli, a young boy just learning what a sandwich is. At an early age, Eli first sees an object with two pieces of bread and something between them, which he hears described as a sandwich.

schema
A concept or mental representation that guides the way a person makes sense of new information.

assimilation
A classification process that makes sense of new information by sorting into already existing schemas.

accommodation
A classification process that makes sense of new information by revising or creating new schemas.

IT'S LIKE...

Assimilation and Accommodation Are Like Sorting Laundry

When you take a basket of laundry out of the dryer, it is a jumbled mess. As you fold it, you categorize it. The first item you pull out of the muddle is a shirt, so you start a shirt pile. The second item is a pair of pants, so you create a pants pile. The third item is a sock, so you start a sock pile. As you make your way through the basket, many of the items fit easily into one of the three piles you've started. For different items, you start a new pile. For example, when you come across your first pair of underwear, it doesn't fit into any of the existing piles, so you start an underwear pile. Eventually, you have separate piles for towels and sheets, and you've divided the pants pile into two piles: long pants and shorts. When you're done folding the laundry, the jumbled mess is now organized and functional.

Each separate pile of clothes—that is, each category—corresponds to what Piaget called a *schema*. When you put an item in a pile you've already started, that is *assimilation*. When you start a new pile for a new item, that is *accommodation*. Without schemas, assimilation, and accommodation, a young child might experience the world like a tangled knot of laundry. However, by using assimilation and accommodation, the world becomes much more orderly and intelligible. ●

At that point, Eli's mind creates a new "sandwich" schema. Later that day, when he sees his sister's PB&J, he shouts, "Sandwich!" The next day, when he sees his mom's turkey on wheat, he shouts, "Sandwich!" Thanks to the schema, Eli can assimilate every sandwich he sees into this new mental box, even though sandwiches had no name or category just a few days earlier (Waxman & Leddon, 2011; Quinn, 2011; Golinkoff et al., 1995).

The next day, Eli sees a taco and says, "Sandwich!" Of course, he's misusing his "sandwich" schema, and his mom kindly corrects him: "No, Eli, that's a taco." So Eli accommodates his system of schemas by creating a new one: the "taco" schema. In upcoming months and years, Eli further accommodates new knowledge by creating separate schemas for "burger," "calzone," "samosa," "empanada," and "knish." And Eli breaks down his original "sandwich" schema into more specific minischemas, such as "BLT," "sub," and "Philly cheesesteak."

As Eli grows up, his collection of schemas develops from simple to complex—not just with sandwiches, but with everything he comes across. Furniture (sofas vs. loveseats vs. armchairs), weather (rain vs. sleet vs. hail), technology (smartphone vs. TV remote vs. video game controller), and feelings (anger vs. jealousy vs. disgust)—these are just a few of the different kinds of things that Eli will use schemas to categorize.

During the sensorimotor stage, which lasts through the first 2 years of life, children understand the world through sensory experience. For example, the way they experience Cheerios involves taste, smell, touch, and sight. DigitalVision/Getty Images

Piaget's Stages of Cognitive Development. Piaget believed that children's thinking progressed through distinct stages. According to his observations, kids stick with the same way of thinking for years, then shift to a new way of thinking in a very short time. He argued that these different stages were biologically determined and only minimally influenced by environment or experience. The idea is that kids around the world move through the same stages in the same order at around the same ages (Keil, 2006; Messerly, 2009; P. H. Miller, 2011). **Table 9.3** offers a summary of Piaget's stages: the *sensorimotor stage*, the *preoperational stage*, the *concrete operational stage*, and the *formal operational stage*. Let's examine each in detail.

Sensorimotor Stage. The **sensorimotor stage** is the first stage in Piaget's theory of development, from birth to about age 2, when babies understand the world through sensory experience. Babies know something is real by seeing, hearing, smelling, touching, or tasting it. That direct experience is crucial because babies can't yet imagine or remember much. For example, consider how babies learn about Cheerios—their taste, texture, color, size, and shape. They don't yet have the brainpower to imagine Cheerios when they're not around or understand someone's description of Cheerios. Babies need to see the Cheerios with their eyes, feel the Cheerios on their fingers, and taste them with their tongues. They need to interact with Cheerios in direct ways to appreciate those crunchy little circles.

Object permanence, which emerges around the age of 1 year, is the ability to realize that an object continues to exist even when you can't see or otherwise sense it. Without a sense of object permanence, a young child (unlike this one, who is removing a cloth to find a hidden toy) would not look for a missing object, because the child would assume that the object was gone. Doug Goodman/Science Source

Does that explain why babies love peek-a-boo so much?

Yes! Peek-a-boo, a favorite of kids during the sensorimotor stage, makes a lot of sense in terms of that need for direct sensory experience (Singer & Revenson, 1996). Think of it this way: If your aunt plays peek-a-boo with you today, you obviously understand that she continues to exist even when she hides her face. But when you were a baby, when she wasn't just momentarily out of sight, she was *gone*. That's what made her reappearance so miraculous and exciting!

Peek-a-boo doesn't work on you anymore because you developed **object permanence**: the ability to realize that an object continues to exist even when you can't see, hear, or otherwise sense it. Piaget argued that object permanence emerges around a child's first birthday, so it is lacking in the first part the sensorimotor stage (Piaget, 1936/1952, 1954). As evidence of young infants' lack of object permanence, Piaget pointed to his experiments in which he hid toys from children in simple ways (under a cloth, for example). The children who had not yet achieved object permanence didn't even look for the toy (remember, it is *gone* to them), but the older children did. The older children knew the toy continued to exist even if they temporarily couldn't see it.

TABLE 9.3: Piaget's Stages of Cognitive Development

STAGE	AGE (APPROX.)	DESCRIPTION	KEY CHALLENGES
Sensorimotor	0–2	Use sensory experience (touch, taste, sight, etc.) to understand the world	Object permanence
Preoperational	2–7	Use language and other symbols but have limited mental operations	Pretend play Conservation Theory of mind Egocentrism
Concrete operational	7–11	Think logically about concrete, but not abstract, things.	Reversibility Transitive reasoning
Formal operational	11–adulthood	Think logically about abstract things.	

Preoperational Stage. After the sensorimotor stage comes the **preoperational stage**, from about age 2 to about age 7, when children can use language and other symbols for real objects but still can't complete many mental operations. This is the period when kids develop the ability to represent things in their mind. They are no longer as dependent upon actual direct sensory experience. One sure sign of the preoperational stage is *pretend play*, which takes place when kids assign fictional roles to people (telling a friend, "You be the mommy and I'll be the little girl…") or give fictional powers to objects (singing into a hairbrush as if it is a microphone) (Müller & Racine, 2010; Müller, 2009). In each of these cases, the child demonstrates the ability to break free of the literal meaning of an object and instead imagine that the object is something or someone else.

During the preoperational stage, children's mathematical abilities bloom. However, through much of this stage, children continue to struggle with **conservation**, a mental operation in which an amount or quantity remains the same regardless of the shape it takes. One of Piaget's best-known observations involved a young child looking at two glasses filled with exactly the same amount of liquid. When one of those glasses was poured into a taller, thinner glass, a child who had not yet attained the ability to conserve would immediately (and mistakenly) say the new glass had "more" (because the liquid was higher in the comparison glass). Likewise, to a child who has not yet mastered conservation, a ball of dough becomes "more" when it is rolled out into a pizza crust (Martí, 2003).

Another hallmark of the preoperational stage is the child's development of **theory of mind**: the understanding of the thoughts, feelings, intentions and other mental activities of oneself and others. Simply put, kids in the preoperational stage gain an ability to "get inside the head" of other people (and themselves) that they did not have when they were younger (Carpenter, 2011; Lewis & Carpendale, 2011; Meltzoff, 2011; Perner, 1999; Wellman et al., 2003). Their language certainly reflects this newfound ability, as they use words to refer to mental events—like *want*, *think*, and *feel*—increasingly during this period (Wellman, 2011; Bartsch & Wellman, 1997).

In one study that illustrates the emergence of theory of mind, a 6- or 18-month-old child sat next to a woman with a toy that the child could see. The woman did not give

The preoperational stage is when children achieve a sense of conservation, or the understanding that an amount or quantity remains the same regardless of the shape it takes. Before developing a sense of conservation, children (like this girl) commonly make the mistake of assuming that a substance becomes "more" or "less" according to its size or shape. Bianca Moscatelli/Worth Publishers

sensorimotor stage
The first stage in Piaget's theory of development, from birth to about age 2, when babies understand the world through sensory experience.

object permanence
The ability to realize that an object continues to exist even when a person can't see, hear, or otherwise sense it.

preoperational stage
The second stage in Piaget's theory of development, from about age 2 to about age 7, when children can use language and other symbols for real objects but still can't complete many mental operations.

conservation
A mental operation in which an amount or quantity remains the same regardless of the shape it takes.

theory of mind
The understanding of the thoughts, feelings, intentions and other mental activities of oneself and others.

the child the toy, either because she accidentally dropped it or because she played with it herself. The older children showed much more impatience and frustration when the woman played with the toy herself than when she dropped it, even though the time the child was kept waiting was the same in both cases. Apparently, the older children were able to read the woman's intentions, so they were more upset by her selfishness than by the accidental mishandling of the toy. Younger children showed no such difference. They were equally mad regardless of the reason for the wait, presumably because they couldn't yet appreciate the woman's intentions (Behne et al., 2005; see also Tomasello et al., 2005; Carpenter et al., 1998).

Some researchers have explored whether an underdeveloped theory of mind relates to autism spectrum disorders, a core characteristic of which is a difficulty socializing with others and seeing the world through others' eyes (Wimmer & Perner, 1983; Perner et al., 1987; Baron-Cohen, 1995; 2000; Bowler, 1992). Several studies of this connection use a research method based on the *false-belief task*, as shown in **Figure 9.6**. The method involves telling children a story about a girl, Sally, who puts an object (usually a toy or a piece of chocolate) in a basket and then leaves the room. While she's out, another girl moves the object from the basket to a box. When Sally comes back, where will she look for the object? Among kids without developmental problems, 85% get it right and say that Sally will look in the basket, where she left it. But among kids with autism spectrum disorder, 80% get it wrong and say that Sally will look in the box, where it is now. (It is important to point out that the kids in this study were well beyond the age of the preoperational stage, so the expectation for some degree of theory of mind was reasonable.)

The researchers interpreted this finding to suggest that kids with autism spectrum disorder (whose IQs were equal or higher to those of the kids without the disorder) lack the theory of mind that would enable them to see the situation as *Sally* would. The suggestion is that kids with autism spectrum disorder assume that the way *they* see the situation is the way everyone (including Sally) must see it (Baron-Cohen et al., 1985, 1997). Other researchers have argued against this interpretation, saying that autism spectrum disorder is more complex than the mere lack of theory of mind. Specifically, they argue that kids with autism spectrum disorder may lack the motivation, along with or instead of the ability, to appreciate the mental activity of others (Chevallier, 2012; Chevallier et al., 2011; Schultz, 2005; Carpendale & Lewis, 2010).

Until kids develop theory of mind, their thinking is dominated by **egocentrism**: the inability to understand a situation from a point of view other than their own. Kids influenced by both egocentrism and theory of mind often show a blend of the two perspectives—they kind of see the world as others see it, but kind of see it their own way too. For example, 3-year-old Kenny's elderly grandfather slips and falls during a visit, breaking his hip. The adults try to make Kenny's grandfather comfortable until the ambulance arrives. Kenny does as well, giving his grandfather his own teddy bear and a Band-Aid, while saying "Here Grandpa, this will make it all better!" Kenny's theory of mind allows him to recognize the pain that his grandpa must be suffering, but Kenny's egocentrism limits him to considering what helps *Kenny* (and not what might help other people) to overcome pain.

FIGURE 9.6 The False-Belief Task. The false-belief task is a research method often used to test for theory of mind. In the false-belief task, the child hears a story about Sally, who puts an object in one container and then leaves the room. When she's gone, another girl moves the object to another container. When Sally returns, where will she look for the object? Kids with an intact theory of mind typically understand that Sally will look in the first container, but kids without an intact theory of mind (including many kids on the autism spectrum) will mistakenly think that Sally will look in the second container. This mistake indicates a failure to appreciate how their own view of a situation differs from another person's view.

Concrete Operational Stage. Piaget's third stage is the **concrete operational stage**, from about age 7 to about age 11, in which children acquire the ability to think logically about concrete things. They master conservation completely. Also, their ability to perform mental manipulations on things, even when those things are just representations in their heads rather than real items in their hands, increases dramatically (Bibok et al., 2009). One such mental manipulation is *reversibility*, which involves an understanding of how certain pairs of mathematical calculations (addition–subtraction or multiplication–division) are opposite. Picture an 11-year-old girl who knows she had \$40 cash in her room but who only counts \$32.50 right now. She does a subtraction problem in her head to calculate that \$7.50 is missing. Later, she finds the missing \$7.50 in the pocket of the jeans she wore a few days ago. To know how much she has after this discovery, she doesn't need to recalculate that 32.50 + 7.50 = 40. Instead, she can jump

immediately to the correct conclusion that she has $40 again, since she understands that addition reverses subtraction.

Another achievement of the concrete operational stage is *transitive reasoning* (Halford & Andrews, 2006). You might remember from a math class that the transitive property goes like this: if A equals B, and B equals C, then A must equal C. In the concrete operational stage, kids come to understand this mathematical version, as well as other versions of transitive reasoning. For example, if Ms. Alexander is as tough a science teacher as Mr. Barker, and Mr. Barker is as tough as Ms. Crawford, then Ms. Alexander must be as tough as Ms. Crawford.

Formal Operational Stage. Piaget's fourth and final stage is the **formal operational stage**, beginning around age 11 and lasting through adulthood, in which the person becomes able to think logically about abstract things. The key difference between this stage and the concrete operational stage is that mental operations don't need to be applied to concrete things. Mental operations can be theoretical, figurative, or conceptual. For example, during the formal operational stage kids develop the ability to appreciate political approaches (such as liberal or conservative), religious beliefs (not just visible objects and symbols of religion), and philosophical points of view. Think about your own experiences. You probably didn't start considering such issues, either in school or with family or friends, until you were well into middle school or high school.

Piaget argued that not everyone reaches the formal operational stage. Several empirical studies indicate that he was correct (Sutherland, 1992; Neimark, 1975; Renner et al., 1976), and one estimates that only about one-third of U.S. high school students fully complete the formal operational stage (Kuhn et al., 1977). More recent research has found that people who can perform this abstract thinking have significant advantages in certain professions, especially those related to math and computer science (Kramer, 2007; Frorer et al., 1997).

Vygotsky's Alternative to Piaget's Theories. Long before contemporary researchers relied on empirical methods to challenge Piaget, Lev Vygotsky countered Piaget with a theory of his own. Vygotsky, who was born in Russia the same year that Piaget was born in Switzerland, argued that social interaction was the primary force behind cognitive development (Vygotsky, 1978, 1986; Daniels, 2011; Yasnitsky, 2012; van der Veer & Valsiner, 1994; Rogoff, 2003). Piaget never denied that children's interactions with the people around them could have some influence on the development of their thinking, but he always considered that influence secondary (Piaget & Inhelder, 1969). Piaget believed biology was the primary force. Vygotsky's theory switched the emphasis, such that kids' interactions with older kids and adults were the main force for changes in thinking. Vygotsky argued that kids' thinking changes because the adults around those kids foster that change.

Vygotsky explained that often, a child's way of thinking was pushed along by **scaffolding**: a process by which a person learns new words, ideas, and ways of thinking by interacting with a more advanced person who provides decreasing levels of help. Consider two children of the same age who live in neighboring apartments, each working on a difficult jigsaw puzzle. The child in apartment A works entirely alone, but the child in apartment B interacts with a parent who is more expert in puzzles. The child in apartment B hears these comments in the process: "That can't be an edge piece. It doesn't have any straight sides." "That has to be a corner piece with its two straight sides." Notice that the parent doesn't do the puzzle for the child, but makes comments that nudge the child to use logic just beyond the child's current level of thinking. Just as scaffolding on a construction site provides a temporary way for people to climb to new heights, Vygotsky's scaffolding allows kids to climb to higher levels of cognition with the help of more advanced people (Langford, 2005; R. Miller, 2011).

Of course, scaffolding won't help if the first step is too high for the child to reach, so Vygotsky also emphasized the *zone of proximal development*, which is essentially the range of learning just above what a kid can do alone (Daniels, 1996; Wersch & Tulviste, 1992; Emerson, 1983, Hedegaard, 1992). This is a particularly important idea for those who work directly with children, like teachers or tutors. They should know

egocentrism
The inability to understand a situation from a point of view other than your own.

concrete operational stage
The third stage in Piaget's theory of development, from about age 7 to about age 11, in which children acquire the ability to think logically about concrete things.

formal operational stage
The final stage in Piaget's theory of development, beginning around age 11 and lasting through adulthood, in which the person becomes able to think logically about abstract things.

scaffolding
A process by which a person learns new words, ideas, and ways of thinking by interacting with a more advanced person who provides decreasing levels of help.

Scaffolding is a process by which a person (like this child) learns new words, ideas, and ways of thinking by interacting with a more advanced person (like this adult) who provides decreasing levels of help. Scaffolding was an idea of Lev Vygotsky, who believed that children's cognitive development was primarily influenced by nurture, or interactions with others. By contrast, Jean Piaget believed that children's cognitive development was primarily influenced by nature, or biologically determined stages. Fancy/Veer/AGE Fotostock

the kid's starting point and then offer challenges a bit beyond it, along with the support to help them meet those challenges (Rose & Fischer, 2009; Fischer & Bidell, 2006). For example, a child who recently mastered addition for one-digit numbers should probably be prodded to try addition problems in which one of the numbers has two digits (as opposed to addition problems in which each number has five digits).

Piaget Now: Empirical Findings. In some ways, Piaget's original theories have held up quite well, especially considering that almost a century has passed since his first ideas. However, more contemporary researchers have tested Piaget's ideas extensively, and some of their results contradict his predictions.

Often, results that don't support Piaget come from studies using methods Piaget didn't use. Modern researchers tested Piaget's theories in different ways than he did, and their tests yielded different results (Kesselring, 2009). As an example, consider Piaget's concept of object permanence. In his own studies, he relied on the method of hiding a toy under a cloth and noticing whether the child moved the cloth in an attempt to find it. His results indicated that kids couldn't develop object permanence until after their first birthday (Piaget, 1952, 1954, 1983). But what if younger babies really did have a sense of object permanence, and they just didn't show it in the way Piaget required? Perhaps younger babies didn't yet have the necessary hand–eye coordination to lift the cloth, or the toy wasn't interesting enough for them to seek it (P. H. Miller, 2011; Müller, 2009; Cohen & Cashon, 2006).

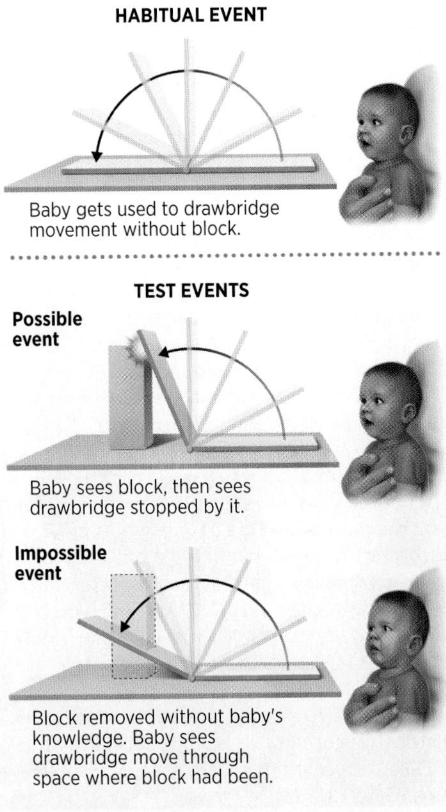

FIGURE 9.7 Testing Object Permanence with the Drawbridge Method. The drawbridge method was developed as a new way to test Piaget's theory of object permanence. The "drawbridge" goes up and down, much as a laptop computer opens and closes. Babies as young as 3.5 months old stared for an extra-long time at the drawbridge when it passed through a space where it should bump into a block—an indication that they knew the block was there, even though they couldn't see it. (Klahr, 2012; Hespos & Baillargeon, 2008; Keen & Berthier, 2004).

Is there a different way that very young babies could show their sense of object permanence?

A group of researchers thought there might be, and they tested Piaget's object permanence idea using an innovative *violation of expectation* method. It was based on the simple idea babies will stare longer at events that surprise them (or violate their expectations) than events that they expect (Mareschal & Kaufman, 2012; Baillargeon et al., 1985, 1990; Baillargeon, 1987, 2004; Baillargeon & Graber, 1987, 1988). Specifically, these researchers showed babies a "drawbridge" video in which they repeatedly saw the moving part of the drawbridge rotate toward them until it hit the ground, then rotate away from them until its opposite side hit the ground. Think of a laptop computer opening and closing all the way across its full 180 degree range. Better yet, see **Figure 9.7** for a side view.

After the babies became used to the opening and closing motion, the researchers inserted the image of a block behind the drawbridge. From that point on, the drawbridge either stopped when it would hit the block (as if your laptop bumped into a short stack of books hidden behind it as you pushed it wide open), or it moved right through that space, as if the block had disappeared. Here's the key finding: babies as young as 3.5 months old stared longer at the drawbridge passing through the block space (a violation of their expectations) than the drawbridge stopping at the point when it would bump into the block (what they expected). This finding suggests that these babies have a sense of object permanence about the block, even though it becomes invisible to them behind the drawbridge, at a much younger age than Piaget claimed (Klahr, 2012; Hespos & Baillargeon, 2008; Keen & Berthier, 2004).

In a different kind of violation-of-expectation study, babies see a doll on a table. Next, they see the researcher cover the doll with a blanket, put a second doll under the blanket, and then remove the blanket. When the blanket is lifted, babies as young as 2.5 months old stare longer if there is only one doll behind the blanket (the other has been secretly removed) than if both dolls are there. This long stare suggests that they expect the second doll to be there even though it was temporarily out of sight—again, at an age far younger than Piaget's methods would have allowed them to display (Wynn, 1992; Baillargeon et al., 2011).

The idea that Piaget's methods underestimated how quickly kids develop object permanence (and other cognitive abilities) is just one of the criticisms that his theories

receive from modern researchers. Two other criticisms are common. One is that Piaget's theory emphasized stages too much. Kids in the real world don't develop their cognitive abilities in the caterpillar-to-butterfly way that Piaget and other stage theorists described. There may be spurts of cognitive growth at certain times, but kids tend to show gradual, continuous change to a greater extent than Piaget described (Bibok et al., 2009).

The second criticism is related to the first: Piaget emphasized that his stages occurred because of biology, or a sequence of changes that was inborn and relatively unaffected by environment. However, as Vygotsky argued, modern research indicates that the environment (especially the interactions kids have with older people) can influence the rate at which their thinking develops (Müller, 2009; Birney et al., 2005; Kingsley & Hall, 1967; Legerstee, 1994). "Screen time" on TV, computers, and other media is another environmental influence: Check the *Watching Psychology* box for how it affects kids' development.

WATCHING PSYCHOLOGY

Screen Time and Kids' Development

Beginning at a very early age, U.S. children spend an enormous amount of time in front of screens (Singer & Singer, 2012; Goldstein, 2011). Elementary-school age kids watch an average of 28 hours of TV per week, and kids aged 2–5 average 32 hours (McDonough, 2009). The average child lives in a home containing 3.8 TVs, 2.3 video game consoles, and 2.0 computers. These numbers don't even include on-the-go screens, like smartphones, tablets, and car headrest monitors. Three-quarters of kids 11–18 and over half of kids 8–10 have a TV in their own bedrooms (Rideout et al., 2010).

How does all of this screen time affect kids' development? Researchers have only begun to explore this question, but some have concluded that it can have both positive and negative effects—effects that will only grow with the increasing integration of media into daily lives (Subrahmanyam & Greenfield, 2012; Huntemann & Morgan, 2012). Certainly, there can be a developmental upside to certain screen activities. For example, some computer games, like Tetris, can enhance kids' ability to pay attention for long periods of time and pay attention to multiple stimuli at the same time. Keep in mind that time kids spend in front of screens is time their parents can get stuff done: working, cooking, cleaning, and so on. Some argue that when used wisely, such screen time can allow parents to cope with busy schedules and be more emotionally available when the screens are off (Rideout & Hamel, 2006).

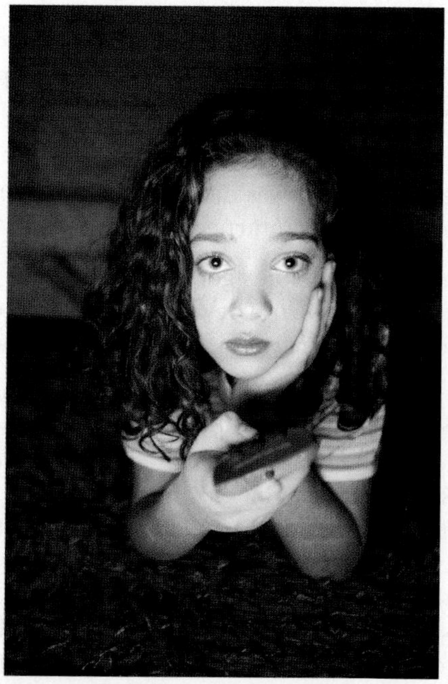

Research suggests that some screen time for children can have positive effects, but when screen time is excessive, the effects tend to be negative. Fuse/Getty Images

On the other hand, excessive screen time can have quite a developmental downside. At the very least, screen time displaces time that could be spent doing other things. More time in front of a screen means less time exercising, sleeping, and socializing in person with friends and family—all essential to healthy growth in childhood (Wartella & Robb, 2007). Also, some studies suggest that kids who text a lot—particularly the use of textisms like *lol* and *brb*—often struggle with the formal writing necessary to succeed in high school, college, and the workplace (Rosen et al., 2010). However, other studies actually suggest that texting correlates with strong literacy skills (Plester et al., 2009; Kemp & Bushnell, 2011).

Another downside to excessive screen time involves TV in particular. TV can expose kids to a much more diverse range of people than they would encounter in real life, but it often promotes stereotypes while doing so (Asamen & Berry, 2012). For example, across all ages of childhood, kids who watch more TV hold more stereotypical views about gender roles (regarding work, child care, etc.) than kids who watch less (Signorielli, 2012). TV stereotypes of ethnic groups have a particular power to shape kids' thinking when kids don't have real-world opportunities to see members of that ethnic group. If the only Indian man a child ever sees on TV or in real life is Raj Koothrappali from *The Big Bang Theory*, he or she may mistakenly come to believe that all Indian men are like him—highly intelligent but socially clueless and petrified of women.

DIVERSITY MATTERS

One last note about the time kids spend watching TV: Much of it is devoted to commercials, which have their own impact on kids' lives. The sheer numbers are eye-popping: kids age 2–7 see over 13,000 ads per year, and the number jumps to about 30,000 ads per year for kids age 8–17 (Gantz et al., 2007). The fact that about a quarter of these are food ads and that the food they promote is overwhelmingly unhealthy undermines kids' physical development. But regardless of what is being advertised, TV ads convince kids that they need the latest, coolest, or otherwise best stuff—and to judge their peers according to the same materialistic standards. TV ads also tend to increase the arguments between kids ("Can I get...?") and parents ("No"), which can create an adversarial family environment that might not otherwise exist (Kunkel & Castonguay, 2012).

Attachment is a close emotional bond between a young child and a caregiver. The first months of life are often crucial to the development of attachment. Chris Ryan/ OJO Images/Getty Images

Psychosocial Development

Just as children's bodies and brains develop, so do their relationships with other people. The first and most fundamental of these relationships are those within the immediate family, so let's begin with concepts related to family: attachment, parenting styles, and temperament. Then, we'll move on to relationships with friends.

Attachment. Attachment is a close emotional bond between two people, particularly a young child and a caregiver. Two researchers—John Bowlby and his one-time student, Mary Ainsworth—devoted their careers to the study of attachment between children and parents. Their work forms the foundation of our understanding of the subject (Ainsworth & Bowlby, 1965; Bowlby, 1969, 1973; Ainsworth, 1989). Their research was based on the notion of the **critical period**: a period of time during which a particular developmental task is especially likely to be influenced by outside events. Of course, there are all kinds of critical periods. For example, the fetus is especially vulnerable to teratogens during pregnancy when particular parts of the body or brain are forming. The focus for these researchers, however, was the critical period of a baby's first months of life for attachment to caregivers.

The primary way researchers examined parent–child attachment was the *strange situation* method. Basically, they observed a baby's reaction when the baby spends a few minutes in a few different situations: with the caregiver (typically mom), with a stranger who enters the room, with both the caregiver and the stranger, or alone. They observed several aspects of the baby's behavior: how much he explored the room (played with toys, etc.), how he reacted when mom left, how he reacted when the stranger approached in mom's absence, and how the baby reacted when mom came back (Bosma & Gerlsma, 2003; Thompson, 2006). Based on these observations, Ainsworth and her colleagues identified three distinct types of attachment—*secure attachment, insecure-avoidant attachment*, and *insecure-resistant attachment* (Ainsworth et al., 1978; Lamb & Lewis, 2005):

- **Secure attachment.** These babies appeared the most stable and well adjusted. When mom was present, they were comfortable enough to explore the new toys and interact with the stranger. In general, these babies seemed to use mom as a secure home base. For the most part, they felt comfortable straying from that secure home base as long as they knew they could return to it. Of course, they did cry at times when mom left or when the stranger spoke to them. All babies exhibit **stranger anxiety**, the fear of unfamiliar people that emerges in children at about 8 months of age. But when securely attached babies got upset, the crying was relatively brief and ended quickly when mom returned. Thankfully, most American babies develop secure attachment (**Figure 9.8**).
- **Insecure-avoidant attachment.** These babies didn't seem to care much when mom left, and they avoided her when she returned.
- **Insecure-resistant attachment.** These babies got quite upset when mom left, and they didn't entirely welcome her return. They had a mixed reaction involving both seeking out mom and angrily resisting the comfort she offered.

Some researchers have also proposed a fourth type of attachment, *disorganized attachment*, in which babies seem confused about how to respond when mom leaves and returns. At different times, these babies may resemble babies in each of the three other types (Main & Solomon, 1986, 1990; Duschinsky, 2015).

In very young children, attachment styles can vary from one time to another and from one caregiver to another. Around the age of 4 or 5, kids generally settle on one attachment style. That attachment style makes a big difference—not just then and there with parents, but for many years to come in many kinds of relationships (Belsky & Fearon, 2002). In fact, Bowlby once wrote that attachment "is a characteristic of human nature throughout our lives—from the cradle to the grave" (1988, p. 82).

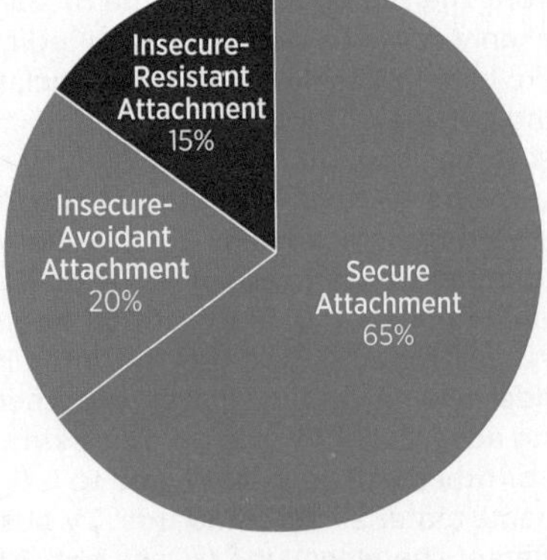

FIGURE 9.8 Attachment Styles of American Babies. Most American babies show a secure attachment to their caregivers. Data from Teti & Teti, 1996; Thompson, 1998.

A secure attachment style yields the most benefits as kids grow up: more self-reliance, a better self-concept, healthier relationships with peers, better at handling unpleasant feelings, more resilient when facing stress, and a happier overall mood

(Sroufe, 2005; Sroufe et al., 2005; Brumariu & Kerns, 2011; Reich & Vandell, 2011; Schore, 2001). One longitudinal study of 1000 kids found that 3-year-olds with secure attachments had the most social success, including the highest-quality friendships, as first- and third-graders (McElwain et al., 2008). A meta-analysis covering over 3500 kids found a strong link between secure mother–child attachment in preschoolers and the number of close friendships in older children (Schneider et al., 2001). Researchers have even found that secure attachment does predict high levels of self-worth and low levels of depression well into adulthood (Kenny & Sirin, 2006).

Attachment, of course, is not uniquely human. It happens in many species, including monkeys, which were the focus of a classic study on the topic. Harry Harlow and colleagues placed infant monkeys in a room containing two fake "mothers"—one made of cold, hard wire mesh, and the other made of soft, warm terry cloth fabric (Harlow & Harlow, 1962; Harlow, 1958; Harlow & Zimmerman, 1958, 1959; Blum, 2002). The wire mesh mother provided a bottle of milk; the terry cloth mother provided no food or drink at all. The researchers' main question was this: With which mother would the young monkeys form an attachment?

The answer was clear: Unless the young monkeys needed nourishment, they attached to the terry cloth mother. They spent much more time with the terry cloth mother, and they explored a new room more eagerly when the terry cloth mother was in the room with them. They even stretched to reach the bottle attached to the wire mesh mother's body while clinging to the terry cloth mother. Their preference for the terry cloth mother was particularly strong when they were frightened. They would run and hold tight to the terry cloth mother, even though it had never provided food. This study was inspired by Harlow's knowledge of orphans raised in institutions where they got little physical attention and became adolescents and adults with significant emotional and behavioral problems. Harlow's research highlights how fundamentally important attachment is in humans and other animals as well (Kobak, 2012).

attachment
A close emotional bond between two people, particularly a young child and a caregiver.

critical period
A period of time during which a particular developmental task is especially likely to be influenced by outside events.

stranger anxiety
The fear of unfamiliar people that emerges in children at about 8 months of age.

authoritarian parenting style
An approach to parenting in which parents require children to obey unquestionable, strict rules.

permissive parenting style
An approach to parenting in which parents place minimal demands and allow children to run their own lives.

authoritative parenting style
An approach to parenting in which parents set rules, but also explain and negotiate those rules with their children.

Parenting Styles. Your own experience with moms and dads—your own parents and your friends'—probably includes some who struck you as terry cloth–ish and others who were more wire-meshy. In fact, based on your experience with various parents, you could probably create numerous categories of *parenting styles* into which most of them could be placed. Developmental psychologists have done the same thing. While researchers acknowledge that each parent has his or her own unique approach, there are three big categories that capture most of them—*authoritarian*, *permissive*, and *authoritative* (Baumrind, 1966, 1967, 1971, 1978, 1996; Laursen & Collins, 2009):

- An **authoritarian parenting style** is an approach to parenting in which parents require children to obey unquestionable strict rules. These "because-I-said-so" parents demand compliance without explanation and with the threat of harsh punishment. When an authoritarian dad tells his 16-year-old newly driver's-licensed son that he must be home by 9 p.m. on a Saturday, there is no negotiation, no discussion, no debate. There is just a respectful "Yes, sir" because any resistance would bring about punishment.
- A **permissive parenting style** is an approach to parenting in which parents place minimal demands on children and allow them to run their own lives. These "whatever" parents either lack the time or energy to involve themselves in their children's lives, or choose to indulge them by agreeing to everything they want. When the new 16-year-old driver goes out on a Saturday night, his permissive parent either tells him to stay out as late as he wants, or says nothing at all.
- An **authoritative parenting style** is an approach to parenting in which parents set rules, but also explain and negotiate those rules with their children. These "here's why" parents are much more engaged in their kids' lives than permissive parents, but not as inflexibly controlling as authoritarian parents. They provide firm boundaries and limits for their kids and exert power at times when parents should. However, these authoritative parents also explain their rationale and consider their kids' input when making decisions. In short, they raise their kids

In classic studies by Harry Harlow and colleagues, infant monkeys formed attachments to soft terry cloth–covered "mothers" even though they did not provide food. The attachment was especially evident when the monkeys were frightened.
Nina Leen/The LIFE Picture Collection/Getty Images

MY TAKE VIDEO 9.1

Parenting Styles

"I think I started out more permissive actually..."

YOUTUBE: http://tiny.cc/mytake
LAUNCHPAD: launchpadworks.com

through balance of clout and cooperation. When the 16-year-old driver of an authoritative dad heads out on a Saturday night, dad might tell him to be home by 10:30. When the son explains that the movie won't end until 10:45, dad extends the deadline to 11, but reminds his son that he'll be grounded if he is late.

Research on parenting styles shows that most often, authoritative parents produce the most well adjusted kids. Compared to kids raised by authoritarian or permissive parents, kids raised by authoritative parents are more independent, autonomous, socially competent, appropriately assertive, academically successful, and unlikely to be anxious, depressed, or delinquent (Baumrind, 1967, 2013; Lamb & Lewis, 2005; Steinberg et al., 1989, 1991, 1992). Teens raised by authoritative parents are also more likely than their peers to maintain healthy eating habits and weight, and to have candid and open discussions of sexual issues (Berge et al., 2010; Askelson et al., 2012).

Some research suggests that this finding is true across many cultures, including African American, Asian, and U.K. families (Chan & Koo, 2011; Cheah et al., 2009; Querido et al., 2002). However, other research suggests that the authoritative style may not yield the same advantages in certain cultures. For example, one study of over 1000 teens in Spain found that children raised by permissive parents (specifically, parents who indulge their children) rate as highly on many desirable characteristics as those raised by authoritative parents (Garcia & Gracia, 2009). Other studies have found that the authoritarian style of parenting may benefit some African American youth as much as the authoritative style (Baumrind, 1972; Deater-Deckard et al., 1996).

DIVERSITY MATTERS

Temperament

Could a mom's or dad's parenting style depend on the type of kid they have?

Absolutely. Parenting is a relationship between two people, so it is not just mom's or dad's behavior that determines its quality. The child's behavior matters too. A major factor in the child's behavior is his or her **temperament**: the basic emotional responsiveness that characterizes a person throughout his or her life span. Ask any mom or dad with several kids and they'll tell you that kids are different from each other from the beginning. In their first days, way before the world around them has had time to exert any real influence, some kids are content and some kids are cranky. Some are easy to soothe, some endlessly fussy, some high-energy, and some relaxed. These qualities are biologically based, noticeable from an early age, and likely to form the foundation of the personalities that will carry through childhood and adulthood (Sanson et al., 2011; Rothbart, 2007; Kagan & Fox, 2006; Caspi & Shiner, 2006; Thomas et al., 1970).

Each kid has his or her own temperament, but classic research by Alexander Thomas and Stella Chess identifies three categories into which most (but certainly not all) kids fall—easy temperament, difficult temperament, and slow-to-warm-up temperament (Thomas & Chess, 1977; Chess & Thomas, 1986):

- Kids with an *easy temperament* are, well, easy-going. They are generally optimistic and positive. They acclimate quickly to new situations and can be calmed in a predictable and manageable way.
- Kids with a *difficult temperament* give their parents a much harder time. They are quick to react negatively (crying, screaming, etc.) to unfamiliar people and things. They don't fall into predictable sleeping or eating patterns. They are also harder to please or comfort when they get upset.
- Kids with a *slow-to-warm-up temperament* take a long time to get used to new people or new situations, and their typical first reaction is to shy away. They are generally quiet and have low levels of activity.

A child with an easy temperament is easy to get along with, especially in comparison to a child with a difficult or slow-to-warm-up temperament. Inti St Clair/Blend Images/Getty Images

More recent research suggests that there are a couple of factors, or basic ingredients, of temperament that underlie these three categories, particularly reactivity and self-regulation. *Reactivity* is a tendency to react with negative emotions such as irritability and anxiety, and *self-regulation* is control over one's own moods and behavior (Rothbart, 2007; Rothbart & Bates, 2006). These basic elements of temperament reflect the way each of us is "wired" and are relatively stable across the life span. For example, numerous studies have found that babies with high levels of reactivity grow up to become grade schoolers, high schoolers, and adults with high odds of experiencing anxiety disorders (Kagan & Snidman, 1999; Rapee et al., 2005; Clark et al., 1994; Fox & Pine, 2012).

But you are not entirely stuck with a particular temperament from birth to death. Your life experiences can alter your temperament a little, or at least loosen it up enough that you can choose to react differently from your first impulse (Kagan & Snidman, 2004; Kagan et al., 1994; Fox et al., 2008). For example, if a highly reactive baby girl's parents make a deliberate effort to challenge her natural anxiety around unfamiliar people, then she is likely to become more comfortable around people than if her parents always shield her from new things. Introducing her to new people and taking her to new places challenges the highly reactive baby girl without overwhelming her.

Goodness-of-fit refers to the match between parenting style and a child's temperament. When goodness-of-fit is poor, conflicts are common. Wavebreakmedia/iStock/Getty Images

As this example illustrates, it is the interaction between parenting styles and temperament that matters, not just the parenting style or the child's temperament. Researchers call this interaction between the natural ways of kids and parents *goodness-of-fit* (Mangelsdorf et al., 1990; Chess & Thomas, 1991). If you've ever played team sports, you've experienced goodness-of-fit with your coach. Coaches who adapt their styles to match the abilities of their players, rather than imposing their preferred style regardless of who is on the roster, are best at fostering the successful development of the team. In the same way parents who adapt their parenting style to the temperament of their kids are best at fostering the successful development of their kids.

Culture can play a significant role in goodness-of-fit between kids and parents.

DIVERSITY MATTERS

One study of 2-year-olds in China and Canada found that mothers from each country reacted differently when the kids acted shy around a stranger (probably demonstrating a difficult or slow-to-warm-up temperament). Canadian moms disapproved of the shyness and encouraged their kids to overcome it, while Chinese moms approved of the shyness and didn't push them to interact with the stranger (Chen et al., 1998). When kids in these countries reach elementary school, they reflect the same preferences toward each other that their moms did toward them as toddlers: Canadian kids dislike shyness in their peers, but Chinese kids like it (Chen et al., 1992).

Friend Relationships. A child's psychosocial development depends not only on family, but on friends too. Developmental psychologists haven't studied friend relationships as much as family relationships. However, the studies conducted confirm the experience you probably had: During childhood, friendships matter a lot (Hymel et al., 2011). Compared to kids without close friendships, kids with close friendships have higher self-esteem and fewer behavioral and emotional problems (Buhrmester, 1990; Ladd et al., 1997). Kids with close friendships experience less loneliness, depression, and victimization by peers (Hodges et al., 1999, Parker & Asher, 1993; Bukowski et al., 1993). They have higher levels of school involvement and earn better grades (Kingery & Erdley, 2007; Kingery et al., 2011). They have decreased chances of dropping out of school and committing criminal acts (Parker & Asher, 1987). Among psychologists who treat kids with ADHD, it is widely recognized that improving the child's social skills often leads to better friendships, which in turn often leads to improvements in ADHD symptoms and other areas of the child's life (Hoza et al., 2003, Mikami, 2010).

Gender matters in childhood friendship, both in who you are likely to befriend and how you are likely to interact. Starting at around age 3 or 4 and lasting until puberty, boys play with boys and girls play with girls. With few exceptions, this is how it happens in cultures around the world (Whiting & Edwards, 1988; Pellegrini et al., 2007). From the same age, boys prefer toy trucks and guns, and girls prefer dolls. Researchers have

temperament
The basic emotional responsiveness that characterizes a person throughout his or her life span.

found these toy preferences in infants as young as 3–8 *months* by tracking eye movements to see which toys they look at longer (Jadva et al., 2010; Alexander et al., 2009). Boys' play is typically more rough-and-tumble, with plenty of physical aggression, and often outside in large groups. Girls' play is typically more cooperative, inside, and in small groups (Pasterski et al., 2011). Girls' play often involves aggression too, but unlike the boys' punches and tackles, girls often hurt each other with gossip or backstabbing—acts of relationship betrayal (Schneider et al., 2011).

Ethnicity matters in childhood friendships too. Kids in Asia tend to be more cooperative with each other, while kids in Europe and the United States tend to be more competitive (Chen et al., 2011; Farver et al., 1995; Orlick et al., 1990). Another Eastern–Western culture distinction is the function of friendship. In the West, kids typically value their friendships because friendships increase their own self-worth. In the East (as well as some African American and Latino groups in the United States), the main benefit of friendship is the opportunity to serve your friends, not yourself. So, Western kids tend to seek friendships for what their friends can do for them, but Eastern kids tend to seek friendships for what they can do for their friends (Rubin et al., 2006; Chen et al., 2004; French et al., 2005; Way, 2006).

DIVERSITY MATTERS

Children from different cultures often value friendships for different reasons. In Western cultures, it is relatively common for children to value friendships for positive impact on their own self-worth. By contrast, in Eastern cultures, it is relatively common for children to value friendships for the opportunity to serve others. Hero Images/Getty Images

As an example, let's say a friendship emerges between two sixth-grade girls in the same science class. In Western countries, it is more likely that the girl with a D– initiated the friendship, with the hope that the girl with an A+ might help her to raise her grade. In an Eastern country, it is more likely that the A+ student initiated the friendship, with the intention of lending a hand to her struggling classmate.

A final note on childhood friendships: Often, the most important friendship is the one with your siblings. Your brothers and sisters are family, but those sibling relationships often double as close friendships, especially if they are close to your age. Sibling relationships are "a natural laboratory for learning about the social world"—a safe place to develop skills in cooperation, assertiveness, conflict resolution, empathy, and many other relationship skills (Howe et al., p. 368).

CHECK YOUR LEARNING:

9.7 Newborn babies' abilities include which senses and reflexes?

9.8 How do nature and nurture influence physical development?

9.9 According to Piaget, how do children use assimilation and accommodation to develop schemas?

9.10 According to Piaget, what is the series of cognitive stages through which children develop?

9.11 In what ways have researchers challenged some of Piaget's conclusions?

9.12 What are three distinct types of attachment, and why is secure attachment to others so important?

9.13 What are the three parenting styles into which most parents can be categorized?

9.14 What is temperament and how early in life does it appear?

Adolescent Development

YOU WILL LEARN:

9.15 how psychologists define adolescence.

9.16 about the changes that occur in girls and boys during puberty.

9.17 how the brain continues to grow during adolescence.

Adolescence is the developmental period that encompasses the transition from childhood to adulthood. Some people define adolescence as the teenage years or the years spent in middle school and high school. This is generally accurate, but adolescence has no official start or end time. Some of your peers (particularly girls) probably showed the physical signs of adolescence while still in elementary school. The cognitive and psychosocial changes of adolescence are less obvious than the physical changes, but some kids go through them earlier than others. At the other end of the timeline, there are those whose adolescence extends well into their 20s or beyond.

Regardless of when adolescence starts or ends, it is marked by the emergence of independence. When you're a younger kid, decisions get made *for* you. As adolescence progresses, decisions increasingly get made *by* you: what food you eat, how you dress, which TV shows you watch, which friends you hang out with, which interests you pursue. (You may have argued with your parents about this very issue—who's in control of the decisions that affect your life—during your own adolescence.) This growing independence means that there is much more variation in development during adolescence than there is in the earlier childhood years. Kids go in different directions once the teenage years hit. Adolescents play different sports, listen to different music, take different classes, and even begin to develop interests in different careers. Even the bodies of adolescents take on different sizes and shapes. This variability makes adolescents a challenging population for developmental psychologists to study. It can be tough to generalize about a group of people branching out in so many different ways. Nonetheless, developmental psychologists have learned a great deal about the physical, cognitive, and psychosocial changes that take place during adolescence (Kuhn & Franklin, 2006; Lerner & Steinberg, 2009).

YOU WILL LEARN: (*Continued*)

9.18 about characteristics of adolescent thinking.

9.19 about Kohlberg's stages of moral thinking.

9.20 how psychologists define identity.

9.21 about Erik Erikson's eight-stage psychosocial theory of development.

9.22 why relationships with both parents and peers are key elements of adolescence.

9.23 about the emerging adulthood stage.

Physical Development

Every time you walked the halls of your middle school and your high school, passing dozens of kids at various points of adolescence, you saw the tremendous range of physical development that takes place during that stage. Let's consider the changes that take place in both the body and the brain.

Bodily Changes. The most observable sign that childhood is ending and adulthood is on the horizon is the beginning of **puberty**, the time period featuring physical changes that mark the onset of adolescence and enable sexual reproduction. You know from your own experience (and your biology or sex ed classes) the outward hallmarks of puberty. Most of them involve **secondary sex characteristics**: the parts of the body that characterize sexual maturation but are not directly involved in reproduction. For example, in girls, hips widen, breasts develop, and body fat increases in certain areas. In boys, shoulders broaden, facial hair grows, muscles develop, and the voice deepens. In both, height surges, underarm and pubic hair appears, and acne does too, at least for some.

Other changes that are not as apparent to the outside observer involve the **primary sex characteristics**: the parts of the body directly involved in sexual reproduction, such as genitals, ovaries, and testes. For example, a boy's penis and testes enlarge, and he experiences his first ejaculation. A girl experiences enlargement of her uterus, clitoris, and labia, and of course **menarche**: her first menstrual period. All of these changes to both primary and secondary sex characteristics are driven by the hormones that the pituitary gland produces.

Girls typically begin puberty about 2 years before boys—around age 10–11 for girls, around age 12–13 for boys. The length of puberty varies a bit, but generally it is complete in 4 or 5 years. The age at which puberty starts actually varies a bit across cultures and across time periods. Girls in many parts of the world now hit puberty sooner than they did about a hundred years ago (Euling et al., 2008). This is true especially for some groups within the United States, such as African American girls. The reasons for this shift are unclear, but some researchers point to obesity, stress, and exposure to chemicals that disrupt endocrine regulation (Walvoord, 2010; Toppari & Juul, 2010; Kaplowitz, 2008).

With puberty comes the child's own emotional reaction to it. Researchers have found that kids who reach puberty before their peers experience a higher rate of unwelcome psychological and behavioral problems. Boys who hit puberty before their male friends are more likely to smoke, use alcohol and drugs, and feel high levels of hostility and stress. Girls who are among the first of their friends to reach puberty have similarly high rates of substance abuse, and also have higher rates of depression and risky behavior (Susman & Dorn, 2009). Possible causes for these

adolescence
The developmental period that encompasses the transition from childhood to adulthood.

puberty
The time period featuring physical changes that mark the onset of adolescence and enable sexual reproduction.

secondary sex characteristics
The parts of the body that characterize sexual maturation but are not directly involved in reproduction.

primary sex characteristics
The parts of the body directly involved in sexual reproduction, such as genitals, ovaries, and testes.

menarche
A girl's first menstrual period.

Experience shapes the brain, especially early in development. In one study, the parts of the brains of violin players that correspond to the four fingers (but not the thumb) of the left hand were larger and more complex than the same brain parts in people who don't play the violin (Elbert et al., 1995).
Bruce Laurance/Blend Image /Getty Images

problems include (1) body image dissatisfaction, primarily for girls who believe they are developing "too soon"; (2) increased odds of hanging out with older kids, whose bodies may be similar, but whose personal activities are far ahead of the younger child; and (3) increased rates of conflict with parents, who may disagree with the child that a grown-up body merits grown-up levels of freedom (Collins & Steinberg, 2006).

Brain Changes. Adolescence means big changes in the brain as well as in the body. The brain's rate of growth can't compare to the prenatal and infancy period, but white matter in particular continues to grow during adolescence (Paus, 2009). In addition to the sheer increase in size, the adolescent brain features a marked increase in *myelination* (insulation, basically) of axons, which enhances the connections between neurons, which in turn improves cognitive ability (see Chapter 2; Zelazo & Lee, 2010).

This increase in myelination is actually part of a larger process taking place. The adolescent brain selects and improves the most often used neuronal pathways, and eliminates the ones that are rarely or never used. This use-it-or-lose-it strategy is another step in the *pruning* process that began in infancy and childhood. Pruning results in the adolescent brain having fewer connections between neurons than the younger brain, but more effective connections (Kuhn, 2009). The primary lesson here is that experience shapes the brain. Adolescents choose their own experiences, which means they determine which neural pathways will flourish and which will waste away (Kuhn & Franklin, 2006; Nelson et al., 2006; Thomas & Johnson, 2008).

For example, consider two classmates, Garrett and Ben, who are 14 years old and finishing eighth grade. Until this time, Garrett's parents and Ben's parents made the big decisions for them, including what they would do during their summer breaks. But this year, the parents allowed the boys to decide for themselves how they would spend their summers. Garrett spends his summer on one thing, video games—no camps, no organized activities, little socialization—just hour after hour in a dark basement playing Minecraft, Madden, or Halo. Ben spends his summer on lots of things: a few weeks at an outdoor sleepaway camp, a week of robotics camp, lots of socializing at the local pool with friends, a couple dozen games with his baseball team, a family trip to the Grand Canyon, a few novels, and a little video game playing of his own. At the end of the summer, an MRI would show connections between neurons in Garrett's brain to have grown extensively in areas that relate to video game playing, but that connections between neurons in other parts of his brain have weakened or wasted away. On the other hand, Ben's brain probably shows many brain areas with significant growth between neurons and far fewer dwindling, but no single type of neuron would be as well developed as Garrett's video game neurons. If Garrett and Ben continue to make similar choices through their teens, their brains will reflect even more drastic differences than what this summer produces.

One study offering empirical support for this idea involves the impact of playing music on the brains of teens. Researchers conducted MRIs on the brains of expert violin players and found that the parts of their cortexes that correspond specifically to the four fingers (but not the thumb) of the left hand (the body parts to which violinists must devote so much attention in order to hit the correct notes at the correct moments) were much larger and involved much richer webs of neurons than those of non–violin players (Elbert et al., 1995). This finding was especially strong for violinists who began playing before the age of 12—that is, those whose violin training likely took place over the course of adolescence.

Cognitive Development

According to Piaget's timetable, adolescents should have entered the last cognitive stage. The formal operational stage enables adolescents to think logically about all kinds of things, both tangible and abstract. Of course, anyone who has spent time

around adolescents knows their thinking is far from fully developed, at least sometimes. Many adolescents think in ways that recall the *egocentrism* they exhibited when they were much younger children (Smetana & Villalobos, 2009; Elkind, 1967, 1985; Frankenberger, 2000; Somerville, 2013).

They are so self-focused that they can only understand the world with themselves at the center of it. For example, many adolescents' thinking features an **imaginary audience**, in which they believe that their lives are continuously being watched and evaluated by other people. If thoughts like "What will people think?" or "I'm so embarrassed!" were prominent during your middle school and high school years, then you know all about the concept of imaginary audience. Often, these concerns are about trivial things—which shoes you wear with a particular outfit, who you sit with at lunch on a given day, whether your friends see you with your parents at the mall. But to adolescents, these events seem hugely important and often spark significant drama, as if a reality show crew is following them with cameras and boom mikes, broadcasting their lives to millions. Today, the not-so-imaginary audiences represented by Twitter and Instagram followers and Facebook friends no doubt reinforce adolescents' sense that their every move is being anticipated and scrutinized.

Another example of egocentrism in adolescence is the **personal fable**: a common way of thinking among adolescents in which they believe themselves to be special or invulnerable. It is as if the adolescent is the hero in a fairy tale that can only have a happy ending, despite the fact that this is real life, in which tragic endings happen too. In fact, kids whose thinking includes the personal fable (as well as other egocentric tendencies) engage in more high-risk behaviors than other kids (Greene et al., 2000; Alberts et al., 2007). For example, the personal fable can convince adolescents that *my* car won't crash if I text while driving or *I* won't get suspended if I steal the chemistry exam from my teacher's desk. In addition to underestimating the chances of bad endings, the personal fable can sway adolescents toward overestimating the chances of good endings. For example, the high school sophomore who's a second-string offensive lineman on the JV football team but is certain that he is a lock for the NFL, or the eighth grade girl who couldn't sing or dance well enough qualify for her middle school talent show but has no doubt she is the next Beyoncé.

Kohlberg and Moral Development. When Piaget examined the development of kids' thinking, he emphasized *logical* thinking. But logic is certainly not the only aspect of thinking that develops. Particularly around the adolescent years, *moral* thinking develops too (Moshman, 2009; Turiel, 2006, 2010; Helwig & Turiel, 2011). Lawrence Kohlberg, a psychologist from New York who was born in 1927 and died in 1987, extended Piaget's work by proposing a theory of moral development that has inspired many developmental researchers (Carpendale, 2009).

Kohlberg's basic idea is that the way we think about moral issues—especially how we determine right and wrong—evolves as we move through childhood and into adulthood. Specifically, Kohlberg argues that we move through three stages of moral reasoning—*preconventional morality*, *conventional morality*, and *postconventional morality* (Kohlberg, 1984, 1973a,b, 1974; Kohlberg & Candee, 1984):

- **Preconventional morality** is a moral decision-making strategy driven by the potential rewards and punishments of the decision. In this stage, what's right is what maximizes benefit and minimizes hardship for *you*. You make decisions to serve your own needs.
- **Conventional morality** is a moral decision-making strategy driven by the desire to follow society's norms and laws. In this stage, what's right is what puts you in line with your culture's expectations of you. You make decisions to ensure that others will approve of you and you realize that the system would fall apart "if everyone did it."
- **Postconventional morality** is a moral decision-making strategy driven by fundamental rights and ethical principles. The personal consequences of the

imaginary audience
A common way of thinking among adolescents in which they believe their lives are continuously being watched and evaluated by other people.

personal fable
A common way of thinking among adolescents in which they believe themselves to be special or invulnerable.

CHAPTER APP 9.2

Imaginary Audience

Twitter

Preview one of the links and consider the following questions.

WEBSITE:
http://tiny.cc/7di7jy

ANDROID:
http://tiny.cc/1277iy

IPHONE:
http://tiny.cc/g277iy

VIDEO DEMO:
http://tiny.cc/chapterapps

You know Twitter. You may be one of the millions who use it every day to share your thoughts with followers.

How does it APPly to your daily life?
When the concept of *imaginary audience* was first proposed, Twitter didn't exist. Now that it does, the imaginary audience of adolescence has been replaced by a real audience of followers. (The same could be said for Facebook friends, Instagram followers, etc.) When you were an adolescent, how did your use of Twitter or other social media affect your sense of imaginary audience—that your life is continuously being watched and evaluated by other people?

How does it APPly to your understanding of psychology?
How do Twitter and other social media help you appreciate the concept of imaginary audience? How might the concept of imaginary audience need to be adapted for today's adolescents?

Adolescents commonly believe in a personal fable, or a way of thinking in which they believe themselves to be special or invulnerable. Personal fables can be dangerous because they make dangerous behaviors, like texting while driving, seem safe. Michael Krinke/iStock/Getty Images

> decision, as well as how well the decision fits with society's preferences, take a backseat at this point. In this stage, what's right is what's *right* in the larger sense. You make decisions because ethical principles that steer all people toward such collective values as justice, dignity, and equality guide you to do so.

Kohlberg (1984, pp. 177–178) offers the example of Joe, a participant in one of his longitudinal studies. Joe answered the same moral question at ages 10, 17, and 24: Why shouldn't you steal from a store? His answers show a progression through Kohlberg's three stages. At 10, Joe explains that "someone could see you and call the police." So, you don't steal because if you do, bad things can happen to *you*. This kind of preconventional moral reasoning is common to children. By 17, adolescent Joe has entered the conventional morality stage. This is shown by his consideration of society's expectations and what it would mean if he and others didn't meet them: "It's one of our rules… If we didn't have these laws, people would steal, they wouldn't have to work for a living and our whole society would get out of kilter." At 24, adult Joe has progressed even further, with reasoning that refers to what is fundamentally and universally right, rather than what the rules or the law say: "It's violating another person's rights, in this case, to property."

For another real-life example of moral decision making, consider the story of a Detroit record shop owner named Jeff Bubeck (Saunders, 2012). Jeff stumbled upon a huge, valuable record and tape collection left behind in a storage unit by J Dilla, a legendary hip-hop producer who had died several years earlier. He knew there was a market for what he had discovered, but he also knew that J Dilla's mother was in deep debt from the medical bills related to her son's lengthy illness. So, he had a moral decision to make: sell his newfound bounty for a profit, or give it to J Dilla's mother. Jeff decided to give the records to J Dilla's mother, and his reasoning reflects Kohlberg's postconventional stage of moral decision making: "I was just trying to do the right thing…it was her son's stuff, you know?…I told her take it with you. It's yours…I was like, 'Yeah, back in the right hands'" (National Public Radio, 2014).

Here are a few other important features of Kohlberg's theory. First, the important thing is not necessarily the decision you make, but the reasoning you use to arrive at that decision. Second, age does not always predict moral thinking. Third, not everyone progresses all the way to the third stage. In fact, Kohlberg labeled the second stage "conventional" because he concluded that moral thinking stops at that level for most people (Kohlberg, 1963, 1984).

Kohlberg believed that moral reasoning should be a focus of the educational system. In addition to the traditional academic subjects, Kohlberg thought schools should offer classes in "character education" to advance the ability to think about issues of right and wrong (Snarey, 2012).

Moral development refers to changes in the way you determine right and wrong. For example, your stage of moral development can influence your decisions about whether or not to steal from a store. Fotosenmeer/Shutterstock

Kohlberg's ideas have been used in educational settings, and have had a powerful impact on the developmental psychology field, but they also have received some sharp criticism. One criticism of Kohlberg's theory is the same that Piaget's theory received: It is too stage-based, and it doesn't reflect the reality that our moral reasoning inches forward gradually rather than leaping forward and then stalling for years (Nucci & Gingo, 2011).

A second criticism points out that moral reasoning and moral behavior—what you think is right and what you actually do in that situation—don't always match. In fact, one study found that the correlation between moral reasoning and moral action is just .3—positive, but far from perfect (Krebs & Denton, 2005).

A third criticism focuses on culture: What seems universally "right" (and therefore underlies the highest level of moral reasoning) may not be universal at all, but dependent upon ethnicity and other variables (Menon, 2003; Turiel, 2006, 2002, 2008). What's "right" in our culture may not be "right" in another. One study posed this moral question to 10- and 11-year-old students: Should you mention your score to your classmates if you did

DIVERSITY MATTERS

much better on an exam than they did? The answer depended heavily on culture: 86% of U.S. kids believed it was right not to mention your own score, because by doing so you were showing off, but 68% of Chinese kids believed it was right to mention your own score, because by doing so you were offering to help your classmates (Heyman et al., 2008).

A fourth criticism focuses not on ethnicity but on gender: Males and females may go about moral reasoning differently. Specifically, males tend to emphasize fair treatment, while females tend to emphasize caring for others in need (Gilligan, 1982, 1987; Gilligan & Wiggins, 1987; Walker, 2006; Eisenberg et al., 2009). This is especially important in light of the fact that the participants in Kohlberg's research were more often male than female, so the stages of moral reasoning that he proposed may describe the process more accurately for males than females (Heyman & Lee, 2012; Jaffee & Hyde, 2000).

J Dilla (James Yancey), a legendary hip-hop producer and DJ, passed away in 2006 after years of illness. Months later, a record store owner named Jeff Bubeck bought a record collection out of an abandoned storage unit. He soon discovered that he had bought J Dilla's records, as well as some of J Dilla's own unreleased beats. Those items were highly collectible and sought after by hip-hop fans. Bubeck faced a moral decision: sell them for a profit, or give them to J Dilla's mom (Maureen Yancey), who was in deep debt because of her son's medical bills. He decided to give them to Ms. Yancey, and his rationale demonstrated moral reasoning that exemplifies Kohlberg's postconventional stage (National Public Radio, 2014; Saunders, 2012). Photo by B+

Psychosocial Development

A primary challenge of adolescence is figuring out who we are as individuals. Erik Erikson, a German psychologist whose developmental theories became prominent in the 1950s and 1960s (and remain influential today), focused extensively on this process of forming an **identity**: a person's stable sense of who he or she is. Actually, identity is just a small part of Erikson's *psychosocial theory of development*, which features eight stages that cover the entire life span (Erikson, 1950, 1959; Erikson & Erikson, 1998; Coles, 2000). Here, we'll focus on the stages most relevant to adolescence, but Table 9.4 offers a description of all eight stages, from birth through late adulthood.

As the table indicates, each stage is characterized by a *crisis*. If the crisis is successfully met, it produces a *virtue* that can benefit the person from that point forward. For example, in the infancy stage (0–18 months), Erikson identifies the crisis as *trust versus mistrust*. Babies can't take care of themselves, so they have to rely on other people for their every need: to feed them, keep them warm, change their diapers, respond to their cries, and so on. Their experience during these early months teaches them whether they can depend upon, or *trust*, other people. If it is a positive experience, they emerge with the virtue of *hope*, or a sense that things will work out and other people will come through for them.

Erikson identified the challenge for adolescence as *identity versus role confusion* (Erikson, 1959, 1968; Marcia, 1966, 1980; Côté, 2009). Our aim during those years is to develop an answer to a fundamental question: Who am I? (see **Table 9.4** on p. 315). That answer, of course, stems from answers to many more specific questions, each crucial to a person's individuality: Who am I in terms of religion? Ethnicity? Politics? Sexual orientation? Career? Style of dress? Social group? Music, sports, and other interests? At first, the options can seem overwhelming, especially as we begin to look beyond our immediate family and see the vast range of choices available not just among our peers but among people across the country or the world. We may "try on" a variety of these options during adolescence, only to replace each one quickly with another. Society seems to allow for these temporary phases of identity during adolescence, at least to a greater extent than if they took place later. For example, a teenager who goes through a new look, a new set of friends, and a new passion every few months probably just gets an eye roll and a head shake from friends and family, but an equally fickle 35-year-old gets more serious disapproval. Erikson called this tolerance of rapidly shifting identities a *moratorium*, suggesting that we suspend judgment of adolescents as they work their way through this process of identity formation.

You probably remember lots of kids from your high school class, perhaps including yourself, who exemplified Erikson's description of an adolescent experiencing role confusion while forming an identity. The best example I've encountered is Steven, a psychotherapy client of mine who was a highly anxious kid. I have seen Steven in short spurts throughout high school—a few sessions when he's struggling, followed by weeks or months of no therapy when he's doing fine. This gave me the unique opportunity

preconventional morality
A moral decision-making strategy driven by the potential rewards and punishments of the decision.

conventional morality
A moral decision-making strategy driven by the desire to follow society's norms and laws.

postconventional morality
A moral decision-making strategy driven by fundamental rights and ethical principles.

identity
A part of Erikson's psychosocial theory of development; a person's stable sense of who he or she is.

CURRENT CONTROVERSY

Social Networking and Computer Gaming: Good or Bad for Adolescent Development?

Adolescents in the United States devote much of their time to technology. Some researchers estimate that kids spend 7.5 hours per day using media, but if you count the time they "double up" (checking Facebook while watching TV, for example), the total amount of time is actually closer to 11 hours (Rideout et al., 2010). Increasingly, that technology time is spent on social networking and computer gaming. Because this phenomenon is still, in the big picture, relatively new (in 1994, only 39% of households with children even *had* a computer), developmental psychologists are now eagerly conducting studies to answer important questions about how these activities might influence development (Roberts et al., 1999).

Research suggests that playing computer games can have both positive and negative effects on adolescents. Filograph/iStock/Getty Images

Studies highlight both the pros and cons of social networking and gaming (Zhao et al., 2012). First, here is the upside: Social networking profiles and computer game avatars give adolescents a way to try out new identities as they move through periods of role confusion on their way to developing a coherent self (James, 2009). At times, gaming can stimulate intellectual development, can be integrated into many school subjects, and can enhance the kinds of visual-spatial skills required for many applications of science, math, and technology (Redecker et al., 2010).

Now, here is the downside: while exploring various identities online, adolescents could inadvertently cause harm to themselves or others. Additionally, the anonymity of the Internet could encourage some adolescents to develop identities that are entirely false, which could hinder their development of a true, coherent identity. This is especially likely to happen to adolescents who are low in self-esteem and social skills and high in anxiety (Harman et al., 2005).

Speaking of social skills, an overreliance on online social networking and gaming can lead to misinterpretation of others' actions or intentions, given that subtle social cues like body language and facial expressions are typically lacking (Bauman & Tatum, 2009). Social networking sites (like Facebook) can also increase loneliness and depression. Despite having hundreds of "friends," an adolescent can feel quite friendless when all of them post photos and descriptions of activities to which he or she was not invited (Chou & Edge, 2012; O'Keeffe & Clarke-Pearson, 2011). One risk of gaming, particularly when an adolescent becomes immersed in one particular game, is that imagination and creativity become stifled. Their cognitive world becomes limited to that virtual world (James, 2009).

For a particular adolescent, the effects of social networking, gaming, and other forms of media depend on the underlying reasons for participation (Roberts et al., 2009). Together, this research suggests a bottom line: If adolescents use media in moderation, and seek it out for healthy reasons, it is likely to positively affect their development. If adolescents let media take over their lives and seek it out for unhealthy reasons, it is likely to negatively affect their development. ●

to get close looks at his life in different stages during his teen years. When I first met Steven, he was intensely academic: lots of advanced classes, lots of concern about standardized test scores, little interest in fashion, friends, or much else. In fact, the original reason for Steven's therapy was intense anxiety about getting into an elite university—pretty early, considering he was just starting ninth grade. "I'm a serious student," he told me. "I'm pretty much all about my grades."

Just 6 months later, Steven was all about something else: skateboarding. He looked different, with a new haircut and new clothes; he spoke differently, with lots of skate lingo. He had plenty of skater friends and spent most of his time at local skate parks or skate shops. His parents were now worried about his grades; Steven was worried about ankle injuries he might get while trying to impress his friends. Skateboard Steven lasted until the summer before tenth grade, at which point his interests shifted to politics. Political Steven joined his high school's chapter of the Young Democrats of America, watched lots of CNN, and planned for a career in office. He hung out with kids on student council and sat at a lunch table where the main topic of conversation (and Steven's main anxiety) was how to help Democratic candidates win their upcoming

elections. The skateboard gear was now in the back of the closet, replaced by a neater, more professional wardrobe and haircut.

Steven's "lifelong" dedication to the Democratic Party lasted through most of tenth grade. At that point a growth spurt got him noticed by the coach of his school's basketball team, who encouraged Steven to attend a summer basketball camp. He did, and then made the varsity team in eleventh grade. Now we had Basketball Steven: hanging with his teammates exclusively, following NCAA and NBA teams enthusiastically, decked out in Nike hoops gear from head to toe, and focusing his worries on his

TABLE 9.4: Erikson's Psychosocial Stages

STAGE	AGE	CRISIS	CENTRAL QUESTION	VIRTUE	
Infancy	0–18 months	Trust vs. mistrust	"Will the people around me take care of me?"	Hope	
Early childhood	2–3 years	Autonomy vs. shame and doubt	"Can I control myself?"	Will	
Preschool	3–5 years	Initiative vs. guilt	"Can I do things on my own?"	Purpose	
Elementary school	6–11	Industry vs. inferiority	"Can I keep up with my peers?"	Competence	
Adolescence	12–18	Identity vs. role confusion	"Can I determine who I am?"	Fidelity	
Young adulthood	19–40	Intimacy vs. isolation	"Can I form a lasting connection with another person?"	Love	
Middle adulthood	40–65	Generativity vs. stagnation	"Can I contribute something valuable?"	Care	
Older adulthood	65+	Ego integrity vs. despair	"Was my life well lived?"	Wisdom	

According to Erik Erikson, at every age from birth through older adulthood, we experience a psychological crisis centering on a question that is particularly relevant at that time in our lives. Ideally, we answer that question in a positive way and develop the corresponding virtue.
(a) oneinchpunch/Shutterstock (b) Jasper Cole/Blend Images/Getty Images (c) Allen Donikowski/Moment Select/Getty Images (d) Juanmonino/iStock/Getty Images (e) lorenzoantonucci/iStock/Getty Images (f) KevinDaugherty/iStock/Getty Images (g) GlobalStock/iStock/Getty Images (h) Jose Luis Pelaez Inc/Blend Images/Getty Images

Achieving intimacy, or long-term emotional closeness with a romantic partner, is a major challenge of young adulthood. Dimitri Otis/Taxi/Getty Images

basketball statistics. All was well until a knee injury prevented Steven from playing basketball during his senior year, but a new passion found him: DJing. Steven bought a starter set of turntables and started making mixes on his laptop. New clothes, friends, and values followed (as did new anxieties, about his ability to get enough paying DJ gigs to pay for upgraded equipment).

Ideally, by the time his adolescence ends, Steven will have developed a coherent sense of who he is to carry him through the rest of his life. If so, he will earn the virtue of *fidelity*, the ability to stay true to who he is even when his life circumstances change. If not, he will remain in a state of role confusion, in which he continues to search for himself and test out different ways of living.

The importance of the outcome of this identity versus role confusion stage is especially clear when you consider Erikson's next stage: *intimacy versus isolation*. **Intimacy** is long-term emotional closeness with a romantic partner. According to Erikson, the intimacy versus isolation stage is when young adults seek monogamous, loving relationships that will last a lifetime. Erikson believed that success at the young adult stage depended heavily on success at the adolescent stage: those who have formed a strong identity are most likely to form successful couples, while those still in a state of role confusion are most likely to struggle. (Would you want to marry someone still unable to commit to a single identity?)

Recent research on Erikson's ideas confirms the importance of identity formation during adolescence. One study found that teens who struggle to form an identity are much more likely to be anxious than their peers (Crocetti et al., 2009). Another study found that teens with low levels of identity development are especially likely to experience high levels of distress or seek psychotherapy (Wiley & Berman, 2013). A longitudinal study followed participants from age 15 to age 25 to see if the teens' levels of identity formation predicted their ability to form intimate romantic relationships 10 years later. These researchers found a significant positive correlation of .33 between these two variables. Correlation doesn't necessarily mean cause (there may be outside factors influencing both identity formation and romantic intimacy), but this correlation supports Erikson's basic idea that success at the adolescent and young adult stages go together (Beyers & Seiffge-Krenke, 2010).

Relationships With Parents. The teenage years are notorious for parent–child conflicts. Certainly, it is a time of tension for everyone involved. After over a decade of dependence, in which young children rely on their parents to do everything from wipe their noses to tie their shoes, adolescents begin to do many big things (driving, dating) and make many big decisions (college, sex) for themselves. But they still can't do everything, so inevitably, there is a push and pull between teens' need for autonomy ("Stop bugging me about my homework!") and their need for help ("Can you help me with my homework?") (McElhaney et al., 2009).

This push-and-pull does not mean that adolescence is doomed to become an all-out conflict between parents and kids. In fact, research suggests that in about 85–95% of families, the level of turmoil is not that severe (Lamb & Lewis, 2005). There is typically a modest increase in conflict around the beginning of adolescence, but these conflicts usually don't threaten the relationships that hold the family together (Branje et al., 2009; Steinberg, 1981, 1990). Families generally find a way to adjust to these adolescent changes and to renegotiate the roles and responsibilities of each member. (This is true especially for families with authoritative parents, who set rules but then alter them in response to the increasing independence of their kids.) Conflict between parents and adolescents is generally less extensive for second-born kids than for first-born kids, suggesting that parents learn from their experiences with the oldest child, then adjust their parenting to minimize conflict with younger siblings (Whiteman et al., 2003).

The few families that are most likely to be torn apart by adolescence are those that were starting to tear well before their kids reached that age (Laursen & Collins, 2009; Stattin & Klackenberg, 1992). From my own psychotherapy practice, I vividly recall the Rollins family, consisting of a mom (Lori), dad (Rick), and 9-year-old nonidentical

twins (Katie and Kyle). The parents brought the twins in for "help with *their* problems," but it was clear from the start that Lori and Rick had problems of their own. They had different parenting philosophies—Lori was a pushover who spoiled the kids, and Rick was a disciplinarian who scared them—and they never compromised about this. Their marriage was also marked by affairs and financial turmoil. When things got especially bad, Lori often fell into deep periods of depression and Rick often fell into the local bar. Neither of these approaches provided any support or attention to the twins, of course.

At 9, the twins were actually holding up quite well, considering the questionable parenting: just occasional skirmishes with each other and a little misbehavior at school. A few years later, the kids' behavior got more troublesome when adolescence hit. Kyle was involved in a couple of fights at school and stealing an occasional beer out of the fridge, while Katie was experimenting with self-inflicted injuries ("cutting"). Their parents blamed each other, responded inconsistently to the kids, and retreated into their own unhealthy coping styles, all of which caused the problems to worsen. At last check, Lori and Rick had divorced when the kids were 15. Katie had two stints in a psychiatric hospital after suicide attempts, and Kyle was on his way to juvenile detention after breaking into a neighbor's house while drunk.

Adolescence is a time when relationships with parents are often tense but not usually overwhelmingly difficult. Monkey Business Images/Shutterstock

The problems that Katie and Kyle experienced illustrate another phenomenon of adolescence: gender differences in psychological disorders. Starting in adolescence, girls (compared to boys) show an increase in *internalizing* disorders. These are disorders in which they direct their distress toward themselves, either bodily (as Katie did by cutting) or more often emotionally, as in mood disorders, especially depression. Adolescent girls also develop much higher levels of body dissatisfaction (typically, seeing themselves as too fat), accompanied by weight control efforts from dieting to bulimia and anorexia (May et al., 2006; Barker & Galambos, 2003; Phelps et al., 1993).

Adolescent boys, on the other hand, demonstrate more *externalizing* disorders—disorders in which they direct their distress toward other people, like conduct disorder, oppositional defiant disorder, and to some extent, attention-deficit/hyperactivity disorder (ADHD). This gender gap in disorders emerges at about age 13, grows until about age 18, and then remains throughout adulthood (Galambos et al., 2009). Keep this in mind: Any of these psychological disorders can be the cause or effect of difficulties in the parent–adolescent relationship. Of course, in some cases, psychological disorders can arise for reasons completely unrelated to parenting.

Researchers who examine adolescents' relationships with their parents often find that teens develop a distinct relationship with each parent. In particular, teens tend to relate differently to their moms than their dads. Of course, it varies from one family to the next, but teens generally spend more time with mom and seek more support from her (Markiewicz et al., 2006; Doyle et al., 2009). Teens also tend to feel closer to mom and share more of their thoughts and feelings with her (Doyle et al., 2009). On the other hand, teens tend to disagree with mom more, showing her less respect and obedience than they do with dad (Maccoby, 1998; McHale et al., 2003; Steinberg & Silk, 2002).

Relationships With Peers. Just as crucial as teens' relationships with their parents are teens' relationships with each other. Adolescents spend twice as much time with peers as with their parents. Compared to early childhood, more of this time is unsupervised, in larger groups, directed by the kids themselves (as opposed to parents determining what kids do), and involves both boys and girls (Rubin et al., 2006).

Researchers have found that these peer relationships have important consequences for functioning and well-being (Hartup, 1999; Rubin et al., 2005). For example, adolescents who struggle socially tend to struggle in lots of other ways: bad grades, poor self-image, depression, delinquency, and substance abuse (Ollendick et al., 1992; Wentzel et al., 2004; Wentzel, 2003; Sandstrom et al., 2003; Gazelle & Ladd,

intimacy
A part of Erikson's psychosocial theory of development; a long-term emotional closeness with a romantic partner.

Relationships with peers become extremely important during the adolescent years. Sam Edwards/OJO Images/Getty Images

2003). Of course, there are exceptions to this rule. Some isolated kids do very well, and some popular kids do quite poorly. And it is often hard to tell which came first: social isolation or the problems (like bad grades, depression, etc.) that often come with it. In many cases, these circumstances feed off of each other. A "loner" kid becomes depressed, which further isolates him from his peers, which worsens his depression, and the cycle continues.

In some cases, the particular group of friends you hang out with—your crowd—can influence the odds of experiencing certain kinds of psychological problems as you move through adolescence. Researchers studied about 250 diverse high school students who labeled themselves as Populars, Jocks, Brains, Burnouts, Nonconformists, or Average kids (Prinstein & La Greca, 2003). They found that Burnouts experience significantly higher rates of depression than Populars and Jocks; Brains experience much higher rates of social anxiety than Populars and Jocks; and Brains, Burnouts, and Average kids experience more loneliness than Populars and Jocks. **Figure 9.9** illustrates some of these findings.

One problem with adolescent crowds and the friendships within them is that they are unstable. Kids tend to move through a number of "BFFs" and peer groups during their middle school and high school years (Jiang & Cillesen, 2005). One study asked adolescents in Montreal once per month to list the names of their friends. The boys' answers were a bit more stable than girls', but both genders demonstrated a high level of instability. Overall, about one-third of the friends on a typical adolescent's list one month didn't make that adolescent's list the very next month (Chan & Poulin, 2007). Over the course of a 9-month school year, that is a high level of turnover, possibly resulting in a different group of friends from the beginning of the year and to the end. Additionally, our self-perceptions of peer relationships are not reliable. This means that teens are likely to overestimate or underestimate how close they are with their friends, which in turn could lead to further social problems (Brown & Larson, 2009).

Friendships take on added importance in adolescence, but another kind of peer relationship—dating—is important as well. As your own experience may reflect, the way kids date changes significantly within just the brief span of high school. Here is a summary of the progression (Connolly & McIsaac, 2009):

- At 14, dating relationships typically last just a few weeks and rarely last more than a few months. Dating often takes place in large groups rather than couples, and social status is often a major motivator. You can become more popular because you're going out with someone popular. There are lots of crushes and infatuations too, the reason for which is often to have something to talk about with your friends as much as it is "true love" with your partner.
- At 16, dating is a bit more serious, with less of it happening in large groups and more of it happening in couples. The average dating relationship lasts 6 months. Couples often get together because their friends broker the relationships by asking "Do you like…?" for each other.
- At 18, dating is again more serious, with the average relationship lasting a full year. Dating activities are almost exclusively couple-based, with only a few big group outings. The relationships are more exclusive, so emotional bonds between couples are more lasting and adult-like. At times, people at this age can find themselves engulfed in romantic relationships, such that they eclipse friends, family, or individual goals. For example, a high school senior limits her college options to the city or the specific school where her partner, whom she has dated all senior year, is going.

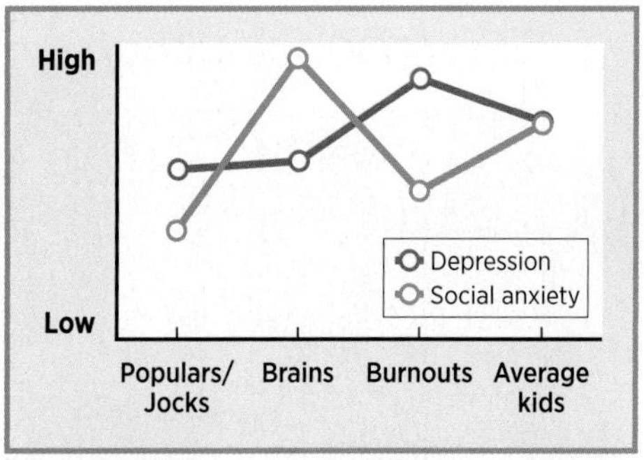

FIGURE 9.9 Your Crowd and Your Mental Health. During adolescence, different crowds experience different psychological problems, like depression and social anxiety, at different rates. Burnouts experience the highest levels of depression, but Brains experience the highest levels of social anxiety. Does this match what you and your classmates experienced in high school? Data from Prinstein & La Greca, 2003.

It is important to keep in mind that the way dating changes throughout adolescence depends on a number of cultural variables, including ethnicity. For example,

DIVERSITY MATTERS

Asian teens tend to start dating relatively late and then progress through the same stages at roughly the same pace as most others. Latino teens tend to start dating relatively late, skipping the early

stages and jumping more quickly to more serious couple-based relationships (Connolly et al., 2004; Raffaelli, 2005).

Most of the data on adolescent dating focuses on heterosexual relationships, but in recent years, research has emerged on homosexual and bisexual relationships among adolescents as well. About 5% of adolescents report same-sex attraction, and they appear to have as many dating experiences as those who are attracted to the opposite sex (Carver et al., 2003; Williams et al., 2003). However, a sizable number of the dating experiences of adolescents who identify as homosexual are actually with opposite sex partners, possibly reflecting a fluctuating sexual orientation during the teen years or pressure from peers to participate in "straight" behaviors (Russell & Consolacion, 2003; Diamond, 2008).

Unfortunately, adolescent dating relationships are not immune to relationship violence (Vagi et al., 2013). Alarmingly, every year about 1 in 10 high school girls experiences violence from a dating partner (Howard et al., 2013). One large-scale longitudinal study of over 600 adolescents identified several factors that predict dating violence: adverse living conditions (poverty, etc.), violence-tolerant attitudes, and perhaps most notably, watching violent media (Connolly et al., 2010). Another study points out the importance of the peer group norms: teens whose friends are violent toward their romantic partners tend to be violent toward their own (Foshee et al., 2013). Child abuse is also a factor. Kids who are abused are at increased likelihood to become perpetrators of dating violence as adolescents (and adults as well) (Gómez, 2011).

On a more uplifting note, some recent research on adolescence has focused on *positive youth development*, efforts to build on teens' strengths by involving them in organized, constructive peer-based activities (Lerner & Steinberg, 2009; Grusec et al., 2011). Kids are offered group activities that allow them to participate in the simultaneous improvement of society and themselves (Snyder et al., 2011; Lerner et al., 2009; Damon, 2004; Larson, 2000). For example, a high school may create a club for kids to boost a community's voter registration or beautify its parks, or a religious institution's youth group may organize a charity drive or a Habitat for Humanity effort.

By design, positive youth development efforts try to enhance the "5 C's": competence, confidence, connection, character, and caring/compassion. Research indicates that these efforts work: High-risk kids experience fewer psychological problems when they participate in these group activities (Holland & Andre, 1987; Masten, 2004, 2006). Of course, the success of any organized activity for teens depends on its availability. Unfortunately, the availability of extracurricular activities of any kind (both at school and elsewhere) depends on socioeconomic status (Fredricks & Eccles, 2006; Theokas & Bloch, 2006). For example, kids from poor families participate in organized sports at a rate far below that for kids from more affluent families, not only because the sports themselves cost money (registration, equipment, etc.), but because they require rides and free time from parents who simply don't have enough of it (Mahoney et al., 2009).

Emerging Adulthood. There is one more question we should consider regarding adolescence: When does it end? Traditionally, adolescence has been roughly defined as the middle school and high school years. The idea was that adolescence is over and adulthood has begun by the time a person graduates, or certainly when he or she hits 20. But some developmental psychologists (Arnett, 2000, 2007) have made the claim for **emerging adulthood**: a recently proposed developmental stage during which the person gradually moves from adolescence to adulthood, typically during the late teens and twenties in modern Western cultures. As an example of emerging adulthood, consider Joshua, who went away to college for a couple of years after high school but returned to his parents' house at the age of 20. He continues to take classes at the local college on a part-time basis, and holds a part-time job as well, but still relies on his parents for money, food, and emotional support. Through his twenties, he occasionally moves into an apartment with friends, but only with his parents' backing. He typically moves back home after a short stint. He's now approaching 30, still striving toward self-sufficiency.

The notion that adulthood *emerges* means that we become adults slowly, little by little. This differs from the conventional idea that we become adults more abruptly,

emerging adulthood
A recently proposed developmental stage during which the person gradually moves from adolescence to adulthood.

Savage Chickens

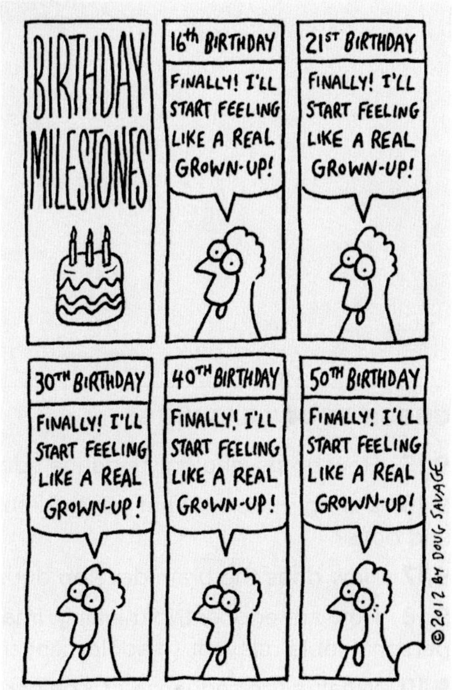

Doug Savage

MY TAKE VIDEO 9.2

Emerging Adulthood

"I think it depends on family, income sometimes, where you are..."

YOUTUBE: http://tiny.cc/mytake
LAUNCHPAD: launchpadworks.com

perhaps around the time we reach a particular birthday (18? 21?) or when we achieve a particular milestone, such as graduation, marriage, or a first job (Kerckhoff, 2003). If adulthood emerges slowly, that means adolescence fades slowly. If a 20-something (or perhaps 30-something or even older in some cases) has not yet fully become an adult, then he or she must remain partially an adolescent, which means that they may still be searching for their own identity, as Erikson described. As a result, emerging adults may delay such tasks as finding a mate and starting a family, and they may stay somewhat dependent on their parents or others for support.

DIVERSITY MATTERS

Some researchers dispute the notion of emerging adulthood as a developmental stage. These researchers argue that emerging adulthood (if it exists at all) exists only in cultures where 20-somethings can afford it and fellow society members endorse it, such as wealthy segments of the United States and other Western countries (Hendry & Kloep, 2007). They suggest we shouldn't necessarily accept emerging adulthood as the norm, even if we accept it as a possibility, since that would imply that making a quicker jump from adolescence to full adulthood is somehow abnormal (Côté & Bynner, 2008). As an illustration, one study of Welsh people in their late teens and early 20s found that they were much more likely to label themselves as full-fledged adults than as emerging adults (Hendry & Kloep, 2010).

CHECK YOUR LEARNING:

9.15 How do psychologists define adolescence?

9.16 During puberty, what physical changes occur in girls and boys?

9.17 How does the brain develop during adolescence?

9.18 How are egocentric thinking, imaginary audience, and personal fable relevant to adolescent thinking?

9.19 What is the sequence of Kohlberg's stages of moral thinking?

9.20 How do psychologists define identity?

9.21 What is Erikson's eight-stage psychosocial theory of development, how does it apply to adolescence?

9.22 What role do relationships with parents and peers play during adolescence?

9.23 What is the proposed stage called emerging adulthood, and how is it relevant to adolescence?

Adulthood

YOU WILL LEARN:

9.24 how the functioning of our bodies and brains changes throughout the stages of adulthood.

9.25 how cognitive performance changes throughout the stages of adulthood.

9.26 about the highlights of psychosocial development throughout adulthood.

Our final phase of development, adulthood, covers a lot of ground: from the late teens or early 20s (or later, according to the idea of emerging adulthood) all the way through the 80s, 90s, and beyond. The earliest developmental psychologists focused exclusively on kids, but the assumption that development stalls in adulthood has been shattered. Current developmental psychologists acknowledge that development continues all the way through the life span (Baltes et al., 2006; Elder & Shanahan, 2006; Moshman, 2003).

One important note about development during the adult years: Age doesn't mean as much as it used to. In the earlier phases of development, age communicates a lot about the developmental tasks of the individual. Any 1-year-old is working on object permanence, any 6-year-old is mastering conservation, and any 12- or 13-year-old is dealing with the physical and psychological effects of the onset of puberty. Of course, the teen years begin to send us in different directions, so we no longer move in lock-step by adulthood. Instead, our paths have diverged to such an extent that people born in the same year might be facing very different developmental challenges (Moen, 2003). For example, 35-year-olds could be single, newlywed, married for 15 years, or divorced. They could be parents or childless, entry-level workers or CEOs. Similarly, a 60-year-old could be cognitively sharp or slipping, physically robust or feeble, retired

or starting a new career. Nonetheless, developmental psychologists have identified common themes for certain periods of adulthood.

menopause
The time in a woman's middle adulthood when she stops having menstrual periods.

Physical Development

Let's consider the physical changes that predictably happen to us as we move through young adulthood, middle adulthood, and older adulthood.

Young Adulthood. In early adulthood, the body and the brain peak. In most sports, elite athletes reach their prime in their 20s, with a quick decline and "retirement" looming in their 30s. (Occasionally, an athlete's stats actually improve in the 30s or 40s, but many of them, like Alex Rodriguez or Mark McGwire, were later found to be using steroids or other illegal drugs to cheat the normal aging process.) Your own athletic prowess might follow a similar path. If you haven't yet experienced it, you will soon learn why rec centers have separate "30 and over" or "40 and over" leagues in so many sports!

The health-related habits of young adulthood are especially important, not just while you're a young adult, but for the rest of your life. The routines that you establish for yourself in your 20s—what you eat, how often you exercise, how much you sleep, how much you smoke, drink, or use drugs—will be hard to break when you're in your 30s, 40s, and beyond (Daniels et al., 2005). You might get by with unhealthy habits while you're younger, but the consequences will probably catch up with you later—often in the form of obesity, high blood pressure, heart disease, or other serious health risks (Mozaffarian et al., 2011).

LIFE HACK 9.2

Make healthy choices about diet, exercise, sleep, and substance use when you're a young adult. Those choices often become habits that continue for decades.

(Daniels et al., 2005; Mozaffarian et al., 2011)

Middle Adulthood. Starting in the 30s and accelerating with every decade, the functioning of our brains and bodies gradually declines. Age spots, wrinkles, thinning hair, creaky joints, and loss of muscle tone creep in. Bone loss causes breaks to happen more easily and heal more slowly. It also causes us to lose height—about 1–2 inches between our 30s and our 70s (Sorkin et al., 1999). We also get fatter, or more specifically, fat comprises much more of our body weight in middle adulthood than it did in adolescence (Kyle et al., 2001). Our need for glasses and contacts increases dramatically in our 40s and 50s due to our eyes' decreased ability to focus. For some, hearing begins to slip too. Of course, healthy habits related to eating, exercise, and sleeping can reduce the rate at which any of these changes take place, at least to some degree. A 40-year old who eats salads, runs 5Ks, and gets a solid 8–10 hours of sleep each night is much more likely to avoid serious physical problems than a 40-year-old who eats burgers and fries, rarely exercises, and pulls all-nighters.

For women, a hallmark of middle adulthood is **menopause**: the time in a woman's life when she stops having menstrual periods. The average age for menopause is 51, but it can take place as early as the upper 30s or as late as the upper 50s (Gold et al., 2001; Morabia & Costanza, 1998). Menopause is associated with a drop in estrogen levels and other physical changes that vary from woman to woman, including hot flashes, fatigue, and stomach and heart irregularities. Typically, these changes do not cause severe or lasting disruption to the woman's life. Some researchers have also found that depression rates increase after menopause, but others have found no such evidence (Llaneza et al., 2012; Hunter, 1990; Matthews et al., 1990). The causes of this increase in depression rates could be the biological changes of menopause themselves, the beliefs they have about menopause and its impact on their identity, or other events in their lives that have nothing to do with menopause, such as children leaving home or health problems in themselves or their partners or friends.

Men don't experience anything quite as definitive as menopause, but they do experience *andropause* starting in their late 30s and continuing through their 50s. The gradual hormonal changes of andropause are centered around lower levels of testosterone (consider the target audience for all of those ads for erectile dysfunction meds). Andropause does not eliminate a man's ability to reproduce, but it does decrease it—a fact that is receiving increased attention among couples and their doctors considering the biological clocks of couples trying to conceive (Lewis et al., 2006).

Exercise and other health-related habits of young adulthood are important because they often extend into middle adulthood and older adulthood. Gary Burchell/DigitalVision/Getty Images

Studies of taxi drivers, who accumulate vast knowledge of a city's streets as they shuttle passengers, show that experience continues to shape the brain even during middle adulthood. Aidon/PhotoDisc/Getty Images

The interaction of nature and nurture—the notion that experience shapes the brain—remains true well into middle adulthood. In an innovative study, researchers used MRIs to examine the brains of London taxi drivers in middle adulthood and found that the volume of their hippocampus was significantly greater than that of control participants (Maguire et al., 2000). This is important because the hippocampus controls spatial representation, which is where we keep maps of streets and other spaces. So, these London taxi drivers' brains actually expanded in such a way that reflects the knowledge they accumulated as they navigated the streets of London during their middle adulthood years. In a 2006 follow-up study, these researchers compared the brains of London taxi drivers to the brains of London bus drivers. Both drive full-time, but the bus drivers follow the same predictable route day after day while the taxi drivers traverse the city on unpredictable routes that they must formulate on the spot. The bus drivers' brains did not show the same increased volume in the hippocampus as the taxi drivers' brains. This finding confirmed that spatial knowledge (which taxi drivers need far more than bus drivers), as opposed to any other aspect of driving, affects brain development.

Older Adulthood. Older adulthood—generally, your 60s and beyond—is a life stage that extends further today than it ever has in the past. With a current life expectancy in the United States of 78 years (about 81 for women, about 75 for men), and with the number of people reaching 100 more than tripling in the last few decades, there is a good chance that your older adulthood will last as long as your young or middle adulthood (National Center for Health Statistics, 2009).

Generally, the decline in physical abilities that began in middle adulthood continues as we move through our 60s and beyond. Just as the body shrinks during older adulthood, the brain does as well, losing about 10–15% of its peak volume by the age of 90 (Shan et al., 2005; Zelazo & Lee, 2010). The parts of the brain that are most likely to shrink include the frontal lobes, a fact that correlates with the decline of memory and other cognitive abilities (Pardo et al., 2007). The sensory abilities weaken, with such vision problems as glaucoma and cataracts increasingly common and deterioration of the cochlea in the inner ear causing an increased need for hearing aids. There are new medical conditions such as arthritis (joint inflammation) and osteoporosis (excessive bone loss). Because of weakening bones and immune systems, simple falls can lead to serious injuries that require extensive recovery time or surgery. More serious and potentially fatal diseases like cancer and cardiovascular disease also become more common. Just as in earlier stages of adult life, healthy habits can reduce the chances of many of these unfortunate events (Mattson, 2012).

Cognitive Development

Like physical functioning, cognitive functioning generally peaks during young adulthood. Memory, speed of information processing, creativity, and other measures that developmental psychologists use to assess the sharpness of our minds all land at their highest levels around our 20s (Verhaeghen & Salthouse, 1997; Park et al., 2002; Salthouse & Babcock, 1991).

Things begin to change during middle adulthood. We process information a bit more slowly, meaning that we need just a bit more time to respond to stimuli that we see and hear. Also, our working memory becomes a bit more restricted, so we take more time to solve problems, formulate responses to other people, and make decisions. As an example, consider a car stopped at a red light, with a stalled truck blocking a lane just past the intersection. If the car takes off the instant the light turns green and makes a quick lane change to avoid the stalled truck, the driver is probably a young adult. If the car hesitates a bit when the light turns green and makes a slow, deliberate lane change while approaching the stalled truck, the driver is likely to have entered middle adulthood.

What happens to intelligence during middle adulthood is more complicated, largely because intelligence consists of so many distinct abilities. Also, age-based comparisons

can be made via either cross-sectional or longitudinal research methods (Salthouse, 2009; O'Connor & Kaplan, 2003). One researcher has conducted the Seattle Longitudinal Study, in which he measured various intelligence-related abilities of thousands of participants over many decades (Schaie, 2012). He concludes that some components of intelligence—particularly processing speed and fluency with words and numbers—seem to peak in early adulthood and decline in middle adulthood, especially toward its tail end (in our 50s). But many other components of intelligence—verbal meaning, reasoning, spatial abilities—seem to remain as high during middle adulthood as they were in young adulthood. Overall, the findings suggest that noticeable declines in intelligence typically don't occur in healthy adults until our 60s or 70s. Most of us will be in our 80s before our intelligence level falls below the middle level for young adults, if it happens at all.

Healthy habits like regular exercise can reduce the chances of serious medical problems during older adulthood.
Jupiterimages/Stockbyte/Getty Images

Of course, diseases of the brain can significantly disrupt the cognitive process. The risk for such diseases—most often, *dementia*—greatly increases during older adulthood. Dementia is a term used to cover any brain disorder in which the main symptom is a steep decline in overall mental functioning. *Alzheimer's disease* is a particular kind of dementia in which basic cognitive functions like memory, language, and reason worsen irreversibly. Alzheimer's disease is devastating and, unfortunately, increasingly common: in the United States; over 10% of people over 65, and 33% of people over 85, have Alzheimer's disease, for a total over 5 million (Alzheimer's Association, 2013). Researchers are actively searching for ways to cure Alzheimer's, or even slow its progress, but with little success. The result is a tremendous burden on families' time, finances, and emotions as they struggle to provide their older loved ones with the care they deserve.

The causes of Alzheimer's disease also remain under investigation. Some of the suspected risk factors are outside of our control (genes), but many other risk factors are at least partially within our control, particularly by exercising and eating right: obesity, smoking, diet, cholesterol levels, and heart health (Daviglus et al., 2011; Li et al., 2011; Ahlskog et al., 2011). One study estimates that half of Alzheimer's disease cases are attributable to these controllable risk factors, and that even moderate improvement in them could prevent millions of cases in the future (Barnes & Yaffe, 2011).

Psychosocial Development

As we move from young adulthood through older age, we also move through a sequence of psychological and social experiences. Let's consider them chronologically, from young adulthood through middle adulthood and older adulthood.

Young Adulthood. As Erik Erikson emphasized, one of the primary tasks of young adulthood is to form loving, lasting couples that will provide intimacy and stave off isolation. Traditionally, this meant marriage, but in recent decades, marriage has been happening less often and later in life (Teachman et al., 2013). In 1980, 64% of men and 53% of women in their 20s were single, but in 2006, those numbers jumped to 73% and 62%, respectively. In the same time period, the average age for a first marriage climbed from 24 to 27.5 for men, and from 21 to 25.6 for women (U.S. Census Bureau, 2006, 2008).

One reason for the differences in marriage patterns is the rise of *cohabitation*, or romantically involved couples living together while unmarried. Since 1970, the number of cohabiting couples has multiplied by 10, and the stigma that once followed "shacking up" is largely gone. Today, at least 75% of young adults will live together with a partner before they get married (Popenoe, 2009). In some cases, cohabitation is a trial run for marriage, but in others, marriage is not at all on the horizon. For those who do eventually get married, divorce rates are higher and marital happiness is lower than for those who did not live together (Jose et al., 2010).

In spite of the trends toward extended singlehood and cohabitation, over 90% of U.S. adults marry, and the vast majority of these marriages take place during young adulthood (Popenoe, 2009). But a sizable number of these marriages end in divorce,

TABLE 9.5: Factors that Increase the Likelihood of Divorce

YOUR SITUATION	YOUR (OR YOUR PARTNER'S) CHARACTERISTICS
Marrying young	Psychological problems
Low education level	Alcohol or substance use
Low socioeconomic status	Violent toward partner
No religious affiliation	Cheating, infidelity
Baby before marriage	Unfair division of household labor
Divorced parents	

Information from Hoelter, 2009.

most often in years 5–10 of the marriage (Amato, 2010). The divorce rate almost tripled between 1980 and 2006, but has stopped growing in more recent years (National Vital Statistics, 2010; Hoelter, 2009). **Table 9.5** lists some of the most powerful predictors of divorce in couples.

Whether married, cohabiting, or single, parenthood is another defining challenge of young adulthood (Azar, 2003). In most cases, young adults rise to the challenge posed by their bundle of joy, but the process can also produce significant distress, especially when the new-baby excitement wears off, helpful relatives leave, and one or both parents increase their work hours (Wallace & Gotlib, 1990). Other studies have found new parents, particularly new moms, are most likely to struggle with depression and other psychological problems when their pre-baby expectations—how much they would enjoy parenthood, how difficult it would be, how much their partner would help—did not match their post-baby experiences (Kalmuss et al., 1992; Hackel & Ruble, 1992; Harwood et al., 2007).

One of my own therapy clients, Marci, illustrated this unhappy reaction to unfulfilled expectations. Early in her first pregnancy, she came to see me for help overcoming some mild OCD (obsessive-compulsive disorder) issues. She had a fear of germs that sent her to the sink to wash her hands about 10–20 times a day. She'd be facing lots of germs when the baby (and dirty diapers) arrived, so she proactively sought my help, and the treatment was successful. A few months before the baby came, Marci no longer washed her hands excessively at all, and she was optimistic that motherhood would be joyful. I didn't hear from her until about 6 months after she had given birth, and when I did, she didn't sound joyful. In fact, she was disillusioned and depressed. Caring for this baby was much more difficult than she anticipated. This wasn't like when she held her friend's babies and made goo-goo eyes at them until she got a big toothless smile. She couldn't hand her own baby back to anyone when he started crying or throwing up. The middle-of-the-night feedings, the fussiness, the never-ending laundry, and more than anything, the limited help she got from her newly promoted husband—none of it was what she expected when she was expecting. We restarted therapy and saw each other for a few more sessions. With some compassion, some adjustments in her expectations, and some suggestions for communicating with her husband about what she needed, she was well on her way to feeling content (if not joyful).

Middle Adulthood. By middle adulthood, most of us have moved past finding partners and becoming parents. We have entered Erikson's *generativity versus stagnation* stage, which means that our work becomes a primary focus (Wapner & Demick, 2003). Work, in this sense, should be understood broadly: not only the kinds of careers or jobs that take us out of the house, but also stay-at-home parenting or other essential roles, whether directly paid or not. In any of these capacities, a goal of work during middle adulthood is to produce something that the individual deems lasting and worthy—perhaps healthy and happy children, or positive change in the world, or a profit.

There is a unique set of circumstances surrounding this pursuit of meaningful work during middle adulthood. In some ways, dedication to work becomes easier in middle adulthood than it was during early adulthood, largely because of family circumstances. Specifically, teenagers require a lot less direct care than babies, preschoolers,

or elementary schoolers, which frees up time and energy for parents to devote to work (Moen & Roehling, 2005; Sterns & Huyck, 2001). On the other hand, middle adulthood comes with its own family stressors that can interfere with work productivity. For example, a 50-year-old working mom might have a 25-year-old son who moves back home, regularly borrows money to pay his student loans, or needs grandma to watch the grandkids on a regular basis. Or, she might have an ailing parent or partner of her own to take care of (Climo & Stewart, 2003). Whether she is an entry-level employee or an executive in the peak earning years of her life, a combination of these factors can detract from her efficiency and add to her stress level (Michel et al., 2011; Simon-Rusinowitz et al., 1996).

Middle adulthood is marked by the stress of multiple obligations, often including work and caring for young children and other family members. monkeybusinessimages/iStock/Getty Images

A large-scale study of workers at various stages of adulthood illustrates the realities of working during middle adulthood. Researchers surveyed over 41,000 male and female employees of a huge corporation (IBM) from 79 countries in North America, Latin America, Europe, and Asia (Erickson et al., 2010). Their main finding was that workers at either end of the spectrum—either no kids or kids grown and out of the house—had the lowest levels of work–family stress. Workers in the middle of the spectrum had the highest levels of work–family stress. These workers are the parents in their 30s and early 40s (the front end of middle adulthood) with young kids—kids who need not only the income that mom or dad brings home but rides to soccer practice, attendance at dance recitals, and quality time reading bedtime books. As these parents move toward the back end of middle adulthood, their kids get more independence (and driver's licenses) and eventually move out. Under most circumstances, this reduces the workers' level of work–family stress.

For example, consider the Tolliver family, which includes Phoebe (mom, age 35), Scott (dad, age 37), Samantha (age 8) and Olivia (age 6). Mom and dad both work full-time, and both kids are quite active: school, piano lessons, basketball and soccer teams, and plenty of birthday parties and play dates too. At this age, Samantha and Olivia need Phoebe and Scott for everything—they simply can't function on their own yet. But as they get older, they gain skills that free up their parents little by little. They start to clean up after themselves, and eventually do the dishes and the laundry. They can stay at home alone, first for just an hour or so, then for longer stretches. They get themselves snacks and eventually cook meals. They soon get to places on their own, either by driving or by arranging rides for themselves. A decade down the road, when their oldest is on the brink of leaving home, Phoebe and Scott will have made it through the period of middle adulthood when the work–parenting combination is at its most demanding.

Speaking of children leaving home, you may be familiar with the *empty nest syndrome*, in which parents in middle adulthood become depressed or otherwise struggle emotionally to adjust to a home without kids. The media and popular literature may portray the empty nest syndrome as universal, but in fact, it is not (Raup & Myers, 1989). In one study of over 300 parents in Vancouver whose kids had recently moved out, only about a quarter (32% of moms and 23% of dads) experienced the negative symptoms associated with the empty nest syndrome (Mitchell & Lovegreen, 2009). In fact, most parents described positive effects of the empty nest, including increased personal growth and leisure time, improved quality of the romantic relationship, and pride in raising and launching their children—a finding that echoes others in similar studies (Dennerstein et al., 2002; Schmidt et al., 2004). When actor Rob Lowe's youngest child was entering college, he described his empty nest this way: "I'm rediscovering my relationship with [my wife] Sheryl. We are like giddy teenagers...I think it is because we're realizing we are going to have a lot of alone time coming up when both the boys are out of the house" (Gomez, 2013).

Culture mattered a lot, with some parents of Eastern descent reporting much higher rates of empty nest syndrome than those of Western descent. Some researchers have speculated that the impact of culture relates to individualism and collectivism. Parents from individualistic cultures may celebrate a child's departure as a graduation to independent life. However, parents from more collectivistic cultures may mourn a child's departure as a betrayal of their family bonds, particularly if it happened sooner than the parents had expected or

DIVERSITY MATTERS

Becoming a grandparent is a significant event that often occurs toward the end of the middle-adulthood phase of life. Ariel Skelley/Blend Images/Getty Images

under adverse circumstances. For example, parents may react this way if their children marry or move in with a partner the parents don't like, or "run away" from family conflicts (Goldscheider & Goldscheider, 1999).

For some middle-aged adults, the nest doesn't become empty soon enough. Increasingly, adult children live at home well into their 20s or beyond. Research suggests that middle-aged adults whose nests remain full often experience a mix of closeness and tension with these adult children (Dor, 2013; Kloep & Hendry, 2010). Many kids return home when economic times are tough, a phenomenon known as "boomerang kids" or "accordion families" (Newman, 2012). These experiences are also likely to bring a blend of renewed attachment and heightened strain to the parent–child relationship (Mitchell & Gee, 1996).

Adding to the caregiving burdens of middle adulthood is *eldercare*, providing help to aging parents or other family members. As life expectancies increase, larger numbers of middle-aged adults give significant time, energy, or money to caring for their own parents. It is especially stressful when the middle generation supports both the generation above (their aging parents) and the generation below (their grown children), known as the "sandwich generation." One study (Fingerman et al., 2011) surveyed over 600 men and women in Philadelphia who ranged in age from 40 to 60 and who had both grown kids and living parents. Results indicated that these middle-aged adults provided frequent support both "upstream" and "downstream," but most provided significantly more support to their kids than their parents. Most participants viewed their kids as more important than their parents and said that their kids were in greater need. Those who supported their parents more than their kids frequently had parents with illness or disability.

An important landmark for middle-aged adults happens the first time their kids have kids of their own: grandparenthood (Brown & Roodin, 2003). Becoming a grandparent brings great joy, but it is not without its challenges (Shlomo et al., 2010). One study followed about 100 first-time grandparents from the time their child (or child's partner) was expecting to 1–2 years after the child was born (Somary & Strieker, 1998). Compared to grandfathers, grandmothers had more of their expectations for grandparenthood fulfilled and found more personal meaning in their relationships with their grandchildren. Grandfathers, however, felt more comfortable offering parenting advice. It also mattered whose mom and dad it was: parents of the baby's mother experienced more satisfaction as grandparents than they expected, but parents of the baby's father did not.

Older Adulthood. At some point, often in our 60s, we move past middle adulthood and into older adulthood. According to Erikson, the crisis we face at this stage is *ego integrity versus despair*, which means that we spend much of our time looking back and deciding if our life was well-lived. Perhaps the best way for a college student to appreciate this reflective experience is to imagine yourself at your graduation ceremony. There may be a moment, between waving to family in the crowd and listening to speeches by university administrators, when you quietly reminisce about the years you just spent in college. Did I make smart decisions? Choose the right school? Choose the right major? Work hard enough? Make good friends? Grow as a person? If your answers are negative, you'll feel regret and anguish about wasting your college years. If your answers are positive, you'll feel gratification and pride because you believe you spent your time intelligently. Now, imagine the power of these feelings if you were looking back not on just your college years, but *all* of your years, from the age of 70, 80, or more.

This looking-back process is so powerful for older adults that clinical psychologists have developed a psychotherapy based on it. Called *life review* (or *reminiscence*), this technique involves asking older adults to recall the major events of their lives, and to reevaluate whether their decisions benefited themselves or others or led to an important life lesson. Meta-analyses of these therapies indicate that they are successful in improving well-being and reducing depression levels in older adults (Bohlmeijer et al., 2003, 2007).

With or without this kind of life review, adults who move successfully through their older years develop *wisdom*, a sense of expertise and good judgment about life decisions that comes from the lessons of their own experiences (Kramer, 2003). Wisdom, therefore, is one cognitive ability in which older adults actually exceed younger adults. In one study, adults of various ages read stories about interpersonal conflicts and were asked to predict how those conflicts would unfold (Grossman et al., 2010). Some of the conflicts involved political or social issues, such as U.S. immigration policies. Other conflicts were more personal, like a sister who bought an expensive headstone for her deceased parents' graves and expected her brothers to pay their share for it even though they had not agreed to it. The oldest group considered the largest number of perspectives on the conflicts (as opposed to being one-sided), which facilitates compromise. The older adults' superiority on this task was so strong that the authors recommended that older adults should be assigned to key roles in high-stakes conflict resolution, such as in negotiations between rival groups or contentious legal cases.

During older adulthood, many older adults enter retirement, a task that can bring both great satisfaction as well as some new stressors. monkeybusinessimages/iStock/Getty Images

Another task that many older adults face is retirement. You might think that *task* is the wrong word to describe retirement, especially if you view it as an ongoing vacation. However, research suggests that retirement can be fraught with its own stressors, even as it brings great satisfaction and new opportunities to many older adults (Kim & Moen, 2001). One study found that for men, being recently retired correlates with higher levels of morale, but being retired for longer periods correlates with more serious depressive symptoms (Kim & Moen, 2002). Of course, it is difficult to know how to interpret this shift as retirement is prolonged. The increase in depressive symptoms could be caused by dissatisfaction with retirement itself, but it could also be caused by deteriorating health, loss of a partner, financial difficulties, or other factors. Other studies have found that those who struggle in retirement are likely not only to encounter these factors but also to have long job histories, strong emotional connections to work, anxiety about retirement, and a lack of control over the retirement process. For example, a worker who developed a strong attachment to a company over a career spanning many decades and who is forced to retire without a plan for his upcoming years may struggle in retirement (Van Solinge & Henkens, 2005, 2007).

Death. For all of us, the older adulthood stage must end in death. Interestingly, death anxiety does not peak in older adulthood. Research indicates that anxiety about death is definitely higher in younger adulthood (perhaps when thoughts of death occur for the first time, or when dependent children enter the picture) and may also be higher in middle adulthood (when heart attacks and other serious health risks increase) (Russac et al., 2007; Gesser et al., 1987). For those older adults who do experience death anxiety, it is less severe when the adult is physically and psychologically healthy, feels a strong sense of gratitude toward life, and has a strong belief in God and the afterlife (Neimeyer et al., 2011; Missler et al., 2011; Lau & Cheng, 2011; Fortner & Neimeyer, 1999; Harding et al., 2005).

Numerous theorists have offered explanations of how we experience the awareness of our own dying. The best-known of these is Elisabeth Kübler-Ross, a psychiatrist who has cared for many dying patients. She identified a common five-stage sequence that begins when we learn that we have a terminal illness (Kübler-Ross, 1969). Here are the five stages, along with an example of what a person diagnosed with terminal cancer might say:

1. Denial: "No way—the test results must be wrong! Let's do them over again."
2. Anger: "It's so unfair! Why should *I* have to die?"
3. Bargaining (often in prayer with a higher power): "If I never drink or smoke again, and I eat healthy and exercise, and I do the chemo, can I stay alive?"
4. Depression: "It's no use. I can't beat it. I'm as good as dead."
5. Acceptance: "I understand that death is inevitable. I'm ready."

The appeal of Kübler-Ross' stages have helped them gain a strong following among health professionals and the general public, but research indicates that they are not universal, especially when multiple ethnicities are involved (Irish et al., 1993; Metzger,

1979; Klass & Hutch, 1985). Instead, there is a wide variety of reactions to impending death, some of which may incorporate some of Kübler-Ross' stages, and some of which may not. In my psychotherapy practice, I have had the privilege of working with a few clients who were facing their own death. One, an 85-year-old woman, worried not about her own limited time, but about how her death would burden those around her after she was gone. A 70-year-old man welcomed the relief from his disease that he expected in heaven. A 30-year-old woman, diagnosed with pancreatic cancer and given six months to live, quickly overcame her initial rage and despair, then bravely vowed to extract joy out of every remaining moment. The variety of these approaches is just a small sample of the variety that we collectively experience.

CHECK YOUR LEARNING:

9.24 How does the level of functioning of our bodies and brains change throughout the stages of adulthood?

9.25 How does the level of cognitive performance change throughout the stages of adulthood?

9.26 What are the highlights of the psychosocial development throughout the stages of adulthood?

CHAPTER SUMMARY

Big Questions About Developmental Psychology

9.1 Developmental psychology is the study of changes to body, mind, and interpersonal interaction across the life span.

9.2 In a cross-sectional research design, people of different ages are compared to each other at the same point in time. In a longitudinal research design, the same group of people is compared to itself at different points in time.

9.3 Developmental psychologists often focus on three big questions: stability versus change, stage development versus continuous development, and nature versus nurture.

Development Before Birth

9.4 The sequence of prenatal development proceeds from conception to zygote to embryo to fetus.

9.5 Teratogens are substances in a pregnant woman's body—such as drugs, pollutants, and diseases—that can harm the embryo or fetus.

9.6 Fetal alcohol syndrome is a pattern of bodily and behavioral problems common in people whose mothers drank heavily during pregnancy.

Infancy and Childhood

9.7 Newborns' abilities include the use of all five senses, as well as a variety of reflexes such as sucking, grasping, rooting, crying, and the Moro reflex.

9.8 Physical development proceeds through predictable stages, but it can be influenced by the amount of stimulation in the environment.

9.9 According to Piaget, children develop schemas (or mental categories) and either assimilate new information into them or accommodate the schemas to account for the new information.

9.10 According to Piaget, children develop through a series of cognitive stages—sensorimotor stage, preoperational stage, concrete operational stage, and formal operational stage—in which their ways of thinking change in predictable ways.

9.11 Researchers have challenged some of Piaget's conclusions, suggesting that cognitive stages may be less rigid and less biologically based than Piaget argued.

9.12 The three distinct types of attachment are secure attachment, insecure-avoidant attachment, and insecure-resistant attachment. Secure attachment to others is essential to healthy psychosocial development.

9.13 The three categories that capture most parenting styles are authoritarian, permissive, and authoritative, each of which can produce distinct outcomes in children.

9.14 Temperament is a person's basic emotional responsiveness, which is typically evident from a very early age and can have a big effect on parent-child relationships.

Adolescent Development

9.15 Psychologists define adolescence as the developmental period that encompasses the transition from childhood to adulthood.

9.16 During puberty, which girls typically reach before boys, both primary and secondary sex characteristics emerge.

9.17 The brain continues to grow during adolescence, including a marked increase in myelination and improved connections between frequently used neurons.

9.18 Adolescent thinking can involve the egocentric thinking of younger children, often featuring an imaginary audience or personal fable.

9.19 Kohlberg's stages of moral thinking progress through preconventional morality to conventional morality and then postconventional morality.

9.20 Psychologists define identity, which often solidifies during adolescence, as a person's stable sense of who he or she is.

9.21 Erik Erikson's eight-stage psychosocial theory of development explains crises faced at every age from infancy through late adulthood. The way an adolescent handles the challenge of identity versus role confusion is important for the next stage, intimacy versus isolation.

9.22 Relationships with both parents and peers are key and often challenging elements of adolescence.

9.23 Some developmental psychologists have recently proposed a new stage, emerging adulthood, as the transition between adolescence and adulthood. The validity of this stage is still being debated.

Adulthood

9.24 The functioning of our bodies and brains typically peaks during young adulthood, starts to decline during middle adulthood, and declines further in older adulthood.

9.25 Cognitive performance typically follows a similar pattern to physical performance: highest during young adulthood and declining through middle adulthood and older adulthood.

9.26 The highlights of psychosocial development through adulthood include forming couples, becoming parents, working, launching children, caring for older relatives, grandparenting, retirement, and facing death.

KEY TERMS

developmental psychology, p. 289
cross-sectional design, p. 289
longitudinal design, p. 289
zygote, p. 290
embryo, p. 290
fetus, p. 290
teratogen, p. 293
fetal alcohol syndrome, p. 293
schema, p. 297
assimilation, p. 297
accommodation, p. 297
sensorimotor stage, p. 299
object permanence, p. 299
preoperational stage, p. 299
conservation, p. 299
theory of mind, p. 299
egocentrism, p. 301
concrete operational stage, p. 301
formal operational stage, p. 301
scaffolding, p. 301
attachment, p. 305
critical period, p. 305
stranger anxiety, p. 305
authoritarian parenting style, p. 305
permissive parenting style, p. 305
authoritative parenting style, p. 305
temperament, p. 307
adolescence, p. 309
puberty, p. 309
secondary sex characteristics, p. 309
primary sex characteristics, p. 309
menarche, p. 309
imaginary audience, p. 311
personal fable, p. 311
preconventional morality, p. 313
conventional morality, p. 313
postconventional morality, p. 313
identity, p. 313
intimacy, p. 317
emerging adulthood, p. 319
menopause, p. 321

SELF-ASSESSMENT

1. In a ______ research design, the same group of people is compared to itself at different points in time.

2. ______ are substances in the pregnant woman's body that harm the embryo or fetus, including alcohol, pesticides, and some prescription drugs.

3. Ben is a newborn baby. When he is surprised, he displays a reflex in which he flings his arms to the side. This reflex is known as
   a. rooting.
   b. grasping.
   c. the Moro reflex.
   d. blinking.

4. ______ is making sense of new information by sorting into already existing schemas, while ______ is making sense of new information by revising or creating new schemas.

5. ______ is a mental operation in which an amount or quantity remains the same regardless of the shape it takes.
   a. Object permanence
   b. Egocentrism
   c. Accommodation
   d. Conservation

6. ______ is a process by which a person learns new words, ideas, and ways of thinking by interacting with a more advanced person who provides decreasing levels of help.
   a. Assimilation
   b. Scaffolding
   c. Accommodation
   d. Attachment

7. Bobby is a parent of two children. He typically sets rules for his kids but also explains the rules and negotiates them with his kids. Bobby's parenting style is best described as
   a. authoritative.
   b. authoritarian.
   c. permissive.
   d. negligent.

8. Sierra is a teenager who makes lots of risky and dangerous decisions, including texting while driving and trying certain drugs, because she believes herself to be special or invulnerable. The term that best describes this decision-making tendency in Sierra and other adolescents is
   a. theory of mind.
   b. assimilation.
   c. object permanence.
   d. personal fable.

9. ______ ______ eight-stage psychosocial theory of development explains crises faced at every age from infancy through late adulthood.
   a. Jean Piaget's
   b. Lev Vygotsky's
   c. Erik Erikson's
   d. Lawrence Kohlberg's

10. The functioning of the body and the brain typically peak in
    a. childhood.
    b. young adulthood.
    c. middle adulthood.
    d. older adulthood.

Research shows quizzing is a highly effective learning tool. Continue quizzing yourself using LearningCurve, the system that adapts to *your* learning.

LaunchPad macmillan learning   LearningCurve macmillan learning

GO TO: launchpadworks.com

Self-Assessment Answers

1. longitudinal, 2. Teratogens, 3. c, 4. Assimilation, accommodation, 5. d, 6. b, 7. a, 8. d, 9. c, 10. b

WHAT'S YOUR TAKE?

1. When Mary Ainsworth created the *strange situation* research design, her intent was to see how babies responded when they found themselves separated from their caretakers, then either left alone or approached by new people. For many first-year college students, arrival on campus might be the young adult version of a strange situation: watching parents drive away from the residence hall after move-in day, left with plenty of moments of solitude and surrounded by plenty of unfamiliar faces. Some researchers noticed this parallel and pointed out the upside: that college can be a time for young adults whose parental attachment gave them a sense of security to explore and master the new environment (Kenny & Barton, 2003). Of course, the downside is that new college students whose parental attachment is not so secure might shy away from exploration (for example, hide out in their rooms) or experience high levels of distress (anxiety, depression, eating disorders, etc.). These researchers have conducted numerous studies that support this connection between parental attachment and well-being in first-year college students (Kenny, 1987; Kenny & Donaldson, 1991; Kenny & Perez, 1996). Do you think your own experience as a first-year college student was influenced by the type of attachment you had to your parents as a young child? What about your siblings, high school friends, or roommates? Did they handle the "strange situation" of college as you would have predicted based on their attachments to their parents?

SHOW ME MORE

9.1 Piaget's Conservation Task

launchpadworks.com LaunchPad

launchpadworks.com LaunchPad

Here is a pair of videos illustrating Piaget's concept of conservation: an older kid whose development allows him to grasp the concept, and a younger kid who is not quite there yet.

© Worth Publishers

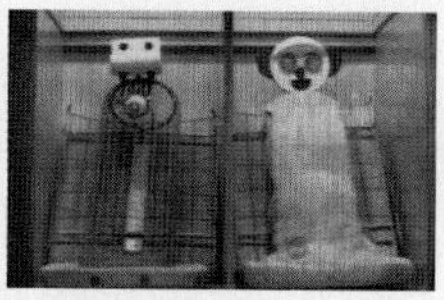

9.2 Attachment and Harlow's Monkeys

http://tiny.cc/showmemore

This vintage footage of Harry Harlow and the monkeys on which he experimented provides a glimpse into early research on attachment.

BBC Worldwide Learning

9.3 Moral Decision Making and a Legendary Producer's Records

http://tiny.cc/lj7njy

This segment from the radio show *Snap Judgment* tells the tale of the moral challenge faced by a record store owner who stumbled across the valuable record collection and original recordings of J Dilla, a legendary DJ and producer.

Africa Studio/Shutterstock

10 Diversity in Psychology: Multiculturalism, Gender, and Sexuality

Aldo Murillo/Getty Images

If you went to see a psychologist who was different from you, would you be concerned about the psychologist's ability to understand you and your issues? A conversation I had with my neighbor, Gabriela, a 20-year-old Hispanic woman, highlights the importance of this question. Knowing that I was a psychologist, Gabriela asked me if I could refer her to another psychologist to help her with some personal issues. I was happy to help and gave her a list of a few names of colleagues I highly recommended. She thanked me, looked down at the list, and asked, "Um, do you know how old they are? And are any of them Hispanic? And this one whose first name is Jordan—is that a man or a woman?" Gabriela explained, "I just want to find someone like me. I'm afraid that someone who is too different—someone who is not Hispanic, someone who is much older than me, someone who is a man—won't appreciate what I'm really going through or where I'm coming from. I just won't be as comfortable talking to them. They might not 'get' me."

Is there truth to what Gabriela was thinking? In your experience, are people of different ethnicities, ages, or genders so different that they can't "get" each other? And if that is true about differences in those variables, is it also true about differences in religion, socioeconomic status, sexual orientation, disability status, and others? If it is true between a client and a therapist, is it true in other kinds of relationships too? Simply put, how different, and how similar, are we?

These are the kinds of questions that underlie the main topic of his chapter, *diversity*. We'll consider lots of issues regarding the diverse range of people that surround you in your town, your city, your country, and your planet. For example, we'll explore what a culture is and the various characteristics of a culture. We'll examine some of the differences that exist between, and within, cultural groups. We'll learn how people adapt when they find themselves immersed in a different culture. We'll investigate ways that you can maximize your ability to ve successfully in a multicultural world. Lastly, we'll take a detailed look at sources of diversity—gender and sexuality—that are especially impactful in all of our lives.

CHAPTER OUTLINE

Diversity Surrounds You

Multiculturalism

Gender and Sexuality: Essential Examples of Diversity

Diversity Surrounds You

YOU WILL LEARN:

10.1 how diverse the United States is in terms of race, ethnicity, language, religion, age, and other variables.

10.2 what a culture is.

10.3 what dynamic sizing is.

10.4 how the definition of *culture* has changed over the years.

DIVERSITY MATTERS

You live in an increasingly diverse world. Whether you define that world narrowly, like your neighborhood or town, or more broadly, like your state or country, the world's population is mixing and mingling like never before. To understand why the field of psychology has devoted so much attention to the issue of diversity, let's consider some of the numbers that show what a varied assortment we have become. (Please note: In most chapters, Diversity Matters tags appear when the material highlights diversity issues. This entire chapter highlights diversity in many forms, so the tags are not used.)

Diversity by the Numbers

According to the U.S. Census Bureau, the following is how U.S. residents collectively answered questions about themselves in terms of race and ethnicity, language, religion, age, education, income, and other topics relating to diversity (United States Census Bureau [USCB], 2011, with specific tables noted; plus other sources as marked):

Race and Ethnicity. The majority (62%) of the U.S. population describes itself as White, 18% as Hispanic, 12% as Black or African American, 6% as Asian, 1% as Native American or Alaska Native, 2% as Native Hawaiian or other Pacific Islander, and 1.7% as multiracial. These numbers are changing, however, with percentages of Hispanic, multiracial, Asian, and Native Hawaiian/Pacific Islander people rising most rapidly (Henry J. Kaiser Family Foundation, 2014; USCB, 2011, Table 6).

Language. With so many ethnic groups, many of which include large numbers of new immigrants, it should come as no surprise that a sizable number of U.S. residents—19.7%, to be specific—speak a language other than English at home (USCB, 2011, Table 54). The number is higher in large U.S. cities, where new immigrants tend to congregate. Of the 25 largest cities in the United States, in only four (Baltimore, Detroit, Indianapolis, and Memphis) do over 90% of residents speak English at home. In about half of those 25 largest cities, at least one-third of residents speak a language other than English at home. Most often, that language is Spanish (USCB, 2011, Table 55). See **Table 10.1** for details.

TABLE 10.1: Linguistic Diversity in the United States

CITY	% OF RESIDENTS WHO SPEAK A LANGUAGE OTHER THAN ENGLISH AT HOME
Los Angeles, CA	60.3
San Jose, CA	53.7
New York, NY	48.0
San Antonio, TX	45.7
Houston, TX	45.3
Dallas, TX	44.5
San Francisco, CA	44.3
Phoenix, AZ	38.9
San Diego, CA	38.2
Chicago, IL	36.1
Boston, MA	35.8
Austin, TX	35.6
Fort Worth, TX	33.8

At least one-third of the population of these 13 cities, each of which is among the 25 largest in the United States, speaks a language other than English (primarily Spanish) at home. Data from the United States Census Bureau, 2011.

Religion. The United States is primarily (81.1%) Christian, but about 1–2% of the population subscribes to each of these religions: Judaism, Islam, Buddhism, and Hinduism. A number of other religious groups are represented in smaller numbers as well. Within Christianity, there is notable diversity: approximately 24% Catholic, 18% Protestant, 22.1% Independent, 12.9% Evangelical, and 15.1% unaffiliated (Keller, 2014). About 12% of people describe themselves as nonreligious. In recent years, the trends among the country's religious diversity have included a decrease in the number of Christians and an increase in the number of non-Christian and nonreligious people (Pew Research Center, 2015).

Age. In the United States, about 5–7% of the population falls into each 5-year age range starting with the youngest children (0–4 years old) and continuing through middle age (54–59 years old). About 18% of the population is over 60, including about 6% over 75. That older demographic has grown in recent decades and is projected to continue to grow in the future. Since 1980, the average age of Americans has risen from 30 to almost 37 (USCB, 2011, Table 7).

Sexual Orientation. Sexual orientation rates depend on who is surveyed and how the surveys are conducted (as described in detail later in this chapter), but experts on

the subject typically agree that about 2–4% of the U.S. population identify as gay, lesbian, or bisexual (Gates & Newport, 2013). Rates differ widely across various parts of the country, with higher gay, lesbian, and bisexual rates in certain cities (for example, San Francisco, Portland, Maine, and Austin, Texas) than in other cities or rural areas (Newport & Gates, 2015; Laumann et al., 2004).

Education. Two significant milestones in U.S. education are high school and college graduation. About 85% of U.S. residents graduate from high school, but only about 28% graduate from college. At the lower end, about 6% don't even finish ninth grade. At the upper end, about 10% earn a graduate degree (USCB, 2011, Table 36).

Income. The median family income in the United States is about $63,000, but the range is tremendous, as illustrated in **Figure 10.1**. The lower end of the range (families making less than $20,000 per year) and the upper end of the range (families making over $150,000 per year) are roughly equal in number: about 11% each. When you consider that the upper end doesn't have an upper limit—it includes some families making many *millions* per year—you realize the tremendous economic diversity within the U.S. population (USCB, 2011, Table 36).

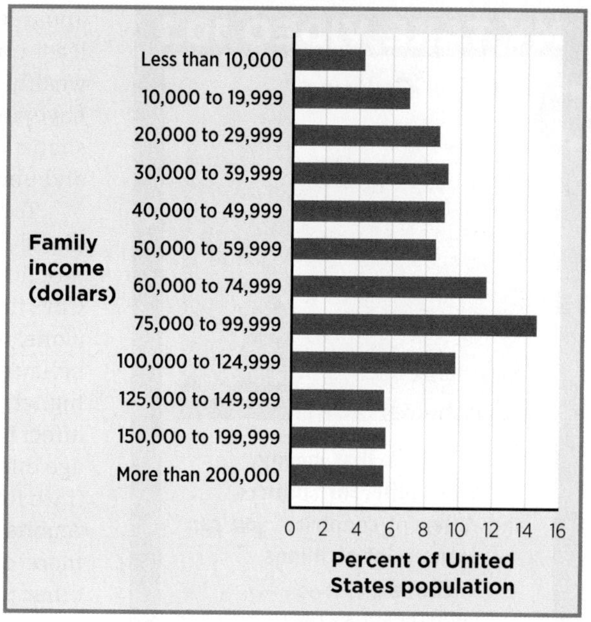

FIGURE 10.1 Economic Diversity in the United States. The economic diversity among U.S. families is great, ranging from extreme poverty to extreme wealth. Data from the United States Census Bureau, 2011, Table 36.

Big City or Small Town. About half of the U.S. population lives in the country's 39 largest cities (governing.com, 2015). Another 30% or so live in towns with at least 2500 people. The remaining approximately 20% live in rural areas, defined as towns with fewer than 2500 people (USCB, 2011, Table 29). That mix of cities, towns, and rural areas also shows up in a state-by-state comparison of population density. The roomiest states—such as Wyoming, Montana, North Dakota, and Alaska—have fewer than 10 people per square mile. The most crowded states—like Massachusetts, New Jersey, Rhode Island, and Connecticut—have over 70 times that many people per square mile (USCB, 2011, Table 13).

We just considered each of these diversity variables separately, but they exist in different combinations in different people. Each of us has a race or ethnicity *and* a religion *and* an economic level *and* a sexual orientation, and so on. To discuss that combination, psychologists often use the term *intersectionality*. The term emphasizes that each person lives at the intersection of his or her own combination of diversity factors. When psychologists (and researchers in other fields) study intersectionality, they often focus on the struggles of people whose combination of diversity factors is the least privileged or most oppressed within a society. For example, researchers might study people who face discrimination (due to race, ethnicity, gender, sexual orientation, etc.) and simultaneously live in poverty. In recent years, psychologists have increasingly explored ways to work toward social justice and equity to minimize the negative psychological consequences experienced by many people living at such unfortunate intersections (Rosenthal, 2016; Cole, 2009; Lewis et al., 2015; Carbado et al., 2013; Crenshaw, 1991).

The main point of all the numbers we reviewed in this section is to demonstrate just how much diversity surrounds you. Each of the diversity variables we considered—race and ethnicity, language, religion, age, sexual orientation, education, money, and population density—all span wide ranges. Collectively, these variables produce an incredibly diverse national profile. All of these variables can contribute to *culture* as well, a topic to which we turn now.

What Constitutes a Culture?

A **culture** is a set of shared beliefs, values, and patterns of behavior within a group of people. The qualities that tie a cultural group together can be any number of things. For example, culture can form around any type of diversity—including sex, gender, race, ethnicity, religion, age, education, and so on. Some of these qualities might seem

culture
A group of similar people who share beliefs, values, and patterns of behavior.

MY TAKE VIDEO 10.1

Culture

"I think that moving from different cultures and different countries, you can learn a lot of things..."

YOUTUBE: http://tiny.cc/mytake
LAUNCHPAD: launchpadworks.com

apparent when you first meet someone. Other qualities might not be so apparent, at least until you get to know them—including religious beliefs, amount of education or wealth, and even race or ethnicity. Any of those qualities, and many others too, can have an important impact on how you live your life. Specifically, those qualities can shape your **worldview**: a comprehensive, culturally influenced way of approaching and understanding the world around you.

To illustrate some real differences in culture and worldview, let's consider two people of different cultural backgrounds. To keep it simple, let's focus on just three characteristics: age, race/ethnicity, and religion. Jasmin is 25 years old, African American, and Christian. Asmita is 75 years old, Indian, and Hindu. Based on these three qualities alone, what differences might you expect between Jasmin's and Asmita's beliefs and behaviors? The religious difference could affect what either woman believes about higher powers and what happens after we die. The race/ethnicity difference could affect the holidays the women celebrate and the roles they fill within their families. The age difference could affect their approaches to dating, education, and technology. Even if we limit ourselves to considering just these three qualities, it is clear that Jasmin and Asmita may have very different cultural experiences. Just imagine if there were even more differences—if one were male and the other female, if one were rich and the other poor, if one lived in a huge city and the other lived in a rural area, or if one were a high school dropout and the other had a graduate degree. Their cultural worlds might be incredibly different.

Wait, if we assume that people are different just because of their cultural qualities, aren't we prejudging them?

Great point. We certainly don't want our efforts to appreciate culture to accidentally morph into prejudice (or stereotyping or discrimination, for that matter). That is why it is so important to use **dynamic sizing**: the ability to simultaneously know the norm for a group *and* recognize that the norm might not apply to every member of that group. When you consider another person's culture, you want to know what is typical for that culture, but you don't want to assume that every person is typical (Sue, 1998, 2006).

There are differences not only between but also *within* cultural groups. Let's consider Jasmin and Asmita again. Without dynamic sizing, someone might look at their ages and assume that they live in different worlds when it comes to technology: Jasmin practically lives online, while Asmita has far less interest in anything computer-related. But with dynamic sizing, you would at least consider the possibility that Jasmin or Asmita doesn't fit the norm for her respective generation. Perhaps Asmita uses Facebook, Twitter, Instagram, and Skype, while Jasmin doesn't even have a smartphone. You can't be sure until you get to know each of them. Dynamic sizing doesn't mean blindness to cultural norms, just flexibility in applying them to specific people.

LIFE HACK 10.1

Use dynamic sizing when you meet someone from a different cultural background. Think of what is common in that person's culture, but remember that the person might be uncommon.

(Sue, 1998, 2006)

Defining Culture. Over the history of psychology, there has been some debate and some change about exactly what constitutes a culture. When psychology began to give cultural issues serious attention (around the 1960s and 1970s), culture was essentially defined as race/ethnicity. In the United States and around the world, race/ethnicity has been a powerful factor in many interpersonal interactions, from education to employment to wars. But as time has gone by, psychologists have expanded the definition of culture (Triandis, 2007; Fukuyama et al., 2014; Pedersen, 1999; Sue et al., 1996; Arredondo et al., 1996).

Today, there are lots of variables besides race/ethnicity that psychologists consider culturally relevant. We discussed many of them earlier in this chapter as we considered the diversity of the population: age, religion, education level, socioeconomic status, sexual orientation, and urban or rural setting. But the list can certainly expand beyond that. Gender, of course, is an important cultural variable (and one to which we will

IT'S LIKE...

Dynamic Sizing Is Like Appreciating Brittney Griner's Height

Women, as a group, are shorter than men. Your experience tells you that, and so do the facts: Average height for grown women in the United States is 5 feet, 3.8 inches, compared to 5 feet, 9.3 inches for men (Centers for Disease Control and Prevention, 2012). But that doesn't mean that every woman falls near the women's average, and every man falls near the men's average. Consider Brittney Griner. She's the 6-foot, 8-inch basketball star who earned All-American honors and won an NCAA championship at Baylor, then became an all-star and a WNBA champion with the Phoenix Mercury. Brittney Griner towers over almost every woman *and* man she meets.

So, two things are true: (1) *As a group*, women tend to be about 5 feet, 4 inches tall; and (2) *as an individual member of that group*, Brittney Griner is much taller than that. Appreciating both of those facts at the same time is just like dynamic sizing.

When psychologists consider culture, they simultaneously consider what is common within that culture and the possibility that a particular member of that culture might not be so common. For example, someone from an individualistic country might be very collectivistic. Or, someone who is old might act very young. Or, someone from a big city might have small-town values. There is lots of variation within any cultural group, just like there is lots of height variation within a gender. Dynamic sizing reminds us that not everyone within a group has characteristics typical of that group, which helps us to avoid stereotyping and prejudice. ●

On average, women tend to be shorter than men. But at 6 ft 8 in, WNBA star Brittney Griner towers above almost all women *and* men. Her exceptional height serves as a reminder of the importance of dynamic sizing: the ability to simultaneously know the norm for a group *and* recognize that the norm might not apply to every member of that group. Dynamic sizing can be especially helpful in appreciating differences within a cultural group. David Sherman/Getty Images

devote significant time later in this chapter). Some have also argued for the importance of other cultural variables too, like disability status and region (within the country).

One way to determine whether a characteristic is culturally important is to ask yourself whether you would experience *culture shock* if you found your situation changed tomorrow. Culture shock is feeling disoriented or bewildered with an unfamiliar situation. For example, consider a 78-year-old man who lives in a retirement home. If he moved to a college residence hall, would he experience culture shock? How about a lifelong resident of the south side of Chicago: Would she experience culture shock if she found herself living in a small mining town in West Virginia? Or a prisoner who has been locked up for years: Does culture shock come with a new life on the outside? There is a good chance that these situations would cause culture shock, at least to some degree, since they would both involve significant change in some fundamental aspects of daily life.

Subcultures. Regarding the question of what constitutes a culture, the list could include what some people would consider *subcultures*: for example, military culture, prison culture, even cultures of specific professions or political parties. In my own therapy practice, I have learned to appreciate not only my clients' cultures, but their subcultures as well. With Dylan, a 19-year-old college sophomore, I learned not to even offer 8 A.M. appointments. The college student culture in which he lived—in the college residence hall where students often stayed up late studying, talking, or partying—made it practically impossible for him. As he once reminded me: "You know 8 A.M. is like the middle of the night for me, right?" With Amy, a stay-at-home mom of twin 6-month-olds, I came to respect the "baby culture" in which she and so many of her friends were immersed. In this baby culture, parents' work, sleep, and sex lives revolved around nap times, bath times, and diaper changes. And, according to Amy, almost everybody had traded in their cool cars for minivans. With David, a high-ranking executive at a Fortune 500 firm, I realized that the overriding expectation in his corporate culture was

worldview
A comprehensive, culturally influenced way of approaching and understanding the world around you.

dynamic sizing
The ability to simultaneously know the norm for a group and recognize that the norm might not apply to every member of that group.

that the job always comes first. David often missed out on important family events and even took phone calls from his coworkers during our therapy sessions. Dylan, Amy, and David each live in a world affected not only by widely recognized cultural variables, but also specific subcultures.

Studies have shown that clients like and benefit from a therapist's cultural sensitivity, because they feel like the therapist respects them, cares about them, and "gets" them (Fuertes et al., 2006; Constantine, 2002; Atkinson et al., 1992; Gim et al., 1991). This cultural appreciation is not just for the benefit of therapists and their clients, however. It is also for anyone who hopes to better understand the factors that influence the lives of everyone.

CHECK YOUR LEARNING:

10.1 In what ways is the United States a diverse nation?

10.2 What is culture, and how does it influence a person's worldview?

10.3 What is dynamic sizing, and why is it important to appreciating differences within a group?

10.4 How has the definition of *culture* changed over the years?

Multiculturalism

YOU WILL LEARN:

10.5 what multiculturalism is and how important it has become in psychology.

10.6 how the understanding of cultural differences has changed over the years.

10.7 how multiculturalism is reflected in psychology today.

10.8 what acculturation is.

10.9 about different acculturation strategies.

10.10 what acculturative stress is.

10.11 about specific ways in which cultures differ from each other.

10.12 about differences that diversity makes in everyday life.

10.13 what cultural intelligence is.

10.14 what microaggressions are.

Multiculturalism is a psychological approach that highlights the importance and value of multiple cultural groups within a society. Let's explore the topic of multiculturalism, beginning with a consideration of the role multiculturalism has played over the years.

The Importance of Multiculturalism in Psychology

In the earliest years of psychology, cultural issues received almost no attention. With rare exceptions, psychology was a science by and for White men (Guthrie, 2004; Hilgard et al., 1991; Scarborough & Furumoto, 1987). In the 1960s and 1970s, issues of culture, especially race/ethnicity and gender, started to appear in the field. This happened, in part, because more ethnic minorities and women were contributing to psychological research, and their contributions were increasingly focused on topics related to their own cultural characteristics. The prominence of cultural issues grew through the 1980s and then exploded in the 1990s and 2000s, as the U.S. population and the members of the psychology profession continued to become more diverse.

Today, multiculturalism is undoubtedly a dominant movement in psychology. In fact, some have called it *the* dominant movement in psychology, going so far as to label it the "fourth force" in psychology's history (Pedersen, 1990, 1999, 2008). The three major forces that came before—Sigmund Freud's psychoanalysis, B. F. Skinner's behaviorism, and Carl Rogers's humanism (all of which are covered in Chapter 12)—can all be enhanced by multiculturalism (Hall, 2014; Bugental, 1964). Multiculturalism blends with other approaches to psychology, enabling them to be adapted and customized for members of diverse cultural groups.

Understanding Cultural Differences. The way that psychologists understand cultural differences has changed as multiculturalism has become more integrated in the field. This change has taken place in four stages (Leong, 2014; Leong et al., 2012a,b). At first, psychologists used a *deficit model* to understand cultural differences. This model suggests that a difference is a deficit—specifically, a difference from the White

male perspective. So, if psychologists recognized that women or members of racial/ethnic minorities did anything differently, that difference was seen as an inherent, built-in shortcoming in comparison to the "right" way—the way that White males did it. The obvious problem with this approach is that no one group does things in an objectively "right" way, which means that other ways shouldn't be viewed as deficits.

The deficit model was replaced by the *culturally disadvantaged model*, which said that the shortcomings were socially created (rather than inherent or built-in). The idea of the deficit was still there, but now the deficit was due to nurture (rather than nature)—including poverty, malnutrition, poor parenting, second-rate schooling, and so on. The same problem still existed, though: No single group's behavior should be seen as "right," with other groups being inferior by comparison.

Thankfully, a big shift came with the *cultural pluralism model*, the basic idea of which is that a cultural difference is *not* a deficiency. According to cultural pluralism, neither the White male way of doing things, nor any other particular way of doing things, is better than any other. Each cultural group brings its own unique approach, and each cultural group represents naturally occurring variation within the human species.

The most recent model is the *positive psychology model*, which not only rejects the idea that cultural difference is deficiency, but goes a step further and argues that the unique qualities of each culture are strengths and virtues worthy of celebration. As an example, consider speech patterns. Specifically, consider how the typical speech patterns of White men might differ from those of women or racial/ethnic minority groups—everything from sentence structure to vocabulary to the underlying purpose of conversations. Decades ago, that different style of speaking would have been viewed as an inborn deficiency, or a bit later, as a deficiency caused by an inferior environment. More recently, those different styles of speaking would be recognized as equally legitimate to any other, or applauded as uniquely impressive and worthy.

Multiculturalism in Contemporary Psychology. Today, the importance of multiculturalism in psychology is obvious. The American Psychological Association now includes quite a few divisions devoted to multicultural or diversity-related topics, including Division 35 (Society for the Psychology of Women), Division 36 (Society for the Psychology of Religion and Spirituality), Division 44 (Society for the Psychological Study of Lesbian, Gay, Bisexual, and Transgender Issues), Division 45 (Society for the Psychological Study of Culture, Ethnicity, and Race), and Division 51 (Society for the Psychological Study of Men and Masculinity). There are dozens of professional psychology journals that regularly publish articles on multicultural topics (see a sampling of journals in **Table 10.2**), and the number of books on multicultural topics is staggering.

Recent revisions of the profession's Code of Ethics have added numerous standards requiring psychologists to do therapy, assessment, and research with sensitivity to

Multiculturalism is a psychological approach that highlights the importance and value of multiple cultural groups within a society. The approach has become increasingly common, and multiculturalism has become an important topic of study in the field of psychology. [a] Susan Chiang/Getty Images [b] Peopleimages/Getty Images [c] Frank Sanchez/Alamy

TABLE 10.2: Psychology Journals That Focus on Multicultural Topics

Cultural Diversity & Ethnic Minority Psychology	*Journal of Gender, Culture, and Health*
Hispanic Journal of Behavioral Sciences	*Journal of Multicultural Counseling and Development*
Journal of Black Psychology	*Journal of Latina/o Psychology*
Journal of Cross-Cultural Psychology	*Psychology of Men and Masculinity*
International Perspectives in Psychology: Research, Practice, Consultation	*Asian American Journal of Psychology*
Psychology of Religion and Spirituality	*Psychology of Sexual Orientation and Gender Diversity*
Psychology of Women Quarterly	*Journal of Rural Mental Health*
Psychology and Aging	*Journal of Language and Social Psychology*

multiculturalism
An approach in psychology that highlights the importance and value of multiple cultural groups within a society.

Sensitivity related to cultural issues is especially crucial for psychologists who do therapy and assessment. The standards of the profession require it, and clients benefit from it. Pressmaster/Shutterstock

cultural issues (American Psychological Association, 2010). For example, if Dr. Yancey (who is Christian) has a therapy session with Aaron (who is Jewish), Dr. Yancey has an ethical obligation to appreciate and respect Aaron's viewpoint and his experience of religiously relevant events. Likewise, if Dr. Yancey (a U.S. psychologist) is going to give an intelligence test to Reka, who recently moved to the United States from Hungary, Dr. Yancey has an ethical obligation to think about several factors as he chooses, administers, and interprets the results of the test: Reka's linguistic abilities, Reka's understanding of the purpose of the test, and how Reka's cultural background might influence some of her answers.

Speaking of tests, the makers of psychology's most widely respected intelligence tests, personality tests, and other assessment tools have gone to great lengths to make their tests more culture-fair than such tests were in the early and mid-1900s. Rather than asking questions that only people with certain cultural backgrounds might answer correctly, or using images only of one cultural group, they have deliberately created questions and images that are more accessible and recognizable to a wider range of people.

The *Diagnostic and Statistical Manual of Mental Disorders* (DSM), the book that lists and defines all of the disorders that psychologists use to diagnose their clients, covers more culture than it ever has too (American Psychiatric Association, 2013). Compared to earlier editions, DSM now includes lots of information about how various disorders might be experienced differently by members of different cultures. For example, in some Asian countries, social anxiety centers on making *others* uncomfortable in social situations rather than feeling uncomfortable yourself.

DSM also gives psychologists a heads-up about certain psychological problems that are unique to certain cultures ("Cultural Concepts of Distress"). For example, *susto* (an experience in which psychological and physical symptoms follow a frightening event that causes the soul to leave the body) is unique to some Latinos. For another example, *maladi moun* (an experience in which a malicious or envious person can "send" depression or other psychological problems to another) is unique to some Haitians. Together, all of these developments across psychology show that multiculturalism has earned a prominent place in the field.

So, is multiculturalism the same thing as the "melting pot" idea?

Not exactly. Think about a melting pot in the literal sense: The fate of the ingredients is to melt away, to lose their unique flavor as they fade into the preexisting contents of the pot (Berry, 2003; Sam, 2006). That is a metaphor that became popular in the United States for quite a while, but a patchwork quilt is a better metaphor for the multicultural approach. In a patchwork quilt, each patch retains its unique identity, while at the same time being an integral part of the whole quilt. In much the same way, multiculturalism encourages members of diverse cultural groups to both join in with the larger society and to hold on to special aspects of their own heritage.

As an example, consider the Zhang family, who immigrated from China to the United States. They might choose to watch fireworks on the Fourth of July, sign their kids up for hockey teams, and eat plenty of burgers and fries. But they might also choose to continue to celebrate the Chinese New Year, play competitive table tennis, and eat seaweed soup and Peking duck. The multicultural approach, more than the melting-pot approach, suggests that there's room for both cultures.

Acculturation: Managing Multiple Cultures

The Zhang family's move from China to the United States raises the issue of **acculturation**: managing a life that involves the coexistence of more than one culture. Acculturation is basically how much to hold on to your old culture and how much

to accept the new one. It is a massive issue for increasing numbers of people in countries around the globe. Some may seek a new home by choice, but many others are forced from their homelands due to conditions made unlivable like natural disasters, war, poverty, or famine (Sam & Berry, 2006).

Acculturation poses a challenge not only for immigrants or refugees looking to permanently relocate, but also for people whose stays are more temporary, like international students, military personnel, expatriate workers, and long-term tourists (van Oudenhoven, 2006; Bochner, 1994; Allen et al., 2006; Donà & Ackermann, 2006). Acculturation can even become relevant to the indigenous population—the people who were already there—especially when many members of another culture arrive together around the same time, bringing their culture with them (Kvernmo, 2006).

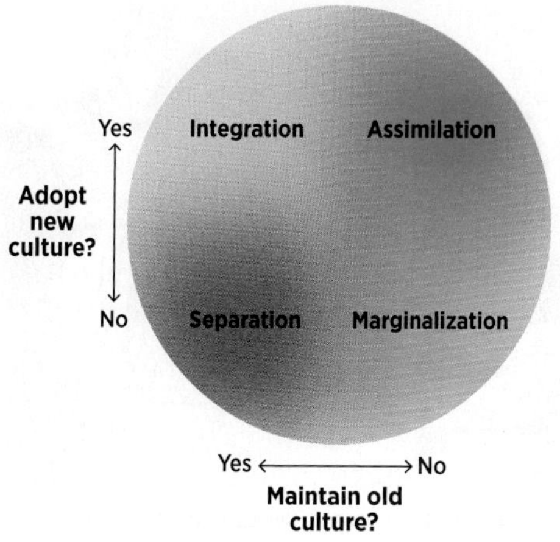

FIGURE 10.2 Acculturation Strategies. There are four assimilation strategies, involving a combination of attitudes toward the old and new cultures. Notice that the boundaries between them are fuzzy—people often choose a middle ground, or drift from one strategy to another. Information from Berry, 2003.

Acculturation Strategies. Acculturation strategies are determined by how the person answers two questions: (1) To what extent will I retain my previous culture? (2) To what extent will I embrace my new culture? As **Figure 10.2** shows, there are four distinct strategies for approaching acculturation: *assimilation, separation, marginalization*, and *integration* (Berry, 1980, 2003; Rivera, 2010):

- **Assimilation** is an acculturation strategy in which the person adopts the new culture and rejects the old culture. For members of the Zhang family, assimilation might mean dropping any connection to language, religion, customs, clothing, food, or other elements of their life in China and entering the U.S. mainstream as much as possible. Assimilation is the acculturation strategy that most closely matches the melting pot idea (Berry, 2006a).
- **Separation** is an acculturation strategy in which the person retains the old culture and rejects the new culture. For the Zhang family, separation might involve choosing to live among Chinese neighbors, to speak Mandarin rather than English, and to eat exactly what they ate in China, all without adopting any part of a more mainstream U.S. lifestyle.
- **Marginalization** is an acculturation strategy in which the person rejects both the new culture and the old culture. For the Zhang family, marginalization might mean not celebrating any U.S. or Chinese holidays, and not forming close connections with the Chinese or mainstream American communities.
- **Integration** is an acculturation strategy in which the person adopts both the new culture and the old culture. For the Zhang family, integration might mean embracing the holidays, sports, food, and other elements of both mainstream U.S. and Chinese lifestyles. Integration is the acculturation strategy that most closely matches the multicultural approach (Berry, 2006a).

Think of these four approaches to acculturation along two dimensions, one that measures attachment to new culture, and another that measures attachment to old culture. Over time, people might adjust their acculturation strategies, moving up or down one of the dimensions, as they spend more time in the new culture (Rudmin & Ahmadzadeh, 2001; Rudmin, 2003; Ryder et al., 2000).

Acculturative Stress. Living between two cultures often causes **acculturative stress**: the physical or psychological stress that comes from acculturation. Acculturative stress can include lots of things that immigrants and other newcomers to cultural groups often experience: language difficulties; pressure to dress, speak, or behave in a certain way; harassment and discrimination; and lack of necessary skills or knowledge (Birman & Simon, 2014; Berry, 1970, 2006b). Most of those stressors come from members of the new, larger group (in the Zhangs' case, mainstream U.S. culture).

There can also be pressure from members of the person's group (in the Zhangs' case, other Chinese or Asian immigrants) to conform and stay true to their roots

acculturation
Managing a life that involves the coexistence of more than one culture.

assimilation
An acculturation strategy in which the person adopts the new culture and rejects the old culture.

separation
An acculturation strategy in which the person retains the old culture and rejects the new culture.

marginalization
An acculturation strategy in which the person rejects both the new culture and the old culture.

integration
An acculturation strategy in which the person adopts both the new culture and the old culture.

acculturative stress
The physical or psychological stress that comes from acculturation.

Acculturative stress takes many forms. Sometimes, it comes from the person's new culture. Other times, it comes from members of the person's culture, such as pressure to stay true to one's roots. mbbirdy/ Getty Images

(Contrada et al., 2001; French & Chavez, 2010). One study found that among Latino college students, pressure to conform to their own group was a significant factor in their overall life satisfaction (Ojeda et al., 2012). These pressures to conform could include dating and hanging out with other Latinos, listening to the music that other Latinos listen to, or dressing like other Latinos dress. Another study found similar results for U.S. college students of Asian descent: The pressure to conform to their own group predicted anxiety better than any other variable the researchers examined, including perceived discrimination and concern about fulfilling stereotypes (French et al., 2013). Similar observations have been made about African American students teasing each other for being "too White" when they get good grades (Contrada et al., 2000).

Among the four acculturation strategies, integration has consistently been linked with the best adaptation to stress and the fewest psychological problems. Marginalization, on the other hand, typically produces the worst results in terms of stress management and overall mental health. The two strategies that involve choosing one culture over the other—assimilation and separation—fall somewhere in between (Nguyen, 2006; Berry et al., 2006b; Berry & Sam, 1997). Other factors that predict good adjustment to acculturation stress include an agreeable, extraverted, stable personality; young age (preschool kids adjust better than older kids and adults); plenty of education and money; and high levels of social support from both the new and the old cultures (Kosic, 2006; Ward et al., 2004; Berry, 2006b; Kealey, 1989; Berry et al., 1987).

How Do Cultures Differ?

It is pretty clear that there are differences between cultures. But how, specifically, do they differ?

Of course, there are the outward signs of culture, like the clothes people wear, the food they eat, the religious texts they read, and the customs they maintain. But what about underlying cultural values that shape those outward signs of culture and the beliefs that maintain them?

One researcher, Geert Hofstede, conducted a massive, long-term study of IBM employees beginning in the late 1960s that answers this question. In the study, Hofstede asked IBM workers from 50 different countries to describe the characteristics they noticed in their colleagues from other countries. From thousands of their responses, he started to piece together the underlying values of people from many different cultures. He then boiled these values down to just four fundamental values that diverse cultures hold (Hofstede, 1980). In recent years, Hofstede and other researchers have continued this line of research with other populations in even more countries, and the more recent research has confirmed the existence of his four original cultural values and added two more (Hofstede et al., 2010; Hofstede & Hofstede, 2001; Minkov & Hofstede, 2010, 2011; Minkov, 2013). Let's discuss each of those six values.

FIGURE 10.3 Individualism and Collectivism Around the World. Individualism is much higher in Western countries such as the United States, Canada, Australia, and some parts of Europe. Collectivism is much higher in Asia, South America, the Middle East, and Africa. (Measurements from many countries are missing, as indicated in white on this map.) Information from Hofstede & Hofstede, 2001.

Individualism Versus Collectivism. **Individualism** is a worldview that emphasizes the well-being of the individual over the well-being of the group. Its opposite, **collectivism**, is a worldview that emphasizes the well-being of the group over the well-being of the individual. As **Figure 10.3** shows, generally, U.S. culture leans toward individualism. By contrast, some other countries, especially many from Asia, lean toward collectivism (Oyserman et al., 2002; Triandis et al., 1988). (Of course, there's plenty of variation *within* the cultural groups too—some people within each culture lean the opposite way.)

The contrast between strongly individualistic cultures and strongly collectivistic cultures is striking. People from individualistic cultures tend to be driven more by this question: "What's best for *me*?" People from collectivistic cultures tend to be driven instead by this question: "What's best for *us*?" For people in collectivistic cultures, *us* can be defined in any number of ways, from a friendship to a romantic relationship to a family or a group of coworkers (Brewer & Chen, 2007; Hui & Triandis, 1986).

At one point in my psychotherapy practice, I had two clients who were each 22-year-old college seniors. Both were applying to law school, and both were equally strong applicants. David, who had more individualistic values, told me about how he decided where to apply: "Here's what I'm looking for: a law school with a great reputation, that specializes in the areas of law I want to practice, and that's in a big city." He applied to about 10 such schools, all around the country, and bought himself a congratulatory new big-screen TV when he got into his top choice, which was a thousand miles away. Mia, who had more collectivistic values, approached her application decisions differently: "I'm only applying to law schools here in town. My parents are nearby, and I might need to help take care of them. They're getting older, you know. Plus, there's that family I nanny for part-time. I don't want to make them go through the hassle of finding someone else. And my boyfriend, he didn't exactly come out and say it, but he made it pretty clear that he doesn't want to do a long-distance thing." She got into a local law school and maintained all of those previous relationships while attending.

Large Versus Small Power Distance. A culture with a large power distance is a power structure, or hierarchy, in which the people on the top have way more power than the people on the bottom. This cultural power structure is much like that at many large corporations: The boss can make big changes that have major effects on lower-level workers and there is nothing the lower-level workers can do about it.

By contrast, in a culture with a small power distance, the distance between people with varying levels of power is much smaller. In fact, in some of these cultures, there is little difference in power: Everyone has nearly the same amount of power, and leadership is often shared or rotating. As an example, consider how a family decides when a child should get their first smartphone. In a family with a large power difference, the decision belongs to the parent absolutely. In a family with a small power difference the decision may ultimately be the parent's to make, but the child may have much more input on the decision.

Assertiveness Versus Caring. Some cultures are much more assertive and cutthroat than others. In these cultures, most interactions are competitions, with clear winners and losers. Strangers are not to be helped, or even trusted. Instead, the best strategy is to remain vigilant and protect yourself. In these cultures, assertiveness is the undercurrent of daily life.

In other cultures, that undercurrent is caring. Strangers are befriended, and even those who might otherwise be called losers because of their low social or economic status are respected. Vigilance is not a pressing need, because other people are trustworthy. Hofstede often referred to the assertive approach as traditionally masculine, and the caring approach as traditionally feminine, but it is worth noting that this cultural value affects members of both genders.

Avoidance Versus Acceptance of Uncertainty. In some cultures, tradition is everything and it pressures people to think, feel, and behave in certain ways, depending on the situation. This way, there is no uncertainty or ambivalence to cause anxiety. Other cultures embrace that uncertainty or ambivalence. They welcome new ideas and novel situations. They have fewer laws and social guidelines (both official and unspoken) to restrict people's behavior. They allow plenty of debate between various viewpoints, rather than insisting that one particular viewpoint is the only truth.

CHAPTER APP 10.1

Multiculturalism

CultureCompass

Preview one of the links and consider the following questions.

WEBSITE: http://tiny.cc/6ei7jy

ANDROID: http://tiny.cc/0a92iy

IPHONE: http://tiny.cc/j582iy

VIDEO DEMO: http://tiny.cc/chapterapps

This app allows you to compare various pairs of countries in terms of many meaningful cultural variables, including individualism versus collectivism.

How does it APPly to your daily life?
How could this app help you gain cultural competence? How can this app help you become more appreciative of diverse cultures? How could psychologists and other therapists benefit from this app in terms of their treatment of clients from various cultures?

How does it APPly to your understanding of psychology?
How does this app affect your appreciation of how cultures differ?

individualism
A worldview that emphasizes the well-being of the individual over the well-being of the group.

collectivism
A worldview that emphasizes the well-being of the group over the well-being of the individual.

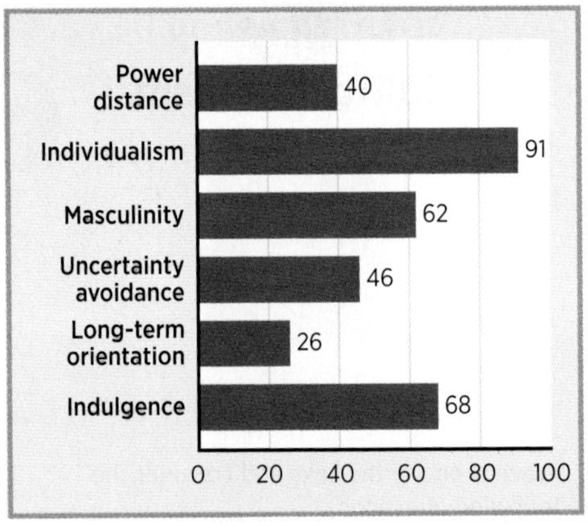

FIGURE 10.4 The Cultural Characteristics of the United States. The United States, according to this profile, has a culture high in individualism and indulgence, and low on long-term orientation. Data from The Hofstede Center (http://geert-hofstede.com/united-states.html).

Long- Versus Short-Term Orientation. People in cultures with a long-term orientation keep an eye on distant goals, and they work hard to reach them, often by saving their money and adapting when the going gets tough. By contrast, in cultures with shorter-term orientations, quick results are more important, and goals that bring immediate results are a high priority. In other words, rather than savers, they are spenders.

Indulgence Versus Restraint. In some cultures, it is all about the current moment and it is OK to indulge in what feels good now. In other cultures, the mentality is much more controlled and reserved. People in these cultures tend to put off immediate pleasure and instead prefer a stoic, muted way of life.

No short list of cultural characteristics can capture all of the complex and subtle differences between cultures, but these six characteristics describe a good portion of those differences. **Figure 10.4** shows a profile for the United States on all six of these cultural characteristics. (You can compare the United States to any other country with Chapter App 10.1.) You'll see that the United States is remarkably high in individualism, has a short-term orientation, and is a bit more indulgent than restrained. If you compare the United States to South Korea (as an example), you'll notice drastic differences in individualism, long-term orientation, and indulgence versus restraint, as well as mild differences on the other variables. The point here is that countries around the world differ widely on some important, measurable cultural characteristics.

What Difference Does Diversity Make?

It is clear that cultural groups differ from each other in many meaningful ways, but what does all that difference mean in your day-to-day life? Which specific behaviors, thoughts, and feelings might relate to your membership in a particular ethnicity, religion, or other cultural group? The answers are actually sprinkled throughout this book. Every chapter offers some information (usually highlighted by a Diversity Matters tag) about how culture influences different experiences. Now let's take a look at a sampling of the many ways that diversity makes a difference.

Differences in Defining Identity. When people from more individualistic cultures are asked to describe themselves, they tend to do so, well, individualistically. On the other hand, when people from more collectivistic cultures are asked to describe themselves, they describe themselves in connection to others (Rhee et al., 1995). In one study, researchers gave both Mexican American and White middle-schoolers the same open-ended prompt: Describe yourself. The Mexican American kids were more likely to use adjectives that implied a relationship to another person, like helpful or cooperative. The White kids were more likely to use adjectives that described personal, independent qualities, like smart and energetic (Dabul et al., 1995).

In another study, people from Malaysia (collectivistic) were compared to people from Australia and Britain (individualistic) in terms of how they finished this sentence: "I am _____." The Malaysians were much more likely to give responses that showed membership in a family or group, like "I am a daughter" or "I am a Muslim." Australians and Brits were more likely to describe their personal traits or characteristics, with no reference to other people: "I am honest," "I am intelligent," and so on (Bochner, 1994). In a similar study, Indian college students were more likely to mention a social role when describing themselves ("I am a student," "I am an Indian"), but Americans were more likely to evaluate themselves ("I am trustworthy," "I am clever," "I am good-looking") (Dhawan et al., 1995).

Differences in Raising Children. Parents with low levels of education and socioeconomic status are more likely to use physical punishment such as spanking

(Dietz, 2000). Physical punishment is also most common in the Southern region of the United States and least common in the Northeast; more common among certain ethnicities (African American and Latinos, in most studies) than others; and more common among people from members of certain conservative religious groups (Gershoff, 2002; Straus & Stewart, 1999). On a separate note, kids in less industrialized countries (like Guatemala and Republic of the Congo) often have very different day-to-day experiences than kids in more industrialized countries such as the United States (Medin et al., 2007). Among other things, their parents often give them more household duties, including babysitting their younger siblings, at a much younger age, even 5–7 years old (Morelli et al., 2003).

Differences in Feelings. Generally speaking, most people in most cultures report feeling happy in most areas of their lives (Biswas-Diener et al., 2005). This overall happiness is reflected in a study that asked residents of 149 nations around the world about their overall happiness and found that only 25% of nations had an average below 5 on a scale of 0–10. But the study revealed significant variability across cultures too. Some countries had averages above 8, and others had averages below 3 (Veenhoven, 2012a,b). (**Table 10.3** has some specific examples.)

There are other cultural differences in happiness too, especially in terms of what makes people happy and just how happy they tend to get (Mesquita & Leu, 2007; Tov & Diener, 2007). For example, in one study, U.S. and Asian students read another student's diary entry that included some positive events, like getting the highest score in the class on a test. When asked what that student is feeling when the positive event happens, U.S. students reported only good feelings. However, Asian students reported a mix of good and bad feelings—with the bad feelings often related to interpersonal consequences like jealousy or envy (Leu et al., 2010).

In another study, U.S. and Asian students filled out questionnaires about their emotions four times a day (3 P.M., 6 P.M., 9 P.M., and midnight) for 8 consecutive days. They were asked to write down and rate the last feeling they had right before completing the questionnaire. Overall, Asian students reported feelings near a neutral level (neither pleasant nor unpleasant), but U.S. students reported feelings significantly above neutral and well into the "pleasant" range (Mesquita & Karasawa, 2002).

Even particular feelings can take on different connotations in different cultures. For example, people in more individualistic cultures like the United States and Australia typically experience pride as a good feeling and guilt as a bad feeling. However, in more collectivistic cultures like China and Taiwan, pride is not always so good, and guilt is not always so bad (Eid & Diener, 2001).

Differences in Memory. When asked to share as many early childhood memories as they could in 5 minutes, people from the United States and Britain came up with about twice as many memories as people from China (Wang et al., 2004). The content of the memories differs as well. People from collectivistic cultures tend to remember group actions and interpersonal relationships, such as a family trip, or a special connection with a teacher. However, people from individualistic cultures tend to remember individual successes and failures, such as winning an award, or performing poorly on a test (Mullen, 1994; Wang & Ross, 2005; Wang & Conway, 2004; Wang, 2006). Also, when asked to remember past emotional experiences, people from individualistic cultures tend to focus on the positive feelings like their team winning a championship, or graduating from high school. People from collectivistic cultures, however, tend to focus more equally on positive and negative feelings (Oishi, 2002; Ross et al., 2002; Wang & Ross, 2005).

Differences in Seeing. People from diverse cultures actually see the world in different ways. For example, consider the *Müller-Lyer illusion*, which demonstrates that the figures attached to the ends of a line can influence how long you estimate the line to be. In **Figure 10.5** the two lines are actually the same length, but one may look

TABLE 10.3: How Happy Are You with Your Life?

COUNTRY	MEAN RATING (0 = UNSATISFIED; 10 = SATISFIED)
Costa Rica	8.5
Denmark	8.3
Iceland	8.2
Switzerland	8.0
Mexico	7.9
Finland	7.9
Norway	7.9
Sweden	7.8
Canada	7.8
Panama	7.8
...	...
Niger	3.8
Madagascar	3.7
Kenya	3.7
Congo (Brazzaville)	3.7
Sierra Leone	3.5
Zimbabwe	3.0
Benin	3.0
Burundi	2.9
Tanzania	2.8
Togo	2.6

On a scale of 0–10, residents of most countries around the world produced a mean above the midpoint of 5 when asked how happy they were with their current lives. The range was wide, however, with some countries producing means well above or below the midpoint. Of the 149 countries surveyed, the top 10 and bottom 10 are listed in the table. The mean for the United States was 7.3.
Data from Veenhoven, 2012a.

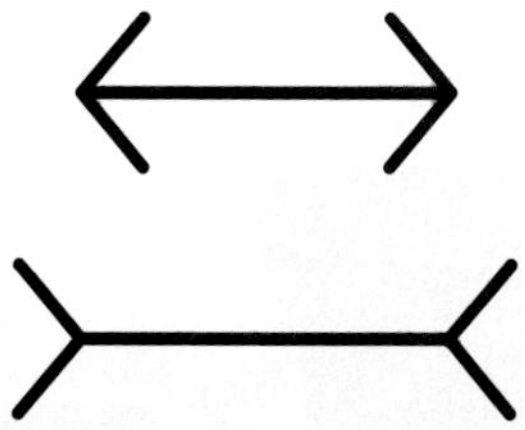

FIGURE 10.5 The Müller-Lyer Illusion. The extent to which these identical lines appear to be of different lengths actually depends on cultural background. People from cultures that are more "carpentered"—that is, people who have spent their lives around buildings and objects that are cut to exact specifications and feature plenty of perfect fits and clean angles—are more susceptible to this illusion than people from less "carpentered" cultures (Segall et al., 1966; Pedersen & Wheeler, 1983; Keith, 2012).

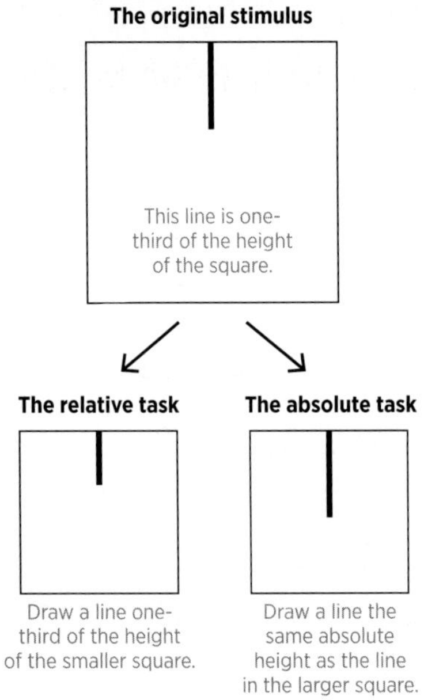

FIGURE 10.6 Seeing Parts in Isolation or in Context. People from collectivistic cultures are better at drawing the hanging line at the same proportion it was in the original square (as shown on the bottom left). However people from individualistic cultures are better at drawing the hanging line at the same absolute height it appeared in the original square, regardless of the size of the second square (as shown on the bottom right). Information from Kitayama et al., 2003.

longer than the other depending on whether the ends fold in (making an arrow shape) or fold out. Actually, the extent to which one looks longer than the other depends on the culture in which you have lived. People who spend their lives in "carpentered" environments—where the buildings feature lots of rectangular walls, doors, and windows, and the rooms feature lots of picture frames, bookshelves, and TVs with right angles—are much more susceptible to this illusion than people from "noncarpentered" environments, where the huts, tepees, and household items are more handmade and less manufactured (Segall et al., 1966; Pedersen & Wheeler, 1983; Keith, 2012; Norenzayan et al., 2007).

Another cultural difference in vision appears when people of Asian or U.S. backgrounds see a square with a small line hanging from the top (see **Figure 10.6**). When given a blank square of a different size and asked to add the hanging line to it, Americans are better at matching the exact length of the first hanging line (regardless of the size of the new square). However, Asians are better at matching the proportion of the hanging line to the new square (one-third the length of a new side). This difference suggests that people from collectivistic cultures tend to see items in context, while people from individualistic cultures tend to see items in isolation (Kitayama et al., 2003).

Differences in Seeking Help. In the United States, when people struggle with mental health problems, the odds that they seek professional help and stick with it depend on ethnicity and race (Meyer & Takeuchi, 2014). In general, ethnic and racial minorities seek help at much lower rates than Whites. Specifically, African Americans and Asian Americans are least likely to seek professional help for mental health problems, with Latinos only slightly higher (Padgett et al., 1994; Virnig et al., 2004; Meyer et al., 2009; Garland et al., 2014; Dobalian & Rivers, 2008).

Ethnic and racial minorities are also more likely than Whites to end treatment early (Wang, 2007). Researchers are trying to uncover the reasons for these differences, but the possibilities are many. The reasons include turning to family, friends, or religious leaders rather than mental health professionals; lack of trust in the mental health system; inability to find therapists culturally or linguistically similar to themselves; cultural values regarding shame and stigma of mental problems; and lack of the necessary money, insurance, transportation, or time (Snowden, 2007, 2012; Snowden & Yamada, 2005; Snowden et al., 2007, 2011).

Differences in Sex Life. Compared to college students in the United States, college students in China are less knowledgeable and experienced with sex. Specifically, Chinese college students lose their virginity later, have less premarital sex, have less oral sex, and participate in a narrower range of sexual activities than their U.S. counterparts (Tang et al., 1997). A study of ethnically diverse medical students found that those from the United States, Canada, Western Europe, and South Africa were much more liberal, while those from the Middle East and Asia were much more conservative (Leiblum et al., 2003).

Culture even impacts *why* people have sex (Hatfield et al., 2010). U.S. and Chinese college students both reported a high motivation to please their partners and strengthen the relationship, but the U.S. college students reported much higher rates of self-centered motives for sex, such as pleasure, stimulation, or stress reduction (Tang et al., 2012).

For "hooking up" on college campuses, ethnicity and race don't seem to matter much, but religion does. Specifically, students of higher levels of religious activity are much less likely to engage in hookups than the rest of their college classmates (Penhollow et al., 2007; Brimeyer & Smith, 2012; Fielder et al., 2013). Similarly, teens who attend religious services or youth activities, or whose families emphasize religion around the house, tend to become sexually active later and have fewer sexual partners (Hernandez et al., 2014; Rostosky et al., 2003; Haglund & Fehring, 2010; Miller & Gur, 2002; Manlove et al., 2008).

Diversity makes a difference in many areas of our lives, including how we feel, what we remember, and how we identify ourselves. It even makes a difference in how we use social media sites like Facebook. Brendan O'Sullivan/Getty Images

Differences in Facebook Pages. People from different cultural and demographic groups handle their Facebook pages in different ways (Alpizar et al., 2012; Park et al., 2012). For example, a study examining Facebook pages of 120 college students found that African American students revealed more about themselves in the About Me section, listed more group affiliations, and offered more extensive self-descriptions than White and Asian American students (DeAndrea et al., 2010).

Whites tend to post fewer selfies than African Americans or Latinos (Williams & Marquez, 2015). The specifics of selfies differ by culture too. Compared to Facebook users in Asia, Facebook users in the United States tend to post photos in which their face takes up a larger proportion of the frame, features of the background are blocked or cropped out, and their face is more emotionally expressive (Huang & Park, 2013). Facebook users in the United States tend to post far more positive self-presentations—photos and messages that emphasize how happy their life is and avoid any mention of negative events or feelings—than Facebook users in South Korea (Lee-Won et al., 2014).

There are Facebook differences with gender and age too. Women tend to disclose more to their Facebook friends than men do (just as they do with in-person relationships) (Sheldon, 2013). Older Facebook users tend to spend more time looking at family pictures and less time looking at posts from their same-age friends than younger Facebook users (McAndrew & Jeong, 2012).

Multicultural Know-How in Your Daily Life

It is great to *have* all of this knowledge about diversity, but it is even better to *use* it. Let's consider some ways you can apply this knowledge to your day-to-day life.

Cultural Intelligence. In other words, your life can be enriched by boosting your **cultural intelligence**: your ability to live and interact effectively in a multicultural society. Also known as *cultural competence*, cultural intelligence is what enables you to get along happily and productively with people of different ethnicities, races, religions, geographic locations, genders, sexual orientations, and more. For many of you, especially if you grew up in diverse neighborhoods or went to diverse schools, cultural intelligence has already been beneficial. For others, these college years are a period of significant cultural expansion, a time when you will meet and form relationships with people from backgrounds different from your own. For others, your postcollege careers will expose you to a variety of places and people far beyond what you've experienced before.

For example, consider Hannah, a White Christian woman who grew up in rural Minnesota. When she was a child, the people in her life were, with rare exceptions, homogeneous—same ethnicity, same religion, same lifestyle. That remained true through high school, but when she went to Rutgers University, a big school with more diversity than Hannah's hometown, she met and developed friendships with students from different parts of the country and different countries around the world.

After college, Hannah got a job in the marketing department at Ford Motor Company. That job not only took her to a big city (Detroit), but also introduced her to an even more diverse array of people, both at her site and on her travels around the United States and to many other parts of the world. At every step of her personal journey, Hannah relied on her cultural intelligence to appreciate the backgrounds of the people with whom she interacted, to form healthy and respectful relationships with them, and to work fruitfully together. In recent years, the realization that workers are more successful and satisfied when they have high levels of cultural intelligence has increasingly found its way into many industries, from business, military, and engineering to education, law enforcement, and health care (Livermore, 2015; Moran et al., 2009; Cushner & Mahon, 2009; Anand & Lahiri, 2009; Grandin & Hedderich, 2009; Earley & Mosakowski, 2004; Dresser, 2005).

CHAPTER APP 10.2

Cultural Intelligence

Vent

Preview one of the links and consider the following questions.

WEBSITE:
http://tiny.cc/egi7jy

ANDROID:
http://tiny.cc/2a92iy

IPHONE:
http://tiny.cc/m582iy

VIDEO DEMO:
http://tiny.cc/chapterapps

This app allows you to express your emotions to a community of others. First, you choose a broad category (fear, sadness, happiness, etc.). Then you choose a specific feeling within that category (within happiness: excited, proud, relieved, etc.) and write a brief post to explain. Other Vent users respond to your emotions by tapping "hug," "same," "omg," "yay," "ugh," or other buttons to express support.

How does it APPly to your daily life?
How valuable would you find this app? Which emotions would you be most likely and least likely to express? How likely would you be to express support for the emotions of others?

How does it APPly to your understanding of psychology?
How might members of different groups (individualistic vs. collectivistic cultures; women vs. men) use this app differently? How does an appreciation of those differences help you understand the ways that people from diverse cultures experience and express feelings? How does that appreciation affect your cultural intelligence?

cultural intelligence
A person's ability to live and interact effectively in a multicultural society.

Cultural intelligence is your ability to live and interact effectively in a multicultural society. Among other things, the appropriate way to greet another person is one behavior that can be informed by cultural intelligence. Image Source/Getty Images

To be culturally intelligent, you need to know information about a cultural group *and* apply that information correctly (Ang & van Dyne, 2008). Imagine Hannah in her first months on the job at Ford. She meets Mohammed, who is Muslim, on a business trip. Should she shake his hand? (Generally, Muslims shun body contact between men and women who are not related.) Her behavior might differ greatly when she meets Javier, from Spain, where not only a handshake but a brief hug and a kiss on the cheek are often customary. Later, Hannah hosts a business dinner, and her guests will include Namit, who is Hindu. What should she consider as she chooses a restaurant? (Generally, Hindus don't eat beef, so a steakhouse is probably a bad idea.) Another time, she interviews Haru, a Japanese applicant for an entry-level position. Haru makes little eye contact with Hannah throughout the interview. Should Hannah consider Haru's behavior rude? (Generally, Japanese people make less eye contact than Americans, especially toward someone in a position of authority, as a sign of respect.) A lack of cultural intelligence in these kinds of situations could offend the people with whom she is interacting, and could damage her relationships with them (Dresser, 2005; Hofstede et al., 2002; Axtell, 2007).

Studies have found that cultural intelligence correlates with all kinds of positive outcomes, including better adjustment in a new culture, more trust in relationships between members of different cultures, better negotiation skills when doing business with a member of another culture, better job performance for international employees, and simply more interactions with members of other cultures (Ng et al., 2012; Templer et al., 2006; Rockstuhl & Ng, 2008; Imai & Gelfland, 2010; Ang et al., 2007; Chen et al., 2012). You can increase your cultural intelligence by reading books or going through training specifically designed to do so. However, just having multicultural encounters—interacting with people different from yourself and learning from those interactions—raises cultural intelligence as well (Shannon & Begley, 2008; Crowne, 2008; Tarique & Takeuchi, 2008).

Microaggressions. One sign of an increase in cultural intelligence is a decrease in **microaggressions**: everyday actions or comments that, often unintentionally, contain hostile or off-putting messages for members of certain cultures. The *micro* in microaggressions refers to the fact that these are typically not grand actions—no physical attacks, no direct slurs, no vandalism or destruction of property. Instead, microaggressions are little things that people do or say that have a negative impact on others, often because they reveal an "ism" (racism, ageism, sexism, heterosexism, weightism, lookism, etc.) that makes the recipient feel insulted, demeaned, or marginalized (Sue, 2010a,b; Sue et al., 2007; Harrell, 2000).

LIFE HACK 10.2

You can boost your own cultural intelligence by reading about different cultures, undergoing multicultural training, or directly interacting with people from cultural groups different from your own.

(Shannon & Begley, 2008; Crowne, 2008; Tarique & Takeuchi, 2008)

Sometimes, microaggressions are explicit, like wearing a T-shirt with a distasteful, potentially offensive joke written across the front. More often, they are subtle, and may even be unconscious to the person delivering it, who believes that they are saying something neutral or kind. For example, consider Sophia, a fourth-grader who just completed her science fair project. A judge evaluating her project says to her, "Nice work! How did *you* get so good at science?" The way the judge emphasizes *you* communicates to Sophia that there is something about her, presumably her gender, that the judge finds incompatible with scientific ability—a message that could damage her self-confidence and discourage her from pursuing science in the future.

As another example, consider Sammy, a 19-year-old college student who has struggled with depression off and on, and finally decided to see a counselor in his university's counseling center. In the first session, Sammy's counselor asks him a series of typical background questions—family, friends, medical history, and so on. The counselor then asks about Sammy's dating life: "Do you have a girlfriend?" By specifying "girlfriend" in the question (rather than asking "Are you dating anyone?" or "Tell me about your dating history"), the counselor subtly communicates to Sammy that heterosexuality is the expectation, the norm, the standard. Sammy, who is gay,

microaggressions
Everyday actions or comments that, often unintentionally, contain hostile or off-putting messages for members of certain cultures.

isn't exactly sure how to respond, but he is sure that he feels uncomfortable with this counselor.

Here is one more example: Joe, a 45-year-old accountant, is having a conversation with coworkers at the office holiday party in mid-December. One coworker shares a fond recollection of a childhood Christmas morning with his parents. The coworker then turns to Joe: "So Joe—what did your mom and dad do for Christmas when you were a kid?" Joe feels slighted for two reasons: When Joe was a kid, he didn't have a mom and a dad, and he is Jewish (he doesn't celebrate Christmas). His coworker's assumptions that everyone has two parents and that everyone celebrates Christmas were part of a well-meaning question, but they communicate an assumption of how things are that might make Joe feel marginalized and "less-than."

Like many microaggressions, these examples are not so blatantly offensive that they would automatically cause the recipient to storm out of the room, burst into tears, or hurl insults (or fists) in retaliation. But being on the receiving end of *many* microaggressions—which is the experience of many members of minority groups—can be hurtful, or as one group of authors put it, "death by a thousand cuts" (Nadal et al., 2011a, p. 234). Numerous studies have examined the accumulated effect of microaggressions on minority groups, including African Americans, Latinos, Asian Americans, multiracial people, women, sexual minorities, and more. The findings are consistent: Higher rates of stress, depression, anxiety, anger, alcohol use, physical illness, and other negative consequences are the result of consistent microaggressions (Wong et al., 2014; Huynh, 2012; McCabe, 2009; Ong et al., 2013; Donovan et al., 2013; Torres et al., 2010; Nadal et al., 2011b, c; Blume et al., 2012; Wang et al., 2011).

MY TAKE VIDEO 10.2

Microaggressions

"It's really important because..."

YOUTUBE: http://tiny.cc/mytake
LAUNCHPAD: launchpadworks.com

So what's the best way to avoid committing microaggressions?

Some people believe that the best strategy is to "bite your tongue." They argue that catching a biased or prejudiced thought before it escapes through your mouth is the way to prevent microaggressions. That can certainly help, but it doesn't get to the root of the problem (and it also discourages you from talking to people who are different from you, which would only lessen your opportunities for increased cultural intelligence). Instead, a better strategy is to explore your underlying beliefs, including any "isms" that might linger in your mind, and change them to be more inclusive of diversity. That is easier said than done, but a noble goal nonetheless. To achieve it, open discussions with others about these issues (including humble admissions of your own less-than-ideal beliefs) and ongoing interactions with a diverse range of people can be quite helpful (Owen et al., 2011, 2014; Hook et al., 2013; Sue & Sue, 2012; Nadal, 2013).

"I have two mommies. I know where the apostrophe goes."

CHECK YOUR LEARNING:

10.5 What is multiculturalism, and how has its importance within psychology changed?

10.6 How has the understanding of cultural differences changed throughout the history of psychology?

10.7 How is the importance of multiculturalism reflected in the profession of psychology today?

10.8 What is acculturation?

10.9 What are the key variables in the various acculturation strategies?

10.10 What is acculturative stress?

10.11 In what specific ways do cultures differ from each other?

10.12 In which areas of daily life can cultural diversity produce differences?

10.13 What is cultural intelligence?

10.14 What are microaggressions?

Gender and Sexuality: Essential Examples of Diversity

YOU WILL LEARN:

10.15 how gender and sex are defined.

10.16 what influences gender development.

10.17 what cisgender, transgender, and transition mean.

10.18 what sexual orientation is, and how some sexual orientations are defined.

10.19 about some factors that relate to sexual orientation.

10.20 about some influences on attitudes toward sexual minorities.

10.21 about some differences that gender makes in daily life.

Any cultural variable could have a meaningful impact in the life of any one person. Some, however, seem especially prominent. Let's take a closer look at two variables—*gender* and *sexuality*—that play central roles in many of our lives.

Defining Gender and Sex

We've already listed many of the qualities around which culture can center, but one of the most fundamental is **gender**: your psychological and behavioral experience of maleness or femaleness. Gender is not necessarily equivalent to **sex**: your biological maleness or femaleness. In casual conversation, you've probably heard people use *gender* and *sex* interchangeably, assuming that the two always match. Maybe you've even filled out forms that ask for either your *gender* or your *sex* but not both, assuming that your answer for one determines your answer for the other. These assumptions are not always correct. A person's sense of being male or female doesn't always match the body parts with which that person was born (Eagly, 2013; Smith et al., 2013; Pryzgoda & Chrisler, 2000).

Gender has been an important characteristic across all cultures and time periods. It is one of the first things we notice about each other, and it is the thing least likely to be forgotten (McCreary & Chrisler, 2010; Fiske et al., 1991). You may not remember exactly what your kindergarten teacher looked like, or the name of the person you met at the party last Saturday night, but you probably still remember if he was a he or she was a she.

Gender plays a prominent role in our languages too. With terms like *he*, *she*, *him*, and *her* to choose from, English doesn't make it easy to refer to a person without identifying gender. Can you imagine seeing your friend's new baby for the first time and saying "*It*'s so cute!" (The newer terms *ze* and *hir* have been offered as gender-neutral options, as has the deliberate use of *they* to refer to one person, but their use is not yet widespread.) English even assigns gender to some nonliving objects, like ships, cars, and countries ("Stand beside her, and guide her…"). In other languages, like Spanish, the names of everyday objects are embedded with gender: el libro (the book) is masculine, but la revista (the magazine) is feminine. And when gender is assigned to an inanimate thing, we often allow it to affect our perception. One study found that there are far more deaths from the average female-named hurricane than the average male-named hurricane, largely because people (perhaps unconsciously) assume the female-named hurricanes are less powerful and evacuate less often (Jung et al., 2014).

MY TAKE VIDEO 10.3

Gender and Sex

"If I were to choose something like design and fashion design…"

YOUTUBE: http://tiny.cc/mytake
LAUNCHPAD: launchpadworks.com

Gender Development

Of course, gender doesn't appear all at once at birth, or puberty, or any other particular point in a person's life. Instead, gender evolves over time through a process called *gender development*, and that process depends on lots of factors beyond simple biology (Bussey, 2013; Zosuls et al., 2011; Ruble & Martin, 1998).

Parents and Gender Development. Parents play a major role in gender development. Some parents would never allow their sons to set foot in the "pink" aisle at Toys "R" Us, or might laugh at their daughters if they were interested in playing or even watching football. Other parents wouldn't mind, and still others would

actively encourage it. These parental responses to interests that don't conform to popular gender norms powerfully shape a child's sense of masculinity or femininity (Bussey & Bandura, 1999). This shaping happens not just with toys and games, but also with occupational interests (engineering vs. nursing) and household responsibilities (cooking vs. lawn mowing).

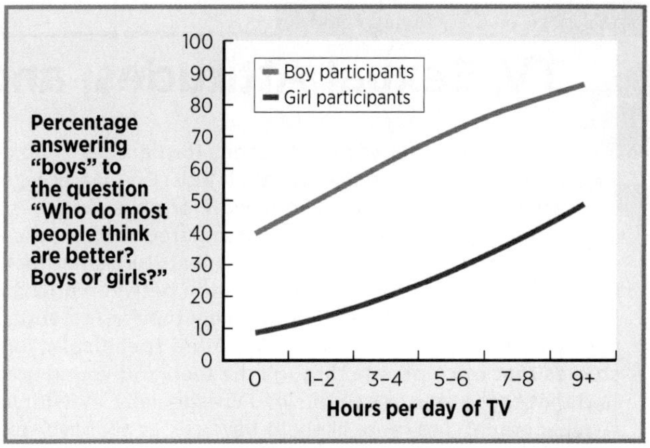

FIGURE 10.7 TV Watching and Gender Development in 4-Year-Olds. When 4-year-old children were asked "Who do most people think are better? Boys or girls?" their answers depended on how much TV they watched per day. For both boys and girls, the more TV they watched, the more likely they were to answer "boys." "Boys" was the answer for less than 10% of the girls who watch no TV, but almost half of the girls who watch 9+ hours of TV per day. Data from Halim et al., 2013.

Peers and Gender Development. Peers influence gender development too, especially as kids enter the preteen years, when fitting in and maintaining popularity become more important (Ruble et al., 2006). How would you respond if you were a fifth-grade boy getting taunted by other fifth-grade boys for your interest in fashion design? Or if you were a seventh-grade girl being teased by other seventh-grade girls for your interest in joining a football team? One study of hundreds of U.S. elementary school students found that getting hit, insulted, left out, or otherwise picked on by peers for doing things that didn't conform to gender stereotypes produced different results for different picked-on kids. Specifically, for kids with many male friends, getting picked on led to more behaviors consistent with gender stereotypes. For boys with many female friends, however, getting picked on led to more behaviors *in*consistent with gender stereotypes (Lee & Troop-Gordon, 2011).

The Media and Gender Development. In addition to parents' and peers' influence on gender development, there is the influence of the media. The way males and females are portrayed on TV, in video games, in magazines, on billboards, and elsewhere has a strong influence on kids' gender development. Let's consider TV as a prime example (see the Watching Psychology box as well). It might be an obvious point, but there is a real difference in the way men and women are typically portrayed on TV. Men are more often portrayed as authoritative, powerful, and physically muscular, while women are more often portrayed as lower in status, helpless, and concerned about sexual attractiveness (Coltrane & Messineo, 2000; Rivadeneyra, 2011; Turow, 2012).

Those TV portrayals make a real difference in how kids see maleness and femaleness. In fact, the more time kids spend watching TV, the more strongly they buy in to the gender stereotypes they see on the screen (Durkin & Nugent, 1998; McGhee & Frueh, 1980; Ward & Friedman, 2006). The effects are evident even before kindergarten. In one study, researchers asked 4-year-old kids this question: "Who do most people think are better? Boys or girls?" The kids' responses depended on how much TV they watched. As **Figure 10.7** shows, the more TV that participants watched, the more likely they were to answer "boys." In fact, a kid who watched 3–4 hours of TV per day was twice as likely to answer "boys" as a kid who watched no TV at all (Halim et al., 2013, p. 130).

The Sexualization of Young Girls. One of the riskiest parts of gender development today involves the sexualization of young girls, which encourages them to use makeup, wear sexy clothing, and behave in flirty or seductive ways well before young adulthood or even puberty (American Psychological Association Task Force on the Sexualization of Girls, 2010; Egan, 2013; Hatch, 2011). Girls who experience this pressure often come to view themselves as sex objects for others rather than independent, strong people (Calogero et al., 2011; Frederickson et al., 1998; Frederickson & Roberts, 1997).

The sexualization of girls has risen drastically in recent decades, as reflected in (and perhaps caused by) the increasing frequency of portrayals of girls as "sexy" (Stankiewicz & Rosselli, 2008; Reichert & Carpenter, 2004). For example, the pictures of girls in *Seventeen* and *Girls' Life* magazines (both read by many girls still in elementary school and middle school) saw a remarkable shift from 1971 to 2011: far fewer childlike outfits, like polka-dot prints and Mary Jane shoes, and far more suggestive outfits, like low-cut shirts, high-heeled shoes, and tight-fitting clothes (Graff et al., 2013).

gender
A person's psychological and behavioral experience of maleness or femaleness.

sex
A person's biological maleness or femaleness.

WATCHING PSYCHOLOGY

TV, Sexual Attitudes, and Sexual Behaviors

There are plenty of good reasons for parents to be concerned about how TV might affect their kids. For example, too much TV could interfere with homework or physical fitness. Recent research highlights another risk associated with excessive TV watching: negative influences on sexual attitudes and behaviors. Generally speaking, there is a correlation between how many hours teens spend watching TV and how likely they are to engage in sexual behaviors (Ward et al., 2014). More specifically, longitudinal studies that track people through the teen and young adult years find that those who watch lots of TV, especially TV with lots of sexual content, are more likely to have sex at all, have sex without a condom, and have sex with multiple partners (Fisher et al., 2009; Collins et al., 2004; O'Hara et al., 2012; Gottfried et al., 2013).

The type of sexual content matters too. When teens watch TV that promotes common sexual stereotypes (women as sex objects, men as driven primarily by sex, casual sex as safe and without negative consequences), they are more likely to believe those stereotypes are true, and also more likely to engage in sexual behaviors (Ward & Friedman, 2006). It is not just TV either. In one study, straight college men who had more exposure to a wide variety of entertainment media (TV, movies, music videos, and men's magazines) had more casual sex partners, less consistent use of condoms, and stronger beliefs that promiscuity and hookups are acceptable (Ward et al., 2011).

It is particularly concerning that some of the common themes in the sex-laden shows targeted toward teens and adults are also common themes in shows targeted toward children and preteens. One study examined multiple episodes of seven popular Nickelodeon and Disney shows from 2004–2012: *Drake and Josh, Suite Life of Zack and Cody, Wizards of Waverly Place, Hannah Montana, iCarly, Sonny with a Chance*, and *Jonas*. The study's results indicated a high frequency of portraying stereotypical heterosexual interactions—in some cases, as often as in shows aimed at an older audience. For example, it was common to find boys objectifying girls and valuing them for their appearance ("she is so hot..."); girls concerned about their own looks ("wait—let me fix my hair...") and offering flirtatious compliments to boys ("my friend didn't tell me how cute you are..."); and boys using material items (gifts) or status (as popular rock stars or TV stars) to impress girls. The shows that relied most heavily on these themes were the ones with male lead characters (Kirsch & Murnen, 2015; Kim et al., 2007). So, even younger TV viewers are being introduced to scripts of sexual interactions that, according to a growing body of research, predict early and risky sexual behavior.

CHAPTER APP 10.3

Transgender

Refuge Restrooms

Preview one of the links and consider the following questions.

WEBSITE: http://tiny.cc/7gi7jy

ANDROID: http://tiny.cc/7a92iy

IPHONE: http://tiny.cc/u582iy

VIDEO DEMO: http://tiny.cc/chapterapps

This app helps users locate public restrooms that are safe and comfortable for transgender people.

How does it APPly to your daily life?
How valuable would this app be to a transgender person? How valuable could it be to someone who is not transgender, in terms of appreciating difficulties that transgender people experience?

How does it APPly to your understanding of psychology?
How does this app help you understand the concepts of gender, transgender, and cisgender?

The consequences of the sexualization of girls, and the self-objectification that accompanies it, are undoubtedly harmful. It contributes to higher rates of many kinds of psychological disorders, including depression, anxiety, and eating disorders (Moradi & Huang, 2008; Grabe et al., 2007, 2008). It also underlies the fact that females' dissatisfaction, anxiety, and shame about their bodies and looks are remarkably high (especially in comparison to males') not only as adults, but as children too (Calogero & Thompson, 2010; Grogan & Wainwright, 1996; Groesz et al., 2002; Tiggemann & Kuring, 2004).

The sexualization of girls also makes other people take them less seriously. One group of researchers took photos of fifth-grade girls and used Photoshop to manipulate the clothes they wore. They created three looks: childlike, somewhat sexualized, or definitely sexualized. College students who viewed the photos rated the definitely sexualized-dressed girls as the least intelligent, competent, capable, moral, and self-respecting (Graff et al., 2012).

Cisgender and Transgender. By adulthood, after gender development is complete, most people have a solid sense of their own gender. When someone's sense of maleness or femaleness corresponds to the biological body parts they received at birth, that person is **cisgender**: a person whose gender and sex match. The opposite of cisgender is **transgender**: a person whose gender and sex do not match. (In Latin, *cis*- means on the same side, and *trans*- means on opposite sides.)

Transgender people are not necessarily *cross-dressers* (people who choose to wear clothes more customary for the other gender), nor are they necessarily attracted to people of the same sex. Transgender people often experience significant distress or unhappiness from feeling female while in a male body, or feeling male while in a female body. In some cases, a person who is transgender will **transition**: choose to take steps to live as the gender that matches their identity rather than their biologically assigned gender. The term *transsexual* has been used to describe people who transition, but its use is on the decline. Transitioning can include name changes, pronoun (he/she) changes, clothing changes, long-term hormone treatments (androgens and estrogens) to cause the body to take on a different shape, or

CURRENT CONTROVERSY

How Does Facebook Affect Body Image?

When you check Facebook, you check out your friends—not only what they're up to, but how they look as well. Recent research suggests that for many Facebook users, especially females, those experiences are often followed by harsh evaluations of their own bodies.

In one study of over 1,000 eighth- and ninth-grade girls, those who used Facebook were more concerned about how thin, pretty, and physically attractive they were (Tiggemann & Slater, 2013). Similarly, among female college students, Facebook time correlates positively with worries about body image, especially among those with strong tendencies to compare their own appearance to the appearance of their friends (Fardouly & Vartanian, 2015).

One study asked women age 17–25 to spend 10 minutes either browsing their own Facebook page or browsing a "neutral" control Web site (a site about handmade crafts and other Etsy-ish ideas). Those who browsed Facebook reported a lower mood and reported more flaws with their own hair, skin, and face (Fardouly et al., 2015). Another study found that among female college students, those who use Facebook to compare and evaluate themselves against others had higher levels of body dissatisfaction as well as more frequent symptoms of bulimia, including binge eating and purging (Smith et al., 2013).

These findings connecting Facebook usage to negative body experiences aren't limited to women. One study found that for both male and female college students, high Facebook usage correlates with self-consciousness and shame about their bodies (Manago et al., 2014). A large-scale study of over 11,000 adults (from their 20s to their 60s) in New Zealand found that both men and women who use a Facebook account have lower levels of body satisfaction than those who don't (Stronge et al., 2015).

A few studies have zoomed in on the link between body image and photo-related activities within Facebook. One study found that it was this photo-related time (posting, viewing, tagging, commenting on photos) that predicted problems with body image and weight dissatisfaction among middle and high school girls (Meier & Gray, 2014). Another found that among seventh-grade girls, those who regularly share selfies on Facebook (or Snapchat, Instagram, or other social media) place much higher value on body shape and weight. And the more they manipulated their selfies (with Photoshop, apps that make skin look smoother or bodies look thinner, etc.), the more body-related worries they had (McLean et al., 2015).

Multiple studies point to a relationship between Facebook usage, including viewing selfies (like this one), and problems with body image. This connection is especially evident among girls and young women. Ivanko_Brnjakovic/Getty Images

surgeries to alter the genitals, chest, face, vocal chords, and other body parts that differ between men and women (Sánchez & Vilain, 2013; National Center for Transgender Equality, 2014).

Jennifer Finney Boylan is an English professor who was born James Boylan. She transitioned male-to-female in her early forties, years after marrying and having two children with a woman. In her memoir *She's Not There*, Boylan explains how her identification with the opposite gender (and the stress that accompanied it) started decades before her sex change hormones and surgeries, when she was a 3-year-old boy (Boylan, 2003, pp. 19–22):

> Since then, the awareness that I was in the wrong body, living the wrong life, was never out of my conscious mind...And at every moment as I lived my life, I countered this awareness with an exasperated companion thought, namely, Don't be an *idiot*. You're *not* a girl. Get over it. But I never got over it...After I grew up and became female, people would often ask me, How did you *know*, when you were a child?...It seemed obvious to me that this was something you understood intuitively, not on the basis of what was between your legs, but because of what you felt in your heart. Remember when you woke up this morning—I'd say to my female friends—and you knew you were female? *That's* how I felt. *That's* how I knew. Of course, knowing with such absolute certainty something that appeared to be both absurd and untrue [was] ...a crushing burden, which was, simultaneously, invisible.

The burden that Jennifer Finney Boylan describes often translates into serious psychological problems for transgender people. One study of over 500 transgender people found that over half were clinically depressed, and about a third had attempted

cisgender
A person whose gender and sex match.

transgender
A person whose gender and sex do not match.

transition
Take steps to live as the gender that matches one's identity rather than one's biologically assigned gender.

Sexual orientations span a wide range. They include heterosexual (straight), homosexual (gay or lesbian), and bisexual (bi), as well as the less widely recognized pansexual, fluid, questioning, and asexual. Doug Menuez/ Getty Images

suicide at some point in their lives—both rates way above those found in the general population (Clements-Nolle et al., 2001). Other studies have found similar results, especially among transgender people who were socially outcast, harassed, or bullied (Bockting et al., 2013; Grant et al., 2010).

Sexual Orientation

Sexual orientation is a person's pattern of romantic attraction to a particular group (or groups) of other people. Your sexual orientation is who you'd like to date. A person with a **heterosexual** orientation is attracted to members of the other sex. A person with a **homosexual** orientation is attracted to members of the same sex. A person with a **bisexual** orientation is attracted to people of both the other and the same sex. The less formal terms *straight*, *gay/lesbian*, and *bi* are often used for heterosexual, homosexual, and bisexual, respectively. You'll see them in this chapter too.

You're probably already familiar with those terms, but it would be a mistake to think that they capture everyone. Sexual orientations can also include *pansexual* (attracted to everyone, regardless of the other person's gender, sexual orientation, etc.), *fluid* (attracted to different people at different times), *questioning* (still in the process of examining or reexamining who is attractive), and *asexual* (sexually attracted to no one) (Zea & Nakamura, 2014). Collectively, people whose sexual orientations differ from that of the majority of the population identify as **LGBTQ**: a community of members of sexual minorities, including lesbian (L), gay (G), bisexual (B), transgender (T), queer/questioning (Q), and other people.

How many people are straight, gay/lesbian, or bisexual?

It depends on both who and how you ask (**Table 10.4**). In terms of *who*, more open-minded cultures in which nonheterosexuality is widely accepted are more likely to produce higher estimates. In terms of *how*, questions that ask how a person labels themselves ("What's your sexual orientation?") produce lower estimates than questions that ask what behaviors a person has done ("Have you ever had sexual interactions with _____?") or who they find attractive ("Have you ever been attracted to _____?"). Also, surveys conducted via the Internet tend to produce higher estimates than those conducted by other means, perhaps because of a higher sense of anonymity (Chandra et al., 2011; Harris Interactive & Witeck-Combs, 2010). But most researchers tend to settle on a range of 2–4% of the general U.S. population (give or take a percentage point or two) as a reasonable estimate of how many of us identify as gay, lesbian, or bisexual (Gates, 2013). That rate also varies from state to state—check **Figure 10.8**.

TABLE 10.4: It Depends How You Ask about Sexual Orientation Rates

	ALL PARTICIPANTS (%)	MEN (%)	WOMEN (%)
Do you *identify* as lesbian, gay, or bisexual?	3.7	2.8	4.6
Do you have any *sexual experience* with a person of same sex?	8.8	5.2	12.5
Do you have any *attraction* to a person of same sex?	11.0	6.5	16.7

Researchers trying to determine how many people are lesbian, gay, or bisexual get different answers when they ask the question in different ways. In this large-scale U.S. study, the rates were lowest when the question asked about *identifying* as lesbian, gay, or bisexual, higher when the question asked about same-sex *behaviors*, and higher still when the question asked about same-sex *attraction*. Data from Chandra et al., 2011; Gates & Newport, 2013.

Within that range, there are gender-based differences. Specifically, men tend to identify as gay more often than bisexual, but women tend to identify as bisexual more often than lesbian (Dworkin, 2013; Herek et al., 2010). In other words, women tend to have a nonexclusive sexuality more often than men. (Here, nonexclusive means that just because a person is attracted to one gender, that doesn't mean that the person isn't also attracted to the other gender (Thompson & Morgan, 2008; Vrangalova & Savin-Williams, 2012; Bailey et al., 2000; Laumann et al., 2004; Dickson et al., 2003).) In one large-scale survey of over 14,000 young adults, the researchers gave the participants several middle ground options to define their sexuality—not just straight or gay, but in-between options like "mostly straight," "bisexual" (presumably around 50/50), and "mostly gay." As **Table 10.5** shows, far more men placed themselves at one end of the scale or the other (definitively straight or gay), and far more women placed themselves in one of the middle categories (Udry & Chantala, 2006).

Another gender-based difference in sexual orientation has to do with *fluid* sexuality, or the likelihood for sexual attraction to change over time. Women are much more

FROM RESEARCH TO REAL LIFE

Does Gaydar Work?

Gaydar, a term that combines the words *gay* and *radar*, is the ability to determine who's gay and who's not without being explicitly told. You may have heard people describe (or even brag about) their own gaydar, but how well does gaydar really work?

Researchers have investigated this question in a variety of ways. The most common method is to present visual information (videos, photos, etc.) to participants and ask them to identify the person as gay or straight. For example, one study found that participants who watched a 6–10-second video of a gay or straight person could correctly identify the person's sexual orientation 81% of the time (87% accuracy for straight targets, 75% accuracy for gay targets) (Rieger et al., 2010).

Another found that participants viewing facial photographs of men and women taken from dating Web sites (where they identified themselves as gay or straight) correctly identified their sexual orientation better than they could if they were blindly guessing (Lyons et al., 2014). Studies have found that the more time you have to look at the person, the better. Participants did better with a 10-second video clip than a 1-second video clip, and worst with a still photo, but the photo still produced better-than-chance accuracy (Ambady et al., 1999). Voice studies have also shown that audio, even without video, produces better-than-chance results (Linville, 1998; Gaudio, 1994; Zimman, 2013). The accuracy of gaydar may depend on some qualities of the person using it. One study found that straight participants who have more real-life experiences with gay men were much more accurate than those with fewer real-life experiences with gay men (Brambilla et al., 2013).

Some researchers have offered more skeptical views about gaydar. An early gaydar study found that participants watching brief videos of gay and straight people did no better than chance when identifying their sexual orientation (Berger et al., 1987). Another study found that gaydar is little more than stereotyping—not so much about physical features or voice, but about interests, careers, and activities that a person reveals (Cox et al., 2016).

The gaydar literature is actually a new development in a long line of research on categorizing people into groups that are visually ambiguous (that is, less than obvious upon first glance). Earlier research of this type has focused on whether a person is Jewish or Mormon, Democrat or Republican. A meta-analysis of 47 articles across all of these categories found that the overall "hit rate"—the odds of correctly determining whether a person fell into the target category—was 64.5% (Tskhay & Rule, 2013). The same meta-analysis found the same rate for gaydar studies specifically. That percentage is significantly above the 50/50 rate you'd expect if gaydar were no better than flipping a coin, but far below the 100% rate you'd expect if gaydar were always accurate. In other words, gaydar works sometimes, but it's far from perfect. ●

likely to experience a fluid sexuality than men over the course of their lives (Peplau & Garnets, 2000; Diamond, 2000). This is especially evident in longitudinal studies, which track people across many years. More often than men, women find their patterns of attraction changing, sometimes dividing their adult lives into two long, distinct periods, and other times dividing them into many briefer periods that involve returning to previous attractions (Diamond, 2005, 2007, 2009; Kinnish et al., 2005). An increasing recognition of the fluidity of sexual orientation has caused many experts in this field to wonder if we should stop thinking of sexual orientation as a trait—something that

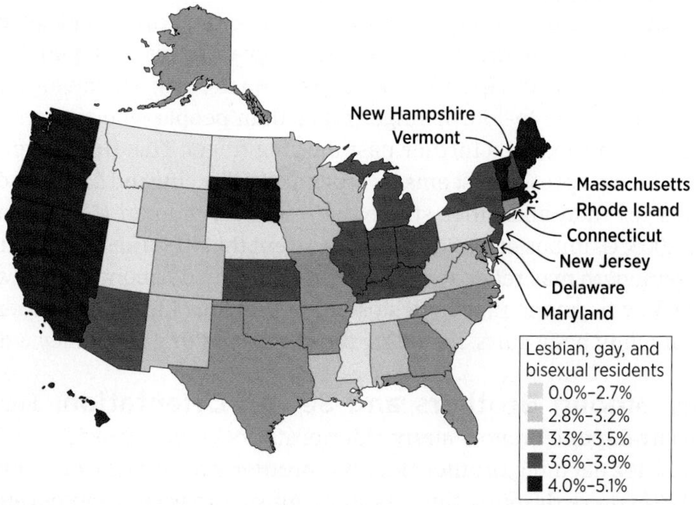

FIGURE 10.8 State-by-State Rates of Lesbian, Gay, and Bisexual Population. States in the Northeast and on the West Coast tend to have higher percentages of lesbian, gay, and bisexual residents than states in the middle of the country. Data from Gates & Newport, 2013.

sexual orientation
A person's pattern of romantic attraction to a particular group or groups of other people.

heterosexual
The sexual orientation of a person who is attracted to members of the other sex.

homosexual
The sexual orientation of a person who is attracted to members of the same sex.

bisexual
The sexual orientation of a person who is attracted to people of both the other and the same sex.

LGBTQ
A community of members of sexual minorities, including lesbian (L), gay (G), bisexual (B), transgender (T), queer/questioning (Q), and other people.

TABLE 10.5: Sexual Orientations of Men and Women

SEXUAL ORIENTATION	MEN (%)	WOMEN (%)
Completely heterosexual	94.03	85.10
Mostly heterosexual	3.18	10.65
Bisexual	0.57	2.55
Mostly homosexual	0.63	0.70
Completely homosexual	1.18	0.47

Often, questions about sexual orientation are worded in all-or-none ways. By contrast, in one large-scale study (about 14,000 participants), there were five options: completely heterosexual, mostly heterosexual, bisexual, mostly homosexual, and completely homosexual. The percentages were higher for men at the two extremes, but higher for women in the three middle-ground categories. Data from Udry & Chantala, 2006.

develops early in life and remains constant—and instead consider that at least for some people, it is a characteristic that can vary throughout the life span (Diamond, 2013).

Genes and Sexual Orientation. The causes of sexual orientation are still being actively researched, but some interesting biological findings have emerged (Hill et al., 2013). Genes appear to play a role in determining sexual orientation (Långström et al., 2010). Studies of siblings have found relatively high rates—7–10%—of the biological brothers of gay men being gay themselves (Bailey et al., 1999).

A twin study found that identical twins had a much higher likelihood to match in terms of same-sex attraction than nonidentical twins (Kendler et al., 2000). For example, if Luke is gay and has a twin brother Jeff, the odds of Jeff being gay are over twice as great as if Jeff and Luke are identical than if Jeff and Luke are not identical. This finding suggests that the more genes you share with a gay or lesbian person, the higher the odds that you will be gay or lesbian. Current research has attempted to get more specific by identifying particular genetic markers (a "gay gene"), generating lots of buzz in the popular media but with only limited success so far (O'Riordan, 2012; Conrad & Markens, 2001; Servick, 2014; Sanders et al., 2015).

Brain Differences and Sexual Orientation. PET scans and other brain-viewing technologies have revealed some interesting differences in brain structure and brain function between gay or lesbian people and straight people. For example, the parts of the hypothalamus are in different proportion. The *suprachiasmatic nucleus*—the part of the hypothalamus that controls your 24-hour circadian rhythms (see Chapter 2)—is 70% larger in gay men than in a random sample of men (Swaab & Hoffman, 1990). Also, one particular region of the *anterior hypothalamus* is about twice as large in straight men as in gay men (LeVay, 1991). Typically, when these kinds of brain differences are found, the differences are such that the brains of gay or lesbian people resemble brains of the opposite sex. In other words, when gay men's brains differ from straight men's brains, they resemble female brains in their differences. Likewise, when lesbians' brains differ from straight women's brains, they resemble male brains (Hill et al., 2013).

Hands, Fingers, and Sexual Orientation. Gay or lesbian people are much less likely to be right-handed than straight people (Lippa, 2003; Peters et al., 2006). Specifically, a meta-analysis found that gay men are 34% more likely to be left-handed or ambidextrous, and lesbian women are 91% more likely to be left-handed or ambidextrous (Lalumière et al., 2000). This non-right-handedness shows up well before puberty, and there is no evidence that parents encourage eventually gay or eventually lesbian kids to use any particular hand. Psychologists and other researchers are still trying to explain this finding.

Another puzzling finding concerns finger size. The ratio of the index finger and the ring finger differs between many (but not all) gay, lesbian, or bisexual people and straight people (Williams et al., 2000). Specifically, people who are gay, lesbian, or bisexual often have higher second-finger-to-fourth-finger ratios than people who are straight. In other words, the index finger extends further past the ring finger. This finding remains somewhat tentative, since its presence seems to depend on ethnicity, and some studies produce stronger results for men and other studies, stronger for women (Manning et al., 2007; Voracek et al., 2005; Grimbos et al., 2010). To the extent that it is true, this finding about difference in finger length may relate to the amount of certain hormones in the womb during pregnancy. The key hormone may be testosterone, which is known to influence physical development of many body parts, including the hands and fingers (Bailey & Hurd, 2005).

Birth Order among Brothers and Sexual Orientation. For a man, the odds of being gay depend on how many older brothers he has. Specifically, the chances go up about 33% for each big brother the little brother has (Blanchard, 2008; Bogaert & Skorska, 2011). If you're thinking this has something to do with the experience of growing up as the baby brother in a house full of older boys, that is not it. This phenomenon doesn't happen with adopted brothers, and it does happen in younger brothers who are raised apart from their older brothers. The key variable seems to be how many boys a

mother has carried through pregnancy rather than anything that happens after those boys arrive, which suggests a strong prenatal (probably hormonal) influence on sexual orientation (Bogeart, 2006; VanderLaan et al., 2015; Blanchard, 2012).

Other Predictors of Sexual Orientation. If prenatal hormones influence sexual orientation, researchers should see some behavioral evidence of those hormones even before puberty—and they do. Kids who act atypical for their gender, even at young ages, are more likely to have nonheterosexual orientations as adults. One study asked adults of diverse sexual orientations how much they agreed or disagreed with statements about their childhood experiences. The more participants endorsed behaviors that didn't conform to traditional gender roles, the more likely they were to be gay, lesbian, or bisexual. For example, gay men (much more than straight men) were likely to agree strongly with this kind of statement: "As a child I disliked competitive sports such as football, baseball, and basketball." And lesbian women (much more than straight women) were likely to agree strongly with this kind of statement: "As a child, I usually avoided feminine clothing such as dresses" (Lippa, 2003).

Another study relied not on memories, but childhood home videos, to illustrate the same point. The researchers asked both gay and straight adults to provide home videos taken when they were young kids. The researchers then showed those videos to undergraduates and asked them to rate how much each kid conformed to gender-typical expectations—how "boyish" the boys acted, and how "girlish" the girls acted. The undergrads found more examples of gender nonconformity (for example, girls assembling trains or boys dancing to music by a female singer) in kids who grew up to be gay or lesbian. They found much more gender conformity (for example, boys fighting with toy swords or girls performing ballet in tutus) in kids who grew up to be straight. So, even when you take out the possibility of memory bias, which might push straight people to remember certain things about their own childhoods and gay or lesbian people to remember other things, the extent to which a child conforms to gender expectations appears to correlate at least slightly with eventual sexual orientation (Rieger et al., 2010). Of course, this doesn't mean that every kid whose behavior is not typical for his or her gender will grow up to be gay, nor does it mean that every kid whose behavior is typical for his or her gender will grow up to be straight. It just means that the odds are greater.

Attitudes Toward Sexual Minorities. Attitudes toward sexual minorities have changed drastically in recent decades—just ask your parents or your grandparents. Not long ago, any kind of same-sex romantic relationship was viewed with disdain by most (but certainly not all) within mainstream U.S. culture. Gay marriage was illegal across the country, and being gay or lesbian was even considered a psychological disorder (American Psychiatric Association, 1952, 1968).

Today's more positive and affirming views toward diverse sexual orientations are not universal, however. According to research, those views depend on a number of factors (many of which could overlap, of course). For example, ethnicity seems to make a difference in the United States. In general, Whites hold more favorable attitudes toward nonheterosexual orientations than African Americans or Latinos. Age seems to make a difference as well, with more positive attitudes held by younger adults (Horn, 2013). Other predictors of negative views toward sexual minorities include conservative religious and political beliefs; traditional beliefs about gender roles (how men and women "should" behave); the belief that sexuality is a choice (and therefore changeable); and lack of direct contact with lesbian women or gay men (Israel & Mohr, 2004; Eliason, 2001; Mohr & Rochlen, 1999; Haslam & Levy, 2006; Hegarty & Pratto, 2001). Negative views of same-sex relationships seem to depend on the sex of the people in those relationships too: Gay men draw more disapproval than lesbian women, especially from straight men (Herek, 2000; Cárdenas & Barrientos, 2008).

Attitudes toward same-sex relationships have generally become more positive and affirming in recent decades, but those attitudes still vary widely and relate to numerous factors such as ethnicity, age, religious and political beliefs, and other factors. Tetra Images/Getty Images

The fact that many people still respond to gay, lesbian, and bisexual orientations with scorn and ridicule contributes to the high rate of mental health problems among sexual minorities (Cochran & Mays, 2013). Depression, anxiety, alcohol and drug problems, and other psychological struggles occur in sexual minorities at two to three times

the rate in the general population (Fergusson et al., 1999, 2005; Cochran et al., 2003; Meyer, 2003). Unsurprisingly, the rates of unpleasant and unfortunate experiences that often contribute to mental disorders—stress, victimization, discrimination, low social support, and hopelessness, among others—are also in greater abundance in the lives of sexual minorities (Hatzenbuehler et al., 2010).

Fortunately, there is a flip side to the finding that a lack of contact with sexual minorities goes along with negative attitudes: Friendships with sexual minorities improve those attitudes. Specifically, high-quality relationships in which a straight person really gets to know a sexual minority as a real person go along with more agreeable attitudes toward sexual minorities overall (Heinze & Horn, 2009; Lemm, 2006; Vonofakou et al., 2007).

Friendship with sexual minorities isn't the only thing that can improve attitudes toward sexual minorities. So can learning about the achievements and fame of sexual minorities. In one study, researchers showed participants pictures of gay celebrities and offered a description of each. For half of the participants, the description included the fact that the celebrity was gay; for the other half, the description omitted that fact. The celebrities—who included filmmaker Pedro Almodovar, author Michael Cunningham, singer Melissa Etheridge, U.S. Congress member Barney Frank, actor Rupert Everett, civil rights leader Bayard Rustin, and tennis star Martina Navratilova—got more favorable ratings from the participants who learned about their sexual orientations (Dasgupta & Rivera, 2008).

Another promising factor for attitudes toward sexual minorities is the presence of *gay–straight alliances* (*GSAs*) in U.S. high schools. GSAs are extracurricular organizations that offer a safe, supportive environment for teens to come together to share experiences, socialize, and engage in advocacy and activism. They welcome students who are (or who think they may be) LGBTQ, as well as students who are straight. GSAs began to appear in a few high schools on the East and West coasts around 1990. Today, there are thousands of GSAs in high schools throughout the United States and in many other countries (Fetner & Kush, 2008).

A growing body of research finds that GSAs have lots of positive effects (Russell et al., 2009). One study found that belonging to a GSA made members more comfortable with diverse sexual orientations, as well as boosted academic performance, family relationships, and a sense of belonging to the school community (Lee, 2002). Another study found that schools with GSAs had lower rates of hopelessness and suicide attempts among sexual minority students (Davis et al., 2014). Other studies have also found a wide range of positive effects—not just for members of GSAs, but also for students who didn't belong to a GSA but simply went to schools that had them (Walls et al., 2010; Toomey et al., 2011).

What Difference Does Gender Make?

There are plenty of ways in which males and females are remarkably similar—overall intelligence, self-esteem, moral reasoning, leadership capabilities, mathematical ability, and other variables (Hyde, 2005, 2014; Hyde et al., 2008; Priess & Hyde, 2010; Bussey, 2013). But there are also plenty of examples of big differences between the genders. As we consider a few of them, remember that just because these differences exist, that doesn't necessarily mean that gender *caused* them. There could be other explanations, and of course, these differences don't apply to *all* members of a gender. These are broad overall trends.

Research indicates that gay-straight alliances, which are increasingly common in U.S. high schools, can have positive effects on attitudes toward sexual minorities.
Custom Life Science Images/Alamy

Differences in Communication. Often, women and men use speech for different reasons. Specifically, women tend to speak to maintain relationships, with an emphasis on listening and compassion. Men, on the other hand, tend to speak to assert dominance or to hold someone else's attention, with an emphasis on taking control or solving problems (Carli, 2013). "For women, a conversation is a chance to make connections; for men, each interaction can result in a winner or a loser" (McHugh & Hambaugh, 2010, p. 386).

For example, picture two pairs of new college roommates meeting each other for the first time on residence hall move-in day: Sean and Alonzo, and Juliana and Zoe. There are lots of decisions to make: who gets which bed, where the mini-fridge should go, whose music plays while they unpack. For Sean and Alonzo, each of those decisions can

feel competitive, a chance to flex some muscle and grab some control. For Juliana and Zoe, each of those decisions can feel cooperative, a chance to team up and join forces. (Of course, the opposite could be true too, but that would be the exception to the rule.)

When researchers examine specific communication behaviors in men and women, they typically find differences that make sense in terms of how men and women use speech. For example, compared to women, men interrupt more often (especially to redirect the conversation) and speak both louder and longer (West & Zimmerman, 1983; Anderson & Leaper, 1998; Mast & Sczesny, 2010). Women, compared to men, apologize more often, offer more compliments, use more verbal reinforcers of others' speech ("mm hm," "right," "yeah," etc.), and sprinkle in more terms to soften their language such as "kinda," "sorta," "like," "I mean," and "y'know?" (Farley et al., 2010; Hannah & Murachver, 2007; Stubbe & Holmes, 1995; Leaper & Robnett, 2011; Carli, 1990; Laserna et al., 2014).

Even nonverbal communication reflects clear gender differences. Women smile, nod, and lean forward more often, while men fidget, stretch out, and demonstrate visual dominance (more eye contact when speaking than when listening) more often (Mast & Sczesny, 2010; Dovidio et al., 1988a,b; Hall, 2006; Hall et al., 2000). **Table 10.6** shows a summary.

Differences in Expressing Emotion. Around the world, women cry more often than men, not only when sad things happen to them, but also when happy things happen, or when they empathize while seeing sad or happy things happen to others (Vingerhoets et al., 2000; Vingerhoets & Scheirs, 2000; De Fruyt, 1997; Peter et al., 2001). Women also smile more often than men, for reasons that may be complex. In some situations, a woman's smile may convey her happiness, but in others, it may communicate agreement, or even submission, in an attempt to build relationships (Fischer & Evers, 2013).

It is not just crying and smiling, either. Women generally demonstrate more emotion through facial expression than men (Kring & Gordon, 1998). People interpret facial expressions of men and women differently too, especially when the feeling being expressed is negative. In one study, researchers showed pictures of the faces of men and women feeling anger, sadness, fear, or disgust. They also offered explanations for why the person might feel that way: got yelled at by boss, heard footsteps in the dark, got some bad news, saw an animal get run over by a car, and so on. Participants were then asked whether the people in the pictures were "emotional" or simply "having a bad day." In other words, they were asked whether their emotions were attributable to their personalities, or to their situation. Women were more often labeled as "emotional," and men were more often labeled as "having a bad day" (Barrett & Bliss-Moreau, 2009).

Differences in Personality. As we will cover in Chapter 12, the most widely accepted model of personality features five separate traits (Costa & McCrae, 1992;

TABLE 10.6: He Says, She Says: Gender Differences in Speaking Behaviors

MEN MORE OFTEN...	WOMEN MORE OFTEN...
Interrupt (especially to change the topic)	Apologize
Speak loudly	Offer compliments
Hold the floor for long periods of time	Use verbal reinforcers like "mm hm" and "right"
Stretch out	Soften language with words like "kinda" and "y'know?"
Fidget	Smile and nod
Maintain visual dominance (more eye contact when speaking than listening)	Lean forward

Women and men often have different motivations for speaking: women to connect, and men to compete. Research on specific speech behaviors (both verbal and nonverbal) reflects this gender difference. Information from Mast & Sczesny, 2010; Carli, 1990, 2013; McHugh & Hambaugh, 2010; West & Zimmerman, 1983; Anderson & Leaper, 1998; Farley et al., 2010; Hannah & Murachver 2007; Stubbe & Holmes, 1995; Leaper & Robnett, 2011; Laserna et al., 2014; Dovidio et al., 1988a, b; Hall, 2006; Hall et al., 2000.

McCrae & Costa, 2003, 2013). In some ways, men and women have equal amounts of these five personality traits. For example, in *conscientiousness* (being organized, responsible, and deliberate), there are no gender differences. But in other traits, there are small but consistent gender differences. Women tend to be slightly higher in *agreeableness* (cooperating and complying with others) and *neuroticism* (experiencing negative emotions like anxiety and depression) (Lynn & Martin, 1997; Rubinstein & Strul, 2007). Men and women have roughly equal levels of *openness to experience* (receptiveness to new things). However, when you break that trait down into its component parts, women have greater openness to feeling new emotions, but men have greater openness to hearing new ideas. In terms of *extraversion* (outgoingness), women are higher in friendliness and warmth toward others, but men are higher in excitement seeking and assertiveness toward others (Stake & Eisele, 2010; Costa et al., 2001; Feingold, 1994; Lodhi et al., 2002).

Differences in Education. In both school and work, females are underrepresented in the *STEM* areas—*s*cience, *t*echnology, *e*ngineering, and *m*ath (Sadler et al., 2012). But that is not because of any inherent gender difference in abilities. The difference occurs because our society has traditionally steered girls away from these "boys'" fields. This has lowered both girls' interest and belief in their capabilities. And it leads to girls fearing that if they struggle in a STEM course they will confirm stereotypes about their gender (Betz et al., 2013; Steele, 1997, 2010; Spencer et al., 1999; Bussey, 2013).

Thankfully, efforts to recruit girls into STEM fields (and women into STEM careers) have increased, but results of these efforts have been mixed (Watt, 2010; Milgram, 2011; Glass & Minnotte, 2010). At the college level, women tend to be underrepresented in STEM majors, but overrepresented in education, nursing, humanities, and social sciences (including psychology) (Basow, 2010). Girls tend to earn slightly better grades throughout school, but boys tend to slightly outperform them on standardized tests (especially in math) (Duckworth & Seligman, 2006; Downey & Vogt Yuan, 2005; Legewie & DiPrete, 2012).

Traditionally, girls and women have been underrepresented in the STEM fields (science, technology, engineering, and math), primarily because of societal norms rather than ability. Recruitment of girls and women into STEM fields has increased in recent years. Jupiterimages, Brand X Pictures/Getty Images

Differences in Following Directions. Researchers haven't shed much light on the old stereotype about men refusing to stop for directions. However, they have found many gender differences in the strategies we use to navigate from place to place (Lawton, 1994; Saucier & Ehresman, 2010). Men tend to rely more on directions that remain constant no matter what, emphasizing distances and compass directions. For example: drive north for 3 miles, then turn east and go 2 miles. Women, on the other hand, tend to rely more on directions that depend on the person's perspective at the time, including landmarks and relative directions. For example: go straight until you see the McDonalds, then turn right and keep going until you see the park on your left (Saucier et al., 2002; Lawton & Kallai, 2002; Choi & Silverman, 2003; Lawton, 1994; Nowak et al., 2015).

When they give directions to others, men and women reveal the same preferences as when they figure out their own routes (Dabbs et al., 1998; MacFadden et al., 2003). This gender difference in using directions shows up as early as middle school (Choi & Silverman, 2003). In one study, about 100 kids age 10–17 completed a walk-through maze set up in a huge room with big, portable wall pieces. The maze included over 30 opportunities to go right or left and over 20 landmarks. After walking through the maze five times, each kid was asked to draw a bird's-eye-view map of the maze or make a written list of step-by-step instructions for navigating it. The girls' drawings and written instructions included far more mentions of landmarks, and far fewer mentions of directions, than the boys' (Schmitz, 1997).

Differences in Sex Life. Men report more interest in sex than women—more frequency, more variety, and more partners (Petersen & Hyde, 2010a; Peplau, 2003). Men also report higher rates of almost every specific sexual activity than women, with masturbation and pornography at the top of the list of things that men do more often (Petersen & Hyde, 2010b; Oliver & Hyde, 1993; Hald et al., 2014). Higher frequency of sex in males is true for gay as well as straight relationships, with gay men reporting higher rates of sex than lesbian couples (Peplau & Fingerhut, 2007). Men also report a higher frequency of orgasm than women during both sex and masturbation (Laumann et al., 1994).

The reasons for sex differ between the genders too: women more often seek emotional and interpersonal connection, while men more often seek physical gratification (Leigh, 1989; Patrick et al., 2007; Meston & Buss, 2007; Baumeister, 2013). Gender differences also apply to *hookups* (one-time sexual encounters between people who don't know each other well). In college, where most hookup research is done, men are more comfortable with hookups than women (Lambert et al., 2003). Women experience more worry and distress after hookups, and they are also more interested in converting their hookups to long-term relationships than men are (Owen & Fincham, 2011; Fielder & Carey, 2010; Townsend & Wasserman, 2011). Hookups also involve a greater risk to women's reputations than to men's. Studies find that the responses of college students to hookup stories depend on who the story is about. If it is about a woman, there is a greater chance that they will lose respect for her. However, if the story is about a man, the odds are lower that such a negative evaluation will take place (Allison & Risman, 2013; Bogle, 2008).

CHECK YOUR LEARNING:

10.15 What is the difference between gender and sex?

10.16 What influences gender development?

10.17 What do cisgender, transgender, and transition mean?

10.18 What is sexual orientation?

10.19 What factors relate to sexual orientation?

10.20 What influences attitudes toward sexual minorities?

10.21 What aspects of daily life can be influenced by gender?

CHAPTER SUMMARY

Diversity Surrounds You

10.1 The United States is a diverse nation in terms of race, ethnicity, language, religion, age, sexual orientation, education, income, and rural or urban location.

10.2 A culture is a group of similar people who share beliefs and patterns of behavior. Culture can powerfully influence worldview, your comprehensive way of understanding the world around you.

10.3 Dynamic sizing is the ability to simultaneously know the norm for a group *and* recognize that the norm might not apply to every member of that group.

10.4 In the early days of psychology, culture was essentially equated to race or ethnicity. Today, psychologists consider many other variables as culturally important, such as gender, age, religion, sexual orientation, and socioeconomic status.

Multiculturalism

10.5 Multiculturalism is a psychological approach that highlights the importance and value of multiple cultural groups within a society. Multiculturalism has become increasingly important in psychology in recent decades. Some call it the dominant movement in contemporary psychology.

10.6 In earlier years, cultural differences were often defined as deficits or disadvantages of one culture compared to another. More recently, the unique qualities of each culture have been viewed as strengths and virtues.

10.7 Today, many areas of psychology reflect an emphasis on multiculturalism, including professional organizations, journals, books, ethical guidelines, assessment tools, and the DSM.

10.8 Acculturation is managing a life that involves the coexistence of more than one culture.

10.9 There are a variety of different acculturation strategies based on how much a person retains their previous culture and how much they embrace their new culture.

10.10 Acculturative stress is the physical or psychological stress that comes from acculturation.

10.11 Specific ways in which cultures differ from each other include individualism and collectivism, power distance, long-term orientation and short-term orientation, and more.

10.12 Cultural diversity can produce differences in many areas of daily life, including how you define your identity, raise children, experience feelings, remember events, and more.

10.13 Cultural intelligence is your ability to live and interact effectively in a multicultural society.

10.14 Microaggressions are everyday actions or comments that, often unintentionally, contain hostile or off-putting messages for members of certain cultures.

Gender and Sexuality: Essential Examples of Diversity

10.15 Gender is your psychological and behavioral experience of maleness or femaleness. Sex is your biological maleness or femaleness.

10.16 Gender development can be influenced by parents, peers, and the media.

10.17 Cisgender refers to a person whose gender and sex match. Transgender refers to a person whose gender and sex do

not match. Transition refers to a person taking steps to live as a member of the sex opposite their sex at birth, often through name changes, pronoun (he/she) changes, clothing changes, or significant biological changes like surgeries or hormone treatments.

10.18 Sexual orientation is a person's pattern of romantic attraction to a particular group (or groups) of other people. Some common sexual orientations include heterosexual (toward members of the other sex), homosexual (toward members of the same sex), and bisexual (toward members of both the other and the same sex).

10.19 Numerous factors can influence or correspond with sexual orientation, including genes, brain differences, handedness, finger size ratio, birth order among brothers, and more.

10.20 Attitudes toward sexual minorities vary widely. They can be influenced by familiarity or friendships with sexual minority members, as well as by involvement in organizations like gay-straight alliances.

10.21 Gender can influence many aspects of daily life, including communication styles, expression of emotion, personality, education, direction following, and sex life.

KEY TERMS

culture, p. 335
worldview, p. 337
dynamic sizing, p. 337
multiculturalism, p. 339
acculturation, p. 341
assimilation, p. 341
separation, p. 341
marginalization, p. 341
integration, p. 341
acculturative stress, p. 341
individualism, p. 343
collectivism, p. 343
cultural intelligence, p. 347
microaggressions, p. 348
gender, p. 351
sex, p. 351
cisgender, p. 353
transgender, p. 353
transition, p. 353
sexual orientation, p. 355
heterosexual, p. 355
homosexual, p. 355
bisexual, p. 355
LGBTQ, p. 355

SELF-ASSESSMENT

1. Language is one way to measure diversity in the United States. Approximately _____% of U.S. residents speak a language other than English at home.
   a. 1
   b. 10
   c. 20
   d. 50

2. A _____ is a group of similar people who share beliefs and patterns of behavior.

3. _____ is the ability to simultaneously know the norm for a group *and* recognize that the norm might not apply to every member of that group.
   a. Dynamic sizing
   b. Microaggression
   c. Culture shock
   d. Acculturation

4. Andrzej moves from Poland to the United States. He retains his Polish culture and also adopts U.S. culture. The acculturation strategy that best describes this behavior is:
   a. assimilation.
   b. separation.
   c. marginalization.
   d. integration.

5. Amber comes from a culture that emphasizes what's best for the individual. Kyong comes from a culture that emphasizes what's best for the group. Which of the following descriptions most accurately characterizes this difference?
   a. Amber's culture is individualistic; Kyong's culture is collectivistic.
   b. Amber's culture has a large power distance; Kyong's culture has a small power distance.
   c. Amber's culture is more caring; Kyong's culture is more assertive.
   d. Amber's culture has a shorter-term orientation; Kyong's culture has a longer-term orientation.

6. _____ is your ability to live and interact effectively in a multicultural society.
   a. Integration
   b. Assimilation
   c. Cultural intelligence
   d. Worldview

7 Travis puts a bumper sticker on his car that makes a joke about a minority group. He intends it to be funny, but his next-door neighbor, who belongs to that group, finds it slightly hostile and offensive. Although he may not realize it, Travis' behavior could be labeled as:

a. acculturative stress.
b. a microaggression.
c. collectivism.
d. dynamic sizing.

8 ______ is your psychological and behavioral experience of maleness or femaleness.

9 Heather is a person whose gender and sex match. Which of these words best describes Heather?

a. transgender
b. transition
c. heterosexual
d. cisgender

10 Which of the following is true regarding surveys of sexual orientation?

a. Most researchers tend to settle on a range of about 2–4% of the general U.S. population as identifying as gay, lesbian, or bisexual.
b. Compared to women, men are more likely to identify as bisexual than homosexual.
c. Compared to women, men tend to have much more fluid sexual orientations, meaning that their sexual orientations change over time.
d. Within the United States, the rates of gay, lesbian, and bisexual people are consistent across all fifty states.

Self-Assessment Answers

1. c, 2. culture, 3. a, 4. d, 5. a, 6. c, 7. b, 8. Gender, 9. d, 10. a

WHAT'S YOUR TAKE?

1. In this chapter, you've read what the experts have to say about cultural differences between different groups. How do your own experiences match with their descriptions? Have you traveled to places, either nearby or far away, where you met people very different from yourself? Did those differences fit into one of the cultural characteristics described in this chapter (for example, individualism vs. collectivism)? Did you notice other important differences besides the ones described in this chapter?

SHOW ME MORE

10.1 Microaggressions

http://tiny.cc/showmemore

In this brief video, Derald Wing Sue, a leading scholar on the topic of microaggressions, offers explanations and illustrations of the concept.

Rawpixel.com/Shutterstock

10.2 Cultural Characteristics of Countries Around the World

http://tiny.cc/vl7njy

This interactive Web site allows you to compare the United States to other countries in terms of individualism/collectivism and other variables on which cultures vary.

Fanatic Studio/Getty Images

11 Stress and Health

bowdenimages/Getty Images

My dentist finishes the tooth cleaning and hands me a mirror. As I check out my bright white grin, she says, "You may notice a little bleeding. Don't worry about it. It's just that sharp-pointed tool I have to use. Happens to everybody."

"No problem," I reply. I leave the dentist's office with glistening teeth but a tiny cut or two around my gums. I don't give it a second thought.

An hour later, I'm writing this chapter, searching for articles about the connection between stress and health. As I run my tongue across one of those tiny cuts in my mouth, I come across a study in which—believe it or not—the researchers gave people those cuts on purpose (Marucha et al., 1998).

I read the study eagerly. The researchers made a 3.5-millimeter cut on the roof of the mouth of each student participant. This happened twice: once during summer break, and once (on the opposite side of the mouth) a couple of months later, just a few days before a major exam during the fall semester. The researchers took close-up photos of each cut every day until it healed. Their findings? For every student, the cut healed much more slowly during exam time than it did during vacation time. It took about a week to disappear during summer, but almost 11 days around exams. The difference was obvious early in the process: After just one or two days, the cut made during summer break was already noticeably smaller than the cut made before the exam. It was the same students, the same mouths, and the same cuts, but different healing rates. What was the researchers' explanation? *Stress*. The high stress brought on by exams made the students' cuts heal much more slowly than identical cuts did during low-stress summer vacation time.

I was amazed at how the healing of such little cuts, just like the ones in my own mouth, could depend so much on stressors like exams. But then I wondered, what if the stakes were higher? What if it wasn't a tiny cut that the body was trying to heal, but a big wound or surgery incision? What if the body was trying to fight off a serious disease, like the flu or HIV? And what if the stressor was bigger and more unpredictable than an exam, like the death of a loved one or a job loss? Especially when the stakes are so high, what can we do to enhance our ability to handle stress well?

This chapter addresses all of those questions and the broad issue that underlies them: how stress affects health. We'll begin by defining stress and identifying some of its common causes. Then we'll explore how stress affects the body and the mind, including the role that culture can play. Finally, we'll finish by discussing the ways we cope with the stress we experience.

CHAPTER OUTLINE

Stress: What Is It and What Causes It?

YOU WILL LEARN:

11.1 how psychologists define stress.

11.2 about the difference between stress and a stressor.

11.3 what the fight-or-flight response is.

11.4 how appraisal is involved in stress.

11.5 how everyday hassles cause significant stress when they accumulate.

Savage Chickens

Doug Savage

Before we explore the connection between stress and health, let's define stress and consider some of the factors that make us feel it.

What Is Stress?

Stress is an unpleasant physical or psychological reaction to circumstances you perceive as challenging. You probably know the reaction well, perhaps too well. Your muscles may tense, your stomach may churn, your pulse may quicken, and your teeth may grind. You may feel anger, irritability, sadness, nervousness, or all of these (Theil & Dretsch, 2011; Folkman, 2011).

It is important to clarify that when psychologists talk about stress, they are talking about that unpleasant reaction, *not* the event or situation that caused it. Sometimes, in everyday speech, we use the word *stress* for both the reaction and the situation, which can get confusing (Monat et al., 2007). You might say, "I'm feeling so much stress about that PowerPoint presentation I have to give" and "That PowerPoint presentation is such a stress." Psychologists make a distinction: The feeling you have about the PowerPoint presentation is indeed stress, but the presentation itself is a *stressor*. We'll examine stressors in more detail a bit later, but for now, the important point is that psychologists use different terms for the feeling of stress and the thing that causes that feeling.

Since the mid-1900s, psychologists have studied stress, along with its effects on health and ways to cope with it. A big reason why the study of stress arose around that time was that soldiers back from World War II were demonstrating the physical and psychological toll of the stress they experienced in battle (Lazarus, 1999; Cooper & Dewe, 2004). Some soldiers were even traumatized by their stress, which eventually led psychologists to create the diagnosis of *posttraumatic stress disorder* (*PTSD*), which we'll discuss later. Of course, psychologists quickly recognized that war wasn't the only thing that caused stress, so their study of stress expanded to include experiences common to all of us.

The Three Categories of Stress. As the study of stress evolved, psychologists identified three broad categories of it: *physiological stress*, *psychological stress*, and *sociocultural stress* (Monat et al., 2007). Physiological stress is the result of something happening directly to a person's body (Cannon, 1953). For example, if Juan gets injured in a car accident or catches a virus, his body feels the stress as he fights to recover. Psychological stress comes from the events in a person's life and the way those events are interpreted. For example, an argument with a romantic partner or the possibility of losing a job are both sources of psychological stress (Lazarus, 1966). Sociocultural stress stems from forces that affect the wider social and cultural groups to which a person belongs. For example, if Grace belongs to a minority group that is likely to experience prejudice, joblessness, or poverty, she is likely to experience sociocultural stress. Of course, most of us experience combinations of these kinds of stress at various points in our lives, and as a single event.

The Fight-or-Flight Response. Underlying all of these categories of stress is the importance of the **fight-or-flight response**: an automatic emotional and physical reaction to a perceived threat that prepares us to either attack it or run away from it. Your fight-or-flight response has long been recognized as a product of evolution (Cannon, 1932). It was essential to the survival of early human beings, and it is still beneficial today. Basically, it is your body quickly gearing up to respond to a perceived danger by taking it on (fight) or taking off (flight). (To be specific, it is your sympathetic nervous system gearing up, as we learned in Chapter 2.) Your heart rate speeds up,

your breathing quickens, you start to sweat, and your muscles tense. When this fight-or-flight response is followed by actual fight or flight—when you actually take on the threat or take off running—your body spends this energy effectively and then calms down naturally. But when the fight-or-flight response is stifled, the result is stress (Taylor, 2011b; McEwen & Lasley, 2002).

Consider this example: David hears someone trying to break into his room at night. At the first sound of this danger, his fight-or-flight response kicks in: He instantly sits up in bed, amped by adrenaline. His body is ready to either confront the intruder or run. But if he does neither, his body will have gotten revved up for nothing. That unnecessary revving won't do much damage if it happens just once. But if it happens over and over, or it never really goes away (as it would if David felt like intruders were constantly after him), it will cause excessive wear and tear on the body. That is the key to how stress, over time, damages health. Repeated wear and tear from the frustration of the fight-or-flight response damages the heart, weakens the immune system, and generally breaks down the health.

stress
An unpleasant physical or psychological reaction to circumstances perceived as challenging.

fight-or-flight response
An automatic emotional and physical reaction to a perceived threat that prepares one to either attack it or run away from it.

stressor
Any event or change in one's life that causes stress.

appraisal
The way you evaluate the things that happen to you.

What Causes Stress?

A **stressor** is any event or change in your life that causes you stress. Anything *can* be a stressor, depending upon what *you* perceive to be challenging. Of course, there are certain events and changes that almost all of us would experience as stressors. Most are big, bad things like the death of a loved one, a divorce or breakup, a serious injury or illness, or a job loss. (There are also a few big, possibly good things on the list of common stressors too, like retiring, getting a new job, finishing school, pregnancy, and starting a romantic relationship.) Back in the 1960s and 1970s, the leading stress researchers made a questionnaire out of these events in which they assigned each event a specific point value (Holmes & Rahe, 1967; Holmes & Masuda, 1974). Participants checked the events that had happened to them in the previous year, added up their points, and then had a stress total that predicted their risk for serious health problems.

Appraisal. That questionnaire, titled the Social Readjustment Rating Scale, did a decent job of predicting stress-related health problems, but it was far from perfect. There were plenty of people who racked up high point totals, but didn't experience much stress or health problems. There were also plenty of people with low point totals, who were stressed out and sick all the time. By the 1980s, researchers had identified at least two reasons why that might happen. As **Figure 11.1** shows, the first reason involves **appraisal**, or the way you evaluate the things that happen to you (Lazarus et al., 1985, 1999; Kemeny, 2011; Benyamini, 2011; Tomaka & Blascovich, 1994). (You may have heard the word *appraisal* when someone is selling a house, or assessing the value of an antique. It means the same thing here—basically, what it is worth—but in terms of stress, not money.) Psychologists actually break down the stress appraisal

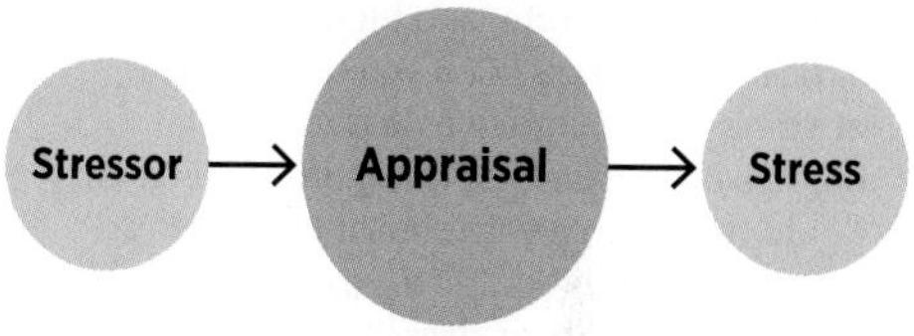

FIGURE 11.1 The Importance of Appraisal. Stressors don't cause stress directly. Between the stressor and the stress, your appraisal—your evaluation of how bad the stressor is and how capable you are of handling it—plays a significant role.

IT'S LIKE...

Stifling Your Fight-or-Flight Response Is Like Stepping on the Gas and Brake at the Same Time

There is a reason you were taught to drive with one foot rather than two. Using two feet would allow you to press the gas and the brake at the same time, which is no good for the car. Especially if both pedals were pushed to the floor, you could expect the simultaneous stop-and-go commands to damage important parts inside your car, like your transmission or your brakes (Magliozzi & Magliozzi, 2011).

The same is true for important parts inside your body when it comes to stress. Your body's natural response to stressors is to *go*, in the form of battling the stressor (fight) or running away (flight). When you prevent yourself from doing either, you are essentially sending a *stop* message at the same time. The problem gets worse as the stressor gets more chronic—which is like keeping a foot on the gas and the brake for days on end.

Realistically, society prevents people from responding as naturally to stressors as other animals do. You *have* to check yourself, or tap the brakes, at least some of the time, in order to get along with others. But it is also important to give yourself an outlet (like regular exercise) for that stifled fight-or-flight response, or to rethink the stressor so the fight-or-flight response doesn't affect you as negatively or last as long as it otherwise might.

CHAPTER APP 11.1

Appraisal

Serenita

Preview one of the links and consider the following questions.

WEBSITE:
http://tiny.cc/qli7jy

ANDROID:
http://tiny.cc/eb92iy

IPHONE:
http://tiny.cc/1582iy

VIDEO DEMO:
http://tiny.cc/chapterapps

This app measures your heart rate pattern, breathing, and blood flow through the tip of your finger, which you place on the camera lens of your smartphone. Serenita then translates those biological measurements into a stress level. (It also offers tips for breathing-based techniques to reduce stress, but our focus here is on how it measures stress.)

How does it APPly to your daily life?
How valid are biological measures like breathing, heart rate, and blood flow as indicators of stress? Can your experience of stress be accurately assessed by such objective measures, or is it more subjective? Could two people with similar heart rates, breathing, and blood flow experience different amounts of stress?

How does it APPly to your understanding of psychology?
How does this app influence your appreciation of *appraisal* of stress, including *primary appraisal* and *secondary appraisal*?

process into two parts, *primary appraisal* and *secondary appraisal*. **Primary appraisal** is determining how stressful an event is to you. **Secondary appraisal** is determining how capable you are of coping with the event. Think of it this way: Primary appraisal is how hard you think the big bad wolf can huff and puff; secondary appraisal is knowing whether your house is built of straw, wood, or brick.

As an example, let's consider Tyler and Chelsea, two single 20-somethings who have worked as sales reps in Peoria, Illinois, for the same big company for several years. They get the same news at the same time: They're being transferred to Chicago. Their reactions are very different. Let's consider their primary appraisals first—what they think about the transfer. Tyler sees the transfer as extremely stressful: "Ugh! I'll have to pack up everything, say goodbye to all my friends, and find a new place to live in Chicago, which is expensive and crowded. Plus, my new job responsibilities might be too much." Chelsea's primary appraisal of the transfer is much more positive: "Cool! I get to live in the big city, make new friends, and have the opportunity for even more success than I've had here."

In terms of secondary appraisal, or what they think about their own abilities to handle the transfer, Tyler and Chelsea differ again. Tyler worries to himself: "I can't handle this. New situations make me nervous, and I'm not the kind of guy who will thrive with a new supervisor in a city I don't know." Chelsea is more confident: "I can do this. I'm good at my job. It may take a little adjusting, but I'm sure I'll find a way to be happy and successful in Chicago. It's a great opportunity." As you can tell, Tyler is in much worse shape than Chelsea in terms of this move. Not only is he likely to experience more stress (due to a big gap between his perception of the stressor and his ability to handle it), he is also more likely to experience physical health problems as a consequence.

Experimental studies have supported the notion that appraisal of stressors influences health (Petrie & Weinman, 2006). For example, one study followed 65 people who had just experienced their first heart attack. All got standard hospital treatment, but half got something extra: three sessions with a psychologist whose goal was to make sure the patients left the hospital with rational and accurate beliefs about their heart condition. Those patients left the hospital thinking something like this: "That heart attack was serious, but I'm recovering, and I can live a long and healthy life." However, patients who didn't get those sessions might think something like this: "That heart attack means I'm going to die soon, and there's nothing I can do about it." The patients whose treatment included their heads as well as their hearts viewed their heart condition as more controllable, less stressful; had fewer ongoing heart-related symptoms; and returned to work faster (Petrie et al., 2002). Other studies have found similar results when the patient's spouse is included in the discussions of beliefs about the illness. In fact, in these cases even the spouse's stress levels are lower (Broadbent et al., 2009a,b).

Appraisal and Culture. Cultural variables like ethnicity, gender, age, and others can influence the way we appraise stressors. For example, while a college entrance exam like the ACT or SAT is probably stressful for most high school students, it might be especially stressful for students from certain cultural groups, including many Asian cultures, who can place unusually high emphasis on academic achievement (Lee & Mock, 2005; Lee, 1997; Sue & Consolacion 2003). A 16-year-old boy who catches the flu may experience less stress than his 75-year-old grandmother who catches the same bug because the boy doesn't worry as much about healing as his grandmother does.

DIVERSITY MATTERS

Hassles. The other reason a simple list of your major stressors doesn't always reflect your total stress level is that the list leaves out **hassles**, the common, minor annoyances or aggravations of day-to-day life. Hassles add up, and cumulatively, they can add significantly to your stress level (Kanner et al., 1981; DeLongis et al., 1988; Serido et al., 2004). Hassles vary from person to person, but some common ones include transportation problems (traffic, car trouble, late buses or subways); losing your keys or wallet; conflict (or "drama") with friends or family members; crowded living conditions

primary appraisal
The way you determine how stressful an event is to you.

secondary appraisal
The way you determine how capable you are of coping with an event.

hassles
The common, minor annoyances or aggravations of day-to-day life.

(including friends crashing on your couch for way too long); a too-long to-do list; and running low on essentials like money, food, or sleep.

A life full of these hassles can provide plenty of stress (and health risk) even in the absence of big events. For example, in my own private practice, I had a therapy client, Makayla, who was a college student with no major stressors to speak of: no losses or breakups; no transferring from one school to another; no car accidents or injuries; and a steady part-time job and family life. But as she walked me through the hassles she experienced the day before our appointment, it was easy to see her stress add up. "My phone dies overnight, so it doesn't wake me up when it's supposed to, and I miss my first class. We had a paper due, so I try to email my professor to explain, but the wireless router in my apartment goes down—again! While I walk to campus to deliver the paper to her office, hoping she'll accept it late, it starts pouring and of course I left my umbrella at home. Later, I'm still drenched and I'm waiting and waiting for my friend to meet me for lunch and she totally stands me up—no text, no call, nothing. I get home later that afternoon and my landlord is waiting for me, saying the rent is past due. My roommate never paid her share, and she's out of town, so now I'm stuck covering for her, which I can't afford. I run over to the pharmacy to pick up my prescription refill because I'm down to my last pill, and they keep me waiting an hour for something that should take a minute. Later that night, I'm trying to study and my mom calls and picks a fight with me about some random comment I made during my last visit home. Then I try to go to bed but my upstairs neighbors with the high-powered speakers decide to blast some death metal. AAGH!" Makayla looks exhausted and frazzled, and she is coming down with a cold. With these accumulated hassles, it is easy to see why.

MY TAKE VIDEO 11.1

Appraisal

"I was trying to stay calm and breathe my way through it..."

YOUTUBE: http://tiny.cc/mytake
LAUNCHPAD: launchpadworks.com

CHECK YOUR LEARNING:

11.1 How do psychologists define stress?

11.2 What is the relationship between stress and stressors?

11.3 What is the flight-or-fight response?

11.4 What is appraisal, and what is the difference between primary appraisal and secondary appraisal?

11.5 What are hassles and how do they relate to stress?

Stress and the Mind-Body Connection

There is no doubt about it: Both mind and body suffer the consequences of stress. As we learned in Chapter 1, psychology has an entire specialization devoted to this connection: *health psychology*, the psychological specialization that focuses on the relationship between mind and body. Most health psychologists are researchers, conducting studies like the ones described in this chapter. Their findings often apply to the practice of psychology and medicine, so health psychology has become increasingly influential in how people are treated for stress-related problems. (As a side note, the term *behavioral medicine* is also used to mean roughly the same thing as *health psychology*.)

Most often, we think of the mind affecting the body, but actually the relationship between mind and body is bidirectional, or a two-way street, as **Figure 11.2** illustrates (Kemeny, 2011). For example, think of the stress Terry would feel in the weeks after breaking his right leg—aggravation with the cast and crutches, difficulty getting around both at home and elsewhere, and an inability to drive. Or consider Jessica's migraine headaches: They come and go without warning, leaving her completely debilitated when they hit. So, not only do these bodily problems cause direct physical pain,

YOU WILL LEARN:

11.6 about the different ways stress damages a person's health.

11.7 what the general adaptation syndrome is.

11.8 how stress affects the immune system and contributes to illness.

11.9 how different personality types experience different levels of stress-related consequences.

11.10 how certain personality traits correlate with high or low stress levels.

11.11 how stress contributes to different psychological disorders.

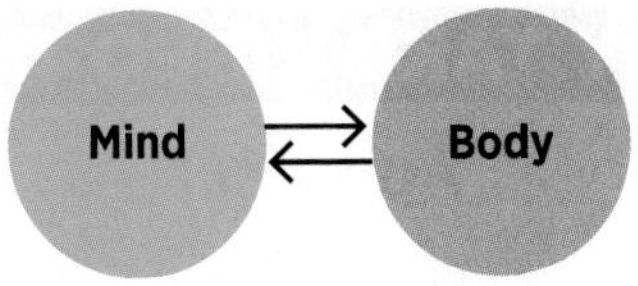

FIGURE 11.2 Mind and Body Influence: A Two-Way Street. In terms of stress, your mind and your body influence each other in a bidirectional way.

they also infuriate and exasperate people with their unpredictability or their power to incapacitate. Sometimes, the mental stress caused by physical problems actually makes the physical problems even worse, creating a cycle of stress.

Both the body and the mind can be affected by stress in this bidirectional, interactive way. To keep things simple, though, we'll separate the body and the mind in the upcoming sections. One section will discuss how stress and the body affect each other, and another section will discuss how stress and the mind affect each other.

How Stress and Your Body Affect Each Other

The notion that stress can affect your physical health has been around for a long time. The ancient Greeks and Romans often included stress-reducing activities like baths and garden strolls in their treatment of diseases. Ancient Indian and Chinese civilizations also emphasized the balance of mind and body, through their respective concepts of Ayurveda and yin–yang (Friedman & Adler, 2011). The idea that lowering stress can improve physical health even appears in Biblical proverbs: "A merry heart does good like a medicine" (Proverbs 17:22; cited in Friedman & Adler, 2011, p. 3). The idea remains strong today: "Humans have long believed that how they think and what they feel may be intimately linked to whether they are healthy or sick" (Pickren & Degni, 2011, p. 15).

In recent years, psychological research has identified many ways in which stress can make you sick. These ways can be grouped into three general categories (Holroyd & Lazarus, 1982; Monat et al., 2007):

1. **Stress damages your health directly.** Earlier, we discussed how repeatedly revving up your fight-or-flight response, without addressing the stress, causes excessive wear and tear on your heart, cardiovascular system, and other important parts of your body.
2. **Reactions to stress can damage your health directly.** This is not about the stress itself, but how a person deals with it. Drinking too much, using illicit drugs, working too much, sleeping too little, or making bad decisions in any of these states can put you at increased risk for injury or illness.
3. **Reactions to stress can damage your health indirectly.** Responding to signs of stress by ignoring them, denying them, or insisting you never need help can heighten the chances that your stress and its negative influence on your body will continue unchecked.

When stressors persist over time, the response follows a predictable pattern. That pattern, first identified by Hungarian medical researcher Hans Selye in the early and mid-1900s (Selye, 1936, 1952, 1956), is known as the **general adaptation syndrome**: a widely accepted understanding of the way bodies respond to ongoing stress, consisting of the sequence of alarm, resistance, and exhaustion. Those first two stages—alarm and resistance—help us to handle short-term stressors (**Figure 11.3**). Again, think of the adrenaline rush that comes with your fight-or-flight response. When you face a one-shot stressor (also known as an *acute* stressor) like a job interview, a big exam, or a speech to a large crowd, your body's built-in strategy of sounding an alarm and resisting the stress is probably enough to get you geared up for the event (while also warding off any long-lasting negative effects). The problems come when the stressor is unrelenting (or *chronic*) rather than short-term. With chronic stressors, the body's alarm keeps sounding, but eventually the resistance wears off (like an army simply overwhelmed by never-ending waves of enemy attacks). The result is exhaustion, which leaves you vulnerable to disease.

general adaptation syndrome
A widely accepted understanding of the way the body responds to ongoing stress, consisting of the sequence of alarm, resistance, and exhaustion.

Chronic Stress: Examples and Evidence. Examples of sources of chronic stress include living in an unstable environment, like a war zone or an extremely

violent neighborhood; living in ongoing poverty, where the next meal is uncertain; living with an abusive partner or parent who could hurt you at any time; and working as a first responder, such as a police officer or paramedic and witnessing terrible things nearly every day (Straker, 2013; Straker et al., 1988; Davies et al., 2013). Consider these examples of evidence linking chronic stress to physical health problems:

- A study of over 9500 adults found that experiencing more chronic stressors during childhood increases the rate of serious medical diseases during adulthood, including heart disease, chronic lung disease, diabetes, and cancer. For adults who grew up experiencing at least four kinds of chronic stressors (like psychological, physical, or sexual abuse; or living in a home with criminal activity, substance abuse, or violence), the risk of serious medical diseases during adulthood was often 2 to 4 times the normal rate (Felitti et al., 1998; see also Shonkoff et al., 2009). (See **Table 11.1** for more details.)
- In Operation Iraqi Freedom (2003–2010), over 83% of the medical evacuations of soldiers were not for battle injuries, but for diseases, including pneumonia and tuberculosis, that increased in likelihood as the soldiers experienced stress-related exhaustion (Fischer, 2013; Wool, 2013).
- Gay men who were "in the closet"—that is, they carried the ongoing stress of hiding their sexual orientation—experienced a much higher rate of serious physical illness over a 5-year period than gay men who were "out," including greater incidence of cancer and infectious diseases like pneumonia and sinusitis (Cole et al., 1996).
- In a study of over 850 elementary-school-age kids with asthma from big U.S. cities, the more the kids were exposed to violence, the greater the amount of

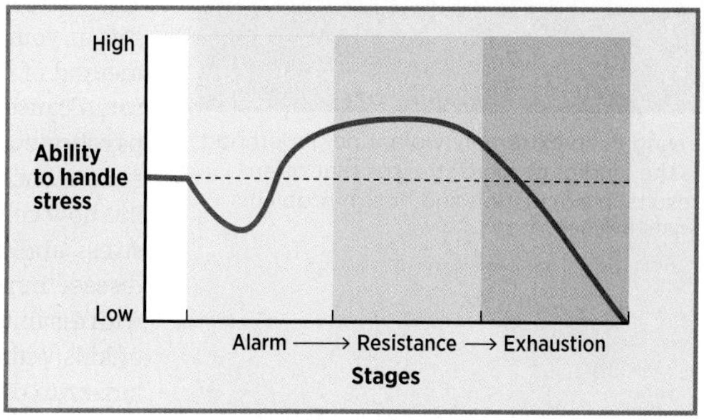

FIGURE 11.3 General Adaptation Syndrome. According to Selye's concept of the general adaptation syndrome, our ability to ward off the effects of stress stays strong for a while (during the resistance stage), but eventually plummets (during the exhaustion phase).

WATCHING PSYCHOLOGY

Sudden Death? The Stress-Related Health Risks of Watching Sports on TV

As a society, we watch *a lot* of sports on TV. The Super Bowl is annually the most watched TV show in the country, typically drawing well over 100 million viewers. In addition to the thrill of victory or the agony of defeat, you may experience something else when you watch your team on TV: stress. Is it possible that the stress of watching the big game is enough to produce big health problems? Numerous researchers have explored this question. Here are some of their findings:

- In the week after the New York Giants dramatically defeated the New England Patriots in the 2008 Super Bowl, deaths in Massachusetts (the Patriots' home state) related to heart or circulatory problems jumped by 20% and deaths related to heart disease jumped by 24% (Schwartz et al., 2013). A similar jump in the same kinds of deaths was noted in Los Angeles after their Rams lost the 1980 Super Bowl (Kloner et al., 2009).
- On days when the German soccer team played during the 2006 World Cup, the number of cardiac emergencies (heart attacks, cardiac arrythmias, etc.) in Munich, Germany, was 2.66 times greater than on ordinary days (Wilbert-Lampen et al., 2008).
- On June 22, 1996, the Netherlands' soccer team was eliminated from the European championship. On that day, there was a much higher rate of fatal heart attacks in the Netherlands than on the 5 days before or after, or during the same calendar day in the previous or next year. Specifically, 14 more people died of heart attacks than expected on that day (Witte et al., 2000). Similar results were found in a study connecting heart attack deaths and home team losses over a 5-year period in English soccer matches (Kirkup & Merrick, 2003).
- On June 30, 1998, England lost its World Cup match to Argentina in a penalty shoot-out. For that day and the 2 days after, rates of hospital admissions for heart attacks in England increased by 25% (Carroll et al., 2002).

Other researchers have disputed the results of studies like these, pointing out methodological flaws (Bauman et al., 2006; Toubiana et al., 2001). It is also worth noting that the worst stress-related health outcomes seem to follow losses rather than wins. Even with those qualifications, these findings suggest that for some fans—most likely, those who already have stress-related health problems and are perhaps a bit overly invested in their team's fate—watching a sporting event on TV can be a dangerous stressor.

Living in an extremely violent neighborhood is the kind of chronic stressor that often results in exhaustion and health problems.
Scott Olson/Getty Images

stress-related asthma symptoms the kids exhibited. Higher stress meant more days of significant wheezing and disrupted play activities for the kids, as well as more lost nights of sleep for the parents. This study controlled for other variables like socioeconomic status and nonviolent negative life events (Wright et al., 2004).

- Kids in the most violent Chicago neighborhoods were twice as likely to *develop* asthma in the first place as kids in the least violent Chicago neighborhoods (Sternthal et al., 2010).

The Immune System. When ongoing stress outlasts your resistance and exhaustion sets in, your *immune system* gets compromised. Your **immune system** is your body's innate method of defending against bacteria, viruses, infections, injuries, and anything else that could cause illness or death. Researchers who focus on this phenomenon call their field **psychoneuroimmunology (PNI)**: the study of the relationship between psychological factors, including stress, and the immune system. Specifically, these researchers examine how certain hormones, like cortisol, epinephrine, and norepinephrine, increase with stress and interfere with the production of *antibodies*, which are the cells that fight off disease in your body (Rabin, 2005; Kaye & Lightman, 2005). In one study, parents of kids with disabilities (whose parenting stress was presumed to be unusually high) and parents of kids without such disabilities were given a vaccination for pneumonia. The parents of kids with disabilities produced fewer pneumonia antibodies, which means that even with the boost of the vaccination their stress levels suppressed the production of the cells that fight off the disease (Gallagher et al., 2009).

Stress and Illness. The physical problems that psychoneuroimmunologists focus on are **psychophysiological illnesses**: any illness that stress can cause, worsen, or maintain. When research on stress and health was in its early stages, in the mid-1900s, it was considered newsworthy when an illness was discovered to be psychophysiological. Now, it is difficult to find an illness that *isn't* psychophysiological. Research has established psychological or stress-related connections to almost every physical malady that you can imagine (Contrada & Baum, 2011). Perhaps the best-established connection is with **coronary heart disease**—a common and often fatal disease in which the arteries that lead to the heart are clogged or blocked—and other cardiovascular conditions (Sparrenberger et al., 2009). Of course, as **Figure 11.4** illustrates, a long list of other diseases have been connected to stress, from the common cold to cancer, from the flu to HIV, from arthritis to pneumonia, from migraines to irritable bowel syndrome, from diabetes to asthma, and many, many more (Vedhara & Irwin, 2005; Irwin, 2008; Segerstrom & Miller, 2004; Cohen & Williamson, 1991; Cohen et al., 1991, 1993).

Even wounds are affected by stress. Wounds are actually a favorite of researchers in this field, since they can be created and measured so much more conveniently than many other diseases or conditions. There are quite a few studies in which the researchers give people wounds of a very specific size and location, measure the decrease in size of the wound over time, and see if stress levels predict how quickly that decrease will happen. (By the way, the word *wound* makes it sound worse than it is—it is typically a small cut or blister that causes the participant very little pain.) Over and over, these studies have found that stress slows wound healing (Gouin & Kiecolt-Glaser, 2011; Ebrecht et al., 2004; Bosch et al., 2007; Walburn et al., 2009). One study found that blisters on the forearm healed less quickly in high-stress people than in low-stress people, and that the high-stress people's bodies also produced fewer of the cell proteins (cytokines) that promote wound healing (Glaser et al., 1999). In another study, researchers gave identical small wounds (near the elbow) to 13 people who take care of a relative with Alzheimer's and to 13 people who don't. The two groups were matched in terms of gender, age, and socioeconomic status. The caregivers' wounds took 9 days longer to heal completely, but the noncaregivers' wounds were noticeably smaller within the first few days, presumably due to the difference in stress levels between the groups (Kiecolt-Glaser et al., 1995).

TABLE 11.1: Multiple Stressors in Childhood Become Health Problems in Adulthood

ADULT HEALTH PROBLEM	INCREASED LIKELIHOOD
severe obesity	1.6 times
diabetes	1.6 times
cancer	1.9 times
heart disease	2.2 times
stroke	2.4 times
chronic lung disease	3.9 times
depression	4.6 times
alcoholism	7.4 times

Researchers found that when people experienced at least four serious chronic stressors during childhood, their risk for serious health problems during adulthood multiplied (Felitti et al., 1998).

Sometimes, these researchers don't need to wound their participants themselves. Instead, they focus on wounds that the participants obtained some other way. For example, one group of researchers tracked people undergoing hernia surgery, which requires an incision. They found that the incisions of patients who were highly stressed about their surgery healed much more slowly than the incisions of patients who were less stressed about the same surgery (Broadbent et al., 2003). Building on that finding, those researchers later developed a technique to lower stress before and after surgery. Patients took part in a 45-minute presurgery meeting with a psychologist who taught them relaxation and deep breathing skills, helped them imagine a successful recovery, and provided them with relaxation recordings that the patients listened to in the days before and after the surgery. They tested this technique on 30 patients having surgery to remove their gallbladders. Compared to 30 patients who underwent the same surgery but did not receive the stress reduction technique, their surgery wounds healed much more quickly (Broadbent et al., 2012). The implications are significant: people undergoing surgery (perhaps any kind of surgery) might be able to mend their bodies more quickly, return home sooner, and spend less on hospital bills, thanks to a simple stress-reduction effort.

immune system
The body's innate method of defending against bacteria, viruses, infections, injuries, and anything else that could cause illness or death.

psychoneuroimmunology (PNI)
The study of the relationship between psychological factors, including stress, and the immune system.

psychophysiological illnesses
Any illness that stress can cause, worsen, or maintain.

coronary heart disease
A common and often fatal disease in which the arteries that lead to the heart are clogged or blocked.

How Stress and Your Mind Affect Each Other

Stress disrupts not only your body, but your mind as well. Think of the most stressful periods in your life. Most likely, your stress eclipsed any chance you had of feeling happiness. For example, if you've been unlucky in love, you know firsthand how the stress of relationship conflict can bring down your mental state. It is no surprise that researchers have found that these kinds of conflicts—even just remembering such

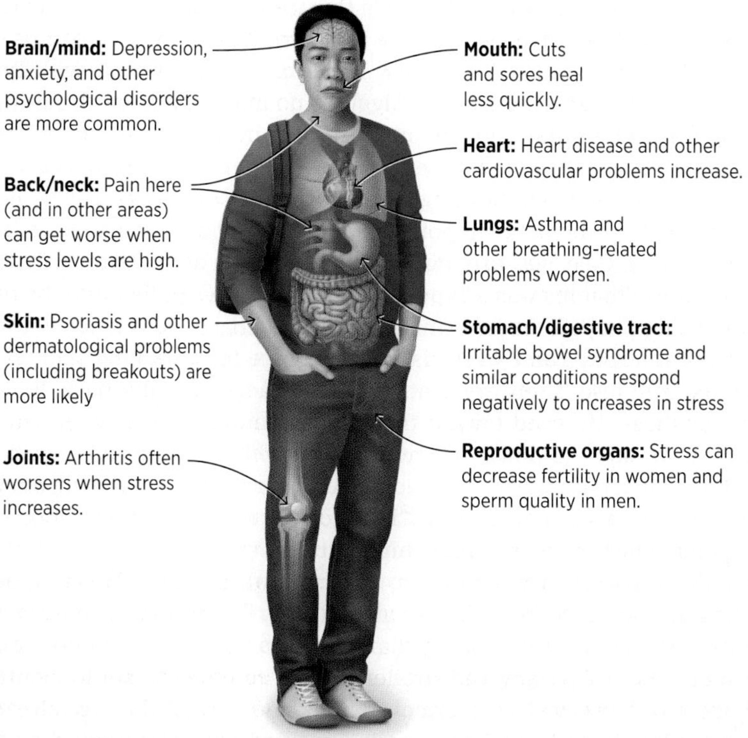

FIGURE 11.4 Stress from Head to Toe. Chronic, severe stress can take its toll on many parts of the body. The conditions listed here, and many more that can affect the whole body (like cancers and viruses), can be worsened by stress. Information from O'Malley et al., 2011; Linton, 2000; Gollenberg et al., 2010; Sanders & Bruce, 1997; Contrada & Baum, 2011; Vedhara & Irwin, 2005; Irwin, 2008; Segerstrom & Miller, 2004; Danoff-Burg & Revenson, 2005.

conflicts long after they've ended—increase levels of stress hormones like epinephrine and norepinephrine (Malarkey et al., 1994; Kiecolt-Glaser et al., 1997). What may be more surprising is that the levels of those hormones in newlywed couples (married less than a year) predict how happy the members of those couples will be with their marriages *10 years later*. In fact, they even predict whether the couple will be married or divorced by that time (Kiecolt-Glaser et al., 2003). So, not only can marital discontent cause stress, stress can cause marital discontent as well.

Let's consider other ways that your mind and your stress level interact, with a focus on the role of your personality and the psychological disorders most closely related to stress.

Personality, Stress, and Health. Back in the late 1800s, a Canadian physician named William Osler was treating people with heart problems. He noticed that many of these heart patients seemed to have similar personalities, most typically "a keen and ambitious [person], the indicator of whose engines are set at full speed ahead" (cited in Chesney & Rosenman, 1980, p. 188). This was one of the first written observations by a medical professional to link a particular personality style with a particular physical illness. As the decades went by, others refined Osler's observation. For example, in the 1930s, Karl and William Menninger (famous U.S. psychiatrists whose Menninger Clinic is now a well-known mental health care institution in Houston) pointed out that many patients with heart problems were also very aggressive.

Stress and Personality Types. In the late 1950s, a cardiologist named Meyer Friedman noticed that in his waiting room, the chairs were showing signs of wear in unusual places—on the front edges of the seats and armrests. He eventually figured out that his patients—who, by definition, had heart trouble—were literally sitting on the edges of their seats and grasping the armrests tensely as they barely tolerated their wait to see the doctor. These impatient patients inspired Friedman and his colleagues to give a formal name to this personality style that predisposed people to heart disease: **Type A personality**, or a personality featuring high levels of competitiveness, drive, impatience, and hostility (Friedman & Rosenman, 1959). People with Type A personality find themselves in a "constant struggle to do more and more things in less and less time, and [are] often quite hostile or aggressive in their efforts to achieve them" (Friedman, 2011, p. 218). They are hurried and cutthroat in their attempts to attain their goals—not just when such qualities might be appropriate or necessary, but all the time.

I once agreed to go holiday shopping in early December with some relatives. My aunt's new boyfriend, Cole, was driving. I didn't know him at all, but it only took a few minutes to recognize that his was a Type A personality. As we pulled into the parking lot of the crowded shopping center, he leaned forward and his hands clenched the steering wheel. A look of intensity came over his face. The race for a parking spot was on, and Cole wasn't about to lose. There were a few open spaces near the back, but he would never settle for those. He sped toward the front, scanning intensely. He patrolled the rows, up and down, up and down. "Come on, *come on*!" he muttered angrily. My aunt pleaded for him to just take one of the spaces open near the back of the lot, but Cole, with a possessed gleam in his eye, cut her off: "Don't distract me. I'll get us a good spot. I can promise you that." She tried to explain to him that we were in no hurry, but her words fell on deaf ears. Eventually, he saw a shopper walking toward her car. He crept behind her until she got to her car in the front row. He immediately put his blinker on and exclaimed "Yes!" as if he had just won the parking championship. It took this shopper a minute to vacate her spot—she had a baby and stroller to load into the car, not to mention lots of shopping bags—so Cole gave her an annoyed honk and barked, "Let's go already!"

Hostility and competitiveness, as illustrated by this coach arguing with the referee, seem to be the most toxic parts of Type A personality. Fuse/Corbis/Getty Images

Through the late 1900s, Type A personality received a lot of attention from researchers, and for good reason: Heart disease had become the greatest cause of premature death in the Western world. According to much of the earlier research, the connection was confirmed: Type A personality was correlated with heart trouble. For example, researchers conducted an 8-year longitudinal study on 3500 men, which found that those with Type A personalities had significantly higher incidence of heart disease (Rosenman et al., 1964; 1975). More recent research has produced results that are not

so definitive, however (Houston & Snyder, 1988; Miller et al., 1991). These recent studies still generally support the link between Type A personality and heart disease, but they try to determine a more particular connection: What, specifically, are the toxic ingredients within Type A personality? Type A personality is a broad cluster of characteristics; perhaps particular characteristics contribute more than others to heart disease (Friedman & Booth-Kewley, 1987). So far, the prime suspects seem to be hostility and competitiveness (Booth-Kewley & Friedman, 1987; Cooper & Bright, 2001; Ganster et al., 1991; Friedman, 2011). Being driven and even impatient are not so bad for your health. In fact, they can be quite productive in many circumstances. However, a constant rivalry with others and an ever-present attitude of anger or nastiness are bad for your health.

When researchers identified Type A personality, they also identified **Type B personality**: a personality very much unlike Type A personality, in which the person is noncompetitive, easygoing, relaxed, and rarely angry (Cooper & Dewe, 2004). People with Type B personalities are more "chill" than their Type A counterparts. For example, unlike Cole, someone with a Type B personality might choose to park in the distant corner of a crowded parking lot to avoid the competition in the front rows—or might even skip the mall on a crowded day altogether.

Other personality types have been identified more recently (Friedman, 2011). **Type C personality** is a personality featuring a low level of emotional expression, a high level of agreeableness with other people, and a tendency to feel helpless. For example, consider Phoebe: Whenever she gets together with her family, she holds her feelings in and goes along with whatever they want to do, but she is bothered by a sense that she doesn't have as much control over her life as she would like. **Type D personality** (sometimes called *distressed personality*) is a personality featuring high levels of negative emotions, like depression and anxiety, and a reluctance to share those emotions with others. For example, consider Ronnie: He worries a lot, and tends to feel blue pretty often, but he keeps these feelings to himself rather than talking about them with his friends or family.

Researchers have hypothesized that Type B personality should correlate with low risk of heart disease, and that Type C personality should correlate with high risk of cancer. However, research testing those hypotheses has not been extensive, and the research that has been done offers little support (Temoshok et al., 1985; Temoshok, 1986). However, there is research support for the hypothesis that Type D personality correlates with high levels of heart disease (Denollet, 2000; Pedersen & Denollet, 2003, 2006; Mols & Denollet, 2010).

Stress and Personality Factors. Most recently, research exploring the link between personality and stress (and health) has focused on *the five-factor model of personality*, or the *Big Five*. We will explore the Big Five in depth in Chapter 12, but for now it is important to know that it is currently the dominant way that psychologists understand personality. The Big Five is based on the idea that each person's personality consists of five fundamental traits. That idea is supported by the work of researchers who have converged upon the finding that there are five basic "ingredients" in human personality, and that what differentiates us from each other is the amount of each ingredient that we have (McCrae & Costa, 1996; Digman, 1990; Hunt, 1993). Those five ingredients are:

- *Neuroticism,* the tendency to experience negative emotions such as anxiety and depression
- *Extraversion,* the tendency to be socially outgoing
- *Openness to experience,* the tendency to be receptive to new or unconventional ideas
- *Conscientiousness,* the tendency to be organized, responsible, and deliberate
- *Agreeableness,* the tendency to cooperate and comply with other people

Lots of studies have found connections between these five personality traits and health-related issues. Conscientiousness and extraversion generally correlate with positive health outcomes. For example, people who are high in conscientiousness as children tend to live longer, healthier lives than people low in conscientiousness (Friedman

Type A personality
A personality featuring high levels of competitiveness, drive, impatience, and hostility.

Type B personality
A personality in which the person is noncompetitive, easygoing, relaxed, and rarely angry.

Type C personality
A personality featuring a low level of emotional expression, a high level of agreeableness with other people, and a tendency to feel helpless.

Type D personality
A personality featuring high levels of negative emotions, like depression and anxiety, and a reluctance to share those emotions with others.

TABLE 11.2: Neuroticism, Stress, and Illness

THE CORRELATION BETWEEN NEUROTICISM AND...	IS...
high blood pressure	.62
heart disease	.61
diabetes	.57
high cholesterol	.53
stroke	.40
obesity	.28
activity and exercise	−.50

Neuroticism, the personality trait defined by a tendency to think and feel negatively, can play a significant role in your experience of stress. It correlates in a strong positive way with stress-related illnesses and in a strong negative way with health-promoting behaviors like exercise. Data from Pesta et al., 2012.

et al., 2003; Kern & Friedman, 2008). In another study, researchers tracked 883 older adults for 5 years, during which 182 died. Those with low conscientiousness were twice as likely to die as those with high conscientiousness (Wilson et al., 2004). High extraversion is also commonly found alongside good health, but can occasionally be harmful to health when it leads to hazardous social behaviors like excessive drinking, risky sex, or long-term smoking (Booth-Kewley & Vickers, 1994; Friedman, 2011). On the other hand, neuroticism has repeatedly been linked to illness and disease. In the study of 883 older adults described earlier, those with high neuroticism were twice as likely to die during the 5-year period as those with low neuroticism. Another study of people from all 50 states found that neuroticism correlated negatively with healthy behaviors like exercise and eating fruits and vegetables, but positively with unhealthy behaviors and outcomes like smoking, obesity, diabetes, high cholesterol, and heart disease (Pesta et al., 2012). (See **Table 11.2** for more on this link between neuroticism and health.)

There is much more to learn about the connection between personality and health, but the collective research findings have proven quite enlightening: People who are generally unhappy and irritated tend to have more health problems (especially heart problems) than people who are generally happy and calm (Cacioppo & Berntson, 2011; Friedman & Martin, 2011; Smith & MacKenzie, 2006). As described by Meyer Friedman, the cardiologist who first identified Type A behavior back in the 1950s and who has spent over half a century studying it, the full body of research on personality and health has taught us:

> ... that a person who is chronically irritated, depressed, hostile, impulsive, bored, frustrated, unstable, lonely, or powerless is indeed more likely to develop illnesses and to die prematurely than is someone who is generally emotionally balanced and effective, ... has stable and supportive social relationships, and is well integrated into the community.—Friedman, 2011, p. 215

Stress-Related Psychological Disorders. Stress can contribute to almost any psychological disorder. Depression, anxiety, eating disorders, attention-deficit/hyperactivity disorder (ADHD), schizophrenia—any of them is worsened in times of high stress. But a few psychological disorders are built around the concept of stress. In the diagnostic manual that psychologists use, the *Diagnostic and Statistical Manual of Mental Disorders* (*DSM;* which we discuss in detail in Chapter 14), those disorders appear in the section "Trauma- and Stress-Related Disorders" in *DSM-5*.

Posttraumatic Stress Disorder. One of the disorders in this section of *DSM-5* describes the lingering stress and other aftereffects caused by traumatic events. That disorder is **posttraumatic stress disorder (PTSD)**: a psychological disorder lasting at least a month characterized by feeling continuously on edge, avoiding reminders of the traumatic event, having difficulty sleeping and concentrating, and frequently recalling or reliving the event. People with PTSD experience a variety of symptoms. Sometimes, they re-experience the trauma through frightening dreams and flashbacks. They may experience hyperarousal, which means they stay keyed up all the time, making sleep difficult. They are highly sensitive to sights or sounds that remind them of the trauma. In some cases, people with PTSD become emotionally numb and seem to "blank out" for periods of time (Keane et al., 2009).

I've been through some very distressing events myself, but I'm not sure if they were traumas. What exactly qualifies as a trauma?

DSM-5 explains that a trauma involves exposure to actual or threatened death, serious injury, or sexual violence (American Psychiatric Association, 2013). The PTSD diagnosis was originally created to capture the "shell shock" experience of soldiers returning from live combat, but people who are diagnosed with PTSD today have experienced a wide range of harrowing events, including acts of violence (shooting incidents, sexual assaults), natural disasters (tornadoes, earthquakes, tsunamis), or accidents (car wrecks, plane crashes) (Resick et al., 2008; Friedman et al.).

CURRENT CONTROVERSY

What Counts as a Trauma?

The first requirement for a diagnosis of PTSD is the *T*, or the trauma. But what, exactly, counts as a trauma? PTSD first appeared as a disorder in the DSM in 1980, after lobbying efforts by people seeking official recognition of what had informally been called *shell shock* or *combat fatigue* in soldiers (Resick et al., 2008; Friedman et al., 2007; Watters, 2010). Undoubtedly, wartime experiences can be traumas. So can other life-changing tragedies, like natural disasters, assaults, bombings, and serious car accidents.

Some events are undoubtedly traumatic. But where should the line be drawn? Scott Olson/Getty Images

But where's the line between a trauma and an event that is merely unfortunate or unpleasant? This question has been at the heart of a controversy among psychologists that continues today (Friedman, 2009). It is important for many reasons, primarily because many things can depend on whether a person is diagnosed with PTSD: health insurance benefits (to pay for treatment), disability benefits, the outcomes of lawsuits for personal injury and worker's compensation, and much more (Sparr & Pitman, 2007).

According to the *DSM-5* definition of PTSD, a trauma consists of "exposure to actual or threatened death, serious injury, or sexual violence" in at least one of these ways (American Psychiatric Association, 2013, p. 271):

- "Directly experiencing the traumatic event"
- "Witnessing, in person, the event as it occurred to others"
- "Learning that the traumatic event occurred to a close family member or close friend"
- "Experiencing repeated or extreme exposure to aversive details of the traumatic event" (like what first responders often see on the job)

This definition is certainly helpful, but a lot of questions remain. How is the phrase "threatened death, serious injury, or sexual violence" defined? (Does it count if you narrowly avoid an oncoming car that could have killed or hurt you?) And who defines the threat? What is threatening to one person might be uneventful or even enjoyable to the next. (Consider skydiving or storm chasing.) Similarly, can words rather than actions constitute such threats? One researcher argues that an individual can experience trauma "simply from a word being spoken," offering the example of certain racial slurs to some African Americans (Brown, 2008, p. 97). On another note, how close does the family member or friend have to be for their trauma to become your trauma when you find out about it? Your second cousin? Someone you used to date? Also, what does the "in person" phrase in the definition mean about witnessing something tragic (like a terrorist attack or a tornado) on live television?

Because of questions like these, psychologists and others continue to debate what constitutes the traumas upon which the PTSD (and acute stress disorder) diagnoses are based. ⬢

Of course, just because a person experiences a trauma does not mean they will develop PTSD (or any other mental disorder, for that matter). Human beings can be quite resilient in the aftermath of horrific events. In fact, as **Figure 11.5** shows, some researchers have estimated that as many as 90% of us will experience some kind of traumatic event in our lifetimes, but only 6.8% of us will develop PTSD in our lifetimes (McFarlane, 2010; Breslau, 2009; Kessler et al., 2005a,b). One study of over 2000 New Yorkers found that more than one-third of the people who lost a loved one in the 9/11 terrorist attacks reported either no symptoms or one symptom of PTSD—a remarkable statistic when you consider that the diagnosis had at least a dozen possible symptoms at the time, and half a dozen were considered the cutoff for qualifying for the diagnosis (Bonanno et al., 2007).

Acute Stress Disorder and Adjustment Disorder. Two additional *DSM-5* disorders represent variations of PTSD. One is **acute stress disorder**: a psychological disorder that takes place in the days and weeks immediately after a trauma in which the person feels dazed and anxious and experiences flashbacks. Essentially, acute stress disorder is like PTSD but more *immediately* after the traumatic stressor. (By definition, acute stress disorder can only be diagnosed 3 days to 1 month after the trauma, and PTSD can only be diagnosed after at least 1 month has passed.) The other related disorder is **adjustment disorder**: a psychological disorder defined by an excessively disruptive stress reaction to an identifiable stressor. Adjustment disorder differs from

posttraumatic stress disorder (PTSD)
A psychological disorder lasting at least a month characterized by feeling continuously on edge, avoiding reminders of the traumatic event, having difficulty sleeping and concentrating, and frequently recalling or reliving the event.

acute stress disorder
A psychological disorder that takes place in the days and weeks immediately after a trauma in which the person feels dazed and anxious and experiences flashbacks.

adjustment disorder
A psychological disorder defined by an excessively disruptive stress reaction to an identifiable stressor.

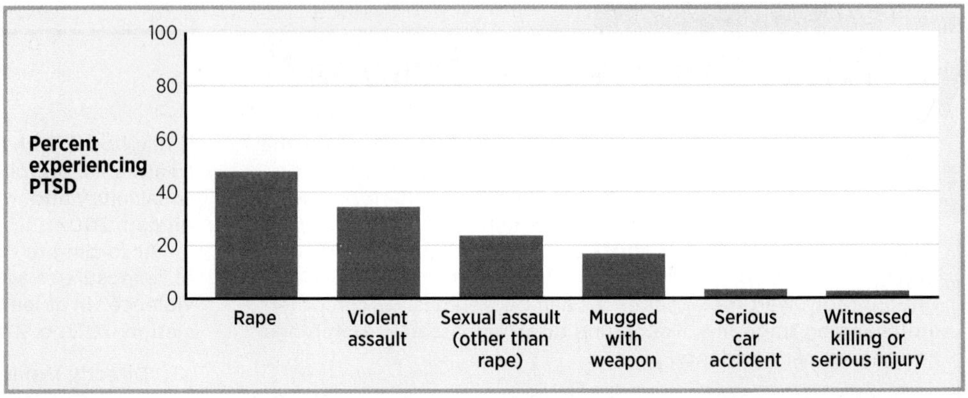

FIGURE 11.5 Resilience after Trauma. Most of us will live through a traumatic event, but only a small portion will go on to experience PTSD. One researcher found that among females who experienced these horrific events, fewer than half—and in some cases, nearly none—developed PTSD (Breslau, 2009).

PTSD and acute stress disorder because it does not require a trauma. Essentially, it is the appropriate diagnosis for a person whose reaction to a nontraumatic or common stressor is way out of proportion, someone who is debilitated by something that most people would overcome more quickly and easily.

Three of my therapy clients, each of whom experienced disruptive levels of stress, illustrate the difference between PTSD, acute stress disorder, and adjustment disorder:

- **Posttraumatic stress disorder.** Holly, a flight attendant, started working with me 5 months after she was assaulted and robbed in the airport parking lot after working a red-eye flight. She told me that since the event, she had a difficult time relaxing at all. She was always nervous, and found it hard to sleep or concentrate on anything. She also had flashbacks almost every day—unwelcome daydreams in which she relived the event—and was scared to park in the same lot or walk alone anywhere inside or outside of the airport. She was going through the motions at work, barely able to get herself to her flights and serve the passengers, in a near-panic state the whole time. Because of the severity and duration of her symptoms, PTSD was the appropriate diagnosis for Holly.
- **Acute stress disorder.** Steven, an attorney, called me 5 days after a terrifying incident in his home. During a thunderstorm, lightning struck a huge, 20-foot tree in his yard, sending it crashing through Steven's house, within feet of crushing Steven, his wife, and their baby, who were in the kitchen at the time. The tree destroyed the kitchen table—"if we had been sitting there, we'd be gone," Steven told me. Steven had been experiencing similar symptoms to Holly's—lots of anxiety and fear, difficulty relaxing and sleeping, flashbacks in which he saw the tree falling over and over again. Every time he saw a big tree near a house, his symptoms got even more intense. Steven was significantly affected by the stress he was experiencing, and he certainly lived through a trauma, but it was so recent—just 5 days ago—that PTSD wasn't an appropriate diagnosis. Instead, acute stress disorder was. (If his symptoms had lasted longer than a month, Steven's diagnosis could have been changed to PTSD. Thankfully, they didn't.)
- **Adjustment disorder.** Grace was a 16-year-old high school sophomore whose Spanish teacher, Ms. Rosales, moved away in the middle of the school year. Now, 6 weeks later, Grace was still absolutely devastated. That is why her parents brought her to me—they couldn't understand why the loss of Ms. Rosales was so upsetting to their daughter, especially because the new Spanish teacher seemed quite competent. Of course, they understood why Grace would be affected a *little*—Ms. Rosales had been an excellent teacher for the first half of the year, and Grace had enjoyed learning from her. But Grace wasn't affected a little,

posttraumatic growth
When people experience trauma and then find a way to benefit, improve, or enrich themselves from that point onward.

she was affected a *lot*. She cried often, worried about her grades and her future. Sometimes, she was so distressed that she passed on opportunities to hang out with friends and missed shifts at her part-time job at Subway. Grace hadn't experienced a trauma, but she was having significant trouble adjusting to a stressor, so the appropriate diagnosis for her was adjustment disorder.

Only a small fraction of people who live through a trauma, such as this soldier's loss of a limb, experience posttraumatic stress disorder. Fortunately, some experience posttraumatic growth by finding a way to benefit, improve, or enrich themselves after the trauma. Scott Olson/Getty Images

Is there any chance that major stressors could actually improve your state of mind?

Posttraumatic growth. Thankfully, yes. In fact, psychologists have recently been paying a lot more attention to the possible upside of the aftermath of traumatic stress. They have found that some trauma survivors actually experience **posttraumatic growth**: when people experience trauma, but find a way to benefit, improve, or enrich themselves from that point forward (Davis & Nolen-Hoeksema, 2009; Zautra & Reich, 2011). Even after the most terrifying experiences, some people prove the line that singer Kelly Clarkson borrowed from philosopher Friedrich Nietzsche: "What does not kill me makes me stronger."

How, exactly, do these people show such resilience? Some psychologists point to *benefit finding*, or deliberately looking for the advantages of the experience of the trauma. For example, although a soldier may lose a leg to a roadside bomb, he may also gain a more appreciative outlook on life, closer relationships with his support network, and greater self-respect for having been tough enough to survive and recover (Pakenham, 2011; Lechner et al., 2009). Benefit finding has actually been linked to increased rates of improvement across a range of health-related stressors (Danoff-Burg & Revenson, 2005; Tennen et al., 2006; Affleck & Tennen, 1996).

Other people who experience a traumatic stressor focus on *meaning making*, trying to create some sense out of what may have made no sense at first (Park, 2011). Sometimes, religion plays an important role in meaning making, as when people accept a stressor as a test that God or another higher power has given them for a good if unknown reason (Pargament, 2011). Researchers also point to positive emotions—love, joy, gratitude, humor, and so on—and say that the more a person feels them, the more they can grow from stressors (Tugade, 2011; Bonanno, 2004, 2009; Folkman & Moskowitz, 2000; Rabkin et al., 2009; Folkman, 1997, 2011). Some therapists have even created interventions designed to foster posttraumatic growth—exercises that deliberately aim to facilitate benefit finding, meaning making, or positive emotions in people who have experienced major distressing events. These interventions show promise, but how well they work isn't clear yet (Moskowitz, 2011).

The idea that a person could find benefit or make meaning from a traumatic event illustrates the more general notion of *eustress*, the interpretation of stress as an opportunity rather than a threat (Simmons & Nelson, 2007; Lazarus, 1993). (The *eu*- in eustress means good, as in *eu*phoria.) Whether the stressor is minor or major, viewing it as a chance to improve yourself, learn something new, or meet a challenge is better for you than viewing it as a looming danger. One study of hundreds of social workers found that those who view their on-the-job responsibilities as eustress report lower levels of exhaustion and cynicism and greater levels of dedication and enthusiasm for their jobs than their colleagues who view those same activities less positively (Kozusznik et al., 2015).

LIFE HACK 11.1

Whenever possible, view stress as eustress—an opportunity rather than a threat. That mindset will increase the chances that you will benefit rather than suffer from the experience.

(Simmons & Nelson, 2007; Lazarus, 1993; Kozusznik et al., 2015)

CHECK YOUR LEARNING:

11.6 What are the different ways that stress damages a person's health?

11.7 What is general adaptation syndrome?

11.8 How does stress affect the immune system and contribute to illness?

11.9 What are the main characteristics of Type A and Type B personality, and how do they relate to the experience of stress?

11.10 How do the personality traits of conscientiousness, extraversion, and neuroticism correlate with stress levels?

11.11 How does stress relate to psychological disorders?

Stress and Culture

YOU WILL LEARN:

11.12 about the different ways males and females experience stress.

11.13 how people of different ethnic backgrounds experience stress.

11.14 how acculturation strategies influence stress level.

11.15 about the ways in which people experience stress at different ages.

Different people experience different stressors. Even when people experience the same stressors, they can experience them differently. The same event can bring about different meanings or challenges for people from diverse groups. Let's consider how some of our diverse characteristics—gender, ethnicity, and age—shape the stress we experience.

Stress and Gender

One way to consider the differences in stressors that males and females face is to find a pair of twins that includes one of each gender and speculate about the stress in each of their lives. For example, did you know that actress Scarlett Johansson has a twin brother named Hunter? Growing up in the same family at the same time, they must have encountered many of the same stressors. But were there differences too? Would you expect that what stressed out Scarlett stressed out Hunter too? Are there some stressors that are more likely to be encountered by one gender than the other? Are there some stressors that they share, but which impact one gender more than the other?

Psychologists have actually collected lots of data on the male and female experiences of stress. In terms of trauma, males experience more traumatic stressors than women, but women experience PTSD more often than men (Olff et al., 2007). Specifically, males are 3.5 times more likely to experience war-related trauma and 1.5 times more likely to experience a physical assault. Females, however, are 6 times more likely to experience sexual assault during adulthood, and 2.5 times more likely to experience sexual assault during childhood (Tolin & Foa, 2006; Basile, 2005; Dallam, 2005). Whether the stress is traumatic or more common, women tend to appraise stressors as more severe than men do (Davis et al., 1999). As a result, the overall self-reported stress level for women tends to be higher than that for men (Matud, 2004). Additionally, women tend to experience stressors that happen *to other people* (especially someone they know) as more stressful than men do (Turner & Avison, 1989). As an example, Jalen is a recent college graduate who tells his mom and dad that he is stressed out about the big job interview he has next week. In this case, Jalen's mom is more likely than Jalen's dad to experience stress herself about Jalen's job interview.

As twins, Scarlett Johansson and her brother, Hunter, have undoubtedly experienced many of the same stressors. As members of opposite genders, however, they have undoubtedly experienced some different stressors too. Jamie McCarthy/ Getty Images for Friends of Rockaway

Males and females also tend to get stressed about different things. In some cases, biology determines the difference: Women are uniquely vulnerable to stressors related to pregnancy and childbirth, while men are uniquely vulnerable to stressors related to impotence (Kendall-Tackett, 2005c). In other cases, as **Table 11.3** shows, social norms play a significant role: females tend to experience much more caregiving-related stress (for their children or elderly or sick relatives) and housework-related stress, while males tend to experience more stress related to money and work (Kendall-Tackett, 2005b, Matud, 2004). In one study, college students experienced two kinds of stressors: achievement stressors (math problems and verbal memorization) and social stressors (avoiding being excluded by two other people in the room who were actually actors told to speak to each other while ignoring the participant). Males had higher levels of cortisol, a hormone that indicates stress, after the achievement stressors, but females had higher levels of cortisol after the social stressors (Stroud et al., 2002).

When males and females experience the same stressor, they often react differently. For example, when married couples argue, women feel more stress, not only by their own description, but also by biological measurements like blood pressure (Kendall-Tackett, 2005a). In one interesting pair of studies, researchers actually put male and female college students through the same stressor—keeping their hand immersed in ice water for 2 minutes—but attached a different description to that stressor for different participants. Researchers told some students that success indicated a high level of qualities that women typically value, like nurturing and forming intimate relationships.

TABLE 11.3: Stressors Endorsed More Often by Women or Men

THIS STRESSOR...	...WAS LISTED BY THIS PERCENTAGE OF WOMEN...	...AND THIS PERCENTAGE OF MEN.
Separation, divorce	**4.4**	2.3
Change in religious attendance or beliefs	**10.0**	7.5
Death in the immediate family	**30.7**	27.0
Birth in family	**27.7**	20.1
Serious illness of a close friend or relative	**18.1**	14.0
Engagement	14.8	**21.6**
Starting a serious relationship (not marriage)	17.8	**25.0**
Ending a serious relationship (not marriage)	11.2	**23.8**
Making new friends	52.7	**57.3**
Major change in financial status	30.6	**37.0**
Change in commitment to work	27.5	**35.3**
Dealings with staff or supervisor	15.1	**19.2**
Change in work pressure	22.6	**29.4**
Increase or decrease in workload	25.2	**30.7**

Data from Matud, 2004.

When over 2800 women and men were given a checklist of 31 stressors that could have happened to any of them over the past 2 years, about half were equally endorsed by both. But the rest of the stressors—listed in this table—were endorsed by one gender significantly more often than the other, emphasizing the reality that gender impacts the stress experience.

They told other students that success indicated a high level of qualities that men typically value, like willpower and physical strength. Researchers found that women experienced more stress (as shown by blood pressure increases) when the task was described as feminine, but men experienced more stress when the task was described as masculine (Lash et al., 1991, 1995). So for both men and women, it is not just the task that causes us stress, but how we perceive the task.

Stress and Ethnicity

DIVERSITY MATTERS Just as people of different genders experience stress differently, so do people of different ethnic backgrounds (Slavin et al., 1991). First of all, minority or immigrant groups in the United States are simply more likely to face certain real-world stressors than people in the majority. For example, Latino(a) families have higher odds of encountering poverty, language barriers, limited education, and unemployment (Padilla & Borrero, 2006). African Americans contend with many of the same experiences at similarly high rates, plus the legacy of racism that remains from the slavery era (McCreary, 2006). That racism can take the form of beliefs held by individuals, policies and customs endorsed by institutions (such as the legal system), or worldviews woven into cultures and passed on from one generation to the next (Jones, 1997). Studies have found that this increased stress due to ethnic or racial factors takes its toll in terms of both physical and mental health (Perry et al., 2013).

One study found that among almost 800 African Americans, the higher the rate of perceived racial discrimination, the higher the rate of psychological distress (Brown et al., 2000). Another study with over 5000 participants found similar connections between perceived racial discrimination and both depression and cardiovascular disease (Chae et al., 2012). Other studies have found that the higher rates of pregnancy- and birth-related complications among African American women—nearly twice that of White women—is due in large part to race-based stress (Rosenthal & Lobel, 2011). Race-related stress may even cause African Americans to age more quickly. One biologically focused study examined *telomeres*—tiny parts of our chromosomes that indicate age like rings on a tree trunk. Researchers found that middle-aged Black women are 7.5 years "older" than White women (according to their telomeres), and

that the difference was due at least in part to stressors that Black women are more likely to experience, like racism and poverty (Geronimus et al., 2010).

Collectivism, Individualism, and Stress. One significant characteristic of an ethnicity is whether it leans toward *collectivism* or *individualism*. Collectivistic ethnicities, which often come from Asian countries (and some African and South American countries), emphasize the well-being of the group over the individual, or *us* over *me*. Individualistic ethnicities, which often come from the United States, Canada, Western Europe, and Australia, emphasize the well-being of the individual over the group, or *me* over *us* (Hofstede, 2001; Hofstede et al., 1997; Kim et al., 1994).

Research shows that people from collectivistic and individualistic cultures often have different experiences of stress (Yeh et al., 2006). For example, people from individualistic cultures are more likely to feel stress about personal achievements, like school or job challenges, while people from collectivistic cultures are more likely to feel stress about family harmony, like how much support they are providing or how agreeable their relationships are (Chun et al., 2006; Heine & Lehman, 1995; Tafarodi & Smith, 2001). Once, in my private practice, I happened to be working with two female therapy clients who were both college seniors applying to medical school. Their credentials, including undergrad GPA and MCAT scores, were nearly identical. The White woman was applying all over the country, and told me quite plainly that she'd choose "the best school that accepts me." The Asian woman was only applying in Los Angeles. Why? Her family, including her aging parents, whose health was declining, lived there. She felt obliged to return home rather than prioritize her own medical school goals. Interestingly, the White woman had ailing family members as well, but they did not factor into her decision-making process.

Another stress-related difference between individualistic and collectivistic cultures involves the issue of "standing out" versus "standing in" (Weisz et al., 1984). Basically, in individualistic cultures, it is considered good to stand out from the crowd, to distinguish yourself by your accomplishments. In collectivistic cultures, however, standing out is more likely to be experienced as highly stressful. Instead, collectivistic cultures tend to favor behavior that is more conventional, or in agreement with others. You know the saying, popular in the United States, that "the squeaky wheel gets the grease"? In Japan, they have a different saying: "The nail that sticks out gets pounded down" (Tweed & Conway, 2006). As an example, imagine that you get a job in which you quickly learn that your supervisor expects you to work a few extra hours without extra pay. You also realize that all of your coworkers are already used to this expectation. If you're from an individualistic culture, your impulse is likely to be to stand up for what is rightfully yours, assert yourself even if you single yourself out as an agitator in the process. In fact, simply accepting the arrangement you see as unfair might cause you stress. However, if you're from a collectivistic culture, it is likely to be *less* stressful to accept the arrangement than to fight it; by fighting it, you threaten harmony in your relationships with your coworkers and your supervisor. If you're from a collectivistic culture you'd likely be willing to sacrifice some personal gains if it meant keeping the peace with those around you.

People from collectivistic cultures (including many from Asia) often have different experiences of stress than people from individualistic cultures. In collectivistic cultures, stress is more likely to come from threats to family harmony than shortcomings in personal achievement. Also, standing out from the crowd is more likely to cause stress for people in collectivistic cultures than people in individualistic cultures. Hill Street Studios/Blend Images/Getty Images

A final note on people from individualistic and collectivistic cultures: Stress affects their bodies and minds differently. Specifically, when people from individualistic cultures get stressed out, they tend to feel it mentally. They tend to complain of unpleasant thoughts and emotions (sadness, despair, anxiety, anger, etc.). On the other hand, when people from collectivistic cultures get stressed out, they tend to feel it physically. They tend to complain of headaches, stomach discomfort, fatigue, and bodily pain. This cultural difference, at least to some degree, appears across a wide range of individualistic and collectivistic cultures (Takeuchi et al., 2002; Chun et al., 1996).

Acculturative Stress. Dealing with stressors from one culture can be tough enough, but we sometimes find ourselves dealing with the stress of managing two cultures. When you find yourself in a new culture, it can be stressful to figure out how to handle both the culture you're already used to and the culture you're now in. Psychologists call this particular challenge **acculturative stress**: stress associated with the process of managing old and new cultures (Berry, 1970, 2006). Acculturative stress

is common in people who move from one part of the world to another, but it can also be present to some extent in people who move from one part of the country or city to another. For example, consider Miguel, a 25-year-old man who moves from his small hometown in Mexico to Minneapolis. In Mexico, Miguel has a familiar way of life: the food he eats, the clothes he wears, the language he speaks, the TV shows he watches, the religion he practices, the holidays he celebrates, and the values he holds. But in Minneapolis, things are different, at least for most people. Of course, some of the people he meets are Mexicans whose cultural backgrounds are somewhat like Miguel's, but most are not. For the most part, Miguel finds himself surrounded by people who eat, dress, speak, and otherwise live differently than he did for his first 25 years.

acculturative stress
Stress associated with the process of managing old and new cultures.

How can Miguel manage this situation? Basically, he's got two decisions to make: how much to hold onto his Mexican culture, and how much to embrace mainstream U.S. (Minneapolis) culture. If you consider that he could be high or low on either of these, that gives him four possible acculturation strategies (Berry, 2003; Rivera, 2008, 2010).

- Abandoning the old culture and embracing the new culture is *assimilation*.
- Keeping the old culture and rejecting the new culture is *separation*.
- Rejecting both the old and the new culture is *marginalization*.
- Keeping the old culture while embracing the new culture is *integration*.

Researchers have found that these four acculturation strategies tend to produce different outcomes in terms of stress. Specifically, integration—in which the person blends an appreciation of both the old and new cultures—produces the least stress. Marginalization—in which the person drops both the old and new cultures—produces the most stress. The other two strategies, in which one culture is retained while the other is rejected, fall somewhere in the middle (Berry & Kim, 1988; Berry, 1997; Berry & Sam, 1997).

So, integrating multiple cultures into your life can actually lower your stress?

Yes—in fact, some researchers argue that integrating multiple cultures provides unique advantages. Being familiar with multiple cultures gives you a wider range of responses to choose from—like a toolbox with twice as many tools in it—and that versatility enhances your ability to deal with a wide range of stressors (Cheng, 2003; Tweed & Conway, 2006). In one study, researchers compared the responses of college students from collectivistic (Malaysian) cultures and from individualistic (U.S., Canadian, and German) cultures to academic pressure—things like exams and papers. It was no surprise to find that the two groups had distinct styles of responding. Generally, the Malaysian students focused on managing their emotions (staying calm, etc.), while the U.S., Canadian, and German students focused on changing the situation (making an effective plan to get the work done, etc.). Surprisingly, researchers found that the students who experienced the least stress were the ones whose responses most closely resembled those of the *other* group. The students from collectivistic cultures who could also think individualistically, and the students from individualistic cultures who could also think collectively, were better equipped to handle stressors than the students who used only a single approach (Essau & Trommsdorff, 1996). So, just as being fluent in more than one language can increase the range of people with whom you can converse, being fluent in more than one culture can increase the range of situations with which you can cope.

Acculturative stress is stress associated with the process of managing both the culture you have known in your past and the culture in which you live now. For example, if this young man recently moved from a small town in Mexico to Minneapolis, Minnesota, he may experience acculturative stress regarding the way he speaks, dresses, eats, and interacts with others, among other things. pkchai/Shutterstock

Stress and Age

What stressed you out when you were 5? 10? 15? What stresses you out now? Perhaps some of your stressors have remained consistent, but undoubtedly, some have changed.

Older adults tend to have lower overall stress levels than younger or middle-aged adults, but when their stress does increase, the health-related consequences can be significant. Anita_Bonita/iStock/Getty Images

At least in mainstream U.S. culture, there are certain sources of stress that are more likely to impact us at various stages (Aldwin, 2011; American Psychological Association, 2014):

- **Preschool**—the behavioral demands of preschool or day care; power struggles with parents ("I want to do it myself!")
- **Elementary school**—academic achievement, making friends
- **Middle school**—academic achievement, starting to date, popularity
- **High school**—academic achievement, dating, arguing with parents, popularity, family financial issues
- **Young adults**—finishing school, committed relationship or marriage, work, money, raising young kids
- **Middle-aged to older adults**—health problems, health problems of loved ones, work, financial issues, divorce, caregiver burdens, death of parents or others

When intensive, chronic stress takes place early in the life span, it can have long-lasting effects. A review of studies on the biological effects of stress on people and animals found that there appear to be certain critical periods of development when this is especially likely, including the prenatal period (when the fetus feels mom's stress), the first year of life (when stress often comes from poor parental care), and adolescence (Lupien et al., 2009). Numerous studies have found that when major stressors—especially family conflict, abuse, and the absence of a father—are persistent throughout a girl's childhood, she is more likely to experience her first period (menarche) earlier than her peers (Belsky et al., 1991; Wierson et al., 1993; Moffitt et al., 1992; Boynton-Jarrett et al., 2013; Romans et al., 2003). Evolutionary theory argues that this would happen because earlier menarche enables earlier childbirth, which might be necessary because girls under perpetually high stress could be expected to have shorter life spans. One study supports this theory quite strongly: Not only did women with high-stress childhoods have their first period sooner, they also had their first baby sooner and expected their own life spans to be shorter than peers with lower-stress childhoods (Chisholm et al., 2005).

Among older adults, stress levels tend to be lower than in younger adults or middle-aged adults (Neupert et al., 2007; Birditt et al., 2005). This may reflect the wisdom of experience, a "been there, done that" attitude that prevents older adults from getting overly upset about day-to-day occurrences. However, when older adults do find themselves facing chronic and unavoidable stressors, the effects can be especially damaging (Esterling et al., 1994). In one study, researchers gave the influenza virus vaccine (flu shots) to older adults, some of whom were taking care of their spouses with dementia. They found that the caregivers' bodies responded more poorly to the vaccine, producing far fewer antibodies and leaving the older adults more susceptible to a disease that could be serious or fatal, especially at that age (Kiecolt-Glaser et al., 1996). Another study of about 400 such spousal caregivers, age 66–96, found that over a 4-year period, they were 63% more likely to die than same-age peers who did not have that ongoing, serious stressor in their lives (Schulz & Beach, 1999). And in a study of older adults caring for their husbands or wives with cancer, these caregivers were significantly more likely to experience heart disease or stroke than peers who were not in similar caregiving situations (Ji et al., 2012).

CHECK YOUR LEARNING:

11.12 How do males and females experience stress in different ways?

11.13 How do people of different ethnic backgrounds, including individualistic and collectivistic cultures, experience stress differently?

11.14 How do acculturation strategies influence stress levels?

11.15 How can age influence the experience of stress?

Coping with Stress: Psychological Strategies and Social Strategies

So far, this chapter has focused heavily on what stresses you out and what effects that stress can have—in other words, what stress does to you. It's time to turn the tables and focus on what you can do about stress. So, we turn to the topic of **coping**: efforts to reduce or manage your experience of stress.

YOU WILL LEARN:

11.16 how psychologists define *coping*.

11.17 how coping styles differ by ethnicity and gender.

11.18 about ways to decrease stress by evaluating it differently.

11.19 how mindfulness can influence stress levels.

11.20 about the importance of social support to emotional and physical health.

11.21 about ways to decrease stress by behaving differently.

Culture and Coping

There is no single formula for how best to cope with stress. What works for your friends or family might not work for you (and vice versa) (Klienke, 2002). In fact, coping strategies often vary according to factors like ethnicity and gender. People from collectivistic ethnicities tend to cope by changing things within themselves, like their own thoughts and feelings (which often allows them to avoid conflict with others). People from individualistic ethnicities tend to cope by changing things outside of themselves, like the stressor itself (Tweed et al., 2004; Chun et al., 2006; Yeh & Inose, 2002). Even when friends and family are available, people from collectivistic cultures may choose not to burden them (which could threaten harmony in the relationship), and they may benefit simply from knowing help is available without actually using it. People from individualistic cultures, on the other hand, are more likely to actually use it, to directly ask friends and family for help, and to take whatever they can get (Kim et al., 2008; Taylor et al., 2004).

DIVERSITY MATTERS

Regarding gender, women tend to cope by talking about their feelings, often repeatedly, with other women; men tend to cope by problem solving and avoid discussing their emotions with anyone (Rose, 2002; Rose et al., 2007; Helgeson, 2011; Brougham et al., 2009; Frydenberg & Lewis, 1993). In fact, some researchers have argued that the classic notion of fight-or-flight as a response to stress actually doesn't fit women's coping strategies as well as it fits men's. Fight-or-flight is good if you're fighting a stressor solo, but not if you're fighting it with your kids in tow, as women have more often found themselves throughout human history. These researchers argue that for women, *tend-and-befriend* is a more accurate description (Taylor, 2002, 2011b; Taylor et al., 2000b; Tamres, 2002). According to the tend-and-befriend theory, evolution would have favored a coping response in women that incorporates their families, especially their kids, since they have typically been the primary caregivers. So, *tending* (or nurturing) relationships with sons and daughters, and *befriending* (or building social connections, especially with other women) creates a safety net big enough to protect women and their children in times of high stress.

MY TAKE VIDEO 11.2

Coping

"I was devastated. Then I started to realize that there were little things I could do about it..."

YOUTUBE: http://tiny.cc/mytake
LAUNCHPAD: launchpadworks.com

In my private practice, I have twice had therapy clients who got laid off. For Yolanda, I was probably the tenth person she had turned to for support, after her mom, her sisters, her cousins, and her friends. Support is what she wanted most from therapy—someone to listen, understand, and empathize. For Greg, I was the only person he had shared the layoff with. He hadn't even told his closest family and friends. What he wanted most from his therapist was not emotional but strategic—a consultant who could advise him best on what actions to take to overcome his feelings of sadness and to secure a new job.

As illustrated previously, there is a wide range of coping strategies, especially among diverse populations. But psychologists have been studying coping strategies for decades, and collectively, their research offers some guidance for ideas that are likely to

coping
Efforts to reduce or manage an experience of stress.

Coping strategies often differ across groups based on ethnicity, gender, or other variables. For example, women tend to cope with stress by talking about their feelings, but men tend to cope with stress by problem solving and avoiding discussion of emotion. BananaStock/Getty Images

LIFE HACK 11.2

Both problem-focused coping (changing the stressor itself) and emotion-focused coping (changing how you feel about the stressor) can be beneficial. Try to use both types of coping, rather than relying too much on only one.

(Carver, 2013)

help you handle your own stress more effectively. **Table 11.4** offers a summary of tips from the American Psychological Association. Next, we examine some of those tactics—thinking differently, improving relationships, and behaving differently—in more detail.

Decreasing Stress by Thinking Differently

Remember earlier in this chapter when we were discussing *appraisal*? We defined it as the way you evaluate the things that happen to you. If you made a deliberate effort to change that evaluation, you could feel less stress. There is a form of psychotherapy, *cognitive therapy*, that is based on the notion of thinking about the things that happen in more realistic and logical ways (see Chapter 15 for more). Actually, you have the opportunity to change the way you think about both kinds of appraisal—how bad the stressor is (*primary appraisal*), and how capable you are to deal with it (*secondary appraisal*). Recall the example from earlier in the chapter—the two sales reps who get transferred to Chicago. One of them, Tyler, considered the stressors huge, focusing on lost friends, financial strain, and added job responsibilities. He also thought about his ability to cope as weak, expecting that he'd crumble under the pressure. But what if Tyler's thoughts are more negative than they need to be? What if he believes that the stressors are tolerable, and that his coping ability is adequate? If he says to himself, "I might actually be OK in Chicago. I may lose some friends, but I'll meet a lot of new people too. Things might be tough financially for a while, but the new job gives me more earning potential. They wouldn't transfer me to this new position if they didn't think I could succeed." These thoughts might be more accurate than the thoughts that first popped into Tyler's head, and his stress will drop to the extent that he believes the more positive thoughts.

Problem-Focused Coping and Emotion-Focused Coping. Changing the way we think also decreases stress if we choose wisely whether to focus on the stressor itself or on our inner reaction to it. Psychologists have names for these two approaches to coping: *problem-focused coping* and *emotion-focused coping*. **Problem-focused coping** is a style of coping with stress that emphasizes changing the stressor itself. This kind of coping involves tackling the problem head-on in an attempt to solve or minimize it (Carroll, 2013). By contrast, **emotion-focused coping** is a style of coping with stress that emphasizes changing your emotional reaction to the stressor (rather than changing the stressor itself). With emotion-focused coping, you basically accept the stressor as unchangeable, so you instead focus on changing the way you feel while facing it (Carver & Connor-Smith, 2010; Carver & Vargas, 2011). The key point is that relying too much on only problem-focused coping or only emotion-focused coping can unnecessarily increase stress. By contrast, allowing yourself the flexibility to switch from one style of coping to the other can decrease stress (Carver, 2013).

TABLE 11.4: Knowing Yourself: Stress Tips

Understand how you stress. What stress signs do you notice in yourself?
Identify your sources of stress. Who or what stresses you out?
Learn your own stress signals. Are they physical symptoms (like headache or muscle tension), mental symptoms (like anger or fatigue), or both?
Recognize how you deal with stress. Do you engage in unhealthy behaviors like overeating or smoking?
Find healthy ways to manage stress. Do you need to exercise, meditate, or talk it out?
Take care of yourself. Get enough sleep, good food, and water. Take breaks or vacations when possible. Make time for things you enjoy.
Reach out for support. Let friends, family, or a mental health professional help you through especially stressful times.

Information from the American Psychological Association, 2007.

FROM RESEARCH TO REAL LIFE

Don't Stress Out about Stress

Stress may contribute to health problems, but *believing* that stress causes health problems can make those problems much worse. A huge study of over 28,000 people examined these two variables—how much stress a person has, and how strongly that person believed that stress affects health—and found that people who were high on both were in the worst shape. They had significantly higher rates of psychological problems, physical health problems, and even death, than those who had high stress but didn't believe that stress harmed their health. Specifically, those who thought stress affected their health "some" were about twice as likely to be in poor physical health, and those who thought stress affected their health "a lot" were about four times as likely to be in poor physical health compared to people who thought that their stress affected their health either hardly or not at all (Keller et al., 2012).

These results point to the tremendous value of thinking positively about stress. Viewing stress as a challenging opportunity or a chance to rise to the occasion, rather than unbeatable pressure that will inevitably harm you, is key. One study examined an intervention designed to change people's thinking in this positive direction. The researchers put people in a series of stressful situations, including delivering a speech in front of an audience of experts. Some of them were taught ahead of time by psychologists to interpret their stress response as "not harmful...and that increased arousal actually aids performance" (Jamieson et al., 2012, p. 418). Others were given no such instructions, or were told to distract themselves by thinking about something else when they felt stressed. Those who got the stress-is-helpful instructions responded to the stressors in a significantly healthier way. So, improving the way you think about stressors—including, perhaps most importantly, the stressor of stress itself—has the power to positively impact your well-being. ●

Switching between coping strategies works best when you consider how *controllable* the stressor is (Aldridge & Roesch, 2007; Clarke, 2006; Penley et al., 2002; Austenfeld & Stanton, 2004). Problem-focused coping tends to work best when the stressor is controllable. For example, let's say you're applying to law school and the LSAT is coming up. (The LSAT is the standardized admission test for law school, roughly the equivalent of the SAT or ACT that you took when applying to college.) If you're stressed about the LSAT, there are lots of things you can do about it. You can buy LSAT study guides, take an LSAT prep course, make a study schedule, search the Web for LSAT tips, take practice tests, or join a study group, among other things. Any of these problem-focused actions has the potential to change your impression of the LSAT, from an overwhelming threat to a challenging opportunity. In problem-focused coping, the point is that you can take action to deal with the situation in a constructive way.

On the other hand, emotion-focused coping tends to work best when the stressor is not so controllable. For example, consider a situation that you will hopefully never have to encounter: A friend from high school dies in a car accident. In this situation, sadly, nothing can change the stressor. The worst has already happened. Your best strategy in terms of managing your stress would be to focus on your own feelings about the event. Some ways of managing those feelings could make this terrible situation more tolerable for you. Perhaps you'd benefit from talking about it with friends, family, or a therapist; or from journaling or blogging about your experience; or from offering kind words about your friend at the funeral; or from engaging in physical exercise to clear your mind. (Other attempts to manage your emotions might be less beneficial, such as drinking excessively, ruminating on the event endlessly, or refusing to acknowledge that it happened at all.) The point here is that once the opportunity for controlling the stressor itself has passed, trying to control it would be futile and maybe even harmful. A better option is to accept it, but manage your feelings as well as possible.

Research indicates that this sequence—consider problem-focused coping first, then resort to emotion-focused coping if necessary—is in fact what people often do (Rothbaum et al., 1982). For example, one study took a close look at the kinds of coping strategies used by people struggling with rheumatoid arthritis. Researchers found that emotion-focused coping was over four times more likely to happen on days when the participants had also tried problem-focused coping. They also found that emotion-focused coping was much more common on days when the previous day featured problem-focused coping. Together, these findings suggest that emotion-focused coping is relatively uncommon as a first-line strategy, but much more common as a follow-up to problem-focused coping that didn't do much good (Tennen et al., 2000).

problem-focused coping
A style of coping with stress that emphasizes changing the stressor itself.

emotion-focused coping
A style of coping with stress that emphasizes changing your emotional reaction to the stressor.

One more note on the controllability of stressors: When stress is *uncontrollable*, it is especially likely to be toxic, both physically and psychologically. In one study, participants received 30 brief, mild electric shocks to their forearms. Half of them decided for themselves when the shocks would happen (controllable stressor); for the other half, the researchers decided when (uncontrollable stressor). Even though the voltage was identical for both groups, the second group reported feeling significantly more intense pain (Müller, 2013). In another study, rats' tails were shocked in a way that they could learn to escape (controllable stressor) or that was inescapable (uncontrollable stressor). Although these shocks took place when the rats were adolescents, serious consequences lasted through adulthood. Specifically, adult rats who had experienced the controllable stressor demonstrated healthier patterns of brain growth throughout their lives. Also, those rats that had experienced the controllable stressor as adolescents were more resilient in the face of uncontrollable stressors when they eventually experienced them as adults (Kubala et al., 2012).

Mindfulness. A final way in which thinking differently can reduce your stress involves *mindfulness*. Mindfulness comes from the Buddhist tradition, but psychologists now typically use it with no connection to religion at all. Mindfulness refers to an increased awareness of what's going on inside of you—your moment-to-moment physical and psychological experiences—with an emphasis on just feeling it rather than analyzing it or avoiding it. People high in mindfulness don't live on autopilot, numbly going through the motions of life. Instead, they actively pay attention to what's happening to them, with full engagement and acceptance of that experience. Whether they face joy or pain, they purposefully stay aware of their emotions rather than repressing them or evading them via distractions (Hick, 2008; Roemer & Orsillo, 2009; Shapiro, 2009a, 2009b; Hayes et al., 2011).

Numerous studies have found that stress decreases as mindfulness increases. Two meta-analyses concluded that mindfulness-based therapies significantly reduce not only stress levels, but all kinds of mental and physical problems associated with stress, like depression, anxiety, chronic pain, and fibromyalgia (Baer, 2003; Grossman et al., 2004; see also Bohlmeijer et al., 2010, and Hoffman et al., 2010). Further, these positive effects of mindfulness often last. One longitudinal study found that organ transplant recipients who received mindfulness training around the time of the transplant were lower in depression, anxiety, and insomnia 6 months later (Kreitzer et al., 2005). Another longitudinal study found that diabetic patients who received mindfulness training were significantly better both medically and psychologically a full year later compared to similar patients who didn't receive the training (Hartmann et al., 2012). So, evidence suggests that making a mindfulness-based change in your thinking can decrease stress and many of its consequences.

Social support—your relationships with friends, family, and others—provides an important buffer from stress and its harmful effects. Hero Images/Getty Images

Decreasing Stress by Improving Relationships

Generally speaking, if the quality of the important relationships in your life is poor—if you're in conflict with your family and friends, or if they've rejected you altogether—your stress level will be high. In fact, researchers have found that prolonged social isolation is one of the most toxic stressors of all, often producing serious physical and psychological health problems (Cohen, 2004; Cacioppo et al. 2003). One study found that widows who were socially isolated were significantly more likely to develop heart disease than those who were well-connected with others (Sorkin et al., 2002). Another study found that a flu shot given to lonely first-year college students produced far fewer antibodies (was much less effective) than the same shot was in first-year college students with more friends (Pressman et al., 2005).

Simply put, staying connected to other people is vitally important to your emotional and physical health. Psychologists call these connections with others **social support**: the relationships you have with friends, family, and others that can benefit you when you experience stress. Social support can take many forms, but it is often categorized in three ways (Taylor, 2011b):

social support
The relationships one has with friends, family, and others that can be beneficial when experiencing stress.

- *Informational social support* occurs when you gain knowledge or understanding from your family and friends. For example, consider Molly, a young adult stressed out about doing her own taxes for the first time. She calls her uncle, her big sister, and an older friend for help. Collectively, they tell her all kinds of things: what forms need to be filled out, what counts as a deduction for her, how much help TurboTax or H&R Block can provide, and more. After those conversations, doing her taxes is no longer the major stressor that Molly first thought it was. It is a chore, but one she can manage without too much worry because of the new information she picked up.
- *Instrumental social support* occurs when you gain something more tangible from your family and friends. For example, let's imagine that Molly loses her job. Informational social support would be helpful (where to find another job, advice on writing a résumé, etc.), but she has more pressing needs right now: a place to live, food to eat, and money to spend on necessities. If her friend Angelina loans Molly some cash and lets her crash at her place for a few weeks, just until Molly can get back on her feet, she will have provided vital instrumental social support.
- *Emotional social support* occurs when you receive warmth, reassurance, or other expressions of feeling from friends and family. If Angelina offered Molly money and a place to stay, but was completely cold and indifferent about doing so, her social support would be incomplete. If, however, she did what good friends do—provide help not only in the form of stuff, but also in the form of compassion and encouragement—she would be supplying Molly with something of great value.

Many studies illustrate the tremendous benefits of social support. Regarding physical health, a high level of social support has been linked to lower risk of heart attack, susceptibility to viruses, diabetes complications, pregnancy problems, and many other conditions (Taylor, 2011b; Uchino, 2006; Schwarzer & Leppin, 1991). A high level of social support also has been shown to slow the progression of diseases after they have been diagnosed, such as HIV and breast cancer (Leung et al., 2014; Leserman et al., 1999). Perhaps the most striking studies on social support and physical health are the longitudinal studies that follow patients for years or decades, which typically find that social support extends the life span. People with continuously high levels of social support are significantly less likely to die early, while continuously low levels of social support predict early death as strongly as chronic health problems like smoking, obesity, or high blood pressure (Seeman, 1996; Rutledge et al., 2004; House et al., 1988; Herbst-Damm & Kulik, 2005). Regarding mental health, social support has been found to be a powerful buffer from depression, anxiety, eating disorders, and many other psychological problems (Stice et al., 2004; Stice, 2002; Rueger et al., 2010; Tiller et al., 1997; Ginter et al., 1994).

Women tend to be more involved in social support (especially emotional social support) than men, both as givers and takers in times of stress (Taylor, 2011a; Taylor et al., 2000b; Tamres et al., 2002). One interesting study followed college students who stayed in their residence halls through the entire winter break—an experience likely to create feelings of loneliness. The researchers found that many students did in fact get lonely, but those who experienced the least loneliness were the ones who had the most contact with women. It didn't matter whether the participants were male or female, and it didn't matter how much contact they had with males. Only contact with females seemed to alleviate loneliness, suggesting that women may have a way of generating social support that is uniquely effective in helping others get through stressful situations (Wheeler et al., 1983). Social support may affect women's health more too: One meta-analysis found that the correlation between social support and health is positive for all of us, but it is stronger for women (.20) than for men (.08) (Schwarzer & Leppin, 1991).

The takeaway message is this: Stress is not something you need to endure alone. The better your relationships with other people, in terms of both quantity and quality, the better your chances of withstanding stressful situations.

CHAPTER APP 11.2

Social Support

ReachOut

Preview one of the links and consider the following questions.

WEBSITE: http://tiny.cc/5li7jy

ANDROID: http://tiny.cc/jb92iy

IPHONE: http://tiny.cc/f682iy

VIDEO DEMO: http://tiny.cc/chapterapps

ReachOut is an app designed to help people give and receive social support for stressors they share. ReachOut users choose a support group for a specific long-term health-related stressor, such as cancer, diabetes, chronic pain, grief, or substance abuse. Within that support group, they "reach out" to the group (which includes both patients and caregivers), and from each other find encouragement, compassion, community, coping skills, and more.

How does it APPly to your daily life?
If you or a loved one were struggling with a long-term health-related stressor, in what ways would you expect an app like ReachOut to be beneficial? What kinds of social support would you expect to find most and least valuable?

How does it APPly to your understanding of psychology?
How does the ReachOut app help you understand the concept of *social support*, and its three specific types: informational social support, instrumental social support, and emotional social support?

LIFE HACK 11.3

Seek social support when you are stressed out. Research strongly suggests that your relationships with friends and family can protect your emotional and physical well-being when stress levels are high.

(Taylor, 2011b; Uchino, 2006; Stice et al., 2004; Stice, 2002; Rueger et al., 2010)

Decreasing Stress by Behaving Differently

There is no substitute for action in the struggle to minimize stress. *Early* action is especially important—the kind of action you take when you anticipate problems before they happen and take measures to prevent them or minimize their impact.

Proactive coping. Psychologists call this kind of coping **proactive coping**: a coping style that focuses on future goals and the stressors that could impede them. The major advantage to proactive coping is that it emphasizes stressors that haven't happened yet. That gives you the chance to either avoid them or prepare for them, either of which can be a more effective strategy than waiting for the stressor to happen (Aspinwall, 2011, 2005, 2003, 1997). Proactive coping means that addressing future problems now takes much less time and effort than waiting for them to arrive (Aspinwall & Taylor, 1997).

To illustrate proactive coping, consider Hannah, a young woman who just found out that she is expecting her first baby. Hannah is a planner. Within hours of the positive pregnancy test, Hannah started thinking about the stressors she would soon face, and what she could do about them in advance. In fact, the first thing Hannah did was order the best-selling pregnancy book *What to Expect When You're Expecting*—a title that fits the proactive coping approach quite well. That book, advice from friends and relatives, and online research provided Hannah with enough information to make a list of pregnancy-related stressors and baby-related stressors. The list included buying maternity clothes, getting baby furniture, finding a pediatrician, and arranging her maternity leave with her employer. At first, the list seemed overwhelming, but Hannah tackled these tasks one by one, *ahead of time*. She borrowed some maternity clothes from her sister and bought some more online; she picked up a gently used crib and changing table from some neighbors whose kindergartner had outgrown them; she selected a pediatrician after meeting with several; and she made specific plans with her boss about how long she'd be off work.

By contrast, consider Hannah's cousin, Taylor, who got pregnant around the same time as Hannah. Taylor knows that pregnancies and babies come with plenty of stressors, but she figures she'll deal with them as they come up. She has always responded well "on the fly" to other challenging situations, and she is confident that she can do the same as she moves through her pregnancy. She might be right, but think of the stress that Taylor will face as she makes last-minute, high-pressure decisions. A proactive coping style makes all the difference.

Proactive coping can certainly have disadvantages, especially if you take it too far. For example, if you worry too much about things that probably won't happen and probably won't be a big deal if they do, then you can cause yourself more work than necessary (Newby-Clark, 2004). Also, if you're too public about your proactive coping efforts, you run the risk of annoying other people by coming across as a worrywart (Ashford et al., 2003; Grant & Ashford, 2008). But overall, a healthy amount of proactive coping has more upside than downside. A little stress now can save a lot of stress later.

Hardiness is a set of behaviors that reflect resilience under stressful circumstances. Hardy people tend to see stress as an opportunity for success rather than a threat of failure. Justin Sullivan/Getty Images

Hardiness and Optimism. Sometimes, there are stressors you can't anticipate, so proactive coping can't help. In such situations, it is beneficial to respond with **hardiness**: behaviors that reflect resilience under stressful circumstances. Hardy people welcome stress. They see it as an opportunity for improvement and success rather than failure and pain. Hardiness is closely related to the concept of *posttraumatic growth* that we discussed earlier in the chapter, but it can emerge even when the stress is less than traumatic. Hardiness has three key ingredients, known by psychologists as the "three C's"—commitment, controlling, and challenge (Maddi, 2002; Maddi & Kobasa, 1984; Maddi & Harvey, 2006; Ouellette & DiPlacido, 2001):

- A *commitment* to staying involved in a tough situation even when it gets stressful, as opposed to looking for an easy escape (or "bailing out")

- *Controlling* the situation as much as possible and exerting whatever influence you can, rather than being passive
- Seeing a stressor as a *challenge* to face courageously rather than a threat to be avoided fearfully

proactive coping
A style of coping that focuses on future goals and the stressors that could impede them.

hardiness
Behaviors that reflect resilience under stressful circumstances.

optimism
An attitude toward the future characterized by hope or expectation of a positive outcome.

Hardiness is not something you are born with (or without)—it can be cultivated. When you face stressors, you can make deliberate efforts to respond with hardy behaviors. In fact, psychologists have successfully used hardiness training to improve this ability in clients (Khoshaba & Maddi, 2001; Maddi, 1987; Maddi et al., 2002). As an example, consider this situation: Due to a mix-up in the campus housing office, Jacob, a college sophomore, is placed in a suite with three other students even though he requested a single room. At first, Jacob might react with frustration, look for ways out of the situation (getting his own apartment instead, or even transferring schools), or experience overwhelming anxiety about getting along with three new roommates. But if Jacob can respond with more hardiness, he might realize that he has the opportunity to turn this mix-up into a blessing in disguise. He can give his suitemates a chance and do his best to build friendships with them rather than just seeing what happens. All the while, he can keep in mind the best possible outcome of this surprise situation: new friends and an enjoyable year living together, when he otherwise would have been living alone. Such a hardy attitude can't guarantee Jacob a great outcome, but it has the potential to lower Jacob's stress level.

Related to hardiness is **optimism**: an attitude toward the future characterized by hope or expectation of a positive outcome. Like hardiness, optimism buffers us from stress (Seligman, 1991). One study of college students found a strongly negative correlation between their optimism levels and the extent to which they experienced about 40 physical symptoms of various kinds. The more optimistic they were, the less they were bothered by headaches, stomachaches, fatigue, aches, and pains (Scheier & Carver, 1985). Additional studies have come to similar conclusions for a wide range of populations, from law school students to middle-aged and older adults (Endrighi et al., 2011; Segerstrom et al., 1998; Smith et al., 2004). Optimism is a key part of the recent movement toward *positive psychology*, a perspective in psychology that emphasizes people's strengths and successes. Such an emphasis (including optimism as well as other aspects of a positive outlook) has been linked to high levels of overall physical health (Taylor et al., 2000a; Gable & Haidt, 2005; Kok et al., 2013; Boehm & Kubzansky, 2012).

As good as optimism is for fending off stress, hardiness may be even better. Both optimistic people and hardy people share a positive outlook even when the future seems bleak, but hardy people tend to work more actively to make that outlook a reality (Maddi & Hightower, 1999). For example, consider Inez and Thomas, two restaurant servers who lose their jobs when their restaurant goes out of business. Inez is an optimist, so she truly believes that "things will work out—I'm sure another job will come along." Thomas is hardy, so he *works* to make sure that things work out and the other job comes along—he checks the help wanted ads online and sends out his résumé more often than Inez does. Of course, there is no reason why optimism and hardiness can't go hand in hand. Expecting a positive outcome *and* working to make it happen may be the best strategy for keeping your stress at bay.

Optimistic people look toward the future with hope and an expectation of a positive outcome. Research has generally found that optimism reduces stress. michaeljung/iStock/Getty Images

CHECK YOUR LEARNING:

11.16 How do psychologists define coping?

11.17 How do coping styles differ by ethnicity and gender?

11.18 What is the difference between problem-focused coping and emotion-focused coping?

11.19 How can mindfulness influence stress levels?

11.20 How can different types of social support be categorized, and what role does social support play in emotional and physical health?

11.21 What kinds of changes in thinking and behavior can decrease stress?

Coping with Stress: Physical Strategies and Medical Strategies

YOU WILL LEARN:

11.22 about the stages of change model.

11.23 how to decrease stress with exercise.

11.24 how to decrease stress with medicine and healing techniques.

You don't need your psychology textbook to tell you this: Taking care of your body is crucial in terms of reducing stress and maintaining physical and mental health. You've heard similar messages a million times before, but most of us could learn more about reducing stress (**Figure 11.6**). Most of us know that getting enough sleep, eating healthy, and exercising are important for reducing stress, but only *half* of us actually do these self-care behaviors at a "very good" or "excellent" level (American Psychological Association, 2014).

Why don't people do healthy things when they know it would decrease their stress?

There are plenty of real-world reasons—we don't have enough time to exercise, healthy food is too expensive or inconvenient, or busy schedules rob us of sleep. But another reason may be that our minds are just not there yet in terms of our readiness to make changes. The *stages of change model* is a way that psychologists think about that readiness to make changes. It is widely accepted by psychologists who focus on health-related issues, and it includes five specific stages that identify how ready someone might be to make major life improvements (Prochaska & Velicer, 1997; DiClemente & Prochaska, 1982; Prochaska et al., 1992; Schwarzer, 2011). **Table 11.5** lists those five stages of change, which basically range from "not even on my radar" to "I've made the change and I want to keep it that way." Research shows that when trying to help someone make major lifestyle changes in diet, exercise, or other health-related behaviors, tailoring efforts to a person's current stage of change helps (Noar et al., 2007). For example, an overweight friend thinking about exercise is at Stage 1 (not even on their radar). The idea is to move them to Stage 2 (starting to think about exercise) rather than trying to push them immediately to Stage 4 (taking action, or committing to an exercise schedule).

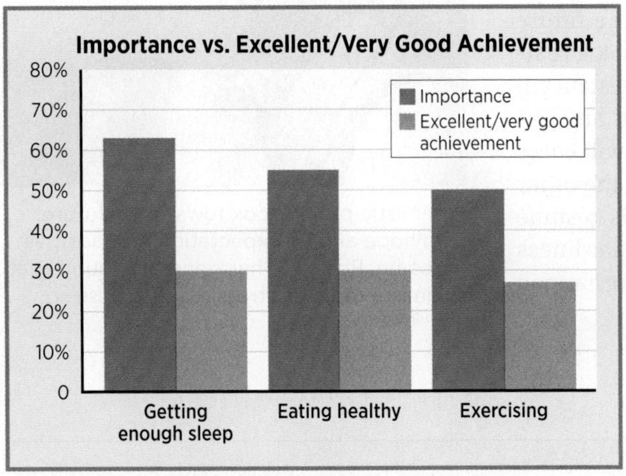

FIGURE 11.6 What We Know Versus What We Do about Managing Stress. Regarding the stress-reducing behaviors of sufficient sleep, healthy eating, and exercising, more of us understand their importance than actually do the behaviors consistently. Data from the American Psychological Association, 2014.

Decreasing Stress with Exercise

Exercising reduces stress and the health risks associated with it (Edenfield & Blumenthal, 2011; Crews & Landers, 1987). Particularly beneficial is **aerobic exercise**: physical exercise that maintains an increased heart rate for a prolonged time. Aerobic exercise brings oxygen to the muscles (*aero-* means air or oxygen). Examples include running, walking, swimming, cycling, rowing, jumping rope, and using an elliptical training machine.

If you think back to the fight-or-flight roots of the stress response, the benefits of aerobic exercise make a lot of sense. The "flight" impulse in particular matches your behavior when you run, bike, swim, or otherwise put your body in continuous motion. (Boxing or MMA forms of exercise probably match the "fight" impulse as well.) This may explain why studies have found that exercise has both immediate and long-term benefits. So, if you look at the big timeline, running several times a week will help you maintain a low stress level over time. But if you zoom in on a more specific point in time, running when you wake up tomorrow will help you feel less stressed through the morning (Forcier et al., 2006; Hamer et al., 2006).

TABLE 11.5: Stages of Change Model

STAGE OF CHANGE	EXAMPLE: THOUGHTS OF AN OVERWEIGHT PERSON CONSIDERING A DAILY EXERCISE ROUTINE
Precontemplation	"Exercise? Why? I'm not even fat. I'm in good shape."
Contemplation	"I just caught a glimpse of myself in the mirror. I also got winded climbing that flight of stairs this morning. Maybe I should lose a few pounds."
Preparation	"It will be tough, but I think I can do it. I'll look at my schedule and see what I can fit in. I'll look into gym membership options too."
Action	"I joined the gym down the street and just had my first session with a trainer there. I'm going three times a week and told my friends and family about it too."
Maintenance	"I've lost 20 pounds so far, and I feel great. I need to keep this up."

Information from Prochaska & Velicer, 1997; DiClemente & Prochaska, 1982; Prochaska et al., 1992; Schwarzer, 2011.

According to the stages of change model, people move through a series of stages in terms of their readiness to make health-related changes in their lives. Matching efforts to help with the person's current stage makes a big difference.

Of course, there is such a thing as too much aerobic exercise (La Gerche & Prior, 2007; Ishikawa-Takata et al., 2003). There is no formula for how much is right for everyone in terms of health benefits and stress reduction. Your exercise habits should be customized to your current fitness and health levels. In the United States, with its increasingly sedentary lifestyle (in other words, we sit too much), most of us could use a boost in our exercise levels. In terms of stress, exercise becomes too much if it generates more stress than it relieves. If your exercise routine becomes a stressor itself (because of pressure or competition), it may be time to take it down a notch (LaCaille & Taylor, 2013).

Aerobic exercise, in which the heart rate stays elevated for a prolonged time, reduces stress. Maridav/Shutterstock

Decreasing Stress with Medical and Healing Techniques

The field of medicine offers countless suggestions for stress reduction. Many of them come from *conventional medicine*—basically, the standard, mainstream Western health care system with its doctors, nurses, and hospitals. But an increasing number of stress-reduction strategies have their origins outside of that system. In some cases, these strategies come from **complementary medicine**: health care that complements conventional medicine. In other cases, these strategies come from **alternative medicine**: health care that is used instead of conventional medicine. Together, complementary medicine and alternative medicine are often called *CAM* (*C*omplementary and *A*lternative *M*edicine). When the best of CAM is combined with the best of conventional medicine, the term *integrative medicine* is often used.

In recent years, mainstream U.S. culture has embraced CAM to a greater extent than ever before. Most U.S. medical schools offer CAM courses as electives, and about a quarter require CAM courses (Jacobs & Gundling, 2009). Rates of CAM usage among cancer patients ranges between 40% and 85% (Bardia et al., 2009). About 60% of HIV patients use CAM, as do about 36% of patients with cardiovascular disease (Tokumoto, 2009; Bloedon & Szapary, 2009). One large-scale survey of over 31,000 U.S. adults found that 36% had used some form of CAM in the past year (excluding prayer, which is sometimes included in such studies as a CAM), mostly for common problems like colds, back pain, neck pain, joint pain, sinus problems, asthma, and hypertension. Those who were most likely to use CAM were female, highly educated, middle-aged, and living in cities (Barnes et al., 2004).

Generally, CAM is more prevention-based than conventional medicine. It also tends to emphasize the idea that what underlies most illness (and stress) is an imbalance

aerobic exercise
Physical exercise that maintains an increased heart rate for a prolonged time.

complementary medicine
Health care that complements, or is used along with, conventional medicine.

alternative medicine
Health care that is used instead of conventional medicine.

CHAPTER APP 11.3

Decreasing Stress with Exercise

Runkeeper

Preview one of the links and consider the following questions.

WEBSITE:
http://tiny.cc/bni7jy

ANDROID:
http://tiny.cc/tc92iy

IPHONE:
http://tiny.cc/o682iy

VIDEO DEMO:
http://tiny.cc/chapterapps

This app allows you to set specific running (or walking, or biking) goals and track your progress over time. It can record your route or suggest a new one according to your preferences. It allows you to share your running achievements on social media, and even tracks your running speed according to the song playing on your phone at the time (in case you want to see which song made you pick up the pace).

How does it APPly to your daily life?
Exercise is a powerful way to decrease stress and maintain health. How can apps like this one influence the amount of exercise you get? How would you improve upon the features of this app?

How does it APPly to your understanding of psychology?
As the textbook mentions, there can be such a thing as too much exercise. In your opinion, what's the best way to use this app to reduce, rather than cause more, stress?

among certain energies or bodily regions, as opposed to the conventional view emphasizing malfunction at the cellular, biochemical, or molecular level (Chiappelli, 2012; Ernst et al., 2006; Micozzi, 2011).

Some of the most common specific CAM practices—*acupuncture, meditation, homeopathic medicine*, and *biofeedback*—are each used for a wide range of stress-related problems. **Acupuncture** is a technique involving the insertion of needles into the skin at specific points to alleviate stress or pain. (Closely related but less popular than acupuncture is *acupressure*, a technique that replaces the insertion of needles with the pressing of fingers or thumbs.) Numerous empirical studies show that acupuncture, which derives from ancient Chinese medical tradition, reduces stress-related symptoms. For example, in one study, acupuncture alleviated the symptoms of PTSD as effectively as cognitive-behavior therapy, and the improvements held up for at least 3 months (Hollifield et al., 2007). In a meta-analysis, acupuncture was found to significantly improve depression symptoms (Wang et al., 2008; see also Zhang et al., 2010). Additional studies suggest that acupuncture may also benefit people with anxiety (Samuels et al., 2008; Pilkington et al., 2007).

Meditation is an activity designed to increase focused attention with the ultimate purpose of improving your mental state. Like acupuncture, meditation originates in Eastern spiritual practice but is now typically practiced in the West without a specific religious emphasis. Meditation takes many forms, but two of the most common are *concentrative meditation* and *mindfulness meditation*. Concentrative meditation involves a focus on a single stimulus, often coming from within the person (breathing patterns, a repeated sound, etc.). *Mindfulness meditation* involves increased attention to all stimuli in the internal and external environment (Shapiro, 2009a). (Mindfulness meditation obviously shares an emphasis with the mindfulness-based thinking described a few pages earlier.) When practiced on a regular basis, meditation lowers stress and the risk of stress-related problems, including anxiety and depression (Oman et al., 2008; Walsh & Shapiro, 2006; MacLean et al., 1997; Beauchamp-Turner & Levinson, 1992). Studies have found that meditating on a regular basis increases the immune system's ability to battle diseases ranging from the flu to cancer (Davidson et al., 2003; Carlson et al., 2003). Another study focused specifically on 91 full-time teachers in elementary, middle, or high schools—a population for whom high stress levels are notoriously common. Its primary finding was that teachers' stress levels dropped significantly when they started practicing meditation, even just twice a week for 20 minutes per session (Anderson et al., 1999).

Homeopathic medicine is health care based on the idea that the human body has the ability to heal itself and characterized by low-dose medications made from natural sources. Homeopathic medicine has been practiced in European countries for hundreds of years but is still considered outside of the mainstream by many in the United States. Homeopathic medicine presumes that your body doesn't need medication made of synthesized ingredients or in large doses, as is common in conventional medicine. (In fact, such medication could worsen your health, according to the homeopathic approach.) Instead, homeopathic medicine believes that your body has an impressive and often underestimated ability to fix itself, but it may need just a little "nudge" from a small dose of a medicine (often made from a plant or mineral) to kick-start the healing process. Advocates of homeopathic medicine believe in it strongly, but there is little empirical evidence that homeopathic medicine improves stress levels and related conditions (Pilkington et al., 2006; Davidson et al., 2011). Also, there is some criticism stating that its benefits are due primarily to the *placebo effect*, or mere expectations of benefit rather than any actual healing properties of the homeopathic medicine (Shang et al., 2005; Smith, 2012).

Biofeedback is using a monitor to see information about your physiological functions (like heartbeat or muscle tension), with the intention of influencing those functions in a healthy direction. If you've ever checked your own heart rate while you're exercising (with a smartphone app, or with the metal sensors on the

acupuncture
A technique involving the insertion of needles into the skin at specific points to alleviate stress or pain.

meditation
An activity designed to increase focused attention with the ultimate purpose of improving your mental state.

homeopathic medicine
Health care based on the idea that the human body has the ability to heal itself and characterized by very low-dose medications made from natural sources.

biofeedback
Use of a monitor that provides information about physiological functions (like heartbeat or muscle tension), with the intention of influencing those functions in a healthy direction.

handles of the treadmill, exercise bike, or elliptical machine at the gym), you have an understanding of biofeedback. For people with stress-related conditions like cardiovascular disease, biofeedback can be an important tool, primarily because knowing your heart rate in real time is the first step to controlling it. Biofeedback allows people to see or hear what their heart is doing (through a graph on a screen, or beeps from the machine), which can prompt them to do something to change it. That "something" might be slowing their breathing, using visual imagery, or taking another deliberate action to bring down a dangerously high heart rate (Schwartz & Andrasik, 2005; Khazan, 2013). Research on the stress-related benefits of biofeedback has been sparse, especially in recent decades, but there are at least a few small-scale supportive studies (Reiner, 2008; Leahy et al., 1997; Teufel et al., 2013).

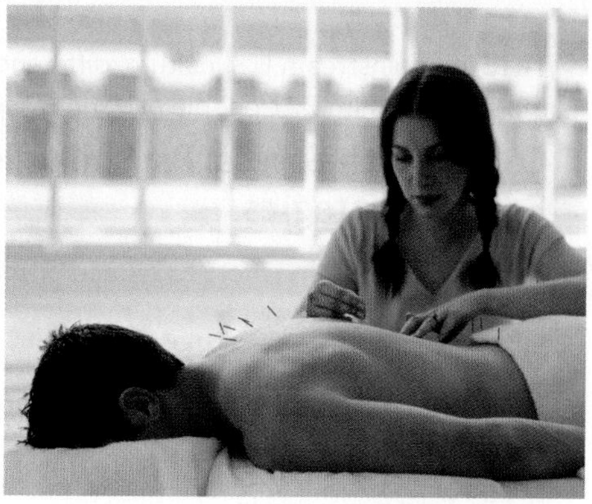

An increasing number of people consider complementary medicine or alternative medicine to reduce stress. A common example of these approaches is acupuncture, a technique involving the insertion of needles into the skin at specific points to alleviate stress or pain. Creatas/Getty Images

CHECK YOUR LEARNING:

11.22 What are the stages in the stages of change model, and how does this model relate to stress reduction efforts?

11.23 What effect does exercise have on stress?

11.24 What are some techniques of complementary medicine and alternative medicine that can decrease stress?

CHAPTER SUMMARY

Stress: What Is It and What Causes It?

11.1 Stress is an unpleasant physical or psychological reaction to circumstances that are perceived as challenging.

11.2 Stressors are the circumstances, such as events or changes in your life, that cause stress.

11.3 The fight-or-flight response is an automatic emotional and physical reaction to a perceived threat that prepares you to either attack or run away.

11.4 Appraisal is how you evaluate the things that happen to you. Primary appraisal determines how stressful the event is and secondary appraisal determines how capable you are to handle it.

11.5 Hassles are the minor annoyances or aggravations of day-to-day life that add up to cause significant stress.

Stress and the Mind-Body Connection

11.6 Both the body and the mind suffer the consequences of stress. The relationship between the body and the mind is bidirectional.

11.7 The general adaptation syndrome is a widely accepted understanding of the way bodies respond to ongoing stress, consisting of the sequence of alarm, resistance, and exhaustion.

11.8 Stress can wear down a person's immune system, which defends the body against bacteria, viruses, infections, injuries, and anything else that could cause illness or death.

11.9 People with Type A personality, who are competitive, driven, and hostile, experience more stress-related health consequences than people with Type B personality, who are noncompetitive, easygoing, and relaxed.

11.10 People with high levels of the personality traits conscientiousness and extraversion tend to experience less stress, while people with high levels of the personality trait neuroticism tend to experience more stress.

11.11 Stress can contribute to almost any psychological disorder, including depression, anxiety, eating disorders, attention-deficit/hyperactivity disorder (ADHD), and schizophrenia.

Stress and Culture

11.12 Men and women often experience different types of stressors and get stressed out about different things. Men and women also tend to react differently to the same stressor, with women appraising stressors as more severe than do men.

11.13 Minority or immigrant groups in the United States are more likely to face certain real-world stressors than people in the majority. People from collectivistic and individualistic cultures often have different experiences of stress.

11.14 The four acculturation strategies tend to produce different outcomes in terms of stress, with integration producing the least stress and marginalization producing the most stress.

11.15 In mainstream U.S. culture, different sources of stress are more likely to impact people at various life stages.

Coping with Stress: Psychological Strategies and Social Strategies

11.16 Coping is any effort to reduce or manage the experience of stress.

11.17 People from collectivistic ethnicities tend to cope by changing things within themselves (like their own thoughts and feelings), while people from individualistic ethnicities tend to cope by changing things outside of themselves (like the stressor itself). Women tend to cope by talking with others about their feelings, while men tend to cope by problem solving and by not discussing their emotions.

11.18 Problem-focused coping emphasizes changing the stressor itself, while emotion-focused coping emphasizes changing one's emotional reaction to the stressor.

11.19 Practicing mindfulness can reduce stress through an increased awareness of moment-to-moment physical and psychological experiences.

11.20 Social support is often categorized in three ways—informational, instrumental, and emotional—and it is important to both emotional and physical health.

11.21 People can decrease stress through positive ways of thinking and behaving such as proactive coping, hardiness, and optimism.

Coping with Stress: Physical Strategies and Medical Strategies

11.22 The stages of change model—which includes precontemplation, contemplation, preparation, action, and maintenance—can explain why people don't always do things that would likely reduce stress.

11.23 Exercise, particularly aerobic exercise, reduces stress and the health risks associated with it.

11.24 Complementary medicine and alternative medicine offer a variety of techniques to decrease stress including acupuncture, meditation, homeopathic medicine, and biofeedback.

KEY TERMS

stress, p. 367
fight-or-flight response, p. 367
stressor, p. 367
appraisal, p. 367
primary appraisal, p. 368
secondary appraisal, p. 368
hassles, p. 368
general adaptation syndrome, p. 370
immune system, p. 373
psychoneuroimmunology (PNI), p. 373
psychophysiological illnesses, p. 373
coronary heart disease, p. 373
Type A personality, p. 375
Type B personality, p. 375
Type C personality, p. 375
Type D personality, p. 375
posttraumatic stress disorder (PTSD), p. 377
acute stress disorder, p. 377
adjustment disorder, p. 377
posttraumatic growth, p. 378
acculturative stress, p. 383
coping, p. 385
problem-focused coping, p. 387
emotion-focused coping, p. 387
social support, p. 388
proactive coping, p. 391
hardiness, p. 391
optimism, p. 391
aerobic exercise, p. 393
complementary medicine, p. 393
alternative medicine, p. 393
acupuncture, p. 394
meditation, p. 394
homeopathic medicine, p. 394
biofeedback, p. 394

SELF-ASSESSMENT

1. Vanessa is about to give a speech to a large group of people. The unpleasant feeling Vanessa has about giving the speech is ______, while the speech itself is ______.
   a. stress; appraisal
   b. a stressor; stress
   c. stress; a stressor
   d. coping; stress

2. ______ is determining how stressful an event is. ______ is determining how capable you are to cope with the stressful event.

3. Isaiah is noncompetitive, easygoing, relaxed, and rarely angry. Which of these personality types best describes him?
   a. Type A personality
   b. Type B personality
   c. Type C personality
   d. Type D personality

4. People whose personalities feature high levels of ______ tend to experience less stress.
   a. anxiety
   b. extraversion

c. neuroticism
d. isolation

5 ______ occurs when people experience trauma but find a way to benefit, improve, or enrich themselves from that point forward.

6 Keeping the old culture while embracing the new culture is the acculturation strategy of ______.

a. assimilation
b. separation
c. marginalization
d. integration

7 ______ is an effort to reduce or manage the experience of stress.

a. Coping
b. Projection
c. Posttraumatic stress disorder
d. Psychoneuroimmunology

8 ______ coping is a style of coping with stress that emphasizes changing the stressor itself, while ______ coping is a style of coping with stress that emphasizes changing your reaction to the stressor.

9 ______ refers to an increased awareness of what's going on inside of a person—the moment-to-moment physical and psychological experiences—with an emphasis on just feeling it rather than analyzing it or avoiding it.

10 ______ is health care based on the idea that the human body can heal itself with low-dose medications made from natural sources.

Research shows quizzing is a highly effective learning tool. Continue quizzing yourself using LearningCurve, the system that adapts to *your* learning.

LaunchPad macmillan learning LearningCurve macmillan learning

GO TO: launchpadworks.com

Self-Assessment Answers

1. c, 2. Primary appraisal; Secondary appraisal, 3. b, 4. b, 5. Posttraumatic growth, 6. d, 7. a, 8. Problem-focused; emotion-focused, 9. Mindfulness, 10. Homeopathic medicine

WHAT'S YOUR TAKE?

1. In my private practice, I've seen quite a few heterosexual couples in therapy whose arguments involve a comparison of who's got it worse, him or her. Typically, she lists her stressors, he lists his, and each comes to the conclusion that the other one has it easier. When couples bring that up, it always gets me thinking: Who *does* have it worse in terms of stress in our society, males or females? What factors might affect your answer to that question—age, ethnicity, socioeconomic status, or other factors? What role does the appraisal of stress play?

SHOW ME MORE

11.1 Human vs. Animal Experience of Stress

launchpadworks.com LaunchPad macmillan learning

This video offers an explanation of important differences between how animals and humans experience stress.

laurien/Getty Images

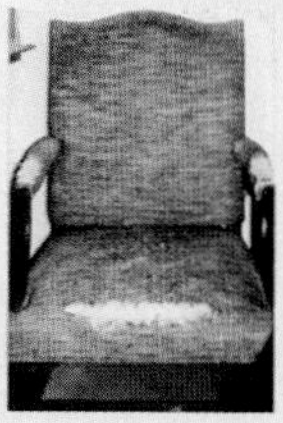

11.2 Type A Personality Explained

launchpadworks.com LaunchPad macmillan learning

This video offers an entertaining version of the origins of Type A personality.

Greater Good Science Center

12 Personality

Eugenio Marongiu/Getty Images

I was doing quite well in my seventh-grade Spanish class. Learning vocabulary words, conjugating verbs, even rolling my r's—everything was *muy bien*. Then we got to the translation for the word *is*, and I found myself quite confused. The textbook had two translations: *está* and *es*. How could a single verb in English translate into two different verbs in Spanish?

My teacher, Señora Fernandez, explained that Spanish speakers make an important distinction between two kinds of *is*. There's the kind of *is* that's momentary and fleeting (*está*), which describes someone's temporary state. There's also the kind of *is* that's more stable and unchanging (*es*), which describes someone's essential character. I started to get it: The two verbs distinguished how someone happens to be right now versus how someone is every day.

Señora Fernandez offered some examples to help us distinguish the two kinds of *is* in Spanish. She started with an English sentence: Miranda is quiet. Does that mean that Miranda is being quiet right now, or that Miranda is generally a quiet person? In Spanish, the choice of verb clarifies it. *Miranda* está *callada* means she's quiet right now; *Miranda* es *callada* means she's usually quiet, an introvert at heart. Here's another example: Alex is happy. Does that mean Alex is happy like he just won a baseball game, or happy like he is always optimistic? Again, the Spanish verbs tell the tale: *Alex* está *feliz* means he's wearing a smile right now; *Alex* es *feliz* means he's a generally cheerful, glass-half-full kind of guy.

I didn't realize it at the time, but when Señora Fernandez explained the difference between those two Spanish verbs, she also taught us an important lesson about personality. Psychologists use the term *personality* to refer to each person's enduring character. It is what Spanish speakers refer to when they describe someone with the verb *es*: what a person *is* at his or her essence, across time and situations. Personality encompasses each person's unique and enduring patterns of thoughts, feelings, and actions. Personality is what makes you *you*.

In this chapter, we will explore numerous theories that psychologists use to explain how your personality developed and how it differs from the personalities of other people. We will also consider the tests and other techniques that psychologists use to measure personality.

CHAPTER OUTLINE

What Is Personality?

YOU WILL LEARN:

12.1 what the definition of personality is.

12.2 how psychologists study personality.

12.3 how twin studies and adoption studies illustrate the biological contributions to personality.

In this section, we will consider three attempts to explain how personality is formed over time: the *psychodynamic* theory, the *humanistic* theory, and the *behavioral and social-cognitive* theory. We will also consider *trait* theory, which emphasizes the ingredients that make personality rather than the way personality is formed over time. But first, let's define personality.

Defining Personality

Personality is a person's distinctive and stable way of thinking, feeling, and behaving. It is the psychological equivalent of your fingerprint: a unique set of characteristics that differentiates you from other people and stays with you long-term. For example, if you've ever gotten together with a friend or relative you haven't seen in years, you can appreciate what personality means. In spite of the time apart, the person rarely surprises you. There may be some superficial changes—a new haircut, a few pounds gained or lost, some wrinkles—but rarely are there changes in who the person *is*. Personality is stable. People's tendencies, their predispositions, their singular way of interacting with the world are generally the same as they have always been.

Personality is a person's distinctive and stable way of thinking, feeling, and behaving. It is the psychological equivalent of your fingerprint: a unique set of characteristics that differentiates you from other people and stays with you long-term.
Thomas Barwick/Stone/Getty Images

A fascinating study illustrates the stability of personality (Nave et al., 2010). Personality researchers found teachers' ratings of students' personalities in an ethnically diverse Hawaii elementary school. The personality ratings were made between 1959 and 1967. *Four decades later*, the researchers located 144 of these students and recruited them for another personality assessment, which involved a video-recorded interview that was scored by trained observers using standardized rating scales. Results indicated that the participants' personalities hadn't changed much. Talkative kids talked a lot as adults; adaptable kids handled new situations well now; humble kids had remained modest; and impulsive kids still acted spontaneously in their 50s. Similar conclusions have come from other studies, including one of almost 1000 people assessed first at age 3 and again at age 26 (Caspi et al., 2003). The conclusion illustrates the way psychologists understand personality:

> [P]ersonality resides *within* people... the same individual... separated by many years... remains recognizably the same person. —Nave et al., 2010, p. 333; italics in original.

Isn't it possible that people think, feel, and act the way they do because of the situation around them rather than the personality within them?

The situation can play a powerful role in how a person behaves. For example, a driver stopped at an intersection is not doing so because she has a timid personality, but because the light is red. Of course, if you spend some time in her passenger seat, you'll notice that personality characteristics influence her driving style too. She might make sudden lane shifts and dart out into busy traffic, suggesting that she's a bold risk taker. She might yield a lot or let other cars take spots in crowded parking lots, both of which suggest a strong tendency to accommodate others and avoid conflict. She might explode with road rage at other drivers for minor infractions, suggesting a deep-seated impatience and self-importance. The main point is that the way you behave depends on an interaction of the situation and what your personality brings to it. What surrounds you can affect behavior, but psychologists recognize that what is *inside* of you—your personality—is also a strong influence on what you do and how you do it.

LIFE HACK 12.1

In relationships, if you think you can easily change the other person's personality, think again. Research suggests that personality generally remains stable over time.

(Nave et al., 2010; Caspi et al., 2003)

Typically, psychologists explain personality with a *theory*. There are plenty of personality theories, offered by Freud, Rogers, Bandura, and others. Unfortunately, we can't crown one personality theory as "correct" and eliminate all the others (Newman & Larsen, 2011; Barenbaum & Winter, 2008). There is a reason why experts still use the term personality *theory* rather than personality *fact*: Psychologists are still figuring out human personality, and will be doing so for many years to come.

Biological Contributions to Personality

Some people believe there is a simple answer to why you have a particular personality: You were born with it. There is certainly some truth to that notion (Krueger, 2008; Kendler et al., 2009; Floderus-Myrhed et al., 1980). The genetic influence is apparent in some aspects of personality from birth (Rothbart et al., 2000; Fish et al., 1991). If you've spent time around newborn babies, you know this firsthand. Some newborns are energetic, others sluggish. Some babies are fussy, others easygoing. Some babies respond to other people, some are oblivious. All of these differences are apparent from day one, before the newborn babies have had any life experiences that might have influenced them.

Twin studies and adoption studies also indicate biological contributions to personality. Such research comes from the field of **behavioral genetics**: the study of the impact of genes (nature) and environment (nurture) on personality and behavior. Numerous studies of behavioral genetics have found that identical twins, who share all of the same genes, have a much higher likelihood of matching each other on many personality traits than fraternal twins, who share only some of the same genes (Segal, 2011; Pedersen et al., 1988; Loehlin & Nichols, 1976; Tellegen et al., 1988). This is true whether the twins are raised together or separated at birth and raised apart. Many adoption studies also show that genes influence personality. Researchers consistently find that adopted kids have personalities that are more similar to their biological parents' than their adoptive parents' (Rhee & Waldman, 2002; Pedersen et al., 1991; Daniels & Plomin, 1985). This is true even though adopted kids spend every day with their adoptive parents and may never have met their biological parents.

Figure 12.1 illustrates the impact of genes on personality characteristics (Jang et al., 1996). Notice how the bars for identical (monozygotic) twins rise much higher than the bars for nonidentical (dizygotic) twins. In many cases, the correlations are

Research on behavioral genetics reveals the strong impact of genes on personality. Identical twins (like the top pair), who share all of their genes, show more similarity in their personalities than nonidentical twins (like the bottom pair), who share only half of their genes. James Woodson/DigitalVision/Getty Images; Jessica Holden Photography/Moment/Getty Images

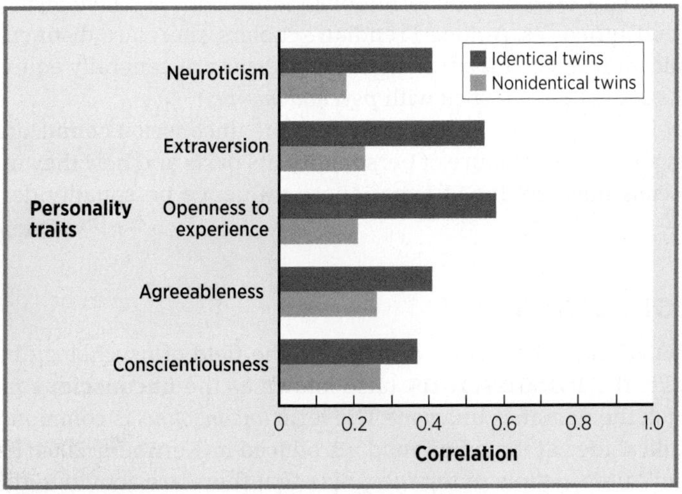

FIGURE 12.1 Correlations of Personality Characteristics Within Twin Pairs. Genes clearly influence personality, as indicated by the longer bars for identical twins than for nonidentical twins. But that space between the ends of the longest bars and the 1.0 line indicates that many nongenetic factors influence personality too. Data from Jang et al., 1996.

personality
A person's distinctive and stable way of thinking, feeling, and behaving.

behavioral genetics
The study of the impact of genes (nature) and environment (nurture) on personality and behavior.

twice as large. This indicates that twins who share all the same genes are more likely to match on personality characteristics than twins who share only half the same genes.

An important fact about the correlations presented in Figure 12.1 is that none of them is even close to the maximum correlation of 1.0. Even the correlations describing identical twins, who are genetic clones, fall far short. If genes completely determined personality—if it were all about biology—the identical twin correlations would be 1.0. The correlations for other relationships would be much higher as well. This is why numerous researchers have estimated that about 50% of personality is determined by genes (Tellegen et al., 1988; Nettle, 2007). That is a sizable amount, but it also means there must be a lot more to personality than biology (Rutter, 2000, 2006, 2011; Tremblay, 2011). That nonbiological contribution is what the theories in this chapter attempt to explain, beginning with the psychodynamic theory of Sigmund Freud.

CHECK YOUR LEARNING:

12.1 What is the definition of personality?

12.2 What is the role of theory in the study of personality?

12.3 What do behavioral genetics studies (twin studies and adoption studies) suggest about the roles of biology and environment in the development of personality?

Psychodynamic Theory of Personality

YOU WILL LEARN:

12.4 what the psychodynamic theory of personality is.

12.5 what the unconscious is and why it is important.

12.6 what the id, ego, and superego are.

12.7 about the psychosexual stages of development.

12.8 how Sigmund Freud's followers offered revised new psychodynamic theories.

12.9 about current thoughts on psychodynamic theory.

The **psychodynamic theory of personality** is an explanation of personality, based on the ideas of Sigmund Freud, that emphasizes unconscious forces and early childhood experiences. The study of personality was founded on Freud's psychodynamic theory. Developed in the late 1800s and early 1900s in Vienna, Austria, it came first historically and has been hugely influential in both academic and popular culture (Routh, 1996, 2011). In fact, many other personality theories were developed because the theorist was dissatisfied with psychodynamic theory (Engel, 2008; Hollon & DiGiuseppe, 2011). (A brief note on terminology—the word *psychoanalytic* is often used to refer to Freud's theories. Among Freudian scholars, there are distinctions between psychodynamic and psychoanalytic, but the two terms are generally equivalent for our purposes. For simplicity, we'll stick with *psychodynamic*.)

We'll start by considering Freud's notion of the unconscious mind, and then move on to his ideas about the structure of personality (its parts and how they interact). After that, we'll discuss how childhood experiences influence personality development at various stages.

The Unconscious

Freud contributed many important concepts to the field of psychology, but one of the most essential is the **unconscious** (also known as the **unconscious mind**): mental activity of which the person is unaware. The term *unconscious* is commonly used today, but it was a radical idea at the time Freud introduced it (Kernberg, 2004; Lane & Harris, 2008). In Freud's time, people didn't recognize that there are activities going on inside our minds that are outside our awareness. And these unconscious activities—thoughts, impulses, wishes, and the like—are not meaningless or negligible. They drive us, influence our thoughts and actions, and affect our lives (Kris, 2012; Karon & Widener, 1995).

According to Freud, the impact of the unconscious is so great that it can explain our actions that are otherwise unexplainable. In other words, "random" things we do

aren't random at all. Instead, they are caused by unconscious thoughts, wishes, or urges. Freud called this idea **psychic determinism**: the belief that all thoughts and behaviors, even those that seem accidental, arbitrary, or mistaken, are determined by psychological forces. For example, consider Jason, a sales rep who has a big presentation today. As he gets into his car to head to the client meeting, he notices his shoe is untied. Jason takes his computer bag off his shoulder, sets it down, and ties his shoe. He then drives off, leaving the computer bag on the ground. Even if Jason can't come up with a conscious reason why he would do that (after all, he needs that laptop for his presentation), that doesn't mean there is no reason for it. According to Freud, the reason lies in Jason's unconscious (Cabaniss et al., 2011; Rycroft, 1968). Perhaps deep down, Jason is terrified about this presentation and desperately wants to avoid it. Or maybe he has some unrecognized hatred for his job. A blown presentation might get him fired and force him to find a new job, which may be exactly what he wants on some level.

Sigmund Freud created the psychodynamic theory of personality, which emphasizes unconscious forces and early childhood experiences. Sigmund Freud Copyrights/ullstein bild via Getty Images

The notion of psychic determinism suggests that your unconscious doesn't do a perfect job of locking in the material that we hope to keep hidden. Sometimes, that unconscious material makes itself evident through errors in your words or actions. Psychologists call such leaks **Freudian slips**: verbal or behavioral mistakes that reveal unconscious thoughts or wishes. If you're a fan of Jennifer Aniston's old TV show *Friends*, you know that her character, Rachel, and Ross (played by David Schwimmer) have had strong feelings for each other since the sitcom began. When Ross is marrying another woman (Emily), he absentmindedly calls her Rachel during the wedding vows ("I, Ross, take thee, Rachel..."). As you can imagine, Emily doesn't laugh it off as if it were a meaningless mistake that Ross just happened to make at the altar. Emily knew exactly where the Freudian slip came from, as did everyone else at the wedding: Ross' unconscious, where he deeply wished that his bride were Rachel instead of Emily.

Psychologists sometimes commit Freudian slips themselves. In my own private practice, I once arrived at my office for a 9 A.M. appointment with a particularly ornery client—Curtis, a physically intimidating man who not only accused me of being incompetent on many occasions, but threatened to sue me during our appointment the week before. I got to my building early and went through my usual routine upon arrival: enter my office through the side door, turn on all the lights, unlock the waiting room door, and wait for my client to arrive. By 9 A.M., he hadn't arrived. I thumbed through a magazine. By 9:05, 9:10, 9:15, still no Curtis. At 9:20, my phone rang. A furious Curtis shouts: "Where are you! I've been outside your office for 20 minutes but the damn door is locked!" Apparently, I had "forgotten" to unlock the waiting room door. In the thousands of times I have arrived at my office to see clients, this was the only time I ever made such a mistake, and also the only time Curtis was my first client of the day. Coincidence? Accident? Freud certainly would say otherwise: My failure to open the waiting room door exposed an unconscious wish—to keep Curtis away from me.

The Structure of Personality

Freud believed that personality was a by-product of the interaction of three components of the mind: the *id*, the *ego*, and the *superego* (**Figure 12.2**). Keep in mind that the three components lie in the unconscious mind, at least partially if not totally hidden. Freud believed that these three components of the mind are engaged in a continuous battle we can't control or even directly observe. He was also confident this battle determines to a significant extent how we think, feel, and behave—our very personalities (Freud, 1923, 1932; Kernberg, 2004; Moore & Fine, 1990; Skelton, 2006).

Id. The first component is the **id**: the animalistic part of the mind that generates our most primal, biologically based impulses such as sex and aggression. For example, imagine a wild animal walking down the hallway outside your psychology classroom, a ferocious bear guided entirely by primal instinct. And it's hungry. How will the bear behave in response to its hunger pangs? Will it kindly ask a student for a small bite of his sandwich? Will the bear patiently slip a dollar into the vending machine? Absolutely not. The bear will devour the student's sandwich (and perhaps devour the

psychodynamic theory of personality
An explanation of personality, based on the ideas of Sigmund Freud, that emphasizes unconscious forces and early childhood experiences.

unconscious (unconscious mind)
Mental activity of which the person is unaware.

psychic determinism
The belief that all thoughts and behaviors, even those that seem accidental, arbitrary, or mistaken, are determined by psychological forces.

Freudian slips
Verbal or behavioral mistakes that reveal unconscious thoughts or wishes.

id
According to Freud, the animalistic part of the mind that generates our most basic, biologically based impulses, such as sex and aggression.

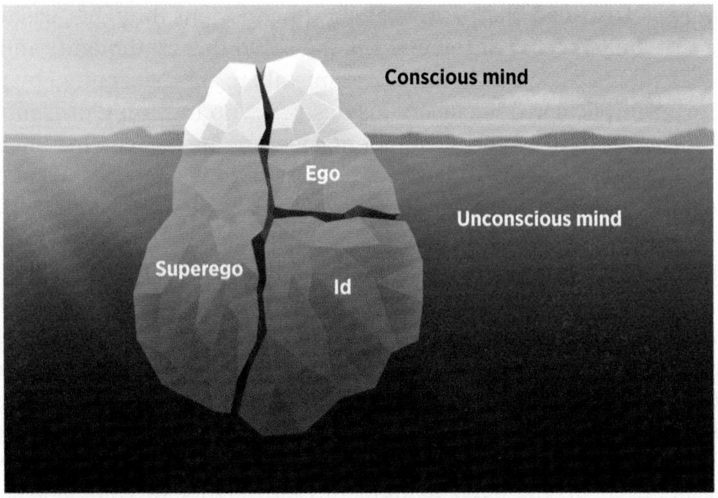

FIGURE 12.2 The Unconscious Nature of the Id, Ego, and Superego. All three of Freud's components of the mind lie at least partially "beneath the surface," in the unconscious mind.

student too). The bear will smash the glass of the vending machine, slash open the packages with its teeth and claws, and gorge on all of the chips, candy, and mini-donuts inside. And it certainly won't feel any need to apologize afterward.

Freud believed that each of us is driven by an id that generates impulses just like those of a wild animal. In fact, he argued that the id is the only component of the mind present at birth. You may never have thought about a cute, cuddly newborn in quite this way before, but it is hard to deny: Babies do seem to be driven solely by their immediate desires. When a newborn wants something—food, a new diaper, a warmer blanket—the baby screams and wails in a selfish attempt to get what would feel good at the moment. The *pleasure principle*—the force that guides the id toward immediate gratification—fuels babies' behavior entirely (Moore & Fine, 1990).

But as babies grow up, they stop acting so selfishly and start being more considerate and socially appropriate. How does that happen?

Superego. As children get older, the people who care for them—parents especially—gradually start to expect them to keep their id impulses in check. The caretakers teach children what is right and wrong, what is acceptable and unacceptable. Those guidelines eventually become a built-in part of the child's mind. So, with the help of others, the child develops a **superego**: the part of the mind that opposes the id by enforcing rules, restrictions, and morality. A toddler who yanks a toy out of another child's hand may be told disapprovingly by a parent (or day care worker, or preschool teacher, or grandparent): "No, Steven. It's not OK to take toys away from your friends. Ask if you can have a turn with it next." As Steven hears comments like this repeatedly, they become part of his own standards of conduct—his own set of "shoulds"—which he carries with him regardless of who (if anyone) may be supervising him in a particular situation. Steven will behave properly not just to gain the approval of those around him, but to gain the approval of himself as well. In this way, Freud's concept of the superego matches the more common notion of the *conscience*, the internal monitor that tells us how acceptable our actions are.

According to psychodynamic theory, the superego is the part of the mind that opposes the id by enforcing the rules, restrictions, and morality learned from caretakers. For example, this child is learning rules about how to treat others on the playground. Maskot/Getty Images

Ego. The job of the superego—to counteract the ongoing stream of powerful id impulses—is certainly a difficult one. This rivalry between the id's drive for gratification and the superego's restraint makes for never-ending conflict within the mind. Freud believed this conflict was managed by the third component of the mind, the **ego**: the part of the mind that serves as a realistic mediator between the id and superego. The ego makes compromises. Its task is to find ways to satisfy both the id and the

superego, while also meeting the demands of the real world (Gabbard, 2005). The ego works according to the *reality principle*: the force that guides a person toward rational, reality-based behavior (Fodor & Gaynor, 1950).

superego
According to Freud, the part of the mind that opposes the id by enforcing rules, restrictions, and morality.

ego
According to Freud, the part of the mind that serves as a realistic mediator between the id and superego.

defense mechanisms
According to Freud, techniques used by the ego to manage conflict between the id and superego.

Defense Mechanisms. Sometimes, the compromises formed by the ego are quite simple: If the id wants to eat a big piece of cake, but the superego says no way, the ego says eat a smaller piece. Other times, the ego resorts to more creative methods to deal with id-versus-superego conflict. Freud and his followers (including his daughter, Anna Freud) identified a number of these **defense mechanisms**: techniques used by the ego to manage conflict between the id and superego. When a person leans heavily on a particular defense mechanism, it can influence or even dominate his or her personality (Dewald, 1964; Freud, 1905, 1936; Sandler & Freud, 1985).

For example, consider Rick, who repeatedly accuses his girlfriend, Mindy, of wanting to cheat on him. There is absolutely no evidence for it, and Mindy steadfastly denies it, but Rick remains sure: Mindy's sick of him and she is actively seeking a fling. Freud would argue that Rick's belief about Mindy wanting to cheat actually began as an id impulse deep within Rick's own unconscious: *Rick* wants to cheat. His superego, of course, rejected that impulse ("Cheating is wrong!"), which left his ego to deal with the resulting id-versus-superego conflict. Rick's ego uses a defense mechanism called *projection*, in which the ego "projects" the id's impulse to cheat onto other people instead of Rick. (Think of it like a movie projector—even though the film is projected onto the screen, the true location of the film is within the projector.) It is as if Rick's ego, in an attempt to deal with this id–versus-superego conflict, converted "*I* want to cheat" into "*She* wants to cheat."

As this example suggests, a person who uses projection as a defense mechanism all the time could develop a distrustful, paranoid personality. Other defense mechanisms handle the id-versus-superego conflict in different ways. For example, when an ego uses *reaction formation*, it does the opposite of the original id impulse—as when a man who is furious at his boss praises her intelligence instead of shouting insults at her. In *displacement*, the ego steers an id impulse to a different, safer target. (This is sometimes known by the nickname "kicking the dog.") For example, an athlete with an impulse to physically assault his coach reroutes his aggression and starts a fight with a teammate who may not deserve it. Psychodynamic theorists consider *sublimation* one of the most successful defense mechanisms: It is just like displacement, but the redirection of the id impulse actually helps other people (Gabbard, 2005; Karon & Widener, 1995). Consider a man who channels his impulses to hurt others into the profession of dentistry—he inflicts pain on others, but in a way that benefits them. **Table 12.1** offers further explanation and examples of many of the defense mechanisms put forth by Freud and his followers.

TABLE 12.1: Selected Defense Mechanisms

DEFENSE MECHANISM	WHAT THE EGO DOES	EXAMPLE
Repression	Hides your id impulse in the unconscious to keep you unaware of it	You have an id impulse to insult your parent, but it never reaches consciousness.
Denial	Blocks external events from consciousness because they are too threatening	You learn that your good friend has a fatal disease but act as if everything is OK.
Regression	Retreats to an earlier time in your life when the current stressor was absent	Soon after you take a stressful new job, you find yourself craving the comfort foods and TV shows you enjoyed as a kid.
Projection	"Projects" your id impulse onto others, so it appears they have it rather than you	You have an id impulse to cheat on your partner, but you accuse your partner of wanting to cheat on you.
Rationalization	Comes up with seemingly acceptable explanations for behaviors actually based on id impulses	You give in to your impulse to order (and eat) many boxes of Girl Scout cookies, but tell yourself that you only did so to support a worthy cause.
Reaction Formation	Overreacts against the id impulse by doing the exact opposite, as if overcompensating	You have an id impulse to damage your friends' new house, but instead you buy them a housewarming gift.
Displacement	Redirects the id impulse toward a safer target in order to minimize the consequences to you	You have an id impulse to scream at your supervisor, but instead you scream at your dog.
Sublimation	Redirects the id impulse in a way that actually benefits others	You have an id impulse to hurt other people, so you become a soldier who can do so for the sake of national security.

The oral stage is the first of Freud's psychosexual stages. It focuses on the long-term psychological consequences of the feeding behavior experienced during infancy. KidStock/Blend Images/Getty Images

TABLE 12.2: Alternative Translations of Freudian Terms

STANDARD TERM	ALTERNATIVE TRANSLATION	MEANING
Id	*It*	Not *he* or *she* (human), but *it* (animal or thing) within you driven toward immediate pleasure
Superego	*Above-me*	The rules that come from those in power over you (parents, etc.)
Ego	*Me*	Your personality, shaped by the way it handles conflict between two other components of the mind

A final note about Freud's three components of the mind may make them easier to understand and remember: Freud wrote in German, and his writings were translated into many languages. When his ideas were translated into English, the translators (for some reason) chose the Latin words *id*, *superego*, and *ego* as the labels for Freud's three components of the mind. As **Table 12.2** shows, if the translators had stuck with ordinary English words instead, the id would be known as the *it*, or the thing inside each of us. (Not *he* or *she*, but *it*—as if referring to an animal or thing, not a human.) The superego would be the *above-me*, that is, the rules and restrictions that came from those in positions of power over each of us. And the ego would be the *me*, the person himself or herself, negotiating between the two powerful forces on either side (Truscott, 2010; Karon & Widener, 1995). Freud intended to say your ego is *you*, which underscores the notion that the way your ego handles conflict defines your personality.

Stages of Development

According to Freud, the experiences we have as young children shape our personalities. He placed special emphasis on the way our parents interacted with us in the earliest years of life. He divided these early years into phases called **psychosexual stages**: the five biologically based developmental stages of childhood during which personality characteristics are formed. **Figure 12.3** presents all of these stages.

According to Freud, each psychosexual stage centers on a particular body part that is the focus of the child's life during that period (Freud, 1905). Kids typically move successfully through each psychosexual stage. However, when a problem arises, a **fixation** can occur: a lingering psychological problem directly related to unsuccessful experience of a particular psychosexual stage. A fixation tends to stay with a person long after the psychosexual stage is over, stirring up psychological problems (and possibly shaping personality) long into adulthood. It is like snagging your sweater as you walk past a doorway: You keep moving forward, but you're caught on something and you can't fully move on until you untether yourself (Westen, Gabbard, & Ortigo, 2008).

Oral Stage. The first of Freud's psychosexual stages is the **oral stage**, which takes place from birth to about 18 months and focuses on the psychological consequences of feeding behavior. Babies experience much of the world through their mouths, and breast-feeding or bottle-feeding is a primary activity. Babies learn what to expect from others by the way their parents respond to their need for food. Most of the time, parents handle feeding just right, and babies learn they can expect to get food when they ask (cry) for it. However, if parents provide too much food too often, then babies may come to expect that others—friends, romantic partners, and so on—will do the same for them as they grow up. This attitude—"Other people are great! They always come through and give me exactly what I need!"—can lead to a naïve and overly optimistic personality. On the other hand, if parents provide too little food too infrequently, babies may come to expect that others will do the same as they grow up. This attitude—"Other people are terrible! They couldn't care less about me!"—can lead to a mistrusting and overly pessimistic personality.

Anal Stage. Freud's second psychosexual stage is the **anal stage**, which lasts from about age 18 months to about age 3, and focuses on the psychological consequences

Stage	Age	Key Issues
Oral	Birth to 18 months	Dependency on caretakers for feeding
Anal	18 months to 3 years	New demands for self-control (toilet training, etc.)
Phallic	3 to 6 years	Self-worth as reflected by parental interest
Latency	Elementary school	None
Genital	Puberty and beyond	Mature sexual relationships

FIGURE 12.3 Freud's Psychosexual Stages. According to the theories of Sigmund Freud, people move through important stages during childhood that impact the formation of their adult personality.

of toilet training. Toilet training is all about control. For the first time, children are expected to control this natural bodily function rather than just letting it happen as they did when they wore diapers. Actually, toilet training is just one of many new demands for self-control placed on kids this age. They are also expected to sit still, be quiet, and behave much more appropriately than they did as babies.

Most parents handle these demands just right, but problems can arise when parents overdo it or underdo it. Parents who demand too much control cause kids to become overly concerned about everything being perfect. It may start in the bathroom, but the demand for perfection can expand—to cleaning up their bedroom, and as the child grows, to personal hygiene, keeping a schedule, and all other aspects of life. Eventually, this child grows into an adult with a "neat freak" personality dominated by the obsessive need to control everything perfectly. On the other hand, parents who demand too little teach their kids that control is unimportant. This attitude can cause not only messes in bathrooms, but disorganization in other areas of life, including messy bedrooms, sloppy appearance, and late schedules.

Phallic Stage. The third psychosexual stage is the **phallic stage**, which runs from 3 to 6 years old and focuses on the psychological consequences of attraction to the opposite-sex parent. Freud believed preschool-aged children strive to have a special relationship with their opposite-sex parent, but see their same-sex parent as a rival. For boys, Freud called this the **Oedipus complex**: the childhood experience of desiring

psychosexual stages
Freud's five biologically based developmental stages of childhood, during which personality characteristics are formed.

fixation
Freud's term for a lingering psychological problem directly related to unsuccessful experience of a particular psychosexual stage.

oral stage
The first of Freud's psychosexual stages, which takes place from birth to about 18 months and focuses on the psychological consequences of feeding behavior.

anal stage
Freud's second psychosexual stage, which lasts from about age 18 months to about age 3, and focuses on the psychological consequences of toilet training.

phallic stage
The third psychosexual stage, which runs from 3 to 6 years old and focuses on the psychological consequences of attraction to the opposite-sex parent.

Oedipus complex
The childhood experience of desiring the mother and resenting the father.

the mother and resenting the father. For girls, he called it the **Electra complex**: the childhood experience of desiring the father and resenting the mother. (Both terms are borrowed from Greek mythology.)

Most parents respond well to their child's wish to have a special relationship with them, but those who respond with too much or too little interest can cause the child psychological problems related to self-worth. Specifically, a parent who drops everything, including his or her partner, to invest in the relationship with the child overinflates the child's self-worth. These children often grow into adults with exaggeratedly wonderful views of themselves—not healthy self-esteem, but conceit. On the other hand, a parent who ignores the child's wish for a special relationship deflates the child's self-worth. These children often grow into adults who undervalue themselves, lack confidence, and feel insecure.

Freud believed that success in the phallic stage was marked by **identification**, in which the child models himself or herself after the undefeatable same-sex parent. Simply put, the child realizes that the parent they desire is already "taken" by the other parent, who is too powerful a foe to overtake. The child then adopts the attitude, "If you can't beat 'em, join 'em." The boy decides to become a protégé of daddy; the girl decides to become a protégé of mommy. That way, the boy and the girl can develop into adults much like their same-sex parents, and eventually find a special opposite-sex partner of their own.

Latency Stage. Freud's fourth psychosexual stage was the **latency stage**, which lasts through the elementary school years, when puberty has not yet kick-started the child's sexual drive, and the child's energies are focused primarily on school and other tasks that have little to do with the sexual or bodily issues that are so prominent in other stages. (As the name of the stage implies, the child's sexuality is *latent* during this time.) As a result, there is relatively little of psychological consequence that takes place during the latency stage, and Freud deemphasized it in his writings (Etchegoyen, 1993).

Genital Stage. The fifth and final psychosexual stage is the **genital stage**, which lasts from puberty through adulthood and focuses on mature, adult sexual relationships. Freud believed that the personality is already set by the time a person enters the genital stage. Freud believed that people who had navigated successfully through the earlier stages (especially the first three) would have the greatest chance of success, which he defined as a long-term romantic relationship with an opposite-sex partner. Those who had become fixated would, by contrast, struggle.

The theories of Alfred Adler regarding birth order influenced much research on the subject. Generally, that research finds that firstborns tend to be more conventional, and laterborns tend to be more unconventional (Sulloway, 2011). Marianna Massey/DigitalVision/Getty Images

Freud's Followers

Sigmund Freud attracted many disciples, many of whom became well-respected personality theorists themselves. Some knew Freud personally; others came along after his death. Their **neo-Freudian theories** revised, but did not entirely reject, the basics of Freud's original psychodynamic theory. Freud's followers held on to his core ideas: the unconscious, the significance of early childhood experiences, and the notion that the mind contained id, ego, and superego. However, his followers let go of some of his ideas too. They deemphasized the biology that was so prominent in Freud's theories, such as the id's bodily drives and the explicit sexuality of the phallic stage (Orlinsky & Howard, 1995; Skelton, 2006; Terman, 2012).

Alfred Adler. Alfred Adler, a psychiatrist colleague of Freud's, offered a different perspective on early child development. He pointed out that young children—particularly in comparison to the stronger, more capable adults they see in their lives—develop an *inferiority complex* that profoundly influences their development. In fact, according to Adler, our primary motivation—which carries past childhood and into adulthood—is to strive for *superiority* over our own perceived weaknesses (Adler, 1927; Mosak & Maniacci, 1999). For example, a man who sees himself as stupid is driven to complete a graduate degree to prove his intelligence, or a woman who sees herself as ugly undergoes multiple plastic surgeries to feel beautiful. Adler's own serious childhood illnesses, including

rickets and a nearly fatal case of pneumonia, undoubtedly prompted him to develop a theory with this emphasis on overcoming perceived weaknesses (Sweeney, 1998).

Adler also shined the light on how personality is influenced by *birth order*, or the place in the family into which a child is born (Adler, 1928). Adler's theories about being the oldest, the middle, the baby, or the only child have spawned hundreds of empirical studies. Collectively, these birth order studies suggest that firstborns tend to be more conservative and conventional, while laterborns (any sibling born into a family with an older brother or older sister) tend to be more liberal and unconventional. "Laterborns seek to discover unique family niches that have not already been taken by older siblings," which requires more out-of-the-box thinking and risk taking (Sulloway, 2011, p. 107). Not surprisingly, laterborns have more open-minded personalities and a greater likelihood to vote for liberal political candidates. Over the course of history, a disproportionately high number of revolutionary thinkers (such as Copernicus, who told us the earth was not the center of the solar system, and Darwin, who told us that humans were just another species produced by evolution) are laterborns. Laterborns are also twice as likely to support a radical political upheaval (Sulloway, 1996, 2001, 2009; Booth & Kee, 2009; Paulhus et al., 1999).

Laterborns are more likely to be risk takers in sports too. As **Figure 12.4** illustrates, laterborns are 1.48 times more likely to play a dangerous sport—football, rugby, ice hockey, lacrosse, gymnastics, boxing, downhill skiing, car racing, and so on—than firstborns. A more detailed analysis of baseball reveals that the difference is even greater when it comes to a particular risky play: stolen-base attempts. Specifically, researchers examined the statistics of 700 Major League Baseball players whose brothers also played in the league and found that younger brothers were 10.6 times more likely to attempt stolen bases than older brothers (Sulloway & Zweigenhaft, 2010). In addition, kid brothers were 4.7 times more likely to be hit by a pitch than big brothers, indicating their increased willingness to risk pain or injury.

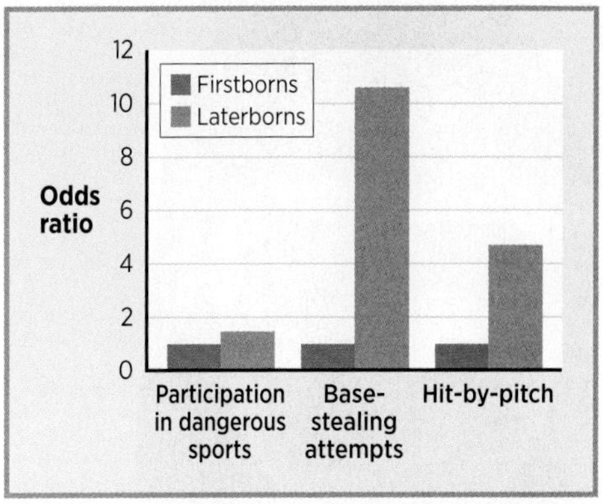

FIGURE 12.4 Birth Order and Risk-Taking in Sports. Laterborns tend to take more dangerous risks than firstborns. As athletes, they more often choose dangerous sports, like boxing or gymnastics. As baseball players, they more often attempt to steal bases, which risks making an out, and to allow pitches to hit them, which risks getting hurt. Data from Sulloway and Zweigenhaft, 2010.

Carl Jung. Carl Jung was once so in line with Freud's way of thinking that Freud personally chose Jung as his successor, but their views eventually diverged so much Freud changed his mind (Bair, 2004; Shiraev, 2011). Among the big differences in their ways of thinking was the understanding of the unconscious. In contrast to Freud's notion that each of us created our own unique unconscious, Jung proposed the **collective unconscious**: common, inherited memories that are present in the minds of people of every culture. The idea is that the collective unconscious equips every person with basic, primal concepts (like a computer comes equipped with basic software) that have become central to human life throughout the ages (Jung, 1963).

Jung called these primal concepts **archetypes**: specific symbols or patterns within the collective unconscious that appear consistently across cultures and time periods. Examples of Jung's archetypes include the child, the hero, the great mother, the devil, the anima (femininity), and the animus (masculinity), among others. He pointed out that these archetypes emerge in some form in the art (paintings, stories, etc.) of cultures from every region and time period (Jung, 1964). For example, the hero archetype appears again and again in different forms from ancient Greece and China to contemporary Western society. Even as the specific appearance of the hero varies so widely, the universal essence of the hero—a courageous, noble person fighting for what they believe is right—remains unchanged.

Jung was also among the first to use the terms *introvert* and *extravert* to describe people with different personality types (Jung, 1971). Introverts are people who tend to focus inward and need little interaction with others. Extraverts are people who tend to focus outward and need lots of interaction with others.

Erik Erikson. Erik Erikson, whose theories we covered in Chapter 9 (Development Across the Life Span), was also a neo-Freudian. His greatest contribution, the eight-stage theory of psychosocial development, was closely related to Freud's five psychosexual stages. Erikson's first five stages correspond directly to Freud's, but the emphasis on biology and sex is replaced by an emphasis on social interaction with significant

Electra complex
The childhood experience of desiring the father and resenting the mother.

identification
Process in which the child models himself or herself after the undefeatable same-sex parent.

latency stage
Freud's fourth psychosexual stage, which lasts through the elementary school years, when the child's energies are focused primarily on school and other tasks that have little to do with sexual or bodily issues.

genital stage
The fifth and final psychosexual stage, which lasts from puberty through adulthood and focuses on mature, adult sexual relationships.

neo-Freudian theories
Theories that revised, but did not entirely reject, the basics of Freud's original psychodynamic theory.

collective unconscious
Common, inherited memories that are present in the minds of people of every culture.

archetypes
Specific symbols or patterns within the collective unconscious that appear consistently across cultures and time periods.

Several theorists, including Karen Horney, Nancy Chodorow, and Carol Gilligan, have emphasized that personality may develop differently for females than males.
Hero Images/Getty Images

others. Erikson's next three stages extend all the way through adulthood, indicating his disagreement with the Freudian idea that personality is completely shaped by the time childhood ends (Erikson, 1946; 1950; Welchman, 2000).

Karen Horney. Karen Horney was one of very few women among the first generation of neo-Freudians. Among her pioneering ideas was the notion that females develop differently than males, and that it would be a mistake to assume that Freud's theories apply equally to both. For example, Horney disagreed with the male emphasis in Freud's psychosexual stage theory, such as the fact that he labeled the third psychosexual stage the "phallic" stage even though half of the people in the world don't have that body part.

Horney's theories served as a springboard for other feminist personality theorists. For example, Nancy Chodorow points out that the primary caretaker for children is typically the mother, which means that boys and girls face different challenges when it comes time to form their own identity. Boys must form their identities by separating from mom and adopting a separate role model (usually dad, if he's available), but girls must form their identities by remaining connected to mom yet developing their own individuality (Chodorow, 1978, 1989).

Similarly, Carol Gilligan highlights that females and males may develop different values and morals as they grow up—with females emphasizing the importance of interpersonal relationships more than males—but both are equally legitimate and normal (Gilligan, 1982, 1992). For example, when faced with the moral dilemma of turning in a friend who has done something wrong, women may focus more on maintaining the relationship, while men may focus more on justice.

Current Thoughts on Psychodynamic Theory

Psychodynamic theory remains a powerful force in psychology, but it is well past its heyday. It has been criticized broadly and sharply, and many different theories have arisen as alternative explanations of personality.

Perhaps the most damaging criticism aimed at psychodynamic theory is that it is not scientific enough (Tallis, 1996). Psychodynamic concepts are not easily defined, which makes it difficult to translate them into hypotheses that can be tested. For example, how can we be sure that the id, ego, and superego actually interact the way Freud said they did? Can we even be sure they exist? The three components certainly don't show up on CAT scans or MRIs of the brain. In Freud's day, when psychology was a younger field, speculations about the inner workings of the mind often went unchallenged. However, as psychology evolved, it has become a field of science rather than guesswork. Today, many psychologists dismiss Freud's theories, at least in part, because they can't be proven true or false. As such, they are often labeled as a faith rather than a science (Gabbard, 2009).

Contemporary psychologists also criticize Freud for overgeneralizing his ideas. He developed theories of personality that may have been an especially good fit for people like Freud himself: White males from Europe who lived during a historical period when sexuality was quite repressed, gender roles were quite rigid, almost every family included a mother and a father, and same-sex attraction was considered a disease. The problem is that when he proposed his theories, he claimed they held true for everyone, everywhere, at every time. The work of Horney, Chodorow, and Gilligan (described previously) underscores the notion that for women and girls, especially women and girls in different times and places from Freud's own, Freud's theories may not apply.

DIVERSITY MATTERS

Even some of Freud's core ideas seem to have softened over the years. Psychodynamic psychologists today are likely to agree with Freud's basic idea that early childhood experiences influence adult personality, but not that they completely determine it (Roberts et al., 2008). Neo-Freudians are likely to agree that the unconscious is an important force, but emphasize that it has numerous roles, including some that Freud didn't identify. For example, contemporary writings on the unconscious are likely to focus on information processing of which we are unaware (for instance, keeping track of how

humanistic theory of personality
A theory based on the ideas of Carl Rogers that emphasizes people's inherent tendencies toward healthy, positive growth and self-fulfillment.

self-actualization
Fully becoming the person you have the potential to become.

positive regard
Warmth, acceptance, and love from those around you.

conditions of worth
Requirements that you must meet to earn a person's positive regard.

frequently events happen to us without trying to do so) in addition to id-versus-superego battles (Kihlstrom, 2008; Power & Brewin, 2011; Stadler & Frensch, 1998; Kaufman et al., 2010). Contemporary psychologists are likely to agree that sexuality is a key element in human motivation, but insist that attraction to the same sex (or both sexes) can be equally healthy as attraction to the opposite sex (Erwin, 2002; Lewes, 1995).

CHECK YOUR LEARNING:

12.4 What is the psychodynamic theory of personality?

12.5 What is the unconscious and why is it important?

12.6 What are the id, superego, and ego?

12.7 What are the psychosexual stages of development?

12.8 How have Sigmund Freud's followers revised psychodynamic theories?

12.9 What is the contemporary view of psychodynamic theory?

Humanistic Theory of Personality

The **humanistic theory of personality**, based on the ideas of Carl Rogers, emphasizes our inherent tendencies toward healthy, positive growth and self-fulfillment. Rogers went to graduate school at a time when the psychodynamic view was dominant, but he (like many others) soon grew weary of Freud's negative view of human nature. He simply didn't see people as fueled by biological, id-based desires like sex, aggression, and an insatiable drive for instant pleasure. Rogers had a much more optimistic view of human nature and believed people to be driven by the desire to reach their full potential (Cain, 2010).

YOU WILL LEARN:

12.10 what the humanistic theory of personality is.

12.11 what self-actualization is

12.12 how positive regard and conditions of worth can affect it.

12.13 how self-concept develops.

12.14 about current thoughts on humanistic theory.

Self-Actualization

Imagine a new plant just peeking out of the ground in the spring. We assume this plant has an inborn tendency to grow, to blossom and bloom. Likewise, Rogers assumed you have an inborn tendency toward **self-actualization**: fully becoming the person you have the potential to become. To grow, the plant needs water and sunlight. To self-actualize, you need what Rogers called **positive regard**: warmth, acceptance, and love from those around you. Rogers liked to use the word *prizing* as a less formal alternative to the term *positive regard*. Prizing captures the tender appreciation of another person (Rogers, 1959). For example, Rogers might say that Dinah, a grandmother, prizes her granddaughter Melissa: she cherishes Melissa without any kind of evaluation, simply because she is Melissa.

Carl Rogers developed the humanistic theory of personality, which emphasizes inherent tendencies toward healthy, positive growth and self-fulfillment.

Why does positive regard matter?

Problems arise when those around you don't provide *unconditional positive regard*, but instead impose **conditions of worth**, or requirements that you must meet to earn their positive regard. For example, some parents' love for their children depends on the grades they get, the sports they play, or the friends they choose. Because the parents' love and approval are so essential, the children will often meet their parents' conditions of worth, even if it means straying from the interests or passions that come naturally to them. Like a plant that only gets sunlight from certain directions, certain "branches" of the child flourish while others wither. So, a child may sacrifice an important part of their true self in order to maintain their parents' approval. Or as Rogers put it, the

Carl Rogers believed that each person—just like a plant emerging from the ground—has an inborn tendency to grow, blossom, and bloom. He called that tendency self-actualization—fully becoming the person you have the potential to become. paladin13/iStock/Getty Images

child's *real self* and *ideal self* would not match. The **real self** is the version of yourself that you actually experience in your day-to-day life. By contrast, the **ideal self** is the self-actualized version of yourself that you naturally strive to become (Cain, 2010).

Incongruence. Rogers believed that this **incongruence**—a mismatch between your real self and your ideal self—leads to unhappiness and mental illness. People experiencing incongruence feel like they can't be true to themselves but instead must edit themselves to gain others' approval (or even pretend to be someone they are not). For example, the third-grader who plays hockey to win dad's affections when he would much rather be practicing his violin; the teenager who does drugs to impress her friends even though she doesn't really want to; the actor who auditions not because she enjoys acting but because her family pushed her into the field—all of these people will eventually sense a disconnect between who they really *are* and who they are *acting like* (Cain, 2010). (Think about that lopsided plant imagining, longingly, how it would feel to have all of its branches blooming.)

Congruence. According to Rogers, the root of mental wellness is **congruence**: a match between your real self and your ideal self. People feel good when they are allowed to grow organically, according to their own natural tendencies. In our plant analogy, congruence happens when the sunlight comes from every direction. In human terms, congruence happens when you get unconditional positive regard from important people in your life, no matter how you behave. That doesn't mean, for example, that your mother and father approve of everything you do, but that they continue to value and appreciate you even when they may disapprove of a particular behavior of yours (Rogers, 1980; Tudor & Worrall, 2006).

The bottom line here is that your personality depends, in large part, on the way the people around you respond to your self-actualization tendency. If they nurture it, and allow all of your branches to flourish, you are likely to fully develop into the person you naturally are. If they stifle it, and allow only some of your branches to flourish, you are likely to develop into a person who only partially resembles your true self (Rogers, 1961, 1980; Bohart & Tallman, 1999). For example, consider Heather, a ninth-grade girl who naturally tends to be cooperative with others. If her parents make their love contingent on Heather defeating others (beating all her rivals at her chess tournament, earning first chair in violin in her school band, winning the election for class president), Heather may develop a competitive streak that betrays her naturally cooperative style.

Abraham Maslow and Self-Actualization

According to Rogers, incongruence is a mismatch between your real self and your ideal self, and it can lead to unhappiness or mental illness. For example, if this young hockey player is pressured for a long time be a competitive athlete when being a musician would feel much more true to himself, he could develop a sense of incongruence. bigjohn36/iStock/Getty Images

Abraham Maslow, whose hierarchy of needs we covered in Chapter 8, was another leading humanistic theorist. Like Rogers, Maslow emphasized that self-actualization is a primary motivation. However, Maslow reminded us that more basic needs (such as food, water, safety, and a feeling of belonging) must be secured before a person attempts to self-actualize (Maslow, 1968). Only when you feel fed, safe, and loved can you move on to fulfilling your full potential as a human being.

Maslow studied the biographies and writings of some famous people he believed to be fully *self-actualized*, such as Abraham Lincoln, Thomas Jefferson, Eleanor Roosevelt, Jane Addams, Albert Schweitzer, and Aldous Huxley. He noticed similarities in their personalities. They judged the world around them, and themselves, realistically and honestly. They were unusually tolerant, creative, and fully engaged in their activities. They had passions that they pursued, and they remained humble no matter how much success they achieved. They were resourceful and independent. They felt strong connections to other people, but were also comfortable being alone. (This list of characteristics offers us a good chance to remember that correlation does not necessarily mean causation. Were they self-actualized because they had these characteristics, or did they have these characteristics because they were self-actualized?)

Maslow also believed that we experience a higher number of *peak experiences* as we move closer to self-actualization. These peak experiences are moments in which we

are overcome with transcendent joy and fulfillment. People often use words like *mystical* or *ecstatic* to describe their peak experiences. They also describe a sense of exceptional harmony with the world around them, as well as a strong sense of purpose. The kinds of activities that bring about peak experiences vary widely, but for many people, art, religion, sports, or intimate interactions are the most likely sparks (Privette, 1983). As Maslow (1968) explained it, a peak experience is "the most wonderful experience or experiences of your life; happiest moments, ecstatic moments, moments of rapture, perhaps from being in love, or from listening to music or suddenly 'being hit' by a book or painting, or from some great creative moment" (p. 83).

real self
The version of yourself that you actually experience in day-to-day life.

ideal self
The self-actualized version of yourself that you naturally strive to become.

incongruence
A mismatch between your real self and your ideal self.

congruence
A match between your real self and your ideal self.

self-concept
Your view of who you are.

Self-Concept

Your **self-concept** is your view of who you are. The way important people in your life treat you, particularly how they respond to your self-actualization tendencies, has tremendous power in shaping that view of yourself. For example, the conditions of worth that others place on you become conditions of worth that you place on yourself (Rogers, 1959; Hattie, 1992). Think again about the fifth-grader whose dad pushes him to excel at hockey despite the boy's lack of passion for the game. The condition he has learned from dad (*You're* a worthy person only if *you* continue to pursue sports over the arts) is likely to become a rule he will apply to himself (*I'm* a worthy person only if *I* continue to pursue sports over the arts). By the same token, someone who receives unconditional positive regard (*You* are a good person no matter what) is likely to internalize that message and have unconditional positive *self*-regard (*I* am a good person no matter what).

According to Rogers, other common terms that refer to our opinions of ourselves—*self-esteem, self-image, self-worth*—all follow the same pattern. The ways we think about ourselves are not inborn, but molded by the opinions of us that we receive from the most important people in our lives. These important people are often parents or other family members when we are kids, but they can also be friends, romantic partners, or coworkers when we grow up. For example, a middle manager whose supervisors repeatedly provide the feedback that "You are lazy" will be hard-pressed not to incorporate that message into her own self-image. A woman whose husband consistently tells her through his words and actions that "You are wonderful" will similarly build that message into her own self-esteem.

Current Thoughts on Humanistic Theory

Like psychodynamic theory, humanistic theory has been hugely influential in both academia and popular culture. Humanistic theory set the stage for the emphasis on self-concept and self-worth, which were largely neglected before its emergence in the 1960s. Now self-concept and self-worth receive attention from parenting experts, educators, and couples counselors. Humanistic theory also gave rise to the positive psychology movement and continues to significantly influence the way that many psychotherapists practice (Cook et al., 2009). More specifically, an increasing number of therapists are now utilizing *positive interventions* or *strength-based counseling*. These treatments differ from more traditional styles, which focus on clients' problems and disorders, by emphasizing and building on clients' assets and abilities (Seligman et al., 2005; Seligman, 2011; Snyder et al., 2011).

The current view of humanistic theory also includes many criticisms. Perhaps the most common critique is that humanistic theory is simply too optimistic and naïve. Remember, the bedrock of humanism is the idea that people are basically good. If this is true, and people simply want to live their own true, full lives, why do horrific crimes committed by one person against another fill our newscasts on a daily basis? Can stifled self-actualization explain rape, murder, and war, or is there something more sinister in human nature than the mere desire to blossom and bloom? Perhaps that plant growing in the sun will not grow into a beautiful rose or even a harmless fern, but a vicious Venus flytrap.

Humanistic theory has also been criticized for being unscientific (like psychodynamic theory). It is difficult to empirically prove or disprove the mere existence of humanism's core concepts—the self-actualization tendency, the real and ideal selves, congruence and incongruence—let alone the way that Rogers proposed they work. Because humanism is so difficult to test, those who endorse it do so as a matter of belief rather than one of scientific evidence.

Humanistic theory is also criticized today for its strong endorsement of individualism. Some argue that Rogers's perception of the healthy individual as someone who follows only his or her own growth potential is a bit self-indulgent. We are individuals, of course, but we are also members of close-knit groups (couples, families, communities, etc.), and we have obligations to balance what fosters our own personal growth with what fosters the well-being of the group. Along the same lines, collectivistic cultures that emphasize harmony in interpersonal relationships and obedience to parents, such as many Asian ethnicities, may have a different take on what Rogers called incongruence. They may view the sacrifice of certain aspects of self-growth as commendable, selfless decisions rather than the source of personal unhappiness (Heine et al., 1999).

DIVERSITY MATTERS

CHECK YOUR LEARNING:

12.10 What is the humanistic theory of personality?

12.11 What is self-actualization?

12.12 What is positive regard, and how does it relate to conditions of worth?

12.13 What is self-concept, and how does it develop?

12.14 What is the contemporary view of humanistic theory?

Behavioral and Social-Cognitive Theories of Personality

YOU WILL LEARN:

12.15 what the behavioral theory of personality is.

12.16 what the social-cognitive theory of personality is.

12.17 about reciprocal determinism, or the interaction of behavior, environment, and cognitions.

12.18 about self-efficacy, or belief about one's abilities.

12.19 about locus of control, or the belief about internal and external influences on one's fate.

12.20 about current thoughts on behavioral and social-cognitive theories.

Behavioral and social-cognitive theories of personality offer a perspective much more grounded in science than either psychodynamic or humanistic theory. The **behavioral theory of personality** emphasizes the influence of the environment and the importance of observable, measurable behavior. The **social-cognitive theory of personality** emphasizes the interaction of environment, thought processes, and social factors.

Behavioral Theory: The Importance of the Environment

You are already quite familiar with behavioral theory. In fact, behaviorism was the main focus of Chapter 6 (Learning), with its emphasis on classical conditioning and operant conditioning as explanations for what we do. Based on what you know about learning, it may come as no surprise that behaviorists think there is no such thing as personality.

Wait—how could they say there's no such thing as personality?

Let's revisit our definition of personality from the beginning of this chapter: "a person's distinctive and stable way of thinking, feeling, and behaving." Behaviorists have trouble with at least a few words in that definition. To begin, thinking and feeling are both activities that take place inside the mind and therefore can't be directly observed or measured. That means they are impossible to study empirically, and that means (to behaviorists) they should not receive our attention. Only behaving *can* be observed and measured, so behaving should define personality by itself (Hunt, 1993; Kazdin, 1978; Watson, 1924). The other word in the definition that behaviorists have a problem with is *stable*, because *stable* implies there is something deep *within* the person—a trait, a characteristic, a quality—that causes them to consistently behave in a certain way. Ivan Pavlov's dogs didn't salivate to the bell because of some internal, stable characteristic; they salivated because of classical conditioning. B. F. Skinner's pigeons didn't peck at a button in the Skinner box because of some internal, stable characteristic; they pecked because of operant conditioning. The animals' behavior changed when the conditioning changed, not because of something internal (Skinner, 1938; Pavlov, 1927, 1928; Evans, 1968).

According to behaviorists, people are no different from Pavlov's dogs or Skinner's pigeons. People behave a certain way because of the conditioning *outside* them rather than any stable force *inside* of them. As long as the conditioning remains the same, the behavior stays the same. If the conditioning changes, then the behavior changes. It is hard to believe that personality exists if behavior is so malleable by external conditions (Skinner, 1971).

For example, consider Josh, a 7-year-old being raised by his father in a single-parent home. Josh whines a lot. A traditional view of personality might suggest that Josh has a deep-seated, unwavering characteristic—whininess—that causes him to whine as much as he does. But behaviorists would point out that Josh's dad reinforces the whining by giving Josh what he wants. Behaviorists would agree that Josh has a *habit* of whining a lot, but this habit developed because Josh received a reinforcing response for it, and it could be reversed if Josh were in an environment that ignored or punished his whining. For example, if Josh's dad decided to pay no attention to Josh's whining, Josh's whining behavior would decrease significantly.

The idea that "personality" is really just habit controlled by external conditions indicates another core idea of the behavioral approach: the absence of free will. For behaviorists, external conditions determine all of your behavior. You do what you do because your conditioning experiences determine it, not because of any "choices" you make based on deep-rooted "personality" characteristics (Skinner, 1938, 1976). According to behaviorists, if you believe in free will, you are kidding yourself.

behavioral theory of personality
A theory that emphasizes the influence of the environment and the importance of observable, measurable behavior.

social-cognitive theory of personality
A theory that emphasizes the interaction of environment, thought processes, and social factors.

reciprocal determinism
The theory that three factors—behavior, environment, and cognitions—continually influence each other.

Social-Cognitive Theory: Social Factors and Thoughts Are Important Too

Even the most diehard behaviorists have to admit that behavior—*human* behavior—can't be entirely explained by external conditions. Compared to rats, pigeons, or dogs, there is a lot more going on between our ears. We don't move through life without thinking, letting reinforcements and punishments shape us as if we were simple California sea slugs. We talk about the things that happen with other people and change our behavior based on what we observe. We form expectations, interpretations, beliefs, and plans rather than just responding automatically to what goes on around us. For social-cognitive theorists, personality blends the behavioral emphasis on external conditioning and these mental activities that involve our interactions with others ("social") and our thought processes ("cognitive"). These social and cognitive ingredients are not as observable and measurable as strict behaviorists would prefer, but social-cognitive theorists recognize that they are powerful influences on personality.

Albert Bandura, Reciprocal Determinism, and Self-Efficacy. Albert Bandura, the most prominent social-cognitive theorist, argues that your personality involves an ongoing *interaction* of multiple forces (Bandura, 1977a, 1986, 2001). He calls this idea **reciprocal determinism**: the theory that three factors—your behavior, your environment, and your cognitions—continually influence each other. **Figure 12.5**

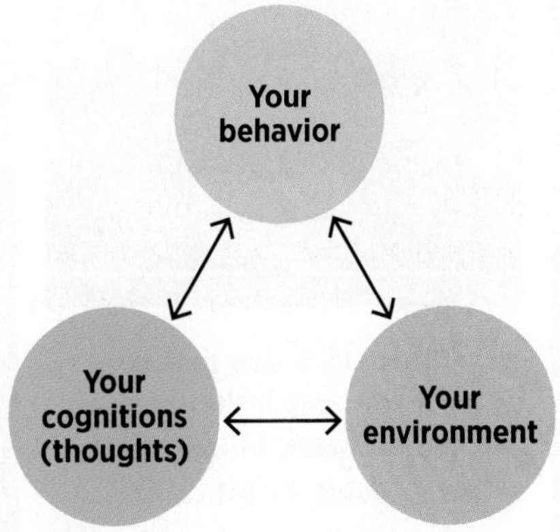

FIGURE 12.5 Reciprocal Determinism. According to Albert Bandura's concept of reciprocal determinism, your thoughts, your environment, and your behavior all influence each other.

Albert Bandura's theory emphasizes the idea of reciprocal determinism, which states that your behavior, your environment, and your cognitions all influence each other.

illustrates this interaction. Notice the double-sided arrows between all three boxes in the figure. These indicate that the relationships between behavior, environment, and cognitions are two-way streets—in other words, they all affect each other. As an example, consider Yolanda, who decides to get in shape by taking a boot-camp exercise class at a nearby gym. By attending that class, Yolanda puts herself in an environment where she receives reinforcement (encouragement from fellow boot-campers) for her exercise behavior and also observes a group of dedicated exercisers who can serve as models. That environment is likely to affect both her cognitions ("this is actually enjoyable," and "I can do this") and her behavior (returning for more classes). She then puts herself in the boot-camp environment even more frequently (that is, her behavior changes), and the cycle continues. The point here is that it is not just your environment that influences your behavior, as behaviorists would argue. Your behavior also shapes the environment in which you find yourself, and your cognitions enter the mix along the way as well.

Speaking of cognitions, Bandura (1977b, 1982, 1997) emphasized one kind especially: **self-efficacy**, or your beliefs about your own capabilities. Yolanda's cognition—"I can do this"—reflects the importance of self-efficacy. If she left the first boot-camp classes overwhelmed and intimidated, thinking, "No way—this is too hard for me," she would be unlikely to return. But she did return, thanks to her belief that she could succeed. The key here is that Yolanda's self-efficacy (what she believes she can do) might be just as important as her actual physical ability or the difficulty level of the class. (I wonder if Bandura's parents read him *The Little Engine That Could* when he was a kid: *"I think I can, I think I can…")*

Julian Rotter and Locus of Control. Julian Rotter, another important social-cognitive theorist, highlighted another kind of cognition that influences personality: **locus of control**, or your belief about how much control you have over what happens to you. The Latin word *locus* is the root of the word *location*, and according to Rotter, there are two locations for locus of control: within yourself and outside yourself. He gave each location a label: An **internal locus of control** is the belief that your life is under the control of forces inside of you, and an **external locus of control** is the belief that your life is under the control of forces outside of you (Rotter, 1966, 1975, 1989).

Locus of control can powerfully influence what we choose to do. Consider bike helmets. Isabella chooses to wear one, demonstrating her internal locus of control: "There are actions I can take to protect myself on this bike ride." Eve chooses not to wear one, demonstrating her external locus of control: "If an accident happens, it happens. I can't really do anything about it." When you consider the vast array of everyday decisions that locus of control can affect—whether to eat healthy, whether to recycle, whether to apply for a better job, whether to vote, whether to try anything at all—it is easy to see how it can shape the behaviors that form Isabella's and Eve's personalities (**Table 12.3**). In Eve's case, if her external locus of control became extreme, it could resemble *learned helplessness*. (Remember Seligman's dogs from Chapter 6?) This in turn could lead to depression based on her belief that any action she might take to help herself will be futile.

Locus of control can also shape personality by powerfully influencing how we explain what happens to us. For example, imagine that both Isabella and Eve were passed over for a promotion in the company where they work. Isabella is more likely to blame herself—"I didn't do enough to earn it"—while Eve is more likely to blame other forces—"Our supervisor is unfair," or "My coworker who got the promotion is a cheater." More recent research on locus of control has indicated that people have not only a general locus of control, but specific ones too. You may feel that you control your fate at work or school, but that your health, finances, and romantic life are not up to you (Ng et al., 2006; Hummer et al., 2011). The From Research to Real Life box explores an additional research finding about how locus of control has shifted over the years.

MY TAKE VIDEO 12.1

Locus of Control

"Their idea was that no matter how much they smoked if they're going to get cancer they're going to get cancer..."

YOUTUBE: http://tiny.cc/mytake
LAUNCHPAD: launchpadworks.com

TABLE 12.3: Internal Locus of Control Versus External Locus of Control

	TO A PERSON WITH AN INTERNAL *LOCUS OF CONTROL*, IT DEPENDS ON...	TO A PERSON WITH AN EXTERNAL *LOCUS OF CONTROL*, IT DEPENDS ON...
"Will I gain weight?"	...whether I eat right and exercise regularly	...the genes my parents passed along, the side effects of my medications, the food industry
"Will I become wealthy?"	...how hard I work and how smartly I invest	...the luck of finding a good-paying job, how generous my friends and relatives are
"Why did my partner and I break up?"	...how much effort I put into the relationship, how I behaved while we were together	...my partner's personality, my partner's behavior, the pressure that others put on us
"How did I get into college?"	...how hard I worked in high school, how much effort I put into my standardized tests	...the college's admission standards, how desperate they were for students

self-efficacy
Your beliefs about your own capabilities.

locus of control
Your belief about how much control you have over what happens to yourself.

internal locus of control
The belief that your life is under the control of forces inside of yourself.

external locus of control
The belief that your life is under the control of forces outside of yourself.

Current Thoughts on Behavioral and Social-Cognitive Theories

Behavioral theories of personality are held in high regard by those who insist that all aspects of psychology should be empirically based. It is, after all, the personality theory most grounded in science. But many current psychologists find that pure behaviorism doesn't tell the whole story. By assuming that people behave just as animals do, it plays up the influence of the environment to the exclusion of uniquely human factors, especially the way we think and interact. And the behavioral notion that personality doesn't exist at all doesn't fly with most current psychologists. Even if conditioning is a major factor in shaping our behavior, few agree that it is the only factor (O'Donohue, 2009; Goldfried, 1995).

Social-cognitive theories of personality consider factors beyond environment, especially the way we think and the social interactions we have. More than other personality theories, social-cognitive theory identifies many possible influences on personality. This "diversified" approach is both a strength and a weakness. On one hand, it

FROM RESEARCH TO REAL LIFE

What's Happening to Our Locus of Control?

How does your locus of control compare to your parents' or grandparents'? Compared to older generations, to what extent do you believe that your actions (rather than outside forces) can impact your life? According to research, your locus of control is probably more external than theirs.

Researchers conducted a massive review of studies conducted since 1930 in which participants' locus of control was measured (Twenge & Campbell, 2008). Combined, these studies included over *1.4 million* participants. The conclusion? Over time, the average score on measures of locus of control has drifted consistently and significantly toward the external extreme. This trend was equally strong in females and males, and appears in children as well as adults. The trend toward a more external locus of control is especially strong in recent decades, such that it is clear in comparisons of studies from the 2000s to studies just two decades earlier (Twenge et al., 2004).

Where does this trend come from? Researchers see a connection between the trend toward external locus of control and societal changes in the United States toward greater individualism, alienation, and cynicism (Twenge et al., 2004). The current generation seems to have some doubt (perhaps a lot of doubt) about the idea that their lives depend on their own actions. Instead, they seem resigned to the notion that their fate is not in their own hands.

This resignation about external locus of control has bad implications for mental health. Researchers combined data from over 40 years of studies across 18 cultures and found positive correlations between locus of control and depression and between locus of control and anxiety (Cheng et al., 2013). Such a connection between locus of control and mental illness, especially depression, has been found by numerous other researchers as well (Richardson et al., 2012; Harrow et al., 2009; Twenge et al., 2010).

Have you noticed any indications of this trend toward external locus of control in your own life, or the corresponding increases in depression? Do your friends accept truths from previous generations such as "Life is what you make it" or "With hard work, anything's possible"? To what extent have those truths been replaced by feelings of apathy and powerlessness? What can we expect for future generations? ⬢

makes social-cognitive theory particularly comprehensive; on the other hand, it makes social-cognitive theory seem less focused than some other theories. It is noteworthy that certain concepts within social-cognitive theory have been quite well supported by empirical literature. Self-efficacy, for example, has been shown to enhance achievement in a wide variety of areas, including memory abilities, work performance, exercise, and even quitting smoking (Beaudoin & Desrichard, 2011; Sadri & Robertson, 1993; Gwaltney et al., 2009; Ashford et al., 2010).

CHECK YOUR LEARNING:

12.15 What is the behavioral theory of personality?

12.16 What is the social-cognitive theory of personality?

12.17 According to the theory of reciprocal determinism, which three factors continually influence each other?

12.18 What is self-efficacy?

12.19 What is locus of control?

12.20 What is the contemporary view of the behavioral theory of personality and the social-cognitive theory of personality?

Trait Theory of Personality

YOU WILL LEARN:

12.21 what the trait theory of personality is.

12.22 how trait theorists strive to identify the basic ingredients of personality.

12.23 about the traits included in the five-factor, or Big Five, model of personality.

12.24 about current thoughts on trait theory.

The **trait theory of personality** emphasizes the discovery and description of the basic components of personality. All other personality theories attempt to explain *why* personality develops the way it does. By contrast, trait theory attempts to explain *what* personality is made of (John et al., 2008).

Many of the other personality theories, especially psychodynamic and humanistic, rely heavily on speculations about the inner workings of the mind that can't be empirically proven or disproven. Trait theory—especially the *five-factor model* (or *Big Five*), which we will examine in detail—has emerged in recent decades as a more scientific alternative. For that reason, while research on some other approaches to personality has dwindled in recent decades, research on trait theory has flourished.

A New Approach to Understanding Personality

When you eat an oatmeal cookie, you probably notice differences between that particular cookie and other oatmeal cookies you have eaten in the past. Why does one taste different from another? All oatmeal cookies are made from the same short list of ingredients—oats, flour, sugar, eggs, butter—but each batch contains a different amount of each ingredient. More sugar in one batch or less butter in another batch will result in a different taste.

Trait theorists believe that human personality is made from a short list of traits, much as oatmeal cookies are made from a short list of ingredients. The difference between one personality and another stems from different amounts of each trait, just as the difference between one oatmeal cookie and another can stem from different amounts of sugar, flour, butter, oats, or eggs.
AnnCason34/iStock/Getty Images

Trait theorists believe that our personalities, like oatmeal cookies, are all made from the same short list of ingredients. The aim of their research is to uncover those ingredients. They call these ingredients **traits**: stable elements of personality that influence thoughts, feelings, and behavior across most situations. Trait theorists assume that varying amounts of each trait account for differences in personality, just as varying amounts of each baking ingredient account for differences in taste. Trait theorists don't concern themselves much with how a particular trait develops over the course of a person's life. (That is a big difference from the psychodynamic, humanistic, behavioral, and social-cognitive theorists who came before them.) Instead, they try to figure out exactly what those traits are, thereby understanding exactly what makes up human personality (Digman, 1996).

One of the main challenges in identifying the basic traits of human personality is narrowing down the massive number of possibilities. Just think of all the words in the English language that could describe the personalities of the people you know. Gordon Allport, an early trait theorist, actually read through the dictionary and found about 18,000 descriptive words (Allport, 1937; Allport & Odbert, 1936). Researchers who followed him took on the task of reducing this enormous number to a more manageable size. (Imagine that you signed up for an online dating service and got 18,000 different personality ratings of each potential date!)

This task—boiling down a huge list of personality traits to a shorter list of "supertraits"—would become a theme of trait theory as the years went by. For example, in the 1940s, Raymond Cattell reduced the personality descriptors to just 16 clusters (Cattell, 1943). From this list, he created a personality questionnaire called the *16PF* that was widely used for some time. As time went by, trait theorists used increasingly sophisticated statistical procedures (and increasingly powerful computers to run them). The most important of these is *factor analysis*, which takes a long list of variables and forms clusters that correlate with each other. Factor analysis shows that certain adjectives that describe personality tend to hang together—for example, *shy*, *reserved*, *introverted*, *bashful*, and *withdrawn*—suggesting that those words all describe the same underlying trait.

MY TAKE VIDEO 12.2

Five-Factor Model of Personality

"I've always been the person who loves to try new things."

YOUTUBE: http://tiny.cc/mytake
LAUNCHPAD: launchpadworks.com

The Five-Factor Model: Universal Human Traits

Today, the leaders of trait theory are Paul Costa and Robert McCrae, who have continued the work of identifying the underlying "supertraits" of personality that was started by Allport and Cattell. Their work, along with related work by other researchers, has produced the **five-factor model of personality** (also known as the **Big Five**): an explanation of personality that emphasizes five fundamental traits present in all people to varying degrees. So, decades after Cattell reduced Allport's list of 18,000 personality ingredients to only 16 clusters, Costa and McCrae further reduced it to just 5 traits (Costa & McCrae, 1985, 1992, 2008; McCrae & Costa, 2003, 2008; Widiger & Costa, 2012).

The Big Five have received so much attention and generated so much research in recent decades that they have become absolutely central to the study of personality (McCrae & Costa, 1996; Digman, 1990). One researcher boldly stated that "most personality psychologists have come to agree that the Big Five *are* the basic dimensions of personality" (Hunt, 1993; italics added). Let's take a close look at those five traits here and in **Figure 12.6**:

- **Neuroticism**—the tendency to experience negative emotions such as anxiety, depression, and stress
- **Extraversion**—the tendency to be socially outgoing
- **Openness to experience**—the tendency to be receptive to new or unconventional ideas
- **Conscientiousness**—the tendency to be organized, responsible, and deliberate
- **Agreeableness**—the tendency to cooperate and comply with other people

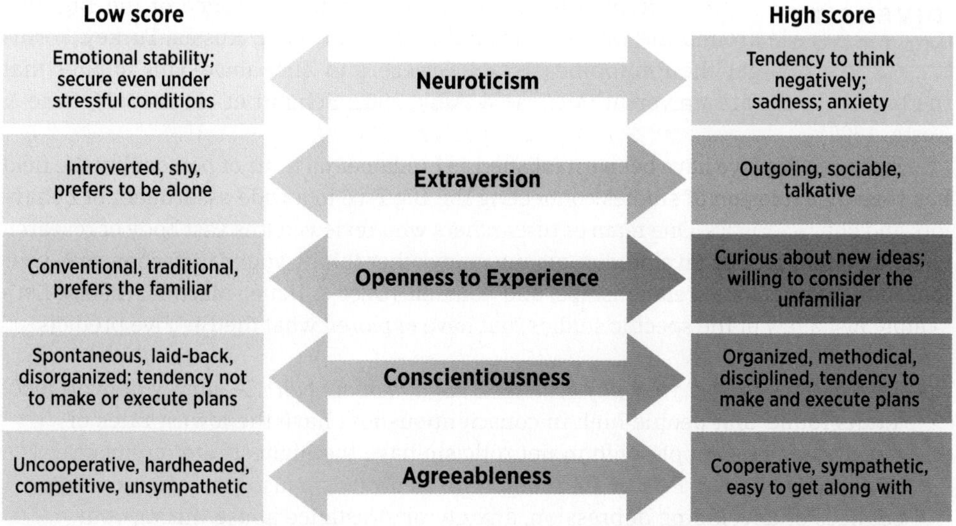

FIGURE 12.6 Descriptions of High and Low Levels of Big Five Personality Traits. Everyone lands somewhere on the dimension of each of the Big Five traits of personality—high, low, or somewhere between.

trait theory of personality
A theory that emphasizes the discovery and description of the basic components of personality.

traits
Stable elements of personality that influence thoughts, feelings, and behavior across most situations.

five-factor model of personality (Big Five)
An explanation of personality that emphasizes five fundamental traits present in all people to varying degrees.

neuroticism
A personality trait emphasizing the tendency to experience negative emotions such as anxiety, depression, and stress.

extraversion
A personality trait emphasizing the tendency to be socially outgoing.

openness to experience
A personality trait emphasizing the tendency to be organized, responsible, and deliberate.

conscientiousness
A personality trait emphasizing the tendency to be organized, responsible, and deliberate.

agreeableness
A personality trait emphasizing the tendency to cooperate and comply with other people.

CURRENT CONTROVERSY

Is There an Upside to Neuroticism?

At first glance, neuroticism seems all bad. The negative thinking, the self-doubt, the worry, the glass-half-empty mentality—who would want it?

Turns out, everybody might, at least a little bit. A number of psychologists have offered a defense of neuroticism, at least in small doses. For example, researchers argue that neuroticism can foster vigilance—a watchfulness or alertness that could provide an early warning of dangerous situations (Watson & Casillas, 2003). Who is more likely to avoid a dimly lit parking lot in a high-crime area or sidestep a doctor's waiting room full of contagious diseases—someone with high or low neuroticism? Viewed this way, a lack of neuroticism could actually leave you more vulnerable.

Other researchers similarly argue that pessimism (again, in moderation) can be a good thing (Norem, 2003, 2008; Norem & Cantor, 1986). The right kind of pessimism—"defensive pessimism"—ensures that you keep your expectations reasonable and don't set yourself up for frustration or disappointment. It also enables you to play out various outcomes in your head, which helps you determine whether a particular option is too risky to your physical or psychological well-being. Compared to an impulsive headfirst dive into a potentially harmful situation, a little defensive pessimism sounds pretty good.

The upside of neuroticism is just one part of the larger picture of pros and cons of the Big Five. High levels of any of these five traits carry advantages and disadvantages (Chang & Sanna, 2003). One researcher contends that these benefits and costs have evolutionary, survival-of-the-fittest connotations (Nettle, 2011). For example, high levels of extraversion probably gave our ancestors increased chances for sexual encounters that could lead to offspring, but also greater risks of infectious diseases or interpersonal conflicts that could lead to bodily harm or death. High levels of openness to experience probably gave our ancestors increased creativity in solving problems (upon which their lives may have depended), but also greater risks of bizarre or disorganized thinking that could lead to life-threatening mistakes. High levels of agreeableness probably gave our ancestors increased ability to form alliances with other individuals and groups (which could enhance survival), but also greater chances of being victimized by dishonest people.

With the Big Five traits (which can be remembered via the acronym OCEAN), the question is not whether a person has them, but to what extent a person has each one. Each trait exists on a continuum, like a light bulb controlled by a dimmer rather than an on–off switch. Consider agreeableness as an example. The question is not whether a person has agreeableness or doesn't have it; it is how much agreeableness the person has. According to this approach, your unique combination of the five traits is what makes your personality different from everyone else's.

The Big Five emerge during childhood and remain rather consistent throughout the life span, suggesting that they may have biological roots (McCrae & Costa, 2003; Soldz & Vaillant, 1999). Additional evidence of the biology behind the Big Five comes from MRI studies, which show that the size of a particular brain region corresponds to the level of each trait. For example, in people with high conscientiousness, the part of the brain that controls planning and voluntary behavior is enlarged. In people with high neuroticism, the part of the brain that processes threat and negative emotions is enlarged (DeYoung et al., 2010).

Every personality displays each of the Big Five traits to some extent. For example, everyone falls somewhere on the continuum for agreeableness—a very high level, a very low level, or somewhere between. So, the question isn't *whether* a person has the trait, but *how much* of the trait that person has.
Portra Images/Taxi/Getty Images

DIVERSITY MATTERS Researchers have also confirmed the presence of the Big Five around the world, including cultures in India, Russia, Turkey, Portugal, the Philippines, Israel, Greece, and Zimbabwe. This implies that the big five traits are universal (McCrae & Allik, 2002; Schmitt et al., 2007; McCrae & Costa, 1997).

Since the Big Five have been established as fundamental traits of personality, the field has seen an explosion of studies connecting the Big Five to a wide assortment of behaviors and characteristics. One team of researchers who reviewed this vast body of research concluded that the Big Five predict, among many other things, your satisfaction with your job, your interpersonal relationships, and yourself (Ozer & Benet-Martinez, 2006). Let's sample just a few of the specific studies that have explored what the Big Five predicts:

- *The Big Five predict your physical health and mental health.* A survey of over 3000 adults found that people high in conscientiousness have the lowest rates of physical illness. People high in neuroticism have the highest rate of physical illness (Goodwin & Friedman, 2006). High neuroticism also predicts increased chances of developing depression, anxiety, or substance abuse during your lifetime (Kendler & Myers, 2010; Kotov et al., 2010). The Big Five even predicts your *beliefs* about your health: people high in neuroticism (and to a lesser extent,

WATCHING PSYCHOLOGY

Personality and Preferences in Movies and TV

Advertisers and marketers in the entertainment field often rely on demographics (age, gender, ethnicity, etc.) to predict who will like particular television shows or movies. Research suggests that psychological variables, especially the Big Five personality traits, may actually do a better job as predictors (Sandy et al., 2013). Among the specific connections made between personality and preferences are these:

- People with high levels of openness to experience tend to like movies and TV shows that present different worlds or provoke new thoughts, such as foreign films, indie movies, artsy pieces, and intellectually challenging documentaries (Chamorro-Premuzic et al., 2014; Kraaykamp & Van Eijck, 2005).
- People with high levels of agreeableness tend to dislike movies in which people have violent disagreements, so they typically avoid action movies and instead choose movies and TV shows where people get along nicely, like romances and comedies (Hall, 2005; Chamorro-Premuzic, et al., 2014).
- People with high levels of neuroticism tend to prefer movies and shows that provide an escape from the real world, like sci-fi films and soap operas (Chamorro-Premuzic et al., 2014; Kraaykamp & Van Eijck, 2005).
- People high in extraversion tend to watch less TV (which is done at home, often alone) and tend to watch more movies (which is often done by going out, usually with others) than people low in extraversion (Krcmar & Kean, 2005; Weaver, 2003). When people high in extraversion do watch TV, they tend to prefer reality TV shows (Shim & Paul, 2007).

people low in agreeableness) believe more strongly than others that they will catch infectious diseases or pick up germs from others if they stand near them, shake their hands, or share a water bottle with them (Duncan et al., 2009).

- *The Big Five predict your grades.* In studies ranging from young children to college students, conscientiousness, agreeableness, and openness correspond with GPA. Conscientiousness was by far the most important of these personality traits; in fact, it predicts grades just as accurately as intelligence does (Poropat, 2009; Caprara et al., 2011). Conscientiousness also predicts academic *motivation*—how badly you want to do well in school—which could certainly be an important part of its link to the grades you get (Komarraju et al., 2009).
- *The Big Five predict your job performance.* Researchers conducted a meta-analysis of studies on Big Five traits and work performance across a wide variety of jobs. Conscientiousness correlated with every kind of job. People with high levels of extraversion performed especially well at jobs that involved lots of social interaction, like managers and salespeople. People who were easiest to train for a new job were high in openness and extraversion (Barrick & Mount, 1991; Hurtz & Donovan, 2000).
- *The Big Five predict satisfaction with your romantic relationship.* According to a meta-analysis, the Big Five recipe for satisfaction in romantic relationships is low neuroticism, high agreeableness, high conscientiousness, and high extraversion (Malouff et al., 2010).

Research has established that the Big Five personality traits describe personality not only in the United States but in many other countries around the world (McCrae & Allik, 2002; Schmitt et al., 2007; McCrae & Costa, 1997). Juanmonino/E+/Getty Images; Cultura RM/Christoffer Askman/Getty Images; Ryan Edy/Photonica World/Getty Images

CHAPTER APP 12.1

Five-Factor Model of Personality

Your Five Basic Personality Traits

Preview one of the links and consider the following questions.

WEBSITE:
http://tiny.cc/9si7jy

ANDROID:
http://tiny.cc/2c92iy

IPHONE:
http://tiny.cc/s682iy

VIDEO DEMO:
http://tiny.cc/chapterapps

This app offers a quick, unverified estimate of your Big Five personality traits. (In a real psychological evaluation, a psychologist would use a more extensive, more verified test with established reliability and validity. Consider the results you get from this app to be an unofficial, rough estimate of where your Big Five scores might truly fall.)

How does it APPly to your daily life?
What scores did you get on each of the Big Five? Do those scores match your expectations?

How does it APPly to your understanding of psychology?
How well do the Big Five traits capture *your* personality? Are there important parts of your personality that those traits don't cover?

- *The Big Five predict what words you use.* A researcher measured the Big Five traits in about 700 bloggers, and then used a computer program to count how often each blogger used particular words. Results show that vocabulary reflects personality. Blogs by people high in neuroticism included an unusually high proportion of words related to fear, sadness, and anger. Blogs by people high in extraversion were full of words related to interpersonal interaction and positive emotions. Blogs by people high in agreeableness contained lots of words about family and friends, as well as the pronouns "*we*" and "*us*," which suggest togetherness with other people (Yarkoni, 2010). Check **Table 12.4** for a telling list of specific words that were common to high levels of each of the Big Five traits.
- *The Big Five predict how likable and popular you are.* Researchers asked 500 teen classmates to rate each other on likability and popularity. The teens also rated themselves on the Big Five. Kids rated most likable and popular by their peers had low levels of neuroticism and high levels of extraversion and agreeableness (van der Linden et al., 2010).
- *The Big Five predict how prejudiced you are.* A meta-analysis of personality and prejudice found that people low in openness to experience and low in agreeableness are most likely to hold prejudices against other groups of people (Sibley & Duckitt, 2008).
- *The Big Five predict how you use Facebook.* People who use Facebook are higher in extraversion and lower in conscientiousness than people who don't use Facebook. People high in extraversion use the social features of Facebook (comments, messaging, and chatting) more than people low in extraversion. People high in neuroticism spend more time on Facebook than people low in neuroticism (Ryan & Xenos, 2011; Gosling et al., 2011). Compared to Twitter users, Facebook users are higher in neuroticism and extraversion (Hughes et al., 2011). By the way, Facebook pages show a stronger match to users' actual Big Five trait ratings than their ideal Big Five trait ratings, suggesting that Facebook pages reflect how people actually are more than how they wish they were (Back et al., 2010).
- *The Big Five predict what kind of dogs you like.* Yes, researchers actually compared people's Big Five ratings with their preferences in dog breeds. People low in agreeableness, high in conscientiousness, and high in neuroticism were most likely to prefer aggressive dogs like pit bulls, German shepherds, and boxers. People with the opposite personality pattern went for cocker spaniels and Labs (Egan & MacKenzie, 2012).

There are even studies indicating that levels of the Big Five vary across the regions of the United States (Rentfrow, 2010; Rentfrow et al., 2008). As **Figure 12.7** shows, you'll find a whole lot more neuroticism in New England than on the West Coast. The West Coast has plenty of openness, though, as do New York and a few of its neighbors. It is interesting to note the connection between high levels of openness and states' voting tendencies: The most open states also tend to be the most liberal or Democratic.

Speaking of politics, researchers conducted an intriguing project in which they asked presidential historians to rate a particular U.S. president on the Big Five (Rubenzer &

TABLE 12.4: Bloggers' Personalities and the Words They Use

BLOGGERS HIGH IN ...	...USE THE WORD _____ UNUSUALLY OFTEN IN THEIR BLOGS.
Neuroticism	awful, worse, stressful, horrible, annoying, ashamed, terrible
Extraversion	bar, drinks, restaurant, dancing, shots, crowd
Openness to experience	art, poet, culture, sexual, films, novel, literature
Agreeableness	together, visiting, share, staying, hug, wonderful
Conscientiousness	completed, adventure

Information from Yarkoni, 2010.

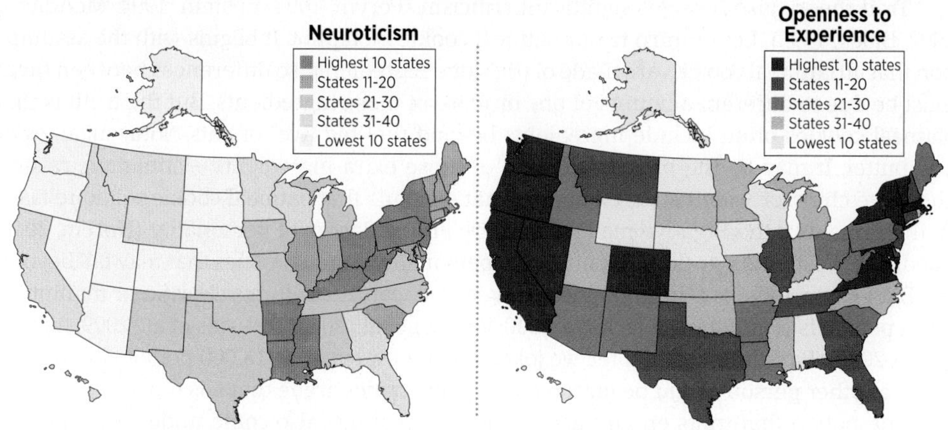

FIGURE 12.7 Distribution of the Big Five Across the United States. Personality traits vary by region. There's a lot of neuroticism in and around New York, but little in the mountain states. California and its neighbors show much higher levels of openness than the Midwest. Data from Rentfrow, 2010; Rentfrow et al., 2008.

Faschingbauer, 2004). (See **Figure 12.8** for the profiles of several selected presidents.) Several points about their ratings are especially interesting. Abraham Lincoln, known for being prone to depression, has the highest neuroticism score of the bunch. The two more politically liberal presidents, Abraham Lincoln and Bill Clinton, are notably higher in openness than the two more politically conservative presidents, Ronald Reagan and George W. Bush. All of these presidents are understandably high in extraversion: it is tough to imagine an introvert choosing the constant media attention that comes along with a campaign and a presidency.

Current Thoughts on Trait Theory

Trait theory dominates current research on personality. Among contemporary psychologists, it is generally viewed quite favorably as a scientifically well-grounded explanation of personality.

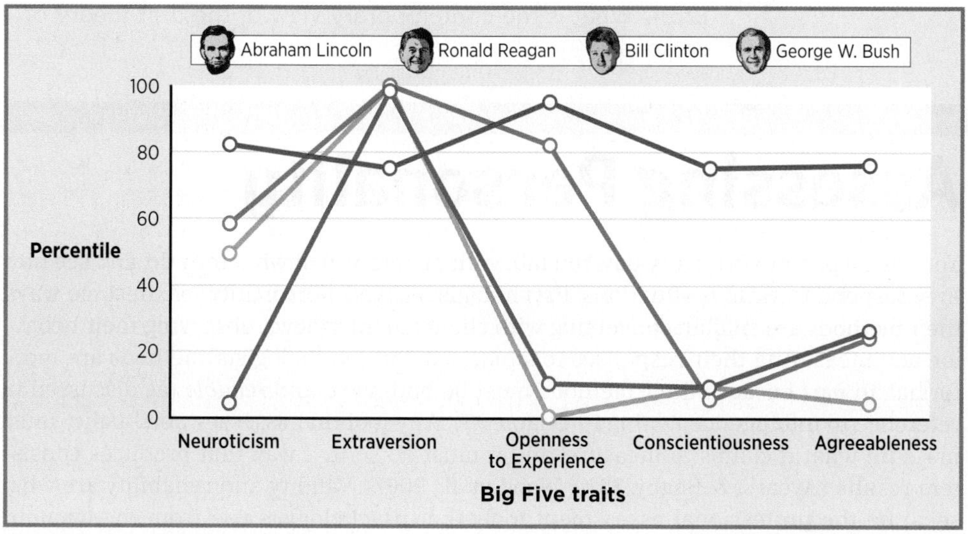

FIGURE 12.8 Big Five Profiles of Selected U.S. Presidents. These measurements of the personalities of U.S. presidents are strikingly similar in some ways (for example, high extraversion) and strikingly different in others (for example, various levels of openness to experience). Data from Rubenzer & Faschingbauer, 2004.

Trait theory also receives significant criticism (Pervin, 1994; Epstein, 1994; McAdams, 1992; Block, 1995). Let's return to our oatmeal cookie metaphor. It begins with the assumption that all oatmeal cookies are made of the same ingredients, so differences between them must be due to different amounts of one or more of those ingredients. But the truth is that oatmeal cookies often include ingredients beyond the "big five" of oats, flour, sugar, eggs, and butter. It may be the presence of one of those extra ingredients—cinnamon, raisins, chocolate chips, or walnuts, for example—that explains that oatmeal cookie's unique taste. In the same way, the Big Five may not capture all the flavors of personality (Norem, 2010; Shedler & Westen, 2004). Some examples of personality characteristics that may fall beyond the Big Five include how funny, honest, religious, cheap, humble, narcissistic, or manipulative a person is (Paunonen & Jackson, 2000; Veselka et al., 2011; De Vries et al., 2009; Ashton & Lee, 2008). Earlier in the chapter, we joked about how learning 18,000 personality ratings about another person would be far too many. Some critics argue that 5 is too few.

The notion that traits endure across the life span has also come under fire. There is significant support for Costa and McCrae's argument that they do endure (McCrae & Costa, 1994), but there is also support for the argument that they don't (Roberts et al., 2006). For example, researchers conducted a huge cross-sectional study of over 132,000 adults aged 21–60 and found that conscientiousness and agreeableness both increased slightly with age (Srivastava et al., 2003). They also found that neuroticism in women decreased slightly with age. The researchers concluded that personality is not "set like plaster" (p. 1041) but changes, at least somewhat, as we enter new phases of life or go through powerful experiences.

A final criticism of trait theory focuses on the overemphasis of the traits themselves, as opposed to external circumstances. If traits were all-powerful, people would behave exactly the same way in all situations. Consider your behavior in your psychology class: You walk in, sit down, stay quiet, take notes, and only speak up after raising your hand and being called on. If traits were the only determinants of behavior, you would behave this way not only in your psychology class, but everywhere all the time. My guess is that your behavior at last Saturday night's party or tomorrow's intramural soccer game would disprove this notion and would confirm the importance of the situation in addition to any of your own traits (Funder, 2008; Mischel & Shoda, 1995; Mischel, 1979).

CHECK YOUR LEARNING:

12.21 What is the trait theory of personality?

12.22 How do trait theorists strive to identify the basic ingredients of personality?

12.23 What is the five-factor model of personality, and which five traits does it include?

12.24 What is the contemporary view of the trait theory of personality?

Assessing Personality

YOU WILL LEARN:

12.25 how and why psychologists assess personality.

12.26 what clinical interviews are, and how psychologists use them.

12.27 what objective personality tests are, and how some specific ones work.

12.28 what projective personality tests are, and how some specific ones work.

12.29 what behavioral assessment is, and how psychologists use it.

You assess personality every day. You talk with people, watch what they do, and see how they respond to various situations. Psychologists assess personality too. In some ways, their methods are similar: conversing with clients in interviews, observing their behavior, and measuring their responses to situations. But psychologists' methods are more formal, in part because their methods must be both *valid* and *reliable* (as discussed in reference to intelligence testing in Chapter 7). Any tool that assesses personality must measure what it claims to measure, and it must do so in a way that produces consistent results (Ayearst & Bagby, 2010; Wood et al., 2007). Validity and reliability are what separate the professional assessment tools that psychologists use from the amateur "personality tests" posted on random Internet sites by people with unknown qualifications (Buchanan, 2002; Buchanan & Smith, 1999).

Psychologists assess personality for a variety of purposes (Butcher, 2010). In many cases, the person being assessed is seeking treatment, and the personality assessment

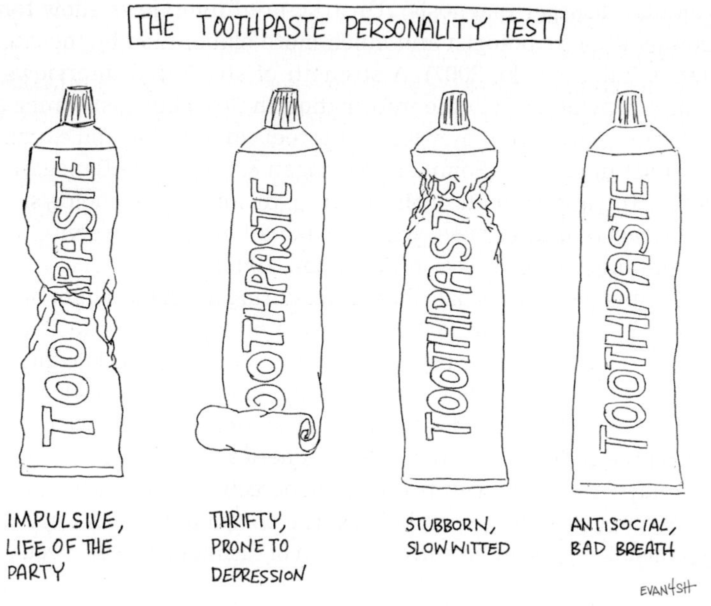

Evan Forsch

helps the psychologist determine the client's issues or diagnoses, which leads to the right treatment or referral. Such personality assessments take place anywhere psychologists practice, including psychiatric institutions, hospitals, clinics, community mental health centers, and private practices. In other cases, the assessment is part of a legal case. This type of psychology practice, in which legal issues are involved, is known as *forensic psychology* (Ogloff, 2002; Marczyk, Krauss, & Burl, 2012). For example, in court cases where the defendant pleads not guilty by reason of insanity, the psychologist may use personality assessment tools to explore whether the defendant was indeed "insane."

Additionally, some psychologists assess personality as part of the employment process, usually to help employers make hiring or placement decisions. This use of personality tests appears to have grown in recent years. Nearly a third of U.S. companies use personality tests for this reason; that number jumps to 40% among Fortune 100 companies, and 100% among the top 100 companies in Great Britain (Rothstein & Goffin, 2006).

Regardless of the purpose, a psychologist typically relies on several tools when assessing a client's personality. Psychologists prefer **multimethod assessment**: an approach to personality assessment that emphasizes the use of multiple methods rather than only one method. Multimethod assessment acknowledges that no single personality assessment tool is perfect. Using more than one assessment tool allows for the methods to offset each other's weaknesses, and in many cases, they converge upon similar conclusions. (In your personal life, as you get to know someone's personality, you are probably more confident if your impressions are based on more than one type of interaction with them.)

DIVERSITY MATTERS

Also, personality assessment depends heavily on the psychologist's **cultural competence**: the ability to work sensitively and expertly with members of a culturally diverse society. For example, let's say Murjanah takes a personality test and scores very low on a measure of extraversion. Murjanah's psychologist should know what is normal and expected for people of Murjanah's ethnicity, gender, and age before making an interpretation of what that low score means, especially if a mental disorder might be diagnosed.

Clinical Interviews

A **clinical interview** is a method of personality assessment in which the psychologist engages in conversation with the client. This conversation varies in terms of its *structure*, or the extent to which it is planned. Highly structured interviews typically follow a scripted list of questions that are asked in a particular order for a particular purpose

LIFE HACK 12.2

Be skeptical of so-called personality tests you find on random Web sites. They often lack the validity and reliability of personality tests used by psychologists.

(Buchanan, 2002; Buchanan & Smith, 1999)

multimethod assessment
An approach to personality assessment that emphasizes the use of multiple methods rather than only one method.

cultural competence
The ability to work sensitively and expertly with members of a culturally diverse society.

clinical interview
A method of personality assessment in which the psychologist engages in conversation with the client.

(such as a mental disorder diagnosis). Unstructured interviews allow for much more improvisation by the psychologist and much more elaboration by the client (Maruish, 2008; O'Brien & Tabaczynski, 2007). A strength of structured interviews is that they are reliable and provide exactly the information the psychologist wants; a strength of unstructured interviews is that they let clients feel comfortable and expand upon what they think is most important (Sommers-Flanagan & Sommers-Flanagan, 2009; Villa & Reitman, 2007). To capture both of these strengths, many psychologists compromise and give *semistructured* interviews, which strike a balance between a predetermined plan and a spontaneous conversation (Morrison, 2008).

Cultural competence is especially important during the clinical interview (Dana, 2005; Hays, 2008; Suzuki & Ponterotto, 2008). In a one-on-one, face-to-face interaction, it is essential for the psychologist to know and appreciate the cultural norms of communication for the client. For example, consider eye contact. The expected behavior could differ according to ethnicity, age, gender, and other variables (Sue & Sue, 2013). Many Asian American clients tend to avoid direct, prolonged eye contact, especially with people they perceive as authority figures (including, perhaps, the psychologist). If the psychologist is ignorant of this tendency, the lack of eye contact could mistakenly be interpreted as a sign of disinterest, disrespect, or dishonesty.

DIVERSITY MATTERS

Objective Personality Tests

Psychologists use a wide variety of personality tests, but they are generally categorized as either *objective* or *projective* personality tests. In **objective personality tests**, the client responds to a standardized set of questions, usually in multiple choice or true–false format. Typically, these are pencil-and-paper tests (although some can be taken on computers as well) in which clients read a list of brief statements about their thoughts, feelings, or behaviors. After each statement, the client marks the response that best describes him or her (Morey & Hopwood, 2008). The response options are often true–false, or a broader range of agreement, such as strongly agree, somewhat agree, neutral, somewhat disagree, strongly disagree. The scoring of objective personality tests is straightforward and can often be done by computer.

Minnesota Multiphasic Personality Inventory-2. The **Minnesota Multiphasic Personality Inventory-2 (MMPI-2)** is a widely used and respected objective personality test that emphasizes mental disorders. It was originally created in 1943; the second edition came out in 1989. It is used with adult clients, but in 1992, a separate version for adolescents (MMPI-Adolescent, or MMPI-A) was published (Butcher & Williams, 2009; Williams & Butcher, 2011). In 2008, a shortened version of the adult form (MMPI-Restructured Form, or MMPI-RF) was also offered (Ben-Porath & Tellegen, 2008).

The MMPI-2 is a list of 567 self-descriptive statements to which the client answers true or false on a separate answer sheet. The statements cover a wide range of behavior, thoughts, and feelings. When the client is finished, the psychologist (perhaps with the help of a computer or answer sheet scanner) tallies up the patterns of true and false responses. These tallies translate into scores on a wide variety of scales. The most important of these are the ten *clinical scales*, which indicate (either alone or in two- or three-scale combinations) the kinds of psychological problems the client is likely to experience (**Table 12.5**). Many additional scales can also be calculated.

The MMPI-2 was made by a process known as **empirical test construction**: a way to create objective personality tests in which items are included only if different groups respond differently to them. The authors of the MMPI-2 originally came up with more than 567 items. Then they gave all the items to people with and without psychological diagnoses. If people with a particular disorder answered an item one way but people without the disorder answered it the other way, the authors considered that item a keeper. This method of test construction is different because items only make the cut if the empirical data—say, a large percent of depressed versus nondepressed people who say "true" to an item—indicates that the item distinguishes one group from another (Ben-Porath & Archer, 2008; Graham, 2012).

TABLE 12.5: Clinical and Validity Scales of the MMPI-2 and MMPI-A

SCALE NAME	WHAT HIGH SCORE INDICATES
CLINICAL SCALES	
Hypochondriasis	Excessive concerns about body, ailments, illness
Depression	Sadness, pessimism
Hysteria	Vague medical reactions to stress, denial of conflict and anger
Psychopathic deviate	Antisocial, rebellious behaviors; uncaring toward others
Masculinity-femininity	Rejection of traditional gender roles
Paranoia	Suspicion of others, guardedness
Psychasthenia	Anxiety, nervousness
Schizophrenia	Bizarre, unconventional, or disorganized thinking; delusions
Mania	Extremely elevated mood; high energy; accelerated speech and thought
Social Introversion	Shyness, preference for solitude
VALIDITY SCALES	
Lying	"Faking good" or denying problems in more obvious way
Defensiveness	"Faking good" or denying problems in less obvious way
Infrequency	"Faking bad" or exaggerating problems
TRIN/VRIN	Random or inconsistent responding

Information from Butcher, 2011; Archer, 2005.

Couldn't the client just fake their way through a test like the MMPI-2?

In some cases, clients may try to respond to MMPI-2 items in ways that would create a false impression (Ziegler et al., 2012; MacCann et al., 2012; Sackett, 2012). For example, a person on trial who has pleaded not guilty by reason of insanity may want to come across as more seriously disturbed than they really are. To address this, the MMPI-2 contains *validity scales* (described in Table 12.5 along with the clinical scales), which assess not the client's personality but their approach to taking this test. These validity scales indicate the likelihood that the client is "faking good," "faking bad," or filling in answers randomly. If any of the validity scales is too high, the psychologist will consider the clinical scales invalid and will not use them to make any interpretations (Butcher, 2011).

The MMPI-2 is the most frequently used personality test for hiring decisions. It has been used for this purpose with the U.S. military since the 1940s, and now it is especially common in the hiring process for jobs that involve public safety, like police officers, airline pilots, and nuclear power plant technicians (Zapata Sola et al., 2009; Sellbom et al., 2007; Butcher & Williams, 2009; Butcher, 2012). It has even been used to screen Roman Catholic clergy. Here's how: The MMPI-2 was administered to clergy members who had credible accusations of sexual misconduct against them. It was later given to new applicants to the clergy, and those applicants who had similar MMPI scores to the clergy members with misconduct accusations were identified (Plante & Aldridge, 2005).

A large number of empirical studies support the reliability and validity of the MMPI-2, and it has been translated into many languages (Butcher et al., 2006; Butcher & Beutler, 2003; Greene & Clopton, 2004; Garrido & Velasquez, 2006).

NEO-Personality Inventory-3. Also widely used is the **NEO-Personality Inventory-3 (NEO-PI-3)**: an objective personality test that measures the Big Five personality factors. Created by the theorists who developed the five-factor model (Paul Costa and Robert McCrae), the NEO-PI-3 emphasizes normal personality traits rather than problematic characteristics like the MMPI-2. For that reason, psychologists do not use the NEO-PI-3 as often as the MMPI-2 when the task is to diagnose a client with a

objective personality tests
Personality tests in which the client responds to a standardized set of questions, usually in multiple choice or true-false format.

Minnesota Multiphasic Personality Inventory-2 (MMPI-2)
A widely used and respected objective personality test that emphasizes mental disorders.

empirical test construction
A way to create objective personality tests in which items are included only if different groups respond differently to them.

NEO-Personality Inventory-3 (NEO-PI-3)
An objective personality test that measures the Big Five personality factors.

IT'S LIKE...

Self-Reports on Personality Questionnaires Are Like Self-Reports in Real Life

You're deciding whether to date someone new. He describes his own personality on Match.com: laid-back and easygoing. You have a mutual friend, and she offers a different description of his personality: uptight and argumentative. Which do you believe?

Your company is deciding whether to hire an applicant for a salesperson job. She offers a description of herself in her cover letter: outgoing and hard-working. One of her reference letters, from a former supervisor, describes her differently: shy and unmotivated. Which is more trustworthy?

The central question in both of these situations is, How accurately do people describe themselves? This is the same question that psychologists face when they consider self-report objective personality tests such as the MMPI-2 or NEO-PI-3. Of course, on Match.com or an employment application, people are motivated to describe themselves in a particular way because they want a particular outcome—the first date or the new job. There are times when people completing a self-report questionnaire for a psychologist might be similarly motivated. For example, a divorced mom or dad who wants custody of the kids might "fake good" to impress the psychologist (and ultimately the judge) as a good parent. On the other hand, a patient with serious mental illness who prefers staying in a mental hospital to returning to an abusive home might "fake bad" to give the impression that he needs more time. Research suggests that motivated test takers, especially when they are intelligent too, can be at least somewhat successful faking self-report objective personality tests (Viswesvaran & Ones, 1999; Tett et al., 2012).

Even when people are not deliberately attempting to fake self-report personality tests, they may simply lack the self-knowledge needed to provide an accurate description of themselves (Connelly & Ones, 2010; Vazire & Carlson, 2010). Seeking input from someone who knows the client might seem like a logical alternative, but that isn't always easy or practical. It requires that the client give permission to talk to the other person. Even if such permission is granted, there is no guarantee that the other will be willing to complete the assessment or will be unbiased. ⬢

disorder. The NEO-PI-3 includes 240 items in a multiple-choice format, with choices ranging from "strongly agree" to "strongly disagree." The NEO-PI-3 lacks the validity scales of the MMPI-2, but it is frequently used by psychologists seeking to assess how much of each of the Big Five traits a person has (Costa & McCrae, 1992, 2008).

Objective personality tests are generally viewed by contemporary psychologists as reliable and valid assessment tools. These tests are standardized, which means the results won't depend on who administers the test, or where or when it is taken.

The primary downside of objective personality tests is their *self-report* format, which means clients answer questions about themselves. As we discussed previously, some clients may knowingly give inaccurate answers in an attempt to deliberately fake a personality, which they may be able to do with some success in spite of validity scales and other attempts to catch them. In other cases, clients simply may not know themselves very accurately, and may unknowingly give answers that do not reflect their true personalities. Researchers have actually compared self-report and *other-report* versions (filled out by family or friends) of Big Five questionnaires, with the intention of discovering how closely the two ratings match and which is a better predictor of behavior. Results indicate that the correlation between self-report and other-report measures of the Big Five is in the .40–.60 range—strongly positive, but far from perfect (Vazire & Carlson, 2010). Of the two, other-report ratings are actually better predictors than self-report ratings of job performance: At least in terms of work-related behavior, the way your friends or family members describe you is more accurate than the way you describe yourself (Connelly & Ones, 2010; Connolly et al., 2007).

Some psychologists believe that personality is revealed by the way a person responds to inkblots like this one, which resembles those in the Rorschach inkblot technique.
Blackspring/Shutterstock

Projective Personality Tests

In **projective personality tests,** clients respond to ambiguous stimuli in a free-form way. Projective personality tests are based on the assumption that the way you interpret what you see reveals something about your personality. You "project" your personality onto the world around you, especially when the world gives you room to make interpretations that may differ from those of others. Rather than forcing clients into a multiple-choice or true–false response, projective tests allow them to respond however they choose, with no restrictions (Tuber, 2012; Smith & Archer, 2008).

Picture yourself guiding a group of sixth-graders on a school field trip to a modern art museum, where many of the paintings are abstract. As you stand in front of a vague

painting, you ask the kids what they see. Kevin says, "The red part is a pool of blood, like after someone has been stabbed." Brooke says, "I see a face laughing at me." Julio points to a tiny black oval in the corner and says, "That little dot looks like a bug." Of course, you wouldn't make much of their responses to this single painting. But as you continue the tour, the same kids make similar responses to painting after painting. Kevin keeps seeing violence, Brooke keeps seeing people persecuting her, and Julio keeps focusing on minuscule details in the painting rather than seeing the big picture. For psychologists who use projective tests, each kid's pattern of responses reveals something important about that kid's personality.

projective personality tests
Personality tests in which clients respond to ambiguous stimuli in a free-form way.

Rorschach inkblot technique
A projective personality test in which the client responds to 10 inkblot images.

Thematic Apperception Test (TAT)
A projective personality test in which the client creates stories in response to cards that show people in undefined situations.

Rorschach Inkblot Technique. An assessment instrument that resembles this abstract art scenario is the **Rorschach inkblot technique**: a projective personality test in which the client responds to 10 inkblot images. Created in 1921 by Hermann Rorschach, a Swiss psychiatrist, it is administered in two phases. In the first phase, the psychologist shows the client each inkblot and asks what the client sees. In the second phase, the psychologist asks the client for an explanation of each response—What was it about the inkblot (its color, its shape, etc.) that made the client offer that response? Later, the psychologist codes the client's responses and calculates a variety of scores to describe the client's personality (Weiner, 2004; Exner, 1986).

Thematic Apperception Test. Inkblots are not the only things ambiguous enough to allow people's personalities to come through. Interpersonal scenes—basically, pictures of people without any caption—can serve the same purpose. That is the approach taken by the **Thematic Apperception Test** (**TAT**): a projective personality test in which the client creates stories in response to cards that show people in undefined situations. The stories a client tells may include what's happening in the scene, what led up to it, what may happen next, and what the people in the scene are thinking or feeling (Morgan & Murray, 1935; Murray, 1943; Ackerman et al., 2008). The administration of the TAT is not standardized. The psychologist can choose any cards and present them in any order. Scoring processes also vary widely, and in many cases, the psychologist simply makes subjective interpretations of the client's stories rather than scoring them in any systematic way (Moretti & Rossini, 2004).

Since the TAT's publication in 1943, a number of other story-telling projective tests have emerged. Most of these offer more standardized scoring procedures and more cultural diversity than the TAT, which emphasizes White people, often in rural settings (Teglasi, 2010; Malgady & Colon-Malgady, 2008).

Projective personality tests are not as popular or respected as they once were, primarily because they lack the validity and reliability of many objective tests. This means that psychologists can't be completely confident that projective tests really measure the personality characteristics they claim to measure. It also means that psychologists can't be sure that the conclusions one psychologist would make about a client's projective test would match the conclusions another psychologist would make. (If a different tour guide heard the sixth-graders' responses in the modern art museum, would that tour guide come up with exactly the same hypotheses as you about the kids' personalities?) This lack of standardization draws significant criticism and controversy for projective tests, and for many psychologists that lack is a deal breaker (Lilienfeld et al., 2010, 2000; Holt, 1999; Wood et al., 2003, 2010).

When psychologists use the Thematic Apperception Test, they present a series of pictures like this one and ask clients to tell a story about each. Some psychologists believe that they can learn a lot about the client's personality by examining the themes of their stories. Kenney Mencher

Supporters of projective tests point out that although there isn't as much data as there is to support their reliability and validity as with objective tests, there is some (Mihura et al., 2015, 2013; Meyer, 2004; Rose et al., 2001). Also, since projective tests do not rely on self-report, they are not as fakeable as objective tests, and this provides a unique way to tap into underlying personality characteristics.

Behavioral Assessment

Objective and projective personality tests both try to uncover something within the person that is presumed to be at the root of their behavior—personality characteristics,

Behavioral assessment assumes client behaviors are themselves the problems, rather than signs of deeper problems. For example, if a child refuses to go to school, the school refusal behavior is not a sign of depression, conduct disorder, or any other deep-rooted problem. Instead, the school refusal behavior *is* the problem.
Steve Debenport/E+/Getty Images

traits, disorders. So why not simply assess the behavior itself? That's the rationale behind **behavioral assessment**: an approach to assessment that assumes client behaviors are themselves the problems, rather than signs of deeper problems. As its name suggests, behavioral assessment is typically conducted by behaviorists—the same psychologists who question whether anything as internal or stable as "personality" even exists. It makes sense that they would devise and use an assessment method that focuses on observable behavior itself rather than any possible "cause" or "source" of it, which couldn't be empirically proven to exist.

For example, let's say Thomas, an 8-year-old third-grader, refuses to go to school. For a behaviorist, the problem is *not* social anxiety, depression, conduct disorder, neuroticism, or anything else inside Thomas' mind. His behavior—his refusal to go to school—*is* the problem, and we shouldn't look any deeper than that. So, a behavioral assessment of Thomas would involve watching the behavior directly, a practice called *behavioral observation*. Ideally, the observation would happen not in the psychologist's office, but in the real-world environment where the problem behavior takes place (Thomas' house on a schoolday morning, his bus stop, or the front door of his school). If such *naturalistic observation* is not possible, the psychologist can try to replicate the situation in the office, or use technology such as video cameras or smartphones to record Thomas' actions as they happen in their natural settings (Ollendick et al., 2004; Heiby & Haynes, 2004; Richard & Lauterbach, 2003).

Behavioral assessment typically involves a precise definition of the problem behavior and a systematic way of measuring how often it happens. It also involves noting the events that happen right before and right after the behavior—in order to understand any conditioning that may maintain the behavior (Cipani & Schock, 2007). (What does Thomas get when he refuses to go to school? Hugs and pancakes? A scolding and a time-out? What does he get when he *does* go to school?) Behavioral assessment may also involve interviewing and questionnaires, but if so, it is geared exclusively toward identifying the problem behavior and its function for the client (Haynes & Kaholokula, 2008).

behavioral assessment
An approach to Assessment that assumes client behaviors are themselves the problems, rather than signs of deeper problems.

CHECK YOUR LEARNING:

12.25 How and why do psychologists assess personality?

12.26 What are clinical interviews?

12.27 How do objective personality tests work?

12.28 How do projective personality tests work?

12.29 What is behavioral assessment, and how do does it differ from other kinds of assessment?

CHAPTER SUMMARY

What Is Personality?

12.1 Personality is a person's distinctive and stable way of thinking, feeling, and behaving.

12.2 Personality is not fully understood by psychologists, so they attempt to explain it with different personality theories.

12.3 Behavioral genetics studies of twins and adoptive families suggest that both biology (nature) and environment (nurture) play important roles in the development of personality.

Psychodynamic Theory of Personality

12.4 The psychodynamic theory of personality is an explanation of personality, based on the ideas of Sigmund Freud, that emphasizes unconscious forces and early childhood experiences.

12.5 The unconscious is the mental activity of which a person is unaware. According to Freud, it can explain actions that are otherwise unexplainable.

12.6 The id is the animalistic part of the mind, which generates primal, biologically based impulses such as sex and aggression. The superego is the part of the mind that opposes the id by enforcing rules, restrictions, and morality. The ego is the part of the mind that serves as a realistic mediator between the id and superego.

12.7 Freud divided early childhood into five phases called psychosexual stages, each of which can have lasting effects on personality: (1) the oral stage, (2) the anal stage, (3) the phallic stage, (4) the latency stage, and (5) the genital stage.

12.8 Neo-Freudians held onto Freud's core ideas—the unconscious, the significance of early childhood experiences, and the notion that

the mind contains the id, ego, and superego—but they deemphasized the biology that was so prominent in Freud's theories.

12.9 Psychodynamic theory is well past its heyday. Contemporary critics point out that it is not scientific enough and that Freud overgeneralized his ideas.

Humanistic Theory of Personality

12.10 The humanistic theory of personality is based on the ideas of Carl Rogers and emphasizes people's inherent tendencies toward healthy, positive growth and self-fulfillment.

12.11 Self-actualization is fully becoming the person one has the potential to become.

12.12 Positive regard is the warmth, acceptance, and love of people around us, while conditions of worth are the requirements that a person must meet to earn positive regard.

12.13 Self-concept is a person's view of who they are, and it develops in response to the ways that other people treat them.

12.14 Humanistic theory gave rise to the positive psychology movement and continues to significantly influence the way that many psychotherapists practice, though it has been criticized for being too optimistic and for being unscientific.

Behavioral and Social-Cognitive Theories of Personality

12.15 The behavioral theory of personality emphasizes the influence of the environment and the importance of observable, measurable behavior.

12.16 The social-cognitive theory of personality emphasizes the interaction of environment, thought processes, and social factors.

12.17 Albert Bandura's theory of reciprocal determinism suggests that three factors—behavior, environment, and cognitions—continually influence each other.

12.18 Bandura emphasized a type of cognition known as self-efficacy, a person's beliefs about his or her own abilities.

12.19 Julian Rotter highlighted a type of cognition known as locus of control, which is a person's belief about how much control they have over what happens in their life.

12.20 Behavioral theories of personality are held in high regard by those who insist that all aspects of psychology should be empirically based, but most current psychologists do not accept the behavioral notion that environment, rather than personality, determines all behavior. More than other personality theories, social-cognitive theory identifies many possible influences on personality, and self-efficacy has been shown to enhance achievement in a wide variety of areas.

Trait Theory of Personality

12.21 The trait theory of personality emphasizes the discovery and description of the basic components of personality.

12.22 Identifying the basic traits of human personality required narrowing down the massive number of possibilities to a much shorter list of "supertraits."

12.23 The five-factor model of personality emphasizes five fundamental traits present in all people to varying degrees—neuroticism, extraversion, openness to experience, conscientiousness, and agreeableness.

12.24 Trait theory dominates current research on personality, but some theorists feel the Big Five may not capture all the aspects of personality, that traits may not endure across the life span, and that trait theory underestimates the impact of external circumstances.

Assessing Personality

12.25 Psychologists assess personality through many valid and reliable methods, including interviews, observation of behavior, and personality tests. Psychologists assess personality for a variety of purposes, including diagnosis and treatment, employment, and forensic (legal or court-related) reasons.

12.26 A clinical interview—which can be structured, unstructured, or semistructured—is a method of personality assessment in which the psychologist engages in conversation with the client.

12.27 In an objective personality test such as the MMPI-2, the client responds to a standardized set of questions, usually in multiple choice or true-false format.

12.28 In projective personality tests like the Rorschach inkblot technique, clients respond to ambiguous stimuli in a free-form way.

12.29 Behavioral assessment is an approach to assessment that assumes client behaviors are the problems (rather than signs of deeper problems).

KEY TERMS

personality, p. 401
behavioral genetics, p. 401
psychodynamic theory of personality, p. 403
unconscious, p. 403
psychic determinism, p. 403
Freudian slips, p. 403
id, p. 403
superego, p. 405
ego, p. 405
defense mechanisms, p. 405
psychosexual stages, p. 407
fixation, p. 407
oral stage, p. 407
anal stage, p. 407
phallic stage, p. 407
Oedipus complex, p. 407
Electra complex, p. 409
identification, p. 409
latency stage, p. 409
genital stage, p. 409

neo-Freudian theories, p. 409
collective unconscious, p. 409
archetypes, p. 409
humanistic theory of personality, p. 410
self-actualization, p. 410
positive regard, p. 410
conditions of worth, p. 410
real self, p. 413
ideal self, p. 413
incongruence, p. 413
congruence, p. 413
self-concept, p. 413
behavioral theory of personality, p. 415
social-cognitive theory of personality, p. 415
reciprocal determinism, p. 415
self-efficacy, p. 417
locus of control, p. 417
internal locus of control, p. 417
external locus of control, p. 417
trait theory of personality, p. 419
traits, p. 419
five-factor model of personality (Big Five), p. 419
neuroticism, p. 419
extraversion, p. 419
openness to experience, p. 419
conscientiousness, p. 419
agreeableness, p. 419
multimethod assessment, p. 425
cultural competence, p. 425
clinical interview, p. 425
objective personality tests, p. 427
Minnesota Multiphasic Personality Inventory-2 (MMPI-2), p. 427
empirical test construction, p. 427
NEO-Personality Inventory-3 (NEO-PI-3), p. 427
projective personality tests, p. 429
Rorschach inkblot technique, p. 429
Thematic Apperception Test (TAT), p. 429
behavioral assessment, p. 430

SELF-ASSESSMENT

1. _____ is a person's distinctive and stable way of thinking, feeling, and behaving.

2. _____ is the study of the impact of genes (nature) and environment (nurture) on personality and behavior.
   a. Self-actualization
   b. Factor analysis
   c. Behavioral genetics
   d. Identification

3. Morgan is working as a cashier, and an extremely attractive customer makes a purchase. Morgan tries to say to the customer, "Your total is six dollars." However, she mistakenly says: "Your total is sex dollars." If this mistake reveals an unconscious wish of Morgan's, the mistake is an example of a(n):
   a. superego.
   b. Freudian slip.
   c. incongruence.
   d. identification.

4. According to Sigmund Freud, the _____ is the animalistic part of the mind that generates our most basic, biologically based impulses such as sex and aggression.
   a. id
   b. ego
   c. superego
   d. ideal self

5. The correct sequence of Freud's five psychosexual stages is:
   a. oral, anal, phallic, latency, genital.
   b. latency, oral, phallic, genital, anal.
   c. phallic, anal, oral, genital, latency.
   d. oral, anal, genital, phallic, latency.

6. According to Carl Rogers, _____ leads to unhappiness and mental illness.
   a. self-actualization
   b. cultural incompetence
   c. extraversion
   d. incongruence

7. The _____ theory of personality emphasizes the interaction of environment, thought processes, and social factors.
   a. social-cognitive
   b. humanistic
   c. behavioral
   d. trait

8. Trina believes that her own actions determine what happens in her life. Troy believes that outside forces, rather than his own actions, determine what happens in his life. Trina has a(n) _____ locus of control, while Troy has a(n) _____ locus of control.

9. The five-factor model of personality emphasizes five fundamental traits present in all people to varying degrees. Which of these is NOT included among those five traits?
   a. Intelligence
   b. Neuroticism
   c. Conscientiousness
   d. Agreeableness

10. Dr. Velsor is a psychologist conducting a personality assessment. If she's using an objective personality test, which of the following might she be using?
    a. Rorschach inkblot technique
    b. Minnesota Multiphasic Personality Inventory-2
    c. Wechsler Adult Intelligence Scale
    d. Thematic Apperception Test

Self-Assessment Answers

1. Personality, 2. c, 3. b, 4. a, 5. a, 6. d, 7. a, 8. internal; external, 9. a, 10. b

WHAT'S YOUR TAKE?

1. When I was a kid, I attended a sports camp. After a few days of track and field week, my best long jump was 9 feet. The next day, the counselor marking our distances in the sand pit laid a stick in the sand and shouted out to me before I started my run up to the pit—"Here's the 9-foot mark!" I landed about a foot short of it. Frustrated, I went back to the starting line, built up more speed, timed my takeoff, and still landed about 6 inches short of the stick. As I walked back for my third try, I told myself, "I *know* I can jump 9 feet. I did it yesterday!" Sure enough, on my third attempt, I cleared that stick. As I smiled and brushed off the sand, my counselor whispered, "Hey, I'll let you in on a little secret. The stick is actually at *10* feet." I had jumped past that stick not because of a new technique or a training regimen, but because I *believed* I could. Bandura would have been proud of my counselor for knowing how to maximize the effects of self-efficacy in his campers. Can you recall any situations in which your own self-efficacy—your belief that you could achieve something—was a primary reason why you were able to actually achieve it?
2. When psychologists do personality assessments, they increasingly offer their services—including clinical interviews—via videoconference (usually via apps similar to Skype). Some celebrate this trend as a step forward with benefits for both client and therapist. Others are more wary about the merging of psychology and Internet-based technology. How about you? If you (or a friend or a family member) called a psychologist to schedule a clinical interview and were offered both videoconference and in-person options, which would you prefer? Why? What circumstances might influence your opinion?

SHOW ME MORE

12.1 Locus of Control and Academic Potential

http://tiny.cc/ip7njy

This article describes how some colleges are now using tests of personality characteristics, including locus of control, to measure academic potential and influence admissions decisions.

Peter Muller/Getty Images

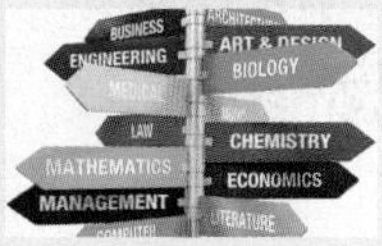

12.2 The Big Five and the Personality of College Majors

http://tiny.cc/0p7njy

This article describes research on the correlation between college students' majors and their big five personality traits.

Nerthuz/Shutterstock

13 Social Psychology

Jose Luis Pelaez Inc/Getty Images

Your neighbor is a famous and espected professor. His list of academic achievements is extraordinary: He has written books, directed research institutes, and done expert appearances on TV shows viewed by millions. *Time* magazine even ncluded him on its list of the "25 Most Influential Americans."

One afternoon, as you look out your window, the professor returns home with a friend. He finds his front door jammed, so he enters through he back door. Once inside, he and his friend work together on the front door to make sure it won't be jammed in the future. Soon, a police car pulls up. A jogger who saw your neighbor and his friend adjusting the ront door called 911 to report what she thought was a burglary attempt. Your neighbor shows the officer his driver's license and university ID, but the officer remains suspicious. As the officer asks your neighbor more questions, the conversation becomes heated. Your neighbor is handcuffed on his porch and ultimately arrested for disorderly conduct.

This story actually happened to Henry Louis Gates, a Harvard professor, in July 2009 (Thompson, 2009). You may have seen Professor Gates as host of the PBS TV show *Finding Your Roots*. Professor Gates is Black. The police officer, Sgt. James Crowley, is White. Their interaction attracted so much media attention—often with "racial profiling" in the headline—that President Barack Obama and Vice President Joe Biden personally intervened. At the president's request, the four men sat down together to discuss the matter (Cooper, 2009). The charges were eventually dropped.

For months following these events, many questions arose on TV, radio, and social media (Phillips, 2009)—almost all of which involve key ssues in *social psychology*. What prompted the jogger to call 911? Why did the police officer behave as he did? Was prejudice, stereotyping, or discrimination involved? What opinions did we form about why he officer responded the way he did—his deep-seated personality characteristics, the demands of that particular situation, or the orders handed down from his superiors? How was President Obama's effort to mprove the relationship between the two men successful? Are there better ways to reduce, or even prevent, such tensions?

Social psychologists study exactly these kinds of questions. Most psychologists explore how each of us behaves as an individual, but social psychologists explore how we behave *together*: how we think about each other, influence each other, and relate to each other. Your day-to-day life s inescapably social, so these are vitally relevant topics.

CHAPTER OUTLINE

Social psychology is the scientific study of how people think about, influence, and relate to each other. skynesher/E+/Getty Images

In the Personality chapter, we zoomed in to focus on the individual. In this chapter, we zoom out to focus on *other people*. Human behavior happens in the context of other humans. Your actions are affected by the people around you, just as their behavior is affected by you (Funder & Fast, 2010; Snyder & Deaux, 2012; Ross et al., 2010). To fully understand behavior, we need to consider **social psychology**: the scientific study of how people think about, influence, and relate to each other.

Sometimes, this scientific study takes place in the lab, where social psychologists design and manipulate situations. Participants are placed among other people and asked to perform a particular task while researchers observe and measure what happens (Crano & Lac, 2012). A social psychologist may place an individual in a group of people performing a particular behavior in a particular way—for example, responding to a puzzle with the same wrong answer—and see whether the individual follows along or resists. Or, they may present individuals with pictures or videos of other people and then assess the individuals' judgments about the other people's attractiveness, personality, or other qualities.

In addition to controlled lab studies, social psychologists conduct real-world (or *naturalistic*) studies, in which researchers observe how people behave in situations from their day-to-day lives (Wilson et al., 2010; Reis & Gosling, 2010). For example, researchers may observe who sits together in a high school cafeteria, or they may observe when and where people are most likely to help on a public street. Together, lab studies and real-world studies by social psychologists shed light on many areas of our lives: how other people affect how we work, play, help, hurt, love, hate, and otherwise behave (Kruglanski & Stroebe, 2012).

The social nature of our lives is not a new phenomenon. In fact, group existence has been a fact of life throughout the evolution of our species (Brewer, 2007; Foley, 1995). For the vast majority of human history, our ancestors lived their whole lives in bands of hunter-gatherers that probably included about 50–200 members (Barrett et al., 2002; Van Vugt & Van Lange, 2006). These bands, and the smaller groups that formed within them, were essential to human survival (Caporael, 2007; Kenrick, 2012). Living among other people has always featured important, even life-saving advantages: they can help you find food, water, and shelter; they can help care for your children (and yourself); and they can protect you against danger. But social relationships have always carried risks too: Other people can hurt you, sicken you, or freeload off you (Neuberg & Cottrell, 2006). Today, as products of our evolution, we find ourselves inextricably connected to the people around us, both for better and for worse. As we'll see, many of social psychology's core concepts remain connected to this evolutionary inheritance.

Social Cognition: How We Think about Each Other

YOU WILL LEARN:

13.1 what social cognition is.

13.2 what attributions are.

13.3 how people often make the fundamental attribution error.

13.4 what attitudes are, and how people try to change them.

13.5 what cognitive dissonance is, and how it can be resolved.

Our thoughts about other people strongly influence our feelings and behavior. Social psychologists use the term **social cognition** to refer to a person's thoughts about other people and the social world. In this section, we focus on forms of social cognition that social psychologists have studied extensively, including *attributions*, *attitudes*, and *cognitive dissonance*.

Attributions

Our thoughts about other people frequently focus on why they behave as they do. We develop an **attribution**: an explanation of the cause of behavior. A single behavior can generate a wide range of attributions. For example, imagine yourself in line at a

coffee shop. As you wait to order, you see a woman walk in, stroll past the line, straight over to the "Pick Up Orders Here" counter, grab a coffee and go. You ask the person in front of you, just to make sure: "Did she really just steal a cup of coffee?" When he confirms that he saw the same thing, you wonder: "*Why*?"

Attribution is an explanation of the cause of behavior. If you saw a woman walk into a coffee shop and take a cup of coffee without paying, multiple attributions could explain her behavior. Westend61/Getty Images

Attribution Theory: Is It the Person or the Situation? Answers to that question could span a wide range, but social psychologists believe that they fall into two distinct categories. These two categories are specified by **attribution theory**: a theory that behavior is caused either by traits within the individual or by the situation surrounding the individual. Sometimes people are driven to behave a certain way because of who they are—their personalities or dispositions, essentially—but other times people are driven to behave a certain way by temporary factors that are outside themselves (Malle, 2006, 2011; Kelley, 1973; Heider, 1958). For example, if we attribute the coffee bandit's behavior to enduring qualities within her—she's cheap, crazy, or a thief—we're pointing at her personality traits. But maybe there's a better explanation based on her situation. Perhaps she's on a new prescription medicine that is causing confusion and erratic behavior. Perhaps she ordered and paid before you came in, then ran out because she saw a friend on the sidewalk, before returning for her coffee. Either of these explanations point to her situation, not her disposition.

The Fundamental Attribution Error. Research on attribution theory has repeatedly found that the way we explain the behavior of other people tends to differ from the way we explain our own behavior (e.g., Ross, 1977; Gilbert & Malone, 1995). Specifically, we often commit the **fundamental attribution error**: overestimating the importance of traits and underestimating the importance of the situation when explaining the behavior of other people. Basically, when *I* do it, it is because of the situation around me, but when *you* do it, it is because of who you are (Funder & Fast, 2010; Ross & Nisbett, 1991). Driving behavior offers some common examples: I'm speeding because the traffic made me late, but he's speeding because he's reckless; I ran the red light because the light is malfunctioning, but she ran it because she's absentminded; I talk on my phone while driving because it's an important call, but you talk on your phone while driving because you're irresponsible. For our own behavior, we can often identify many extenuating circumstances that caused us to behave as we did. For ourselves, "it's complicated." For others, we assume it is simple: their personality traits explain it all.

LIFE HACK 13.1

It is called the fundamental attribution *error* for a reason. You might be making a mistake if you judge other people by considering only their personality traits and overlooking their circumstances.

(Funder & Fast, 2010; Ross & Nisbett, 1991; Jones & Harris, 1967)

In a classic experiment, researchers had participants read "pro" or "con" essays about controversial topics of the time—for example, segregation (Jones & Harris, 1967). Then participants were asked for their opinions about why the authors wrote the essays. Participants overwhelmingly attributed the content of the essays to the authors' personalities, not any external circumstances—even when the experimenters told them that the authors had been *assigned* to take the viewpoint.

Since the early days of research on fundamental attribution error, evidence has suggested that it characterizes some cultural groups more than others. In particular,

DIVERSITY MATTERS

the fundamental attribution error occurs more often in individualistic cultures (like the United States and most other Western countries) than in collectivistic cultures (like most Asian countries) (Crittenden, 1991; Shweder & Bourne, 1982). In one study, researchers read sports articles and editorials in newspapers from the United States (including the *New York Times* and the *Boston Globe*) and Hong Kong (the *South China Morning Post*) (Lee et al., 1996). They then categorized each article in terms of how it attributed the action described: to the personalities of the people who did it, or to the circumstances surrounding those people. The results indicated that the Asian newspapers made far more attributions to the situation and far fewer attributions to personalities. This difference may stem from the fact that in collectivistic cultures, there is a general understanding that people often do things for the sake of others, and that actions

social psychology
The scientific study of how people think about, influence, and relate to each other.

social cognition
A person's thoughts about other people and the social world.

attribution
An explanation of the cause of behavior.

attribution theory
A theory that behavior is caused either by traits within the individual or by the situation surrounding the individual.

fundamental attribution error
Overestimating the importance of traits and underestimating the importance of the situation when explaining the behavior of other people.

MY TAKE VIDEO 13.1

Fundamental Attribution Error

"Someone rudely cut in front of me and took my parking spot. I thought they were mean, but in reality..."

YOUTUBE: http://tiny.cc/mytake
LAUNCHPAD: launchpadworks.com

done for this reason may not accurately reflect the personality of the person who does them.

At times, people in power may commit the fundamental attribution error, at least according to some of their critics. For example, an expert on education argues that educational administrators who blame bad student test scores on bad teachers often fail to appreciate the importance of the situation in which teachers work. This situation often includes overcrowded classrooms, poor equipment, little parental support, and unprepared students (Kennedy, 2010).

Attitudes

An **attitude** is a viewpoint, often influenced by both thoughts and emotions, that affects your responses to people, things, or situations. Attitudes (often called *preferences* by social psychologists) land somewhere between what you know and how you feel (Banaji & Heiphetz, 2010; Petty et al., 1997, 2009a). Consider your attitude toward capital punishment (the death penalty). It certainly consists of more than mere facts, such as whether capital punishment decreases crime rates, or the financial costs of capital punishment versus life in prison. It is also certainly more than pure emotion, such as your gut reaction to the idea of a convicted criminal being put to death. Instead, your attitude is a hybrid of thoughts and emotions, both informed by facts and infused with sentiment.

As **Figure 13.1** shows, the importance of attitudes lies in their connection to behavior. Attitudes predict action (Fazio, 1990; Kraus, 1995). Consider Ronald, an overweight 40-year-old man with a very negative attitude toward exercising. The whole idea of working out seems unpleasant to Ronald: It is a hassle and a burden, an unpleasant, sweaty, boring, time-consuming chore. Not surprisingly, he hasn't worked out in years. But if Ronald's wife, friends, or coworkers can effectively persuade him that exercise is enjoyable and rejuvenating, then it is much more likely Ronald will go to the gym. And it works the other way too: Actions predict attitudes. Let's imagine that Ronald gets some scary news about the condition of his heart from his doctor at his annual checkup. As a result, he drags himself to the gym, forcing himself to exercise. His attitude toward exercise is likely to shift in a positive direction to match his new exercise behavior.

Attitudes and actions correlate strongly, but they don't always match (Wallace et al., 2005; Ajzen, 2000). There are instances in which a person's stated attitudes disagree with the behaviors they perform. A meta-analysis of research on the attitude–action link found that attitudes are least likely to predict behavior when the person lacks confidence in the attitude, the attitude is unstable, and contradictory attitudes are also present (Glasman & Albarracín, 2006). In a classic study of the disconnect between attitudes and actions, a Chinese couple traveled by car through the United States during the early 1930s (a time when prejudice in the United States toward Chinese people was high), seeking food and lodging at many stops along the way. Almost every restaurant and hotel welcomed them. Six months later, the same restaurants and hotels received a survey in the mail asking if they would serve Chinese customers, and most said they would *not*—an attitude opposite of the behavior they had just exhibited (LaPiere, 1934). The explanation for this discrepancy is not entirely clear, but it could involve social pressures against admitting to a hospitable attitude toward certain minority groups at that time in U.S. history. The disconnect also might be explained by the difficulty of turning down any paying customer in tough economic times, regardless of attitudes toward them.

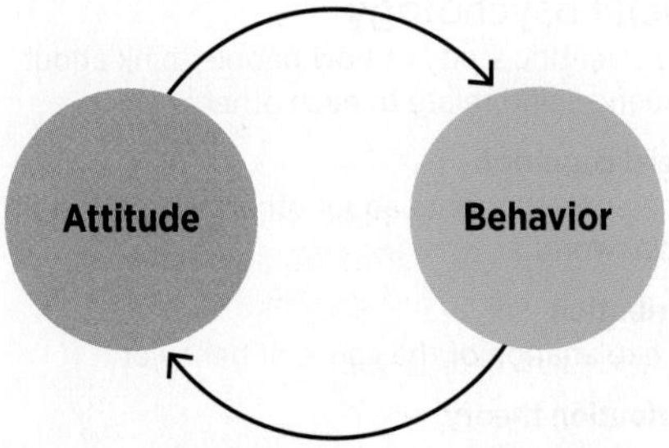

FIGURE 13.1 Reciprocal Influence of Attitude and Behavior. Attitudes and behavior influence each other. For example, consider exercising. Positive attitudes toward exercising can increase exercise frequency, and increased exercise frequency can improve attitudes toward exercising.

Explicit Attitudes and Implicit Attitudes.

Social psychologists distinguish between *explicit* attitudes and *implicit* attitudes (Albarracín & Vargas, 2010). Explicit attitudes are the attitudes we know we have, the ones we can easily and accurately describe. Implicit attitudes are much more automatic and involuntary, lying a bit below the surface of our awareness, a bit more difficult to acknowledge (Petty et al., 2009b). As an example of explicit and implicit attitudes, consider your attitude toward people

of a race different from your own. It is possible that your explicit and implicit attitudes differ a bit. Perhaps you like to see yourself as open-minded, but you are actually more closed-minded than you would like to admit. As **Figure 13.2** illustrates, the biology of explicit and implicit thoughts reflects this distinction: They take place in different parts of the brain. Neuroimaging studies show that explicit attitudes come from the frontal cortex (specifically, the orbitofrontal cortex region), which allows for deliberate cognitive processing, but implicit attitudes emerge straight from the amygdala, which processes emotion (Wright et al., 2008; Phan et al., 2002).

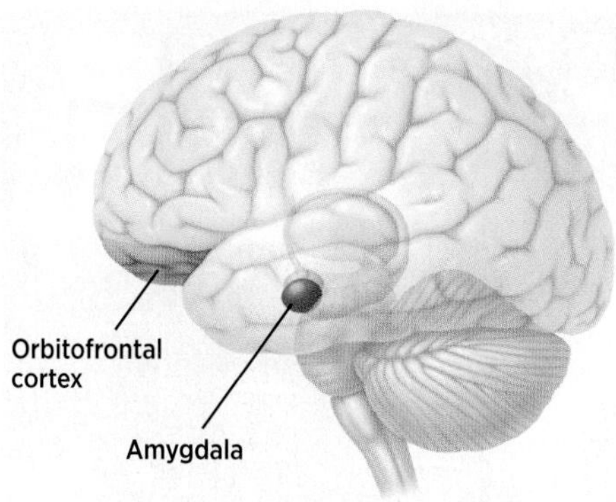

FIGURE 13.2 Implicit and Explicit Attitudes in the Brain. Explicit attitudes, which we have consciously thought through, activate the orbitofrontal cortex, where cognition takes place. Implicit attitudes, which we may not be so aware of, activate the amygdala, which processes emotion. Information from Wright et al., 2008; Phan et al., 2002.

Which would you expect to be a better predictor of behavior—explicit attitudes or implicit attitudes? Social psychologists were somewhat surprised to find that the two are roughly equivalent in predicting behavior. They expected implicit attitudes to be better predictors, "truer" indicators, of how a person genuinely thinks and feels toward a topic than explicit attitudes (Ajzen, 2012; Greenwald et al., 2009). An important exception to this equivalence was found in the area of racial attitudes and discrimination. In numerous experiments, implicit racial attitudes were better predictors than explicit racial attitudes of nonverbal behaviors—making eye contact, smiling at, sitting near people of different races (Fazio & Olson, 2003; Olson & Fazio, 2009).

Why are we covering attitudes in a chapter on *social* psychology?

Attitudes are important to social psychologists for a couple of reasons. First, many of our attitudes are social and are important influences on our behavior. We hold many attitudes toward other people (as individuals or groups), and they hold many attitudes toward us. Second, social psychologists study attitudes because we spend so much time and effort trying to *change* each other's attitudes. Just think of how often someone tries to alter your attitude on a daily basis. Your roommates plead with you that a bigger TV really would be worth the money. Your neighbor's yard sign tries to sway your vote toward their preferred candidate. The voiceover on a commercial tries to convince you that your current Internet speed is too slow and you need to upgrade.

Attitude Persuasion Strategies. Social psychologists have identified a variety of specific strategies that we use in attempts to change the attitudes of those around us. For example, **central route persuasion** is a persuasion strategy that emphasizes the message's content. By contrast, **peripheral route persuasion** is a persuasion strategy that emphasizes factors other than the message's content. Advertisers have undoubtedly made you familiar with both persuasion strategies. For example, when you see a TV commercial that directly explains the advantages of a particular car—good gas mileage, high safety rating, plenty of leg room—the advertisers are using central route persuasion. However, when you see a TV commercial for another car that simply pairs the car with a hot celebrity or trendy music, the advertisers are using peripheral route persuasion. The first ad, because of its direct approach, is more likely to be effective in the long run, especially if it gets the viewer to think about the advantages mentioned in its message.

Social psychologists use the term *elaboration* to refer to this "thinking about it" process by the listener, and the more elaboration, the more effective the message (Petty & Briñol, 2012; Petty et al., 1995). When the strategy emphasizes stuff around the message (in its "periphery") rather than the message itself, elaboration tends to be minimal, so any attitude change tends to be superficial and short-term (Wagner & Petty, 2011; Petty & Cacioppo, 1986).

Other strategies for attitude change resemble sales tactics even more closely. The **foot-in-the-door technique** is a persuasion strategy in which one person gets another person to agree to a small request before asking for a bigger one. Of course, the bigger request is the target, the change the first person wanted all along (Hogg, 2010; Dolinski, 2000; Cialdini & Trost, 1998; Gorassini & Olson, 1995). For example,

attitude
A viewpoint, often influenced by both thoughts and emotions, that affects a person's responses to people, things, or situations.

central route persuasion
A persuasion strategy that emphasizes the message's content.

peripheral route persuasion
A persuasion strategy that emphasizes factors other than the message's content.

foot-in-the-door technique
A persuasion strategy in which one person gets another person to agree to a small request before asking for a bigger one.

This car salesperson is using central route persuasion, a strategy to emphasize the message's content—for example, the car's fuel economy, warranty, or roominess. A TV commercial for the same car might use peripheral route persuasion by emphasizing factors other than the message's content—for example, pairing the car with beautiful people or well-liked celebrities. Echo/Cultura/Getty Images

let's imagine that you want to borrow your friend's car for an overnight trip to a city several hours away. Asking for such a big favor out of the blue may strike your friend as a bit much. But if you start by asking your friend to borrow his car for a 2-mile trip to the grocery store, he's more likely to say yes. Once he's agreed to the little request, he's more likely to say yes to a medium-sized request—say, a 20-mile trip to the doctor's office. Ultimately, he might even agree to a large request like the overnight trip.

In one study of the foot-in-the-door technique, researchers sent emails to about 1000 participants asking them to click a link to a Web site designed to help children who had been injured by land mines in war zones (Guéguen & Jacob, 2001). For half, clicking the link in the email immediately brought up a "donation" Web page. For the other half, clicking the link first brought up a petition against land mines that participants were asked to sign, which then was followed by the same "donation" Web page. Results indicated that getting participants to sign the petition—a foot-in-the-door—more than tripled the likelihood that the participant would click to donate.

Opposite to the foot-in-the-door technique is the **door-in-the-face technique**: a persuasion strategy in which one person gets another person to reject a large request before making a smaller one. In this case, the smaller request is the target that the first person has in mind from the beginning. The name of this term reflects the second person slamming the door in the face of the first person, only to reopen it when the more reasonable request follows. For example, a teenage girl who wants a $100 pair of shoes for her birthday might begin by asking her parents for a $300 pair. When they respond "Absolutely not!" her subsequent request for the $100 gift may seem much more reasonable by comparison.

Researchers studying the door-in-the-face technique asked participants for a big, long-term commitment—to be a voluntary counselor at a juvenile detention center for 2 hours a week for 2 years—and almost none of them said yes. But when they followed that request with a smaller one—taking kids from the juvenile detention center on a single trip to the zoo—half agreed to do so. Other participants simply received the zoo request alone, and only 17% complied (Cialdini et al., 1975).

A final persuasion strategy used both on the sales floor and in day-to-day interactions is the **lowball technique**: a persuasion strategy in which one person quotes another person a low price to get an initial agreement and then raises the price. Car dealers are notorious for lowballing customers—luring them in to the dealership with a low advertised price and then nonchalantly adding hundreds or thousands for undercoating, delivery, and various mysterious fees. It happens elsewhere too. A friend moving to a new apartment invites you to help him move his couch and promises free pizza as a reward. You agree, but once you finish with the couch, he asks for help with the bed, the furniture, the TV, and the dozens of boxes of clothes, books, and other stuff. Hours later, sweaty and exhausted, you realize that you've worked much harder and longer than expected to earn that "free" pizza.

As a summary of these attitude persuasion strategies, **Table 13.1** uses as an example how a real estate agent might try to convince someone to buy a house.

Social Role. Our attitudes are also shaped by our sense of who we are and what we are supposed to do. Our attitudes and ultimately our actions are often influenced by our **social role**: a title, position, or status that carries expectations for acceptable behavior. The power of the social role is often most evident right after our role changes. When a person becomes something new—a college graduate, an employee, a parent, a boss, a retiree—he or she often feels a new pressure to behave as someone with that label should behave (Hogg et al., 1995; Stryker & Statham, 1986). A recent college graduate starts to rethink the clothes he wears and the music he listens to, eventually graduating to something a bit more "grown-up." A woman who becomes pregnant begins to reconsider her eating habits, swears off alcohol altogether, and suddenly views her subcompact car as far too unsafe. After all, she's now in a position of being doubly responsible.

TABLE 13.1: Attitude Persuasion Strategies as a Real Estate Agent Might Use Them

ATTITUDE PERSUASION STRATEGY	DESCRIPTION	HOW A REAL ESTATE AGENT MIGHT USE IT
Central route persuasion	Directly explain the actual benefits.	This house has 3 bedrooms, 2 bathrooms, 2000 square feet, and a 2-car garage.
Peripheral route persuasion	Use "smoke and mirrors" to make it seem great.	Several local celebrities live near this neighborhood.
Foot-in-the-door technique	Get them to agree to something little before asking for something big.	Will you come to the open house and look inside?
Door-in-the-face technique	Ask for something way too big first; then what I actually want will seem reasonable.	I've got a nice house available for $1 million. Not interested? How about this one for a fraction of that price?
Lowball technique	Get them to agree, then jack up the price.	Sign the contract right now and we'll waive all closing costs. (I won't show them the taxes, fees, and other add-ons until later.)

A well-known and disturbing study from the 1970s illustrates the power that social roles can have on our attitudes and behavior. Social psychologist Phillip Zimbardo asked a couple of dozen male college students to volunteer to spend time in a fake prison. It was actually a basement in a Stanford University building, but the researchers randomly assigned some of the men to be guards, while the others were randomly assigned to be inmates. The guards got uniforms, clubs, and mirrored sunglasses; the inmates got prison outfits, ID numbers, and cells.

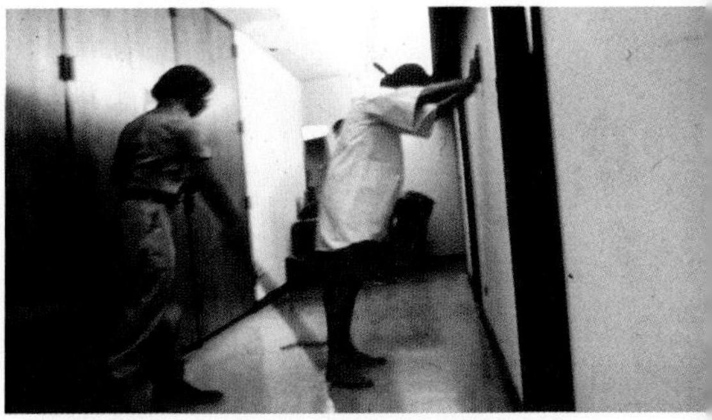

The Stanford Prison Experiment, conducted in the 1970s, demonstrated the power of social roles. College students randomly assigned to play the roles of prisoners or guards allowed those roles to impact their behavior to such an extent that even the researchers were surprised. Philip G. Zimbardo, Inc.

The experiment was scheduled to go on for weeks, but within a few days, the guards' behavior became degrading, humiliating, and abusive toward the prisoners. At times, they punished prisoners' behavior by denying them food and access to bathrooms; stripping their clothes off; spraying them with fire extinguishers; taking their beds away; and forcing them to clean toilets with their bare hands. When the complaints from the inmates about mistreatment by the guards intensified into rebellion—not to mention their physical and psychological health was at risk—the experimenters stopped the study after only 6 days (Zimbardo, 1972; Zimbardo et al., 1973; Banuazizi & Movahedi, 1975). The important point here is that the guards were just *playing the role* of prison guard. In real life, they were Stanford University students, but the role of prison guard altered their attitudes and behaviors to the point of intimidating and endangering their own classmates.

A real-life version of the Stanford prison experiments seemed to unfold in 2003, when photos were revealed of U.S. soldiers' treatment of Iraqi prisoners at Abu Ghraib prison near Baghdad. Humiliation, degradation, and abuse were on display. The soldiers took prisoners' clothes away, posed them in demeaning positions, blindfolded them, and piled them on top of each other. Among the most disturbing images in these photos were the expressions of approval and even joy on the faces of the soldiers, most of whom had no record of similar behavior before being put into this situation. Like the Stanford experiments, the Abu Ghraib photos highlighted the influence of the social role.

Let's remember that social role can push people to perform wonderful behaviors too. We often see people performing heroic actions that are expected of people in certain positions. For example, first responders of all kinds, including firefighters and police officers, ran into the twin towers on 9/11 when thousands were running out, giving their lives in the name of their roles. Sully Sullenberger, the pilot who saved all 155 aboard by landing his powerless plane on the Hudson River in January 2009, walked up and down the passenger aisle to make sure all passengers and crew

door-in-the-face technique
A persuasion strategy in which one person gets another person to reject a large request before making a smaller one.

lowball technique
A persuasion strategy in which one person quotes another person a low price to get an initial agreement and then raises the price.

social role
A title, position, or status that carries expectations for acceptable behavior.

were out safely. He did this *twice* before exiting the plane himself, all in the name of doing his job.

Cognitive Dissonance: Attitudes in Conflict

Cognitive dissonance is the discomfort caused by having an attitude that contradicts another attitude or a behavior (**Figure 13.3**). You may be familiar with "dissonance" in music: a pair of sounds that are not in harmony with each other, and can be unpleasant to experience. The same holds true for cognitive dissonance. We prefer for our attitudes (or our attitude–behavior combinations) to be in harmony with each other. At times, however, we sense that they are not, and that experience is indeed unpleasant. Like saying one thing when you believe another, it is an inner hypocrisy that demands to be resolved (Nail & Boniecki, 2011; Cooper, 2012; Aronson, 1999).

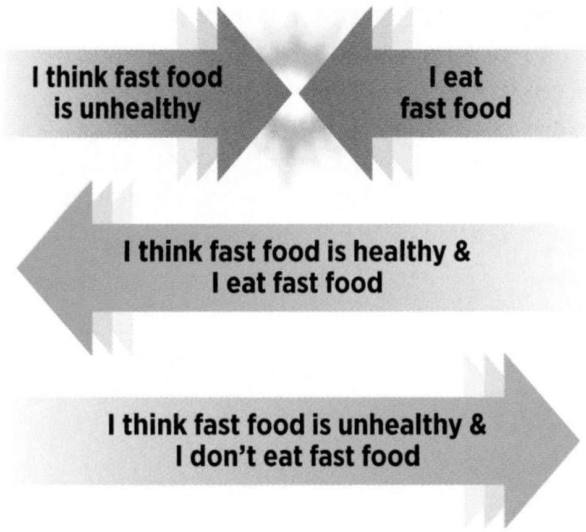

FIGURE 13.3 Cognitive Dissonance. The first row illustrates cognitive dissonance: an attitude and a behavior at odds with each other. The next two rows show two ways that cognitive dissonance could be resolved—either a change in the attitude or a change in the behavior.

For example, consider Keith, a serious long-distance runner and new father. Since completing college on a cross-country scholarship, he has trained 6 days a week year-round and has completed two marathons per year. This commitment reflects Keith's attitude toward his sport: "Running is my life. It's my top priority." A few months ago, Keith's wife gave birth to their first child, a daughter. Keith has long wanted to have children, and is thrilled about the baby's arrival. His attitude about fatherhood? "Fatherhood is my life. It's my top priority." Obviously, the baby's arrival has caused Keith some cognitive dissonance. He can't have two top priorities, and the coexistence of his commitments to his daughter and his sport has him stressed out. When he chooses running, he feels bad about neglecting his daughter; when he chooses his daughter, he feels bad about neglecting his running.

How can Keith resolve his cognitive dissonance? Social psychologists see three solutions: (1) Change Attitude A; (2) change Attitude B; or (3) come up with an Attitude C to resolve the tension between A and B (Harmon-Jones & Mills, 1999; Cooper, 1999). In Keith's case, changing Attitude A would mean that he drops running as his top priority and becomes a fully devoted father. Changing Attitude B would mean that he drops being a father as his top priority and becomes a fully devoted runner. Attitude C could take a number of forms, each of which is effective only if it is believable: "I should keep running, for my daughter's sake. It keeps me happy and healthy as a dad, and sets a great example for her." Or, "Not running 6 days a week doesn't mean I'm not dedicated to the sport. I'm just taking a break, for a good reason." Or, "I'll invest in a good jogging stroller and take her along with me!"

The study of cognitive dissonance has a long history, stretching back to the classic 1950s work of Leon Festinger (1957, 1964). This field of study centers on the question that begins one of Festinger's most famous studies: "What happens to a person's private opinion if he is forced to do or say something contrary to that opinion?" (Festinger & Carlsmith, 1959, p. 203). In this study, participants were required to do monotonous, hour-long tasks that involved placing wooden pegs into slots over and over. The task was boring by design, but when it was over, the researchers asked each participant to tell the participants waiting outside the room that the task was enjoyable. Half of the participants were paid $1 to offer this false opinion; the other half were paid $20. Guess which group had a more positive attitude about the task? You might expect the $20 group, since they were paid so much more, but the results indicated that the $1 group actually had a much more positive attitude about the task. Researchers suggested the $1 group had to convince themselves that they actually liked the task to resolve the cognitive dissonance between "I thought that task was boring" and "I'm not a liar." The $20 group didn't experience cognitive dissonance, because they could rationalize their behavior with the large sum of money.

In the decades since Festinger's studies, many other researchers have reconfirmed the power of cognitive dissonance to motivate changes in attitude and behavior (Cooper, 2007). In many cases, this cognitive dissonance has pushed individuals not toward lying, but toward more desirable behaviors (Stone & Fernandez, 2008). The basic idea is that confronting an incompatibility between your good attitude

and your bad behavior can inspire you to change the behavior for the better. For example, researchers asked college women to perform actions inconsistent with eating disorders—such as speaking highly of their own bodies while in front of a mirror—later had lower levels of attitudes consistent with eating disorders than college women who did not (Becker et al., 2010). Also, people recycle more when they are made aware of the cognitive dissonance between their positive attitude toward recycling and their lack of recycling at times, such as throwing aluminum cans or plastic bottles in the trash rather than finding a recycling bin (Fried & Aronson, 1995). Similarly, people who see themselves as financially responsible but notice some out-of-control spending on their credit card statements can be motivated to spend more responsibly (Davies & Lea, 1995).

Some clever researchers have even found neurological evidence of cognitive dissonance. They slid participants into an uncomfortable fMRI scanner and asked them to convince the next participants that they were actually comfortable. fMRI images taken during the process showed that a particular part of the brain's frontal lobe (the anterior cingulate cortex) was activated during the process. The same part of the brain was not activated in participants who were paid to make the fake positive statements, and so experienced less cognitive dissonance (van Veen et al., 2009).

There is an alternative explanation for the attitude change found with cognitive dissonance. *Self-perception theory* states that our attitudes form after our actions, rather than before them (Bem, 1967). People behave in a particular way, then work backward to figure out what attitude they held before performing that behavior. For example, if you find yourself driving way over the speed limit and weaving through traffic without wearing a seatbelt, you conclude, "I guess I value excitement over safety." Self-perception theory is quite consistent with the "fake it till you make it" approach to life: Behave like the kind of person you wish you were, and soon enough, you'll become that person.

cognitive dissonance
The discomfort caused by having an attitude that contradicts another attitude or a behavior.

social influence
Any way in which the presence of other people influences one's thoughts, feelings, or behavior.

CHECK YOUR LEARNING:

13.1 What is social cognition?

13.2 What are attributions?

13.3 What is the fundamental attribution error?

13.4 What are attitudes, and how do people try to change them?

13.5 What is cognitive dissonance, and how can people resolve it?

Social Influence: How We Influence Each Other

Intentionally or unintentionally, human beings influence each other's behavior. In some cases, a group sways you. In other cases, one person commands you. In still others, your mere awareness of other people modifies how you think and act. To illustrate, imagine yourself spending a full week completely *alone*. You are absolutely inaccessible, with no contact (in person, on the phone, online) with anyone else. The difference between the way you would behave in such isolation and the way you behave in your usual, day-to-day life illustrates **social influence**: any way in which the presence of other people influences your thoughts, feelings, or behavior. Let's explore some ways that having others around you could cause you to conform, obey, or otherwise affect what you do.

YOU WILL LEARN:

13.6 what social influence is.

13.7 what conformity is, and when and why it happens.

13.8 what obedience is

13.9 to what extent people obey authority.

YOU WILL LEARN: (*Continued*)

13.10 how groups can help or hinder individual performance.

13.11 what processes affect group decision making.

Conformity: Going Along with the Group

You walk into the psychology experiment and take a seat. There are other participants in the room with you, about a half dozen or so. The experimenter explains that he will show you a straight line of a particular length (the "standard" line), and then show you three "comparison" lines of varying lengths. Your job is to identify which comparison line is closest in length to the standard line. No problem, you say to yourself. You take a look at the first set of lines and the correct answer is obvious: Line A. The experimenter calls on four other participants first, and gets the same response four times in a row: "Line A, Line A, Line A, Line A." It's your turn now. You say Line A. It's a no-brainer.

The second set of lines has an equally obvious correct answer: Line B. (**Figure 13.4**). The experimenter calls on participants in the same order as before. The first participant answers: Line C. You're surprised. You take a closer look, and the answer is still obviously Line B. The next participant agrees with the first participant: Line C. Now you're puzzled. The next two participants concur with the first two: Line C, Line C. Now it's your turn, and you're bewildered. Your eyes are telling you that absolutely, without question, Line B is correct. But the group has spoken: unanimously, they say Line C. How do you answer? Do you go with what you think you know, despite being the only one in the group to do so, or do you go along with the consensus?

MY TAKE VIDEO 13.2

Conformity

"I tend to witness a lot of conformity using social media..."

YOUTUBE: http://tiny.cc/mytake
LAUNCHPAD: launchpadworks.com

This is precisely the methodology used by Solomon Asch in his classic 1950s studies (Asch, 1951, 1955, 1956). Asch was examining **conformity**: changes in an individual's behavior to correspond to the behavior of a group of other people. In these studies, Asch made it seem like there was a roomful of participants. In reality, there was only one participant: you. The others were actors (confederates, as psychology researchers call them) whom Asch had instructed to provide answers to set you up for the decision about conforming. His findings were quite interesting. About 37% of the time, participants conformed. They went along with the group's opinion even when that opinion was obviously wrong. Only about 25% of participants never conformed to any of the 12 situations in which all the confederates answered incorrectly.

Asch's studies apply to many situations in our daily lives, most of which are much more consequential than choosing among straight lines. For example, Phoebe, a 16-year-old high school junior, knows very well the dangers of bulimia. She fully realizes that the pattern of bingeing on huge amounts of food and then purging to prevent weight gain is associated with great physical and psychological dangers. But many of the girls on her cheerleading squad binge and purge. Some make themselves vomit, some exercise excessively, and one even abuses laxatives. They all see it as the right way to stay thin. What will Phoebe do? What would you do? Researchers have found

FIGURE 13.4 Asch's Classic Studies of Conformity. The person in the middle of the photo is the actual participant in Asch's classic study. The other two are actors (confederates) instructed to provide the same incorrect answer when asked to choose a line (A, B, or C) that matches the length of the target line (to the left). Source: Asch, 1951, 1955, 1956.

that for young women who develop bulimia, conformity to peers' behavior is often a powerful reason why (Mason & Chaney, 1996).

A recent study creatively adapted Asch's method of studying conformity, using medical students as the participants (Beran et al., 2013). The medical students' task was to choose the right location to insert a needle. Specifically, the students were learning to insert a syringe into a specific spot near the kneecap to draw fluid, which is commonly done when testing for arthritis. Some students practiced on a fake knee that was brand new; others practiced on a fake knee that already had holes—in an incorrect location—supposedly from previous students working on the same task. The results? Students working on the "used" knee were more than 50% more likely than students working on the "new" knee to make an insertion in the wrong location. Those preexisting holes served the same function as the confederates' answers in Asch's original experiment: They caused the participants to doubt their own judgment and feel pressure to go along with what others had done.

Why do people conform? Why don't they just do what they want and ignore the group?

One explanation for conformity is that it helps us belong to social groups and avoid the pain and loneliness of a solitary life.
PeopleImages.com/DigitalVision/Getty Images

Inclusion in social groups is such a primary, vital human need that it often outweighs other demands (Baumeister & Leary, 1995; Fiske, 2010). We touched on group inclusion under a different name—*belongingness*—in our discussion of Abraham Maslow's hierarchy of needs back in Chapter 8 (Motivation and Emotion). This need may have evolved from our prehistoric ancestors, for whom exclusion from the social group could mean exclusion from food, shelter, and possibly even life itself. Our brains certainly reveal biological indicators of the importance of group inclusion: Getting kicked out of a group activates the same pain-related brain areas as getting kicked in the shin, and forming friendships produces the same pain-killing substance (opioids) as morphine (Eisenberger et al., 2003; MacDonald & Leary, 2005; Panksepp et al., 1985). No wonder the drive to stay connected to the group makes us question our own better judgment.

The deep-seated, evolutionary nature of the drive for inclusion in the social group doesn't exclude more conscious thoughts about the benefits of staying "in" with the group and the drawbacks of being ousted (Levine & Kerr, 2007). For example, Joe, a 21-year-old college junior and fraternity member, is being asked to participate in a hazing ritual for new pledges. His frat brothers are all in favor of the hazing, but Joe finds it distasteful and dangerous. Joe calculates what he stands to lose if he refuses to go along and his frat brothers then turn on him: friends, dating opportunities, social status, academic assistance, self-esteem, and more. He also calculates what he stands to gain: staying true to his own judgment, possibly helping out a new pledge. For many Joes, the pros outweigh the cons, and they choose to conform to the group. Asch and many more recent researchers have identified certain factors that can increase or decrease the chances that a person will conform to a group. **Table 13.2** summarizes their findings.

Another reason why people may conform is that they don't know how to behave, so they mimic those around them. This type of conformity stems from a different kind of situation from the one in the Asch studies. If you were a participant in the Asch studies, you would know which line was correct, but you might choose to override that knowledge to fit in with the norm of the group. That kind of conformity is *normative conformity*.

In other situations, you are clueless about what is correct. There is no knowledge to override. You seek information from those around you about how to behave, and by following their lead, you conform to their way of behaving. Your main goal isn't so much to be liked by everyone else as simply to do what you need to do to get through the situation. That kind of conformity is *informational conformity* (Madon et al., 2008; Cialdini & Goldstein, 2004; Deutch & Gerard, 1955; Sherif, 1936). For example, imagine

conformity
Changes in an individual's behavior to correspond to the behavior of a group of other people.

TABLE 13.2: Conformity Is Most Likely When...
the group includes at least 3–5 members.
the group contains no other dissenting members.
the group is highly valued by the person.
the group is working toward a single, shared goal.
the person has low self-esteem.
the person has low status within the group.
the person's behaviors are visible to the group.
the person's alternatives outside the group are minimal.

(As summarized in Levine & Kerr, 2007, and Hogg, 2010).

yourself visiting downtown Chicago for the first time. It is lunchtime, there are dozens of restaurants within walking distance, but you don't know which to choose. How will you decide? You might walk a few blocks, noticing which restaurants seem busy (a good sign) and which seem abandoned (a bad sign). You might use the Yelp app on your phone to read reviews others have posted about nearby restaurants. You might text your cousin who used to live in downtown Chicago and could offer a suggestion. Any of these strategies help you learn where the locals like to eat. If you then use that information to make your decision, you are likely to conform to their preferences by choosing a restaurant they endorse.

A final note about conformity: It may be a universal human need, but it varies from one culture to the next. Researchers looked back on 133 conformity studies from 17 countries that used similar methodologies to Asch's line judgment task (Bond & Smith, 1996). They found that conformity levels were consistently higher in collectivist countries than in individualistic countries. This should come as no surprise, since collectivist cultures (such as China, Japan, and other Asian countries) emphasize group harmony and value compliance to a greater extent than individualistic cultures (like the United States, England, and other Western countries). It has also been found that conformity rates in the United States have dropped since the 1950s, when Asch's studies were conducted, presumably because the values of our society have moved toward greater individualism (Bond & Smith, 1996; Lalancette & Standing, 1990; Nicholson et al., 1985).

DIVERSITY MATTERS

Obedience: Following Orders

Solomon Asch had a graduate student, Stanley Milgram, whose own research in social psychology became even more widely known than that of his mentor (Prislin & Crano, 2012). Milgram studied **obedience**: changes in an individual's behavior to comply with the demands of an authority figure. Obedience differs from conformity in important ways. We conform to groups of peers, whose status is equal to ours. We obey superiors, who hold positions of power over us (Hogg, 2010). Milgram's obedience studies focused on following orders.

As a Jewish person whose parents grew up during the Holocaust, Milgram felt compelled to understand how Nazi soldiers could have committed so many heartless, vicious murders of Jewish people. Many presumed these Nazi soldiers were driven by pure evil, but Milgram wondered about the role of obedience to authority. His idea seems consistent with the comments of Adolf Eichmann, a prominent Nazi who was responsible for the death of millions. Eichmann later explained that he was "just following orders" (Blass, 2004; Cesarani, 2004).

Milgram's method of studying obedience was both ingenious and controversial (Milgram, 1963, 1965, 1974; Lunt, 2009). (In fact, his studies, which took place in the 1960s, deceived and distressed participants; they would almost certainly not be allowed today.) Here's how the Milgram experiments worked, step by step, from the participants' point of view:

1. You respond to a newspaper ad for a study at Yale University involving "memory and learning." As a participant, you will be paid $4.00 plus 50¢ for travel expenses.
2. When you arrive, you meet two men. One, wearing a white coat, is clearly in charge of the study; we'll call him the Authority. The other appears to be another participant, just like you. The Authority explains that one of the participants will be the "Teacher" and the other the "Learner" in this study. You randomly choose slips of paper to determine who will play each role, and you get "Teacher."
3. What you don't realize at this point is that the slips of paper were rigged, and the "Learner" is actually an actor (confederate) who is in on Milgram's scheme. The study actually has nothing to do with memory or learning, but everything to do with obedience to authority.
4. The Authority explains that you will read pairs of words to the Learner. Then you will quiz him by saying the first word and expecting him to say the second (for example, "table/chair," or "solid/striped"). When the Learner gets a pair right, you do nothing. When he gets a pair wrong, you jolt him with electric shock as punishment.
5. You see the Authority take the Learner into the next room and attach his arm to a metal plate that delivers the shock. (In reality, no shock is delivered, but you don't know that yet.) The Learner mentions that he has a slight heart condition; the Authority replies that the shocks will be painful but not cause permanent damage. In your room, you sit before an electric shock generator that can deliver a range of shocks, labeled both in numbers (15–450 volts) and in words (from "slight" to "danger: severe" to the highest level, "XXX," as shown in **Figure 13.5**). You can't see the Learner in the next room, but you can hear him.
6. The Authority instructs you to begin the word-pair learning exercise. You do so, and the Learner gets the first few correct. But then he starts making mistakes. The Authority tells you to deliver the lowest level of shock for the first mistake; with each additional mistake, he tells you to increase the voltage by 15 volts. If you resist, the Authority insists, stating, "It is absolutely essential that you continue," or "You have no other choice; you must go on."
7. As the voltage increases, so do the Learner's reactions to the shock you deliver (all of which, of course, are simulated and performed according to a script of which you are unaware). At 75 volts, he grunts in pain; at 150 volts, he says "Experimenter! That's all. Get me out of here…My heart's starting to bother me. I refuse to go on." At 300 volts, the Learner screams, "I absolutely refuse to answer any more…You can't hold me here." At 330 volts, he shrieks, "Let me out of here. My heart's bothering me… Let me out of here! Let me out!" From 330 volts all the way up to 450 volts, he's completely silent, leaving you to perhaps wonder if he's still conscious or even alive.

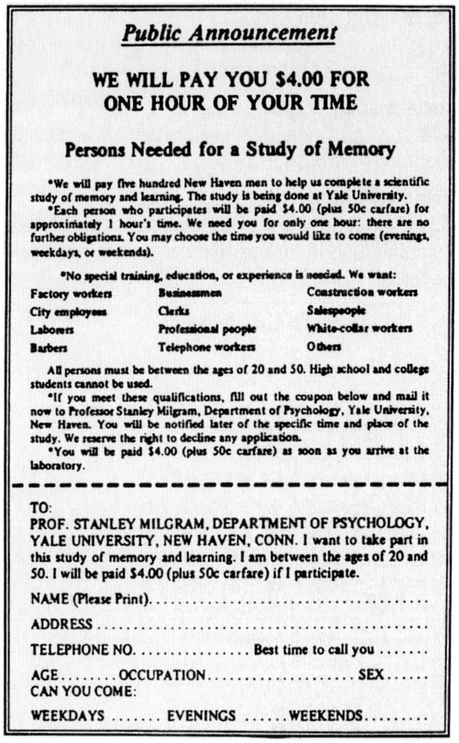

Public Announcement

WE WILL PAY YOU $4.00 FOR ONE HOUR OF YOUR TIME

Persons Needed for a Study of Memory

*We will pay five hundred New Haven men to help us complete a scientific study of memory and learning. The study is being done at Yale University.

*Each person who participates will be paid $4.00 (plus 50c carfare) for approximately 1 hour's time. We need you for only one hour: there are no further obligations. You may choose the time you would like to come (evenings, weekdays, or weekends).

*No special training, education, or experience is needed. We want:

Factory workers	Businessmen	Construction workers
City employees	Clerks	Salespeople
Laborers	Professional people	White-collar workers
Barbers	Telephone workers	Others

All persons must be between the ages of 20 and 50. High school and college students cannot be used.

*If you meet these qualifications, fill out the coupon below and mail it now to Professor Stanley Milgram, Department of Psychology, Yale University, New Haven. You will be notified later of the specific time and place of the study. We reserve the right to decline any application.

*You will be paid $4.00 (plus 50c carfare) as soon as you arrive at the laboratory.

TO:
PROF. STANLEY MILGRAM, DEPARTMENT OF PSYCHOLOGY, YALE UNIVERSITY, NEW HAVEN, CONN. I want to take part in this study of memory and learning. I am between the ages of 20 and 50. I will be paid $4.00 (plus 50c carfare) if I participate.

NAME (Please Print)…………

ADDRESS…………

TELEPHONE NO. ………… Best time to call you ……

AGE…… OCCUPATION………… SEX……
CAN YOU COME:

WEEKDAYS …… EVENINGS …… WEEKENDS……

This is the ad that Stanley Milgram used to recruit participants for his famous study in the early 1960s. Although the ad claimed that the study focused on memory, it actually focused on obedience. Its results illustrated that people often obey authority figures even when their behaviors appear to hurt other people.

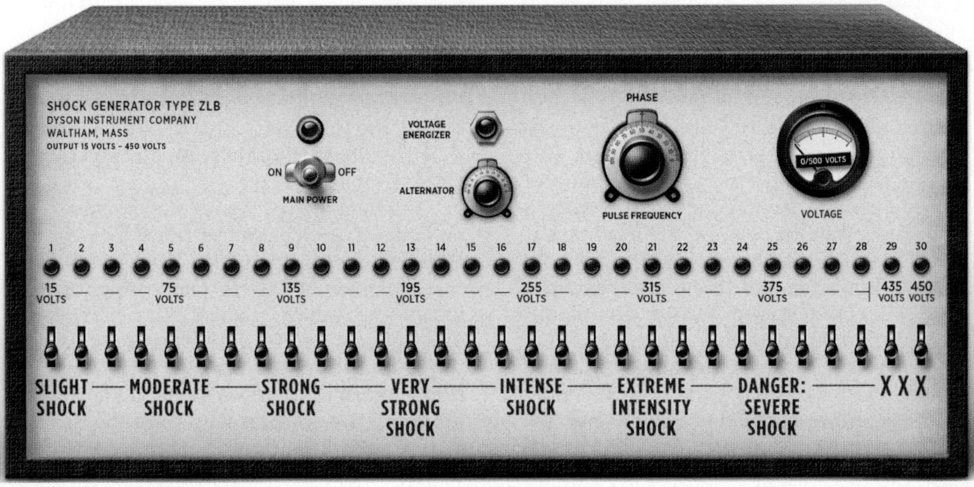

FIGURE 13.5 Milgram's "Shock Generator." Most participants in Milgram's famous study obeyed orders to shock another person all the way up to the XXX level on the far right of this machine.

obedience
Changes in an individual's behavior to comply with the demands of an authority figure.

social facilitation
An increase in individual performance caused by the presence of other people.

social loafing
A decrease in individual performance when tasks are done in groups.

deindividuation
A loss of identity and accountability experienced by individuals in groups that can lead to atypical behavior.

The big question, of course, was how far the Teacher would go in delivering the electric shocks to the Learner. At what point would the Teacher refuse to obey? Prior to the study, Milgram posed this question to mental health professionals and college students, and they unanimously agreed that no participants would obey all the way to the maximum shock. Many predicted that they would disobey as soon as the Learner made his first request to stop (Milgram, 1974; Funder & Fast, 2010). Those predictions were shockingly wrong. The vast majority of the Teachers went well past the Learner's first request to stop. None of them stopped before 300 volts. Only 38% stopped at all—which means that 62% shocked the Learner all the way to the maximum, 450-volt, XXX level! Many participants tried to reason or argue with the Authority, and some showed signs of anxiety or anguish, but still did not stop obeying the Authority (Milgram, 1974).

Later studies by Milgram and others (often using methods that were more humane to participants) found similar results under similar conditions, confirming Milgram's original findings (Milgram, 1965; Blass, 1999a, b, 2009; Burger, 2009). They did, however, identify some factors that influence the likelihood of obedience. Some factors related to the person being ordered to act. For example, people who have progressed to high levels of Kohlberg's moral development scale (as covered in Chapter 9) were more likely to disobey the authority figure than those whose sense of morality was less developed (Kohlberg, 1981; Feather, 1988).

Other factors that influenced obedience relate to the authority figure. Obedience is greater when the authority figure is physically close and visible (as opposed to far away or invisible), viewed as an expert possessing legitimate power (as opposed to being a fraud), and associated with a respected institution, as Yale was for Milgram's studies (Blass, 1999a; Blass & Schmidt, 2001). Still other factors that influence obedience relate to the situation. Disobedience grows when others disobey, the victim can be seen and heard, or the authority figure is challenged by another authority figure (Milgram, 1974).

Obedience research has enlightened us about the process by which people do despicable things. To place all the blame on the cruelty of the perpetrators would be a mistake. In fact, it is an example of the fundamental attribution error we discussed just a few pages ago—emphasizing a person's traits over the situation when explaining the behavior of others. At times, those people may be following the orders of authority figures rather than their own beliefs when they commit monstrous acts such as the Holocaust killings, which inspired Milgram's experiments. Of course, this explanation makes it difficult to know exactly whom to hold responsible: the people who do the deed, or the people who order it. (See the From Research to Real Life box for a contemporary example of this debate.)

FROM RESEARCH TO REAL LIFE

Milgram, Obedience, and the NFL's Bounty Scandal

From 2009–2011, defensive players on the New Orleans Saints deliberately tried to injure players on opposing teams. Their primary goals were to deliver "knock out" or "cart off" hits to offensive stars, typically running backs and quarterbacks. It is believed that the players received cash bonuses for such hits. For example, there was supposedly a $10,000 bounty for a hit on Minnesota Vikings quarterback Brett Favre.

After an investigation, the NFL commissioner's office handed down significant punishments to all the players and coaches involved. Four players received suspensions, including one for a full season. Coaches who orchestrated the bounty system were also punished. Defensive coordinator Gregg Williams was thought to be the primary force behind the plot, and he received a suspension for an indefinite period of time. Head coach Sean Payton was presumed to be in on the bounties as well, and he was suspended for a full year.

Months later, after the players appealed, the NFL commissioner's office completely overturned the player's suspensions. However, the coaches' penalties remained unchanged. Essentially, the reversal implied that the players should not suffer any consequences because they were following orders, doing their best to perform the behaviors that their superiors expected of them. Some sportswriters even made explicit connections between the players' behavior, the behavior of Nazi soldiers during the Holocaust, and the behavior of participants in Milgram's obedience study (Miller & Igel, 2012).

The behavior of Saints players and coaches, as well as the responses by the NFL commissioner's office, raise important questions about who is responsible for loathsome behavior when that behavior was commanded by authority figures. Some argue that the NFL's final decision was right—those players were only doing their jobs, and the coaches who gave the orders deserve all of the punishment. Others argue that the players should receive some of the blame as well: They could have collectively rejected the bounty system or reported it to league authorities rather than accepting and complying with it.

Performing Tasks in Groups

Performing a behavior alone can be different from performing the same behavior in front of other people. Sometimes, the company of others helps.

Social Facilitation. Social psychologists call this boost **social facilitation**: an increase in individual performance caused by the presence of other people. Social facilitation is most likely to occur when the task is easy and simple (Levine & Moreland, 2012; Hackman & Katz, 2010). For example, runners typically run faster times at meets, surrounded by spectators and other runners, than they do on solo training runs (Strube et al., 1981; Worringham & Messick, 1983). Call it adrenaline or simply being hyped up: The energy of the other people causes an arousal that translates into improved performance.

But don't people sometimes choke when they perform in front of crowds?

People do choke sometimes, but that's typically when the task is challenging, and something they haven't fully mastered yet. In those cases, arousal causes them to stumble rather than pick up the pace. For example, consider people chosen to sing the national anthem before sporting events. Some are experienced vocalists who have sung the anthem in similar circumstances many times; others are novices singing live in front of a big crowd for the first time. Any guess who's more likely to fumble through it?

Social Loafing. Related to choking is **social loafing**: a decrease in individual performance when tasks are done in groups. The difference between choking and social loafing is that choking takes place when we feel we are being watched and evaluated by an audience, but social loafing takes place when we simply find ourselves in a group of people that is collectively responsible for the task (Karau & Williams , 1993; Latané et al., 1979; Ingham et al., 1974). Think about group projects you've worked on with classmates for which all members of the group will receive the same grade. Or when you and your siblings were collectively told to clean up the house, with no individual chores assigned. Those are the kinds of situations much more likely to produce social loafing—slacking off, basically.

Researchers have found that social loafing is especially likely to take place when the individual feels his or her output is not distinguishable from the output of others (Harkins & Jackson, 1985). For example, when participants in one study were asked to shout as loudly as possible, the volume of each individual shouter depended significantly on the number of people in his or her group of shouters and whether the experimenters said they were being measured as a group or as individuals. Specifically, they shouted less loudly when they were in large groups and when they were told the volume was going to be measured only as a group rather than individually (Williams et al., 1981).

Deindividuation. Sometimes, we find ourselves in groups in which we don't stand out in any particular way, just another face in the crowd. Such situations are likely to produce **deindividuation**: a loss of identity and accountability experienced by individuals in groups that can lead to atypical behavior. For example, imagine being at a stand-up comedy show in which the house lights are down but the stage is brightly lit. A heckler's voice emerges, an unidentifiable voice shrouded by the darkness. He heckles the comedian unmercifully until suddenly the comedian breaks from his routine, points, and tells the spotlight operator, "Shine some light over here. Let's find this guy." Not surprisingly, the heckling stops. His bravery was fueled by his anonymity, but now that he can be identified, he is silent.

Deindividuation inspires other behaviors that are far more sinister than bothering a comedian. Soldiers often feel deindividuated in their uniforms and short haircuts, which make them difficult to distinguish from their fellow fighters and therefore more likely to behave aggressively. Ku Klux Klan hoods and warrior face paint common in

CHAPTER APP 13.1

Social Facilitation

CoachMe Habit Tracker

Preview one of the links and consider the following questions.

WEBSITE: http://tiny.cc/mvi7jy

ANDROID: http://tiny.cc/gab8iy

IPHONE: http://tiny.cc/O9a8iy

VIDEO DEMO: http://tiny.cc/chapterapps

There are many apps designed to help you track a behavior you want to do more often: work out, eat healthy, practice a musical instrument, speak a new language, etc. With CoachMe Habit Tracker, when you choose your target behavior, you become part of a community that shares the same target behavior. Users within your community can see your progress, congratulate you when you succeed, encourage you when you struggle, and offer helpful suggestions at any time. Of course, you can do the same for others in the community.

How does it APPly to your daily life?
If you were trying to increase a particular behavior, how much of a difference would it make to know that you were part of a community of people who shared the same goal? Would you expect to do better or worse if you tried to increase your behavior alone?

How does it APPly to your understanding of psychology?
How does this app affect your appreciation of *social facilitation*? In your opinion, what, *specifically*, about the presence of other people doing the same thing as you is most likely to facilitate your behavior?

Social facilitation is an increase in individual performance caused by the presence of other people. It is most likely to happen when the task is easy and simple, such as running alongside others rather than running alone. © Yon Marsh/Alamy

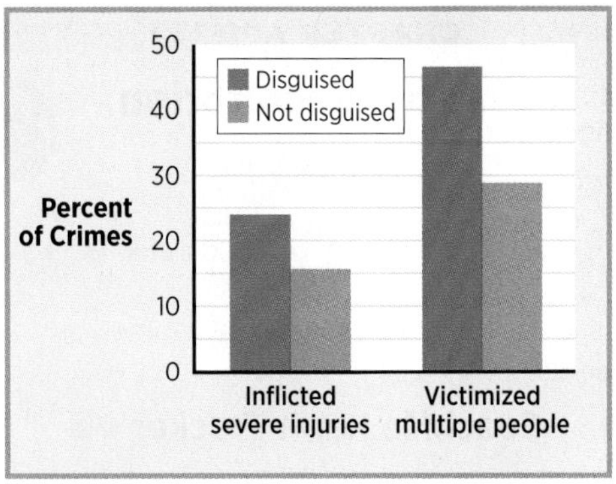

FIGURE 13.6 Deindividuation and Crime. Compared to violent criminals whose identities were visible, those in disguise—in other words, those more likely to experience *deindividuation*—are more likely to hurt multiple victims and to hurt them severely.
Data from Silke, 2003.

many tribal communities serve the same purpose (Watson, 1973). **Figure 13.6** shows data from a study of violent crimes in Ireland, which found that attackers in disguises hurt more people more severely and made more threats for future harm than those without disguises (Silke, 2003). People who pirate music, movies, and other materials online may be similarly fueled by a sense of anonymity (Hinduja, 2008). The common thread to all of these examples is the lack of inhibition that we often place on our own behavior, which can occur when we perceive ourselves as an indistinguishable member of a crowd. When we know we can't get caught or punished, we sometimes act in ways we never would otherwise (Bushman & Huesmann, 2010).

Group Decision Making

When groups work together, they often make decisions quite different from what any individual member might have made. For example, picture a city council meeting in which seven council members discuss how to spend the money in their budget: new playground equipment, a new police cruiser, improvements to highway signs, better exercise equipment at the community center, or something else?

Groupthink. The obvious goal for the city council just described is to make a wise decision, but another goal (often unspoken) is for the group to be cooperative toward each other. Usually, both goals can be accomplished, but if cooperation starts to outweigh wise decision making, we get **groupthink**: a phenomenon that occurs when group members value getting along with each other more than finding the best solution. If this happened in the city council meeting, there is a good chance that the first suggestion—"Let's get the kids a new playground!"—will be met by one "yes" after another. Eventually, the group is unanimous and happy, and the meeting is adjourned. Never mind that the police force needed that new car much more desperately than the kids needed a new playground. Pushing for the new police car would have caused a clash at the meeting, and that's to be avoided at all costs when groupthink is involved.

LIFE HACK 13.2

When you are part of a group, remember the potential problems of groupthink. Allow everyone to voice their opinions, even if those opinions differ from the opinions of others.

(Janis, 1982; Nemeth et al., 2001; Nemeth & Rogers, 2011)

When groupthink happens at higher levels of government, the consequences can be severe. The term *groupthink* was actually coined as a description of the massive Bay of Pigs debacle that President John F. Kennedy and his inner circle collectively decided upon in 1961. The idea was to enlist hundreds of Cuban immigrants to invade Cuba and overthrow Fidel Castro, but it failed miserably. Many of the invaders were captured or killed, and no political ground was gained by the United States. In retrospect, it seems obvious that someone in the room should have spoken up about the plan's flaws, but no one did. They were too concerned with maintaining the unity and togetherness they felt as a group to raise a different point of view (Janis, 1982).

Groupthink happens in the workplace as well. In 1985, Coca-Cola decided to change its formula and replace one of the most successful products in history with "New Coke." It was a disaster. Loyal Coke drinkers resented the company for changing their beloved drink, and many flocked to rival Pepsi. (Shortly, "New Coke" was gone, and Coca-Cola classic was back.) Prior to the switch to "New Coke," there were signs in the market research that a backlash might happen, but the executives at Coca-Cola remained in agreement and a bad group decision was made (Schindler, 1992).

To combat groupthink, it is wise to encourage disagreement within a group, and to reassure members that they will be valued, rather than shunned, for offering opposing opinions. It is also helpful to run a group's decision past other experts on the subject—outsiders for whom getting along with those group members is unimportant—to see if they too would give it the go-ahead (Janis, 1982; Nemeth et al., 2001; Nemeth & Rogers, 2011).

Group Polarization. Another common occurrence in group decision making is **group polarization**: the tendency for a group's attitudes to become more extreme as a result of group discussions. For example, at first, a group of neighbors

kind of lean toward a particular candidate for mayor, but then become that candidate's most hardworking campaigners after several chats on the subject. At first, a group of people are *kind of* prejudiced, but then become even more prejudiced after sharing their opinions with each other (Myers & Bishop, 1970; Myers & Lamm, 1976).

Group polarization can happen to two opposing groups at the same time, causing them to distance themselves from each other even more. (The term *polarization*, after all, refers to *poles*, or extreme opposites, like the North Pole or South Pole on a globe.) For example, politics today are much more polarized than they were a generation ago, largely because of the growth of media in which people can immerse themselves in exclusively one side of the debate. Web sites, talk show hosts, and even entire news organizations filter in their own opinion and filter out any viewpoint that doesn't conform. As a result, conservatives get more conservative, liberals get more liberal, and the middle ground becomes barren (Evans, 2009).

groupthink
A phenomenon that occurs when group members value getting along with each other more than finding the best solution.

group polarization
The tendency for a group's attitudes to become more extreme as a result of group discussions.

impression formation
The initial appraisal, or "first impression," that a person makes of another person.

CHECK YOUR LEARNING:

13.6 What is social influence?

13.7 What is conformity, and how does it differ between cultures?

13.8 What is obedience?

13.9 What did the classic obedience studies by Stanley Milgram reveal about the extent to which people obey authority?

13.10 How can the presence of other people help or hinder individual performance?

13.11 How can groupthink or group polarization influence group decision making?

Social Relations: How We Relate to Each Other

Love, hate, and everything in between: We form all kinds of relationships with each other. Social psychologists study how these relationships develop, and uncover the reasons why we help or hurt each other. Specifically, they examine how we form *first impressions*, how we develop (and fight against) *prejudices*, why we behave *aggressively*, and why we feel *attraction* and *romantic love*.

YOU WILL LEARN:

13.12 how first impressions are made.

13.13 what prejudice, stereotypes, and discrimination are.

13.14 how prejudice, stereotypes, and discrimination develop.

13.15 how to overcome prejudice.

13.16 why people behave aggressively.

13.17 what attracts people to one another.

First Impressions

All relationships begin with **impression formation**: the initial appraisal, or "first impression," that a person makes of another person. You know from firsthand experience how quickly you form impressions of other people, and how strong those impressions can be. Imagine meeting a woman at a party. Within seconds, you've gathered a massive amount of information (Kelley, 1950; Eiser, 2012; Uleman & Saribay; 2012). You realize that this information—her clothes, her hairstyle, her attractiveness, her age, her voice, the way she carries herself—is all superficial and preliminary. You don't really *know* her, but you can't help but to start form an opinion.

According to research by social psychologists, the factors that influence that first impression are quite predictable. Physical attractiveness, for example, is a powerful predictor of a positive first impression. Compared to less attractive people, highly attractive people have more money, more jobs, and more sex (Macrae & Quadflieg, 2010). These findings may relate to the fact that good looks enable a person to make a good first impression with people who might provide these benefits. Your attractiveness is defined in large part by your face, which people may size up in as little as

As Chris Rock has joked about impression formation, "You can't get nobody being *you*. You got to *lie* to get somebody. You can't get nobody looking like you look, acting like you act, sounding like you sound. That's right—when you meet somebody for the first time, you're not meeting *them*: you're meeting their *representative*." Source: Chris Rock, "Women Lie". Kevin Mazur/Getty Images for KCA

one-tenth of a second (Locher et al., 1993; Olson & Marshuetz, 2005). (This high-speed face processing is undoubtedly another evolutionary gift from our ancestors—the quicker you can assess the face of another person, the quicker you can react if that face indicates danger [Neuberg et al., 2010; Kenrick, 2012]). In general, the attractiveness of a face depends upon its bilateral symmetry (how equivalent the left and right halves are) and the extent to which each facial feature falls close to the average or prototype for the person's age, gender, and ethnicity (Rhodes, 2006; Thornhill & Gangestad, 1999). Other key facial features include healthy skin and teeth, good grooming, and a friendly expression (Willis et al., 2008; Jones et al., 2004).

DIVERSITY MATTERS

Of course, your body is important too. Culturally, there is quite a bit of variation in terms of bodily attractiveness. Across genders, ethnicities, countries, and time periods, different body types have been preferred (Anderson et al., 1992). However, in contemporary Western culture, people who are obese or overweight are often viewed in unflattering ways. The extra weight creates a negative physical impression, as well as a negative interpersonal impression. Specifically, obese and overweight people receive higher ratings of laziness, incompetence, and boringness than physically fit people (Hebl & Turchin, 2005; Brochu & Morrison, 2007; Puhl & Brownell, 2012). The attractiveness of your body depends not only on its size and shape, but also on how it moves. In particular, men with a masculine gait and women with a feminine gait are viewed more positively than those whose walking style doesn't match their gender (Johnson & Tassinary, 2007).

We know the power of first impressions from both sides—as the person *forming* the first impression of someone else, and as the person *making* the first impression on someone else. As the maker of first impressions, we often engage in *impression management*, or attempts to improve the way we strike other people in an effort to enhance our first impression (Koslowsky & Pindek, 2011). In those crucial first seconds, we control whatever we can about what others will think of us: our hairstyle and color, our clothes, our posture, our greeting, our facial expression, and more.

Prejudice: Us Versus Them

Sometimes, our impression of a person is defined by the group to which he or she belongs. In these cases, we have preconceived ideas about the group that prevent us from appreciating the person as an individual (Dovidio et al., 2012; Yzerbyt & Demoulin, 2010). This prejudgment is better known as **prejudice**: an often negative attitude toward a social group that is formed before getting to know group members. As an example, Justine is a 20-year-old with a prejudice against older adults that wrongly casts all older adults as forgetful.

Stereotypes. Once a prejudice is in place, it produces **stereotypes**: beliefs about a group's characteristics that are applied generally, and often inaccurately, to group members. Prejudice is a general bias toward the group as a whole; stereotyping is a specific application of that bias to a person within the group. For example, Justine's prejudice against older adults becomes a stereotype when she meets 65-year-old Hannah and presumes that Hannah is forgetful before giving Hannah a chance to prove otherwise.

Stereotypes can focus on any number of characteristics, but the surface characteristics that can't be hidden—especially gender, race, and age—are the most common targets (Brewer, 1988; Fiske & Neuberg, 1990). We typically don't realize when we stereotype others. This may relate to the fact that stereotyping occurs largely in the amygdala, a part of the brain dedicated to emotional (rather than cognitive) processing. This suggests that we don't explicitly "think" stereotypes as much as we implicitly "feel" them (Andersen et al., 2007; Schultheiss & Pang, 2007; Lieberman et al., 2005; Amodio et al., 2004).

Discrimination. Together, these kinds of biased thinking cause **discrimination**: action based on prejudice or stereotypes toward a social group. Justine's prejudice and stereotyping toward Hannah produce discrimination when Justine visits the restaurant

prejudice
An often negative attitude toward a social group that is formed before getting to know group members.

stereotypes
Beliefs about a group's characteristics that are applied very generally, and often inaccurately, to group members.

discrimination
Action based on prejudice or stereotypes toward a social group.

ingroup
A social group to which a person believes he or she belongs ("us").

outgroup
A social group to which a person believes he or she does not belong ("them").

ingroup bias
The tendency to hold a more positive attitude toward the ingroup than the outgroup.

outgroup homogeneity
The assumption that all members of an outgroup are essentially similar.

where Hannah works as a server and assumes that Hannah will make mistakes with Justine's food order. Prejudice and stereotypes occur inside the mind, and might remain unknown to others. Discrimination is a behavior that others can see (Dovidio & Gaertner, 2010; Allport, 1954). Prejudice is "Black people are dangerous." Stereotyping is "DeMarko is dangerous because he's Black." Discrimination is stepping off the elevator when DeMarko steps in.

In our contemporary society, we like to think that we have progressed past prejudice, stereotypes, and discrimination. Our society is much more open-minded than it once was, but at various times in U.S. history our government has enslaved African Americans, locked Japanese citizens in internment camps, and denied women the right to vote. Today, there is evidence of more subtle bias in attitudes, beliefs, and actions all around us (Pager & Shepherd, 2008; Ross et al., 2010). For example, researchers sent résumés to companies in Chicago and Boston on which the job qualifications were equivalent, but the first names suggested African American or White ethnicity. "Brett" and "Allison" received 50% more callbacks than "Rasheed" and "Tamika" (Bertrand & Mullainathan, 2003). In another study (called "Shopping While Black"), shoppers in high-end retail stores asked a White salesperson to remove the security tag from a pair of sunglasses so they could try them on (**Figure 13.7**). The salesperson always removed the security tag, but Black shoppers were three times more likely to be stared at or followed to the mirror than White shoppers (Schreer et al., 2009).

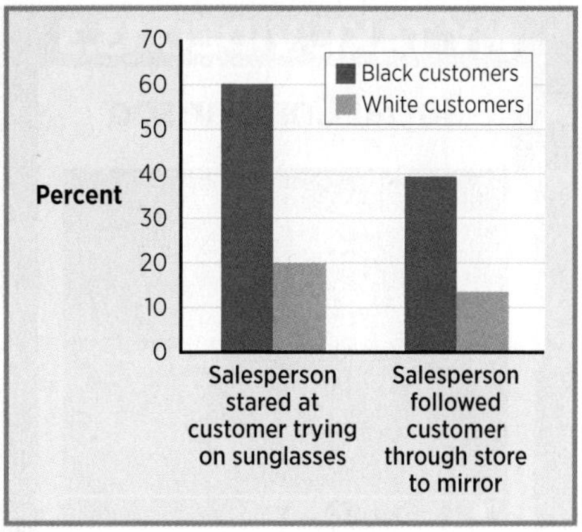

FIGURE 13.7 Shopping While Black. Salespeople at high-end stores stared at and followed a far greater percentage of Black customers than White customers, suggesting prejudice, stereotyping, and discrimination.
Data from Schreer et al., 2009.

How do people become prejudiced?

In order for prejudice to have the opportunity to form in the first place, there has to be an "us" and a "them." Social psychologists use the terms *ingroup* and *outgroup* to refer to these classifications.

Ingroups and Outgroups. An **ingroup** is a social group to which you believe you belong ("us"). An **outgroup** is a social group to which you believe you do not belong ("them"). Each of us identifies with many ingroups; for example, Michelle Obama may consider herself part of the ingroups of Americans, African Americans, women, wives, moms, Christians, Chicagoans, and first ladies.

People have a natural tendency to favor the groups to which they belong (Mullen et al., 1992; Brewer & Silver, 2006). Social psychologists call this **ingroup bias**: the tendency to hold a more positive attitude toward the ingroup than the outgroup. At the same time, we tend to overlook the diversity within outgroups, mistakenly presuming that all of its members are alike (Mullen & Hu, 1989; Simon & Mummendey, 2012). This misperception is called **outgroup homogeneity**: the assumption that all members of an outgroup are essentially similar. Social psychologists have argued that of these two biases, ingroup bias comes first, and that any outgroup homogeneity occurs only when that outgroup is perceived as a threat (Brewer, 2007; Stephan & Stephan, 2000). In other words, it is more about rooting for your own group to succeed than rooting for the other group to fail, unless the other group is directly challenging something your group holds dear, such as resources, values, or well-being. This is why most sports fans cheer for their own team to win much more often than they cheer for an opposing team to lose.

One reason why sports fans may root for their team is the ingroup bias: the tendency to hold a more positive attitude toward the ingroup (often their hometown team) than the outgroup (other teams). Leon Halip/ Getty Images

Once the ingroup–outgroup distinction breeds prejudice, additional factors allow it to thrive. One factor that enables prejudice is the natural human tendency to think *categorically* (Allport, 1954; Blashfield & Burgess, 2007). Thinking categorically means making sense of the world by placing everything and everyone we encounter in separate "boxes." For example, we categorize just about everything: vehicles (car/truck/SUV), computers (PC/Mac), dogs (beagles/greyhounds/poodles), music (pop/rap/country/R&B/metal/jazz/classical), seasons (winter/spring/summer/fall), and so on. But people are all unique, and when we engage in social categorization, we tend to overlook that uniqueness (Fiske, 2012; Crisp & Maitner, 2011; Dovidio & Gaertner, 2010).

MY TAKE VIDEO 13.3

Social Comparison

"Social media has a big imprint on social comparison, because people see other people being happy..."

YOUTUBE: http://tiny.cc/mytake
LAUNCHPAD: launchpadworks.com

A second factor that fosters prejudice when judging other people is the *smoke detector principle*—the notion that it is better to be oversensitive and produce many "false alarms" than to be undersensitive and allow even one catastrophe to take place. This oversensitivity is not a conscious decision, but a deep-seated tendency rooted in evolution (Nesse, 2005). Think about it from the point of view of your ancestor living thousands of years ago. Life in the hunter-gatherer band is good. The immediate and extended family helps to provide you with everything you need. When an unknown face appears—which was not as common as it is now—should you take a chance and get to know the person before making any judgments? There could be an upside—form a new alliance that might help to provide resources and share responsibilities. But the downside is too great to take the chance. The new person could hurt you or the others in your hunter-gatherer band. It is wiser to err on the side of prejudice.

No wonder humans still have a tendency to prejudge negatively other people who look unhealthy or dirty (and could sicken us), those who have angry facial expressions (and could injure us), and those who are unfamiliar (and could threaten the ingroup) (Neuberg & Cottrell, 2006). That last example—negatively prejudging people who are unfamiliar—goes a long way toward explaining the roots of racism, or any other prejudice based on obvious physical differences (Kurzban et al., 2001).

A third factor that promotes prejudice is **social comparison**: assessing yourself by determining how you measure up to other people. When you prejudge outgroups negatively, you seem better by contrast (Suls & Wheeler, 2012; Carrillo et al., 2011; Festinger, 1954). If you pigeonhole other people as dishonest, you seem more truthful; if you write other people off as lazy, you seem more energetic. Research has shown that we compare ourselves to other people in many ways, from our weight to our health to our looks to our relationship satisfaction (Corcoran et al., 2011; Buunk et al., 1990; Poran, 2002).

Rationalizing Prejudices. When individuals realize that they hold prejudices, they often try to rationalize them, or explain why they are justified in thinking that way. One such rationalization is the **just-world hypothesis**: the notion that the world is fair and that unfortunate events happen to those who deserve them (Dalbert, 2009; Lerner, 1965; Lerner & Miller, 1978; Hafer & Bègue, 2005). For example, consider Kevin, who hears that his neighbor Louisa lost her job. Kevin says to his brother, "I guess Louisa must have made a lot of mistakes at work." Kevin's assumption that Louisa caused the job loss, and his failure to consider that the job loss might have nothing to do with Louisa's behavior, illustrate the just-world hypothesis. Others who similarly "blame the victim" with "just-world" thinking often target members of particular ethnicities, genders, or age groups.

Another rationalization for prejudice is the **scapegoat hypothesis**: the notion that prejudice can be fueled by the need to find someone to blame. By pawning off negative characteristics onto other groups, we try to convince ourselves that we couldn't have any such negative characteristics. History is full of examples of such scapegoating, including the blame that Germans wrongly piled on Jews during the Holocaust and the blame that Americans wrongly piled on Muslims after the attacks of September 11, 2001. More recently, some have argued that certain American politicians scapegoat Hispanics, particularly those who immigrated illegally, as being solely responsible for high levels of unemployment and other economic woes within the country (Hohmann, 2012). Such scapegoating overlooks the complexity of the U.S. economy and promotes prejudice toward Hispanics.

Toward Fairness and Cooperation: Fighting Prejudice

Thankfully, social psychologists' efforts to understand prejudice have generated strategies for overcoming it. Let's take a look at some of them.

social comparison
Assessing oneself by determining how one measures up to other people.

just-world hypothesis
The notion that the world is fair and that unfortunate events happen to those who deserve them.

scapegoat hypothesis
The notion that prejudice can be fueled by the need to find someone to blame.

intergroup contact
A strategy for fighting prejudice based on direct interpersonal interaction between members of multiple groups.

common group identity
A strategy for fighting prejudice based on the creation of a larger group that includes multiple smaller groups.

Intergroup Contact. **Intergroup contact** is a strategy for fighting prejudice based on direct interpersonal interaction between members of multiple groups. People who hold strong prejudices against certain groups have, in many cases, never even met someone from that group. When they do, those prejudices often dissolve (Pettigrew & Tropp, 2006). To illustrate, researchers followed 2000 White, Asian, Latino, and African American students through their college years. They found that first-year students with more outgroup friendships showed less anxiety about outgroups, as well as less ingroup bias, by the end of college (Levin et al., 2003). The same researchers also found that students who had a first-year roommate of a different ethnicity were less prejudiced about that ethnicity, and usually about other ethnicities as well, by the end of college than students who shared the same ethnicity as their first-year roommate (Laar et al., 2005).

A key to intergroup contact is equal status between the groups. Such equality allows each group to recognize the value that the other brings, and how they can work together to realize shared goals (Brown & Hewstone, 2005; Brewer, 1996). If one group clearly holds greater power than the other group, that difference will hinder the ability of both groups to cooperate, respect, and trust each other, and the prejudices may remain despite contact with each other (Tropp & Molina, 2012). For example, let's say a group of Jews and a group of Muslims hope to decrease prejudice toward each other by sharing an activity. They would be better off meeting at a neutral site and working together in small, leaderless groups rather than meeting at one of their houses of worship and placing members of the host group in charge of members of the visiting group.

Intergroup contact is a strategy for fighting prejudice based on direct interpersonal interaction between members of multiple groups. monkeybusinessimages/iStock/Getty Images

Common Group Identity. **Common group identity** is a strategy for fighting prejudice based on the creation of a larger group that includes multiple smaller groups. Think of the U.S. Men's Olympic basketball team. Members of different professional teams—players who typically view each other as opponents—come together to play for a bigger common goal. They are no longer the Warriors versus the Cavaliers, or Kevin Durant versus Kyrie Irving. The antagonism disappears as competitors become teammates to form a single team representing their country.

When members of religious, ethnic, or cultural groups come together for a common cause, they too can overcome prejudice in the process. For example, after one of the most devastating tornadoes in U.S. history hit Joplin, Missouri, in May 2011, religious organizations came together to help. They all had a common group identity now: survivors. The interfaith experience was so successful that a year later, they planned an interfaith remembrance service involving Christian, Jewish, and Muslim congregations. An organizer commented, "One of the things that struck me after the tornado was how different groups of people, who don't normally do things together, were cooperating and working together…It was really inspiring." (Kennedy, 2012).

IT'S LIKE...

Fighting Prejudice Is Like Treating Phobias

The intergroup contact approach to overcoming prejudice is a lot like the way psychologists help a client overcome a phobia. We'll discuss phobia treatment in more detail in Chapter 15 (Therapy), but the best way to treat a phobia is gradually to *expose* yourself to the source of your anxiety. In other words, you face your fear. People can conquer a fear of dogs, for example, by choosing to face dogs instead of avoiding them. Little by little, the fear goes away through repeated exposure.

Intergroup contact works the same way: through *exposure*. People with strong prejudices toward a group of people typically avoid that group as much as possible, just as a person with a dog phobia avoids dogs. In both cases, the avoidance denies the person the chance to disprove their irrational belief. Avoidance of dogs makes it impossible for the person to learn that they're wrong about dogs being dangerous. Similarly, avoidance of an ethnic, racial, or other group makes it impossible for the person to learn that they're wrong about that group having the unfavorable quality they presumed.

Meeting someone from an unfamiliar group serves the same purpose as that first step in phobia treatment: a shift from avoidance to *exposure*, which gives real-life experience a chance to prevail over any ignorance-based prejudices (Pettigrew & Tropp, 2006). This might mean that prejudice (and the stereotyping and discrimination that it initiates) is an irrational fear at its core, just like any phobia.

Common group identity is a strategy for fighting prejudice based on the creation of a larger group that includes multiple smaller groups—for example, when NBA stars who typically play on opposing teams, like LeBron James and Kevin Durant, join forces during the Olympics. Streeter Lecka/Getty Images

The odds of success for common group identity are highest when the larger group is just as important and meaningful as the smaller groups, and when none of the smaller groups rank above the other in terms of power or prestige (Gaertner & Dovidio, 2012; Dovidio et al., 2009; Hornsey & Hogg, 2000). The common group identity approach has been found successful in numerous studies. For example, executives from two competing banks who suddenly found themselves working together after a merger cooperated most effectively when they identified with the new, larger bank (Gaertner et al., 1996). Similarly, members of blended families get along better if they see themselves as one big family rather than two separate, cohabiting families (Banker & Gaertner, 1998).

Education. Straightforward information about an outgroup can be helpful in reducing prejudice. Sources like books, videos, and Web sites that present accurate, unbiased information enhance knowledge and challenge negative assumptions. This kind of education can also prepare people for the intergroup contact described previously.

Interestingly, prejudice can also fade when you educate yourself about your own group—particularly the opinions and experiences of your fellow ingroup members. In one study, researchers found that when a person learned that an ingroup friend was friends with an outgroup member, that person became less prejudiced toward that outgroup (Wright et al., 1997). For example, if a conservative who holds negative biases about liberals finds out that a conservative friend socializes with a liberal buddy on the weekends, that conservative is likely to be less biased. (For example, "If Steve hangs out with a liberal, liberals must not be so bad.") Another researcher found that cross-group friendships actually decrease prejudice toward outgroups in general, not just the outgroup to which the friend belongs (Pettigrew, 1997). In other words, venturing out of your ingroup for even one meaningful relationship can have a ripple effect on your openness to people of all kinds.

LIFE HACK 13.3

To reduce your own prejudices, spend time and develop relationships with people different from yourself.

(Pettigrew, 1997; Pettigrew & Tropp, 2006; Levin et al., 2003)

Jigsaw Classroom. The **jigsaw classroom** is a strategy for reducing prejudice by giving each student in a diverse group an essential part of the solution to a problem that must be solved via group interaction. Essentially, the jigsaw classroom forces students who are different from each other to cooperate on a shared project, and their success hinges on each student's participation. For example, a group of diverse science students is learning about the parts of a cell. Each student is assigned to become an expert on a particular part of the cell (nucleus, mitochondria, cell wall, protoplasm, etc.). For the group to be successful, they must share and integrate what each has learned. Such an interdependent assignment requires the students to work as partners toward a collective goal—something they might not otherwise do during the regular school routine. Jigsaw classroom exercises have been found effective in a wide range of educational settings, from young children to adult learners (Aronson, 1978, 2002; Walker & Crogan, 1998; Perkins & Saris, 2001).

Aggression

Two of the forces that most passionately draw human beings together are complete opposites of one another, *aggression* and *interpersonal attraction*. **Aggression** is behavior intended to cause harm or death. In *interpersonal attraction*, people who like or love each other feel a desire to enhance their relationship. Let's consider both in detail, beginning with aggression.

Biological Influences on Aggression. Whether or not we want to admit it, aggression is inherent to human behavior. Some of the earliest historical evidence of interaction between people includes irrefutable evidence of lethal brutality. Consider this evidence: archeologists in Egypt uncovered a group of 59 human skeletons dating back 12,000–14,000 years. Almost half had stone projectiles embedded in their bones. Many had multiple broken bones, most of which were on the left side of the

skull and rib cage, where right-handed attackers would have most likely landed their punches and weapon strikes (Buss, 2005). There is little doubt that these archeologists had stumbled into an ancient war zone. Similarly, some traditional, indigenous tribes living in Venezuela, Africa, and Australia—groups that have certainly never experienced *Grand Theft Auto* video games, *Saw* movies, or Eminem records—actually have higher homicide rates than many U.S. cities (Buss & Duntley, 2006; Daly & Wilson, 1988; Chagnon, 1988).

More evidence that aggression is part of our nature comes from the fact that it appears as soon as we are physically capable of producing it. Before our first birthday, well before we fully soak up the influences around us, we behave aggressively. In fact, some psychologists have argued that the toddler years (age 1–3) are the most aggressive of any during the life span: A full 25% of interactions between kids at this age are aggressive (Bushman & Huesmann, 2010; Tremblay & Nagin, 2005). Thankfully, young kids can't do much damage, but that doesn't mean we should discount their hitting, kicking, biting, scratching, hair pulling, and name calling. All of it supports the idea that aggression is innate in human beings.

The role of biology in aggression is supported by the fact that toddlers, and even babies, often behave aggressively even though they have had little time to be influenced by other factors. Alexey Losevich/Shutterstock

Aggressive kids tend to become aggressive adults, too (Huesmann & Moise, 1998). Researchers tracked 230 people from a small town in New York state for 40 years, measuring their aggressiveness at four points: ages 8, 19, 30, and 48 (Huesmann et al., 2009). Their primary finding was that aggressiveness at age 8 was a strong predictor of aggressiveness at every later age, especially for males. By the time participants reached 48, they were much more likely to have committed a wide variety of aggressive acts (from spousal abuse to dangerous traffic violations) if they were highly aggressive 8-year-olds. These results imply that aggression is more of a stable trait within each of us than a temporary state caused solely by external variables.

There are also twin and adoption studies that find genes to be major contributing factors to aggression. A meta-analysis of 24 studies found that genes account for up to 50% of each person's level of aggressiveness (Miles & Carey, 1997). A more recent large-scale study found similar results, and specified that they apply to both impulsive ("heat-of-the-moment") aggression and premeditated ("cold and calculated") aggression (Baker et al., 2008).

Psychological Influences on Aggression. Genetics may form the foundation of aggression, but psychological factors play a role too. For example, certain personality traits have been linked to aggressive behavior. People low in *empathy* (the capacity to feel compassion for another person) tend to be highly aggressive (Castano, 2012; Miller & Eisenberg, 1988; Sergeant et al., 2006). Low-empathy people tend to dehumanize others, leading to callous behaviors that hurt them.

Being impulsive is another personality variable that correlates with aggressiveness. Highly impulsive people lack the self-control, or "brakes," that less impulsive people use to stop themselves from committing acts of aggression. As a result, highly impulsive people find themselves lashing out with spur-of-the-moment aggressiveness at a high frequency (Hinshaw et al., 1992). Among the specific aggressive behaviors linked to both low empathy and high impulsivity is bullying, which is discussed in the Current Controversy box in more detail (Endresen & Olweus, 2001; Mayberry & Espelage, 2007; Jagers et al., 2007; Jolliffe & Farrington, 2011).

Aggressive behavior is also influenced by observational learning (Chapter 6). Just as kids in Albert Bandura's studies imitated models' behavior toward a Bobo doll, they also imitate parents' behavior (Bandura, 1977, 1986). Whether the parents' aggressive behavior is aimed at the child, at each other, or at others, it becomes one of the child's behavioral options. In fact, the model of the aggression doesn't even need to be a parent. Aggressive behavior by any family member or friend, especially if it appears to produce benefits and no cost, is likely to be imitated by children. Monkey see aggression, monkey do aggression.

jigsaw classroom
A strategy for reducing prejudice by giving each student in a diverse group an essential part of the solution to a problem that must be solved via group interaction.

aggression
Behavior intended to cause harm or death.

Situational Influences on Aggression. Biological factors and psychological factors are both internal, but external circumstances play a role in aggressiveness too. For

CURRENT CONTROVERSY

Cyberbullying and Social Psychology

Cyberbullying is a major social problem. It involves intentional harm of another person via computers, smartphones, or other Internet-connected devices, and is typically done to and by teenagers. Facebook, Twitter, YouTube, Instagram, texts, and emails are just some of the media used by cyberbullies. Specific acts of cyberbullying can include posting humiliating videos or photos, spreading rumors about the victim to a wide circle of peers, and sending cruel written messages directly to the victim.

Cyberbullying, typically done by and to teenagers, has become a major social problem. AntonioGuillem/iStock/Getty Images

Cyberbullying is startlingly widespread. One survey asked 4400 kids age 11–18 if they had ever experienced repeated cyberbullying, and about 20% said yes. About the same percentage admitted to doing the cyberbullying (Hinduja & Patchin, 2010).

Significant controversy exists over how our society should address cyberbullying. Indeed, it is difficult to know where to start: with the kids who might commit cyberbullying, the schools that foster social environments that lead to it, or parents who could discourage it (but in many cases lag behind their children in technical expertise). Many key concepts in social psychology are relevant to choosing strategies to combat cyberbullying:

- First and foremost, cyberbullying is a form of *aggression*. It can be direct (when insults or threats are texted straight to the victim) or indirect (when one teen starts a rumor about another who initially knows nothing about it).
- Unlike older forms of bullying, in which the behavior took place face-to-face, cyberbullying often happens anonymously. The ability to hide behind a screen name or a hidden identity is a form of *deindividuation*, which heightens aggressiveness.
- *Social comparison* may play a role in cyberbullying behavior. Cyberbullies may attempt to pull someone else down to make themselves seem better by contrast.
- Teens have always been concerned with *ingroups* and *outgroups* among their peers, and cyberbullying may be seen as a way to get themselves included among a sought-after social group or get a rival ousted from theirs.
- The *scapegoat theory* suggests that people tend to look for someone to blame, and by doing so, they protect themselves from receiving such blame. Victimizing a peer via cyberbullying can serve exactly the scapegoat function.
- When an act of cyberbullying represents a group effort rather than one teen's idea, *groupthink* can be a factor. For example, one friend might say to a few others, "Hey, should I start a rumor about Tina?" If the others respond with a chorus of yeses, because they value their friendship with each other more than doing the right thing, then Tina is likely to get bullied.
- Cyberbullying could be motivated by revenge, especially if a bully believes the *reciprocity norm* has been violated. For example, 13-year-old Zach invites his friend Jake to spend the night. Jake never reciprocates, and in fact, he ignores Zach entirely after the sleepover. Feeling wronged, Zach sends a threatening email to Jake from a new account with a mysterious address that Zach created solely for that purpose.
- The *bystander effect* is also applicable here. How many of us know about cyberbullying, or even know someone who has been victimized by it, but have done nothing to reduce it?

example, unpleasant events often trigger angry action (Berkowitz, 1989, 1993; Berkowitz & Harmon-Jones, 2004). Some unpleasant events seem like minor nuisances, but these "little things" can be maddening when they are long-lasting, uncontrollable, and produce frustration (Donnerstein & Wilson, 1976; Green & McCown, 1984; Fernandez & Turk, 1995). Second-hand smoke, bad smells, overcrowded spaces, nagging pain, and loud noises are all examples of negative situational factors that might trigger aggression.

Other unpleasant events that might produce aggression are "big things." For example, social rejection often results in angry outbursts. A friend who has been ostracized from the group, a player who has been kicked off the team, or a romantic partner who has been dumped—any of these people is at increased likelihood for hostility, especially if they are sensitive to rejection (Ayduk et al., 2008; Warburton et al., 2006; MacDonald & Leary, 2005). Social rejection may play a role in "going postal," the slang term for workplace violence that takes place after an employee has been let go. (Of course, loss of a paycheck is a major factor too.) Many of the gunmen who have committed mass murders in schools and other public places, such as the shooters at Columbine High School in 1999, had experienced social rejection (Leary et al., 2003).

TABLE 13.3: Temperature and Violence: The Possible Effects of Global Warming

Average annual temperature increase	2 Degrees	4 Degrees	6 Degrees	8 Degrees
Predicted increase in murders per 100,000 people	9	18	27	36
Predicted increase in total murders for U.S. population	24,000	48,000	72,000	96,000

Data from Anderson, 2001.

Even the weather can be a situational contributor to aggression. The most well-established weather-related predictor of aggression is temperature: When the weather gets hotter, so do people's tempers (Anderson et al., 2000; Agnew, 2012). This holds true not only in terms of crime statistics, but even in Major League Baseball. Pitchers hit more batters with pitches on hot days than cooler days, particularly as retaliation after one of their own teammates has been hit (Reifman et al., 1991; Larrick et al., 2011). Some social psychologists have pointed out that among the other risks of global warming, a hotter Earth is likely to be a more violent one. They predict that by the mid-2100s, the United States could see nearly 100,000 more serious assaults per year if global warming continues (**Table 13.3**) (Anderson et al., 1997; Anderson, 2001).

The presence of weapons encourages aggressive behavior as well. In fact, in study after study, just the *sight* of weapons serves as a cue that translates into increased aggressive behavior (Carlson et al., 1990; Anderson et al., 1998). In one innovative real-world study from the 1970s, researchers had the driver of a pickup truck intentionally remain stopped when a red light turned green (Turner et al., 1975). The researchers then measured aggressive behavior in the driver behind the pickup, which they defined as honking the horn. In some cases, the pickup truck had a visible rifle in a gun rack and a bumper sticker that read "Vengeance." In others, it had neither. Drivers who saw the gun and sticker honked more often—a finding that defies logic (at least given today's possibility of road rage), but indicates the power that weapons have to prime feelings of anger.

In a more recent study on how exposure to weapons increases aggressiveness, researchers had male participants hold either a gun (a replica of a Desert Eagle automatic handgun) or a children's toy (the game Mouse Trap) for 15 minutes (Klinesmith et al., 2006). They were then instructed to add as much hot sauce as they wanted to a glass of water that another person (unseen by the participant) would have to drink. The gun holders added three times as much hot sauce as the toy holders—a finding the experimenters interpreted as a sign of aggressiveness (**Table 13.4**).

No discussion of the situational causes of aggression would be complete without mention of alcohol. Many studies have found a link between alcohol consumption and aggressive behavior, including domestic violence and violence outside of the home (Bushman & Cooper, 1990; Lipsey et al., 1997; Miller & Pollock, 1996). In fact, over half of violent crimes are committed by people who were under the influence of alcohol (Pernanen, 1991; Innes, 1988). In another creative study using the "hot sauce" method described earlier, researchers illustrated that it's not only how much alcohol you consumed, but how much alcohol you *think* you consumed—how intoxicated you expect to be, that is—that affects aggressiveness. Researchers gave participants either a nonalcoholic, weak, or strong drink. They also told participants that they just had a nonalcoholic, weak, or strong drink, but what they were told had nothing to do with what they actually drank. The result? Hot sauce levels depended directly upon what the participants were told they drank, but not at all upon how much alcohol they actually drank. The participants who *thought* they drank the most alcohol added the most hot sauce to the glass of water (Bègue et al., 2009).

Violence in the media also contributes to aggressive behavior. As mentioned in Chapter 6, there are some studies that cast doubt on the connection between violence in the media and aggressive behavior (Ferguson & Kilburn, 2009), but there are

TABLE 13.4: Just Holding a Gun Increases Aggression

PARTICIPANTS WHO HELD A ____ FOR 15 MINUTES...	ANONYMOUSLY ADDED ____ OF HOT SAUCE TO WATER THAT ANOTHER PERSON WAS REQUIRED TO DRINK
Children's game	4.23 grams
Gun	13.61 grams

Data from Klinesmith et al., 2006.

many more that establish that connection strongly (Anderson et al., 2010; Anderson & Bushman, 2001; Huesmann & Kirwil, 2007). Particularly when the people experiencing the violent TV, movies, and video games are kids, the link can be powerful and troubling. Some social psychologists have examined the short-term effects of media violence on behavior. For example, one researcher had 9-year-old boys watch either a violent or a nonviolent movie before they played floor hockey against each other. Those who watched the violent movie committed acts of aggression during the hockey game—hitting, tripping, elbowing, and so on—much more often than those who watched the nonviolent movie (Josephson, 1987).

Other researchers have taken a more long-term approach, and have typically found that exposure to violence in the media desensitizes people to real-world aggression and makes them more likely to behave aggressively (Carnagey et al., 2007). For example, researchers who studied a group of males from age 8 through age 30 found that those who viewed the most violence on TV as youngsters were most likely to act aggressively and commit criminal acts, even after controlling for other factors that could predict aggressiveness (Eron et al., 1972; Huesmann, 1986; Huesmann & Miller, 1994).

Among the various forms of violent media, violent video games may be especially potent in terms of stimulating aggressive behavior. They involve active participation in violence rather than just passive observation, and they offer direct rewards for violent behavior, including points, progression to the next level of the game, and even verbal praise ("Great shot!") (Bushman & Huesmann, 2010). In one study, boys around 14 years old played either a violent or nonviolent video game for 20 minutes and then competed against a partner in a reaction-time task (pressing a button as quickly as possible after a signal). The winner of the reaction-time task was allowed to blast the loser with noise through headphones. Boys who had played the violent video game chose to blast their opponents with much louder noises than boys who had played the nonviolent video game, even though the researchers told the boys that such loud noises could cause permanent hearing damage (Konijn et al., 2007).

In an innovative study of the role of active participation in violent video games, one group of 10–13-year-old kids played violent video games, while another group watched (but did not play) the same games. When they were then sent out to recess, those who had played the games behaved much more violently than those who merely watched (Polman et al., 2008).

Beginning in the school years and continuing into adulthood, boys and men behave with more physical aggression, while girls and women behave with more relational aggression. a) Lopolo/Shutterstock; b) KidStock/Blend Images/Getty Images

Cultural Influences on Aggression. Aggression varies across cultural and demographic groups in terms of how often it occurs and whether it is *direct* or *indirect* (Bond, 2004). Consider gender, for example. By the time children enter kindergarten, boys are more physically aggressive than girls (Loeber & Hay, 1997). Physical aggression such as punching or kicking is called *direct* aggression: the person you hurt is right there, and his or her reaction is immediately obvious. As boys begin to engage in more direct aggression, girls begin to engage in more *indirect* or *relational* aggression, in which the victim is not present (Card et al., 2008; Archer & Coyne, 2005). Many examples of indirect or relational aggression involve social "drama" such as telling rumors or gossiping. This divergence—males toward direct physical aggression, and females toward indirect and relational aggression—increases throughout the school years and continues into adulthood (Lagerspetz et al., 1988, Crick & Grotpeter, 1995).

DIVERSITY MATTERS

When we compare homicide rates across countries, a wide range emerges, suggesting that aggression (at least in its most lethal form) characterizes some cultures more than others. The United States has a relatively high homicide rate, especially in comparison to many other Western countries: four times higher than in France, Spain, or Germany; three times higher than in the United Kingdom, more than double that of Canada. However, the U.S. homicide rate is only half the rate of Bolivia, one-third of the rate of Nicaragua, and one-tenth of the rate of Venezuela. Asian countries are known for their extremely low rates of homicide and other violent crimes. Japan, for example,

has a population about 40% of the size of the U.S. population, but had only 3% of the murders that the United States did in 2011 (United Nations Office on Drugs and Crime, 2012).

interpersonal attraction
The desire to enhance a relationship with another person.

mere exposure effect
An increase in the attractiveness of a person (or object) resulting from nothing more than repeated contact.

Attraction

After so much focus on people hurting each other, it's refreshing to remember that we often like or even love each other! Social psychologists place liking, loving, and any similarly warm and fuzzy reaction into the broad category of **interpersonal attraction**: the desire to enhance a relationship with another person. Lots of factors influence the attractiveness of one person to another, from nearness to sameness to beauty to the odds of being liked back. Let's consider them one by one.

Proximity. Physical closeness produces emotional closeness. If you are like most people, some of your best friendships and most serious romantic relationships began when you were neighbors of one kind or another. For example, maybe you lived in the same apartment building, sat near each other in the same classes, or played on the same sports teams. In one study, four equally attractive women were instructed to attend a college class (but not interact with actual students) at different rates: 15 times, 10 times, 5 times, or not at all. When the semester ended, students in the class were given photos of the four women and asked to rate the attractiveness of each. The more often they had been in class, the higher their attractiveness was rated (Moreland & Beach, 1992).

What is it about proximity that causes people to become attracted to each other? Seeing them (often) may actually be the key. Social psychologists call this the **mere exposure effect**: an increase in the attractiveness of a person (or object) resulting from nothing more than repeated contact. Many studies point to the fact that we feel positive toward what is familiar—not just people, but things too, including shapes, words, photographs, songs, and sounds (Bornstein, 1989; Albarracín & Vargas, 2010; Zajonc, 1968; Kunst-Wilson & Zajonc, 1980).

Advertisers certainly know how to take advantage of the mere exposure effect. Consider Intel as an example. How many (hundreds of) times have you seen the Intel logo on computers? Or TV ads that include the Intel logo and the quick sound that accompanies it? With the exception of the computer geeks among us, most of us have little specific knowledge of whether Intel's semiconductor chips are better than those of its competitors. (In fact, some of us don't even know what part of the computer Intel makes.) But when we see that familiar, recognizable logo on a computer, it creates a feeling of familiarity—perhaps just enough to nudge us toward buying that computer rather than one with a less well known logo. (No wonder computer manufacturers like to include that little sticker.) The mere exposure effect works with the people we see in ads too. That's why companies pay so much for spokespeople whom we recognize easily. For a fraction of the cost, Covergirl could find someone just as beautiful as Ellen DeGeneres, and Calvin Klein could find someone just as good-looking as Justin Beiber, but we *know* Ellen and Justin, and knowing them translates into attraction toward the products they endorse.

Physical Attractiveness. We like beautiful people. We may like to tell ourselves that we are attracted to a person's inner beauty, but outward beauty (*looks*) has generated much more social psychology research.

As the saying goes, beauty is in the eye of the beholder, but men and women behold it quite differently. One researcher surveyed over 10,000 men and women from 33 countries on 6 continents—an absolutely massive, culturally diverse sample—to determine what each gender finds attractive in the opposite sex (Buss, 1989). Results indicate that there are some undeniable universal themes. Across cultures, men place a higher premium on physical attractiveness in women. Specifically, men around the world seek women who appear youthful, healthy, and have appealing figures (waist-to-hip ratio especially)—all features that

DIVERSITY MATTERS

The mere exposure effect is an increase in the attractiveness of a person (or object) resulting from nothing more than repeated contact. If you've seen this Intel logo many times before—on advertisements or on computers themselves—you are more likely to view it favorably than if you've never seen it before. Antoine Antoniol/Bloomberg via Getty Images

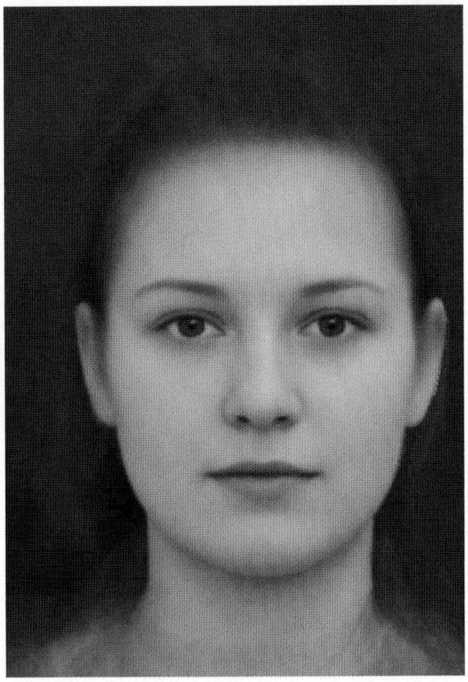

This is a composite of photos of over 50 young Latvian women (Jakobsen, 2013; Rantala et al., 2013). Although researchers call it an "average" of those women's faces, it is typically rated as significantly above average in studies of facial attractiveness. The reasons for high attractiveness ratings of "average" faces may include the fact that they lack any idiosyncratic features—scars or blemishes, for example—that could signal illness or injury. Markus J. Rantala

suggest fertility, or the ability to conceive, give birth to, and nurture a child. On the other hand, women around the world place less emphasis on a man's physical appearance and instead prefer men who have wealth, status, and power—all features that suggest the ability to provide resources.

These results have been confirmed by other large-scale, cross-cultural studies (Shackelford et al., 2005). The primary explanation for the male–female difference has been evolutionary: Assuming heterosexuality, the male strategy for passing along his genes is to mate with any woman who can successfully bear his child. The female strategy was to selectively choose mates with the means to feed, clothe, and protect the family once the children had arrived (Buss, 1994, 1995).

Some fascinating research results provide support for this evolutionary explanation. For example, heterosexual men and women tend to experience jealousy for different reasons. Generally, a man is more likely to become jealous if a woman cheats on him sexually, because it could mean that she will focus on another man's child instead of their own. Generally, a woman is more likely to become jealous if a man cheats on her emotionally, because it could mean that he will develop a connection with another woman that will steer his resources away from them and their children (Buss et al., 1992; Sagarin et al., 2003; Buunk et al., 1996). Along the same lines, when asked to describe their greatest regrets, men more often wished they had slept with more women, but women more often wished they had slept with fewer men (Roese et al., 2006).

Other studies have extended the conversation about male versus female attractiveness. For example, researchers have found that gender differences in mate preferences occur only if men or women have to prioritize. In other words, everyone actually values *both* physical attractiveness and resourcefulness, but if forced to choose, men go with physical attractiveness and women go with resourcefulness (Li et al., 2002). Additionally, some researchers have found that both men and women highly value some other qualities just as much as physical attractiveness and resourcefulness—intelligence, kindness, honesty, sense of humor (Fletcher et al., 2006; Lippa, 2007). Also, *social role theory* suggests that any difference in what men and women find attractive actually stems from the more basic desire to find a partner who can bring things to the relationship that we can't bring ourselves. A traditional man may seek a traditional woman, and vice versa, but if either is untraditional—a man who sees himself as a homemaker, or a woman who sees herself as a breadwinner—he or she may adjust his or her mate preferences accordingly (Wood & Eagly, 2010; Eagly & Wood, 1999).

One last point on physical attractiveness: when it comes to faces, we tend to rate "average" way above average. That is, a person's facial attractiveness depends upon how unremarkable its features are within his or her age group, gender, and ethnicity (Langlois & Roggman, 1990). This may be counterintuitive, since we often think of "average" looking people as plain or run-of-the-mill. But in this kind of research, social psychologists define "average" as the computerized combination of multiple faces, and

WATCHING PSYCHOLOGY

The Voice, American Idol, and Attractiveness

The Voice and *American Idol* each feature aspiring singers trying to impress celebrity judges. The shows are similar in many ways, but one of their most obvious differences is also one of the most intriguing to anyone with an interest in social psychology: the judges on *The Voice* can't see their contestants, but the judges on the *American Idol* can.

What influence might this difference have on the judges' decisions, such as who advances past the first round, who makes the finals, and even who wins the top prize? Facial attractiveness could make a big difference, especially in the first round of *American Idol*. Considering how quickly people tend to form first impressions based on facial attractiveness, the judges could be leaning toward or away from sending a contestant to Hollywood before they sing their first note. What about contestants' bodies? From time to time, *American Idol* judges during the first round have made side comments to each other about how "hot" a particular contestant was. (A Season 9 sensation, "Bikini Girl," seemed to sway some judges quite a bit with her nonvocal qualities.)

To social psychologists, the way new contestants are judged on *The Voice*—with the judges facing the opposite direction, able to hear but not see them—is a more valid way to select the best voices. Looks, in this case, might confuse judgment of the singer's voice. ●

an "average" face could have a real upside. There are no idiosyncratic facial features that might be unappealing. There are no signs of possible illness or injury (scars, sores, blemishes). This "average" face has been found preferable in a wide range of cultures (Gangestad & Scheyd, 2005; Rhodes, 2006; Jones & Hill, 1993).

DIVERSITY MATTERS

Similarity. "Opposites attract" is common wisdom for how we form friendships and romantic partnerships. But according to social psychology research, it is wrong (Montoya & Horton, 2012). A much more accurate account is that "birds of a feather flock together."

Many studies have found that we like other people if they are like us. For example, one study of newlyweds found that people have a strong likelihood to choose a marriage partner who is equal to them in terms of both educational level and facial attractiveness (Stevens et al., 1990). A meta-analysis of similarity studies found that both *perceived* similarity and actual similarity predict attraction, meaning that you are likely to find yourself drawn to those who you think are similar to you just as much as those who are in fact like you (Montoya et al., 2008).

Reciprocal Liking. Remember your days in middle school, when you told your friends who you "liked" and then sent them across the lunchroom to find out if your crush "liked you back"? Social psychologists have examined the same concern—the likelihood that the other person is attracted to *you*—and have found that it makes quite a difference in your attraction toward the other person. If they like you, your attraction to them rises; if they don't, it drops (Curtis & Miller, 1986; Knobloch et al., 2008). One study found that in speed-dating situations, knowing that the other person is interested in you significantly increases your chances of reporting interest in them (Eastwick et al., 2007).

Romantic Love

Most of our discussion of attraction so far has covered all kinds of liking or loving. But one kind of love—*romantic love*—deserves special attention. Social psychologists have distinguished two distinct types of romantic love, one more typical of the early stages of a relationship, and the other more typical of long-term commitment. Let's explore both.

Passionate love is characterized by arousal and desire, and often experienced early in relationships. Couples feeling passionate love *burn* for each other. They are smitten by the thought of each other, by being together, and are distraught at the thought of being apart (Hatfield & Rapson, 1993).

Sometimes, couples who burn for each other burn out. But when they don't, their passionate love often evolves to a more mature love in which the raging fire becomes a steady warm flame (**Figure 13.8**). This is **companionate love**: love characterized by deep commitment and affection, and often experienced later in long-term relationships. These companion couples still describe themselves as being "in love," but the love they share is different than it was when they initially dated: less exhilarating, perhaps, but more stable and secure (Sprecher & Regan, 2007; Hatfield & Sprecher, 1986).

Researchers have identified a key reason why companionate love develops: *equity*, or the belief by each partner that he or she is giving and getting a fair amount in the relationship (Polk, 2011). Actually, equity is important at every stage of a romantic relationship, but in the early stages, passion can hide many relationship flaws. As things get more serious, equity becomes even more important, and the perception by either partner that he or she is being treated unfairly can be a deal breaker (Hatfield & Rapson, 1993). *Self-disclosure*, or openness about yourself to your partner, is another important ingredient of lasting romantic relationships. It tends to be a mutual process: As one partner shares private thoughts and feelings, so does the other, but if one partner clams up, the other does as well (Sprecher, 1987; Kito, 2005).

Savage Chickens

Doug Savage

passionate love
Love characterized by arousal and desire, and often experienced early in relationships.

companionate love
Love characterized by deep commitment and affection, and often experienced later in long-term relationships.

FIGURE 13.8 Passionate Love and Companionate Love in Popular Music. Kesha's lyrics capture the passionate love common in early stages of relationships, while John Legend's lyrics capture the companionate love common in more mature relationships. [a] Scott Dudelson/Getty Images [b] Scott Dudelson/Getty Images

Passionate love and companionate love certainly cover a lot of ground, but there may be more to love than those two terms describe. Robert Sternberg's *triangular theory of love* suggests that love can include up to three ingredients: passion, intimacy, and commitment (Sternberg, 1986, 2007; Sternberg & Barnes, 1989). The first two of Sternberg's ingredients line up quite well with passionate and companionate love, but the third, commitment, adds a new dimension. Sternberg calls a love built on all three ingredients *consummate love*, the ideal love that couples seek. A couple experiencing consummate love may disagree from time to time, but they do so respectfully and resolve their disputes constructively. Expressing love, letting your partner know how you feel, is essential if consummate love is to last.

CHECK YOUR LEARNING:

13.12 When we create first impressions, how long does it take and what role does physical attractiveness play?

13.13 What is the difference between a prejudice, a stereotype, and discrimination?

13.14 How are each of these concepts relevant to prejudice: ingroup bias, outgroup homogeneity, categorical thinking, and social comparison?

13.15 How can people overcome prejudice?

13.16 What is aggression, and why do people behave aggressively?

13.17 What attracts people to one another?

Prosocial Behavior: Helping Each Other

YOU WILL LEARN:

13.18 what altruism is.

13.19 why people help others.

13.20 why people *don't* help others.

Prosocial behavior is behavior intended to help others. Social psychologists have explored many questions surrounding prosocial behavior, but two of these questions—*why* people help others and why people *don't* help others—have received the most attention. The sections below cover both.

Altruism

The purest motivation for prosocial behavior is **altruism**: completely unselfish concern for others. Earlier in this chapter, we recognized the extent to which aggression comes naturally to human beings. Thankfully, altruism seems to come naturally too. After Hurricane Sandy hit the New York and New Jersey area in October 2012, thousands of people offered their displaced neighbors a place to stay and food to eat. Within 3 weeks, the American Red Cross had received $145 million in donations from around the world (Ellis & Anthony, 2012). Speaking of the Red Cross, over 9 million people donate blood every year (http://www.redcrossblood.org/learn-about-blood/blood-facts-and-statistics).

But *why*? Psychologists and philosophers have long considered altruism a paradox. It is hard to understand why the person is being altruistic, since his or her actions are entirely selfless. Or are they? Some have argued that any apparently altruistic act, if examined closely enough, actually brings a selfish payoff (Maner et al., 2002; Ghiselin, 1974). Let's consider Hurricane Sandy again. You watch the events unfold on TV—people in New York and New Jersey losing their homes, their cars, in some cases their loved ones—and you call the 800 number to donate $50. This is a completely selfless act, right? Maybe not. Maybe your donation relieves your guilt. Maybe it makes you feel proud of yourself. Maybe it makes you feel, vicariously, the same hopefulness that the recipients of that donation will feel (Smith et al., 1989; Schaller & Cialdini, 1988). In any of these cases, *you* benefit. Of course, this doesn't lessen the positive impact of the donation—$50 is $50 to the recipient, regardless of what the donor gets out of it—but it does cast some doubt on the utter selflessness of altruism.

Altruism, such as helping others by providing food after a natural disaster, is completely unselfish concern for others.
Ramin Talaie/Getty Images

Social Exchange Theory. Whether the altruistic motivation is pure or not, people provide help to others all the time. Social psychologists have put forth a number of theories to explain why people help others. One explanation is **social exchange theory**: the comparison of benefits and costs to the individual for helping. This explanation emphasizes what you get out of the helping behavior in comparison to what you give away. Imagine Scott and Lori, a couple out on a dinner date. They leave the restaurant with their leftovers boxed up. Outside the restaurant, they pass a homeless person. Scott gives the leftovers to the homeless person—a truly kind act, but not without some benefit to Scott. As he recounted to his friend the next day, "That box was gonna spill all over my car. Plus, Lori smiled and told me I was sweet when I did it." By helping, he lost half an order of pasta but kept his car clean and got a compliment from his girlfriend—not a bad exchange for Scott.

Reciprocity Norm. Another theory of helping is the **reciprocity norm**: the expectation that those who provide help will receive help in the future. Remember why Bill Withers invites you to "Lean on Me": "...for it won't be long 'til I'm gonna need somebody to lean on." You may be the one providing help now, but you'll be the one seeking it in the future, so it can't hurt to bank some good will. The key difference between the

prosocial behavior
Behavior intended to help others.

altruism
Completely unselfish concern for others.

social exchange theory
An explanation of helping that emphasizes the comparison of benefits and costs to the individual for helping.

reciprocity norm
An explanation of helping that emphasizes the expectation that those who provide help will receive help in the future.

When New York City Police Officer Lawrence DePrimo bought a brand-new pair of boots for a barefoot homeless man on a frigid night, his act of kindness was front page news. The officer's explanation captured the essence of the social responsibility norm: "It was freezing out...I don't care what the price is. We just got to help him out" (2012). (See Show Me More 13.3 at the end of the chapter for a TV interview in which Officer DePrimo explains his actions.) Richard B. Levine/Newscom

reciprocity norm and social exchange theory is how certain the repayment is. In social exchange theory, the repayment happens right away—it's a sure thing. When you bank on reciprocity, however, you're taking a chance that if you help others, they'll return the favor in the future. Restaurant servers who bring candies or mints with the bill know all about the reciprocity norm. As **Figure 13.9** shows, providing this small gift can increase tips by 20% (Strohmetz et al., 2006). Special interest groups who donate to a candidate's fundraising efforts and poor people (usually in big cities) who voluntarily clean the windows of stopped cars are also hoping that their act of kindness prompts a payback.

Is it possible that an act of kindness stimulates an act of kindness by the recipient, but not necessarily back to the original helper? In other words, when nice things happen to us, do we "pay it forward" to someone else entirely? In an innovative study, researchers had two actors (confederates) walk through a supermarket, one a few steps behind the other (Guéguen & De Gail, 2003). The first actor smiled at half of the 800 strangers they passed, and did not smile at the other half. The second actor then dropped a pile of computer parts, scattering them all over the floor. The primary question was this: Would those customers who just received a smile be more likely to help clean up a stranger's mess than those who did not receive a smile? The answer was yes. In fact, smile getters helped about 50% more often than the control group.

Social Responsibility Norm. A third theory of helping is the **social responsibility norm**: the notion of duty to help those who need it, regardless of any potential payback to the helper. According to the social responsibility norm, you help because you are supposed to, period. It is your job as a citizen of your city, country, or the world to take care of other people who can't take care of themselves. New York City Police Officer Lawrence DePrimo illustrated the social responsibility norm when, on a particularly frigid night, he bought a brand-new pair of boots for a homeless, barefoot man. He explained: "It was freezing out and you could see the blisters on the man's feet...I said, I don't care what the price is. We just got to help him out" (Kim, 2012).

Kinship Theory. A fourth theory of helping is more evolutionary in nature. **Kinship theory** emphasizes the importance of passing your genes on to future generations. To whom would you be most likely to donate a kidney? For most of us, a relative would definitely outrank a stranger, and the closer the relative, the higher they are on our list. The tendency to help family first is evident throughout the animal kingdom. Bees, ants,

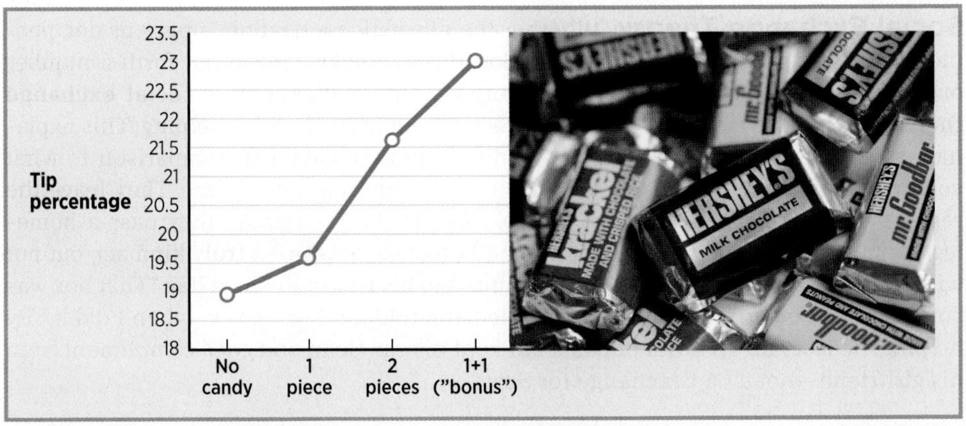

FIGURE 13.9 If You Give (Candy), You Shall Receive (Bigger Tips). Diners reciprocated with larger tips when servers offered mini Hershey bars with the bill. The highest tips came when the server offered one piece and then returned to offer a second "bonus" piece, which diners may have perceived as a particularly kind gesture. Data from Strohmetz et al., 2006; © Kristoffer Tripplaar/Alamy.

and termites routinely give up their own lives for the sake of their colonies of relatives (Crawford, 1998; Hamilton, 1964). We similarly feel the impulse to help when doing so could benefit someone who carries at least some of our genes, such as our siblings, children, or cousins. By helping them survive, we help part of ourselves survive (Van Vugt & Van Lange, 2006; Neyer & Lang, 2003). Even if it is not a life-or-death situation, some impulse to help kin remains, which can extend to those with whom we feel a closeness. Good friends and adopted relatives essentially qualify as family somewhere deep in our minds, whether or not we share genetic material (Korchmoros & Kenney, 2001, 2006).

Why *Don't* People Help?

We've seen a lot of explanations for helping, but often, people choose not to help when the opportunity arises. Why not?

In some cases, it is because you're not the only one around. This is the **bystander effect**: the decrease in likelihood that you will help another person caused by the presence of others also available to help. Research on the bystander effect was triggered by the murder of Kitty Genovese in Queens, New York, in 1964. According to news reports, Kitty was stabbed repeatedly over a half-hour period outside her own apartment building. Many of Kitty's neighbors watched the 3 A.M. crime unfold from their own apartments, hearing her cries for help the whole time. However, nobody intervened, and only some even called police. (The facts of the case, including the number of bystanders and the lack of help offered, have since come into question [Cook, 2014; Manning et al., 2007].)

Especially because of the attention this case attracted at the time, social psychologists began exploring the possible reasons behind onlookers' decisions to help or not help in similar situations (Latané & Darley, 1970). In a classic study, participants were filling out questionnaires when smoke began to fill the room (Latané & Darley, 1968). When participants were alone, they reported the smoke 75% of the time. When they had two other participants with them, the percentage dropped to 38%. When they had two actors (confederates) with them who noticed the smoke but did nothing, the percentage plummeted to 10%. This research generated a list of the five steps necessary for a bystander to intervene (**Table 13.5**) (Darley and Latané, 1968). Keep in mind that failure to take *any* single step would stop the bystander from helping.

Cases like Kitty Genovese's continue to occur. Some are smaller crimes against individuals (a purse is snatched, a car is broken into), but others are large-scale crimes against humanity (genocides, country-wide oppression of women or exploitation of children). Why do some people choose to stand by and do nothing? The reason may involve a **diffusion of responsibility**: a decreased sense of obligation to help when others are present. People presume that others will take care of it, and dismiss any sense of obligation. The larger the group, the greater the diffusion of responsibility, and the lower the chances that people will help.

TABLE 13.5: Five Steps Necessary for Bystander Intervention

STEP	EXAMPLE
Notice the event	I hear my elderly next-door neighbor screaming in pain.
Interpret it as an emergency	I think she has fallen and hurt herself.
Assume responsibility to intervene	Whether other people hear this or not, I need to do something to help her.
Decide how to intervene	I'm going to call 911 and go next door to help.
Take action	Call 911, enter neighbor's apartment, offer help.

Information from Latané & Darley, 1968; Darley & Latané, 1968.

CHAPTER APP 13.2

Prosocial Behavior/Altruism

Waze

Preview one of the links and consider the following questions.

WEBSITE:
http://tiny.cc/1vi7jy

ANDROID:
http://tiny.cc/fe92iy

IPHONE:
http://tiny.cc/3682iy

VIDEO DEMO:
http://tiny.cc/chapterapps

There are lots of apps to help you drive from Point A to Point B, but Waze is unique among them. As its Web site describes, Waze is "community-based," which means that drivers share info about the roads with each other. For example, Waze users can alert each other to the specific locations of police cars, accidents, traffic jams, cars on the shoulder, and even cheap gas stations they encounter. The Web site explains that Waze users are "outsmarting traffic, together" by getting a "heads-up from a few million of your friends on the road."

How does it APPly to your daily life?
Would you use an app like Waze? If so, would you share road information with other drivers, or only use the road information they shared with you?

How does it APPly to your understanding of psychology?
Which explanation of *prosocial behavior* (or *altruism*) best explains the decision by a Waze user to voluntarily give a heads-up to other drivers without any external reward (money, etc.)?

social responsibility norm
An explanation of helping that emphasizes the notion of duty to help those who need it, regardless of any potential payback to the helper.

kinship theory
An explanation of helping that emphasizes the importance of passing genes on to future generations.

bystander effect
The decrease in likelihood that one person will help another person caused by the presence of others also available to help.

diffusion of responsibility
A decreased sense of obligation to help when others are present.

Another reason why people choose not to help relates closely to the concept of *attribution* that we covered earlier in this chapter. In this case, however, the crucial question is whether the bystander feels the need for help is deserved (Rudolph et al., 2004; Weiner, 1993). Consider the victims of Hurricane Katrina in New Orleans in 2005. Some who saw the thousands of people ravaged by the storm and left with nothing thought, "Those poor people! It's terrible that this disaster happened to them." Others thought, "They deserve it! They chose to live in an area susceptible to flooding, and they ignored multiple warnings to evacuate." Of course, the first attribution is more likely to lead to donations of time or money.

In one study regarding attribution and helping, researchers gave participants fake news reports about the underlying causes of obesity. For some participants, the news report said obesity was genetic, which implied that obese people "can't help it." For other participants, the news report said obesity was behavioral, which implied that obese people choose to behave in ways that make them obese (overeating, not exercising). Participants who heard the genetic explanation were much more willing to help obese people (Jeong, 2007). Research has also shown that people are more willing to help a sick person than a drunk person, and an Alzheimer's patient more than a drug-addicted person (Weiner et al., 1988; Piliavin et al., 1969).

CHECK YOUR LEARNING:

13.18 What is altruism?

13.19 Why do people help others?

13.20 Why don't people help others?

CHAPTER SUMMARY

Social Cognition: How We Think about Each Other

13.1 Social cognition refers to your thoughts about other people, including attributions, attitudes, and cognitive dissonance.

13.2 An attribution is an explanation for the cause of behavior, and social psychologists put them into two distinct categories, the person or the situation.

13.3 When explaining the behavior of other people, we often make the fundamental attribution error, in which we overestimate the importance of traits and underestimate the importance of the situation.

13.4 An attitude is a viewpoint, often influenced by both thoughts and emotions, that affects a person's responses toward people, things, or situations. Social psychologists have identified a variety of strategies people use to change other people's attitudes, including central route persuasion, peripheral route persuasion, foot-in-the-door technique, door-in-the-face technique, and lowball technique.

13.5 Cognitive dissonance is the discomfort caused by having an attitude that contradicts another attitude or a behavior. Social psychologists see three solutions to cognitive dissonance: (1) changing the first attitude, (2) changing the second attitude, or (3) creating a third attitude to resolve the tension between the first and second attitudes.

Social Influence: How We Influence Each Other

13.6 Social influence is any way in which the presence of other people influences a person's thoughts, feelings, or behavior.

13.7 Conformity occurs when a person changes his or her behavior to correspond to the behavior of a group of other people. Conformity may occur out of a universal human need for group inclusion, but it varies from one culture to the next. Conformity levels are consistently higher in collectivist cultures than in individualistic cultures.

13.8 Obedience occurs when a person changes his or her behavior to comply with the demands of an authority figure.

13.9 Classic studies by Stanley Milgram revealed that many people will obey authority figures to a surprising extent.

13.10 Social facilitation is an increase in individual performance caused by the presence of other people, while social loafing is a decrease in individual performance when tasks are done in groups.

13.11 Groupthink is a phenomenon that occurs when group members value getting along with each other more than finding the best solution. Group polarization is the tendency for a group's attitudes to become more extreme as a result of group discussions.

Social Relations: How We Relate to Each Other

13.12 First impressions are made in the first seconds of meeting a person and are influenced by physical attractiveness.

13.13 A prejudice is an often negative attitude toward a social group that is formed before getting to know group members. Once a prejudice is in place, it produces stereotypes, which are beliefs about a group's characteristics that are applied to group members. Discrimination is any action based on prejudice or stereotypes toward a social group.

13.14 People's tendency to favor the groups to which they belong is known as ingroup bias, and people's tendency to overlook the diversity within outgroups is known as outgroup homogeneity. Prejudice is enabled by the natural tendency to think categorically, the predisposition to negatively prejudge people who are unfamiliar, and social comparison.

13.15 People can overcome prejudice through intergroup contact, common group identity, education about outgroups, and working together in settings like the jigsaw classroom.

13.16 Aggression is behavior intended to cause harm or death, and is influenced by genetics, personality traits, external circumstances, and cultural influences.

13.17 People are attracted to one another for a variety of reasons, including proximity, physical attractiveness, similarity, and reciprocal liking.

Prosocial Behavior: Helping Each Other

13.18 Altruism is completely unselfish concern for others.

13.19 Social psychologists have put forth a number of theories to explain why people help others, including social exchange theory, the reciprocity norm, the social responsibility norm, and kinship theory.

13.20 Social psychologists have suggested a number of explanations for why people don't help others, including the bystander effect and diffusion of responsibility.

KEY TERMS

social psychology, p. 437
social cognition, p. 437
attribution, p. 437
attribution theory, p. 437
fundamental attribution error, p. 437
attitude, p. 439
central route persuasion, p. 439
peripheral route persuasion, p. 439
foot-in-the-door technique, p. 439
door-in-the-face technique, p. 441
lowball technique, p. 441
social role, p. 441
cognitive dissonance, p. 443
social influence, p. 443
conformity, p. 445
obedience, p. 447
social facilitation, p. 448
social loafing, p. 448
deindividuation, p. 448
groupthink, p. 451
group polarization, p. 451
impression formation, p. 451
prejudice, p. 452
stereotypes, p. 452
discrimination, p. 452
ingroup, p. 452
outgroup, p. 452
ingroup bias, p. 452
outgroup homogeneity, p. 452
social comparison, p. 454
just-world hypothesis, p. 454
scapegoat hypothesis, p. 454
intergroup contact, p. 454
common group identity, p. 454
jigsaw classroom, p. 457
aggression, p. 457
interpersonal attraction, p. 461
mere exposure effect, p. 461
passionate love, p. 463
companionate love, p. 463
prosocial behavior, p. 465
altruism, p. 465
social exchange theory, p. 465
reciprocity norm, p. 465
social responsibility norm, p. 467
kinship theory, p. 467
bystander effect, p. 467
diffusion of responsibility, p. 467

SELF-ASSESSMENT

1. Yolanda is driving and sees another driver run a red light. According to the ______, Yolanda is likely to overestimate the importance of the situation and underestimate the importance of that driver's traits when explaining why that driver made that driving error.

2. An ______ is a viewpoint, often influenced by both thoughts and emotions, that affects your responses to people, things, or situations.
   a. attribution
   b. attitude
   c. action
   d. None of the answers is correct.

3. Which of the following is a persuasion technique?
   a. foot-in-the-door technique
   b. lowball technique
   c. door-in-the-face technique
   d. All of the answers are correct.

4. ______ is the discomfort caused by having an attitude that contradicts another attitude or behavior.
   a. Implicit attitude
   b. Social role
   c. Cognitive dissonance
   d. Group polarization

5. When a person changes his or her behavior to comply with the demands of an authority figure, that person is ______.
   a. conforming
   b. obeying
   c. attributing
   d. discriminating

6. ______ is an increase in individual performance caused by the presence of other people.
   a. Social facilitation
   b. Social cognition
   c. Social loafing
   d. The smoke detector principle

7. ______ is the tendency for a group's attitudes to become more extreme as a result of group discussions.
   a. Social loafing
   b. Group polarization
   c. Groupthink
   d. Obedience

8. Inez believes that the world is fair and that unfortunate events happen to people who deserve them. Her belief illustrates:
   a. common group identity.
   b. reciprocal liking.
   c. diffusion of responsibility.
   d. the just-world hypothesis.

9. ______ love is characterized by arousal and passion, while ______ love is characterized by deep commitment and affection.

10. The idea that people help others because of a duty to do so, regardless of any potential payback to the helper, is known as the ______.
    a. reciprocity norm
    b. social exchange norm
    c. social responsibility norm
    d. none of the above

Research shows quizzing is a highly effective learning tool. Continue quizzing yourself using LearningCurve, the system that adapts to *your* learning.

LaunchPad macmillan learning   LearningCurve macmillan learning

GO TO: launchpadworks.com

Self-Assessment Answers

1. fundamental attribution error, 2. b, 3. d, 4. c, 5. b, 6. a, 7. b, 8. d, 9. Passionate, companionate, 10. c

WHAT'S YOUR TAKE?

1. We've all experienced salespeople who try many strategies to make a sale. A bicycle shop once tried to lowball me by advertising an unbelievably low price for a nice mountain bike and then, after they had my credit card in hand, mentioned that a few things were "extra"—including pedals and tires! Another time, I was shopping for a TV and the salesperson started with the biggest, most expensive TV in the store. After I said no, he showed me one at about half the price, which I bought. I thought I was getting quite a deal, but I actually spent more than I had planned because it seemed so cheap. Turns out he had used the door-in-the-face strategy on me: The model he sold me had a high profit margin, and it was the one he hoped to sell me all along. Have you had any experiences with salespeople who tried to use any of the strategies described in this section? Be sure to label the strategy (central route persuasion, peripheral route persuasion, foot-in-the-door, door-in-the-face, lowball technique), and describe how effective it was on you.
2. The research on attraction patterns comes to some pretty strong conclusions about what attracts us to each other as couples. Some of the biggest findings: Men who seek women prioritize looks; women who seek men prioritize ability to provide resources; and everyone prioritizes intelligence, kindness, honesty, and sense of humor. How does your own personal experience match with these research results? Do these findings describe who you are attracted to? Do they describe who your friends find themselves attracted to? Do they describe the reasons why others are attracted to you?

SHOW ME MORE

13.1 Social Roles in the Stanford Prison Experiment

http://tiny.cc/1d5dly

This video offers more details about the Stanford Prison Experiment.

Phillip G. Zimbardo, Inc.

13.2 The Give and Take of the Reciprocity Norm

http://tiny.cc/gq7njy

This radio clip (which is also presented in written form) offers detailed explanation, and additional examples, of the reciprocity norm theory.

Carolyn Franks/Shutterstock

13.3 An Act of Kindness

launchpadworks.com LaunchPad macmillan learning

This news clip features an interview of a New York City police officer who gained fame on social media for a prosocial act he performed for a homeless man on a frigid night.

© ABC News

14 Psychological Disorders

Kerkez/Getty Images
Licensed material is being used for illustrative purposes only; any person depicted in the licensed material is a model.

Have you ever been in love? If so, you might describe that feeling in much the same way that psychologist Frank Tallis described one of his therapy clients (Tallis, 2004, pp. ix–x):

> He collapsed on the couch and allowed his body to slide from a seated to an almost horizontal position...The shadows beneath his eyes betrayed a week of sleepless nights—long hours, worrying in darkness.
>
> Only a few weeks earlier he had been a different person. He had burst through the door like a hurricane, shaking my hand vigorously and illuminating the room with a broad, fixed smile... His enthusiasm was feverish. He was boiling over with plans, schemes, and ideas.
>
> Yet, some fourteen days later, the hurricane had blown itself out. He was inert, cheerless, and exhausted. His face had dropped like melted wax and his eyes were made of glass.
>
> What was wrong with him? Was he clinically depressed? Had his preoccupations turned into obsessions? Had he been manic the last time I saw him?

Dr. Tallis soon learned what was wrong with his client: He was in love, but his partner was having doubts. Dr. Tallis uses this tale to start a book in which he proposes that being in love should be considered a mental disorder. *Love Sick: Love as a Mental Illness* details the common "symptoms" of being in love: extreme mood swings, uncontrollable and obsessive thoughts, difficulty concentrating, impaired judgment, changes in sleeping and eating habits, and more. It compares these symptoms to the symptoms of established disorders, especially depression, and concludes that being in love often causes just as much impairment and disruption in the lives of those it afflicts.

Of course, this psychologist's argument was unsuccessful: Being in love is *not* a mental illness. But the idea raises some interesting questions about psychological disorders that we explore in this chapter. First, what is abnormal? The question may seem simple, but distinguishing normal from abnormal is remarkably difficult—as illustrated by the experience of Tallis' lovesick client (and perhaps your own experiences as well). Next, how do experts define psychological disorders? To address this question, we discuss the diagnostic manual that describes all psychological disorders and is used by psychologists and other mental health professionals. Finally, what are some specific psychological disorders? We focus on quite a few, including anxiety disorders, depressive disorders, bipolar disorder, schizophrenia, eating disorders, disorders of childhood, dissociative disorders, and personality disorders.

CHAPTER OUTLINE

What's Abnormal?

YOU WILL LEARN:

14.1 what the definition of a psychological disorder is.

14.2 about the criteria psychologists use to distinguish normal from abnormal.

14.3 about the strengths and weaknesses of these criteria.

A **psychological disorder** is a pattern of behavior that interferes with a person's life by causing significant distress or dysfunction. Some psychological disorders are so common in our society that you have undoubtedly come into contact with them, either through people you know or people you've seen on TV or in movies: depression, phobias, anorexia, and attention deficit/hyperactivity disorder (ADHD), among others. Other disorders may be somewhat familiar to you, but their exact definitions remain a bit uncertain: borderline personality disorder, generalized anxiety disorder, schizophrenia, or bipolar disorder, perhaps.

In this chapter, you will learn about all of these psychological disorders and many more. For each disorder, you'll come to understand *what* it is (its characteristics, symptoms, etc.), *who* has it, and *why* it occurs. You will also consider important issues that surround these disorders—including how they are defined, how those definitions have changed over the years, and controversies that swirl around many of them.

Medical Student Syndrome: How This Chapter Might Affect You

Before we dive into psychological disorders, let's start with a quick note of caution about an effect this material may have on you. The effect is quite well known among medical students as well. In fact, it is called **medical student syndrome**: an experience common among medical students, and perhaps psychology students, in which they start to believe that they have the illnesses about which they are learning. They study ulcers and suddenly feel sharp stomach pains; they study skin cancer and become convinced that their freckles are fatal. Fortunately, the medical students do not usually have the diseases they are studying, despite any fleeting phantom symptoms they might experience (Candel & Merckelbach, 2003).

Your experience learning about psychological disorders might be similar. At some point in this chapter, you are likely to say to yourself, "I've felt that way at times," or even "That's me! I have that disorder!" At those moments, remember medical student syndrome. Even if a few of your symptoms are real, they may not be severe or long-lasting enough to qualify as a psychological disorder (Deo & Lymburner, 2011; Hardy & Calhoun, 1997).

Of course, it would be a mistake to dismiss serious symptoms of a psychological disorder. Some students may truly be struggling with a disorder they read about in this chapter, but keep in mind there are plenty of false alarms. If you find yourself in need of reassurance, seek another opinion from family, friends, your college's counseling center, or a mental health professional.

Distinguishing Abnormal from Normal

You may know people who you would label as abnormal. In fact, you may use a sort of personal radar for abnormality, or a sense that another person's behavior falls outside the normal range. For example, if your friend's grief over her aunt's death consisted of days or weeks of sadness, you would probably view that reaction as normal. However, if her sadness lasted years, included suicidal thoughts or behaviors, and prevented her from working, studying, or socializing, you would begin to view her reaction as abnormal. Likewise, you can make a distinction between your slightly shy neighbor and your neighbor whose shyness is so severe that he lives completely alone and panics at the thought of going outside.

Psychologists have long faced the challenge of distinguishing normal from abnormal (Zachar & Kendler, 2010; Maddux et al., 2005). In fact, over the years,

psychological disorder
A pattern of behavior that interferes with a person's life by causing significant distress or dysfunction.

medical student syndrome
An experience common among medical students, and perhaps psychology students, in which they start to believe that they have the illnesses about which they are learning.

psychologists have changed their minds about whether certain problems fall outside of the range of normal human experience. For example, homosexuality was once considered a psychological disorder, but now it is not (Drescher, 2010). Until the 1980s, social anxiety disorder didn't exist as a psychological disorder: Such individuals were simply thought to be extremely shy, not mentally ill (Wessely, 2008). The fact that psychologists have reversed their thinking on numerous disorders highlights how difficult it is to differentiate normal from abnormal. Let's consider some of the standards that psychologists use to make that distinction. Abnormality can be based on infrequency, deviation from social norms, personal distress, or impairment in daily functioning.

MY TAKE VIDEO 14.1

Abnormal vs. Normal

"I felt a little bit of relief, honestly..."

YOUTUBE: http://tiny.cc/mytake
LAUNCHPAD: launchpadworks.com

Infrequency. The simplest way to determine if a behavior is abnormal is to consider how statistically infrequent it is. By this definition, infrequent means abnormal and common means normal. This distinction makes sense for most psychological problems, such as the hallucinations of schizophrenia or the food refusal of anorexia, since these behaviors are quite infrequent. However, lots of behaviors that are not problematic (or are even desirable) would be classified as abnormal if infrequency were the only factor. For instance, a person with an unusually good memory or a great capacity to handle stress would be considered abnormal. Generally, psychologists do not categorize desirable rare qualities as disorders. So, infrequency is a useful, but imperfect, way to define abnormality. It only works with certain qualities.

Deviation from Social Norms. Abnormality can also be defined by the extent to which it deviates from social norms. For example, the social norm is to wash your hands several times a day. However, some people who suffer from obsessive-compulsive disorder (OCD) wash their hands dozens or even hundreds of times a day. In those cases, the handwashing behavior would be abnormal. Of course, people can deviate from social norms and not be called abnormal. For instance, an athlete who trains excessively for an upcoming big game, neglecting school and friends in the process, is usually described as dedicated or committed rather than abnormal. Like infrequency, deviation from social norms can help to identify abnormality, but by itself it is an imperfect standard.

Here's another complication regarding deviation from social norms: Our society is so varied that what is normal within one group might vary widely from what is normal in another group. What's normal among men might be abnormal among women; what's normal in the Bronx might be abnormal in rural South Dakota; what's normal among African Americans might be abnormal among Asian Americans. As a specific example, consider a behavior as simple as two men greeting each other: For most American men of European descent, a firm handshake is the norm, but in more traditional Italian or Spanish cultures, kissing on the cheek may be expected, and in many Asian cultures, the greeting may include a bow or nod rather than any kind of verbal exchange or physical contact. The norms get even more complicated when we consider a woman greeting a man or another woman. For this reason, it is crucial to consider the cultural context of behaviors before labeling a deviation from social norms as abnormal (Gone & Kirmayer, 2010; McGoldrick et al., 2005).

DIVERSITY MATTERS

For judging whether a behavior deviates from social norms, whose social norms should apply? In some social groups, this woman's tattoos would be abnormal, but in others, they would be completely normal.
moodboard/Getty Images

Personal Distress. It is often assumed that personal distress accompanies most psychological disorders. It is true that people genuinely *suffer* from depressive disorders, anxiety disorders, and eating disorders—aching to escape or overcome them, seeking out treatment to alleviate their symptoms. This is not true of all psychological disorders, though. For example, a person with antisocial disorder might rob or even kill another person without the slightest trace of anxiety or anguish before or after the act.

Impairment in Daily Functioning. The definition of abnormality also includes the extent to which a thought, feeling, or behavior interferes with day-to-day life, the

It is difficult to distinguish abnormality from normality. Impairment with daily functioning is one way to make the distinction, but even that way is not always accurate. In the years before his suicide in 2014, Robin Williams reportedly struggled with various psychological disorders and substance abuse, yet he continued to work extensively as an actor. CBS Photo Archive/Getty Images

amount it impairs work, school, and relationships. The hopelessness and weariness of depression certainly interfere with daily life, as do the restlessness and impulsiveness of attention-deficit/hyperactivity disorder (ADHD). Most other disorders involve a similar level of impairment. However, there are exceptions. Some people with psychological disorders actually function at a high level. For example, prior to his suicide in 2014, actor Robin Williams reportedly struggled off and on for decades with substance abuse and various psychological disorders (Itzkoff, 2014). Yet during that time, he became a major movie and TV star, earning millions of dollars and winning an Academy Award for Best Supporting Actor in *Good Will Hunting*. J. K. Rowling wrote the first *Harry Potter* book while suffering through depression: "I was very depressed…I simply felt like a nonperson. I was very low and I felt I had to achieve something" (Shapiro, 2000, p. 54). So even impairment in daily functioning is, by itself, an imperfect standard.

Seems like none of these criteria is a perfect rule for determining what's abnormal. So how do the experts decide?

That's right: None of these four criteria is perfect. Each of them applies to many, but not all, psychological disorders. Experts consider each of the four factors when defining abnormality, but the last two factors (personal distress and impairment in daily functioning) are generally given more weight than the first two factors (infrequency or deviation from social norms). This emphasis is reflected in the definition of mental disorder offered by the American Psychiatric Association in its manual of mental disorders, DSM, which is used by many mental health professions. Mental disorders "are usually associated with significant distress or disability in social, occupational, or other important activities" (American Psychiatric Association, 2013, p. 20).

CHECK YOUR LEARNING:

14.1 What is a psychological disorder?

14.2 What are the criteria that psychologists use to distinguish between normal and abnormal?

14.3 What are the strengths and weaknesses of the criteria that psychologists use to define abnormality?

What Causes Abnormality?

YOU WILL LEARN:

14.4 about the biological theory of abnormality.

14.5 about the psychological theory of abnormality.

14.6 about the sociocultural theory of abnormality.

14.7 about the biopsychosocial theory of abnormality.

Why do people develop psychological disorders? Centuries ago, explanations centered on forces that we largely dismiss today: evil spirits inhabiting the body or soul, witches casting spells, or the consequences of sin leading to a person's suffering (George, 2007; Stone, 1997). In historical periods when more than one explanation existed, leaders in the field often argued about which explanation was most accurate (Shorter, 1997; Fancher, 1995). In a sense, the same is true today. A variety of explanations for abnormality compete with each other, each with researchers and other experts offering support. Four theories dominate contemporary discussions of what causes abnormality: (1) *biological*, (2) *psychological*, (3) *sociocultural*, and (4) *biopsychosocial*.

The Biological Theory of Abnormality

The **biological theory of abnormality** asserts that biological factors within the human body, such as brain structures, neurochemicals, and genes, are the primary causes of psychological disorders. This theory fits well with a medical approach, in which psychological disorders are viewed as diseases of the brain (Howland, 2005; Clinton &

Hyman, 1999; Kihlstrom, 2002). For that reason, psychiatrists and other medically trained experts tend to agree with this way of understanding abnormality.

Let's consider the example of Jamie, a person with major depressive disorder (defined later in this chapter). Psychologists who favor the biological theory of abnormality would assume that Jamie's major depressive disorder is an illness in her brain. They would suggest that the disorder stems perhaps from too much or too little of a particular neurochemical, or a malfunction in a particular region of Jamie's brain, or a genetic tendency toward depression. These psychologists would also argue that biological treatment methods—such as medications—are necessary to treat Jamie's biological condition.

Contemporary explanations for abnormality differ greatly from explanations from centuries ago, when evil spirits or spells were often assumed to be the root cause.
UniversalImagesGroup/Getty Images

The Psychological Theory of Abnormality

The **psychological theory of abnormality** asserts that psychological factors—including emotions, thoughts, behaviors, and traits—are the primary causes of psychological disorders. When the inner workings of our minds are flawed in a significant way, they can produce psychological disorders. Within the psychological theory of abnormality, there are a variety of different explanations, namely *psychodynamic*, *behavioral*, *cognitive*, and *trait* explanations.

One type of psychological theory of abnormality is the psychodynamic explanation. Psychodynamic explanations emphasize the influence of unconscious feelings and thoughts, much of which stems from early childhood experiences and primal instincts that focus on sex and aggression (Mitchell & Black, 1995). As Sigmund Freud suggested, unconscious feelings and thoughts can affect our lives even though they are out of our awareness. Sometimes, these feelings and thoughts affect our lives in such a way that we develop a psychological disorder (Freud, 1922). According to the psychodynamic approach, Jamie's major depressive disorder might represent feelings of anger that she has turned inward toward herself—rather than directing the feelings at the person toward whom she truly (but unconsciously) feels anger.

Behavioral explanations of abnormality emphasize learning and conditioning (discussed in Chapter 6). According to behavioral approaches, psychological disorders are behaviors that have been shaped by the reinforcements and punishments an individual has experienced as a result of his or her own behaviors (Skinner, 1974). From this point of view, Jamie's major depressive disorder consists of specific actions on her part that have brought about reinforcements she finds valuable. For example, her crying has elicited compassion and attention from friends and family, and her absences from work have resulted in the opportunity to sleep in and watch TV.

Cognitive explanations of abnormality point to the way we think, particularly our illogical thoughts, as major contributors to psychological disorders. If we don't think logically about the events that happen to us, then we are susceptible to feelings that are more unpleasant than they need to be (Beck, 1976). In Jamie's case, her depressive feelings may stem from the way she thinks about her recent failed job application. Let's say she thinks, "I'm completely unemployable. I'll never be able to get a job and I'll end up homeless." Of course, such negative thoughts are not justified by one failed attempt to get a job. These kinds of illogical thoughts may lead Jamie to feel much more dejected than she needs to.

Trait explanations highlight extremely high or low levels of a particular personality trait as the main reason behind a psychological disorder. The five-factor model of personality (see Chapter 12) offers a short list of broad and enduring personality traits—neuroticism, openness, extraversion, conscientiousness, and agreeableness—too much or too little of which could make a person vulnerable to certain psychological disorders (Costa & Widiger, 2001; Claridge, 1995). In this way, Jamie's major depressive disorder could be viewed as a by-product of very high levels of neuroticism, a personality trait that centers on a generally negative, pessimistic outlook on life.

The Sociocultural Theory of Abnormality

The **sociocultural theory of abnormality** asserts that social and cultural factors surrounding the person, rather than factors within the person, are the primary causes of

biological theory of abnormality
A theory of abnormality asserting that biological factors within the human body, such as brain structures, neurochemicals, and genes, are the primary causes of psychological disorders.

psychological theory of abnormality
A theory of abnormality asserting that psychological factors, including emotions, thoughts, behaviors, and traits, are the primary causes of psychological disorders.

sociocultural theory of abnormality
A theory of abnormality asserting that social and cultural factors surrounding the person, rather than factors within the person, are the primary causes of psychological disorders.

psychological disorders. Abnormality may show itself within an individual person, but the problem actually lies within the social or cultural context in which that person lives (Eshun & Gurung, 2009; Caplan, 1995). That context can be large, such as the person's city or country, or it can be small, such as the person's family. Regardless of the scope, those who promote the sociocultural theory of abnormality believe that a faulty system will produce psychological problems in the individuals who live within it. Common social and cultural factors that are thought to contribute to psychological disorders include poverty, oppression, political unrest, prejudice, and abuse. From this viewpoint, Jamie's major depressive disorder doesn't originate within Jamie. Instead, the depression may be a consequence of her economic hardship stemming from widespread unemployment in a weak economy.

The Biopsychosocial Theory of Abnormality

The **biopsychosocial theory of abnormality** is a contemporary theory of abnormality acknowledging that a combination of biological, psychological, and sociocultural factors contribute to psychological disorders. Our best attempt to explain psychological disorders is a comprehensive theory such as the biopsychosocial theory. Neither the body (biological), mind (psychological), nor life circumstances (sociocultural) of a person should be ignored in attempts to explain abnormality. Often, all three factors interact to cause psychological disorders (Campbell & Rohrbaugh, 2006). As **Figure 14.1** shows, the biopsychosocial theory has become widely accepted in recent decades. Today, most psychologists recognize that each of these three perspectives offer important insights into psychological disorders.

Psychologists often use the *diathesis–stress model* as a specific explanation of how biological, psychological, and social factors interact to produce abnormality (Belsky & Pluess, 2009; Zuckerman, 1999; Monroe & Simmons, 1991). In this model, *diathesis* refers to a vulnerability with which a person is born; *stress* is an event (or series of events) that turns that vulnerability into a full-blown psychological problem.

According to the biopsychosocial theory, multiple factors underlie Jamie's major depressive disorder. She may have inherited a slight genetic predisposition to depression (biological), think a bit illogically about events in her life (psychological), and struggle economically due to a shortage of available jobs (sociocultural).

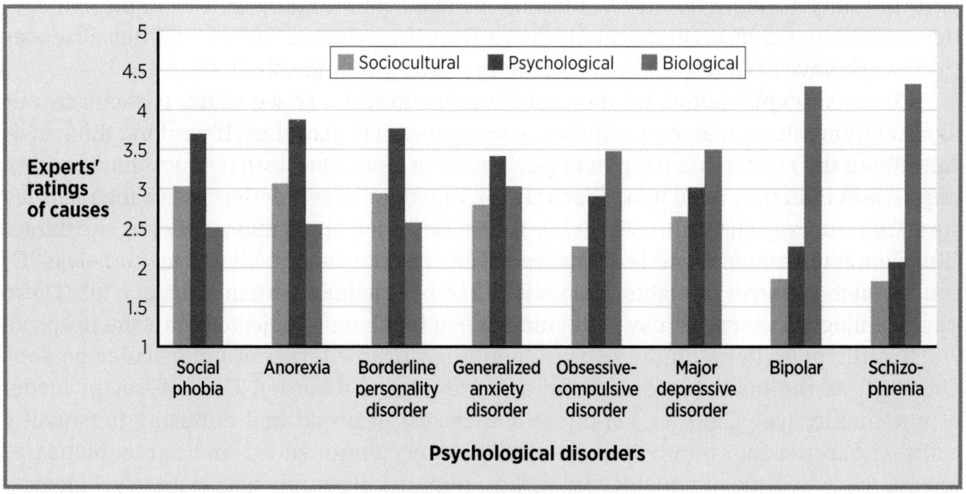

FIGURE 14.1 Experts' Beliefs about the Causes of Psychological Disorders. Researchers asked psychologists and other mental health professionals to rate, on a scale of 1 (lowest) to 5 (highest), whether various disorders were caused by biological, psychological, or sociocultural factors (Ahn et al., 2009). Different disorders received very different ratings. However, even for disorders that received a high rating in one of the three categories, the other two categories were still endorsed. For example, schizophrenia was rated as highly biological, but its ratings for psychological and sociocultural factors were above the bottom of the scale. In general, this pattern endorses a biopsychosocial model, in which neither biology, psychology, nor sociocultural context is ruled out as a contributing factor to any disorder. Data from Ahn et al., 2009.

biopsychosocial theory of abnormality
A contemporary theory of abnormality acknowledging that a combination of biological, psychological, and sociocultural factors contribute to psychological disorders.

***Diagnostic and Statistical Manual of Mental Disorders* (DSM)**
The book in which mental disorders are officially defined.

CHECK YOUR LEARNING:

14.4 According to the biological theory of abnormality, what factors are primary causes of psychological disorders?

14.5 According to the psychological theory of abnormality, what factors are primary causes of psychological disorders?

14.6 According to the sociocultural theory of abnormality, what factors are primary causes of psychological disorders?

14.7 How does the biopsychosocial theory of abnormality combine the other three theories of abnormality?

The Diagnostic Manual: DSM

YOU WILL LEARN:

14.8 what DSM is.

14.9 who uses DSM and for what purposes.

14.10 how DSM is organized and how it has changed over the years.

14.11 about the difference between the categorical and dimensional models of psychopathology.

DSM (full name: ***Diagnostic and Statistical Manual of Mental Disorders***) is the book in which mental disorders are officially defined. DSM is used by psychiatrists, psychologists, social workers, counselors, even physicians and nurses—anyone who might diagnose or treat an individual with a mental disorder. (Outside the United States, mental health professionals often use other manuals, like the *International Classification of Diseases* or the *Chinese Classification of Mental Disorders*.) Likewise, when health insurance companies pay for a person's psychological treatment, including therapy or medication, they typically do so because the person has been given a DSM diagnosis. With so many professionals using it and so many of our lives affected by it, DSM has become a powerful force in U.S. society (Widiger, 2005). Its contents determine the psychological diagnoses professionals can assign to us, which in turn influences not only the treatments we might receive, but our own views of ourselves as well (Eriksen & Kress, 2005; Langenbucher & Nathan, 2006).

The current (fifth) edition of DSM is a hefty book—over 900 pages describing hundreds of psychological disorders (American Psychiatric Association, 2013). It organizes these psychological disorders into 19 categories based on similar characteristics and common themes. Within each category, specific disorders are named and defined (see **Table 14.1**). For example, within the eating disorders category, DSM lists the specific disorders anorexia nervosa, bulimia nervosa, and binge eating disorder. Within the category anxiety disorders, DSM lists panic disorder, specific phobia, social anxiety disorder, generalized anxiety disorder, and others.

For each disorder it names, DSM describes criteria for the disorder, how common it is, how it may appear differently across cultures, and how it may develop over time. At the end of this description, DSM lists the diagnostic criteria for the disorder, an itemized list of exactly what symptoms are necessary to qualify for the diagnosis. The criteria are presented as a checklist, with rules regarding how many symptoms must be checked for the diagnosis to apply. For example, the diagnostic criteria for borderline personality disorder include nine possible symptoms, and the person must have at least five of them to qualify. As another example, the diagnostic criteria for generalized anxiety disorder include six possible symptoms, and the person must have at least three of them to qualify.

How has DSM changed over the years?

DSM wasn't always such a big book. When it was originally published in 1952, it included only 106 disorders—a small fraction of the number the current edition includes. As new editions of DSM came out, sometimes a single disorder was split into many, and sometimes entirely different problems were included as new disorders. Among the disorders that weren't included in the original DSM are many of today's most common or familiar disorders, including attention-deficit/hyperactivity disorder (ADHD), social anxiety disorder, bulimia nervosa, and posttraumatic stress disorder (PTSD) (Blashfield et al., 2010; Langenbucher & Nathan, 2006).

TABLE 14.1: Disorders in DSM-5

CATEGORY	EXAMPLES OF DISORDERS
Neurodevelopmental disorders	Autism spectrum disorders, specific learning disorder, intellectual disability, attention-deficit/ hyperactivity disorder
Schizophrenia spectrum and other psychotic disorders	Schizophrenia, brief psychotic disorder, schizoaffective disorder
Bipolar and related disorders	Bipolar disorder, cyclothymic disorder
Depressive disorders	Major depressive disorder, persistent depressive disorder (dysthymia), premenstrual dysphoric disorder
Anxiety disorders	Specific phobia, social anxiety disorder, panic disorder, generalized anxiety disorder
Obsessive-compulsive and related disorders	Obsessive-compulsive disorder, hoarding disorder, body dysmorphic disorder
Trauma- and stressor-related disorders	Posttraumatic stress disorder, acute stress disorder, adjustment disorder
Dissociative disorders	Dissociative identity disorder, dissociative amnesia
Somatic symptom and related disorders	Somatic symptom disorder, illness anxiety disorder, conversion disorder
Feeding and eating disorders	Anorexia nervosa, bulimia nervosa, binge eating disorder
Elimination disorders	Enuresis, encopresis
Sleep–wake disorders	Insomnia, narcolepsy
Sexual dysfunctions	Erectile disorder, female orgasmic disorder
Gender dysphoria	Gender dysphoria in children, gender dysphoria in adolescents and adults
Disruptive, impulse control, and conduct disorders	Oppositional defiant disorder, conduct disorder, intermittent explosive disorder
Substance-related and addictive disorders	Alcohol use disorder, cannabis use disorder
Neurocognitive disorders	Major neurocognitive disorder, mild neurocognitive disorder
Personality disorders	Antisocial personality disorder, borderline personality disorder, narcissistic personality disorder
Paraphilic disorders	Voyeuristic disorder; exhibitionistic disorder

Information from DSM-5, American Psychiatric Association, 2013.

The Current Edition: DSM-5

The fifth and most recent edition of DSM was published in May 2013. As the first revision of the definitions of mental disorders in almost 20 years, this was a major event for the field of psychology. The new edition of DSM was the culmination of an extensive, multistep process that lasted more than a decade and involved hundreds of experts from at least a dozen countries (American Psychiatric Association, 2013; Kupfer et al., 2013; Regier et al., 2013; Paris, 2013a,b).

At first, DSM-5 authors considered a significant overhaul to the way psychological disorders are defined. Specifically, they looked into the possibility of defining disorders biologically or neurologically (Blashfield et al., 2014). That would have meant that psychological disorders would be defined by something physical within the brain instead of (or perhaps in addition to) lists of symptoms based on behaviors, thoughts, and feelings. This shift would have made psychology more similar to other areas of health care that rely on PET scans, x-rays, blood tests, biopsies, or similar tests to access hard evidence from inside the body to determine whether a person has a disease. However, it soon became clear to DSM-5 authors that the mental health field hasn't reached that point yet. In spite of recent brain research and improvements in technology, there aren't enough definite connections between specific brain abnormalities and corresponding disorders to shift the way we define those disorders yet (Paris, 2013a,b; Pierre, 2013; Stringaris, 2013).

There are plenty of changes in DSM-5, though. Many of these involve introducing new disorders or changing the criteria for old disorders. The new disorders include these:

- *Premenstrual dysphoric disorder* is a severe form of premenstrual syndrome (PMS). It requires a combination of at least five emotional symptoms and physical symptoms to occur during most menstrual cycles. Those symptoms must

cause clinically significant distress or interfere with work, school, social life, or relationships with others (American Psychiatric Association, 2013; Paris, 2013a; Wakefield, 2013; Regier et al., 2013).

- *Disruptive mood dysregulation disorder* occurs in children 6–18 years old who have an excessive number of temper tantrums per week over the course of a year. The tantrums must take place in at least two settings (like home and school), and the children are often irritable or angry between the tantrums (American Psychiatric Association, 2013; Pierre, 2013; Copeland et al., 2013; Frances & Bastra, 2013).
- *Binge eating disorder* involves at least one out-of-control food binge per week for 3 months. The binges often feature rapid eating, eating alone, and feelings of guilt (American Psychiatric Association, 2013; Ornstein et al., 2013; Stice et al., 2013). (We discuss this disorder in more detail later in this chapter.)
- *Mild neurocognitive disorder* is a less intense version of more serious neurocognitive problems like amnesia or dementia. It features minor problems with cognitive functions like memory or attention—for example, forgetting what you wanted to buy at the grocery store, or losing track of the plot of a movie—but nothing serious enough that it prevents the person from living independently (American Psychiatric Association, 2013; Blazer, 2013; Frances, 2013).

MY TAKE VIDEO 14.2

Categorical vs. Dimensional Models of Psychopathology

"The dimensional model of psychopathology is like a dimmer on a light switch..."

YOUTUBE: http://tiny.cc/mytake
LAUNCHPAD: launchpadworks.com

Criticisms of DSM

Some people have criticized DSM authors for its continued expansion with each new edition (Blashfield et al., 2014). Such criticism was especially common around the time DSM-5 was released in 2013, when there were letters of protest from numerous mental health organizations and plenty of media coverage regarding its controversial

CURRENT CONTROVERSY

Premenstrual Dysphoric Disorder?

For some women, the symptoms of premenstrual syndrome (PMS) can be quite severe. If these symptoms significantly disrupt daily life or cause substantial distress, is the person experiencing a psychological disorder? In the most recent edition of DSM, the authors added a new disorder: *premenstrual dysphoric disorder* (PMDD). PMDD is not "ordinary" PMS, but a premenstrual experience that substantially interferes with aspects of life such as work, school, and relationships with others (American Psychiatric Association, 2013). PMDD is much less common and more severe than PMS. Its psychological symptoms include depression, anxiety, mood swings, and decreased interest in activities. (Some physical symptoms are also included.)

Is it a good thing or a bad thing that PMDD is now included in DSM as a psychological disorder? On the good side, women with severe premenstrual symptoms may finally receive some acknowledgment that their experience is legitimate. They may receive more compassion and understanding from those around them, who otherwise might have thought they were complaining about "nothing" or "making up" their problem (Gallant & Hamilton, 1988). Also, these women will be more likely to receive treatment and less likely to be misdiagnosed with a different disorder.

Those who have argued that adding PMDD as a psychological disorder is a bad thing tend to focus on the idea that premenstrual symptoms, as unpleasant as they may be, are a part of normal life. They suggest that people who experience them are not psychologically disordered, but simply going through a difficult experience, and not all difficult experiences are psychological disorders. Receiving a diagnosis of PMDD might cause some to see themselves differently, to change their self-image from "I'm normal" to "I'm mentally ill." There could be some practical, real-world consequences to the disorder too. Consider a woman in a custody battle whose ex-husband's lawyer points out to the judge that the woman is mentally ill because she has received a PMDD diagnosis. This could not happen if PMDD were not a DSM diagnostic category in the first place (Caplan, 1992; Caplan & Cosgrove, 2004; Eriksen & Kress, 2005).

Again, the question here is not whether anyone experiences severe, life-disrupting premenstrual symptoms. Unfortunately, we know that to be true for at least a few people. The question is whether those people should be diagnosed with a psychological disorder. Perhaps the larger question is where we should draw the line between normal (but troubling) life experiences and mental illness. After all, PMDD is just one example. Other new disorders added to DSM-5 include disorders based on excessive or out-of-control versions of some common experiences, like temper tantrums (disruptive mood dysregulation disorder), overeating (binge eating disorder), and concern about physical illnesses (somatic symptom disorder).

IT'S LIKE...

The Categorical Model Is Like an HIV Test, and the Dimensional Model Is Like a Blood Pressure Test

Some medical tests give you definitive yes-or-no, black-or-white, all-or-none results. An HIV test is a great example: It comes back either positive or negative. These possible results match the underlying nature of what is being tested. HIV is a virus that is either in your body or not.

For other medical tests, the results might not be so either-or. They might tell you where you fall within a range, or how high or low your scores are. A blood pressure test is a great example: It comes back as a pair of numbers that indicate how forcefully your heart is pumping blood through your veins. These results match the underlying nature of what is being tested. Blood pressure is something that is present in all of us, so the issue is not whether we have blood pressure or not, but how much blood pressure we have.

The contrast between yes-or-no tests (like HIV) and how-much tests (like blood pressure) is a lot like the contrast between the categorical model and the dimensional model of psychopathology. The categorical model resembles an HIV test: It places individuals in either the yes category or the no category regarding a particular disorder. DSM has always used a categorical model, and you can hear categorical thinking reflected in the common language we use to discuss psychological problems: "He *has* bipolar disorder," "She *doesn't have* obsessive-compulsive disorder." On the other hand, the dimensional model resembles a blood pressure test: it asks how much, or to what extent, the problem is present in a person's life. Just like blood pressure scores are points on a continuum, people would receive ratings for psychological problems on, say, a 1–10 scale rather than being placed in a yes-or-no category.

Are psychological disorders something that we either have or don't have, like a virus? Or are psychological disorders something that we all have but in different amounts, like blood pressure? Is the answer different for different disorders? DSM has always used a categorical approach, but in recent years, many researchers have pushed for changes toward a dimensional model (Widiger & Trull, 2007; Widiger & Edmundson, 2011; Blashfield et al., 2009). ●

new disorders (Whooley & Horwitz, 2013; Greenberg, 2013; Caccavale, 2013). One of the most outspoken critics of DSM-5 was Allen Frances, the psychiatrist in charge of the previous DSM revision, DSM-IV (Frances, 2012). One of Frances' main complaints, shared by many other critics as well, is that the problems DSM-5 labels as new disorders might actually fall within the range of normal life (Frances, 2013). Critics made similar complaints about previous revisions of DSM as well (Caplan, 1995; Kutchins & Kirk, 1997). The critics' point is that not every unpleasant or problematic human experience should qualify as a mental disorder.

DSM has received other criticisms too. Some find fault with the all-or-nothing way it defines disorders, which is similar to the way physicians define many medical problems. Typically, with medical diseases, you either have it or you don't. For example, you either have cancer or you don't. Likewise, you either have the flu virus or you don't. It is a black-or-white question rather than a shades-of-gray question. Does the same logic apply to psychological problems? According to DSM, it does. DSM says *whether or not* a person has a particular disorder. This approach illustrates a **categorical model of psychopathology**: a model in which psychological problems exist as either totally present or totally absent, as opposed to present to a certain extent. Some psychologists think that this categorical model of psychopathology, with its distinct "yes" and "no" categories, doesn't fit psychological problems as well as it fits many medical problems.

Recently, some psychologists have promoted an alternative to the categorical model of psychopathology: the **dimensional model of psychopathology**, in which psychological problems exist on a continuum as opposed to being fully present or absent. If the categorical model is a light switch—either totally on or totally off— then the dimensional model is a dimmer. The dimensional model of psychopathology suggests that rather than determining *whether or not* a person has a disorder, DSM should help psychologists determine *the extent to which* a person has its symptoms (Widiger & Trull, 2007; Simonsen, 2010; Kraemer, 2010). The authors of DSM-5 considered a more dimensional diagnostic system, especially for the personality disorders, but ultimately stuck with the categorical model that previous editions of DSM used (De Fruyt et al., 2013; Phillips, 2013; Gore & Widiger, 2013; Whooley & Horwitz, 2013). Check out the "It's Like ..." box for further discussion.

categorical model of psychopathology
A model in which psychological problems exist as either totally present or totally absent, as opposed to present to a certain extent.

dimensional model of psychopathology
A model of psychopathology in which psychological problems exist on a continuum, as opposed to being fully present or absent.

anxiety disorders
The group of DSM disorders in which the experience of excessive, unjustified anxiety is the primary symptom.

generalized anxiety disorder
A disorder involving anxiety symptoms that persist for a long time across a wide range of situations and activities.

CHECK YOUR LEARNING:

14.8 What is DSM?

14.9 Who uses DSM and why?

14.10 How is DSM organized and how has it changed over the years?

14.11 What is the difference between the categorical and dimensional models of psychopathology?

Anxiety Disorders and Obsessive-Compulsive Disorder

YOU WILL LEARN:

14.12 what anxiety disorders are.

14.13 what generalized anxiety disorder is.

14.14 what specific phobia is.

14.15 what social anxiety disorder is.

14.16 what panic disorder is.

14.17 what obsessive-compulsive disorder is.

14.18 who gets anxiety disorders and obsessive-compulsive disorder.

14.19 why anxiety disorders and obsessive-compulsive disorder develop.

Anxiety disorders are the group of DSM disorders in which the experience of excessive, unjustified anxiety is the primary symptom. Although the focus of this section is anxiety gone awry, it is important to keep in mind that often, anxiety can be a good thing. Anxiety is a built-in alarm system that alerts you to danger so you can react, perhaps by avoiding it or fighting against it (Hofer, 2010; Blanchard et al., 2008). You can probably recall many times when a touch of anxiety served you well. At the time, you may have called the feeling nervousness, worry, apprehension, or just plain fear. Sometimes people get these feelings before a big test, a big date, or a big game. In these cases, a little anxiety may improve your performance by arousing you, keeping you focused, and motivating you to perform well.

Anxiety becomes problematic when it occurs needlessly or in excess—that is, when there is more of it than the situation calls for (Craske et al., 2009). DSM-5 includes quite a few anxiety disorders, all of which share the same core of physical symptoms (heart racing, palms sweating) and psychological symptoms (worry, fear). Let's examine four of them: *generalized anxiety disorder*, *specific phobia*, *social anxiety disorder*, and *panic disorder*. We'll also examine *obsessive-compulsive disorder*, which used to fall within the anxiety disorders category of DSM, but was placed in a new category of its own with DSM-5. (*Posttraumatic stress disorder*, which also features anxiety as a prominent symptom, was covered in Chapter 11.)

Generalized Anxiety Disorder

Generalized anxiety disorder (GAD) involves anxiety symptoms that persist for a long time across a wide range of situations and activities (Brown & Lawrence, 2009). People with generalized anxiety disorder worry—about almost everything. Even when there isn't an obvious reason, as **Figure 14.2** shows, a person with GAD worries about work, school, family, friends, health, money, appearance, life decisions, and world events. This never-ending worry leaves a person with GAD feeling continually nervous and stressed.

Wait, I worry about a lot of that stuff. Do I have GAD?

What separates most people from those with GAD is that those with GAD worry excessively—far more than they need to, to the point that it significantly interferes with their lives (Papp, 2010; Hazlett-Stevens et al., 2009). People with GAD often describe their worry as out of control. When they consider things that may happen in the future,

LIFE HACK 14.1

A little bit of anxiety is not necessarily a bad thing. As long as it is not excessive, anxiety can work to your benefit by alerting you to danger or improving your performance.

(Hofer, 2010; Blanchard et al., 2008)

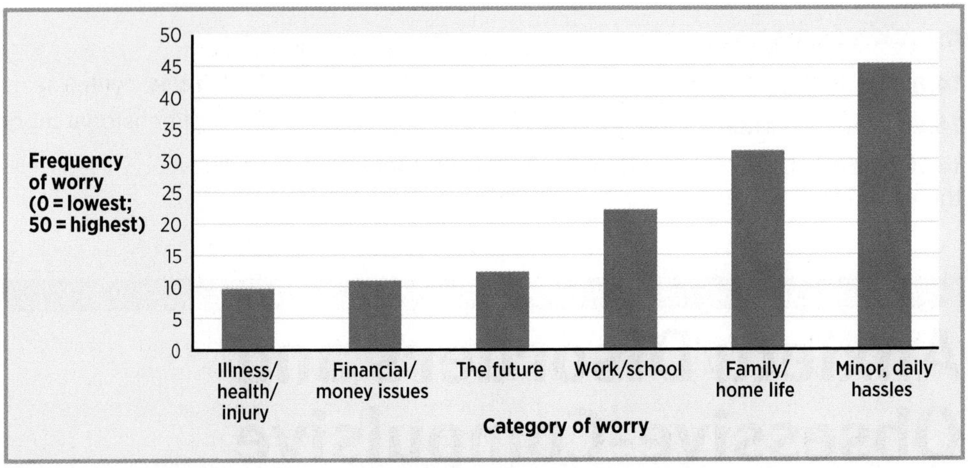

FIGURE 14.2 What Do People with Generalized Anxiety Disorder Worry About? Researchers interviewed almost 100 people with GAD and asked them what they worry about. Their answers spanned a remarkably wide range from the minor hassles of daily life to physical illness, from family and home life to travel, from finances to the future. Data from Roemer et al., 1997.

"When I can't sleep, I find that it sometimes helps to get up and jot down my anxieties."

they fear the worst despite knowing that the worst is extremely unlikely to happen (Holmes & Newman, 2006).

Consider your own experience as you approach a big exam. Your mind might generate a few worrisome thoughts: "What if I bomb it?" You can probably calm those worrisome thoughts, though, by reminding yourself that you have attended class, read the assigned material, and studied for the test. However, the student with GAD can't stop the barrage of what-ifs no matter how prepared for the test: "What if I bomb it? What if that bad grade makes me fail this class? What if failing this class makes me drop out of college? What if I do OK on this test, but I bomb the next one? Wait, I think I'm getting a headache: What if it's actually a brain tumor?" With GAD, the worry doesn't stop.

Patricia Pearson, a news journalist, wrote a book about her struggle with generalized anxiety disorder that reveals the psychological disorder's almost unlimited reach into a person's life:

> I would prefer not to be afraid of the following: phone bills, ovarian cancer, black bears, climate change, walking on golf courses at night, being blundered into by wild insects; unseemly heights, running out of gas, having the mole on my back that I can feel, but not see, secretly morph into a malignant melanoma. Plus, flying. This is a big problem. Also, on occasion, the prospect that the supervolcano underlying Yosemite National Park will erupt and kill us all. Certainly, in addition, unexpected liver failure. And cows. Also, but only occasionally, when I'm really over the edge with anxiety, the fear that the car I'm driving will simply explode. —Pearson, 2008, pp. 1–2

Like all anxiety disorders, the signs of GAD are physical as well as psychological. Bodily symptoms like muscle tension, fatigue, restlessness, and difficulty sleeping accompany the worried thought processes. Even more serious problems like ulcers and heart disease are common among people with GAD (Rygh & Sanderson, 2004).

Specific Phobia

Aretha Franklin, the legendary R&B performer who sang at President Obama's inauguration, has a serious fear of airplanes. She traces the fear back to 1983, when she was on a small plane that experienced severe turbulence:

> We were bouncing all over the sky, and, to say the least, I had an anxiety attack...I kiddingly told my road manager... "You don't have to worry

> about getting me on another plane soon." However, I didn't feel it would be permanent. All I needed was a little time and I'd start flying again. But that never happened...My fear of flying has had an impact on my tour scheduling. I haven't been back to California since I left in the early eighties. It's been even longer since I've been in Europe. I have had to turn down hundreds of offers to appear all over the world. Africa, Japan, Egypt, Australia, and China are just a few of the places I did not go.... —Franklin & Ritz, 1999, pp. 200–201

Aretha Franklin's fear of airplanes provides an excellent illustration of a **specific phobia**: a disorder characterized by excessive anxiety toward a specific object or situation. A specific phobia involves intense anxiety triggered by a single known stimulus (unlike GAD, in which anxiety can stem from almost any situation). People with specific phobias may live without much disruption as long as they avoid the feared object or situation. But that avoidance can itself become a major hassle—or in Aretha Franklin's case, disruption to her career and her life—and when the avoidance fails, the anxiety can be overwhelming (Gamble et al., 2010; Hofmann et al., 2009a).

You are probably quite familiar with some of the most common phobias, such as fear of heights (acrophobia), fear of snakes (ophidiophobia), fear of thunder and lightning (astraphobia), fear of dogs (cynophobia), fear of spiders (arachnophobia), fear of germs (mysophobia), or fear of enclosed spaces (claustrophobia). Thousands more specific phobias—some common, most very rare—have been identified.

Social Anxiety Disorder

People with **social anxiety disorder** (also called *social phobia*) have an intense and irrational fear of situations in which they may be judged or scrutinized. Some people with social anxiety disorder are anxious across most social situations—one-on-one conversations, small group interactions, parties, and many others. For others, social anxiety disorder is more limited, occurring only when they must perform in front of others in such situations as public speaking, athletic contests, or theater events. In both cases, they worry excessively about doing something in front of other people that will cause them embarrassment or humiliation. The anxiety this disorder produces includes both psychological symptoms (like worry and dread) and physical symptoms (like sweating, quickened breathing, and a racing heart) (Taylor et al., 2009; Beidel & Turner, 2007).

Emily Ford, a high school English teacher, wrote a memoir about her experience with social anxiety disorder. Here, she recalls a typical day from her own experience as an eleventh-grader, ruled by the imagined criticisms of everyone around her:

> In first-period chemistry, I was up to my ears in dread...The imagined thoughts of my classmates bombarded me from all sides: "Her hair is so ugly." "Yeah, but did you see those yellow teeth?" "Look at what she's wearing." "She's covered in cat hair." "She's covered in her own hair. Did you see her arms?" "She better not be my lab partner."
>
> Meanwhile, Mrs. H. set a pile of graded papers on the edge of her desk, ready to return them to the class. *What did she think of my answers?* I wondered. *Were they silly, messy, too long, too short, too precise, or just plain wrong? Did my work look like I was trying too hard or not hard enough?*
>
> I was the only one in my class not to fly to Disney World for the senior class trip...I dreaded having to team up with roommates who would undoubtedly cringe at the thought of rooming with me...It seemed simpler to stay home...
> —Ford, 2007, pp. 28–29, 35

As this example illustrates, people with social anxiety disorder pay close attention to their behavior and are critical of themselves, often condemning themselves much more than others around them do (Hofmann et al., 2009b). As a result, people with social anxiety disorder often choose to avoid social interaction, which costs them friends and dating relationships (Ledley et al., 2008).

specific phobia
An anxiety disorder characterized by excessive anxiety toward a specific object or situation.

social anxiety disorder
An anxiety disorder characterized by an intense and irrational fear of situations in which one may be judged or scrutinized.

I know some very shy people, and this social anxiety disorder diagnosis sounds like it would fit them pretty well. What's the difference between social anxiety disorder and extreme shyness?

Actually, that's a tough distinction, and one that has caused some controversy. Some people question whether social anxiety disorder should be considered a disorder at all, since it is essentially a very high level of a personality trait—shyness, or introversion—that is considered normal (Moynihan & Cassels, 2005; Lane, 2007). As with other disorders, DSM emphasizes that its symptoms must cause significant distress or disruption to qualify for the diagnosis.

Panic Disorder

People with phobias know when the anxiety is coming. However, there is no identifiable trigger for people with **panic disorder**: an anxiety disorder characterized by sudden, intense, unpredictable brief bursts of anxiety. In panic disorder, no object or situation sets off the fear reaction. And these episodes are called panic *attacks* for a reason: The reaction is unexpected and overwhelming, with powerful physical components (heart pounding, profuse sweating, gasping for air, dizziness) accompanying equally scary thoughts like "I'm having a heart attack!" or "I'm going to die!" (Craske & Barlow, 2008).

If panic attacks happened to me, I'd become totally preoccupied about when the next attack might come.

That actually happens to many people with panic disorder. Sometimes, they become so concerned about the next panic attack they develop *agoraphobia*. With agoraphobia, the person avoids situations from which escape might be difficult or impossible if they feel a panic attack coming on. This leaves people with agoraphobia essentially imprisoned at home, so scared of having a panic attack at the grocery store, the movie theater, or a friend's house that they don't venture out at all (Arch & Craske, 2008; Smits et al., 2006). Robert Rand, a dancer who wrote a memoir about his struggles with panic disorder, describes both the terrifying attacks (which landed him in the emergency room on at least one occasion) and the paralyzing agoraphobia that came along with it:

> The [panic attacks]...struck with increasingly terrible persistence. Day in and day out, for weeks at a time...the racing heart, the imploded mind, a feeling that surely I would faint or, even worse, would die—all this poked and jabbed at my mind...
>
> My fear of panic attacks had become overwhelming. Anticipatory anxiety controlled every single aspect of my life... Working, shopping, driving, socializing, even exercising—I gauged these activities by their potential to trigger uncontrollable, terrifying panic. There was much, very much, I didn't do for fear of bringing on attacks. —Rand, 2004, pp. 28–29, 33

People with panic disorder often become worried about when the next panic attack might occur. Sometimes, they become agoraphobic, or afraid to leave home.
ARENA Creative/Shutterstock

Many people with panic disorder also experience a hypersensitivity to small changes within their own bodies—slight increases in heart rate, light perspiration, a second or two of light-headedness, or a few heavy breaths. These sorts of bodily changes might happen to you if you climb a few flights of stairs or even stand up too quickly, but if you notice them at all, you can probably dismiss them easily. However, a person with panic disorder often misinterprets these sensations as early signs of an impending panic attack. Unfortunately, this misinterpretation often intensifies the anxiety, which in turn increases the physical sensations, which actually brings on a panic attack (Pollack et al., 2010).

Obsessive-Compulsive Disorder

Obsessive-compulsive disorder (OCD) is a disorder characterized by unwanted, repetitive thoughts and uncontrollable actions done in response to those thoughts. OCD can make the simple tasks of daily life remarkably difficult. Such difficulties filled every day of high school for Jenny Traig, as she explained in her memoir:

> Head toward locker to retrieve calculus book. En route, accidentally brush against classmate. Pause. Is this classmate...unclean? What do you know about this classmate? ... Head to girls' room to wash...Wash hands for a count of one hundred and eighty Mississippi's. On the way out, accidentally touch the door handle. Go back inside and wash three minutes more. Proceed to locker. Realize you forgot paper towels you'll need to touch locker with. Return to girls' room... —Traig, 2004, pp. 221–222

As Jenny's ordeal illustrates, OCD centers on the interaction of two things: obsessions and compulsions. Obsessions are thoughts—unwanted, intrusive, anxiety-provoking thoughts that seem to appear out of nowhere. Compulsions are actions—actions done with the intention of reducing the anxiety caused by the obsessions. It is a cycle: The obsession causes anxiety, and the compulsion reduces that anxiety. The problem is that the obsession occurs again, and again, and again, which makes the person feel the need to perform the compulsion again, and again, and again. A person with OCD can't stop the obsession from popping up, and then can't resist performing the compulsion that soothes the anxiety that the obsession caused (Abramowitz & Mahaffey, 2011; Eisen et al., 2010; Mathews, 2009).

Here's a more detailed description of the process of Jenny's OCD. She has a thought that involves some kind of threat, such as, "My hands have germs on them. I might get sick." That thought makes her feel anxious, and the only behavior that calms the anxiety is washing her hands at the sink. She washes her hands and feels better, but only temporarily. The next time that thought about germs on her hands occurs to her—which might be just a few minutes later—she will again feel the anxiety, and again feel the need to wash her hands to relieve the anxiety. If this pattern happens a lot, she may find her life—work, school, relationships, and everything else—continually interrupted.

Other common forms of OCD—checking to see if the door is locked, making sure the stove is turned off—follow similar patterns. An anxiety-provoking obsession ("I left the stove on and the house is going to burn down") is followed by a ritualized compulsion (checking the stove). With less common versions of OCD, the link between obsession and compulsion can be a senseless (but powerful) superstition. In these cases, the compulsions can be strange. For example, some people with OCD believe that they can perform a ritual involving a certain pattern of tapping or touching to "undo" the anxiety caused by an obsessive thought. They might feel the need to tap a table, say, five times with each index finger. Or, the ritual might be entirely mental and undetectable by others, such as when a person with OCD counts in a particular way—for example, counting by fours to 100. When friends and family learn of these compulsive behaviors, the person with OCD can appear quite eccentric. Nonetheless, the person can't seem to overcome the belief that those compulsions are the only option for undoing the anxiety caused by the recurring obsessions.

CHAPTER APP 14.1

Anxiety Disorders

MindShift

Preview one of the links and consider the following questions.

WEBSITE:
http://tiny.cc/wwi7jy

ANDROID:
http://tiny.cc/ne92iy

IPHONE:
http://tiny.cc/6682iy

VIDEO DEMO:
http://tiny.cc/chapterapps

This app enables users to enter your anxiety symptoms and get help in the form of breathing exercises, challenges to irrational thoughts, and actions that can provide immediate help. It describes itself as "your portable coach helping you face challenging situations and take charge of your life."

How does it APPly to your daily life?
In your opinion, to what extent can apps like this replace face-to-face help that might otherwise come from family or friends? Or from a psychologist or another mental health professional?

How does it APPly to your understanding of psychology?
In your opinion, what distinguishes abnormal anxiety—the kind that underlies *generalized anxiety disorder*, *specific phobia*, *social anxiety disorder*, *panic disorder*, and other anxiety disorders—from the kind of anxiety we all feel as part of normal life?

Who Gets Anxiety Disorders and Obsessive-Compulsive Disorder?

Lots of people develop anxiety disorders, especially in comparison to other types of psychological disorders. In fact, anxiety disorders are the single most common category of psychological disorders. In the U.S. population, 28.8% will experience some anxiety disorder at some point in their lifetime, and almost 18.1% will experience some anxiety disorder within any calendar year. Specific phobia and social anxiety disorder

panic disorder
An anxiety disorder characterized by sudden, intense, unpredictable brief bursts of anxiety.

obsessive-compulsive disorder (OCD)
A disorder characterized by unwanted, repetitive thoughts and uncontrollable actions done in response to those thoughts.

each occur at some point in the lives of more than 12% of people, which puts those disorders at the top of the list not only for anxiety disorders but for all psychological disorders (Kessler et al., 2009, 2005a,b).

Are certain people more likely than others to get anxiety disorders?

Anxiety disorders happen to people of all ages, from young children to older adults (Moore et al., 2010; Rapee et al., 2009; Ayers et al., 2009). Anxiety disorders occur two to three times more often in females than males (Tolin et al., 2010). Interestingly, specific phobias occur twice as often in females as in males, but only after the age of 10. Some experts have speculated that socialization may play a role in the development of specific phobias. They suggest that society allows boys and girls to experience fear equally when kids are young, but then encourages boys to behave more fearlessly than girls around the time kids reach age 10 (Emmelkamp & Wittchen, 2009; Woody & Nosen, 2009).

DIVERSITY MATTERS

Anxiety disorders happen across all ethnicities, both in the United States and around the world. In fact, the lifetime prevalence rates for anxiety disorders tends to hover around 25–30% in most countries, which is remarkably consistent with the rate for the U.S. population (Clark & Beck, 2010). In many cases, anxiety disorders look similar across cultures, but sometimes anxiety can take on unique forms. In many non-Western cultures, the experience of anxiety emphasizes physical discomfort rather than mental discomfort (Asmal & Stein, 2009). For example, GAD in Nigeria and some other African countries often involves the sensation that an insect is crawling inside the person's head or body (Stein & Williams, 2010). In Cambodia, panic attacks can feature neck pain and a sensation in the ears as if wind is shooting out (Good & Hinton, 2009; Hinton et al., 2009). Additionally, some specific phobias have emerged as common in certain parts of the world but remain unheard of elsewhere. For example, in parts of Asia (including Thailand and China), many people have experienced *koro*, a sudden and intense fear that a part of the body (the penis in men, the vulva or nipples in women) will retract into the body and possibly cause death.

Why Do Anxiety Disorders and Obsessive-Compulsive Disorder Develop?

Psychologists are still exploring the reasons behind anxiety disorders, but numerous factors have emerged. The most prominent are psychological factors and biological factors. Specific psychological factors that underlie anxiety disorders include illogical thoughts, learned reinforcements and punishments, the personality trait of neuroticism, and overprotective parenting.

Illogical thoughts can contribute to anxiety disorders. For example, if a person illogically thinks that a harmless dog will viciously attack, that person is more likely to develop a specific phobia of dogs. sanjagrujic/Getty Images

Illogical Thoughts. Illogical thoughts (also known as illogical or irrational cognitions) often take the form of if-then statements that are not true and lead to unnecessary anxiety (Clark & Beck, 2010). For example, a person with a specific phobia might think: "If I go near a dog, then it will viciously attack me." A person with a social anxiety disorder might think: "If I go to the party, then I'll humiliate myself." A person with OCD might think: "If I don't check the stove, then the house will burn down."

Learned Reinforcements and Punishments. In addition to illogical thoughts, learned reinforcements and punishments can also contribute to the development of anxiety disorders. Behavioral psychologists argue that people learn anxiety-related behaviors through experience, just like we learn any other behavior (Lissek et al., 2005; Lissek & Grillon, 2010). For example, if a young man learns that going into elevators is terrifying, then he may choose to avoid elevators. That choice prevents the terror, which the man experiences as reinforcing. As he repeats this behavior for months and years, he develops a specific phobia to elevators.

Neuroticism. Anxiety disorders are also the by-product of the personality trait of neuroticism (Pagura et al., 2009). Neuroticism is a personality trait that we all have to some degree: the tendency to think and react negatively to the events that happen to us. Individuals with high levels of neuroticism tend to remain so from childhood through the life span, and are more susceptible to developing anxiety disorders (Zinbarg et al., 2009; Lawrence et al., 2009). Consider, for example, a group of friends on their way to watch a baseball game who hear on the radio a weather forecast calling for rain. Those with low or moderate levels of neuroticism might think, "It's probably not even going to happen," or "Maybe we'll get a little bit wet, or we'll have to wait through a rain delay—no big deal." But the friend high in neuroticism will react in a much more anxious way: "We could get hit by lightning! We could slip and fall as we walk to our seats! The roads could flood, and we could end up stranded at the stadium!"

Overprotective Parenting. Overprotective parenting can also cause anxiety-related problems to arise in childhood and perhaps persist into adulthood (Hudson & Rapee, 2009). When parents prevent or discourage their kids from experiencing any anxiety, they deny the kids the chance to realize how resilient they may be, and how much control they might have over a situation. Instead, the kids may get the message that even the smallest amount of anxiety can be overwhelming, which could lead to a lifetime of avoidance and fear. For example, 10-year-old Elbia expresses excitement about going to a 1-week sleep-away camp during the summer. At the same time, she mentions that she might feel slightly homesick if she goes. If Elbia's parents respond in an overprotective manner and deny Elbia the chance to attend summer camp, then they communicate to her that the homesickness might devastate her. In reality, being homesick may have been an issue that she could have handled and grown from.

Genetic Factors. Biological factors that underlie anxiety disorders include genetics, brain abnormalities, and evolution. The genetic link is simple: Anxious parents tend to have anxious kids. The biological heritability of anxiety disorders has been estimated around 20–40%. This suggests that the likelihood of developing an anxiety disorder depends to a significant extent on the genes inherited from biological parents (Eley, 2009; Gelernter & Stein, 2009). It seems unlikely, however, that the genetic transmission is specific. Instead, what happens is that parents pass on a generally anxious disposition to their kids. This anxious disposition then reveals itself in any number of ways, rather than in any particular disorder (Maron et al., 2008; Smoller et al., 2008). For example, a mother with panic disorder would pass along to her kids a broad tendency to be anxious rather than panic disorder specifically. If her kids develop an anxiety disorder, their disorder could be a specific phobia or generalized anxiety disorder as easily as panic disorder.

Brain Abnormalities. Brain abnormalities are also evident in people with anxiety disorders. In fact, most of the anxiety disorders share the same physiological abnormalities of the brain. Specifically, as **Figure 14.3** shows, researchers have found that in people with anxiety disorders, the amygdala, a part of the brain that "sounds the alarm" when danger approaches, is overactive, and the prefrontal cortex, which opposes the amygdala by signaling that all is well, is underactive (Britton & Rauch, 2009; Fischer & Tsai, 2009). Additionally, certain neurochemicals tend to function abnormally in the brains of people with anxiety disorders. These neurochemicals include serotonin, dopamine, norepinephrine, and GABA. The particular problem with these neurochemicals is the subject of ongoing research (Bremmer & Charney, 2010; Malizia & Nutt, 2008).

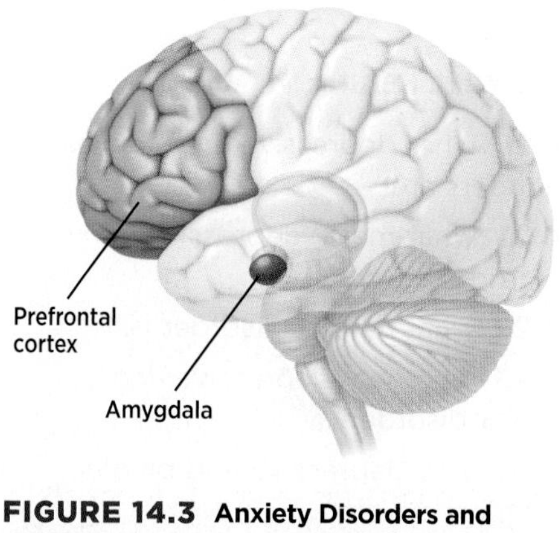

FIGURE 14.3 Anxiety Disorders and the Brain. In people with anxiety disorders, the amygdala is often overactive, and the prefrontal cortex is often underactive.

Evolution. Evolution—in the natural selection, survival-of-the-fittest sense—is also widely recognized as a factor in the development of anxiety disorders (Debiec & LeDoux, 2009; Bracha & Maser, 2008). Our brains and bodies have evolved over the course of human history to predispose us to anxious responses. Think of it this way: If there ever were primitive tribes of humans who were *not* equipped with at least a little anxiety, they didn't survive. They weren't afraid of much and were therefore killed off at a faster rate

than people with a little anxiety. The anxious ones survived, and we are their descendants. The problem with anxiety arises when our evolved tendencies are exaggerated or applied at the wrong times. When that happens, we go into fight-or-flight mode unnecessarily.

For example, throughout human history it has been adaptive to panic when immediate danger emerges. In ancient times, the danger may have been a wild animal attacking or an enemy tribe approaching. Today, it might be a tornado siren wailing or car tires screeching. In any of these cases, people actually benefit from the rush of adrenaline that panic disorders bring: It gears them up to do battle or run away. However, when panic attacks occur in the absence of any apparent threat, the attacks are disruptive rather than helpful.

The best understanding of the cause of anxiety disorders would take both psychological and biological factors into account. A leading theory does exactly that. **Triple vulnerability theory** is an explanation for anxiety disorders that emphasizes the interaction of biological factors, general psychological factors, and specific psychological factors. According to David Barlow, the theory's primary author, the "recipe" for an anxiety disorder consists of three "ingredients": (1) a biological predisposition based on genes and brain abnormalities; (2) a general perceived lack of control over life events that may be caused by parenting styles or illogical thoughts; and (3) life experience that teaches the individual what, exactly, is threatening. For example, if that third factor turns out to be dogs, a specific phobia to dogs may develop; or, if it turns out to be judgment by other people, social anxiety disorder may develop (Barlow, 2002; Barlow et al., 2007; Suarez et al., 2009; Liverant et al., 2007).

CHECK YOUR LEARNING:

14.12 What are anxiety disorders?

14.13 What is generalized anxiety disorder?

14.14 What is specific phobia?

14.15 What is social anxiety disorder?

14.16 What is panic disorder?

14.17 What is obsessive-compulsive disorder?

14.18 How common are anxiety disorders, and in which groups are they most frequently diagnosed?

14.19 Why do anxiety disorders and obsessive-compulsive disorder develop?

Depressive and Bipolar Disorders

YOU WILL LEARN:

14.20 what depressive and bipolar disorders are.

14.21 what major depressive disorder is.

14.22 what bipolar disorder is.

14.23 who gets depressive and bipolar disorders.

14.24 why depressive and bipolar disorders develop.

Depressive and bipolar disorders are the category of psychological disorders based on extreme moods or emotional states. Of course, some variation in mood is entirely normal. We experience good moods or bad moods every day, and we casually use terms like *down* or *blue* to describe our state of mind when things are not going well. There is a difference, however, between these common, passing struggles with mood and full-fledged depressive or bipolar disorders. For people with these disorders, the emotional experiences are so intense or long-lasting that they significantly disrupt daily life (Craighead et al., 2008; Klein et al., 2006). According to DSM, these disorders can occur in one of two specific ways: when a person becomes stuck at the low end of the mood range, where sadness prevails, or when a person skips over the middle range of mood and alternates between the lowest lows and the highest highs (American Psychiatric Association, 2013). Let's focus on four specific disorders in this category: *major depressive disorder*, *persistent depressive disorder* (*dysthymia*), *bipolar disorder*, and *cyclothymic disorder*.

Among well-known people who have struggled with depressive disorders or bipolar disorder are Abraham Lincoln (left), Kid Cudi (middle), and Sheryl Crow (right).
[a] Stock Montage/Getty Images [b] Robin Platzer/Twin Images/Newscom/Photoshot Images/New York/New York/United States of America [c] Ethan Miller/Getty Images

Danny Evans was a young man with a wife, a baby, and a good job in advertising. He was living a happy, healthy life in Southern California—until he rather suddenly found himself experiencing a serious depressive episode. In his book (Evans, 2009, pp. 42–47), he captures depression's powerful impact:

> ...the energy depletion that overcame me as I awoke that morning was far beyond anything I'd ever known. [The depression] must have tripped on an electrical cord that connected me to anything in life that gave me energy or optimism or pleasure. My mind felt physically heavy. I had an all-consuming sense of desolation, as though my soul was made of lead, but it also left me feeling empty. Vacant. It was as though I was dying from the inside out...
>
> ...Only a few months earlier I was playing full-court basketball for forty minutes straight. I was fit. I was strong....Yet there I was that morning, maybe a hundred days later, struggling just to get up...
>
> ...sadness duplicated itself so many times over that every fiber of my emotional fabric was occupied by this single sensation. My spirit was so heavy that the emotions one would normally summon to pull oneself out of depression—hope, enthusiasm, pride—had nowhere to go. They atrophied. They shriveled up and died. And that was sad, too...

Danny's experience vividly illustrates **major depressive disorder**: a psychological disorder in which a person experiences at least 2 weeks of depressed mood and a loss of interest in most activities. Major depressive disorder goes by many other names among mental health professionals and the general public: clinical depression, unipolar depression, or simply depression. Although major depressive disorder has many possible symptoms, its cornerstone is sadness—an unshakable, persistent, relentless sadness that pervades all parts of the person's life. Activities that used to bring pleasure now bring none. Weight changes are common, either because the person has little appetite or because they become unusually inactive while eating more than usual. Sleep is also frequently disrupted—sometimes more, sometimes less than normal. Energy levels, physical activity, and the ability to concentrate tend to dwindle, while feelings of worthlessness and thoughts of death often increase (American Psychiatric Association, 2013; Thase, 2006; Mondimore, 2006).

I feel sad sometimes. Pretty often, actually. And some of those other symptoms have happened to me too. Could I be depressed?

We probably throw around the word *depressed* more than we should. The sadness that characterizes major depressive disorder is much more than common, everyday

triple vulnerability theory
An explanation for anxiety disorders that emphasizes the interaction of biological factors, general psychological factors, and specific psychological factors.

depressive and bipolar disorders
The category of psychological disorders based on extreme moods or emotional states.

major depressive disorder
A depressive disorder in which a person experiences at least 2 weeks of depressed mood and a loss of interest in most activities.

CHAPTER APP 14.2

Depressive and Bipolar Disorders

Moodtrack Diary

Preview one of the links and consider the following questions.

WEBSITE:
http://tiny.cc/cxi7jy

ANDROID:
http://tiny.cc/ue92iy

IPHONE:
http://tiny.cc/q782iy

VIDEO DEMO:
http://tiny.cc/chapterapps

This app allows users to input mood information with unlimited frequency, in the form of both a numeric rating and a verbal description. It provides charts and other kinds of feedback to show how mood changes over the course of days, weeks, or months.

How does it APPly to your daily life?
How could this be helpful to people with or without psychological disorders? How could this be helpful to psychologists seeing clients with depressive disorders or bipolar disorder?

How does it APPly to your understanding of psychology?
How does this app affect your appreciation of the difficulty in drawing the line between normality and abnormality? For example, how low would a person's mood need to be, and for how long, before that person should be considered seriously depressed (as opposed to just feeling blue or down)?

FIGURE 14.4 The Poles of Bipolar Disorder. People with bipolar disorder alternate between the poles of mood: the highs of mania and the lows of depression.

sadness. It is more forceful, resulting in genuine distress and real disruption in day-to-day life. Going to class, driving to work, hanging out with friends, even getting out of bed can seem like insurmountable challenges to the person with major depressive disorder. Also, it is important to remember that for most of us, even intense feelings of sadness tend to last hours or days, falling far short of the 2-week duration that is required by the DSM definition of major depressive disorder. Having said that, if you do experience sadness or depression that is especially intense or long-lasting, seeking help is a good idea.

Speaking of duration, DSM also includes a separate disorder that shares the same core of sadness as major depressive disorder, but it is much longer-lasting. **Persistent depressive disorder (dysthymia)** is a psychological disorder characterized by a chronic, relatively low-intensity depressed mood. The diagnosis of persistent depressive disorder requires the symptoms to be present for 2 *years* rather than 2 weeks, and many people with persistent depressive disorder can't remember a time in their lives when they didn't feel blue. It is essentially a perpetual mild gloominess that eclipses any memories of happier times. Meri Nana-Ama Danquah, a native of Ghana and a poet, playwright, performance artist, and social activist, captures the essence of this disorder in her description of her own struggle:

> There are times when I feel like I've known depression longer than I've known myself. It has been with me since the beginning, I think. Long before I learned to spell my name. No, even longer than that. I'm sure that before I could even speak my own name or learn to love the color of my skin, this hollow heartache was following me, patiently awaiting the inevitable crossing of our paths, planning my future unhappiness…this terrible sickness…has cost me lovers and friendships, money and opportunities, time and more time. So much wasted time. —Danquah, 2002, pp. 174–175; see also Danquah, 1999

Bipolar Disorder

The term *bipolar* refers to the two poles of mood. Picture them as the North Pole of elation and the South Pole of sadness. We all experience mood swings that take us back and forth between the Northern Hemisphere and the Southern Hemisphere, but most of us rarely stray far from the equator in the middle. Some people, however, don't spend much time in the middle at all. These people may have **bipolar disorder** (formerly known as *manic depression*): a psychological disorder characterized by alternating between extremely high moods and extremely low moods. As **Figure 14.4** illustrates, their emotional state fluctuates back and forth from elation to sadness, and with little explanation or control over the shifts from one emotional extreme to the other (Otto & Applebaum, 2011).

You are already familiar with one of the poles of bipolar disorder—depression—from our discussion of major depressive disorder. (Remember that one of the terms for major depressive disorder is *unipolar* depression.) The other pole is **mania**, an emotional state of excessively elated mood and overabundant energy (Johnson et al., 2009; Miklowitz & Johnson, 2008; Miklowitz & Craighead, 2007). There are two variations of bipolar disorder, distinguished largely by the intensity and length of the mania experience. *Bipolar I disorder* features full-fledged manic episodes that last at least a week and cause significant impairment in daily functioning; in *bipolar II disorder*, the mania symptoms are typically briefer and less debilitating (and are called hypomanic episodes rather than manic episodes).

If mania is the opposite of depression, wouldn't mania be a good thing? I wouldn't mind feeling elated and energetic all the time.

Actually, people with bipolar disorder find their manic episodes quite disturbing. In small doses, periods of intense energy can be great: Imagine your reaction when you scratch off a winning lottery ticket, or land the job of your dreams, or score backstage passes to a concert by your favorite band. But mania can make a person feel out of control if the elation doesn't have an identifiable reason behind it, or goes on far too long.

During manic episodes, which last for days on end, people can't seem to hit the brakes: They feel continuously full of energy, with little need for sleep. They are without inhibition, and may find themselves engaging in behaviors with harmful consequences, like indiscriminate talking, spending, working, or sex. If this uninhibited behavior goes on for a while, serious problems can arise. Consider the experience of Terri Cheney, an entertainment lawyer with bipolar disorder who wrote a book about her disorder in which she offers this first-hand description of a manic episode:

> The mania came at me in four-day spurts. Four days of not eating, not sleeping, barely sitting in place for more than a few minutes at a time. Four days of constant shopping...and four days of indiscriminate, nonstop talking: first to everyone I knew on the West Coast, then to anyone still awake on the East Coast, then to Santa Fe itself, whoever would listen...Mostly, however, I talked to men. Canyon Road has a number of extremely lively, extremely friendly bars and clubs.... It wasn't hard for a redhead with a ready smile and a feverish glow in her eyes to strike up a conversation and then continue that conversation well into the early-morning hours, at his place or mine. —Cheney, 2009, pp. 6–7

Many people with bipolar disorder experience extreme manic episodes like Terri, but some people describe milder episodes. In these milder cases, the ongoing up-and-down mood cycle can still interfere with daily life in significant ways, particularly when the ups and downs continue for a prolonged period. DSM has a different diagnostic label for this experience: **cyclothymic disorder**, a long-term, lower-intensity version of bipolar disorder. Essentially, cyclothymic disorder is to bipolar disorder what persistent depressive disorder is to major depressive disorder—the same core symptoms, but less intense and longer lasting. A person with cyclothymic disorder alternates between emotional ups that aren't quite manic and emotional downs that aren't quite depressive for 2 years or more (Ketter & Wang, 2010; Newman, 2006; Stewart et al., 2006).

In serious cases, the despair brought on by bipolar disorder or depressive disorders can drive people to contemplate or commit acts of self-harm. The most serious concern, of course, is suicide. Compared to the general public, people with major depressive disorder are 20 times more likely to commit suicide. For people with bipolar disorder, the ratio is even higher (Osby et al., 2001; Swartz, 2007; Newman, 2006). Thankfully, in spite of these statistics, the majority of people who struggle with depressive and bipolar disorders don't make suicide attempts.

persistent depressive disorder (dysthymia)
A depressive disorder characterized by a chronic, relatively low-intensity depressed mood.

bipolar disorder
A psychological disorder characterized by alternating between extremely high moods and extremely low moods.

mania
An emotional state of excessively elated mood and overabundant energy.

cyclothymic disorder
A long-term, lower-intensity version of bipolar disorder.

Who Gets Depressive and Bipolar Disorders?

Depressive and bipolar disorders are remarkably common. In fact, only anxiety disorders are more widespread. Among Americans, 20.8% have been diagnosed with a depressive or bipolar disorder at some point in their lives, and 9.5% have been diagnosed in the last year (Kessler et al., 2008). As **Figure 14.5** shows, these disorders take a tremendous toll: Including treatment costs, lost productivity at work, and other expenses, the price tag for major depressive disorder and bipolar disorder in the United States alone is $100 billion annually (Wang & Kessler, 2006). Dollars are not the only costs: People with depressive and bipolar disorders suffer through higher rates of marital conflict, divorce, and job loss than the general public (Newman, 2006; Kessler & Wang, 2009; Murray & Lopez, 1996; Constantino et al., 2006; Thase, 2006).

Within the depressive disorders and bipolar disorders categories, specific disorders occur at different rates. For example, major depressive disorder is far more common than bipolar disorder. Major depressive disorder has a lifetime prevalence rate of 17%, and a 1-year prevalence rate of 6.6%. For bipolar disorder, those numbers are just 3.9% and 2.6%, respectively (Kessler et al., 2008; Kessler & Wang, 2009; Kessler et al., 2005a, b). Major depressive disorder is about twice as common in females as in males, but bipolar disorder is diagnosed with about equal frequency across the sexes (Goodwin et al., 2006; Kornstein & Sloan, 2006). As with phobias, the sex difference in rates of major depressive disorder occurs only after the age of about 12 or 13. Experts have offered many possible explanations, including socialization that encourages women to

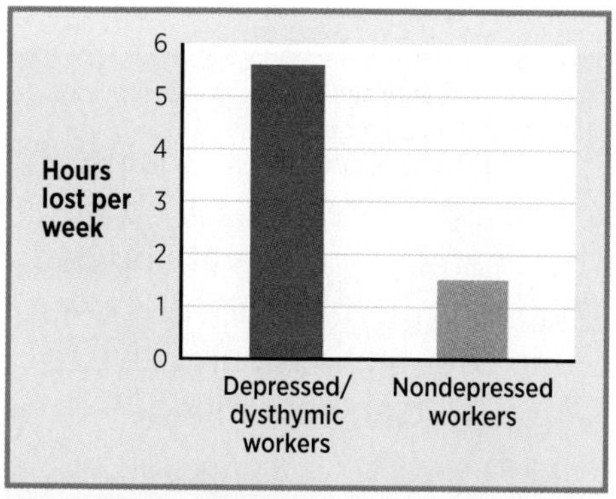

FIGURE 14.5 The Costs of Depression and Persistent Depressive Disorder (Dysthymia) at Work. Workers with depressive disorders cost their employers much more than similar workers without depressive disorders. Researchers found that U.S. workers with major depressive disorder or persistent depressive disorder (dysthymia) experience over three times as many hours of lost production (either absent, or present but not fully productive) as their peers, costing their employers over three times as much money (Stewart et al., 2003).

express sadness but men to hide it, and greater pressure on women to take on multiple responsibilities (Nolen-Hoeksema & Hilt, 2009; Lara, 2008; Hankin et al., 2008).

Some version of major depressive disorder happens in every society around the world. However, the way people experience it appears to vary greatly. Generally, non-Western cultures tend to experience depression as more physical than psychological, just as they do anxiety disorders. In some African countries, depression is often expressed as a sensation of heat in the head; in Iran, as a heavy heart or tightness in the chest; and in India, a sinking feeling (Kirmayer & Jarvis, 2006). Additionally, non-Western cultures may not view the experience of sadness as a sign of disorder; in fact, in Japan, sadness is often viewed as an important part of human experience that produces self-understanding and gives meaning to life (Watters, 2010). Depression is experienced and defined in different ways around the world, which might explain why it occurs at different rates in different places: very low in Japan, China, and Nigeria, but very high in the Netherlands, the United Kingdom, and Chile (Ustun & Sartorius, 1995).

DIVERSITY MATTERS

Why Do Depressive and Bipolar Disorders Develop?

Like anxiety disorders, depressive and bipolar disorders can develop for a variety of reasons. Research suggests that both biological factors and psychological factors play a role.

The biological factors that underlie these disorders include genetics, brain abnormalities, and neurochemicals. In terms of genetics, bipolar disorder appears to be one of the most heritable psychological disorders, and major depressive disorder is not far behind (Miklowitz & Johnson, 2008). Brain abnormalities are also present in both major depressive disorder and bipolar disorder, especially in the parts of the brain that process emotions, including the hippocampus, amygdala, and prefrontal cortex. So, when people with one of these disorders experience an unfortunate event, their brains may generate more intensely negative emotions than the brains of those without such disorders.

The focus on biological factors underlying depressive and bipolar disorders often takes the form of the *chemical imbalance* theory, which states that the levels of certain brain chemicals are awry in people with these disorders. The chemical imbalance theory is quite popular, but many scientists who study it have some reservations about how completely or accurately it explains these disorders. So, levels of serotonin, norepinephrine, and dopamine may play some role in major depressive disorder and bipolar disorder; however, their exact role remains under investigation (Johnson et al., 2009; Delgado & Moreno, 2006; Hammen & Watkins, 2008).

The most prominent psychological factor behind depressive and bipolar disorders is the presence of illogical thoughts, especially pessimistic and cynical ones. For people with depressive disorders, illogical thinking stems from a *depressive schema*, which is a mental framework that biases a person toward viewing the environment in a negative way (Joorman, 2009; Beck, 1976; Beck et al., 1979). A depressive schema can darken the experience of life like sunglasses that never come off. They cause a person to believe that they are worthless, unlikable, or a failure, even if those beliefs are actually false (Beck, 1976; McBride et al., 2007). For people who struggle with depression, negative thoughts tend to stick around once they get in. Depressed people tend to *ruminate*, or think about their perceived shortcomings and failures over and over again, unable to let them go, which further worsens their mood (Nolen-Hoeksema et al., 2007; Beevers, 2005).

LIFE HACK 14.2

To protect yourself against feeling depressed, try not to ruminate. When something bad happens, thinking about it over and over again is only likely to worsen your mood.

(Nolen-Hoeksema et al., 2007; Beevers, 2005).

CHECK YOUR LEARNING:

14.20 What are depressive and bipolar disorders?

14.21 What is major depressive disorder?

14.22 What is bipolar disorder?

14.23 How common are depressive and bipolar disorders, and in which groups are they most frequently diagnosed?

14.24 Why do depressive and bipolar disorders develop?

Eating Disorders

Food is central to human survival, and the drive to obtain it may be our most primal instinct. But there is also psychological and social meaning attached to food that can derail even this most fundamental drive. Food means weight, and weight can have powerful consequences, especially in our culture. For some people, weight and body image translate into attractiveness and self-worth. These people are especially vulnerable to **eating disorders**: the category of psychological disorders that involve significant disturbances in behaviors related to eating or food.

Eating disorders, like other psychological disorders, range in severity. In some cases, they become so severe that the person with the eating disorder must stay for days or weeks in a hospital. There, mental health professionals work with physicians and dieticians toward the primary goal of ensuring that the person takes in enough calories to stay alive and healthy. Let's examine the three most common disorders within this category: anorexia nervosa, bulimia nervosa, and binge eating disorder.

YOU WILL LEARN:

14.25 what eating disorders are.
14.26 what anorexia nervosa is.
14.27 what bulimia nervosa is.
14.28 what binge eating disorder is.
14.29 who gets eating disorders.
14.30 why eating disorders develop.

Anorexia Nervosa

Anorexia nervosa (often called simply **anorexia**) is an eating disorder based on a refusal to eat enough food to maintain a minimally normal body weight, based on the person's height and age. This refusal to eat usually starts with a distorted view of one's own body as fat. Additionally, people with anorexia typically base their self-image on their physical appearance, with thinness at the top of the list of desirable physical qualities. People with anorexia are shockingly thin—sometimes to the point that they risk starving themselves to death—but refuse to eat adequately because they wrongly see themselves as overweight (Keel & McCormick, 2010; Steiger & Bruce, 2009).

Lisa Himmel's memoir tells the story of her fight against anorexia. In this excerpt, Lisa describes going out to lunch with her mom during her senior year of high school. In particular, notice the inflexibility in her thinking about food and her strategy for tricking her mom into thinking she ate more than she did:

> They had plenty of suitable menu items: fresh soups, large salads, and fancy sandwiches. But I freaked out. Nothing appealed to me—or rather nothing fit in the strictures of my rigid diet plan.
>
> I know she just wanted to have a pleasant lunch with her daughter. But I stared at the menu board overhead, while she carefully made suggestions, and I said, "No! That will make me fat, Mom!" She read out one option after the other, and I rejected everything. I wanted to give up, and let my hunger wallow in my tiny stomach, but I could tell I was acting like a child. I settled on a grilled vegetable sandwich on wheat bread, which I broke apart around the edges. The sandwich was fine, but I left most of it on the plate...
>
> ...As I got older I began to stray from family dinners and my formerly adventurous appetite. My weight dropped and I seemed to become more noticeable to those who before had never or rarely acknowledged my presence. Words like "fit" and "thin" joined in their compliments of my body... receiving praise about my body was better than a fancy restaurant meal. Even when praise turned into worry as I lost more weight, I only heard "skinny" or "thin"... and I had to keep going. —Himmel & Himmel, 2009, pp. 116–117

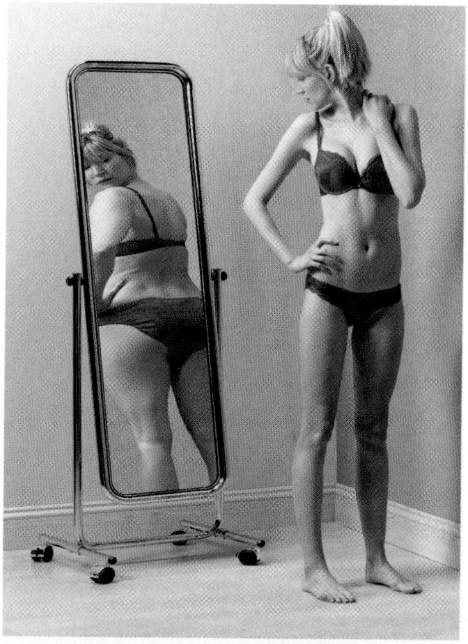

People with anorexia have a distorted view of their own bodies as fatter than they really are, and often highly value that body image. As a result, they refuse to eat enough to maintain a minimally healthy body weight.
Peter Dazeley/Getty Images

eating disorders
The category of psychological disorders that involve significant disturbances in behaviors related to eating or food.

anorexia nervosa
An eating disorder based on a refusal to eat enough food to maintain a minimally normal body weight, based on the person's height and age.

Anorexia sounds like a psychological disorder that could have some serious physical consequences. Does it?

There are many dangerous consequences for the body when there is prolonged malnutrition from anorexia: irregular heart rate, chest pain, hypothermia, hair loss, dry skin, and constipation, among others. It is also common for women with anorexia to stop having menstrual periods (Mitchell & Crow, 2010; Katzman et al., 2010). Unfortunately, anorexia proves to be fatal in about 5% of cases, whether due directly to self-starvation or indirectly to medical complications (Keel, 2010).

Bulimia Nervosa and Binge Eating Disorder

Bulimia nervosa (often called simply **bulimia**) is an eating disorder in which an individual exhibits a pattern of overeating followed by drastic attempts to prevent weight gain. Originally, bulimia was considered a variation of anorexia, but for decades it has been recognized as a distinct disorder (Russell, 1979). People with bulimia are overly concerned about their weight, but find themselves trapped in a pattern of binging and purging (rather than flatly refusing food, as people with anorexia do). They overeat (binge) and then try to undo that overeating by quickly subtracting those calories from their bodies (purge). The overeating episode feels out of control and involves eating far more than others would eat in the same situation, at least once per week for 3 months. Often, the foods that people with bulimia choose to binge on are high-calorie sweets, like cakes, cookies, or ice cream. Also, people with bulimia often feel quite embarrassed by their binges, and only do so when they are alone or can hide the evidence (wrappers, packages, etc.). The most common form of purging is self-induced vomiting, but other forms include excessive exercise, misuse of laxatives or other medications, and temporary fasting (Sysko & Wilson, 2011).

People with bulimia are not necessarily underweight. As a result, people with bulimia may be able to keep their symptoms undetected for longer periods of time than skeleton-thin people with anorexia. Frank Bruni's memoir about his struggles with disordered eating describe the desire to hide bulimic symptoms from friends and family. This passage is about a dinner with friends while he was a freshman at University of North Carolina:

> I'd eaten too much... No way was I going to let all of that linger in my stomach. The bathroom at Sadlack's was for one person only, and it locked, so I had the privacy I needed. I ran the water from the sink to camouflage any sound I might make. I got to work immediately. I kept getting speedier and speedier at this.
>
> Within forty-five seconds the sandwich was gone. I flushed the toilet, then went to the sink and scooped some cold water into my mouth to rinse it. I splashed some water on my face. I studied myself in the mirror. I needed to wait a bit longer before returning to the booth. I was still too red.
>
> After a minute, I made a fresh appraisal: pink now. Much better. Almost there.
>
> Thirty seconds later, I was good to go. My eyes were still watery, and faintly bloodshot. But how much of a giveaway, really, was that? Eyes could look the way mine did for any number of reasons... —Bruni, 2009, pp. 94, 98

In Fiji, eating disorders such as anorexia and bulimia were essentially nonexistent until its residents were able to watch American television. Soon after, some girls and women started evaluating their bodies in more negative ways, and there was a rise in eating disorders. testing/Shutterstock

The physical toll of bulimia is severe. Not only can people with bulimia experience any of the medical problems associated with anorexia, but they may also experience problems specifically tied to the purging method. Forcing yourself to throw up on a regular basis does serious damage to your body, in the form of dental problems, chronic sore throat, heartburn, fluid retention, and swelling of the glands involved in salivation and vomiting (Mehler et al., 2010).

Binge eating disorder is an eating disorder with the overeating pattern of bulimia but without the purging. Binge eating disorder is an appropriate diagnosis for people who binge on food at least once a week for 3 months but do not engage in calorie-subtracting behaviors like self-induced vomiting, overexercising, using laxatives, or fasting. Like people with bulimia, people with binge eating disorder feel a lack of

control over their eating, and often choose to binge alone to avoid embarrassment. Binge eating disorder has been informally recognized by clinicians for many years, often as a variation of bulimia, but it became an official disorder of its own with the release of DSM-5 in 2013 (Fairburn et al., 2000; Kessler et al., 2013; Hudson et al., 2012).

bulimia nervosa
An eating disorder in which an individual exhibits a pattern of overeating followed by drastic attempts to prevent weight gain.

binge eating disorder
An eating disorder with the overeating pattern of bulimia but without the purging.

Who Gets Eating Disorders?

Eating disorders typically develop around the middle school, high school, or young adult years. They are not exclusive to females, but the female-to-male ratio is about 10:1 (Gordon, 2000; Keel, 2010). Eating disorders are relatively rare. In the United States, the combined rate for all three eating disorders is less than 2% of the population, with anorexia less common than bulimia and binge eating disorder (Agras, 2010; Crow & Brandenburg, 2010; Kessler et al., 2013).

There is no doubt that Western cultural influences such as the glorification of thin female celebrities push people, especially young women, toward eating disorders, but versions of eating disorders have been found elsewhere in the world (Keel, 2010). In some cases, the rise of eating disorders in a particular location happened right after people there gained access to Western media. There is actually quite a list of countries—Ukraine, Belize, South Korea, South Africa, and others—in which eating disorders quickly jumped from nonexistent to prevalent as soon as the country was exposed to U.S. pop culture (Levine & Smolak, 2010). Consider this example: The island nation of Fiji (in the South Pacific, east of Australia)—where full-figured, robust women were traditionally viewed as symbols of beauty—had virtually no eating disorders until 1995. That year, U.S. and British television, with its exceedingly thin female stars, reached the island. Within a few years, 74% of teenage girls in Fiji reported that they viewed themselves as too fat, and 15% reported that they had intentionally vomited to lose weight (Becker et al., 2002).

DIVERSITY MATTERS

Why Do Eating Disorders Develop?

The development of eating disorders involves biological, psychological, and social factors. A small amount of research, including twin studies, points to biological factors, such as heritability (Wade, 2010; Bulik et al., 2006; Klump et al., 2001). There is also a small body of evidence from neuropsychological research suggesting that people with eating disorders may have disturbances in the regions of the brain responsible for taste and reward processing (Kaye & Oberndorfer, 2010).

Psychological factors that play a role in the development of eating disorders include a tendency toward perfectionism, especially among people with anorexia. This perfectionism often translates into an all-or-none attitude toward one's weight: either perfectly

FROM RESEARCH TO REAL LIFE

How Powerful Are Magazines in the Development of Eating Disorders?

Researchers conducted a large-scale study exploring magazine images and other possible causes of body dissatisfaction, which is a major contributor to the development of eating disorders (van den Berg et al., 2007). The researchers surveyed over 2500 participants in middle school, high school, and early adulthood. They used numerous questionnaires to measure body dissatisfaction and many of the variables that could contribute to it. These variables included how often they read magazines that feature images of underweight women and articles about weight loss and dieting.

But lots of other variables were measured as well, including:

- How many hours of TV they watch per week
- Their level of self-esteem
- Their level of depression
- How much their parents diet or encourage dieting
- How much their friends diet
- How often they were teased about their weight
- Their body mass index (essentially, a height-weight comparison that indicates how underweight or overweight a person is)

The researchers then determined how closely each of these factors related to body dissatisfaction. They found that exposure to magazines featuring underweight women correlates strongly with body dissatisfaction, especially for females. But most of the other variables were strongly related also, including self-esteem, friend dieting, and body mass index. ●

thin or unacceptably fat, with no in-between. In this way, the idea that "you can never be too thin," which is all too widely accepted in the United States, becomes a dangerous obsession (Jacobi & Fittig, 2010; Vogele & Gibson, 2010). Among people with bulimia, impulsiveness is a much higher risk than perfectionism. Acting on impulses can result in binging, and those binges, of course, lead to purging (Couturier & Lock, 2006).

By far, social and cultural influences (such as those related to Western media) have received the most attention as possible causes of eating disorders. Our TV shows, films, and magazines convince young females that thinness equals beauty. A never-ending parade of slender female models and movie stars, combined with harsh criticism of those who gain a few pounds, encourages some females to pursue thinness at all costs (Grabe et al., 2008; Levine & Murmen, 2009). In fact, some studies have found a strong correspondence between how often young females read magazines that feature extremely thin women and their dissatisfaction with their own bodies, which can lead to an eating disorder (van den Berg et al., 2007; Groesz et al., 2002; Field et al., 1999a,b). See the From Research to Real Life box for a detailed discussion of one of these studies.

All of the girls and women I know watch TV, see movies, and read magazines, but only a small number of them develop eating disorder symptoms. Why does the media affect some people differently than others?

The media message that thinness equals beauty is especially toxic when it is combined with another belief: Beauty is everything. For people whose self-concept is built around the way their bodies look—not their intelligence, or abilities, or relationships, or anything else—the quest to lose weight can become life's primary goal.

This belief that beauty is everything can come from a variety of sources. For example, researchers have found that girls whose parents overemphasize their daughters' physical appearance and criticize their weight are much more likely to develop eating disorders than girls who do not (Davison et al., 2000; Field et al., 2005). Also, girls whose mothers or friends are role models for eating disorders are at an increased risk (Stice, 2002; Eisenberg et al., 2005). Culture plays a powerful role too: Women from ethnicities in which body dissatisfaction rates are relatively low, such as African Americans, tend to have low rates of eating disorders. By contrast, European women tend to have among the highest rates of both body image dissatisfaction and eating disorders (Roberts et al, 2006; Field & Kitos, 2010).

DIVERSITY MATTERS

CHECK YOUR LEARNING:

14.25 What are eating disorders?

14.26 What is anorexia nervosa?

14.27 What is bulimia nervosa?

14.28 What is binge eating disorder?

14.29 How common are eating disorders, and in which groups are they most frequently diagnosed?

14.30 Why do eating disorders develop?

Schizophrenia

YOU WILL LEARN:

14.31 what schizophrenia is.

14.32 about the differences between positive, negative, and cognitive symptoms of schizophrenia.

14.33 who gets schizophrenia.

14.34 why schizophrenia develops.

Schizophrenia is a severe psychological disorder in which the person exhibits bizarre disturbances in thinking, perception, feelings, and behavior.

Wait—isn't schizophrenia the disorder in which the person has multiple personalities?

No—that's a common belief, but it is wrong (Duckworth et al., 2003). (Dissociative identity disorder, which comes up later in this chapter, comes closest to that description.)

An accurate description of a person with schizophrenia centers on the fact that he or she has a take on reality that is blatantly unrealistic. This obvious break from reality differs from the slight distortions of reality common in other disorders. It is more extreme than in the person with a phobia who overestimates the danger of a friendly dog or the person with major depressive disorder who views a recent job interview in an unjustifiably negative way. To describe this blatantly unrealistic way of perceiving the world, psychologists use the word **psychosis**: a significant impairment in the basic ability to tell the difference between the real world and imagination. As a result, people with schizophrenia often seem to have created their own personal fantasy world. They see things others don't see, hear things others don't hear, think things others don't think, and believe things others don't believe. In short, people with schizophrenia don't live in the same reality as those around them (Mueser & Duva, 2011; Lieberman et al., 2006).

Consider Elyn Saks, a law professor at the University of Southern California who has schizophrenia. In her book, she describes the experience of living with schizophrenia, including this striking passage in which she discusses an assignment with fellow law students at the library. Notice how her grip on reality appears to slip, and how her speech reveals an illogical and bizarre thought process:

> "I don't know if you're having the same experience of words jumping around the pages as I am," I say. "I think someone's infiltrated my copies of the cases. We've got to case the joint. I don't believe in joints. But they do hold your body together." I glance up from my papers to see my two colleagues staring at me. "I...I have to go," says one. "Me, too," says the other...

Later, Elyn finds herself in her professor's office, discussing the assignment:

> "The memo materials have been infiltrated," I tell him. "They're jumping around. I used to be good at the broad jump, because I'm tall. I fall. People put things in and then say it's my fault. I used to be God, but I got demoted." I begin to sing my little Florida juice jingle, twirling around his office, my arms thrust out like bird wings. —Saks, 2007, pp. 1–3

Elyn's episodes illustrate just some of the more obvious symptoms of schizophrenia, including seeing things that aren't really there, believing in ideas that are bizarre and untrue, and thinking that jumps from one topic to another without obvious connections. The many symptoms of schizophrenia can be divided into three types: positive symptoms, negative symptoms, and cognitive symptoms (Lewis & Buchanan, 2007).

Positive Symptoms of Schizophrenia

Positive symptoms of schizophrenia are experiences that are present or excessive in people with schizophrenia but largely absent in people without it. Positive symptoms are the most visible signs of schizophrenia, especially delusions and hallucinations.

Delusions. **Delusions** are completely false beliefs that a person with schizophrenia believes to be reality. It doesn't matter that no one else in the person's family or culture holds those beliefs, or that they seem magical or peculiar to others, or that they defy logic. In spite of all of this, the person with schizophrenia accepts these beliefs as completely legitimate, usually without questioning them at all. For example, one man with schizophrenia believed that the streetlights (and presumably the people who control them) were communicating directly with him, threatening him as he drove under them. When his family members tried to convince him otherwise, he not only refused to believe them, but suspected that they were in on the streetlights' plot (McLean, 2003).

Certain types of delusions can be especially prominent in certain cases of schizophrenia (Lindenmayer & Khan, 2006; Vahia & Cohen, 2008). For example, those with *delusions of persecution* believe that others are out to get them. ("My neighbors are all spying on me, plotting to steal everything I own.") Those with *delusions of grandeur* believe that they have superhuman powers, or that they are a famous person such as a past president or a religious icon. ("I am George Washington, and I will start a new

schizophrenia
A severe psychological disorder in which the person exhibits bizarre disturbances in thinking, perception, feelings, and behavior.

psychosis
A significant impairment in the basic ability to tell the difference between the real world and imagination.

positive symptoms
Experiences that are present or excessive in people with schizophrenia but largely absent in people without it.

delusions
Completely false beliefs that a person with schizophrenia believes to be reality.

country.") And those with *delusions of reference* believe that random events have personal meaning specifically intended for them. ("A bluebird just flew by—that must be a warning for me not to leave the house.")

Hallucinations. **Hallucinations** are false sensations or perceptions. Hallucinations are sounds, images, scents, or other physical sensations that the person with schizophrenia experiences even though those sensations do not exist in reality (Castle & Buckley, 2008; Guillin et al., 2007).

The most common type of hallucination is auditory, often described as "voices." Hearing voices is quite different from the common experience of a train of thought or even a two-sided argument going back and forth within your mind. Instead, during an auditory hallucination, the person with schizophrenia hears the voice as entirely separate. The voice is like another person talking to them, but the person with schizophrenia can't recognize that the voice is in fact coming from within their own head. They have a hard time dismissing what these voices say, and often respond to them aloud, which can strike observers as odd or disturbing.

For example, I once worked in a psychiatric hospital with Janet, a patient with schizophrenia who repeatedly heard a voice telling her that her "insides" were dirty, so she should drink liquid soap to cleanse herself. Any attempt to convince Janet that the voice wasn't real was hopeless. To Janet, that voice was real, as believable as any. I vividly recall one quiet evening when the patients were in the lounge watching TV, only to be suddenly interrupted by Janet. "No! I just drank soap this morning! I don't need to drink more tonight!" she shouted out of the blue. She paused for a few seconds, apparently listening. "I said NO!" Another pause. Finally, she gave in. "Fine—I'll drink some, if it will shut you up." Defeated by the voice inside her head, she stomped in the direction of the soap dispensers in the restroom, only to be intercepted by hospital staff.

Visual hallucinations involve seeing something that isn't actually there. No one else sees it, yet the person with schizophrenia sees it, accepts it as real, and interacts with it accordingly. In the same psychiatric hospital where I worked with Janet, another patient, Morris, had frequent visual hallucinations. For a while, he "saw" holes spontaneously open up in solid walls. On more than one occasion, he repeatedly tried to move his hand through the apparent hole, only to grow increasingly frustrated and confused as it proved impossible. When hospital staff asked him what he was doing, Morris was quite surprised that the holes were not obvious to them too. Another patient, Tony, often "saw" cats come into the room, when in fact there were no cats in the hospital at all. It was quite clear when Tony had one of his cat hallucinations, because he also happened to be allergic to cats: He would suddenly jump back in fright or scurry from the room in response to nothing that anyone else could see.

Beyond auditory and visual hallucinations, there are less common types of hallucination as well. These include olfactory hallucinations (involving false smells) and tactile hallucinations (involving false feelings of an object touching one's body). In one case, a person with schizophrenia described an olfactory hallucination in which he detected a foul body odor on himself so often that he felt the need to take six showers a day (O'Neal, 1984). Additionally, another patient with whom I worked in the psychiatric hospital often experienced a tactile hallucination in which bugs were crawling up and down his arm, when there were in fact no bugs at all.

Negative Symptoms of Schizophrenia

Negative symptoms of schizophrenia are behaviors that are lacking in people with schizophrenia, but that are usually present in people without the disorder. In general, negative symptoms don't draw as much attention as positive symptoms, but their impact on day-to-day functioning can be quite strong. Usually, negative symptoms involve a withdrawal from life's activities, especially interpersonal interaction and emotional involvement. People with schizophrenia often find themselves disengaged, not only from others, but from their own emotions as well.

hallucinations
False sensations or perceptions.

negative symptoms
Behaviors that are lacking in people with schizophrenia, but that are usually present in people without the disorder.

flat affect
The absence of appropriate emotion.

One specific negative symptom of schizophrenia is **flat affect**, the absence of appropriate emotion. For example, a person with schizophrenia may be the only one who doesn't laugh during a funny movie or cry at a funeral. Instead, this person may stare vacantly, expressing no emotion through words or facial expressions. When people with schizophrenia do express emotion, it can be way off-base. For example, they might be angry at a drinking fountain, surprised by a flower, or joyful about a tornado.

People with schizophrenia also exhibit some negative symptoms involving an absence of certain social behaviors. They may display *alogia*, an almost complete absence of speaking. They may also demonstrate *avolition*, a lack of initiative to take even the smallest action. Or, they may find themselves exhibiting *anhedonia*, an inability to experience happiness even when in the most joyful situations. Together, these negative symptoms can strongly hinder social interactions for people with schizophrenia (Nisenson et al., 2001; Andia et al., 1995). (Imagine trying to have a friendship, or even a conversation, with a person who displays all of these symptoms.) These negative social impairments are often the first signs of schizophrenia, appearing long before the more obvious hallucinations and delusions (Hollis, 2003).

WATCHING PSYCHOLOGY

A Beautiful Mind

A Beautiful Mind won the 2002 Academy Award for Best Picture. The film is based on the true life of John Nash, a mathematician with schizophrenia who won the Nobel Prize in 1994. Early in the movie, Nash (played by Russell Crowe) is a graduate student at Princeton whose brilliance is matched only by his peculiarity. As he moves through graduate school and academic jobs (in real life, he taught at both MIT and Princeton), his grip on reality becomes increasingly loose and his thoughts and perceptions become increasingly psychotic.

The award-winning 2002 film *A Beautiful Mind* tells the story of John Nash, a mathematician with schizophrenia who won a Nobel Prize. Everett Collection, Inc

Nash's psychosis revolves around feelings of paranoia, which are shown in his hallucinations and delusions. At one point, the movie depicts Nash interacting with U.S. government officials who recruit him to work as a secret agent decoding Russian messages. Soon, Nash is chased and shot at by Russians who learn of his activities. Only later in the movie (spoiler alert) do we learn that the whole thing—his conversations with government agents, the pursuit by Russians, all of it—was an elaborate delusion. We also learn that Nash's relationships with a close friend and a beloved niece were hallucinations: Despite his many seemingly real conversations with them, those people did not exist at all.

To the moviemakers' credit, the film is shot in such a way that it is difficult to tell the differences between the scenes involving real people and those people who exist only in hallucinations. Nash's emotions appear equally genuine whether he is conversing with his wife (who is real) or a government agent (who is not real). This inability to distinguish between reality and fantasy closely mimics the actual experiences of people with schizophrenia every day.

Many other Hollywood films portray schizophrenia in an insensitive or blatantly inaccurate way. For example, in Jim Carrey's *Me, Myself, and Irene*, "schizophrenia" is wrongly portrayed as a split personality (Owen, 2012). *A Beautiful Mind*, however, captures many of the realities of living with schizophrenia. In addition to positive symptoms such as hallucinations and delusions, we see some evidence of negative symptoms when Nash withdraws socially and emotionally from colleagues and family. We also see cognitive symptoms when Nash's thought processes and speech become idiosyncratic and illogical. We see Nash spend time in mental institutions and receive treatment for his disorder (both of which have changed in the years since Nash's experience). We also see the effect that schizophrenia can have on the people who care about the person with the disorder. For example, Nash's wife struggles to find a balance between supporting her husband and challenging his unrealistic thoughts and beliefs.

Of course, *A Beautiful Mind* is a Hollywood film, so not all of its depictions are accurate. In Nash's real life, he and his wife were divorced for many years before getting remarried (Nassar, 1998). Also, in real life, most people with schizophrenia are not as professionally accomplished as Nash. But in all, *A Beautiful Mind* is a vivid and effective introduction to the experience of schizophrenia (Rosenstock, 2003).

Schizophrenia typically arises in adolescence or early adulthood, but in many cases, negative symptoms are evident even at younger ages. Among the negative symptoms seen in children who eventually develop schizophrenia are a lack of positive emotion and low levels of social responsiveness. Images by Victoria J Baxter/Moment Select/Getty Images

In a fascinating study illustrating the early appearance of social impairment in schizophrenia, researchers obtained the childhood family home movies of people who went on to develop the disorder as adults. (Of course, these family home movies included footage of not only the person who developed schizophrenia, but many other family members as well.) Then, they showed these movies to viewers who did not know which member of the family developed schizophrenia. The viewers guessed, with remarkable accuracy, which family member it was. When the researchers asked them how they knew, the viewers cited many negative symptoms, including lack of positive emotion, social responsiveness, and other interpersonal behaviors (Walker & Lewine, 1990).

Cognitive Symptoms of Schizophrenia

Cognitive symptoms of schizophrenia involve the disturbed, illogical ways that people with schizophrenia think. The behavior and speech of people with schizophrenia often seems blatantly disorganized and disordered to others (Keefe & Eesley, 2006). For example, people with schizophrenia often display loose associations, thoughts that proceed with little apparent logical connection from one to the next. People with schizophrenia may jump nonsensically from a casual comment about last night's baseball game to a harsh criticism of their neighbors to a list of their favorite foods. If there is an identifiable reason for jumping from one sentence to the next, it may be the sounds of the words rather than their meaning. Some psychologists use the word *derailment* as a synonym for loose associations, which offers a visual image of a train (of thought) going off the tracks.

Sometimes, the speech or writing of someone with schizophrenia is so jumbled that even a single sentence is baffling, a phenomenon known as word salad. For example, a person exhibiting word salad might say something like this: "This pillow empowers the rejection of every word of those who fall behind. The difference? The streets order blue pencils for the animals." At other times, the speech of a person with schizophrenia may be sprinkled with neologisms, entirely new words of their own creation (Noll, 2007; Minzenberg et al., 2008). Loose associations, word salad, and neologisms are all on display in this excerpt from the writings of Pamela Spiro Wagner, an award-winning poet who developed schizophrenia:

> I am seeking truth and seeing it, which is Holy See-ing, a sacred pun, meaning I'd been given a nod of approval from the Vatican, the Vat-I-Can. I can see that I am at sea, that I will get Cs in all my classes, the gentlewoman's Cs, for good attendance and sitting for every test, though I am no Ladybird Johnson, I don't wear white gloves or send invitations for tea. I don't garden or beautify America's highways. But there is the matter of the piano's high C and canned orange juice drink, and high seas and...seven seas and...seize the day and...Eat drink be merry for tomorrow we die, and...konk [sic] out.
> —Wagner & Spiro, 2005, pp. 104–105

Schizophrenia sounds like a pretty devastating disorder. How can a person with schizophrenia function in the real world with such serious symptoms?

Schizophrenia—which typically arises in late adolescence or early adulthood and can endure for years or even a lifetime—is an especially incapacitating psychological disorder (Hafner & an der Heiden, 2008; Kopelowicz et al., 2007; Mueser & Jeste, 2008). In many cases, people with schizophrenia don't function well in the real world. Many are so impaired that they must spend time—often long periods—in mental institutions. Some can live independently in the community, but they often struggle to hold jobs, maintain relationships, or take basic care of themselves (Hooley, 2009).

There is some reason for optimism regarding the treatment of schizophrenia, however. Antipsychotic medication provides significant improvement for some (especially regarding positive symptoms). In some cases, people with schizophrenia can lead self-sufficient and productive lives. In fact, the movie *A Beautiful Mind* (which won the Academy Award for Best Picture in 2002) tells the true story of John Nash, a man with

schizophrenia who earned a doctoral degree at Princeton, married, and became a Nobel Prize–winning mathematician and economist.

When people with schizophrenia create art, their works often suggest the unusual perceptions and thought patterns that characterize the symptoms of the disorder. For example, consider this self-portrait by Bryan Charnley. He explains the inclusion of a second "mouth" covering his forehead by suggesting that his brain was sending messages to others in a way that he could not control: "My mind seemed to be thought broadcasting very severely and it was beyond my will to do anything about it. I summed this up by painting my brain as an enormous mouth, acting independently of me" (Charnley, 1991). Copyright Estate of Bryan Charnley

Who Gets Schizophrenia?

Thankfully, schizophrenia is not a common psychological disorder. It occurs in around 1% of individuals, a finding that has been rather consistent across countries and cultures (Mueser et al., 2006; Cornblatt et al., 2009). Schizophrenia is about equally common in females and males, but far more common and long-lasting in urban areas than nonurban areas (Saha et al., 2005; Eaton & Chen, 2006). In fact, the bigger the city, the greater the likelihood of schizophrenia (Van Os et al., 2001, 2003). The reasons for this finding are unclear, but a leading theory focuses on the work role. Specifically, when people in a rural area or developing country suffer from schizophrenia, there is a good chance they can still work in some capacity, primarily because of employers' willingness to adjust responsibilities to match abilities. By contrast, in a big city, people suffering from schizophrenia are likely to simply get fired and replaced. The resulting unemployment, possible homelessness, and other stressors may increase the likelihood of schizophrenia (or worsen its symptoms) in a way that doesn't happen in less urban areas (Warner, 2004).

DIVERSITY MATTERS

There has been some debate about the schizophrenia rates of various ethnic groups in the United States. Specifically, African Americans have a greater risk of a schizophrenia diagnosis—in some studies, four times greater—than European Americans (Barnes, 2004; Blow et al., 2004). However, some research suggests that the diagnoses of African Americans have historically been mistaken, with mental health professionals overestimating the severity of symptoms or failing to follow diagnostic criteria (Lawson, 2008).

Why Does Schizophrenia Develop?

The number of studies devoted to exploring the cause of schizophrenia is huge. Collectively, they point to two main conclusions: (1) There are many causes of schizophrenia, and (2) the most prominent of these causes are biological (Mueser & Roe, 2016).

We know that schizophrenia has biological roots because of a couple of different lines of research—research on genetics and research on the brain itself. Genetic studies typically examine psychiatric records of people who are related to each other in some way to calculate the odds that a particular person will develop schizophrenia. The primary findings of these studies? An adopted child who develops schizophrenia is far more likely to have biological parents with schizophrenia than adoptive parents with schizophrenia (Kendler & Diehl, 1993). This finding strongly suggests that genes contribute to schizophrenia.

Another way researchers have examined the genetics of schizophrenia is through twin studies. Basically, twin studies center on the fact that monozygotic (identical) twins are much more genetically similar than dizygotic (fraternal) twins. Twin studies consistently find that the odds of a person developing schizophrenia are much higher if their monozygotic twin has the disorder than if their dizygotic twin has the disorder. This finding actually extends to other relatives too, as illustrated in **Figure 14.6**: The more genes you share with a person with schizophrenia, the greater the odds that you will develop the disorder (Gottesman, 1991; Cardno & Gottesman, 2000).

A second line of research that highlights biological causes of schizophrenia focuses on the physical brain itself. Brain studies involving MRI, fMRI, and other imaging technologies have consistently found some structural differences in the brains of people with schizophrenia. For example, the ventricles—basically, fluid-filled spaces within the brain—tend to be larger in the brains of people with schizophrenia than in people without it. A few other areas, including the hippocampus, amygdala, thalamus, and whole brain, are slightly smaller in people with schizophrenia than in people without it (Stewart & Davis, 2008; Eyler, 2008; Schmajuk, 2001).

cognitive symptoms
The disturbed, illogical ways that people with schizophrenia think.

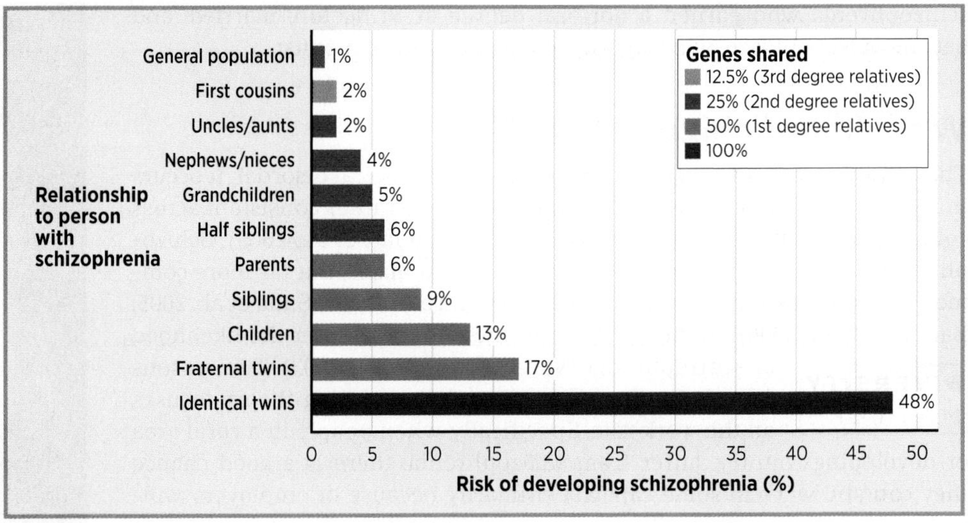

FIGURE 14.6 Shared Genes and Schizophrenia. The odds that a person will develop schizophrenia increase significantly with the percentage of genes that person shares with someone else who has schizophrenia. Data from Gottesman, 2001.

Researchers have also found that there are unusual amounts of certain neurochemicals in the brains of people with schizophrenia. One neurochemical that has received a lot of attention in studies of this type is dopamine, but its exact role is still being determined. Through the 1970s and 1980s, research suggested that excess dopamine caused schizophrenia (Javitt & Laruelle, 2006; Baumeister & Francis, 2002). Later, that theory was revised to state that too much dopamine in certain (subcortical) regions of the brain caused positive symptoms of schizophrenia, while too little dopamine in other (prefrontal cortex) regions of the brain caused negative symptoms (Downar & Kapur, 2008; Guillin et al., 2007). Still, this revised dopamine theory cannot explain why some people with schizophrenia experience no change in symptoms when they take medication that changes their dopamine level (Noll, 2007).

Biological causes are not entirely responsible for schizophrenia (Mueser et al., 2013). Certain patterns of interaction in families also contribute to the disorder. This is true especially when family members are overinvolved in each other's lives and openly hostile toward each other. Researchers call this pattern of interaction *expressed emotion*, and it seems to be a factor in the relapse of people with schizophrenia. When a person hospitalized with schizophrenia returns home, they are 2.5 times more likely to relapse if the family shows high levels of expressed emotion than if the family shows low levels of expressed emotion (Bebbington & Kuipers, 2008; Butzlaff & Hooley, 1998).

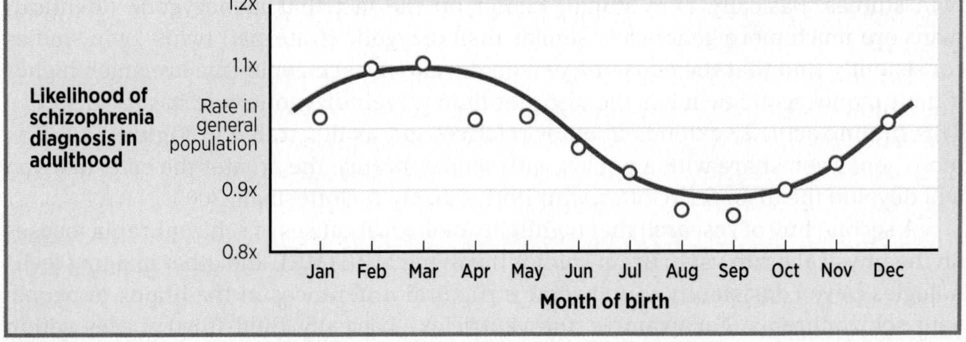

FIGURE 14.7 Birthdays of People with Schizophrenia. The month in which a person is born influences the risk of developing schizophrenia, with spring births at the highest risk. The underlying reason may be the increased risk of flu in expectant mothers during the middle months of pregnancy. Data from Mortensen et al., 1999.

Other factors that play a role in the development of schizophrenia occur even before the person is born. Children of pregnant women who are malnourished or have a viral infection are at increased risk of eventually developing schizophrenia (Susser & Opler, 2006; Brown et al., 2004). Interestingly, as **Figure 14.7** shows, the birthdays of people with schizophrenia fall disproportionately in winter and early spring. This means their mothers went through months 4–6 of their pregnancies, when fetal brain development is especially crucial, during the height of flu season (Bradbury & Miller, 1985; Mortensen et al., 1999; Tramer, 1929; Torrey et al., 1997).

CHECK YOUR LEARNING:

14.31 What is schizophrenia?

14.32 What is the difference between the positive, negative, and cognitive symptoms of schizophrenia?

14.33 How common is schizophrenia, and in which groups is it most frequently diagnosed?

14.34 Why does schizophrenia develop?

Disorders of Childhood

Many psychological disorders can occur in children, but there are some that emerge during childhood by definition. In DSM-5, these disorders fall in the category of *neurodevelopmental disorders*. These disorders include school-related problems such as specific learning disorders (formerly called learning disabilities) and developmental delays such as intellectual disability (formerly called mental retardation). Let's focus on two well-known disorders of childhood: *attention-deficit/hyperactivity disorder* (ADHD) and *autism spectrum disorder*.

YOU WILL LEARN:

14.35 what disorders of childhood are.

14.36 what attention-deficit/hyperactivity disorder (ADHD) is.

14.37 what autism spectrum disorder is.

14.38 who gets disorders of childhood.

14.39 why disorders of childhood develop.

Attention-Deficit/Hyperactivity Disorder

Attention-deficit/hyperactivity disorder (ADHD) is a disorder emerging in childhood that features significant problems with attention, hyperactivity/impulsivity, or both. Symptoms must be present before the age of 12 (even if the diagnosis comes later) and must occur in at least two settings, such as school and home. For some people with ADHD, the main problem is inattention: They are easily distracted or sidetracked, struggle to listen effectively, forget things easily, and make careless mistakes. For other people with ADHD, the main problem is hyperactivity or impulsivity: They have trouble staying seated or still, waiting their turn, and preventing themselves from interrupting others' words or actions (American Psychiatric Association, 2013; Roberts et al., 2015).

For many kids with ADHD, the core symptoms of the disorder often lead to additional problems (Beauchaine & Hayden, 2016). For example, ADHD symptoms can cause problems in relationships with important people: teachers who want students to sit still and follow rules, parents who expect kids to display patience and self-control, and other kids who prefer peers to wait their turn and use appropriate social skills. Turbulent relationships can in turn increase the likelihood of anxiety, depression, and rule-breaking behavior (Pliszka, 2015). Given the nature of the symptoms, academic struggles are understandably common in kids with ADHD, and rates of substance abuse are high as well (Pfiffner & Haack, 2015; Kent et al., 2011).

Katherine Ellison, a Pulitzer Prize–winning journalist, wrote a book about raising a son with ADHD. Here, she describes some of his struggles, beginning with core symptoms of inattentiveness but eventually expanding into interpersonal difficulties common in kids with ADHD (Ellison, 2010, pp. 7–8):

attention-deficit/hyperactivity disorder (ADHD) A disorder emerging in childhood that features significant problems with attention, hyperactivity/impulsivity, or both.

Actor Channing Tatum was diagnosed with ADHD as a child. Samir Hussein/Getty Images

> Buzz was an eager, successful student right up until second grade… It was then that he started forgetting to write down his assignments, or to do them, or to get them back to school. He lost permission slips, field trip forms, bulletins, thermoses, notebooks, sweaters, coats, and lunch boxes. Worst of all: he also lost every single member of his former pack of friends.
>
> By sixth grade…he refused to do chores or his homework, and wouldn't stop pinching and punching [his brother] Max. Our conflicts escalated. Bribes failed; "consequences" backfired. Sent to his room, Buzz roared obscenities and threw shoes at the door.

By contrast to Buzz's inattentive version of ADHD, consider this firsthand account of a more hyperactive/impulsive version. It was written by Blake Taylor as he neared the end of high school and looked back on his childhood with ADHD. (Taylor has since graduated from the University of California–Berkeley and started medical school at Columbia University.) In this description of a day when he was in second grade, notice his inability to put the brakes on his own behavior at dinnertime, even when his caretaker insists (Taylor, 2007, pp. 7–8):

> I am building a section of a robot on the family room floor. It is dinnertime, and Gloria, our babysitter, calls from the kitchen.
>
> "Blakey, come back and sit down and eat…You are eight years old. It is time to behave…"
>
> I return to the table for one bite … I chew it, then get up and leave the dinner table again.
>
> "Blake! Come and eat [your] dinner!" Gloria commands this time.
>
> "I don't want to," I whine. I am thinking, "I don't want to sit down, and I have better things to do." I reluctantly return for another bite.
>
> …[my food] is getting cold on its plate—it has been on the dinner table for an hour—and I have been continually leaving the table to play with my K'nex and Legos on the family room floor.
>
> Finally…with the help of Gloria…I am actually able to sit still long enough to finish dinner.

What happens to kids with ADHD when they grow up?

For many years, the assumption was that kids commonly grow out of ADHD. Research strongly suggests that such an outcome is, unfortunately, not so common (Resnick, 2005). Many adults who struggled with ADHD as kids continue to struggle well into adulthood (Kessler et al., 2006). When the disorder persists into adulthood, it correlates with many of the same problems that correlate with childhood ADHD, including anxiety, depression, and substance abuse (Uchida et al., 2015). It also correlates with some uniquely adult problems: Adults with ADHD lose jobs, experience marital problems, and engage in partner violence at unusually high rates (Kuriyan et al., 2013; Wymbs et al., 2012; Eakin et al., 2004).

Autism Spectrum Disorder

Autism spectrum disorder is a disorder emerging in childhood that features significant social interaction deficits and rigid, repetitive patterns of behavior. Autism spectrum disorder was introduced in DSM-5 as a combination of several disorders

that were listed separately in previous editions of DSM, including autistic disorder and Asperger's disorder. The inclusion of the word *spectrum* in the name of the disorder reflects the fact that its severity can vary greatly from one child to another. (It is also the root of the term *on the spectrum*, often informally used to describe children with this diagnosis.) Symptoms of autism spectrum disorder typically appear before the child turns 2 years old (American Psychiatric Association, 2013; Matson et al., 2013).

autism spectrum disorder
A disorder emerging in childhood that features significant social interaction deficits and rigid, repetitive patterns of behavior.

The social struggles of kids with autism spectrum disorder span a wide range. Frequently, they show little or no interest in approaching others to begin an interaction, or don't respond receptively when others approach them. When interactions do happen, the conversation often lacks a natural back-and-forth or any real sharing of interests or emotions. Nonverbal cues are typically impaired too, with minimal eye contact, facial expression, or body language.

In terms of rigid, repetitive patterns of behavior, many kids with autism make the same physical movements over and over again—for example, spinning in a circle, flapping their hands, or opening and closing a door. In rare cases, the rigid, repetitive behavior can be dangerous to the child—for example, a girl slapping herself or a boy hitting his head against a wall. The preference for rigid, repetitive behavior often extends to routines in which the child is involved. For example, kids with autism spectrum disorder may react with extreme displeasure if they have to ride in an unfamiliar car or eat meals at an unusual time or place.

When they reach adulthood, some people with autism spectrum disorder do live independent lives, while others continue to require help and support.

Who Gets Disorders of Childhood?

When researchers conduct surveys to determine how many kids actually qualify for the ADHD diagnosis according to DSM criteria, the results consistently show a rate of about 5–7%. However, the actual rate of kids receiving the diagnosis in the community is much higher—around 11–15% overall (Wilcutt, 2012; Schwarz, 2016; Polanczyk et al., 2007, 2014). The rate is even higher in certain populations, including boys, Whites, and kids in the South and Midwest (Visser et al., 2014; Owens et al., 2015). The reason for this discrepancy between the smaller number of kids who *should* get the diagnosis and the larger number of kids who *do* get the diagnosis is not entirely clear. It may relate to the fact that parents, teachers, and kids are familiar with the diagnosis, so when they seek help from a professional, "Is it ADHD?" may be the question that guides the conversation. Also, despite the need for a thorough evaluation, too often pediatricians diagnose ADHD after a brief visit including just a handful of questions about the child's behavior (Hinshaw & Scheffler, 2014; Hinshaw & Ellison, 2016).

Autism spectrum disorder affects about 1–2% of kids, with about 5 times as many boys as girls receiving the diagnosis (Centers for Disease Control and Prevention, 2014). The rate is relatively consistent throughout most countries in the world (Baxter et al., 2015). Autism rates are significantly higher now than they were decades ago, a finding that may be attributed to a number of factors, including increased awareness of the disorder, changes in the way it is defined, and changes in the way it is assessed (Dawson, 2013; Hansen et al., 2015).

Why Do Disorders of Childhood Develop?

The factors behind both ADHD and autism spectrum disorders remain the focus of extensive research. For ADHD, it is clear that there is no single cause. Genes are likely a powerful factor, as are brain abnormalities (especially in parts of the brain involved in inhibition, like the frontal lobe), low birth weight, and prenatal exposure to toxins such as lead and nicotine (Thapar et al., 2013; Cortese et al., 2012; Beauchaine & Hayden, 2016). Environmental factors such as excessive video game use, excessive TV watching, and abusive parenting styles can worsen ADHD in kids who already have it, but do not cause the disorder in otherwise healthy kids (Barkley, 2015). Factors such as these

combine to create a brain that struggles with working memory (doing multiple things at once, rather than needing to drop attention from one thing to attend to another), executive functioning (planning future actions and considering consequences), and behavioral inhibition (stopping an action before it starts) (Barkley, 1997; Hinshaw & Ellison, 2016).

Genetics seems to play a significant role in the development of autism spectrum disorder, especially genes related to the development of brain regions that influence social interaction (Lichtenstein et al., 2010; Dawson, 2008). Prenatal problems (including the mother's use of certain drugs) and childbirth complications also increase the risk. Certain members of the popular media have promoted theories that autism spectrum disorder can be caused by vaccines, but extensive research debunks this claim (Madsen et al., 2002; Hupp & Jewell, 2015; Donovan & Zucker, 2016).

CHECK YOUR LEARNING:

14.35 What are disorders of childhood?

14.36 What is ADHD?

14.37 What is autism spectrum disorder?

14.38 How common are ADHD and autism spectrum disorder, and in which groups are they most frequently diagnosed?

14.39 Why do ADHD and autism spectrum disorder develop?

Dissociative Disorders

YOU WILL LEARN:

14.40 what dissociative disorders are.

14.41 what dissociative identity disorder is.

14.42 what dissociative amnesia and dissociative fugue are.

14.43 who gets dissociative disorders.

14.44 why dissociative disorders develop.

Dissociative disorders are the category of psychological disorders in which the person loses awareness of, or becomes disconnected from, essential parts of the self such as memories, emotions, or identity. When people dissociate in this way, they lose touch with some component of their own mental processes to such an extent that their day-to-day lives are significantly impacted. Their minds become fragmented rather than integrated, with certain facets seemingly split off from others (American Psychiatric Association, 2013; van der Hart & Nijenhuis, 2009).

Dissociative Identity Disorder

The most widely known and sensational dissociative disorder is **dissociative identity disorder** (or DID), in which a person exhibits two or more distinct personalities. (It is perhaps better known by its former name, *multiple personality disorder*.) Instead of having a single coherent "self," a person with dissociative identity disorder has two or more selves that are not integrated. These are entirely separate selves that seemingly share nothing other than the body in which they are located. These personalities typically alternate, with only one operating at a time. The shifts from one personality to the next are often sudden and unpredictable, and the contrast between personalities is often striking. When any particular personality is in control, the person finds it difficult or impossible to remember any details, or even the existence, of the other personalities. Most people with DID also experience a more general memory impairment for events that took place before the onset of DID (Lilienfeld & Lynn, 2003). For example, some have no recollection of long periods of their childhood.

A particularly well-publicized case of dissociative identity disorder is that of "Sybil," a client whose real name was Shirley A. Mason. In the early 1970s, her case was the subject of a bestselling book and TV movie that brought this psychological condition to the awareness of the general public. Sybil had 16 personalities (or *alters*, as they are often called), including a whiny toddler, two devious young boys, two girls in elementary school, and a sad older woman. Her various personalities were so fractured that each

dissociative disorders
The category of psychological disorders in which the person loses awareness of, or becomes disconnected from, essential parts of the self such as memories, emotions, or identity.

dissociative identity disorder
A psychological disorder in which a person exhibits two or more distinct personalities.

was unaware of what the others did. For example, when Sybil looked in her closet, she often found clothes that she didn't remember buying and didn't even like because she had purchased them while a different personality was in control. She also struggled to do arithmetic at times, because the personality that was present when she learned to do arithmetic didn't share that ability with the others (Nathan, 2011; Schreiber, 1973).

This is Shirley A. Mason, otherwise known as Sybil. In the early 1970s, Sybil's experience with dissociative identity disorder—which, in her case, featured 16 different personalities—was the focus of a bestselling book and TV movie. The fame of Sybil's case increased awareness of the disorder, but since that time, dissociative identity disorder has been so rare that some experts have wondered whether it really exists. The fact that some therapists (including Sybil's) may encourage clients to experience dissociative identity disorder also casts doubt on the validity of the disorder. MBR/Newscom/Tribune News Service/RIO GRANDE/OH/USA

Dissociative Amnesia

Dissociative amnesia occurs when a person becomes unable to recall important information from their past. Essentially, they blank out regarding a particular period of their lives. In most cases, dissociative amnesia represents a gap in an otherwise intact memory, and almost always, the gap includes something horrific that happened to (or perhaps was done by) the person with the disorder. As an example, a person involved in a terrible car wreck may be unable to recall anything from the day of the accident. Or, a person who violently attacks a loved one may have no recollection of the episode (American Psychiatric Association, 2013).

Now imagine a case of dissociative amnesia that is accompanied by unplanned and unexplained travel to a new location. That is a *dissociative fugue*. You may have heard occasional stories of dissociative fugues on the news, involving people who turn up in a random, unfamiliar location and can't explain to the locals who they are or offer any other personal details. A captivating 2009 case involved Hannah Emily Upp, a 23-year-old middle school teacher who went for a jog in one section of New York on August 28 and was found swimming in a harbor in a completely different part of the city on September 16—with no memories at all of what happened between. Security cameras at Apple computer stores, Starbucks coffee shops, and several gyms showed that Hannah had visited those places, but she had no recollection of those events. As she put it, "It was like 10 minutes had passed, but it was almost three weeks" (Marx & Didziulis, 2009).

Who Gets Dissociative Disorders?

Dissociative disorders are extremely rare, with estimates of their frequency typically falling no higher than about 1% of the population (Johnson et al., 2006). There was a surge of reports of DID in the 1970s and 1980s, but current researchers believe that verifiable cases of the disorder are exceedingly scarce. In fact, some experts have argued that DID may not even be a valid disorder at all (Arrigo & Pezdek, 1998). These experts suggest that many patients who report multiple personalities are actually responding to a psychotherapist's subtle encouragement to do so. A psychotherapist who is motivated to have a client with such a fascinating disorder might ask leading questions to convince a client that he or she in fact has multiple personalities, even if multiple personalities are not part of the client's original presenting problem (McHugh, 1995). In fact, Sybil's therapist has been criticized for persuading Sybil to understand her own problem in this way (Nathan, 2011). The controversy over the status of this phenomenon continues today.

Why Do Dissociative Disorders Develop?

When dissociative disorders do occur, the people receiving the diagnosis almost always have personal histories featuring severe abuse or trauma. In the case of dissociative identity disorder, the abuse or trauma often happened during childhood, in some cases decades before the emergence of the dissociative symptoms. For example, Sybil's mother, according to Sybil's therapist, committed acts of unspeakable physical and psychological abuse. With dissociative amnesia, the abuse or trauma is often a recent event that served as an immediate trigger for the dissociation, such as assaults, acts of war, or natural disasters (American Psychiatric Association, 2013). In any of these cases, the person's coping skills seem to be overwhelmed by their horrific experiences. Because of this, they disconnect from their own identities, either by forgetting themselves or reinventing themselves as a collection of other people because they can't function as the person they originally were (Gleaves et al., 2001; Ross, 1997).

Hannah Upp is a New York schoolteacher who experienced a dissociative fugue. Nicole Bengiveno/The New York Times/Redux

CHECK YOUR LEARNING:

14.40 What are dissociative disorders?

14.41 What is dissociative identity disorder?

14.42 What is dissociative amnesia?

14.43 How common are dissociative disorders?

14.44 Why do dissociative disorders develop?

Personality Disorders

YOU WILL LEARN:

14.45 what personality disorders are.

14.46 what borderline personality disorder is.

14.47 what antisocial personality disorder is.

14.48 who gets personality disorders.

14.49 why personality disorders develop.

As we discussed in Chapter 12, your personality is your unique way of behaving, thinking, and feeling—and personality traits are stable across long periods of time. In some people, however, these longstanding traits are the very qualities that are disordered. According to DSM, these people have **personality disorders**: the category of psychological disorders based on an enduring pattern of inflexible and maladaptive behavior that appears across a wide range of situations and interferes with interpersonal interaction (Sperry, 2016; South et al., 2011; Widiger & Lowe, 2010; Millon, 2004).

People with personality disorders can be frustrating or exasperating to friends, family members, and coworkers. They often have trouble getting along with others because their personality traits are so rigid. People with personality disorders lack the ability to vary their typical perception and reaction to the world, no matter how blatantly it doesn't work in a given situation. They usually have a hard time seeing their own role in interpersonal problems, even though people around them point it out repeatedly (Millon, 2009; Widiger & Mullins-Sweatt, 2008). Personality disorders are evident by late childhood or early adulthood and become woven into the person's enduring character (American Psychiatric Association, 2013).

From my own psychotherapy practice, one client with a personality disorder, Fran, was especially memorable. Fran's problematic traits were evident not only in the stories she told, but also in the way she interacted during the sessions. On the day I met this 28-year-old woman, she took over from the first minute of the initial interview. "Get rid of that list of questions," she barked as she scowled at my clipboard. "*I'll* decide what you need to know." What I needed to know, apparently, was that Fran was furious with both her husband and an employee. She explained why: "So, for the last 6 months I've been cheating on my husband with this guy who worked for me. No big deal, right? But neither one of them can get over it! I ended it as soon as my husband found out three days ago, but he's *still* upset. I did what *he* wanted by ending it, and he doesn't even appreciate it! And my employee—he's upset too! I fired him when I ended the affair, and now he's saying that I treated him unfairly! I mean, I give this guy a paycheck for years, and this is the thanks I get. They both need to get over this *now*. They are making my life too difficult." Throughout her explanation, Fran interrupted me repeatedly, and when I told her we were running out of time, she shot me a glare and corrected me: "*I'll* tell you when we're done."

Obviously, Fran thought the world revolved around her. Feelings of privilege and self-importance dominated her personality. She believed that she had the right to cheat on her husband, mistreat her employee, decide how each of them should react to the situation, and even tell her psychologist how to conduct the interview. I eventually learned that Fran had been like this since childhood (she was quite a bully in elementary school), and that almost all of her meaningful relationships had suffered because her personality was so inflexible. In short, she had a personality disorder—narcissistic personality disorder, to be specific—that interfered significantly with her ability to get along with other people (Ronningstam, 2009).

Narcissistic personality disorder is just one of 10 separate personality disorders included in DSM-5, each distinct in its emphasis. Each personality disorder focuses on a different personality trait, but in each case that trait is inflexible and causes problems in relationships with others. **Table 14.2** includes a brief description of all 10 personality

TABLE 14.2: DSM Personality Disorders: A Brief Summary

PERSONALITY DISORDER	DOMINANT TRAITS, CHARACTERISTICS, BEHAVIORS
Antisocial personality disorder	Exploits others; self-serving; frequent illegal behaviors
Avoidant personality disorder	Socially fearful; self-conscious; easily embarrassed in front of others; sees self as incompetent and likely to be criticized or rejected by others
Borderline personality disorder	Unstable and unpredictable; rapidly and drastically changing view of self and others; impulsive and tumultuous
Dependent personality disorder	Submissive; needs others' reassurance and approval; follows others' lead rather than act independently
Histrionic personality disorder	Excessive and dramatic display of emotions; seeks to be the center of attention; theatrical but emotionally shallow
Narcissistic personality disorder	Egotistical, entitled, and self-important; sees self as superior to others; needs others to admire him/her
Obsessive-compulsive personality disorder	Orderly, a perfectionist; overly controlling and detail-oriented; rigid and stubborn
Paranoid personality disorder	Distrustful and suspicious; feels justified in never letting guard down; views others as dangerous or deceptive
Schizoid personality disorder	Solitary; loner with little or no desire for relationships with others; detached and unemotional
Schizotypal personality disorder	Eccentric, quirky, peculiar, odd; blurred line between reality and fantasy; engages in magical thinking

Information from Millon, 2004; Sperry, 2016; American Psychiatric Association, 2013.

disorders. Let's focus on 2 personality disorders that are especially well known and well researched: borderline personality disorder and antisocial personality disorder.

Borderline Personality Disorder

Borderline personality disorder is a psychological disorder based on instability in many areas of the person's life, including interpersonal relationships, mood, and self-image. For people with borderline personality disorder, everything is tumultuous—their view of themselves, their relationships with others, and their emotional reactions to the world around them. As a result of this instability, life feels chaotic and uncertain, as if things could change drastically at any moment, not only for the person with borderline personality disorder but for others around that person as well (Hooley & St. Germain, 2008; Paris, 2007). A leading expert in the disorder, Marsha Linehan, explains it this way: People with borderline personality disorder are "the psychological equivalent of third-degree burn patients. They simply have, so to speak, no emotional skin. Even the slightest touch or movement can create immense suffering" (Linehan, 1993, p. 69).

In relationships, people with borderline personality disorder may love the other person at times, perhaps in an unrealistic, idealized way, and then hate the same person soon after with no reason for the dramatic shift other than an unjustified sense of abandonment. This tendency toward *splitting*, or seeing others as all good or all bad, is also applied to other people and events, making the emotional lives of people with borderline personality disorder volatile and unpredictable (Clarkin et al., 2006).

As a clinical psychologist, I once worked with Bianca, a woman with borderline personality disorder. Bianca was a bright 25-year-old unmarried woman whose family referred her to me after she made suicide threats. This was not the first time she had openly discussed suicide. In fact, on numerous occasions since her teens, Bianca had made similar threats and had overdosed on pills. Most of these attempts happened after she became upset with a family member, friend, or boyfriend and then plummeted into a state of extreme rage and sadness. The latest suicide threats fell into the same pattern. She had been dating David for about a month and was madly in love with him, but his slight hesitation when she began discussing marriage sent her quickly in the opposite

dissociative amnesia
A psychological disorder in which a person becomes unable to recall important information from their past.

personality disorders
The category of psychological disorders based on an enduring pattern of inflexible and maladaptive behavior that appears across a wide range of situations and interferes with interpersonal interaction.

borderline personality disorder
A psychological disorder based on instability in many areas of the person's life, including interpersonal relationships, mood, and self-image.

direction. Within minutes, she went from adoring David to despising him, and from feeling wonderful about her future to feeling hopeless.

As Bianca shared these experiences with me, I noticed that she was relating to me in a way that paralleled the way she had related to David. Just a few sessions in, she told me I was the most caring and competent therapist she had ever had. She felt much happier, and was confident that her life would stay on course. Her happiness and optimism were encouraging to me, but they felt fragile. Sure enough, a few sessions later, a power outage in my office building caused me to reschedule all of my appointments for the day, including one with Bianca. She responded furiously, screaming through tears that I had deserted her and accusing me of being uncaring and incompetent. She spiraled downward for some time after that, bogged down in the false belief that she was worthless and no one cared about her.

As Bianca's case illustrates, people with borderline personality disorder require significant care from mental health professionals. In fact, this single disorder accounts for a whopping 20% of hospitalized psychiatric patients (Bradley et al., 2007). Bianca's case is also typical in that people with borderline personality disorder have a high likelihood of self-harm. In fact, about 75% of people with this diagnosis have a history of at least one attempt to hurt or kill themselves (Paris, 2009; Clarkin et al., 1983).

Antisocial Personality Disorder

Antisocial personality disorder is a psychological disorder based on a disregard for, and violation of, the rights of other people (American Psychiatric Association, 2013; Patrick, 2007). In this diagnosis, *antisocial* does not mean that a person prefers not to be social, or would choose to stay home alone rather than go to a party. Instead, *antisocial* means *antisociety*—a threat to society and the people living in it. Essentially, having antisocial personality disorder is like having no conscience, particularly regarding the welfare of others. To someone with antisocial personality disorder, other people are tools to be used for one's own benefit, with no concern or empathy for what happens to those people in the process.

People with antisocial personality disorder have long histories of deceiving, exploiting, and ripping off other people. If someone stands in the way of what the person with antisocial personality disorder wants, that someone might get manipulated, assaulted, or even killed. Extreme cases have probably caught your attention on the news: stories of people, often labeled as psychopaths, who commit heinous crimes against others yet seem to feel no remorse about it.

You mean they don't feel guilty about these acts afterward?

No, they don't feel guilty. That is the most striking characteristic of people with antisocial personality disorder: They show a heartless lack of guilt, as if they have committed their crimes against inanimate objects rather than human beings. Unfortunately, U.S. history is full of people with antisocial personality disorder, including serial killers Jeffrey Dahmer, Charles Manson, and Ted Bundy. Hollywood has also generated several fictional examples of cold-blooded characters, such as the title character from the TV series *Dexter* and Lord Voldemort from the *Harry Potter* series (DePaullo, 2010; Murakami, 2006).

Who Gets Personality Disorders?

Each of the 10 personality disorders occurs at its own rate, with specific rates for each hovering between 1% and 5% of the population. Collectively, about 10% of the population could be diagnosed with a personality disorder (Lenzenweger et al., 2007; Coker & Widiger, 2005). Borderline personality disorder occurs in about 1–2% of the population, and about 75% of those who receive the diagnosis are female (Lenzenweger et al., 2007; Coid et al., 2006; Gunderson, 2001). Antisocial personality disorder occurs in about 2% of the population, and about two-thirds of those who receive the diagnosis are male. There are also some

small gender differences among the other personality disorders, but none as exaggerated as borderline personality disorder and antisocial personality disorder (Paris, 2004).

antisocial personality disorder
A psychological disorder based on a disregard for, and violation of, the rights of other people.

Why Do Personality Disorders Develop?

The causes of personality disorders are still largely unknown, but research continues. Regarding borderline personality disorder, some evidence points to both a genetic predisposition and a serious disruption in the parent–child relationship—such as abuse, loss of a parent, or poor attachment in early childhood (Lenzenweger & Clarkin, 2005; Hooley & St. Germain, 2008). Genetics also appears to play a role in antisocial personality disorder, but other factors do as well. For example, people with antisocial personality disorder are quite insensitive to punishments that would discourage a behavior (such as legal consequences like arrest or jail), but quite sensitive to rewards that would encourage a behavior (such as money or thrills). Additionally, people with antisocial personality disorder were often raised in families in which exploitation and manipulation of others was modeled by parents, while empathy and remorse were met with disapproval (Patrick, 2007; Coker & Widiger, 2005).

CHECK YOUR LEARNING:

14.45 What are personality disorders?

14.46 What is borderline personality disorder?

14.47 What is antisocial personality disorder?

14.48 How common are borderline and antisocial personality disorders, and in which groups are they most frequently diagnosed?

14.49 Why do personality disorders develop?

CHAPTER SUMMARY

What's Abnormal?

14.1 A psychological disorder is a pattern of behavior that interferes with a person's life by causing significant distress or dysfunction.

14.2 The task of distinguishing abnormal from normal behavior is a significant challenge for psychologists. At times, psychologists have reversed their opinions regarding the status of particular human experiences as either abnormal or normal. Multiple criteria are used to define abnormality, including infrequency, deviation from social norms, personal distress, and impairment in daily functioning.

14.3 None of these criteria is perfect, but personal distress and impairment in daily functioning are most clearly emphasized by the authors of DSM. Culture should play an important role when considering whether a behavior is normal or abnormal.

What Causes Abnormality?

14.4 A variety of explanations offer answers to the question of what causes psychological disorders. The biological theory proposes that factors such as brain structures, neurochemicals, and genes are the primary causes of psychological disorders.

14.5 The psychological theory proposes that factors such as emotions, thoughts, behaviors, and traits are the primary causes of psychological disorders. Different psychological theories—including psychodynamic, behavioral, cognitive, and trait theories—emphasize particular psychological factors.

14.6 The sociocultural theory proposes that the social and cultural context in which a person lives, rather than factors within the person, are the primary causes of psychological disorders.

14.7 The biopsychosocial theory proposes that all of these factors—biological, psychological, and sociocultural—contribute to psychological disorders, often in an interactive way. This theory is particularly comprehensive and widely accepted by contemporary psychologists.

The Diagnostic Manual: DSM

14.8 DSM (*Diagnostic and Statistical Manual of Mental Disorders*) is the book in which mental disorders are officially defined.

14.9 In the United States, DSM is used by all major mental health professions and all other professionals who diagnose or treat mental disorders.

14.10 The most recent edition of DSM, DSM-5, was published in 2013. It includes a number of new disorders and revised definitions of existing disorders. Since it was originally published in the 1950s, DSM has expanded greatly. The great increase in the number of psychological disorders has been criticized by some as labeling common, normal experiences as abnormal.

14.11 DSM uses a categorical model of psychological disorders, in which psychologists provide a yes-or-no answer to the question of

whether a person has a particular disorder. The dimensional model is an alternative approach that poses questions about psychopathology such as "How much?" rather than "Yes or no?"

Anxiety Disorders and Obsessive-Compulsive Disorder

14.12 Anxiety disorders are the category of DSM disorders in which the primary symptom is anxiety, which is also known as worry, apprehension, nervousness, or fear.

14.13 Generalized anxiety disorder is characterized by anxiety, particularly in the form of worry, about a wide range of situations and activities.

14.14 Specific phobia is characterized by excessive anxiety toward a specific, identifiable object or situation.

14.15 Social anxiety disorder is characterized by an intense and irrational fear of the scrutiny of others and the embarrassment or humiliation that would follow.

14.16 Panic disorder is characterized by sudden, intense, unpredictable brief bursts (*attacks*) of anxiety that lack an identifiable trigger.

14.17 Obsessive-compulsive disorder is characterized by unwanted recurring anxiety-producing thoughts (obsessions) and uncontrollable actions (compulsions) done to reduce the anxiety produced by the obsessions.

14.18 Anxiety disorders are more common than any other category of psychological disorder. They are similarly common in the United States and other parts of the world. They occur two to three times more often in females than males.

14.19 Anxiety disorders and obsessive-compulsive disorder develop for a variety of reasons, often in combination. The reasons involve psychological factors—such as illogical thinking, learned reinforcements and punishments, neuroticism, and overly protective parenting—and biological factors—such as genes, brain abnormalities, and evolution.

Depressive and Bipolar Disorders

14.20 Depressive disorders and bipolar disorders are a category of psychological disorders characterized by extreme moods or emotional states that significantly disrupt daily functioning.

14.21 Major depressive disorder is characterized by depressed mood, loss of interest in most activities, and an assortment of other symptoms lasting at least 2 weeks. A much longer, less intensive version of these symptoms is known as persistent depressive disorder (dysthymia).

14.22 Bipolar disorder, formerly known as manic depressive disorder, is characterized by alternating between extremely high moods and low moods (the "poles" of emotion).

14.23 Collectively, depressive disorders and bipolar disorders are quite common, second only to anxiety disorders. Major depressive disorder is more common in females than males, and far more common than bipolar disorder.

14.24 Depressive disorders and bipolar disorders develop for a variety of reasons, including biological factors—such as genetics, brain abnormalities, and neurochemicals—and psychological factors—such as illogical thinking stemming from a depressive schema.

Eating Disorders

14.25 Eating disorders are a category of psychological disorders that involve significant disturbances in behaviors related to eating or food.

14.26 Anorexia nervosa is characterized by a refusal to eat enough food to maintain a normal body weight. It almost always stems from a distorted, inaccurate view of one's own body as fat.

14.27 Bulimia nervosa is characterized by a pattern of overeating (bingeing) followed by dangerous or drastic attempts to prevent weight gain (purging).

14.28 Binge eating disorder is essentially the bingeing pattern of bulimia without the purging. Eating disorders are relatively rare, but they occur about 10 times more often in females than males. They typically develop in young women who live in the United States or countries similarly influenced by Western values.

14.29 Biological and psychological factors can also play a role in the development of eating disorders, but sociocultural factors have received much more attention from researchers.

14.30 Specifically, the emphasis in Western TV, movies, and magazines that thinness determines female beauty, and to some extent worth, contributes to eating-related problems.

Schizophrenia

14.31 Schizophrenia is a severe psychological disorder characterized by bizarre disturbances in thinking, perception, feelings, and behavior. It involves a blatantly unrealistic take on reality that is held only by the person with the disorder.

14.32 Positive symptoms of schizophrenia are experiences that are present or excessive in people with the disorder but largely absent in people without the disorder. They include the most visible signs of schizophrenia, such as delusions (false beliefs) and hallucinations (false sensations or perceptions). Negative symptoms of schizophrenia are behaviors that are lacking in people with schizophrenia, but usually present in people without the disorder. A specific negative symptom is flat affect, the absence of feelings appropriate to a situation or being disengaged from social and emotional aspects of life. Cognitive symptoms of schizophrenia involve the disturbed, illogical ways that people with the disorder think, speak, and behave, all of which are often disorganized and disordered.

14.33 Schizophrenia is rare, but occurs around the world and at approximately equal rates in males and females. It occurs more often in urban areas than rural areas.

14.34 Biological factors loom large as primary contributors to the development of schizophrenia. These factors include genes, structural differences in the brain, and possibly neurochemical

abnormalities. Other factors include hostile, overinvolved family interaction and prenatal complications during fetal development.

Disorders of Childhood

14.35 Many psychological disorders can occur during childhood, but disorders of childhood are those that begin during childhood by definition. They include specific learning disorders, intellectual disability, attention-deficit/hyperactivity disorder (ADHD), and autism spectrum disorder.

14.36 Attention-deficit/hyperactivity disorder (ADHD) is a disorder emerging in childhood that features significant problems with attention, hyperactivity/impulsivity, or both.

14.37 Autism spectrum disorder is a disorder emerging in childhood that features significant social interaction deficits and rigid, repetitive patterns of behavior.

14.38 Research suggests that 5–7% of children meet criteria for ADHD, but rates of actual diagnosis in the community are significantly higher. Rates of autism spectrum disorder are lower—around 1–2%. Both disorders are much more common in boys than girls.

14.39 The reasons why ADHD and autism spectrum disorder arise continue to be investigated. Genes appear heavily involved in both, but multiple causes are likely.

Dissociative Disorders

14.40 Dissociative disorders are a category of psychological disorders in which the person loses awareness of, or becomes disconnected from, essential parts of themselves such as memories, emotions, or identity.

14.41 Dissociative identity disorder, formerly known as multiple personality disorder, involves a person exhibiting two or more distinct personalities rather than a single, coherent self.

14.42 Dissociative amnesia is characterized by an inability to recall important information from one's past. The particular period about which the person blanks out almost always includes a horrific occurrence.

14.43 Dissociative disorders are exceptionally rare; in fact, some experts doubt whether some of these disorders, particularly dissociative identity disorder, are valid diagnoses at all.

14.44 The primary reason for the development of most dissociative disorders appears to be severe abuse or trauma, either immediately before or long before the onset of the disorder.

Personality Disorders

14.45 Personality disorders are psychological disorders characterized by an enduring pattern of inflexible, maladaptive behavior occurring across a wide range of situations and interfering with interpersonal interaction. People with personality disorders have unbending, rigid personality traits in spite of the problems those traits cause in various situations.

14.46 Borderline personality disorder centers on instability in many areas of the person's life, including interpersonal relationships, mood, and self-image. It is characterized by a view of the self, relationships with others, and emotional reactions that are tumultuous and volatile.

14.47 Antisocial personality disorder centers on a disregard for, and violation of, the rights of other people. It often involves the exploitation or use of others for one's own benefit, with no concern or empathy for how those others are hurt or otherwise affected.

14.48 Each personality disorder occurs at its own rate. Borderline and antisocial personality disorders are both relatively uncommon. Borderline personality disorder occurs more often in females; antisocial personality disorder occurs more often in males.

14.49 The reasons why personality disorders develop are still largely undetermined. For borderline personality disorder, a serious disruption in the parent-child relationship appears to be a factor. For antisocial personality disorder, an insensitivity to punishment and a family background in which exploitation of others was modeled or encouraged appears to be a factor. Genes may also play a role in the development of personality disorders.

KEY TERMS

SELF-ASSESSMENT

1. The ______ theory of abnormality asserts that factors within the human body—such as brain structures, neurochemicals, and genes—are the primary causes of psychological disorders.
   a. sociocultural
   b. biological
   c. psychological
   d. categorical

2. The book used by U.S. mental health professionals to diagnose or treat mental disorders is ______.

3. The number of psychological disorders has ______ since the mid-1900s.
   a. increased
   b. decreased
   c. remained the same
   d. alternated each decade between about a dozen and about 100

4. Joseph has an anxiety disorder. Which of these specific diagnoses could Joseph have?
   a. social anxiety disorder, panic disorder, or generalized anxiety disorder
   b. schizophrenia or dissociative identity disorder
   c. anorexia nervosa or bipolar disorder
   d. All of the answers are correct.

5. ______ is characterized by an intense and irrational fear of the scrutiny of others and the embarrassment or humiliation that would follow.

6. Hector has bipolar disorder. His mood goes back and forth between the two emotional "poles" of bipolar disorder, which are ______ and ______.

7. Which of the following is true?
   a. Eating disorders occur equally often in males and females.
   b. Binge eating disorder involves a pattern of overeating followed by drastic attempts to avoid weight gain.
   c. Both a and b
   d. Neither a nor b

8. Hallucinations, delusions, flat affect, and loose associations are all symptoms of:
   a. anorexia nervosa.
   b. major depressive disorder.
   c. schizophrenia.
   d. obsessive-compulsive disorder.

9. ______ are psychological disorders in which the person loses awareness of, or becomes disconnected from, essential parts of themselves such as memories, emotions, or identity.
   a. Eating disorders
   b. Dissociative disorders
   c. Personality disorders
   d. Anxiety disorders

10. The core characteristic of antisocial personality disorder is ______.
   a. excessive shyness
   b. a very high level of anxiety
   c. a very high level of sadness
   d. a disregard for, and violation of, the rights of other people

Self-Assessment Answers

1. b, 2. *Diagnostic and Statistical Manual of Mental Disorders* (DSM), 3. a, 4. a, 5. Social anxiety disorder, 6. depression, mania, 7. d, 8. c, 9. b, 10. d

WHAT'S YOUR TAKE?

1. Psychologists and other experts in mental health work hard to create definitions of psychological disorders. They might use infrequency, deviation from social norms, personal distress, or impairment in daily functioning as a way to draw the line between normal and abnormal. In your opinion, how should that line be drawn? What criteria should be used to distinguish abnormal from normal?

2. Do you agree with the hypothesis that gender-specific socialization influences the rates of anxiety disorders for males and females? Imagine two soccer games on adjacent fields—one between teams of 7-year-old girls, the other between teams of 7-year-old boys. Each game happens to include a player with a specific phobia of lightning and thunder. When dark clouds appear and the first thunderclap sounds, how do you think parents and coaches will react to the terrified boy and girl? What if the kids were 15 years old rather than 7? What does your response suggest about the influence of socialization on the development of anxiety disorders, and possibly other psychological disorders as well?

SHOW ME MORE

14.1 Eating Disorders in Fiji

Link: http://tiny.cc/2q7njy

This article explains how the arrival of American TV in Fiji influenced the ways that girls and women viewed their own bodies, and the subsequent rise in eating disorders.

AnastasiaN/Shutterstock

14.2 Hannah Upp's Dissociative Amnesia and Dissociative Fugue

Link: http://tiny.cc/is7njy

This article tells the story of Hannah Emily Upp, a 23-year-old New Yorker who experienced dissociative amnesia and a dissociative fugue.

Nicole Bengiveno/The New York Times/Redux

15 Therapy

For many of the psychological disorders we discussed in Chapter 14, there are psychological treatments that work. Every year, therapy improves the lives of millions of people, including, perhaps, you or someone close to you. Some who benefit from therapy have diagnosed disorders, while others simply have problems in daily living. In one eye-opening study, 60 clients with a wide range of disorders offered an insider's view of the positive impact therapy can have (Kassan, 1999). Some clients emphasized how they benefited from the accepting and caring relationship with a therapist:

- "It's having someone accept you, whatever you're saying, without judgment, that allows you to accept yourself." (p. 407)
- "It was her warmth. She really gave off such humanity and sincere caring. It made it possible for me to be so trusting of her as to visit some very dark places. I felt very safe." (p. 370)

Some clients achieved insight during therapy, realizing something new and important about themselves:

- "I got more of an understanding of why I do what I do. I've become more aware of how I am." (p. 396)
- "She made me aware of relationships in my childhood that very much affected my adult relationships. She helped me realize a lot of things that I was just oblivious to." (p. 360)

Some clients overcame specific symptoms or improved a particular behavior:

- "I got over my fear of flying..." (p. 398)
- "I'm less anxious when presenting things in public..." (p. 397)

Treatments for psychological disorders have the potential to enhance the lives of most who seek it. In this chapter, we will explore a variety of styles and formats of psychotherapy, including many you might be likely to encounter if you seek therapy yourself. We will also consider how well treatments work, how cultural variables can impact treatment, ethical issues that can arise during treatment, the impact of modern technology on treatment, and biomedical treatments including psychiatric medications.

CHAPTER OUTLINE

History of Treatment of Psychological Disorders

YOU WILL LEARN:

15.1 how psychological disorders were treated centuries ago.

15.2 how and when the treatment of psychological disorders began to change toward the current approach.

15.3 about the definitions of psychotherapy and biomedical therapy.

Treatment for psychological problems has existed in one form or another since ancient times (Benjamin, 2005, 2007; Alexander & Selesnick, 1966). Early treatments were often bizarre and brutal. People suffering from psychological disorders were often thought to be possessed by the devil or evil spirits. They were often imprisoned in dungeon-like conditions or subjected to torturous interventions designed to rid their bodies of these spirits—including bloodletting and cutting holes in their skulls (Routh, 2011; Tallis, 1998). In many cases, the treatment was far worse than the disorder. In fact, in some cases, the treatment was fatal.

Thankfully, in the late 1700s and early 1800s, a new sentiment toward people with psychological problems began to grow—one that recognized them as human beings deserving real treatment and humane living conditions. In England, philanthropist William Tuke was so appalled by the miserable living conditions in homes for the mentally ill that he raised funds to open York Retreat. There, residents found more day-to-day freedoms, better food, more opportunities for physical exercise, and staff members who actually cared about them (Reisman, 1991).

In France, as **Figure 15.1** illustrates, physician Philippe Pinel convinced those in power that the mentally ill deserved better treatment than they had been receiving (Ehrenwald, 1991). Among other things, Pinel successfully argued that staff members should create a case history for each patient, which included treatment notes and a label for the patient's psychological illness. These tasks were unheard of at the time, but now are commonplace. These changes reflected a changing attitude toward the mentally ill, one focused on improving their lives rather than simply locking them away (Cautin, 2011; Weiner, 1994). As Pinel himself wrote in 1801, "The mentally sick, far from being guilty people deserving punishment, are sick people whose miserable state deserves all the consideration that is due to suffering humanity" (cited in Zilboorg & Henry, 1941).

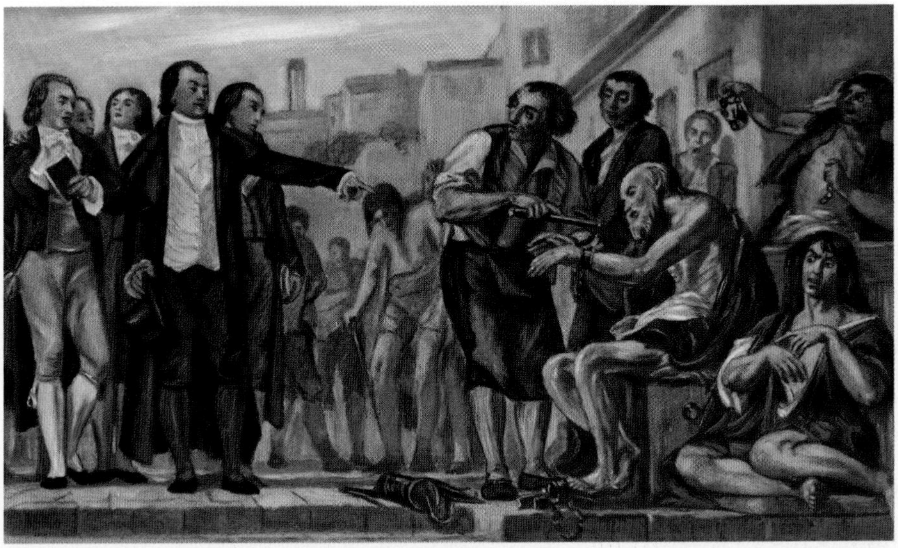

FIGURE 15.1 Philippe Pinel and Better Treatment. The title of this 1849 painting by Charles Müller—*Pinel Orders the Removal of Iron Shackles from the Insane Men at Bicêtre Hospice*—captures the role that Philippe Pinel and others played in promoting more humane treatment of the mentally ill in the late 1700s and early 1800s. Bettmann/Getty Images

psychotherapy
A treatment that involves a mental health professional using various techniques to help a person overcome a psychological disorder or improve some aspect of emotional, cognitive, or behavioral functioning.

biomedical therapy
A treatment for psychological problems that involves medications or medical procedures to directly change the biology of the brain.

In the United States, the Connecticut physician Eli Todd was inspired by progress being made in Europe. Todd's own sister had committed suicide, and he believed that a better system of mental health treatment might have saved her life. Unfortunately, effective treatment was scarce in those days. In fact, before 1800 only three states had mental hospitals at all (Reisman, 1991). For decades, Todd campaigned for improved treatment of the mentally ill, and his efforts resulted in the first mental hospital in Connecticut opening in 1824 (Goodheart, 2003). For the first time, many families of mentally ill individuals had a place where they could seek around-the-clock care for their loved ones.

Like Todd, Dorothea Dix recognized the need for mental hospitals. Dix was a Sunday school teacher in a Boston jail where she noticed that many of her students had been imprisoned because of mental illness rather than criminal activity. The authorities simply had nowhere else to take people with mental illnesses, so they often threw them in jail alongside convicts. Dix devoted the rest of her life to solving this problem. She traveled to city after city pleading with local community leaders to provide more adequate treatment to the mentally ill. Her efforts were remarkably successful: Dix was responsible for the creation of 30 state institutions for the mentally ill in various states throughout the 1800s.

Dorothea Dix was one of numerous pioneers who worked to provide more resources for the mentally ill. Her efforts sparked the creation of dozens of state institutions for the mentally ill in various U.S. states throughout the 1800s.

Collectively, the efforts of reformers like Tuke, Pinel, Todd, and Dix changed society's attitude toward the treatment of the mentally ill—from shunning and punishment to compassion and respect (Cautin, 2011). This movement paved the way for the two primary forms of treatment used today—*psychotherapy* and *biomedical therapy*—that will be the focus of the rest of this chapter. **Psychotherapy** involves techniques used by a mental health professional to help a person overcome a psychological disorder or improve some aspect of emotional, cognitive, or behavioral functioning. **Biomedical therapy** involves medications or medical procedures that treat psychological problems by directly changing the biology of the brain.

CHECK YOUR LEARNING:

15.1 How were psychological disorders treated centuries ago?

15.2 When and how did the treatment of psychological disorders begin to change toward the current approach?

15.3 What are the differences between psychotherapy and biomedical therapy?

Psychotherapies for Individual Clients

Psychotherapy often goes by the name *talk therapy* to distinguish it from treatments that involve medications. The most common type of psychotherapy is individual therapy—in which only the client and the therapist are in the room (Norcross et al., 2005).

YOU WILL LEARN:

15.4 who seeks psychotherapy.

15.5 about the basics of psychodynamic therapy, including transference.

15.6 about the basics of person-centered therapy, including empathy, unconditional positive regard, and genuineness.

Who seeks psychotherapy?

Lots of people seek psychotherapy for lots of reasons. Over half of Americans will undergo some form of psychotherapy in their lifetimes—some to treat a psychological

YOU WILL LEARN: (*Continued*)

15.7 about the basics of behavior therapy, including exposure techniques and token economies.

15.8 about the basics of cognitive therapy, including the ABCDE model and cognitive distortions.

15.9 how therapies can be combined, including eclectic and integrative approaches.

disorder, and others to help with day-to-day struggles with emotions, behaviors, or relationships (Engel, 2008). As shown in **Figure 15.2**, psychotherapy clients come from all backgrounds, but those most likely to enter therapy are female, white, middle-aged, highly educated, and with above-average income (Hunsley et al., 1999; Vessey & Howard, 1993).

There are many varieties of individual psychotherapy, but we will focus on the major ones—*psychodynamic therapy*, *person-centered therapy*, *behavior therapy*, and *cognitive therapy*. We'll start with psychodynamic therapy, which stems from Sigmund Freud's theories. Historically, Freud came first. In fact, until the mid-1900s, Freud's therapy was the only kind of therapy. The other therapies that you'll read about came along later, often as an attempt to offer something different than Freud did (Hollon & DiGiuseppe, 2011; Guadiano, 2008; Routh, 1996).

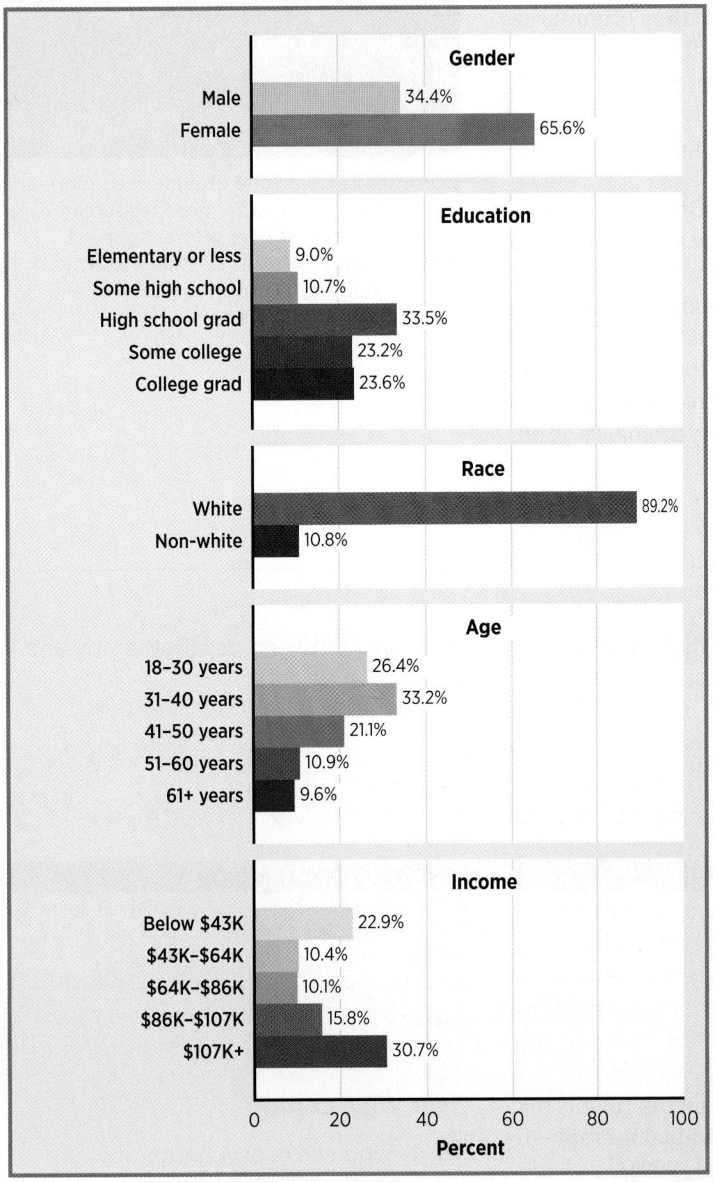

FIGURE 15.2 Who Seeks Psychotherapy? People of all kinds seek psychotherapy, but a large proportion of adult clients are female, White, educated, and affluent.

Data from Vessey & Howard, 1993. Note: Data based on adult clients making at least one mental health visit. Income levels converted from 1975 dollars as reported in Vessey & Howard, 1993, to 2012 dollars via http://www.coinnews.net/tools/cpi-inflation-calculator/.

Psychodynamic Therapy

Sigmund Freud, whose theory of personality we explored in Chapter 12, was a pioneer of psychotherapy in the late 1800s and early 1900s. He developed **psychoanalysis**: an approach to psychotherapy in which the main goal is to make the unconscious conscious—that is, helping the client become more aware of thoughts and feelings of which he or she was unaware at the start of therapy (Cabaniss et al., 2011; Karon & Widener, 1995). *Insight* is a single word often used to describe this process of looking inside oneself and seeing something that had previously gone unnoticed (McAleavey & Castonguay, 2014; Lacewing, 2014; Gibbons et al., 2007). For example, clients in psychoanalysis might realize for the first time that their low self-esteem today stems from an early childhood relationship with a parent who ignored or belittled them.

In the 100-plus years since Freud created psychoanalysis, the treatment has been revised many times, usually to make the approach to therapy a quicker, more direct way of addressing psychological problems (and so more in tune with contemporary society). Collectively, we now call all of these revisions of Freud's original approach **psychodynamic therapy**: therapy that retains the goal of making the unconscious conscious, but compared to psychoanalysis, it is briefer and more focused on the client's current life than the past. Although classic psychoanalysis is rarely practiced today, many forms of psychodynamic therapy are very common (Gabbard, 2009a).

Psychodynamic therapists face two big challenges as they help their clients become more aware of unconscious thoughts and feelings. First, the therapist needs to "get at" the unconscious material, the innermost workings of the client's mind that are outside of even the client's awareness. Second, the therapist needs to help the client recognize this unconscious material and deal with it consciously.

To deal with the first of these challenges—gaining access to the client's unconscious—psychodynamic therapists use a variety of techniques, including *free association*, *dream analysis*, working with a client's *resistance*, and working with a client's *transference*.

Free Association. In **free association**, the therapist encourages the client to say whatever comes to mind without any censoring (Skelton, 2006). It seems simple enough, but it is actually difficult to do. Even at your most candid and uninhibited, could you let yourself speak completely freely, expressing your most raw, unedited thoughts? A client who can free-associate might jump from one topic to another in a way that seems

random or nonsensical. Their train of thought might travel from one rude thought to another, and reveal some sexual or aggressive impulses that are usually kept hidden from others. For example, a client who is able to truly free-associate may openly admit to a deeply guarded attraction to a married friend, or a wish to hurt their seemingly loving parent.

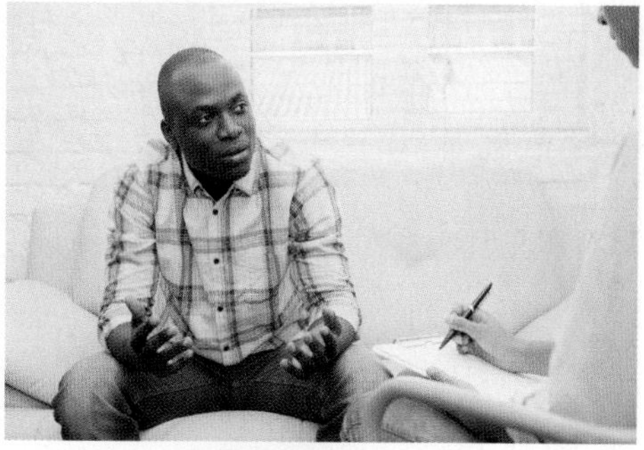

There are many kinds of individual therapy, including psychodynamic therapy, person-centered therapy, behavior therapy, and cognitive therapy. Wavebreakmedia/Getty Images

Dream Analysis. In **dream analysis**, the therapist and client attempt to find the underlying meaning of the client's dreams. Many psychodynamic therapists see dreams as symbolic expressions of unconscious wishes (Kernberg, 2004; Freud, 1900). So, consider a client who shares a dream in which a dog scratches and whines desperately to escape from a small locked cage. The therapist may encourage the client to consider the dog as a symbol for herself and think about what part of her life—her job, her romantic relationship, her family—represents the cage from which she wants to be freed.

Resistance. In addition to free association and dream analysis, the way the client relates to the therapist can reveal some of the client's unconscious issues. For example, when difficult or challenging issues come up during therapy, clients often find a way to steer clear of discussing them. They change the subject to a safer topic, or suddenly think of an entirely different problem that demands immediate attention. If the next session promises to include more discussion of the difficult issue, clients arrive late or don't show up at all. Psychodynamic therapists call this **resistance**: client behavior that blocks discussion or conscious awareness of anxiety-provoking topics. The client is typically unaware of the reason behind the resistance, and in some cases, the resistant behavior itself. It is up to the psychodynamic therapist to point it out to the client, to help make it conscious (LaFarge, 2012; Dewald, 1964; Gabbard, 2009b; Karon & Widener, 1995; Lane & Harris, 2008).

One of my own psychotherapy clients, whom I'll call Ana, provided me with a real-life example of resistance. Ana was in her early 20s, and the main reason she sought therapy was to deal with feelings of sadness and low self-esteem that had lingered since she was a young child. She spent several early sessions expressing a bitter anger toward her older brother, who mistreated her as they grew up. This was more than mere sibling rivalry: Ana's brother insulted her relentlessly, hit her until she was bruised, and sometimes fondled her. During our third session, I listened to Ana offer more details of what her brother had done and how it had affected her. Then I asked her if anyone else in her family knew about her brother's mistreatment of her. At that moment, she abruptly changed the subject to some new responsibilities her boss had given her at work, and proceeded to talk about that until we ran out of time. She missed our next appointment altogether, and was 15 minutes late to the one after that.

A psychodynamic explanation of Ana's behavior would go something like this: She was OK discussing her brother, despite his abusive behavior, but the idea of other people in her family being aware of it made Ana so uncomfortable that she resisted talking about it. Much later in therapy, Ana revealed that their mother knew about her brother's abusive behavior toward Ana, but did nothing to protect her. Ana was so scared to acknowledge her feelings of anger toward her mother during that third session that she prevented the conversation from going there without realizing why.

Transference. Perhaps the most powerful tool that psychodynamic therapists have for accessing the client's unconscious is *transference* (Galatzer-Levy et al., 2000; Karon & Widener, 1995). **Transference** happens when the client unconsciously and unrealistically expects the therapist to behave like an important person from the client's past. Without realizing it, the client *transfers* what they learned from previous relationships onto the relationship with the therapist. In a way, they unconsciously prejudge the therapist to be a certain kind of person—usually like mom, dad, or some other "big" figure from the client's own past—when in reality, they don't have enough evidence to know whether it is true at all (S. H. Goldberg, 2012; A. Harris, 2012; Gabbard, 2005). For example, a client who grew up with a critical, fault-finding mom might—without

psychoanalysis
An approach to psychotherapy developed by Sigmund Freud in which the main goal is to make the unconscious conscious—that is, helping the client become more aware of thoughts and feelings of which he or she was unaware at the start of therapy.

psychodynamic therapy
A therapy that retains psychoanalysis' goal of making the unconscious conscious, but is briefer and more focused on the client's current life (as opposed to his or her past) than psychoanalysis.

free association
A psychodynamic technique in which the therapist encourages the client to simply say whatever comes to mind without any censoring at all.

dream analysis
A psychodynamic technique in which the therapist and client attempt to find the underlying meaning of the client's dreams.

resistance
Client behavior that blocks discussion or conscious awareness of anxiety-provoking topics.

transference
A client's unconscious and unrealistic expectations for the therapist to behave like an important person from the client's past.

Transference happens when the client unconsciously and unrealistically expects the therapist to behave like an important person from the client's past. Psychodynamic therapists try to help clients become aware of their transference tendencies, which may affect many of the client's other relationships outside of therapy. Wavebreakmedia Ltd/Getty Images

realizing it—presume from the start that his new therapist will have the same qualities (especially if the therapist is female). Or, a client whose dad always demanded that she keep her opinions to herself might enter a relationship with a therapist (especially a male therapist) assuming—without being aware of it—that the therapist will make similar demands on her.

So, when clients experience transference, are they hallucinating? Do they actually think that their therapist is their mom or dad?

No, transference is not a hallucination at all. There is nothing bizarre about it. In fact, transference is a common experience in all kinds of relationships, not just therapy. You have probably been on the receiving end of transference yourself. For example, maybe you dated someone who suspected you of cheating, despite the fact that they had no real reason to think so. Or maybe you worked for a supervisor who thought you were trying to steal his or her job, despite the fact that you had no such intentions at all. Why would these people have these false beliefs? According to psychodynamic therapists, the answer lies in their previous relationships. If their previous romantic partners cheated or their previous employees stole their jobs, then they may have a hard time expecting you not to do the same. They transferred what they learned from earlier relationships onto their relationship with you.

Psychodynamic therapists are good at noticing the "leftovers" from previous relationships that their clients transfer onto them during their sessions. Again, one of my own clients comes to mind as an example. Juan was a 30-year-old man who came to see me for mild anxiety and occasional panic attacks. As we began our initial session together, Juan offered some background about his job and his family, then started to describe his symptoms. About 10 minutes in, he stopped himself and, to my surprise, apologized to me: "I'm so sorry. I can tell you are bored, and that I am wasting your time. You are probably thinking, 'I wish this guy would shut up so I could go home.'" With that, he stood up to leave. I encouraged Juan to stay and assured him that I was very interested in him. After a moment's hesitation, he did. But then, 15 minutes later, he again interrupted himself, apologized for wasting my time, and started to leave. Altogether, Juan interrupted himself and started to leave four times during the first session.

It is important to note that I did nothing to cause Juan's behavior. I didn't glance at my cell phone, stare at the clock, gaze out the window, or yawn as he spoke. So why did Juan presume that I was so uninterested and annoyed by him? The psychodynamic explanation goes like this: Without realizing that he was doing so, Juan presumed that I would be like some other important person in his life who did, in fact, find him uninteresting and annoying. He jumped to the conclusion that I would too, despite the fact that there was no evidence that I felt that way. As therapy progressed, Juan shared many more details about his family, including his father who—you guessed it—found Juan to be an uninteresting and annoying nuisance throughout Juan's whole childhood.

Interpretation. Once psychodynamic therapists have gained access to clients' unconscious material, their next challenge is helping the client recognize it too. The primary technique for this is **interpretation**: the psychodynamic therapist's attempt to make a connection between the client's unconscious material and his or her current behavior, thoughts, or feelings (P. Goldberg, 2012; Johansson et al., 2010). Let's consider again the examples of my clients Ana and Juan. Ana won't benefit if I just notice the way she resists talking about her mother's role in the abuse, but I don't make Ana aware of it. Likewise, Juan won't benefit if I simply notice the way he expects me to relate to him like his dad did, but don't make Juan aware of it. In both cases, good interpretations could provide the client with an "aha" moment, a powerful insight in which they come to know something about themselves that they didn't know before. Ana would recognize her hidden feelings toward her mother and Juan would understand his tendency to transfer expectations of his father onto others.

Working Through. Of course, this interpretation may not have an immediate impact. Even the most powerful insight takes some getting used to. So, after a psychodynamic therapist offers an insight, there is typically a need for **working through**: a lengthy phase of therapy in which interpretations are repeated, reconsidered, and given a chance to gradually sink in (Gabbard, 2009b). Over time, both Ana and Juan worked through my interpretations and incorporated them into their way of thinking and their views of themselves. Little by little, Ana accepted her feelings of anger and disappointment toward her mother, as well as how avoiding them had been interfering with her life. Bit by bit, Juan recognized that he transferred expectations of his father onto me, and, more importantly, onto other people in his life, including his friends and his supervisor at work. From that point on, he caught himself when he started to do so, and reminded himself to relate to other people for who they actually were. In many cases, people were far more accepting than his father.

Psychodynamic Therapy Today. The number of therapists practicing traditional, "old school" psychoanalysis is dwindling, but the number practicing "new school" variations of psychodynamic therapy remains high (Gabbard, 2009a). One particular form of psychodynamic therapy, *interpersonal therapy*, is especially highly regarded. Studies have shown that it is especially beneficial for clients with depression, and perhaps some with other disorders as well (Markowitz & Weissman, 2012; Swartz & Markowitz, 2009). Interpersonal therapy is a short-term therapy (usually 14–18 sessions) built around the assumption that depression grows out of stressful interpersonal relationships. The therapist therefore attempts to improve the client's ability to form healthy relationships, particularly by making the client more aware of his or her own thoughts, feelings, and expectations regarding those relationships (Didie, 2015; Frank & Levenson, 2011; Klerman et al., 1984; Weissman, 1995). Interpersonal therapists specify four issues that cause many of these relationship problems: (1) role transitions, such as when a grown child moves out; (2) role disputes, such as figuring out who does what in a new marriage; (3) interpersonal deficits, such as a lack of meaningful friendships; and (4) grief, such as the death of a loved one (Blanco & Weissman, 2005; Lipsitz, 2009).

Person-Centered Therapy

Person-centered therapy is an approach based on the theories of Carl Rogers that emphasizes the tendency toward healthy growth inherent in each person (a tendency we labeled *self-actualization* in Chapter 12). Person-centered therapy has also been called *humanistic therapy* and *client-centered therapy*. Person-centered therapists believe that most psychological problems are caused by the self-actualization tendency being blocked. Therapy, then, is focused on helping clients return to their own self-actualization tendencies, which will guide them back to happiness and psychological health (Watson & Bohart, 2015; Erekson & Lambert, 2015; Cain, 2002, 2010; Maslow, 1968; Rogers, 1957).

The notion that clients have the capacity within themselves to overcome their own psychological problems is a unique characteristic of person-centered therapy. Other forms of therapy typically assume that the client needs a special technique to be applied to them by the therapist. In person-centered therapy, the therapist's role is more of a facilitator, someone who helps clients help themselves by reconnecting with their own tendencies toward healthy growth. As a result, person-centered therapists tend to conduct **nondirective therapy**: a style of therapy in which the client, rather than the therapist, determines the course of therapy. Person-centered therapists trust that if the therapist follows the client's lead, rather than vice versa, the client's own tendency toward self-actualization will guide them wisely.

How, exactly, do person-centered therapists accomplish this? According to Rogers, it is all about the relationship that the therapist forms with the client. Specifically, there are three essential characteristics, or "ingredients," that the therapist must bring to the therapeutic relationship in order to foster the client's self-actualization: *empathy*, *unconditional positive regard*, and *genuineness* (Cain, 2002, 2010; Tudor & Worrall, 2006; Rogers, 1959).

interpretation
The psychodynamic therapist's attempt to make a connection between the client's unconscious material and his or her current behavior, thoughts, or feelings.

working through
A lengthy phase of psychodynamic therapy in which interpretations are repeated, reconsidered, and given a chance to gradually sink in.

person-centered therapy
An approach based on the theories of Carl Rogers that emphasizes the tendency toward healthy growth inherent in each person.

nondirective therapy
A style of therapy in which the client, rather than the therapist, determines the course of therapy.

Empathy. **Empathy** is the therapist's ability to sense the client's emotions just as the client would, and to then respond compassionately. Empathy is a deep, nonjudgmental understanding of "what it's like" to be the client (Bozarth, 1997; Rogers, 1980). This means the client doesn't have to worry about the other person forming negative opinions or finding fault in him or her (as in other relationships). Empathy makes clients feel supported and helps them clarify their own feelings (Gillon, 2007).

Unconditional Positive Regard. The second essential ingredient that the person-centered therapist provides is **unconditional positive regard**, or full acceptance of the client "no matter what," without any conditions or limitations. Rogers liked to say that the therapist should *prize* the client (Rogers, 1959). Regardless of what the client does, thinks, or feels, the person-centered therapist accepts him or her as a human being. Such full acceptance communicates to clients that they can be themselves completely; they need not pick and choose which aspects of themselves they can show and which they must hide. Such a relationship is quite unique. (With how many friends or family members can you be completely yourself, with no need to monitor or edit what you say and do, and with no concern that you might be rejected?) Over time, unconditional positive regard from the therapist can convince the client to have unconditional positive regard for himself or herself, which can lead to self-actualization and psychological well-being.

Genuineness. The third essential ingredient of the therapeutic relationship that the person-centered therapist offers is **genuineness**: the therapist's truthfulness, realness, and honesty, as opposed to falsely playing the therapist role. (Genuineness is also known as *congruence*.) Simply put, empathy and unconditional positive regard are worthless if they are fake. You've probably been the recipient of phony empathy before, and you've probably had others pretend to accept you no matter what. If so, you know how those experiences left you feeling—poorly understood and not valued for who you really are. Person-centered therapists aren't acting or otherwise faking it; they truly feel compassion for their clients and sincerely offer them complete acceptance. Such genuineness by the therapist encourages clients to be more engaged in the therapy process (Rogers, 1961; Gillon, 2007).

Rogers was extremely confident about the combined power of empathy, unconditional positive regard, and genuineness. In fact, he boldly claimed that a therapist who provided those three ingredients, without any additional specific techniques, could help any client no matter what the problem might be—depression, anxiety, eating disorder, whatever (Rogers, 1957). Research generally supports the notion that these three ingredients are requirements for a good therapeutic relationship, which is a key factor in any kind of therapy (Zuroff et al., 2010; Elliott et al., 2011; Farber & Doolin, 2011; Kolden et al., 2011). However, the three ingredients alone are not sufficient to help all types of clients.

In person-centered therapy, one of the key elements is empathy, or the therapist's ability to sense the client's emotions and respond compassionately and nonjudgmentally. wavebreakmedia/Shutterstock

So, what exactly do person-centered therapists *do* during a session? What techniques do they use?

Actually, person-centered therapy is less about techniques than attitudes. Person-centered therapists believe that *how they are* with clients—not *what they do* to them—is the source of the benefit in psychotherapy. Most other approaches emphasize the use of particular techniques by the therapist rather than the power of a compassionate, accepting attitude (Bozarth et al., 2002).

Reflection. The only element of person-centered therapy that resembles a technique is *reflection*. In **reflection**, the therapist listens closely and actively, then restates the client's words in a way that highlights the client's feelings. *Reflection* is actually a shortened form of Rogers's preferred term, *reflection of feeling* (Rogers, 1986). When done appropriately, reflections have the ability to communicate the empathy, unconditional positive regard, and genuineness that are so central to the person-centered

therapy approach. They help clients recognize their own feelings more deeply, and consider the possibility that any feelings they have are important and acceptable.

As an illustration of not only reflection but all of the components of person-centered therapy, consider my client, Talia. Talia grew up as an only child, and her single mother was loving but domineering. From an early age, Talia's mother told Talia how her life should go: go to college, major in nursing, get a job, get married, and have children. Whenever Talia voiced any doubt about this life path, her mom dismissed her thoughts as nonsense: "Oh Talia, that's not you." But Talia sensed that there was, in fact, more to her than the nurse, wife, and mom roles her mother had laid out for her. Now 23, Talia had followed the first few of her mother's preapproved steps. She had graduated from college with a nursing degree and held a good job in a hospital. But she was frustrated and unfulfilled. She wanted to take her life in directions that her mother didn't even know about, she told me, and would certainly frown upon if she did.

Little by little, as our relationship strengthened, Talia revealed to me an astonishing array of yet-unexplored interests: She wanted to join a roller-derby team, create first-person shooter video games, and open a sushi restaurant. She yearned to travel through Australia, study architecture, and volunteer for a pet rescue organization. Hesitantly, she even shared that she might never want to get married or have children—decisions that would definitely stray from her mother's master plan for her.

It seemed clear to me that Talia's self-actualization was stifled. Following her mother's orders had provided Talia with a steady job, but thwarted many of her other interests, leaving her quite unhappy. As I worked with Talia, I did a number of things that were characteristic of person-centered therapists. I expressed empathy for her situation, often through reflection: "It sounds like you're OK with your job, but you have all of these other passions that seem 'against the rules,' like you're not allowed to pursue them. It seems like that could leave you frustrated or depressed. Is that how you feel?" I practiced unconditional regard and was careful to accept her no matter what. I prized Talia as a human being—whether she was a mild-mannered nurse, a roller-derby bruiser, or an Australian adventurer. And I did all of this genuinely: I honestly felt empathy and unconditional positive regard toward her, rather than merely acting as if I did.

Over time, these therapeutic ingredients blended to create a therapy relationship in which Talia felt she could be herself completely. This was a new, liberating experience for Talia. In therapy, she didn't need to follow anyone's preapproved path or censor any of her thoughts or wishes—she could simply say what she really felt, and be who she really was. Eventually, Talia felt more free to be who she actually was—not only with her therapist, but with everyone else, including herself. As our therapy wrapped up, she had signed up for a roller-derby class and had booked a trip to Australia—with no concern about disapproval by her mother or herself!

Motivational Interviewing. In recent years, *motivational interviewing*, a contemporary variation of person-centered therapy, has become more prominent. (Don't let the word *interviewing* in the name mislead you: This is a form of psychotherapy that lasts multiple sessions, not just an approach to the initial interview.) Motivational interviewing was originally developed to help people with addiction problems (for example, substance abuse), but its use has expanded to many other problems.

A key element of motivational interviewing is tapping into the client's own motivation to change (Dennhardt et al., 2015; Miller & Rose, 2009; Hettema et al., 2005). Too often, the need to change has been imposed by the therapist on the client. For example, picture a rehab center where therapists tell clients that the clients have to stop drinking or taking drugs. Clients often resist such orders from outsiders. They are more likely to make genuine, long-lasting change if the desire to do so comes from within themselves.

Therapists who use motivational interviewing openly discuss the mixed feelings the clients may have about a big change in their behavior or lifestyle, such as giving up alcohol, drugs, overeating, or any other unhealthy behavior. In fact, therapists

empathy
The therapist's ability to sense the client's emotions just as the client would, and to then respond compassionately.

unconditional positive regard
The therapist's full acceptance of the client without any conditions or limitations.

genuineness
The therapist's truthfulness, realness, and honesty, as opposed to falsely playing the therapist role.

reflection
A technique in which the therapist listens closely and actively, then restates the client's words in a way that highlights the client's feelings.

empathize with their client's ambivalence about changing, as any good person-centered therapist would. They also highlight discrepancies between the client's real life and the client's values to enhance the motivation to change. For example, the therapist might highlight how they value their family and work but have put both at risk by substance use. After compassionately listening to the client's own struggle between the pros and cons of changing, the therapist essentially asks how the client would like to proceed. If the client decides to take the steps necessary to make the change, the motivation is the client's own, and success is more likely than if the therapist had strong-armed the client into it (Miller & Rollnick, 2013; Miller & Rose, 2015; Arkowitz et al., 2015).

Behavior Therapy

Behavior therapy is the application of operant and classical conditioning to change outward behavior, with little to no emphasis on the mental processes affecting that behavior. One of the primary reasons behavior therapy developed was to provide a more observable, measurable alternative to the therapies that came before it (Shikatani et al., 2015; Hunt, 1993; Watson, 1924). After all, many of the core concepts of psychodynamic therapy—the unconscious, resistance, transference, and so on—are impossible to observe or measure in an objective way. And progress in psychodynamic therapy—the extent to which the client's unconscious has been made conscious—is also impossible to directly see or calculate. Similarly, a person-centered therapist would have a difficult time measuring the effects of empathy, unconditional positive regard, or genuineness in a concrete way. All of these concepts are inside the mind. Behavior therapy shifts the focus from inner mental processes that can't be seen to behaviors—outward, visible actions—that can. As a result, behavior therapy lends itself to scientific testing to a greater extent than other kinds of psychotherapy (Grant et al., 2005; Kazdin, 1978).

The first step of behavior therapy is to define the problem that the client brings to therapy in behavioral terms—words that refer to observable, measurable behaviors, rather than inside-the-mind experiences that can't be seen. This process differs drastically from how problems are often defined in other kinds of therapy (Spiegler & Guevremont, 2010; Truax, 2002). For example, consider Jamal, who seeks therapy from Dr. Lin, a behavior therapist. Jamal initially defines his problem as "social anxiety." When Dr. Lin asks Jamal to describe his social anxiety, Jamal says that he "feels really nervous around other people" and he "always thinks that other people are being critical of me." To Dr. Lin, those descriptions don't do much good, because they are all inside of Jamal's head. Jamal's *feelings* of nervousness and his *thoughts* about others' attitudes toward him can't be directly observed or measured, so they aren't good targets for therapy. So, Dr. Lin asks Jamal: "What *behaviors* do you want to change? What do you want to *do* differently?" After struggling with the question, Jamal provides some answers—he wants to call friends more often, go out to restaurants with friends and coworkers more often, and attend more parties on weekends. These are outward, observable, and measurable behaviors that Jamal and Dr. Lin can easily count. As such, they are much better goals for behavior therapy. After determining a *baseline*—the number of times that Jamal already performs each of those behaviors—Jamal and Dr. Lin can work toward increasing those numbers, and measure Jamal's progress at any point during therapy.

As Jamal's case illustrates, behavior therapists don't see unwanted behaviors (such as his avoidance of social situations) as symptoms of some deeper, underlying problem. Instead, they believe the unwanted behaviors *are* the problem to be fixed in therapy. Think of it this way: If your dog developed the bad habit of chewing your shoes, would you need to explain that behavior by labeling it an underlying disorder in the dog's mind? Or would you simply try to change your dog's shoe-chewing behavior with no regard to where it may have come from? Behavior therapists find it as unproductive to look within the human mind as most of us do to look within the canine mind.

Once they define problems behaviorally, behavior therapists use a variety of techniques to change the frequency or intensity of that behavior. All of these techniques are

behavior therapy
The application of operant and classical conditioning to change outward behavior, with little to no emphasis on the mental processes affecting that behavior.

exposure therapy
A form of behavior therapy based on classical conditioning in which anxiety is treated by gradually exposing the client to the thing or situation that causes the anxiety.

based on either classical conditioning or operant conditioning (see Chapter 12). The idea is that classical conditioning or operant conditioning shaped the problem behavior, so classical conditioning or operant conditioning can be used to modify it (Craske, 2010).

Techniques Based on Classical Conditioning. **Exposure therapy** is a form of behavior therapy based on classical conditioning in which anxiety is treated by gradually exposing the client to the thing or situation that causes the anxiety. In short, exposure therapy makes clients face their fears (Foa & McLean, 2015; Abramowitz et al., 2015; Hazlett-Stevens & Craske, 2008). Consider Ronnie, a client who was seriously bitten by a dog many years ago, an incident that involved blood, stitches, and plenty of terror on her part. She has fearfully avoided dogs ever since. Now, she finds herself engaged to a man who has been a dog lover his whole life, so Ronnie is motivated to change. Her fear (phobia, actually) is the result of classical conditioning: Through real-life experience, the feared object (dogs) was paired with unpleasant outcomes (the pain of a dog bite). If Ronnie has new real-life experiences with dogs in which dogs are not paired with pain, that pairing will weaken, and dogs will not evoke such a strong fear reaction in her. Exposure therapy provides that new real-world experience.

It is important to note that the exposure to the anxiety-producing object or situation happens in small steps, each of which causes slightly more anxiety than the one before it. That is, clients face their fears little by little, rather than all at once. (*Flooding*, a behavioral treatment in which clients do face their worst fears all at once, is rarely practiced today because it can be traumatic ([Levis, 2008; Zoellner et al., 2008; Taylor, 2002].) Clients, together with their behavior therapists, define those small steps by creating an *anxiety hierarchy*. An anxiety hierarchy is a list of situations that involve the feared object or situation, ranked in order of least to most frightening. The first item on the list causes only mild anxiety, and is often seen by the client as quite achievable; the last item on the list causes significant anxiety, and achieving it would indicate that the treatment has been successful. The items in between are like rungs on a ladder—evenly spaced and within reach from the previous step.

As an illustration, **Table 15.1** shows the anxiety hierarchy used in the treatment of Ronnie's dog phobia. Notice that the first few items on the list don't involve real dogs at all. They involve Ronnie thinking about or imagining dog-related sights and sounds. These are known as *imaginal exposures*, and they are often good initial steps for clients to take when actual exposure of any kind would be overwhelming. Eventually, Ronnie

MY TAKE VIDEO 15.1

Exposure Therapy

"At first we started with just me sitting in the car..."

YOUTUBE: http://tiny.cc/mytake
LAUNCHPAD: launchpadworks.com

TABLE 15.1: Example of an Anxiety Hierarchy Used in Treatment of Phobia of Dogs

EXPOSURE	RONNIE'S DISTRESS RATING (0 = NO FEAR; 100 = MAXIMUM FEAR)	TYPE OF EXPOSURE
1. Visualizing a dog on a leash far away	5	Imaginal
2. Visualizing a dog on a leash nearby	15	Imaginal
3. Visualizing an unleashed dog nearby	25	Imaginal
4. Hearing a dog bark in the next room	35	In vivo
5. Seeing a dog through a window	45	In vivo
6. Standing in the same room with a dog 20 feet away	55	In vivo
7. Standing in the same room with a dog 3 feet away	65	In vivo
8. Petting a dog for 1 second	75	In vivo
9. Petting a dog for 10 seconds	85	In vivo
10. Petting a dog for 1 minute	95	In vivo

Behavior therapists use anxiety hierarchies like this one to help clients take small steps toward facing and overcoming their fears. Notice that some of the exposures take place only in the client's mind (*imaginal*), and others take place in real life (*in vivo*).

does start to interact with real dogs—first at a distance, then closer, then in physical contact. These are *in vivo exposures*, meaning that they happen in real life as opposed to Ronnie's imagination.

For Ronnie, successful exposure therapy would mean that dogs are paired with no emotional response instead of being paired with anxiety (which is a big improvement!). Sometimes, instead of replacing anxiety with no emotional response, behavior therapists try to replace the anxious feeling with a more pleasant feeling, such as relaxation. In Ronnie's case, the sights and sounds of dogs would gradually become linked to relaxation rather than fear, a difference that would make interaction with dogs much more possible in her day-to-day life. This is known as **systematic desensitization**: a form of exposure therapy, primarily for phobias, in which the client experiences the new pairing of relaxation (rather than anxiety) with the thing or situation that previously caused the anxiety.

Systematic desensitization is a therapeutic application of **counterconditioning**: a classical conditioning technique in which the trigger for an unwanted response is paired with a new stimulus that prevents the unwanted response (Head & Gross, 2008; McGlynn, 2002; Wolpe, 1958, 1969). Systematic desensitization takes advantage of the fact that relaxation and anxiety are mutually exclusive, meaning you can't feel both at the same time. In moments of deep relaxation, you are immune from anxiety. If an anxiety-provoking object were to appear in such a moment, you would have the experience of pairing that object with the relaxation you were feeling rather than the anxiety you used to feel. In Ronnie's case, seeing a dog while in a relaxed state creates a new link between dogs and relaxation rather than the old link of dogs and anxiety.

The first step of systematic desensitization is *relaxation training*, which can take a variety of forms. Sometimes the therapist instructs the client to tense and then release various muscles in the body; sometimes the therapist helps the client envision a calming scene such as a beach or meadow; sometimes the therapist plays soothing music. Once clients can relax themselves during the session, the therapist exposes them to the items on their anxiety hierarchy while they remain in that relaxed state. The result is that the client experiences things that were previously feared—snakes, airplanes, germs, and so on—in combination with relaxation, a new association that eclipses the old one in which those things were associated with fear.

A token economy is a behavior therapy strategy in which clients earn tokens for performing target behavior and then exchange those tokens for rewards. Token economies are typically used in settings where the client's behavior is being constantly monitored, like inpatient psychiatric hospitals, prisons, and schools. If you have ever spent time at Chuck E. Cheese's, Dave & Buster's, or any other arcade in which certain behaviors earn you tickets (or points on a card) that you can cash in for prizes, you have a first-hand appreciation of how token economies can shape behavior. Stephen Barnes/Entertainment/Alamy

Techniques Based on Operant Conditioning. Operant conditioning is all about the consequences that follow a behavior (see Chapter 12) (Sturmey et al., 2007). If those consequences are good, we learn to do the behavior more often. If those consequences are bad, we learn to do the behavior less often. Behavior therapists often attempt to change those consequences, an approach known as *contingency management*. Contingencies are those personal "if..., then..." rules that we have each learned through our life experiences. Behaviors that turn out to be problematic are often learned in this way. For example, a boy's experience may have taught him that if he insults classmates (the problem behavior), then he gets laughs from classmates (the reinforcement). If behavior therapists can change these contingencies—particularly, the consequences (or the "then..." part) that follow the behavior—the problem behaviors will change as well (Petry et al., 2013; Drossel et al., 2008; Kearney & Vecchio, 2002; Villamar et al., 2008).

One technique that behavior therapists use to change clients' contingencies is the **token economy**, in which clients earn tokens that are exchangeable for rewards when they perform target behaviors. (If you ever played games for tickets or points at Dave & Buster's or Chuck E. Cheese's, then traded them in for prizes, you temporarily experienced a token economy.) Token economies work best in settings where the client's behavior is under constant watch, like inpatient psychiatric hospitals, prisons, and schools. In these environments, supervisors pinpoint a target behavior for a particular person, and they provide a token (or chip, or ticket, or point) every time the behavior is performed (Ghezzi et al., 2008). As an example, consider Jeffrey, a man with severe depression staying in a residential psychiatric facility. Jeffrey refuses to leave his room to participate in group activities, exercise, or socialize. However, the staff has noticed that he enjoys the cookies served in the cafeteria, so they set up this token economy:

Every time Jeffrey leaves his room, he gets a token. He can "buy" an extra cookie with three tokens. Soon, Jeffrey leaves his room more often, enticed by the reward of the cookies.

An issue with token economies is generalizability, the idea that what the client learns in one setting will transfer to other settings (Stuve & Salinas, 2002). In Jeffrey's case, the goal isn't simply to get him to leave his room when he's in the facility, but to continue to do so after he returns home. If Jeffrey becomes too dependent on a cookie contingency that doesn't exist in the real world, any improvement he shows in the facility may disappear when he returns home.

Token economies are based on reinforcement, but punishment is also a powerful consequence to behavior. **Aversive conditioning** is a form of behavior therapy that aims to reduce unwanted behavior by pairing it with an unpleasant experience. Aversive conditioning punishes undesired behaviors. Typically, the punishment used in aversive conditioning is a physically unpleasant sensation such as nausea or electric shock. It is delivered immediately after the client performs a clearly defined unwanted behavior, such as drinking alcohol, smoking, or self-injury (Emmelkamp & Kamphuis, 2002).

As an example, consider the treatment known as *rapid smoking* (Gifford & Shoenberger, 2009; Lichtenstein & Rodrigues, 1977). Rapid smoking is a technique designed to reduce smoking behavior by forcing people to smoke rapidly until they become physically ill. Clients are instructed to take a puff from a cigarette every 6 seconds and the therapist monitors the clients to make sure they are, in fact, inhaling. The clients continue inhaling once every 6 seconds until they are about to vomit or feel very lightheaded. Once the clients reach that point, they are given a 5-minute break and then instructed to start smoking rapidly again. When it works, a treatment such as rapid smoking teaches clients a new consequence to a familiar behavior—in this case, that puffing on a cigarette makes you sick.

It is important to note that in rapid smoking or any therapy involving punishment, therapists must be extremely careful to use it ethically and with concern for the client's overall well-being. Typically, it is only considered after reinforcement-based strategies have failed (Poling et al., 2002).

A final point about behavior therapy based on operant conditioning: A client's behavior can change significantly as a result of observing other people's behavior. Seeing another person receive reinforcements or punishments for a particular action can have powerful effects (Spiegler & Guevremont, 2010; Freeman, 2002; Bandura, 1977). Behavior therapists call the therapeutic use of this kind of observation **participant modeling**: a technique in which a client watches a model (in some cases, the therapist) perform the target behavior with the intent of the client imitating the model.

As an example of participant modeling, consider Terrence, a client struggling with a fear of elevators. His elevator phobia became a significant problem when his company transferred him to a major city, where his office was located on the thirty-third floor of a high-rise office building. Terrence's behavior therapist, who specializes in this issue, has a video recording of an actor successfully riding an elevator. They watch it repeatedly, discussing the particular components of the behavior that the model displays. Terrence's therapist also models the behavior himself, live in front of Terrence. His therapist makes sure that Terrence notices not only the behaviors involved in riding the elevator (button pressing, entering, waiting, exiting, etc.), but the absence of any negative consequences to any of the models. Then, it is Terrence's turn: With his therapist's encouragement and support, he initially rides the elevator in the therapist's building, with his therapist along for the ride, just one floor at a time. Soon, he applies his newly acquired behavior to the real world and finds himself independently riding up to and down from his thirty-third-floor office every day.

Cognitive Therapy

Cognitive therapy is a psychotherapy approach in which therapists help clients change the way they think about life events. What we think about the things that happen to us—our *cognitions* about them—have a huge impact on the way we feel. In

systematic desensitization
A form of behavior therapy, primarily for phobias, in which the client experiences the new pairing of relaxation (rather than anxiety) with the thing or situation that previously caused the anxiety.

counterconditioning
A classical conditioning therapy technique in which the trigger for an unwanted response is paired with a new stimulus that prevents the unwanted response.

token economy
A behavior therapy technique in which clients earn tokens that are exchangeable for rewards when they perform target behaviors.

aversive conditioning
A form of behavior therapy that aims to reduce unwanted behavior by pairing it with an unpleasant experience.

participant modeling
A technique in which a client watches a model (in some cases, the therapist) perform the target behavior with the intent of the client imitating the model.

cognitive therapy
A psychotherapy approach in which therapists help clients change the way they think about life events.

CHAPTER APP 15.1

Cognitive Therapy

SAM: Self-Help for Anxiety Management

Preview one of the links and consider the following questions.

WEBSITE:
http://tiny.cc/zyi7jy

ANDROID:
http://tiny.cc/ze92iy

IPHONE:
http://tiny.cc/xt87iy

VIDEO DEMO:
http://tiny.cc/chapterapps

This app is designed to help people (with or without anxiety disorders) cope with feelings of anxiety. It offers many resources, including physical relaxation tips and suggestions for anxiety-reducing behaviors such as exercise and deep breathing. One of its main resources is essentially a version of cognitive therapy. If you click "Thinking and Anxiety," you learn about cognitive distortions (which the app calls "anxious thinking"), then are prompted to enter your negative thoughts and replace them with more positive thoughts.

How does it APPly to your daily life?
If you were struggling with anxiety, could the cognitive therapy emphasis of an app like this be helpful? Could it complement or replace a human therapist?

How does it APPly to your understanding of psychology?
Consider the various anxiety disorders you learned about in the previous chapter. Which, in your opinion, would be most and least treatable with a cognitive therapy approach as utilized by this app?

fact, some of the feelings that underlie psychological disorders (especially sadness and anxiety) are often caused by the way we think about the events that take place in our lives, rather than the events themselves (Beck & Haigh, 2014; Dozois & Brinker, 2015; Hofmann et al., 2013; Dobson, 2012; Bermudes et al., 2009; Clark et al., 2009; Beck, 2002, 1995, 1976). (See **Figure 15.3** for a cognitive model of emotions.)

We tend to overlook the importance of our cognitions about events, and mistakenly believe that the events themselves caused our emotions. For example, I once had a client, Tina, whose depression had lasted for weeks and had significantly interfered with her work and social life. She explained her reason for seeking therapy this way: "I'm miserable because my application for a promotion at work got rejected." According to cognitive therapists, a statement like that overlooks the middle step that occurs between the event and the feeling. A more complete explanation might go like this: "I'm miserable *because I see myself as a complete failure* because my application for a promotion got rejected." Here, it is easy to see that the thought about the rejection is the link between the rejection and Tina's misery about it.

Cognitive therapy tends to be rather short-term and structured, qualities it shares with behavior therapy (Olatunji & Feldman, 2008; Pretzer & Beck, 2004; Roth et al., 2002). Cognitive therapy started as an outgrowth of behavior therapy, after some behavior therapists realized that behavior therapy didn't always work as predicted. They recognized that mental processes, as difficult as they can be to define and measure, do in fact play a powerful role in determining people's behavior. Techniques based on classical conditioning and operant conditioning often failed because they didn't take into account what the client was thinking. For that reason, cognitions were given much more attention (O'Donohue, 2009; Goldfried, 1995). The relationship between cognitive and behavioral forms of therapy is reflected in the fact that many therapists today describe themselves as practicing **cognitive-behavioral therapy**, a hybrid therapy approach that combines an emphasis on logical thinking with the use of conditioning principles to directly change behavior.

There are two pioneers of cognitive therapy, Albert Ellis and Aaron Beck (Rosner, 2015; Dryden, 2015). Their approaches differ a bit, but both emphasize improving psychological well-being by changing thought processes.

Rational-Emotive Behavior Therapy. Albert Ellis's approach is called **rational-emotive behavior therapy (REBT)**: a form of cognitive therapy in which the therapist challenges the client's illogical beliefs and encourages the client to adopt more logical beliefs (Ellis & Ellis, 2011; Ellis, 1962, 2008). Therapists who use REBT argue with clients—respectfully, but forcefully—pointing out when clients' thoughts are unreasonable or irrational. Therapists also point out how those thoughts may contribute to their depression, anxiety, or other psychological symptoms. They encourage clients to challenge their own thoughts, with the ultimate goal of replacing those thoughts with more sensible ones (Dryden, 2009).

Rational-emotive behavior therapy utilizes the **ABCDE model of cognitive therapy**, in which the therapist and client identify the sequence that leads from illogical thinking to logical thinking about particular life events. In the ABCDE model, each letter stands for a step in the therapeutic sequence: *activating event*,

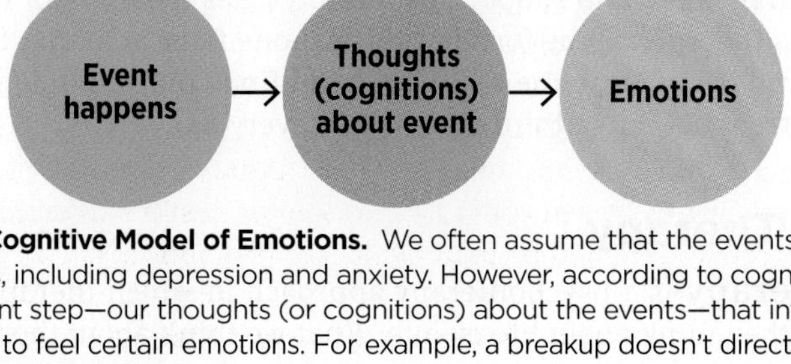

FIGURE 15.3 Cognitive Model of Emotions. We often assume that the events in our lives lead directly to feelings, including depression and anxiety. However, according to cognitive therapists, there's an important step—our thoughts (or cognitions) about the events—that intervenes and actually causes us to feel certain emotions. For example, a breakup doesn't directly cause sadness—the *thoughts* about the breakup do.

Activating event	Belief	Consequence (emotional)	Dispute	Effective new belief
My heart was pounding when I got to my seat at the concert.	"I'm probably having a heart attack."	Anxiety, panic	My seat was way up in the nosebleed section, so it's normal for my heart to pound a little after all that stair climbing.	"I'm fine—it's just a slightly stronger heartbeat, and it'll go away in a few minutes."
My brakes squeaked when I stopped at that stop sign.	"My brakes will go out completely at any minute, and I'll die in a car crash."	Anxiety, panic	One little squeak does not mean the brakes are completely shot.	"The squeak is cause for a little concern, but not too much. I'll take the car to the mechanic to fix it before it gets dangerous."

FIGURE 15.4 Sample ABCDE Form for Cognitive Therapy Clients. This form shows how a client in cognitive therapy might learn to identify and dispute the beliefs that lead to anxiety or other troublesome emotions and replace them with new beliefs that are more logical.

belief, consequence (emotional), dispute, and *effective new belief* (Dryden, 1995, 2009; Ellis & Grieger, 1977; Ellis & Harper, 1975). Often, to teach clients to use this model, therapists ask clients to fill out a five-column form with each of these letters at the top of a column (**Figure 15.4**). Let's go back to Tina's case as an example. The *activating event* for Tina was getting turned down for the job. Her *belief* about this event was, "I see myself as a complete failure." This belief caused the *consequence (emotional)* of misery in Tina's case. Steps A, B, and C illustrate how Tina's problem developed: The job rejection led to her belief about being a complete failure, which led to the feeling of misery.

Steps D and E are where the therapeutic change happens. The *dispute* was the argument I made (with Tina's help) against the illogical belief that she was a "complete failure." We disputed it with accurate arguments like, "Just because you didn't get this particular promotion, that doesn't mean you are complete failure," and "Many aspects of your life are actually very successful, even without that promotion." Finally, we moved on to the *effective new belief*—a way of thinking about what happened that replaces the original belief (from step B). As Tina put it, her effective new belief was this: "Losing that promotion is a letdown, but it doesn't mean I'm a failure at all. Actually, I'm a success in many ways, and I'll have many more chances to succeed too."

Cognitive Distortions. In Aaron Beck's approach to cognitive therapy, therapists teach their clients terminology to label their **cognitive distortions**: descriptive, memorable names for various kinds of irrational thinking (Beck, 1976, 2002; Leahy, 2003; Beck et al., 1979). Let's highlight some of the cognitive distortions that apply to Tina's case. **All-or-nothing thinking** is a cognitive distortion in which the client mistakenly evaluates events as either absolutely flawless or completely awful, with no middle ground in between. Tina's belief that she was a complete failure for not receiving the promotion could fall into the all-or-nothing category. Tina's illogical belief of being a complete failure might also be an example of **overgeneralization**, in which the client comes to a very broad-based conclusion based on just a single unfortunate event. After all, Tina's misery stemmed from just one lost promotion, not an endless series of them. Allowing that single event to define her as a complete failure simply isn't logical.

Another of Beck's cognitive distortions, **catastrophizing**, occurs when the client exaggerates the negative consequences of an event, or makes a "catastrophe" out of

cognitive-behavioral therapy
A hybrid therapy approach that combines an emphasis on logical thinking with the use of conditioning principles to directly change behavior.

rational-emotive behavior therapy (REBT)
A form of cognitive therapy in which the therapist challenges the client's illogical beliefs and encourages the client to adopt more logical beliefs.

ABCDE model of cognitive therapy
A type of rational-emotive behavior therapy in which the therapist and client identify the sequence that leads from illogical thinking to logical thinking about particular life events.

cognitive distortions
Descriptive names for various kinds of irrational thinking.

all-or-nothing thinking
A cognitive distortion in which the client mistakenly evaluates events as either absolutely flawless or completely awful, with no middle ground in between.

overgeneralization
A cognitive distortion in which the client comes to a very broad-based conclusion based on just a single unfortunate event.

catastrophizing
A cognitive distortion in which the client exaggerates the negative consequences of an event, or makes a "catastrophe" out of a minor mishap.

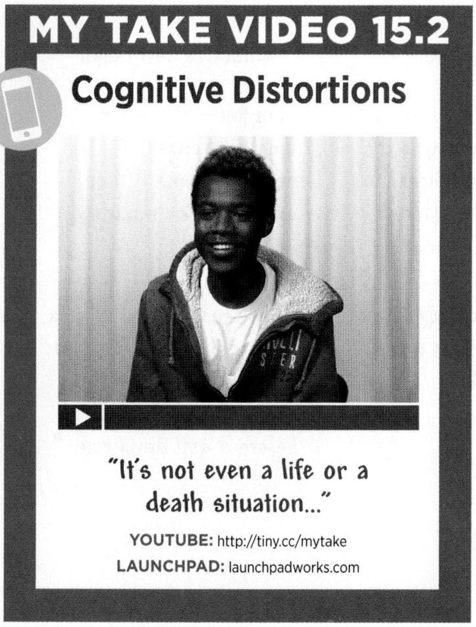

a minor mishap. Maybe a lost promotion isn't quite minor, but it is certainly not life or death. **Mental filtering** describes the client's tendency to ignore, or "filter out," the positive while focusing excessively on the negative. Tina had actually been promoted several times to obtain her current position, but ignored those promotions when she labeled herself a failure. When the client takes too much of the blame and responsibility for unfortunate events, that is called **personalization**. That promotion may have gone to someone else for any number of reasons, only some of which have anything to do with Tina.

When clients understand cognitive distortions, they can reexamine their initial thoughts about life events and quickly label them as illogical in a particular way. By doing so, clients discredit that illogical thought, and give themselves the opportunity to replace it with a more rational one. That, in turn, improves their emotional and psychological well-being.

Another trademark of cognitive therapy (particularly Aaron Beck's approach) is the idea that our beliefs about ourselves are actually just hypotheses waiting to be tested (Dobson & Hamilton, 2008; Kuehlwein, 1993). Too often, we accept our beliefs as proven facts when, actually, we have not tested them at all. For that reason, cognitive therapists often encourage clients to put their beliefs to the test in real life. Just as scientists conduct experiments in a lab to test their hypotheses about chemistry or physics, clients should conduct experiments in their real lives to test their hypotheses about themselves.

For example, one of my clients, Elbia, was a 65-year-old grandmother who lived a sad, lonely life despite having two children and five grandchildren in town. "I'm a nuisance," she told me. "My kids and grandkids are busy with their own lives. They don't want to be bothered with this old lady." "How do you know that?" I kindly asked. At first, she was very confident about it, but as I repeated the question, she realized that she had no proof for her belief. Bravely, she decided to test it. In our next session, Elbia told me that she had asked her daughter if she and her kids might want to have dinner together, and her daughter happily accepted. Soon, she asked her son the same question, and he responded positively too. Within weeks, she was seeing her kids and grandkids frequently. Most importantly, Elbia felt much happier. Had she never tested her belief—the hypothesis that she was a nuisance to her family members—she would have never given herself the chance to prove it false.

How do cognitive therapists determine which cognitions are logical and which are illogical?

One of the challenges that cognitive therapists face centers on exactly that question: What's logical? It may seem like a simple question, but it can get quite complex. Just consider the many conflicting beliefs held by people of different ethnicities, religions, and other cultural groups (Ridley et al., 2008; Pargament, 2007; Hays & Iwamasa, 2006; Paradis et al., 2006; Koenig, 2005). I once had a client from the West Indies who was terrified that she would have a miscarriage because another woman had cast a spell on her. Another client, a teenage boy whose family belonged to a conservative religion, was convinced that he would go to Hell because he had a brief homosexual impulse about a male friend. At first, it occurred to me to challenge the logic of these clients' beliefs—it doesn't make sense that a spell can cause a miscarriage, and it doesn't make sense that a quick same-sex kiss would condemn a person to Hell. But then I realized, those things don't make sense *to me* because I come from a different cultural background than either of these clients. It would have been culturally insensitive for me to presume that the way *I* think is logical, just because I'm the psychologist, and to impose that logic on all clients, regardless of their own backgrounds. A better strategy is to remember that my definition of logic is just one of many, and to consider the logic of the client's thoughts and beliefs in the context of his or her own cultural background.

DIVERSITY MATTERS

Cognitive therapists help clients to recognize their own cognitive distortions, including catastrophizing, which happens when the client exaggerates the negative consequences of an event. Robert Llewellyn/Getty Images

Third-Wave Therapies. The most recent versions of cognitive therapy are collectively known as *third-wave therapies*, following behavior therapy as the first wave and traditional cognitive therapy as the second wave. One of the core elements of third-wave therapies is *mindfulness*, an increased awareness of internal experiences with an emphasis on just feeling them rather than analyzing or avoiding them (as we discussed in Chapter 11). Therapists who promote mindfulness in their clients help them pay attention to and fully accept their emotions, rather than relying on distractions or numbness to get them through their days (Morgan & Roemer, 2015; Dimidjian & Linehan, 2009).

A big difference between third-wave therapists and traditional cognitive therapists is how they encourage clients to relate to their thoughts (Olatunji & Feldman, 2008). For traditional cognitive therapists, the strategy is to dispute irrational thoughts, with the intent of preventing the unpleasant emotions they may bring. For third-wave therapists, the strategy is to let those irrational thoughts run their course, and not to react against them. Those irrational thoughts will pass, and any feelings they bring will subside as well. With third-wave therapies, clients learn that they don't have to avoid these irrational thoughts or feelings: They are resilient enough to experience them and emerge unscathed.

There are many specific varieties of third-wave therapies. One popular third-wave therapy is *acceptance and commitment therapy* (ACT), which helps people with anxiety and other disorders to focus on accepting emotions and thoughts, as well as committing to one's own personal values (Hayes, 2004; Hayes et al., 2011, 2012; Forman et al., 2015; Swain et al., 2013; Linehan, 1993a,b). Another well-established third-wave therapy is *dialectical behavior therapy*, which helps people with borderline personality disorder and other disorders to regulate and tolerate intense emotional experiences (Koerner, 2012; Cameron, 2015).

Combining Therapies: Eclectic and Integrative Approaches

Psychodynamic therapy, person-centered therapy, behavior therapy, and cognitive therapy are the major approaches to psychotherapy. You might have gotten the impression that a therapist has to choose one of these and abandon the others. That is not the case at all. In fact, most clinical psychologists combine approaches. Each therapy approach has its "purebreds," but there are even more "mutts," whose therapy involves a combination of various approaches (Cook et al., 2010; Norcross et al., 2005).

These combinations of approaches take two distinct forms, *eclectic* and *integrative*. In the **eclectic approach to therapy**, the psychotherapist selects the best treatment for a particular client based on evidence from studies of similar clients (Stricker, 2010; Gold, 1996). These eclectic therapists rely heavily on studies of "what works" for specific diagnoses to determine what kind of therapy they will conduct. The therapists' own preferred style is not the determining factor. Instead, eclectic therapists must master a variety of different approaches, and must shift gears between them as they work with clients with various problems. For example, an eclectic therapist might practice exposure therapy with her 9:00 A.M. client because that client has a specific phobia and the scientific studies suggest that exposure therapy works best for phobias. If the therapist's next client has generalized anxiety disorder, the therapist may shift to cognitive therapy, because that is what the evidence supports for that disorder. The eclectic approach has also been called the *prescriptive* approach because it resembles the way that physicians prescribe particular medications for particular illnesses (Antony & Barlow, 2010).

In contrast to the eclectic approach, some therapists adopt an **integrative approach to therapy**: a strategy in which the psychotherapist blends styles or techniques to create a new form of psychotherapy. Integrative therapists recognize that psychodynamic, person-centered, behavioral, and cognitive therapies need not be mutually exclusive. Their components can complement each other quite well. When they are expertly

mental filtering
A cognitive distortion in which the client ignores, or "filters out," the positive while focusing excessively on the negative.

personalization
A cognitive distortion in which the client takes too much of the blame and responsibility for unfortunate events.

eclectic approach to therapy
A strategy in which the psychotherapist selects the best treatment for a particular client based on evidence from studies of similar clients.

integrative approach to therapy
A strategy in which the psychotherapist blends styles or techniques to create a new form of psychotherapy.

IT'S LIKE...

Eclectic Therapy Is Like Fruit Salad, and Integrative Therapy Is Like a Smoothie

When you eat a fruit salad, each bite delivers a distinct flavor: pineapple first, strawberry second, raspberry third. When you drink a smoothie, the same ingredients blend into a unique flavor that comes through in every sip.

An eclectic approach to psychotherapy is a lot like a fruit salad. Eclectic therapists bring a distinct approach to each client, based on the empirical evidence for what works best with that client's disorder. During the course of a workday, an eclectic therapist may be behavioral with her first client, psychodynamic with her second, and cognitive with her third.

On the other hand, an integrative approach to psychotherapy is a lot like a smoothie. Rather than offering them separately, the therapist blends these same ingredients—for example, behavioral, psychodynamic, and cognitive approaches—to form a unique combined type of therapy that comes through with every client. Like a well-mixed smoothie, the flavor of this type of therapy remains more constant from client to client, as opposed to the contrasting flavors of an eclectic therapist shifting therapy approaches for each client.

In an eclectic approach to therapy, the therapist provides each client with a single form of psychotherapy based on evidence that it works for a particular disorder—similar to a fruit salad in which each bite contains a single piece of fruit, each has just one taste. In an integrative approach to therapy, the therapist blends styles or techniques to create a new form of psychotherapy—similar to a sip of a smoothie that contains tastes of several blended fruits. Indochina studio/Shutterstock; Africa Studio/Shutterstock

combined, the hybrid can be especially effective for a variety of clients (Beitman & Manring, 2009; Norcross, 2005; Wachtel, 1977).

For example, I once saw a client, Bobby, a shy man who struggled with a combination of anxiety and depression. He was 30 years old and interested in dating, but had never asked anyone out on a date and felt increasingly hopeless about his difficulty doing so. My therapy with Bobby included, at various times, elements of each of the major approaches to therapy. I expressed genuine empathy with his nervousness about asking someone out and the subsequent hopelessness, as a person-centered therapist would. I offered interpretations about how his early relationships with his parents may contribute to difficulty trying to start new relationships—ideas of which he had been unconscious—as a psychodynamic therapist would. I helped him create and progress through an anxiety hierarchy—including many behaviorally defined "baby steps" along the way to asking someone out—as a behavior therapist would. And I challenged the logic of his thinking about asking someone out—he might not get rejected, after all, and if rejection did happen, it wouldn't destroy him—as a cognitive therapist would. (Check the "It's Like ..." box for further explanation about the difference between eclectic and integrative approaches.)

CHECK YOUR LEARNING:

15.4 Who seeks psychotherapy?

15.5 What is the main goal of psychodynamic therapy, and what techniques do therapists use to help the client reach that goal?

15.6 What are the most important aspects of person-centered therapy, including its three essential characteristics?

15.7 How do behavior therapists use techniques based on classical conditioning (like exposure techniques) and techniques based on operant conditioning (like token economies) to help clients?

15.8 What is the main goal of cognitive therapy, and how are the ABCDE model and cognitive distortions relevant to that goal?

15.9 What are the similarities and differences between the eclectic and integrative approaches to psychotherapy?

Psychotherapies for Groups and Families

So far, we have focused exclusively on forms of psychotherapy in which there is only one client in the room. Let's now shift our focus to therapies that involve multiple clients, *group therapy* and *family therapy*.

YOU WILL LEARN:

15.10 about the basics of group therapy.

15.11 about the basics of family therapy.

Group Therapy

Group therapy is psychotherapy conducted with a group of clients and with an emphasis on interpersonal interaction. Group therapy can follow any of the approaches discussed as individual therapies, but it offers the additional unique opportunity to focus on interpersonal interaction, the way people get along with each other (Markin & Kasten, 2015; Burlingame & Baldwin, 2011; Yalom, 1983, 2005). Many group therapists assume that a client's difficulties with interpersonal interaction are major reasons for the psychological disorder. People whose relationships with close friends and family members are full of conflict, tension, and mistreatment are especially vulnerable to developing psychological disorders. Group therapy gives these clients the chance to relate to new people (fellow group members), get feedback from them about the interaction, and then decide if they want to change it (Goldberg & Hoyt, 2015; Brabender, 2002; Ormont, 1992).

For example, I once led a group that included Steven, an extremely insecure 30-year-old client with social phobia, and Monique, a 48-year-old woman diagnosed with depression following a recent divorce. Steven didn't speak up in the group for many sessions. He was timid and thought others would be angry at him for taking up valuable group time when they had problems of their own to discuss. On the other hand, Monique did not hesitate to dominate the conversation. In fact, she seemed to presume that the group revolved around her. More than any other client, she discussed her personal problems at great length and volume—including the four divorces she had experienced, and the many other friends who had moved on from her, leaving her lonely.

As one session started, Steven surprised us all by meekly saying that he would like to spend a minute discussing his issues, "if that's OK." Most of us encouraged Steven to speak, but Monique rolled her eyes and exhaled disapprovingly. Steven tearfully began describing how he had few friends and had never made efforts to meet new people because he was terrified to "put himself out there:" He was sure that others would reject him, and he wouldn't be able to handle it. Most of us were on the edge of our seats as we listened to Steven, but Monique was checking her watch. After just a few minutes, she interrupted Steven mid-sentence: "Are you about done? Can someone else have a turn to talk? I have important stuff to bring up."

Steven apologized, returned to his silence, and let Monique take over. Before she did, though, I posed a question to the whole group: "What do you think of the way Monique and Steven communicate with each other?" One by one, the group members shared their opinions, which formed a consensus: Monique's behavior was too domineering, which made them dislike her; Steven's behavior was too unassertive, which made them lose respect for him. Neither Monique nor Steven had ever received such candid feedback. With further discussion, both Monique and Steven realized that the interpersonal tendencies they showed in the group were exactly the same ones that contributed to their problems in their real lives: Monique's failed marriages and friendships were due to her domineering behavior; Steven's loneliness was due to his lack of assertiveness. I then posed another question to Monique and Steven: "Do you want to change your interpersonal tendency?" They both agreed that they did, and our group spent the remaining group sessions practicing

group therapy
Psychotherapy conducted with a group of clients and with an emphasis on interpersonal interaction.

Group therapy is psychotherapy conducted with a group of clients and with an emphasis on interpersonal interaction. wavebreakmedia/Shutterstock

different styles of interacting. The goal was for Monique and Steven (and the others) to develop healthier interaction skills with their fellow group members, but, more importantly, to translate those skills to their real lives (which, I'm happy to say, they did!).

As this example illustrates, some groups include clients with a variety of diagnoses. Other groups include clients who share similar diagnoses (for example, bulimia groups, substance abuse groups, bipolar groups). Both types of groups have unique advantages (Yalom, 2005). Groups with a variety of diagnoses offer a wider variety of individuals with whom to interact; those with similar diagnoses offer a more immediate sense of *universality*, or the feeling that "we're all in the same boat." The number of clients in groups varies, but in most cases, falls between 5 and 10 (Brabender, 2002). The number of therapists can vary as well—sometimes one, sometimes two. The presence of two therapists allows for two perspectives on clients' problems, as well as two sets of eyes and ears to capture clients' many verbal and nonverbal messages (Shapiro, 1999).

In other cases, the group is a **self-help group**, in which the group members run the session without a professional therapist leading them. Self-help groups typically center around a particular problem—alcohol or drug use, for example—and often consist of low-cost or free meetings organized by a veteran member of the group.

Family Therapy

Family therapy is psychotherapy that aims to improve how the family system functions, which in turn will improve the problems of its individual members. In family therapy, the idea is that the entire family system is flawed—even if only one person shows symptoms (Davis et al., 2015; Kaslow, 2011; Rolland & Walsh, 2009; Goldenberg & Goldenberg, 2007). This is why family therapy focuses on improving the ways family members communicate and relate to each other.

Think of it this way: If something was wrong with a wheel on your car, would you take the wheel off the car and take the tire to a mechanic to repair it? The mechanic might tell you that was a bad idea. The same problem could occur again after you put the repaired wheel back on the same car, because the problem may actually be in the car, not the wheel. Perhaps the car's suspension or axles are bad, or perhaps the alignment is off. Repairing the car's system more broadly could address the problem better than a narrow-minded focus on just the wheel alone. Family therapists think in much the same way. For example, treating any individual—a teenage girl with anorexia, a fourth-grade boy with panic disorder, a husband or wife with major depression—in isolation from the family system in which they live is like taking the wheel off the car.

Family therapists utilize a wide range of styles, including family versions of individual therapies (psychodynamic, person-centered, behavioral, cognitive). But they also try to take advantage of opportunities that are available only when the family participates in treatment. For example, family therapists often examine the family's *structure*, the rules by which it operates (Minuchin, 1974). Family rules are rarely explicit (they aren't posted on the refrigerator door), but they are still powerful influences on how individuals behave within families. Think of the eye-opening experience you had when you first slept over at a friend's house. You probably got an insider's view on your friend's family structure and realized just how different it was from your own family's structure. For example, some families encourage children to become independent thinkers who might disagree with parents; others encourage children to behave obediently and agree with parents at all times. The unspoken rule in family A might be "Always think for yourself," while the unspoken rule in family B might be "Do as you're told—because I said so." Regardless of the particular family rules, they may not be working if a member of the family develops a psychological disorder. With the whole family in the room, a family therapist has the unique chance to help clarify and change the family rules.

self-help group
A type of group therapy in which the group members run the session without a professional therapist leading them.

family therapy
Psychotherapy that aims to improve how the family system functions, which in turn will improve the problems of its individual members.

CHECK YOUR LEARNING:

15.10 What is group therapy, and how does its emphasis differ from the emphasis of individual therapy?

15.11 What is the main goal of family therapy?

How Well Does Psychotherapy Work?

YOU WILL LEARN:

15.12 about the challenges involved in testing the results of psychotherapy.

15.13 how well psychotherapy works.

15.14 how the outcomes of different kinds of psychotherapy compare to each other.

15.15 what makes psychotherapy work.

In the early days of psychotherapy, there weren't many questions about how well it worked. Those who practiced psychotherapy or received it generally assumed that it was beneficial, and that was that (Weissmark & Giacomo, 1998). But in 1952, a prominent researcher named Hans Eysenck wrote a summary of the small amount of research on the outcome of psychotherapy available at that time. His conclusion was surprising and controversial: Psychotherapy *didn't* work, at least not any better than working through one's problems without psychotherapy (Eysenck, 1952). It turns out that Eysenck's methods were flawed, and his conclusion was wrong: Thousands of later studies of psychotherapy support the conclusion that it *is* helpful, but his claim did inspire many researchers to examine how well psychotherapy works (Routh, 2011; Wampold, 2010a).

When researchers examine how well psychotherapy works, they face a number of important questions in terms of the scientific methods they use. For example, whom should they ask? The client, the therapist, or an outside observer (Strupp, 1996; Strupp & Hadley, 1977)? When should they ask? During therapy, right when it ends, or long afterward (Lambert, 2011)? How should they ask? Questionnaires, interviews, or even brain scans? (See the From Research to Real Life box for more on how therapy changes the brain.) The point here is that determining how well psychotherapy works is a complex undertaking, full of methodological choices that can have a powerful influence on the results researchers obtain.

FROM RESEARCH TO REAL LIFE

Psychotherapy Changes the Brain

A fascinating way to measure the outcome of therapy—in addition to the more common methods of asking the client, asking the therapist, or observing the client's behavior—is to see how psychotherapy changes the brain itself. Studies using functional magnetic resonance imaging (fMRI) and positron emission tomography (PET) neuroimaging technologies to view clients' brains have shown that psychotherapy produces biological changes in the brain. In many cases, psychotherapy and medication appear to change the brain in similar ways. These studies typically compare clients with the same diagnosis, half of whom get therapy and half of whom get drugs. Among their findings:

- For clients with OCD, behavior therapy and Prozac *both* resulted in decreased metabolism in the right caudate nucleus, which corresponds with clients' reports of decreased anxiety (Baxter et al., 1992).
- For clients with social phobia, cognitive-behavior therapy and Celexa *both* resulted in decreased activation in the amygdala and hippocampus, which corresponds to lower anxiety levels (Furmark et al., 2002).
- For clients with major depressive disorder, interpersonal therapy and Paxil *both* resulted in decreased activation in the prefrontal cortex and increased activation in the inferior temporal lobe and insula, brain changes that suggest an improvement in mood (Brody et al., 2001).

For many, it comes as no surprise that medication changes the brain: After all, it is a biological intervention. But accumulating evidence suggests that psychotherapy changes the brain as well, often in much the same way as the corresponding medication (Roffman et al., 2005; Arden & Linford, 2009; Viamontes & Beitman, 2009). Some forward-thinking researchers have speculated that, if the technology becomes less expensive, psychotherapy could involve routine fMRI or PET scans to examine the effects that the therapy has had on the client's brain (Cozolino, 2010). For now, most measurements of therapy outcome continue to rely on the tried-and-true (and inexpensive) methods of surveys or behavior observations, but it will be interesting to see how brain scans are involved in the future. ●

MY TAKE VIDEO 15.3

Understanding Psychotherapy

"I feel like it helped me a lot..."

YOUTUBE: http://tiny.cc/mytake
LAUNCHPAD: launchpadworks.com

Fortunately, the thousands of studies on the benefits of psychotherapy involve all of these methodological choices. Together, these studies point to one undeniable conclusion: Psychotherapy works. Large-scale reviews of psychotherapy outcome studies have repeatedly confirmed this finding for decades (Wampold, 2010a; Lambert & Simon, 2008; Luborsky et al., 2002; Lipsey & Wilson, 1993; Shapiro & Shapiro, 1982; Smith & Glass, 1977). The average person who receives psychotherapy for a particular issue is better off afterward than 80% of people who did not receive psychotherapy for a similar issue (Smith et al., 1980). Researchers have also repeatedly found that the benefits of psychotherapy tend to last for long periods of time, and that those benefits represent real-world improvement in the quality of the clients' lives (Lambert & Ogles, 2004). Of course, psychotherapy is not a cure-all. Some psychotherapy clients don't benefit, others drop out, and a very small number actually get worse over the course of therapy (Lebow, 2006; Striano, 1988). However, these negative outcomes are the exception to the rule of successful outcome.

Studies showing that psychotherapy works generally fall into two categories: *efficacy* studies and *effectiveness* studies (Dalrymple et al., 2015; Spokas et al., 2008; Truax & Thomas, 2003). (See the Current Controversy box for more on efficacy studies.) Efficacy studies examine how well psychotherapy works in controlled studies, with textbook-case clients and therapy manuals directing therapists' actions—in other words, how well it works "in the lab" (Durand & Wang, 2011; Rosqvist et al., 2011). In an efficacy study, researchers test a specific type of therapy for a specific type of problem. For example, researchers might recruit people who meet the diagnostic criteria for obsessive-compulsive disorder and treat them with a behavior therapy known as *exposure and response prevention* (*ERP*). ERP is a specific version of the exposure therapy in which the therapist also prevents clients from responding as they typically would—for example, making clients touch dirt and then preventing them from washing their hands. Numerous studies of this type have shown success, so psychologists now recognize ERP as a therapy that works for obsessive-compulsive disorder (Nathan & Gorman, 2007; Carr, 2008; Roth & Fonagy, 2005).

The notion of using "therapy that works" for a particular problem is a cornerstone of **evidence-based practice**: an approach to psychotherapy in which the therapist makes decisions based on a combination of three factors: research evidence, therapist expertise, and client characteristics (APA Presidential Task Force on Evidence-Based Practice, 2006; Barlow et al., 2013; Buscemi & Spring, 2015). Increasingly, psychologists rely on evidence-based practice to help their clients. They consider "what works"

CURRENT CONTROVERSY

Therapies That Work...For Whom?

Efficacy studies are a great way to determine how well a particular form of psychotherapy works for a particular disorder. In efficacy studies, researchers carefully recruit only those clients who definitely meet the criteria for the disorder (and are often "textbook cases," with no other problems to complicate the diagnosis). Such research methods create a tightly controlled study in which there is a clear link between the therapy and the outcome.

But there are drawbacks to efficacy studies as well, especially for real-world psychotherapists—those who practice in clinics, hospitals, and private practices rather than in universities, where most efficacy studies are conducted—and their clients. Consider these issues:

- The clients in real-world settings often have messier diagnoses than those in the efficacy studies: Textbook cases are quite rare (Durand & Wang, 2011). For example, some clients may not have enough symptoms of major depressive disorder to qualify for the diagnosis. Or, if clients do have enough symptoms, they may also have symptoms of anxiety disorders, eating disorders, or personality disorders, which complicate the diagnosis.
- The clients in real-world settings often come from a wider range of cultural backgrounds than those in the efficacy studies (Rosqvist et al., 2011). Few efficacy studies include significant numbers of clients from diverse backgrounds in terms of ethnicity, disability status, or sexual orientation; in fact, most clients in these studies are White and at least middle class (Sue & Zane, 2006; Olkin & Taliaferro, 2006; Brown, 2006; Munoz & Mendelson, 2005).

DIVERSITY MATTERS

These drawbacks are among the reasons that certain therapies gain empirical support, but are not automatically adopted by all therapists (Safran et al., 2011; Boswell et al., 2011). As a result, there is a gap between the findings that psychotherapy researchers make and the way that many psychotherapists actually practice (Gyani et al., 2014).

according to efficacy studies, but also their own unique abilities as therapists and the unique characteristics of their clients as well—not just their diagnosis, but their ethnicity, age, socioeconomic status, religion, sexual orientation, and other cultural variables (Norcross et al., 2011; Spring & Neville, 2011).

DIVERSITY MATTERS

In contrast to efficacy studies, effectiveness studies examine how well psychotherapy works in the real world, the clinics, hospitals, and private practices where clients are rarely textbook cases of any particular disorder (Garske & Anderson, 2003; Chambless et al., 1998). Effectiveness studies are less tightly controlled than efficacy studies. They involve clients with varied diagnoses, and a range of therapies rather than just one manualized technique. However, they often do a better job of capturing the hodgepodge of clients that actual therapists see and the medley of treatment methods that they use in their day-to-day practices. A large-scale effectiveness study appeared in *Consumer Reports* magazine, in which readers described their experiences as psychotherapy clients (Seligman, 1995; "Mental Health," 1995). Of course, the respondents had a tremendous range of psychotherapy experiences—different types, lengths, therapist professions, and so on—but the results were very positive. The overwhelming majority reported feeling much better at the time of the survey than they were at the time they started psychotherapy. Effectiveness studies such as this one suggest that the benefits of psychotherapy are evident in real-world settings as well as lab studies.

evidence-based practice
An approach to psychotherapy in which the therapist makes decisions based on a combination of three factors: research evidence, therapist expertise, and client characteristics.

dodo bird verdict
A nickname (from *Alice in Wonderland*) for the research finding that different forms of psychotherapy are equally effective.

common factors
Elements found in all forms of effective psychotherapy that play an important role in client improvement.

Which Therapy Works Best?

After researchers established that psychotherapy works, the battle over which type of psychotherapy works best began (Lambert, 2011; Smith et al., 1980). Psychodynamic therapists, person-centered therapists, behavioral therapists, cognitive therapists—all of them claimed that their approach was uniquely beneficial. To settle the score, researchers designed studies in which clients were divided into two groups, one of which received Therapy A and the other of which received Therapy B. Over and over again, these studies yielded an unexpected result: a tie. The competing therapies both worked, with about equal rates of success (Wampold, 2010b; Lambert & Ogles, 2004; Luborsky et al., 2002; Norcross & Newman, 1992). Researchers called this finding the **dodo bird verdict**—a nickname (from *Alice in Wonderland*) for the research finding that different forms of psychotherapy are equally effective (Luborsky et al., 1975; Elliott et al., 2015). (As **Figure 15.5** illustrates, in *Alice in Wonderland*, the dodo bird character watches a race between many contestants and utters the line, "Everybody has won and all must have prizes.")

Psychotherapy researchers have confirmed the dodo bird verdict many times, but it is not without controversy (Wampold, 2001). Some researchers point to recent studies that are specifically targeted—specific techniques for specific problems—in which the findings are not equal across therapies (Antony & Barlow, 2010; Siev & Chambless, 2007; Chambless, 2002; Chambless & Ollendick, 2001). Some of these specifically targeted studies have found that particular therapies (most often behavioral techniques) have benefits with particular diagnoses (most often anxiety disorders) that other therapies have not been able to match. As a result, the major forms of therapy are all recognized as beneficial in general, while many psychotherapists also recognize that certain therapies may have advantages for certain problems (Paul, 2007; Norcross, 2005).

FIGURE 15.5 Dodo Bird Verdict. In *Alice in Wonderland*, the dodo bird character judges a race and declares, "Everybody has won and all must have prizes." In studies comparing the outcome of various kinds of therapy, the finding has often been similar: All of the therapies generally produce positive results at about the same rate. That finding has been nicknamed the *dodo bird verdict*. Universal History Archive/Getty Images

What Makes Therapy Work?

The finding that various forms of psychotherapy are all about equally beneficial highlights the presence of **common factors**: elements found in all forms of effective psychotherapy that play an important role in client improvement (Huibers & Cuijpers, 2015; Wampold, 2010b; Stricker, 2010; Messer & Wampold, 2002). The idea that different therapies all work because of the same underlying mechanisms has actually been around since the 1930s, but only in the last few decades has the scientific study of psychotherapy been able to back it up with data (Rosenzweig, 1936; Frank, 1961; Torrey, 1986).

IT'S LIKE...

Common Factors in Therapy Are Like the Common Active Ingredient in Toothpaste

All toothpastes work about equally well, though their advertisements suggest otherwise. Those ads try to convince us that some special ingredient—baking soda, whiteners, sparkles—makes their brand uniquely effective. But the truth is that the various flavors of Crest, Colgate, Aim, and Aquafresh all prevent cavities quite well (and equivalently). That is because these toothpastes all share the same active ingredient: fluoride.

Toothpaste is like psychotherapy in this way. As the dodo bird verdict indicates, all major forms of psychotherapy work about equally well. The reason for this equality is the same as well: Common factors are what makes various kinds of therapy work. This is true in spite of the fact that the supporters of each kind of therapy usually point to its unique qualities—the ingredients that set it apart from the others. They may be important in terms of making the therapy palatable to certain clients, but they are not the active ingredients. So, what is the common active ingredient—the fluoride—of psychotherapy? The therapeutic relationship seems to be the leading contender for active ingredient. However, therapy seems to have a few active ingredients rather than just one (including positive expectations and attention to problems).

It is the common, active ingredient fluoride that makes toothpaste work rather than any of its other features. And it is the common, active ingredients—a good therapeutic relationship, hope, and attention—that make psychotherapy work across so many different approaches. ●

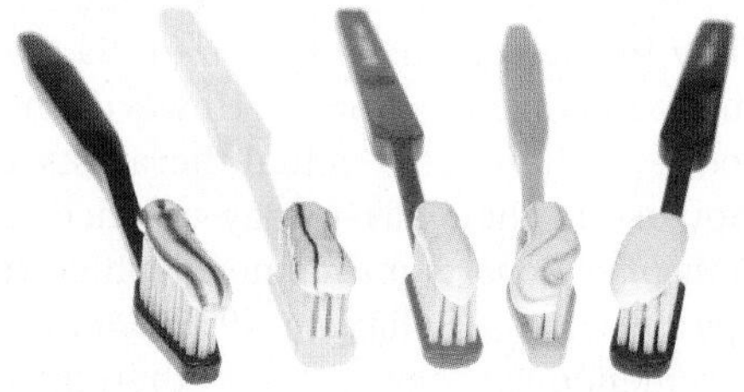

Across brands of toothpaste, fluoride is a common factor, an active ingredient that makes them all effective. Research suggests that there are common factors across types of psychotherapy too: a good therapeutic alliance, positive expectations, and attention to problems. pixelman/Shutterstock

The best-supported common factor in psychotherapy is the **therapeutic alliance**: a trusting and collaborative relationship in which therapist and client work toward shared goals (Alavi & Sanderson, 2015; Norcross & Wampold, 2011; Norcross & Lambert, 2011; Horvath et al., 2011; Crits-Christoph et al., 2011). The therapeutic alliance is the single best predictor of success in psychotherapy. If you want to know whether therapy is going to work, it is more important to know about the strength of the therapeutic alliance than it is to know what type of therapy is being conducted, how much experience the therapist has, what type of training the therapist has, or anything else about the therapy (Laska & Wampold, 2014; Beitman & Manring, 2009; Wampold, 2010a). The therapeutic alliance is especially important from the client's point of view. It is crucial for the client to experience this sense of coalition and partnership as a foundation of therapy (Rosenfeld, 2009; Wampold, 2001).

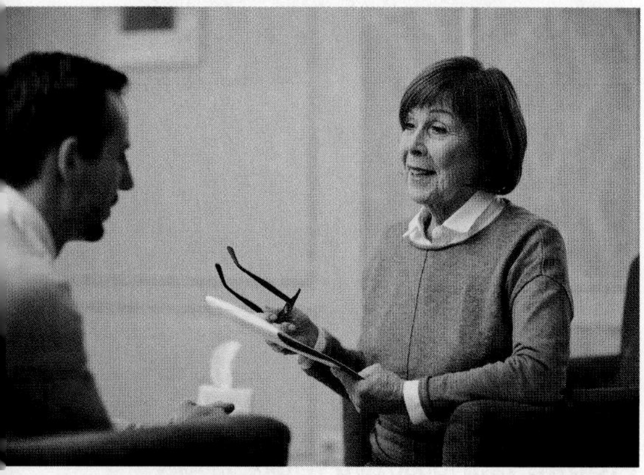

The therapeutic alliance is a trusting and collaborative relationship in which therapist and client work toward shared goals. It is a common factor across various types of psychotherapy and the single best predictor of success in psychotherapy. Pressmaster/Shutterstock

Other common factors of effective psychotherapy have been recognized as well. For example, *positive expectations* (or, more simply, *hope*) are provided by good therapists across all styles of therapy. The idea that things will change for the better, by whatever techniques the therapist uses, can be therapeutic in and of itself (Constantino et al., 2011). When a physician tells you what is wrong and hands you a prescription, you may start to feel better immediately—even before you go to the drugstore to get the medication. When a mechanic diagnoses your car's malfunction, and tells you it is fixable, you may feel relief—even while the car is still up on the lift. In both cases, improvement begins when hope replaced despair. The same is true in psychotherapy, regardless of the therapist's particular approach.

A final common factor across therapies is *attention*—simply focusing on a problem rather than ignoring or neglecting it offers an opportunity for improvement. Any kind of therapy involves attention to the client's problem (Prochaska & Norcross, 2010). For example, consider Kelly, a 15-year-old girl who developed bulimia nervosa. Kelly and her family may initially find her bingeing and purging so difficult to accept that they pretend it isn't so bad, convince themselves that it will simply go away on its own, or deny it altogether—anything to avoid dealing with it. On the other hand, taking her to any competent therapist would require, at the very least,

that Kelly and her family acknowledge the problem. That mere decision to address to her bulimic behavior rather than disregard it would provide Kelly the opportunity for improvement.

CHECK YOUR LEARNING:

15.12 When they research how well psychotherapy works, how do researchers address the issues of who, when, and how to ask?

15.13 According to research, does psychotherapy work?

15.14 How do different types of psychotherapy generally compare to each other in terms of effectiveness?

15.15 What are the common factors that make various kinds of psychotherapy work?

The Importance of Culture in Psychotherapy

YOU WILL LEARN:

15.16 what cultural competence is, and why it is important in the practice of psychotherapy.

15.17 what cultural self-awareness is, and why it is important for psychotherapists to have.

Good therapists recognize the importance of their clients' cultural backgrounds. They know that culture can influence the way clients interact with others, the meanings they attach to life events, and their expectations of psychotherapy as well. As a result, they use psychotherapy in a way that honors each client's unique combination of cultural qualities.

Psychotherapists practice in an increasingly diverse population. One-fifth of U.S. schoolchildren speak a language other than English at home (Roberts, 2004). Within 40 years, half of the U.S. population will at least partially identify as African American, American Indian, Asian American, or Latino/Latina (U.S. Census Bureau, 2008). Psychotherapists have an ethical and moral responsibility to work with diverse clients in a way that respects their cultural background, values, and practices (Comas-Díaz, 2011, 2012; Vasquez, 2010; Pedersen, 2008). Essential to the success of therapy is **cultural competence**: a therapist's ability to work sensitively and expertly with clients from diverse backgrounds.

DIVERSITY MATTERS

Without cultural competence, a client might feel misunderstood and could miss out on the gains that therapy might bring (Sue & Sue, 2008; McGoldrick et al., 2005; Owen et al., 2011; Huey et al., 2014). For example, consider Saalim, a Muslim man who is in regularly scheduled therapy with Dr. Martels, a Christian psychologist. Saalim's upcoming appointment happens to fall at the end of Ramadan, a month in which Muslims traditionally fast during daylight hours. Specifically, the appointment conflicts with Eid al-Fitr, a three-day celebration marking the end of Ramadan during which the fast is broken with family and friends. Ideally, Dr. Martels would foresee this scheduling conflict and gladly offer Saalim a different appointment. At the very least, he should be respectful and receptive if Saalim points out the scheduling conflict. He certainly should not become annoyed about the time conflict or belittle the religious observance—to do so would indicate an insensitivity that could jeopardize his relationship with Saalim, possibly resulting in a premature end to therapy (Brown & Pomerantz, 2011).

LIFE HACK 15.1

If you ever seek therapy, make sure to choose a therapist who "gets" your cultural background. It is important to the success of therapy.

(Sue & Sue, 2008; McGoldrick et al., 2005; Owen et al., 2011)

An important component of cultural competence is **cultural self-awareness**: the therapist's recognition that his or her perspective is not necessarily that of others. Cultural self-awareness also requires the therapist to understand his or her own cultural background and the values and beliefs it has influenced (Graham & Roemer, 2015; Nezu, 2010; Mirsalimi, 2010; Gelso, 2010; Fouad & Arredondo, 2007). To illustrate the importance of cultural self-awareness, consider the experience I had with my client, Kumar, who moved to the United States from India as a child. Now 32, he was married to an Indian woman and they had two young children. In large part, they

therapeutic alliance
A trusting and collaborative relationship in which therapist and client work toward shared goals.

cultural competence
A therapist's ability to work sensitively and expertly with clients from diverse backgrounds.

cultural self-awareness
The therapist's recognition that his or her perspective is not necessarily that of others.

Cultural competence is a therapist's ability to work sensitively and expertly with clients from diverse backgrounds. Rawpixel Ltd/Getty Images

held traditional Indian beliefs about many things, including the roles of husbands and wives within families. Kumar sought therapy for depressive symptoms. Rather quickly, he had gone from a happy, productive man to a man who felt sad most of the time, lost all interest in his pastimes, and had trouble eating and sleeping. At first, he was reluctant to offer any explanations for his sudden downturn, but as our relationship grew stronger, he told me about the event that devastated him: His wife had received a raise. In fact, his wife (who happened to work for the same large company as Kumar) had been promoted to a higher position than Kumar, with correspondingly higher pay. As he told me of her promotion, Kumar was filled with shame and embarrassment. In traditional Indian culture (as in many others), the expectation is for the husband to be the primary (or only) breadwinner. To be out-earned by one's wife is to be emasculated.

My own cultural beliefs differed from Kumar's. As far as I'm concerned, my wife's promotion would be cause for celebration, regardless of whether (or especially if!) her new position or pay exceeded my own. But thankfully, I had enough cultural self-awareness to recognize that my reaction to that situation was just my own, and not necessarily Kumar's (or anyone else's, for that matter). My responsibility was to recognize Kumar's experience through his eyes, not mine.

CHECK YOUR LEARNING:

15.16 Why is cultural competence important in the practice of psychotherapy, and how is it valuable to clients?

15.17 Why is cultural self-awareness important for psychotherapists?

WATCHING PSYCHOLOGY

Psychotherapists in Movies and on TV

Think of the psychotherapists you have seen in movies and TV shows. How many of them behave ethically?

Unfortunately, too many do not. Too often, the fictional psychotherapists display behaviors that violate the ethical guidelines that they should follow. They date or socialize with their clients, break their clients' confidentiality, or otherwise act in ways that violate the ethical guidelines that they are supposed to maintain. A pair of film (and therapy) buffs watched over 5000 movies featuring psychotherapists and discovered a few findings. The number of movies portraying psychotherapists has increased dramatically, but the percentage in which the therapist is portrayed positively has dropped, as illustrated by **Figure 15.6**.

The therapists in *Numb*, *What About Bob?*, and *Analyze This* (and its sequels) all form multiple relationships with clients (or people close to clients), and several commit other ethical violations as well. Collectively, popular movies such as these can communicate to the public that such behavior from therapists is OK when it is not. Thankfully, there are others in which the therapists' behavior is at least somewhat closer to the ethical standard, including the HBO TV series *The Sopranos* and *In Therapy*, as well as the movies *Antwone Fisher*, *Lars and Real Girl*, and *Good Will Hunting* (Wedding et al., 2010). Hopefully, those who write and produce movies and TV shows will portray psychotherapists behaving ethically, or at least include some negative consequences for them (and their clients) when they don't. This could have a powerful impact on expectations of people who become therapy clients.

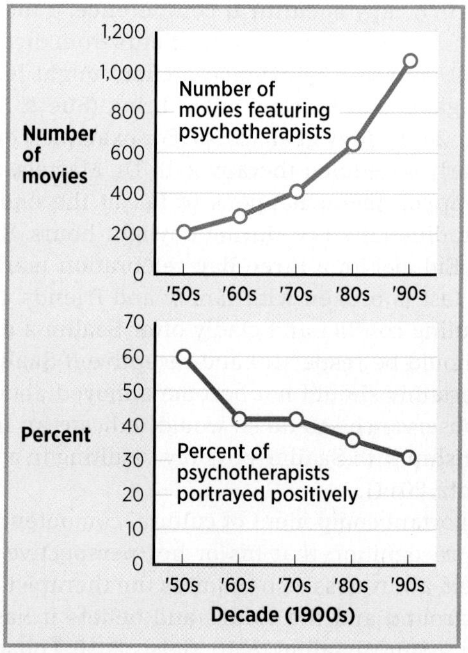

FIGURE 15.6 Portrayal of Psychotherapists in Movies. Over a 50-year period, the number of movies featuring psychotherapists increased fivefold, but the percent of psychotherapists portrayed positively dropped by half. Data from Flowers & Frizler, 2004. Note: Movies include both theatrical and television releases.

Ethics in Psychotherapy

The responsibility to be culturally competent is just one of many ethical duties that psychotherapists uphold. Every mental health profession lists these ethical duties in its own *ethical code*, a document that sets the expectations for ethical behavior within that profession (Pope & Vasquez, 2011; Koocher & Keith-Spiegel, 2008). The American Psychological Association, for example, originally published an ethical code in the 1950s, and has updated it on a regular basis since that time (Vasquez, 2015; Behnke & Jones, 2012; American Psychological Association, 2010). The vast majority of psychotherapists maintain consistently high ethical standards. Those who violate their ethical obligations run the risk of harming clients, as well as the reputation of the profession.

Confidentiality—maintaining the privacy of client information—is among the most essential ethical responsibilities of psychotherapists, without which the practice of psychotherapy might be impossible (Fisher, 2012). Clients expect psychotherapists to keep the content of their sessions secret; in fact, they often believe that confidentiality is absolute (Miller & Thelen, 1986). Clients often perceive psychotherapy as a "vault" from which therapists never release any of their information. They are right for the most part, but not entirely. In the vast majority of cases, confidentiality is maintained, but on rare occasions, therapists are obligated to break confidentiality to protect the well-being of the client or someone else. For example, state laws require therapists to break confidentiality to report ongoing child abuse (Koocher & Daniel, 2012; Knapp & VandeCreek, 2006; Tribbensee & Claiborn, 2003). Also, if the therapist learns that the client intends to harm someone—including himself or herself—the therapist is required to break confidentiality to warn those who may be at risk (Pope, 2011; Welfel et al., 2012). (Imagine that the Virginia Tech murderer had told a therapist ahead of time about his intent to go on a killing spree.)

Psychotherapists are also ethically required to obtain **informed consent**: permission given by the client, after the therapist educates him or her about the therapy process, to move forward with the therapy. As you take this psychology course, you may have the opportunity to participate in research studies, and if so, you probably read informed consent forms before those studies begin. The forms give you a description of what the research entails and give you the option of going ahead or backing out. The process is quite similar with psychotherapy, but it can involve different methods. For example, informed consent for psychotherapy often involves both a written form and a verbal discussion. This discussion gives the client the chance to receive answers to any questions about the therapy process, and also gives the therapist the opportunity to begin to form a therapeutic alliance with the client by ensuring that the client truly understands what therapy might involve (Pomerantz, 2012, 2015; Pomerantz & Handelsman, 2004). Additionally, informed consent to therapy is often more of an ongoing process than a one-time event. Researchers usually know exactly what participation in an experiment will involve, but therapists can't always have such foresight. They don't always know at the outset how long therapy will last, or exactly what techniques might be included, or even what all of the goals will be. So, psychotherapists often provide as much information as they can at the very beginning, and then more as they get to know the client and his or her issues in greater detail (Pomerantz, 2005).

Psychotherapists are often experts in a wide range of diagnoses and therapy techniques, but no one is expert in everything. Therefore, they have the ethical obligation to stay within their **boundaries of competence**: the limits of a therapist's expertise and abilities. Just having a particular degree, or a professional license, does not make a psychotherapist capable of providing every service to every possible type of client. It is important for a therapist to know his or her limits, and to be aware of other mental

YOU WILL LEARN:

15.18 why confidentiality is crucial to psychotherapy, and when psychotherapists might break it.

15.19 what informed consent is, and why it is important to psychotherapy.

15.20 why it is important for psychotherapists to stay within their boundaries of competence.

15.21 what multiple relationships are, and how they can be harmful to clients.

No therapist is expert in everything. Therefore, therapists have an ethical obligation to stay within their boundaries of competence: the limits of a therapist's expertise and abilities. For example, therapists should not work with young children unless they have the appropriate training and experience. KatarzynaBialasiewicz/Getty Images

confidentiality
When a therapist maintains the privacy of client information.

informed consent
Permission given by the client, after the therapist educates him or her about the therapy process, to move forward with the therapy.

boundaries of competence
The limits of a therapist's expertise and abilities.

multiple relationship
A situation in which a therapist has both a professional relationship and a nonprofessional relationship with the same person.

cybertherapy
Psychotherapy that takes place via technological devices over the Internet.

virtual reality exposure therapy
A form of exposure therapy in which clients use electronic means to experience simulations of the situations that cause them anxiety.

health professionals with different areas of expertise to whom he or she can refer clients if necessary (Nagy, 2012; Salter & Salter, 2012).

For example, Dr. Barton, a clinical psychologist trained in a doctoral program that specialized in clinical work with children, receives a call from Ryan, a 47-year-old man struggling with symptoms of borderline personality disorder. It would be an ethical mistake for Dr. Barton to think that because she is a licensed clinical psychologist, she can treat anyone; indeed, Ryan's treatment is outside of her boundaries of competence. Of course, Dr. Barton could seek additional training beyond her degree, but until she does, it is her duty to recognize that she is not a qualified therapist for Ryan and to refer him to someone who is.

A particularly treacherous ethical issue that psychotherapists face is the **multiple relationship**: a situation in which a therapist has both a professional relationship and a nonprofessional relationship with the same person. The nonprofessional part of the multiple relationship can involve sexual interaction, nonsexual friendship, or a business partnership (Cohen-Filipic, 2015; Sommers-Flanagan, 2012; Zur, 2007; Anderson & Kitchener, 1996). Not every multiple relationship is unethical; in small towns where everyone knows everyone, for example, they can be unavoidable (Werth et al., 2010; Schank et al., 2010). In many cases, however, multiple relationships are avoidable, especially when they have the potential to exploit the client or impair the therapist's ability to function competently and objectively (Zur, 2009; Gutheil & Brodsky, 2008; Schank et al., 2003). Unfortunately, the media have often depicted therapists engaging in multiple relationships: sleeping with clients, becoming friends with them, or getting involved in their business endeavors. While movies and TV shows may portray such multiple relationships as normal or even helpful to clients, in the real world they pose significant risk to clients' well-being, and they are definitely not part of standard treatment by competent professionals (Sonne, 2012; Pope, 1994). The Watching Psychology box explores this issue in more detail.

CHECK YOUR LEARNING:

15.18 Why is confidentiality crucial to psychotherapy, and under what circumstances might psychotherapists break it?

15.19 What is informed consent and why is it important to psychotherapy?

15.20 Why is it important for psychotherapists to stay within their boundaries of competence?

15.21 How can multiple relationships be harmful to psychotherapy clients?

Cybertherapy: Psychotherapy via Modern Technology

YOU WILL LEARN:

15.22 what cybertherapy is.

15.23 what the pros and cons of cybertherapy are.

15.24 how one example of cybertherapy, virtual reality exposure therapy, works.

Traditional, face-to-face, in-person psychotherapy now has a rapidly growing counterpart: **cybertherapy**, psychotherapy that takes place via technological devices over the Internet. Cybertherapy can take a variety of forms, including videoconferencing (like Skype) and email-, or app-based interactions. It can also take place via computer, tablet, or smartphone (Andersson, 2015, 2016; Dimeff et al., 2011; Eonta et al., 2011; Marks & Cavanagh, 2009). Cybertherapy has a few undeniable advantages (Maheu et al., 2005). For example, it allows people who live a great distance from a psychotherapist specializing in their problem to access the help they need. It also brings therapy to the relatively small number of people whose disorders prevent them from leaving the house to go to a therapist's office, including those with agoraphobia, severe social phobia, or debilitating depression (Nelson & Bui, 2010; Kraus, 2004).

Cybertherapy also has significant limitations (Koocher, 2009; Fisher & Fried, 2003; Naglieri et al., 2004). For example, the ability to disguise one's identity on the Internet makes it possible for impostors to present themselves as legitimately trained therapists. Even when cybertherapists are legitimate, they must be expert enough in the technology to deal with computer problems when they arise. Without any glitches at all, cybertherapy still cannot match in-person visits in terms of picking up on nonverbal communication (Rummell & Joyce, 2010). Especially when therapy is conducted in written form (email or text), it can be easy for a therapist or a client to misunderstand each other's tone or emotional state. (That's why we so often resort to emoticons or emojis when emailing and texting, but sometimes those still fail to do the trick.)

A number of recent studies have found that traditional therapies and cybertherapies work equally well for the same diagnoses. For example, researchers found that for anxiety disorders in children, cybertherapy was as effective as face-to-face therapy (Spence et al., 2011). Other researchers found the same results with cybertherapy for anxiety disorders in adults (Reger and Gahm, 2009). One particular form of cybertherapy that has earned positive reviews is **virtual reality exposure therapy**: a form of exposure therapy in which clients use electronic means to experience simulations of the situations that cause them anxiety. Perhaps the best way to describe virtual reality exposure therapy is to compare it to a video game that has been created with the specific goal of gradually helping clients face what they fear. For example, a client with a phobia of spiders can see virtual 3D spiders at decreasing distances. A child afraid of thunderstorms can see and hear virtual storms at increasing levels of intensity. A military veteran with posttraumatic stress disorder (PTSD) can experience virtual flashbacks of the trauma until the power of those flashbacks to cause anxiety wears off. A number of initial studies on virtual reality exposure therapy have demonstrated positive effects (Reger et al., 2011; Gerardi et al., 2008). It will be interesting to see the role that virtual reality exposure therapy and other forms of therapy that depend on technology plays in the future of psychotherapy.

Videoconferencing with a therapist is one of many forms of the increasingly popular cybertherapy: psychotherapy that takes place via technological devices over the Internet.
Sandy Huffaker/The New York Times/Redux Pictures

CHECK YOUR LEARNING:

15.22 How is cybertherapy different from face-to-face, in-person therapy?

15.23 What are the pros and cons of cybertherapy?

15.24 What is virtual reality exposure therapy?

Biomedical Therapies

In addition to psychotherapy, biomedical therapies are frequently used to treat psychological disorders by directly altering the biology of the brain. *Drug therapies* are by far the most common form of biomedical therapy, but others include *psychosurgery* and electric or magnetic forms of *brain stimulation*.

YOU WILL LEARN:

15.25 who prescribes psychiatric drugs.

15.26 about antipsychotic drugs, including their benefits and drawbacks.

15.27 about antianxiety drugs, including their benefits and drawbacks.

15.28 about antidepressant drugs, including their benefits and drawbacks.

15.29 about mood-stabilizing drugs, including their benefits and drawbacks.

15.30 about brain stimulation techniques and psychosurgery, including their benefits and drawbacks.

Can psychologists prescribe drugs?

In recent years, some psychologists have tried to obtain the privilege to prescribe drugs, but they have been successful only in a few states. Even in those states, prescribing psychologists are very rare (DeLeon et al., 2011; McGrath, 2010; Burns et al., 2008; Tryon, 2008). So, generally speaking, psychologists do not prescribe drugs. *Psychiatrists* do. They are trained as medical doctors, and their approach to mental disorders emphasizes the biological abnormalities of the brain. Other medical doctors—family physicians, pediatricians, OB-GYNs, and so on—also prescribe drugs for psychological

problems. Actually, these nonpsychiatrist medical doctors write more prescriptions for psychiatric medications than psychiatrists do, as illustrated in **Figure 15.7**. Psychologists often work collaboratively with these prescribers to provide comprehensive treatment for their clients (Ruddy et al., 2008).

Drug Therapies

Psychopharmacology is the treatment of psychological disorders with medications. Often, clients who receive such medication also receive psychotherapy, and some studies have indicated that this combination can be better than either medication or therapy alone. Medication can be especially helpful in the reduction of psychological symptoms, often rather quickly. However, symptoms often come back after the medication is discontinued, especially if the client has not addressed underlying issues that contributed to the problem. As **Figure 15.8** shows, there are four primary types of drugs used to treat psychological disorders: *antipsychotic*, *antianxiety*, *antidepressant*, and *mood-stabilizing* drugs.

Antipsychotic Drugs. **Antipsychotic drugs** are medications used to reduce psychotic symptoms such as delusions, hallucinations, and bizarre behavior. Common brand names of antipsychotics include Risperdal, Zyprexa, Abilify, and Haldol. They are prescribed primarily to clients with schizophrenia, but can also benefit clients with other disorders whose symptoms involve a loss of connection with reality. They work primarily by affecting the levels of dopamine in the brain. Most antipsychotics lower dopamine levels, but some recently introduced antipsychotics actually raise them—a finding that researchers are still trying to explain (Kutscher, 2008). Some antipsychotics also affect serotonin levels (Sharif et al., 2007).

When the first antipsychotic drugs were discovered in the 1950s, they transformed the lives of many people who had been debilitated by schizophrenia their entire lives. There was a drastic drop in the population of U.S. mental hospitals after these drugs enabled people with schizophrenia to function well enough to manage their own lives. Consider this: From 1955 to 2006, when the U.S. population nearly doubled, from 164 million to nearly 300 million, the number of people in public mental hospitals *dropped* drastically, from 558,000 to 40,00 (Torrey, 2008). Many of these "deinstitutionalized" people lived on their own, held jobs, and formed meaningful relationships. Today, antipsychotics remain the treatment of choice for schizophrenia for all of these reasons (Sajatovic et al., 2008; Castle & Buckley, 2008).

In spite of their upside, antipsychotics have a significant downside as well. For example, they do not help everyone with schizophrenia. Researchers have estimated that only half of those treated with antipsychotics improve significantly (Hopper et al., 2007; Hegarty et al., 1994). For those who do benefit, the gains are often limited to the positive symptoms of schizophrenia, with the less obvious negative symptoms, such as social withdrawal, remaining unaffected. The side effects of antipsychotics are often quite severe (Kingdon & Turkington, 2005). For example, the earliest antipsychotics disrupt the way the central nervous system coordinates bodily movements. As a result, people taking these drugs often have involuntary restless movement in their legs and feet; tremors that resemble Parkinson's disease; and *tardive dyskinesia*, a condition that involves spastic, repetitive movements of the mouth, face, trunk, or extremities (Dolder, 2008; Stroup et al., 2006). A newer generation of antipsychotics has lessened these movement-related side effects to some extent, but they (like the first generation) often cause significant weight gain (and the health risks that accompany it, like diabetes and heart disease), as well as dangerous cholesterol levels (Lehman et al., 2004; Lieberman et al., 2005). With side effects like these, it is not surprising that many people who receive a prescription for antipsychotics don't stay on their meds. Some studies have found that 40–50% of clients on antipsychotics stop taking their medication before instructed to do so (Taylor, 2006).

CHAPTER APP 15.2

Cybertherapy

Dr

Doctor On Demand

Preview one of the links and consider the following questions.

WEBSITE: http://tiny.cc/0zi7jy

ANDROID: http://tiny.cc/9e92iy

IPHONE: http://tiny.cc/p982iy

VIDEO DEMO: http://tiny.cc/chapterapps

This app enables users to schedule and have an appointment with a psychologist (or medical doctor) through their device—essentially, a videoconference with a therapist (*cybertherapy*). (To understand this app and answer the questions, you don't need to actually have an appointment or a videoconference. Exploring the features of the app and reading about it here will be enough.)

How does it APPly to your daily life?
If you decided to see a therapist, would you prefer meeting via videoconference/cybertherapy or meeting in person? Why?

How does it APPly to your understanding of psychology?
In your opinion, how do the pros and cons of videoconference/cybertherapy reflect the essential ingredients of successful therapy?

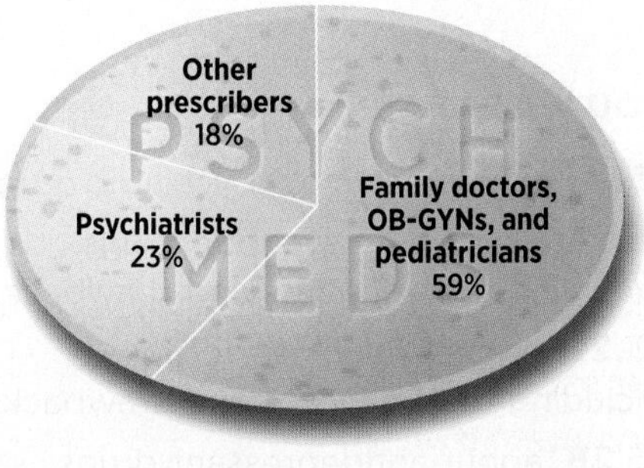

FIGURE 15.7 Who Prescribes Psychiatric Medications? The majority of prescriptions for psychiatric medications are written not by psychiatrists, but by the "first line" of physicians that patients most often see: general practitioners, OB/GYNs, pediatricians, and the nurses and assistants who often work in their offices. Data from Mark et al., 2009. Note: Data collected from U.S. prescribers from August 2006 to July 2007.

Prescriptions in the United States in 2009

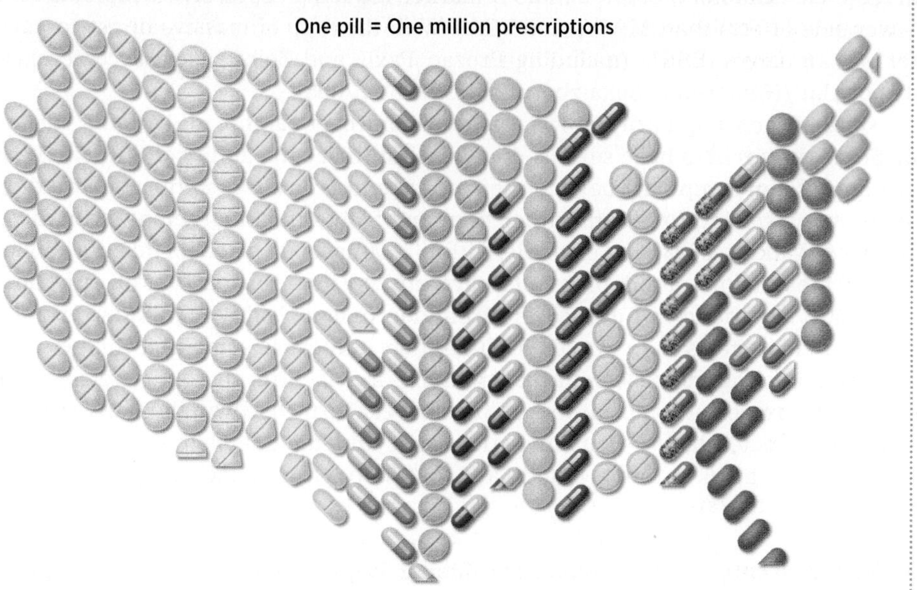

Brand name	Category	Prescriptions
Xanax	Antianxiety	44.0 million
Lexapro	Antidepressant	27.7 million
Ativan	Antianxiety	25.9 million
Zoloft	Antidepressant	19.5 million
Prozac	Antidepressant	19.5 million
Desyrel	Antidepressant	18.9 million
Cymbalta	Antidepressant	16.6 million
Seroquel	Antipsychotic	15.8 million
Effexor XR	Antidepressant	15.0 million
Valium	Mood stabilizer	14.0 million
Amphetamine salts (generic)	Stimulant (primarily for ADHD)	10.8 million
Risperdal	Antipsychotic	10.6 million
Vistaril	Antianxiety	9.8 million
Buproprion	Antidepressant	9.0 million
Abilify	Antipsychotic	8.2 million

FIGURE 15.8 Commonly Prescribed Psychiatric Medications. Psychiatric medications, especially antianxiety and antidepressant medications, are prescribed millions of times per year in the United States. Information from Grohol, 2010.

Antianxiety Drugs. **Antianxiety drugs** are medications used to reduce anxiety symptoms. Common brand names include Xanax, Ativan, and Valium. Early in their history, drugs in this category were called *tranquilizers*, from the word *tranquil*, meaning calm or relaxed.

Antianxiety drugs are benzodiazepines, which means that they have an immediate sedating effect on the central nervous system. So, they tend to bring relief from anxiety rather quickly, and are often used successfully in the treatment of anxiety disorders such as generalized anxiety disorder, social phobia, and panic disorder (Bandelow & Baldwin, 2010; Pollack & Simon, 2009; Blanco et al., 2010; Ledley et al., 2008; Van Ameringen et al., 2009).

A particular danger associated with antianxiety drugs is addiction, both physical and psychological. Indeed, many people have experienced withdrawal symptoms such as insomnia and physical illness when they discontinued antianxiety medications after taking them for a long time. Antianxiety medications can also be abused to produce a high.

Antianxiety drugs are not the only type of drugs prescribed to people with anxiety symptoms. Although the name may suggest otherwise, *antidepressant* drugs are actually even more common than antianxiety drugs in the treatment of anxiety. The success of antidepressants for people with anxiety symptoms highlights the overlap between depression and anxiety, and indicates that the two problems may be nearly indistinguishable biologically.

Antidepressant Drugs. **Antidepressant drugs** are medications used to reduce depression symptoms, and are also sometimes effective in reducing some anxiety symptoms. Common brand names include Prozac, Paxil, Zoloft, Effexor, Wellbutrin, and Elavil. Antidepressants improve mood by increasing the activity of serotonin or norepinephrine, both of which are underactive in the brains of people diagnosed with depression.

The first widely used antidepressants were MAOIs (monoamine oxidase inhibitors), followed closely by TCAs (tricyclic antidepressants). Both treated the symptoms of depression with some success, but side effects were a significant problem: MAOIs have serious interactions with certain common foods, drinks, and other drugs; and TCAs can cause heart irregularities and can be quite toxic in overdoses (Potter et al.,

psychopharmacology
The treatment of psychological disorders with medications.

antipsychotic drugs
Medications used to reduce psychotic symptoms such as delusions, hallucinations, and bizarre behavior.

antianxiety drugs
Medications used to reduce anxiety symptoms.

antidepressant drugs
Medications used to reduce depression symptoms (which are also sometimes effective in reducing some anxiety symptoms).

2006; Denko & Thase, 2006). In the late 1980s and early 1990s, SSRIs (selective serotonin reuptake inhibitors) entered the U.S. market, reducing depressive symptoms with far fewer side effects than MAOIs and TCAs. With the help of massive direct-to-consumer ad campaigns, SSRIs (including Prozac, Paxil, and Zoloft) have become massively popular (Nemeroff & Schatzberg, 2007; Barber, 2008).

In spite of their popularity, SSRIs remain a controversial topic (Shelton & Lester, 2006). Some researchers have serious doubts about the actual ability of SSRIs to help reduce depression symptoms beyond the *placebo effect*, or the benefits generated by the expectation for improvement rather than any truly active ingredient in the drug (Hammen & Watkins, 2008). For example, Gitlin (2009) makes the claim that only about 60–65% of those taking antidepressants have any positive response at all, and only about 25–40% experience a full recovery from depression. And while SSRIs certainly cause fewer side effects than MAOIs or TCAs, they still cause some that can be quite significant, including increased suicidal thinking or self-harm in youth, weight gain, and sexual desire performance problems (Kaslow et al., 2009). Given these iffy success rates and these potentially serious side effects, it is understandable that 40% of people stop taking their meds within a month, and 75% stop within 3 months (Olfson et al., 2006).

Mood-Stabilizing Drugs. **Mood-stabilizing drugs** are medications used to lessen the extreme emotional highs and lows of bipolar disorder. *Lithium* is by far the most common mood stabilizer, and has been for about half a century. Lithium is a salt-based substance that affects sodium neurons. Lithium helps people with bipolar disorder stay closer to the middle of the mood spectrum during all phases of the disorder: when depression or mania are in full swing, or as a preventive measure between episodes (Keck & McElroy, 2006; Ketter & Wang, 2010). People with bipolar disorder often take other drugs in addition to lithium, including antidepressants during depressive episodes and antipsychotics during manic episodes (Keck & McElroy, 2007; Sachs, 2004; Strakowski & Shelton, 2006).

The drawbacks of lithium include a number of side effects, including weight gain, sedation, hand tremors, and extreme thirst (Miklowitz, 2009; Miklowitz & Johnson, 2008). Occasionally, anticonvulsant medications—the kind more often used to treat seizure disorders like epilepsy—can be used to treat people with bipolar disorder (Muzina & Calabrese, 2006).

Brain Stimulation and Psychosurgery

More drastic and controversial options are available when psychotherapy and medication have repeatedly failed as treatment efforts. One such option is **electroconvulsive therapy** (**ECT**): a biomedical therapy for severe disorders in which an electric current passes through the brain of the client (**Figure 15.9**). The current is delivered via electrodes attached to the patient's head as the patient lies in a hospital bed, and it causes a seizure or a convulsion. ECT is used primarily for severe depression, but it has also been used for severe schizophrenia and some other conditions (Fink, 2009; Carney et al., 2003).

Contemporary ECT is nowhere near as brutal as its earliest versions (Shorter & Healy, 2007). When it began in the 1930s, patients received no anesthetic, no protection from injury induced by the seizure or convulsion (such as broken bones and bitten tongues), and sometimes excessive voltages of electric shock. In 1975, *One Flew Over the Cuckoo's Nest* (which won five Academy Awards, including Best Picture) popularized the harsh image of ECT when a rather uncaring mental hospital staff administered ECT to Jack Nicholson's character (Kneeland & Warren, 2002; Abrams, 2002). Today, any patient receiving ECT is far more safeguarded before any volts of electricity cross their brains. Now patients get anesthesia, muscle relaxant (to lessen the extremity of the bodily seizure, which can cause injuries), and attention from a full team of medical personnel (Fink, 2001, 2009).

mood-stabilizing drugs
Medications used to lessen the extreme emotional highs and lows of bipolar disorder.

electroconvulsive therapy (ECT)
A biomedical therapy for severe disorders in which an electric current passes through the brain of the client.

transcranial magnetic stimulation (TMS)
A treatment for depression in which weak electric current repeatedly pulses through a paddle-shaped magnetic coil just outside the person's head.

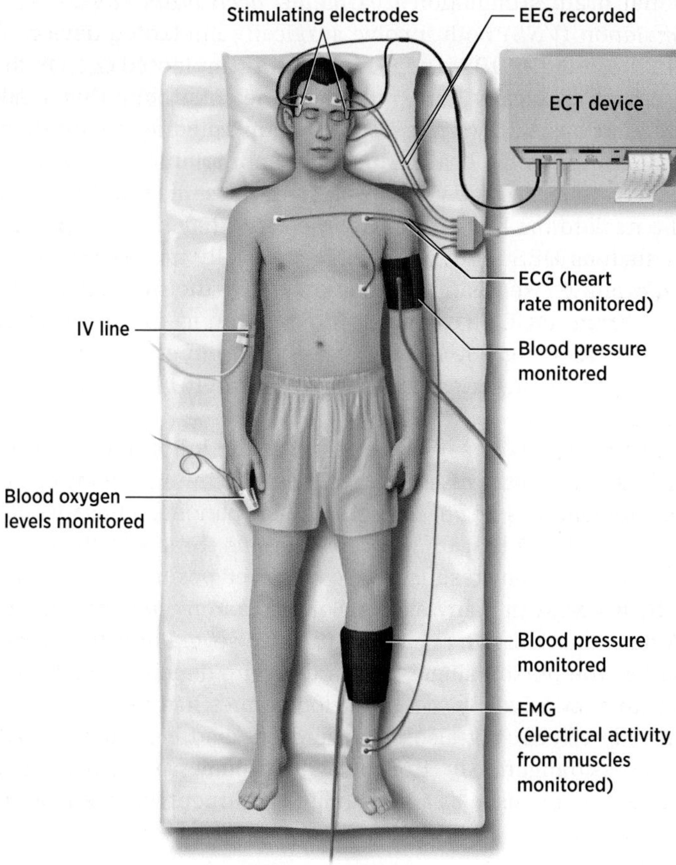

FIGURE 15.9 Electroconvulsive Therapy. Electroconvulsive therapy (ECT) is a biomedical therapy for severe disorders in which an electric current passes through the brain of the client.

ECT seems to work rather well in terms of alleviating severe symptoms of depression and schizophrenia. This can seem miraculous for clients who have been completely debilitated or suicidal despite ongoing therapy and medication. However, researchers are not sure why this happens (Nobler & Sackeim, 2006; Carney et al., 2003). Researchers know that the jolt of electricity causes a seizure or convulsion, but they can't make a definitive connection between the seizure or convulsion and the subsequent improvement in mood or overall functioning (McClintock et al., 2008). Other drawbacks to ECT include short-lived gains (many patients who improve relapse weeks or months later) and memory loss for the period (in some cases, weeks or months) immediately before and after the treatment (Fink, 2009; Kneeland & Warren, 2002). It remains a highly controversial treatment (Andre, 2009; Breggin, 2008).

In recent years, alternatives to ECT have emerged. They offer different kinds of brain stimulation in forms that are less objectionable to some people, largely because they lack the seizures and convulsions inherent in ECT (Shorter & Healy, 2007; Abrams, 2002). They include **transcranial magnetic stimulation (TMS)**: a treatment for depression in which weak electric current repeatedly pulses through a paddle-shaped magnetic coil just outside the person's head (**Figure 15.10**). (The precise location of the coil depends on the client's symptoms and is still being explored by researchers.) TMS is noninvasive. It does not cause pain, memory loss, or any of the other side effects common in ECT, and a few early studies suggest it can alleviate symptoms of severe depression (Fink, 2009). Like ECT, how TMS works is not entirely clear.

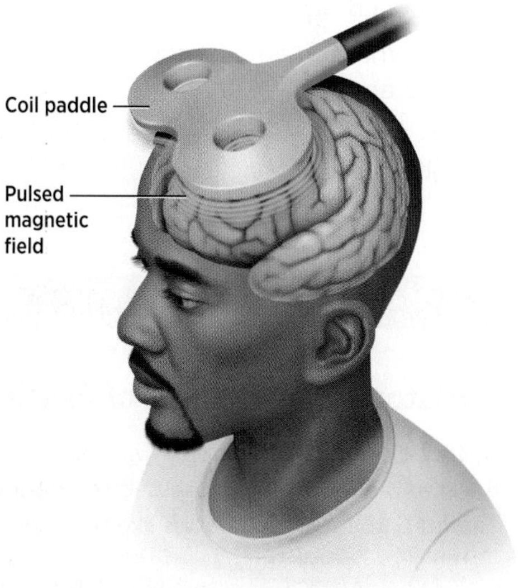

FIGURE 15.10 Transcranial Magnetic Stimulation. Transcranial magnetic stimulation is a treatment for depression in which weak electric current repeatedly pulses through a paddle-shaped magnetic coil just outside the person's head.

psychosurgery
Surgery performed directly on the brain in an effort to improve severe psychological disorders.

lobotomy
A psychosurgery in which the prefrontal lobes are disconnected from the inner regions of the brain that control emotions.

Two additional brain stimulation treatments, *deep brain stimulation* (*DBS*) and *vagal nerve stimulation* (*VNS*) both involve surgically implanted devices that deliver electricity within the body. In DBS, a wire is surgically implanted deep in the brain and connected to a device surgically implanted near the collarbone that sends electrical impulses on a regular basis. In VNS, a surgically implanted device on the vagal nerve delivers electrical energy to the brain. Much like an implanted pacemaker stimulates the heart with electric charges, the VNS device does the same to the vagal nerve, which runs through the neck to the brainstem (George et al., 2006; Nobler & Sackeim, 2006).

Treatments such as DBS and VNS involve surgically implanting devices that are connected to the brain. These treatments do not involve the surgeon directly accessing and changing the brain itself. That kind of intervention is known as **psychosurgery**: surgery performed directly on the brain in an effort to improve severe psychological disorders. In many psychosurgeries, surgeons deliberately remove or disable particular parts of the brain.

One of the original forms of psychosurgery was the **lobotomy**: a psychosurgery in which the prefrontal lobes were disconnected from the inner regions of the brain that control emotions. Lobotomies began in the 1930s on patients whose moods or violent behavior were so disordered that they became serious threats to themselves or other people (Andre, 2009). Lobotomy results were considered positive in some cases, but they were undoubtedly negative in many others. Some lobotomy patients didn't survive the surgery at all. Among survivors, the changes included severe and permanent personality changes that left the person sluggish, unintelligent, dependent, and in some cases emotionless and unresponsive. By the 1960s, lobotomies had ceased, not only because of these horrific side effects, but also because drugs had been discovered that could control symptoms less dangerously (Braslow, 1997). Today, psychosurgeries of any kind are extremely rare and only used as a last-chance treatment when all else has failed.

CHECK YOUR LEARNING:

15.25 Who prescribes psychiatric drugs?

15.26 What are antipsychotic drugs and what are their benefits and drawbacks?

15.27 What are antianxiety drugs, and what are their benefits and drawbacks?

15.28 What are antidepressant drugs, and what are their benefits and drawbacks?

15.29 What are mood-stabilizing drugs, and what are their benefits and drawbacks?

15.30 What are electroconvulsive therapy (ECT), transcranial magnetic stimulation (TMS), and psychosurgery, and when might each be used?

CHAPTER SUMMARY

History of Treatment of Psychological Disorders

15.1 Centuries ago, people with psychological disorders were often thought to be possessed by evil spirits and were treated with barbaric interventions like bloodletting and cutting holes in the skulls of patients.

15.2 The treatment of psychological disorders started to become more humane in the late 1700s, changing the attitude toward the mentally ill from shunning and punishment to compassion and respect.

15.3 Psychotherapy involves techniques used by a mental health professional to help a person overcome a psychological disorder or improve some aspect of emotional, cognitive, or behavioral functioning. Biomedical therapy involves medications and medical procedures that treat psychological problems by directly changing the biology of the brain.

Psychotherapies for Individual Clients

15.4 Psychotherapy clients come from all backgrounds, and about half of Americans will undergo some form of psychotherapy in their lifetimes.

15.5 In psychodynamic therapy, the main goal is to make the unconscious conscious through a process that results in insight. Psychodynamic therapists use a variety of techniques, including

free association, dream analysis, working with the client's resistance, and working with the client's transference.

15.6 In person-centered therapy, the therapist-client relationship is especially important. Person-centered therapists conduct nondirective therapy and emphasize the tendency toward healthy growth that exists in every person. The three essential characteristics of person-centered therapy are empathy, unconditional positive regard, and genuineness.

15.7 Behavior therapy is the application of operant conditioning and classical conditioning to change outward behavior. Behavior therapists use exposure therapy (a technique based on classical conditioning) and token economies (a technique based on operant conditioning).

15.8 Cognitive therapy is a psychotherapy approach in which a therapist helps clients change the way they think about life events. In the ABCDE model of cognitive therapy, the therapist helps the client identify illogical thinking and replace it with more logical thinking. Cognitive therapists teach their clients to recognize cognitive distortions such as all-or-nothing thinking, overgeneralization, catastrophizing, mental filtering, and personalization.

15.9 In the eclectic approach to therapy, the therapist selects the best treatment for a particular client based on evidence from studies of similar clients. In the integrative approach to therapy, the therapist blends different therapeutic techniques to create a new form of psychotherapy.

Psychotherapies for Groups and Families

15.10 Group therapy is psychotherapy conducted with a group of clients and an emphasis on interpersonal interaction.

15.11 Family therapy is psychotherapy that aims to improve how the family system functions, which in turn will improve the problems of its individual members.

How Well Does Psychotherapy Work?

15.12 To determine how well psychotherapy works, researchers have varied whom they ask (clients, therapists, or outside observers), when they ask (during, right after, or long after therapy), and how they ask (questionnaires, interviews, or other methods).

15.13 Thousands of studies on the benefits of psychotherapy point to one undeniable conclusion: Psychotherapy works.

15.14 Generally, different types of therapy have about equal rates of success, a finding that researchers call the dodo bird verdict. However, particular therapies can be especially beneficial for particular diagnoses.

15.15 There are a few common factors in all forms of effective therapy, including the therapeutic alliance, positive expectations, and attention.

The Importance of Culture in Psychotherapy

15.16 Cultural competence is a therapist's ability to work sensitively and expertly with clients from diverse backgrounds. If the therapist lacks cultural competence, the client might feel misunderstood and could miss out on the benefits of therapy.

15.17 With cultural self-awareness, a therapist recognizes that his or her perspective is not necessarily that of others. Having cultural self-awareness helps a therapist to recognize that a client's culture can influence his or her experience.

Ethics in Psychotherapy

15.18 Confidentiality is maintaining the privacy of client information. Therapy might be impossible without that trust between a client and a therapist. Therapists are obligated to break confidentiality to protect the well-being of the client or another person.

15.19 After the therapist explains the therapy process, the client gives informed consent, which is permission to move forward with the therapy. Providing informed consent is important to therapy because it allows the client to ask questions about the process and gives the therapist the opportunity to begin forming a therapeutic alliance.

15.20 It is important for therapists to stay within their boundaries of competence—the limits of their expertise and abilities—and refer clients to other mental health professionals as necessary.

15.21 A multiple relationship is a situation in which a therapist has both a professional relationship and a nonprofessional relationship with the same person. A multiple relationship can impair the therapist's ability to function competently and objectively.

Cybertherapy: Psychotherapy via Modern Technology

15.22 Cybertherapy is psychotherapy that takes place via technological devices like computers or smartphones over the Internet, including videoconferencing (similar to Skype) and email.

15.23 Cybertherapy has a couple of significant benefits, in particular allowing people who live a great distance from a psychotherapist to access help, as well as providing people with disorders that prevent them from leaving the house an opportunity to see a therapist.

15.24 Limitations of cybertherapy include the risk of impostors posing as legitimate therapists and the burden on the therapist to be technologically proficient. A form of cybertherapy, virtual reality exposure therapy, allows the client to experience the situation that causes him or her anxiety via electronic means.

Biomedical Therapies

15.25 Psychiatrists and other medical doctors prescribe drugs for psychological problems. Psychologists, with the exception of a very small number with extra training in a couple of U.S. states, do not prescribe medication.

15.26 Antipsychotic drugs are used to reduce psychotic symptoms such as delusions, hallucinations, and bizarre behavior. They have transformed the lives of people suffering from schizophrenia, but the side effects can be severe.

15.27 Antianxiety drugs are used to reduce anxiety symptoms and bring relief quickly, but they can be addictive.

15.28 Antidepressant drugs are used to reduce depression symptoms (as well as some anxiety symptoms), but their success rate is questionable, and they can have serious side effects, including increased suicidal thinking.

15.29 Mood-stabilizing drugs are used to lessen the extreme emotional highs and lows of bipolar disorder, but they can have significant side effects.

15.30 Electroconvulsive therapy (ECT) is a biomedical therapy for severe depression in which an electric current passes through the brain of the client. Unfortunately, the gains can be short-lived and the side effects include memory loss. In transcranial magnetic stimulation (TMS), a weak electric current repeatedly pulses though a coil outside the client's head. It is a noninvasive treatment for depression and doesn't have the severe side effects of ECT. When other efforts prove ineffective, psychosurgery can be performed directly on the brain in an effort to improve severe psychological disorders. Decades ago, some lobotomy patients didn't survive the surgery, and survivors often had severe personality changes.

KEY TERMS

psychotherapy, p. 520
biomedical therapy, p. 520
psychoanalysis, p. 523
psychodynamic therapy, p. 523
free association, p. 523
dream analysis, p. 523
resistance, p. 523
transference, p. 523
interpretation, p. 525
working through, p. 525
person-centered therapy, p. 525
nondirective therapy, p. 525
empathy, p. 527
unconditional positive regard, p. 527
genuineness, p. 527
reflection, p. 527
behavior therapy, p. 528
exposure therapy, p. 528
systematic desensitization, p. 531
counterconditioning, p. 531
token economy, p. 531
aversive conditioning, p. 531
participant modeling, p. 531
cognitive therapy, p. 531
cognitive-behavioral therapy, p. 533
rational-emotive behavior therapy (REBT), p. 533
ABCDE model of cognitive therapy, p. 533
cognitive distortions, p. 533
all-or-nothing thinking, p. 533
overgeneralization, p. 533
catastrophizing, p. 533
mental filtering, p. 535
personalization, p. 535
eclectic approach to therapy, p. 535
integrative approach to therapy, p. 535
group therapy, p. 537
self-help group, p. 538
family therapy, p. 538
evidence-based practice, p. 541
dodo bird verdict, p. 541
common factors, p. 541
therapeutic alliance, p. 543
cultural competence, p. 543
cultural self-awareness, p. 543
confidentiality, p. 545
informed consent, p. 545
boundaries of competence, p. 545
multiple relationship, p. 546
cybertherapy, p. 546
virtual reality exposure therapy, p. 546
psychopharmacology, p. 549
antipsychotic drugs, p. 549
antianxiety drugs, p. 549
antidepressant drugs, p. 549
mood-stabilizing drugs, p. 550
electroconvulsive therapy (ECT), p. 550
transcranial magnetic stimulation (TMS), p. 550
psychosurgery, p. 552
lobotomy, p. 552

SELF-ASSESSMENT

1. Psychodynamic therapists use a variety of techniques including:
   a. transference, dream analysis, and self-actualization.
   b. dream analysis, catastrophizing, and interpretation.
   c. free association, token economy, and working with a client's resistance.
   d. transference, dream analysis, and interpretation.

2. Person-centered therapy emphasizes the tendency toward healthy growth inherent in each person, which is also known as ______.
   a. self-actualization
   b. cognition
   c. exposure
   d. participant modeling

3. ______ is a form of exposure therapy primarily used to treat phobias in which the client experiences relaxation and the anxiety-provoking thing or situation at the same time.

4. ______ is a psychotherapy in which therapists help clients change the way they think about life events.

5 There are various types of cognitive distortions, including:

a. all-or-nothing thinking, mental filtering, and operant conditioning.
b. personalization, overgeneralization, and unconditional positive regard.
c. all-or-nothing thinking, overgeneralization, and catastrophizing.
d. personalization, effectiveness, and catastrophizing.

6 There are two types of studies concerning how well psychotherapy works: ______ studies that focus on how well it works in a highly controlled study, and ______ studies that focus on how well it works with real clients and real therapists.

7 ______ are elements found in all forms of effective psychotherapy that play an important role in client improvement.

8 ______ is a therapist's ability to work sensitively and expertly with clients from diverse backgrounds.

a. Operant conditioning
b. Token economy
c. Cultural competence
d. Counterconditioning

9 ______ is maintaining the privacy of client information and an essential ethical responsibility of a psychotherapist.

10 The four primary types of drugs used to treat psychological disorders are:

a. antipsychotic, antianxiety, antidepressant, and antidissociative.
b. anticognitive, antianxiety, mood-stabilizing, and antipersonality.
c. antipsychotic, antianxiety, antidepressant, and mood-stabilizing.
d. anticognitive, antianxiety, antidepressant, and antidissociative.

Self-Assessment Answers

1. d, 2. a, 3. systematic desensitization, 4. cognitive therapy, 5. c, 6. efficacy, effectiveness, 7. common factors, 8. c, 9. confidentiality, 10. c

WHAT'S YOUR TAKE?

1. As technology improves and psychotherapists become more competent using it, the option of seeing a therapist via a videoconference app (similar to Skype or FaceTime) is increasingly available. In my own clinical practice, I've received that question—"Do you do sessions online?"—quite a few times in recent years from prospective clients. If you were the client, which would you prefer: in-person meetings or cybertherapy? For you, what are the most important pros and cons of each? How important would the cybertherapy option be when choosing a therapist?

SHOW ME MORE

15.1 Judith Beck and Cognitive Therapy

Link: launchpadworks.com LaunchPad macmillan learning

In this video, prominent cognitive therapist Judith Beck explains the cognitive approach to therapy.

Courtesy Freedom from Fear

15.2 Virtual Reality Exposure Therapy for Phobias

Link: launchpadworks.com LaunchPad macmillan learning

This video provides a peek into virtual reality exposure therapy.

Courtesy CNN

A Appendix: An Introduction to Statistics in Psychological Research

Measures of Central Tendency

YOU WILL LEARN:

A.1 about measures of central tendency, including mean, median, and mode.

A.2 about variability, including range and standard deviation

A.3 about types of distributions of data, including normal distribution, positively skewed distributions, and negatively skewed distributions.

A.4 about statistical significance and practical significance.

In Chapter 1, we discussed the three types of psychological research: *descriptive research, correlational research,* and *experimental research*. In descriptive research, it is important to describe the main characteristic of your population with one number. So, psychological researchers often include a **measure of central tendency**: a single number used to summarize or represent a group of numbers. Let's recall the descriptive study we considered in Chapter 1: how many hours per day college students spend on social media. If you collect data on daily social media hours from many students, you'll want a single number that shows how many hours per day, on average, that group of students spent on social media. The most commonly used measure of central tendency is the **mean**: the average of a group of numbers.

Another common measure of central tendency is the **median**: the number that falls at the midpoint in a group of numbers listed in order, such that half the numbers fall above it and half the numbers fall below it. The median of a list of numbers does the same thing as the median of a highway—divides it in half, with an equal amount of numbers (or lanes) on either side. The median is a good measure of central tendency when a handful of extremely high or low numbers might pull the mean in one direction, possibly making the mean deceptive. For example, if a few of your participants reported an extremely high number of hours per day on social media—15 or more hours, perhaps—those few participants could push the mean up to a number that gives a misleading impression of the overall group. The median—the line that splits the population in half—doesn't get pulled up or down by extreme numbers.

A final measure of central tendency often used in descriptive psychological research is the **mode**: in a group of numbers, the one that occurs most often. The mode is easy to find: it is just a matter of counting, with no calculations needed. In our study of daily social media usage among college students, if the most common response is 2 hours, then the mode is 2.

The median of a group of numbers performs the same function as the median of a highway: split the numbers (or lanes) such that the same amount falls on either side.
junyyeung/iStock/Getty Images

measure of central tendency
A single number used to summarize or represent a group of numbers.

mean
The average of a group of numbers.

median
The number that falls at the midpoint in a group of numbers listed in order, such that half fall above it and half fall below it.

mode
The number that occurs the most often in a group of numbers.

variability
The degree to which numbers in a group differ from the mean.

range
The difference between the highest score and the lowest score in a group of numbers.

standard deviation
A statistic that measures the variability around a mean.

normal distribution
A symmetrical distribution of numbers in which the mean, median, and mode all fall exactly in the middle.

skewed distribution
A distribution of numbers that is not symmetrical around the mean.

negatively skewed distribution
A distribution of numbers that includes more numbers in the low end (toward the left on a graph) than in a normal distribution.

positively skewed distribution
A distribution of numbers that includes more numbers in the high end (toward the right on a graph) than in a normal distribution.

Variability

The mean (and other measures of central tendency) is important, but so is the scatter around the mean. Psychologists call that scatter **variability**: the degree to which numbers in a group differ from the mean. The most basic measure of variability is **range**: the difference between the highest score and the lowest score in a list of numbers. A large range suggests a lot of scatter around the mean, and a small range suggests little scatter around the mean. However, range can be deceptive, since it takes just one high number or one low number to extend it in either direction.

A more sophisticated measure of variability is **standard deviation**: a statistic, commonly used in psychology research, that measures the variability around a mean. Standard deviation is basically the mean of the difference (or deviation) between each number in the list and the mean of that list. (Actually, if you consider the mathematical details, standard deviation is slightly more complicated. To calculate standard deviation, you have to square the difference between each number and the mean; otherwise, the positive differences and the negative differences would simply cancel each other out for a total of zero. When the differences are squared, however, they become positive. You then add together those positive numbers and divide that total by the number of items in the list. Finally, you take the square root of that number and you have the standard deviation.)

For example, let's say that among the students who provided data, the mean was 3 hours per day spent on social media. That mean of 3 could come from a list of numbers that consistently fall close to 3, such as this: 3, 3, 2, 3, 3, 4, 2, 3, 4, 5, 3, 2, 1, 3, 4, 3, 3, and 3. That list has little variability, so it produces a small standard deviation (about 0.9). It also has a small range, 4 (the difference between the highest score, of 5, and the lowest score, of 1). By contrast, that same mean of 3 could come from a list of numbers with much more scatter, such as this: 10, 3, 0, 1, 1, 9, 0, 1, 2, 5, 11, 1, 1, 2, 0, 1, 1, and 5. That list has much more variability, so it produces a much larger standard deviation (about 3.4). It also has a much larger range, of 11 (the difference between the highest score, of 11, and the lowest score, of 0). (See **Figure A.1**.)

One of the benefits of knowing the variability and standard deviation around a mean involves making sense of *outliers*, or numbers in a list that fall far from the mean. If your mean of 3 came from the first list, and you meet Austin, a college student who spends 9 hours a day on social media, then you can be sure that Austin's behavior is rare. But if your mean of 3 came from the second list, Austin's social media time is not quite so out of the ordinary. It is quite high, but he is clearly not the only one in the second list spending that much time on social media.

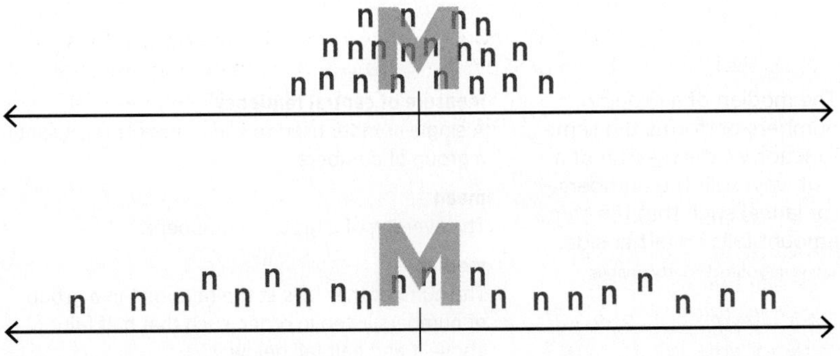

FIGURE A.1 Mean, Variability, and Standard Deviation. When a list of numbers clusters closely around their mean, as they do in the top scatterplot, the variability and standard deviation are small. When the list of numbers is spread widely around their mean, as they do in the bottom scatterplot, the variability and standard deviation are large. So, even if two lists of numbers produce the same mean, they can produce different variabilities and standard deviations, which indicate the amount of scatter.

Distribution of Data

The research data that psychologists collect can be distributed in various ways. Those distributions can be symmetrical around the mean, lean toward the high end, or lean toward the low end. The first of those distributions is the **normal distribution**: a symmetrical distribution of numbers in which the mean, median, and mode all fall exactly in the middle. The normal distribution is also called a *normal curve,* or *bell curve,* because in graph form it resembles a perfectly symmetrical bell (**Figure A.2**).

A common example of a normal distribution is height. The mean height for women in the United States is 5 feet, 4 inches. Lots of women are exactly that height, and many are within an inch of that height (5′3″ or 5′5″). As you move away from the mean toward shorter or taller heights, the number of women at each

IT'S LIKE...

Standard Deviation Is Like the Variation in Daily High Temperature

Sometimes, the standard deviation tells us more than the mean does. In May, the mean high temperature in Los Angeles is about 75°F. In May, the mean high temperature in St. Louis is also about 75°F. But what about the standard deviation? In LA, the standard deviation is small. LA has such predictable temperatures that if the high fell outside the 70s in May, it would be shocking. But St. Louis has a much larger standard deviation. In May, the temperature in St. Louis is all over the place. It could be a cool day with a high in the 50s, a scorcher that reaches the 90s, or anywhere between. That unpredictability is important to know if you're planning a May trip to one city or the other!

When psychologists conduct descriptive research, they routinely report the standard deviation along with the mean. Researchers know that the mean is generally a good use of a single number to summarize a group of numbers, but they know that the mean tells us a lot more when it is accompanied by a measure of how closely that group of numbers clusters around it. For example, imagine that a psychologist measured the overall anxiety levels of college students on two different campuses with a scale that ranged from 0 (no anxiety) to 100 (extreme anxiety). The two colleges produce the same mean of 20, not bad. But one has a tiny standard deviation, meaning that almost everybody lands right around 20. The other has a huge standard deviation, meaning that students land all over the place—some around 20, but some much lower and some (gulp) much higher. If you were a high school senior, where would you want to apply? ●

height declines. When you get to the extremes—many standard deviations above and below the mean—women at those heights are quite rare. Among psychological variables, IQ (intelligence quotient) comes closest to a normal distribution, with most of us clustered at or around the mean level of IQ, and fewer and fewer of us landing at each score that is increasingly above or below the mean.

As illustrated in Figure A.2, in a normal distribution, we know the percentage of numbers that fall in each section as defined by standard deviations. Specifically, about 68% fall within one standard deviation of the mean, and roughly another 28% fall between one and two standard deviations from the mean. That is about 96%, meaning that only about 4% fall more than two standard deviations above or below the mean. The main point here is just how uncommon it is, within a normal distribution, for a number to far fall from the mean. That's why it's so noteworthy when you see a woman who is nearly 6 feet tall, or meet someone with gifted-level IQ.

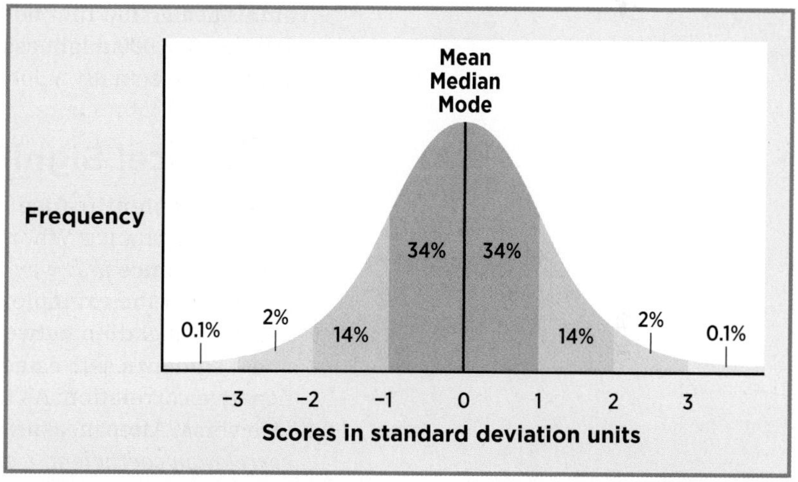

FIGURE A.2 The Normal Distribution. In a normal distribution, numbers are symmetrically distributed around a midpoint at which the mean, median, and mode all fall. Over two-thirds of the numbers fall within one standard deviation of the mean, and fewer than 5% fall more than two standard deviations away from the mean.

In psychological research, not all distributions are normal. Many distributions lean one way or the other. Psychologists call this a **skewed distribution**: a distribution of numbers that is not symmetrical around the mean. There are two types of skewed distributions, negative and positive. A **negatively skewed distribution** is a distribution of numbers that includes more numbers in the low end (toward the left on a graph) than in a normal distribution. A **positively skewed distribution** is a distribution of numbers that includes more numbers in the high end (toward the right on a graph) than in a normal distribution.

In a skewed distribution, the mean, median, and mode do not coincide. Instead, the skew (or the tail of the graph) pulls the mean, and to a lesser extent the median, in its direction. The mode remains at the peak of the graph (**Figure A.3**). The lesson to be learned here is that the mean can be a misleading statistic when the

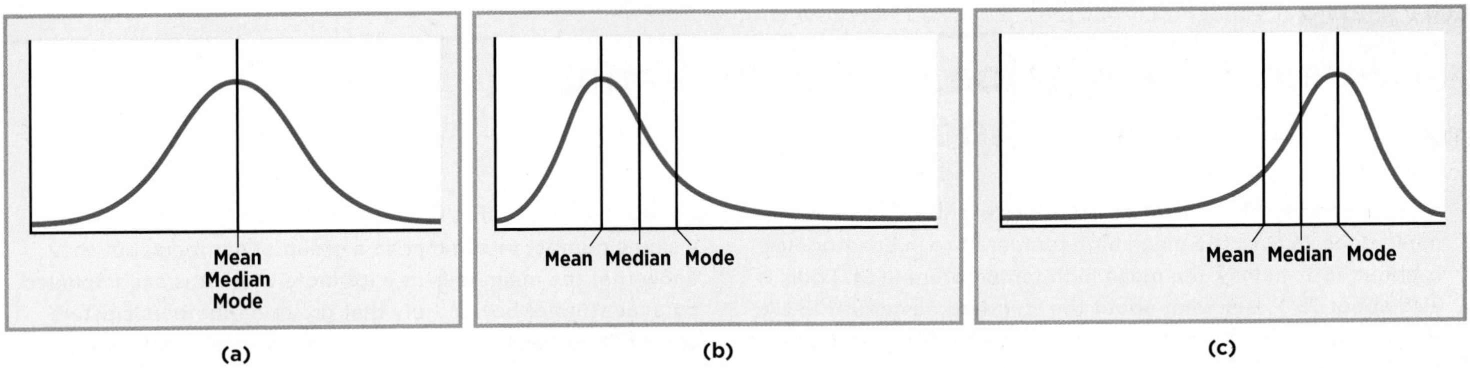

FIGURE A.3 Skewed Distributions. In a normal distribution, the mean, median, and mode are all the same. However, in a skewed distribution, extreme values at one end of the distribution pull the mean, and to a lesser extent the median, in their direction.

distribution is skewed. As an example, imagine that a used car dealership had 50 cars for sale. The vast majority of cars—45 out of 50—were priced between $10,000 and $12,000, with the most common price being $11,000. But the other five cars were high-end luxury cars, with price tags of $30,000, $40,000, $50,000, $60,000, and $70,000. That is a positively skewed distribution. Those five expensive cars would raise the mean price quite a bit. In fact, that mean price would fall several thousand dollars above the mode, $11,000. Used-car shoppers who see the mean price of cars at this dealership (but not the mode or median) and who have a budget of about $10,000–$12,000 might assume that cars there are out of their price range, when most of them are actually a good fit.

Statistical Significance

Statistical significance is the probability that a statistic could have been obtained by random chance. When psychologists conduct research, they consider statistical significance as a way to determine whether their hypotheses were supported. Let's revisit the example of correlational research in Chapter 1, a study examining the correlation between the number of hours students spend on social media and a student's self-esteem. Let's also assume that we expect (or hypothesize) a negative correlation: As time spent online goes up, self-esteem goes down, and vice versa. After measuring those two variables in our participants, we calculate a *correlation coefficient,* a statistic (as described in detail in Chapter 1) that ranges from +1.0 to −1.0. Let's say we get a correlation coefficient of −0.3. That is a negative correlation, but is it a strong enough correlation to support our hypothesis? Someone skeptical of our study might claim that a correlation of −0.3 could have been obtained with random numbers. After all, −0.3 isn't far from 0, and 0 signifies no correlation at all.

statistical significance
The probability that a statistic could have been obtained by random chance.

That is where statistical significance comes in. Statistical significance is essentially a percentage of chance, or a *probability,* that the statistic happened by chance. The lower that probability, the higher the statistical significance. A low probability means that getting a statistic that strong rarely happens by chance, but a high *probability* means that getting a statistic that strong often happens by chance. Statistical significance is shades of gray rather than black and white, but psychologists have generally settled on 5% as a cutoff: If the statistical significance is less than 5% (often written as $p < 0.05$, with the p standing for probability), the result is considered statistically significant. In our example, if our correlation coefficient of −0.3 was accompanied by a statistical significance of 0.65, that would indicate a 65% probability of a correlation of that strength happening by chance. That is not impressive, and suggests no link between our two variables. However, if our correlation coefficient of −0.3 had a statistical significance of 0.02, that would indicate just a 2% probability of a

correlation of that strength happening by chance. That is more impressive, and suggests a link between our two variables.

Statistical significance can be affected by many factors, but a major influence is *sample size*, the number of participants in the study (a number that psychologists abbreviate as n). Think of flipping a coin. You always expect 50% heads and 50% tails, but sometimes your results differ. If you flip just 10 coins, getting 70% tails is not noteworthy. In fact, it could be a fluke. But if you flip 1000 coins, getting 70% tails is noteworthy. It is different from what you would expect for such a large number of coin flips, and it suggests the influence of a factor other than just luck. In our study, a correlation of –0.3 would be more likely to have the statistical significance of 0.65 if we had a small number of participants, but the statistical significance of 0.02 if we had a much larger number of participants.

In addition to statistical significance, it is important for psychologists to consider *practical significance*. Practical significance is essentially real-world significance, or the impact of a statistic on the real lives of real people. Statistical significance and practical significance don't always match. As an example, imagine that a team of clinical psychologists creates a new therapy for panic disorder, and they test their new therapy on real clients who actually have panic disorder. Before the therapy starts, the mean number of panic attacks per week is 16. After the therapy ends, the mean number of panic attacks per week is 11. The psychologists run statistics (in this case, a comparison of pretherapy and posttherapy means known as a *t-test*) and find that this decrease of 5 panic attacks per week is a result with a less than 5% probability of happening by chance. That's impressive statistical significance, but what about practical significance? Clients who achieve this outcome would still be having about two-thirds of the panic attacks they had before they started, and would still average well over one panic attack per day. Many of them might argue that the therapy had only minimal practical significance in their day-to-day lives.

CHECK YOUR LEARNING:

A.1 What is the difference between the mean, median, and mode?

A.2 What do range and standard deviation measure, and how are they different from each other?

A.3 How does a normal distribution differ from positively and negatively skewed distributions?

A.4 What is statistical significance, and how does it differ from practical significance?

APPENDIX SUMMARY

A.1 For any group of numbers, the mean is the average, the median is the number that falls at the midpoint of the numbers listed in order, and the mode is the number that occurs most often.

A.2 Range and standard deviation are measures of variance. Range is the difference between the highest score and the lowest score in a group of numbers; standard deviation is a statistic that measures the variability around a mean.

A.3 In a normal distribution, the mean, median, and mode all fall exactly in the middle. In a negatively skewed distribution, there are more numbers in the low end, so the mean and median fall below the mode. In a positively skewed distribution, there are more numbers in the high end, so the mean and median fall above the mode.

A.4 Statistical significance is the probability that a statistic could have been obtained by random chance. By contrast, practical significance is the impact of a statistic on the real lives of real people.

KEY TERMS

measure of central tendency, p. A-1
mean, p. A-1
median, p. A-1
mode, p. A-1
variability, p. A-2
range, p. A-2
standard deviation, p. A-2
normal distribution, p. A-2
skewed distribution, p. A-2
negatively skewed distribution, p. A-2
positively skewed distribution, p. A-2
statistical significance, p. A-4

Glossary

ABCDE model of cognitive therapy A type of rational-emotive behavior therapy in which the therapist and client identify the sequence that leads from illogical thinking to logical thinking about particular life events.

absolute threshold The minimum level of a stimulus necessary for a person to detect its presence at least half of the time.

accommodation A classification process that makes sense of new information by revising or creating new schemas.

acculturation Managing a life that involves the coexistence of more than one culture.

acculturative stress Stress associated with the process of managing old and new cultures.

acculturative stress The physical or psychological stress that comes from acculturation.

achievement goal theory A theory of motivation stating that when the person is motivated to achieve a goal, certain goals (mastery goals) produce better outcomes than other goals (performance goals).

achievement test An assessment technique used by psychologists to numerically measure the level of learning a person has attained.

acquisition The point in the learning process at which the neutral stimulus becomes a conditioned stimulus because of its link to the conditioned response.

action potential The release, or firing, of an electrical impulse that travels through the axon.

acupuncture A technique involving the insertion of needles into the skin at specific points to alleviate stress or pain.

acute stress disorder A psychological disorder that takes place in the days and weeks immediately after a trauma in which the person feels dazed and anxious and experiences flashbacks.

addiction Problematic drug use that persists in spite of serious negative consequences.

adjustment disorder A psychological disorder defined by an excessively disruptive stress reaction to an identifiable stressor.

adolescence The developmental period that encompasses the transition from childhood to adulthood.

adrenal glands The glands located on top of the kidneys that produce hormones to arouse the body in response to stress.

aerobic exercise Physical exercise that maintains an increased heart rate for a prolonged time.

affect heuristic An educated guess in which the worth of something is strongly influenced by how a person feels toward it.

affective forecasting Predicting how a person will feel about the outcomes of his or her decisions.

aggression Behavior intended to cause harm or death.

agreeableness A personality trait emphasizing the tendency to cooperate and comply with other people.

algorithm A formula-like method of problem solving.

all-or-nothing thinking A cognitive distortion in which the client mistakenly evaluates events as either absolutely flawless or completely awful, with no middle ground in between.

alternative medicine Health care that is used instead of conventional medicine.

altruism Completely unselfish concern for others.

amnesia The inability to remember some or all information, either temporarily or permanently.

amygdala The part of the limbic system involved most directly in emotion, especially fear.

anal stage Freud's second psychosexual stage, which lasts from about age 18 months to about age 3, and focuses on the psychological consequences of toilet training.

anchoring heuristic An educated guess in which the starting point has a strong influence on the conclusion that is ultimately reached.

anorexia nervosa An eating disorder based on a refusal to eat enough food to maintain a minimally normal body weight, based on the person's height and age.

anterograde amnesia The inability to form new memories after a certain point in time.

antianxiety drugs Medications used to reduce anxiety symptoms.

antidepressant drugs Medications used to reduce depression symptoms (which are also effective in reducing some anxiety symptoms).

antipsychotic drugs Medications used to reduce psychotic symptoms such as delusions, hallucinations, and bizarre behavior.

antisocial personality disorder A psychological disorder based on a disregard for, and violation of, the rights of other people.

anxiety disorders The group of DSM disorders in which the experience of excessive, unjustified anxiety is the primary symptom.

applied psychology specializations Areas in which psychologists apply their expertise to real-world problems, using their knowledge of mind and behavior to enhance some important aspect of their clients' lives.

appraisal The way you evaluate the things that happen to you.

archetypes Specific symbols or patterns within the collective unconscious that appear consistently across cultures and time periods.

arousal theory A theory of motivation stating that the person is motivated to obtain and maintain an optimal level of arousal.

assimilation A classification process that makes sense of new information by sorting into already existing schemas.

assimilation An acculturation strategy in which the person adopts the new culture and rejects the old culture.

association areas Brain material that is devoted to synthesizing and interpreting information rather than merely taking information in.

attachment A close emotional bond between two people, particularly a young child and a caregiver.

attention-deficit/hyperactivity disorder (ADHD) A disorder emerging in childhood that features significant problems with attention, hyperactivity/impulsivity, or both.

attitude A viewpoint, often influenced by both thoughts and emotions, that affects a person's responses to people, things, or situations.

attribution An explanation of the cause of behavior.

attribution theory A theory that behavior is caused either by traits within the individual or by the situation surrounding the individual.

audition The sense of hearing.

authoritarian parenting style An approach to parenting in which parents require children to obey unquestionable, strict rules.

authoritative parenting style An approach to parenting in which parents set rules, but also explain and negotiate those rules with their children.

autism spectrum disorder A disorder emerging in childhood that features significant social interaction deficits and rigid, repetitive patterns of behavior.

automatic processing The entrance of some information into long-term memory without any conscious processing.

autonomic nervous system The part of the peripheral nervous system that connects the central nervous system to the parts of the body controlled involuntarily.

availability heuristic An educated guess based on the information that most quickly and easily comes to mind.

aversive conditioning A form of behavior therapy that aims to reduce unwanted behavior by pairing it with an unpleasant experience.

axon The part of the neuron that carries information toward other neurons.

axon terminals The small branches at the end of an axon that form connections with the next neuron.

babbling An early stage of speech development during which the baby vocalizes a wide variety of nonword sounds.

basic research psychology specializations Areas in which psychologists conduct research for the sake of enhancing the understanding of behavior and mental processes.
behavior therapy The application of operant and classical conditioning to change outward behavior, with little to no emphasis on the mental processes affecting that behavior.
behavioral assessment An approach to assessment that assumes client behaviors are themselves the problems, rather than signs of deeper problems.
behavioral genetics The study of the impact of genes (nature) and environment (nurture) on personality and behavior.
behavioral theory of personality A theory that emphasizes the influence of the environment and the importance of observable, measurable behavior.
behaviorism A psychological perspective that emphasizes observable behavior over internal mental processes.
belief perseverance A tendency to maintain a belief even when evidence suggests it is incorrect.
binge eating disorder An eating disorder with the overeating pattern of bulimia but without the purging.
binocular depth cues The qualities of visual stimuli that indicate depth when using both eyes.
biofeedback Use of a monitor that provides information about physiological functions (like heartbeat or muscle tension), with the intention of influencing those functions in a healthy direction.
biological preparedness An animal's evolutionary predisposition to learn that which is most relevant to the survival of that species.
biological theory of abnormality A theory of abnormality asserting that biological factors within the human body, such as brain structures, neurochemicals, and genes, are the primary causes of psychological disorders.
biomedical therapy A treatment for psychological problems that involves medications and medical procedures to directly change the biology of the brain.
biopsychosocial theory A uniquely comprehensive psychological perspective that emphasizes biological, psychological, and social factors as influences on behavior.
biopsychosocial theory of abnormality A contemporary theory of abnormality acknowledging that a combination of biological, psychological, and sociocultural factors contribute to psychological disorders.
bipolar disorder A psychological disorder characterized by alternating between extremely high moods and extremely low moods.
bisexual The sexual orientation of a person who is attracted to people of both the other and the same sex.
blind spot The part of the retina that contains no rods or cones and is therefore unable to sense light.
body mass index (BMI) A number calculated from a person's height and weight that indicates body fat and overall fitness level.
borderline personality disorder A psychological disorder based on instability in many areas of the person's life, including interpersonal relationships, mood, and self-image.
bottom-up processing A way of processing information in which what a person senses becomes a perception with no influence of expectations or previous experiences.
boundaries of competence The limits of a therapist's expertise and abilities.
brainstem The part of the brain that connects to the spine and controls the functions most essential to staying alive.
Broca's aphasia The speech dysfunction caused by damage to Broca's area.
Broca's area The part of the left side of the frontal lobe heavily involved in speaking.
bulimia nervosa An eating disorder in which an individual exhibits a pattern of overeating followed by drastic attempts to prevent weight gain.
bystander effect The decrease in likelihood that one person will help another person caused by the presence of others also available to help.
Cannon–Bard theory A theory of emotion stating that the person experiences emotion by simultaneously becoming aware of bodily changes and feelings.
catastrophizing A cognitive distortion that occurs when the client exaggerates the negative consequences of an event, or makes a "catastrophe" out of a minor mishap.
categorical model of psychopathology A model in which psychological problems exist as either totally present or totally absent, as opposed to present to a certain extent.
cell body (soma) The large central region of a neuron that performs the basic activities, including the production of energy, to keep the neuron functional.
central nervous system The brain and the spinal cord.
central route persuasion A persuasion strategy that emphasizes the message's content.
cerebellum The part of the brain near the bottom and the back, primarily involved in balance and the coordination of movement.
cerebral cortex The outer layer of the cerebrum, where sensory information is processed.
cerebral hemispheres The left and right halves of the cerebrum.
cerebrum (forebrain) The front and upper part of the brain, consisting of two hemispheres and involved in sophisticated, often uniquely human, abilities.
change blindness The failure to notice changes in the visual field simply because a person expects otherwise.
chunking Grouping pieces of information together in a meaningful way to enhance memory.
cilia Tiny scent-seeking threads that extend from olfactory receptor cells through the mucus of your nose.
circadian rhythm The 24-hour cycle on which the brain and body function.
cisgender A person whose gender and sex match.
classical conditioning A form of learning in which animals or people make a connection between two stimuli that have occurred together, such that one predicts the other.
clinical interview A method of personality assessment in which the psychologist engages in conversation with the client.
clinical psychology An applied specialization in which psychologists focus on psychological disorders.
cochlea The spiral fluid-filled structure in the inner ear that sends sound waves to the brain via the auditory nerve.
cocktail party effect The ability to attend to certain stimuli within one sense (such as hearing) over other stimuli within the same sense.
cognition What the brain does with information, including understanding it, organizing it, analyzing it, and communicating it.
cognitive appraisal theory A theory of emotion stating that what the person thinks about a stimulus causes the emotion.
cognitive dissonance The discomfort caused by having an attitude that contradicts another attitude or a behavior.
cognitive distortions Descriptive names for various kinds of irrational thinking.
cognitive map A mental diagram of the physical environment as it is initially explored when no reinforcement is available.
cognitive psychology A psychological perspective that emphasizes cognitive processes such as thinking, language, attention, memory, and intelligence.
cognitive symptoms The disturbed, illogical ways that people with schizophrenia think.
cognitive therapy A psychotherapy approach in which therapists help clients change the way they think about life events.
cognitive-behavioral therapy A hybrid therapy approach that combines an emphasis on logical thinking with the use of conditioning principles to directly change behavior.
collective unconscious Common, inherited memories that are present in the minds of people of every culture.
collectivism A worldview that emphasizes the well-being of the group over the well-being of the individual.
common factors Elements found in all forms of effective psychotherapy that play an important role in client improvement.
common group identity A strategy for fighting prejudice based on the creation of a larger group that includes multiple smaller groups.
community psychology An applied specialization in which psychologists focus on the wellness of entire communities.
companionate love Love characterized by deep commitment and affection, and often experienced later in long-term relationships.

comparative psychology A basic research specialization in which psychologists focus on the behavior of species other than humans.
complementary medicine Health care that complements, or is used along with, conventional medicine.
computed tomography (CT) A technique in which multiple x-rays are combined to make a 3D image of the brain.
concept A mental representation of a category of similar things, actions, or people.
concrete operational stage The third stage in Piaget's theory of development, from about age 7 to about age 11, in which children acquire the ability to think logically about concrete things.
conditioned response The response to a conditioned stimulus acquired through learning.
conditioned stimulus A formerly neutral stimulus that now causes a response because of its link to an unconditioned stimulus.
conditions of worth Requirements that you must meet to earn a person's positive regard.
cones Receptor cells in the retina that detect color when light is plentiful.
confidentiality When a therapist maintains the privacy of client information.
confirmation bias A tendency to prefer information that confirms what a person thought in the first place.
conformity Changes in an individual's behavior to correspond to the behavior of a group of other people.
congruence A match between your real self and your ideal self.
conscientiousness A personality trait emphasizing the tendency to be organized, responsible, and deliberate.
consciousness A person's awareness of his or her self and surroundings.
conservation A mental operation in which an amount or quantity remains the same regardless of the shape it takes.
continuous reinforcement A pattern by which a behavior is reinforced every time it occurs.
control group The group of participants in experimental research who do not receive the treatment that is the focus of the study.
conventional morality A moral decision-making strategy driven by the desire to follow society's norms and laws.
convergent thinking A problem-solving strategy in which a person uses logic to deduce the single best solution.
coping Efforts to reduce or manage an experience of stress.
cornea The thin transparent cover for the whole eye.
coronary heart disease A common and often fatal disease in which the arteries that lead to the heart are clogged or blocked.
corpus callosum The bundle of neurons that connects and allows communication between the two cerebral hemispheres.
correlation coefficient A statistic that shows the relationship between two variables, ranging from highly positive (+1) to highly negative (–1).
correlational research A type of research in which the goal is to determine the relationship between two variables.
correlation–causation fallacy A mistaken belief that when two variables correlate strongly with each other, one must cause the other.
co-sleeping Sleeping in the same room or same bed with another person (usually a caregiver).
counseling psychology An applied specialization in which psychologists focus on improving the functioning of people who are struggling through difficult times in their lives.
counterconditioning A classical conditioning therapy technique in which the trigger for an unwanted response is paired with a new stimulus that prevents the unwanted response.
creativity The capacity to come up with original ideas or approaches to a problem.
critical period A period of time during which a particular developmental task is especially likely to be influenced by outside events.
critical thinking An inquisitive, challenging approach to ideas and assumptions.
cross-sectional design A research design in which people of different ages are compared to each other at the same point in time.
cultural competence A therapist's ability to work sensitively and expertly with clients from diverse backgrounds.
cultural competence The ability to work sensitively and expertly with members of a culturally diverse society.
cultural intelligence A person's ability to live and interact effectively in a multicultural society.
cultural self-awareness The therapist's recognition that his or her perspective is not necessarily that of others.
culture A group of similar people who share beliefs, values, and patterns of behavior.
culture-fair intelligence tests Intelligence tests that aim to reduce or remove any cultural factors that could lead to bias.
cybertherapy Psychotherapy that takes place via technological devices over the Internet.
cyclothymic disorder A long-term, lower-intensity version of bipolar disorder.
decay The dwindling or loss of information from memory due to the passing of time.
decision making Using cognition to choose between available options.
defense mechanisms According to Freud, techniques used by the ego to manage conflict between the id and superego.
deindividuation A loss of identity and accountability experienced by individuals in groups that can lead to atypical behavior.
déjà vu An experience that feels vaguely like it has already happened even though it has not.
delusions Completely false beliefs that a person with schizophrenia believes to be reality.
dendrites The branches at the end of neurons that receive signals from other neurons.
dependent variable (DV) A variable in experimental research that is expected to depend upon the independent variable.
depressants Drugs that slow bodily functions.
depressive and bipolar disorders The category of psychological disorders based on extreme moods or emotional states.
depth perception The ability to judge the distance and depth of objects.
descriptive research A type of research in which the goal is simply to describe a characteristic of the population.
developmental psychology A basic research specialization in which psychologists focus on how people change throughout the lifespan.
developmental psychology The study of the changes to body, mind, and interpersonal interaction that people experience across the life span.
***Diagnostic and Statistical Manual of Mental Disorders* (DSM)** The book in which mental disorders are officially defined.
dialect A group's particular version of a language with its own unique characteristics.
difference threshold (just noticeable difference) The smallest change in a stimulus necessary for a person to detect it at least half of the time.
diffusion of responsibility A decreased sense of obligation to help when others are present.
dimensional model of psychopathology A model of psychopathology in which psychological problems exist on a continuum, as opposed to being fully present or absent.
discrimination Action based on prejudice or stereotypes toward a social group.
discrimination The learning process by which stimuli that are different from the conditioned stimulus fail to cause the same conditioned response.
discriminative stimulus A signal indicating that a particular behavior will be followed by a particular consequence.
display rules Norms within a group about the acceptable verbal and nonverbal expression of emotion.
dissociative amnesia A psychological disorder in which a person becomes unable to recall important information from their past.
dissociative disorders The category of psychological disorders in which the person loses awareness of, or becomes disconnected from, essential parts of the self such as memories, emotions, or identity.
dissociative identity disorder A psychological disorder in which a person exhibits two or more distinct personalities.
divergent thinking A problem-solving strategy in which a person comes up with lots of different possible solutions.
dodo bird verdict A nickname (from *Alice in Wonderland*) for the research finding that different forms of psychotherapy are equally effective.

door-in-the-face technique A persuasion strategy in which one person gets another person to reject a large request before making a smaller one.

double-blind procedure A way of conducting experimental research in which neither the participants nor the researchers are aware of which participants are in the experimental group and which are in the control group.

dream analysis A psychodynamic technique in which the therapist and client attempt to find the underlying meaning of the client's dreams.

drive reduction theory A theory of motivation stating that unmet biological drives cause unpleasant sensations that motivate the person to meet those needs.

dual-process theory The notion that every person possesses two separate types of thinking, one automatic and one deliberate.

durability bias The overestimation of the expected length of the feeling produced by the outcome of a decision.

dynamic sizing The ability to simultaneously know the norm for a group and recognize that the norm might not apply to every member of that group.

eating disorders The category of psychological disorders that involve significant disturbances in behaviors related to eating or food.

echoic memory The auditory sensory memory, or all the information the ears took in during the previous few seconds.

eclectic approach to therapy A strategy in which the psychotherapist selects the best treatment for a particular client based on evidence from studies of similar clients.

educational psychology An applied specialization in which psychologists focus on learning and teaching.

ego According to Freud, the part of the mind that serves as a realistic mediator between the id and superego.

egocentrism The inability to understand a situation from a point of view other than your own.

elaborative rehearsal Adding meaning or associations to information to enhance memory.

Electra complex The childhood experience of desiring the father and resenting the mother.

electroconvulsive therapy (ECT) A biomedical therapy for severe disorders in which an electric current passes through the brain of the client.

electroencephalography (EEG) A technique in which electrodes are placed on the scalp to record electrical activity in the brain.

embryo The prenatal human organism from about 2 weeks to about 2 months after conception.

emerging adulthood A recently proposed developmental stage during which the person gradually moves from adolescence to adulthood.

emotion All aspects of feeling, including changes to the body, behavior, and consciousness.

emotion regulation The ability to manage the type, intensity, length, and expression of one's own emotions.

emotional intelligence A person's ability to sense and manage his or her own emotions as well as the emotions of others.

emotion-focused coping A style of coping with stress that emphasizes changing your emotional reaction to the stressor.

empathy The therapist's ability to sense the client's emotions just as the client would, and to then respond compassionately.

empirical test construction A way to create objective personality tests in which items are included only if different groups respond differently to them.

encoding specificity The effect that contextual information that was present when memory was encoded, such as physical surroundings, has on retrieval.

encoding The entering of information into memory.

endocrine system The set of glands that send hormones throughout the body via the bloodstream.

endorphins The neurotransmitters involved in reducing pain and increasing pleasure.

episodic memory A type of explicit memory consisting of personal firsthand experiences.

evidence-based practice An approach to psychotherapy in which the therapist makes decisions based on a combination of three factors: research evidence, therapist expertise, and client characteristics.

evolutionary psychology A psychological perspective that emphasizes Charles Darwin's theory of evolution as an influence on behavior.

experimental group The group of participants in experimental research who receive the treatment that is the focus of the study.

experimental research A type of research in which the goal is to determine the cause-and-effect relationship between two variables by manipulating one and observing changes in the other.

explicit memory Memory of which one is consciously aware.

exposure therapy A form of behavior therapy based on classical conditioning in which anxiety is treated by gradually exposing the client to the thing or situation that causes the anxiety.

external locus of control The belief that your life is under the control of forces outside of yourself.

extinction The point in the learning process at which the conditioned stimulus no longer causes the conditioned response because it is no longer linked to the unconditioned stimulus.

extralinguistic information Components of language other than the literal meaning of the words.

extrasensory perception (ESP) The debatable notion of perception without sensation.

extraversion A personality trait emphasizing the tendency to be socially outgoing.

extrinsic motivation A desire to perform a behavior to obtain an external reward.

facial feedback theory A theory of emotion stating that one's brain can influence one's emotions by monitoring one's facial expressions.

family therapy Psychotherapy that aims to improve how the family system functions, which in turn will improve the problems of its individual members.

fetal alcohol syndrome A pattern of physical and behavioral abnormalities common in people whose mothers drank alcohol excessively during pregnancy.

fetus The prenatal human organism from about 2 months after conception to birth.

fight-or-flight response An automatic emotional and physical reaction to a perceived threat that prepares one to either attack it or run away from it.

figure–ground organization The tendency to visually distinguish between an object and its background.

five-factor model of personality (Big Five) An explanation of personality that emphasizes five fundamental traits present in all people to varying degrees.

fixation Freud's term for a lingering psychological problem directly related to unsuccessful experience of a particular psychosexual stage.

fixed-interval schedule A reinforcement schedule in which a behavior can be reinforced after a time interval that is consistent and predictable.

fixed-ratio schedule A reinforcement schedule in which a behavior is reinforced after a consistent, predictable number of occurrences.

flashbulb memory A distinctively clear and vivid memory of an emotionally charged and novel event.

flat affect The absence of appropriate emotion.

flow Performing a behavior with complete immersion and enjoyment, or feeling like one is "in the zone."

foot-in-the-door technique A persuasion strategy in which one person gets another person to agree to a small request before asking for a bigger one.

forensic psychology An applied specialization in which psychologists focus on legal and criminal justice issues.

formal operational stage The final stage in Piaget's theory of development, beginning around age 11 and lasting through adulthood, in which the person becomes able to think logically about abstract things.

fovea The area in the center of the retina that contains many cones but no rods.

framing The particular way a question or problem is presented, which can influence how a person responds to it.

free association A psychodynamic technique in which the therapist encourages the client to simply say whatever comes to mind without any censoring at all.
frequency theory The explanation of pitch perception based on the idea that a person hears different pitches because nerve impulses travel with different frequencies through the auditory nerve.
Freudian slips Verbal or behavioral mistakes that reveal unconscious thoughts or wishes.
frontal lobe The part of the cerebral cortex right behind the forehead, involved in complex thinking tasks, planning, purposeful actions, and other advanced functions.
functional fixedness Thinking about something in only the way it is most typically used rather than other possible uses.
functional magnetic resonance imaging (fMRI) A technique in which magnetic fields are used to make images of brain activity.
functionalism A perspective from the early history of psychology that focused on the function of our mental processes and behaviors.
fundamental attribution error Overestimating the importance of traits and underestimating the importance of the situation when explaining the behavior of other people.
gender A person's psychological and behavioral experience of maleness or femaleness.
general adaptation syndrome A widely accepted understanding of the way the body responds to ongoing stress, consisting of the sequence of alarm, resistance, and exhaustion.
general intelligence (*g*) Overall intelligence that applies across all tasks and situations.
generalization The learning process by which stimuli that are similar to the conditioned stimulus cause the same conditioned response.
generalized anxiety disorder A disorder involving anxiety symptoms that persist for a long time across a wide range of situations and activities.
genital stage The fifth and final psychosexual stage, which lasts from puberty through adulthood and focuses on mature, adult sexual relationships.
genuineness The therapist's truthfulness, realness, and honesty, as opposed to falsely playing the therapist role.
gestalt An organized whole that is perceived as different than just the sum of its parts.
ghrelin A hormone that signals feelings of hunger.
giftedness Significantly above-average intelligence.
glial cells The cells that support and protect neurons throughout the brain.
grammar The set of rules within a language.
group polarization The tendency for a group's attitudes to become more extreme as a result of group discussions.
group therapy Psychotherapy conducted with a group of clients and with an emphasis on interpersonal interaction.
groupthink A phenomenon that occurs when group members value getting along with each other more than finding the best solution.
gustation The sense of taste.
hallucinations False sensations or perceptions.
hallucinogens Drugs that produce unrealistic sensations such as hallucinations.
hardiness Behaviors that reflect resilience under stressful circumstances.
hassles The common, minor annoyances or aggravations of day-to-day life.
health psychology A basic research specialization in which psychologists focus on the relationship between mind and body.
heterosexual The sexual orientation of a person who is attracted to members of the other sex.
heuristic An educated guess or rule-of-thumb method of problem solving.
hierarchy of needs An explanation of motivation created by Abraham Maslow based on the idea that certain needs must be satisfied before others.
higher-order conditioning Classical conditioning that involves three or more stimuli.
hippocampus The part of the limbic system involved in memory, especially spatial memory and long-term memory.
homeopathic medicine Health care based on the idea that the human body has the ability to heal itself and characterized by very low-dose medications made from natural sources.
homeostasis Steadiness or balance in the person's bodily state.
homosexual The sexual orientation of a person who is attracted to members of the same sex.
hormones The chemicals made by the glands of the endocrine system that affect certain tissues throughout the body.
hue The color of light, as determined by its wavelength.
humanism A psychological perspective that emphasizes the notion that human nature is generally good and people are naturally motivated to grow toward their own potential.
humanistic theory of personality A theory based on the ideas of Carl Rogers that emphasizes people's inherent tendencies toward healthy, positive growth and self-fulfillment.
hypnosis An altered state of consciousness in which one person, the participant, becomes very suggestible to another person, the hypnotist.
hypothalamus The part of the limbic system involved in maintaining a steadiness in bodily functions.
hypothesis A prediction, typically based on a theory, that can be tested.
iconic memory The visual sensory memory, or all the information the eyes took in during the previous fraction of a second.
id According to Freud, the animalistic part of the mind that generates our most basic, biologically based impulses, such as sex and aggression.
ideal self The self-actualized version of yourself that you naturally strive to become.
identification Process in which the child models himself or herself after the undefeatable same-sex parent.
identity A part of Erikson's psychosocial theory of development; a person's stable sense of who he or she is.
imaginary audience A common way of thinking among adolescents in which they believe their lives are continuously being watched and evaluated by other people.
immune system The body's innate method of defending against bacteria, viruses, infections, injuries, and anything else that could cause illness or death.
implicit memory Memory of which one is not consciously aware.
impression formation The initial appraisal, or "first impression," that a person makes of another person.
inattentional blindness The failure to notice something in your visual field simply because your attention was focused elsewhere.
incentive An object or situation outside the person that the person is motivated to acquire.
incongruence A mismatch between your real self and your ideal self.
independent variable (IV) A variable in experimental research that is manipulated by the researcher.
individualism A worldview that emphasizes the well-being of the individual over the well-being of the group.
industrial/organizational (I/O) psychology An applied specialization in which psychologists focus on the workplace.
information processing model A model of memory that involves the three steps of encoding, storage, and retrieval.
informed consent Permission given by the client, after the therapist educates him or her about the therapy process, to move forward with the therapy.
informed consent to research An ethical requirement for psychologists by which they must inform people about the research and obtain their consent before participation can occur.
ingroup A social group to which a person believes he or she belongs ("us").
ingroup bias The tendency to hold a more positive attitude toward the ingroup than the outgroup.
insight The perception of a solution to a problem that results from cognitive understanding rather than from trial and error.
insomnia A sleep disorder featuring consistent difficulty falling asleep, staying asleep, or achieving high-quality sleep.
instinct A motivation that is biologically innate.
instinct theory A theory of motivation stating that humans, like all other animals, are motivated primarily by instinct.

instinctive drift The tendency of animals' behavior to return to innate, genetically programmed patterns.
integration An acculturation strategy in which the person adopts both the new culture and the old culture.
integrative approach to therapy A strategy in which the psychotherapist blends styles or techniques to create a new form of psychotherapy.
intellectual disability A mental disorder based on significantly below-average intelligence and impaired day-to-day functioning.
intelligence quotient (IQ) A single number used to represent a person's overall intelligence.
intelligence test An assessment technique used by psychologists to numerically measure intelligence.
intelligence The ability to gain knowledge and learn from experience.
intergroup contact A strategy for fighting prejudice based on direct interpersonal interaction between members of multiple groups.
internal locus of control The belief that your life is under the control of forces inside of yourself.
interneurons The neurons that serve only to connect to other nearby neurons, rather than reaching farther out into the body.
interpersonal attraction The desire to enhance a relationship with another person.
interpretation The psychodynamic therapist's attempt to make a connection between the client's unconscious material and his or her current behavior, thoughts, or feelings.
intimacy A part of Erikson's psychosocial theory of development; a long-term emotional closeness with a romantic partner.
intrinsic motivation A desire to perform a behavior because the behavior itself is rewarding.
involuntary memory The spontaneous retrieval of information in the absence of any intention to retrieve it.
iris The colored, circular muscle situated in the center of the eye.
James–Lange theory A theory of emotion stating that the person experiences emotion by noticing bodily changes first and then interpreting them as particular feelings.
jigsaw classroom A strategy for reducing prejudice by giving each student in a diverse group an essential part of the solution to a problem that must be solved via group interaction.
just-world hypothesis The notion that the world is fair and that unfortunate events happen to those who deserve them.
kinesthetic sense The sense of the position and movement of the body parts.
kinship theory An explanation of helping that emphasizes the importance of passing genes on to future generations.
language acquisition device A specific capacity within a person's brain that provides the ability to use language.
language The ability to communicate with others using words or other symbols combined and arranged according to rules.
latency stage Freud's fourth psychosexual stage, which lasts through the elementary school years, when the child's energies are focused primarily on school and other tasks that have little to do with sexual or bodily issues.
latent learning A type of learning that has taken place but cannot be directly observed.
law of effect The observation that a behavior is more likely to be repeated if its effects are desirable but less likely to be repeated if its effects are undesirable.
learned helplessness The absence of any attempt to help oneself that results from previously learning that such attempts are useless.
learning The process by which life experience causes change in the behavior or thinking of an organism.
lens The clear layer beneath the surface of the eye that maintains focus on an object by varying its own shape.
leptin A hormone that signals feelings of fullness.
lesion The damage or destruction of brain tissue.
level of processing How deeply information is processed.
LGBTQ A community of members of sexual minorities, including lesbian (L), gay (G), bisexual (B), transgender (T), queer/questioning (Q), and other people.
limbic system The cluster of brain areas involved primarily in emotion, located near the center of the brain and surrounding the thalamus.
linguistic relativity The theory that language influences thought.
literature review A step in scientific research during which a researcher learns what previous research on the topic already exists.
lobotomy A psychosurgery in which the prefrontal lobes are disconnected from the inner regions of the brain that control emotions.
localization The idea that specific parts of the brain do specific things.
locus of control Your belief about how much control you have over what happens to yourself.
longitudinal design A research design in which the same group of people is compared to itself at different points in time.
long-term memory A seemingly limitless amount of information being held for extensive periods of time.
long-term potentiation The increased connectivity between simultaneously stimulated neurons that forms the biological basis of memory.
lowball technique A persuasion strategy in which one person quotes another person a low price to get an initial agreement and then raises the price.
lucid dreaming A dreaming experience in which a person has some control over the dream while remaining asleep.
magnetic resonance imaging (MRI) A technique in which magnetic fields and radio waves are used to make images of brain structures.
maintenance rehearsal Information repeated in exactly the same form as it was originally encoded.
major depressive disorder A depressive disorder in which a person experiences at least 2 weeks of depressed mood and a loss of interest in most activities.
mania An emotional state of excessively elated mood and overabundant energy.
marginalization An acculturation strategy in which the person rejects both the new culture and the old culture.
medical student syndrome An experience common among medical students, and perhaps psychology students, in which they start to believe that they have the illnesses about which they are learning.
meditation An activity designed to increase focused attention with the ultimate purpose of improving a person's mental state.
medulla The part of the brainstem most specifically involved in heartbeat and breathing.
memory The process of taking in information, saving it over time, and calling it to mind later.
menarche A girl's first menstrual period.
menopause The time in a woman's middle adulthood when she stops having menstrual periods.
mental filtering A cognitive distortion in which the client ignores, or "filters out," the positive while focusing excessively on the negative.
mental set The limits a person places on an approach to problem solving based on what has worked in the past.
mere exposure effect An increase in the attractiveness of a person (or object) resulting from nothing more than repeated contact.
metabolic rate (or metabolism) The rate at which one's body burns energy.
microaggressions Everyday actions or comments that, often unintentionally, contain hostile or off-putting messages for members of certain cultures.
mindfulness Awareness of one's moment-to-moment experiences fully, deliberately, and without distraction.
Minnesota Multiphasic Personality Inventory-2 (MMPI-2) A widely used and respected objective personality test that emphasizes mental disorders.
mirror neurons Neurons that are thought to underlie empathy and imitation and that activate when a person performs or observes a particular behavior.
misinformation effect The tendency of false or misleading information presented after the fact to be mistakenly incorporated into memory.
mnemonic A specific technique or strategy deliberately used to enhance memory.

monocular depth cues The qualities of visual stimuli that indicate depth when using only one eye.
mood-stabilizing drugs Medications used to lessen the extreme emotional highs and lows of bipolar disorder.
morpheme The smallest meaningful unit of a language.
motivation A desire that stimulates and steers behavior.
motor cortex The strip of brain matter near the back of the frontal lobe, involved in voluntary movement.
motor neurons The cells that carry messages from the brain to the muscles.
multiculturalism A psychological perspective that emphasizes the influences of culture on behavior and mental processes.
multiculturalism An approach in psychology that highlights the importance and value of multiple cultural groups within a society.
multimethod assessment An approach to personality assessment that emphasizes the use of multiple methods rather than only one method.
multiple relationship A situation in which a therapist has both a professional relationship and a nonprofessional relationship with the same person.
myelin sheath A protective sleeve of fatty material that surrounds the axon.
narcolepsy A disorder of "sleep attacks" characterized by immediate and unexpected shifts from wakefulness to REM sleep.
nativist theory A theory of language development that says the ability to use language is inborn.
near-death experience An altered state of consciousness caused by the belief that death is about to happen.
negative reinforcement A type of reinforcement that involves removing something undesirable.
negative symptoms Behaviors that are lacking in people with schizophrenia, but that are usually present in people without the disorder.
neo-Freudian theories Theories that revised, but did not entirely reject, the basics of Freud's original psychodynamic theory.
NEO-Personality Inventory-3 (NEO-PI-3) An objective personality test that measures the Big Five personality factors.
nervous system The full set of nerves that connect the brain with all other parts of the body.
neurogenesis The creation of new neurons.
neurons The cells that facilitate communication within the nervous system.
neuroscience A psychological perspective that emphasizes the link between behavior and the biological functioning of the brain.
neuroticism A personality trait emphasizing the tendency to experience negative emotions such as anxiety, depression, and stress.
neurotransmitters The chemical messengers that travel across synapses from one neuron to the next.
neutral stimulus A stimulus that causes no response at all.
nondirective therapy A style of therapy in which the client, rather than the therapist, determines the course of therapy.
non-REM sleep Any sleep other than REM sleep, when rapid eye movement, intense brain activity, and dreams are unlikely to occur.
normal curve A graph showing that the frequency of scores on a test is greatest in the middle and decreases toward the extremes.
obedience Changes in an individual's behavior to comply with the demands of an authority figure.
obesity A BMI of 30 or higher.
object permanence The ability to realize that an object continues to exist even when a person can't see, hear, or otherwise sense it.
objective personality tests Personality tests in which the client responds to a standardized set of questions, usually in multiple choice or true–false format.
observational learning A type of learning that occurs as a result of observing others' behavior and consequences rather than our own.
obsessive-compulsive disorder (OCD) A disorder characterized by unwanted, repetitive thoughts and uncontrollable actions done in response to those thoughts.
occipital lobe The lower back part of the brain, involved in vision.
Oedipus complex The childhood experience of desiring the mother and resenting the father.
olfaction The sense of smell.
olfactory bulbs Brain structures located on the underside of your brain (behind the bridge of your nose) that receive scent information from cilia.
olfactory cortex A collection of brain regions involved in smell, including the amygdala and parts of the cerebral cortex.
one-word stage A stage of speech development during which the young child uses a single word as a full sentence.
openness to experience A personality trait emphasizing the tendency to be organized, responsible, and deliberate.
operant conditioning A form of learning in which the consequences of a voluntary behavior affect the likelihood that the behavior will recur.
operational definition A specific, measurable definition of a variable for the purpose of a scientific study.
opiates Drugs made from the poppy plant that relieve pain.
opponent-process theory of color vision An explanation of color vision based on the idea that the cones are specialized to sense specific opposite pairs of colors (like red–green and blue–yellow).
optimism An attitude toward the future characterized by hope or expectation of a positive outcome.
oral stage The first of Freud's psychosexual stages, which takes place from birth to about 18 months and focuses on the psychological consequences of feeding behavior.
ossicles A chain of very small bones connected in ball-and-socket fashion on the inner side of the tympanic membrane.
outgroup A social group to which a person believes he or she does not belong ("them").
outgroup homogeneity The assumption that all members of an outgroup are essentially similar.
oval window membrane A membrane between the ossicles of the middle ear and the inner ear.
overgeneralization A cognitive distortion in which the client comes to a very broad-based conclusion based on just a single unfortunate event.
overweight A BMI between 25 and 29.9.
panic disorder An anxiety disorder characterized by sudden, intense, unpredictable brief bursts of anxiety.
parapsychology The study of topics that fall outside the range of mainstream psychology.
parasympathetic division The part of the autonomic nervous system that calms the body down when stressors decrease.
parietal lobe The part of the brain near the top and back of the head, involved in touch and perception.
partial reinforcement (intermittent reinforcement) A pattern by which a behavior is reinforced only some of the times it occurs.
participant modeling A technique in which a client watches a model (in some cases, the therapist) perform the target behavior with the intent of the client imitating the model.
passionate love Love characterized by arousal and desire, and often experienced early in relationships.
peak experience A moment of self-actualization that produces strong, often mystical, feelings of personal fulfillment.
peer review process The appraisal of research by people who are at least as expert on the subject as the researcher.
perception The ability of the brain to interpret the raw sensations it has taken in.
perceptual constancy The brain's ability to maintain the same perception of an object even when conditions around it cause it to produce different sensations.
perceptual set The tendency to perceive things in a certain way because of a person's previous experiences or attention strategy.
peripheral nervous system The neurons that connect the central nervous system to other parts of the body.
peripheral route persuasion A persuasion strategy that emphasizes factors other than the message's content.
permissive parenting style An approach to parenting in which parents place minimal demands and allow children to run their own lives.
persistent depressive disorder (dysthymia) A depressive disorder characterized by a chronic, relatively low-intensity depressed mood.

personal fable A common way of thinking among adolescents in which they believe themselves to be special or invulnerable.
personality A person's distinctive and stable way of thinking, feeling, and behaving.
personality disorders The category of psychological disorders based on an enduring pattern of inflexible and maladaptive behavior that appears across a wide range of situations and interferes with interpersonal interaction.
personality psychology A basic research specialization in which psychologists focus on people's personality traits.
personalization A cognitive distortion in which the client takes too much of the blame and responsibility for unfortunate events.
person-centered therapy An approach based on the theories of Carl Rogers that emphasizes the tendency toward healthy growth inherent in each person.
phallic stage The third psychosexual stage, which runs from 3 to 6 years old and focuses on the psychological consequences of attraction to the opposite-sex parent.
phoneme The smallest distinct unit of speech.
physical dependence A bodily need for a particular drug in order to function normally
physiological psychology A basic research specialization in which psychologists focus on the neural basis of behavior.
pinna The outer ear.
pitch The description of how "high" or "low" a sound is.
pituitary gland The "master gland" in the brain that produces human growth hormone and controls all of the other glands in the body.
place theory The explanation of pitch perception based on the idea that a person hears different pitches because tiny hairs in different places within the cochlea are stimulated.
placebo effect The effect of expectations in experimental research rather than the effect of experimental manipulations.
plasticity The ability of the brain to adapt its structure or function in response to damage or experience.
pons The part of the brainstem involved in transmitting information, sleep, breathing, swallowing, and equilibrium.
population The whole range of people on whom a study's research is focused.
positive psychology A perspective in psychology that emphasizes people's strengths and successes.
positive regard Warmth, acceptance, and love from those around a person.
positive reinforcement A type of reinforcement that involves getting something desirable.
positive symptoms Experiences that are present or excessive in people with schizophrenia but largely absent in people without it.
positron emission tomography (PET) A technique in which activity in various brain structures is illustrated by a radioactive sugar injected into the body.
postconventional morality A moral decision-making strategy driven by fundamental rights and ethical principles.
posttraumatic growth When people experience trauma and then find a way to benefit, improve, or enrich themselves from that point onward.
posttraumatic stress disorder (PTSD) A psychological disorder lasting at least a month characterized by feeling continuously on edge, avoiding reminders of the traumatic event, having difficulty sleeping and concentrating, and frequently recalling or reliving the event.
preconventional morality A moral decision-making strategy driven by the potential rewards and punishments of the decision.
prejudice An often negative attitude toward a social group that is formed before getting to know group members.
preoperational stage The second stage in Piaget's theory of development, from about age 2 to about age 7, when children can use language and other symbols for real objects but still can't complete many mental operations.
primacy effect The tendency to remember the first items in a series particularly well.
primary appraisal The way you determine how stressful an event is to you.
primary reinforcer An innate reinforcer that requires no learning to have a reinforcing effect because it satisfies a biological need.
primary sex characteristics The parts of the body directly involved in sexual reproduction, such as genitals, ovaries, and testes.
priming When recent experiences cause an increased likelihood of recalling certain memories.
proactive coping A style of coping that focuses on future goals and the stressors that could impede them.
proactive interference Problems remembering newer information caused by older information.
problem solving Using cognition to find a way to achieve a goal.
problem-focused coping A style of coping with stress that emphasizes changing the stressor itself.
procedural memory A type of implicit memory consisting of how to perform tasks that are done automatically.
projective personality tests Personality tests in which clients respond to ambiguous stimuli in a free-form way.
prosocial behavior Behavior intended to help others.
prototype The most typical or best example within a concept.
pseudopsychology Psychological information that is not supported by science but may appear to be.
psychiatry The medical specialization that focuses on the brain and its disorders.
psychic determinism The belief that all thoughts and behaviors, even those that seem accidental, arbitrary, or mistaken, are determined by psychological forces.
psychoactive drugs Substances that alter mental functioning.
psychoanalysis A psychological perspective created by Sigmund Freud that emphasizes unconscious mental activity and the long-lasting influence of childhood experiences.
psychoanalysis An approach to psychotherapy developed by Sigmund Freud in which the main goal is to make the unconscious conscious—that is, helping the client become more aware of thoughts and feelings of which he or she was unaware at the start of therapy.
psychodynamic theory of personality An explanation of personality, based on the ideas of Sigmund Freud, that emphasizes unconscious forces and early childhood experiences.
psychodynamic therapy A therapy that retains psychoanalysis' goal of making the unconscious conscious, but is briefer and more focused on the client's current life (as opposed to his or her past) than psychoanalysis.
psychological dependence A mental need for a particular drug in order to function normally
psychological disorder A pattern of behavior that interferes with a person's life by causing significant distress or dysfunction.
psychological theory of abnormality A theory of abnormality asserting that psychological factors, including emotions, thoughts, behaviors, and traits, are the primary causes of psychological disorders.
psychology The scientific study of behavior and mental processes.
psychoneuroimmunology (PNI) The study of the relationship between psychological factors, including stress, and the immune system.
psychopharmacology The treatment of psychological disorders with medications.
psychophysiological illnesses Any illness that stress can cause, worsen, or maintain.
psychosexual stages Freud's five biologically based developmental stages of childhood, during which personality characteristics are formed.
psychosis A significant impairment in the basic ability to tell the difference between the real world and imagination.
psychosurgery Surgery performed directly on the brain in an effort to improve severe psychological disorders.
psychotherapy A treatment that involves a mental health professional using various techniques to help a person overcome a psychological disorder or improve some aspect of emotional, cognitive, or behavioral functioning.
puberty The time period featuring physical changes that mark the onset of adolescence and enable sexual reproduction.

punishment Any consequence of a behavior that makes that behavior less likely to recur.
pupil The opening in the middle of the iris.
random assignment A procedure in experimental research by which the assignment of participants into either the experimental or control group happens entirely by chance.
rational-emotive behavior therapy (REBT) A form of cognitive therapy in which the therapist challenges the client's illogical beliefs and encourages the client to adopt more logical beliefs.
real self The version of yourself that you actually experience in day-to-day life.
recall A type of retrieval in which stored information is accessed without any comparison to external information.
recency effect The tendency to remember the last items in a series particularly well.
receptor sites The openings in dendrites that match specific neurotransmitters like a lock fits a specific key.
reciprocal determinism The theory that three factors—behavior, environment, and cognitions—continually influence each other.
reciprocity norm An explanation of helping that emphasizes the expectation that those who provide help will receive help in the future.
recognition A type of retrieval in which stored information is compared to external information to determine if it matches.
reflection A technique in which the therapist listens closely and actively, then restates the client's words in a way that highlights the client's feelings.
reflex An automatic motor response to sensory input.
refractory period A waiting time, during which the neuron is reset before another action potential can begin.
regulatory focus theory A theory of motivation stating that there are two primary motivation systems—promotion and prevention—that affect different people in different ways.
rehearsal Deliberately repeating information to enhance memory.
reinforcement schedule A pattern by which reinforcements occur in response to a particular behavior.
reinforcement Any consequence of a behavior that makes that behavior more likely to recur.
reliability The extent to which an assessment technique provides consistent, repeatable results.
REM Rapid eye movement, or the flitting of the eyeballs behind the eyelids during sleep.
REM paralysis Temporary immobility during REM sleep.
REM rebound An increase in REM sleep after a period of REM sleep deprivation.
REM sleep The stage of sleep in which intense brain activity and vivid dreams are most likely to occur.
replication Conducting a study again to confirm or disconfirm the results.
representativeness heuristic An educated guess based on similarity to a prototype.
resistance Client behavior that blocks discussion or conscious awareness of anxiety-provoking topics.
resting potential The low-level electrical charge in a neuron that is not firing.
reticular activating system The collection of neurons in the brainstem involved in arousal.
retina The rear part of the eyeball, which receives visual stimulation and sends it to the brain via the optic nerve.
retinal disparity (stereopsis) The brain's measurement of the difference between the images of a single object sent by each of the two eyes.
retrieval cues Reminders that facilitate retrieval of information from memory.
retrieval Pulling information out of memory.
retroactive interference Problems remembering older information caused by newer information.
retrograde amnesia The inability to retrieve information that took place before a certain point in time.
reuptake The process when a neurotransmitter is taken back up by the sending neuron after failing to land in a receptor site in the receiving neuron.
rods Receptor cells in the retina that detect shades of gray and allow a person to see in low light.
Rorschach inkblot technique A projective personality test in which the client responds to 10 inkblot images.
sample The subset of the population who actually participate in the research.
scaffolding A process by which a person learns new words, ideas, and ways of thinking by interacting with a more advanced person who provides decreasing levels of help.
scapegoat hypothesis The notion that prejudice can be fueled by the need to find someone to blame.
Schachter–Singer theory A theory of emotion stating that the label one assigns to one's bodily reaction determines one's mental reaction.
schema A concept or mental representation that guides the way a person makes sense of new information.
schizophrenia A severe psychological disorder in which the person exhibits bizarre disturbances in thinking, perception, feelings, and behavior.
scientific method A way of asking and answering questions that follows a predetermined series of steps: posing a question, conducting a literature review, developing a hypothesis, testing the hypothesis by collecting data, and analyzing the data and drawing conclusions.
secondary appraisal The way you determine how capable you are of coping with an event.
secondary reinforcer A reinforcer that requires a learned link to a primary reinforcer to have a reinforcing effect.
secondary sex characteristics The parts of the body that characterize sexual maturation but are not directly involved in reproduction.
selective attention When the brain pays more attention to one sensory channel than others.
self-actualization Fully becoming the person an individual has the potential to become.
self-concept Your view of who you are.
self-determination theory A theory of motivation stating that the strongest and healthiest motivations are those that come from within the person.
self-efficacy Your beliefs about your own capabilities.
self-help group A type of group therapy in which the group members run the session without a professional therapist leading them.
semantic memory A type of explicit memory consisting of facts, figures, word meanings, and other general information.
semantics The rules by which a person extracts meaning from words and sentences.
sensation The ability of the sensory organs to pick up energy in the environment around the body and transmit it to the brain.
sensorimotor stage The first stage in Piaget's theory of development, from birth to about age 2, when babies understand the world through sensory experience.
sensory adaptation The tendency of a person's sensation of a stimulus to decrease when the stimulus remains constant.
sensory conflict theory The theory that explains motion sickness as a byproduct of sensory interaction.
sensory interaction The idea that the senses can influence each other.
sensory memory The earliest part of the memory process, in which the senses take in and very briefly hold information.
sensory neurons The cells that carry information to the brain from the senses (sight, hearing, smell, taste, touch).
separation An acculturation strategy in which the person retains the old culture and rejects the new culture.
serial position effect The tendency to remember the first and last items in a series better than the items in the middle.
set point A particular weight to which the person's body tends to return after increases or decreases.
sex A person's biological maleness or femaleness.
sexual orientation A person's pattern of romantic attraction to a particular group or groups of other people.
shaping The process of gradually learning a complex behavior through the reinforcement of each small step that is a part of the complex behavior.
short-term memory A limited amount of new information being held briefly until it is either discarded or encoded into long-term memory.

Skinner box (originally called an operant chamber) A container into which animals such as pigeons or rats could be placed for the purpose of observing and recording their behavior in response to consequences.
sleep apnea A sleep disorder caused by interruptions of breathing that cause repeated waking.
sleep deprivation The failure to get enough sleep, regardless of the reason.
sleep hygiene Routine behaviors that promote healthy sleep.
sleep terrors Brief, sudden awakenings in which the person feels frightened and confused.
sleepwalking Walking while asleep, or somnambulism.
social anxiety disorder An anxiety disorder characterized by an intense and irrational fear of situations in which one may be judged or scrutinized.
social cognition A person's thoughts about other people and the social world.
social comparison Assessing oneself by determining how one measures up to other people.
social exchange theory An explanation of helping that emphasizes the comparisons of benefits and costs to the individual for helping.
social facilitation An increase in individual performance caused by the presence of other people.
social influence Any way in which the presence of other people influences one's thoughts, feelings, or behavior.
social loafing A decrease in individual performance when tasks are done in groups.
social psychology A basic research specialization in which psychologists focus on how people think about, influence, and relate to each other.
social psychology The scientific study of how people think about, influence, and relate to each other.
social responsibility norm An explanation of helping that emphasizes the notion of duty to help those who need it, regardless of any potential payback to the helper.
social role A title, position, or status that carries expectations for acceptable behavior.
social support The relationships one has with friends, family, and others that can be beneficial when one is experiencing stress.
social-cognitive theory of hypnosis A theory of hypnosis that emphasizes pressure to play the role assigned to a person being hypnotized
social-cognitive theory of personality A theory that emphasizes the interaction of environment, thought processes, and social factors.
social-pragmatic theory Suggests that a child's use of language develops from a desire to interact socially.
sociocultural theory of abnormality A theory of abnormality asserting that social and cultural factors surrounding the person, rather than factors within the person, are the primary causes of psychological disorders.
solitary sleeping Sleep in which only one person is in the bed or in the room.
somatic nervous system The part of the peripheral nervous system that connects the central nervous system to the parts of the body controlled voluntarily.
somatosenses The senses experienced through the skin, primarily touch, temperature, and pain.
somatosensory cortex The strip of brain matter near the front of the parietal lobe, involved in receiving information from the senses.
sound localization The ability to perceive the location from which a sound originates.
source amnesia The inability to remember the source of a particular memory (but not the memory itself) or how it was obtained.
spacing effect The tendency to have better long-term memory for information when attempts to study it are spaced apart rather than crammed together.
specific intelligences (*s*) Intelligences that apply to only a particular area.
specific learning disorder A mental disorder in which achievement in reading, writing, or math is significantly below age expectations.
specific phobia An anxiety disorder characterized by excessive anxiety toward a specific object or situation.
split-brain surgery A surgical procedure in which the corpus callosum is cut, typically to reduce epileptic seizures.
spontaneous recovery After a temporary period of inactivity, the return of a conditioned response that had become extinct.
Stanford-Binet Intelligence Test A widely used and highly respected intelligence test originally developed by Alfred Binet and revised by Lewis Terman and appropriate across the life span.
stem cells Cells that have not yet specialized, and therefore can become a variety of different cells as the need arises.
stereotype threat The expectation that others may judge you according to stereotypes about a group to which you belong.
stereotypes Beliefs about a group's characteristics that are applied very generally, and often inaccurately, to group members.
stimulants Drugs that speed up bodily functions.
storage Retaining information in memory.
stranger anxiety The fear of unfamiliar people that emerges in children at about 8 months of age.
stress An unpleasant physical or psychological reaction to circumstances perceived as challenging.
stressor Any event or change in one's life that causes stress.
structuralism A perspective from the early history of psychology that focused on breaking down mental processes into their structure or basic parts.
superego According to Freud, the part of the mind that opposes the id by enforcing rules, restrictions, and morality.
sympathetic division The part of the autonomic nervous system that revs the body up in response to stressors.
synapse The gap between two connecting neurons.
synaptic vesicles The tiny, saclike containers for neurotransmitters.
syntax The rules by which words are put together to make phrases and sentences.
systematic desensitization A form of behavior therapy, primarily for phobias, in which the client experiences the new pairing of relaxation (rather than anxiety) with the thing or situation that previously caused the anxiety.
temperament The basic emotional responsiveness that characterizes a person throughout his or her life span.
temporal lobe The lower middle part of the brain, involved in hearing and speech production.
teratogen Any substance that harms the embryo or fetus.
test bias The tendency of a test to produce scores in a consistently inaccurate way for members of particular groups.
thalamus The brain's main sensory processing center, located near the center of the brain.
Thematic Apperception Test (TAT) A projective personality test in which the client creates stories in response to cards that show people in undefined situations.
theory A proposed explanation for observed events.
theory of mind The understanding of the thoughts, feelings, intentions and other mental activities of oneself and others.
therapeutic alliance A trusting and collaborative relationship in which therapist and client work toward shared goals.
threshold The level of electrical charge required to trigger an action potential.
token economy A behavior therapy technique in which clients earn tokens that are exchangeable for rewards when they perform target behaviors.
tolerance Decreased effectiveness of a particular amount of a drug.
top-down processing A way of processing information in which expectations or previous experiences influence what a person perceives.
trait theory of personality A theory that emphasizes the discovery and description of the basic components of personality.
traits Stable elements of personality that influence thoughts, feelings, and behavior across most situations.
transcranial magnetic stimulation (TMS) A treatment for depression in which weak electric current repeatedly pulses through a paddle-shaped magnetic coil just outside the person's head.
transduction The conversion of energy outside the body, like light or sound, into neural energy, like brain activity.

transference A client's unconscious and unrealistic expectations for the therapist to behave like an important person from the client's past.
transgender A person whose gender and sex do not match.
transition To take steps to live as the gender that matches one's identity rather than one's biologically assigned gender.
trichromatic theory of color vision An explanation of color vision based on the idea that the cones are specialized to sense either red, green, or blue.
triple vulnerability theory An explanation for anxiety disorders that emphasizes the interaction of biological factors, general psychological factors, and specific psychological factors.
tympanic membrane A surface stretched taut across the ear canal to form the boundary between the outer ear and the middle ear.
Type A personality A personality featuring high levels of competitiveness, drive, impatience, and hostility.
Type B personality A personality in which the person is noncompetitive, easygoing, relaxed, and rarely angry.
Type C personality A personality featuring a low level of emotional expression, a high level of agreeableness with other people, and a tendency to feel helpless.
Type D personality A personality featuring high levels of negative emotions, like depression and anxiety, and a reluctance to share those emotions with others.
unconditional positive regard The therapist's full acceptance of the client without any conditions or limitations.
unconditioned response The automatic response to a stimulus that occurs naturally, without any need for learning.
unconditioned stimulus A stimulus that causes a response automatically, without any need for learning.
unconscious (unconscious mind) Mental activity of which the person is unaware.
validity The extent to which an assessment technique measures what it claims to measure.
variable-interval schedule A reinforcement schedule in which a behavior can be reinforced after a time interval that is inconsistent and unpredictable.
variable-ratio schedule A reinforcement schedule in which a behavior is reinforced after an inconsistent, unpredictable number of occurrences.
vestibular sense The sense of balance.
vicarious conditioning Conditioning that takes place via observation of others' life experiences rather than one's own.
virtual reality exposure therapy A form of exposure therapy in which the client experiences the situation that causes him or her anxiety via electronic means.
vision The sense of sight.
visual accommodation The process by which the lens changes shape to focus on objects at varying distances from the eyes.
Wechsler Intelligence Tests A widely used and highly respected set of intelligence tests originally developed by David Wechsler.
Wernicke's aphasia The dysfunction in understanding or creating coherent speech caused by damage to Wernicke's area.
Wernicke's area The part of the temporal lobe specifically involved in understanding speech.
withdrawal Stressful and uncomfortable symptoms caused by discontinuing a drug that had become habitual.
working memory A type of memory in which processing, or work, is done on briefly held information.
working through A lengthy phase of psychodynamic therapy in which interpretations are repeated, reconsidered, and given a chance to gradually sink in.
worldview A comprehensive, culturally influenced way of approaching and understanding the world around you.
Yerkes–Dodson law The finding that moderate levels of arousal are linked to higher levels of performance than high or low levels of arousal.
zygote The prenatal human organism from the moment the egg is fertilized by sperm to about 2 weeks.

transference A client's unconscious and irrational reactions toward the therapist as though the therapist were a significant figure from the client's past.

transduction The process by which the sensory receptors convert stimuli into neural impulses that are sent to the brain.

trichromatic theory A theory of color vision that proposes there are three kinds of cones.

triarchic theory of intelligence A theory that proposes three kinds of intelligence.

tympanic membrane The eardrum; a membrane located between the outer ear and the middle ear.

Type A personality A personality type characterized by high levels of competitiveness, impatience, and hostility.

Type B personality A person with a relatively relaxed, easygoing personality.

Type C personality A personality type characterized by being cooperative, unassertive, and patient.

Type D personality A personality type characterized by high levels of negative affectivity and social inhibition.

unconditional positive regard The therapist's unconditional acceptance of the client.

unconditioned response An unlearned response to an unconditioned stimulus.

unconditioned stimulus A stimulus that naturally produces a response without learning.

unconscious In Freud's theory, the part of the mind that holds thoughts and feelings outside of awareness.

variable-interval schedule A reinforcement schedule in which the first correct response after a variable amount of time is reinforced.

variable-ratio schedule A reinforcement schedule in which reinforcement follows a variable number of correct responses.

vestibular sense The sense of balance.

vicarious conditioning Conditioning that occurs through observing others.

virtual reality exposure therapy A form of exposure therapy in which the client is exposed to the feared stimulus in a computer-generated environment.

vision The sense of sight.

visual accommodation The process in which the lens changes shape to focus light on the retina.

Wechsler Intelligence Tests A widely used and highly respected series of intelligence tests developed by David Wechsler.

Wernicke's aphasia A language disorder caused by damage to Wernicke's area.

Wernicke's area An area in the temporal lobe of the brain involved in understanding language.

withdrawal The physical and psychological symptoms that occur when a person stops using a drug.

working memory A type of memory in which information is actively processed.

working through A healing process in psychoanalytic therapy.

worldview A framework or set of beliefs through which a person views the world.

Yerkes-Dodson law The principle that performance is best at moderate levels of arousal.

zygote The single cell formed when a sperm fertilizes an ovum.

References

Abar, B., LaGasse, L. L., Derauf, C., Newman, E., Shah, R., Smith, . . ., Lester, B. M. (2013). Examining the relationships between prenatal methamphetamine exposure, early adversity, and child neurobehavioral disinhibition. *Psychology of Addictive Behaviors, 27*(3), 662.

Abbey, A., & McAuslan, P. (2004). A longitudinal examination of male college students' perpetration of sexual assault. *Journal of Consulting and Clinical Psychology, 72*(5), 747–756.

Abbey, A., McAuslan, P., & Ross, L. T. (1998). Sexual assault perpetration by college men: The role of alcohol, misperception of sexual intent, and sexual beliefs and experiences. *Journal of Social and Clinical Psychology, 17*(2), 167–195.

Abbey, A., McAuslan, P., Zawacki, T., Clinton, A. M., & Buck, P. O. (2001). Attitudinal, experiential, and situational predictors of sexual assault perpetration. *Journal of Interpersonal Violence, 16*(8), 784–807.

Abbey, A., Ross, L. T., McDuffie, D., & McAuslan, P. (1996). Alcohol and dating risk factors for sexual assault among college women. *Psychology of Women Quarterly, 20*(1), 147–169.

Abbey, A., Wegner, R., Woerner, J., Pegram, S. E., & Pierce, J. (2014). Review of survey and experimental research that examines the relationship between alcohol consumption and men's sexual aggression perpetration. *Trauma, Violence, & Abuse, 15*(4), 265–282.

Abbey, A., Zawacki, T., Buck, P. O., Clinton, A. M., & McAuslan, P. (2004). Sexual assault and alcohol consumption: What do we know about their relationship and what types of research are still needed? *Aggression and Violent Behavior, 9*(3), 271–303.

Abe, K., Amatomi, M., & Oda, N. (1984). Sleepwalking and recurrent sleeptalking in children of childhood sleepwalkers. *The American Journal of Psychiatry, 141*, 800–801.

Abe, K., Oda, N., Ikenaga, K., & Yamada, T. (1993). Twin study on night terrors, fears and some physiological and behavioural characteristics in childhood. *Psychiatric Genetics, 3*(1), 39–44.

Abel, E. L., & Kruger, M. L. (2010). Smile intensity in photographs predicts longevity. *Psychological Science, 21*(4), 542–544.

Abraham, R. (2005). Emotional intelligence in the workplace: A review and synthesis. In R. Schulze and R. D. Roberts, *Emotional intelligence: An international handbook* (pp. 255–270). Cambridge, MA: Hogrefe & Huber Publishers.

Abramowitz, J. S., & Mahaffey, B. L. (2011). The obsessive-compulsive disorder spectrum. In D. H. Barlow (Ed.), *The Oxford handbook of clinical psychology* (pp. 311–333). New York, NY: Oxford University Press.

Abramowitz, J. S., Fabricant, L. E., & Jacoby, R. J. (2015). Exposure-based therapies. In R. L. Cautin & S. O. Lilienfeld (Eds.), *The Encyclopedia of Clinical Psychology* (pp. 1183–1189). West Sussex, UK: Wiley-Blackwell.

Abrams, M. T., Patchan, K. M., Boat, T. F., & Institute of Medicine (U.S.). (2003). *Research training in psychiatry residency: Strategies for reform*. Washington, D.C: National Academies Press.

Abrams, R. (2002). *Electroconvulsive therapy* (4th ed.). New York, NY: Oxford University Press.

Ackerman, P. L. (2013). Personality and cognition. In S. Kreitler (Ed.), *Cognition and motivation: Forging an interdisciplinary perspective* (pp. 62–75). Cambridge, UK: Cambridge University Press.

Ackerman, P. L., & Heggestad, E. D. (1997). Intelligence, personality, and interests: Evidence for overlapping traits. *Psychological Bulletin, 121*(2), 219–245.

Ackerman, S. J., Fowler, J. C., & Clemence, A. J. (2008). TAT and other performance-based assessment techniques. In R. P. Archer & S. R. Smith (Eds.), *Personality assessment* (pp. 337–378). New York, NY: Routledge.

Adams, K. F., Schatzkin, A., Harris, T. B., Kipnis, V., Mouw, T., Ballard-Barbash, R., . . . Leitzmann, M. F. (2006). Overweight, obesity, and mortality in a large prospective cohort of persons 50 to 71 years old. *New England Journal of Medicine, 355*(8), 763–778.

Ader, R., & Cohen, N. (1982). Behaviorally conditioned immunosuppression and murine systemic lupus erythematosus. *Science, 215*(4539), 1534–1536.

Ader, R., Mercurio, M. G., Walton, J., James, D., Davis, M., Ojha, V., . . . Fiorentino, D. (2010). Conditioned pharmacotherapeutic effects: A preliminary study. *Psychosomatic Medicine, 72*(2), 192–197.

Adler, A. (1927). *Understanding human nature*. New York, NY: Greenburg.

Adler, A. (1928). *The practice and theory of individual psychology*. New York, NY: Greenburg.

Adler, A., Bliese, P., & Castro, C. (Eds.) (2011). *Deployment psychology: Evidence-based strategies to promote mental health in the military*. Washington, DC: American Psychological Association.

Adolph, K. E., & Berger, S. E. (2005). Physical and motor development. In M. H. Bornstein & M. E. Lamb (Eds.), *Developmental science: An advanced textbook* (5th ed., pp. 223–281). Mahwah, NJ: Lawrence Erlbaum.

Adolph, K. E., & Berger, S. E. (2006). Motor development. In D. Kuhn & R. Siegler (Vol. Eds.), *Handbook of child psychology* (6th ed., Vol. 2, pp. 161–213). Hoboken, NJ: Wiley.

Adolphs, R., Tranel, D., Damasio, H., & Damasio, A. (1994). Impaired recognition of emotion in facial expressions following bilateral damage to the human amygdala. *Nature, 372*(6507), 669–672.

Adolphs, R., Tranel, D., Hamann, S., Young, A. W., Calder, A. J., Phelps, E. A., . . . Damasio, A. R. (1999). Recognition of facial emotion in nine individuals with bilateral amygdala damage. *Neuropsychologia, 37*(10), 1111–1117.

Affleck, G., & Tennen, H. (1996). Construing benefits from adversity: Adaptational significance and dispositional underpinnings. *Journal of Personality, 64*(4), 899–922.

Afifi, T. O., Mota, N. P., Dasiewicz, P., MacMillan, H. L., & Sareen, J. (2012). Physical punishment and mental disorders: Results from a nationally representative U.S. sample. *Pediatrics, 130*, 184–192.

Agnew, R. (2012). Dire forecast: A theoretical model of the impact of climate change on crime. *Theoretical Criminology, 16*(1), 21–42.

Agras, W. S. (2010). Introduction and overview. In W. S. Agras (Ed.), *The Oxford handbook of eating disorders* (pp. 1–6). New York, NY: Oxford University Press.

Agrawal, Y., Platz, E. A., & Niparko, J. K. (2008). Prevalence of hearing loss and differences by demographic characteristics among U.S. adults: Data from the National Health and Nutrition Examination Survey, 1999–2004. *Archives of Internal Medicine, 168*(14), 1522–1530.

Agrawal, Y., Platz, E. A., & Niparko, J. K. (2009). Risk factors for hearing loss in U.S. adults: Data from the National Health and Nutrition Examination Survey, 1999 to 2002. *Otology & Neurotology, 30*(2), 139–145.

Ahlskog, J. E., Geda, Y. E., Graff-Radford, N. R., & Petersen, R. C. (2011, September). Physical exercise as a preventive or disease-modifying treatment of dementia and brain aging. *Mayo Clinic Proceedings, 86*(9), 876–884.

Ahn, W., Proctor, C. C., & Flanagan, E. H. (2009). Mental health clinicians' beliefs about the biological, psychological, and environmental bases of mental disorders. *Cognitive Science, 33*(2), 147–182.

Ainsworth, M. D. S., Blehar, M. C., Waters, E., & Wall, S. (1978). *Patterns of attachment*. Hillsdale, NJ: Lawrence Erlbaum.

Ainsworth, M. S. (1989). Attachments beyond infancy. *American Psychologist, 44*, 709–716.

Ainsworth, M., and Bowlby, J. (1965). *Child care and the growth of love*. London, UK: Penguin Books.

Aitchison, J. 1996. *The seeds of speech: Language origin and evolution*. Cambridge, UK: Cambridge University Press.

Ajzen, I. (2000). Nature and operation of attitudes. *Annual Review of Psychology, 52*, 27–58

Ajzen, I. (2012). Attitudes and persuasion. In K. Deaux & M. Snyder (Eds.), *The Oxford handbook of personality and social psychology* (pp. 367–393). New York, NY: Oxford University Press.

Åkerstedt, T., & Kecklund, G. (2012). Sleep, work, and occupational stress. In C. M. Morin & C. A. Espie (Eds.), *The Oxford handbook of sleep and sleep disorders* (pp. 248–265). Oxford, UK: Oxford University Press.

Akmajian, A., Demers, R. A., Farmer, A. K., & Harnish, R. M. (2010). *Linguistics: An introduction to language and communication* (6th ed.). Cambridge, MA: MIT Press.

Alavi, S. B., & Sanderson, W. C. (2015). Mechanisms of action in psychotherapy. In R. L. Cautin & S. O. Lilienfeld (Eds.), *The encyclopedia of clinical psychology* (pp. 1745–1751). West Sussex, UK: Wiley-Blackwell.

Albarracín, D., & Vargas, P. (2010). Attitudes and persuasion: From biology to social responses to persuasive intent. In S. T. Fiske, D. T. Gilbert, & G. Lindzey (Eds.), *Handbook of social psychology* (5th ed., Vol. 1, pp. 394–427). Hoboken, NJ: Wiley.

Alberts, A., Elkind, D., & Ginsberg, S. (2007). The personal fable and risk-taking in early adolescence. *Journal of Youth and Adolescence, 36*(1), 71–76.

Albright, T. D. (2013). High-level visual processing: Cognitive influences. In E. R. Kandel, J. H. Schwartz, T. M. Jessell, S. A. Siegelbaum, & A. J. Hudspeth (Eds.), *Principles of neural science* (5th ed., pp. 621–637). New York, NY: McGraw-Hill.

Aldridge, A. A., & Roesch, S. C. (2007). Coping and adjustment in children with cancer: A meta-analytic study. *Journal of Behavioral Medicine, 30*(2), 115–129.

Aldwin, C. (2011). Stress and coping across the lifespan. In S. Folkman, *Oxford handbook of stress, health, and coping* (pp. 15–34). Oxford, UK: Oxford University Press.

Aleman, A., Hijman, R., de Haan, E. H., & Kahn, R. S. (1999). Memory impairment in schizophrenia: A meta-analysis. *American Journal of Psychiatry, 156*(9), 1358–1366.

Alexander, F., & Selesnick, S. T. (1966). *The history of psychiatry: An evaluation of psychiatric thought and practice from prehistoric times to the present*. New York, NY: Harper & Row.

Alexander, G. M., Wilcox, T., & Woods, R. (2009). Sex differences in infants' visual interest in toys. *Archives of Sexual Behavior, 38*(3), 427–433.

Alfredo Martínez, J., Enríquez, L., Moreno-Aliaga, M. J., & Marti, A. (2007). Genetics of obesity. *Public Health Nutrition, 10*(10A), 1138–1144.

Allard, F., & Burnett, N. (1985). Skill in sport. *Canadian Journal of Psychology, 39*, 294–312.

Allen, J., Vaage, A. B., & Hauff, E. (2006). Refugees and asylum seekers in societies. In D. L. Sam, & J. W. Berry (Eds.), *The Cambridge handbook of acculturation psychology* (pp. 198–217). New York, NY: Cambridge University Press.

Allen, M., Witt, P. L., & Wheeless, L. R. (2006). The role of teacher immediacy as a motivational factor in student learning: Using meta-analysis to test a causal model. *Communication Education, 55*(1), 21–31.

Allen, P., Larøi, F., McGuire, P. K., & Aleman, A. (2008). The hallucinating brain: A review of structural and functional neuroimaging studies of hallucinations. *Neuroscience & Biobehavioral Reviews, 32*(1), 175–191.

Allison, R., & Risman, B. J. (2013). A double standard for "hooking up": How far have we come toward gender equality? *Social Science Research, 42*(5), 1191–1206.

Alloway, T. P. (2011). *Training your brain for dummies*. Chichester, UK: Wiley.

Alloway, T. P., & Alloway, R. (2013). *The working memory advantage: Train your brain to function stronger, smarter, faster*. New York, NY: Simon & Schuster.

Alloway, T. P., & Gathercole, S. (2005). Working memory and short-term sentence recall in young children. *European Journal of Cognitive Psychology, 17*(2), 207–220.

Alloway, T. P., Gathercole, S. E., Adams, A. M., Willis, C., Eaglen, R., & Lamont, E. (2005). Working memory and phonological awareness as predictors of progress towards early learning goals at school entry. *British Journal of Developmental Psychology, 23*(3), 417–426.

Allport, G. W. (1937). *Personality: A psychological interpretation.* New York, NY: Holt, Rinehart, & Winston.

Allport, G. W. (1954). *The nature of prejudice*. New York, NY: Addison-Wesley.

Allport, G. W., & Odbert, H. S. (1936). Trait-names: A psycho-lexical study. *Psychological Monographs, 47*(1), i–171.

Alpizar, K., Islas-Alvarado, R., Warren, C. R., & Fiebert, M. S. (2012). Gender, sexuality and impression management on Facebook. *International Review of Social Sciences and Humanities, 4*(1), 121–125.

Altus, D. E., & Morris, E. K. (2009). B. F. Skinner's utopian vision: Behind and beyond *Walden Two*. *Journal of Applied Behavioral Analysis, 32*, 319–335.

Alzheimer's Association (2013). Fact Sheet, March 2013. Retrieved July 13, 2013, from http://www.alz.org/documents_custom/2013_facts_figures_fact_sheet.

Amaral, D. G. (2013). The functional organization of perception and movement. In E. R. Kandel, J. H. Schwartz, T. M. Jessell, S. A. Siegelbaum, & A. J. Hudspeth (Eds.), *Principles of neural science* (5th ed., pp. 356–369). New York, NY: McGraw-Hill.

Amaral, D. G., & Strick, P. L. (2013). The organization of the central nervous system. In E. R. Kandel, J. H. Schwartz, T. M. Jessell, S. A. Siegelbaum, & A. J. Hudspeth (Eds.), *Principles of neural science* (5th ed., pp. 337–355). New York, NY: McGraw-Hill.

Amato, P. R. (2010). Research on divorce: Continuing trends and new developments. *Journal of Marriage and Family, 72*(3), 650–666.

Ambady, N., Hallahan, M., & Conner, B. (1999). Accuracy of judgments of sexual orientation from thin slices of behavior. *Journal of Personality and Social Psychology, 77*(3), 538–547.

Amen, D., Hanks, C., Prunella, J., & Green, A. (2007). An analysis of regional cerebral blood flow in impulsive murderers using single photon emission computed tomography. *Journal of Neuropsychiatry and Clinical Neurosciences, 19*(3), 304–309.

American Psychiatric Association. (1952). *Diagnostic and statistical manual of mental disorders.* Washington, DC: American Psychiatric Association Publishing.

American Psychiatric Association. (1968). *Diagnostic and statistical manual of mental disorders: DSM-II.* Washington, DC: American Psychiatric Association Publishing.

American Psychiatric Association (2013). *Diagnostic and statistical manual of mental disorders: DSM-5.* Washington, DC: American Psychiatric Association.

American Psychological Association. (2002). Ethical principles of psychologists and code of conduct. *American Psychologist, 57,* 1060–1073.

American Psychological Association. (2005). *Guidelines and principles for accreditation of programs in professional psychology*. Retrieved from www.apa.org/ed/G&P052.pdf

American Psychological Association (2007). *APA guidelines for the undergraduate psychology major*. Washington, DC: American Psychological Association.

American Psychological Association (2007). Stress tip sheet. Retrieved from http://www.apa.org/helpcenter/stress-tips.aspx

American Psychological Association. (2007). *Getting in: A step-by-step plan for gaining admission to graduate school in psychology* (2nd ed.). Washington, DC: American Psychological Association.

American Psychological Association. (2010). *Ethical principles of psychologists and code of conduct, including 2010 amendments*. Retrieved from http://apa.org/ethics/code/index.aspx

American Psychological Association. (2013). APA guidelines for the undergraduate psychology major: Version 2.0. Washington, DC: American Psychological Association.

American Psychological Association (2014). Stress in America: Are teens adopting adults' stress habits? Retrieved from http://www. apa.org/news/press/releases/stress/2013/stress-report.pdf

American Psychological Association (2014). *Who we are*. Retrieved from http://www.apa.org/about/apa/index.aspx

American Psychological Association Task Force on the Sexualization of Girls. (2010). *Report of the APA Task Force on the Sexualization of Girls*. Retrieved from http://www.apa.org/pi/women/programs/girls/report-full.pdf.

American Sleep Apnea Association (2015). Personal stories: Bill's story—it was a big deal after all. Retrieved from http://www.sleepapnea.org/learn/personal-stories/bills-story.html

Ames, C. (1992). Classrooms: Goals, structures, and student motivation. *Journal of Educational Psychology, 84*(3), 261–271.

Ames, C., & Archer, J. (1987). Mothers' beliefs about the role of ability and effort in school learning. *Journal of Educational Psychology, 79*(4), 409–414.

Ames, C., & Archer, J. (1988). Achievement goals in the classroom: Students' learning strategies and motivation processes. *Journal of Educational Psychology, 80*(3), 260–267.

Aminoff, E. M., Balslev, D., Borroni, P., Bryan, R. E., Chua, E. F., Cloutier, J., . . . Yamada, M. (2009). The landscape of cognitive neuroscience: Challenges, rewards, and new perspectives. In M. S. Gazzaniga (Ed.), *The cognitive neurosciences* (4th ed., pp. 1255–1292). Cambridge, MA: MIT Press.

Amodio, D. M., Harmon-Jones, E., Devine, P. G., Curtin, J. J., Hartley, S. L., & Covert, A. E. (2004). Neural signals for the detection of unintentional race bias. *Psychological Science, 15*(2), 88–93.

Amrutkar, C., Woodward, M., Shah, H., Benedict, R., Rajakrishnan, S., Doody, R., . . . Szigeti, K. (2015). Validation of olfactory deficit as a biomarker of Alzheimer's disease, *Neurology, 84*(14 Suppl. P2-170).

Anand, R., & Lahiri, I. (2009). Intercultural competence in health care. In D. K. Deardorff (Ed.), *The SAGE handbook of intercultural competence* (pp. 387–402). Thousand Oaks, CA: SAGE.

Anderman, E. M., Griesinger, T., & Westerfield, G. (1998). Motivation and cheating during early adolescence. *Journal of Educational Psychology, 90*(1), 84–93.

Andersen, M. L., Poyares, D., Alves, R. S., Skomro, R., & Tufik, S. (2007). Sexsomnia: Abnormal sexual behavior during sleep. *Brain Research Reviews, 56*(2), 271–282.

Andersen, S. M., Moskowitz, G. B., Blair, I. V., & Nosek, B. A. (2007). Automatic thought. In A. W. Kruglanski & E. T. Higgins (Eds.), *Social psychology: Handbook of basic principles* (2nd ed., pp. 138–175). New York, NY: Guilford Press.

Anderson, C. A. (2001). Heat and violence. *Current Directions in Psychological Science, 10*(1), 33–38.

Anderson, C. A., Anderson, K. B., Dorr, N., DeNeve, K. M., & Flanagan, M. (2000). Temperature and aggression. *Advances in Experimental Social Psychology, 32*, 63–133.

Anderson, C. A., Arciniegas, D. B., Hall, D. A., & Filley, C. M. (2013). Behavioral neuroanatomy. In D. B. Arciniegas, C. A. Anderson, & C. M. Filley (Eds.), *Behavioral neurology & neuropsychiatry* (pp. 12–31). Cambridge, UK: Cambridge University Press.

Anderson, C. A., Benjamin, A. J., Jr., & Bartholow, B. D. (1998). Does the gun pull the trigger? Automatic priming effects of weapon pictures and weapon names. *Psychological Science, 9*(4), 308–314.

Anderson, C. A., Bushman, B. J., & Groom, R. W. (1997). Hot years and serious and deadly assault: Empirical tests of the heat hypothesis. *Journal of Personality and Social Psychology, 73*(6), 1213–1223.

Anderson, C. A., & Bushman, B. J. (2001). Effects of violent video games on aggressive behavior, aggressive cognition, aggressive affect, physiological arousal, and prosocial behavior: A meta-analytic review of the scientific literature. *Psychological Science, 12*(5), 353–359.

Anderson, C. A., Shibuya, A., Ihori, N., Swing, E. L., Bushman, B. J., Sakamoto, A., . . . Saleem, M. (2010). Violent video game effects on aggression, empathy, and prosocial behavior in eastern and western countries: A meta-analytic review. *Psychological Bulletin, 136*(2), 151–173.

Anderson, J. L., Crawford, C. B., Nadeau, J., & Lindberg, T. (1992). Was the Duchess of Windsor right? A cross-cultural review of the socioecology of ideals of female body shape. *Ethology and Sociobiology, 13*(3), 197–227.

Anderson, K. J., & Leaper, C. (1998). Meta-analyses of gender effects on conversational interruption: Who, what, when, where, and how. *Sex Roles, 39*(3–4), 225–252.

Anderson, N. D., & Craik, F. I. M. (2000). Memory in the aging brain. In E. Tulving & F. I. M. Craik (Eds.), *The Oxford handbook of memory* (pp. 411–425). Oxford, UK: Oxford University Press.

Anderson, S. E., Cohen, P., Naumova, E. N., Jacques, P. F., & Must, A. (2007). Adolescent obesity and risk for subsequent major depressive disorder and anxiety disorder: Prospective evidence. *Psychosomatic Medicine, 69*(8), 740–747.

Anderson, S. K., & Kitchener, K. S. (1996). Nonromantic, nonsexual posttherapy relationships between psychologists and former clients: An exploratory study of critical incidents. *Professional Psychology: Research and Practice, 27*(1), 59–66.

Anderson, S. W., & Rizzo, M. (1994). Hallucinations following occipital lobe damage: The pathological activation of visual representations. *Journal of Clinical and Experimental Neuropsychology, 16*(5), 651–663.

Anderson, V. L., Levinson, E. M., Barker, W., & Kiewra, K. R. (1999). The effects of meditation on teacher perceived occupational stress, state and trait anxiety, and burnout. *School Psychology Quarterly, 14*(1), 3–25.

Andersson, G. (2015). Computerized psychotherapy. In R. L. Cautin & S. O. Lilienfeld (Eds.), *The encyclopedia of clinical psychology* (pp. 712–716). West Sussex, UK: Wiley-Blackwell.

Andersson, G. (2016). Internet-delivered psychological treatments. *Annual Review of Clinical Psychology, 12*, 157–179.

Andia, A. N., Zisook, S., Heaton, R. K., Hesselink, J., Jernigan, T., Kuck, J., . . . Braff, L. (1995). Gender differences in schizophrenia. *Journal of Nervous and Mental Disease, 183*(8), 522–528.

Andrade, M., & Menna-Baretto, L. (2002). Sleep patterns of high school students living in Sao Paulo, Brazil. In M. A. Carskadon (Ed.), *Adolescent sleep patterns:*

Biological, social, and psychological factors (pp. 118–131). New York, NY: Cambridge University Press.
Andre, L. (2009). *Doctors of deception: What they don't want you to know about shock treatment*. New Brunswick, NJ: Rutgers University Press.
Andreasen, N. C. (1987). Creativity and mental illness. *American Journal of Psychiatry, 144*(10), 1288–1292.
Ang, S., & Van Dyne, L. (2008). Conceptualization of cultural intelligence: Definition, distinctiveness, and nomological networks. In S. Ang & L. Van Dyne (Eds.), *Handbook of cultural intelligence: Theory, measurement, and applications* (pp. 3–15). New York, NY: M. E. Sharpe.
Ang, S., Van Dyne, L., & Ling Tan, M. (2011). Cultural intelligence. In R. J. Sternberg & S. B. Kaufman (Eds.), *The Cambridge handbook of intelligence* (pp. 582–602). Cambridge, UK: Cambridge University Press.
Ang, S., Van Dyne, L., Koh, C., Ng, K.-Y., Templer, K. J., Tay, C., & Chandrasekar, N. A. (2007). Cultural intelligence: Its measurement and effects on cultural judgment and decision making, cultural adaptation and task performance. *Management and Organization Review, 3*(3), 335–371.
Angell, J. R. (1907). The province of functional psychology. *Psychological Review, 14*(2), 61–91.
Anglin, J. M. (1993). Vocabulary development: A morphological analysis. *Monographs of the Society for Research in Child Development, 58*, 1–165.
Angrilli, A., Mauri, A., Palomba, D., Flor, H., Birbaumer, N., Sartori, G., & di Paola, F. (1996). Startle reflex and emotion modulation impairment after a right amygdala lesion. *Brain, 119*(6), 1991–2004.
Antony, M. M., & Barlow, D. H. (Eds.). (2010). *Handbook of assessment and treatment planning for psychological disorders* (2nd ed.). New York, NY: Guilford Press.
Anzman, S. L., Rollins, B. Y., & Birch, L. L. (2010). Parental influence on children's early eating environments and obesity risk: Implications for prevention. *International Journal of Obesity, 34*, 1116–1124.
APA Presidential Task Force on Evidence-Based Practice. (2006). Evidence-based practice in psychology. *American Psychologist, 61*, 271–285.
Arber, S., Bote, M., & Meadows, R. (2009). Gender and socio-economic patterning of self-reported sleep problems in Britain. *Social Science & Medicine, 68*(2), 281–289.
Arber, S., Meadows, R., & Venn, S. (2012). Sleep and society. In C. M. Morin & C. A. Espie (Eds.), *The Oxford handbook of sleep and sleep disorders* (pp. 223–247). Oxford, UK: Oxford University Press.
Arch, J., & Craske, M. G. (2008). Panic disorder. In W. E. Craighead, D. J. Milkowitz, & L. W. Craighead (Eds.), *Psychopathology: History, diagnosis, and empirical foundations* (pp. 115–158). Hoboken, NJ: Wiley.
Arch, J. J., & Landy, L. N. (2015). Emotional benefits of mindfulness. In K. W. Brown, J. D. Creswell, & R. M. Ryan (Eds.), *Handbook of mindfulness: Theory, research, and practice* (pp. 208–224). New York, NY: Guilford Press.
Archer, J., & Coyne, S. M. (2005). An integrated review of indirect, relational, and social aggression. *Personality and Social Psychology Review, 9*(3), 212–230.
Archer, R. P. (2005). MMPI-A: Assessing adolescent psychopathology (3rd ed.). Mahwah, NJ: Lawrence Erlbaum.
Archer, R. P., & Newsom, C. R. (2000). Psychological test usage with adolescent clients: Survey update. *Assessment, 7*(3), 227–235.
Arciniegas, D. B. (2013). Executive function. In D. B. Arciniegas, C. A. Anderson, & C. M. Filley (Eds.), *Behavioral neurology & neuropsychiatry* (pp. 225–249). Cambridge, UK: Cambridge University Press.
Arden, J. B., & Linford, L. (2009). *Brain-based therapy with adults: Evidence-based treatment for everyday practice*. Hoboken, NJ: Wiley.
Ariely, D., Loewenstein, G., & Prelec, D. (2003). Coherent arbitrariness: Stable demand curves without stable preferences. *Quarterly Journal of Economics, 118*, 73–105.
Arkes, H. R. (1991). Costs and benefits of judgment errors: Implications for debiasing. *Psychological Bulletin, 110*(3), 486–498.
Arkowitz, H., Miller, W. R., & Rollnick, S. (2015). *Motivational interviewing in the treatment of psychological problems* (2nd ed.) New York, NY: Guilford Press.
Arnett, J. J. (2000). Emerging adulthood: A theory of development from the late teens through the twenties. *American Psychologist, 55*(5), 469.
Arnett, J. J. (2007). Emerging adulthood: What is it, and what is it good for? *Child Development Perspectives, 1*(2), 68–73.
Aronson, E. (1978). *The jigsaw classroom*. Beverly Hills: SAGE.
Aronson, E. (1999). Dissonance, hypocrisy, and the self-concept. In E. Harmon-Jones & J. Mills (Eds.), *Cognitive dissonance: Progress on a pivotal theory in social psychology* (pp. 103–126). Washington, DC: American Psychological Association.
Aronson, E. (2002). Building empathy, compassion, and achievement in the jigsaw classroom. In J. Aronson (Ed.), *Improving academic achievement: Impact of psychological factors on education* (pp. 209–225). San Diego, CA: Academic Press.
Aronson, E., Wilson, T. D., & Akert, R. M. (2013). *Social psychology* (8th ed.). Boston: Pearson.
Arredondo, P., Toporek, R., Brown, S. P., Jones, J., Locke, D. C., Sanchez, J., & Stadler, H. (1996). Operationalization of the multicultural counseling competencies. *Journal of Multicultural Counseling and Development, 24*(1), 42–78.
Arrigo, J. M., & Pezdek, K. (1998). Textbook models of multiple personality: Source, bias, and social consequences. In S. J. Lynn & K. M. McConkey (Eds.), *Truth in memory* (pp. 372–393). New York, NY: Guilford Press.
Artal, P. (2010). Eye: Structure and optics. In E. B. Goldstein (Ed.), *Encyclopedia of perception*(pp. 413–416). Thousand Oaks, CA: SAGE.
Artal, P., Benito, A., & Tabernero, J. (2006). The human eye is an example of robust optical design. *Journal of Vision, 6*(1), 1–7.
Artman, L. K., & Daniels, J. A. (2010). Disability and psychotherapy practice: Cultural competence and practical tips. *Professional Psychology: Research and Practice, 41*(5), 442–448.
Arzi, A., & Sobel, N. (2010). Spatial perception: Time tells where a smell comes from. *Current Biology, 20*(13), R563–R564.
Asamen, J. K., & Berry, G. L. (2012). Television, children, and multicultural awareness: Comprehending the medium in a complex multimedia society. In D. G. Singer & J. L. Singer (Eds.), *Handbook of children and the media* (2nd ed., pp. 363–377). Los Angeles, CA: SAGE.
Asch, S. E. (1951). Effects of group pressure upon the modification and distortion of judgments. In M. Henle (Ed.), *Documents of Gestalt psychology* (pp. 222–236). Berkeley, CA: University of California Press.
Asch, S. E. (1955). Opinions and social pressure. *Scientific American,193*(5), 31–35.
Asch, S. E. (1956). Studies of independence and conformity: I. A minority of one against a unanimous majority. *Psychological Monographs: General and Applied, 70*(9), 1–70.
Aschoff, J. (1965). Circadian rhythms in man: A self-sustained oscillator with an inherent frequency underlies human 24-hour periodicity. *Science, 148*, 1427–1432.
Aserinsky, E., & Kleitman, N. (1953). Regularly occurring periods of eye motility, and concomitant phenomena, during sleep. *Science, 118*(3062), 273–274.
Asher, G., & Sassone-Corsi, P. (2015). Time for food: The intimate interplay between nutrition, metabolism, and the circadian clock. *Cell, 161*(1), 84–92.
Ashford, S. J., Blatt, R., & VandeWalle, D. (2003). Reflections on the looking glass: A review of research on feedback-seeking behavior in organizations. *Journal of Management, 29*, 769–799.
Ashford, S., Edmunds, J., and French, D. P. (2010). What is the best way to change self-efficacy to promote lifestyle and recreational physical activity? A systematic review with meta-analysis. *British Journal of Health Psychology, 15*, 265–288. doi:10.1348/135910709X461752
Ashton, M. C., & Lee, K. (2008). The HEXACO model of personality structure. In G. J. Boyle, G. Matthews, & D. H. Saklofske (Eds.), *The SAGE handbook of personality theory and assessment* (Vol. 2, pp. 239–260). Thousand Oaks, CA: SAGE.
Askelson, N. M., Campo, S., & Smith, S. (2012). Mother–daughter communication about sex: The influence of authoritative parenting style. *Health Communication, 27*(5), 439–448.
Asmal, L., & Stein, D. J. (2009). Anxiety and culture. In M. M. Antony & M. B. Stein (Eds.), *Oxford handbook of anxiety and related disorders* (pp. 657–664). New York, NY: Oxford University Press.
Aspinwall, L. G. (1997). Where planning meets coping: Proactive coping and the detection and management of potential stressors. In S. L. Friedman & E. K. Scholnick (Eds.), *The developmental psychology of planning: Why, how, and when do we plan?* (pp. 285–320). Hillside, NJ: Lawrence Erlbaum.
Aspinwall, L. G. (2003). Dealing with adversity: Self-regulation, coping, adaptation, and health. In A. Tesser & N. Schwarz (Eds.), *Blackwell handbook of social psychology: Intraindividual processes* (pp. 591–614). Malden: MA: Wiley-Blackwell.
Aspinwall, L. G. (2005). The psychology of future-oriented thinking: From achievement to proactive coping, adaptation, and aging. *Motivation and Emotion, 29*(4), 203–235.
Aspinwall, L. G. (2011). Future-oriented thinking, proactive coping, and the management of potential threats to health and well-being. In S. Folkman (Ed.), *Oxford handbook of stress, health, and coping* (pp. 334–365). Oxford, UK: Oxford University Press.
Aspinwall, L. G., & Taylor, S. E. (1997). A stitch in time: Self-regulation and proactive coping. *Psychological Bulletin, 121*(3), 417–436.
Athappilly, G. K., Greyson, B., & Stevenson, I. (2006). Do prevailing societal models influence reports of near-death experiences?: A comparison of accounts reported before and after 1975. *The Journal of Nervous and Mental Disease, 194*(3), 218–222.
Atkinson, D. R., Casas, A., & Abreu, J. (1992). Mexican-American acculturation, counselor ethnicity and cultural sensitivity, and perceived counselor competence. *Journal of Counseling Psychology, 39*(4), 515–520.
Atkinson, J. W. (1964). *An introduction to motivation.* Princeton, NJ: Van Nostrand.
Atkinson, R. C., & Shiffrin, R. M. (1968). Human memory: A proposed system and its control processes. *The Psychology of Learning and Motivation, 2*, 89–195.
Ator, N. A. (1991). Subjects and instrumentation. In I. H. Iverson & K. A. Lattal (Eds.), *Experimental analysis of behavior* (Pt. 1, pp. 1–62). Amsterdam, Netherlands: Elsevier.
Au, R., Appleman, E. R., & Stavitsky, K. (2013). Systematic strategies: Case of school start times. In A. R. Wolfson & H. Montgomery-Downs (Eds.), *The Oxford handbook of infant, child, and adolescent sleep and behavior* (pp. 559–571). New York, NY: Oxford University Press.
Aubin, T., & Jouventin, P. (1998). Cocktail-party effect in king penguin colonies. *Proceedings of the Royal Society of London. Series B: Biological Sciences, 265*(1406), 1665–1673.
Aubin, T., & Jouventin, P. (2002). How to vocally identify kin in a crowd: The penguin model. *Advances in the Study of Behavior, 31*, 243–277.
Auger, R. R. (2006). Sleep-related eating disorders. *Psychiatry (Edgmont), 3*(11), 64–70.
Auger, R. R., & Morgenthaler, T. I. (2006). Sleep-related eating disorders. In T. L. Lee-Chiong (Ed.), *Sleep: A comprehensive handbook* (pp. 457–462). Hoboken, NJ: Wiley-Liss.
Augustine, A. A., Larsen, R. J., & Lee, H. (2013). Affective personality traits and cognition: Interactions between extraversion/neuroticism, affect, and cognition.

In M. D. Robinson, E. Watkins, & E. Harmon-Jones, *Handbook of cognition and emotion* (pp. 312–328). New York, NY: Guilford Press.

Auld, M. C., & Powell, L. M. (2009). Economics of food energy density and adolescent body weight. *Economica, 76*(304), 719–740.

Austenfeld, J. L., & Stanton, A. L. (2004). Coping through emotional approach: A new look at emotion, coping, and health-related outcomes. *Journal of Personality, 72*(6), 1335–1364.

Austin, E. J., & Saklofske, D. H. (2005). Far too many intelligences? On the communalities and differences between social, practical, and emotional intelligences. In R. Schulze and R. D. Roberts (Eds.), *Emotional intelligence: An international handbook* (pp. 107–128). Cambridge, MA: Hogrefe & Huber Publishers.

Averbach, E., & Sperling, G. (1961). Short-term storage of information in vision. In C. Cherry (Ed.), *Information theory* (pp. 196–211). London, UK: Butterworth.

Awh, E., Jonides, J., & Reuter-Lorenz, P. A. (1998). Rehearsal in spatial working memory. *Journal of Experimental Psychology: Human Perception and Performance, 24*(3), 780–790.

Awh, E., Jonides, J., Smith, E. E., Buxton, R. B., Frank, L. R., Love, T., . . . Gmeindl, L. (1999). Rehearsal in spatial working memory: Evidence from neuroimaging. *Psychological Science, 10*(5), 433–437.

Axtell, R. E. (2007). *Essential do's and taboos: The complete guide to international business and leisure travel.* Hoboken, NJ: Wiley.

Ayduk, Ö., Gyurak, A., & Luerssen, A. (2008). Individual differences in the rejection–aggression link in the hot sauce paradigm: The case of rejection sensitivity. *Journal of Experimental Social Psychology, 44*(3), 775–782.

Ayearst, L. E. & Bagby, R. M. (2010). Evaluating the psychometric properties of psychological measures. In M. M. Antony & D. H. Barlow (Eds.), *Handbook of assessment and treatment planning for psychological disorders* (2nd ed., pp. 23–61). New York, NY: Guilford Press.

Ayers, C. R., Thorp, S. R., & Wetherell, J. L. (2009). Anxiety disorders and hoarding in older adults. In M. M. Antony & M. B. Stein (Eds.), *Oxford handbook of anxiety and related disorders* (pp. 625–635). New York, NY: Oxford University Press.

Azar, S. T. (2003). Adult development and parenthood: A social-cognitive perspective. In J. Demick & C. Andreoletti (Eds.), *Handbook of adult development* (pp. 417–431). New York, NY: Kluwer.

Aziz-Zadeh, L., Kaplan, J. T., & Iacoboni, M. (2009). "Aha!": The neural correlates of verbal insight solutions. *Human Brain Mapping, 30*(3), 908–916.

Babkin, B. P. (1949). *Pavlov: A biography*. Chicago, IL: University of Chicago Press.

Back, M. D., Stopfer, J. M., Vazire, S., Gaddis, S., Schmukle, S. C., Egloff, B., & Gosling, S. D. (2010). Facebook profiles reflect actual personality, not self-idealization. *Psychological Science, 21*(3), 372–374.

Baddeley, A. (1994). The magical number seven: Still magic after all these years? *Psychological Review, 101*(2), 353–356.

Baddeley, A. (2000). Short-term and working memory. In E. Tulving & F. I. M. Craik (Eds.), *The Oxford handbook of memory* (pp. 77–92). Oxford, UK: Oxford University Press.

Baddeley, A. D. (2002). The psychology of memory. In A. D. Baddeley, M. D. Kopelman, & B. A. Wilson (Eds.), *The handbook of memory disorders* (2nd ed., pp. 3–15). Chichester, UK: Wiley.

Baddeley, A. (2003). Working memory: Looking back and looking forward. *Nature Reviews Neuroscience, 4*(10), 829–839.

Baddeley, A. D. (2004). *Your memory: A user's guide*. London, UK: Carlton.

Baddeley, A. (2007). Working memory: Multiple models, multiple mechanisms. In H. L. Roediger, Y. Dudai, & S. M. Fitzpatrick (Eds.), *Science of memory: Concepts* (pp. 151–153). Oxford, UK: Oxford University Press.

Baddeley, A. D., & Hitch, G. (1974). Working memory. *The Psychology of Learning and Motivation, 8*, 47–89.

Baddeley, A. D., Eysenck, M. W., & Anderson, M. C. (2009). *Memory*. Hove, UK: Psychology Press.

Baer, J., Kaufman, J. C., & Baumeister, R. F. (Eds.). (2008). Are we free? *Psychology and free will*. New York, NY: Oxford University Press.

Baer, R. A. (2003). Mindfulness training as a clinical intervention: A conceptual and empirical review. *Clinical Psychology: Science and Practice, 10*(2), 125–143.

Baer, R. A. (Ed.). (2006) *Mindfulness-based treatment approaches: Clinician's guide to evidence base and applications*. Amsterdam, Netherlands: Elsevier, Academic Press.

Bahrick, H. P. (2000). Long-term maintenance of knowledge. In E. Tulving & F. I. M. Craik (Eds.), *The Oxford handbook of memory* (pp. 347–362). Oxford, UK: Oxford University Press.

Bailey, A. A., & Hurd, P. L. (2005). Finger length ratio (2D: 4D) correlates with physical aggression in men but not in women. *Biological Psychology, 68*(3), 215–222.

Bailey, D. R. (2006). Oral devices therapy for obstructive sleep apnea. In T. L. Lee-Chiong (Ed.), *Sleep: A comprehensive handbook* (pp. 373–379). Hoboken, NJ: Wiley-Liss.

Bailey, J. M., Dunne, M. P., & Martin, N. G. (2000). Genetic and environmental influences on sexual orientation and its correlates in an Australian twin sample. *Journal of Personality and Social Psychology, 78*(3), 524–536.

Bailey, J. M., Pillard, R. C., Dawood, K., Miller, M. B., Farrer, L. A., Trivedi, S., & Murphy, R. L. (1999). A family history study of male sexual orientation using three independent samples. *Behavior Genetics, 29*(2), 79–86.

Baillargeon, R. (1987). Object permanence in 3½- and 4½-month-old infants. *Developmental Psychology, 23*(5), 655–664.

Baillargeon, R. (2004). Infants' reasoning about hidden objects: Evidence for event-general and event-specific expectations. *Developmental Science, 7*(4), 391–414.

Baillargeon, R., & Graber, M. (1987). Where's the rabbit? 5-month-old infants' representation of the height of a hidden object. *Cognitive Development, 2*(4), 375–392.

Baillargeon, R., & Graber, M. (1988). Evidence of location memory in 8-month-old infants in a nonsearch AB task. *Developmental Psychology, 24*(4), 502–511.

Baillargeon, R., Graber, M., DeVos, J., & Black, J. (1990). Why do young infants fail to search for hidden objects? *Cognition, 36*(3), 255–284.

Baillargeon, R., Li, J., Gertner, Y., & Wu, D. (2011). How do infants reason about physical events? In U. Goswami (Ed.), *The Wiley-Blackwell handbook of childhood cognitive development* (2nd ed., pp. 11–48). Malden, MA: Wiley-Blackwell.

Baillargeon, R., Spelke, E. S., & Wasserman, S. (1985). Object permanence in five-month-old infants. *Cognition, 20*(3), 191–208.

Bair, D. (2004). *Jung: A biography*. New York, NY: Back Bay Books.

Baker, D. B., & Benjamin, L. T., Jr. (2012). Concluding thoughts on internationalizing the history of psychology. In D. B. Baker (Ed.), *The Oxford handbook of the history of psychology: Global perspectives* (pp. 616–624). New York, NY: Oxford University Press.

Baker, F. C., & Driver, H. S. (2004). Self-reported sleep across the menstrual cycle in young, healthy women. *Journal of Psychosomatic Research, 56*(2), 239–243.

Baker, F. C., & Driver, H. S. (2007). Circadian rhythms, sleep, and the menstrual cycle. *Sleep Medicine, 8*(6), 613–622.

Baker, J. R., Bezance, J. B., Zellaby, E., & Aggleton, J. P. (2004). Chewing gum can produce context-dependent effects upon memory. *Appetite, 43*(2), 207–210.

Baker, L. A., Raine, A., Liu, J., & Jacobson, K. C. (2008). Differential genetic and environmental influences on reactive and proactive aggression in children. *Journal of Abnormal Child Psychology, 36*(8), 1265–1278.

Baker, L. D., Frank, L. L., Foster-Schubert, K., Green, P. S., Wilkinson, C. W., McTiernan, A.,. . . & Craft, S. (2010). Effects of aerobic exercise on mild cognitive impairment: A controlled trial. *Archives of Neurology, 67*(1), 71.

Baker, M. C. (2001). Syntax. In M. Aronoff & J. Rees-Miller (Eds.), *The handbook of linguistics* (pp. 265–294). Malden, MA: Blackwell.

Balch, W. R., Bowman, K., & Mohler, L. A. (1992). Music-dependent memory in immediate and delayed word recall. *Memory & Cognition, 20*(1), 21–28.

Balch, W. R., & Lewis, B. S. (1996). Music-dependent memory: The roles of tempo change and mood mediation. *Journal of Experimental Psychology: Learning, Memory, and Cognition, 22*(6), 1354–1363.

Baldwin, D., & Meyer, M. (2007). How inherently social is language? In E. Hoff & M. Shatz (Eds.), *Blackwell handbook of language development* (pp. 87–106). Malden, MA: Blackwell.

Ball, H. L., Hooker, E., & Kelly, P. J. (1999). Where will the baby sleep? Attitudes and practices of new and experienced parents regarding cosleeping with their newborn infants. *American Anthropologist, 101*(1): 143–151.

Balon, R., Martini, S., & Singareddy, R. K. (2004). Patient perspective on collaborative treatment. *Psychiatric Services, 55*, 945–946.

Baltes, P. B., Lindenberger, U., & Staudinger, U. M. (2006). Life span theory in developmental psychology. In R. M. Lerner (Vol. Ed.), *Handbook of child psychology* (6th ed., Vol. 1, pp. 569–664). Hoboken, NJ: Wiley.

Banaji, M. R., & Heiphetz, L. (2010). Attitudes. In S. T. Fiske, D. T. Gilbert, & G. Lindzey (Eds.), *Handbook of social psychology* (5th ed., Vol. 1, pp. 353–393). Hoboken, NJ: Wiley.

Bandelow, B., & Baldwin, D. S. (2010). Pharmacotherapy for panic disorder. In D. J. Stein, E. Hollander, & B. O. Rothbaum (Eds.), *Textbook of anxiety disorders* (2nd ed., pp. 399–416). Washington, D.C.: American Psychiatric Publishing.

Bandettini, P. A. (2012). Twenty years of functional MRI: The science and the stories. *Neuroimage, 62*(2), 575–588.

Bandura, A. (1965). Influence of models' reinforcement contingencies on the acquisition of imitative responses. *Journal of Social Psychology, 1*, 589–595.

Bandura, A. (1977a). Self-efficacy: Toward a unifying theory of behavioral change. *Psychological Review, 84*(2), 191–215.

Bandura, A. (1977b). *Social learning theory*. Englewood Cliffs, NJ: Prentice Hall.

Bandura, A. (1982). Self-efficacy mechanism in human agency. *American Psychologist, 37*(2), 122–147.

Bandura, A. (1986). *Social foundations of thought and action: A social-cognitive theory*. Englewood Cliffs, NJ: Prentice-Hall.

Bandura, A. (1997). *Self-efficacy: The exercise of control*. New York, NY: W. H. Freeman.

Bandura, A. (2001). Social-cognitive theory: An agentic perspective. *Annual Review of Psychology, 52*, 1–26.

Bandura, A., Ross, D., & Ross, S. A. (1961). Transmission of aggression through imitation of aggressive models. *Journal of Abnormal and Social Psychology, 63*, 575–582.

Bandura, A., Ross, D., & Ross, S. A. (1963). Imitation of film-mediated aggressive models. *Journal of Abnormal and Social Psychology, 66*, 3–11.

Banich, M. T. (2009). Executive function: The search for an integrated account. *Current Directions in Psychological Science, 18*(2), 89–94.

Banker, B. S., & Gaertner, S. L. (1998). Achieving stepfamily harmony: An intergroup-relations approach. *Journal of Family Psychology, 12*(3), 310–325.

Banuazizi, A., & Movahedi, S. (1975). Interpersonal dynamics in a simulated prison: A methodological analysis. *American Psychologist, 30*, 152–160.

Barabasz, A. F., & Barabasz, M. (2008). Hypnosis and the brain. In M. R. Nash & A. J. Barnier (Eds.), *The Oxford handbook of hypnosis: Theory, research, and practice* (pp. 337–364). Oxford, UK: Oxford University Press.

Barad, M. (2005). Fear extinction in rodents: Basic insight to clinical promise. *Current Opinion in Neurobiology, 15*(6), 710–715.

Barash, D. P. (1983). *Sociobiology and behavior*. New York, NY: Elsevier.

Barber, C. (2008). *Comfortably numb: How psychiatry is medicating a nation*. New York, NY: Pantheon.

Bard, P. (1928). A diencephalic mechanism for the expression of rage with special reference to the central nervous system. *American Journal of Physiology, 84*, 490–513.

Bard, P. (1934). The neuro-humoral basis of emotional reactions. In C. Murchinson (Ed.), *Handbook of general experimental psychology* (pp. 264–311). Worcester, MA: Clark University Press.

Bard, P., & Rioch, D. M. (1937). A study of four cats deprived of neocortex and additional portions of the forebrain. *The Johns Hopkins Medical Journal, 60*, 73–153.

Bardia, A., Bauer, B. A., & Loprinzi, C. L. (2009). Cancer. In B. P. Jacobs & K. Gundling (Eds.), *The ACP evidence-based guide to complementary and alternative medicine* (pp. 77–100). Philadelphia, PA: American College of Physicians.

Barenbaum, N. B., & Winter, D. G. (2008). History of modern personality theory and research. In O. P. John, R. W. Robins, & L. A. Pervin (Eds.), *Handbook of personality: Theory and research* (3rd ed., pp. 3–27). New York, NY: Guilford.

Barker, E. T., & Galambos, N. L. (2003). Body dissatisfaction of adolescent girls and boys: Risk and resource factors. *The Journal of Early Adolescence, 23*(2), 141–165.

Barkley, R. A. (1997). Behavioral inhibition, sustained attention, and executive functions: Constructing a unifying theory of ADHD. *Psychological Bulletin, 121*(1), 65–94.

Barkley, R. A. (2015). Etiologies of ADHD. In R. A. Barkley (Ed.). Attention-deficit *hyperactivity disorder: A handbook for diagnosis and treatment* (4th ed., pp. 356–390). New York, NY: Guilford Press.

Barlow, D. H. (2002). *Anxiety and its disorders: The nature and treatment of anxiety and panic* (2nd ed.). New York, NY: Guilford Press.

Barlow, D. H., Allen, L. B., & Basden, S. L. (2007). Psychological treatments for panic disorders, phobias, and generalized anxiety disorder. In P. E. Nathan & J. M. Gorman (Eds.), *A guide to treatments that work* (3rd ed., pp. 351–394). New York, NY: Oxford University Press.

Barlow, D. H., Bullis, J. R., Comer, J. S., & Ametaj, A. A. (2013). Evidence-based psychological treatments: An update and a way forward. *Annual Review of Clinical Psychology, 9*, 1–27.

Barnes, A. (2004). Race, schizophrenia, and admission to state psychiatric hospitals. *Administration and Policy in Mental Health, 31*(3), 241–252.

Barnes, D. E., & Yaffe, K. (2011). The projected effect of risk factor reduction on Alzheimer's disease prevalence. *The Lancet: Neurology, 10*(9), 819–828.

Barnes, P. M., Powell-Griner, E., McFann, K., & Nahin, R. L. (2004, June). Complementary and alternative medicine use among adults: United States, 2002. *Seminars in Integrative Medicine, 2*(2), 54–71.

Barnes, S., Brown, K. W., Krusemark, E., Campbell, W. K., & Rogge, R. D. (2007). The role of mindfulness in romantic relationship satisfaction and responses to relationship stress. *Journal of Marital and Family Therapy, 33*(4), 482–500.

Barnier, A. J., & McConkey, K. M. (1998). Posthypnotic responding: Knowing when to stop helps to keep it going. *International Journal of Clinical and Experimental Hypnosis, 46*(2), 204–219.

Barnier, A. J., & Nash, M. R. (2008). Introduction: A roadmap for explanation, a working definition. In M. R. Nash & A. J. Barnier (Eds.), *The Oxford handbook of hypnosis: Theory, research, and practice* (pp. 1–20). Oxford, UK: Oxford University Press.

Baron-Cohen, S. (1995). *Mindblindness: An essay on autism and theory of mind*. Cambridge, MA: MIT Press.

Baron-Cohen, S. (2000). Theory of mind and autism: A review. *International Review of Research in Mental Retardation, 23*, 169–184.

Baron-Cohen, S., Jolliffe, T., Mortimore, C., and Robertson, M. (1997). Another advanced test of theory of mind: Evidence from very high functioning adults with autism or Asperger syndrome. *Journal of Child Psychology and Psychiatry, 38*, 813–822.

Baron-Cohen, S., Leslie, A. M., & Frith, U. (1985). Does the autistic child have a "theory of mind"? *Cognition, 21*(1), 37–46.

Barr, H., Bookstein, F., O'Malley, K., Connor, P., Huggins, J., & Streissguth, A. (2006). Binge drinking during pregnancy as a predictor of psychiatric disorders on the Structured Clinical Interview for DSM-IV in young adult offspring. *American Journal of Psychiatry, 163*(6), 1061–1065.

Barr, J. T. (2005). History and development of contact lenses. In E. S. Bennett & B. A. Weissman (Eds.), *Clinical contact lens practice* (pp. 1–10). Philadelphia, PA: Lippincott Williams & Wilkins.

Barrash, J., Tranel, D., & Anderson, S. W. (2000). Acquired personality disturbances associated with bilateral damage to the ventromedial prefrontal region. *Developmental Neuropsychology, 18*(3), 355–381.

Barrett, L. F., & Bliss-Moreau, E. (2009). She's emotional. He's having a bad day: Attributional explanations for emotion stereotypes. *Emotion, 9*(5), 649–658.

Barrett, L., Dunbar, R., & Lycett, J. (2002). *Human evolutionary psychology*. Basingstoke, UK: Palgrave.

Barrick, M. R., & Mount, M. K. (1991). The big five personality dimensions and job performance: A meta-analysis. *Personnel Psychology, 44*(1), 1–26.

Barringer, M., & Saenz, A. (2007). Promoting positive school environments: A career in school psychology. In R. J. Sternberg (Ed.), *Career paths in psychology: Where your degree can take you* (2nd ed., pp. 227–248). Washington, DC: American Psychological Association.

Barrouillet, P., Gavens, N., Vergauwe, E., Gaillard, V., & Camos, V. (2009). Working memory span development: A time-based resource-sharing model account. *Developmental Psychology, 45*(2), 477.

Barsaglini, A., Sartori, G., Benetti, S., Pettersson-Yeo, W., & Mechelli, A. (2014). The effects of psychotherapy on brain function: A systematic and critical review. *Progress in Neurobiology, 114*, 1–14.

Barsalou, L. W. (1983). Ad hoc categories. *Memory Cognition, 11*(3), 211–227.

Barsalou, L. W. (1985). Ideals, central tendency, and frequency of instantiation as determinants of graded structure in categories. *Journal of Experimental Psychology: Learning, Memory, and Cognition, 11*(4), 629–654.

Barsalou, L. W. (2003). Situated simulation in the human conceptual system. *Language and Cognitive Processes, 18*(5–6), 513–562.

Barsalou, L. W. (2012). The human conceptual system. In M. Spivey, K. McRae, & M. Joanisse (Eds.), *The Cambridge handbook of psycholinguistics* (pp. 239–258). New York, NY: Cambridge University Press.

Bartels, M., Rietveld, M. J. H., Van Baal, G. C. M., & Boomsma, D. I. (2002). Genetic and environmental influences on the development of intelligence. *Behavior Genetics, 32*(4), 237–249.

Bartoshuk, L. M., Duffy, V. B., & Miller, I. J. (1994). PTC/PROP tasting: Anatomy, psychophysics, and sex effects. *Physiology & Behavior, 56*(6), 1165–1171.

Bartsch, K., & Wellman, H. M. (1997). *Children talk about the mind*. New York, NY: Oxford University Press.

Barušs, I. (2003). *Alterations of consciousness: An empirical analysis for social scientists*. Washington, DC: American Psychological Association.

Basile, K. C. (2005). Sexual violence in the lives of girls and women. In K. A. Kendall-Tackett (Ed.), *Handbook of women, stress, and trauma* (pp. 101–122). New York, NY: Brunner-Routledge.

Basow, S. A. (2010). Gender in the classroom. In J. C. Chrisler & D. R. McCreary (Eds.), *Handbook of gender research in psychology* (pp. 277–295). New York, NY: Springer Science+Business Media.

Bassok, M., & Novick, L. R. (2012). Problem solving. In K. J. Holyoak and R. G. Morrison (Eds.), *The Oxford handbook of thinking and reasoning* (pp. 413–432). Oxford, UK: Oxford University Press.

Bates, C. J., Prentice, A., & Finch, S. (1999). Gender differences in food and nutrient intakes and status indices from the National Diet and Nutrition Survey of people aged 65 years and over. *European Journal of Clinical Nutrition, 53*(9), 694–699.

Batey, M., & Furnham, A. (2008). The relationship between measures of creativity and schizotypy. *Personality and Individual Differences, 45*(8), 816–821.

Batson, C. D., & Shaw, L. L. (1991). Evidence for altruism: Toward a pluralism of prosocial motives. *Psychological Inquiry, 2*(2), 107–122.

Batty, G. D., Deary, I. J., & Gottfredson, L. S. (2007). Premorbid (early life) IQ and later mortality risk: Systematic review. *Annals of Epidemiology, 17*(4), 278–288.

Bauer, P. J., Larkina, M., & Deocampo, J. (2011). Early memory development. In U. Goswami (Ed.), *The Wiley-Blackwell handbook of childhood cognitive development* (2nd ed., pp. 153–179). Malden, MA: Wiley-Blackwell.

Bauman, A. E., van der Ploeg, H. P., Chey, T., & Sholler, G. (2006). The hazards of watching football—are Australians at risk? *Medical Journal of Australia, 185*(11/12), 684–686.

Bauman, S., & Tatum, T. (2009). Web sites for young children: Gateway to online social networking? *Professional School Counseling, 13*(1), 1–10.

Baumann, N., & Pham Dinh, D. (2001). Biology of oligodendrocyte and myelin in the mammalian central nervous system. *Physiological, 81*(2), 871–927.

Baumeister, A., & Francis, J. (2002). Historical development of the dopamine hypothesis of schizophrenia. *Journal of the History of the Neurosciences, 11*(3), 265–277.

Baumeister, R. F. (2013). Writing a literature review. In M. J. Prinstein (Ed.), *The portable mentor: Expert guide to a successful career in psychology* (pp. 119–132). New York, NY: Springer.

Baumeister, R. F., & Leary, M. R. (1995). The need to belong: Desire for interpersonal attachments as a fundamental human motivation. *Psychological Bulletin, 117*(3), 497–529.

Bäuml, K. H. (1996). Revisiting an old issue: Retroactive interference as a function of the degree of original and interpolated learning. *Psychonomic Bulletin & Review, 3*(3), 380–384.

Baumrind, D. (1966). Effects of authoritative parental control on child behavior. *Child Development, 37*(4), 887–907.

Baumrind, D. (1967). Child care practices anteceding three patterns of preschool behavior. *Genetic Psychology Monographs, 75*, 43–88.

Baumrind, D. (1971). Current patterns of parental authority. *Developmental Psychology Monographs, 4*, 1–103.

Baumrind, D. (1972). An exploratory study of socialization effects on black children: Some black-white comparisons. *Child Development, 43*(1), 261–267.

Baumrind, D. (1978). Parental disciplinary patterns and social competence in children. *Youth & Society, 9*(3), 239–76.

Baumrind, D. (1996). The discipline controversy revisited. *Family Relations, 45*, 405–414.

Baumrind, D. (2013). Authoritative parenting revisited: History and current status. In R. E. Larzelere, A. S. Morris, & A. W. Harrist (Eds.), *Authoritative parenting: Synthesizing nurturance and discipline for optimal child development* (pp. 11–34). Washington, DC: American Psychological Association.

Baxendale, S. (2004). Memories aren't made of this: Amnesia at the movies. *BMJ, 329*(7480), 1480–1483.

Baxter, A. J., Brugha, T. S., Erskine, H. E., Scheurer, R. W., Vos, T., & Scott, J. G. (2015). The epidemiology and global burden of autism spectrum disorders. *Psychological Medicine, 45*(3), 601–613.

Baxter, L. R., Schwartz, J. M., Bergman, K. S., Szuba, M. P., Guze, B. H., Mazziotta, J. C., . . . Phelps, M. E. (1992). Caudate glucose metabolic rate changes with both drug and behavior therapy for obsessive-compulsive disorder. *Archives of General Psychiatry, 49*(9), 681–689.

Bazin, N., & Perruchet, P. (1996). Implicit and explicit associative memory in patients with schizophrenia. *Schizophrenia Research, 22*, 241–248.

Bear, M. F., & Abraham, W. C. (1996). Long-term depression in hippocampus. *Annual Review of Neuroscience, 19*(1), 437–462.

Beauchaine, T. P., & Hayden, E. P. (2016). Child and adolescent disorders. In J. C. Norcross, G. R. VandenBox, & D. K. Freedheim (Eds.), *APA Handbook of Clinical Psychology* (Vol. 4, pp. 135–171). Washington, DC: American Psychological Association.

Beauchaine, T. P., Hinshaw, S. P., & Gatzke-Kopp, L. (2008). Genetic and environmental influences on behavior. In T. P. Beauchaine & S. P. Hinshaw (Eds.), *Child and adolescent psychopathology* (pp. 58–90). Hoboken, NJ: Wiley.

Beauchamp-Turner, D. L., & Levinson, D. M. (1992). Effects of meditation on stress, health, and affect. *Medical Psychotherapy: An International Journal, 5*, 123–131.

Beaudoin, M., & Desrichard, O. (2011). Are memory self-efficacy and memory performance related? A meta-analysis. *Psychological Bulletin, 137(2)*, 211–241

Bebbington, P., & Kuipers, E. (2008). Psychosocial factors. In K. T. Meuser & D. V. Jeste (Eds.), *Clinical handbook of schizophrenia* (pp. 74–81). New York, NY: Guilford Press.

Bechara, A., & Damasio, A. R. (2005). The somatic marker hypothesis: A neural theory of economic decision. *Games and Economic Behavior, 52*(2), 336–372.

Bechara, A., Damasio, H., Tranel, D., & Damasio, A. R. (1997). Deciding advantageously before knowing the advantageous strategy. *Science, 275*(5304), 1293–1295.

Beck, A. T. (1976). *Cognitive therapy and the emotional disorders*. New York, NY: International Universities Press.

Beck, A. T., & Haigh, E. A. (2014). Advances in cognitive theory and therapy: The generic cognitive model. *Annual Review of Clinical Psychology, 10*, 1–24.

Beck, A. T., Rush, A. J., Shaw, B. F., & Emery, G. (1979). *Cognitive therapy of depression*. New York, NY: Guilford Press.

Beck, H. P., Levinson, S., & Irons, G. (2009). Finding Little Albert: A journey to John B. Watson's infant laboratory. *American Psychologist, 64*, 605–614.

Beck, J. S. (1995). *Cognitive therapy: Basics and beyond*. New York, NY: Guilford Press.

Beck, J. S. (2002). Beck therapy approach. In M. Hersen & W. Sledge (Eds.), *Encyclopedia of psychotherapy* (Vol. 1, pp. 155–163). San Diego, CA: Academic Press.

Beck, R. C., & McBee, W. (1995). Mood-dependent memory for generated and repeated words: Replication and extension. *Cognition & Emotion, 9*(4), 289–307.

Becker, A. E., Burwell, R. A., Gilman, S. E., Herzog, D. B., & Hamburg, P. (2002). Eating behaviours and attitudes following prolonged exposure to television among ethnic Fijian adolescent girls. *British Journal of Psychiatry, 180*, 509–514.

Becker, C. B., Wilson, C., Williams, A., Kelly, M., McDaniel, L., & Elmquist, J. (2010). Peer-facilitated cognitive dissonance versus healthy weight eating disorders prevention: A randomized comparison. *Body Image, 7*(4), 280–288.

Becker, J. T., & Overman, A. A. (2002). The memory deficit in Alzheimer's disease. In A. D. Baddeley, M. D. Kopelman, & B. A. Wilson (Eds.), *The handbook of memory disorders* (2nd ed., pp. 569–589). Chichester, UK: Wiley.

Bee, M. A., & Micheyl, C. (2008). The "cocktail party problem": What is it? How can it be solved? And why should animal behaviorists study it? *Journal of Comparative Psychology, 122*(3), 235–251.

Beer-Borst, S., Hercberg, S., Morabia, A., Bernstein, M. S., Galan, P., Galasso, R., . . . & Northridge, M. E. (2000). Dietary patterns in six European populations: Results from EURALIM, a collaborative European data harmonization and information campaign. *European Journal of Clinical Nutrition, 54*(3), 253–262.

Beevers, C. G. (2005). Cognitive vulnerability to depression: A dual process model. *Clinical Psychology Review, 25*, 975–1002.

Bègue, L., Subra, B., Arvers, P., Muller, D., Bricout, V., & Zorman, M. (2009). A message in a bottle: Extrapharmacological effects of alcohol on aggression. *Journal of Experimental Social Psychology, 45*(1), 137–142.

Behne, T., Carpenter, M., Call, J., & Tomasello, M. (2005). Unwilling versus unable: Infants' understanding of intentional action. *Developmental Psychology, 41*(2), 328–337.

Behnke, S. H., & Jones, S. E. (2012). Ethics and ethics codes for psychologists. In S. J. Knapp (Ed.), *APA handbook of ethics in psychology* (Vol. 1, pp. 43–74). Washington, DC: American Psychological Association.

Beidel, D. C., & Turner, S. M. (2007). *Shy children, phobic adults: Nature and treatment of social anxiety disorder* (2nd ed.). Washington, DC: American Psychological Association.

Beins, B. C. (2012). Jean Piaget: Theorist of the child's mind. In W. E. Pickren, D. A. Dewsbury, & M. Wertheimer (Eds.), *Portraits of pioneers in developmental psychology* (pp. 89–107). New York, NY: Psychology Press.

Beins, B., & Beins, A. (2008). *Effective writing in psychology: Papers, posters, and presentations*. Malden, MA: Blackwell.

Beitman, B. D., & Manring, J. (2009). Theory and practice of psychotherapy integration. In G. O. Gabbard (Ed.), *Textbook of psychotherapeutic treatments* (pp. 705–726). Washington, DC: American Psychiatric Publishing.

Bekkers, R. (2007). Intergenerational transmission of volunteering. *Acta Sociologica, 50*, 99–114.

Belanger, H. G., Spiegel, E., & Vanderploeg, R. D. (2010). Neuropsychological performance following a history of multiple self-reported concussions: A meta-analysis. *Journal of the International Neuropsychological Society, 16*(2), 262–267.

Bélanger, L., Vallières, A., Ivers, H., Moreau, V., Lavigne, G., & Morin, C. M. (2007). Meta-analysis of sleep changes in control groups of insomnia treatment trials. *Journal of Sleep Research, 16*(1), 77–84.

Belgrave, F. Z., & Allison, K. W. (2014). *African American psychology: From Africa to America* (3rd ed.). Thousand Oaks, CA: SAGE.

Belicki, D., & Belicki, K. (1982). Nightmares in a university population. *Sleep Research, 11*, 116.

Belicki, K. (1992a). Nightmare frequency versus nightmare distress: Relations to psychopathology and cognitive style. *Journal of Abnormal Psychology, 101*(3), 592–597.

Belicki, K. (1992b). The relationship of nightmare frequency to nightmare suffering with implications for treatment and research. *Dreaming, 2*(3), 143–148.

Bell, C. G., Walley, A. J., & Froguel, P. (2005). The genetics of human obesity. *Nature Reviews Genetics, 6*(3), 221–234.

Bellieni, C. V., Severi, F., Bocchi, C., Caparelli, N., Bagnoli, F., Buonocore, G., & Petraglia, F. (2005). Blink-startle reflex habituation in 30–34-week low-risk fetuses. *Journal of Perinatal Medicine, 33*(1): 33–37.

Belsky, J., & Fearon, R. P. (2002). Early attachment security, subsequent maternal sensitivity, and later child development: Does continuity in development depend upon continuity of caregiving? *Attachment & Human Development, 4*(3), 361–387.

Belsky, J., & Pluess, M. (2009). Beyond diathesis stress: Differential susceptibility to environmental influences. *Psychological Bulletin, 135*(6), 885–908.

Belsky, J., Steinberg, L., & Draper, P. (1991). Childhood experience, interpersonal development, and reproductive strategy: An evolutionary theory of socialization. *Child Development, 62*(4), 647–670.

Bem, D. J. (1967). Self-perception: An alternative interpretation of cognitive dissonance phenomena. *Psychological Review, 74*(3), 183–200.

Beniczky, S., Kéri, S., Vörös, E., Ungureán, A., Benedek, G., Janka, Z., & Vécsei, L. (2002). Complex hallucinations following occipital lobe damage. *European Journal of Neurology, 9*(2), 175–176.

Benjafield, J. G. (2012). *Psychology: A concise history*. Toronto, Canada: Oxford University Press.

Benjafield, J. G. (2015). *A history of psychology* (3rd. ed.). Toronto, Canada: Oxford University Press.

Benjamin, L. T. (2006). *A history of psychology in letters*. Malden, MA: Blackwell

Benjamin, L. T. (2007). *A brief history of modern psychology*. Malden, MA: Blackwell

Benjamin, L. T., Jr. (2005). A history of clinical psychology as a profession in America (and a glimpse at its future). *Annual Review of Clinical Psychology, 1*, 1–30.

Benjamin, L. T., Jr. (2007). *A brief history of modern psychology*. Malden, MA: Blackwell.

Benjamin, L. T., Jr., & Baker, D. B. (2012). The internationalization of psychology: A history. In D. B. Baker (Ed.), *The Oxford handbook of the history of psychology: Global perspectives* (pp. 1–17). New York, NY: Oxford University Press.

Benjamin, L. T., Jr., & Crouse, E. M. (2002). The American Psychological Association's response to Brown v. Board of Education: The case of Kenneth B. Clark. *American Psychologist, 57*(1), 38–50.

Bennett, M. (1999). Introduction. In M. Bennett (Ed.), *Developmental psychology: Achievements and prospects* (pp. 1–12). New York, NY: Psychology Press.

Ben-Porath, Y. S., & Archer, R. P. (2008). The MMPI-2 and MMPI-A. In R. P. Archer & S. R. Smith (Eds.), *Personality assessment* (pp. 81–131). New York, NY: Routledge.

Ben-Porath, Y. S., & Tellegen, A. (2008). *Minnesota Multiphasic Personality Inventory-2: Restructured Form manual*. New York, NY: Pearson.

Bensmaia, S. (2010). Tactile acuity. In E. B. Goldstein (Ed.), *Encyclopedia of perception* (pp. 947–950). Thousand Oaks, CA: SAGE.

Benson, K., Flory, K., Humphreys, K. L., & Lee, S. S. (2015). Misuse of stimulant medication among college students: A comprehensive review and meta-analysis. *Clinical Child and Family Psychology Review, 18*(1), 50–76.

Benware, C. A., & Deci, E. L. (1984). Quality of learning with an active versus passive motivational set. *American Educational Research Journal, 21*(4), 755–765.

Benyamani, Y. (2011). Health and illness perception. In H. S. Friedman (Ed.), *The Oxford handbook of health psychology* (pp. 281–314). Oxford, UK: Oxford University Press.

Beran, T. N., McLaughlin, K., Al Ansari, A., & Kassam, A. (2013). Conformity of behaviors among medical students: Impact on performance of knee arthrocentesis in simulation. *Advances in Health Sciences Education: Theory and Practice, 18*(4), 589–596.

Berge, J. M., Wall, M., Loth, K., & Neumark-Sztainer, D. (2010). Parenting style as a predictor of adolescent weight and weight-related behaviors. *Journal of Adolescent Health, 46*(4), 331–338.

Berger, G., Hank, L., Rauzi, T., & Simkins, L. (1987). Detection of sexual orientation by heterosexuals and homosexuals. *Journal of Homosexuality, 13*(4), 83–100.

Bering, J. M., & Bjorklund, D. F. (2007). The serpent's gift: Evolutionary psychology and consciousness. In P. D. Zelazo, M. Moscovitch, & E. Thompson (Eds.), *The Cambridge handbook of consciousness* (pp. 597–630). Cambridge, UK: Cambridge University Press.

Berk, E. (2008a). Leptin. In K. Keller (Ed.), *Encyclopedia of obesity* (Vol. 2, pp. 425–426). Los Angeles, CA: SAGE.

Berk, E. (2008b). Thrifty gene hypothesis. In K. Keller (Ed.), *Encyclopedia of obesity* (Vol. 2, pp. 743–745). Los Angeles, CA: SAGE.

Berkowitz, L. (1989). Frustration-aggression hypothesis: Examination and reformulation. *Psychological Bulletin, 106*(1), 59–73.

Berkowitz, L. (1993). *Aggression: Its causes, consequences, and control*. New York, NY: McGraw-Hill.

Berkowitz, L., & Harmon-Jones, E. (2004). Toward an understanding of the determinants of anger. *Emotion, 4*(2), 107–130.

Berlin, B. O., & Kay, P. D. (1969). *Basic color terms*. Berkeley. CA: University of California Press.

Berlyne, D. E. (1960). *Conflict, arousal, and curiosity*. New York, NY: McGraw-Hill.

Bermudes, R. A., Wright, J. H., & Casey, D. (2009). Techniques of cognitive-behavioral therapy. In G. O. Gabbard (Ed.), *Textbook of psychotherapeutic treatments* (pp. 201–237). Washington, DC: American Psychiatric Publishing.

Bernal, G., Jiménez-Chafey, M. I., & Domenech Rodríguez, M. M. (2009). Cultural adaptation of treatments: A resource for considering culture in evidence-based practice. *Professional Psychology: Research and Practice, 40*(4), 361–368. doi:10.1037/a0016401

Bernstein, I. L. (1978). Learned taste aversions in children receiving chemotherapy. *Science, 200*, 1302–1303.

Bernstein, I. L. (1999). Taste aversion learning: A contemporary perspective. *Nutrition, 15*(3), 229–234.

Bernstein, I. L., & Webster, M. M. (1985). Learned food aversions: A consequence of cancer chemotherapy. In T. G. Burish, S. M. Levy, & B. E. Meyerowitz (Eds.), *Cancer, nutrition, and eating behavior* (pp. 103–116). Hillsdale, NJ: Lawrence Erlbaum.

Berntsen, D. (1996). Involuntary autobiographical memories. *Applied Cognitive Psychology, 10*(5), 435–454.

Berntsen, D. (2001). Involuntary memories of emotional events: Do memories of traumas and extremely happy events differ? *Applied Cognitive Psychology, 15*(7), S135–S158.

Berry, J. W. (1970). Marginality, stress and ethnic identification in an acculturated Aboriginal community. *Journal of Cross-Cultural Psychology, 1*(3), 239–252.

Berry, J. W. (1980). Acculturation as varieties of adaptation. In A. Padilla (Ed.), *Acculturation: Theory, models and findings* (pp. 9–25). Boulder, CO: Westview Press.

Berry, J. W. (1997). Immigration, acculturation, and adaptation. *Applied Psychology, 46*(1), 5–34.

Berry, J. W. (2003). Conceptual approaches to acculturation. In K. M. Chun, P. B. Organista, & G. Marin (Eds.), *Acculturation: Advances in theory, measurement, and applied research* (pp. 17–37). Washington, DC: American Psychological Association.

Berry, J. W. (2006). Acculturative stress. In P. T. P. Wong and L. C. J Wong (Eds.), *Handbook of multicultural perspectives on stress and coping* (pp. 287–298). New York, NY: Springer Science+Business Media.

Berry, J. W. (2006a). Contexts of acculturation. In D. L. Sam & J. W. Berry (Eds.), *The Cambridge Handbook of Acculturation Psychology* (pp. 27–42). New York, NY: Cambridge University Press.

Berry, J. W. (2006b). Stress perspectives on acculturation. In D. L. Sam, & J. W. Berry (Eds.), *The Cambridge Handbook of Acculturation Psychology* (pp. 43–57). New York, NY: Cambridge University Press.

Berry, J. W., & Kim, U. (1988). Acculturation and mental health. In P. R. Dasen, J. W. Berry, & N. Sartorius (Eds.), *Health and cross-cultural psychology: Toward applications* (pp. 207–236). Thousand Oaks, CA: SAGE.

Berry, J. W., & Sam, D. L. (1997). Acculturation and adaptation. In J. W. Berry, M. H. Segal, & C. Kagitçibasi (Eds.), *Handbook of cross-cultural psychology* (Vol. 3, pp. 293–326). Needham Heights, MA: Allyn & Bacon.

Berry, J. W., Kim, U., Minde, T., & Mok, D. (1987). Comparative studies of acculturative stress. *International Migration Review, 21*(3), 491–511.

Berry, J. W., Phinney, J. S., Sam, D. L., & Vedder, P. (2006). Immigrant youth: Acculturation, identity, and adaptation. *Applied Psychology, 55*(3), 303–332.

Bertrand, M., & Mullainathan, S. (2003). Are Emily and Greg more employable than Lakisha and Jamal? A field experiment on labor market discrimination. *American Economics Review, 94*(4), 991–1013.

Betz, D. E., Ramsey, L. R., & Sekaquaptewa, D. (2013). Gender stereotype threat among women and girls. In M. K. Ryan & N. R. Branscombe (Eds.), *The SAGE Handbook of Gender and Psychology* (pp. 428–450). Thousand Oaks, CA: SAGE.

Beyers, W., & Seiffge-Krenke, I. (2010). Does identity precede intimacy? Testing Erikson's theory on romantic development in emerging adults of the 21st century. *Journal of Adolescent Research, 25*(3), 387–415.

Bhattacharyya, D., Ranjan, R., Alisherov, F., & Choi, M. (2009). Biometric authentication: A review. *International Journal of u- and e-Service, Science and Technology, 2*(3), 13–28.

Bibok, M. B., Müller, U., & Carpendale, J. I. M. (2009). Childhood. In U. Müller, J. I. M. Carpendale, & L. Smith (Eds.), *The Cambridge companion to Piaget* (pp. 229–254). New York, NY: Cambridge University Press.

Bickerton, D. (1992). *Language and species*. Chicago, IL: University of Chicago Press.

Bickerton, D. (2009). *Adam's tongue: How humans made language, how language made humans*. New York, NY: Hill and Wang.

Bickerton, D. (2013). The evolution of language. In D. Reisberg, *The Oxford handbook of cognitive psychology* (pp. 524–538). Oxford, UK: Oxford University Press.

Bickerton, D., & Szathmáry, E. (Eds.). (2009). *Biological foundations and origin of syntax*. Cambridge, MA: MIT Press.

Birbiglia, M. (2011). *Sleepwalk with me: And other painfully true stories*. New York: Simon & Schuster.

Birditt, K. S., & Fingerman, K. L. (2005). Do we get better at picking our battles? Age group differences in descriptions of behavioral reactions to interpersonal tensions. *The Journals of Gerontology Series B: Psychological Sciences and Social Sciences, 60*(3), P121–P128.

Birditt, K. S., Fingerman, K. L., & Almeida, D. M. (2005). Age differences in exposure and reactions to interpersonal tensions: A daily diary study. *Psychology and Aging, 20*(2), 330.

Birman, D., & Simon, C. D. (2014). Acculturation research: Challenges, complexities, and possibilities. In F. T. L. Leong (Ed.), *APA Handbook of Multicultural Psychology* (Vol. 1, pp. 207–230). Washington, DC: American Psychological Association.

Birney, D. P., Citron-Pousty, J. H., Lutz, D. J., & Sternberg, R. J. (2005). The development of cognitive and intellectual abilities. In M. H. Bornstein & M. E. Lamb (Eds.), *Developmental science: An advanced textbook* (5th ed., pp. 327–358). Mahwah, NJ: Lawrence Erlbaum.

Bishop, S. R., Lau, M., Shapiro, S., Carlson, L., Anderson, N. D., Carmody, J., Devins, G. (2004). Mindfulness: A proposed operational definition. *Clinical Psychology: Science and Practice, 11*(3), 230–241.

Biswas-Diener, R., & Diener, E. (2001). Making the best of a bad situation: Satisfaction in the slums of Calcutta. *Social Indicators Research, 55*(3), 329–352.

Biswas-Diener, R., Vittersø, J., & Diener, E. (2005). Most people are pretty happy, but there is cultural variation: The Inughuit, the Amish, and the Maasai. *Journal of Happiness Studies, 6*(3), 205–226.

Bjerkeset, O., Romundstad, P., Evans, J., & Gunnell, D. (2008). Association of adult body mass index and height with anxiety, depression, and suicide in the general population: The HUNT Study. *American Journal of Epidemiology, 167*(2), 193–202.

Bjork, E. L., Bjork, R. A., & Anderson, M. C. (1998). Varieties of goal-directed forgetting. In J. M. Golding & C. Macleod (Eds.), *Intentional forgetting: Interdisciplinary approaches* (pp. 103–137). Hillsdale, NJ: Erlbaum.

Bjork, R. A. (1972). Theoretical implications of directed forgetting. In A. W. Melton & E. Martin (Eds.), *Coding processes in human memory* (pp. 217–235). Washington, DC: V. M. Winston.

Bjork, R. A. (1978). The updating of human memory. In G. H. Bower (Ed.), *The psychology of learning and motivation* (Vol. 12, pp. 235–259). New York, NY: Academic Press.

Bjork, R. A. (1989). Retrieval inhibition as an adaptive mechanism in human memory. In H. L. Roediger & F. I. M. Craik (Eds.), *Varieties of memory and consciousness: Essays in honor of Endel Tulving* (pp. 309–330). Hillsdale, NJ: Erlbaum.

Bjork, R. A. (2011). On the symbiosis of remembering, forgetting, and learning. In A. S. Benjamin (Ed.), *Successful remembering and successful forgetting: A Festschrift in honor of Robert A. Bjork* (pp. 1–22). New York, NY: Psychology Press.

Blackwell, L. S., Trzesniewski, K. H., & Dweck, C. S. (2007). Implicit theories of intelligence predict achievement across an adolescent transition: A longitudinal study and an intervention. *Child Development, 78*(1), 246–263.

Blair, R. J. R. (2007). The amygdala and ventromedial prefrontal cortex in morality and psychopathy. *Trends in Cognitive Sciences, 11*(9), 387–392.

Blanchard, R. (2008). Sex ratio of older siblings in heterosexual and homosexual, right-handed and non-right-handed men. *Archives of Sexual Behavior, 37*(6), 977–981.

Blanchard, R. (2012). A possible second type of maternal–fetal immune interaction involved in both male and female homosexuality. *Archives of Sexual Behavior, 41*(6), 1507–1511.

Blanchard, R. J., Blanchard, D. C., Griebel, G., & Nutt, D. (2008). Introduction to the handbook on fear and anxiety. In R. J. Blanchard, D. C. Blanchard, G. Griebel, & D. Nutt (Eds.), *Handbook of anxiety and fear* (pp. 3–7). Amsterdam, The Netherlands: Elsevier.

Blanco, C., Schneier, F. R., Vesga-Lopez, O., & Liebowitz, M. R. (2010). Pharmacotherapy for social anxiety disorder. In D. J. Stein, E. Hollander, & B. O. Rothbaum (Eds.), *Textbook of anxiety disorders* (2nd ed., pp. 471–499). Washington, D.C.: American Psychiatric Publishing.

Blanco, C., & Weissman, M. M. (2005). Interpersonal psychotherapy. In G. O. Gabbard, J. S. Beck, & J. Holmes (Eds.), *Oxford textbook of psychotherapy* (pp. 27–34). New York, NY: Oxford University Press.

Blanton, J. S. (2007) In the halls of business: Consulting psychology as a career. In R. J. Sternberg (Ed.), *Career paths in psychology: Where your degree can take you* (2nd ed., pp. 259–278). Washington, DC: American Psychological Association.

Blashfield, R. K., & Burgess, D. R. (2007). Classification provides an essential basis for organizing mental disorders. In S. O. Lilienfeld & W. T. O'Donohue (Eds.), *The great ideas of clinical science: 17 principles that every mental health professional should understand* (pp. 93–117). New York, NY: Routledge.

Blashfield, R. K., Flanagan, E., & Raley, K. (2010). Themes in the evolution of the 20th-century DSMs. In T. Millon, R. F. Krueger, & E. Simonsen (Eds.), *Contemporary directions in psychopathology: Scientific foundations of the DSM-IV and ICD-11* (pp. 53–71). New York, NY: Guilford Press.

Blashfield, R. K., Keeley, J. W., & Burgess, D. R. (2009). Classification. In P. H. Blaney & T. Millon (Eds.), *Oxford textbook of psychopathology* (pp. 35–57). New York, NY: Oxford University Press.

Blashfield, R. K., Keeley, J. W., Flanagan, E. H., & Miles, S. R. (2014). The cycle of classification: DSM-I through DSM-5. *Annual Review of Clinical Psychology, 10*, 25–51.

Blass, T. (Ed.). (1999a). *Obedience to authority: Current perspectives on the Milgram paradigm*. Mahwah, NJ: Lawrence Erlbaum.

Blass, T. (1999b). The Milgram paradigm after 35 years: Some things we now know about obedience to authority. *Journal of Applied Social Psychology, 29*(5), 955–978.

Blass, T. (2004). *The man who shocked the world: The life and legacy of Stanley Milgram*. New York, NY: Basic Books.

Blass, T. (2009). *The man who shocked the world: The life and legacy of Stanley Milgram.* New York, NY: Basic Books.

Blass, T., & Schmitt, C. (2001). The nature of perceived authority in the Milgram paradigm: Two replications. *Current Psychology, 20*(2), 115–121.

Blazer, D. (2013). Neurocognitive disorders in DSM-5. *American Journal of Psychiatry, 170*(6), 585–587.

Bliss, T. V., & Collingridge, G. L. (1993). A synaptic model of memory: Long-term potentiation in the hippocampus. *Nature, 361*(6407), 31–39.

Block, Jack. (1995). A contrarian view of the five-factor approach to personality description. *Psychological Bulletin, 117*(2), 187–215.

Bloedon, L. T., & Szapary, P. O. (2009). Coronary heart disease. In B. P. Jacobs & K. Gundling, *The ACP evidence-based guide to complementary and alternative medicine* (pp. 161–200). Philadelphia, PA: American College of Physicians.

Blood, A. J., & Zatorre, R. J. (2001). Intensely pleasurable responses to music correlate with activity in brain regions implicated in reward and emotion. *Proceedings of the National Academy of Sciences, 98*(20), 11818–11823.

Bloom, P. (2002). *How children learn the meanings of words*. Cambridge, MA: MIT press.

Blow, F. C., Zeber, J. E., McCarthy, J. F., Valenstein, M., Gillon, L., & Bingham, C. R. (2004). Ethnicity and diagnostic patterns in veterans with psychoses. *Social Psychiatry and Psychiatric Epidemiology, 39*, 841–851.

Blowers, G. (2006). Origins of scientific psychology in China 1899–1949. In A. C. Brock (Ed.), *Internationalizing the history of psychology* (pp. 94–111). New York, NY: New York University Press.

Bluck, S., Alea, N., & Demiray, B. (2010). You get what you need: The psychosocial functions of remembering. In J. H. Mace (Ed.), *The act of remembering* (pp. 284–307). Chichester, UK: Wiley-Blackwell.

Blum, D. (2002). *Love at Goon Park: Harry Harlow and the science of affection*. Cambridge, MA: Perseus.

Blume, A. W., Lovato, L. V., Thyken, B. N., & Denny, N. (2012). The relationship of microaggressions with alcohol use and anxiety among ethnic minority college students in a historically White institution. *Cultural Diversity and Ethnic Minority Psychology, 18*(1), 45–54.

Blumenthal, A. L. (1997). Wilhelm Wundt. In W. G. Bringmann, H. E. Lück, R. Miller, & C. E. Early (Eds.), *A pictorial history of psychology* (pp. 117–125). Carol Stream, IL: Quintessence Publishing.

Blumenthal, A. L. (2002). A reappraisal of Wilhelm Wundt. In W. E. Pickren & D. A. Dewsbury (Eds.), *Evolving perspectives on the history of psychology* (pp. 65–78). Washington, DC: American Psychological Association.

Bochner, S. (1994). Cross-cultural differences in the self-concept: A test of Hofstede's individualism/collectivism distinction. *Journal of Cross-Cultural Psychology, 25*(2), 273–283.

Bockting, W. O., Miner, M. H., Swinburne Romine, R. E., Hamilton, A., & Coleman, E. (2013). Stigma, mental health, and resilience in an online sample of the U.S. transgender population. *American Journal of Public Health, 103*(5), 943–951.

Bodade, R. M., & Talbar, S. N. (2014). *Iris analysis for biometric recognition systems*. New Delhi, India: Springer.

Boden, M. A. (2004). *The creative mind: Myths and mechanisms* (2nd ed.). New York, NY: Routledge.

Boecker, H., Sprenger, T., Spilker, M. E., Henriksen, G., Koppenhoefer, M., Wagner, K. J., . . . Tolle, T. R. (2008). The runner's high: Opioidergic mechanisms in the human brain. *Cerebral Cortex, 18*(11), 2523–2531

Boehm, J. K., & Kubzansky, L. D. (2012). The heart's content: The association between positive psychological well-being and cardiovascular health. *Psychological Bulletin, 138*(4), 655–691.

Boehm, J. K., Lyubomirsky, S., & Sheldon, K. M. (2011). A longitudinal experimental study comparing the effectiveness of happiness-enhancing strategies in Anglo Americans and Asian Americans. *Cognition & Emotion, 25*(7), 1263–1272.

Bogaert, A. F. (2006). Biological versus nonbiological older brothers and men's sexual orientation. *Proceedings of the National Academy of Sciences, 103*(28), 10771–10774.

Bogaert, A. F., & Skorska, M. (2011). Sexual orientation, fraternal birth order, and the maternal immune hypothesis: A review. *Frontiers in Neuroendocrinology, 32*(2), 247–254.

Bogdan, A., Bouchareb, B., & Touitou, Y. (2001). Ramadan fasting alters endocrine and neuroendocrine circadian patterns. Meal-time as a synchronizer in humans? *Life Sciences, 68*(14), 1607–1615.

Bogle, K. (2008). *Hooking up*. New York, NY: New York University Press.

Bohart, A. C., & Tallman, K. (1999). *How clients make therapy work: The process of active self-healing*. Washington, DC: American Psychological Association.

Bohlmeijer, E., Prenger, R., Taal, E., & Cuijpers, P. (2010). The effects of mindfulness-based stress reduction therapy on mental health of adults with a chronic medical disease: A meta-analysis. *Journal of Psychosomatic Research, 68*(6), 539–544.

Bohlmeijer, E., Roemer, M., Cuijpers, P., & Smit, F. (2007). The effects of reminiscence on psychological well-being in older adults: A meta-analysis. *Aging and Mental Health, 11*(3), 291–300.

Bohlmeijer, E., Smit, F., & Cuijpers, P. (2003). Effects of reminiscence and life review on late-life depression: A meta-analysis. *International Journal of Geriatric Psychiatry, 18*(12), 1088–1094.

Bolger, D. J., Perfetti, C. A., & Schneider, W. (2005). Cross-cultural effect on the brain revisited: Universal structures plus writing system variation. *Human Brain Mapping, 25*(1), 92–104.

Bolzan, S., Bolzan, J., & Rother, C. (2011). *My life, deleted: A memoir*. New York, NY: Harper Collins.

Bonanno, G. A. (2004). Loss, trauma, and human resilience: Have we underestimated the human capacity to thrive after extremely aversive events? *American Psychologist, 59*(1), 20–28.

Bonanno, G. A. (2009). *The other side of sadness: What the new science of bereavement tells us about life after loss*. New York, NY: Basic Books.

Bonanno, G. A., Galea, S., Bucciarelli, A., & Vlahov, D. (2007). What predicts psychological resilience after disaster? The role of demographics, resources, and life stress. *Journal of Consulting and Clinical Psychology, 75*(5), 671–682.

Bonanno, G. A., Goorin, L., & Coifman, K. G. (2008). Sadness and grief. In M. Lewis, J. M. Haviland-Jones, & L. F. Barrett (Eds.), *Handbook of emotions* (3rd ed., pp. 797–810). New York, NY: Guilford Press.

Bond, M. H. (2004). Culture and aggression—from context to coercion. *Personality and Social Psychology Review, 8*(1), 62–78.

Bond, R., & Smith, P. B. (1996). Culture and conformity: A meta-analysis of studies using Asch's (1952b, 1956) line judgment task. *Psychological Bulletin, 119*(1), 111.

Bonnet, M. H., & Arand, D. L. (1995). We are chronically sleep deprived. *Sleep, 18*(10), 908–911.

Bonnie, R. J., & Scott, E. S. (2013). The teenage brain: Adolescent brain research and the law. *Current Directions in Psychological Science, 22*(2), 158–161.

Booth, A. L., & Kee, H. J. (2009). Birth order matters: The effect of family size and birth order on educational attainment. *Journal of Population Economics, 22*(2), 367–397.

Booth-Kewley, S., & Friedman, H. S. (1987). Psychological predictors of heart disease: A quantitative review. *Psychological Bulletin, 101*(3), 343–362.

Booth-Kewley, S., & Vickers, R. R. (1994). Associations between major domains of personality and health behavior. *Journal of Personality, 62*(3), 281–298.

Borbély, A. A. (1982). A two-process model of sleep regulation. *Human Neurobiology, 1*(3): 195–204.

Born, J., Rasch, B., & Gais, S. (2006). Sleep to remember. *Neuroscientist, 12*(5), 410–424.

Bornstein, M. H. (1999). Human infancy: Past, present, future. In M. Bennett (Ed.), *Developmental psychology: Achievements and prospects* (pp. 13–35). Philadelphia, PA: Psychology Press.

Bornstein, M. H., Arterberry, M. E., & Mash, C. (2005). Perceptual development. In M. H. Bornstein & M. E. Lamb (Eds.), *Developmental science: An advanced textbook* (5th ed., pp. 283–325). Mahwah, NJ: Lawrence Erlbaum.

Bornstein, M. H., & Bradley, R. H. (2003). *Socioeconomic status, parenting, and child development*. Mahwah, NJ: Lawrence Erlbaum.

Bornstein, R. F. (1989). Exposure and affect: Overview and meta-analysis of research, 1968–1987. *Psychological Bulletin, 106*(2), 265–289.

Boroditsky, L. (2011). How language shapes thought. *Scientific American, 304*(2), 62–65

Boroditsky, L. (2012). How the languages we speak shape the ways we think: The FAQs. In M. Spivey, M. Joanisse., & K. McRae (Eds.), *The Cambridge handbook of psycholinguistics* (pp. 615–632). New York, NY: Cambridge University Press.

Boroditsky, L., & Gaby, A. (2006). East of Tuesday: Representing time in absolute space. In *Proceedings of the 28th Annual Meeting of the Cognitive Science Society, Vancouver, BC, Canada*.

Boroditsky, L., Schmidt, L. S., & Phillips, W. (2003). In Gentner, D., & Goldin-Meadow, S. (Eds.), *Language in mind: Advances in the study of language and thought*. Cambridge, MA: MIT Press.

Bos, J. E., Bles, W., & Groen, E. L. (2008). A theory on visually induced motion sickness. *Displays, 29*(2), 47–57.

Bosch, J. A., Engeland, C. G., Cacioppo, J. T., & Marucha, P. T. (2007). Depressive symptoms predict mucosal wound healing. *Psychosomatic Medicine, 69*(7), 597–605.

Bosma, H., & Gerlsma, C. (2003). From early attachment relations to the adolescent and adult organization of self. In J. Valsiner & K. Connolly (Eds.), *Handbook of developmental psychology* (pp. 450–488). Thousand Oaks, CA: SAGE.

Boswell, J. F., Sharpless, B. A., Greenberg, L. S., Heatherington, L., Huppert, J. D., Barber, J. P., . . . Castonguay, L. G. (2011). Schools of psychotherapy and the beginnings of a scientific approach. In D. H. Barlow (Ed.), *The Oxford handbook of clinical psychology* (pp. 98–127). New York, NY: Oxford University Press.

Both, S., Brauer, M., & Laan, E. (2011). Classical conditioning of sexual response in women: A replication study. *The Journal of Sexual Medicine, 8*, 3116–3131.

Bottoms, B. L., Shaver, P. R., & Goodman, G. S. (1996). An analysis of ritualistic and religion-related child abuse allegations. *Law and Human Behavior, 20*(1), 1–34.

Bouchard, C., Tremblay, A., Després, J. P., Thériault, G., Nadeauf, A., Lupien, P. J., . . . Fournier, G. (1994). The response to exercise with constant energy intake in identical twins. *Obesity Research, 2*(5), 400–410.

Bouchard, G. (2014). How do parents react when their children leave home? An integrative review. *Journal of Adult Development, 21*(2), 69–79.

Bouchard, T. J. (2013). The Wilson effect: The increase in heritability of IQ with age. *Twin Research and Human Genetics, 16*(05), 923–930.

Bouchard, T. J., & McGue, M. (1981). Familial studies of intelligence: A review. *Science, 212*(4498), 1055–1059.

Bouchard, T. J., & McGue, M. (2003). Genetic and environmental influences on human psychological differences. *Journal of Neurobiology, 54*(1), 4–45.

Bouchard, T. J., Lykken, D. T., McGue, M., Segal, N. L., & Tellegen, A. (1990). Sources of human psychological differences: The Minnesota study of twins reared apart. *Science, 250*(4978), 223–228.

Boulougouris, J. C., Marks, I. M., & Marset, P. (1971). Superiority of flooding (implosion) to desensitisation for reducing pathological fear. *Behaviour Research and Therapy, 9*(1), 7–16.

Bowen, S., Vietan, C., Witikiewitz, K., & Carroll, H. (2015). A mindfulness-based approach to addiction. In K. W. Brown, J. D. Creswell, & R. M. Ryan (Eds.), *Handbook of mindfulness: Theory, research, and practice* (pp. 387–404). New York, NY: Guilford Press.

Bower, G. H. (1981). Mood and memory. *American Psychologist, 36*(2), 129–148.

Bower, G. H. (2000). A brief history of memory research. In E. Tulving & F. I. M. Craik, *The Oxford handbook of memory* (pp. 3–32). Oxford, UK: Oxford University Press.

Bowers, J. S., & Davis, C. J. (2004). Is speech perception modular or interactive? *Trends in Cognitive Sciences, 8*(1), 3–5.

Bowlby, J. (1969). *Attachment and loss* (Vol. 1). New York, NY: Basic Books.

Bowlby, J. (1973). *Attachment and loss* (Vol. 2). New York, NY: Basic Books.

Bowlby, J. (1988). *A secure base.* New York, NY: Basic Books.

Bowler, D. M. (1992), "Theory of mind" in Asperger's syndrome. *Journal of Child Psychology and Psychiatry, 33*(5), 877–893.

Boyce, J. A., & Kuijer, R. G. (2015). Perceived stress and freshman weight change: The moderating role of baseline body mass index. *Physiology & Behavior, 139*, 491–496.

Boylan, J. F. (2003). *She's not there: A life in two genders*. New York, NY: Broadway Books.

Boyland, E. J., & Whalen, R. (2015). Food advertising to children and its effects on diet: Review of recent prevalence and impact data. *Pediatric Diabetes, 16*(5), 331–337.

Boynton-Jarrett, R., Wright, R. J., Putnam, F. W., Lividoti Hibert, E., Michels, K. B., Forman, M. R., & Rich-Edwards, J. (2013). Childhood abuse and age at menarche. *Journal of Adolescent Health, 52*(2), 241–247.

Bozarth, J. D. (1997). Empathy from the framework of client-centered theory and the Rogerian hypothesis. In A. C. Bohart & L. S. Greenberg (Eds.), *Empathy reconsidered: New directions in psychotherapy* (pp. 81–102). Washington, DC: American Psychological Association.

Bozarth, J. D., Zimring, F. M., & Tausch, R. (2002). Client-centered therapy: The evolution of a revolution. In D. J. Cain & J. Seeman (Eds.), *Humanistic psychotherapies: Handbook of research and practice* (pp. 147–188). Washington, DC: American Psychological Association.

Brabender, V. A. (2002). *Introduction to group therapy*. New York, NY: Wiley.

Bracha, H. S., & Maser, J. D. (2008). Anxiety and posttraumatic stress disorder in the context of human brain evolution: A role for theory in DSM-V? *Clinical Psychology: Science and Practice, 15*, 91–97.

Bracken, B. A., & McCallum, S. (2009). Universal Nonverbal Intelligence Test (UNIT). In J. A. Naglieri & S. Goldstein (Eds.), *Practitioner's guide to assessing intelligence and achievement* (pp. 291–313). Hoboken, NJ: Wiley.

Bradbury, T. N., & Miller, G. A. (1985). Season of birth in schizophrenia: A review of evidence, methodology, and etiology. *Psychological Bulletin, 98*(3), 569–594.

Bradley, R., Conklin, C. Z., & Westen, D. (2007). Borderline personality disorder. In W. O'Donohue, K. A. Fowler, & S. O. Lilienfeld (Eds.), *Personality disorders: Toward the DSM-V* (pp. 167–201). Thousand Oaks, CA: SAGE.

Brambilla, M., Riva, P., & Rule, N. O. (2013). Familiarity increases the accuracy of categorizing male sexual orientation. *Personality and Individual Differences, 55*(2), 193–195.

Brand, A., Behrend, O., Marquardt, T., McAlpine, D., & Grothe, B. (2002). Precise inhibition is essential for microsecond interaural time difference coding. *Nature, 417*(6888), 543–547.

Brand, M., Eggers, C., Reinhold, N., Fujiwara, E., Kessler, J., Heiss, W. D., & Markowitsch, H. J. (2009). Functional brain imaging in 14 patients with dissociative amnesia reveals right inferolateral prefrontal hypometabolism. *Psychiatry Research: Neuroimaging, 174*(1), 32–39.

Brand, M., & Markowitsch, H. J. (2010). Aspects of forgetting in psychogenic amnesia. In S. Della Sala (Ed.), *Forgetting* (pp. 239–251). East Sussex, UK: Psychology Press.

Branje, S. J., van Doorn, M., van der Valk, I., & Meeus, W. (2009). Parent-adolescent conflicts, conflict resolution types, and adolescent adjustment. *Journal of Applied Developmental Psychology, 30*(2), 195–204.

Braslow, J. (1997). *Mental ills and bodily cures: Psychiatric treatment in the first half of the twentieth century*. Berkeley, CA: University of California Press.

Bray, G. A. (2004). Medical consequences of obesity. *The Journal of Clinical Endocrinology & Metabolism, 89*(6), 2583–2589.

Brazelton, T. B., Koslowski, B., Main, M., Lewis, M., & Rosenblum, L. A. (1974). *The origins of reciprocity: The early mother-infant interaction.* Oxford, UK: Wiley-Interscience.

Brebion, G., Amador, X., Smith, M. J., & Gorman, J. M. (1997). Mechanisms underlying memory impairment in schizophrenia. *Psychological Medicine, 27*, 383–393.

Breggin, P. R. (2008). *Brain-disabling treatments in psychiatry: Drugs, electroshock, and the psychopharmaceutical complex* (2nd ed.). New York, NY: Springer Publishing.

Breinbauer, H. A., Anabalón, J. L., Gutierrez, D., Cárcamo, R., Olivares, C., & Caro, J. (2012). Output capabilities of personal music players and assessment of preferred listening levels of test subjects: Outlining recommendations for preventing music-induced hearing loss. *The Laryngoscope, 122*(11), 2549–2556.

Breland, K. & Breland, M. (1961). The misbehavior of organisms. *American Psychologist, 16*, 661–664.

Bremner, J. D., & Charney, D. S. (2010). Neural circuits in fear and anxiety. In D. J. Stein, E. Hollander, & B. O. Rothbaum (Eds.), *Textbook of anxiety disorders* (2nd ed., pp. 55–71). Washington, DC: American Psychiatric Publishing.

Bremner, J. D. (1999). Does stress damage the brain? *Biological Psychiatry, 45*(7), 797–805.

Brennan, P. A. (2010). Pheromones. In E. B. Goldstein (Ed.), *Encyclopedia of perception* (pp. 801–805). Thousand Oaks, CA: SAGE Publications.

Brenner, R. A., Simons-Morton, B. G., Bhaskar, B., Revenis, M., Das, A., & Clemens, J. D. (2003). Infant-parent bed sharing in an inner-city population. *Archives of Pediatrics & Adolescent Medicine, 157*(1), 33–39.

Breslau, N. (2009). The epidemiology of trauma, PTSD, and other posttrauma disorders. *Trauma, Violence, & Abuse, 10*, 198–210.

Breslau, N., Kessler, R. C., Chilcoat, H. D., Schultz, L. R., Davis, G. C., & Andreski, P. (1998). Trauma and posttraumatic stress disorder in the community: The 1996 Detroit area survey of trauma. *Archives of General Psychiatry, 55*(7), 626–632.

Brewer, M. B. (1988). A dual-process model of impression formation. In R. S. Wyer, Jr. & T. K. Srull (Eds.), *Advances in social cognition* (Vol. 1, pp. 1–36). Mahwah, NJ: Lawrence Erlbaum.

Brewer, M. B. (1996). When contact is not enough: Social identity and intergroup cooperation. *International Journal of Intercultural Relations, 20*(3), 291–303.

Brewer, M. B. (2007). The social psychology of intergroup relations: Social categorization, ingroup bias, and outgroup prejudice. In A. W. Kruglanski & E. T. Higgins (Eds.), *Social psychology: Handbook of basic principles* (2nd ed., pp. 695–715). New York, NY: Guilford Press.

Brewer, M. B., & Chen, Y. R. (2007). Where (who) are collectives in collectivism? Toward conceptual clarification of individualism and collectivism. *Psychological Review, 114*(1), 133–151.

Brewer, M. B., & Silver, M. (2006). Ingroup bias as a function of task characteristics. *European Journal of Social Psychology, 8*(3), 393–400.

Brick, J., & Erickson, C. K. (2013). *Drugs, the brain, and behavior: The pharmacology of drug use disorders*. New York, NY: Routledge.

Brimeyer, T. M., & Smith, W. L. (2012). Religion, race, social class, and gender differences in dating and hooking up among college students. *Sociological Spectrum, 32*(5), 462–473.

Bringmann, W. G., Voss, U., & Ungerer, G. A. (1997). Wundt's laboratories. In W. G. Bringmann, H. E. Lück, R. Miller, & C. E. Early (Eds.), *A pictorial history of psychology* (pp. 126–132). Carol Stream, IL: Quintessence Publishing.

Briton, N. J., & Hall, J. A. (1995). Beliefs about female and male nonverbal communication. *Sex Roles, 32*(1–2), 79–90.

Britton, J. C., & Rauch, S. L. (2009). Neuroanatomy and neuroimaging of anxiety disorders. In M. M. Antony & M. B. Stein (Eds.), *Oxford handbook of anxiety and related disorders* (pp. 97–110). New York, NY: Oxford University Press.

Broadbent, D. E., & Gregory, M. (1964). Accuracy of recognition for speech presented to the right and left ears. *Quarterly Journal of Experimental Psychology, 16*(4), 359–360.

Broadbent, E., Ellis, C. J., Thomas, J., Gamble, G., & Petrie, K. J. (2009a). Further development of an illness perception intervention for myocardial infarction patients: A randomized controlled trial. *Journal of Psychosomatic Research, 67*(1), 17–23.

Broadbent, E., Ellis, C. J., Thomas, J., Gamble, G., & Petrie, K. J. (2009b). Can an illness perception intervention reduce illness anxiety in spouses of myocardial infarction patients? A randomized controlled trial. *Journal of Psychosomatic Research, 67*(1), 11–15.

Broadbent, E., Kahokehr, A., Booth, R. J., Thomas, J., Windsor, J. A., Buchanan, C. M., . . . Hill, A. G. (2012). A brief relaxation intervention reduces stress and improves surgical wound healing response: A randomised trial. *Brain, Behavior, and Immunity, 26*(2), 212–217.

Broadbent, E., Petrie, K. J., Alley, P. G., & Booth, R. J. (2003). Psychological stress impairs early wound repair following surgery. *Psychosomatic Medicine, 65*(5), 865–869.

Broberg, D. J., & Bernstein, I. L. (1987). Candy as a scapegoat in the prevention of food aversions in children receiving chemotherapy. *Cancer, 60*(9), 2344–2347.

Brochu, P. M., & Morrison, M. A. (2007). Implicit and explicit prejudice toward overweight and average-weight men and women: Testing their correspondence and relation to behavioral intentions. *The Journal of Social Psychology, 147*(6), 681–706.

Brock, A. C. (2006). Introduction. In A. C. Brock (Ed.), *Internationalizing the history of psychology* (pp. 1–15). New York, NY: New York University Press.

Brod, J. H. (1997). Creativity and schizotypy. In G. Claridge (ed.), *Schizotypy: Implications for illness and health* (pp. 274–298). New York, NY: Oxford University Press.

Brodal, P. (2010). *The central nervous system: Structure and function*. New York, NY: Oxford University Press.

Brody, A. L., Saxena, A. L., Saxena, S., Stoessel, P., Gillies, L. A., Alborzian, S., . . . Baxter, L. R. (2001). Regional brain metabolic changes in patients with major depression treated with either paroxetine or interpersonal therapy: Preliminary findings. *Archives of General Psychiatry,* 58(7), 631–640.

Brody, L. R. (2000). The socialization of gender differences in emotional expression: Display rules, infant temperament, and differentiation. In A. H. Fischer (Ed.), *Gender and emotion: Social psychological perspectives* (pp. 24–47). Cambridge, UK: Cambridge University Press.

Brody, L. R., & Hall, J. A. (2008). Gender and emotion in context. In M. Lewis, J. M. Haviland-Jones, & L. F. Barrett (Eds.), *Handbook of emotions* (3rd ed., pp. 395–408). New York, NY: Guilford Press.

Brody, N. (2000). History of theories and measurements of intelligence. In R. J. Sternberg (Ed.), *Handbook of intelligence* (pp. 16–33). Cambridge, UK: Cambridge University Press.

Brooks, D. (2007, October 26). The outsourced brain. The *New York Times*.

Brooks, L. R. (1978). Nonanalytic concept formation and memory for instances. In E. Rosch & B. B. Lloyd (Eds.), *Cognition and categorizations* (pp. 169–211). New York, NY: Erlbaum.

Brooks, R., & Meltzoff, A. N. (2005). The development of gaze following and its relation to language. *Developmental Science, 8*(6), 535–543.

Brose, A., Scheibe, S., & Schmiedek, F. (2013). Life contexts make a difference: Emotional stability in younger and older adults. *Psychology and Aging, 28*(1), 148–159.

Brougham, R. R., Zail, C. M., Mendoza, C. M., & Miller, J. R. (2009). Stress, sex differences, and coping strategies among college students. *Current Psychology, 28*(2), 85–97.

Brown, A. S. (2003). A review of the déjà vue experience. *Psychological Bulletin, 129*, 394–413.

Brown, A. S. (2004). *The déjà vu experience*. New York, NY: Psychology Press.

Brown, A. S., Begg, M. D., Gravenstein, S., Schaefer, C. A., Wyatt, R. J., Bresnahan, M., . . . Susser, E. S. (2004). Serologic evidence of prenatal influenza in the etiology of schizophrenia. *Archives of General Psychiatry, 61*(8), 774–780.

Brown, B. B., & Larson, J. (2009). Peer relationships in adolescence. In R. M. Lerner & L. Steinberg (Eds.), *Handbook of adolescent psychiatry* (3rd ed., Vol. 2, pp. 74–103). Hoboken, NJ: Wiley.

Brown, D. L., & Pomerantz, A. M. (2011). Multicultural incompetence and other unethical behaviors: Perceptions of therapist practices. *Ethics & Behavior, 21*(6), 498–508.

Brown, G. D. A., & Lewandowsky, S. (2010). Forgetting in memory models: Arguments against trace decay and consolidation failure. In S. Della Sala (Ed.), *Forgetting* (pp. 49–75). East Sussex, UK: Psychology Press.

Brown, G. D., Neath, I., & Chater, N. (2007). A temporal ratio model of memory. *Psychological Review, 114*(3), 539–576.

Brown, J. (1958). Some tests of the decay theory of immediate memory. *Quarterly Journal of Experimental Psychology, 10*(1), 12–21.

Brown, J. S. (1965). Generalization and discrimination. In D. I. Mostofsky (Ed.), *Stimulus generalization* (pp. 7–23). Stanford, CA: Stanford University Press.

Brown, K. W. (2015). Mindfulness training to enhance positive functioning. In K. W. Brown, J. D. Creswell, & R. M. Ryan (Eds.), *Handbook of mindfulness: Theory, research, and practice* (pp. 311–328). New York, NY: Guilford Press.

Brown, K. W., & Ryan, R. M. (2004). Perils and promise in defining and measuring mindfulness: Observations from experience. *Clinical Psychology: Science and Practice, 11*(3), 242–248.

Brown, K. W., Creswell, J. D., & Ryan, R. M. (2015). Introduction: The evolution of mindfulness science. In K. W. Brown, J. D. Creswell, & R. M. Ryan (Eds.), *Handbook of mindfulness: Theory, research, and practice* (pp. 1–8). New York, NY: Guilford Press.

Brown, K. W., Goodman, R. J., & Inzlicht, M. (2012). Dispositional mindfulness and the attenuation of neural responses to emotional stimuli. *Social Cognitive and Affective Neuroscience, 8*(1), 93–99.

Brown, L. H., & Roodin, P. A. (2003). Grandparent-grandchild relationships and the life-course perspective. In J. Demick & C. Andreoletti (Eds.), *Handbook of adult development* (pp. 459–474). New York, NY: Springer Science+Business Media.

Brown, L. S. (2006). The neglect of lesbian, gay, bisexual, and transgendered clients. In J. C. Norcross, L. E. Beutler, & R. F. Levant (Eds.), *Evidence-based practices in mental health: Debate and dialogue on the fundamental questions* (pp. 346–353). Washington, DC: American Psychological Association.

Brown, L. S. (2008). *Cultural competence in trauma therapy: Beyond the flashback*. Washington, DC: American Psychological Association.

Brown, L. S. (2011). Psychotherapy patients: Client diversity in psychotherapy. In J. C. Norcross, G. R. Vandenbos, & D. K. Freedheim (Eds.), *History of psychotherapy: Continuity and change* (2nd ed., pp. 475–483). Washington, DC: American Psychological Association.

Brown, R. H., Cannon, S. C., & Rowland, L. P. (2013). Diseases of the nerve and motor unit. In E. R. Kandel, J. H. Schwartz, T. M. Jessell, S. A. Siegelbaum, & A. J. Hudspeth (Eds.), *Principles of neural science* (5th ed., pp. 307–331). New York, NY: McGraw-Hill.

Brown, R. J., & Hewstone, M. (2005). An integrative theory of intergroup contact. In M. Zanna (Ed.), *Advances in experimental social psychology* (Vol. 37, pp. 256–343). New York, NY: Elsevier.

Brown, R., & Kulik, J. (1977). Flashbulb memories. *Cognition, 5*, 73–99.

Brown, S. C., & Craik, F. I. M. (2000). Encoding and retrieval of information. In E. Tulving & F. I. M. Craik (Eds.), *The Oxford handbook of memory* (pp. 93–107). Oxford, UK: Oxford University Press.

Brown, T. (2011). School-based interventions. In J. H. Cawley (Ed.), *The Oxford handbook of the social science of obesity* (pp. 665–682). New York, NY: Oxford University Press.

Brown, T. A., & Lawrence, A. E. (2009). Generalized anxiety disorder and obsessive-compulsive disorder. In P. H. Blaney & T. Millon (Eds.), *Oxford textbook of psychopathology* (2nd ed., pp. 146–175). New York, NY: Oxford University Press.

Brown, T. N., Williams, D. R., Jackson, J. S., Neighbors, H. W., Torres, M., Sellers, S. L., & Brown, K. T. (2000). "Being black and feeling blue": The mental health consequences of racial discrimination. *Race and Society, 2*(2), 117–131.

Browne, K. D., & Hamilton-Giachritsis, C. (2005). The influence of violent media on children and adolescents: A public-health approach. *The Lancet, 365*(9460), 702–710.

Brownell, K. D. (2004). *The LEARN program for weight management* (10th ed.). Dallas, TX: American Health Publishing Company.

Brownell, K. D., & Salovey, P. (2007). Health psychology: Where psychological, biological, and social factors intersect. In R. J. Sternberg (Ed.), *Career paths in psychology: Where your degree can take you* (2nd ed., pp. 307–327). Washington, DC: American Psychological Association.

Bruce, J. M., & Echemendia, R. J. (2009). History of multiple self-reported concussions is not associated with reduced cognitive abilities. *Neurosurgery, 64*(1), 100–106.

Bruder, K. J. (1997). William James: America's premier psychologist. In W. G. Bringmann, H. E. Lück, R. Miller, & C. E. Early (Eds.), *A pictorial history of psychology* (pp. 66–70). Carol Stream, IL: Quintessence Publishing.

Brugger, P. (2010). Phantom limb. In E. B. Goldstein (Ed.), *Encyclopedia of perception* (pp. 796–799). Thousand Oaks, CA: SAGE Publications.

Bruine de Bruin, W. (2005). Save the last dance for me: Unwanted serial position effects in jury evaluations. *Acta Psychologica, 118*(3), 245–260.

Bruine de Bruin, W. (2006). Save the last dance II: Unwanted serial position effects in figure skating judgments. *Acta Psychologica, 123*(3), 299–311.

Brumariu, L. E., & Kerns, K. A. (2011). Parent-child attachment in early and middle childhood. In P. K. Smith & C. H. Hart (Eds.), *The Wiley-Blackwell handbook of childhood social development* (2nd ed., pp. 319–336). Malden, MA: Wiley-Blackwell.

Brumm, H., & Slabbekoorn, H. (2005). Acoustic communication in noise. *Advances in the Study of Behavior, 35*(35), 151–209.

Bruner, J. (1981). The social context of language acquisition. *Language & Communication, 1*(2), 155–178.

Bruner, J. S. (1975). The ontogenesis of speech acts. *Journal of Child Language, 2*(1), 1–19.

Bruni, F. (2009). *Born round: The secret history of a full-time eater*. New York, NY: Penguin.

Brunt, L. (2008). Sote hue log: In and out of sleep in India. In L. Brunt & B. Steger (Eds.), *Worlds of sleep* (pp. 153–174). Berlin, Germany: Frank & Timme.

Bruschi, T. (2014). From Super Bowl to stroke—And back again. *Men's Health*, June 10, 2014. Retrived from http://www.menshealth.com/health/tedy-bruschi-stroke.

Bryant, P. A., Trinder, J., & Curtis, N. (2004). Sick and tired: Does sleep have a vital role in the immune system? *Nature Reviews Immunology, 4*(6), 457–467.

Bryant, R. A. (2008). Hypnosis and anxiety: Early interventions. In M. R. Nash & A. J. Barnier (Eds.), *The Oxford handbook of hypnosis: Theory, research, and practice* (pp. 535–548). Oxford, UK: Oxford University Press.

Brzezinski, A., Vangel, M. G., Wurtman, R. J., Norrie, G., Zhdanova, I., Ben-Shushan, A., & Ford, I. (2005). Effects of exogenous melatonin on sleep: A meta-analysis. *Sleep Medicine Reviews, 9*(1), 41–50.

Buchanan, T. (2002). Online assessment: Desirable or dangerous? *Professional Psychology: Research and Practice, 33*(2), 148–154.

Buchanan, T., & Smith, J. L. (1999). Using the Internet for psychological research: Personality testing on the World Wide Web. *British Journal of Psychology, 90*(1), 125–144.

Buchsbaum, G., & Gottschalk, A. (1983). Trichromacy, opponent colours coding and optimum colour information transmission in the retina. *Proceedings of the Royal Society of London. Series B: Biological Sciences, 220*(1218), 89–113.

Buck, R. (1980). Nonverbal behavior and the theory of emotion: The facial feedback hypothesis. *Journal of Personality and Social Psychology, 38*(5), 811–824.

Buckley, K. W. (1989). *Mechanical man: John B. Watson and the beginnings of behaviorism*. New York, NY: The Guilford Press.

Buddin, R. (2014). Gender gaps in high school GPA and ACT scores. ACT Research & Policy Information Brief 2014-12. Retrieved from http://www.act.org/research/researchers/briefs/pdf/2014-12.pdf

Budson, A. E., & Gold, C. A. (2009). Flashbulb, personal, and event memories in clinical populations. In O. Luminet & A. Curci (Eds.), *Flashbulb memories: New issues and new perspectives* (pp. 141–161). East Sussex, UK: Psychology Press.

Bugental, J. F. (1964). The third force in psychology. *Journal of Humanistic Psychology, 4*(1), 19–25.

Bühner, M., König, C. J., Pick, M., & Krumm, S. (2006). Working memory dimensions as differential predictors of the speed and error aspect of multitasking performance. *Human Performance, 19*(3), 253–275.

Buhrmester, D. (1990). Intimacy of friendship, interpersonal competence, and adjustment during preadolescence and adolescence. *Child Development, 61*(4), 1101–1111.

Buijzen, M., van der Molen, J. H. W., & Sondij, P. (2007). Parental mediation of children's emotional responses to a violent news event. *Communication Research, 34*(2), 212–230.

Bukowski, W. M., Hoza, B., & Boivin, M. (1993). Popularity, friendship, and emotional adjustment during early adolescence. *New Directions for Child and Adolescent Development, 1993*(60), 23–37.

Bulik, C. M., Sullivan, P. F., Tozzi, F., Furberg, H., Lichtenstein, P., & Pedersen, N. L. (2006). Prevalence, heritability, and prospective risk factors for anorexia nervosa. *Archives of General Psychiatry, 63*(3), 305–312.

Burger, J. M. (2009). Replicating Milgram: Would people still obey today? *American Psychologist, 64*(1), 1–11.

Burke, D. M., Locantore, J. K., Austin, A. A., & Chae, B. (2004). Cherry pit primes Brad Pitt: Homophone priming effects on young and older adults' production of proper names. *Psychological Science, 15*(3), 164–170.

Burke, J., O'Campo, P., Salmon, C., & Walker, R. (2009). Pathways connecting neighborhood influences and mental well-being: Socioeconomic position and gender differences. *Social Science & Medicine, 68*(7), 1294–1304.

Burke, M. J., & Bowyer, K. W. (Eds.) (2013). *Handbook of iris recognition*. London, UK: Springer.

Burlingame, G. M., & Baldwin, S. (2011). Treatment modalities: Group therapy. In J. C. Norcross, G. R. Vandenbos, & D. K. Freedheim (Eds.), *History of psychotherapy: Continuity and change* (2nd ed., pp. 505–515). Washington, DC: American Psychological Association.

Burnett, D. (2013, November 29). Online IQ tests: Are they valid? *The Guardian*. Retrieved from http://www.theguardian.com/science/2013/nov/29/iq-tests-online-are-they-valid

Burnham, M. M. (2013). Co-sleeping and self-soothing during infancy. In A. R. Wolfson & H. Montgomery-Downs (Eds.), *The Oxford handbook of infant, child, and adolescent sleep and behavior* (pp. 127–139). New York, NY: Oxford University Press.

Burnham, M. M., & Gaylor, E. E. (2011). Sleep environment of young children in post-industrial societies. In M. El-Sheikh (Ed.), *Sleep and development: Familial and socio-cultural considerations* (pp. 195–218). New York, NY: Oxford University Press.

Burns, W. J., Rey, J., & Burns, K. A. (2008). Psychopharmacology as practiced by psychologists. In M. Hersen & A. M. Gross (Eds.), *Handbook of clinical psychology* (Vol. 1, pp. 663–692). Hoboken, NJ: Wiley.

Burt, D. B., Zembar, M. J., & Niederehe, G. (1995). Depression and memory impairment: A meta-analysis of the association, its pattern, and specificity. *Psychological Bulletin, 117*(2), 285–305.

Burton, R. A. (2013). *A skeptic's guide to the mind: What neuroscience can and cannot tell us about ourselves*. New York, NY: St. Martin's Press.

Bus, A. G., Van Ijzendoorn, M. H., & Pellegrini, A. D. (1995). Joint book reading makes for success in learning to read: A meta-analysis on intergenerational transmission of literacy. *Review of Educational Research, 65*(1), 1–21.

Buscemi, J., & Spring, B. (2015). Evidence-based practice in psychology. In R. L. Cautin & S. O. Lilienfeld (Eds.), *The encyclopedia of clinical psychology* (pp. 1147–1153). West Sussex, UK: Wiley Blackwell.

Bush, N. E. (1983). The near-death experience in children: Shades of the prison-house reopening. *Anabiosis: The Journal of Near-Death Studies*, 3, 177–193.

Bushdid, C., Magnasco, M. O., Vosshall, L. B., & Keller, A. (2014). Humans can discriminate more than 1 trillion olfactory stimuli. *Science, 343*(6177), 1370–1372.

Bushman, B. J., & Anderson, C. A. (2001). Media violence and the American public: Scientific facts versus media misinformation. *American Psychologist, 56*, 477–489.

Bushman, B. J., & Cooper, H. M. (1990). Effects of alcohol on human aggression: An integrative research review. *Psychological Bulletin, 107*(3), 341–354.

Bushman, B. J., & Huesmann, L. R. (2010). Aggression. In S. T. Fiske, D. T. Gilbert, & G. Lindzey (Eds.), *Handbook of social psychology* (5th ed., Vol. 2, pp. 833–863). Hoboken, NJ: Wiley.

Bushnell, I. W. R. (2001). Mother's face recognition in newborn infants: Learning and memory. *Infant and Child Development, 10*(1–2), 67–74.

Bushnell, I. W. R., Sai, F., and Mullin, J. T. (1989). Neonatal recognition of the mother's face. *British Journal of Developmental Psychology, 7*(1), 3–15.

Buss, D. M. (1989). Sex differences in human mate preferences: Evolutionary hypotheses tested in 37 cultures. *Behavioral and Brain Sciences, 12*(1), 1–49.

Buss, D. M. (1994). *The evolution of desire: Strategies of human mating*. New York, NY: Basic Books.

Buss, D. M. (1995). Psychological sex differences: Origins through sexual selection. *American Psychologist, 50*, 164–168.

Buss, D. M. (2005). *The murderer next door: Why the mind is designed to kill*. New York, NY: Penguin Press.

Buss, D. M., & Duntley, J. D. (2006). The evolution of aggression. In M. Schaller, J. A. Simpson, & D. T. Kenrick (Eds.), *Evolution and social psychology* (pp. 263–285). New York, NY: Psychology Press.

Buss, D. M., Larsen, R. J., Westen, D., & Semmelroth, J. (1992). Sex differences in jealousy: Evolution, physiology, and psychology. *Psychological Science, 3*(4), 251–255.

Bussey, K. (2013). Gender development. In M. K. Ryan & N. R. Branscombe (Eds.), *The SAGE handbook of gender and psychology* (pp. 81–99). Thousand Oaks, CA: SAGE.

Bussey, K., & Bandura, A. (1999). Social cognitive theory of gender development and differentiation. *Psychological Review, 106*(4), 676–713.

Butcher, J. N. (2010). Personality assessment from the nineteenth to the early twenty-first century: Past achievements and contemporary challenges. *Annual Review of Clinical Psychology, 6*, 1–20.

Butcher, J. N. (2011). *A beginner's guide to the MMPI-2* (3rd ed.). Washington, DC: American Psychological Association.

Butcher, J. N. (2012). 25 historical highlights: Significant contributions for use of the MMPI/MMPI-2 in personnel applications retrieved from http://www.umn.edu/mmpi.

Butcher, J. N., & Beutler, L. E. (2003). The MMPI-2. In L. E. Beutler & G. Groth-Marnat (Eds.), *Integrative assessment of adult personality* (2nd ed., pp. 157–191). New York, NY: Guilford Press.

Butcher, J. N., Mosch, S. C., Tsai, J., & Nezami, E. (2006). Cross-cultural applications of the MMPI-2. In J. N. Butcher (Ed.), *MMPI-2: A practitioner's guide* (pp. 505–537). Washington, DC: American Psychological Association.

Butcher, J. N., & Williams, C. L. (2009). Personality assessment with the MMPI-2: Historical roots, international adaptations, and current challenges. *Applied Psychology: Health and Well-being, 1*(1), 105–135.

Butler, E. A., Egloff, B., Wilhelm, F. H., Smith, N. C., Erickson, E. A., & Gross, J. J. (2003). The social consequences of expressive suppression. *Emotion, 3*(1), 48–67.

Butzlaff, R. L., & Hooley, J. M. (1998). Expressed emotion and psychiatric relapse: A meta-analysis. *Archives of General Psychiatry, 55*(6), 547–552.

Buunk, B. P., Angleitner, A., Oubaid, V., & Buss, D. M. (1996). Sex differences in jealousy in evolutionary and cultural perspective: Tests from the Netherlands, Germany, and the United States. *Psychological Science, 7*(6), 359–363.

Buunk, B. P., Collins, R. L., Taylor, S. E., VanYperen, N. W., & Dakof, G. A. (1990). The affective consequences of social comparison: Either direction has its ups and downs. *Journal of Personality and Social Psychology, 59*(6), 1238–1249.

Bybee, J., & McClelland, J. L. (2005). Alternatives to the combinatorial paradigm of linguistic theory based on domain general principles of human cognition. *The Linguistic Review, 22*(2–4), 381–410.

Cabaniss, D. L., Cherry, S., Douglas, C. J., & Schwartz, A. R. (2011). *Psychodynamic psychotherapy: A clinical manual*. New York, NY: Wiley.

Caccavale, J. (2013). Mental healthcare professionals need to boycott the DSM-5. *The Clinical Practitioner, 8*(4), 1–3.

Cacciari, C., & Padovani, R. (2012). The development of figurative language. In M. Spivey, M. Joanisse, & K. McRae, *The Cambridge handbook of psycholinguistics* (pp. 505–522). New York, NY: Cambridge University Press.

Caceres, A., Hall, D. L., Zelaya, F. O., Williams, S. C., & Mehta, M. A. (2009). Measuring fMRI reliability with the intra-class correlation coefficient. *Neuroimage, 45*(3), 758–768.

Cacioppo, J. T., & Berntson, G. C. (2011). The brain, homeostasis, and health: Balancing demands of the internal and external milieu. In H. S. Friedman (Ed.), *The Oxford handbook of health psychology* (pp. 121–137). Oxford, UK: Oxford University Press.

Cacioppo, J. T., Hawkley, L. C., & Berntson, G. G. (2003). The anatomy of loneliness. *Current Directions in Psychological Science, 12*(3), 71–74.

Cadinu, M., Maass, A., Rosabianca, A., & Kiesner, J. (2005). Why do women underperform under stereotype threat? Evidence for the role of negative thinking. *Psychological Science, 16*(7), 572–578.

Cain, D. J. (2002). Defining characteristics, history, and evolution of humanistic psychotherapies. In D. J. Cain & J. Seeman (Eds.), *Humanistic psychotherapies: Handbook of research and practice* (pp. 3–54). Washington, DC: American Psychological Association.

Cain, D. J. (2010). *Person-centered psychotherapies*. Washington, DC: American Psychological Association.

Cain, W. S. (1982). Odor identification by males and females: Predictions vs performance. *Chemical Senses, 7*(2), 129–142.

Cairns, R. B., & Cairns, B. D. (2006). The making of developmental psychology. In R. M. Lerner (Vol. Ed.), *Handbook of child psychology* (6th ed., Vol. 1, pp. 89–165). Hoboken, NJ: Wiley.

Calfee, R. (2007). Learning about learning: Psychologists in schools of education. In R. J. Sternberg (Ed.), *Career paths in psychology: A guide for graduate students and research assistants* (pp. 35–49). Washington, DC: American Psychological Association.

Calle, E. E., Rodriguez, C., Walker-Thurmond, K., & Thun, M. J. (2003). Overweight, obesity, and mortality from cancer in a prospectively studied cohort of U.S. adults. *New England Journal of Medicine, 348*(17), 1625–1638.

Calogero, R. M., & Thompson, J. K. (2010). Gender and body image. In J. C. Chrisler & D. R. McCreary (Eds.), *Handbook of gender research in psychology* (Vol. 1, pp. 153–184). New York, NY: Springer Science+Business Media.

Calogero, R. M., Tantleff-Dunn, S., & Thompson, J. K. (Eds.) (2011). *Self-objectification in women: Causes, consequences, and counteractions*. Washington, DC: American Psychological Association.

Camara, W. J., Nathan, J. S., & Puente, A. E. (2000). Psychological test usage: Implications in professional psychology. *Professional Psychology: Research and Practice, 31*(2), 141–154.

Cameron, A. Y. (2015). Dialectical behavior therapy. In R. L. Cautin & S. O. Lilienfeld (Eds.), *The encyclopedia of clinical psychology* (pp. 873–878). West Sussex, UK: Wiley-Blackwell.

Campbell, W. H., & Rohrbaugh, R. M. (2006). *The biopsychosocial formulation manual: A guide for mental health professionals*. New York, NY: Routledge.

Camras, L. A., Malatesta, C., & Izard, C. E. (1991). The development of facial expression in infancy. In R. Feldman & B. Rime (Eds.), *Fundamentals of nonverbal behavior* (pp. 73–105). New York, NY: Cambridge University Press.

Candel, I., & Merckelbach, H. (2003). Fantasy proneness and thought suppression as predictors of Medical Student Syndrome. *Personality and Individual Differences, 35*(1), 519–524.

Cannon, W. B. (1927). The James-Lange theory of emotions: A critical examination and an alternative theory. *American Journal of Psychology, 39*, 106–124.

Cannon, W. B. (1931). Against the James–Lange and the thalamic theories of emotions. *Psychological Review, 38*(4), 281–295.

Cannon, W. B. (1932). *The wisdom of the body*. New York, NY: Norton.

Cantor, J. (2004). "I'll never have a clown in my house"—Why movie horror lives on. *Poetics Today, 25*(2), 283–304.

Cantor, J. (2011). Fear reactions and the mass media. In K. Döveling, C. Sheve, & E. Konijn (Eds.), *The Routledge handbook of emotions and mass media* (pp. 148–165). London, UK: Routledge.

Cantor, J., Byrne, S., Moyer-Gusé, E., & Riddle, K. (2010). Descriptions of media-induced fright reactions. *Journal of Children and Media, 4*(1), 1–17.

Capaldi, E. J., & Proctor, R. W. (2003). Current and future trends in experimental psychology. In S. F. Davis (Ed.), *Handbook of research methods in experimental psychology* (pp. 24–38). Malden, MA: Blackwell

Capellini, I., Nunn, C. L., McNamara, P., Preston, B. T., & Barton, R. A. (2008). Energetic constraints, not predation, influence the evolution of sleep patterning in mammals. *Functional Ecology, 22*(5), 847–853.

Caplan, P. J. (1992). Gender issues in the diagnosis of mental disorder. *Women & Therapy, 12*(4), 71–82.

Caplan, P. J. (1995). *They say you're crazy: How the world's most powerful psychiatrists decide who's normal*. Reading, MA: Addison-Wesley.

Caplan, P. J., & Cosgrove, L. (Eds.) (2004). *Bias in psychiatric diagnosis*. Lanham, MD: Jason Aronson.

Caporael, L. R. (2007). Evolutionary theory for social and cultural psychology. In A. W. Kruglanski & E. T. Higgins (Eds.), *Social psychology: Handbook of basic principles* (2nd ed., pp. 3–18). New York, NY: Guilford Press.

Caprara, G. V., Vecchione, M., Alessandri, G., Gerbino, M., & Barbaranelli, C. (2011). The contribution of personality traits and self-efficacy beliefs to academic achievement: A longitudinal study. *British Journal of Educational Psychology, 81*(1), 78–96.

Carbado, D. W., Crenshaw, K. W., Mays, V. M., & Tomlinson, B. (2013). Intersectionality. *Du Bois Review: Social Science Research on Race, 10*(2), 303–312.

Card, N. A., & Little, T. D. (2007). Longitudinal modeling of developmental processes. *International Journal of Behavioral Development, 31*(4), 297–302.

Card, N. A., Stucky, B. D., Sawalani, G. M., & Little, T. D. (2008). Direct and indirect aggression during childhood and adolescence: A meta-analytic review of gender differences, intercorrelations, and relations to maladjustment. *Child Development, 79*(5), 1185–1229.

Cárdenas, M., & Barrientos, J. E. (2008). The attitudes toward lesbians and gay men scale (ATLG): Adaptation and testing the reliability and validity in Chile. *Journal of Sex Research, 45*(2), 140–149.

Cardno, A. G., & Gottesman, I. I. (2000). Twin studies of schizophrenia: From bow-and-arrow concordances to Star Wars Mx and functional genomics. *American Journal of Medical Genetics, 97*(1), 12–17.

Carew, T. J., Hawkins, R. D., & Kandel, E. R. (1983). Differential classical conditioning of a defensive withdrawal reflex in *Aplysia californica*. *Science, 219*, 397–400.

Carew, T. J., Walters, E. T., & Kandel, E. R. (1981). Classical conditioning in a simple withdrawal reflex in *Aplysia californica*. *The Journal of Neuroscience, 1*, 1426–1437.

Carli, L. L. (1990). Gender, language, and influence. *Journal of Personality and Social Psychology, 59*(5), 941–951.

Carli, L. L. (2013). Gendered communication and social influence. In M. K. Ryan & N. R. Branscombe (Eds.), *The SAGE handbook of gender and psychology* (pp. 199–215). Thousand Oaks, CA: SAGE.

Carlson, L. A. (2010). Top-down and bottom-up processing. In E. B. Goldstein (Ed.), *Encyclopedia of perception* (pp. 1011–1014). Thousand Oaks, CA: SAGE.

Carlson, L. E. (2015). Mindfulness-based interventions for physical conditions: A selective review. In K. W. Brown, J. D. Creswell, & R. M. Ryan (Eds.), *Handbook of mindfulness: Theory, research, and practice* (pp. 405–425). New York, NY: Guilford Press.

Carlson, L. E., Speca, M., Patel, K. D., & Goodey, E. (2003). Mindfulness-based stress reduction in relation to quality of life, mood, symptoms of stress, and immune parameters in breast and prostate cancer outpatients. *Psychosomatic Medicine, 65*(4), 571–581.

Carlson, M., Marcus-Newhall, A., & Miller, N. (1990). Effects of situational aggression cues: A quantitative review. *Journal of Personality and Social Psychology, 58*(4), 622–633.

Carmody, J. (2015). Reconceptualizing mindfulness: The psychological principles of attending in mindfulness practice and their role in well-being. In K. W. Brown, J. D. Creswell, & R. M. Ryan (Eds.), *Handbook of mindfulness: Theory, research, and practice* (pp. 62–80). New York, NY: Guilford Press.

Carnagey, N. L., Anderson, C. A., & Bushman, B. J. (2007). The effect of video game violence on physiological desensitization to real-life violence. *Journal of Experimental Social Psychology, 43*(3), 489–496.

Carney, S. Cowen, P., Geddes, J., Goodwin, G., Rogers, R., Dearness, K., . . . Scott, A. (2003). Efficacy and safety of electroconvulsive therapy in depressive disorders: A systematic review and meta-analysis. *The Lancet, 361*(9360), 799–808.

Carpendale, J. I. M. (2009). Piaget's theory of moral development. In U. Müller, J. I. M. Carpendale, & L. Smith (Eds.), *The Cambridge companion to Piaget* (pp. 270–286). New York, NY: Cambridge University Press.

Carpendale, J. I. M., & Lewis, C. (2010). The development of social understanding: A relational perspective. In W. F. Overton (Ed.), *Handbook of life-span development* (Vol. 1, pp. 584–627). Hoboken, NJ: Wiley.

Carpenter, M. (2011). Social cognition and social motivations in infancy. In U. Goswami (Ed.), *The Wiley-Blackwell handbook of childhood cognitive development* (2nd ed., pp. 106–128). Malden, MA: Wiley-Blackwell.

Carpenter, M., Akhtar, N., & Tomasello, M. (1998). Fourteen- through 18-month-old infants differentially imitate intentional and accidental actions. *Infant behavior and development, 21*(2), 315–330.

Carpenter, R. J. (1997). Margaret Floy Washburn. In W. G. Bringmann, H. E. Lück, R. Miller, & C. E. Early (Eds.), *A pictorial history of psychology* (pp. 187–190). Carol Stream, IL: Quintessence Publishing

Carr, A. (2008). *What works with children, adolescents, and adults? A review of research on the effectiveness of psychotherapy*. New York, NY: Routledge.

Carr, N. (2008). Is Google making us stupid? *The Atlantic*, July 1, 2008. Retrieved from http://www.theatlantic.com/magazine/archive/2008/07/is-google-making-us-stupid/306868/ on September 7, 2013.

Carraher, T. N., Carraher, D. W., & Schliemann, A. D. (1985). Mathematics in the streets and in schools. *British Journal of Developmental Psychology, 3*(1), 21–29.

Carrier, M., & Pashler, H. (1992). The influence of retrieval on retention. *Memory & Cognition, 20*(6), 633–642.

Carrillo, J., Corning, A. F., Dennehy, T. C., & Crosby, F. J. (2011). Relative deprivation: Understanding the dynamics of discontent. In D. Chadee (Ed.), *Theories in social psychology* (pp. 140–160). West Sussex, UK: Wiley-Blackwell.

Carroll, D., Ebrahim, S., Tilling, K., Macleod, J., & Smith, G. D. (2002). Admissions for myocardial infarction and World Cup football: Database survey. *BMJ: British Medical Journal, 325*(7378), 1439–1442.

Carroll, J. B. (1993). *Human cognitive abilities: A survey of factor-analytic studies*. Cambridge, UK: Cambridge University Press.

Carroll, L. (2013). Problem-focused coping. In M. D. Gellman & J. R. Turner (Eds.), *Encyclopedia of Behavioral Medicine* (pp. 1540–1541). New York, NY: Springer Science+Business Media.

Carskadon, M. A., Acebo, C., & Jenni, O. G. (2004). Regulation of adolescent sleep: Implications for behavior. *Annals of the New York Academy of Sciences, 1021*(1), 276–291.

Carskadon, M. A. & Dement, W. C. (1996). Normal human sleep: An overview. In M. H. Kryger, T. Roth, & W. C. Dement (Eds.), *Principles and practice of sleep medicine* (pp. 16–25). Philadelphia, PA: Saunders.

Carskadon, M. A., & Tarokh, L. (2013). Developmental changes in circadian timing and sleep: Adolescence and emerging adulthood. In A. R. Wolfson & H. Montgomery-Downs (Eds.), *The Oxford handbook of infant, child, and adolescent sleep and behavior* (pp. 70–79). New York, NY: Oxford University Press.

Carskadon, M. A., Vieira, C., & Acebo, C. (1993). Association between puberty and delayed phase preference. *Sleep, 16*, 258–262.

Carson, J. W., Carson, K. M., Gil, K. M., & Baucom, D. H. (2004). Mindfulness-based relationship enhancement. *Behavior Therapy, 35*(3), 471–494.

Carson, S. H., Peterson, J. B., & Higgins, D. M. (2005). Reliability, validity, and factor structure of the creative achievement questionnaire. *Creativity Research Journal, 17*(1), 37–50.

Carstairs-McCarthy, A. (2001). Origins of language. In M. Aronoff & J. Rees-Miller (Eds.), *The handbook of linguistics* (pp. 1–18). Malden, MA: Blackwell.

Carstens, E. (2010). Itch, tickle, and tingle. In E. B. Goldstein (Ed.), *Encyclopedia of perception* (pp. 509–512). Thousand Oaks, CA: SAGE.

Carstensen, L. L., Pasupathi, M., Mayr, U., & Nesselroade, J. R. (2000). Emotional experience in everyday life across the adult life span. *Journal of Personality and Social Psychology, 79*(4), 644–655.

Carstensen, L. L., Turan, B., Scheibe, S., Ram, N., Ersner-Hershfield, H., Samanez-Larkin, G. R., . . . Nesselroade, J. R. (2011). Emotional experience improves with age: Evidence based on over 10 years of experience sampling. *Psychology and Aging, 26*(1), 21–33.

Carter, N., Ulfberg, J., Nyström, B., & Edling, C. (2003). Sleep debt, sleepiness and accidents among males in the general population and male professional drivers. *Accident Analysis & Prevention, 35*(4), 613–617.

Cartwright, M., Wardle, J., Steggles, N., Simon, A. E., Croker, H., & Jarvis, M. J. (2003). Stress and dietary practices in adolescents. *Health Psychology, 22*(4), 362–369.

Cartwright, R. (2005). Dreaming as a mood regulation system. In M. Kryger, T. Roth, & W. Dement (Eds.), *Principles and practice of sleep medicine* (4th ed., pp. 565–572). Philadelphia, PA: Elsevier Saunders.

Cartwright, R. D. (2006). Sleepwalking. In T. L. Lee-Chiong (Ed.), *Sleep: A comprehensive handbook* (pp. 429–434). Hoboken, N.J: Wiley-Liss.

Cartwright, R., Luten, A., Young, M., Mercer, P., & Bears, M. (1998a). Role of REM sleep and dream affect in overnight mood regulation: A study of normal volunteers. *Psychiatry Research, 81*(1), 1–8.

Cartwright, R., Young, M. A., Mercer, P., & Bears, M. (1998b). Role of REM sleep and dream variables in the prediction of remission from depression. *Psychiatry Research, 80*(3), 249–255.

Carver, C. (2013). Coping. In M. D. Gellman & J. R. Turner (Eds.), *Encyclopedia of behavioral medicine* (pp. 496–500). New York, NY: Springer Science+Business Media.

Carver, C. S., & Connor-Smith, J. (2010). Personality and coping. *Annual Review of Psychology, 61*, 679–704.

Carver, C. S., & Vargas, S. (2011). Stress, coping, and health. In H. S. Friedman (Ed.), *The Oxford handbook of health psychology* (pp. 162–188). Oxford, UK: Oxford University Press.

Carver, K., Joyner, K., & Udry, J. R. (2003). National estimates of adolescent romantic relationships. In P. Florsheim (Ed.), *Adolescent romantic relations and sexual behavior: Theory, research, and practical implications* (pp. 23–56). Mahwah, NJ: Lawrence Erlbaum.

Cashel, M. L. (2002). Child and adolescent psychological assessment: Current clinical practices and the impact of managed care. *Professional Psychology: Research and Practice, 33*(5), 446–453.

Caskey-Sirmons, L. A., & Hickerson, N. P. (1977). Semantic shift and bilingualism: Variation in the color terms of five languages. *Anthropological Linguistics, 19*(8), 358–367.

Caspi, A., & Shiner, R. L. (2006). Personality development. In N. Eisenberg (Vol. Ed.), *Handbook of child psychology* (6th ed., Vol. 3, pp. 300–365). Hoboken, NJ: Wiley.

Caspi, A., Harrington, H., Milne, B., Amell, J., Theodore, R. F., & Moffitt, T. E. (2003). Children's behavioral styles at age 3 are linked to their adult personality traits at age 26. *Journal of Personality, 71*, 495–514.

Castano, E. (2012). Antisocial behavior in individuals and groups: An empathy-focused approach. In K. Deaux & M. Snyder (Eds.), *The Oxford handbook of personality and social psychology* (pp. 419–445). New York, NY: Oxford University Press.

Castle, D. J., & Buckley, P. F. (2008). *Schizophrenia*. New York, NY: Oxford University Press.

Castro, F. G., Barrera, M., Jr., & Holleran Steiker, L. K. (2010). Issues and challenges in the design of culturally adapted evidence-based interventions. *Annual Review of Clinical Psychology, 6*, 213–239.

Cattell, J. McK. (1895). Proceedings of the Third Annual Meeting of the American Psychological Association. *Psychological Review, 2*, 149–172.

Cattell, R. B. (1943). The description of personality: Basic traits resolved into clusters. *The Journal of Abnormal and Social Psychology, 38*(4), 476–506.

Cattell, R. B. (1971). *Abilities: their structure, growth, and action*. Boston, MA: Houghton Mifflin.

Cautin, R. L. (2011). A century of psychotherapy, 1860–1960. In J. C. Norcross, G. R. Vandenbos, & D. K. Freedheim (Eds.), *History of psychotherapy: Continuity and change* (2nd ed., pp. 3–38). Washington, DC: American Psychological Association.

Cavanaugh, J. C., & Whitbourne, S. K. (2003). Research methods in adult development. In J. Demick & C. Andreoletti (Eds.), *Handbook of adult development* (pp. 85–100). New York, NY: Springer Science+Business Media.

Cawley, J. (2011). The economics of obesity. In J. H. Cawley (Ed.), *The Oxford handbook of the social science of obesity* (pp. 120–137). New York, NY: Oxford University Press.

Ceci, S. J., Peters, D., & Plotkin, J. (1985). Human subjects review, personal values, and the regulation of social science research. *American Psychologist, 40*(9), 994–1002.

Centers for Disease Control and Prevention (2012). Fast stats: Body measurements. Retrieved from: http://www.cdc.gov/nchs/fastats/body-measurements.htm

Centers for Disease Control and Prevention (2015). About adult BMI. Retrieved from http://www.cdc.gov/healthyweight/assessing/bmi/adult_bmi/#Definition.

Centers for Disease Control and Prevention (2014). Prevalence of autism spectrum disorder among children aged 8 years—Autism and developmental disabilities monitoring network, 11 sites, United States, 2010. *Morbidity and Mortality Weekly Report, Surveillance Summaries, 63*(2), 1–21.

Cerasoli, C. P., Nicklin, J. M., & Ford, M. T. (2014). Intrinsic motivation and extrinsic incentives jointly predict performance: A 40-year meta-analysis. *Psychological Bulletin, 140*(4), 980–1008.

Cernoch, J. M., & Porter, R. H. (1985). Recognition of maternal axillary odors by infants. *Child Development, 56*(6)1593–1598.

Cervero, F. (2013). III. Pain research: What have we learned and where are we going. *British Journal of Anaesthesia, 111*(1), 6–8.

Cesarani, D. (2004). *Eichmann: His life and crimes*. London, UK: Heinemann.

Chae, D. H., Nuru-Jeter, A. M., Lincoln, K. D., & Jacob Arriola, K. R. (2012). Racial discrimination, mood disorders, and cardiovascular disease among black Americans. *Annals of Epidemiology, 22*(2), 104–111.

Chagnon, N. A. (1988). Life histories, blood revenge, and warfare in a tribal population. *Science, 239*(4843), 985–992.

Chakravarthy, M. V., & Booth, F. W. (2004). Eating, exercise, and "thrifty" genotypes: Connecting the dots toward an evolutionary understanding of modern chronic diseases. *Journal of Applied Physiology, 96*(1), 3–10.

Chaloupka, F. J. (2011). Lessons for obesity policy from the tobacco wars. In J. H. Cawley (Ed.), *The Oxford handbook of the social science of obesity* (pp. 620–638). New York, NY: Oxford University Press.

Chambless, D. L, & Ollendick, T. H. (2001). Empirically supported psychological interventions: Controversies and evidence. *Annual Review of Psychology, 52*, 685–716.

Chambless, D. L. (2002). Beware the dodo bird: The dangers of overgeneralization. *Clinical Psychology: Science and Practice, 9*(1), 13–16.

Chambless, D. L., Baker, M. J., Baucom, D. H., Beutler, L. E., Calhoun, K. S., Crits-Christoph, P., . . . Woody, S. R. (1998). Update on empirically validated therapies, II. *The Clinical Psychologist, 51*(1), 3–13.

Chamorro-Premuzic, T., Kallias, A., & Hsu, A. (2014). What type of movie person are you? Understanding individual differences in film preferences and uses: A psychographic approach. In J. C. Kaufman & D. K. Simonton (Eds.), *The social science of cinema* (pp. 87–122). New York, NY: Oxford University Press.

Chan, A. S., & Cistulli, P. A. (2009). Oral appliance treatment of obstructive sleep apnea: An update. *Current Opinion in Pulmonary Medicine, 15*(6), 591–596.

Chan, A., & Poulin, F. (2007). Monthly changes in the composition of friendship networks in early adolescence. *Merrill-Palmer Quarterly, 53*(4), 578–602.

Chan, T. W., & Koo, A. (2011). Parenting style and youth outcomes in the UK. *European Sociological Review, 27*(3), 385–399.

Chance, S., Gaunet, F., Beall, A., & Loomis, J. (1998). Locomotion mode affects the updating of objects encountered during travel: The contribution of vestibular and proprioceptive inputs to path integration. *Presence, 7*(2), 168–178.

Chandler, J., & Schwarz, N. (2009). How extending your middle finger affects your perception of others: Learned movements influence concept accessibility. *Journal of Experimental Social Psychology, 45*(1), 123–128.

Chandra, A, Mosher, W. D., & Copen, C. (2011). Sexual behavior, sexual attraction, and sexual identity in the United States: Data from the 2006–2008 National Survey of Family Growth. *National Health Statistics Report, 36*, 1–36.

Chang, E. C. & Sanna, L. J. (2003). Introduction: Beyond virtue and vice in personality: Classical themes and current trends. In E. C. Chang & L. J. Sanna (Eds.), *Virtue, vice, and personality: The complexity of behavior* (pp. xix–xxvi). Washington, DC: American Psychological Association.

Changizi, M. A., Zhang, Q., & Shimojo, S. (2006). Bare skin, blood and the evolution of primate colour vision. *Biology Letters, 2*(2), 217–221.

Chaplin, T. M., & Aldao, A. (2013). Gender differences in emotion expression in children: A meta-analytic review. *Psychological Bulletin, 139*(4), 735–765.

Charles, S. T., Luong, G., Almeida, D. M., Ryff, C., Sturm, M., & Love, G. (2010). Fewer ups and downs: Daily stressors mediate age differences in negative affect. *The Journals of Gerontology Series B: Psychological Sciences and Social Sciences, 65*(3), 279–286.

Charnley, B. (1991). Self portrait series 18th May 1991. Retrived from http://www.bryancharnley.info/self-portraits-2/charnley_self_portrait_series_09/

Chase, W. G., & Simon, H. A. (1973). Perception in chess. *Cognitive Psychology, 4*(1), 55–81.

Chater, N., Heit, E., & Oaksford, M. (2005). Reasoning. In K. Lamberts & R. L. Goldstone, *Handbook of cognition* (pp. 297–320). London: SAGE.

Chatfield, T. (2012, July 4). Google Glass and the rise in outsourcing our memories. *BBC Future*. Retrieved from http://www.bbc.com/future/story/20120703-outsourcing-our-memories on September 7, 2013.

Cheah, C. S., Leung, C. Y., Tahseen, M., & Schultz, D. (2009). Authoritative parenting among immigrant Chinese mothers of preschoolers. *Journal of Family Psychology, 23*(3), 311–320.

Chen, C., Xue, G., Mei, L., Chen, C., & Dong, Q. (2009). Cultural neurolinguistics. *Progress in Brain Research, 178*, 159–171.

Chen, H. (2006). Flow on the net—detecting Web users' positive affects and their flow states. *Computers in Human Behavior, 22*(2), 221–233.

Chen, H., Wigand, R. T., & Nilan, M. (2000). Exploring web users' optimal flow experiences. *Information Technology & People, 13*(4), 263–281.

Chen, H., Wigand, R. T., & Nilan, M. S. (1999). Optimal experience of web activities. *Computers in Human Behavior, 15*(5), 585–608.

Chen, X. P., Liu, D., & Portnoy, R. (2012). A multilevel investigation of motivational cultural intelligence, organizational diversity climate, and cultural sales: Evidence from U.S. real estate firms. *Journal of Applied Psychology, 97*(1), 93–106.

Chen, X., Chung, J., Lechcier-Kimel, R., & French, D. (2011). Culture and social development. In P. K. Smith & C. H. Hart (Eds.), *The Wiley-Blackwell handbook of childhood social development* (2nd ed., pp. 141–160). Malden, MA: Wiley-Blackwell.

Chen, X., Hastings, P. D., Rubin, K. H., Chen, H., Cen, G., & Stewart, S. L. (1998). Child-rearing attitudes and behavioral inhibition in Chinese and Canadian toddlers: A cross-cultural study. *Developmental Psychology, 34*(4), 677–686.

Chen, X., Kaspar, V., Zhang, Y., Wang, L., & Zheng, S. (2004). Peer relationships among Chinese and North American boys: A cross-cultural perspective. In N. Way & J. Chu (Eds.), *Adolescent boys: Exploring diverse cultures of boyhood* (pp. 197–218). New York, NY: New York University Press.

Chen, X., Rubin, K. H., and Sun, Y. (1992). Social reputation and peer relationships in Chinese and Canadian children: A cross-cultural study. *Child Development, 63*, 1336–1343.

Cheney, T. (2009). *Manic: A Memoir*. New York: HarperCollins.

Cheng, C. (2003). Cognitive and motivational processes underlying coping flexibility: A dual-process model. *Journal of Personality and Social Psychology, 84*(2), 425–438.

Cheng, C., Cheung, S.-F., Chio, J. H., & Chan, M.-P. (2013) Cultural meaning of perceived control: A meta-analysis of locus of control and psychological symptoms across 18 cultural regions. *Psychological Bulletin, 139*(1), 152–188.

Cheng, Y. H., Roach, G. D., & Petrilli, R. (2014). Current and future directions in clinical fatigue management: An update for emergency medicine practitioners. *Emergency Medicine Australasia, 26*(6), 640–644.

Cherry, E. C. (1953). Some experiments on the recognition of speech, with one and with two ears. *The Journal of the Acoustical Society of America, 25*(5), 975–979.

Chesney, M. A. & Rosenman, R. H. (1980). Type A behavior in the work setting. In C. L. Cooper & R. Payne (Eds.), *Current concerns in occupational stress*, (pp. 187–212). New York, NY: John Wiley.

Chess, S., & Alexander, T. (1991) Temperament and the concept of goodness of fit. In J. Strelau & A. Angleitner (Eds.), *Explorations in temperament: International perspectives on theory and measurement* (pp. 15–28). New York, NY: Plenum Press.

Chess, S., & Thomas, A. (1986). *Temperament in clinical practice*. New York, NY: Guilford.

Chevallier, C. (2012). Theory of mind and autism: Revisiting Baron-Cohen et al.'s Sally-Anne study. In A. M. Slater & P. C. Quinn (Eds.), *Developmental psychology: Revisiting the classic studies* (pp. 148–163). Los Angeles, CA: SAGE.

Chevallier, C., Noveck, I., Happé, F., & Wilson, D. (2011). What's in a voice? Prosody as a test case for the theory of mind account of autism. *Neuropsychologia, 49*(3), 507–517.

Chiao, J., & Harada, T. (2008). Cultural neuroscience of consciousness: From visual perception to self-awareness. *Journal of Consciousness Studies, 15*(10–11), 58–69.

Chida, Y., & Steptoe, A. (2008). Positive psychological well-being and mortality: A quantitative review of prospective observational studies. *Psychosomatic Medicine, 70*(7), 741–756.

Chiesa, A., & Serretti, A. (2011). Mindfulness-based cognitive therapy for psychiatric disorders: A systematic review and meta-analysis. *Psychiatry Research, 187*(3), 441–453.

Chihuly, D. (2007). *Team Chihuly*. Seattle, WA: Portland Press.

Chisholm, J. S., Quinlivan, J. A., Petersen, R. W., & Coall, D. A. (2005). Early stress predicts age at menarche and first birth, adult attachment, and expected lifespan. *Human Nature, 16*(3), 233–265.

Chiu, L. H. (1972). A cross-cultural comparison of cognitive styles in Chinese and American children. *International Journal of Psychology, 7*(4), 235–242.

Chodorow, N. J. (1978). *The reproduction of mothering*. Berkeley, CA: University of California Press.

Chodorow, N. J. (1989). *Feminism and psychoanalytic theory*. New Haven, CT: Yale University Press.

Choi, S., Kim, S., Yang, J. S., Lee, J. H., Joo, C., & Jung, H. I. (2014). Real-time measurement of human salivary cortisol for the assessment of psychological stress using a smartphone. *Sensing and Bio-Sensing Research, 2*, 8–11.

Choi, J., & Silverman, I. (2003). Processes underlying sex differences in route-learning strategies in children and adolescents. *Personality and Individual Differences, 34*(7), 1153–1166.

Cholewiak, R. W., & Cholewiak, S. A. (2010). Cutaneous perception. In E. B. Goldstein (Ed.), *Encyclopedia of perception* (pp. 343–348). Thousand Oaks, CA: SAGE.

Chomsky, N. (1959). A review of B. F. Skinner's verbal behavior. *Language, 35*(1), 26–58.

Chomsky, N. (1988). *Aspects of the theory of syntax* (Vol. 11). Cambridge, MA: MIT Press.

Chomsky, N. (1993). *Lectures on government and binding: The Pisa lectures* (No. 9). Berlin, Germany: Walter de Gruyter.

Chomsky, N. (1995). *The minimalist program* (Vol. 28). Cambridge, MA: MIT press.

Chou, H. T. G., & Edge, N. (2012). "They are happier and having better lives than I am": The impact of using Facebook on perceptions of others' lives. *Cyberpsychology, Behavior, and Social Networking, 15*(2), 117–121.

Christiansen, M. H., & Kirby, S. (Eds.). (2003). *Language evolution*. Oxford, UK: Oxford University Press.

Christie, B. R., Swann, S. E., Fox, C. J., Froc, D., Lieblich, S. E., Redila, V., & Webber, A. (2005). Voluntary exercise rescues deficits in spatial memory and long-term potentiation in prenatal ethanol-exposed male rats. *European Journal of Neuroscience, 21*(6), 1719–1726.

Chrysikou, E. G. (2006). When shoes become hammers: Goal-derived categorization training enhances problem-solving performance. *Journal of Experimental Psychology: Learning, Memory, and Cognition, 32*(4), 935–942.

Chua, H. F., Boland, J. E., & Nisbett, R. E. (2005). Cultural variation in eye movements during scene perception. *Proceedings of the National Academy of Sciences of the United States of America, 102*(35), 12629–12633.

Chun, C. A., Enomoto, K., & Sue, S. (1996). Health care issues among Asian Americans. In P. M. Kato & T. Mann (Eds.), *Handbook of diversity issues in health psychology* (pp. 347–365). New York, NY: Springer Science+Business Media.

Chun, C., Moos R. H., & Cronkite, R. C. (2006). Culture: A fundamental context for the stress and coping paradigm. In P. T. P. Wong and L. C. J. Wong (Eds.), *Handbook of multicultural perspectives on stress and coping* (pp. 29–54). New York, NY: Plenum Press.

Chun, M. M., & Wolfe, J. M. (2001). Visual attention. In E. B. Goldstein (Ed.), *Blackwell handbook of perception* (pp. 272–310). Oxford, UK: Blackwell.

Chung, F. F., Yao, C. C. C., & Wan, G. H. (2005). The associations between menstrual function and life style/working conditions among nurses in Taiwan. *Journal of Occupational Health, 47*(2), 149–156.

Cialdini, R. B., & Goldstein, N. J. (2004). Social influence: Compliance and conformity. *Annual Review of Psychology, 55*, 591–621.

Cialdini R. B., & Trost, M. R. (1998). Social influence: Social norms, conformity, and compliance. In D. T. Gilbert, S. T. Fiske, & G. Lindzey (Eds.), *The handbook of social psychology* (4th ed., Vol. 2, pp. 151–192). Boston, MA: McGraw-Hill.

Cialdini, R. B., Vincent, J. E., Lewis, S. K., Catalan, J., Wheeler, D., & Darby, B. L. (1975). Reciprocal concessions procedure for inducing compliance: The door-in-the-face technique. *Journal of Personality and Social Psychology, 31*(2), 206–215.

Cipani, E., & Schock, K. M. (2007). *Functional behavioral assessment, diagnosis, and treatment*. New York, NY: Springer.

Claparède, E. (1911). Recognition et moiité. *Archives de Psychologie, 11*, 79–90.

Claridge, G. (1995). *Origins of mental illness: Temperament, deviance, and disorder*. Cambridge, MA: Malor.

Clark, D. A., & Beck, A. T. (2010). *Cognitive therapy of anxiety disorders*. New York, NY: Guilford Press.

Clark, D. A., Hollifield, M., Leahy, R., & Beck, J. (2009). Theory of cognitive therapy. In G. O. Gabbard (Ed.), *Textbook of psychotherapeutic treatments* (pp. 165–200). Washington, DC: American Psychiatric Publishing.

Clark, H. H. (1992). *Arenas of language use*. Chicago, IL: University of Chicago Press.

Clark, L. A., Watson, D., & Mineka, S. (1994). Temperament, personality, and the mood and anxiety disorders. *Journal of Abnormal Psychology, 103*(1), 103–116.

Clarke, A. T. (2006). Coping with interpersonal stress and psychosocial health among children and adolescents: A meta-analysis. *Journal of Youth and Adolescence, 35*(1), 10–23.

Clarkin, J. F., Widiger, T. A., Frances, A., Hurt, S. W., & Gilmore, M. (1983). Prototypic typology and the borderline personality disorder. *Journal of Abnormal Psychology, 92*(3), 263–275.

Clarkin, J., Yeomanns, F., & Kernberg, O. (2006). *Psychotherapy for borderline personality disorder: Focusing on object relations*. Washington, DC: American Psychiatric Association Publishing.

Cleary, A. M. (2008). Recognition memory, familiarity, and déjà vu experiences. *Current Directions in Psychological Science, 17*(5), 353–357.

Clements-Nolle, K., Marx, R., Guzman, R., & Katz, M. (2001). HIV prevalence, risk behaviors, health care use, and mental health status of transgender persons: Implications for public health intervention. *American Journal of Public Health, 91*(6), 915–921.

Climo, A. H., & Stewart, A. J. (2003). Eldercare and personality development in middle age. In J. Demick & C. Andreoletti (Eds.), *Handbook of adult development* (pp. 443–458). New York, NY: Kluwer.

Clinton, H. R., & Hyman, S. (1999). Mental illness is a disease. In T. I. Rodeff & L. K. Egendorf (Eds.), *How should mental illness be defined?* (pp. 37–41). San Diego, CA: Greenhaven Press.

Coburn, K., Lauterbach, E., Boutros, N., Black, K., Arciniegas, D., & Coffey, C. (2006). The value of quantitative electroencephalography in clinical psychiatry: A report by the Committee on Research of the American Neuropsychiatric Association. *Journal of Neuropsychiatry and Clinical Neurosciences, 18*(4), 460–500.

Cochran, S. D. & Mays, V. M. (2013). Sexual orientation and mental health. In C. J. Patterson & A. R. D'Augelli (Eds.), *Handbook of psychology and sexual orientation* (pp. 204–222). New York, NY: Oxford University Press.

Cochran, S. D., Sullivan, J. G., & Mays, V. M. (2003). Prevalence of mental disorders, psychological distress, and mental health services use among lesbian, gay, and bisexual adults in the United States. *Journal of Consulting and Clinical Psychology, 71*(1), 53–61.

Cohen, D. & Gunz, A. (2002). As seen by the other. . .: Perspectives on the self in the memories and emotional perceptions of Easterners and Westerners. *Psychological Science, 13*(1), 55–59.

Cohen, L. B., & Cashon, C. H. (2006). Infant cognition. In D. Kuhn & R. Siegler (Vol. Eds.), *Handbook of child psychology* (6th ed., Vol. 2, pp. 214–251). Hoboken, NJ: Wiley.

Cohen, L. L., Greco, L., & Martin, S. (2013). Presenting your research. In M. J. Prinstein (Ed.), *The portable mentor: Expert guide to a successful career in psychology* (pp. 133–143). New York, NY: Springer.

Cohen, N., Moynihan, J. A., & Ader, R. (1994). Pavlovian conditioning of the immune system. *International Archives of Allergy and Immunology, 105*(2), 101–106.

Cohen, S. (2004). Social relationships and health. *American Psychologist, 59*(8), 676–684.

Cohen, S., Doyle, W. J., Turner, R., Alper, C. M., & Skoner, D. P. (2003). Sociability and susceptibility to the common cold. *Psychological Science, 14*(5), 389–395.

Cohen, S., & Pressman, S. D. (2006). Positive affect and health. *Current Directions in Psychological Science, 15*(3), 122–125.

Cohen, S., Tyrrell, D. A., & Smith, A. P. (1991). Psychological stress and susceptibility to the common cold. *New England Journal of Medicine, 325*(9), 606–612.

Cohen, S., Tyrrell, D. A., & Smith, A. P. (1993). Negative life events, perceived stress, negative affect, and susceptibility to the common cold. *Journal of Personality and Social Psychology, 64*(1), 131–140.

Cohen, S., & Williamson, G. M. (1991). Stress and infectious disease in humans. *Psychological Bulletin, 109*(1), 5–24.

Cohen-Filipic, J. (2015). Dual relationship/conflict of interest. In R. L. Cautin & S. O. Lilienfeld (Eds.), *The encyclopedia of clinical psychology* (pp. 978–984). West Sussex, UK: Wiley-Blackwell.

Cohn, A. (2001). Phonology. In M. Aronoff & J. Rees-Miller (Eds.), *The handbook of linguistics* (pp. 180–212). Malden, MA: Blackwell.

Coid, J., Yang, N., Tyrer, P., Roberts, S., & Ullrich. S. (2006). Prevalence and correlates of personality disorder in Great Britain. *British Journal of Psychiatry, 188*, 423–431.

Coker, L. A., & Widiger, T. A. (2005). Personality disorders. In J. E. Maddux & B. A. Winstead (Eds.), *Psychopathology: Foundations for a contemporary understanding* (pp. 223–252). Mahway, NJ: Lawrence Erlbaum.

Colcombe, S. J., Erickson, K. I., Scalf, P. E., Kim, J. S., Prakash, R., McAuley, E., . . . & Kramer, A. F. (2006). Aerobic exercise training increases brain volume in aging humans. *The Journals of Gerontology Series A: Biological Sciences and Medical Sciences, 61*(11), 1166–1170.

Cole, E. R. (2009). Intersectionality and research in psychology. *American Psychologist, 64*(3), 170–180.

Cole, M. (2005). Culture in development. In M. H. Bornstein & M. E. Lamb (Eds.), *Developmental science: An advanced textbook* (5th ed., pp. 45–101). Mahwah, NJ: Lawrence Erlbaum.

Cole, M. (2006). Culture and cognitive development in phylogenic, historical, and ontogenic perspective. In D. Kuhn & R. Siegler (Vol. Eds.), *Handbook of child psychology* (6th ed., Vol. 2, pp. 636–683). Hoboken, NJ: Wiley.

Cole, S. W., Kemeny, M. E., Taylor, S. E., & Visscher, B. R. (1996). Elevated physical health risk among gay men who conceal their homosexual identity. *Health Psychology, 15*(4), 243–251.

Coleman, S. R. (1997). B. F. Skinner: Maverick, inventor, behaviorist, critic. In W. G. Bringmann, H. E. Lück, R. Miller, & C. E. Early (Eds.), *A pictorial history of psychology* (pp. 206–213). Carol Stream, IL: Quintessence Publishing
Coles, R. (Ed.). (2000). *The Erik Erikson reader*. New York, NY: W. W. Norton.
Collins, R. L., Elliott, M. N., Berry, S. H., Kanouse, D. E., Kunkel, D., Hunter, S. B., & Miu, A. (2004). Watching sex on television predicts adolescent initiation of sexual behavior. *Pediatrics, 114*(3), e280–e289.
Collins, W. A., & Steinberg, L. (2006). Adolescent development in interpersonal context. In N. Eisenberg (Vol. Ed.), *Handbook of child psychology* (6th ed., Vol. 3, pp. 1003–1067). Hoboken, NJ: Wiley.
Colom, R., Martínez-Molina, A., Shih, P. C., & Santacreu, J. (2010). Intelligence, working memory, and multitasking performance. *Intelligence, 38*(6), 543–551.
Coltheart, M. (1980). Iconic memory and visible persistence. *Perception & Psychophysics, 27*(3), 183–228.
Comas-Diaz, L. (2011). Multicultural approaches to psychotherapy. In J. C. Norcross, G. R. Vandenbos, & D. K. Freedheim (Eds.), *History of psychotherapy: Continuity and change* (2nd ed., pp. 243–268). Washington, DC: American Psychological Association.
Comas-Diaz, L. (2012). *Multicultural care: A clinician's guide to cultural competence*. Washington, DC: American Psychological Association.
Committee on Sleep Medicine and Research (2006). *Sleep disorders and sleep deprivation: An unmet public health problem*. Washington, DC: National Academies Press.
Compton, R. P., & Berning, A. (2015, February). *Drug and alcohol crash risk*. (Traffic Safety Facts, Research Note. DOT HS 812 117). Washington, DC: National Highway Traffic Safety Administration.
Cone, J. E., Vaughan, L. M., Huete, A., & Samuels, S. J. (1998). Reproductive health outcomes among female flight attendants: An exploratory study. *Journal of Occupational and Environmental Medicine, 40*(3), 210–216.
Connelly, B. S., & Ones, D. S. (2010). An other perspective on personality: Meta-analytic integration of observers' accuracy and predictive validity. *Psychological Bulletin, 136*(6), 1092.
Connolly, J., Craig, W., Goldberg, A., & Pepler, D. (2004). Mixed-gender groups, dating, and romantic relationships in early adolescence. *Journal of Research on Adolescence, 14*(2), 185–207.
Connolly, J., Friedlander, L., Pepler, D., Craig, W., & Laporte, L. (2010). The ecology of adolescent dating aggression: Attitudes, relationships, media use, and socio-demographic risk factors. *Journal of Aggression, Maltreatment & Trauma, 19*(5), 469–491.
Connolly, J. A., & McIsaac, C. (2009). Romantic relationships in adolescence. In R. M. Lerner & L. Steinberg (Eds.), *Handbook of adolescent psychology* (3rd ed., Vol. 2, pp. 104–151). Hoboken, NJ: Wiley.
Connolly, J. J., Kavanagh, E. J., & Viswesvaran, C. (2007). The convergent validity between self and observer ratings of personality: A meta-analytic review. *International Journal of Selection and Assessment, 15*(1), 110–117.
Conover, E. A., & Polifka, J. E. (2011, August). The art and science of teratogen risk communication. *American Journal of Medical Genetics Part C: Seminars in Medical Genetics 157*(3), 227–233.
Conrad, P., & Markens, S. (2001). Constructing the "gay gene" in the news: Optimism and skepticism in the U.S. and British press. *Health, 5*(3), 373–400.
Constantine, M. G. (2002). Predictors of satisfaction with counseling: Racial and ethnic minority clients' attitudes toward counseling and ratings of their counselors' general and multicultural counseling competence. *Journal of Counseling Psychology, 49*(2), 255–263.
Constantino, M. J., Glass, C. R., Arnkoff, D. B., Ametrano, R. M., & Smith, J. Z. (2011). Expectations. In J. C. Norcross (Ed.), *Psychotherapy relationships that work: Evidence-based responsiveness* (2nd ed., pp. 354–376). New York, NY: Oxford University Press.
Constantino, M. J., Lembke, A., Fischer, C., & Arnow, B. A. (2006). Adult depression: Features, burdens, models, and interventions. In T. G. Plante (Ed.), *Mental disorders of the new millennium* (Vol. 1, pp. 139–166). Westport, CT: Praeger.
Contrada, R. J., & Baum, A. (2011). *The handbook of stress science: Biology, psychology, and health*. New York, NY: Springer Publishing.
Contrada, R. J., Ashmore, R. D., Gary, M. L., Coups, E., Egeth, J. D., Sewell, A., . . . Chasse, V. (2000). Ethnicity-related sources of stress and their effects on well-being. *Current Directions in Psychological Science, 9*(4), 136–139.
Contrada, R. J., Ashmore, R. D., Gary, M. L., Coups, E., Egeth, J. D., Sewell, A., . . . Chasse, V. (2001). Measures of ethnicity-related stress: Psychometric properties, ethnic group differences, and associations with well-being. *Journal of Applied Social Psychology, 31*(9), 1775–1820.
Conway, M. A. (2008). Exploring episodic memory. In E. Dere, A. Easton, L. Nadel, & J. P. Huston (Eds.), *Handbook of episodic memory* (pp. 19–29). Amsterdam, Netherlands: Elsevier Science.
Conway, M. A., Wang, Q., Hanyu, K., & Haque, S. (2005). A cross-cultural investigation of autobiographical memory on the universality and cultural variation of the reminiscence bump. *Journal of Cross-Cultural Psychology, 36*(6), 739–749.
Cook, E. W., Hodes, R. L., & Lang, P. J. (1986). Preparedness and phobia: Effects of stimulus content on human visceral conditioning. *Journal of Abnormal Psychology, 95*, 195–207.
Cook, J. M., Biyanova, T., & Coyne, J. C. (2009). Influential psychotherapy figures, authors, and books: An Internet survey of over 2,000 psychotherapists. *Psychotherapy: Theory, Research, Practice, Training, 46*(1), 42–51.
Cook, J. M., Biyanova, T., Elhai, J., Schnurr, P. P., & Coyne, J. C. (2010). What do psychotherapists really do in practice? An Internet study of over 2,000 practitioners. *Psychotherapy: Theory, Research, Practice, Training, 47*(2), 260–267.
Cook, K. (2014). *Kitty Genovese: The murder, the bystanders, the crime that changed America*. New York, NY: W. W. Norton.
Coolidge, F. L., & Wynn, T. (2012) Cognitive prerequisites for the evolution of indirect speech. In M. Tallerman & K. R. Gibson (Eds.), *The Oxford handbook of language evolution* (pp. 216–223). Oxford, UK: Oxford University Press.
Cooper, C. L. & Dewe, P. (2004). *Stress: A brief history*. Malden, MA: Blackwell.
Cooper, H., & Goodnough, A. (2009, July 30). "Over Beers, No Apologies, But Plans to Have Lunch." The *New York Times*. http://www.nytimes.com/2009/07/31/us/politics/31obama.html
Cooper, J. (1999). Unwanted consequences and the self: In search of the motivation for dissonance reduction. In E. Harmon-Jones & J. Mills (Eds.), *Cognitive dissonance: Progress on a pivotal theory in social psychology* (pp. 149–173). Washington, DC: American Psychological Association.
Cooper, J. (2007). *Cognitive dissonance: 50 years of a classic theory*. Thousand Oaks, CA: SAGE.
Cooper, J. (2012). Cognitive dissonance theory. In P. A. M. Van Lange, A. W. Kruglanski, & E. T. Higgins (Eds.), *Handbook of theories of social psychology* (Vol. 1, pp. 377–397). Thousand Oaks, CA: SAGE.
Cooper, L., & Bright, J. (2001). Individual differences in reactions to stress. In F. Jones & J. Bright (Eds.), *Stress: Myth, theory and research* (pp. 111–131). Essex, UK: Pearson Education Ltd.
Copeland, W. E., Angold, A., Costello, E. J., & Egger, H. (2013). Prevalence, comorbidity, and correlates of DSM-5 proposed disruptive mood dysregulation disorder. *American Journal of Psychiatry, 170*(2), 173–179.
Corballis, M. C. (2007). The evolution of consciousness. In P. D. Zelazo, M. Moscovitch, & E. Thompson (Eds.), *The Cambridge handbook of consciousness* (pp. 571–596). Cambridge, UK: Cambridge University Press.
Corcoran, K., Crusius, J., & Mussweiler, T. (2011). Social comparison: Motives, standards, and mechanisms. In D. Chadee (Ed.), *Theories in social psychology* (pp. 119–139). West Sussex, UK: Wiley-Blackwell.
Corkin, S. (2013). *Permanent present tense: The unforgettable life of the amnesic patient, H. M.* New York, NY: Basic Books.
Cornblatt, B. A., Green, M. F., Walker, E. F., & Mittal, V. A. (2009). Schizophrenia: Etiology and neurocognition. In P. H. Blaney & T. Millon (Eds.), *Oxford textbook of psychopathology* (2nd ed., pp. 298–332). New York, NY: Oxford University Press.
Cornette, M. M., Strauman, T. J., Abramson, L. Y., & Busch, A. M. (2009). Self-discrepancy and suicidal ideation. *Cognition and Emotion, 23*(3), 504–527.
Cortese, S., Kelly, C., Chabernaud, C., Proal, E., Adriana Di Martino, M. D., Milham, M. P., & Castellanos, F. X. (2012). Toward systems neuroscience of ADHD: A meta-analysis of 55 fMRI studies. *American Journal of Psychiatry, 169*(10), 1038–1055.
Costa, P., Jr., Terracciano, A., & McCrae, R. R. (2001). Gender differences in personality traits across cultures: Robust and surprising findings. *Journal of Personality and Social Psychology, 81*(2), 322–331.
Costa, P. T., & McCrae, R. R. (1985). *The NEO personality inventory*. Odessa, FL: Psychological Assessment Resources.
Costa, P. T., & McCrae, R. R. (1992). Four ways five factors are basic. *Personality and Individual Differences, 13*(6), 653–665.
Costa, P. T., & McCrae, R. R. (1992). *Revised NEO personality inventory (NEO) PI-R) and NEO five-factor inventory: Professional manual*. Odessa, FL: Psychological Assessment Resources.
Costa, P. T., & Widiger, T. A. (2001). *Personality disorders and the five-factor model of personality* (2nd ed.). Washington, DC: American Psychological Association.
Costa, P. T., Jr., & McCrae, R. R. (2008). The NEO inventories. In R. P. Archer & S. R. Smith (Eds.), *Personality assessment* (pp. 213–246). New York, NY: Routledge.
Côté, J. E. (2009). Identity formation and self-development in adolescence. In R. M. Lerner & L. Steinberg (Eds.), *Handbook of adolescent psychology* (3rd ed., Vol. 1, pp. 266–304). Hoboken, NJ: Wiley.
Côté, J., & Bynner, J. M. (2008). Changes in the transition to adulthood in the UK and Canada: The role of structure and agency in emerging adulthood. *Journal of Youth Studies, 11*(3), 251–268.
Côté, S., Lopes, P. N., Salovey, P., & Miners, C. T. (2010). Emotional intelligence and leadership emergence in small groups. *The Leadership Quarterly, 21*(3), 496–508.
Cotton, J. L. (1981). A review of research on Schachter's theory of emotion and the misattribution of arousal. *European Journal of Social Psychology, 11*(4), 365–397.
Couturier, J., & Lock, J. (2006). Eating disorders: Anorexia nervosa, bulimia nervosa, and binge eating disorder. In T. G. Plante (Ed.), *Mental disorders of the new millennium* (Vol. 3, pp. 135–156). Westport, CT: Praeger.
Cowan, N. (1988). Evolving conceptions of memory storage, selective attention, and their mutual constraints within the human information-processing system. *Psychological Bulletin, 104*(2), 163–191.
Cowan, N. (2001). The magical number 4 in short-term memory: A reconsideration of mental storage capacity. *Behavioral and Brain Sciences, 24*(1), 87–114.
Cowan, N. (2005). *Working memory capacity*. New York, NY: Psychology Press.
Cowan, N. (2008). What are the differences between long-term, short-term, and working memory? *Progress in Brain Research, 169*, 323–338.
Cowan, N. (2010). The magical mystery four: How is working memory capacity limited, and why? *Current Directions in Psychological Science, 19*(1), 51–57.
Cowart, B. J., & Rawson, N. E. (2001). Olfaction. In E. B. Goldstein (Ed.), *Blackwell handbook of perception* (pp. 567–635). Oxford, UK: Blackwell.

Cox, W. T., Devine, P. G., Bischmann, A. A., & Hyde, J. S. (In Press). Inferences about sexual orientation: The role of stereotypes, faces, and the gaydar myth. *Journal of Sex Research*.

Cozolino, L. J. (2008). *The healthy aging brain: Sustaining attachment, attaining wisdom*. New York, NY: W. W. Norton.

Cozolino, L. J. (2010). *The neuroscience of psychotherapy: Healing the social brain*. New York, NY: W. W. Norton.

Craddock, N., & Jones, I. (1999). Genetics of bipolar disorder. *Journal of Medical Genetics, 36*(8), 585–594.

Craighead, W. E., Ritschel, L. A., Arnarson, E. O., & Gillespie, C. F. (2008). Major depressive disorder. In W. E. Craighead, D. J. Milkowitz, & L. W. Craighead (Eds.), *Psychopathology: History, diagnosis, and empirical foundations* (pp. 279–328). Hoboken, NJ: Wiley.

Craik, F. I. M. (2002). Levels of processing: Past, present... and future? *Memory, 10*(5–6), 305–318.

Craik, F. I. M. (2007). Encoding: A cognitive perspective. In H. L. Roediger, Y. Dudai, & S. M. Fitzpatrick (Eds.), *Science of memory: Concepts* (pp. 129–135). Oxford, UK: Oxford University Press.

Craik, F. I. M., & Lockhart, R. S. (1972). Levels of processing: A framework for memory research. *Journal of Verbal Learning and Verbal Behavior, 11*(6), 671–684.

Craik, F. I. M., & Tulving, E. (1975). Depth of processing and the retention of words in episodic memory. *Journal of Experimental Psychology: General, 104*(3), 268–294.

Craik, F. I. M. & Watkins, M. J. (1973). The role of rehearsal in short-term memory. *Journal of Verbal Learning and Verbal Behavior, 12*(6), 599–607.

Crano, W. D., & Lac, A. (2012). The evolution of research methodologies in social psychology: A historical analysis. In A. W. Kruglanski & W. Stroebe (Eds.), *Handbook of the history of social psychology* (pp. 159–174). New York, NY: Psychology Press.

Craske, M. G. (2010). *Cognitive-behavioral therapy*. Washington, DC: American Psychological Association.

Craske, M. G., & Barlow, D. H. (2008). Panic disorder and agoraphobia. In D. H. Barlow (Ed.), *Clinical handbook of psychological disorders: A step-by-step treatment manual* (4th ed., pp. 1–64). New York, NY: Guilford Press.

Craske, M. G., Rauch, S. L., Ursano, R., Prenoveau, J., Pine, D. S., & Zinbarg, R. E. (2009). What is an anxiety disorder? *Depression and Anxiety, 26*(12), 1066–1085.

Crawford, C. (1998). The theory of evolution in the study of human behavior: An introduction and overview. In C. Crawford & D. L. Krebs (Eds.), *Handbook of evolutionary psychology: Ideas, issues, and applications* (pp. 3–43). Mahwah, NJ: Lawrence Erlbaum.

Credé, M., Roch, S. G., & Kieszczynka, U. M. (2010). Class attendance in college: A meta-analytic review of the relationship of class attendance with grades and student characteristics. *Review of Educational Research, 80*(2), 272–295.

Crenshaw, K. (1991). Mapping the margins: Intersectionality, identity politics, and violence against women of color. *Stanford Law Review, 43*(6), 1241–1299.

Crespo, C. J., Smit, E., Troiano, R. P., Bartlett, S. J., Macera, C. A., & Andersen, R. E. (2001). Television watching, energy intake, and obesity in U.S. children: Results from the third National Health and Nutrition Examination Survey, 1988–1994. *Archives of Pediatrics & Adolescent Medicine, 155*(3), 360–365.

Creswell, J. D., Way, B. M., Eisenberger, N. I., & Lieberman, M. D. (2007). Neural correlates of dispositional mindfulness during affect labeling. *Psychosomatic Medicine, 69*(6), 560–565.

Crews, D. J., & Landers, D. M. (1987). A meta-analytic review of aerobic fitness and reactivity to psychosocial stressors. *Medicine & Science in Sports & Exercise, 19*, 114–120.

Crick, N. R., & Grotpeter, J. K. (1995). Relational aggression, gender, and social-psychological adjustment. *Child Development, 66*(3), 710–722.

Crisler, M. C., Brooks, J. O., Ogle, J. H., Guirl, C. D., Alluri, P., & Dixon, K. K. (2008). Effect of wireless communication and entertainment devices on simulated driving performance. *Transportation Research Record: Journal of the Transportation Research Board, 2069*(1), 48–54.

Crisp, R. J., & Maitner, A. T. (2011). Social categorization theories: From culture to cognition. In D. Chadee (Ed.), *Theories in social psychology* (pp. 232–249). West Sussex, UK: Wiley-Blackwell.

Crits-Christoph, P., Gibbons, M. B. C., Hamilton, J., Ring-Kurtz, S., & Gallop, R. (2011). The dependability of alliance assessments: The alliance–outcome correlation is larger than you might think. *Journal of Consulting and Clinical Psychology, 79*, 267–278.

Crittenden, K. S. (1991). Asian self-effacement or feminine modesty? Attributional patterns of women university students in Taiwan. *Gender & Society, 5*(1), 98–117.

Crocetti, E., Klimstra, T., Keijsers, L., Hale, W. W., III, & Meeus, W. (2009). Anxiety trajectories and identity development in adolescence: A five-wave longitudinal study. *Journal of Youth and Adolescence, 38*(6), 839–849.

Crocker, J., & Park, L. E. (2004). The costly pursuit of self-esteem. *Psychological Bulletin, 130*(3), 392–414.

Croizet, J. C., & Claire, T. (1998). Extending the concept of stereotype threat to social class: The intellectual underperformance of students from low socioeconomic backgrounds. *Personality and Social Psychology Bulletin, 24*(6), 588–594.

Crow, S. J., & Brandenburg, B. (2010). Diagnosis, assessment, and treatment planning for bulimia nervosa. In C. M. Grilo & J. E. Mitchell (Eds.), *The treatment of eating disorders: A clinical handbook* (pp. 28–43). New York, NY: Guilford Press.

Crowder, R. G., & Green, R. L. (2000). Serial learning: Cognition and behavior. In E. Tulving & F. I. M. Craik (Eds.), *The Oxford handbook of memory* (pp. 125–135). Oxford, UK: Oxford University Press.

Crowe, E., & Higgins, E. T. (1997). Regulatory focus and strategic inclinations: Promotion and prevention in decision-making. *Organizational Behavior and Human Decision Processes, 69*(2), 117–132.

Crowe, S. F., Matthews, C., & Walkenhorst, E. (2007). Relationship between worry, anxiety and thought suppression and the components of working memory in a non-clinical sample. *Australian Psychologist, 42*(3), 170–177.

Crowne, K. A. (2008). What leads to cultural intelligence? *Business Horizons, 51*(5), 391–399.

Crystal, D. (2008). *Txtng: The gr8 db8*. Oxford, UK: Oxford University Press.

Csikszentmihalyi, M. (1975). *Beyond boredom and anxiety*. San Francisco, CA: Jossey-Bass.

Csikszentmihalyi, M. (1990). *Flow: The psychology of optimal experience* (Vol. 3, pp. 13–36). New York, NY: Harper & Row.

Cummings, N. A. (2007). Treatment and assessment take place in an economic context, always. In S. O. Lilienfeld & W. T. O'Donohue (Eds.), *The great ideas of clinical science: 17 principles that every mental health professional should understand* (pp. 163–184). New York: Routledge.

Curci, A. & Luminet, O. (2009). General conclusions. In O. Luminet & A. Curci (Eds.), *Flashbulb memories: New issues and new perspectives* (pp. 269–276). East Sussex, UK: Psychology Press.

Curcio, G., Ferrara, M., & De Gennaro, L. (2006). Sleep loss, learning capacity and academic performance. *Sleep Medicine Reviews, 10*(5), 323–337.

Curtis, R. C., & Miller, K. (1986). Believing another likes or dislikes you: Behaviors making the beliefs come true. *Journal of Personality and Social Psychology, 51*(2), 284.

Cury, F., Da Fonseca, D., Zahn, I., & Elliot, A. (2008). Implicit theories and IQ test performance: A sequential mediational analysis. *Journal of Experimental Social Psychology, 44*(3), 783–791.

Cushner, K., & Mahon, J. (2009). Intercultural competence in teacher education. In D. K. Deardorff (Ed.), *The SAGE handbook of intercultural competence* (pp. 304–320). Thousand Oaks, CA: SAGE.

Czeisler, C. A., & Dijk, D.-J. (2001). Human circadian physiology and sleep–wake regulation. In J. S. Takahashi, F. W. Turek, & R. Y. Moore (Eds.), *Circadian clocks* (pp. 531–569). New York: Kluwer Academic/Plenum Publishers.

Czeisler, C. A., Duffy, J. F., Shanahan, T. L., Brown, E. N., Mitchell, J. F., Rimmer, D. W., Kronauer, R. E. (1999). Stability, precision, and near 24-hour period of the human circadian pacemaker. *Science, 284*, 2177–2181.

Da Fonseca, D., Cury, F., Fakra, E., Rufo, M., Poinso, F., Bounoua, L., & Huguet, P. (2008). Implicit theories of intelligence and IQ test performance in adolescents with Generalized Anxiety Disorder. *Behaviour Research and Therapy, 46*(4), 529–536.

Dabbs, J. M., Chang, E. L., Strong, R. A., & Milun, R. (1998). Spatial ability, navigation strategy, and geographic knowledge among men and women. *Evolution and Human Behavior, 19*(2), 89–98.

Dabul, A. J., Bernal, M. E., & Knight, G. P. (1995). Allocentric and idiocentric self-description and academic achievement among Mexican American and Anglo American adolescents. *The Journal of Social Psychology, 135*(5), 621–630.

Dalbert, C. (2009). Belief in a just world. In M. R. Leary & R. H. Hoyle (Eds.), *Handbook of individual differences in social behavior* (pp. 288–297). New York, NY: Guilford Press.

Daley, A. (2008). Exercise and depression: A review of reviews. *Journal of Clinical Psychology in Medical Settings, 15*(2), 140–147.

Daley, C. E., & Onwuegbuzie, A. J. (2011). Race and intelligence. In R. J. Sternberg & S. B. Kaufman (Eds.), *The Cambridge handbook of intelligence* (pp. 293–308). Cambridge, UK: Cambridge University Press.

Dalgleish, T. (2004). The emotional brain. *Nature Reviews Neuroscience, 5*(7), 583–589.

Dalgleish, T., & Cox, S. G. (2002). Memory and emotional disorder. In A. D. Baddeley, M. D. Kopelman, & B. A. Wilson (Eds.), *The handbook of memory disorders* (2nd ed., pp. 437–449). Chichester, UK: Wiley.

Dallam, S. J. (2005). Health issues associated with violence against women. In K. A. Kendall-Tackett (Ed.), *Handbook of women, stress, and trauma* (pp. 159–180). New York, NY: Brunner-Routledge.

Dalrymple, K. L., Guadiano, B. A., & Weinstock, L. M. (2015). Efficacy versus effectiveness research. In R. L. Cautin & S. O. Lilienfeld (Eds.), *The encyclopedia of clinical psychology* (pp. 1015–1021). West Sussex, UK: Wiley-Blackwell.

Dalton, M. A., Beach, M. L., Adachi-Mejia, A. M., Longacre, M. R., Matzkin, A. L., Sargent, J. D., . . . Titus-Ernstoff, L. (2009). Early exposure to movie smoking predicts established smoking by older teens and young adults. *Pediatrics, 123*, 551–558.

Daly, M., & Wilson, M. (1988). *Homicide*. Piscataway, NJ: Aldine Transaction.

Damasio, A. R. (1994). *Descartes' error: Emotion, rationality and the human brain*. New York, NY: Putnam.

Damasio, H., Grabowski, T., Frank, R., Galaburda, A. M., & Damasio, A. R. (1994). The return of Phineas Gage: Clues about the brain from the skull of a famous patient. *Science, 264*(5162), 1102–1105.

Damon, W. (2004). What is positive youth development? *The ANNALS of the American Academy of Political and Social Science, 591*(1), 13–24.

Dana, R. H. (2005). *Multicultural assessment: Principles, applications, and examples*. Mahwah, NJ: Lawrence Erlbaum.

Daniels, D., & Plomin, R. (1985). Origins of individual differences in infant shyness. *Developmental Psychology, 21*(1), 118–121.

Daniels, H. (1996). Introduction: Psychology in a social world. In H. Daniels (Ed.), *An introduction to Vygotsky* (pp. 1–27). New York, NY: Routledge.

Daniels, H. (2011). Vygotsky and psychology. In U. Goswami (Ed.), *The Wiley-Blackwell handbook of childhood cognitive development* (2nd ed., pp. 673–696). Malden, MA: Wiley-Blackwell.

Daniels, S. R., Arnett, D. K., Eckel, R. H., Gidding, S. S., Hayman, L. L., Kumanyika, S., . . . Williams, C. L. (2005). Overweight in children and adolescents: Pathophysiology, consequences, prevention, and treatment. *Circulation, 111*(15), 1999–2012.

Danion, J., Huron, C., Rizzo, L., & Vidaihet, P. (2004). Emotion, memory, and conscious awareness in schizophrenia. In D. Reisberg & P. Hertel (Eds.), *Memory and emotion* (pp. 217–241). Oxford, UK: Oxford University Press.

Danner, F., & Phillips, B. (2008). Adolescent sleep, school start times, and teen motor vehicle crashes. *Journal of Clinical Sleep Medicine: Official Publication of the American Academy of Sleep Medicine, 4*(6), 533.

Danoff-Burg, S., & Revenson, T. A. (2005). Benefit-finding among patients with rheumatoid arthritis: Positive effects on interpersonal relationships. *Journal of Behavioral Medicine, 28*(1), 91–103.

Danquah, M. N. (1999). *Willow weep for me: A black woman's journey through depression*. New York, NY: One World/Ballantine.

Danquah, M. N. (2002). Writing the wrongs of identity. In N. Casey (Ed.), *Unholy ghost: Writers on depression* (pp. 173–180). New York, NY: Perennial.

Danziger, K. (2006). Universalism and indigenization in the history of modern psychology. In A. C. Brock (Ed.), *Internationalizing the history of psychology* (pp. 208–225). New York, NY: New York University Press.

Danziger, K., & Ballantyne, P. (1997). Psychological experiments. In W. G. Bringmann, H. E. Lück, R. Miller, & C. E. Early (Eds.), *A pictorial history of psychology* (pp. 233–239). Carol Stream, IL: Quintessence Publishing.

Darcangelo, S. (2012). Fetishism: Psychotherapy and theory. In D. R. Laws & W. T. O'Donohue (Eds.), *Sexual deviance: Theory, assessment, and treatment* (2nd ed., pp. 108–118). New York, NY: Guilford Press.

Darley, J. M., & Latané, B. (1968). Bystander intervention in emergencies: Diffusion of responsibility. *Journal of Personality and Social Psychology, 8*(4, Pt. 1), 377–383.

Darwin, C. (1877). Biographical sketch of an infant. *Mind, 2*, 285–294.

Das, J. P. (2014). *Consciousness quest: Where East meets West: On mind, meditation, and neural correlates*. New Delhi, India: SAGE.

Dasgupta, N., & Rivera, L. M. (2008). When social context matters: The influence of long-term contact and short-term exposure to admired outgroup members on implicit attitudes and behavioral intentions. *Social Cognition, 26*(1), 112–123.

Dauvilliers, Y., & Bayard, S. (2012). Hypersomnia and narcolepsy. In C. M. Morin & C. A. Espie (Eds.), *The Oxford handbook of sleep and sleep disorders* (pp. 690–706). Oxford, UK: Oxford University Press.

Dauvilliers, Y., Arnulf, I., & Mignot, E. (2007). Narcolepsy with cataplexy. *The Lancet, 369*(9560), 499–511.

Dauvilliers, Y., Montplaisir, J., Molinari, N., Carlander, B., Ondze, B., Besset, A., & Billiard, M. (2001). Age at onset of narcolepsy in two large populations of patients in France and Quebec. *Neurology, 57*(11), 2029–2033.

Davidson, J. E., & Kemp, I. A. (2011). Contemporary models of intelligence. In R. J. Sternberg & S. B. Kaufman (Eds.), *The Cambridge handbook of intelligence* (pp. 58–84). Cambridge, UK: Cambridge University Press.

Davidson, J. R., Crawford, C., Ives, J. A., & Jonas, W. B. (2011). Homeopathic treatments in psychiatry: A systematic review of randomized placebo-controlled studies. *The Journal of Clinical Psychiatry, 72*(6), 795–805.

Davidson, K. W., Mostofsky, E., & Whang, W. (2010). Don't worry, be happy: Positive affect and reduced 10-year incident coronary heart disease: The Canadian Nova Scotia Health Survey. *European Heart Journal, 31*(9), 1065–1070.

Davidson, P. S. R. (2008). The cognitive and neural bases of flashbulb memories. In E. Dere, A. Easton, L. Nadel, & J. P. Huston (Eds.), *Handbook of episodic memory* (pp. 81–97). Amsterdam, Netherlands: Elsevier Science.

Davidson, R. J., Kabat-Zinn, J., Schumacher, J., Rosenkranz, M., Muller, D., Santorelli, S. F., & Sheridan, J. F. (2003). Alterations in brain and immune function produced by mindfulness meditation. *Psychosomatic Medicine, 65*(4), 564–570.

Davies, E., & Lea, S. E. (1995). Student attitudes to student debt. *Journal of Economic Psychology, 16*(4), 663–679.

Davies, G., & Hine, S. (2007). Change blindness and eyewitness testimony. *The Journal of Psychology, 141*(4), 423–434.

Davies, P. T., Sturge-Apple, M. L., & Martin, M. J. (2013). Family discord and child health: An emotional security formulation. In N. S. Landale, S. M. McHale, & A. Booth (Eds.), *Families and child health* (National Symposium on Family Issues) (pp. 45–74). New York, NY: Springer Science+Business Media.

Daviglus, M. L., Plassman, B. L., Pirzada, A., Bell, C. C., Bowen, P. E., Burke, J. R., . . . Williams Jr, J. W. (2011). Risk factors and preventive interventions for Alzheimer disease: State of the science. *Archives of Neurology, 68*(9), 1185–1190.

Davis, B., Stafford, M. B. R., & Pullig, C. (2014). How gay-straight alliance groups mitigate the relationship between gay-bias victimization and adolescent suicide attempts. *Journal of the American Academy of Child & Adolescent Psychiatry, 53*(12), 1271–1278.

Davis, C. G., & Nolen-Hoeksema, S. (2009). Making sense of loss, perceiving benefits, and posttraumatic growth. In S. J. Lopez & C. R. Snyder (Eds.), *Oxford handbook of positive psychology* (pp. 641–651). Oxford, UK: Oxford University Press.

Davis, D., & Loftus, E. F. (2007). Internal and external sources of misinformation in adult witness memory. In M. P. Toglia, J. D. Read, D. F. Ross, & R. C. L. Lindsay (Eds.), *The Handbook of eyewitness psychology* (pp. 195–237). Mahwah, NJ: Lawrence Erlbaum.

Davis, J. H., & Thompson, E. (2015). Developing attention and decreasing affective bias: Toward a cross-cultural cognitive science of mindfulness. In K. W. Brown, J. D. Creswell, & R. M. Ryan (Eds.), *Handbook of mindfulness: Theory, research, and practice* (pp. 42–61). New York, NY: Guilford Press.

Davis, J. I., Senghas, A., & Ochsner, K. N. (2009). How does facial feedback modulate emotional experience? *Journal of Research in Personality, 43*(5), 822–829.

Davis, K., Christodoulou, J., Seider, S., & Gardner, H. (2011). The theory of multiple intelligences. In R. J. Sternberg & S. B. Kaufman (Eds.), *The Cambridge handbook of intelligence* (pp. 485–503). Cambridge, UK: Cambridge University Press.

Davis, M. C., Matthews, K. A., & Twamley, E. W. (1999). Is life more difficult on Mars or Venus? A meta-analytic review of sex differences in major and minor life events. *Annals of Behavioral Medicine, 21*(1), 83–97.

Davis, S. D., Dattilio, F. M., & Gonzalez, A. (2015). Family therapies. In R. L. Cautin & S. O. Lilienfeld (Eds.), *The encyclopedia of clinical psychology* (pp. 1239–1246). West Sussex, UK: Wiley-Blackwell.

Davison, G. C., & Lazarus, A. A. (2007). Clinical case studies are important in the science and practice of psychotherapy. In S. O. Lilienfeld & W. T. O'Donohue (Eds.), *The great ideas of clinical science: 17 principles that every mental health professional should understand* (pp. 149–162). New York, NY: Routledge.

Davison, K. K., Markey, C., & Birch, L. (2000). Etiology of body dissatisfaction and weight concerns among 5-year-old girls. *Appetite, 35*(2), 143–151.

Davy, B. M., Van Walleghen, E. L., & Orr, J. S. (2007). Sex differences in acute energy intake regulation. *Appetite, 49*(1), 141–147.

Dawson, G. (2008). Early behavioral intervention, brain plasticity, and the prevention of autism spectrum disorder. *Development and Psychopathology, 20*(3), 775–803.

Dawson, G. (2013). Dramatic increase in autism prevalence parallels explosion of research into its biology and causes. *JAMA, 70*(1), 9–10.

De Fruyt, F. (1997). Gender and individual differences in adult crying. *Personality and Individual Differences, 22*(6), 937–940.

De Fruyt, F., De Clercq, B., De Bolle, M., Wille, B., Markon, K., & Krueger, R. F. (2013). General and maladaptive traits in a five-factor framework for DSM-5 in a university student sample. *Assessment, 20*(3), 295–307.

De Houwer, J., Thomas, S., & Baeyens, F. (2001). Association learning of likes and dislikes: A review of 25 years of research on human evaluative conditioning. *Psychological Bulletin, 127*(6), 853–869.

De Koninck, J. D. (2012). Sleep, dreams, and dreaming. In C. M. Morin & C. A. Espie (Eds.), *The Oxford handbook of sleep and sleep disorders* (pp. 150–171). Oxford, UK: Oxford University Press.

de Mejia, E. G., & Ramirez-Mares, M. V. (2014). Impact of caffeine and coffee on our health. *Trends in Endocrinology & Metabolism, 25*(10), 489–492.

De Vries, R. E., de Vries, A., de Hoogh, A., & Feij, J. (2009). More than the Big Five: Egoism and the HEXACO model of personality. *European Journal of Personality, 23*(8), 635–654.

de Waal, F. B. (2008). Putting the altruism back into altruism: The evolution of empathy. *Annual Review of Psychology, 59*, 279–300.

Dean, M. L. (1980). Presentation order effects in product taste tests. *The Journal of Psychology, 105*(1), 107–110.

DeAndrea, D. C., Shaw, A. S., & Levine, T. R. (2010). Online language: The role of culture in self-expression and self-construal on Facebook. *Journal of Language and Social Psychology, 29*(4), 425–442.

Deary, I. J., Spinath, F. M., & Bates, T. C. (2006). Genetics of intelligence. *European Journal of Human Genetics, 14*(6), 690–700.

Deary, I. J., Strand, S., Smith, P., & Fernandes, C. (2007). Intelligence and educational achievement. *Intelligence, 35*(1), 13–21.

Deater-Deckard, K., Dodge, K. A., Bates, J. E., & Pettit, G. S. (1996). Physical discipline among African American and European American mothers: Links to children's externalizing behaviors. *Developmental Psychology, 32*(6), 1065–1072.

Debarnot, U., Castellani, E., Valenza, G., Sebastiani, L., & Guillot, A. (2011). Daytime naps improve motor imagery learning. *Cognitive, Affective, & Behavioral Neuroscience, 11*(4), 541–550.

Debiec, J., & LeDoux, J. E. (2009). The amygdala networks of fear: From animal models to human psychopathology. In D. McKay, J. S. Abramowitz, S. Taylor, & G. J. G. Asmundson (Eds.), *Current perspectives on the anxiety disorders: Implications for DSM-V and beyond* (pp. 107–126). New York, NY: Springer Publishing.

DeCasper, A. J., & Fifer, W. P. (1980). Of human bonding: Newborns prefer their mothers' voices. *Science, 208*(4448), 1174–1176.

DeCasper, A. J., & Spence, M. J. (1986). Prenatal maternal speech influences newborns' perception of speech sounds. *Infant Behavior and Development, 9*(2), 133–150.

Deci, E. L. (1971). Effects of externally mediated rewards on intrinsic motivation. *Journal of Personality and Social Psychology, 18*(1), 105–115.

Deci, E. L., Koestner, R., & Ryan, R. M. (1999). A meta-analytic review of experiments examining the effects of extrinsic rewards on intrinsic motivation. *Psychological Bulletin, 125*(6), 627–668.

Deci, E. L., & Ryan, R. M. (2012). Motivation, personality, and development within embedded social contexts: An overview of self-determination theory. In R. M. Ryan (Ed.), *The Oxford handbook of human motivation* (pp. 85–110). New York, NY: Oxford University Press.

Dehaene, S. (2011). *The number sense: How the mind creates mathematics*. New York, NY: Oxford University Press

Dehaene, S., Spelke, E., Pinel, P., Stanescu, R., & Tsivkin, S. (1999). Sources of mathematical thinking: Behavioral and brain-imaging evidence. *Science, 284* (5416), 970–974.
Dehaene-Lambertz, G., Dehaene, S., & Hertz-Pannier, L. (2002). Functional neuroimaging of speech perception in infants. *Science, 298*(5600), 2013–2015
Dehn, M. J. (2008). *Working memory and academic learning: Assessment and intervention*. Hoboken, NJ: John Wiley
DeLeon, P. H., Kenkel, M. B., Gray, J. M. O., & Sammons, M. T. (2011). Emerging policy issues for psychology: A key to the future of the profession. In D. H. Barlow (Ed.), *The Oxford handbook of clinical psychology* (pp. 34–51). New York, NY: Oxford University Press.
Delgado, M. R., Labouliere, C. D., & Phelps, E. A. (2006). Fear of losing money? Aversive conditioning with secondary reinforcers. *Social Cognitive and Affective Neuroscience, 1*, 250–259.
Delgado, M. R., Olsson, A., & Phelps, E. A. (2006). Extending animal models of fear conditioning to humans. *Biological Psychology, 73*(1), 39–48.
Delgado, P. L., & Moreno, F. A. (2006). Neurochemistry of mood disorders. In D. J. Stein, D. J. Kupfer, & A. F. Schatzberg (Eds.), *The American Psychiatric Publishing textbook of mood disorders* (pp. 101–116). Washington, DC: American Psychiatric Association Publishing.
Dell, D. M., Schmidt, L. D., & Meara, N. M. (2006). Applying for approval to conduct research with human participants. In F. T. L. Leong & J. T. Austin (Eds.), *The psychology research handbook: A guide for graduate students and research assistants* (2nd ed., pp. 175–185). Thousand Oaks: SAGE Publications.
Dellis, N. (2012). Watch memory champion trick his brain. YouTube video retrieved September 6, 2013. http://www.youtube.com/watch?v=KxD_XQ7ItyA
DeLongis, A., Folkman, S., & Lazarus, R. S. (1988). The impact of daily stress on health and mood: Psychological and social resources as mediators. *Journal of Personality and Social Psychology, 54*(3), 486–495.
Demaree, H. A., Schmeichel, B. J., Robinson, J. L., Pu, J., Everhart, D. E., & Berntson, G. G. (2006). Up- and down-regulating facial disgust: Affective, vagal, sympathetic, and respiratory consequences. *Biological Psychology, 71*(1), 90–99.
DeMatteo, D., Marczyk, G., Krauss, D. A., & Burl, J. (2009). Educational and training models in forensic psychology. *Training and Education in Professional Psychology, 3*, 184–201.
Dement, W. (1960). The effect of dream deprivation. *Science, 131*(3415),1705–1707.
Dement, W., & Kleitman, N. (1957). The relation of eye movement during sleep to dream activity: An objective method for the study of dreaming. *Journal of Experimental Psychology, 53*, 330–346.
Denes-Raj, V., & Epstein, S. (1994). Conflict between intuitive and rational processing: When people behave against their better judgment. *Journal of Personality and Social Psychology, 66*(5), 819–829.
Deng, W., Aimone, J. B., & Gage, F. H. (2010). New neurons and new memories: How does adult hippocampal neurogenesis affect learning and memory? *Nature Reviews Neuroscience, 11*(5), 339–350.
Denko, T. C., & Thase, M. E. (2006). Psychopharmacological interventions. In M. Hersen & J. C. Thomas (Eds.), *Comprehensive handbook of personality and psychopathology* (Vol. 2, pp. 503–518). Hoboken, NJ: Wiley.
Dennerstein, L., Dudley, E., & Guthrie, J. (2002). Empty nest or revolving door: A prospective study of women's quality of life in midlife during the phase of children leaving and reentering the home. *Psychological Medicine, 32*(3), 545–550.
Dennhardt, A. A., Yurasek, A. M., & Murphy, J. G. (2015). Motivational interviewing. In R. L. Cautin & S. O. Lilienfeld (Eds.), *The encyclopedia of clinical psychology* (pp. 1908–1913). West Sussex, UK: Wiley-Blackwell.
Denollet, J. (2000). Type D personality: A potential risk factor refined. *Journal of Psychosomatic Research, 49*(4), 255–266.
Deo, M. S., & Lymburner, J. A. (2011). Personality traits and psychological health concerns: The search for Psychology Student Syndrome. *Teaching of Psychology, 38*(3), 155–157.
DePaullo, B. (2010). *The Psychology of Dexter*. Dallas, TX: Smart Pop.
DePrince, A. P., Brown, L. S., Cheit, R. E., Freyd, J. J., Gold, S. N., Pezdek, K., & Quina, K. (2012). Motivated forgetting and misremembering: Perspectives from betrayal trauma theory. In R. F. Belli (Ed.), *True and false recovered memories: Toward a reconciliation of the debate,* 193–242. New York: Springer.
DeRubeis, R. J., Siegle, G. J., & Hollon, S. D. (2008). Cognitive therapy versus medication for depression: Treatment outcomes and neural mechanisms. *Nature Reviews Neuroscience, 9*(10), 788–796.
DeSantis, A. D., Webb, E. M., & Noar, S. M. (2008). Illicit use of prescription ADHD medications on a college campus: A multimethodological approach. *Journal of American College Health, 57*(3), 315–324.
Deutsch, M., & Gerard, H. B. (1955). A study of normative and informative social influences upon individual judgment. *Journal of Abnormal and Social Psychology, 51*(3), 629–636.
Dewald, P. A. (1964). *Psychotherapy: A dynamic approach*. New York, NY: Basic Books.
Dewar, M., Cowan, N., & Della Sala, S. (2010). Forgetting due to retroactive interference in amnesia: Findings and implications. In S. Della Sala (Ed.), *Forgetting* (pp. 185–209). East Sussex, UK: Psychology Press.
DeYoung, C. G., Hirsh, J. B., Shane, M. S., Papademetris, X., Rajeevan, N., & Gray, J. R. (2010). Testing predictions from personality neuroscience brain structure and the Big Five. *Psychological Science, 21*(6), 820–828.
Dhawan, N., Roseman, I. J., Naidu, R. K., Thapa, K., & Rettek, S. I. (1995). Self-concepts across two cultures: India and the United States. *Journal of Cross-Cultural Psychology, 26*(6), 606–621.
Di Lorenzo, P. M., & Rosen, A. M. (2010). Taste. In E. B. Goldstein (Ed.), *Encyclopedia of perception* (pp. 952–957). Thousand Oaks, CA: SAGE.
Diamond, L. M. (2000). Sexual identity, attractions, and behavior among young sexual-minority women over a 2-year period. *Developmental Psychology, 36*(2), 241–250.
Diamond, L. M. (2005). A new view of lesbian subtypes: Stable versus fluid identity trajectories over an 8-year period. *Psychology of Women Quarterly, 29*(2), 119–128.
Diamond, L. M. (2007). A dynamical systems approach to the development and expression of female same-sex sexuality. *Perspectives on Psychological Science, 2*(2), 142–161.
Diamond, L. M. (2008). Female bisexuality from adolescence to adulthood: Results from a 10–year longitudinal study. *Developmental Psychology, 44*(1), 5.
Diamond, L. M. (2009). *Sexual fluidity: Understanding women's love and desire*. Cambridge, MA: Harvard University Press.
Diamond, L. M. (2013). Concepts of female sexual orientation. In C. J. Patterson & A. R. D'Augelli (Eds.), *Handbook of psychology and sexual orientation* (pp. 3–17). New York, NY: Oxford University Press.
Diamond, M. C., Law, F., Rhodes, H., Lindner, B., Rosenzweig, M. R., Krech, D., & Bennett, E. L. (1966). Increases in cortical depth and glia numbers in rats subjected to enriched environment. *Journal of Comparative Neurology, 128*(1), 117–125.
Diamond, M. C., Lindner, B., Johnson, R., Bennett, E. L., & Rosenzweig, M. R. (1975). Difference in occipital cortical synapses from environmentally enriched, impoverished, and standard colony rats. *Journal of Neuroscience Research, 1*(2), 109–119.
Dickerson, B. C. (2007). Advances in functional magnetic resonance imaging: Technology and clinical applications. *Neurotherapeutics, 4*(3), 360–370.
Dickson, N., Paul, C., & Herbison, P. (2003). Same-sex attraction in a birth cohort: Prevalence and persistence in early adulthood. *Social Science & Medicine, 56*(8), 1607–1615.
Dickter, D. N. (2006). Basic statistical analyses. In F. T. L. Leong & J. T. Austin (Eds.), *The psychology research handbook* (pp. 293–305). Thousand Oaks: SAGE.
DiClemente, C. C., & Prochaska, J. O. (1982). Self-change and therapy change of smoking behavior: A comparison of processes of change in cessation and maintenance. *Addictive Behaviors, 7*(2), 133–142.
Didie, E. R. (2015). Interpersonal psychotherapy (IPT). In R. L. Cautin & S. O. Lilienfeld (Eds.), *The encyclopedia of clinical psychology* (pp. 1540–1545). West Sussex, UK: Wiley-Blackwell.
Diekelmann, S., & Born, J. (2010). The memory function of sleep. *Nature Reviews Neuroscience, 11*(2), 114–126.
Diekman, A. B., & Eagly, A. H. (2008). Of men, women, and motivation: A role congruity account. In J. Y. Shah & W. L. Gardner, *Handbook of motivation science* (pp. 434–447). New York, NY: Guilford Press.
Diekman, A. B., Brown, E. R., Johnston, A. M., & Clark, E. K. (2010). Seeking congruity between goals and roles: A new look at why women opt out of science, technology, engineering, and mathematics careers. *Psychological Science, 21*(8), 1051–1057.
Diener, E., & Biswas-Diener, R. (2002). Will money increase subjective well-being? *Social Indicators Research, 57*(2), 119–169.
Diener, E., & Chan, M. Y. (2011). Happy people live longer: Subjective well-being contributes to health and longevity. *Applied Psychology: Health and Well-Being, 3*(1), 1–43.
Diener, E., & Diener, M. (2009). Cross-cultural correlates of life satisfaction and self-esteem. In E. Diener (Ed.), *Culture and well-being: The collected works of Ed Diener* (pp. 71–91). New York, NY: Springer Science+Business Media.
Diener, E., & Suh, E. (2003). National differences in subjective well-being. In D. Kahneman, E. Diener, & N. Schwarz (Eds.), *Well-being: The foundations of hedonic psychology* (pp. 434–450). New York, NY: Russell Sage Foundation.
Diener, E., Sandvik, E., Seidlitz, L., & Diener, M. (1993). The relationship between income and subjective well-being: Relative or absolute? *Social Indicators Research, 28*(3), 195–223.
Dietz, T. L. (2000). Disciplining children: Characteristics associated with the use of corporal punishment. *Child Abuse & Neglect, 24*(12), 1529–1542.
Digman, J. M. (1990). Personality structure: Emergence of the five-factor model. *Annual Review of Psychology, 41*, 417-440.
Digman, J. M. (1996). The curious history of the five-factor model. In J. S. Wiggins (Ed.), *The five-factor model of personality: Theoretical perspectives* (pp. 1–20). New York, NY: Guilford Press.
Dijk, D.-J., Duffy, J. F., Riel, E., Shanahan, T. L., & Czeisler, C. A. (1999). Ageing and the circadian and homeostatic regulation of human sleep during forced desynchrony of rest, melatonin and temperature rhythms. *The Journal of Physiology, 516*(2), 611–627.
Dijk, D.-J., Groeger, J. A., Stanley, N., & Deacon, S. (2010). Age-related reduction in daytime sleep propensity and nocturnal slow wave sleep. *Sleep, 33*(2), 211.
Dijk, D.-J., & Lazar, A. S. (2012). The regulation of human sleep and wakefulness: Sleep homeostasis and circadian rhythmicity. In C. M. Morin & C. A. Espie (Eds.), *The Oxford handbook of sleep and sleep disorders* (pp. 38–60). Oxford, UK: Oxford University Press.
Dimberg, U., & Lundquist, L. O. (1990). Gender differences in facial reactions to facial expressions. *Biological Psychology, 30*(2), 151–159.
Dimberg, U., & Thunberg, M. (2012). Empathy, emotional contagion, and rapid facial reactions to angry and happy facial expressions. *PsyCh Journal, 1*(2), 118–127.

Dimberg, U., Andréasson, P., & Thunberg, M. (2011). Emotional empathy and facial reactions to facial expressions. *Journal of Psychophysiology, 25*(1), 26–31

Dimeff, L. A., Paves, A. P., Skutch, J. M., & Woodcock, E. A. (2011). Shifting paradigms in clinical psychology: How innovative technologies are shaping treatment delivery. In D. H. Barlow (Ed.), *The Oxford handbook of clinical psychology* (pp. 618–648). New York, NY: Oxford University Press.

Dimidjian, S., & Linehan, M. M. (2009). Mindfulness practice. In W. T. O'Donohue & J. E. Fisher (Eds.), *General principles and empirically supported techniques of cognitive behavior therapy* (pp. 425–434). Hoboken, NJ: Wiley.

Dinehart, M. E., Hayes, J. E., Bartoshuk, L. M., Lanier, S. L., & Duffy, V. B. (2006). Bitter taste markers explain variability in vegetable sweetness, bitterness, and intake. *Physiology & Behavior, 87*(2), 304–313.

Dinges, D. F., & Broughton, R. (1989). *Sleep and alertness: Chronobiological, behavioral, and medical aspects of napping*. New York, NY: Raven Press.

Dinges, D. F., Pack, F., Williams, K., Gillen, K. A., Powell, J. W., Ott, G. E., . . . Pack, A. I. (1997). Cumulative sleepiness, mood disturbance and psychomotor vigilance performance decrements during a week of sleep restricted to 4–5 hours per night. *Sleep: Journal of Sleep Research & Sleep Medicine, 20*(4), 267–277.

Dirix, C. E. H., Nijhuis, J. G., Jongsma, H. W., and Hornstra, G. (2009). Aspects of fetal learning and memory. *Child Development, 80*, 1251–1258. doi:10.1111/j.1467-8624.2009.01329.x

do Nascimento, I. C., & Ulrich, H. (2015). Basic studies on neural stem cells in the brain. In L. Zhao & J. H. Zhang (Eds.), *Cellular therapy for stroke and CNS injuries* (pp. 3–16). New York, NY: Springer International Publishing.

Dobalian, A., & Rivers, P. A. (2008). Racial and ethnic disparities in the use of mental health services. *The Journal of Behavioral Health Services & Research, 35*(2), 128–141.

Dobson, K. S. (2012). *Cognitive therapy*. Washington, DC: American Psychological Association.

Dobson, K. S., & Hamilton, K. E. (2008). Cognitive restructuring: Behavioral tests of negative cognitions. In W. T. O'Donohue & J. E. Fisher (Eds.), *Cognitive behavior therapy: Applying empirically supported techniques in your practice* (2nd ed., pp. 96–100). Hoboken, NJ: Wiley.

Dodgen, D., Fowler, R. D., & Williams-Nickelson, C. (2013). Getting involved in professional organizations: A gateway to career advancement. In M. J. Prinstein (Ed.), *The portable mentor: Expert guide to a successful career in psychology* (pp. 257–267). New York, NY: Springer.

Doherty, R. W. (1997). The emotional contagion scale: A measure of individual differences. *Journal of Nonverbal Behavior, 21*(2), 131–154.

Dolder, C. R. (2008). Side effects of antipsychotics. In K. T. Mueser & D. V. Jeste (Eds.), *Clinical handbook of schizophrenia* (pp. 168–177). New York, NY: Guilford Press.

Dolinski, D. (2000). On inferring one's beliefs from one's attempt and consequences for subsequent compliance. *Journal of Personality and Social Psychology, 78*(2), 260–272.

Dollinger, S. J., Urban, K. K., & James, T. A. (2004). Creativity and openness: Further validation of two creative product measures. *Creativity Research Journal, 16*(1), 35–47.

Domínguez D. J. F., Lewis, E. D., Turner, R., & Egan, G. F. (2009). The brain in culture and culture in the brain: A review of core issues in neuroanthropology. *Progress in Brain Research, 178*, 43–64.

Dominy, N. J., & Lucas, P. W. (2001). Ecological importance of trichromatic vision to primates. *Nature, 410*(6826), 363–366.

Donà, G., & Ackermann, L. (2006). Refugees in camps. In D. L. Sam, & J. W. Berry (Eds.), *The Cambridge handbook of acculturation psychology* (pp. 218–232). New York, NY: Cambridge University Press.

Donahoe, J. W. (1998). Positive reinforcement: The selection of behavior. In W. O'Donohue (Ed.), *Learning and behavior therapy* (pp. 169–187). Boston, MA: Allyn and Bacon.

Donnerstein, E., & Wilson, D. W. (1976). Effects of noise and perceived control on ongoing and subsequent aggressive behavior. *Journal of Personality and Social Psychology, 34*(5), 774–781.

Donoghue, J. P., Suner, S., & Sanes, J. N. (1990). Dynamic organization of primary motor cortex output to target muscles in adult rats. II. Rapid reorganization following motor nerve lesions. *Experimental Brain Research, 79*(3), 492–503.

Donovan, J., & Zucker, C. (2016). *In a different key: The story of autism*. New York, NY: Crown Publishers.

Donovan, R. A., Galban, D. J., Grace, R. K., Bennett, J. K., & Felicié, S. Z. (2013). Impact of racial macro-and microaggressions in black women's lives: A preliminary analysis. *Journal of Black Psychology, 39*(2), 185–196.

Dor, A. (2013). Don't stay out late! Mom, I'm twenty-eight: Emerging adults and their parents under one roof. *International Journal of Social Science Studies, 1*(1), 37–46.

Dorofaeff, T. F., & Denny, S. (2006). Sleep and adolescence. Do New Zealand teenagers get enough? *Journal of Paediatrics and Child Health, 42*(9), 515–520.

Dosher, B., & Lu, Z-L. (2010). Attention: Selective. In E. B. Goldstein (Ed.), *Encyclopedia of perception* (pp. 100–103). Thousand Oaks, CA: SAGE.

Doty, R. L. (2010). Olfaction. In E. B. Goldstein (Ed.), *Encyclopedia of perception* (pp. 657–661). Thousand Oaks, CA: SAGE.

Doty, R. L. (2012). Olfactory dysfunction in Parkinson disease. *Nature Reviews Neurology, 8*(6), 329–339.

Doty, R. L., Applebaum, S., Zusho, H., & Settle, R. G. (1985). Sex differences in odor identification ability: A cross-cultural analysis. *Neuropsychologia, 23*(5), 667–672.

Doty, R. L., & Kamath, V. (2014). The influences of age on olfaction: A review. *Frontiers in Psychology, 5*, 20. doi:10.3389/fpsyg.2014.00020

Dovidio, J. F., Brown, C. E., Heltman, K., Ellyson, S. L., & Keating, C. F. (1988a). Power displays between women and men in discussions of gender-linked tasks: A multichannel study. *Journal of Personality and Social Psychology, 55*(4), 580–587.

Dovidio, J. F., Ellyson, S. L., Keating, C. F., Heltman, K., & Brown, C. E. (1988b). The relationship of social power to visual displays of dominance between men and women. *Journal of Personality and Social Psychology, 54*(2), 233–242.

Dovidio, J. F., Gaertner, S. L., & Saguy, T. (2009). Commonality and the complexity of "we": Social attitudes and social change. *Personality and Social Psychology Review, 13*(1), 3–20.

Dovidio, J. F., & Gaertner, S. L. (2010). Intergroup bias. In S. T. Fiske, D. T. Gilbert, & G. Lindzey (Eds.), *Handbook of social psychology* (5th ed., Vol. 2, pp. 1084–1121). Hoboken, NJ: Wiley.

Dovidio, J. F., Newheiser, A., & Leyens, J. (2012). A history of intergroup relations research. In A. W. Kruglanski & W. Stroebe (Eds.), *Handbook of the history of social psychology* (pp. 407–429). New York, NY: Psychology Press.

Dowling, W. J. (2001). Perception of music. In E. B. Goldstein (Ed.), *Blackwell handbook of perception* (pp. 469–498). Oxford, UK: Blackwell.

Downar, J., & Kapur, S. (2008). Biological theories. In K. T. Meuser & D. V. Jeste (Eds.), *Clinical handbook of schizophrenia* (pp. 25–34). New York. NY: Guilford Press.

Downey, D. B., & Vogt Yuan, A. S. (2005) Sex differences in school performance during high school: Puzzling patterns and possible explanations. *The Sociological Quarterly, 46*(2), 299–321.

Doyle, A. B., Lawford, H., and Markiewicz, D. (2009). Attachment style with mother, father, best friend, and romantic partner during adolescence. *Journal of Research on Adolescence, 19*, 690–714.

Dozois, D. J. A. & Brinker, J. K. (2015). Cognitive therapies. In R. L. Cautin & S. O. Lilienfeld (Eds.), *The encyclopedia of clinical psychology* (pp. 656–665). West Sussex, UK: Wiley Blackwell.

Draaisma, D. (2000). *Metaphors of memory: A history of ideas about the mind*. Cambridge, UK: Cambridge University Press.

Drake, C. L., Roehrs, T., Richardson, G., Walsh, J. K., & Roth, T. (2004). Shift work sleep disorder: Prevalence and consequences beyond that of symptomatic day workers. *Sleep, 27*(8), 1453–1462.

Drescher, J. (2010). Queer diagnoses: Parallels and contrasts in the history of homosexuality, gender variance, and the Diagnostic and Statistical Manual. *Archives of Sexual Behavior, 39*, 427–460.

Dresser, N. (2005). *Multicultural manners: Essential rules of etiquette for the 21st century*. Hoboken, N.J: John Wiley.

Drews, F. A., Yazdani, H., Godfrey, C. N., Cooper, J. M., & Strayer, D. L. (2009). Text messaging during simulated driving. *Human Factors: The Journal of the Human Factors and Ergonomics Society, 51*(5), 762–770.

Dreyfuss, J. H. (2010). Thirdhand smoke identified as potent, enduring carcinogen. *CA: A Cancer Journal for Clinicians, 60*(4), 203–204.

Driver, H. S. (2012). Sleep and gender: The paradox of sex and sleep? In C. M. Morin & C. A. Espie (Eds.), *The Oxford handbook of sleep and sleep disorders* (pp. 266–288). Oxford, UK: Oxford University Press.

Dror, O. E. (2014). The Cannon–Bard thalamic theory of emotions: A brief genealogy and reappraisal. *Emotion Review, 6*(1), 13–20.

Drossel, C., Garrison-Diehn, C. G., & Fisher, J. E. (2008). Contingency management interventions. In W. T. O'Donohue & J. E. Fisher (Eds.), *Cognitive behavior therapy: Applying empirically supported techniques in your practice* (2nd ed., pp. 116–122). Hoboken, NJ: Wiley.

Drotar, D., Wu, Y. P., & Rohan, J. M. (2013). How to write an effective journal article review. In M. J. Prinstein (Ed.), *The portable mentor: Expert guide to a successful career in psychology* (pp. 163–173). New York, NY: Springer.

Drouin, M. A. (2011). College students' text messaging, use of textese and literacy skills. *Journal of Computer Assisted Learning, 27*(1), 67–75.

Dryden, W. (1995). *Brief rational emotive behaviour therapy*. Chichester, UK: Wiley.

Dryden, W. (2009). *Understanding emotional problems: The REBT perspective*. New York, NY: Routledge.

Dryden, W. (2015). Albert Ellis. In R. L. Cautin & S. O. Lilienfeld (Eds.), *The encyclopedia of clinical psychology* (pp. 1025–1027). West Sussex, UK: Wiley-Blackwell.

Duboué, E. R., Keene, A. C., & Borowsky, R. L. (2011). Evolutionary convergence on sleep loss in cavefish populations. *Current Biology, 21*(8), 671–676.

Duckworth, A. L., & Seligman, M. E. (2006). Self-discipline gives girls the edge: Gender in self-discipline, grades, and achievement test scores. *Journal of Educational Psychology, 98*(1), 198–208.

Duckworth, K., Halpern, J. H., Schutt, R. K., & Gillespie, C. (2003). Use of schizophrenia as a metaphor in U.S. newspapers. *Psychiatric Services, 54*(10), 1402–1404.

Duclos, S. E., Laird, J. D., Schneider, E., Sexter, M., Stern, L., & Van Lighten, O. (1989). Emotion-specific effects of facial expressions and postures on emotional experience. *Journal of Personality and Social Psychology, 57*(1), 100–108.

Dudai, Y. (1997). How big is human memory, or, on being just useful enough. *Learning & Memory, 3*, 341–365.

Duffy, J. F., & Dijk, D.-J. (2002). Getting through to circadian oscillators: Why use constant routines? *Journal of Biological Rhythms, 17*(1), 4–13.

Duffy, J. F., Rimmer, D. W., & Czeisler, C. A. (2001). Association of intrinsic circadian period with morningness–eveningness, usual wake time, and circadian phase. *Behavioral Neuroscience, 115*(4), 895–899.

Duffy, J. F., & Wright, K. P. (2005). Entrainment of the human circadian system by light. *Journal of Biological Rhythms, 20*(4), 326–338.
Duffy, V. B., & Bartoshuk, L. M. (2000). Food acceptance and genetic variation in taste. *Journal of the American Dietetic Association, 100*(6), 647–655.
Dum, R. P., & Strick, P. L. (2009). Basal ganglia and cerebellar circuits with the cerebral cortex. In M. S. Gazzaniga (Ed.), *The cognitive neurosciences* (4th ed., pp. 553–564). Cambridge, MA: MIT Press.
Duncan, L. A., Schaller, M., & Park, J. H. (2009). Perceived vulnerability to disease: Development and validation of a 15-item self-report instrument. *Personality and Individual Differences, 47*(6), 541–546.
Dunn, E. W., Wilson, T. D., & Gilbert, D. T. (2003). Location, location, location: The misprediction of satisfaction in housing lotteries. *Personality and Social Psychology Bulletin, 29*(11), 1421–1432.
Durand, V. M., & Wang, M. (2011). Clinical trials. In J. C. Thomas & M. Hersen (Eds.), *Understanding research in clinical and counseling psychology* (2nd ed., pp. 201–227). New York, NY: Taylor & Francis.
Durkin, K., & Nugent, B. (1998). Kindergarten children's gender-role expectations for television actors. *Sex Roles, 38*(5–6), 387–402.
Durlach, P. J. (2004). Change blindness and its implications for complex monitoring and control systems design and operator training. *Human–Computer Interaction, 19*(4), 423–451.
Duschinsky, R. (2015). The emergence of the disorganized/disoriented (D) attachment classification, 1979–1982. *History of Psychology, 18*(1), 32–46.
Dweck, C. S., & Grant, H. (2008). Self-theories, goals, and meaning. In J. Y. Shah & W. L. Gardner (Eds.), *Handbook of motivation science* (pp. 405–416). New York, NY: Guilford Press.
Dweck, C. S., & Leggett, E. L. (1988). A social-cognitive approach to motivation and personality. *Psychological Review, 95*(2), 256–273.
Dworkin, S. H. (2013). Bisexual identities. In C. J. Patterson & A. R. D'Augelli (Eds.), *Handbook of psychology and sexual orientation* (pp. 31–41). New York, NY: Oxford University Press.
Eagly, A. H. (1987). *Sex differences in social behavior: A social-role interpretation*. Hillsdale, NJ: Lawrence Erlbaum.
Eagly, A. H. (2013). The science and politics of comparing women and men: A reconsideration. In M. K. Ryan & N. R. Branscombe (Eds.), *The SAGE handbook of gender and psychology* (pp. 11–28). Thousand Oaks, CA: SAGE.
Eagly, A. H., & Crowley, M. (1986). Gender and helping behavior: A meta-analytic review of the social psychological literature. *Psychological Bulletin, 100*(3), 283–308.
Eagly, A. H., & Diekman, A. B. (2003). The malleability of sex differences in response to changing social roles. In L. G. Aspinwall & U. M. Staudinger (Eds.), *A psychology of human strengths* (pp. 103–115). Washington DC: American Psychological Association.
Eagly, A. H., & Wood, W. (1999). The origins of sex differences in human behavior: Evolved dispositions versus social roles. *American Psychologist, 54*(6), 408–423.
Eagly, A. H., Wood, W., & Diekman, A. B. (2000). Social role theory of sex differences and similarities: A current appraisal. In T. Eckes & H. M. Trautner (Eds.), *The developmental social psychology of gender* (pp. 123–174). Mahwah, NJ: Lawrence Erlbaum.
Eakin, L., Minde, K., Hechtman, L., Ochs, E., Krane, E., Bouffard, R., . . . Looper, K. (2004). The marital and family functioning of adults with ADHD and their spouses. *Journal of Attention Disorders, 8*(1), 1–10.
Earley, P. C., & Ang, S. (2003). *Cultural intelligence: Individual interactions across cultures*. Palo Alto, CA: Stanford University Press.
Earley, P. C., & Mosakowski, E. (2004). Cultural intelligence. *Harvard Business Review, 82*(10), 139–146.
Eastwick, P. W., Finkel, E. J., Mochon, D., & Ariely, D. (2007). Selective versus unselective romantic desire: Not all reciprocity is created equal. *Psychological Science, 18*(4), 317–319.
Eatock, R. A. (2010). Auditory receptors and transduction. In E. B. Goldstein (Ed.), *Encyclopedia of perception* (pp. 183–186). Thousand Oaks, CA: SAGE.
Eaton, W. W., & Chen, C. (2006). Epidemiology. In J. A. Lieberman, T. S. Stroup, & D. O. Perkins (Eds.), *The American Psychiatric Publishing textbook of schizophrenia* (pp. 17–37). Washington, DC: American Psychiatric Association Publishing.
Ebbinghaus, H. (1885). *Memory: A contribution to experimental psychology*. New York, NY: Dover.
Eberth, J., & Sedlmeier, P. (2012). The effects of mindfulness meditation: A meta-analysis. *Mindfulness, 3*(3), 174–189.
Ebner, N. C. (2008). Age of face matters: Age-group differences in ratings of young and old faces. *Behavior Research Methods, 40*(1), 130–136.
Ebner, N. C., Freund, A. M., & Baltes, P. B. (2006). Developmental changes in personal goal orientation from young to late adulthood: From striving for gains to maintenance and prevention of losses. *Psychology and Aging, 21*, 664–678.
Ebrecht, M., Hextall, J., Kirtley, L. G., Taylor, A., Dyson, M., & Weinman, J. (2004). Perceived stress and cortisol levels predict speed of wound healing in healthy male adults. *Psychoneuroendocrinology, 29*(6), 798–809.
Eccleston, C., & Crombez, G. (1999). Pain demands attention: A cognitive–affective model of the interruptive function of pain. *Psychological Bulletin, 125*(3), 356–366.
Eckert, D. J., Malhotra, A., & Jordan, A. S. (2009). Mechanisms of apnea. *Progress in Cardiovascular Diseases, 51*(4), 313–323.
Economos, C. D., Brownson, R. C., DeAngelis, M. A., Foerster, S. B., Foreman, C. T., Gregson, J., . . . Pate, R. R. (2001). What lessons have been learned from other attempts to guide social change? *Nutrition Reviews, 59*(3), S40–S56.
Economos, C. D., & Sliwa, S. A. (2011). Community interventions. In J. H. Cawley (Ed.), *The Oxford handbook of the social science of obesity* (pp. 713–740). New York, NY: Oxford University Press.
Edenfield, T. M., & Blumenthal, J. A. (2011). Exercise and stress reduction. In A. Baum & R. Contrada (Eds.), *The handbook of stress science: Biology, psychology, and health* (pp. 301–319). New York, NY: Springer.
Egan, R. D. (2013). *Becoming sexual: A critical appraisal of the sexualization of girls*. Cambridge, MA: Polity Press.
Egan, V., & MacKenzie, J. (2012). Does personality, delinquency, or mating effort necessarily dictate a preference for an aggressive dog? *Anthrozoos: A Multidisciplinary Journal of the Interactions of People & Animals, 25*(2), 161–170.
Egger, G., & Swinburn, B. (1997). An "ecological" approach to the obesity pandemic. *BMJ: British Medical Journal, 315*(7106), 477–479.
Ehlers, A. (1993). Somatic symptoms and panic attacks: A retrospective study of learning experiences. *Behaviour Research and Therapy, 31*(3), 269–278.
Ehrenwald, J. (Ed.). (1991). *The history of psychotherapy*. Northvale, NJ: Aronson.
Ehrlich, P., & Feldman, M., (2003). Genes and cultures. *Current Anthropology, 44*(1), 87–107.
Eibl-Eibesfeldt, I. (1973). The expressive behaviour of the deaf-and-blind born. In M. von Cranach & I. Vine (Eds.), *Social communication and movement* (pp. 163–194). London, UK: Academic Press.
Eich, E. (1995a). Searching for mood dependent memory. *Psychological Science, 6*(2), 67–75.
Eich, E. (1995b). Mood as a mediator of place dependent memory. *Journal of Experimental Psychology: General, 124*(3), 293–308.
Eich, E. (2007). Context: Mood, memory, and the concept of context. In H. L. Roediger, Y. Dudai, & S. M. Fitzpatrick (Eds.). *Science of memory: Concepts* (pp. 107–110). Oxford, UK: Oxford University Press.
Eichenbaum, H. (2010). Memory systems. *Wiley Interdisciplinary Reviews: Cognitive Science, 1*(4), 478–490.
Eichstaedt, J. C., Schwartz, H. A., Kern, M. L., Park, G., Labarthe, D. R., Merchant, R. M., . . . Seligman, M. E. (2015). Psychological language on Twitter predicts county-level heart disease mortality. *Psychological Science, 26*(2), 159–169.
Eid, M., & Diener, E. (2001). Norms for experiencing emotions in different cultures: Inter-and intranational differences. *Journal of Personality and Social Psychology, 81*(5), 869–885.
Eisen, J. L., Yip, A. G., Mancebo, M. C., Pinto, A., & Rasmussen, S. A. (2010). Phenomenology of obsessive-compulsive disorder. In D. J. Stein, E. Hollander, & B. O. Rothbaum (Eds.), *Textbook of anxiety disorders* (2nd ed., pp. 261–286). Washington, D.C.: American Psychiatric Association Publishing.
Eisenberg, A. E., Baron, J., & Seligman, M. E. (1998). Individual differences in risk aversion and anxiety. *Psychological Bulletin, 87*, 245–251.
Eisenberg, M. E., Neumark-Sztainer, M. S., & Perry, C. (2005). The role of social norms and friends' influences on unhealthy weight-control behaviors among adolescent girls. *Social Science & Medicine, 60*, 1165–1173.
Eisenberg, N., Fabes, R. A., Miller, P. A., Fultz, J., Shell, R., Mathy, R. M., & Reno, R. R. (1989). Relation of sympathy and distress to prosocial behavior: A multimethod study. *Journal of Personality and Social Psychology, 57*(1), 55–66.
Eisenberg, N., Morris, A. S., McDaniel, B., & Spinrad, T. L. (2009). Moral cognitions and prosocial responding in adolescence. In R. M. Lerner & L. Steinberg (Eds.), *Handbook of adolescent psychology* (3rd ed., Vol. 1, pp. 229–265). Hoboken, NJ: Wiley.
Eisenberger, N. I., Lieberman, M. D., & Williams, K. D. (2003). Does rejection hurt? An fMRI study of social exclusion. *Science, 302*(5643), 290–292
Eiser, J. R. (2012). A history of social judgment research. In A. W. Kruglanski & W. Stroebe (Eds.), *Handbook of the history of social psychology* (pp. 219–241). New York, NY: Psychology Press.
Ekman, P. (1972). Universal and cultural differences in facial expression of emotion. In J. R. Cole (Ed.), *Nebraska symposium on motivation* (Vol. 19, pp. 207–283). Lincoln, NE: University of Nebraska Press.
Ekman, P. (Ed.). (1974). *Darwin and facial expression*. New York, NY: Academic Press.
Ekman, P. (1993). Facial expression and emotion. *American Psychologist, 48*(4), 384–392.
Ekman, P. (2003). *Emotions revealed: Recognizing faces and feelings to improve communication and emotional life*. New York, NY: Times Books.
Ekman, P., & Cordaro, D. (2011). What is meant by calling emotions basic. *Emotion Review, 3*(4), 364–370.
Ekman, P., & Friesen, W. (1971). Constants across culture in the face and emotion. *Journal of Personality and Social Psychology, 17*(2), 124–129.
Ekman, P., Friesen, W. V., O'Sullivan, M., Chan, A., Diacoyanni-Tarlatiz, I., & Heider, K., . . . Ricci-Pitti, P. E. (1987). Universals and cultural differences in the judgements of facial expressions of emotion, *Journal of Personality and Social Psychology, 53*(4), 712–717.
Ekstrand, B. R. (1972). To sleep, perchance to dream: About why we forget. In C. Duncan, P. L. Sechrest, & A. W. Melton (Eds.), *Human memory; Festschrift for Benton J. Underwood* (pp. 59–82). East Norwalk, CT: Appleton-Century-Crofts.
Elbert, T., Pantev, C., Wienbruch, C., Rockstroh, B., & Taub, E. (1995). Increased cortical representation of the fingers of the left hand in string players. *Science, 270*(5234), 305–307.
Elder, G. H. Jr., & Shanahan, M. J. (2006). The life course and human development. In R. M. Lerner (Vol. Ed.), *Handbook of child psychology* (6th ed., Vol. 1, pp. 665–715). Hoboken, NJ: Wiley.

Eley, T. C. (2009). The genetic basis of anxiety disorders. In G. Andrews, D. S. Charney, P. J. Sirovatka, & D. A. Regier (Eds.), *Stress-induced and fear circuitry disorders: Refining the research agenda for DSM-V* (pp. 145–158). Arlington, VA: American Psychiatric Association.

Elfenbein, H. A., & Ambady, N. (2002). On the universality and cultural specificity of emotion recognition: A meta-analysis. *Psychological Bulletin, 128*(2), 203–235.

Eliason, M. J. (2001). Substance abuse counselor's attitudes regarding lesbian, gay, bisexual, and transgendered clients. *Journal of Substance Abuse, 12*(4), 311–328.

Elkind, D. (1967). Egocentrism in adolescence. *Child Development, 38*(4), 1025–1034.

Elkind, D. (1985). Egocentrism redux. *Developmental Review, 5*(3), 218–226.

Elkins, G., & Perfect, M. (2008). Hypnosis for health-compromising behaviors. In M. R. Nash & A. J. Barnier (Eds.), *The Oxford handbook of hypnosis: Theory, research, and practice* (pp. 569–592). Oxford, UK: Oxford University Press.

Ellenbogen, J. M., Hulbert, J. C., Stickgold, R., Dinges, D. F., & Thompson-Schill, S. L. (2006). Interfering with theories of sleep and memory: Sleep, declarative memory, and associative interference. *Current Biology, 16*(13), 1290–1294.

Elliot, A. J., McGregor, H. A., & Gable, S. (1999). Achievement goals, study strategies, and exam performance: A mediational analysis. *Journal of Educational Psychology, 91*(3), 549–563.

Elliott, E. S., & Dweck, C. S. (1988). Goals: An approach to motivation and achievement. *Journal of Personality and Social Psychology, 54*(1), 5–12.

Elliott, J. L., & Gentile, J. R. (1986). The efficacy of a mnemonic technique for learning disabled and nondisabled adolescents. *Journal of Learning Disabilities, 19*, 237–241.

Elliott, K., Barker, K. K., & Hunsley, J. (2015). Dodo bird verdict in psychotherapy. In R. L. Cautin & S. O. Lilienfeld (Eds.), *The encyclopedia of clinical psychology* (pp. 944–948). West Sussex, UK: Wiley-Blackwell.

Elliott, R., Bohart, A. C., Watson, J. C., & Greenberg, L. S. (2011). Empathy. In J. C. Norcross (Ed.), *Psychotherapy relationships that work: Evidence-based responsiveness* (2nd ed., pp. 132–152). New York, NY: Oxford University Press.

Ellis, A. (1962). *Reason and emotion in psychotherapy*. New York, NY: Lyle Stuart.

Ellis, A. (2008). Cognitive restructuring of the disputing of irrational beliefs. In W. T. O'Donohue & J. E. Fisher (Eds.), *Cognitive behavior therapy: Applying empirically supported techniques in your practice* (2nd ed., pp. 91–95). Hoboken, NJ: Wiley.

Ellis, A., & Ellis, D. J. (2011). *Rational emotive behavior therapy*. Washington, DC: American Psychological Association.

Ellis, A., & Grieger, R. (1977). *Handbook of rational-emotive therapy*. New York, NY: Springer Publishing.

Ellis, A., & Harper, R. A. (1975). *A new guide to rational living*. North Hollywood, CA: Wilshire.

Ellis, B., & Anthony, J. (2012, November 16). Red Cross donations hit $145 million for Sandy relief. CNN Money. http://money.cnn.com/2012/11/16/pf/sandy-donations-red-cross/index.html

Ellison, C. G. (1991). Religious involvement and subjective well-being. *Journal of Health and Social Behavior, 32*(1), 80–99.

Ellison, K. (2010). *Buzz: A year of paying attention*. New York, NY: Voice.

Elman, J. L., Bates, E. A., Johnson, M. H., Karmiloff-Smith, A., Parisi, D., & Plunkett, K. (1996). *Rethinking innateness*. Cambridge, MA: MIT Press.

Emerson, C. (1983). The outer word and inner speech: Bakhtin, Vygotsky, and the internalization of language. *Critical Inquiry, 10*(2), 245–264.

Emmelkamp, P. M. G., & Kamphuis, J. H. (2002). Aversion relief. In M. Hersen & W. Sledge (Eds.), *Encyclopedia of psychotherapy* (Vol. 1, pp. 139–143). San Diego, CA: Academic Press.

Emmelkamp, P. M. G., & Wittchen, H. (2009). Specific phobias. In G. Andrews, D. S. Charney, P. J. Sirovatka, & D. A. Regier (Eds.), *Stress-induced and fear circuitry disorders: Refining the research agenda for DSM-V* (pp. 77–101). Arlington, VA: American Psychiatric Association.

Emmelkamp, P. M., & Wessels, H. (1975). Flooding in imagination vs flooding in vivo: A comparison with agoraphobics. *Behaviour Research and Therapy, 13*(1), 7–15.

Emmons, R. A., & McCullough, M. E. (2003). Counting blessings versus burdens: An experimental investigation of gratitude and subjective well-being in daily life. *Journal of Personality and Social Psychology, 84*(2), 377–389.

Encinosa, W. E., Bernard, D. M., Du, D., & Steiner, C. A. (2009). Recent improvements in bariatric surgery outcomes. *Medical Care, 47*(5), 531–535.

Encinosa, W., Du, D., & Bernard, D. (2011). Anti-obesity drugs and bariatric surgery. In J. H. Cawley (Ed.), *The Oxford handbook of the social science of obesity* (pp. 792–807). New York, NY: Oxford University Press.

Endo, T., Roth, C., Landolt, H. P., Werth, E., Aeschbach, D., Achermann, P., & Borbély, A. A. (1998). Selective REM sleep deprivation in humans: Effects on sleep and sleep EEG. *American Journal of Physiology – Regulatory, Integrative and Comparative Physiology, 274*(4), R1186–R1194.

Endo, Y., Heine, S. J., & Lehman, D. R. (2000). Culture and positive illusions in close relationships: How my relationships are better than yours. *Personality and Social Psychology Bulletin, 26*(12), 1571–1586.

Endresen, I. M., & Olweus, D. (2001). Self-reported empathy in Norwegian adolescents: Sex differences, age trends, and relationship to bullying. In A. C. Bohart, & D. J. Stipek (Eds.), *Constructive & destructive behavior: Implications for family, school, and society* (pp. 147–165). Washington, DC: American Psychological Association.

Endrighi, R., Hamer, M., & Steptoe, A. (2011). Associations of trait optimism with diurnal neuroendocrine activity, cortisol responses to mental stress, and subjective stress measures in healthy men and women. *Psychosomatic Medicine, 73*(8), 672–678.

Engel, J. (2008). *American therapy: The rise of psychotherapy in the United States*. New York, NY: Gotham Books.

Engle, R. W. (2002). Working memory capacity as executive attention. *Current Directions in Psychological Science, 11*(1), 19–23.

English, T., John, O. P., & Gross, J. J. (2013). Emotion regulation in close relationships. In J. A. Simpson & L. Campbell (Eds.), *The Oxford handbook of close relationships* (pp. 500–513). New York, NY: Oxford University Press.

Eonta, A. M., Christon, L. M., Hourigan, S. E., Ravindran, N., Vrana, S. R., Southam-Gerow, M. A. (2011). Using everyday technology to enhance evidence-based treatments. *Professional Psychology: Research and Practice, 42*(6), 513–520.

Epstein, S. (1991). Cognitive-experiential self-theory: An integrative theory of personality. In R. Curtis (Ed.), *The self with others: Convergences in psychoanalytic, social, and personality psychology* (pp. 111–137). New York, NY: Guilford Press.

Epstein, S. (1994). Trait theory as personality theory: Can a part be as great as the whole? *Psychological Inquiry, 5*(2), 120–122.

Er, N. (2003). A new flashbulb memory model applied to the Marmara earthquake. *Applied Cognitive Psychology, 17*, 503–517.

Erekson, D. M., & Lambert, M. J. (2015). Client-centered therapy. In R. L. Cautin & S. O. Lilienfeld (Eds.), *The encyclopedia of clinical psychology* (pp. 532–537). West Sussex, UK: Wiley-Blackwell.

Erhart, S. M., Young, A. S., Marder, S. R., & Mintz, J. (2005). Clinical utility of magnetic resonance imaging radiographs for suspected organic syndromes in adult psychiatry. *Journal of Clinical Psychiatry, 66*(8), 968–973.

Erickson, J. J., Martinengo, G., & Hill, E. J. (2010). Putting work and family experiences in context: Differences by family life stage. *Human Relations, 63*(7), 955–979.

Erickson, K. I., & Kramer, A. F. (2009). Aerobic exercise effects on cognitive and neural plasticity in older adults. *British Journal of Sports Medicine, 43*(1), 22–24.

Erickson, K. I., Voss, M. W., Prakash, R. S., Basak, C., Szabo, A., Chaddock, L., . . . Kramer, A. F. (2011). Exercise training increases size of hippocampus and improves memory. *Proceedings of the National Academy of Sciences, 108*(7),

Eriksen, K. & Kress, V. E. (2005). *Beyond the DSM story: Ethical quandaries, challenges, and best practices*. Thousand Oaks, CA: SAGE.

Erikson, E. H. (1946). Ego development and historical change—clinical notes. *Psychoanalytic Study of the Child, 2*, 359–396.

Erikson, E. H. (1950). *Childhood and society*. New York, NY: Norton.

Erikson, E. H. (1950). Growth and crises of the "healthy personality." In M. J. E. Senn (Ed), *Symposium on the healthy personality* (pp. 91–146). Oxford, UK: Josiah Macy, Jr. Foundation.

Erikson, E. H. (1959). *Identity and the life cycle.* New York, NY: International Universities Press.

Erikson, E. H. (1968) *Identity, youth and crisis*. New York, NY: Norton.

Erikson, E. H., & Erikson, J. M. (1998). The life cycle completed (extended version). New York, NY: Norton.

Erikson, Erik H. (1959) *Identity and the life cycle*. New York, NY: International Universities Press.

Eriksson, P. S., Perfilieva, E., Björk-Eriksson, T., Alborn, A. M., Nordborg, C., Peterson, D. A., & Gage, F. H. (1998). Neurogenesis in the adult human hippocampus. *Nature Medicine, 4*(11), 1313–1317.

Erlacher, D. (2012). Lucid dreaming in sports. In D. Barrett & P. McNamara (Eds.), *Encyclopedia of sleep and dreams* (pp. 400–401). Santa Barbara, CA: Greenwood.

Ernsberger, P. (2008). Set or setting point. In K. Keller (Ed.), *Encyclopedia of obesity* (Vol. 2, p. 683). Los Angeles, CA: SAGE.

Ernst, E., Pittler, M. H., & Wider, B. (2006). *The desktop guide to complementary and alternative medicine: An evidence-based approach* (2nd ed.). London, UK: Mosby Elsevier.

Eron, L. D., Huesmann, L. R., Lefkowitz, M. M., & Walder, L. O. (1972). Does television violence cause aggression? *American Psychologist, 27*(4), 253–263.

Erwin, E. (Ed.). (2002). *The Freud encyclopedia: Theory, therapy, and culture*. New York, NY: Routledge.

Eshun, S., & Gurung, R. A. R. (Eds.) (2009). *Culture and mental health: Sociocultural influences, theory, and practice*. Malden, MA: Wiley-Blackwell.

Espie, C. A., & Morin, C. M. (2012). Introduction: Historical landmarks and current status of sleep research and practice. In C. M. Morin & C. A. Espie (Eds.), *The Oxford handbook of sleep and sleep disorders* (pp. 1–9). Oxford, UK: Oxford University Press.

Essau, C. A., & Trommsdorff, G. (1996). Coping with university-related problems: A cross-cultural comparison. *Journal of Cross-Cultural Psychology, 27*(3), 315–328.

Esterling, B. A., Kiecolt-Glaser, J. K., Bodnar, J. C., & Glaser, R. (1994). Chronic stress, social support, and persistent alterations in the natural killer cell response to cytokines in older adults. *Health Psychology, 13*(4), 291–298.

Etchegoyen, A. (1993). Latency: A reappraisal. *International Journal of Psychoanalysis, 74*(Pt. 2), 347–357.

Etkin, A., Pittenger, C., Polan, H. J., & Kandel, E. R. (2005). Toward a neurobiology of psychotherapy: Basic science and clinical applications. *Journal of Neuropsychiatry and Clinical Neurosciences, 17*(2), 145–158.

Euling, S. Y., Selevan, S. G., Pescovitz, O. H., & Skakkebaek, N. E. (2008). Role of environmental factors in the timing of puberty. *Pediatrics, 121*(Suppl. 3), S167–S171.

Evans, D. (2009) *Rage against the meshugenah: Why it takes balls to go nuts: A memoir*. New York, NY: Penguin Books.

Evans, J. H. (2009). Have Americans' attitudes become more polarized?—An update. *Social Science Quarterly, 84*(1), 71–90.

Evans, J. St. B. T. (2012). Dual-process theories of deductive reasoning: Facts and fallacies. In K. J. Holyoak and R. G. Morrison (Eds.), *The Oxford handbook of thinking and reasoning* (pp. 115–133). Oxford, UK: Oxford University Press.

Evans, J. St. B. T. (2012). Dual-process theories of deductive reasoning: Facts and fallacies. In K. J. Holyoak and R. G. Morrison (Eds.), *The Oxford handbook of thinking and reasoning* (pp. 115–133). Oxford, UK: Oxford University Press.

Evans, J. St. B. T. (2013). Reasoning. In D. Reisberg (Ed.), *The Oxford handbook of cognitive psychology* (pp. 635–649). Oxford, UK: Oxford University Press.

Evans, J. St. B. T., & Over, D. E. (1996) *Rationality and reasoning*. Hove, UK: Psychology Press.

Evans, J. St. B. T., & Stanovich, K. E. (2013). Dual-process theories of higher cognition advancing the debate. *Perspectives on psychological science, 8*(3), 223–241.

Evans, R. I. (1968). *B. F. Skinner: The man and his ideas*. New York, NY: Dutton.

Everitt, B. J., & Robbins, T. W. (2005). Neural systems of reinforcement for drug addiction: From actions to habits to compulsion. *Nature Neuroscience, 8*(11), 1481–1489.

Ewert, J. P. (1987). Neuroethology of releasing mechanisms: Prey-catching in toads. *Behavioral Brain Science, 10*(3), 337–405.

Exner, J. E., Jr. (1986). *The Rorschach: A comprehensive system* (2nd ed.). New York, NY: Wiley.

Exton, M. S., von Auer, A. K., Buske-Kirschbaum, A., Stockhorst, U., Göbel, U., & Schedlowski, M. (2000). Pavlovian conditioning of immune function: Animal investigation and the challenge of human application. *Behavioural Brain Research, 110*(1), 129–141.

Eyde, L, D. (2000). Other responsibilities to participants. In B. D. Sales, & S. Folkman (Eds.), *Ethics in research with human participants* (pp. 61–73). Washington, D.C: American Psychological Association.

Eysenck, H. J. (1952). The effects of psychotherapy: An evaluation. *Journal of Consulting Psychology, 16*(6), 319–324.

Eysenck, H. J. (1995). *Genius: The natural history of creativity*. Cambridge, UK: Cambridge University Press.

Eysenck, M. W. (2013). The impact of anxiety on cognitive performance. In S. Kreitler (Ed.), *Cognition and motivation: Forging an interdisciplinary perspective* (pp. 96–108). Cambridge, UK: Cambridge University Press.

Eysenck, M. W., & Calvo, M. G. (1992). Anxiety and performance: The processing efficiency theory. *Cognition & Emotion, 6*(6), 409–434.

Eysenck, M. W., Derakshan, N., Santos, R., & Calvo, M. G. (2007). Anxiety and cognitive performance: Attentional control theory. *Emotion, 7*(2), 336–353.

Fabbri-Destro, M., & Rizzolatti, G. (2008). Mirror neurons and mirror systems in monkeys and humans. *Physiology, 23*, 171–179.

Fabel, K., & Kempermann, G. (2008). Physical activity and the regulation of neurogenesis in the adult and aging brain. *Neuromolecular Medicine, 10*(2), 59–66.

Fairburn, C. G., Cooper, Z., Doll, H. A., Norman, P., & O'Connor, M. (2000). The natural course of bulimia nervosa and binge eating disorder in young women. *Archives of General Psychiatry, 57*(7), 659–665.

Faith, M. S., Butryn, M., Wadden, T. A., Fabricatore, A., Nguyen, A. M., & Heymsfield, S. B. (2011). Evidence for prospective associations among depression and obesity in population-based studies. *Obesity Reviews, 12*(5), e438–e453.

Falk, D. (2012). The role of hominin mothers and infants in prelinguistic evolution. In M. Tallerman & K. R. Gibson (Eds.), *The Oxford handbook of language evolution* (pp. 318–321). Oxford, UK: Oxford University Press.

Falls, W. A. (1998). Extinction: A review of the theory and the evidence suggesting that memories are not erased with nonreinforcement. In W. O'Donohue (Ed.), *Learning and behavior therapy* (pp. 205–229). Boston, MA: Allyn and Bacon.

Famy, C., Streissguth, A. P., & Unis, A. S. (1998). Mental illness in adults with fetal alcohol syndrome or fetal alcohol effects. *American Journal of Psychiatry, 155*(4), 552–554.

Fancher, R. E., & Rutherford, A. (2012). *Pioneers of psychology: A history* (4th ed.). New York, NY: Norton.

Fancher, R. T. (1995). *Cultures of healing: Correcting the image of American mental health care*. New York, NY: W. H. Freeman.

Fantz, R. L., Fagan, J. F., & Miranda, S. B. (1975). Early visual selectivity: As function of pattern variables, previous exposure, age from birth and conception, and expected cognitive deficit. In L. B. Cohen & P. Salapatek (Eds.), *Infant perception: From sensation to cognition* (Vol. 1, pp. 249–346). New York, NY: Elsevier.

Farah, M. J. (2010). *Neuroethics: An introduction with readings*. Cambridge, MA: MIT Press.

Faravelli, C., Furukawa, T. A., & Truglia, E. (2009). Panic disorder. In G. Andrews, D. S. Charney, P. J. Sirovatka, & D. A. Regier (Eds.), *Stress-induced and fear circuitry disorders: Refining the research agenda for DSM-V* (pp. 31–58). Arlington, VA: American Psychiatric Association.

Farber, B. A., & Doolin, E. M. (2011). Positive regard and affirmation. In J. C. Norcross (Ed.), *Psychotherapy relationships that work: Evidence-based responsiveness* (2nd ed., pp. 168–186). New York, NY: Oxford University Press.

Fardouly, J. & Vartanian, L. R. (2015). Negative comparisons about one's appearance mediate the relationship between Facebook usage and body image concerns. *Body Image, 12*, 82–88.

Fardouly, J., Diedrichs, P. C., Vartanian, L. R., & Halliwell, E. (2015). Social comparisons on social media: The impact of Facebook on young women's body image concerns and mood. *Body Image, 13*, 38–45.

Farley, S. D., Ashcraft, A. M., Stasson, M. F., & Nusbaum, R. L. (2010). Nonverbal reactions to conversational interruption: A test of complementarity theory and the status/gender parallel. *Journal of Nonverbal Behavior, 34*(4), 193–206.

Farley, S. D., Hughes, S. M., & LaFayette, J. N. (2013). People will know we are in love: Evidence of differences between vocal samples directed toward lovers and friends. *Journal of Nonverbal Behavior, 37*(3), 123–138.

Farver, J. A. M., Kim, Y. K., & Lee, Y. (1995). Cultural differences in Korean- and Anglo-American preschoolers' social interaction and play behaviors. *Child Development, 66*(4), 1088–1099.

Fast, D. K., & Conry, J. (2009). Fetal alcohol spectrum disorders and the criminal justice system. *Developmental Disabilities Research Reviews, 15*(3), 250–257.

Fast, D. K., Conry, J., & Loock, C. A. (1999). Identifying fetal alcohol syndrome among youth in the criminal justice system. *Journal of Developmental and Behavioral Pediatrics, 20*(5), 370–372.

Fast, D. K., & Conry, J. (2004). The challenge of fetal alcohol syndrome in the criminal legal system. *Addiction Biology, 9*(2), 161–166.

Fazio, R. H. (1990). Multiple processes by which attitudes guide behavior: The MODE model as an integrative framework. In M. P. Zanna (Ed.), *Advances in experimental social psychology* (pp. 75–109). New York, NY: Academic Press.

Fazio, R. H., & Olson, M. A. (2003). Implicit measures in social cognition research: Their meaning and use. *Annual Review of Psychology, 54*(1), 297–327.

Feather, N. T. (1988). Moral judgement and human values. *British Journal of Social Psychology, 27*, 239–246.

Federman, J. (Ed.) (1998). *National television violence study: Executive summary*. Santa Barbara, CA: The Center for Communication and Social Policy.

Federn, E. (1997). Sigmund Freud: A biographical sketch. In W. G. Bringmann, H. E. Lück, R. Miller, & C. E. Early (Eds.), *A pictorial history of psychology* (pp. 391–394). Carol Stream, IL: Quintessence Publishing

Feigenbaum, E. A., & Simon, H. A. (1962). A theory of the serial position effect. *British Journal of Psychology, 53*(3), 307–320.

Feinberg, I., & Campbell, I. G. (2010). Sleep EEG changes during adolescence: An index of a fundamental brain reorganization. *Brain and Cognition, 72*(1), 56–65.

Feinberg, I., & Floyd, T. C. (1979). Systematic trends across the night in human sleep cycles. *Psychophysiology, 16*(3), 283–291.

Feingold, A. (1994). Gender differences in personality: A meta-analysis. *Psychological Bulletin, 116*(3), 429–456.

Feist, G. J. (1998). A meta-analysis of personality in scientific and artistic creativity. *Personality and Social Psychology Review, 2*(4), 290–309.

Feist, G. J. (1999). The function of personality in creativity: The nature and nurture of the creative personality. In R. J. Sternberg (Ed.), *The Cambridge handbook of creativity* (pp. 113–130). Cambridge, UK: Cambridge University Press.

Felitti, V. J., Anda, R. F., Nordenberg, D., Williamson, D. F., Spitz, A. M., Edwards, V., . . . Marks, J. S. (1998). Relationship of childhood abuse and household dysfunction to many of the leading causes of death in adults: The Adverse Childhood Experiences (ACE) Study. *American Journal of Preventive Medicine, 14*(4), 245–258.

Fenson, L., Dale, P. S., Reznick, J. S., Bates, E., Thal, D. J., & Pethick, S. J. (1994). *Variability in early communicative development*. Monographs of the Society for Research in Child Development, 59, 1–173.

Ferber, S., & Karnath, H. O. (1999). Parietal and occipital lobe contributions to perception of straight ahead orientation. *Journal of Neurology, Neurosurgery & Psychiatry, 67*(5), 572–578.

Ferdenzi, C., Roberts, S. C., Schirmer, A., Delplanque, S., Cekic, S., Porcherot, C., . . . & Grandjean, D. (2013). Variability of affective responses to odors: Culture, gender, and olfactory knowledge. *Chemical Senses, 38*(2), 175–186.

Ferdowsian, H., Durham, D., Brüne, M. (2013). Mood and anxiety disorders in chimpanzees (*pan* troglodytes): A response to Rosati et al. (2012). *Journal of Comparative Psychology, 127*(3), 337–40. doi:10.1037/a0032823

Ferguson, C. J. (2013). Spanking, corporal punishment and negative long-term outcomes: A meta-analytic review of longitudinal studies. *Clinical Psychology Review, 33*, 196–208

Ferguson, C. J., & Kilburn, J. (2009). The public health risks of media violence: A meta-analytic review. *The Journal of Pediatrics, 154*, 759–763.

Ferguson, C. J., & Kilburn, J. (2010). Much ado about nothing: The misestimation and overinterpretation of violent video game effects in eastern and western nations: Comment on Anderson et al. (2010). *Psychological Bulletin, 136*, 182–187.

Ferguson, C. J., Miguel, C. S., Garza, A., & Jerabeck, J. M. (2012). A longitudinal test of video game violence influences on dating and aggression: A 3-year longitudinal study of adolescents. *Journal of Psychiatric Research, 46*, 141–146.

Ferguson, C. J., & Savage, J. (2012). Have recent studies addressed methodological issues raised by five decades of television violence research? A critical review. *Aggression and Violent Behavior, 17*, 129–139.

Ferguson, K. A., Cartwright, R., Rogers, R., & Schmidt-Nowara, W. (2006). Oral appliances for snoring and obstructive sleep apnea: A review. *Sleep, 29*(2), 244.

Fergusson, D. M., Horwood, L. J., & Beautrais, A. L. (1999). Is sexual orientation related to mental health problems and suicidality in young people? *Archives of General Psychiatry, 56*(10), 876–880.

Fergusson, D. M., Horwood, L. J., Ridder, E. M., & Beautrais, A. L. (2005). Sexual orientation and mental health in a birth cohort of young adults. *Psychological Medicine, 35*(7), 971–981.

Fernald, A. (1994). Human material vocalizations to infants as biologically relevant signals: An evolutionary perspective. In P. Bloom (Ed.), *Language acquisition: Core readings* (pp. 51–94). Cambridge, MA: MIT Press.

Fernandez, E., & Turk, D. C. (1995). The scope and significance of anger in the experience of chronic pain. *Pain, 61*(2), 165–175.

Ferracioli-Oda, E., Qawasmi, A., & Bloch, M. H. (2014). Meta-analysis: Melatonin for the treatment of primary sleep disorders. *FOCUS, 12*(1), 73–79.

Festinger, L. (1954). A theory of social comparison processes. *Human Relations, 7*, 117–140.
Festinger, L. (1957). *A theory of cognitive dissonance*. Evanston, IL: Row, Peterson.
Festinger, L. (1964). *Conflict, decision, and dissonance*. Stanford, CA: Stanford University Press.
Festinger, L., & Carlsmith, M. M. (1959). Cognitive consequences of forced compliance. *Journal of Abnormal and Social Psychology, 58*(2), 203–210.
Fetner, T., & Kush, K. (2008). Gay-straight alliances in high schools social predictors of early adoption. *Youth & Society, 40*(1), 114–130.
Fiechtner, L., Block, J., Duncan, D. T., Gillman, M. W., Gortmaker, S. L., Melly, S. J., . . . Taveras, E. M. (2013). Proximity to supermarkets associated with higher body mass index among overweight and obese preschool-age children. *Preventive Medicine, 56*(3), 218–221.
Field, A. E., Austin, S. B., Strigel-Moore, R., Taylor, C. B., Camargo, C. A., Jr., Laird, N., & Colditz, G. (2005). Weight concerns and weight control behaviors of adolescents and their mothers. *Archives of Pediatric and Adolescent Medicine, 159*(12), 1121–1126.
Field, A. E., Camargo, C. A., Taylor, C. B., Berkey, C. S., & Colditz, G. A. (1999a). Relation of peer and media influence to the development of purging behaviors among preadolescent and adolescent girls. *Archives of Pediatric & Adolescent Medicine, 153*(11), 1184–1189.
Field, A., Cheung, L., Wolf, A., Herzog, D., Gortmaker, S., & Colditz, G. (1999b). Exposure to the mass media and weight concerns among girls. *Pediatrics, 103*(3), E36.
Field, A. E., & Kitos, N. (2010). Eating and weight concerns in eating disorders. In W. S. Agras (Ed.), *The Oxford handbook of eating disorders* (pp. 206–222). New York, NY: Oxford University Press.
Field, T. M. (1979). Visual and cardiac responses to animate and inanimate faces by young term and preterm infants. *Child Development, 50*(1), 188–194.
Fielder, R. L., & Carey, M. P. (2010). Predictors and consequences of sexual "hookups" among college students: A short-term prospective study. *Archives of Sexual Behavior, 39*(5), 1105–1119.
Fielder, R. L., Walsh, J. L., Carey, K. B., & Carey, M. P. (2013). Predictors of sexual hookups: A theory-based, prospective study of first-year college women. *Archives of Sexual Behavior, 42*(8), 1425–1441.
Fields, H. L. (2011). The doctor's dilemma: Opiate analgesics and chronic pain. *Neuron, 69*(4), 591–594.
Filley, C. M. (2013). White matter. In D. B. Arciniegas, C. A. Anderson, & C. M. Filley (Eds.), *Behavioral Neurology & Neuropsychiatry* (pp. 47–58). Cambridge, UK: Cambridge University Press.
Finer, L. B., & Zolna, M. R. (2011). Unintended pregnancy in the United States: Incidence and disparities, 2006. *Contraception, 84*(5), 478–485.
Fingerman, K. L., Pitzer, L. M., Chan, W., Birditt, K., Franks, M. M., & Zarit, S. (2011). Who gets what and why? Help middle-aged adults provide to parents and grown children. *The Journals of Gerontology Series B: Psychological Sciences and Social Sciences, 66*(1), 87–98.
Fink, M. (2001). Convulsive therapy: A review of the first 55 years. *Journal of Affective Disorders, 63*(1-3), 1–15.
Fink, M. (2009). *Electroconvulsive therapy: A guide for professionals and their patients*. New York, NY: Oxford University Press.
Finkelstein, E. A., Trogdon, J. G., Cohen, J. W., & Dietz, W. (2009). Annual medical spending attributable to obesity: Payer- and service-specific estimates. *Health Affairs, 28*(5), w822–w831.
Finkelstein, E., & Yang, H. K. (2011). Obesity and medical costs. In J. H. Cawley (Ed.), *The Oxford handbook of the social science of obesity* (pp. 495–501). New York, NY: Oxford University Press.
Finucane, M. L., Alhakami, A., Slovic, P., & Johnson, S. M. (2000). The affect heuristic in judgments of risks and benefits. *Journal of Behavioral Decision Making, 13*(1), 1–17.
Fischer, A., & Evers, C. (2013). The social basis of emotion in men and women. In M. K. Ryan & N. R. Branscombe (Eds.), *The SAGE handbook of gender and psychology* (pp. 183–198). Thousand Oaks, CA: SAGE.
Fischer, A. H., & Manstead, A. S. (2000). The relation between gender and emotions in different cultures. In A. Fischer (Ed.), *Gender and emotion: Social psychological perspectives* (pp. 71–94). Cambridge, UK: University of Cambridge Press.
Fischer, A. H., & Manstead, A. S. R. (2008). Social functions of emotion. In M. Lewis, J. M. Haviland-Jones, & L. F. Barrett (Eds.), *Handbook of emotions* (3rd ed., pp. 456–468). New York, NY: Guilford Press.
Fischer, A., & Tsai, L. (2009). Counteracting molecular pathways regulating the reduction of fear: Implications for the treatment of anxiety disorders. In P. J. Shiromani, T. M. Keane, & J. E. LeDoux (Eds.), *Post-traumatic stress disorder: Basic science and clinical practice* (pp. 79–104). New York, NY: Humana Press.
Fischer, B., Gooch, J., Goldman, B., Kurdyak, P., & Rehm, J. (2014). Non-medical prescription opioid use, prescription opioid-related harms and public health in Canada: An update 5 years later. *The Canadian Journal of Public Health, 105*(2), e146–e149.
Fischer, H. 2013. *U.S. Military casualty statistics: Operation New Dawn, Operation Iraqi Freedom, and Operation Enduring Freedom*. RS22452. Washington DC: Congressional Research Service.
Fischer, K. W. & Bidell, T. R. (2006). Dynamic development of action and thought. In R. M. Lerner (Vol. Ed.), *Handbook of child psychology* (6th ed., Vol. 1, pp. 313–399). Hoboken, NJ: Wiley.
Fischman, M. W. (2000). Informed consent. In B. D. Sales & S. Folkman (Eds.), *Ethics in research with human participants* (pp. 35–48). Washington, D.C: American Psychological Association.
Fish, M., Stifter, C. A., & Belsky, J. (1991). Conditions of continuity and discontinuity in infant negative emotionality: Newborn to five months. *Child Development, 62*(6), 1525–1537.
Fisher, C. B., & Fried, A. A. (2003). Internet-mediated psychological services and the American Psychological Association ethics code. *Psychotherapy: Theory, Research, Practice, Training, 40*(1-2), 103–111.
Fisher, C. B., & Vacanti-Shova, K. (2012). The responsible conduct of psychological research: An overview of ethical principles, APA ethics code standards, and federal regulations. In S. J. Knapp (Ed.), *APA handbook of ethics in psychology, Vol. 2*, pp. 335–369). Washington, DC: American Psychological Association.
Fisher, D. A., Hill, D. L., Grube, J. W., Bersamin, M. M., Walker, S., & Gruber, E. L. (2009). Televised sexual content and parental mediation: Influences on adolescent sexuality. *Media Psychology, 12*(2), 121–147.
Fisher, M. A. (2012). Confidentiality and record keeping. In S. J. Knapp (Ed.), *APA handbook of ethics in psychology* (Vol. 1, pp. 333–375). Washington, DC: American Psychological Association.
Fisher, R. P., & Craik, F. I. M. (1977). Interaction between encoding and retrieval operations in cued recall. *Journal of Experimental Psychology: Human Learning and Memory, 3*(6), 701.
Fiske, A. P., Haslam, N., & Fiske, S. T. (1991). Confusing one person with another: What errors reveal about the elementary forms of social relations. *Journal of Personality and Social Psychology, 60*(5), 656–674.
Fiske, D. W., & Maddi, S. R. (1961). A conceptual framework. In D. W. Fiske & S. R. Maddi (Eds.), *Function of varied experience* (pp. 11–56). Homewood, IL: Dorsey.
Fiske, S. T. (2008). Core social motivations: Views from the couch, consciousness, classroom, computers and collectives. In J. Y. Shah & W. L. Gardner (Ed.), *Handbook of motivation science* (pp. 3–27). New York, NY: Guilford Press.
Fiske, S. T. (2010). *Social beings: Core motives in social psychology* (2nd ed.). Hoboken, NJ: Wiley.
Fiske, S. T. (2012). The continuum model and the stereotype content model. In P. A. M. Van Lange, A. W. Kruglanski, & E. T. Higgins (Eds.), *Handbook of theories of social psychology* (Vol. 1, pp. 267–288). Thousand Oaks, CA: SAGE.
Fiske, S. T., & Neuberg, S. L. (1990). A continuum of impression formation, from category-based to individuating process: Influences of information and motivation on attention and interpretation. *Advances in Experimental Social Psychology, 23*(C), 1–74.
Fitch, W. T. (2012). Innateness and human language: A biological perspective. In M. Tallerman & K. R. Gibson (Eds.), *The Oxford handbook of language evolution* (pp. 143–156). Oxford, UK: Oxford University Press.
Fitzpatrick, J. F., & Bringmann, W. G. (1997). Charles Darwin and psychology. In W. G. Bringmann, H. E. Lück, R. Miller, & C. E. Early (Eds.), *A pictorial history of psychology* (pp. 51–52). Carol Stream, IL: Quintessence Publishing.
Fivush, R., Bohanek, J. B., Marin, K., & Sales, J. M. (2009). Emotional memory and memory for emotions. In O. Luminet & A. Curci (Eds.), *Flashbulb memories: New issues and new perspectives* (pp. 163–184). East Sussex, UK: Psychology Press.
Flanagan, D. P., McGrew, K. S., & Ortiz, S. O. (2000). *The Wechsler Intelligence Scales and Gf-Gc theory: A contemporary approach to interpretation*. Boston, MA: Allyn & Bacon.
Flanagan, D. P., Ortiz, S. O., & Alfonso, V. C. (2013). *Essentials of cross-battery assessment*. Hoboken, NJ: John Wiley & Sons.
Flash, G., & Ritz, D. (2008). *The adventures of Grandmaster Flash: My life, my beats*. New York, NY: Broadway Books.
Fletcher, G. J., Simpson, J. A., & Boyes, A. D. (2006). Accuracy and bias in romantic relationships: An evolutionary and social psychological analysis. In M. Schaller, J. A. Simpson, & D. T. Kenrick (Eds.), *Evolution and social psychology* (pp. 189–209). New York, NY: Psychology Press.
Flier, J. S. (2004). Obesity wars: Molecular progress confronts an expanding epidemic. *Cell, 116*(2), 337–350.
Floderus-Myrhed, B., Pedersen, N., & Rasmuson, I. (1980). Assessment of heritability for personality, based on a short-form of the Eysenck personality inventory: A study of 12,898 twin pairs. *Behavioral Genetics, 10*(2), 153–162. doi:10.1007/BF01066265
Flor, H. (2002). Phantom-limb pain: Characteristics, causes, and treatment. *The Lancet Neurology, 1*(3), 182–189.
Flor, H., Nikolajsen, L., & Jensen, T. S. (2006). Phantom limb pain: A case of maladaptive CNS plasticity? *Nature Reviews Neuroscience, 7*(11), 873–881.
Flora, S. R. (2004). *The power of reinforcement*. Albany, NY: State University of New York Press.
Flowers, J., & Frizler, P. (2004). *Psychotherapists on film, 1899–1999: A worldwide guide to over 5000 films*. Jefferson, NC: McFarland.
Flynn, C. P. (1986). *After the beyond: Human transformation and the near-death experience*. Upper Saddle River, NJ: Prentice-Hall.
Flynn, J. R. (1984). The mean IQ of Americans: Massive gains 1932 to 1978. *Psychological Bulletin, 95*(1), 29–51.
Flynn, J. R. (1987). Massive IQ gains in 14 nations: What IQ tests really measure. *Psychological Bulletin, 101*(2), 171–191.
Flynn, J. R. (2011). Secular changes in intelligence. In R. J. Sternberg & S. B. Kaufman (Eds.), *The Cambridge handbook of intelligence* (pp. 647–665). Cambridge, UK: Cambridge University Press.

Foa, E. B., & McLean, C. P. (2015). The efficacy of exposure therapy for anxiety-related disorders and its underlying mechanisms: The case of OCD and PTSD. *Annual Review of Clinical Psychology, 12*, 1–28.

Fodor, N., & Gaynor, F. (1950). *Freud: Dictionary of psychoanalysis*. New York, NY: Barnes & Noble Books.

Foell, J., & Flor, H. (2013). Phantom limb pain. In R. J. Moore (Ed.), *Handbook of pain and palliative care* (pp. 417–430). New York, NY: Springer.

Foer, J. (2011). *Moonwalking with Einstein: The art and science of remembering everything*. New York, NY: Penguin Press.

Foley, D., Ancoli-Israel, S., Britz, P., & Walsh, J. (2004). Sleep disturbances and chronic disease in older adults: Results of the 2003 National Sleep Foundation Sleep in America Survey. *Journal of Psychosomatic Research, 56*(5), 497–502.

Foley, R. (1995). The adaptive legacy of human evolution: A search for the environment of evolutionary adaptedness. *Evolutionary Anthropology: Issues, News, and Reviews, 4*(6), 194–203.

Folkman, S. (1997). Positive psychological states and coping with severe stress. *Social Science & Medicine, 45*(8), 1207–1221.

Folkman, S. (2011). Stress, health, and coping: An overview. In S. Folkman, *Oxford handbook of stress, health, and coping* (pp. 3–11). Oxford, UK: Oxford University Press.

Folkman, S., Chesney, M. A., & Christopher-Richards, A. (1994). Stress and coping in caregiving partners of men with AIDS. *Psychiatric Clinics of North America. 17*(1), 35–53.

Folkman, S., Lazarus, R. S., Dunkel-Schetter, C., DeLongis, A., & Gruen, R. J. (1986). Dynamics of a stressful encounter: Cognitive appraisal, coping, and encounter outcomes. *Journal of Personality and Social Psychology, 50*(5), 992–1003.

Folkman, S., & Moskowitz, J. T. (2000). Positive affect and the other side of coping. *American Psychologist, 55*(6), 647–654.

Fong, J. (2012, December 7). Eye-opener: Why do pupils dilate in response to emotional states? *Scientific American*. Retrieved on May 24, 2015 from http://www.scientificamerican.com/article/eye-opener-why-do-pupils-dilate.

Forcier, K., Stroud, L. R., Papandonatos, G. D., Hitsman, B., Reiches, M., Krishnamoorthy, J., & Niaura, R. (2006). Links between physical fitness and cardiovascular reactivity and recovery to psychological stressors: A meta-analysis. *Health Psychology, 25*(6), 723–739.

Ford, E. (2007). *What you must think of me: A firsthand account of one teenager's experience with social anxiety disorder*. New York, NY: Oxford University Press.

Forman, E. M., Juarascio, A. S., Martin, L. M., & Herbert, J. D. (2015). Acceptance and commitment therapy (ACT). In R. L. Cautin & S. O. Lilienfeld (Eds.), *The encyclopedia of clinical psychology* (pp. 10–17). West Sussex, UK: Wiley-Blackwell.

Forsyth, J. P., Fuse, T., & Acheson, D. T. (2009). Interoceptive exposure for panic disorder. In W. O'Donohue & J. E. Fisher (Eds.), *General principles and empirically supported techniques of cognitive behavior therapy* (pp. 394–406). Hoboken, NJ: Wiley.

Fortner, B. V., and Neimeyer, R. A. (1999). Death anxiety in older adults: A quantitative review. *Death Studies, 23*(5), 387–411.

Foshee, V. A., Benefield, T. S., Reyes, H. L. M., Ennett, S. T., Faris, R., Chang, L. Y., . . . & Suchindran, C. M. (2013). The peer context and the development of the perpetration of adolescent dating violence. *Journal of Youth and Adolescence, 42*(4), 471–486.

Foster, G. D., Wadden, T. A., Makris, A. P., Davidson, D., Sanderson, R. S., Allison, D. B., & Kessler, A. (2003). Primary care physicians' attitudes about obesity and its treatment. *Obesity Research, 11*(10), 1168–1177.

Foster, J. K. (2009). *Memory: A very short introduction*. Oxford, UK: Oxford University Press.

Fouad, N. A., & Arredondo, P. (2007). *Becoming culturally oriented: Practical advice for psychologists and educators*. Washington, DC: American Psychological Association.

Fowler, C. A., & Magnuson, J. S. (2012). Speech perception. In M. J. Spivey, K. McRae, & M. F. Joanisse (Eds.), *The Cambridge handbook of psycholinguistics* (pp. 3–25). New York, NY: Cambridge University Press.

Fox, N. A., Henderson, H. A., Pérez-Edgar, K., & White, L. K. (2008). The biology of temperament: An integrative approach. In C. A. Nelson & M. Luciana (Eds.), *Handbook of developmental cognitive neuroscience* (2nd ed., pp. 839–853). Cambridge, MA: MIT Press.

Fox, N. A., & Pine, D. S. (2012). Temperament and the emergence of anxiety disorders. *Journal of the American Academy of Child and Adolescent Psychiatry, 51*(2), 125–128.

Fox, R., Lehmkuhle, S. W., & Bush, R. C. (1977). Stereopsis in the falcon. *Science, 197*(4298), 79–81.

Frances, A. (2012, December 2). DSM-5 is guide not bible—ignore its ten worst changes. Retrieved from http://www.psychologytoday.com/blog/dsm5-in-distress/201212/dsm-5-is-guide-not-bible-ignore-its-ten-worst-changes.

Frances, A. (2013). *Saving normal: An insider's revolt against out-of-control psychiatric diagnosis, DSM-5, Big Pharma, and the medicalization of ordinary life*. New York, NY: HarperCollins.

Frances, A., & Batstra, L. (2013). Why so many epidemics of childhood mental disorder? *Journal of Developmental & Behavioral Pediatrics, 34*(4), 291–292.

Francis, L. A., Ventura, A. K., Marini, M., & Birch, L. L. (2007). Parent overweight predicts daughters' increase in BMI and disinhibited overeating from 5 to 13 years. *Obesity, 15*, 1544–1553.

Frank, E., & Levenson, J. C. (2011). *Interpersonal psychotherapy*. Washington, DC: American Psychological Association.

Frank, J. D. (1961). *Persuasion and healing*. Baltimore. MD: Johns Hopkins University Press.

Frank, M. G. (2006a). The function of sleep. In T. L. Lee-Chiong (Ed.), *Sleep: A comprehensive handbook* (pp. 45–48). Hoboken, NJ: Wiley-Liss.

Frank, M. G. (2006b). The mystery of sleep function: Current perspectives and future directions. *Reviews in the Neurosciences, 17*(4), 375–392.

Frank, M. G. (2010). The function(s) of sleep. In J. W. Winkelman & D. T. Plante (Eds.), *Foundations of psychiatric sleep medicine* (pp. 59–78). New York, NY: Cambridge University Press.

Frankenberger, K. D. (2000). Adolescent egocentrism: A comparison among adolescents and adults. *Journal of Adolescence, 23*(3), 343–354.

Franklin, A., & Ritz, D. (1999). *Aretha: From these roots*. New York: Villard.

Fraser, S. (1995). (Ed.) *The bell curve wars: Race, intelligence, and the future of America*. New York, NY: Basic Books.

Fredricks, J. A., & Eccles, J. S. (2006). Is extracurricular participation associated with beneficial outcomes? Concurrent and longitudinal relations. *Developmental Psychology, 42*(4), 698.

Fredrickson, B. L. (2001). The role of positive emotions in positive psychology: The broaden-and-build theory of positive emotions. *American Psychologist, 56*(3), 218–226.

Fredrickson, B. L., & Branigan, C. (2005). Positive emotions broaden the scope of attention and thought-action repertoires. *Cognition & Emotion, 19*(3), 313–332.

Fredrickson, B. L., & Cohn, M. A. (2008). Positive emotions. In M. Lewis, J. M. Haviland-Jones, & L. F. Barrett (Eds.), *Handbook of emotions* (3rd ed., pp. 777–796). New York, NY: Guilford Press.

Fredrickson, B. L., & Roberts, T. A. (1997). Objectification theory. *Psychology of Women Quarterly, 21*(2), 173–206.

Fredrickson, B. L., Roberts, T. A., Noll, S. M., Quinn, D. M., & Twenge, J. M. (1998). That swimsuit becomes you: Sex differences in self-objectification, restrained eating, and math performance. *Journal of Personality and Social Psychology, 75*(1), 269–284.

Freeman, J. B., Rule, N. O., Adams, R. B. Jr., & Ambady, N. (2009a). Culture shapes a mesolimbic response to signals of dominance and subordination that associates with behavior. *Neuroimage, 47*(1), 353–359.

Freeman, J. B., Rule, N. O., & Ambady, N. (2009b). The cultural neuroscience of person perception. *Progress in Brain Research, 178*, 191–201.

Freeman, K. A. (2002). Modeling. In M. Hersen & W. Sledge (Eds.), *Encyclopedia of psychotherapy* (Vol. 2, pp. 147–154). San Diego, CA: Academic Press.

Freeman, K. A., & Eagle, R. F. (2011). Single-subject research designs. In J. C. Thomas & M. Hersen (Eds.), *Understanding research in clinical and counseling psychology* (2nd ed., pp. 129–154). New York, NY: Taylor & Francis.

French, D., Pidada, S., & Victor, A. (2005). Friendships of Indonesian and United States youth. *International Journal of Behavioral Development, 29*(4), 304–313.

French, S. E., & Chávez, N. R. (2010). The relationship of ethnicity-related stressors and Latino ethnic identity to well-being. *Hispanic Journal of Behavioral Sciences, 32*(3), 410–428.

French, S. E., Tran, N., & Chávez, N. R. (2013). Exploring the effect of in-group and out-group race-related stressors on anxiety among Asian Pacific Islander American students. *Journal of Applied Social Psychology, 43*(S2), E339–E350.

Freud, A. (1936). *The ego and the mechanisms of defense*. New York, NY: International Universities Press.

Freud, S. (1900). *The interpretation of dreams*. London, UK: Hogarth Press.

Freud, S. (1905). *Three essays on the theory of sexuality*. London, UK: Hogarth Press.

Freud, S. (1914/1989). On narcissism: An introduction. In P. Gay (Ed.), *The Freud Reader* (pp. 545–561). New York, NY: W. W. Norton.

Freud, S. (1922). *A general introduction to psychoanalysis*. New York, NY: Boni and Liveright.

Freud, S. (1923/1990). *The ego and the id* (Standard Edition) (pp. 1–66). New York, NY: W. W. Norton.

Freud, S. (1932/1990). *New introductory lectures on psycho-analysis* (Standard Edition) (pp. 1–182). New York, NY: W. W. Norton.

Freund, A. M., & Ebner, N. C. (2005). The aging self: Shifting from promoting gains to balancing losses. In W. Greve, K. Rothermund, & D. Wentura (Eds.), *The adaptive self: Personal continuity and intentional self-development* (pp. 185–202). Ashland, OH: Hogrefe & Huber.

Freund, A. M., Hennecke, M., & Mustafić, M. (2012). On gains and losses, means, and ends: Goal orientation and goal focus across adulthood. In R. M. Ryan (Ed.), *The Oxford handbook of human motivation* (pp. 280–302). New York, NY: Oxford University Press.

Freund, A. M., Hennecke, M., & Riediger, M. (2010). Age-related differences in outcome and process goal focus. *European Journal of Developmental Psychology, 7*(2), 198–222.

Fridlund, A. J., Beck, H. P., Goldie, W. D., & Irons, G. (2012). Little Albert: A neurologically impaired child. *History of Psychology*. doi:10.1037/a0026720.

Fried, A. L. (2012). Ethics in psychological research: Guidelines and regulations. In H. Cooper (Ed.), *APA handbook of research methods in psychology* (Vol. 1, pp. 55–74). Washington, DC: American Psychological Association.

Fried, C. B., & Aronson, E. (1995). Hypocrisy, misattribution, and dissonance reduction. *Personality and Social Psychology Bulletin, 21*(9), 925–933.

Friedlander, J. W., & Sarbin, T. R. (1938). The depth of hypnosis. *The Journal of Abnormal and Social Psychology, 33*(4), 453–475.

Friedman, E. M., Love, G. D., Rosenkranz, M. A., Urry, H. L., Davidson, R. J., Singer, B. H., & Ryff, C. D. (2007). Socioeconomic status predicts objective and subjective sleep quality in aging women. *Psychosomatic Medicine, 69*(7), 682–691.

Friedman, H. S. (2011). Personality, disease, and self-healing. In H. S. Friedman (Ed.), *The Oxford handbook of health psychology* (pp. 215–240). Oxford, UK: Oxford University Press.

Friedman, H. S., & Adler, N. E. (2011). The intellectual roots of health psychology. In H. S. Friedman (Ed.), *The Oxford handbook of health psychology* (pp. 3–14). Oxford, UK: Oxford University Press.

Friedman, H. S., & Booth-Kewley, S. (1987). The "disease-prone personality": A meta-analytic view of the construct. *American Psychologist, 42*(6), 539–555.

Friedman, H., & Martin, L. R. (2011). *The Longevity Project: Surprising discoveries for health and long life from the landmark eight-decade study*. New York, NY: Hudson Street Press.

Friedman, H. S., Tucker, J. S., Tomlinson-Keasey, C., Schwartz, J. E., Wingard, D. L., & Criqui, M. H. (2003). Does childhood personality predict longevity? *Journal of Personality and Social Psychology, 65*(1), 176–185.

Friedman, M. J. (2009). PTSD and other posttraumatic syndromes. In D. McKay, J. S. Abramowitz, S. Taylor, & G. J. G. Asmundson (Eds.), *Current perspectives on the anxiety disorders: Implications for DSM-V and beyond* (pp. 377–410). New York, NY: Springer.

Friedman, M. J., Resick, P. A., & Keane, T. M. (2007). PTSD: Twenty-five years of progress and challenges. In M. J. Friedman, T. M. Keane, & P. A. Resick (Eds.), *Handbook of PTSD: Science and practice* (pp. 3–18). New York, NY: Guilford Press.

Friedman, M., and Rosenman, R. H. (1959). Association of specific overt behavior pattern with blood and cardiovascular findings: Blood cholesterol level, blood clotting time, incidence of arcus senilis, and clinical coronary artery disease. *JAMA,169*, 1286–1296.

Frijda, N. H. (2008). The psychologists' point of view. In M. Lewis, J. M. Haviland-Jones, & L. F. Barrett (Eds.), *Handbook of emotions* (3rd ed., pp. 68–87). New York, NY: Guilford Press.

Frishman, L. J. (2001). Basic visual processes. In E. B. Goldstein (Ed.), *Blackwell handbook of perception* (pp. 53–91). Oxford, UK: Blackwell.

FritoLay (2016). Tostitos Original Restaurant Style Tortilla Chips. See the Nutrition Info. Retrieved from http://www.fritolay.com/snacks/product-page/tostitos.

Froh, J. J., Kashdan, T. B., Ozimkowski, K. M., & Miller, N. (2009). Who benefits the most from a gratitude intervention in children and adolescents? Examining positive affect as a moderator. *The Journal of Positive Psychology, 4*(5), 408–422.

Froh, J. J., Sefick, W. J., & Emmons, R. A. (2008). Counting blessings in early adolescents: An experimental study of gratitude and subjective well-being. *Journal of School Psychology, 46*(2), 213–233.

Fromm-Reichmann, F. (1948). Notes on the development of treatment of schizophrenics by psychoanalytic psychotherapy. *Psychiatry, 11*, 263–274.

Frorer, P., Hazzan, O., and Manes, M. (1997). Revealing the faces of abstraction. *International Journal of Computers for Mathematical Learning, 2*(3), 217–228. New York, NY: Kluwer Academic Publishers.

Froy, O. (2010). Metabolism and circadian rhythms—implications for obesity. *Endocrine Reviews, 31*(1), 1–24.

Frydenberg, E., & Lewis, R. (1993). Boys play sport and girls turn to others: Age, gender and ethnicity as determinants of coping. *Journal of Adolescence, 16*(3), 253–266.

Fryer, S. L., Crocker, N. A., & Mattson, S. N. (2008). Exposure to teratogenic agents as a risk factor for psychopathology. In T. P. Beauchaine & S. P. Hinshaw (Eds.), *Child and adolescent psychopathology* (pp. 180–207). Hoboken, NJ: Wiley.

Fryer, S. L., McGee, C. L., Matt, G. E., Riley, E. P., & Mattson, S. N. (2007). Evaluation of psychopathological conditions in children with heavy prenatal alcohol exposure. *Pediatrics, 119*(3), e733–e741.

Fuchs, A. H. (2002). Contributions of American mental philosophers to psychology in the United States. In W. E. Pickren & D. A. Dewsbury (Eds.), *Evolving perspectives on the history of psychology* (pp. 79–100). Washington, DC: American Psychological Association.

Fuertes, J. N., Stracuzzi, T. I., Bennett, J., Scheinholtz, J., Mislowack, A., Hersh, M., & Cheng, D. (2006). Therapist multicultural competency: A study of therapy dyads. *Psychotherapy: Theory, Research, Practice, Training, 43*(4), 480–490.

Fukuyama, M., Puig, A., Baggs, As., &Wolf, C. P. (2014). Religion and spirituality. In F. T. L. Leong (Ed.), *APA handbook of multicultural psychology* (Vol. 1, pp. 519–534). Washington, DC: American Psychological Association.

Fuligni, A. J., & Hardway, C. (2006). Daily variation in adolescents' sleep, activities, and psychological well-being. *Journal of Research on Adolescence, 16*(3), 353–378.

Funder, D. C. (2008). Persons, situations, and person-situation interactions. In O. P. John, R. W. Robins, & L. A. Pervin (Eds.) *Handbook of personality: Theory and research* (3rd ed., pp. 568–580). New York, NY: Guilford Press.

Funder, D. C., & Fast, L. A. (2010). Personality in social psychology. In S. T. Fiske, D. T. Gilbert, & G. Lindzey (Eds.), *Handbook of social psychology* (5th ed., Vol. 1, pp. 668–697). Hoboken, NJ: Wiley.

Fung, J. (2011). Cultural psychological perspectives on social development in childhood. In P. K. Smith & C. H. Hart (Eds.), *The Wiley-Blackwell handbook of childhood social development* (2nd ed., pp. 100–118). Malden, MA: Wiley-Blackwell.

Furmark, T., Tillfors, M., Marteinsdottir, I., Fischer, H., Pissiota, A., Långström, B., & Fredrikson, M. (2002). Common changes in cerebral blood flow in patients with social phobia treated with citalopram or cognitive-behavioral therapy. *Archives of General Psychiatry, 59*(5), 425–433.

Furumoto, L., & Scarborough, E. (2002). Placing women in the history of psychology: The first American women psychologists. In W. E. Pickren & D. A. Dewsbury (Eds.), *Evolving perspectives on the history of psychology* (pp. 527–543). Washington, DC: American Psychological Association.

Gabbard, G. O. (2001). Psychotherapy in Hollywood cinema. *Australasian Psychiatry, 9*(4), 365–369.

Gabbard, G. O. (2005). Major modalities: Psychoanalytic/psychodynamic. In G. O. Gabbard, J. S. Beck, & J. Holmes (Eds.), *Oxford textbook of psychotherapy* (pp. 3–14). New York, NY: Oxford University Press.

Gabbard, G. O. (2009a). Foreword. In R. A. Levy & J. S. Ablon (Eds.), *Handbook of evidence-based psychodynamic psychotherapy: Bridging the gap between science and practice* (pp. vii–ix). New York, NY: Humana.

Gabbard, G. O. (2009b). Techniques of psychodynamic psychotherapy. In G. O. Gabbard (Ed.), *Textbook of psychotherapeutic treatments* (pp. 43–67). Washington, DC: American Psychiatric Publishing.

Gabig, C. S. (2014). Language development in middle and late childhood and adolescence. In S. Levey, *Introduction to language development* (pp. 211–246). San Diego, CA: Plural Publishing.

Gable, S. L., & Haidt, J. (2005). What (and why) is positive psychology? *Review of General Psychology, 9*(2), 103–110.

Gabrieli, J. D., Poldrack, R. A., & Desmond, J. E. (1998). The role of left prefrontal cortex in language and memory. *Proceedings of the National Academy of Sciences, 95*(3), 906–913.

Gaddy, C. D., Charlot-Swilley, D., Nelson, P. D., & Reich, J. N. (1995). Selected outcomes of accredited programs. *Professional Psychology: Research and Practice, 26*, 507–513.

Gaertner, S. L., Dovidio, J. F., & Bachman, B. A. (1996). Revisiting the contact hypothesis: The induction of a common ingroup identity. *International Journal of Intercultural Relations, 20*(3), 271–290.

Gaertner. S. L., & Dovidio, J. F. (2012). The common ingroup identity model. In P. A. M. Van Lange, A. W. Kruglanski, & E. T. Higgins (Eds.), *Handbook of theories of social psychology* (Vol. 2, pp. 439–457). Thousand Oaks, CA: SAGE.

Gage, F. H. (2000). Mammalian neural stem cells. *Science, 287*(5457), 1433–1438.

Gais, S., Lucas, B., & Born, J. (2006). Sleep after learning aids memory recall. *Learning and Memory, 13*(3), 259–262.

Galambos, N. L. Berenbaum, S. A., & McHale, S. M. (2009). Gender development in adolescence. In R. M. Lerner & L. M. Steinberg (Eds.), *Handbook of adolescent psychology* (3rd ed., Vol. 1, pp. 305–357). Hoboken, NJ: Wiley.

Galambos, N. L., Dalton, A. L., & Maggs, J. L. (2009). Losing sleep over it: Daily variation in sleep quantity and quality in Canadian students' first semester of university. *Journal of Research on Adolescence, 19*(4), 741–761.

Galatzer-Levy, R. M., Bachrach, H., Skolnikoff, A., & Waldron, S. (2000). *Does psychoanalysis work?* New Haven, CT: Yale University Press.

Gallagher, S., Phillips, A. C., Drayson, M. T., & Carroll, D. (2009). Parental caregivers of children with developmental disabilities mount a poor antibody response to pneumococcal vaccination. *Brain, Behavior, and Immunity, 23*(3), 338–346.

Gallant, S. J., & Hamilton, J. A. (1988). On a premenstrual psychiatric diagnosis: What's in a name? *Professional Psychology: Research and Practice, 19*(3), 271–278.

Gallo, K. P., Comer, J. S., & Barlow, D. H. (2013). Single-case experimental designs and small pilot trial designs. In J. S. Comer & P. C. Kendall (Eds.), *The Oxford handbook of research strategies for clinical psychology* (pp. 24–39). Oxford, UK: Oxford University Press.

Gamble, A. L., Harvey, A. G., & Rapee, R. M. (2010). Specific phobia. In D. J. Stein, E. Hollander, & B. O. Rothbaum (Eds.), *Textbook of anxiety disorders* (2nd ed., pp. 525–543). Washington, DC: American Psychiatric Association.

Gandour, J. (2005). Neurophonetics of tone. In K. Brown (Ed.), *Encyclopedia of language and linguistics* (2nd ed.). Oxford, UK: Elsevier.

Gangestad, S. W., & Scheyd, G. J. (2005). The evolution of human physical attractiveness. *Annual Review of Anthropology, 34*, 523–548.

Ganster, D. C., Schaubroeck, J., Sime, W. E., & Mayes, B. T. (1991). The nomological validity of the Type A personality among employed adults. *Journal of Applied Psychology, 76*(1), 143–168.

Gantz, W., Schwartz, N., Angelini, J. R., & Rideout, V. (2007). *Food for thought: Television food advertising to children in the United States*. Menlo Park, CA: Henry J. Kaiser Family Foundation.

Garcia, F., & Gracia, E. (2009). Is always authoritative the optimum parenting style? Evidence from Spanish families. *Adolescence, 44*(173), 101–131.

Garcia, J., & Gustavson, A. R. (1997). Carl R. Gustavson (1946–1996): Pioneering wildlife psychologist. *APS Observer, 10*(1), 34–35.

Garcia, J., & Koelling, R. A. (1966). Relation of cue to consequence in avoidance learning. *Psychonomic Science, 4*, 123–124.

Garcia, J., Brett. L. P., & Rusiniak, K. W. (1989). Limits of Darwinian conditioning. In S. B. Klein & R. R. Mowrer (Eds.), *Contemporary learning theories: Instrumental conditioning theory and the impact of biological constraints on learning* (pp. 237–275). Hillsdale, NJ: Lawrence Erlbaum.

Garcia, J., Ervin, F. R., & Koelling, R. A. (1966). Learning with prolonged delay of reinforcement. *Psychonomic Science, 5*, 121–122.

Gardiner, J. M. (2007). Retrieval: On its essence and related concepts. In H. L. Roediger, Y. Dudai, & S. M. Fitzpatrick (Eds.), *Science of memory: Concepts* (pp. 221–224). Oxford, UK: Oxford University Press.

Gardiner, J. M., & Atema, J. (2010). The function of bilateral odor arrival time differences in olfactory orientation of sharks. *Current Biology, 20*(13), 1187–1191.

Gardiner, J. M., Gawlik, B., & Richardson-Klavehn, A. (1994). Maintenance rehearsal affects knowing, not remembering; elaborative rehearsal affects remembering, not knowing. *Psychonomic Bulletin & Review, 1*(1), 107–110.

Gardner, E. P., & Johnson, K. O. (2013). The somatosensory system: Receptors and central pathways. In E. R. Kandel, J. H. Schwartz, T. M. Jessell, S. A. Siegelbaum, & A. J. Hudspeth (Eds.), *Principles of neural science* (5th ed., pp. 475–497). New York, NY: McGraw-Hill.

Gardner, H. (1985). *Frames of mind: The theory of multiple intelligences*. New York, NY: Basic Books.

Gardner, H. (1995). Cracking open the IQ box. In S. Fraser (Ed.), *The bell curve wars: Race, intelligence, and the future of America* (pp. 23–35). New York, NY: Basic Books.

Gardner, H. (1999). *The disciplined mind: What all students should understand*. New York, NY: Simon & Schuster.

Gardner, H. (2006). *Multiple intelligences: New horizons in theory and* practice. New York, NY: Basic Books.

Garland, A. F., Lau, A. S., Yeh, M., McCabe, K. M., Hough, R. L., & Landsverk, J. A. (2014). Racial and ethnic differences in utilization of mental health services among high-risk youths. *American Journal of Psychiatry, 162*(7), 1336–1343.

Garland, D. J., & Barry, J. R. (1990). Sport expertise: The cognitive advantage. *Perceptual and Motor Skills, 70*(3 Pt 2), 1299–1314.

Garland, D. J., & Barry, J. R. (1991). Cognitive advantage in sport: The nature of perceptual structures. *The American Journal of Psychology, 104*(2), 211–228.

Garn, S. N., & Newton, R. A. (1988). Kinesthetic awareness in subjects with multiple ankle sprains. *Physical Therapy, 68*(11), 1667–1671.

Garnham, A. (2005). Language comprehension. In K. Lamberts & R. L. Goldstone (Eds.), *Handbook of cognition* (pp. 241–254). London, UK: SAGE.

Garrett, B. (2009). *Brain & behavior: An introduction to biological psychology* (2nd ed.). Los Angeles, CA: SAGE.

Garrido, M., & Velasquez, R. (2006). Interpretation of Latino/Latina MMPI-2 profiles: Review and application of empirical findings and cultural-linguistic considerations. In J. N. Butcher (Ed.), *MMPI-2: A practitioner's guide* (pp. 477–504). Washington, DC: American Psychological Association.

Garske, J. P., & Anderson, T. (2003). Toward a science of psychotherapy research: Present status and evaluation. In S. O. Lilienfeld, S. J. Lynn, & J. M. Lohr (Eds.), *Science and pseudoscience in clinical psychology* (pp. 145–175). New York: NY: Guilford Press.

Gates, G. J. (2013). Demographic perspectives on sexual orientation. In C. J. Patterson & A. R. D'Augelli (Eds.), *Handbook of psychology and sexual orientation* (pp. 69–86). New York, NY: Oxford University Press.

Gates, G. J., & Newport, F. (2013). Gallup Special Report: New estimates of the LGBT population in the United States. Retrieved from http://williamsinstitute.law.ucla.edu/research/census-lgbt-demographics-studies/gallup-lgbt-pop-feb-2013/

Gathercole, S. E. (2007). Working memory: What it is, and what it is not. In H. L. Roediger, Y. Dudai, & S. M. Fitzpatrick (Eds.), *Science of memory: Concepts* (pp. 155–158). Oxford, UK: Oxford University Press.

Gathercole, S. E., & Alloway, T. (2008). Working memory and classroom learning. In S. K. Thurman & C. A. Fiorello (Eds.), *Applied cognitive research in K-3 classrooms* (pp. 17–40). New York, NY: Routledge.

Gathercole, S. E., Pickering, S. J., Knight, C., & Stegmann, Z. (2004). Working memory skills and educational attainment: Evidence from national curriculum assessments at 7 and 14 years of age. *Applied Cognitive Psychology, 18*(1), 1–16.

Gau, S. F., & Suen Soong, W. T. (1999). Psychiatric comorbidity of adolescents with sleep terrors or sleepwalking: A case-control study. *Australian and New Zealand Journal of Psychiatry, 33*(5), 734–739.

Gauci, M., Husband, A. J., Saxarra, H., and King, M. G. Pavolovian conditioning of nasal tryptase release in human subjects with allergic rhinitis. *Physiology & Behavior, 55*(5), 823–825.

Gaudio, R. P. (1994). Sounding gay: Pitch properties in the speech of gay and straight men. *American Speech, 69*(1), 30–57.

Gauthier, I. (2010). Face perception: Physiological. In E. B. Goldstein (Ed.), *Encyclopedia of perception* (pp. 449–452). Thousand Oaks, CA: SAGE.

Gay, P. (Ed.). (1995). *The Freud reader.* New York, NY: W. W. Norton.

Gay, P., Weaver, T., Loube, D., & Iber, C. (2006). Evaluation of positive airway pressure treatment for sleep-related breathing disorders in adults. *Sleep, 29*(3), 381–401.

Gazelle, H., & Ladd, G. W. (2003). Anxious solitude and peer exclusion: A diathesis–stress model of internalizing trajectories in childhood. *Child Development, 74*(1), 257–278.

Gazzaniga, M. S. (1995). Principles of human brain organization derived from split-brain studies. *Neuron, 14*(2), 217–228

Gazzaniga, M. S. (1998). The split brain revisited. *Scientific American, 279*(1), 50–55.

Gazzaniga, M. S. (2005). Forty-five years of split-brain research and still going strong. *Nature Reviews Neuroscience, 6*(8), 653–659

Gazzaniga, M. S., Bogen, J. E., & Sperry, R. W. (1962). Some functional effects of sectioning the cerebral commissures in man. *Proceedings of the National Academy of Sciences of the United States of America, 48*(10), 1765–1769.

Geen, R. G., & McCown, E. J. (1984). Effects of noise and attack on aggression and physiological arousal. *Motivation and Emotion, 8*(3), 231–241.

Gegenfurtner, K. (2010). Color perception: Physiological. In E. B. Goldstein, *Encyclopedia of perception* (pp. 270–275). Thousand Oaks, CA: SAGE.

Gegenfurtner, K. R., & Kiper, D. C. (2003). Color vision. *Annual Review of Neuroscience, 26*(1), 181–206.

Gehrman, P., Findley, J., & Perlis, M. (2012). Insomnia I: Etiology and conceptualization. In C. M. Morin & C. A. Espie (Eds.), *The Oxford handbook of sleep and sleep disorders* (pp. 405–427). Oxford, UK: Oxford University Press.

Gelernter, J., & Stein, M. B. (2009). Heritability and genetics of anxiety disorders. In M. M. Antony & M. B. Stein (Eds.), *Oxford handbook of anxiety and related disorders* (pp. 87–96). New York, NY: Oxford University Press.

Gelman, S. A., & Kalish, C. W. (2006). Conceptual development. In D. Kuhn & R. Siegler (Vol. Eds.), *Handbook of child psychology* (6th ed., Vol. 2, pp. 687–733). Hoboken, NJ: Wiley.

Gelso, C. J. (2006). Applying theories to research: The interplay of theory and research in science. In F. T. L. Leong & J. T. Austin (Eds.), *The psychology research handbook: A guide for graduate students and research assistants* (2nd ed., pp. 455–464). Thousand Oaks: SAGE Publications.

Gelso, C. J. (2010). The diversity status of the psychotherapist: Editorial introduction. *Psychotherapy: Theory, Research, Practice, Training, 47*(2), 143.

Gentner, D., & Kurtz, K. J. (2005). Relational categories. In W. K. Ahn, R. L. Goldstone, B. C. Love, A. B. Markman, & P. Wolff (Eds.), *Categorization inside and outside the laboratory: Essays in honor of Douglas L. Medin* (pp. 151–175). Washington, DC: American Psychological Association.

George, J. M. (2000). Emotions and leadership: The role of emotional intelligence. *Human Relations, 53*(8), 1027–1055.

George, L. (2007). Foreword: The haunted animal. In R. Noll (Ed.), *The encyclopedia of schizophrenia and other psychotic disorders* (3rd ed., iv–vi). New York, NY: Facts on File.

George, M. S., Hahas, Z., Bohning, D. E., Kozel, A., Anderson, B., . . . Li, X. (2006). Vagus nerve stimulation and deep brain stimulation. In D. J. Stein, D. J. Kupfer, & A. F. Schatzberg (Eds.), *The American Psychiatric Publishing textbook of mood disorders* (pp. 337–349). Washington, DC: American Psychiatric Publishing.

Gerardi, M., Rothbaum, B. O., Ressler, K., Heekin, M. and Rizzo, A. (2008). Virtual reality exposure therapy using a virtual Iraq: Case report. *Journal of Traumatic Stress, 21*(2), 209–213.

Gerber, A. J., & Gonzalez, M. Z. (2013). Structural and functional brain imaging in clinical psychology. In J. S. Comer & P. C. Kendall (Eds.), *The Oxford handbook of research strategies for clinical psychology* (pp. 165–187). Oxford, UK: Oxford University Press.

Gerdes, A. B. M., Uhl, G., & Alpers, G. W. (2009). Spiders are special: Fear and disgust evoked by pictures of arthropods. *Evolution and Human Behavior, 30*, 66–73.

Gerend, M. A., & Maner, J. K. (2011). Fear, anger, fruits, and veggies: Interactive effects of emotion and message framing on health behavior. *Health Psychology, 30*(4), 420–423.

Gerhardt, H. C., & Bee, M. A. (2006). Recognition and localization of acoustic signals. In P. M. Narins, A. S. Feng, R. R. Fay, & A. N. Popper (Eds.), *Hearing and sound communication in amphibians* (pp. 113–146). New York, NY: Springer.

Gerken, L. (2007). Acquiring linguistic structure. In E. Hoff & M. Shatz (Eds.), *Blackwell handbook of language development* (pp. 173–190). Malden, MA: Blackwell.

Germain, A. (2012). Parasomnias I: Nightmares. In C. M. Morin & C. A. Espie (Eds.), *The Oxford handbook of sleep and sleep disorders* (pp. 555–576). Oxford, UK: Oxford University Press.

Germer, C. K. (2005). Mindfulness: What is it? What does it matter? In C. K. Germer, R. D. Siegel, & P. R. Fulton (Eds.), *Mindfulness and psychotherapy* (pp. 3–27). New York, NY: Guilford Press.

Geronimus, A. T., Hicken, M. T., Pearson, J. A., Seashols, S. J., Brown, K. L., & Cruz, T. D. (2010). Do U.S. black women experience stress-related accelerated biological aging? *Human Nature, 21*(1), 19–38.

Gershoff, E. T. (2010). More harm than good: A summary of scientific research on the intended and unintended effects of corporal punishment on children. *Law and Contemporary Problems, 73*, 31–56.

Gershoff, E. T. (2002). Corporal punishment by parents and associated child behaviors and experiences: A meta-analytic and theoretical review. *Psychological Bulletin, 128*(4), 539–579.

Gershoff, E. T. (2002). Physical punishment by parents and associated child behaviors and experiences: A meta-analytic and theoretical review. *Psychological Bulletin, 128*, 539–579.

Gershoff, E. T. (2008). *Report on physical punishment in the United States: What research tells us about its effects on children*. Columbus OH: Center for Effective Discipline.

Gershoff, E. T., & Bitensky, S. H. (2007). The case against corporal punishment of children: Converging evidence from social science research and international human rights law and implications for U.S. public policy. *Psychology, Public Policy, and Law, 13*(4), 231–272.

Gershowitz, A. M. (2012). Texting while driving meets the Fourth Amendment: Deterring both texting and warrantless cell phone searches. *Arizona Law Review, 54*, 577–829.

Gerstorf, D., Ram, N., Mayraz, G., Hidajat, M., Lindenberger, U., Wagner, G. G., & Schupp, J. (2010). Late-life decline in well-being across adulthood in Germany, the United Kingdom, and the United States: Something is seriously wrong at the end of life. *Psychology and Aging*, *25*(2), 477.

Gessen, M. (2015, March 10). At the Boston Marathon bombing trial, prosecutors evoke the scent of horror. *Washington Post*. Retrieved from http://www.washingtonpost.com/news/post-nation/wp/2015/03/10/at-the-boston-marathon-bombing-trial-prosecutors-evoke-the-scent-of-horror/

Gesser, G., Wong, P. T., & Reker, G. T. (1987). Death attitudes across the life-span: The development and validation of the Death Attitude Profile (DAP). *OMEGA—Journal of Death and Dying*, *18*(2), 113–128.

Gethin, R. (2015). Buddhist conceptualizations of mindfulness. In K. W. Brown, J. D. Creswell, and R. M. Ryan (Eds.), *Handbook of mindfulness: Theory, research, and practice* (pp. 9–41). New York, NY: Guilford Press.

Gharaibeh, N. M. (2005). The psychiatrist's image in commercially available American movies. *Acta Psychiatrica Scandinavica*, *111*(4), 316–319.

Ghezzi, P. M., Wilson, G. R., Tarbox, R. S. F., & MacAlesse, K. R. (2008). Guidelines for developing and managing a token economy. In W. T. O'Donohue & J. E. Fisher (Eds.), *Cognitive behavior therapy: Applying empirically supported techniques in your practice* (2nd ed., pp. 565–570). Hoboken, NJ: Wiley.

Ghiselin, M. T. (1974). *The economy of nature and the evolution of sex*. Berkeley, CA: University of California Press.

Giannotti, F., Cortesi, F., Sebastiani, T., & Vagnoni, C. (2008). Sleep practices and habits in children across different cultures. In A. Ivanenkno (Ed.), *Sleep and psychiatric disorders in children and adolescents* (pp. 37–48). New York, NY: Informa Healthcare USA.

Gibbons, M. B. C., Crits-Christoph, P., Barber, J. P., & Schamberger, M. (2007). Insight in psychotherapy: A review of empirical literature. In L. G. Castonguay & C. E. Hill (Eds.), *Insight in psychotherapy* (pp. 143–165). Washington, DC: American Psychological Association.

Gibbs, Jr. R. W., Wilson, N. L. & Bryant, G. A. (2012). Figurative language: Normal adult cognitive research. In M. Spivey, M. Joanisse, & K. McRae, *The Cambridge handbook of psycholinguistics* (pp. 465–484). New York, NY: Cambridge University Press.

Gibson K. R., & Tallerman, M. (2012). Introduction to part III: The prehistory of language: When and why did language evolve? In M. Tallerman & K. R. Gibson (Eds.), *The Oxford handbook of language evolution* (pp. 239–249). Oxford, UK: Oxford University Press.

Gibson, E. S., Powles, A. C., Thabane, L., O'Brien, S., Molnar, D. S., Trajanovic, N., Chilcott-Tanser, L. (2006). "Sleepiness" is serious in adolescence: Two surveys of 3235 Canadian students. *BMC Public Health*, *6*(116), 1–9.

Gibson, K. R. (2012). Tool-dependent foraging strategies and the origin of language. In M. Tallerman & K. R. Gibson (Eds.), *The Oxford handbook of language evolution* (pp. 340–342). Oxford, UK: Oxford University Press.

Gifford, E. V., & Shoenberger, D. (2009). Rapid smoking. In W. T. O'Donohue & J. E. Fisher (Eds.), *General principles and empirically supported techniques of cognitive behavior therapy* (pp. 513–519). Hoboken, NJ: Wiley.

Gil, K. M., Carson, J. W., Porter, L. S., Scipio, C., Bediako, S. M., & Orringer, E. (2004). Daily mood and stress predict pain, health care use, and work activity in African American adults with sickle-cell disease. *Health Psychology*, *23*(3), 267–274.

Gilbert, A. N. (2008). *What the nose knows: The science of scent in everyday life*. New York, NY: Crown Publishers.

Gilbert, D. (2006). *Stumbling on happiness*. New York, NY: Knopf.

Gilbert, D. T., & Malone, P. S. (1995). The correspondence bias. *Psychological Bulletin*, *117*(1), 21.

Gilbert, D. T., & Wilson, T. D. (2000). Miswanting. In J. P. Forgas (Ed.), *Feeling and thinking: The role of affect in social cognition* (pp. 178–197). New York, NY: Cambridge University Press.

Gilbert, D. T., & Wilson, T. D. (2007). Prospection: Experiencing the future. *Science*, *317*(5843), 1351–1354.

Gilbert, D. T., Pinel, E. C., Wilson, T. D., Blumberg, S. T., & Wheatley, T. P. (1998). Durability bias in affective forecasting. *Journal of Personality and Social Psychology*, *75*, 617–638.

Gillespie, G. (1997). Hypnopompic imagery and visual dream experience. *Dreaming*, *7*(3), 187–194.

Gillespie, W. H. (1971). Aggression and instinct theory. *The International Journal of Psychoanalysis*, *52*, 155–160.

Gilligan, C. (1982). *In a different voice: Psychological theory and women's development*. Cambridge, MA: Harvard University Press.

Gilligan, C. (1987). Moral orientation and moral development. In E. F. Kittay & D. T. Meyers (Eds.), *Women and moral theory* (pp. 19–33). Totowa, NJ: Rowman & Littlefield.

Gilligan, C. (1992). *Meeting at the crossroads: Women's psychology and girls' development*. Cambridge, MA: Harvard University Press.

Gilligan, C., & Wiggins, G. (1987). The origins of morality in early childhood relationships. In J. Kagan & S. Lamb, *The emergence of morality in young children* (pp. 277–305). Chicago, IL: University of Chicago Press.

Gillon, W. (2007). *Person-centered counseling psychology: An introduction*. Thousand Oaks, CA: SAGE.

Gilman, S. E., Rende, R., Boergers, J., Abrams, D. B., Buka, S. L., & Clark, M. A., et al. (2009). Parental smoking and adolescent initiation: An intergenerational perspective on tobacco control. *Pediatrics*, *123*, 274–281.

Gilovich, T., & Savitsky, K. (2002). Like goes with like: The role of representativeness in erroneous and pseudo-scientific beliefs. In T. Gilovich, D. W. Griffin, & D. Kahneman (Eds.), *Heuristics and biases: The psychology of intuitive judgment* (pp. 617–624). New York, NY: Cambridge University Press.

Gim, R. H., Atkinson, D. R., & Kim, S. J. (1991). Asian-American acculturation, counselor ethnicity and cultural sensitivity, and ratings of counselors. *Journal of Counseling Psychology*, *38*(1), 57–62.

Ginter, E., Glauser, A., & Richmond, B. O. (1994). Loneliness, social support, and anxiety among two South Pacific cultures. *Psychological Reports*, *74*(3), 875–879.

Girz, L., Polivy, J., Provencher, V., Wintre, M. G., Pratt, M. W., Pancer, S. M., . . . Adams, G. R. (2013). The four undergraduate years. Changes in weight, eating attitudes, and depression. *Appetite*, *69*, 145–150.

Gitlin, M. J. (2009). Pharmacotherapy and other somatic treatments for depression. In I. H. Gotlib & C. L. Hammen (Eds.), *Handbook of depression* (2nd ed., pp. 554–585). New York, NY: Guilford Press.

Glaser, R., Kiecolt-Glaser, J. K., Marucha, P. T., MacCallum, R. C., Laskowski, B. F., & Malarkey, W. B. (1999). Stress-related changes in proinflammatory cytokine production in wounds. *Archives of General Psychiatry*, *56*(5), 450–456.

Glasman, L. R., & Albarracín, D. (2006). Forming attitudes that predict future behavior: A meta-analysis of the attitude-behavior relation. *Psychological Bulletin*, *132*(5), 778–822.

Glass, C., & Minnotte, K. L. (2010). Recruiting and hiring women in STEM fields. *Journal of Diversity in Higher Education*, *3*(4), 218–229.

Gleaves, D. H., May, M. C., & Cardena E. (2001). An examination of the diagnostic validity of dissociative identity disorder. *Clinical Psychology Review*, *21*(4), 577–608.

Gleeson, S. (1991). Response acquisition. In I. H. Iverson & K. A. Lattal (Eds.), *Experimental analysis of behavior* (Pt. 1, pp. 63–86). Amsterdam, Netherlands: Elsevier.

Gleitman, L., & Papafragou, A. (2012). New perspectives on language and thought. In K. J. Holyoak and R. G. Morrison (Eds.), *The Oxford handbook of thinking and reasoning* (pp. 543–568). Oxford, UK: Oxford University Press.

Gleitman, L., & Papafragou, A. (2013). Relations between language and thought. In D. Reisberg (Ed.), *The Oxford handbook of cognitive psychology* (pp. 504–523). Oxford, UK: Oxford University Press.

Glisky, M. L., Tataryn, D. J., Tobias, B. A., Kihlstrom, J. F., & McConkey, K. M. (1991). Absorption, openness to experience, and hypnotizability. *Journal of Personality and Social Psychology*, *60*(2), 263–272.

Globus, A., Rosenzweig, M. R., Bennett, E. L., & Diamond, M. C. (1973). Effects of differential experience on dendritic spine counts in rat cerebral cortex. *Journal of Comparative and Physiological Psychology*, *82*(2), 175.

Glucksberg, S. (1989). Metaphors in conversation: How are they understood? Why are they used? *Metaphor and Symbol*, *4*(3), 125–143.

Glucksberg, S., & Weisberg, R. W. (1966). Verbal behavior and problem solving: Some effects of labeling in a functional fixedness problem. *Journal of Experimental Psychology*, *71*(5), 659–664.

Gobet, F., & Clarkson, G. (2004). Chunks in expert memory: Evidence for the magical number four. . . or is it two? *Memory*, *12*(6), 732–747.

Gobet, F., & Simon, H. A. (1998). Expert chess memory: Revisiting the chunking hypothesis. *Memory*, *6*(3), 225–255.

Gobet, F., Lane, P. C., Croker, S., Cheng, P. C., Jones, G., Oliver, I., & Pine, J. M. (2001). Chunking mechanisms in human learning. *Trends in Cognitive Sciences*, *5*(6), 236–243.

Godden, D. R., & Baddeley, A. D. (1975). Context-dependent memory in two natural environments: On land and underwater. *British Journal of Psychology*, *66*(3), 325–331.

Godijn, R., & Theeuwes, J. (2012). Overt is no better than covert when rehearsing visuo-spatial information in working memory. *Memory & Cognition*, *40*(1), 52–61.

Goebel, M. U., Meykadeh, N., Kou, W., Schedlowski, M., & Hengge, U. R. (2008). Behavioral conditioning of antihistamine effects in patients with allergic rhinitis. *Psychotherapy and Psychosomatics*, *77*(4), 227–234.

Goetz, T., Frenzel, A., Pekrun, R., & Hall, N. (2005). Emotional intelligence in the context of learning and achievement. In R. Schulze & R. D. Roberts (Eds.), *Emotional intelligence: An international handbook* (pp. 233–253). Cambridge, MA: Hogrefe & Huber.

Goetzel, R. Z., Kowlessar, N., Rormer, E. C., Pei, X., Tabrizi, M., Liss-Levinson, R. C., . . . Waddell, J. (2011). Workplace obesity prevention programs. In J. H. Cawley (Ed.), *The Oxford handbook of the social science of obesity* (pp. 683–712). New York, NY: Oxford University Press.

Gold, E. B., Bromberger, J., Crawford, S., Samuels, S., Greendale, G. A., Harlow, S. D., & Skurnick, J. (2001). Factors associated with age at natural menopause in a multiethnic sample of midlife women. *American Journal of Epidemiology*, *153*(9), 865–874.

Gold, J. R. (1996). *Key concepts in psychotherapy integration*. New York, NY: Plenum Press.

Goldapple, K., Segal, Z., Garson, C., Lau, M., Bieling, P., Kennedy, S., & Mayberg, H. (2004). Modulation of cortical-limbic pathways in major depression: Treatment-specific effects of cognitive behavior therapy. *Archives of General Psychiatry*, *61*(1), 34–41.

Goldberg, P. (2012). Process, resistance, and interpretation. In G. O. Gabbard, B. E. Litowitz, & P. Williams (Eds.), *Textbook of psychoanalysis* (2nd ed., pp. 283–302). Washington, DC: American Psychiatric Publishing.

Goldberg, S. B., & Hoyt, W. T. (2015). Group as social microcosm: Within-group interpersonal style is congruent with outside group relational tendencies. *Psychotherapy*, *52*(2), 195–204.

Goldberg, S. H. (2012). Transference. In G. O. Gabbard, B. E. Litowitz, & P. Williams (Eds.), *Textbook of psychoanalysis* (2nd ed., pp. 65–78). Washington, DC: American Psychiatric Publishing.

Goldberg, W. A., and Keller, M. A. (2007). Co-sleeping during infancy and early childhood: Key findings and future directions. *Infant and Child Development, 16*(4), 457–469. doi:10.1002/icd.522

Goldenberg, H., & Goldenberg, I. (2007). *Family therapy: An overview* (7th ed.). Pacific Grove, CA: Brooks/Cole.

Goldfried, M. R. (1995). *From cognitive-behavior therapy to psychotherapy integration: An evolving view*. New York, NY: Springer Publishing.

Goldin-Meadow, S. (2005). *The resilience of language: What gesture creation in deaf children can tell us about how all children learn language*. New York, NY: Psychology Press.

Goldscheider, F., & Goldscheider, C. (1999). *The changing transition to adulthood: Leaving and returning home*. Thousand Oaks, CA: SAGE.

Goldstein, E. B. (2001a). Cross-talk between psychophysics and physiology in the study of perception. In E. B. Goldstein (Ed.), *Blackwell handbook of perception* (pp. 1–23. Oxford, UK: Blackwell.

Goldstein, E. B. (2001b). Pictorial perception and art. In E. B. Goldstein (Ed.), *Blackwell handbook of perception* (pp. 344–378). Oxford, UK: Blackwell.

Goldstein, E. B. (2010a). Constancy. In E. B. Goldstein (Ed.), *Encyclopedia of perception* (pp. 309–313). Thousand Oaks, CA: SAGE.

Goldstein, E. B. (2010b). Vision. In E. B. Goldstein (Ed.), *Encyclopedia of perception* (pp. 1044–1048). Thousand Oaks, CA: SAGE.

Goldstein, G. (2008). Intellectual evaluation. In M. Hersen & A. M. Gross (Eds.), *Handbook of clinical psychology* (Vol. 1, pp. 395–421). Hoboken, NJ: Wiley.

Goldstein, J. (2011). Technology and play. In A. D. Pellegrini (Ed.), *The Oxford handbook of the development of play* (pp. 322–337). New York, NY: Oxford University Press.

Goldstein, M. H., King, A. P., & West, M. J. (2003). Social interaction shapes babbling: Testing parallels between birdsong and speech. *Proceedings of the National Academy of Sciences, 100*(13), 8030–8035.

Goldstein, M. H., & Schwade, J. A. (2008). Social feedback to infants' babbling facilitates rapid phonological learning. *Psychological Science, 19*(5), 515–523.

Goldstein, M. H., & West, M. J. (1999). Consistent responses of human mothers to prelinguistic infants: The effect of prelinguistic repertoire size. *Journal of Comparative Psychology, 113*(1), 52–58.

Goldwater, M. B., Markman, A. B., & Stilwell, C. H. (2011). The empirical case for role-governed categories. *Cognition, 118*(3), 359–376

Goleman, D. (1998). *Working with emotional intelligence*. New York, NY: Random House.

Goleman, D. (2006). *Emotional intelligence: Why it can matter more than IQ*. New York, NY: Random House LLC.

Golinkoff, R. M., Shuff-Bailey, M., Olguin, R., & Ruan, W. (1995). Young children extend novel words at the basic level: Evidence for the principle of categorical scope. *Developmental Psychology, 31*(3), 494–507.

Gollenberg, A. L., Liu, F., Brazil, C., Drobnis, E. Z., Guzick, D., Overstreet, J. W., . . . Swan, S. H. (2010). Semen quality in fertile men in relation to psychosocial stress. *Fertility and Sterility, 93*(4), 1104–1111.

Gomersall, P., & Baguley, D. (2010). Audition: Disorders. In E. B. Goldstein (Ed.), *Encyclopedia of perception* (pp. 141–145). Thousand Oaks, CA: SAGE.

Gómez, A. M. (2011). Testing the cycle of violence hypothesis: Child abuse and adolescent dating violence as predictors of intimate partner violence in young adulthood. *Youth & Society, 43*(1), 171–192.

Gomez, P. (2013, November 18). Rob Lowe: Loving life at 49. *People Magazine, 80*(21). Retrieved from http://www.people.com/people/archive/article/0,20758135,00.html

Gómez, R. L., & Gerken, L. (2000). Infant artificial language learning and language acquisition. *Trends in Cognitive Sciences, 4*(5), 178–186.

Gone, J. P., & Kirmayer, L. J. (2010). On the wisdom of considering culture and context in psychopathology. In T. Millon, R. F. Krueger, & E. Simonsen (Eds.), *Contemporary directions in psychopathology: Scientific foundations of the DSM-V and ICD-11* (pp. 72–96). New York, NY: Guilford Press.

Gonzales, A. L., & Hancock, J. T. (2011). Mirror, mirror on my Facebook wall: Effects of exposure to Facebook on self-esteem. *Cyberpsychology, Behavior, and Social Networking, 14*(1–2), 79–83.

Gonzales, P. M., Blanton, H., & Williams, K. J. (2002). The effects of stereotype threat and double-minority status on the test performance of Latino women. *Personality and Social Psychology Bulletin, 28*(5), 659–670.

Good, B. J., & Hinton, D. E. (2009). Introduction: Panic disorder in cross-cultural and historical perspective. In D. E. Hinton & B. J. Good (Eds.), *Culture and panic disorder* (pp. 1–28). Stanford, CA: Stanford University Press.

Goodale, M. A. (2011). Transforming vision into action. *Vision Research, 51*(13), 1567–1587.

Goodale, M. A., & Humphrey, G. K. (2001). Separate visual systems for action and perception. In E. B. Goldstein (Ed.), *Blackwell handbook of perception* (pp. 311–343). Oxford, UK: Blackwell.

Goodale, M. A., & Milner, A. D. (1992). Separate visual pathways for perception and action. *Trends in Neurosciences, 15*(1), 20–25.

Goodale, M. A., & Milner, A. D. (2013). *Sight unseen: An exploration of conscious and unconscious vision* (2nd ed.). Oxford, UK: Oxford University Press.

Goodale, M. A., & Westwood, D. A. (2004). An evolving view of duplex vision: Separate but interacting cortical pathways for perception and action. *Current Opinion in Neurobiology, 14*(2), 203–211

Goodheart, L. B. (2003). *Mad Yankees: The Hartford Retreat for the Insane and nineteenth-century psychiatry*. Amherst, MA: University of Massachusetts Press.

Goodman, G. S., Magnussen, S., Andersson, J., Endestad, T., Løkken, L., & Moestue, A. C. (2007). Memory illusions and false memories in the real world. In S. Magnussen & T. Helstrup (Eds.), *Everyday memory* (pp. 157–182). East Sussex, UK: Psychology Press.

Goodwin, C. J. (2003). Psychology's experimental foundations. In S. F. Davis (Ed.), *Handbook of research methods in experimental psychology* (pp. 3–23). Malden, MA: Blackwell.

Goodwin, C. J. (2012). United States. In D. B. Baker (Ed.), *The Oxford handbook of the history of psychology: Global perspectives* (pp. 571–593). New York, NY: Oxford University Press.

Goodwin, R. D., & Friedman, H. S. (2006). Health status and the five-factor personality traits in a nationally representative sample. *Journal of Health Psychology, 11*(5), 643–654.

Goodwin, R. D., Jocobi, F., Bittner, A., & Wittchen, H. (2006). Epidemiology of mood disorders. In D. J. Stein, D. J. Kupfer, & A. F. Schatzberg (Eds.), *The American Psychiatric Publishing textbook of mood disorders* (pp. 33–54). Washington, DC: American Psychiatric Association Publishing.

Gopinath, B., Sue, C. M., Kifley, A., & Mitchell, P. (2012). The association between olfactory impairment and total mortality in older adults. *The Journals of Gerontology, Series A: Biological Sciences and Medical Sciences, 67*(2), 204–209.

Gopnik, A., & Meltzoff, A. N. (1997). *Words, thoughts, and theories*. Cambridge, MA: MIT Press.

Gorassini, D. R., & Olson, J. M. (1995). Does self-perception change explain the foot-in-the-door effect? *Journal of Personality and Social Psychology, 69*(1), 91–105.

Gordon, J., & Abramov, I. (2001). Color vision. In E. B. Goldstein (Ed.), *Blackwell handbook of perception* (pp. 92–127). Oxford, UK: Blackwell.

Gordon, R. A. (2000). *Eating disorders: Anatomy of a social epidemic* (2nd ed.). Malden, MA: Blackwell.

Gore, W. L., & Widiger, T. A. (2013). The DSM-5 dimensional trait model and five-factor models of general personality. *Journal of Abnormal Psychology, 122*(3), 816–821.

Goren, C. C., Sarty, M., & Wu, P. Y. (1975). Visual following and pattern discrimination of face-like stimuli by newborn infants. *Pediatrics, 56*(4), 544–549.

Gosling, S. D., Augustine, A. A., Vazire, S., Holtzman, N., & Gaddis, S. (2011). Manifestations of personality in online social networks: Self-reported Facebook-related behaviors and observable profile information. *Cyberpsychology, Behavior, and Social Networking, 14*(9), 483–488.

Gottesman, I. I. (1991). *Schizophrenia genesis: The origins of madness*. New York, NY: W. H. Freeman.

Gottesman, I. I. (2001). Psychopathology through a life span–genetic prism. *American Psychologist, 56*(11), 867–878.

Gottesmann, C. (2013). *Henri Piéron and Nathaniel Kleitman, two major figures of 20th century sleep research*. New York, NY: Nova Biomedical.

Gottfredson, L. S., & Deary, I. J. (2004). Intelligence predicts health and longevity, but why? *Current Directions in Psychological Science, 13*(1), 1–4.

Gottfried, J. A., Vaala, S. E., Bleakley, A., Hennessy, M., & Jordan, A. (2013). Does the effect of exposure to TV sex on adolescent sexual behavior vary by genre? *Communication Research, 40*(1), 73–95.

Gouin, J. P., & Kiecolt-Glaser, J. K. (2011). The impact of psychological stress on wound healing: Methods and mechanisms. *Immunology and Allergy Clinics of North America, 31*(1), 81–93.

Gould, J. L., & Gould, C. G. (1994). *The animal mind*. New York: Scientific American Library.

Governing.com (2015). Half of US population map. Retrieved from http://www.governing.com/gov-data/census/half-of-usa-population-map-metro-areas.html.

Grabe, S., Hyde, J. S., & Lindberg, S. M. (2007). Body objectification and depression in adolescents: The role of gender, shame, and rumination. *Psychology of Women Quarterly, 31*(2), 164–175.

Grabe, S., Ward, L. M., & Hyde, J. S. (2008). The role of the media in body image concerns among women: A meta-analysis of experimental and correlational studies. *Psychological Bulletin, 134*(3), 460–476.

Grabe, S., Ward, L., & Hyde, J. (2008). The role of the media in body image concerns among women: A meta-analysis of experimental and correlational studies. *Psychological Bulletin, 134*(3), 460–476.

Gradisar, M., & Short, M. A. (2013). Sleep hygiene and environment: Role of technology. In A. R. Wolfson and H. Montgomery-Downs (Eds.), *The Oxford handbook of infant, child, and adolescent sleep and behavior* (pp. 113–126). New York, NY: Oxford University Press.

Graff, K. A., Murnen, S. K., & Krause, A. K. (2013). Low-cut shirts and high-heeled shoes: Increased sexualization across time in magazine depictions of girls. *Sex Roles, 69*(11-12), 571–582.

Graff, K., Murnen, S. K., & Smolak, L. (2012). Too sexualized to be taken seriously? Perceptions of a girl in childlike vs. sexualizing clothing. *Sex Roles, 66*(1112), 764–775.

Graham, J. R. (2012). *MMPI-2: Assessing personality and psychopathology* (5th ed.). New York, NY: Oxford University Press.

Graham, J. R., & Roemer, L. (2015). Multicultural issues in training and practice. In R. L. Cautin & S. O. Lilienfeld (Eds.), *The encyclopedia of clinical psychology* (pp. 1921–1926). West Sussex, UK: Wiley-Blackwell.

Grandin, J. M., & Hedderich, N. (2009). International competence in engineering. In D. K. Deardorff (Ed.), *The SAGE handbook of intercultural competence* (pp. 362–373). Thousand Oaks, CA: SAGE.
Grant, A. M., & Ashford, S. J. (2008). The dynamics of proactivity at work. *Research in Organizational Behavior, 28,* 3–34.
Grant, J. M., Mottet, L. A., Tanis, J., Herman, J. L., Harrison, J., & Keisling, M. (2010). National Transgender Discrimination Survey Report on health and health care (pp. 1–23). Washington, DC: *National Center for Transgender Equality and National Gay and Lesbian Task Force.*
Grant, P., Young, P. R., & DeRubeis, R. J. (2005). Cognitive and behavioral therapies. In G. O. Gabbard, J. S. Beck, & J. Holmes (Eds.), *Oxford textbook of psychotherapy* (pp. 15–25). New York, NY: Oxford University Press.
Gray, J. A. (1979). *Ivan Pavlov.* New York, NY: Viking Press.
Gray, J. A. (1987). *The psychology of fear and stress* (2nd ed.). Cambridge, UK: Cambridge University Press.
Green, B. G. (2004). Temperature perception and nociception. *Journal of Neurobiology, 61*(1), 13–29.
Green, C. D., & Groff, P. R. (2003). *Early psychological thought: Ancient accounts of mind and soul.* Westport, CT: Praeger.
Green, C. S., & Bavelier, D. (2003). Action video game modifies visual selective attention. *Nature, 423*(6939), 534–537.
Green, D., Callands, T. A., Radcliffe, A. M., Luebbe, A. M., & Klonoff, E. A. (2009). Clinical psychology students' perceptions of diversity training: A study of exposure and satisfaction. *Journal of Clinical Psychology, 65*(10), 1056–1070.
Green, J. P., & Lynn, S. J. (2000). Hypnosis and suggestion-based approaches to smoking cessation: An examination of the evidence. *International Journal of Clinical and Experimental Hypnosis, 48*(2), 195–224.
Greenberg, G. (2013). *The book of woe: The DSM and the unmaking of psychiatry.* New York, NY: Blue Rider Press.
Greene, G. (2008). *Insomniac.* Berkeley, CA: University of California Press.
Greene, K., Krcmar, M., Walters, L. H., Rubin, D. L., & Hale, L. (2000). Targeting adolescent risk-taking behaviors: The contributions of egocentrism and sensation-seeking. *Journal of Adolescence, 23*(4), 439–461.
Greene, R. L. (1986). Sources of recency effects in free recall. *Psychological Bulletin, 99*(2), 221–228.
Greene, R. L. (1987). Effects of maintenance rehearsal on human memory. *Psychological Bulletin, 102*(3), 403–413.
Greene, R. L., & Clopton, J. R. (2004). Minnesota Multiphasic Personality Inventory-2 (MMPI-2). In M. W. Maruish (Ed.), *The use of psychological testing for treatment planning and outcomes assessment* (3rd ed., Vol. 3, pp. 449–477). Mahwah, NJ: Lawrence Erlbaum.
Greeno, C. G., & Wing, R. R. (1994). Stress-induced eating. *Psychological Bulletin, 115*(3), 444–464.
Greenwald, A. G., Poehlman, T. A., Uhlmann, E. L., & Banaji, M. R. (2009). Understanding and using the Implicit Association Test: III. Meta-analysis of predictive validity. *Journal of Personality and Social Psychology, 97*(1), 17–41.
Grey, N., & Holmes, E. A. (2008). "Hotspots" in trauma memories in the treatment of post-traumatic stress disorder: A replication. *Memory, 16*(7), 788–796.
Greyson, B. (1985). A typology of near-death experiences. *American Journal of Psychiatry, 142*(8), 967–969.
Greyson, B. (1991). Near-death experiences precipitated by suicide attempt: Lack of influence of psychopathology, religion, and expectations. *Journal of Near-Death Studies, 9,* 183–188.
Greyson, B. (2012). The psychology of near-death experiences and spirituality. In L. J. Miller (Ed.), *The Oxford handbook of psychology and spirituality* (pp. 514–529). New York, NY: Oxford University Press.
Greyson, B., & Stevenson, I. (1980). The phenomenology of near-death experiences. *The American Journal of Psychiatry. 137*(10), 1193–1196.
Griffin, D. W., Gonzalez, R., Koehler, D. J., & Gilovich, T. (2012). Judgmental heuristics: A historical overview. In K. J. Holyoak and R. G. Morrison (Eds.), *The Oxford handbook of thinking and reasoning* (pp. 322–345). Oxford, UK: Oxford University Press.
Griffiths, B. (2001). Have you paxiled lately? *Annals of the American Psychotherapy Association, 4,* 9.
Grigorenko, E. L. (2007). Working as a psychologist in a medical school. In R. J. Sternberg (Ed.), *Career paths in psychology: Where your degree can take you* (2nd ed., pp. 69–81). Washington, DC: American Psychological Association.
Grimbos, T., Dawood, K., Burriss, R. P., Zucker, K. J., & Puts, D. A. (2010). Sexual orientation and the second to fourth finger length ratio: A meta-analysis in men and women. *Behavioral Neuroscience, 124*(2), 278–287.
Griner, D., & Smith, T. B. (2006). Culturally adapted mental health intervention: A meta-analytic review. *Psychotherapy: Theory, Research, Practice, Training, 43*(4), 531–548.
Groeger, J. A., Zijlstra, F. R. H., & Dijk, D.-J. (2004). Sleep quantity, sleep difficulties and their perceived consequences in a representative sample of some 2000 British adults. *Journal of Sleep Research, 13*(4), 359–371.
Groesz, L. M., Levine, M. P., & Murnen, S. K. (2002). The effect of experimental presentation of thin media images on body satisfaction: A meta-analytic review. *International Journal of Eating Disorders, 31*(1), 1–16.
Grogan, S., & Wainwright, N. (1996). Growing up in the culture of slenderness: Girls' experiences of body dissatisfaction. *Women's Studies International Forum, 19*(6), 665–673.
Grohol, J. (2010). Top 25 psychiatric prescriptions for 2009. *PsychCentral.* Retrieved on May 26, 2012, from http://psychcentral.com/lib/2010/top-25–psychiatric-prescriptions-for-2009/
Gros-Louis, J., West, M. J., Goldstein, M. H., & King, A. P. (2006). Mothers provide differential feedback to infants' prelinguistic sounds. *International Journal of Behavioral Development, 30*(6), 509–516.
Gross, J. J. (1998a). Antecedent-and response-focused emotion regulation: Divergent consequences for experience, expression, and physiology. *Journal of Personality and Social Psychology, 74*(1), 224–237.
Gross, J. J. (1998b). The emerging field of emotion regulation: An integrative review. *Review of General Psychology, 2*(3), 271–299.
Gross, J. J. (2008). Emotion regulation. In M. Lewis, J. M. Haviland-Jones, & L. F. Barrett (Eds.), *Handbook of emotions* (3rd ed., pp. 497–512). New York, NY: Guilford Press.
Gross, J. J. (2014). Emotion regulation: Conceptual and empirical foundations. In J. J. Gross (Ed.), *Handbook of emotion regulation* (2nd ed., pp. 3–20). New York, NY: Guilford Press.
Gross, J. J., & John, O. P. (2003). Individual differences in two emotion regulation processes: Implications for affect, relationships, and well-being. *Journal of Personality and Social Psychology, 85*(2), 348–362.
Gross, J. J., & Levenson, R. W. (1993). Emotional suppression: Physiology, self-report, and expressive behavior. *Journal of Personality and Social Psychology, 64*(6), 970.
Gross, J. J., & Levenson, R. W. (1997). Hiding feelings: The acute effects of inhibiting negative and positive emotion. *Journal of Abnormal Psychology, 106*(1), 95–103.
Grossman, P. (2011). Defining mindfulness by how poorly I think I pay attention during everyday awareness and other intractable problems for psychology's (re)invention of mindfulness: Comment on Brown et al. (2011). *Psychological Assessment, 23*(4), 1034–1040.
Grossman, P., Niemann, L., Schmidt, S., & Walach, H. (2004). Mindfulness-based stress reduction and health benefits: A meta-analysis. *Journal of Psychosomatic Research, 57*(1), 35–43.
Grossman, P., Niemann, L., Schmidt, S., & Walach, H. (2004). Mindfulness-based stress reduction and health benefits: A meta-analysis. *Journal of Psychosomatic Research, 57*(1), 35–43.
Grossman, P., & Van Dam, N. T. (2011). Mindfulness, by any other name. . .: Trials and tribulations of *sati* in western psychology and science. *Contemporary Buddhism, 12*(01), 219–239.
Grossmann, I., Na, J., Varnum, M. E., Park, D. C., Kitayama, S., & Nisbett, R. E. (2010). Reasoning about social conflicts improves into old age. *Proceedings of the National Academy of Sciences, 107*(16), 7246–7250.
Groth-Marnat, G. (2009). *Handbook of psychological assessment* (5th ed.). Hoboken, NJ: Wiley.
Grusec, J. E., Hastings, P., & Almas, A. (2011). Prosocial behavior. In P. K. Smith & C. H. Hart (Eds.), T*he Wiley-Blackwell handbook of childhood social development* (2nd ed., pp. 549–566). Malden, MA: Wiley-Blackwell.
Gu, J., Strauss, C., Bond, R., & Cavanagh, K. (2015). How do mindfulness-based cognitive therapy and mindfulness-based stress reduction improve mental health and wellbeing? A systematic review and meta-analysis of meditation studies. *Clinical Psychology Review, 37,* 1–12.
Guadiano, B. A. (2008). Cognitive behavioural therapies: Achievements and challenges. *Evidence-Based Mental Health, 11*(1), 5–7.
Guéguen, N., & De Gail, M. A. (2003). The effect of smiling on helping behavior: Smiling and good Samaritan behavior. *Communication Reports, 16*(2), 133–140.
Guéguen, N., & Jacob, C. (2001). Fund-raising on the web: The effect of an electronic foot-in-the-door on donation. *CyberPsychology & Behavior, 4*(6), 705–709.
Guilleminault, C., Moscovitch, A., Yuen, K., & Poyares, D. (2002). Atypical sexual behavior during sleep. *Psychosomatic Medicine, 64*(2), 328–336.
Guillin, O., Abi-Dargham, A., & Laruelle, M. (2007). Neurobiology of dopamine in schizophrenia. In A. Abi-Dargham & O. Guillin (Eds.), *Integrating the neurobiology of schizophrenia* (pp. 1–39). San Diego, CA: Elsevier.
Gulerce, A. (2006). History of psychology in Turkey as a sign of diverse modernization and global psychologization. In A. C. Brock (Ed.), *Internationalizing the history of psychology* (pp. 75–93). New York, NY: New York University Press.
Gunaratana, B. H. (2014). *Mindfulness in plain English (20th anniversary edition).* Somerville, MA: Wisdom Publications.
Gunderson, J. G. (2001). *Borderline personality disorder: A clinical guide.* Washington, DC: American Psychiatric Association Press.
Günsoy, C., Cross, S. E., Sarıbay, A., Olcaysoy Ökten, I., & Kurutaş, M. (2015). Would you post that picture and let your dad see it? Culture, honor, and Facebook. *European Journal of Social Psychology, 45*(3), 323–335.
Gupta, A., Elheis, M., & Pansari, K. (2004). Imaging in psychiatric illnesses. *International Journal of Clinical Practice, 58*(9): 850–858.
Gupta, P., & Cohen, N. J. (2002). Theoretical and computational analysis of skill learning, repetition priming, and procedural memory. *Psychological Review, 109*(2), 401–448.
Gurstelle, E. B., & De Oliveira, J. L. (2004). Daytime parahypnagogia: A state of consciousness that occurs when we almost fall asleep. *Medical Hypotheses, 62*(2), 166–168.
Gurung, R. A. R. (2014). *Health psychology: A cultural approach.* (3rd ed.). Belmont, CA: Wadsworth Cengage Learning.
Gustavson, C. R., Garcia, J., Hankins, W. G., & Rusiniak, K. W. (1974). Coyote predation control by aversive conditioning. *Science, 184,* 581–583.
Gustavson, C. R., Holzer, G. A., Gustavson, J. C., & Vakoch, D. L. (1982). An evaluation of phenol methylcarbamates as taste aversion producing agents in caged blackbirds. *Applied Animal Ethology, 8,* 551–559.

Gustavson, C. R., Kelly, D. J., Seeney, M., & Garcia, J. (1976). Prey lithium aversions I: Coyotes and wolves. *Behavioral Biology, 17*, 61–72.

Gutheil, T. G., & Brodsky, A. (2008). *Preventing boundary violations in clinical practice*. New York, NY: Guilford Press.

Guthrie, R. V. (2004). *Even the rat was white: A historical view of psychology* (2nd ed.) Boston, MA: Allyn and Bacon.

Gwaltney, C. J., Metrik, J., Kahler, C. W., & Shiffman, S. (2009). Self-efficacy and smoking cessation: A meta-analysis. *Psychology of Addictive Behaviors, 23*(1), 56–66.

Gyani, A., Shafran, R., Myles, P., & Rose, S. (2014). The gap between science and practice: How therapists make their clinical decisions. *Behavior Therapy, 45*(2), 199–211.

Hackel, L. S., & Ruble, D. N. (1992). Changes in the marital relationship after the first baby is born: Predicting the impact of expectancy disconfirmation. *Journal of Personality and Social Psychology, 62*(6), 944.

Hackman, J. R., & Katz, N. (2010). Group behavior and performance. In S. T. Fiske, D. T. Gilbert, & G. Lindzey (Eds.), *Handbook of social psychology* (5th ed., Vol. 2, pp. 1208–1251). Hoboken, NJ: Wiley.

Hackney, C. M. (2010). Auditory processing: Peripheral. In E. B. Goldstein (Ed.), *Encyclopedia of perception* (pp. 180–183). Thousand Oaks, CA: SAGE.

Hafer, C. L., & Begue, L. (2005). Experimental research on just-world theory: Problems, developments, and future challenges. *Psychological Bulletin, 131*(1), 128–167.

Hafner, H., & an der Heiden, W. (2008). Course and outcome. In K. T. Mueser & D. V. Jeste (Eds.), *Clinical handbook of schizophrenia* (pp. 100–113). New York, NY: Guilford Press.

Hagenauer, M. H., Perryman, J. I., Lee, T. M., & Carskadon, M. A. (2009). Adolescent changes in the homeostatic and circadian regulation of sleep. *Developmental Neuroscience, 31*(4), 276–284.

Haggbloom, S. J., Warnick, R., Warnick, J. E., Jones, V. K., Yarbrough, G. L., Russell, T. M., . . . Monte, E. (2002). The 100 most eminent psychologists of the 20th century. *Review of General Psychology, 6*(2), 139–152.

Haglund, K. A., & Fehring, R. J. (2010). The association of religiosity, sexual education, and parental factors with risky sexual behaviors among adolescents and young adults. *Journal of Religion and Health, 49*(4), 460–472.

Hald, G. M., Seaman, C., & Linz, D. (2014). Sexuality and pornography. In D. Tolman, L. Diamond, J. Bauermeister, W. George, J. Pfaus, & M. Ward (Eds.), *APA handbook of sexuality and psychology: Contextual approaches* (Vol. 2, pp. 3–35). Washington, DC: American Psychological Association.

Halford, G. S., & Andrews, G. (2006). Reasoning and problem solving. In D. Kuhn & R. Siegler (Vol. Eds.), *Handbook of child psychology* (6th ed., Vol. 2, pp. 557–608). Hoboken, NJ: Wiley.

Halim, M. L., Ruble, D. N., & Tamis-LeMonda, C. S. (2013). Four-year-olds' beliefs about how others regard males and females. *British Journal of Developmental Psychology, 31*(1), 128–135.

Hall, A. (2005). Audience personality and the selection of media and media genres. *Media Psychology, 7*(4), 377–398.

Hall, C. C. I. (2014). The evolution of the revolution: The successful establishment of multicultural psychology. In F. T. L. Leong (Ed.), *APA handbook of multicultural psychology* (Vol. 1, pp. 3–18). Washington, DC: American Psychological Association.

Hall, J. A. (2006). Women's and men's nonverbal communication: Similarities, differences, stereotypes, and origins. In V. Manusov & M. L. Patterson (Eds.), *The SAGE handbook of nonverbal communication* (pp. 201–218). Thousand Oaks, CA: SAGE.

Hall, J. A., Carter, J. D., & Horgan, T. G. (2000). Gender differences in nonverbal communication of emotion. In A. H. Fischer (Ed.), *Gender and emotion: Social psychological perspectives* (pp. 97–117). Cambridge, UK: Cambridge University Press.

Hall, M., Levenson, J., & Hasler, B. (2012). Sleep and emotion. In C. M. Morin & C. A. Espie (Eds.), *The Oxford handbook of sleep and sleep disorders* (pp. 131–149). Oxford, UK: Oxford University Press.

Haller, D. L., & Acosta, M. C. (2010). Characteristics of pain patients with opioid-use disorder. *Psychosomatics, 51*(3), 257–266.

Halpern, D. F. (2012). *Sex differences in cognitive abilities*. (4th ed). New York, NY: Psychology Press.

Halpern, D. F., Beninger, A. S., & Straight, C. A. (2011). Sex differences in intelligence. In R. J. Sternberg & S. B. Kaufman (Eds.), *The Cambridge handbook of intelligence* (pp. 253–272). Cambridge, UK: Cambridge University Press.

Hamann, S., Herman, R. A., Nolan, C. L., & Wallen, K. (2004). Men and women differ in amygdala response to visual sexual stimuli. *Nature Neuroscience, 7*(4), 411–416.

Hambrick, D. Z., Kane, M. J., & Engle, R. W. (2005). The role of working memory in higher-level cognition: Domain-specific versus domain-general perspectives. In R. Sternberg, & J. E. Pretz (Eds.), *Cognition and intelligence: Identifying the mechanisms of the mind* (pp. 104–121). New York, NY: Cambridge University Press.

Hambrick, D. Z., & Meinz, E. J. (2011). Limits on the predictive power of domain-specific experience and knowledge in skilled performance. *Current Directions in Psychological Science, 20*(5), 275–279.

Hambrick, D. Z., Oswald, F. L., Darowski, E. S., Rench, T. A., & Brou, R. (2010). Predictors of multitasking performance in a synthetic work paradigm. *Applied Cognitive Psychology, 24*(8), 1149–1167.

Hamer, M., Taylor, A., & Steptoe, A. (2006). The effect of acute aerobic exercise on stress related blood pressure responses: A systematic review and meta-analysis. *Biological Psychology, 71*(2), 183–190.

Hamilton, W. D. (1964). The genetical evolution of social behaviour. I. *Journal of Theoretical Biology, 7*(1), 1–16.

Hammen, C., & Watkins, E. (2008). *Depression* (2nd ed.). New York, NY: Psychology Press.

Hampton, J. A. (1995). Testing the prototype theory of concepts. *Journal of Memory and Language, 34*(5), 686–708.

Haninger, K., & Thompson, K. M. (2004). Content and ratings of teen-rated video games. *The Journal of the American Medical Association, 291*, 856–865.

Hankin, B. L., Wetter, E., & Cheely, C. (2008). Sex differences in child and adolescent depression: A developmental psychopathological approach. In J. R. Z. Abela & B. L. Hankin (Eds.), *Handbook of depression in children and adolescents* (pp. 377–414). New York, NY: Guilford Press.

Hanley, G., Piazza, C., Fisher, W., & Maglieri, K. (2005). On the effectiveness of and preference for punishment and extinction components of function-based interventions. *Journal of Applied Behavior Analysis, 38*, 51–65.

Hannah, A., & Murachver, T. (2007). Gender preferential responses to speech. *Journal of Language and Social Psychology, 26*(3), 274–290.

Hannon, E. E., & Trainor, L. J. (2007). Music acquisition: Effects of enculturation and formal training on development. *Trends in Cognitive Sciences, 11*(11), 466–472.

Hannon, E. E., & Trehub, S. E. (2005a). Metrical categories in infancy and adulthood. *Psychological Science, 16*(1), 48–55.

Hannon, E. E., & Trehub, S. E. (2005b). Tuning in to musical rhythms: Infants learn more readily than adults. *Proceedings of the National Academy of Sciences of the United States of America, 102*(35), 12639–12643.

Hansen, S. N., Schendel, D. E., & Parner, E. T. (2015). Explaining the increase in the prevalence of autism spectrum disorders: The proportion attributable to changes in reporting practices. *JAMA Pediatrics, 169*(1), 56–62.

Hansen, T. (2010). Color naming. In E. B. Goldstein (Ed.), *Encyclopedia of perception* (pp. 264–266). Thousand Oaks, CA: SAGE.

Hanson, J., & Hackman, D. A. (2012). Cognitive neuroscience and disparities in socioeconomic status. In B. Wolfe (Ed.), *The biological consequences of socioeconomic inequalities* (pp. 158–186). New York, NY: Russell Sage Foundation.

Hanson, J., Hair, N., Chandra, A., Moss, E., Bhattacharya, J., Pollak, S. D., & Wolfe, B. (2012). Brain development and poverty: A first look. In B. Wolfe (Ed.), *The biological consequences of socioeconomic inequalities* (pp. 187–214). New York, NY: Russell Sage Foundation.

Harackiewicz, J. M., Barron, K. E., Tauer, J. M., & Elliot, A. J. (2002). Predicting success in college: A longitudinal study of achievement goals and ability measures as predictors of interest and performance from freshman year through graduation. *Journal of Educational Psychology, 94*(3), 562.

Harackiewicz, J. M., Barron, K. E., Tauer, J. M., Carter, S. M., & Elliot, A. J. (2000). Short-term and long-term consequences of achievement goals: Predicting interest and performance over time. *Journal of Educational Psychology, 92*(2), 316–330.

Harackiewicz, J. M., Barron, K. E., Pintrich, P. R., Elliot, A. J., & Thrash, T. M. (2002a). Revision of achievement goal theory: Necessary and illuminating. *Journal of Educational Psychology, 94*, 638–645.

Harackiewicz, J. M., Barron, K. E., Tauer, J. M., & Elliot, A. J. (2002b). Predicting success in college: A longitudinal study of achievement goals and ability measures as predictors of interest and performance from freshman year through graduation. *Journal of Educational Psychology, 94*(3), 562–575.

Harding, S. R., Flannelly, K. J., Weaver, A. J., & Costa, K. G. (2005). The influence of religion on death anxiety and death acceptance. *Mental Health, Religion & Culture, 8*(4), 253–261.

Hardy, M. S., & Calhoun, L. G. (1997). Psychological distress and the "medical student syndrome" in abnormal psychology students. *Teaching of Psychology, 24*(3), 192–193.

Harkins, S. G., & Jackson, J. M. (1985). The role of evaluation in eliminating social loafing. *Personality and Social Psychology Bulletin, 11*(4), 457–465.

Harlow, H. F. (1958). The nature of love. *American Psychologist, 13*, 673–685.

Harlow, H. F., & Harlow, M. (1962). Social deprivation in monkeys. *Scientific American, 207*, 136–146.

Harlow, H. F., & Zimmerman, R. (1958). The development of affection in infant monkeys. *Proceedings of the American Philosophical Society, 102*, 501–509.

Harlow, H. F., & Zimmerman, R. (1959). Affectional responses in the infant monkey. *Science, 130*, 421–432.

Harman, J. P., Hansen, C. E., Cochran, M. E., & Lindsey, C. R. (2005). Liar, liar: Internet faking but not frequency of use affects social skills, self-esteem, social anxiety, and aggression. *CyberPsychology & Behavior, 8*, 1–6.

Harmon-Jones, E., & Mills, J. (1999). An introduction to cognitive dissonance theory and an overview of current perspectives on the theory. In E. Harmon-Jones & J. Mills (Eds.), *Cognitive dissonance: Progress on a pivotal theory in social psychology* (pp. 3–21). Washington, DC: American Psychological Association

Harrell, S. P. (2000). A multidimensional conceptualization of racism-related stress: Implications for the well-being of people of color. *American Journal of Orthopsychiatry, 70*(1), 42–57.

Harrington, A. (2008). *The cure within: A history of mind-body medicine*. New York, NY: W. W. Norton.

Harris Interactive & Witeck-Combs (2010). The lesbian, gay, bisexual, and transgender population at a glance. Washington, DC: Harris Interactive, Inc.

Harris, A. (2012). Transference, countertransference, and the real relationship. In G. O. Gabbard, B. E. Litowitz, & P. Williams (Eds.), *Textbook of psychoanalysis* (2nd ed., pp. 255–268). Washington, DC: American Psychiatric Publishing.

Harris, C., & Alvarado, N. (2005). Facial expressions, smile types, and self-report during humour, tickle, and pain. *Cognition & Emotion, 19*(5), 655–669.

Harris, G. (2011, March 5). Talk doesn't pay, so psychiatry turns instead to drug therapy. *New York Times*. Retrieved from http://www.nytimes.com/2011/03/06/health/policy/06 doctors.html?_r=1&pagewanted=all

Harris, J. A. (2004). Measured intelligence, achievement, openness to experience, and creativity. *Personality and Individual Differences, 36*(4), 913–929.

Harris, J. E. (2012). Multicultural counseling in a multitheoretical context: New applications for practice. In M. E. Gallardo, C. J. Yeh, J. E. Trimble, & T. A. Parham (Eds.), *Culturally adaptive counseling skills: Demonstrations of evidence-based practices* (pp. 287–312). Thousand Oaks, CA: SAGE.

Harris, J. L., Bargh, J. A., & Brownell, K. D. (2009). Priming effects of television food advertising on eating behavior. *Health Psychology, 28*(4), 404–413.

Harrison, K., & Cantor, J. (1999). Tales from the screen: Enduring fright reactions to scary media. *Media Psychology, 1*(2), 97–116.

Harrison, M. A. (2011). College students' prevalence and perceptions of text messaging while driving. *Accident Analysis & Prevention, 43*(4), 1516–1520.

Harrison, Y. (2012). The functions of sleep. In C. M. Morin & C. A. Espie (Eds.), *The Oxford handbook of sleep and sleep disorders*, (pp. 61–74). Oxford, UK: Oxford University Press.

Harrow, M., Hansford, B. G., & Astrachan-Fletcher, E. B. (2009). Locus of control: Relation to schizophrenia, to recovery, and to depression and psychosis—A 15-year longitudinal study. *Psychiatry Research, 168*(3), 186–192.

Hartmann, M., Kopf, S., Kircher, C., Faude-Lang, V., Djuric, Z., Augstein, F., . . . & Nawroth, P. P. (2012). Sustained effects of a mindfulness-based stress-reduction intervention in type 2 diabetic patients: Design and first results of a randomized controlled trial (the Heidelberger Diabetes and Stress-Study). *Diabetes Care, 35*(5), 945–947.

Hartup, W. W. (1999). Peer experience and its developmental significance. In M. Bennett (Ed.), *Developmental psychology: Achievements and prospects* (pp. 106–125). Philadelphia, PA: Psychology Press.

Hartwell, C. E. (1996). The schizophrenogenic mother concept in American psychiatry. *Psychiatry,* 59(3), 274–297.

Hartz, A. J., Rupley, D. C., Kalkhoff, R. D., & Rimm, A. A. (1983). Relationship of obesity to diabetes: Influence of obesity level and body fat distribution. *Preventive Medicine, 12*(2), 351–357.

Hartzler, B. M. (2014). Fatigue on the flight deck: The consequences of sleep loss and the benefits of napping. *Accident Analysis & Prevention, 62*, 309–318.

Harwood, K., McLean, N., & Durkin, K. (2007). First-time mothers' expectations of parenthood: What happens when optimistic expectations are not matched by later experiences? *Developmental Psychology, 43*(1), 1–12.

Hasher, L., & Zacks, R. T. (1979). Automatic and effortful processes in memory. *Journal of Experimental Psychology: General, 108*(3), 356–388.

Hasher, L., & Zacks, R. T. (1984). Automatic processing of fundamental information: The case of frequency of occurrence. *American Psychologist, 39*(12), 1372–1388.

Haslam, N., & Levy, S. R. (2006). Essentialist beliefs about homosexuality: Structure and implications for prejudice. *Personality and Social Psychology Bulletin, 32*(4), 471–485.

Hatch, L. (2011). The American Psychological Association Task Force on the Sexualization of Girls: A review, update and commentary. *Sexual Addiction & Compulsivity, 18*(4), 195–211.

Hatfield, E., Luckhurst, C., & Rapson, R. L. (2010). Sexual motives: Cultural, evolutionary, and social psychological perspectives. *Sexuality & Culture, 14*(3), 173–190.

Hatfield, E., & Rapson, R. (1993). *Love, sex, and intimacy: The psychology, biology, and history*. New York, NY: HarperCollins.

Hatfield, E., & Sprecher, S. (1986). Measuring passionate love in intimate relationships. *Journal of Adolescence, 9*(4), 383–410.

Hattie, J. (1992). *Self-concept*. Hillsdale, NJ: Lawrence Erlbaum.

Hatzenbuehler, M. L., McLaughlin, K. A., Keyes, K. M., & Hasin, D. S. (2010). The impact of institutional discrimination on psychiatric disorders in lesbian, gay, and bisexual populations: A prospective study. *American Journal of Public Health, 100*(3), 452–459.

Hauck, F. R., Signore, C., Fein, S. B., & Raju, T. N. (2008). Infant sleeping arrangements and practices during the first year of life. *Pediatrics, 122*(Suppl. 2), S113–S120.

Haus, E. L., & Smolensky, M. H. (2013). Shift work and cancer risk: Potential mechanistic roles of circadian disruption, light at night, and sleep deprivation. *Sleep Medicine Reviews, 17*(4), 273–284.

Hawkins, R. D., Clark, G. A., & Kandel, E. R. (2006). Brief communications: Operant conditioning of gill withdrawal in *Aplysia*. *The Journal of Neuroscience, 26*, 2443–2448.

Hayashi, M., Watanabe, M., & Hori, T. (1999). The effects of a 20 min nap in the mid-afternoon on mood, performance and EEG activity. *Clinical Neurophysiology, 110*(2), 272–279.

Haycock, D. A. (2014). *Murderous minds: Exploring the criminal psychopathic brain: Neurological imaging and the manifestation of evil*. New York, NY: Pegasus Books.

Hayes, J. P., Morey, R. A., Petty, C. M., Seth, S., Smoski, M. J., McCarthy, G., & LaBar, K. S. (2010). Staying cool when things get hot: Emotion regulation modulates neural mechanisms of memory encoding. *Frontiers in Human Neuroscience, 4*, 1–10.

Hayes, S. C. (2004). Acceptance and commitment therapy and the new behavior therapies: Mindfulness, acceptance, and relationship. In S. C. Hayes, V. M. Follette, & M. M. Linehan (Eds.), *Mindfulness and acceptance: Expanding the cognitive-behavioral tradition* (pp. 1–29). New York, NY: Guilford Press.

Hayes, S. C., Strosahl, K., & Wilson, K. G. (2012). *Acceptance and commitment therapy: The process and practice of mindful change*. (2nd ed.) New York, NY: Guilford Press.

Hayes, S. C., Villatte, M., Levin, M., & Hildebrandt, M. (2011). Open, aware, and active: Contextual approaches as an emerging trend in the behavioral and cognitive therapies. *Annual Review of Clinical Psychology, 7*, 141–168.

Hayes, S. C., Villatte, M., Levin, M., & Hildebrandt, M. (2011). Open, aware, and active: Contextual approaches as an emerging trend in the behavioral and cognitive therapies. *Annual Review of Clinical Psychology, 7*, 141–168.

Hayes, S., Hirsch, C., & Mathews, A. (2008). Restriction of working memory capacity during worry. *Journal of Abnormal Psychology, 117*(3), 712– 717.

Hayes-Skelton, J. A., & Wadsworth, L. P. (2015). Mindfulness in the treatment of anxiety. In K. W. Brown, J. D. Creswell, & R. M. Ryan (Eds.), *Handbook of mindfulness: Theory, research, and practice* (pp. 367–386). New York, NY: Guilford Press.

Haynes, S. N., & Kaholokula, J. K. (2008). Behavioral assessment. In M. Hersen & A. M. Gross (Eds.), *Handbook of clinical psychology* (Vol. 1, pp. 495–522). Hoboken, NJ: Wiley.

Hays, P. A. (2008). *Addressing cultural complexities in practice: Assessment, diagnosis, and therapy* (2nd ed.). Washington, DC: American Psychological Association.

Hays, P. A., & Iwamasa, G. Y. (Eds.). (2006). *Culturally responsive cognitive-behavioral therapy: Assessment, practice, and supervision*. Washington, DC: American Psychological Association.

Hazlett-Stevens, H., & Craske, M. G. (2008). Live (in vivo) exposure. In W. T. O'Donohue & J. E. Fisher (Eds.), *Cognitive behavior therapy: Applying empirically supported techniques in your practice* (2nd ed., pp. 309–316). Hoboken, NJ: Wiley.

Hazlett-Stevens, H., Pruitt, L. D., & Collins, A. (2009). Phenomenology of generalized anxiety disorder. In M. M. Antony & M. B. Stein (Eds.), *Oxford handbook of anxiety and related disorders* (pp. 47–55). New York, NY: Oxford University Press.

He, S. (2010). Selective adaptation. In E. B. Goldstein (Ed.), *Encyclopedia of perception* (pp. 879–881). Thousand Oaks, CA: SAGE.

Head, L. S., & Gross, A. M. (2008). Systematic desensitization. In W. T. O'Donohue & J. E. Fisher (Eds.), *Cognitive behavior therapy: Applying empirically supported techniques in your practice* (2nd ed., pp. 542–549). Hoboken, NJ: Wiley.

Head, L. S., & Gross, A. M. (2009). Systematic desensitization. In W. O'Donohue & J. E. Fisher (Eds.), *General principles and empirically supported techniques of cognitive behavior therapy* (pp. 640–647). Hoboken, NJ: Wiley.

Heaps, C. M., & Nash, M. (2001). Comparing recollective experience in true and false autobiographical memories. *Journal of Experimental Psychology: Learning, Memory, and Cognition, 27*(4), 920–930.

Heatherton, T. F., & Sargent, J. D. (2009). Does watching smoking in movies promote teenage smoking. *Current Directions in Psychological Science, 18*(2), 63–67.

Hebl, M. R., & Turchin, J. M. (2005). The stigma of obesity: What about men? *Basic and Applied Social Psychology, 27*(3), 267–275.

Hedegaard, M. (1992). The zone of proximal development as basis for instruction. In L. C. Moll (Ed.), *Vygotsky and education: Instructional implications and applications of sociohistorical psychology* (pp. 349–371). New York, NY: Cambridge University Press.

Hedges, L. V., & Nowell, A. (1995). Sex differences in mental test scores, variability, and numbers of high-scoring individuals. *Science, 269*(5220), 41–45.

Hegarty, J. D., Baldessarine, R. J., Tohen, M., Waternaux, C., & Oepen, G. (1994). One hundred years of schizophrenia: A meta-analysis of the outcome literature. *American Journal of Psychiatry, 151*(10), 1409–1416.

Hegarty, M., & Waller, D. A. (2005). Individual differences in spatial abilities. In A. Miyake & P. Shah (Eds.), *The Cambridge handbook of visuospatial thinking* (pp. 121–169). Cambridge, UK: Cambridge University Press.

Hegarty, P., & Pratto, F. (2001). Sexual orientation beliefs: Their relationship to anti-gay attitudes and biological determinist arguments. *Journal of Homosexuality, 41*(1), 121–135.

Heiby, E. M., & Haynes, S. N. (2004). Introduction to behavioral assessment. In S. N. Haynes & E. M. Heiby (Eds.), *Comprehensive handbook of psychological assessment: Behavioral assessment* (Vol. 3, pp. 3–18). Hoboken, NJ: Wiley.

Heider, E. R., & Olivier, D. C. (1972). The structure of the color space in naming and memory for two languages. *Cognitive Psychology, 3*(2), 337–354.

Heider, F. (1958). *The psychology of interpersonal relations*. New York, NY: Wiley.

Heine, S. J., Kitayama, S., Lehman, D. R., Takata, T., Ide, E., Leung, C., & Matsumoto, H. (2001). Divergent consequences of success and failure in Japan and North America: An investigation of self-improving motivations and malleable selves. *Journal of Personality and Social Psychology, 81*(4), 599–615.

Heine, S. J., & Lehman, D. R. (1995). Cultural variation in unrealistic optimism: Does the West feel more vulnerable than the East? *Journal of Personality and Social Psychology, 68*(4), 595–607.

Heine, S. J., Lehman, D. R., Markus, H. R., & Kitayama, S. (1999). Is there a universal need for positive self-regard? *Psychological Review, 106*(4), 766–794.

Heinze, J. E., & Horn, S. S. (2009). Intergroup contact and beliefs about homosexuality in adolescence. *Journal of Youth and Adolescence, 38*(7), 937–951.

Helgeson, V. S. (2011). Gender, stress, and coping. In S. Folkman, *Oxford handbook of stress, health, and coping* (pp. 63–85). Oxford, UK: Oxford University Press.

Helmholtz, H. V. (1852). LXXXI. On the theory of compound colours. *Philosophical Magazine Series 4*, *4*(28), 519–534.

Helms, J. E. (2006). Fairness is not validity or cultural bias in racial-group assessment: A quantitative perspective. *American Psychologist*, *61*(8), 845–859.

Helms, J. L., & Rogers, D. T. (2015). *Majoring in psychology: Achieving your educational and career goals* (2nd ed.) Malden, MA: Wiley-Blackwell.

Helstrup, T., De Beni, R., Cornoldi, C., & Koriat, A. (2007). Memory pathways: Involuntary and voluntary processes in retrieving personal memories. In S. Magnussen & T. Helstrup (Eds.), *Everyday memory* (pp. 291–315). East Sussex, UK: Psychology Press.

Helwig, C. C., & Turiel, E. (2011). Children's social and moral reasoning. In P. K. Smith & C. H. Hart (Eds.), *The Wiley-Blackwell handbook of childhood social development* (2nd ed., pp. 567–583). Malden, MA: Wiley-Blackwell.

Helzner, E. P., Cauley, J. A., Pratt, S. R., Wisniewski, S. R., Zmuda, J. M., Talbott, E. O., . . . Newman, A. B. (2005). Race and sex differences in age-related hearing loss: The Health, Aging and Body Composition Study. *Journal of the American Geriatrics Society*, *53*(12), 2119–2127.

Hembree, R. (1988). Correlates, causes, effects, and treatment of test anxiety. *Review of Educational Research*, *58*(1), 47–77.

Henderlong, J., & Lepper, M. R. (2002). The effects of praise on children's intrinsic motivation: A review and synthesis. *Psychological Bulletin*, *128*(5), 774–795.

Henderson, V. R., & Kelly, B. (2005). Food advertising in the age of obesity: Content analysis of food advertising on general market and African American television. *Journal of Nutrition Education and Behavior*, *37*(4), 191–196.

Hendry, L. B., & Kloep, M. (2007). Conceptualizing emerging adulthood: Inspecting the emperor's new clothes? *Child Development Perspectives*, *1*(2), 74–79.

Hendry, L. B., & Kloep, M. (2010). How universal is emerging adulthood? An empirical example. *Journal of Youth Studies*, *13*(2), 169–179.

Henry J. Kaiser Family Foundation (2014). Population distribution by race/ethnicity. Retrieved from http://kff.org/other/state-indicator/distribution-by-raceethnicity/

Henry, L. A. (2001). How does the severity of a learning disability affect working memory performance? *Memory*, *9*(4–6), 233–247.

Hepper, P. (2003). Prenatal psychological and behavioural development. In J. Valsiner & K. Connolly (Eds.), *Handbook of developmental psychology* (pp. 91–113). Thousand Oaks, CA: SAGE.

Hepper, P. G., Dornan, J. C., & Lynch, C. (2012). Sex differences in fetal habituation. *Developmental Science*, *15*(3), 373–383.

Herbst-Damm, K. L., & Kulik, J. A. (2005). Volunteer support, marital status, and the survival times of terminally ill patients. *Health Psychology*, *24*(2), 225–229.

Herek, G. M. (2000). Sexual prejudice and gender: Do heterosexuals' attitudes toward lesbians and gay men differ? *Journal of Social Issues*, *56*(2), 251–266.

Herek, G. M., Norton, A. T., Allen, T. J., & Sims, C. L. (2010). Demographic, psychological, and social characteristics of self-identified lesbian, gay, and bisexual adults in a U.S. probability sample. *Sexuality Research and Social Policy*, *7*(3), 176–200.

Hering, E. (1878). *Zur lehre vom lichtsinne* (Vol. 68). K. Akademie der Wissenschaften.

Hering, E. (1964). *Outlines of a theory of the light sense* (L. M. Hurvich & D. Jameson, Trans.). Cambridge, MA: Harvard University Press.

Herman, C. P., & Polivy, J. S. (2010). Sex and gender differences in eating behavior. In J. C. Chrisler & D. R. McCreary (Eds.), *Handbook of gender research in psychology* (Vol. 1, pp. 455–469). New York, NY: Springer Science+Business Media.

Hernandez, K. M., Mahoney, A., & Pargament, K. I. (2014). Sexuality and religion. In D. L. Tolman & L. M. Diamond (Eds.), *APA handbook of sexuality and psychology* (Vol. 2, pp. 425–447). Washington, DC: American Psychological Association.

Hernández-Díaz, S., Werler, M. M., Walker, A. M., & Mitchell, A. A. (2000). Folic acid antagonists during pregnancy and the risk of birth defects. *New England Journal of Medicine*, *343*(22), 1608–1614.

Herrnstein, R. J., & Murray, C. (1994). *Bell curve: Intelligence and class structure in American life*. New York, NY: Free Press.

Hershey, D. A., Jacobs-Lawson, J. M., & Wilson, T. L. (2006). Research as a script. In F. T. L. Leong & J. T. Austin, *The psychology research handbook: A guide for graduate students and research assistants* (2nd ed., pp. 3–22). Thousand Oaks: SAGE Publications.

Hershey, D. A., Wilson, T. L., & Mitchell-Copeland, J. (1996). Conceptions of the psychological research process: Script variation as a function of training and experience. *Current Psychology*, *14*(4), 293–312.

Hershner, S. (2013). Impact of sleep on the challenges of safe driving in young adults. In A. R. Wolfson & H. Montgomery-Downs (Eds.), *The Oxford handbook of infant, child, and adolescent sleep and behavior* (pp. 441–455). New York, NY: Oxford University Press.

Hertel, P. (2004). Memory for emotional and nonemotional events in depression: A question of habit? In D. Reisberg & P. Hertel (Eds.), *Memory and emotion* (pp. 186–216). Oxford, UK: Oxford University Press.

Herz, R. S. (1997). The effects of cue distinctiveness on odor-based context-dependent memory. *Memory & Cognition*, *25*(3), 375–380.

Herzog, D. B., & Herrin, J. T. (1985). Near-death experiences in the very young. *Critical Care Medicine*, *13*(12), 1074–1075.

Hespos, S. J., & Baillargeon, R. (2008). Young infants' actions reveal their developing knowledge of support variables: Converging evidence for violation-of-expectation findings. *Cognition*, *107*(1), 304–316.

Hess, T. M., Auman, C., Colcombe, S. J., & Rahhal, T. A. (2003). The impact of stereotype threat on age differences in memory performance. *The Journals of Gerontology Series B: Psychological Sciences and Social Sciences*, *58*(1), P3–P11.

Hess, U., Adams, R. B., Simard, A., Stevenson, M. T., & Kleck, R. E. (2012). Smiling and sad wrinkles: Age-related changes in the face and the perception of emotions and intentions. *Journal of Experimental Social Psychology*, *48*(6), 1377–1380.

Hess, U., & Thibault, P. (2009). Darwin and emotion expression. *American Psychologist*, *64*(2), 120–128.

Hettema, J., Steele, J., & Miller, W. R. (2005). Motivational interviewing. *Annual Review of Clinical Psychology*, *1*, 91–111.

Heyes, C. (2010). Where do mirror neurons come from? *Neuroscience & Biobehavioral Reviews*, *34*(4), 575–583.

Heyman, G. D., & Dweck, C. S. (1992). Achievement goals and intrinsic motivation: Their relation and their role in adaptive motivation. *Motivation and Emotion*, *16*(3), 231–247.

Heyman, G. D., Fu, G., & Lee, K. (2008). Reasoning about the disclosure of success and failure to friends among children in the United States and China. *Developmental Psychology*, *44*(4), 908.

Heyman, G. D., & Lee, K. (2012). Moral development: Revisiting Kohlberg's stages. In A. M. Slater & P. C. Quinn (Eds.), *Developmental psychology: Revisiting the classic studies* (pp. 164–175). Thousand Oaks, CA: SAGE.

Hick, S. F. (2008). Cultivating therapeutic relationships: The role of mindfulness. In S. F. Hick & T. Bien (Eds.), *Mindfulness and the therapeutic relationship* (pp. 3–18). New York, NY: Guilford Press.

Hickok, G., & Poeppel, D. (2007). The cortical organization of speech processing. *Nature Reviews Neuroscience*, *8*(5), 393–402.

Higgins, E. T. (1997). Beyond pleasure and pain. *American Psychologist*, *52*(12), 1280–1300.

Higgins, E. T. (2000). Making a good decision: Value from fit. *American Psychologist*, *55*(11), 1217–1230.

Higgins, E. T. (2002). How self-regulation creates distinct values: The case of promotion and prevention decision making. *Journal of Consumer Psychology*, *12*(3), 177–191.

Higgins, E. T. (2008). Regulatory fit. In J. Y. Shah & W. L. Gardner (Ed.), *Handbook of motivation science* (pp. 356–372). New York, NY: Guilford Press.

Higgins, E. T. (2011). *Beyond pleasure and pain: How motivation works*. New York, NY: Oxford University Press.

Hilbig, B. E. (2008). Individual differences in fast-and-frugal decision making: Neuroticism and the recognition heuristic. *Journal of Research in Personality*, *42*(6), 1641–1645.

Hilgard, E. R., Leary, D. E., & McGuire, G. R. (1991). The history of psychology: A survey and critical assessment. *Annual Review of Psychology*, *42*(1), 79–107.

Hill, A. K., Dawood, K., & Puts, D. A. (2013). Biological foundations of sexual orientation. In C. J. Patterson & A. R. D'Augelli (Eds.), *Handbook of psychology and sexual orientation* (pp. 55–68). New York, NY: Oxford University Press.

Hill, L. C. (2013). *When the beat was born: DJ Kool Herc and the creation of hip hop*. New York, NY: Roaring Book Press.

Himmel, S., & Himmel, L. (2009). *Hungry: A mother and daughter fight anorexia*. New York, NY: Berkley Books.

Hinduja, S. (2008). Deindividuation and Internet software piracy. *CyberPsychology & Behavior*, *11*(4), 391–398.

Hinduja, S., & Patchin, J. W. (2010) Cyberbullying identification, prevention, and response. http://www.cyberbullying.us/Cyberbullying_Identification_Prevention_Response_Fact_Sheet.pdf

Hinshaw, S. P., & Ellison, K. (2016). *ADHD: What everyone needs to know*. New York, NY: Oxford University Press.

Hinshaw, S. P., & Scheffler, R. M. (2014). *The ADHD explosion: Myths, medication, money, and today's push for performance*. New York, NY: Oxford University Press.

Hinshaw, S. P., Heller, T., & McHale, J. P. (1992). Covert antisocial behavior in boys with attention-deficit hyperactivity disorder: External validation and effects of methylphenidate. *Journal of Consulting and Clinical Psychology*, *60*(2), 274–281.

Hinton, D. E., Hsia, C., Park, L., Rasmussen, A., & Pollack, M. H. (2009). Cultural anthropology and anxiety diagnoses. In D. McKay, J. S. Abramowitz, S. Taylor, & G. J. G. Asmundson (Eds.), *Current perspectives on the anxiety disorders: Implications for DSM-V and beyond* (pp. 245–274). New York, NY: Springer Publishing.

Hirshkowitz, M., & Lee-Chiong, T. (2006). Positive airway pressure therapy for obstructive sleep apnea. In T. L. Lee-Chiong (Ed.), *Sleep: A comprehensive handbook* (pp. 355–364). Hoboken, N.J: Wiley-Liss.

His Holiness the Dalai Lama. (2011). *Beyond religion: Ethics for a whole world*. Boston, MA: Houghton-Mifflin.

Hoagland, H. (1930). The Weber–Fechner law and the all-or-none theory. *The Journal of General Psychology*, *3*(3), 351–373.

Hobson, J. A. (2009). REM sleep and dreaming: Towards a theory of protoconsciousness. *Nature Reviews Neuroscience*, *10*(11), 803–813.

Hobson, J. A., & McCarley R. W. (1977). The brain as a dream state generator: An activation-synthesis hypothesis of the dream process. *American Journal of Psychiatry*, *134*, 1335–1348.

Hock, R. R. (2013). Preface. In R. R. Hock, *Forty studies that changed psychology: Explorations into the history of psychological research* (7th ed., pp. xi–xviii). Upper Saddle River, NJ: Pearson.

Hodapp, R. M., Evans, D. W., and Gray, F. L. (1999). Intellectual development in children with Down syndrome. In J. Rondal, J. Perera, & L. Nadel (Eds.), *Down syndrome: A review of current knowledge* (pp. 124–132). London, UK: Whurr.

Hodapp, R. M., Griffin, M. M., Burke, M. M., & Fisher, M. H. (2011). Intellectual disabilities. In R. J. Sternberg & S. B. Kaufman, *The Cambridge handbook of intelligence* (pp. 193–209). Cambridge, UK: Cambridge University Press.

Hodges, E. V., Boivin, M., Vitaro, F., & Bukowski, W. M. (1999). The power of friendship: Protection against an escalating cycle of peer victimization. *Developmental Psychology, 35*(1), 94–101.

Hodges, J. R. (2000). Memory in the dementias. In E. Tulving & F. I. M. Craik, *The Oxford handbook of memory* (pp. 441–459). Oxford, UK: Oxford University Press.

Hoekstra, S. J., Harris, R. J., & Helmick, A. L. (1999). Autobiographical memories about the experience of seeing frightening movies in childhood. *Media Psychology, 1*(2), 117–140.

Hoelter, L. (2009). Divorce and separation. In D. Carr (Ed.), *Encyclopedia of the life course and human development* (Vol. 2, pp. 100–104). Boston, MA: Gale/Cengage.

Hofer, M. A. (2010). Evolutionary concepts of anxiety. In D. J. Stein, E. Hollander, & B. O. Rothbaum (Eds.), *Textbook of anxiety disorders* (2nd ed., pp. 129–145). Washington, DC: American Psychiatric Association.

Hoffmann, H., Janssen, E., & Turner, S. L. (2004). Classical conditioning of sexual arousal in women and men: Effects of varying awareness and biological relevance of the conditioned stimulus. *Archives of Sexual Behavior, 33*(1), 43–53.

Hofmann, S. G., Alpers, G. W., & Pauli, P. (2009a). Phenomenology of panic and phobic disorders. In M. M. Antony & M. B. Stein (Eds.), *Oxford handbook of anxiety and related disorders* (pp. 34–46). New York, NY: Oxford University Press.

Hofmann, S. G., Asmundson, G. J., & Beck, A. T. (2013). The science of cognitive therapy. *Behavior Therapy, 44*(2), 199–212.

Hofmann, S. G., Richey, J. A., Sawyer, A., Asnaani, A., & Rief, W. (2009b). Social anxiety disorder and the DSM-V. In D. McKay, J. S. Abramowitz, S. Taylor, & G. J. G. Asmundson (Eds.), *Current perspectives on the anxiety disorders: Implications for DSM-V and beyond* (pp. 411–430). New York, NY: Springer Publishing.

Hofmann, S. G., Sawyer, A. T., Witt, A. A., & Oh, D. (2010). The effect of mindfulness-based therapy on anxiety and depression: A meta-analytic review. *Journal of Consulting and Clinical Psychology, 78*(2), 169–183.

Hofstede, G. (1980). *Culture's consequences*. Beverly Hills, CA: SAGE.

Hofstede, G. H. (2001). *Culture's consequences: Comparing values, behaviors, institutions and organizations across nations* (2nd ed.). Thousand Oaks, CA: SAGE.

Hofstede, G. H., Hofstede, G. J., & Minkov, M. (2010). *Cultures and organizations: Software of the mind: International cooperation and its importance for survival* (3rd ed., rev. and expanded). New York, NY: McGraw-Hill.

Hofstede, G. J., Pedersen, P., & Hofstede, G. H. (2002). *Exploring culture: Exercises, stories, and synthetic cultures*. Yarmouth, ME: Intercultural Press.

Hofstede, G., Hofstede, G. J., & Minkov, M. (1997). *Cultures and organizations*. New York, NY: McGraw-Hill.

Hogg, M. A. (2010). Influence and leadership. In S. T. Fiske, D. T. Gilbert, & G. Lindzey (Eds.), *Handbook of social psychology* (5th ed., Vol. 2, pp. 1166–1207). Hoboken, NJ: Wiley.

Hogg, M. A., Terry, D. J., & White, K. M. (1995). A tale of two theories: A critical comparison of identity theory with social identity theory. *Social Psychology Quarterly*, 58(4), 255–269.

Hohmann, J. (2012) Ron Paul says Latinos are being made "scapegoats." http://www.politico.com/news/stories/0212/72336.html#ixzz2L6KVJoXW

Holland, A., & Andre, T. (1987). Participation in extracurricular activities in secondary school: What is known, what needs to be known? *Review of Educational Research, 57*(4), 437–466

Holland, P. C., & Rescorla, R. A. (1975). Second-order conditioning with food unconditioned stimulus. *Journal of Comparative & Physiological Psychology, 88*, 459–467.

Holliday, B. G. (2009). The history and visions of African American psychology: Multiple pathways to place, space, and authority. *Cultural Diversity and Ethnic Minority Psychology, 15*(4), 317–337.

Hollifield, M., Sinclair-Lian, N., Warner, T. D., & Hammerschlag, R. (2007). Acupuncture for posttraumatic stress disorder: A randomized controlled pilot trial. *The Journal of Nervous and Mental Disease, 195*(6), 504–513.

Hollingworth, A. (2009). Memory for real-world scenes. In J. R. Brockmole (Ed.), *The visual world in memory* (pp. 89–116). New York, NY: Psychology Press.

Hollins, M. (2010). Texture perception: Tactile. In E. B. Goldstein (Ed.), *Encyclopedia of perception* (pp. 987–991). Thousand Oaks, CA: SAGE.

Hollis, C. (2003). Developmental precursors of child- and adolescent-onset schizophrenia and affective psychoses: Diagnostic specificity and continuity with symptom dimensions. *British Journal of Psychiatry, 182*, 37–44.

Hollon, S. D., & DiGiuseppe, R. (2011). Cognitive theories of psychotherapy. In J. C. Norcross, G. R. Vandenbos, & D. K. Freedheim (Eds.), *History of psychotherapy: Continuity and change* (2nd ed., pp. 203–242). Washington, DC: American Psychological Association.

Holmes, E. A., Grey, N., & Young, K. A. (2005). Intrusive images and "hotspots" of trauma memories in posttraumatic stress disorder: An exploratory investigation of emotions and cognitive themes. *Journal of Behavior Therapy and Experimental Psychiatry, 36*(1), 3–17.

Holmes, M., & Newman, M. G. (2006). Generalized anxiety disorder. In M. Hersen & J. C. Thomas (Eds.), *Comprehensive handbook of personality and psychopathology* (Vol. 2, pp. 101–120). Hoboken, NJ: Wiley.

Holmes, T. H., & Masuda, M. (1973). Life changes and illness susceptibility. In J. Scott & E. Senay (Eds.) *Separation and depression: Clinical and research aspects* (pp. 161–186). Washington, DC: American Association for the Advancement of Science.

Holmes, T. H., & Rahe, R. H. (1967). The social readjustment rating scale. *Journal of Psychosomatic Research, 11*(2), 213–218.

Holroyd, K. A., & Lazarus, R. S. (1982). Stress, coping, and somatic adaptation. In L. Goldberger & S. Breznitz (Eds.), *Handbook of stress: Theoretical and clinical aspects* (pp. 21–35). New York, NY: Free Press.

Holt, R. R. (1999). Empiricism and the Thematic Apperception Test: Validity is the payoff. In L. Gieser & M. I. Stein (Eds.), *Evocative images: The Thematic Apperception Test and the art of projection* (pp. 99–105). Washington, DC: American Psychological Association.

Hong, J. H., Omur-Ozbek, O., Stanek, B. T., Dietrich, A. M., Duncan, S. E., Lee, Y. W., et al. & Lesser, G. (2009). Taste and odor abnormalities in cancer patients. *The Journal of Supportive Oncology, 7*, 58–65.

Hook, J. N., Davis, D. E., Owen, J., Worthington, E. L., Jr., & Utsey, S. O. (2013). Cultural humility: Measuring openness to culturally diverse clients. *Journal of Counseling Psychology, 60*(3), 353–366.

Hooley, J. M. (2009). Schizophrenia: Interpersonal functioning. In P. H. Blaney & T. Millon (Eds.), *Oxford textbook of psychopathology* (2nd ed., pp. 333–360). New York, NY: Oxford University Press.

Hooley, J. M., & St. Germain, S. (2008). Borderline personality disorder. In W. E. Craighead, D. J. Miklowitz, & L. W. Craighead (Eds.), *Psychopathology: History, diagnosis, and empirical foundations* (pp. 598–630). New York, NY: Wiley.

Hopper, K., Harrison, G., Janca, A., Sartorius, N., & Wiersman, D. (2007). Conclusion. In K. Hopper, G. Harrison, A. Janca, & N. Sartorius (Eds.), Recovery from schizophrenia: An international perspective (pp. 277–282). New York, NY: Oxford University Press.

Horn, J. L., & Cattell, R. B. (1966). Refinement and test of the theory of fluid and crystallized general intelligences. *Journal of Educational Psychology, 57*(5), 253–270.

Horn, J. L., & Noll, J. (1997). Human cognitive capabilities: Gf-Gc theory. In D. P. Flanagan, J. L. Genshaft, & P. L. Harrison (Eds.), *Contemporary intellectual assessment: Theories, tests, and issues* (pp. 53–91). New York, NY: Guilford Press.

Horn, J. P., & Swanson, L. W. (2013). The autonomic motor system and the hypothalamus. In E. R. Kandel, J. H. Schwartz, T. M. Jessell, S. A. Siegelbaum, & A. J. Hudspeth (Eds.), *Principles of neural science* (5th ed., pp. 1056–1078). New York, NY: McGraw-Hill.

Horn, S. S. (2013). Attitudes about sexual orientation. In C. J. Patterson & A. R. D'Augelli (Eds.), *Handbook of psychology and sexual orientation* (pp. 239–251). New York, NY: Oxford University Press.

Horne, J., & Reyner, L. (1999). Vehicle accidents related to sleep: A review. *Occupational and Environmental Medicine, 56*(5), 289–294.

Hornsey, M. J., & Hogg, M. A. (2000). Subgroup relations: A comparison of mutual intergroup differentiation and common ingroup identity models of prejudice reduction. *Personality and Social Psychology Bulletin, 26*(2), 242–256.

Horowitz, S. S. (2012). *The universal sense: How hearing shapes the mind*. New York, NY: Bloomsbury.

Horsley, R. R., Osborne, M., Norman, C., & Wells, T. (2012). High-frequency gamblers show increased resistance to extinction following partial reinforcement. *Behavioural Brain Research, 229*, 438–442.

Horvath, A. O., Del Re, A. C., Flückiger, C., & Symonds, D. (2011). Alliance in individual psychotherapy. In J. C. Norcross (Ed.), *Psychotherapy relationships that work: Evidence-based responsiveness* (2nd ed., pp. 25–69). New York NY: Oxford University Press.

Hosking, S. G., Young, K. L., & Regan, M. A. (2009). The effects of text messaging on young drivers. *Human Factors: The Journal of the Human Factors and Ergonomics Society, 51*(4), 582–592.

Hothersall, D. (2004). *History of psychology*. (4th ed.). New York, NY: Random House.

House, J. S., Landis, K. R., & Umberson, D. (1988). Social relationships and health. *Science, 241*(4865), 540–545.

Houston, B., & Snyder, C. R. (1988). *Type A behavior pattern: Research, theory, and intervention*. Hoboken, NJ: Wiley.

Houston, D. M., Hay-McCutcheon, M. J., Bergeson, T. R., & Miyamoto, R. T. (2010). Cochlear implants: Technology. In E. B. Goldstein (Ed.), *Encyclopedia of perception* (pp. 245–249). Thousand Oaks, CA: SAGE.

Howard, D. E., Debnam, K. J., & Wang, M. Q. (2013). Ten-year trends in physical dating violence victimization among U.S. adolescent females. *Journal of School Health, 83*(6), 389–399.

Howard, M. E., Desai, A. V., Grunstein, R. R., Hukins, C., Armstrong, J. G., Joffe, D., . . . Pierce, R. J. (2004). Sleepiness, sleep-disordered breathing, and accident risk factors in commercial vehicle drivers. *American Journal of Respiratory and Critical Care Medicine, 170*(9), 1014–1021.

Howe, M. L., & Malone, C. (2011). Mood-congruent true and false memory: Effects of depression. *Memory, 19*(2), 192–201.

Howell, M. J., Schenck, C. H., & Crow, S. J. (2009). A review of nighttime eating disorders. *Sleep Medicine Reviews, 13*(1), 23–34.

Howland, R. H. (2005). Biological bases of psychopathology. In J. E. Maddux & B. A. Winstead (Eds.), *Psychopathology* (pp. 109–124). Mahwah, NJ: Lawrence Erlbaum.

Hoza, B., Mrug, S., Pelham, W. E., Greiner, A. R., & Gnagy, E. M. (2003). A friendship intervention for children with attention-deficit/hyperactivity disorder: Preliminary findings. *Journal of Attention Disorders, 6*(3), 87–98.

Hsiao, S. (2010). Cutaneous perception: Physiology. In E. B. Goldstein (Ed.), *Encyclopedia of perception* (pp. 348–354). Thousand Oaks, CA: SAGE.

Hsueh, Y. & Guo, B. (2012). China. In D. B. Baker (Ed.), *The Oxford handbook of the history of psychology: Global perspectives* (pp. 81–124). New York: Oxford University Press.

Huang, C. M., & Park, D. (2013). Cultural influences on Facebook photographs. *International Journal of Psychology, 48*(3), 334–343.

Huang, W., Ramsey, K. M., Marcheva, B., & Bass, J. (2011). Circadian rhythms, sleep, and metabolism. *The Journal of Clinical Investigation, 121*(6), 2133–2141.

Huber, L., & Wilkinson, A. (2010). Evolutionary approach. In E. B. Goldstein (Ed.), *Encyclopedia of perception* (pp. 401–405). Thousand Oaks, CA: SAGE.

Hublin, C., & Kaprio, J. (2003). Genetic aspects and genetic epidemiology of parasomnias. *Sleep Medicine Reviews, 7*(5), 413–421.

Hublin, C., Kaprio, J., Partinen, M., Heikkila, K., & Koskenvuo, M. (1997). Prevalence and genetics of sleepwalking: A population-based twin study. *Neurology, 48*(1), 177–181.

Hudson, J. I., Coit, C. E., Lalonde, J. K., & Pope, H. G. (2012). By how much will the proposed new DSM-5 criteria increase the prevalence of binge eating disorder? *International Journal of Eating Disorders, 45*(1), 139–141.

Hudson, J. L., & Rapee, R. M. (2009). Familial and social environments in the etiology and maintenance of anxiety disorders. In M. M. Antony & M. B. Stein (Eds.), *Oxford handbook of anxiety and related disorders* (pp. 173–189). New York, NY: Oxford University Press.

Huesmann, L. R. (1986). Psychological processes promoting the relation between exposure to media violence and aggressive behavior by the viewer. *Journal of Social Issues, 42*(3), 125–139.

Huesmann, L. R. (2010). Nailing the coffin shut on doubts that violent video games stimulate aggression: Comment on Anderson et al. (2010). *Psychological Bulletin, 136*, 179–181.

Huesmann, L. R., Dubow, E. F., & Boxer, P. (2009). Continuity of aggression from childhood to early adulthood as a predictor of life outcomes: Implications for the adolescent-limited and life-course-persistent models. *Aggressive Behavior, 35*(2), 136–149.

Huesmann, L. R., & Kirwil, L. (2007). Why observing violence increases the risk of violent behavior by the observer. In D. J. Flannery, A. T. Vazsonyi, & I. D. Waldman (Eds.), *The Cambridge handbook of violent behavior and aggression* (pp. 545–570). New York, NY: Cambridge University Press.

Huesmann, L. R., & Miller, L. S. (1994). Long-term effects of repeated exposure to media violence in childhood. In L. R. Huesmann (Ed.), *Aggressive behavior: Current perspective* (pp. 153–186). New York, NY: Plenum Press.

Huesmann, L. R., & Moise, J. (1998). The stability and continuity of aggression from early childhood to young adulthood. In D. J. Flannery & C. R. Huff (Eds.), *Youth violence: Prevention, intervention, and social policy* (pp. 73–95). Washington, DC: American Psychiatric Press.

Huesmann, L. R., Moise-Titus, J., Podolski, C., & Eron, L. D. (2003). Longitudinal relations between children's exposure to TV violence and their aggressive and violent behavior in young adulthood. *Developmental Psychology, 39*, 201–221.

Huey, S. J., Jr., Tilley, J. L., Jones, E. O., & Smith, C. A. (2014). The contribution of cultural competence to evidence-based care for ethnically diverse populations. *Annual Review of Clinical Psychology, 10*, 305–338.

Hughes, D. J., Rowe, M., Batey, M., & Lee, A. (2011). A tale of two sites: Twitter vs. Facebook and the personality predictors of social media usage. *Computers in Human Behavior, 28*(2), 561–562.

Hui, C. H., & Triandis, H. C. (1986). Individualism-collectivism: A study of cross-cultural researchers. *Journal of Cross-Cultural Psychology, 17*(2), 225–248.

Huibers, M. J. H., & Cuijpers, P. (2015). Common (nonspecific) factors in psychotherapy. In R. L. Cautin & S. O. Lilienfeld (Eds.), *The encyclopedia of clinical psychology* (pp. 681–687). West Sussex, UK: Wiley-Blackwell.

Hull, C. (1943). *Principles of behavior*. New York, NY: Appleton-Century-Crofts.

Hull, C. L. (1952). *A behavior system*. New Haven, CT: Yale University Press.

Hulse, S. H. (2002). Auditory scene analysis in animal communication. *Advances in the Study of Behavior, 31*, 163–200.

Hummer, K., Vannatta, J., & Thompson, D. (2011). Locus of control and metabolic control of diabetes: A meta-analysis. *The Diabetes Educator, 37*(1), 104–110.

Hummert, M. L. (2014). Age changes in facial morphology, emotional communication, and age stereotyping. In P. Verhaeghen & C. K. Hertzog (Ed.), *The Oxford handbook of emotion, social cognition, and problem solving in adulthood* (pp. 47–60). New York, NY: Oxford University Press.

Humphreys, G. W., & Riddoch, M. J. (2001). The neuropsychology of visual object and space perception. In E. B. Goldstein (Ed.), *Blackwell handbook of perception* (pp. 204–236). Oxford, UK: Blackwell.

Hunsley, J., Lee, C. M., & Aubry, T. (1999). Who uses psychological services in Canada? *Canadian Psychology, 40*, 232–240.

Hunt, J. M. (1965). Intrinsic motivation and its role in psychological development. In D. Levine (Ed.), *Nebraska symposium on motivation* (Vol. 13, pp. 189–282). Lincoln, NE: University of Nebraska Press.

Hunt, M. H. (1993). *The story of psychology*. New York, NY: Doubleday.

Hunt, M. M. (2007). *The story of psychology* (2nd ed.). New York: Anchor Books.

Huntemann, N., & Morgan, M. (2012). Media and identity development. In D. G. Singer & J. L. Singer (Eds.), *Handbook of children and the media* (2nd ed., pp. 303–319). Los Angeles, CA: SAGE.

Hunter, M. S. (1990). Psychological and somatic experience of the menopause: A prospective study. *Psychosomatic Medicine, 52*(3), 357–367.

Hupp, S., & Jewell, J. (2015). *Great myths of child development*. Malden, MA: Wiley-Blackwell.

Hurley, R., Flashman, L., Chow, T., & Taber, K. (2010). The brainstem: Anatomy, assessment, and clinical syndromes. *Journal of Neuropsychiatry and Clinical Neurosciences, 22*(1), iv–7.

Hurley, R. A., Lucas, D. M., & Taber, K. H. (2013). Structural neuroimaging. In D. B. Arciniegas, C. A. Anderson, & C. M. Filley, *Behavioral neurology & neuropsychiatry* (pp. 415–429). Cambridge, UK: Cambridge University Press.

Hurley, R. A., Taber, K. H., Zhang, & Hayman, L. A. (1999). Neuropsychiatric presentation of multiple sclerosis. *Journal of Neuropsychiatry and Clinical Neurosciences, 11*(1), 5–7.

Hurtz, G. M., & Donovan, J. J. (2000). Personality and job performance: The Big Five revisited. *Journal of Applied Psychology, 85*(6), 869–879.

Huttenlocher, P. R., & Dabholkar, A. S. (1997). Regional differences in synaptogenesis in human cerebral cortex. *Journal of Comparative Neurology, 387*(2), 167–178.

Huynh, V. W. (2012). Ethnic microaggressions and the depressive and somatic symptoms of Latino and Asian American adolescents. *Journal of Youth and Adolescence, 41*(7), 831–846.

Hyde, J. S. (2005). The gender similarities hypothesis. *American Psychologist, 60*(6), 581–592.

Hyde, J. S. (2014). Gender similarities and differences. *Annual Review of Psychology, 65*, 373–398.

Hyde, J. S., Lindberg, S. M., Linn, M. C., Ellis, A. B., & Williams, C. C. (2008). Gender similarities characterize math performance. *Science, 321*(5888), 494–495.

Hymel, S., Closson, L. M., Caravita, S. C. S., & Vaillancourt, T. (2011). Social status among peers: From sociometric attraction to peer acceptance to perceived popularity. In P. K. Smith & C. H. Hart (Eds.), *The Wiley-Blackwell handbook of childhood social development* (2nd ed., pp. 375–392). Malden, MA: Wiley-Blackwell.

Iacoboni, M. (2009). Imitation, empathy, and mirror neurons. *Annual Review of Psychology, 60*, 653–670.

Ibrahim, J. K., Anderson, E. D., Burris, S. C., & Wagenaar, A. C. (2011). State laws restricting driver use of mobile communications devices: Distracted-driving provisions, 1992–2010. *American Journal of Preventive Medicine, 40*(6), 659–665.

If you HAD to give up a sense, which would it be? http://www.quibblo.com/quiz/1JoM1SK/If-you-HAD-to-give-up-a-sense-which-would-it-be. Retrieved May 24, 2015.

Ikeda, M., Iwanaga, M., & Seiwa, H. (1996). Test anxiety and working memory system. *Perceptual and Motor Skills, 82*, 1223–1231.

Illes, J., Moser, M. A., McCormick, J. B., Racine, E., Blakeslee, S., Caplan, A., . . . Weiss, S. (2009). Neurotalk: Improving the communication of neuroscience research. *Nature Reviews Neuroscience, 11*(1), 61–69.

Imai, L., & Gelfand, M. J. (2010). The culturally intelligent negotiator: The impact of cultural intelligence (CQ) on negotiation sequences and outcomes. *Organizational Behavior and Human Decision Processes, 112*(2), 83–98.

Ingham, A. G., Levinger, G., Graves, J., & Peckham, V. (1974). The Ringelmann effect: Studies of group size and group performance. *Journal of Experimental Social Psychology, 10*(4), 371–384.

Ingraham, C. (2015, February 9). How just a couple drinks make your odds of a car crash skyrocket. *Washington Post*. Retrieved from http://www.washingtonpost.com/blogs/wonkblog/wp/2015/02/09/how-just-a-couple-drinks-make-your-odds-of-a-car-crash-skyrocket/

Innes, C. A. (1988). *Drug use and crime*. Washington, DC: U.S. Department of Justice.

Institute of Medicine, (2006). *Food marketing to children and youth: Threat or opportunity?* Washington, DC: National Academies Press.

Ippolito, P. M. (2011). Regulation of food advertising. In J. H. Cawley (Ed.), *The Oxford handbook of the social science of obesity* (pp. 741–751). New York, NY: Oxford University Press.

Irish, D. P., Lundqvist, K. F., & Nelsen, V. J. (Eds.). (1993). *Ethnic variations in dying, death, and grief: Diversity in universality*. New York, NY: Routledge.

Irving, J. A., Farb, N. A. S., & Segal, Z. V. (2015). Mindfulness-based cognitive therapy for chronic depression. In K. W. Brown, J. D. Creswell, & R. M. Ryan (Eds.), *Handbook of mindfulness: Theory, research, and practice* (pp. 348–366). New York, NY: Guilford Press.

Irwin, D. E., & Thomas, L. E. (2008). Visual sensory memory. In S. J. Luck & A. Hollingworth (Eds), *Visual memory* (pp. 9–41). Oxford, UK: Oxford University Press.

Irwin, M. R. (2008). Human psychoneuroimmunology: 20 years of discovery. *Brain, Behavior, and Immunity, 22*(2), 129–139.

Isen, A. M. (2008). Some ways in which positive affect influences decision making and problem solving. In M. Lewis, J. M. Haviland-Jones, & L. F. Barrett (Eds.), *Handbook of emotions* (3rd ed., pp. 548–573). New York, NY: Guilford Press.

Ishikawa-Takata, K., Ohta, T., & Tanaka, H. (2003). How much exercise is required to reduce blood pressure in essential hypertensives: A dose–response study. *American Journal of Hypertension, 16*(8), 629–633.

Israel, T., & Mohr, J. J. (2004). Attitudes toward bisexual women and men: Current research, future directions. *Journal of Bisexuality, 4*(12), 117–134.

Itzkoff, D. (2014, August 11). Robin Williams, Oscar-winning comedian, dies at 63. *New York Times*.

Ivanenko, A., & Larson, K. (2013). Nighttime distractions: Fears, nightmares, and parasomnias. In A. R. Wolfson & H. Montgomery-Downs (Eds.), *The Oxford handbook of infant, child, and adolescent sleep and behavior* (pp. 347–361). New York, NY: Oxford University Press.

Iverson, G. L., Brooks, B. L., Lovell, M. R., & Collins, M. W. (2006). No cumulative effects for one or two previous concussions. *British Journal of Sports Medicine, 40*(1), 72–75.

Iverson, G. L., Gaetz, M., Lovell, M. R., & Collins, M. W. (2004). Cumulative effects of concussion in amateur athletes. *Brain Injury, 18*(5), 433–443.

Jackendoff, R. (2012). Language. In K. Frankish & W. M. Ramsey (Eds.), *The Cambridge handbook of cognitive science* (pp. 171–192). Cambridge, UK: Cambridge University Press.

Jackson, D. D. (1960). *The etiology of schizophrenia*. New York: Basic Books.

Jackson, S. A. (1995). Factors influencing the occurrence of flow state in elite athletes. *Journal of Applied Sport Psychology, 7*(2), 138–166.

Jackson, S. A. (2012). Flow. In R. M. Ryan (Ed.), *The Oxford handbook of human motivation* (pp. 127–140). New York, NY: Oxford University Press.

Jackson, S. A., & Csikszentmihalyi, M. (1999). *Flow in sports: The keys to optimal experiences and performances*. Champaign, IL: Human Kinetics.

Jacobellis v. Ohio, 378 U.S. 184 (1964).

Jacobi, C., & Fittig, E. (2010). Psychosocial risk factors for eating disorders. In W. S. Agras (Ed.), *The Oxford handbook of eating disorders* (pp. 123–136). New York, NY: Oxford University Press.

Jacobs, B., & Gundling, K. (2009). Complementary and alternative medicine: Definitions and patterns of use. In B. P. Jacobs & K. Gundling (Eds.), *The ACP evidence-based guide to complementary and alternative medicine* (pp. 3–22). Philadelphia, PA: American College of Physicians.

Jacobs, G. D., Pace-Schott, E. F., Stickgold, R., & Otto, M. W. (2004). Cognitive behavior therapy and pharmacotherapy for insomnia: A randomized controlled trial and direct comparison. *Archives of Internal Medicine, 164*(17), 1888–1896.

Jacobs, G. H. (2009). Evolution of colour vision in mammals. *Philosophical Transactions of the Royal Society B: Biological Sciences, 364*(1531), 2957–2967.

Jacobson, B. H., Chen, H. C., Cashel, C., & Guerrero, L. (1997). The effect of T'ai Chi Chuan training on balance, kinesthetic sense, and strength. *Perceptual and Motor Skills, 84*(1), 27–33.

Jadva, V., Hines, M., & Golombok, S. (2010). Infants' preferences for toys, colors, and shapes: Sex differences and similarities. *Archives of Sexual Behavior, 39*(6), 1261–1273.

Jaffee, S., & Hyde, J. S. (2000). Gender differences in moral orientation: A meta-analysis. *Psychological Bulletin, 126*(5), 703–726.

Jagers, R. J., Morgan-Lopez, A. A., Howard, T. L., Browne, D. C., & Flay, B. R. (2007). Mediators of the development and prevention of violent behavior. *Prevention Science, 8*(3), 171–179.

Jakobsen, K. V. (2012). Applying for academic positions. In P. J. Giordano, S. F. Davis, & C. A. Licht (Eds.), *Your graduate training in psychology: Effective strategies for success* (pp. 279–294). Los Angeles: SAGE Publications.

James, C. (2009). *Young people, ethics, and the new digital media: A synthesis from the GoodPlay Project*. Cambridge, MA: MIT Press.

James, W. (1884). What is an emotion? *Mind, 9*, 188–205.

James, W. (1890), *The principles of psychology*. Cambridge, MA: Harvard University Press.

James, W. (1981). *The principles of psychology* (Vols. 1–2). Cambridge, MA: Harvard University Press. (Original work published in 1890.)

Jamieson, J. P., Nock, M. K., & Mendes, W. B. (2012). Mind over matter: Reappraising arousal improves cardiovascular and cognitive responses to stress. *Journal of Experimental Psychology: General, 141*(3), 417–422.

Jamison, K. R. (1989). Mood disorders and patterns of creativity in British writers and artists. *Psychiatry: Interpersonal and Biological Processes, 52*(2), 125–134.

Jamison, K. R. (1993). *Touched with fire: Manic-depressive illness and the artistic temperament*. New York, NY: Free Press.

Jang, K. L., Livesley, W. J., & Vernon, P. A. (1996). Heritability of the Big Five personality dimensions and their facets: A twin study. *Journal of Personality, 64*(3), 577–591.

Janis, I. L. (1982). *Groupthink: Psychological studies of policy decisions and fiascoes*. Boston: Houghton Mifflin.

Javitt, D. C., & Laruelle, M. (2006). Neurochemical theories. In J. A. Lieberman, T. S. Stroup, & D. O. Perkins (Eds.), *The American Psychiatric Publishing textbook of schizophrenia* (pp. 85–116). Washington, DC: American Psychiatric Association.

Jeffery, R. W., Wing, R. R., Sherwood, N. E., & Tate, D. F. (2003). Physical activity and weight loss: Does prescribing higher physical activity goals improve outcome? *The American Journal of Clinical Nutrition, 78*(4), 684–689.

Jenni, O. G., & O'Connor, B. B. (2005). Children's sleep: An interplay between culture and biology. *Pediatrics, 115*(Suppl. 1), 204–216.

Jensen, M. P, & Patterson, D. R. (2008). Hypnosis in the relief of pain and pain disorders. In M. R. Nash & A. J. Barnier (Eds.), *The Oxford handbook of hypnosis: Theory, research, and practice* (pp. 503–534). Oxford, UK: Oxford University Press.

Jeong, S. H. (2007). Effects of news about genetics and obesity on controllability attribution and helping behavior. *Health Communication, 22*(3), 221–228.

Jessell, T. M., & Sanes, J. R. (2013). Differentiation and survival of nerve cells. In E. R. Kandel, J. H. Schwartz, T. M. Jessell, S. A. Siegelbaum, & A. J. Hudspeth (Eds.), *Principles of neural science* (5th ed., pp. 1187–1208). New York, NY: McGraw-Hill.

Jewett, M. E., Wyatt, J. K., Ritz-De Cecco, A., Khalsa, S. B., Dijk, D.-J., & Czeisler, C. A. (1999). Time course of sleep inertia dissipation in human performance and alertness. *Journal of Sleep Research, 8*(1), 1–8.

Ji, J., Zöller, B., Sundquist, K., & Sundquist, J. (2012). Increased risks of coronary heart disease and stroke among spousal caregivers of cancer patients. *Circulation, 125*(14), 1742–1747.

Ji, L. J., Peng, K., & Nisbett, R. E. (2000). Culture, control, and perception of relationships in the environment. *Journal of Personality and Social Psychology, 78*(5), 943–955.

Ji, L. J., Zhang, Z., & Nisbett, R. E. (2004). Is it culture or is it language? Examination of language effects in cross-cultural research on categorization. *Journal of Personality and Social Psychology, 87*(1), 57–65.

Jiang, X. L., & Cillessen, A. H. (2005). Stability of continuous measures of sociometric status: A meta-analysis. *Developmental Review, 25*(1), 1–25.

Jiang, Y. V., Makovski, T., & Shim, W. M. (2009). Visual memory for features, conjunctions, objects, and locations. In J. R. Brockmole (Ed.), *The visual world in memory* (pp. 33–65). New York, NY: Psychology Press.

Johanson, A., Risberg, J., Tucker, D. M., & Gustafson, L. (2006). Changes in frontal lobe activity with cognitive therapy for spider phobia. *Applied Neuropsychology, 13*(1), 34–41.

Johansson, P., Høglend, P., Ulberg, R., Amlo, S., Marble, A., Bøgwald, K., . . . Heyerdahl, O. (2010). The mediating role of insight for long-term improvements in psychodynamic therapy. *Journal of Consulting and Clinical Psychology, 78*(3), 438–448.

John, O. P., & Gross, J. J. (2004). Healthy and unhealthy emotion regulation: Personality processes, individual differences, and life span development. *Journal of Personality, 72*(6), 1301–1334.

John, O. P., Naumann, L. P., & Soto, C. J. (2008). Paradigm shift to the integrative Big Five trait taxonomy: History, measurement, and conceptual issues. In O. P. John, R. W. Robins, & L. A. Pervin (Eds.) *Handbook of personality: Theory and research* (3rd ed., pp. 114–158). New York, NY: Guilford Press.

Johnson, J. G., Cohen, P., Kasen, S., & Brook, J. S. (2006). Dissociative disorders among adults in the community, impaired functioning, and axis I and II comorbidity. *Journal of Psychiatric Research, 40*(2), 131–140.

Johnson, K. E. (2013). Culture, expertise, and mental categories. In D. Reisberg (Ed.), *The Oxford handbook of cognitive psychology* (pp. 330–345). Oxford, UK: Oxford University Press.

Johnson, K. E., & Mervis, C. B. (1997). Effects of varying levels of expertise on the basic level of categorization. *Journal of Experimental Psychology: General, 126*(3), 248–277.

Johnson, K. J., & Fredrickson, B. L. (2005). "We all look the same to me": Positive emotions eliminate the own-race bias in face recognition. *Psychological Science, 16*(11), 875–881.

Johnson, K. L., & Tassinary, L. G. (2007). Compatibility of basic social perceptions determines perceived attractiveness. *Proceedings of the National Academy of Sciences, 104*(12), 5246–5251.

Johnson, M. H., Dziurawiec, S., Ellis, H., & Morton, J. (1991). Newborns' preferential tracking of face-like stimuli and its subsequent decline. *Cognition, 40*(1), 1–19.

Johnson, M. K., Hashtroudi, S., & Lindsay, D. S. (1993). Source monitoring. *Psychological Bulletin, 114*(1), 3–28.

Johnson, S. L., Cuellar, A. K., & Miller, C. (2009). Bipolar and unipolar depression: A comparison of clinical phenomenology, biological vulnerability, and psychosocial predictors. In I. H. Gotlib & C. L. Hammen (Eds.), *Handbook of depression* (2nd ed., pp. 142–162). New York, NY: Guilford Press.

Johnson, T. P., Shavitt, S., & Holbrook, A. L. (2011). Survey response styles across cultures. In D. Matsumoto & F. J. R. van de Vijver (Eds.), *Cross-cultural research methods in psychology* (pp. 130–177). New York, NY: Cambridge University Press.

Johnston, J. M. (1972). Punishment of human behavior. *American Psychologist, 27*(11), 1033.

Johnstone, T., Somerville, L. H., Alexander, A. L., Oakes, T. R., Davidson, R. J., Kalin, N. H., & Whalen, P. J. (2005). Stability of amygdala BOLD response to fearful faces over multiple scan sessions. *Neuroimage, 25*(4), 1112–1123

Jolliffe, D., & Farrington, D. P. (2006). Examining the relationship between low empathy and bullying. *Aggressive Behavior, 32*(6), 540–550.

Jolliffe, D., & Farrington, D. P. (2011). Is low empathy related to bullying after controlling for individual and social background variables? *Journal of Adolescence, 34*(1), 59–71.

Jones, B. C., Little, A. C., Burt, D. M., & Perrett, D. I. (2004). When facial attractiveness is only skin deep. *Perception, 33*(5), 569–576.

Jones, C. M. (2013). Heroin use and heroin use risk behaviors among nonmedical users of prescription opioid pain relievers – United States, 2002–2004 and 2008–2010. *Drug and Alcohol Dependence, 132*(1), 95–100.

Jones, D., & Hill, K. (1993). Criteria of facial attractiveness in five populations. *Human Nature, 4*(3), 271–296.

Jones, E. E., & Harris, V. A. (1967). The attribution of attitudes. *Journal of Experimental Social Psychology, 3*(1), 1–24.

Jones, G. V., & Martin, M. (2004). Orientation illusions in memory. In R. F. Pohl (Ed.), *Cognitive illusions: A handbook on fallacies and biases in thinking, judgement, and memory* (pp. 293–308). East Sussex, UK: Psychology Press.

Jones, J. M. (1997). *Prejudice and racism*. New York, NY: McGraw-Hill.

Jones, K. L., & Streissguth, A. P. (2010). Fetal alcohol syndrome and fetal alcohol spectrum disorders: A brief history. *Journal of Psychiatry and Law, 38*, 373–382.

Jones, L. A. (2010). Temperature perception. In E. B. Goldstein (Ed.), *Encyclopedia of perception* (pp. 983–987). Thousand Oaks, CA: SAGE.

Jones-Corneille, L. R., Stack, R. M., & Wadden, T. A. (2011). Behavioral treatment of obesity. In J. H. Cawley (Ed.), *The Oxford handbook of the social science of obesity* (pp. 771–791). New York, NY: Oxford University Press.

Joormann, J. (2009). Cognitive aspects of depression. In I. H. Gotlib & C. L. Hammen (Eds.), *Handbook of depression* (2nd ed., pp. 298–321). New York, NY: Guilford Press.

Joormann, J., & Siemer, M. (2004). Memory accessibility, mood regulation, and dysphoria: Difficulties in repairing sad mood with happy memories? *Journal of Abnormal Psychology*, *113*(2), 179–188.

Jorm, A. F., Korten, A. E., Jacomb, P. A., Rodgers, B., & Pollitt, P. (1997). Beliefs about the helpfulness of interventions for mental disorders: A comparison of general practitioners, psychiatrists and clinical psychologists. *Australian and New Zealand Journal of Psychiatry*, *31*(6), 844–851.

Jose, A., O'Leary, K. D., Moyer, A., & Buehler, C. (2010). Does premarital cohabitation predict subsequent marital stability and marital quality? A meta-analysis. *Journal of Marriage and Family*, *72*(1), 105–116.

Josephson, B. R. (1996). Mood regulation and memory: Repairing sad moods with happy memories. *Cognition & Emotion*, *10*(4), 437–444.

Josephson, W. L. (1987). Television violence and children's aggression: Testing the priming, social script, and disinhibition predictions. *Journal of Personality and Social Psychology*, *53*(5), 882–890.

Jouvet, M., Michel, F., & Courjon, J. (1959). On a stage of rapid cerebral electrical activity in the course of physiological sleep. *Comptes Rendus des Seances de la Societe de Biologie et de Ses Filiales*, *153*, 1024–1028.

Joy, J., McClure, N., Hepper, P. G., & Cooke, I. (2012). Fetal habituation in assisted conception. *Early Human Development*, *88*(6), 431–436.

Junco, R. (2012). Too much face and not enough books: The relationship between multiple indices of Facebook use and academic performance. *Computers in Human Behavior*, *28*(1), 187–198.

Junco, R. (2013a). Inequalities in Facebook use. *Computers in Human Behavior*, *29*(6), 2328–2336.

Junco, R. (2013b). Comparing actual and self-reported measures of Facebook use. *Computers in Human behavior*, *29*(3), 626–631.

Jung, C. G. (1963). *Memories, dreams, reflections*. New York, NY: Random House.

Jung, C. G. (1964). *Man and his symbols*. New York, NY: Doubleday.

Jung, C. G. (1971). *Psychological types*. Princeton, NJ: Princeton University Press.

Jung, K., Shavitt, S., Viswanathan, M., & Hilbe, J. M. (2014). Female hurricanes are deadlier than male hurricanes. *Proceedings of the National Academy of Sciences*, *111*(24), 8782–8787.

Kabat-Zinn, J. (1994). *Wherever you go, there you are: Mindfulness meditation in everyday life*. New York, NY: Hyperion.

Kagan, J., & Fox, N. A. (2006). Biology, culture, and temperamental biases. In N. Eisenberg (Vol. Ed.), *Handbook of child psychology* (6th ed., Vol. 3, pp. 167–225). Hoboken, NJ: Wiley.

Kagan, J., & Snidman, N. (1999). Early childhood predictors of adult anxiety disorders. *Biological Psychiatry*, *46*(11), 1536–1541.

Kagan, J., & Snidman, N. C. (2004). *The long shadow of temperament*. Cambridge, MA: Belknap Press of Harvard University Press.

Kagan, J., Snidman, N., Arcus, D., & Reznick, J. S. (1994). *Galen's prophecy: Temperament in human nature*. New York, NY: Basic Books.

Kahana, M. J. (2000). Contingency analyses of memory. In E. Tulving & F. I. M. Craik, *The Oxford handbook of memory* (pp. 59–72). Oxford, UK: Oxford University Press.

Kahneman, D. (1999). Objective happiness. In D. Kahneman, E. Diener, & N. Schwarz (Eds.), *Well-being: The foundations of hedonic psychology* (pp. 758–774). New York, NY: Russell Sage Foundation.

Kahneman, D. (2000). New challenges to the rationality assumption. In D. Kahneman & A. Tversky (Eds.), *Choices, values, and frames* (pp. 758–774). New York: Russell Sage Foundation.

Kahneman, D. (2011). *Thinking, fast and slow*. New York, NY: Farrar, Straus, and Giroux.

Kahneman, D., & Fredrick, S. (2002). Representativeness revisited: Attribute substitution in intuitive judgement. In T. Gilovich, D. W. Griffin, & D. Kahneman (Eds.), *Heuristics and biases: The psychology of intuitive judgment* (pp. 49–81). New York, NY: Cambridge University Press.

Kahneman, D., & Fredrick, S. (2005). A model of heuristic judgement. In K. J. Holyoak & R. G. Morrison (Eds.), *The Cambridge handbook of thinking and reasoning* (pp. 267–293). New York, NY: Cambridge University Press.

Kahneman, D., Fredrickson, B. L., Schreiber, C. A., & Redelmeier, D. A. (1993). When more pain is preferred to less: Adding a better end. *Psychological Science*, *4*(6), 401–405.

Kahneman, D., & Tversky, A. (1972). Subjective probability: A judgment of representativeness. *Cognitive Psychology*, *3*(3), 430–454.

Kahneman, D., & Tversky, A. (1973). On the psychology of prediction. *Psychology Review*, *80*, 237–251.

Kahneman, D., & Tversky, A. (1979). Prospect theory: An analysis of decision under risk. *Econometrica: Journal of the Econometric Society*, *47*(2), 263–291.

Kahneman, D., & Tversky, A. (1996). On the reality of cognitive illusions. *Psychological Review*, *103*(3), 582–591.

Kahneman, D., & Tversky, A. (2000). *Choices, values, and frames*. New York, NY: Cambridge University Press.

Kalaska, J. F. & Rizzolatti, G. (2013). Voluntary movement: The primary motor cortex. In E. R. Kandel, J. H. Schwartz, T. M. Jessell, S. A. Siegelbaum, & A. J. Hudspeth (Eds.), *Principles of neural science* (5th ed., pp. 835–864). New York. NY: McGraw-Hill.

Kalmuss, D., Davidson, A., & Cushman, L. (1992). Parenting expectations, experiences, and adjustment to parenthood: A test of the violated expectations framework. *Journal of Marriage and the Family*, *54*(3), 516–526.

Kalpidou, M., Costin, D., & Morris, J. (2011). The relationship between Facebook and the well-being of undergraduate college students. *Cyberpsychology, Behavior, and Social Networking*, *14*(4), 183–189.

Kälviäinen, R., Salmenperä, T., Partanen, K., Vainio, P., Riekkinen, P., & Pitkänen, A. (1998). Recurrent seizures may cause hippocampal damage in temporal lobe epilepsy. *Neurology*, *50*(5), 1377–1382.

Kamphaus, R. W., & Kroncke, A. P. (2004). "Back to the future" of the Stanford-Binet Intelligence Scales. In M. Hersen (Ed.-in-Chief), *Comprehensive handbook of psychological assessment* (Vol. 1, pp. 77–86). New York, NY: Wiley.

Kandel, E. R., Barres, B. A., & Hudspeth, A. J. (2013). Nerve cells, neural circuitry, and behavior. In E. R. Kandel, J. H. Schwartz, T. M. Jessell, S. A. Siegelbaum, & A. J. Hudspeth (Eds.), *Principles of neural science* (5th ed., pp. 21–38). New York, NY: McGraw-Hill.

Kandel, E. R., & Hudspeth, A. J. (2013). The brain and behavior. In E. R. Kandel, J. H. Schwartz, T. M. Jessell, S. A. Siegelbaum, & A. J. Hudspeth (Eds.), *Principles of neural science* (5th ed., pp. 5–20). New York, NY: McGraw-Hill.

Kandel, E. R., & Siegelbaum, S. A. (2013). Cellular mechanisms of implicit memory storage and the biological basis of individuality. In E. R. Kandel, J. H. Schwartz, T. M. Jessell, S. A. Siegelbaum, & A. J. Hudspeth (Eds.), *Principles of neural science* (5th ed., pp. 1461–1486). New York, NY: McGraw-Hill.

Kanner, A. D., Coyne, J. C., Schaefer, C., & Lazarus, R. S. (1981). Comparison of two modes of stress measurement: Daily hassles and uplifts versus major life events. *Journal of Behavioral Medicine*, *4*(1), 1–39.

Kanwisher, N., McDermott, J., & Chun, M. M. (1997). The fusiform face area: A module in human extrastriate cortex specialized for face perception. *The Journal of Neuroscience*, *17*(11), 4302–4311.

Kapen, S. (2006). Medical treatment of obstructive sleep apnea: Life-style changes, weight reduction, and postural therapy. In T. L. Lee-Chiong (Ed.), *Sleep: A comprehensive handbook* (pp. 33–346). Hoboken, NJ: Wiley-Liss.

Kaplan, A., & Midgley, C. (1997). The effect of achievement goals: Does level of perceived academic competence make a difference? *Contemporary Educational Psychology*, *22*(4), 415–435.

Kaplan, K. A., & Harvey, A. G. (2013). Behavioral treatment of insomnia in bipolar disorder. *American Journal of Psychiatry*, *170*(7), 716–720.

Kaplowitz, P. B. (2008). Link between body fat and the timing of puberty. *Pediatrics*, *121*(Suppl. 3), S208–S217.

Kapur, N., Thompson, P., Kartsounis, L. D., & Abbott, P. (1998). Retrograde amnesia: Clinical and methodological caveats. *Neuropsychologia*, *37*(1), 27–30.

Kapur, S., Craik, F. I., Tulving, E., Wilson, A. A., Houle, S., & Brown, G. M. (1994). Neuroanatomical correlates of encoding in episodic memory: Levels of processing effect. *Proceedings of the National Academy of Sciences*, *91*(6), 2008–2011.

Karau, S. J., & Williams, K. D. (1993). Social loafing: A meta-analytic review and theoretical integration. *Journal of Personality and Social Psychology*, *65*(4), 681–706.

Karni, A., Tanne, D., Rubenstein, B. S., Askenasy, J. J., & Sagi, D. (1994). Dependence on REM sleep of overnight improvement of a perceptual skill. *Science*, *265*(5172), 679–682.

Karon, B. P., & Widener, A. J. (1995). Psychodynamic therapies in historical perspective: "Nothing human do I consider alien to me." In B. Bongar & L. E. Beutler (Eds.), *Comprehensive textbook of psychotherapy: Theory and practice* (pp. 24–47). New York, NY: Oxford University Press.

Kaslow, F. W. (2011). Treatment modalities: Family therapy. In J. C. Norcross, G. R. Vandenbos, & D. K. Freedheim (Eds.), *History of psychotherapy: Continuity and change* (2nd ed., pp. 497–504). Washington, DC: American Psychological Association.

Kaslow, N. J., Davis, S. P., & Smith, C. O. (2009). Biological and psychosocial interventions for depression in children and adolescents. In I. H. Gotlib & C. L. Hammen (Eds.), *Handbook of depression* (2nd ed., pp. 642–671). New York, NY: Guilford Press.

Kassan, L. D. (1999). *Second opinions: Sixty psychotherapy patients evaluate their therapists*. Northvale, NJ: Aronson.

Kasser, T., & Ryan, R. M. (1993). A dark side of the American dream: Correlates of financial success as a central life aspiration. *Journal of Personality and Social Psychology*, *65*(2), 410.

Kasser, T., & Ryan, R. M. (1996). Further examining the American dream: Differential correlates of intrinsic and extrinsic goals. *Personality and Social Psychology Bulletin*, *22*(3), 280–287.

Katzman, D. K., Kanbur, N. O., & Steinegger, C. M. (2010). Medical screening and management of eating disorders in adolescents. In W. S. Agras (Ed.), *The Oxford handbook of eating disorders* (pp. 267–291). New York, NY: Oxford University Press.

Kaufman, J. C., & Beghetto, R. A. (2009). Beyond big and little: The Four C model of creativity. *Review of General Psychology*, *13*(1), 1–12.

Kaufman, J. C., Kaufman, S. B., & Plucker, J. A. (2013). Contemporary theories of intelligence. In D. Reisberg (Ed.), *The Oxford handbook of cognitive psychology* (pp. 811–822). Oxford, UK: Oxford University Press.

Kaufman, S. B., DeYoung, C. G., Gray, J. R., Jiménez, L., Brown, J., & Mackintosh, N. (2010). Implicit learning as an ability. *Cognition*, *116*(3), 321–340.

Kaufman, S. B., Reynolds, M. R., Liu, X., Kaufman, A. S., & McGrew, K. S. (2012). Are cognitive *g* and academic achievement *g* one and the same *g*: An exploration on the Woodcock–Johnson and Kaufman tests. *Intelligence, 40*(2), 123–138.

Kavanau, J. L. (2004). Sleep researchers need to bring Darwin on board: Elucidating functions of sleep via adaptedness and natural selection. *Medical Hypotheses, 62*(2), 161–165.

Kavanau, J. L. (2005). Evolutionary approaches to understanding sleep. *Sleep Medicine Reviews, 9*(2), 141–152.

Kavanau, J. L. (2006). Is sleep's "supreme mystery" unraveling? An evolutionary analysis of sleep encounters no mystery; nor does life's earliest sleep, recently discovered in jellyfish. *Medical Hypotheses, 66*(1), 3-9.

Kavanau, J. L. (2008). Sleepless in the sea. *Science* (Letters), *322*(5901), 527.

Kay, P., & Regier, T. (2006). Language, thought and color: Recent developments. *Trends in Cognitive Sciences, 10*(2), 51–54.

Kay, P., & Regier, T. (2007). Color naming universals: The case of Berinmo. *Cognition, 102*(2), 289–298.

Kaye, J. M., & Lightman, S. L. (2005). Psychological stress and endocrine axes. In K. Vedhara & M. Irwin (Eds.), *Human psychoneuroimmunology* (pp. 25–52). New York, NY: Oxford University Press.

Kaye, W. H., & Oberndorfer, T. (2010). Appetitive regulation in anorexia nervosa and bulimia nervosa. In W. S. Agras (Ed.), *The Oxford handbook of eating disorders* (pp. 75–102). New York, NY: Oxford University Press.

Kayyal, M. H., & Russell, J. A. (2013). Americans and Palestinians judge spontaneous facial expressions of emotion. *Emotion, 13*(5), 891–904.

Kazdin, A. E. (1978). *History of behavior modification: Experimental foundations of contemporary research*. Baltimore, MD: University Park Press.

Kazdin, A. E. (1978). *History of behavior modification: Experimental foundations of contemporary research*. Baltimore, MD: University Park Press.

Kazdin, A. E. (2011). *Single-case research designs: Methods for clinical and applied settings* (2nd ed.). New York, NY: Oxford University Press.

Kazdin, A. E. (2013). Publishing your research. In M. J. Prinstein (Ed.), *The portable mentor: Expert guide to a successful career in psychology* (pp. 145–161). New York, NY: Springer.

Kealey, D. J. (1989). A study of cross-cultural effectiveness: Theoretical issues, practical applications. *International Journal of Intercultural Relations, 13*(3), 387–428.

Keane, T. M., Fairbank, J. A., Caddell, J. M., & Zimering, R. T. (1989). Implosive (flooding) therapy reduces symptoms of PTSD in Vietnam combat veterans. *Behavior Therapy, 20*(2), 245–260.

Keane, T. M., Marx, B. P., & Sloan, D. M. (2009). Post-traumatic stress disorder: Definition, prevalence, and risk factors. In P. J. Shiromani, T. M. Keane, & J. E. LeDoux (Eds.), *Post-traumatic stress disorder: Basic science and clinical practice*, (pp.1–19). New York, NY: Humana.

Kearney, C. A., & Vecchio, J. (2002). Contingency management. In M. Hersen & W. Sledge (Eds.), *Encyclopedia of psychotherapy* (Vol. 1, pp. 525–532). San Diego, CA: Academic Press.

Keck, P. E., Jr. & McElroy, S. L. (2006). Lithium and mood stabilizers. In D. J. Stein, D. J. Kupfer, & A. F. Schatzberg (Eds.), *The American Psychiatric Publishing textbook of mood disorders* (pp. 281–290). Washington, DC: American Psychiatric Publishing.

Keck, P. E., Jr. & McElroy, S. L. (2007). Pharmacological treatments for bipolar disorder. In P. E. Nathan & J. M. Gorman (Eds.), *A guide to treatments that work* (3rd ed., pp. 323–350). New York, NY: Oxford University Press.

Keefe, R. S. E., & Eesley, C. E. (2006). Neurocognitive impairments. In J. A. Lieberman, T. S. Stroup, & D. O. Perkins (Eds.), *The American Psychiatric Publishing textbook of schizophrenia* (pp. 245–260). Washington, DC: American Psychiatric Association Publishing.

Keel, P. K. (2010). Epidemiology and course of eating disorders. In W. S. Agras (Ed.), *The Oxford handbook of eating disorders* (pp. 25–32). New York, NY: Oxford University Press.

Keel, P. K., & McCormick, L. (2010). Diagnosis, assessment, and treatment planning for anorexia nervosa. In C. M. Grilo & J. E. Mitchell (Eds.), *The treatment of eating disorders: A clinical handbook* (pp. 3–27). New York, NY: Guilford Press.

Keen, E. (2001). *A history of ideas in American psychology*. Westport, CT: Praeger.

Keen, R. E., & Berthier, N. E. (2004). Continuities and discontinuities in infants' representation of objects and events. In R. V. Kail (Ed.), *Advances in Child Development and Behavior, 32*, 243–279.

Keeney, R. L., & Raiffa, H. (1993). *Decisions with multiple objectives: Preferences and value trade-offs*. Cambridge, UK: Cambridge University Press.

Keeping, J. (2006). How does the bird build its nest? Instincts as embodied meaning. *Phenomenology and the Cognitive Sciences, 5*(2), 171–195.

Kegl, J., Senghas, A., and Coppola, M. (1999). Creations through contact: Sign language emergence and sign language change in Nicaragua. In M. DeGraff (Ed.), *Language creation and language change* (pp. 179–237). Cambridge, MA: MIT Press.

Kehoe, E. J., & Macrae, M. (1998). Classical conditioning. In W. O'Donohue (Ed.), *Learning and behavior therapy* (pp. 36–58). Boston, MA: Allyn and Bacon.

Keil, F. (2006). Cognitive science and cognitive development. In D. Kuhn & R. Siegler (Vol. Eds.), *Handbook of child psychology* (6th ed., Vol. 2, pp. 609–635). Hoboken, NJ: Wiley.

Keith, K. D. (2012). Visual illusions and ethnocentrism: Exemplars for teaching cross-cultural concepts. *History of Psychology, 15*(2), 171–176.

Keller, A., Litzelman, K., Wisk, L. E., Maddox, T., Cheng, E. R., Creswell, P. D., & Witt, W. P. (2012). Does the perception that stress affects health matter? The association with health and mortality. *Health Psychology, 31*(5), 677–684.

Keller, M. A., & Goldberg, W. A. (2004). Co-sleeping: Help or hindrance for young children's independence? *Infant and Child Development, 13*(5), 369–388.

Keller, M. C., & Miller, G. (2006). Resolving the paradox of common, harmful, heritable mental disorders: Which evolutionary genetic models work best? *Behavioral and Brain Sciences, 29*(4), 385–404.

Keller, R. R. (2014). Religious diversity in North America. In P. S. Richards and A. E. Bergin (Eds.), *Handbook of psychotherapy and religious diversity* (2nd ed., pp. 21–50). Washington, DC: American Psychological Association.

Kelley, A. E., & Berridge, K. C. (2002). The neuroscience of natural rewards: relevance to addictive drugs. *The Journal of Neuroscience, 22*(9), 3306–3311.

Kelley, H. H. (1950). The warm-cold variable in first impressions of persons. *Journal of Personality, 18*(4), 431–439.

Kelley, H. H. (1973). The processes of causal attribution. *American Psychologist, 28*(2), 107–128.

Kellman, P. J. & Arterberry, M. E. (2006). Infant visual perception. In D. Kuhn & R. Siegler (Vol. Eds.), *Handbook of child psychology* (6th ed., Vol. 2, pp. 109–160). Hoboken, NJ: Wiley.

Keltner, D., & Kring, A. M. (1998). Emotion, social function, and psychopathology. *Review of General Psychology, 2*(3), 320–342.

Kemeny, M. E. (2011). Psychoneuroimmunology. In H. S. Friedman (Ed.), *The Oxford handbook of health psychology* (pp. 138–161). Oxford, UK: Oxford University Press.

Kemp, N. (2010). Texting versus txtng: Reading and writing text messages, and links with other linguistic skills. *Writing Systems Research, 2*(1), 53–71.

Kemp, N., & Bushnell, C. (2011). Children's text messaging: Abbreviations, input methods, and links with literacy. *Journal of Computer Assisted Learning, 27*(1), 18–27.

Kempermann, G., Kuhn, H. G., & Gage, F. H. (1997). More hippocampal neurons in adult mice living in an enriched environment. *Nature, 386*(6624), 493–495.

Kendall-Tackett, K. A. (2005a). Introduction: Women's experiences of stress and trauma. In K. A. Kendall-Tackett (Ed.), *Handbook of women, stress, and trauma* (pp. 1–5). New York, NY: Brunner-Routledge.

Kendall-Tackett, K. A. (2005b). Caught in the middle: Stress in the lives of young adult women. In K. A. Kendall-Tackett (Ed.), *Handbook of women, stress, and trauma* (pp. 33–52). New York, NY: Brunner-Routledge.

Kendall-Tackett, K. A. (2005c). Trauma associated with perinatal events: Birth experience, prematurity, and childbearing loss. In K. A. Kendall-Tackett, *Handbook of women, stress, and trauma* (pp. 53–74). New York, NY: Brunner-Routledge.

Kendler, K. S., & Diehl, S. R. (1993). The genetics of schizophrenia: A current genetic-epidemiologic perspective. *Schizophrenia Bulletin, 19*(2), 261–285.

Kendler, K. S., Myers, J., Potter, J., & Opalesky, J. (2009). A Web-based study of personality, psychopathology and substance use in twin, other relative and relationship pairs. *Twin Research and Human Genetics, 12*, 137–141.

Kendler, K. S., & Myers, J. (2010). The genetic and environmental relationship between major depression and the five-factor model of personality. *Psychological Medicine, 40*(5), 801–806.

Kendler, K. S., Thornton, L. M., Gilman, S. E., & Kessler, R. C. (2000). Sexual orientation in a U.S. national sample of twin and nontwin sibling pairs. *American Journal of Psychiatry, 157*(11), 1843–1846.

Keng, S. L., Smoski, M. J., & Robins, C. J. (2011). Effects of mindfulness on psychological health: A review of empirical studies. *Clinical Psychology Review, 31*(6), 1041–1056.

Kennedy, M. M. (2010). Attribution error and the quest for teacher quality. *Educational Researcher, 39*, 591–598.

Kennedy, W. (2012, May 12). Congregations find themselves stronger after storm. *The Joplin Globe*. http://www.joplinglobe.com/topstories/x1640795676/Congregations-find-themselves-stronger-after-storm

Kenny, M. E. (1987). The extent and function of parental attachment among first-year college students. *Journal of Youth and Adolescence, 16*(1), 17–29.

Kenny, M. E., & Barton, C. E. (2003). Attachment theory and research: Contributions for understanding late adolescent and young adult development. In J. Demick & C. Andreoletti (Eds.), *Handbook of adult development* (pp. 371–390). New York, NY: Springer Science+Business Media.

Kenny, M. E., & Donaldson, G. A. (1991). Contributions of parental attachment and family structure to the social and psychological functioning of first-year college students. *Journal of Counseling Psychology, 38*(4), 479.

Kenny, M. E., & Perez, V. (1996). Attachment and psychological well-being among racially and ethnically diverse first-year college students. *Journal of College Student Development. 37*(5), 527–535.

Kenny, M. E., & Sirin, S. R. (2006). Parental attachment, self-worth, and depressive symptoms among emerging adults. *Journal of Counseling & Development, 84*(1), 61–71.

Kenrick, D. T. (2012). Evolutionary theory and human social behavior. In P. A. M. Van Lange, A. W. Kruglanski, & E. T. Higgins (Eds.), *Handbook of theories of social psychology* (Vol. 1, pp. 11–31). Thousand Oaks, CA: SAGE.

Kent, K. M., Pelham, W. E., Jr., Molina, B. S., Sibley, M. H., Waschbusch, D. A., Yu, J., . . . Karch, K. M. (2011). The academic experience of male high school students with ADHD. *Journal of Abnormal Child Psychology, 39*(3), 451–462.

Keppel, G., & Underwood, B. J. (1962). Proactive inhibition in short-term retention of single items. *Journal of Verbal Learning and Verbal Behavior, 1*(3), 153–161.

Kerckhoff, A. C. (2003). From student to worker. In J. T. Mortimer & M. J. Shanahan (Eds.), *Handbook of the life course* (pp. 251–267). New York, NY: Kluwer.

Kern, L., & Kokina, A. (2008). Using positive reinforcement to decrease challenging behavior. In J. K. Luiselli, D. C. Russo, W. P. Christian, & S. W. Wilczynski (Eds.), *Effective practices for children with autism* (pp. 413–432). New York, NY: Oxford University Press.

Kern, M. L., & Friedman, H. S. (2008). Do conscientious individuals live longer? A quantitative review. *Health Psychology, 27*(5), 505–512.

Kernberg, O. F. (2004). *Contemporary controversies in psychoanalytic theories, techniques, and their applications*. New Haven, CT: Yale University Press.

Kersh, R., & Morone, J. (2011). Obesity politics and policy. In J. H. Cawley (Ed.), *The Oxford handbook of the social science of obesity* (pp. 158–172). New York, NY: Oxford University Press.

Kesselring, T. (2009). The mind's staircase revisited. In U. Müller, J. I. M. Carpendale, & L. Smith (Eds.), *The Cambridge companion to Piaget* (pp. 371–399). New York, NY: Cambridge University Press.

Kessler, R. C., & Berglund, P., et al. (2005a). Lifetime prevalence and age-of-onset distributions of DSM-IV disorders in the National Comorbidity Survey Replication. *Archives of General Psychiatry, 62*, 593–602.

Kessler, R. C., & Berglund, P., Demler, O., Jin. R., Merikangas, K. R., & Walters, E. E. (2005). Lifetime prevalence and age-of-onset distributions of DSM-IV disorders in the National Comorbidity Survey Replication. *Archives of General Psychiatry, 62*(7), 593–602.

Kessler, R. C., & Wang, P. S. (2009). Epidemiology of depression. In I. H. Gotlib & C. L. Hammen (Eds.), *Handbook of depression* (2nd ed., pp. 5–22). New York, NY: Guilford Press.

Kessler, R. C., Adler, L., Barkley, R., Biederman, J., Conners, C. K., Demler, O., . . . Spencer, T. (2006). The prevalence and correlates of adult ADHD in the United States: Results from the National Comorbidity Survey Replication. *American Journal of Psychiatry, 163*(4), 716–723.

Kessler, R. C., Berglund, P. A., Chiu, W. T., Deitz, A. C., Hudson, J. I., Shahly, V., . . . Xavier, M. (2013). The prevalence and correlates of binge eating disorder in the World Health Organization World Mental Health Surveys. *Biological Psychiatry, 73*(9), 904–914.

Kessler, R. C., Berglund, P. A., Chiu, W., Demler, O., Glantz, M., Lane, M. C. . . . Wells, K. B. (2008). The national comorbidity survey replication (NCS-R): Cornerstone in improving mental health and mental health care in the United States. In R. C. Kessler & T. B. Ustun (Eds.), *The WHO World Mental Health Surveys: Global perspectives on the epidemiology of mental disorders* (pp. 165–209). New York, NY: Cambridge University Press.

Kessler, R. C., Chiu, W. T., Demler, O., & Walters, E. E. (2005). Prevalance, severity, and comorbidity of 12-month DSM-IV disorders in the National Comorbidity Survey Replication (NCS-R). *Archives of General Psychiatry, 62*(6), 617–709.

Kessler, R. C., Ruscio, A. M., Shear, K., & Wittchen, H. (2009). Epidemiology of anxiety disorders. In M. M. Antony & M. B. Stein (Eds.), *Oxford handbook of anxiety and related disorders* (pp. 19–33). New York, NY: Oxford University Press.

Ketter, T. A., & Wang, P. W. (2010). DSM-IV-TR diagnosis of bipolar disorders. In T. A. Ketter (Ed.), *Handbook of diagnosis and treatment of bipolar disorders* (pp. 11–37). Washington, DC: American Psychiatric Publishing.

Kharkhurin, A. V., & Samadpour Motalleebi, S. N. (2008). The impact of culture on the creative potential of American, Russian, and Iranian college students. *Creativity Research Journal, 20*(4), 404–411.

Khazan, I. Z. (2013). *The clinical handbook of biofeedback: A step-by-step for training and practice with mindfulness*. Malden, MA: Wiley-Blackwell.

Khoshaba, D. M., & Maddi, S. R. (2001). *HardiTraining*. Newport Beach, CA: Hardiness Institute.

Khoury, B., Lecomte, T., Fortin, G., Masse, M., Therien, P., Bouchard, V., Hofmann, S. G. (2013). Mindfulness-based therapy: A comprehensive meta-analysis. *Clinical Psychology Review, 33*(6), 763–771.

Kidd, G., Jr. (2010). Auditory thresholds. In E. B. Goldstein (Ed.), *Encyclopedia of perception* (pp. 197–200). Thousand Oaks, CA: SAGE.

Kiecolt-Glaser, J. K., Bane, C., Glaser, R., & Malarkey, W. B. (2003). Love, marriage, and divorce: Newlyweds' stress hormones foreshadow relationship changes. *Journal of Consulting and Clinical Psychology, 71*(1), 176–188.

Kiecolt-Glaser, J. K., Glaser, R., Cacioppo, J. T., MacCallum, R. C., Snydersmith, M., Kim, C., & Malarkey, W. B. (1997). Marital conflict in older adults: Endocrinological and immunological correlates. *Psychosomatic Medicine, 59*(4), 339–349.

Kiecolt-Glaser, J. K., Glaser, R., Gravenstein, S., Malarkey, W. B., & Sheridan, J. (1996). Chronic stress alters the immune response to influenza virus vaccine in older adults. *Proceedings of the National Academy of Sciences, 93*(7), 3043–3047.

Kiecolt-Glaser, J. K., Marucha, P. T., Mercado, A. M., Malarkey, W. B., & Glaser, R. (1995). Slowing of wound healing by psychological stress. *The Lancet, 346*(8984), 1194–1196.

Kihlstrom, J. F. (2002). To honor Kraepelin...: From symptoms to pathology in the diagnosis of mental illness. In L. E. Beutler & M. L. Malik (Eds.), *Rethinking the DSM: A psychological perspective* (pp. 279–303). Washington, DC: American Psychological Association.

Kihlstrom, J. F. (2005). Is hypnosis an altered state of consciousness or what? *Contemporary Hypnosis, 22*(1), 34–38.

Kihlstrom, J. F. (2007). Consciousness in hypnosis. In P. D. Zelazo, M. Moscovitch, & E. Thompson (Eds.), *The Cambridge handbook of consciousness* (pp. 445–480). Cambridge, UK: Cambridge University Press.

Kihlstrom, J. F. (2008). The domain of hypnosis, revisited. In M. R. Nash & A. J. Barnier (Eds.), *The Oxford handbook of hypnosis: Theory, research, and practice* (pp. 21–52). Oxford, UK: Oxford University Press.

Kihlstrom, J. F. (2008). The psychological unconscious. In O. P. John, R. W. Robins, & L. A. Pervin (Eds.), *Handbook of personality: Theory and research* (3rd ed., pp. 583–602. New York, NY: Guilford Press.

Kihlstrom, J. F., Diaz, W. A., McClellan, G. E., Ruskin, P. M., Pistole, D. D., & Shor, R. E. (1980). Personality correlates of hypnotic susceptibility: Needs for achievement and autonomy, self-monitoring, and masculinity-femininity. *American Journal of Clinical Hypnosis, 22*(4), 225–230.

Kilmer, J. R., Geisner, I. M., Gasser, M. L., & Lindgren, K. P. (2015). Normative perceptions of non-medical stimulant use: Associations with actual use and hazardous drinking. *Addictive Behaviors, 42*, 51–56.

Kim, E. K. (2012, November 30). Cop who bought shoes for homeless man "really didn't think about the money." *Today News*. http://todaynews.today.com/news/2012/11/30/15568550-cop-who-bought-shoes-for-homeless-man-really-didnt-think-about-the-money?lite

Kim, H. S., Sherman, D. K., & Taylor, S. E. (2008). Culture and social support. *American Psychologist, 63*(6), 518–526.

Kim, J. E., & Moen, P. (2001). Is retirement good or bad for subjective well-being? *Current Directions in Psychological Science. 10*(3), 83–86.

Kim, J. E., & Moen, P. (2002). Retirement transitions, gender, and psychological well-being: A life-course, ecological model. *The Journals of Gerontology Series B: Psychological Sciences and Social Sciences, 57* (3), P212–P222.

Kim, J. L., Lynn Sorsoli, C., Collins, K., Zylbergold, B. A., Schooler, D., & Tolman, D. L. (2007). From sex to sexuality: Exposing the heterosexual script on primetime network television. *Journal of Sex Research, 44*(2), 145–157.

Kim, U. E., Triandis, H. C., Kâğitçibaşi, Ç. E., Choi, S. C. E., & Yoon, G. E. (Eds.). (1994). *Individualism and collectivism: Theory, method, and applications*. Thousand Oaks, CA: SAGE.

Kim, Y. J. (2006). The role of regulatory focus in message framing in antismoking advertisements for adolescents. *Journal of Advertising, 35*(1), 143–151.

Kimble, G. A. (1981). *Biological and cognitive constraints on learning*. Washington, D. C.: American Psychological Association.

Kimura, D. (1967). Functional asymmetry of the brain in dichotic listening. *Cortex, 3*(2), 163–178.

King, L. A. (2001). The health benefits of writing about life goals. *Personality and Social Psychology Bulletin, 27*(7), 798–807.

Kingdon, D. G., & Turkington, D. (2005). *Cognitive therapy of schizophrenia*. New York, NY: Guilford Press.

Kingery, J. N., & Erdley, C. A. (2007). Peer experience as predictors of adjustment across the middle school transition. *Education and Treatment of Children, 30*(2), 73–88.

Kingery, J. N., Erdley, C. A., & Marshall, K. C. (2011). Peer acceptance and friendship as predictors of early adolescents' adjustment across the middle school transition. *Merrill-Palmer Quarterly, 57*(3), 215–243.

Kingsley, R. C., & Hall, V. C. (1967). Training conservation through the use of learning sets. *Child Development, 38*(4), 1111–1126.

Kinnish, K. K., Strassberg, D. S., & Turner, C. W. (2005). Sex differences in the flexibility of sexual orientation: A multidimensional retrospective assessment. *Archives of Sexual Behavior, 34*(2), 173–183.

Kirby, M., Maggi, S., & D'Angiulli, A. (2011). School start times and the sleep–wake cycle of adolescents: A review and critical evaluation of available evidence. *Educational Researcher, 40*(2), 56–61.

Kirkup, W., & Merrick, D. W. (2003). A matter of life and death: Population mortality and football results. *Journal of Epidemiology and Community Health, 57*(6), 429–432.

Kirmayer, L. J., & Jarvis, G. E. (2006). Depression across cultures. In D. J. Stein, D. J. Kupfer, & A. F. Schatzberg (Eds.), *The American Psychiatric Publishing textbook of mood disorders* (pp. 699–716). Washington, DC: American Psychiatric Association Publishing.

Kirsch, A. C., & Murnen, S. K. (2015). "Hot" girls and "cool dudes": Examining the prevalence of the heterosexual script in American children's television media. *Psychology of Popular Media Culture, 4*(1), 18–30.

Kirsch, I., & Braffman, W. (2001). Imaginative suggestibility and hypnotizability. *Current Directions in Psychological Science, 10*(2), 57–61.

Kirschbaum, C., & Hellhammer, D. H. (1994). Salivary cortisol in psychoneuroendocrine research: Recent developments and applications. *Psychoneuroendocrinology, 19*(4), 313–333.

Kirschbaum, C., Tietze, A., Skoluda, N., & Dettenborn, L. (2009). Hair as a retrospective calendar of cortisol production—increased cortisol incorporation into hair in the third trimester of pregnancy. *Psychoneuroendocrinology, 34*(1), 32–37.

Kirsh, S. J. (2012). *Children, adolescents, and media violence: A critical look at the research*. Thousand Oaks, CA: SAGE.

Kisilevsky, B. S., Stack, D. M., & Muir, D. W. (1991). Fetal and infant response to tactile stimulation. In M. J. S. Weiss & P. R. Zelazo (Eds.), *Newborn attention: Biological constraints and the influence of experience* (pp. 63–98). Norwood, NJ: Ablex.

Kitayama, S., Duffy, S., Kawamura, T., & Larsen, J. T. (2003). Perceiving an object and its context in different cultures: A cultural look at new look. *Psychological Science, 14*(3), 201–206.

Kito, M. (2005). Self-disclosure in romantic relationships and friendships among American and Japanese college students. *The Journal of Social Psychology, 145*(2), 127–140.

Klahr, D. (2012). Revisiting Piaget: A perspective from studies of children's problem-solving abilities. In A. M. Slater & P. C. Quinn (Eds.), *Developmental psychology: Revisiting the classic studies* (pp. 56–70). Los Angeles, CA: SAGE.

Klass, D., & Hutch, R. A. (1985). Elisabeth Kubler-Ross as a religious leader. *OMEGA—Journal of Death and Dying, 16*(2), 89–109.

Klatzky, R. L., & Lederman, S. J. (2010). Haptics. In E. B. Goldstein (Ed.), *Encyclopedia of perception* (pp. 477–481). Thousand Oaks, CA: SAGE.

Klein, D. N., Shankman, S. A., & McFarland, B. R. (2006). Classification of mood disorders. In D. J. Stein, D. J. Kupfer, & A. F. Schatzberg (Eds.), *The American Psychiatric Publishing textbook of mood disorders* (pp. 17–32). Washington, DC: American Psychiatric Association Publishing.

Klein, R. P., & Jennings, K. D. (1979). Responses to social and inanimate stimuli in early infancy. *The Journal of Genetic Psychology, 135*(1), 3–9.

Kleinke, C. (2002). *Coping with life challenges*. Prospect Heights, IL: Waveland Press.

Kleinman, N. L., Brook, R. A., Doan, J. F., Melkonian, A. K., & Baran, R. W. (2009). Health benefit costs and absenteeism due to insomnia from the employer's perspective: A retrospective, case-control, database study. *The Journal of Clinical Psychiatry, 70*(8), 1098–1104.

Kleitman, N. (1963). *Sleep and wakefulness*. Chicago, IL: University of Chicago Press.

Kleitman, N., & Kleitman, E. (1953). Effect of non-twenty-four-hour routines of living on oral temperature and heart rate. *Journal of Applied Physiology, 6*(5), 283–291.

Klenk, M. M., Strauman, T. J., & Higgins, E. T. (2011). Regulatory focus and anxiety: A self-regulatory model of GAD-depression comorbidity. *Personality and Individual Differences, 50*(7), 935–943.

Klerman, G. L., Weissman, M. M., Rounsaville, B. J., & Chevron, E. S. (1984). *Interpersonal psychotherapy of depression*. New York, NY: Basic Books.

Klinesmith, J., Kasser, T., & McAndrew, F. T. (2006). Guns, testosterone, and aggression: An experimental test of a mediational hypothesis. *Psychological Science, 17*(7), 568–571.

Kloep, M., & Hendry, L. B. (2010). Letting go or holding on? Parents' perceptions of their relationships with their children during emerging adulthood. *British Journal of Developmental Psychology, 28*, 817–834. doi:10.1348/026151009X480581

Kloner, R. A., McDonald, S., Leeka, J., & Poole, W. K. (2009). Comparison of total and cardiovascular death rates in the same city during a losing versus winning super bowl championship. *The American Journal of Cardiology, 103*(12), 1647–1650.

Klump, K. L., Miller, K., Keel, P., McGue, M., & Iacono, W. (2001). Genetic and environmental influence on anorexia nervosa symptoms in a population-based twin sample. *Psychological Medicine, 31*(4), 737–740.

Knapp, S. J., & VandeCreek, L. D. (2006). *Practical ethics for psychologists: A positive approach*. Washington, DC: American Psychological Association.

Kneeland, T. W., & Warren, C. A. B. (2002). *Pushbutton psychiatry: A history of electroshock in America*. Westport, CT: Praeger.

Knobloch, L. K., Miller, L. E., Sprecher, S., Wenzel, A., & Harvey, J. (2008). Uncertainty and relationship initiation. In S. Sprecher, A. Wenzel, & J. Harvey (Eds.), *Handbook of relationship initiation* (pp. 121–134). New York, NY: Psychology Press.

Knutsson, A. (2003). Health disorders of shift workers. *Occupational Medicine, 53*(2), 103–108.

Kobak, R. (2012). Attachment and early social deprivation: Revisiting Harlow's monkey studies. In A. M. Slater & P. C. Quinn (Eds.), *Developmental psychology: Revisiting the classic studies* (pp. 10–23). Los Angeles, CA: SAGE.

Koenig, H. G. (2005). *Faith and mental health: Religious resources for healing*. Philadelphia, PA: Templeton Foundation Press.

Koenig, M., & Cole, C. (2013). Early word learning. In D. Reisberg (Ed.), *The Oxford handbook of cognitive psychology* (pp. 492–503). Oxford, UK: Oxford University Press.

Koerner, K. (2012). *Doing dialectical behavior therapy: A practical guide*. New York, NY: Guilford Press.

Koester, J., & Siegelbaum, S. A. (2013a). Membrane potential and the passive electrical properties of the neuron. In E. R. Kandel, J. H. Schwartz, T. M. Jessell, S. A. Siegelbaum, & A. J. Hudspeth (Eds.), *Principles of neural science* (5th ed., pp. 126–147). New York, NY: McGraw-Hill.

Koester, J., & Siegelbaum, S. A. (2013b). Propagated signaling: The action potential. In E. R. Kandel, J. H. Schwartz, T. M. Jessell, S. A. Siegelbaum, & A. J. Hudspeth (Eds.), *Principles of neural science* (5th ed., pp. 148–171). New York, NY: McGraw-Hill.

Koestner, R., Zuckerman, M., & Koestner, J. (1987). Praise, involvement, and intrinsic motivation. *Journal of Personality and Social Psychology, 53*(2), 383–390.

Kohlberg, L. (1963). The development of children's orientations toward a moral order. *Human Development, 51*(1), 8–20.

Kohlberg, L. (1973a). The claim to moral adequacy of a highest stage of moral judgment. *The Journal of Philosophy, 70*(18), 630–646.

Kohlberg, L. (1973b). The contribution of developmental psychology to education—examples from moral education. *Educational Psychologist, 10*(1), 2–14.

Kohlberg, L. (1974). Education, moral development and faith. *Journal of Moral Education, 4*(1), 5–16.

Kohlberg, L. (1981). *The philosophy of moral development: Moral stages and the idea of justice*. New York, NY: Harper & Row.

Kohlberg, L. (1984). *Essays on moral development* (Vol. II). New York, NY: Harper & Row.

Kohlberg, L., & Candee, D. (1984). The relationship of moral judgment to moral action. In W. Kirtines & J. Gerwitz (Eds.), *Morality, moral behavior, and moral development* (pp. 52–73). New York, NY: Wiley.

Kohler, W. (1924). *The mentality of apes*. Oxford, UK: Harcourt.

Kohout, J. L. & Pate, W. E. II (2013). Employment and trends in psychology. In M. J. Prinstein (Ed.), *The portable mentor: Expert guide to a successful career in psychology* (pp. 343–361). New York, NY Springer.

Kok, B. E., Coffey, K. A., Cohn, M. A., Catalino, L. I., Vacharkulksemsuk, T., Algoe, S. B., . . . Fredrickson, B. L. (2013). How positive emotions build physical health: Perceived positive social connections account for the upward spiral between positive emotions and vagal tone. *Psychological Science, 24*(7), 1123–1132.

Kolb, B., & Gibb, R. (2011). Brain plasticity and behaviour in the developing brain. *Journal of the Canadian Academy of Child and Adolescent Psychiatry, 20*(4), 265.

Kolb, B., & Whishaw, I. Q. (1998). Brain plasticity and behavior. *Annual Review of Psychology, 49*(1), 43–64.

Kolden, G. G., Klein, M. H., Wang, C., & Austin, S. B. (2011). Congruence/genuineness. In J. C. Norcross (Ed.), *Psychotherapy relationships that work: Evidence-based responsiveness* (2nd ed., 187–202). New York, NY: Oxford University Press.

Koltko-Rivera, M. E. (1998). Maslow's "transhumanism": Was transpersonal psychology conceived as "a psychology without people in it"? *Journal of Humanistic Psychology, 38*(1), 71–80.

Koltko-Rivera, M. E. (2006). Rediscovering the later version of Maslow's hierarchy of needs: Self-transcendence and opportunities for theory, research, and unification. *Review of General Psychology, 10*(4), 302–317.

Komarraju, M., Karau, S. J., & Schmeck, R. R. (2009). Role of the Big Five personality traits in predicting college students' academic motivation and achievement. *Learning and Individual Differences, 19*(1), 47–52.

Konijn, E. A., Bijvank, M. N., & Bushman, B. J. (2007). I wish I were a warrior: The role of wishful identification in effects of violent video games on aggression in adolescent boys. *Developmental Psychology, 43*(4), 1038–1044.

Koocher, G. P. (2009). Any minute now but far far away: Electronically mediated mental health. *Clinical Psychology: Science and Practice, 16*(3), 339–342.

Koocher, G. P. (2013). Ethical considerations in clinical psychology research. In J. S. Comer & P. C. Kendall (Eds.), *The Oxford handbook of research strategies for clinical psychology* (pp. 395–412). Oxford, UK: Oxford University Press.

Koocher, G. P., & Daniel, J. H. (2012). Treating children and adolescents. In S. J. Knapp (Ed.), *APA handbook of ethics in psychology* (Vol. 2, pp. 3–14). Washington, DC: American Psychological Association.

Koocher, G. P., & Keith-Spiegel, P. (2008). *Ethics in psychology and the mental health professions* (3rd ed.). New York, NY: Oxford University Press.

Koole, S. L. (2009). The psychology of emotion regulation: An integrative review. *Cognition and Emotion, 23*(1), 4–41.

Kopelman, M. D. (2002). Psychogenic amnesia. In A. D. Baddeley, M. D. Kopelman, & B. A. Wilson (Ed.), *The handbook of memory disorders* (2nd ed., pp. 451–471). Chichester, UK: Wiley.

Kopelman, M. D. (2002). Retrograde amnesia. In A. D. Baddeley, M. D. Kopelman & B. A. Wilson (Eds.), *The handbook of memory disorders* (2nd ed., pp. 189–207). Chichester, UK: Wiley.

Kopelowicz, A., Liberman, R. P., & Zarate, R. (2007). Psychosocial treatments for schizophrenia. In P. E. Nathan & J. M. Gorman (Eds.), *A guide to treatments that work* (3rd ed., pp. 243–269). New York, NY: Oxford University Press.

Korchmaros, J. D., & Kenny, D. A. (2001). Emotional closeness as a mediator of the effect of genetic relatedness on altruism. *Psychological Science, 12*(3), 262–265.

Korchmaros, J. D., & Kenny, D. A. (2006). An evolutionary and close-relationship model of helping. *Journal of Social and Personal Relationships, 23*(1), 21–43.

Koriat, A. (2000). Control processes in remembering. In E. Tulving & F. I. M. Craik, *The Oxford handbook of memory* (pp. 333–346). Oxford, UK: Oxford University Press.

Kornstein, S. G., & Sloan, D. M. E. (2006). Depression and gender. In D. J. Stein, D. J. Kupfer, & A. F. Schatzberg (Eds.), *The American Psychiatric Publishing textbook of mood disorders* (pp. 687–698). Washington, DC: American Psychiatric Association Publishing.

Kosic, A. (2006). Personality and individual factors in acculturation. In D. L. Sam, & J. W. Berry (Eds.), *The Cambridge handbook of acculturation psychology* (pp. 113–128). New York, NY: Cambridge University Press.

Koslowsky, M., & Pindek, S. (2011). Impression management: Influencing perceptions of self. In D. Chadee (Ed.), *Theories in social psychology* (pp. 280–296). West Sussex, UK: Wiley-Blackwell.

Kotov, R., Gamez, W., Schmidt, F., & Watson, D. (2010). Linking "big" personality traits to anxiety, depressive, and substance use disorders: A meta-analysis. *Psychological Bulletin, 136*(5), 768–821.

Kottler, J. A. (2005). *Divine madness: Ten stories of creative struggle*. New York, NY: John Wiley.

Kounios, J., & Beeman, M. (2009). The *Aha!* moment: The cognitive neuroscience of insight. *Current Directions in Psychological Science, 18*(4), 210–216.

Kowler, E., & Collewijin, H. (2010). Eye movements: Behavioral. In E. B. Goldstein (Ed.), *Encyclopedia of perception* (pp. 421–425). Thousand Oaks, CA: SAGE.

Kozusznik, M. W., Rodríguez, I., & Peiró, J. M. (2015). Eustress and distress climates in teams: Patterns and outcomes. *International Journal of Stress Management, 22*(1), 1–23.

Kraaykamp, G., & Van Eijck, K. (2005). Personality, media preferences, and cultural participation. *Personality and Individual Differences, 38*(7), 1675–1688.

Kraemer, H. C. (2010). Concepts and methods for researching categories and dimensions in psychiatric diagnosis. In T. Millon, R. F. Krueger, & E. Simonsen (Eds.), *Contemporary directions in psychopathology: Scientific foundations of the DSM-V and ICD-11* (pp. 337–349). New York, NY: Guilford Press.

Krakow, B., Hollifield, M., Johnston, L., Koss, M., Schrader, R., Warner, T. D., Prince, H. (2001). Imagery rehearsal therapy for chronic nightmares in sexual assault survivors with posttraumatic stress disorder: A randomized controlled trial. *The Journal of the American Medical Association, 286*(5), 537–545.

Krakow, B., & Zadra, A. (2006). Clinical management of chronic nightmares: Imagery rehearsal therapy. *Behavioral Sleep Medicine, 4*(1), 45–70.

Kramer, D. (2003). The ontogeny of wisdom in its variations. In J. Demick & C. Andreoletti (Eds.), *Handbook of adult development* (pp. 131–152). New York, NY: Kluwer.

Kramer, J. (2007). Is abstraction the key to computing? *Communications of the ACM, 50*(4), 36–42.

Kramer, M. (2006). Biology of dreaming. In T. L. Lee-Chiong (Ed.), *Sleep: A comprehensive handbook* (pp. 31–36). Hoboken, NJ: Wiley-Liss.

Krans, J., Woud, M. L., Näring, G., Becker, E. S., & Holmes, E. A. (2010). Exploring involuntary recall in posttraumatic stress disorder from an information processing perspective: Intrusive images of trauma. In J. H. Mace (Ed.), *The act of remembering* (pp. 311–336). Chichester, UK: Wiley-Blackwell.

Kraus, M. W., Huang, C., & Keltner, D. (2010). Tactile communication, cooperation, and performance: An ethological study of the NBA. *Emotion, 10*(5), 745–749.

Kraus, R. (2004). Ethical and legal considerations for providers of mental health services online. In R. Kraus, J. Zack, & G. Stricker (Eds.), *Online counseling: A handbook for mental health professionals* (pp. 123–144). San Diego, CA: Elsevier.

Kraus, S. J. (1995). Attitudes and the prediction of behavior: A meta-analysis of the empirical literature. *Personality and Social Psychology Bulletin, 21*(1), 58–75.

Krcmar, M., & Kean, L. G. (2005). Uses and gratifications of media violence: Personality correlates of viewing and liking violent genres. *Media Psychology, 7*(4), 399–420.

Krebs, D. L., & Denton, K. (2005). Toward a more pragmatic approach to morality: A critical evaluation of Kohlberg's model. *Psychological Review, 112*(3), 629.

Krech, D., Rosenzweig, M. R., & Bennett, E. L. (1966). Environmental impoverishment, social isolation and changes in brain chemistry and anatomy. *Physiology & Behavior, 1*(2), 99–104.

Kreitzer, M. J., Gross, C. R., Ye, X., Russas, V., & Treesak, C. (2005). Longitudinal impact of mindfulness meditation on illness burden in solid-organ transplant recipients. *Progress in Transplantation, 15*(2), 166–172.

Kreuger, K. A., & Dayan, P. (2009). Flexible shaping: How learning in small steps helps. *Cognition, 110*, 380–394.

Kring, A. M., & Gordon, A. H. (1998). Sex differences in emotion: Expression, experience, and physiology. *Journal of Personality and Social Psychology, 74*(3), 686–703.

Kris, A. O. (2012). Unconscious processes. In G. O. Gabbard, B. E. Litowitz, & P. Williams (Eds.), *Textbook of psychoanalysis* (2nd ed., pp. 53–64). Washington, DC: American Psychiatric Publishing.

Krueger, R. F. (2008). Behavioral genetics and personality: A new look at the integration of nature and nurture. In O. P. John, R. W. Robins, & L. A. Pervin (Eds.) *Handbook of personality: Theory and research* (3rd ed., pp. 287–310). New York, NY: Guilford Press.

Kruglanski, A. W., & Stroebe, W. (2012). The making of social psychology. In A. W. Kruglanski & W. Stroebe (Eds.), *Handbook of the history of social psychology* (pp. 3–18). New York, NY: Psychology Press.

Krumbholz, K., Patterson, R. D., & Pressnitzer, D. (2000). The lower limit of pitch as determined by rate discrimination. *The Journal of the Acoustical Society of America, 108*(3), 1170–1180.

Kruschke, J. K. (2005). Category learning. In K. Lamberts & R. L. Goldstone, *Handbook of cognition* (pp. 183–201). London, UK: SAGE.

Kubala, K. H., Christianson, J. P., Kaufman, R. D., Watkins, L. R., & Maier, S. F. (2012). Short-and long-term consequences of stressor controllability in adolescent rats. *Behavioural Brain Research, 234*(2), 278–284.

Kübler-Ross, E. (1969). *On death and dying*. New York, NY: Macmillan.

Kuehlwein, K. T. (1993). A survey and update of cognitive therapy systems. In K. T. Kuehlwein & H. Rosen (Eds.), *Cognitive therapies in action* (pp. 1–32). San Francisco, CA: Jossey-Bass.

Kuh, G. D., Cruce, T. M., Shoup, R., Kinzie, J., & Gonyea, R. M. (2008). Unmasking the effects of student engagement on first-year college grades and persistence. *The Journal of Higher Education, 79*(5), 540–563.

Kuhl, P. K. (2004). Early language acquisition: Cracking the speech code. *Nature Reviews Neuroscience, 5*(11), 831–843.

Kuhl, P. K., & Damasio, A. R. (2013). Language. In E. R. Kandel, J. H. Schwartz, T. M. Jessell, S. A. Siegelbaum, & A. J. Hudspeth (Eds.), *Principles of neural science* (5th ed., pp. 1353–1372). New York, NY: McGraw-Hill.

Kuhn, D. (2009). Adolescent thinking. In R. M. Lerner & L. Steinberg (Eds.), *Handbook of adolescent psychology* (3rd ed., Vol. 1, pp. 152–186). Hoboken, NJ: Wiley.

Kuhn, D., & Franklin, S. (2006). The second decade: What develops (and how). In D. Kuhn & R. Siegler (Vol. Eds.), *Handbook of child psychology* (6th ed., Vol. 2, pp. 953–993). Hoboken, NJ: Wiley.

Kuhn, D., Langer, J., Kohlberg, L., & Haan, N. S. (1977). The development of formal operations in logical and moral judgment. *Genetic Psychology Monographs*, 95, 97–188.

Kunkel, D., & Castonguay, J. (2012). Children and advertising: Content, comprehension, and consequences. In D. G. Singer & J. L. Singer (Eds.), *Handbook of children and the media* (2nd ed., pp. 395–418). Los Angeles, CA: SAGE.

Kunst-Wilson, W. R., & Zajonc, R. B. (1980). Affective discrimination of stimuli that cannot be recognized. *Science, 207*(4430), 557–558.

Kuo, W. H., & Tsai, Y. M. (1986). Social networking, hardiness and immigrant's mental health. *Journal of Health and Social Behavior, 27*(2), 133–149.

Kupfer, D. J., Kuhl, E. A., & Regier, D. A. (2013). DSM-5—the future arrived. *JAMA, 309*(16), 1691–1692.

Kuriyan, A. B., Pelham, W. E., Jr., Molina, B. S., Waschbusch, D. A., Gnagy, E. M., Sibley, M. H., . . . Kent, K. M. (2013). Young adult educational and vocational outcomes of children diagnosed with ADHD. *Journal of Abnormal Child Psychology, 41*(1), 27–41.

Kurtz, K. J., Boukrina, O., & Gentner, D. (2013). Comparison promotes learning and transfer of relational categories. *Journal of Experimental Psychology: Learning, Memory, and Cognition, 39*(4), 1303–1310.

Kurzban, R., Tooby, J., & Cosmides, L. (2001). Can race be erased? Coalitional computation and social categorization. *Proceedings of the National Academy of Sciences, 98*(26), 15387–15392.

Kutchins, H., & Kirk, S. A. (1997). *Making us crazy: DSM: The psychiatric bible and the creation of mental disorders.* New York, NY: Free Press.

Kuther, T. L., & Morgan, R. D. (2013). *Careers in psychology: Opportunities in a changing world* (4th ed.). Australia: Thomson/Wadsworth.

Kutscher, E. C. (2008). Antipsychotics. In K. T. Mueser & D. V. Jeste (Eds.), *Clinical handbook of schizophrenia* (pp. 159–167). New York, NY: Guilford Press.

Kvavilashvili, L., & Mandler, G. (2004). Out of one's mind: A study of involuntary semantic memories. *Cognitive Psychology, 48*(1), 47–94.

Kvernmo, S. (2006). Indigenous peoples. In D. L. Sam, & J. W. Berry (Eds.), *The Cambridge handbook of acculturation psychology* (pp. 233–250). New York, NY: Cambridge University Press.

Kyle, U. G., Genton, L., Slosman, D. O., & Pichard, C. (2001). Fat-free and fat mass percentiles in 5225 healthy subjects aged 15 to 98 years. *Nutrition, 17*(7), 534–541.

La Gerche, A., & Prior, D. L. (2007). Exercise—is it possible to have too much of a good thing? *Heart, Lung and Circulation, 16*, S102–S104.

Laar, C. V., Levin, S., Sinclair, S., & Sidanius, J. (2005). The effect of university roommate contact on ethnic attitudes and behavior. *Journal of Experimental Social Psychology, 41*(4), 329–345.

Laberge, S. (1985). *Lucid dreaming*. New York, NY: Ballantine.

LaBerge, S. (1988). The psychophysiology of lucid dreaming. In J. Gackenbach & S. LaBerge (Eds.), *Conscious mind, sleeping brain: Perspectives on lucid dreaming* (pp. 135–153). New York, NY: Plenum Press.

LaBerge, S. (2000). Lucid dreaming: Evidence and methodology. *Behavioral and Brain Sciences, 23*(06), 962–964.

LaBerge, S. (2007). Lucid dreaming. In D. Barrett & P. McNamara (Eds.), *The new science of dreaming* (Vol. 2, pp. 307–328). Westport, CT: Praeger.

LaBerge, S., Levitan, L., Rich, R., & Dement, W. C. (1988). Induction of lucid dreaming by light stimulation during REM sleep. *Sleep Research, 17*, 104.

Labov, W., Ash, S., & Boberg, C. (2006). *The Atlas of North American English: Phonetics, phonology, and sound change.* Berlin, Germany: Mouton de Gruyter.

Labyak, S., Lava, S., Turek, F., & Zee, P. (2002). Effects of shiftwork on sleep and menstrual function in nurses. *Health Care for Women International, 23*(6–7), 703–714.

LaCaille, R., & Taylor, M. (2013). Stress, exercise. In M. D. Gellman & J. R. Turner (Eds.) *Encyclopedia of behavioral medicine* (pp. 1908–1910). New York, NY: Springer Science+Business Media.

Lacewing, M. (2014). Psychodynamic psychotherapy, insight, and therapeutic action. *Clinical Psychology: Science and Practice, 21*(2), 154–171.

Lack, L. C., & Wright, H. R. (2012). Circadian rhythm disorders I: Phase-advanced and phase-delayed syndromes. In C. M. Morin & C. A. Espie (Eds.), *The Oxford handbook of sleep and sleep disorders* (pp. 597–625). Oxford, UK: Oxford University Press.

Lackner, J. R. (2010a). Kinesthesia. In E. B. Goldstein (Ed.), *Encyclopedia of perception* (pp. 513–517). Thousand Oaks, CA: SAGE.

Lackner, J. R. (2010b). Proprioception. In E. B. Goldstein (Ed.), *Encyclopedia of perception* (pp. 832–836). Thousand Oaks, CA: SAGE.

Lackner, J. R. (2010c). Vestibular system. In E. B. Goldstein (Ed.), *Encyclopedia of perception* (pp. 1025–1029). Thousand Oaks, CA: SAGE.

Lacks, P., Bertelson, A. D., Sugerman, J., & Kunkel, J. (1983). The treatment of sleep-maintenance insomnia with stimulus-control techniques. *Behaviour Research and Therapy, 21*(3), 291–295.

Ladd, G. W., Kochenderfer, B. J., & Coleman, C. C. (1997). Classroom peer acceptance, friendship, and victimization: Distinct relational systems that contribute uniquely to children's school adjustment? *Child Development, 68*(6), 1181–1197.

Laessle, R. G., Lehrke, S., & Dückers, S. (2007). Laboratory eating behavior in obesity. *Appetite, 49*(2), 399–404.

LaFarge, L. (2012). Defense and resistance. In G. O. Gabbard, B. E. Litowitz, & P. Williams (Eds.), *Textbook of psychoanalysis* (2nd ed., pp. 93–104). Washington, DC: American Psychiatric Publishing.

LaGasse, L. L., Derauf, C., Smith, L. M., Newman, E., Shah, R., Neal, C., . . . Lester, B. M. (2012). Prenatal methamphetamine exposure and childhood behavior problems at 3 and 5 years of age. *Pediatrics, 129*(4), 681–688.

Lagerspetz, K. M., Björkqvist, K., & Peltonen, T. (1988). Is indirect aggression typical of females? Gender differences in aggressiveness in 11- to 12-year-old children. *Aggressive Behavior, 14*(6), 403–414.

Laird-Johnson, P. N. (2012). Inference in mental models. In K. J. Holyoak and R. G. Morrison (Eds.), *The Oxford handbook of thinking and reasoning* (pp. 134–154). Oxford, UK: Oxford University Press.

Lalancette, M. F., & Standing, L. (1990). Asch fails again. *Social Behavior and Personality: An International Journal, 18*(1), 7–12.

Lalumière, M. L., Blanchard, R., & Zucker, K. J. (2000). Sexual orientation and handedness in men and women: A meta-analysis. *Psychological Bulletin, 126*(4), 575–592.

Lalumiere, M. L., & Quinsey, V. L. (1998). Pavlovian conditioning of sexual interests in human males. *Archives of Sexual Behavior, 27*(3), 241–252.

Lam, S. P., Fong, S. Y., Ho, C. K., Yu, M. W., & Wing, Y. K. (2008). Parasomnia among psychiatric outpatients: A clinical, epidemiologic, cross-sectional study. *The Journal of Clinical Psychiatry, 69*(9), 1374–1382.

Lamb, M. E., & Lewis, C. (2005). The role of parent-child relationships in child development. In M. H. Bornstein & M. E. Lamb (Eds.), *Developmental science: An advanced textbook* (5th ed., pp. 429–468). Mahwah, NJ: Lawrence Erlbaum.

Lambert, M. J. (2011). Psychotherapy research and its achievements. In J. C. Norcross, G. R. Vandenbos, & D. K. Freedheim (Eds.), *History of psychotherapy: Continuity and change* (2nd ed., pp. 299–332). Washington, DC: American Psychological Association.

Lambert, M. J., & Ogles, B. M. (2004). The efficacy and effectiveness of psychotherapy. In M. J. Lambert (Ed.), *Bergin and Garfield's handbook of psychotherapy and behavior change* (5th ed., pp. 139–193). New York, NY: Wiley.

Lambert, M. J., & Simon, W. (2008). The therapeutic relationship: Central and essential in psychotherapy outcome. In S. F. Hick & T. Bien (Eds.), *Mindfulness and the therapeutic relationship* (pp. 19–33). New York, NY: Guilford Press.

Lambert, T. A., Kahn, A. S., & Apple, K. J. (2003). Pluralistic ignorance and hooking up. *Journal of Sex Research, 40*(2), 129–133.

Landauer, T. K. (2011). Distributed learning and the size of memory: A 50-year spacing odyssey. In A. S. Benjamin (Ed.), *Successful remembering and successful forgetting: A Festschrift in honor of Robert A. Bjork* (pp. 49–69). New York, NY: Psychology Press.

Landauer, T. K., & Bjork, R. A. (1978). Optimum rehearsal patterns and name learning. In M. Gruneberg, P. E. Morris, & R. N. Sykes (Eds.), *Practical aspects of memory* (pp. 625–632). London, UK: Academic Press.

Landrine, H., & Klonoff, E. A. (1996). Traditional African-American family practices: Prevalence and correlates. *The Western Journal of Black Studies, 20*, 59–62.

Landrum, R. E., & Gurung, R. A. (2013). The memorability of introductory psychology revisited. *Teaching of Psychology, 40*(3), 222–227.

Lane, C. (2007). *Shyness: How normal behavior became a sickness*. New Haven, CT: Yale University Press.

Lane, R. C., & Harris, M. (2008). Psychodynamic psychotherapy. In M. Hersen & A. M. Gross (Eds.), *Handbook of clinical psychology* (Vol. 1, pp. 525–550). Hoboken, NJ: Wiley.

Lang, P. J. (1994). The varieties of emotional experience: A meditation on James–Lange theory. *Psychological Review, 101*(2), 211–221.

Lang, P. J., Greenwald, M. K., Bradley, M. M., & Hamm, A. O. (1993). Looking at pictures: Affective, facial, visceral, and behavioral reactions. *Psychophysiology, 30*(3), 261–273.

Lange, B. P., Zaretsky, E., Schwarz, S., & Euler, H. A. (2013). Words won't fail: Experimental evidence on the role of verbal proficiency in mate choice. *Journal of Language and Social Psychology, 33*(5), 482–499.

Langenbucher, J., & Nathan, P. E. (2006). Diagnosis and classification. In M. Hersen & J. C. Thomas (Eds.), *Comprehensive handbook of personality and psychopathology* (Vol. 2, pp. 3–20). Hoboken, NJ: Wiley.

Langford, P. E. (2005). *Vygotsky's developmental and educational psychology*. New York, NY: Psychology Press.

Langlois, J. H., & Roggman, L. A. (1990). Attractive faces are only average. *Psychological Science, 1*(2), 115–121.

Långström, N., Rahman, Q., Carlström, E., & Lichtenstein, P. (2010). Genetic and environmental effects on same-sex sexual behavior: A population study of twins in Sweden. *Archives of Sexual Behavior, 39*(1), 75–80.

LaPiere, R. T. (1934). Attitudes vs. actions. *Social Forces, 13*(2), 230–237.

LaPointe, L. L. (2013). *Paul Broca and the origins of language in the brain*. San Diego, CA: Plural Publishing.

Lappin, S. (2001). An introduction to formal semantics. In M. Aronoff & J. Rees-Miller (Eds.), *The handbook of linguistics* (pp. 369–393). Malden, MA: Blackwell.

Lara, M. A. (2008). Women and depression: The influence of gender in major depressive disorder. In S. A. Aguilar-Gaxiola & T. P. Gullotta (Eds.), *Depression in Latinos: Assessment, treatment, and prevention* (pp. 239–261). New York, NY: Springer Science+Business Media.

Larrick, R. P., Timmerman, T. A., Carton, A. M., & Abrevaya, J. (2011). Temper, temperature, and temptation: Heat-related retaliation in baseball. *Psychological Science, 22*(4), 423–428.

Larsen, R. J., Kasimatis, M., & Frey, K. (1992). Facilitating the furrowed brow: An unobtrusive test of the facial feedback hypothesis applied to unpleasant affect. *Cognition & Emotion, 6*(5), 321–338.

Larson, M. C., Gunnar, M. R., & Hertsgaard, L. (1991). The effects of morning naps, car trips, and maternal separation on adrenocortical activity in human infants. *Child Development, 62*(2), 362–372.

Larson, R. W. (2000). Toward a psychology of positive youth development. *American Psychologist, 55*(1), 170.

Larzelere, R. E., & Kuhn, B. R. (2005). Comparing child outcomes of physical punishment and alternative disciplinary tactics: A meta-analysis. *Clinical Child and Family Psychology Review, 8*(1), 1–37.

Laserna, C. M., Seih, Y. T., & Pennebaker, J. W. (2014). Um... Who like says you know: Filler word use as a function of age, gender, and personality. *Journal of Language and Social Psychology, 33*(3), 328–338.

Lash, S. J., Eisler, R. M., & Southard, D. R. (1995). Sex differences in cardiovascular reactivity as a function of the appraised gender relevance of the stressor. *Behavioral Medicine, 21*(2), 86–94.

Lash, S. J., Gillespie, B. L., Eisler, R. M., & Southard, D. R. (1991). Sex differences in cardiovascular reactivity: Effects of the gender relevance of the stressor. *Health Psychology, 10*(6), 392–398.

Laska, K. M., & Wampold, B. E. (2014). Ten things to remember about common factor theory. *Psychotherapy, 51*(4), 519–524.

Latané, B., & Darley, J. M. (1968). Group inhibition of bystander intervention in emergencies. *Journal of Personality and Social Psychology, 10*(3), 215–221.

Latané, B., & Darley, J. M. (1970). *The unresponsive bystander: Why doesn't he help?* New York, NY: Appleton-Century Crofts.

Latané, B., Williams, K., & Harkins, S. (1979). Many hands make light the work: The causes and consequences of social loafing. *Journal of Personality and Social Psychology, 37*(6), 822–832.

Lattal, K. A. (1991). Scheduling positive reinforcers. In I. H. Iverson & K. A. Lattal (Eds.), *Experimental analysis of behavior* (Pt. 1, pp. 87–134). Amsterdam, Netherlands: Elsevier.

Latz, S., Wolf, A. W., & Lozoff, B. (1999). Cosleeping in context: Sleep practices and problems in young children in Japan and the United States. *Archives of Pediatrics & Adolescent Medicine, 153*(4), 339–346.

Lau, R. W., & Cheng, S. T. (2011). Gratitude lessens death anxiety. *European Journal of Ageing, 8*(3), 169–175.

Laumann, E. O. (1994). *The social organization of sexuality: Sexual practices in the United States*. Chicago, IL: University of Chicago Press.

Laumann, E. O., Ellingson, S., Mahay, J., Paik, A., Youm, Y. (2004). *Sexual organization of the city*. Chicago, IL: University of Chicago Press.

Laurence, J-R, Beaulieu-Prévost, D., du Chéné, T. (2008). Measuring and understanding individual differences in hypnotizability. In M. R. Nash & A. J. Barnier (Eds.), *The Oxford handbook of hypnosis: Theory, research, and practice* (pp. 225–254). Oxford, UK: Oxford University Press.

Lauriola, M., & Levin, I. P. (2001). Personality traits and risky decision-making in a controlled experimental task: An exploratory study. *Personality and Individual Differences, 31*(2), 215–226.

Laursen, B., & Collins, W. A. (2009). Parent-child relationships during adolescence. In R. M. Lerner & L. Steinberg (Eds.). *Handboook of adolescent psychology* (3rd ed., Vol. 2, pp. 3–42). Hoboken, NJ: Wiley.

Lavie, C. J., Milani, R. V., & Ventura, H. O. (2009). Obesity and cardiovascular disease: Risk factor, paradox, and impact of weight loss. *Journal of the American College of Cardiology, 53*(21), 1925–1932.

LaVoie, D. J., Mertz, H. K., & Richmond, T. L. (2007). False memory susceptibility in older adults: Implications for the elderly eyewitness. In M. P. Toglia, J. D. Read, D. F. Ross, & R. C. L. Lindsay (Eds.), *The handbook of eyewitness psychology: Memory for events* (Vol. I, pp. 605–625). East Sussex, UK: Psychology Press.

Lawless, H. T. (2001). Taste. In E. B. Goldstein (Ed.), *Blackwell handbook of perception* (pp. 601–635). Oxford, UK: Blackwell.

Lawrence, A. E., Rosellini, A. J., & Brown, T. A. (2009). Classification of anxiety disorders: Treatment implications. In J. Abramowitz, D. McKay, S. Taylor, & G. Asmundson (Eds.), *Current perspectives on the anxiety disorders: Implications for DSM-V and beyond* (pp. 453–475). New York, NY: Springer Publishing.

Lawrence, K., Campbell, R., & Skuse, D. (2015). Age, gender and puberty influence the development of facial emotion recognition. *Frontiers in Psychology, 6*, 761.

Lawson, T. J. (2007). *Scientific perspectives on pseudoscience and the paranormal: Readings for general psychology*. Upper Saddle River, N.J: Pearson Prentice Hall.

Lawson, W. B. (2008). Schizophrenia in African Americans. In K. T. Mueser & D. V. Jeste (Eds.), *Clinical handbook of schizophrenia* (pp. 616–623). New York, NY: Guilford Press.

Lawton, C. A. (1994). Gender differences in way-finding strategies: Relationship to spatial ability and spatial anxiety. *Sex Roles, 30*(1112), 765–779.

Lawton, C. A., & Kallai, J. (2002). Gender differences in wayfinding strategies and anxiety about wayfinding: A cross-cultural comparison. *Sex Roles, 47*(910), 389–401.

Layous, K., Nelson, S. K., & Lyubomirsky, S. (2013). What is the optimal way to deliver a positive activity intervention? The case of writing about one's best possible selves. *Journal of Happiness Studies, 14*(2), 635–654.

Lazarus, R. S. (1964). A laboratory approach to the dynamics of psychological stress. *American Psychologist, 19*(6), 400–411.

Lazarus, R. S. (1966). *Psychological stress and the coping process*. New York, NY: McGraw-Hill.

Lazarus, R. S. (1982). Thoughts on the relations between emotion and cognition. *American Psychologist, 37*(9), 1019–1024.

Lazarus, R. S. (1984). On the primacy of cognition. *American Psychologist, 39*(2), 124–129.

Lazarus, R. S. (1993). From psychological stress to the emotions: A history of changing outlooks. *Annual Review of Psychology, 44*, 1–22.

Lazarus, R. S. (1999). *Stress and emotion: A new synthesis*. New York, NY: Springer.

Lazarus, R. S., & Alfert, E. (1964). Short-circuiting of threat by experimentally altering cognitive appraisal. *The Journal of Abnormal and Social Psychology, 69*(2), 195–205.

Lazarus, R. S., DeLongis, A., Folkman, S., & Gruen, R. (1985). Stress and adaptational outcomes: The problem of confounded measures. *American Psychologist, 40*(7), 770–779.

Le Grand, R., Mondloch, C. J., Maurer, D., & Brent, H. P. (2001). Neuroperception: Early visual experience and face processing. *Nature, 410*(6831), 890–890.

Le Grand, R., Mondloch, C. J., Maurer, D., & Brent, H. P. (2004). Impairment in holistic face processing following early visual deprivation. *Psychological Science, 15*(11), 762–768.

Leach, M. J., & Page, A. T. (2015). Herbal medicine for insomnia: A systematic review and meta-analysis. *Sleep Medicine Reviews, 24*, 1–12.

Leahy, A., Clayman, C., Mason, I., Lloyd, G., & Epstein, O. (1997). Computerised biofeedback games: A new method for teaching stress management and its use in irritable bowel syndrome. *Journal of the Royal College of Physicians of London, 32*(6), 552–556.

Leahy, R. L. (2003). *Cognitive therapy techniques: A practitioner's guide*. New York, NY: Guilford Press.

Leaper, C., & Robnett, R. D. (2011). Women are more likely than men to use tentative language, aren't they? A meta-analysis testing for gender differences and moderators. *Psychology of Women Quarterly, 35*(1), 129–142.

Leary, D. E. (2002). William James and the art of human understanding. In W. E. Pickren & D. A. Dewsbury (Eds.), *Evolving perspectives on the history of psychology* (pp. 101–120). Washington, DC: American Psychological Association.

Leary, D. E. (2003). A profound and radical change: How William James inspired the reshaping of American psychology. In R. J. Sternberg (Ed.), *The anatomy of impact: What makes the great works of psychology great* (pp. 19–42). Washington, DC: American Psychological Association.

Leary, M. R., & Cox, C. B. (2008). Belongingness motivation: A mainspring of social action. In J. Y. Shah & W. L. Gardner (Eds.), *Handbook of motivation science* (pp. 27–40). New York, NY: Guilford Press.

Leary, M. R., Koch, E. J., & Hechenbleikner, N. R. (2001). Emotional response to interpersonal responses to interpersonal rejections. In M. R. Leary (Ed.), *Interpersonal rejection* (pp. 145–166). New York, NY: Oxford University Press.

Leary, M. R., Kowalski, R. M., Smith, L., & Phillips, S. (2003). Teasing, rejection, and violence: Case studies of the school shootings. *Aggressive Behavior, 29*(3), 202–214.

LeBoeuf, R. A., & Shafir, E. (2012). Decision making. In K. J. Holyoak and R. G. Morrison (Eds.), *The Oxford handbook of thinking and reasoning* (pp. 301–321). Oxford, UK: Oxford University Press.

Lebow, J. (2006). *Research for the psychotherapist: From science to practice*. New York, NY: Routledge.

Lechner, S. C., Tennen, H., & Affleck, G. (2009). Benefit-finding and growth. In S. J. Lopez & C. R. Snyder (Eds.), *Oxford handbook of positive psychology*, 633–640. New York, NY: Oxford University Press.

Ledley, D. R., Erwin, B. A., & Heimberg, R. G. (2008). Social anxiety disorder. In W. E. Craighead, D. J. Milkowitz, & L. W. Craighead (Eds.), *Psychopathology: History, diagnosis, and empirical foundations* (pp. 198–233). Hoboken, NJ: Wiley.

LeDoux, J. E. (1996). *The emotional brain: The mysterious underpinnings of emotional life*. New York, NY: Simon & Schuster.

LeDoux, J. E. (2007). Consolidation: Challenging the traditional view. In H. L. Roediger, Y. Dudai, & S. M. Fitzpatrick (Eds.), *Science of memory: Concepts* (pp. 171–175). Oxford, UK: Oxford University Press.

LeDoux, J. E. & Damasio, A. R. (2013). Emotions and feelings. In E. R. Kandel, J. H. Schwartz, T. M. Jessell, S. A. Siegelbaum, & A. J. Hudspeth (Eds.), *Principles of neural science* (5th ed., pp. 1079–1094). New York, NY: McGraw-Hill.

LeDoux, J. E., Schiller, D., & Cain, C. (2009). Emotional reaction and action: From threat processing to goal-directed behavior. In M. S. Gazzaniga (Ed.), *The cognitive neurosciences* (4th ed., pp. 905–924). Cambridge, MA: MIT Press.

Lee, B. B. (2010). Retinal anatomy. In E. B. Goldstein (Ed.), *Encyclopedia of perception* (pp. 868–871). Thousand Oaks, CA: SAGE.

Lee, C. (2002). The impact of belonging to a high school gay/straight alliance. *The High School Journal, 85*(3), 13–26.

Lee, E. (Ed.). (1997). *Working with Asian Americans: A guide for clinicians*. New York, NY: Guilford Press.

Lee, E. A. E., & Troop-Gordon, W. (2011). Peer processes and gender role development: Changes in gender atypicality related to negative peer treatment and children's friendships. *Sex Roles, 64*(12), 90–102.

Lee, E., & Mock, M. R. (2005). Asian families: An overview. In M. McGoldrick, J. Giordano, & N. Garcia-Preto (Eds.), *Ethnicity and family therapy* (3rd ed., pp. 269–289). New York, NY: Guilford Press.

Lee, F., Hallahan, M., & Herzog, T. (1996). Explaining real-life events: How culture and domain shape attributions. *Personality and Social Psychology Bulletin, 22*, 732–741.

Lee, J. J., & Pinker, S. (2010). Rationales for indirect speech: The theory of the strategic speaker. *Psychological Review, 117*(3), 785–807.

Lee, K. A., & Rosen, L. A. (2012). Sleep and human development. In C. M. Morin & C. A. Espie (Eds.), *The Oxford handbook of sleep and sleep disorders* (pp. 75–94). Oxford, UK: Oxford University Press.

Lee-Chiong, T., & Sateia, M. (2006). Pharmacologic therapy of insomnia. In T. L. Lee-Chiong (Ed.), *Sleep: A comprehensive handbook* (pp. 125–132). Hoboken, NJ: Wiley-Liss.

Lee-Won, R. J., Shim, M., Joo, Y. K., & Park, S. G. (2014). Who puts the best "face" forward on Facebook?: Positive self-presentation in online social networking and the role of self-consciousness, actual-to-total Friends ratio, and culture. *Computers in Human Behavior, 39*, 413–423.

Leger, D. (1994). The cost of sleep-related accidents: A report for the National Commission on Sleep Disorders Research. *Sleep, 17*(1), 84–93.

Leger, D. (2012). A socioeconomic perspective of sleep disorders (insomnia and obstructive sleep apnea). In C. M. Morin & C. A. Espie (Eds.), *The Oxford handbook of sleep and sleep disorders* (pp. 324–3470). Oxford, UK: Oxford University Press.

Legerstee, M. (1992). A review of the animate-inanimate distinction in infancy: Implications for models of social and cognitive knowing. *Early Development and Parenting, 1*(2), 59–67.

Legerstee, M. (1994), The role of familiarity and sound in the development of person and object permanence. *British Journal of Developmental Psychology, 12*, 455–468. doi:10.1111/j.2044-835X

Legerstee, M., Pomerleau, A., Malcuit, G., & Feider, H. (1987). The development of infants' responses to people and a doll: Implications for research in communication. *Infant Behavior and Development, 10*(1), 81–95.

Legewie, J., & DiPrete, T. A. (2012). School context and the gender gap in educational achievement. *American Sociological Review, 77*(3), 463–485.

Lehman, A. F., Kreyenbuhl, J., Buchanan, R. W., Dickerson, F. B., Dixon, L. B., Goldberg, R., . . . Steinwachs, D. M. (2004). The schizophrenia patient outcomes research team (PORT): Updated treatment recommendations 2003. *Schizophrenia Bulletin, 30*(2), 193–217.

Leiblum, S., Wiegel, M., & Brickle, F. (2003). Sexual attitudes of U.S. and Canadian medical students: The role of ethnicity, gender, religion and acculturation. *Sexual and Relationship Therapy, 18*(4), 473–491.

Leigh, B. C. (1989). Reasons for having and avoiding sex: Gender, sexual orientation, and relationship to sexual behavior. *Journal of Sex Research, 26*(2), 199–209.

Leigh, E., & Hirsch, C. R. (2011). Worry in imagery and verbal form: Effect on residual working memory capacity. *Behaviour Research and Therapy, 49*(2), 99–105.

Leighty, K. A., Grand, A. P., Pittman Courte, V. L., Maloney, M. A., & Bettinger, T. L. (2013) Relational responding by eastern box turtles (*Terrapene carolina*) in a series of color discrimination tasks. *Journal of Comparative Psychology, 127*.256–264.

Lemm, K. M. (2006). Positive associations among interpersonal contact, motivation, and implicit and explicit attitudes toward gay men. *Journal of Homosexuality, 51*(2), 79–99.

Lenzenweger, M. F., & Clarkin, J. F. (Eds.) (2005). *Major theories of personality disorder*. New York, NY: Guilford Press.

Lenzenweger, M. F., Lane, M. C., Loranger, A. W., & Kessler, R. C. (2007). DSM-IV personality disorders in the National Comorbidity Survey Replication (NCS-R). *Biological Psychiatry, 62*(6), 553–564.

Leone, R., & Barowski, L. (2011). A longitudinal analysis of the PG-13 rating category in U.S. movies. *Journal of Children and Media, 5*, 53–68.

Leong, F. T. L. (2009). Guest editor's introduction: History of racial and ethnic minority psychology. *Cultural Diversity and Ethnic Minority Psychology, 15*(4), 315–316.

Leong, F. T. L. (2014). Introduction. In F. T. L. Leong (Ed.), *APA handbook of multicultural psychology* (Vol. 1, pp. xxi–xxvii). Washington, DC: American Psychological Association.

Leong, F. T. L., Holliday, B. G., Trimble, J. E., Padilla, A., & McCubbin, L. (2012a). Ethnic minority psychology. In I. Weiner (Ed.-in-Chief) & D. Freedheim (Vol. Ed.), *Handbook of psychology* (2nd ed., Vol. 1). New York, NY: Wiley.

Leong, F. T. L. & Kalibetseva, Z. (2013). Clinical research with culturally diverse populations. In J. S. Comer & P. C. Kendall (Eds.), *The Oxford handbook of research strategies for clinical psychology* (pp. 413–433). Oxford: Oxford University Press.

Leong, F. T. L. & Okazaki, S. (2009). History of Asian American psychology. *Cultural Diversity and Ethnic Minority Psychology, 15*(4), 352–362.

Leong, F. T., Pickren, W. E., & Tang, L. C. (2012b). A history of cross-cultural clinical psychology, and its importance to mental health today. In E. C. Chang & C. A. Downey (Eds.), *Handbook of race and development in mental health* (pp. 11–26). New York, NY: Springer Science+Business Media.

Leong, F. T. L., Schmitt, N., & Lyons, B. J. (2012). Developing testable and important research questions. In H. Cooper (Ed.), *APA handbook of research methods in psychology*: Vol. 1. Foundations, *planning, measures, and psychometrics* (pp. 119–132). Washington, DC: American Psychological Association.

Lepper, M. R., Ross, L., & Lau, R. R. (1986). Persistence of inaccurate beliefs about the self: Perseverance effects in the classroom. *Journal of Personality and Social Psychology, 50*, 482–491.

Lerman, D. C., & Toole, L. M. (2011). Developing function-based punishment procedures for problem behavior. In W. W. Fisher, C. C. Piazza, & H. S. Roane (Eds.), *Handbook of applied behavior analysis* (pp. 348–369). New York, NY: Guilford.

Lerner, J. V., Phelps, E., Forman, Y., & Bowers, E. P. (2009). Positive youth development. In R. M. Lerner & L. Steinberg (Eds.), *Handbook of adolescent psychology* (3rd ed., Vol. 1, pp. 524–558). Hoboken, NJ: Wiley.

Lerner, M. J. (1965). Evaluation of performance as a function of performer's reward and attractiveness. *Journal of Personality and Social Psychology, 1*(4), 355–360.

Lerner, M. J., & Miller, D. T. (1978). Just world research and the attribution process: Looking back and ahead. *Psychological Bulletin, 85*(5), 1030–1051.

Lerner, R. M. & Steinberg, L. (2009). The scientific study of adolescent development: Historical and contemporary perspectives. In R. M. Lerner & L. Steinberg (Eds.), *Handbook of adolescent psychology* (3rd ed., Vol. 1, pp. 3–14. Hoboken, NJ: Wiley.

Lerner, R. M. (2006). Developmental science, developmental systems, and contemporary theories of human development. In R. M. Lerner (Vol. Ed.), *Handbook of child psychology* (6th ed., Vol. 1, pp. 1–17). Hoboken, NJ: Wiley.

Lerner, R. M., Theokas, C., & Bobek, D. L. (2005). Concepts and theories of human development: Historical and contemporary dimensions. In M. H. Bornstein & M. E. Lamb (Eds.), *Developmental science: An advanced textbook* (5th ed., pp. 3–44). Mahwah, NJ: Lawrence Erlbaum.

Leserman, J., Jackson, E. D., Petitto, J. M., Golden, R. N., Silva, S. G., Perkins, D. O., . . . Evans, D. L. (1999). Progression to AIDS: The effects of stress, depressive symptoms, and social support. *Psychosomatic Medicine, 61*(3), 397–406.

Lesku, J. A., Rattenborg, N. C., & Amlaner Jr., C. J. (2006). The evolution of sleep: A phylogenetic approach. In T. L. Lee-Chiong (Ed.), *Sleep: A comprehensive handbook* (pp. 49–62). Hoboken, NJ: Wiley-Liss.

Leu, J., Mesquita, B., Ellsworth, P. C., ZhiYong, Z., Huijuan, Y., Buchtel, E., . . . Masuda, T. (2010). Situational differences in dialectical emotions: Boundary conditions in a cultural comparison of North Americans and East Asians. *Cognition and Emotion, 24*(3), 419–435.

Leung, A. K. Y., & Cohen, D. (2007). The soft embodiment of culture: Camera angles and motion through time and space. *Psychological Science, 18*(9), 824–830.

Leung, A. K. Y., Maddux, W. W., Galinsky, A. D., & Chiu, C. Y. (2008). Multicultural experience enhances creativity: The when and how. *American Psychologist, 63*(3), 169–181.

Leung, J., Pachana, N. A., and McLaughlin, D. (2014), Social support and health-related quality of life in women with breast cancer: A longitudinal study. *Psycho-oncology*. doi:10.1002/pon.3523

LeVay, S. (1991). A difference in hypothalamic structure between heterosexual and homosexual men. *Science, 253*(5023), 1034–1037.

Levey, S. (2013). *Introduction to language development*. San Diego, CA: Plural Publishing.

Levin, D. S., Thurman, S. K., & Kiepert, M. H. (2010). More than just a memory: The nature and validity of working memory in educational settings. In G. M. Davies & D. B. Wright (Eds.), *Current issues in applied memory research* (pp. 72–95). East Sussex, UK: Psychology Press.

Levin, H. S., & Hanten, G. (2002). Posttraumatic amnesia and residual memory deficit after closed head injury. In A. D. Baddeley, M. D. Kopelman, & B. A. Wilson (Eds.), *The handbook of memory disorders* (2nd ed., pp. 381–411). Chichester, UK: Wiley.

Levin, I. P. (1987). Associative effects of information framing. *Bulletin of the Psychonomic Society, 25*(2), 85–86.

Levin, I. P., Schnittjer, S. K., & Thee, S. L. (1988). Information framing effects in social and personal decisions. *Journal of Experimental Social Psychology, 24*(6), 520–529.

Levin, S., Van Laar, C., & Sidanius, J. (2003). The effects of ingroup and outgroup friendships on ethnic attitudes in college: A longitudinal study. *Group Processes & Intergroup Relations, 6*(1), 76–92.

Levine, J. M., & Kerr, N. L. (2007). Inclusion and exclusion: Implications for group processes. In A. W. Kruglanski & E. T. Higgins (Eds.), *Social psychology: Handbook of basic principles* (2nd ed., pp. 759–784). New York, NY: Guilford Press.

Levine, J. M., & Moreland, R. L. (2012). A history of small group research. In A. W. Kruglanski & W. Stroebe (Eds.), *Handbook of the history of social psychology* (pp. 383–405). New York, NY: Psychology Press.

Levine, M. P., & Murnen, S. K. (2009). "Everybody knows that mass media are/are not [pick one] a cause of eating disorders": A critical review of evidence for a causal link between media, negative body image, and disordered eating in females. *Journal of Social & Clinical Psychology, 28*(1), 9–42.

Levine, M. P., & Smolak, L. (2010). Cultural influences on body image and the eating disorders. In W. S. Agras (Ed.), *The Oxford handbook of eating disorders* (pp. 223–246). New York, NY: Oxford University Press.

Levine, M. W. (2001). Principles of neural processing. In E. B. Goldstein (Ed.), *Blackwell handbook of perception* (pp. 24–52). Oxford, UK: Blackwell.

Levis, D. J. (2008). The prolonged exposure techniques of implosive (flooding) therapy. In W. T. O'Donohue & J. E. Fisher (Eds.), *Cognitive behavior therapy: Applying empirically supported techniques in your practice* (2nd ed., pp. 272–282). Hoboken, NJ: Wiley.

Levis, D. J., & Carrera, R. (1967). Effects of ten hours of implosive therapy in the treatment of outpatients: A preliminary report. *Journal of Abnormal Psychology, 72*(6), 504.

Levitin, D. J., & Tirovolas, A. K. (2010). Music cognition and perception. In E. B. Goldstein (Ed.), *Encyclopedia of perception* (pp. 599–606). Thousand Oaks, CA: SAGE.

Levorato, M. C., & Cacciari, C. (2002). The creation of new figurative expressions: Psycholinguistic evidence in Italian children, adolescents and adults. *Journal of Child Language, 29*(01), 127–150.

Levorato, M. C., Nesi, B., & Cacciari, C. (2004). Reading comprehension and understanding idiomatic expressions: A developmental study. *Brain and Language, 91*(3), 303–314.

Lewes, K. (1995). *Psychoanalysis and male homosexuality*. Lanham, MD: Jason Aronson.

Lewis, B. H., Legato, M., & Fisch, H. (2006). Medical implications of the male biological clock. *JAMA: The Journal of the American Medical Association, 296*(19), 2369–2371.

Lewis, C., & Carpendale, J. (2011). Social cognition. In P. K. Smith & C. H. Hart (Eds.), *The Wiley-Blackwell handbook of childhood social development* (2nd ed., pp. 531–548). Malden, MA: Wiley-Blackwell.

Lewis, M. (2008). The emergence of human emotions. In M. Lewis, J. M. Haviland-Jones, & L. F. Barrett (Eds.), *Handbook of emotions* (3rd ed., pp. 304–319). New York, NY: Guilford Press.

Lewis, M. B. (2012). Exploring the positive and negative implications of facial feedback. *Emotion, 12*(4), 852–859.

Lewis, M., & Thomas, D. (1990). Cortisol release in infants in response to inoculation. *Child Development, 61*(1), 50–59.

Lewis, M., Takai-Kawakami, K., Kawakami, K., & Sullivan, M. W. (2010). Cultural differences in emotional responses to success and failure. *International Journal of Behavioral Development, 34*(1), 53–61.

Lewis, S. W., & Buchanan, R. W. (2007). *Fast facts: Schizophrenia* (3rd ed.). Oxford, UK: Health Press.

Lewis, T. T., Cogburn, C. D., & Williams, D. R. (2015). Self-reported experiences of discrimination and health: Scientific advances, ongoing controversies, and emerging issues. *Annual Review of Clinical Psychology, 11*, 407–440.

Lewkowicz, D. J. (2010). Nature and nurture in perception. In E. B. Goldstein (Ed.), *Encyclopedia of perception* (pp. 610–615). Thousand Oaks, CA: SAGE.

Li, J., Wang, Y. J., Zhang, M., Xu, Z. Q., Gao, C. Y., Fang, C. Q., . . . Zhou, H. D. (2011). Vascular risk factors promote conversion from mild cognitive impairment to Alzheimer disease. *Neurology, 76*(17), 1485–1491.

Li, N. P., Bailey, J. M., Kenrick, D. T., & Linsenmeier, J. A. (2002). The necessities and luxuries of mate preferences: Testing the tradeoffs. *Journal of Personality and Social Psychology, 82*(6), 947–955.

Li, P., & Ma, H. (2012). Iris recognition in non-ideal imaging conditions. *Pattern Recognition Letters, 33*(8), 1012–1018.

Li, P., Jin, Z., & Tan, L. H. (2004). Neural representations of nouns and verbs in Chinese: An fMRI study. *NeuroImage, 21*(4), 1533–1541.

Li, W., Luxenberg, E., Parrish, T., & Gottfried, J. A. (2006). Learning to smell the roses: Experience-dependent neural plasticity in human piriform and orbitofrontal cortices. *Neuron, 52*(6), 1097–1108.

Li, Y., & Epley, N. (2009). When the best appears to be saved for last: Serial position effects on choice. *Journal of Behavioral Decision Making, 22*(4), 378–389.

Libby, D., & Chaparro, A. (2009, October). Text messaging versus talking on a cell phone: A comparison of their effects on driving performance. *Proceedings of the Human Factors and Ergonomics Society Annual Meeting, 53*(18), 1353–1357.

Lichstein, K. L., Durrence, H. H., Riedel, B. W., Taylor, D. J., & Bush, A. J. (2004). *Epidemiology of sleep: Age, gender, and ethnicity*. Mahwah, NJ: Lawrence Erlbaum.

Lichstein, K. L., Vander Wal, G. S., & Dillon, H. R. (2012). Insomnia III: Therapeutic approaches. In C. M. Morin & C. A. Espie (Eds.), *The Oxford handbook of sleep and sleep disorders* (pp. 453–470). Oxford, UK: Oxford University Press.

Lichtenberger, E. O., & Kaufman, A. S. (2009). *Essentials of WAIS-IV assessment*. Hoboken, NJ: Wiley.

Lichtenstein, E., & Rodrigues, M. P. (1977). Long-term effects of rapid smoking treatment for dependent cigarette smokers. *Addictive Behaviors, 2*(2-3), 109–112.

Lichtenstein, P., Carlström, E., Råstam, M., Gillberg, C., & Anckarsäter, H. (2010). The genetics of autism spectrum disorders and related neuropsychiatric disorders in childhood. *American Journal of Psychiatry, 167*(11), 1357–1363.

Lichtenstein, P., Yip, B. H., Björk, C., Pawitan, Y., Cannon, T. D., Sullivan, P. F., & Hultman, C. M. (2009). Common genetic determinants of schizophrenia and bipolar disorder in Swedish families: A population-based study. *The Lancet, 373*(9659), 234–239.

Lidz, T., Cornelison, A. R., & Fleck, S. (1965). *Schizophrenia and the family*. New York, NY: International Universities Press.

Lieberman, J. A., Stroup, T. S., & Perkins, D. O. (2006). Preface. In J. A. Lieberman, T. S. Stroup, & D. O. Perkins (Eds.), *The American Psychiatric Publishing textbook of schizophrenia* (p. xvii). Washington, DC: American Psychiatric Association Publishing.

Lieberman, J. A., Stroup, T. S., McEvoy, J. P., Swartz, M. S., Rosenheck, R. A., Perkins, D. O., . . . Hsaiao, J. K. (2005). Effectiveness of antipsychotic drugs in patients with chronic schizophrenia. *New England Journal of Medicine*, 353(12), 1209–1223.

Lieberman, M. D., Hariri, A., Jarcho, J. M., Eisenberger, N. I., & Bookheimer, S. Y. (2005). An fMRI investigation of race-related amygdala activity in African-American and Caucasian-American individuals. *Nature Neuroscience, 8*(6), 720–722.

Liepert, J., Bauder, H., Miltner, W. H., Taub, E., & Weiller, C. (2000). Treatment-induced cortical reorganization after stroke in humans. *Stroke, 31*(6), 1210–1216.

Lilienfeld, S. O. (2010). *50 great myths of popular psychology: Shattering widespread misconceptions about human behavior*. Malden, MA: Wiley-Blackwell.

Lilienfeld, S. O., & Lynn, S. J. (2003). Dissociative identity disorder: Multiple personalities, multiple controversies. In S. O. Lilienfeld, S. J. Lynn, & J. M. Mohr (Eds.), *Science and pseudoscience in clinical psychology* (pp. 109–142). New York, NY: Guilford Press.

Lilienfeld, S. O., Lynn, S. J., & Lohr, J. M. (Eds.) (2015). *Science and pseudoscience in clinical psychology* (2nd ed.). New York, NY: Guilford Press.

Lilienfeld, S. O., Lynn, S. J., Ruscio, J., & Beyerstein, B. L. (2010). *50 great myths of popular psychology*. Malden, MA: Wiley-Blackwell.

Lilienfeld, S. O., Wood, J. M., & Garb, H. N. (2000). The scientific status of projective techniques. *Psychological Science in the Public Interest, 1*(2), 27–66.

Lim, J., & Dinges, D. F. (2010). A meta-analysis of the impact of short-term sleep deprivation on cognitive variables. *Psychological Bulletin, 136*(3), 375–389.

Lima, S. L., Rattenborg, N. C., Lesku, J. A., & Amlaner, C. J. (2005). Sleeping under the risk of predation. *Animal Behaviour, 70*(4), 723–736.

Lind, M. (1995). Brave new right. In S. Fraser (Ed.) *The bell curve wars: Race, intelligence, and the future of America* (pp. 172–178). New York, NY: Basic Books.

Linden, D. (2012). *The biology of psychological disorders*. Basingstoke, UK: Palgrave Macmillan.

Linden, D. E. J. (2006). How psychotherapy changes the brain: The contribution of functional neuroimaging. *Molecular Psychiatry, 11*(6), 528–538.

Linden, D. J. (1994). Long-term synaptic depression in the mammalian brain. *Neuron, 12*(3), 457–472.

Linden, D. J. (2015). *Touch: The science of hand, heart, and mind*. New York, NY: Penguin.

Linden, D. J. & Connor, J. A. (1995). Long-term synaptic depression. *Annual Review of Neuroscience, 18*(1), 319–357.

Lindenmayer, J. P., & Khan, A. (2006). Psychopathology. In J. A. Lieberman, T. S. Stroup, & D. O. Perkins (Eds.), *The American Psychiatric Publishing textbook of schizophrenia* (pp. 187–221). Washington, DC: American Psychiatric Association.

Lindsey, D. T., & Brown, A. M. (2002). Color naming and the phototoxic effects of sunlight on the eye. *Psychological Science, 13*(6), 506–512

Lindsey, D. T., & Brown, A. M. (2006). Universality of color names. *Proceedings of the National Academy of Sciences of the United States of America, 103*(44), 16608–16613.

Linehan, M. M. (1993a). *Cognitive-behavioral treatment of borderline personality disorder*. New York, NY: Guilford Press.

Linehan, M. M. (1993b). *Skills training manual for treating borderline personality disorder*. New York, NY: Guilford Press.

Linton, S. J. (2000). A review of psychological risk factors in back and neck pain. *Spine, 25*(9), 1148–1156.

Linville, S. E. (1998). Acoustic correlates of perceived versus actual sexual orientation in men's speech. *Folia Phoniatrica et Logopaedica, 50*(1), 35–48.

Lippa, R. A. (2003). Handedness, sexual orientation, and gender-related personality traits in men and women. *Archives of Sexual Behavior, 32*(2), 103–114.

Lippa, R. A. (2007). The preferred traits of mates in a cross-national study of heterosexual and homosexual men and women: An examination of biological and cultural influences. *Archives of Sexual Behavior, 36*(2), 193–208.

Lipsey, M. W., & Wilson, D. B. (1993). The efficacy of psychological, educational, and behavioral treatment: Confirmation from meta-analysis. *American Psychologist, 48*(12), 1181–1209.

Lipsey, M. W., Wilson, D. B., Cohen, M. A., & Derzon, J. H. (1997). Is there a causal relationship between alcohol use and violence. *Recent Developments in Alcoholism, 13,* 245–282.

Lipsitz, J. D. (2009). Theory of interpersonal psychotherapy. In G. O. Gabbard (Ed.), *Textbook of psychotherapeutic treatments* (pp. 289–307). Washington, DC: American Psychiatric Publishing.

Lipton, M. L., Kim, N., Zimmerman, M. E., Kim, M., Stewart, W. F., Branch, C. A., & Lipton, R. B. (2013). Soccer heading is associated with white matter microstructural and cognitive abnormalities. *Radiology, 268*(3), 850–857.

Lisberger, S. G., & Thach, W. T. (2013). The cerebellum. In E. R. Kandel, J. H. Schwartz, T. M. Jessell, S. A. Siegelbaum, & A. J. Hudspeth (Eds.), *Principles of neural science* (5th ed., pp. 960–981). New York, NY: McGraw-Hill.

Lissek, S., & Grillon, C. (2010). Overgeneralization of conditioned fear in the anxiety disorders: Putative memorial mechanisms. *Journal of Psychology, 218*(2), 146–148.

Lissek, S., Powers, A. S., McClure, E. B., Phelps, E. A., Woldehawariat, G., Gillon, C., & Pine, D. S. (2005). Classical fear conditioning in the anxiety disorders: A meta-analysis. *Behaviour Research and Therapy, 43*(11), 1391–1424.

Little, D. M., Arciniegas, D. B., & Hart Jr., J. (2013). Electroencephalography. In D. B. Arciniegas, C. A. Anderson, & C. M. Filley (Eds.), *Behavioral neurology & neuropsychiatry* (pp. 442–458). Cambridge, UK: Cambridge University Press.

Little, T. D., Card, N. A., Preacher, K. J., & McConnell, E. (2009). Modeling longitudinal data from research on adolescence. In R. M. Lerner & L. Steinberg (Eds.), *Handbook of adolescent psychology* (3rd ed., Vol. 1, pp. 15–54). Hoboken, NJ: Wiley.

Liverant, G. I., Stoddard, J. A., Meuret, A. E., & Barlow, D. H. (2007). Clinical science and the revolution in psychological treatment: The example of anxiety disorders. In T. A. Treat, R. R. Bootzin, & T. B. Baker (Eds.), *Psychological clinical science: Papers in honor of Richard M. McFall* (pp. 77–103). New York, NY: Routledge.

Livermore, D. A. (2015). *Leading with cultural intelligence: The real secret to success.* New York, NY: AMACOM.

Livingstone, M. (2014). *Vision and art: The biology of seeing*. New York, NY: Abrams.

Llaneza, P., García-Portilla, M. P., Llaneza-Suárez, D., Armott, B., & Pérez-López, F. R. (2012). Depressive disorders and the menopause transition. *Maturitas, 71*(2), 120–130.

Locher, P., Unger, R., Sociedade, P., & Wahl, J. (1993). At first glance: Accessibility of the physical attractiveness stereotype. *Sex Roles, 28*(11), 729–743.

Locke, J. L. (2012). Displays of vocal and verbal complexity: A fitness account of language, situated in development. In M. Tallerman & K. R. Gibson (Eds.), *The Oxford handbook of language evolution* (pp. 328–339). Oxford, UK: Oxford University Press.

Lockhart, R. S. (2000). Methods of memory research. In E. Tulving & F. I. M. Craik, *The Oxford handbook of memory* (pp. 45–57). Oxford, UK: Oxford University Press.

Lodhi, P. H., Deo, S., & Belhekar, V. M. (2002). The five-factor model of personality. In R. R. McCrae & J. Allik (Eds.), *The five-factor model of personality across cultures* (pp. 227–248). New York, NY: Springer Science+Business Media.

Loebach, J. L., Conway, C. M., & Pisoni, D. B. (2010). Attention: Cognitive influences. In E. B. Goldstein (Ed.), *Encyclopedia of perception* (pp. 138–141). Thousand Oaks, CA: SAGE.

Loeber, R., & Hay, D. (1997). Key issues in the development of aggression and violence from childhood to early adulthood. *Annual Review of Psychology, 48*(1), 371–410.

Loehlin, J. C., & Nichols, R. C. (1976). *Heredity, environment, & personality: A study of 850 sets of twins*. Austin, TX: University of Texas Press.

Loewenstein, G. (1994). The psychology of curiosity: A review and reinterpretation. *Psychological Bulletin, 116*(1), 75–98.

Loftus, E. F. (1979). *Eyewitness testimony*. Cambridge, MA: Harvard University Press.

Loftus, E. F. (2005). Planting misinformation in the human mind: A 30-year investigation of the malleability of memory. *Learning & Memory, 12*(4), 361–366.

Loftus, E. F., & Cahill, L. (2007). Memory distortion: From misinformation to rich false memory. In H. L. Roediger & J. S. Nairne (Eds.), *The foundation of remembering* (pp. 413– 425). New York, NY: Psychology Press.

Loftus, E. F., & Palmer, J. C. (1974). Reconstruction of automobile destruction: An example of the interaction between language and memory. *Journal of Verbal Learning and Verbal Behavior, 13*(5), 585–589.

Loftus, E. F., & Pickrell, J. E. (1995). The formation of false memories. *Psychiatric Annals, 25*(12), 720–725.

Logue, A. W. (1979). Taste aversion and the generality of the laws of learning. *Psychological Bulletin, 86*(2), 276–296.

Lohmann, R. I. (2007). Dreams and ethnography. In D. Barrett & P. McNamara (Eds.), *The new science of dreaming* (Vol. 3, pp. 35–70). Westport, CT: Praeger.

Long, G. M. (1980). Iconic memory: A review and critique of the study of short-term visual storage. *Psychological Bulletin, 88*(3), 785–820.

Long, J. E., Jr. (2005). Power to prescribe: The debate over prescription privileges for psychologists and the legal issues implicated. *Law and Psychology Review, 29,* 243–260.

Longo, D. L., Duffey, P. L., Kopp, W. C., Heyes, M. P., Alvord, W. G., Sharfman, W. H., . . . Rosenstein, D. L. (1999). Conditioned immune response to interferon-γ in humans. *Clinical Immunology, 90*(2), 173–181.

Lotze, M., Grodd, W., Birbaumer, N., Erb, M., Huse, E., & Flor, H. (1999). Does use of a myoelectric prosthesis prevent cortical reorganization and phantom limb pain? *Nature Neuroscience, 2*(6), 501–502.

Lowe, R. (2011). *Stories I only tell my friends: An autobiography.* New York, NY: Henry Holt.

Lubart, T. (1999). Cross-cultural perspectives on creativity. In R. J. Sternberg (Ed.), *The Cambridge handbook of creativity* (pp. 265–278). Cambridge, UK: Cambridge University Press.

Luborsky, L., Rosenthal, R., Diguer, L., Andrusyna, T. P., Berman, J. S., Levitt, J. T., . . . Krause, E. (2002). The dodo bird verdict is alive and well—mostly. *Clinical Psychology: Science and Practice, 9*(1), 2–12.

Luborsky, L., Singer, J., & Luborsky, L. (1975). Comparative studies of psychotherapies: Is it true that "everyone has won and all must have prizes"? *Archives of General Psychiatry, 32*(8), 995–1008.

Lucas, R. E., Clark, A. E., Georgellis, Y., & Diener, E. (2003). Reexamining adaptation and the set point model of happiness: Reactions to changes in marital status. *Journal of Personality and Social Psychology, 84*(3), 527–539.

Lucas, R. E., & Diener, E. (2008). Subjective well-being. In M. Lewis, J. M. Haviland-Jones, & L. F. Barrett (Eds.), *Handbook of emotions* (3rd ed., pp. 471–484). New York, NY: Guilford Press.

Luders, E., Narr, K. L., Thompson, P. M., & Toga, A. W. (2009). Neuroanatomical correlates of intelligence. *Intelligence, 37*(2), 156–163.

Ludwig, A. M. (1994). Mental illness and creative activity in female writers. *American Journal of Psychiatry, 151*(11), 1650–1656.

Ludwig, A. M. (1995). *The price of greatness: Resolving the creativity and madness controversy*. New York, NY: Guilford Press.

Ludwig, A. M. (1997). Creative achievement and psychopathology: Comparison among professions. In M. A. Runco & R. Richards (Eds.), *Eminent creativity, everyday creativity, and health* (pp. 33–60). Greenwich, CT: Ablex.

Lukatela, G., & Turvey, M. T. (1994a). Visual lexical access is initially phonological: I. Evidence from associative priming by words, homophones, and pseudohomophones. *Journal of Experimental Psychology: General, 123*(2), 107–128.

Lukatela, G., & Turvey, M. T. (1994b). Visual lexical access is initially phonological: 2. Evidence from phonological priming by homophones and pseudohomophones. *Journal of Experimental Psychology: General, 123*(4), 331–353.

Luminet, O., & Curci, A. (2009). Introduction. In O. Luminet & A. Curci (Eds.), *Flashbulb memories: New issues and new perspectives* (pp. 1–9). East Sussex, UK: Psychology Press.

Lundström, J. N., Gonçalves, M., Esteves, F., & Olsson, M. J. (2003). Psychological effects of subthreshold exposure to the putative human pheromone 4, 16-androstadien-3-one. *Hormones and Behavior, 44*(5), 395–401.

Lunt, P. (2009). *Stanley Milgram: Shaper of obedience*. New York, NY: Palgrave Macmillan

Lupien, S. J., de Leon, M., De Santi, S., Convit, A., Tarshish, C., Nair, N. P. V., . . . Meaney, M. J. (1998). Cortisol levels during human aging predict hippocampal atrophy and memory deficits. *Nature Neuroscience, 1*(1), 69–73.

Lupien, S. J., McEwen, B. S., Gunnar, M. R., & Heim, C. (2009). Effects of stress throughout the lifespan on the brain, behaviour and cognition. *Nature Reviews Neuroscience, 10*(6), 434–445.

Lyamin, O. I., Manger, P. R., Ridgway, S. H., Mukhametov, L. M., & Siegel, J. M. (2008). Cetacean sleep: An unusual form of mammalian sleep. *Neuroscience & Biobehavioral Reviews, 32*(8), 1451–1484.

Lynch, M. P., & Eilers, R. E. (1991). Children's perception of native and nonnative musical scales. *Music Perception: An Interdisciplinary Journal, 9*(1), 121–131.

Lynch, M. P., & Eilers, R. E. (1992). A study of perceptual development for musical tuning. *Perception & Psychophysics, 52*(6), 599–608.

Lynn, R., Harvey, J., & Nyborg, H. (2009). Average intelligence predicts atheism rates across 137 nations. *Intelligence, 37*(1), 11–15.

Lynn, R., & Martin, T. (1997). Gender differences in extraversion, neuroticism, and psychoticism in 37 nations. *The Journal of Social Psychology, 137*(3), 369–373.

Lyons, H. Z., Bieschke, K. J., Dendy, A. K., Worthington, R. L., & Georgemiller, R. (2010). Psychologists' competence to treat lesbian, gay and bisexual clients: State of the field and strategies for improvement. *Professional Psychology: Research and Practice, 41*(5), 424–434.
Lyons, M., Lynch, A., Brewer, G., & Bruno, D. (2014). Detection of sexual orientation ("gaydar") by homosexual and heterosexual women. *Archives of Sexual Behavior, 43*(2), 345–352.
Lyubomirsky, S., Dickerhoof, R., Boehm, J. K., & Sheldon, K. M. (2011). Becoming happier takes both a will and a proper way: An experimental longitudinal intervention to boost well-being. *Emotion, 11*(2), 391–402.
Lyubomirsky, S., King, L., & Diener, E. (2005). The benefits of frequent positive affect: Does happiness lead to success? *Psychological Bulletin, 131*(6), 803–855.
Lyubomirsky, S., & Layous, K. (2013). How do simple positive activities increase well-being? *Current Directions in Psychological Science, 22*(1), 57–62.
Lyubomirsky, S., Sheldon, K. M. & Schkade, D. (2005). Pursuing happiness: The architecture of sustainable change. *Review of General Psychology, 9*(2), 111–131.
MacCann, C., Ziegler, M., & Roberts, R. D. (2012). Faking in personality assessments: Reflections and recommendations. In M. Ziegler, C. MacCann, & R. D. Roberts (Eds.), *New perspectives on faking in personality assessment* (pp. 309–329). New York, NY: Oxford University Press.
Maccoby, E. E. (1998). *The two sexes: Growing up apart, coming together.* Cambridge, MA: Harvard University Press.
MacDonald, G., & Leary, M. R. (2005). Why does social exclusion hurt? The relationship between social and physical pain. *Psychological Bulletin, 131*(2), 202–223.
Mace, J. H. (2004). Involuntary autobiographical memories are highly dependent on abstract cuing: The Proustian view is incorrect. *Applied Cognitive Psychology, 18*(7), 893–899.
Mace, J. H. (2010). The act of remembering the past: An overview. In J. H. Mace (Ed.), *The act of remembering: Toward an understanding of how we remember the past* (pp. 3–10). Chichester, UK: Wiley-Blackwell.
MacFadden, A., Elias, L., & Saucier, D. (2003). Males and females scan maps similarly, but give directions differently. *Brain and Cognition, 53*(2), 297–300.
Mack, A. (2003). Inattentional blindness: Looking without seeing. *Current Directions in Psychological Science, 12*(5), 180–184.
Mackintosh, N. J. (2011). History of theories and measurement of intelligence. In R. J. Sternberg & S. B. Kaufman (Eds.), *The Cambridge handbook of intelligence* (pp. 3–19). Cambridge, UK: Cambridge University Press.
Macknik, S. L., & Martinez-Conde, S. (2010). *Sleights of mind: What the neuroscience of magic reveals about our everyday deceptions.* New York, NY: Henry Holt.
MacLean, C. R., Walton, K. G., Wenneberg, S. R., Levitsky, D. K., Mandarino, J. P., Waziri, R., . . . Schneider, R. H. (1997). Effects of the transcendental meditation program on adaptive mechanisms: Changes in hormone levels and responses to stress after 4 months of practice. *Psychoneuroendocrinology, 22*(4), 277–295.
MacLeod, C. M. (1988). Forgotten but not gone: Savings for pictures and words in long-term memory. *Journal of Experimental Psychology: Learning, Memory, and Cognition, 14*(2), 195–212.
MacLeod, C., & Mathews, A. (2004). Selective memory effects in anxiety disorders: An overview of research findings and their implications. In D. Reisberg & P. Hertel (Eds.), *Memory and emotion* (pp. 155–185). Oxford, UK: Oxford University Press.
Macleod, M. D., & Hulbert, J. C. (2011). Sleep, retrieval inhibition, and the resolving power of human memory. In A. S. Benjamin (Eds.), *Successful remembering and successful forgetting: A Festschrift in honor of Robert A. Bjork* (pp. 133–152). New York, NY: Psychology Press.
Macmillan, M. (2000a). *An odd kind of fame: Stories of Phineas Gage.* Cambridge, MA: MIT Press.
Macmillan, M. (2000b). Restoring Phineas Gage: A 150th retrospective. *Journal of the History of the Neurosciences, 9*(1), 46–66.
Macrae, C. N., & Quadflieg, S. (2010). Perceiving people. In S. T. Fiske, D. T. Gilbert, & G. Lindzey (Eds.), *Handbook of social psychology* (5th ed., Vol. 1, pp. 428–463). Hoboken, NJ: Wiley.
MacWhinney, B. (2001). First language acquisition. In M. Aronoff & J. Rees-Miller (Eds.), *The Handbook of linguistics* (pp. 466–487). Malden, MA: Blackwell.
Maddi, S. R. (1987). Hardiness training at Illinois Bell Telephone. In J. P. Opatz (Ed.), *Health Promotion Evaluation* (pp. 101–115). Stevens Point, WI: National Wellness Institute.
Maddi, S. R. (2002). The story of hardiness: Twenty years of theorizing, research, and practice. *Consulting Psychology Journal: Practice and Research, 54*(3), 173–185.
Maddi, S. R., & Harvey, R. H. (2006). Hardiness considered across cultures. In P. T. P. Wong and L. C. J. Wong (Eds.), *Handbook of multicultural perspectives on stress and coping* (pp. 409–426). New York: Springer Science+Business Media.
Maddi, S. R., & Hightower, M. (1999). Hardiness and optimism as expressed in coping patterns. *Consulting Psychology Journal: Practice and Research, 51*(2), 95–105.
Maddi, S. R., & Kobasa, S. C. (1984). *The hardy executive: Health under stress.* Homewood, IL: Dow Jones-Irwin.
Maddi, S. R., Khoshaba, D. M., Jensen, K., Carter, E., Lu, J. L., & Harvey, R. H. (2002). Hardiness training for high risk undergraduates. *NACADA Journal, 22*, 45–55.
Maddock, J. (2004). The relationship between obesity and the prevalence of fast food restaurants: State-level analysis. *American Journal of Health Promotion, 19*(2), 137–143.
Maddux, J. E., Gosselin, J. T., & Winstead, B. A. (2005). Conceptions of psychopathology: A social constructionist perspective. In J. E. Maddux & B. A. Winstead (Eds.), *Psychopathology* (pp. 3–18). Mahwah, NJ: Lawrence Erlbaum.
Madon, S., Guyll, M., Buller, A. A., Scherr, K. C., Willard, J., & Spoth, R. (2008). The mediation of mothers' self-fulfilling effects on their children's alcohol use: Self-verification, informational conformity, and modeling processes. *Journal of Personality and Social Psychology, 95*(2), 369–384.
Madsen, K. M., Hviid, A., Vestergaard, M., Schendel, D., Wohlfahrt, J., Thorsen, P., . . . Melbye, M. (2002). A population-based study of measles, mumps, and rubella vaccination and autism. *New England Journal of Medicine, 347*(19), 1477–1482.
Maehr, M. L., & Midgley, C. (1991). Enhancing student motivation: A schoolwide approach. *Educational Psychologist, 26*(3–4), 399–427.
Maes, H. H., Neale, M. C., & Eaves, L. J. (1997). Genetic and environmental factors in relative body weight and human adiposity. *Behavior Genetics, 27*(4), 325–351.
Magai, C. (2001). Emotions over the lifespan. In J. E. Birren & K. W. Schaie (Eds.), *Handbook of the psychology of aging* (5th ed., pp. 310–344). San Diego, CA: Academic Press.
Magai, C. (2008). Long-lived emotions: A life course perspective on emotional development. In M. Lewis, J. M. Haviland-Jones, & L. F. Barrett (Eds.), *Handbook of emotions* (3rd ed., pp. 376–392). New York, NY: Guilford Press.
Magga, O. H. (2006). Diversity in Saami terminology for reindeer, snow, and ice. *International Social Science Journal, 58*(157), 25–34.
Magliozzi, T., & Magliozzi, R. (2011, February 25). Hitting brake and gas is bad move. Retrieved from http://blog. nwautos. com/2011/02/hitting_brake_and_gas_is_bad_move. html
Magnus, A., Haby, M. M., Carter, R., & Swinburn, B. (2009). The cost-effectiveness of removing television advertising of high-fat and/or high-sugar food and beverages to Australian children. *International Journal of Obesity, 33*(10), 1094–1102.
Magnusson, D. & Stattin, H. (2006). The person in context: A holistic-interactionistic approach. In R. M. Lerner (Vol. Ed.), *Handbook of child psychology* (6th ed., Vol. 1, pp. 400–464). Hoboken, NJ: Wiley.
Maguire, E. A., Gadian, D. G., Johnsrude, I. S., Good, C. D., Ashburner, J., Frackowiak, R. S., & Frith, C. D. (2000. Navigation-related structural change in the hippocampi of taxi drivers. *Proceedings of the National Academy of Sciences, 97*(8), 4398–4403.
Maheu, M. M., Pulier, M. L., Wilhelm, F. H., McMenamin, J. P., & Brown-Connolly, N. E. (2005). *The mental health professional and the new technologies: A handbook for practice today.* Mahwah, NJ: Lawrence Erlbaum.
Mahoney, J. L., Vandell, D. L., Simpkins, S., & Zarrett, N. (2009). Adolescent out-of-school activities. In R. M. Lerner & L. Steinberg (Eds.), *Handbook of adolescent psychology* (3rd ed., Vol. 2, pp. 228–269). Hoboken, NJ: Wiley.
Mahoney, M. M. (2010). Shift work, jet lag, and female reproduction. *International Journal of Endocrinology*, doi:10.1155/2010/813764
Maier, S. F., Seligman, M. E. P., & Solomon, R. L. (1969). Pavlovian fear conditioning and learned helplessness. In B. A. Campbell & R. M. Church (Eds.), *Punishment and aversive behavior* (pp. 299–343). New York, NY: Appleton-Century-Crofts.
Main, M., & Solomon, J. (1986). Discovery of a new, insecure-disorganized/disoriented attachment pattern. In M. Yogman & T. B. Brazelton (Eds.), *Affective development in infancy* (pp. 95–124). Norwood, NJ: Ablex.
Main, M., & Solomon, J. (1990). Procedures for identifying infants as disorganised/disoriented during the Ainsworth strange situation. In M. T. Greenberg, D. Cicchetti, & E. M. Cummings (Eds.), *Attachment in the preschool years* (pp. 121–160). Chicago, IL: University of Chicago Press.
Majid, A., Bowerman, M., Kita, S., Haun, D. B., & Levinson, S. C. (2004). Can language restructure cognition? The case for space. *Trends in Cognitive Science, 8*(3), 108–114.
Malarkey, W. B., Kiecolt-Glaser, J. K., Pearl, D., & Glaser, R. (1994). Hostile behavior during marital conflict alters pituitary and adrenal hormones. *Psychosomatic Medicine, 56*(1), 41–51.
Malatesta, C. Z., & Haviland, J. M. (1982). Learning display rules: The socialization of emotion expression in infancy. *Child Development, 53*(4), 991–1003.
Malenka, R. C., & Bear, M. F. (2004). LTP and LTD: An embarrassment of riches. *Neuron, 44*(1), 5–21.
Malenka, R. C. & Nicoll, R. A. (1999). Long-term potentiation—a decade of progress? *Science, 285*(5435), 1870–1874.
Malgady, R. G., & Colon-Malgady, G. (2008). Building community test norms: Considerations for ethnic minority populations. In L. A. Suzuki & J. G. Ponterotto (Eds.), *Handbook of multicultural assessment: Clinical, psychological, and educational applications* (3rd ed., pp. 34–51). Hoboken, NJ: Wiley.
Malizia, A. L., & Nutt, D. (2008). Principles and findings from human imaging of anxiety disorders. In R. J. Blanchard, D. C. Blanchard, G. Griebel, & D. Nutt (Eds.), *Handbook of anxiety and fear* (pp. 437–454). Amsterdam, The Netherlands: Elsevier.
Malle, B. F. (2006). The actor-observer asymmetry in attribution: A (surprising) meta-analysis. *Psychological Bulletin, 132*(6), 895–919.
Malle, B. F. (2011). Attribution theories: How people make sense of behavior. In D. Chadee (Ed.), *Theories in social psychology* (pp. 72–95). West Sussex, UK: Wiley-Blackwell.
Malleret, G., Alarcon, J. M., Martel, G., Takizawa, S., Vronskaya, S., Yin, D., . . . Shumyatsky, G. P. (2010). Bidirectional regulation of hippocampal long-term synaptic plasticity and its influence on opposing forms of memory. *Journal of Neuroscience, 30*(10), 3813–3825.

Malone, J. C. (2009). *Psychology: Pythagoras to present*. Cambridge, Mass: MIT Press.

Malouff, J. M., Thorsteinsson, E. B., Schutte, N. S., Bhullar, N., & Rooke, S. E. (2010). The Five-Factor Model of personality and relationship satisfaction of intimate partners: A meta-analysis. *Journal of Research in Personality, 44*(1), 124–127.

Malouff, J., Thorsteinsson, E., Schutte, N., & Rooke, S. E. (2009). Effects of vicarious punishment: A meta-analysis. *The Journal of General Psychology, 136*(3), 271–286.

Manago, A. M., Ward, L. M., Lemm, K. M., Reed, L., & Seabrook, R. (2014). Facebook involvement, objectified body consciousness, body shame, and sexual assertiveness in college women and men. *Sex Roles, 72*(12), 1–14.

Manber, R., & Bootzin, R. R. (1997). Sleep and the menstrual cycle. *Health Psychology, 16*(3), 209–214.

Mandell, B., & Pherwani, S. (2003). Relationship between emotional intelligence and transformational leadership style: A gender comparison. *Journal of Business and Psychology, 17*(3), 387–404.

Mandelman, S. D., & Grigorenko, E. L. (2011). Intelligence: Genes, environments, and their interactions. In R. J. Sternberg & S. B. Kaufman (Eds.), *The Cambridge handbook of intelligence* (pp. 85–106). Cambridge, UK: Cambridge University Press.

Mandler, G. (1980). Recognizing: The judgment of previous occurrence. *Psychological Review, 87*(3), 252–271.

Manenschijn, L., van Kruysbergen, R. G., de Jong, F. H., Koper, J. W., & van Rossum, E. F. (2011). Shift work at young age is associated with elevated long-term cortisol levels and body mass index. *The Journal of Clinical Endocrinology & Metabolism, 96*(11), E1862–E1865.

Maner, J. K., Luce, C. L., Neuberg, S. L., Cialdini, R. B., Brown, S., & Sagarin, B. J. (2002). The effects of perspective taking on motivations for helping: Still no evidence for altruism. *Personality and Social Psychology Bulletin, 28*(11), 1601–1610.

Maner, J. K., Richey, J. A., Cromer, K., Mallott, M., Lejuez, C. W., Joiner, T. E., & Schmidt, N. B. (2007). Dispositional anxiety and risk-avoidant decision-making. *Personality and Individual Differences, 42*(4), 665–675.

Mangan, M. A. (2004). A phenomenology of problematic sexual behavior occurring in sleep. *Archives of Sexual Behavior, 33*(3), 287–293.

Mangelsdorf, S., Gunnar, M., Kestenbaum, R., Lang, S., & Andreas, D. (1990). Infant proneness-to-distress temperament, maternal personality, and mother–infant attachment: Associations and goodness of fit. *Child Development, 61*(3), 820–831.

Manlove, J., Logan, C., Moore, K. A., & Ikramullah, E. (2008). Pathways from family religiosity to adolescent sexual activity and contraceptive use. *Perspectives on Sexual and Reproductive Health, 40*(2), 105–117.

Manning, J. T., Churchill, A. J., & Peters, M. (2007). The effects of sex, ethnicity, and sexual orientation on self-measured digit ratio (2D: 4D). *Archives of Sexual Behavior, 36*(2), 223–233.

Manning, R., Levine, M., & Collins, A. (2007). The Kitty Genovese murder and the social psychology of helping: The parable of the 38 witnesses. *American Psychologist, 62*(6), 555–562.

Manson, J. H., & Perry, S. (2013) Personality structure, sex differences, and temporal change and stability in wild white-faced capuchins (*Cebus capucinus*). *Journal of Comparative Psychology, 127*(3), 299–311. doi:10.1037/a0031316

Manto, M. (2010). *Cerebellar disorders: A practical approach to diagnosis and management*. Cambridge, UK: Cambridge University Press.

Mantonakis, A., Rodero, P., Lesschaeve, I., & Hastie, R. (2009). Order in choice effects of serial position on preferences. *Psychological Science, 20*(11), 1309–1312.

Maquet, P., Péters, J. M., Aerts, J., Delfiore, G., Degueldre, C., Luxen, A., & Franck, G. (1996). Functional neuroanatomy of human rapid-eye-movement sleep and dreaming. *Nature, 383*(6596), 163–166.

Marcia, J. E. (1966). Development and validation of ego-identity status. *Journal of Personality and Social Psychology, 3*(5), 551.

Marcia, J. E. (1980). Identity in adolescence. *Handbook of Adolescent Psychology, 9*, 159–187.

Marcus, G. (2004). *The birth of the mind: How a tiny number of genes creates the complexities of human thought*. New York, NY: Basic Books.

Marcus, G. F., Vijayan, S., Rao, S. B., & Vishton, P. M. (1999). Rule learning by seven-month-old infants. *Science, 283*(5398), 77–80.

Marczyk, G. R., DeMatteo, D., & Festinger, D. (2005). *Essentials of research design and methodology*. Hoboken, NJ: John Wiley & Sons.

Marczyk, G., Krauss, D. A., & Burl, J. (2012). Educational and training models in forensic psychology. In C. R. Bartol & A. M. Bartol (Eds.), *Current perspectives in forensic psychology and criminal behavior* (pp. 2–10). Thousand Oaks, CA: SAGE.

Mareschal, D., & Kaufman, J. (2012). Object permanence in infancy: Revisiting Baillargeon's drawbridge study. In A. M. Slater & P. C. Quinn (Eds.), *Developmental psychology: Revisiting the classic studies* (pp. 86–100). Los Angeles, CA: SAGE.

Margetic, S., Gazzola, C., Pegg, G. G., & Hill, R. A. (2002). Leptin: A review of its peripheral actions and interactions. *International Journal of Obesity*, 26(11), 1407–1433.

Marian, V., & Kaushanskaya, M. (2004). Self-construal and emotion in bicultural bilinguals. *Journal of Memory and Language, 51*(2), 190–201.

Marian, V., & Neisser, U. (2000). Language-dependent recall of autobiographical memories. *Journal of Experimental Psychology: General, 129*(3), 361.

Mark, T. L., Levit, K. R., & Buck, J. A. (2009). Datapoints: Psychotropic drug prescriptions by medical speciality. *Psychiatric Services, 60*(9), 1167. Retrieved from http://ps.psychiatryonline.org/data/Journals/PSS/3889/09ps1167.pdf

Markiewicz, D., Lawford, H., Doyle, A. B., & Haggart, N. (2006). Developmental differences in adolescents' and young adults' use of mothers, fathers, best friends, and romantic partners to fulfill attachment needs. *Journal of Youth and Adolescence, 35*(1), 121–134.

Markin, R. D., & Kasten, J. (2015). Group psychotherapy. In R. L. Cautin & S. O. Lilienfeld (Eds.), *The encyclopedia of clinical psychology* (pp. 1358–1363). West Sussex, UK: Wiley-Blackwell.

Markman, A. B. (1999). *Knowledge representation*. Mahwah, NJ: Lawrence Erlbaum.

Markman, A. B., & Rein, J. R. (2013). The nature of mental concepts. In D. Reisberg (Ed.), *The Oxford handbook of cognitive psychology* (pp. 321–329). Oxford, UK: Oxford University Press.

Markowitz, J. C., & Weissman, M. M. (2012). Interpersonal psychotherapy: Past, present and future. *Clinical Psychology and Psychotherapy, 19*(2), 99–105.

Marks, I., & Cavanagh, K. (2009). Computer-aided psychological treatments: Evolving issues. *Annual Review of Clinical Psychology, 5*, 121–141.

Maron, E., Hettema, J. M., & Shilk, J. (2008). The genetics of human anxiety disorders. In R. J. Blanchard, D. C. Blanchard, G. Griebel, & D. Nutt (Eds.), *Handbook of anxiety and fear* (pp. 475–510). Amsterdam, The Netherlands: Elsevier.

Marr, M. J. (2011). Has radical behaviorism lost its right to privacy? *The Behavior Analyst, 34*, 213–219.

Marsh, A. A., & Blair, R. J. R. (2008). Deficits in facial affect recognition among antisocial populations: A meta-analysis. *Neuroscience & Biobehavioral Reviews, 32*(3), 454–465.

Marsh, A. A., Stoycos, S. A., Brethel-Haurwitz, K. M., Robinson, P., VanMeter, J. W., & Cardinale, E. M. (2014). Neural and cognitive characteristics of extraordinary altruists. *Proceedings of the National Academy of Sciences, 111*(42), 15036–15041.

Marshall, G. D., & Zimbardo, P. G. (1979). Affective consequences of inadequately explained physiological arousal. *Journal of Personality and Social Psychology, 37*(6), 970–988.

Marshall, L., & Born, J. (2007). The contribution of sleep to hippocampus-dependent memory consolidation. *Trends in Cognitive Sciences, 11*(10), 442–450.

Marshall, W. L. (1985). The effects of variable exposure in flooding therapy. *Behavior Therapy, 16*(2), 117–135.

Martell, B. A., O'Connor, P. G., Kerns, R. D., Becker, W. C., Morales, K. H., Kosten, T. R., & Fiellin, D. A. (2007). Systematic review: Opioid treatment for chronic back pain: Prevalence, efficacy, and association with addiction. *Annals of Internal Medicine, 146*(2), 116–127.

Marti, A., Moreno-Aliaga, M. J., Hebebrand, J., & Martinez, J. A. (2004). Genes, lifestyles and obesity. *International Journal of Obesity, 28*(Suppl. 3), S29–S36.

Martí, E. (2003). Strengths and weaknesses of cognition over preschool years. In J. Valsiner & K. Connolly (Eds.), *Handbook of developmental psychology* (pp. 114–140). Thousand Oaks, CA: SAGE.

Martin, A., & Chao, L. L. (2001). Semantic memory and the brain: Structure and processes. *Current Opinion in Neurobiology, 11*(2), 194–201.

Martin, R. A. (2011). *The psychology of humor: An integrative approach*. Burlington, MA: Elsevier Academic Press.

Marucha, P. T., Kiecolt-Glaser, J. K., & Favagehi, M. (1998). Mucosal wound healing is impaired by examination stress. *Psychosomatic Medicine, 60*(3), 362–365.

Maruish, M. E. (2008). The clinical interview. In R. P. Archer & S. R. Smith (Eds.), *Personality assessment* (pp. 37–80). New York, NY: Routledge.

Marx, R. F., & Didziulis, V. (2009, February 27). A life, interrupted. *New York Times*. Retrieved from http://www.nytimes.com/2009/03/01/nyregion/thecity/01miss.html?pagewanted=1&_r=3&ref=nyregion.

Maslach, C. (1979). Negative emotional biasing of unexplained arousal. *Journal of Personality and Social Psychology, 37*(6), 953–969.

Maslow, A. H. (1943). A theory of human motivation. *Psychological Review, 50*(4), 370–396.

Maslow, A. H. (1954). *Motivation and personality*. New York, NY: Harper.

Maslow, A. H. (1967). A theory of metamotivation: The biological rooting of the value-life. *Journal of Humanistic Psychology, 7*, 93–127.

Maslow, A. H. (1968). *Toward a psychology of being* (2nd ed.). New York: Van Nostrand.

Maslow, A. H. (1968). *Toward a psychology of being* (3rd ed.). New York: John Wiley.

Maslow, A. H. (1969). The farther reaches of human nature. *Journal of Transpersonal Psychology, 1*(1), 1–9.

Maslow, A. H. (1970). *Religions, values, and peak-experiences*. New York, NY: Viking Press.

Maslow, A. H. (1971). *The farther reaches of human nature*. New York, NY: Viking.

Mason, N. S., & Chaney, J. M. (1996). Bulimia nervosa in undergraduate women: Factors associated with internalization of the sociocultural standard of thinness. *Applied and Preventive Psychology, 5*(4), 249–259.

Massen, C., & Vaterrodt-Plunnecke, B. (2006). The role of proactive interference in mnemonic techniques. *Memory, 14*, 189–196.

Mast, M. S., & Sczesny, S. (2010). Gender, power, and nonverbal behavior. In J. C. Chrisler & D. R. McCreary (Eds.), *Handbook of gender research in psychology* (Vol. 1, pp. 411–425). New York, NY: Springer Science+Business Media.

Masten, A. S. (2004). Regulatory processes, risk, and resilience in adolescent development. *Annals of the New York Academy of Sciences, 1021*(1), 310–319.

Masten, A. S. (2006). Developmental psychopathology: Pathways to the future. *International Journal of Behavioral Development, 30*(1), 47–54.

Masuda, T. (2010). Cultural effects on visual perception. In E. B. Goldstein (Ed.), *Encyclopedia of perception* (pp. 339–343). Thousand Oaks, CA: SAGE.
Masuda, T., & Nisbett, R. E. (2001). Attending holistically versus analytically: Comparing the context sensitivity of Japanese and Americans. *Journal of Personality and Social Psychology, 81*(5), 922–934.
Masuda, T., & Nisbett, R. E. (2006). Culture and change blindness. *Cognitive Science, 30*(2), 381–399.
Mather, G. (2011). *Essentials of sensation and perception*. London, UK: Routledge.
Mathers, C., Smith, A., & Concha, M. (2000). Global burden of hearing loss in the year 2000. *Global Burden of Disease, 18*, 1–30.
Matheson, D. M., Killen, J. D., Wang, Y., Varady, A., & Robinson, T. N. (2004). Children's food consumption during television viewing. *The American Journal of Clinical Nutrition, 79*(6), 1088–1094.
Mathews, C. A. (2009). Phenomenology of obsessive-compulsive disorder. In M. M. Antony & M. B. Stein (Eds.), *Oxford handbook of anxiety and related disorders* (pp. 56–64). New York, NY: Oxford University Press.
Mathias, K. C., Rolls, B. J., Birch, L. L., Kral, T. V., Hanna, E. L., Davey, A., & Fisher, J. O. (2012). Serving larger portions of fruits and vegetables together at dinner promotes intake of both foods among young children. *Journal of the Academy of Nutrition and Dietetics, 112*(2), 266–270.
Mathy, F., & Feldman, J. (2012). What's magic about magic numbers? Chunking and data compression in short-term memory. *Cognition, 122*(3), 346–362.
Matser, J. T., Kessels, A. G. H., Lezak, M. D., & Troost, J. (2001). A dose-response relation of headers and concussions with cognitive impairment in professional soccer players. *Journal of Clinical and Experimental Neuropsychology, 23*(6), 770–774.
Matson, J. L., Rieske, R. D., & Williams, L. W. (2013). The relationship between autism spectrum disorders and attention-deficit/hyperactivity disorder: An overview. *Research in Developmental Disabilities, 34*(9), 2475–2484.
Matsumoto, D. (1990). Cultural similarities and differences in display rules. *Motivation and Emotion, 14*(3), 195–214.
Matsumoto, D. (2003). Cross-cultural research. In S. F. Davis (Ed.), *Handbook of research methods in experimental psychology* (pp. 189–208). Malden, MA: Blackwell.
Matsumoto, D., & Willingham, B. (2006). The thrill of victory and the agony of defeat: Spontaneous expressions of medal winners of the 2004 Athens Olympic Games. *Journal of Personality and Social Psychology, 91*(3), 568–581.
Matsumoto, D., & Willingham, B. (2009). Spontaneous facial expressions of emotion of congenitally and noncongenitally blind individuals. *Journal of Personality and Social Psychology, 96*(1), 1–10.
Matsumoto, D., Consolacion, T., Yamada, H., Suzuki, R., Franklin, B., Paul, S., . . . Uchida, H. (2002). American-Japanese cultural differences in judgements of emotional expressions of different intensities. *Cognition & Emotion, 16*(6), 721–747.
Matsumoto, D., Keltner, D., Shiota, M. N., O'Sullivan, M., & Frank, M. (2008a). Facial expressions of emotion. In M. Lewis, J. M. Haviland-Jones, & L. F. Barrett (Eds.), *Handbook of emotions* (3rd. ed., pp. 211–234). New York, NY: Guilford Press.
Matsumoto, D., Yoo, S. H., & Fontaine, J. (2008b). Mapping expressive differences around the world: The relationship between emotional display rules and individualism versus collectivism. *Journal of Cross-Cultural Psychology, 39*(1), 55–74.
Matsumoto, D., Yoo, S. H., & Nakagawa, S. (2008c). Culture, emotion regulation, and adjustment. *Journal of Personality and Social Psychology, 94*(6), 925–937.
Matt, G. E., Quintana, P. J., Fortmann, A. L., Zakarian, J. M., Galaviz, V. E., Chatfield, D. A., . . . Winston, C. (2014). Thirdhand smoke and exposure in California hotels: Non-smoking rooms fail to protect non-smoking hotel guests from tobacco smoke exposure. *Tobacco Control, 23*(3), 264–272.
Matt, G. E., Quintana, P. J., Zakarian, J. M., Fortmann, A. L., Chatfield, D. A., Hoh, E., . . . Hovell, M. F. (2010). When smokers move out and non-smokers move in: Residential thirdhand smoke pollution and exposure. *Tobacco Control*, doi:1136/tc.2010.037382.
Matt, G. E., Vazquez, C., & Campbell, W. K. (1992). Mood-congruent recall of affectively toned stimuli: A meta-analytic review. *Clinical Psychology Review, 12*, 227–255.
Mattes, R. D. (1997). The taste for salt in humans. *The American Journal of Clinical Nutrition, 65*(2), 692S–697S.
Matthews, J. R., & Matthews, L. H. (2012). Applying for clinical and other applied positions. In P. J. Giordano, S. F. Davis, & C. A. Licht (Eds.), *Your graduate training in psychology: Effective strategies for success* (pp. 295–306). Los Angeles: SAGE.
Matthews, K. A., Wing, R. R., Kuller, L. H., Meilahn, E. N., Kelsey, S. F., Costello, E. J., & Caggiula, A. W. (1990). Influences of natural menopause on psychological characteristics and symptoms of middle-aged healthy women. *Journal of Consulting and Clinical Psychology, 58*(3), 345–351.
Mattson, M. P. (2012). Energy intake and exercise as determinants of brain health and vulnerability to injury and disease. *Cell Metabolism, 16*(6), 706–722.
Mattson, S. N., & Riley, E. P. (1998). A review of the neurobehavioral deficits in children with fetal alcohol syndrome or prenatal exposure to alcohol. *Alcoholism: Clinical and Experimental Research, 22*(2), 279–294.
Mattys, S. L. (2013). Speech perception. In D. Reisberg (Ed.), *The Oxford handbook of cognitive psychology* (pp. 391–411). Oxford, UK: Oxford University Press.
Matud, M. P. (2004). Gender differences in stress and coping styles. *Personality and Individual Differences, 37*(7), 1401–1415.
Maurer, D., Lewis, T. L., & Mondloch, C. J. (2005). Missing sights: Consequences for visual cognitive development. *Trends in Cognitive Sciences, 9*(3), 144–151.
Maury, E., Ramsey, K. M., & Bass, J. (2010). Circadian rhythms and metabolic syndrome from experimental genetics to human disease. *Circulation Research, 106*(3), 447–462.
Mauss, I. B., Levenson, R. W., McCarter, L., Wilhelm, F. H., & Gross, J. J. (2005). The tie that binds? Coherence among emotion experience, behavior, and physiology. *Emotion, 5*(2), 175–190.
May, A. L., Kim, J. Y., McHale, S. M., & Crouter, A. (2006). Parent–adolescent relationships and the development of weight concerns from early to late adolescence. *International Journal of Eating Disorders, 39*(8), 729–740.
Mayberry, M. L., & Espelage, D. L. (2007). Associations among empathy, social competence, & reactive/proactive aggression subtypes. *Journal of Youth and Adolescence, 36*(6), 787–798.
Mayer, J. D., Roberts, R. D., & Barsade, S. G. (2008). Human abilities: Emotional intelligence. *Annual Review of Psychology, 59*, 507–536.
Mayer, J. D., & Salovey, P. (1997). What is emotional intelligence? In P. Salovey & D. J. Sluyter (Eds.), *Emotional development and emotional intelligence: Educational implications* (pp. 3–31). New York, NY: Basic Books.
Mayer, J. D., Salovey, P., & Caruso, D. R. (2008). Emotional intelligence: New ability or eclectic traits? *American Psychologist, 63*(6), 503–517.
Mayer, R. E. (2011). Intelligence and achievement. In R. J. Sternberg & S. B. Kaufman (Eds.), *The Cambridge handbook of intelligence* (pp. 738–747). Cambridge, UK: Cambridge University Press.
Mayer, R. E. (2013). Problem solving. In D. Reisberg (Ed.), *The Oxford handbook of cognitive psychology* (pp. 769–778). Oxford, UK: Oxford University Press.
Mayes, A. R. (2000). Selective memory disorders. In E. Tulving & F. I. M. Craik, *The Oxford handbook of memory* (pp. 427–440). Oxford, UK: Oxford University Press.
Mayes, A. R. (2002). Theories of anterograde amnesia. In A. D. Baddeley, M. D. Kopelman, & B. A. Wilson (Eds.), *The handbook of memory disorders* (2nd ed., pp. 167–187). Chichester, UK: Wiley.
Mayhew, G., & Harris, F. (1979). Decreasing self-injurious behavior: Punishment with citric acid and reinforcement of alternative behavior. *Behavior Modification, 3*(3), 322–336.
Mayo Clinic Staff (2014, May 13). Caffeine content for coffee, tea, soda and more. Retrieved from http://www.mayoclinic.org/healthy-lifestyle/nutrition-and-healthy-eating/in-depth/caffeine/art-20049372?pg=1
Mazer, J. P. 2015. Teacher immediacy in the classroom. *The International Encyclopedia of Interpersonal Communication*. Doi:10.1002/9781118540190.wbeic038
McAdams, D. P. (1992). The five-factor model in personality: A critical appraisal. *Journal of Personality, 60*(2), 329–361.
McAleavey, A. A., & Castonguay, L. G. (2014). Insight as a common and specific impact of psychotherapy: Therapist-reported exploratory, directive, and common factor interventions. *Psychotherapy, 51*(2), 283–294.
McAlpine, D. (2010). Auditory localization: Physiology. In E. B. Goldstein (Ed.), *Encyclopedia of perception* (pp. 167—170). Thousand Oaks, CA: SAGE.
McAndrew, F. T., & Jeong, H. S. (2012). Who does what on Facebook? Age, sex, and relationship status as predictors of Facebook use. *Computers in Human Behavior, 28*(6), 2359–2365.
McBride, C., Farvolden, P., & Swallow, S. R. (2007). Major depressive disorder and cognitive schemas. In L. P. Riso, P. L. du Toit, D. J. Stein, & J. E. Young (Eds.), *Cognitive schemas and core beliefs in psychological problems: A scientist-practitioner guide*, 11–39. Washington, DC: American Psychological Association.
McBurney, D. H. (2010a). Evolutionary approach: Perceptual adaptations. In E. B. Goldstein (Ed.), *Encyclopedia of perception* (pp. 405–407). Thousand Oaks, CA: SAGE.
McBurney, D. H. (2010b). Extrasensory perception. In E. B. Goldstein (Ed.), *Encyclopedia of perception* (pp. 411–413). Thousand Oaks, CA: SAGE.
McCabe, D. P., & Castel, A. D. (2008). Seeing is believing: The effect of brain images on judgments of scientific reasoning. *Cognition, 107*(1), 343–352.
McCabe, J. (2009). Racial and gender microaggressions on a predominantly-White campus: Experiences of Black, Latina/o and White undergraduates. *Race, Gender & Class, 16* (1/2), 133–151.
McCallum, R. S., & Bracken, B. A. (2005). The Universal Nonverbal Intelligence Test: A multidimensional measure of intelligence. In D. P. Flanagan & P. L. Harrison (Eds.), *Contemporary intellectual assessment: Theories, tests, and issues* (2nd ed., pp. 425–440). New York, NY: Guilford Press.
McCann, L. I., Immel, K. R., Kadah-Ammeter, T. L., & Adelson, S. K. (2016). The importance and interest of introductory psychology textbook topics: Student opinions at technical college, 2-, and 4-year institutions. *Teaching of Psychology, 43*(3), 215–220.
McCleery, A., Lee, J., Joshi, A., Wynn, J. K., Hellemann, G. S., & Green, M. F. (2015). Meta-analysis of face processing event-related potentials in schizophrenia. *Biological Psychiatry, 77*(2), 116–126.
McClellan, J., & King, M. C. (2010). Genomic analysis of mental illness. *JAMA, 303*(24), 2523–2524.
McClelland, D. C. (1961). *Achieving society*. Princeton, NJ: Van Nostrand.
McClenon, J. (1994). *Wondrous events: Foundations of religious belief*. Philadelphia, PA: University of Pennsylvania Press.
McClintock, M. K. (2010). Olfaction and reproductive behavior. In E. B. Goldstein (Ed.), *Encyclopedia of perception* (pp. 671–674). Thousand Oaks, CA: SAGE.
McClintock, S. M., Ranginwala, N., & Husain, M. M. (2008). Electroconvulsive therapy. In K. T. Mueser & D. V. Jeste (Eds.), *Clinical handbook of schizophrenia* (pp. 196–204). New York, NY: Guilford Press.
McCloskey, M. E., & Glucksberg, S. (1978). Natural categories: Well defined or fuzzy sets? *Memory & Cognition, 6*(4), 462–472.

McConkey, K. M. (2008). Generations and landscapes of hypnosis: Questions we've asked, questions we should ask. In M. R. Nash & A. J. Barnier (Eds.), *The Oxford handbook of hypnosis: Theory, research, and practice* (pp. 53–79). Oxford, UK: Oxford University Press.
McCrae, R. R. (1987). Creativity, divergent thinking, and openness to experience. *Journal of Personality and Social Psychology, 52*(6), 1258–1265.
McCrae, R. R. (2001). Traits through time. *Psychological Inquiry, 12*(2), 85–87.
McCrae, R. R. & Costa, P. T. (1996). Toward a new generation of personality theories: Theoretical contexts for the five-factor model. In J. S. Wiggins (Ed.). *The five-factor model of personality: Theoretical perspectives* (pp. 51–87). New York, NY: Guilford Press.
McCrae, R. R. & Costa, P. T. (2003). *Personality in adulthood: A five-factor theory perspective* (2nd ed.). New York, NY: Guilford Press.
McCrae, R. R., & Allik, I. U. (2002). *The five-factor model of personality across cultures*. New York, NY: Kluwer Academic/Plenum.
McCrea, R. R., & Costa, P. T., Jr. (1997). Personality trait structure as a human universal. *American Psychologist, 52*(5), 509–516.
McCrae, R. R., & Costa, P. T. (2003). *Personality in adulthood* (2nd ed.) New York, NY: Guilford Press.
McCrae, R. R., & Costa, P. T. Jr. (2008). The five-factor theory of personality. In O. P. John, R. W. Robins, & L. A. Pervin (Eds.) *Handbook of personality: Theory and research* (3rd ed., pp. 159–181). New York, NY: Guilford Press.
McCrae, R. R., & Costa, P. T. (2013). Introduction to the empirical and theoretical status of the five-factor model of personality traits. In T. A. Widiger & P. T. Costa (Eds.), *Personality disorders and the five-factor model of personality* (3rd ed., pp. 15–27). Washington, DC: American Psychological Association.
McCreary, D. R., & Chrisler, J. C. (2010). Introduction. In J. C. Chrisler & D. R. McCreary (Eds.), *Handbook of gender research in psychology* (Vol. 1, pp. 1–17). New York, NY: Springer Science+Business Media.
McCreary, M. L., Cunningham, J. N., Ingram, K. M., & Fife, J. E. (2006). Stress, culture, and racial socialization: Making an impact. In P. T. P. Wong and L. C. J. Wong (Eds.), *Handbook of multicultural perspectives on stress and coping* (pp. 487–514). New York, NY: Springer Science+Business Media.
McCroskey, J. C., & Richmond, V. P. (1992). Increasing teacher influence through immediacy. In V. P. Richmond & J. C. McCroskey (Eds.), *Power in the classroom: Communication, control, and concern* (pp. 101–119). Hillside, NJ: Lawrence Erlbaum.
McDonough, P. (2009). TV viewing among kids at an eight-year high. *Nielsenwire*. October 26, 2009. Retrieved from http://blog. nielsen.com/nielsenwire/media_entertainment/tv-viewing-among-kids-at-an-eight-year-high/
McElhaney, K. B., Allen, J. P., Stephenson, J. C., & Hare, A. L. (2009). Attachment and autonomy during adolescence. In R. M. Lerner & L. Steinberg (Eds.), *Handbook of adolescent psychology* (3rd ed., Vol. 1, pp. 358–403). Hoboken, NJ: Wiley.
McElwain, N. L., Booth-LaForce, C., Lansford, J. E., Wu, X., & Justin Dyer, W. (2008). A process model of attachment–friend linkages: Hostile attribution biases, language ability, and mother–child affective mutuality as intervening mechanisms. *Child Development, 79*(6), 1891–1906.
McEwen, B. S. (1999). Stress and hippocampal plasticity. *Annual Review of Neuroscience, 22*(1), 105–122.
McEwen, B. S. (2004). How sex and stress hormones regulate the structural and functional plasticity of the hippocampus. In M. S. Gazzaniga (Ed.), *The new cognitive neurosciences III* (pp. 171–182). Cambridge, MA: MIT Press.
McEwen, B., & Lasley, E. N. (2002). Allostatic load: When protection gives way to damage. In B. McEwen, and E. N. Lasley, *The end of stress as we know it* (pp. 99–109). Washington DC: National Academies Press.
McFarlane, A. C. (2010). Phenomenology of posttraumatic stress disorder. In D. J. Stein, E. Hollander, & B. O. Rothbaum (Eds.), *Textbook of anxiety disorders* (2nd ed., pp. 547–565). Washington, DC: American Psychiatric Publishing.
McGhee, P. E., & Frueh, T. (1980). Television viewing and the learning of sex-role stereotypes. *Sex Roles, 6*(2), 179–188.
McGilchrist, I. (2009). *The master and his emissary: The divided brain and the making of the Western world*. New Haven, CT: Yale University Press.
McGilchrist, I. (2010). Reciprocal organization of the cerebral hemispheres. *Dialogues in Clinical Neuroscience, 12*(4), 503.
McGlynn, F. D. (2002). Systematic desensitization. In M. Hersen & W. Sledge (Eds.), *Encyclopedia of psychotherapy* (Vol. 2, pp. 755–764). San Diego, CA: Academic Press.
McGoldrick, M., Giordano, J., & Garcia-Preto, N. (Eds.). (2005). *Ethnicity and family therapy* (3rd ed.). New York, NY: Guilford Press.
McGrath, R. E. (2004). Saving our psychosocial souls. *American Psychologist,59*, 644–645.
McGrath, R. E. (2010). Prescriptive authority for psychologists. *Annual Review of Clinical Psychology, 6*, 21–47.
McGuire, P. K., Murray, R. M., & Shah, G. M. S. (1993). Increased blood flow in Broca's area during auditory hallucinations in schizophrenia. *The Lancet, 342*(8873), 703–706.
McHale, S. M., Crouter, A. C., & Whiteman, S. D. (2003). The family contexts of gender development in childhood and adolescence. *Social Development, 12*(1), 125–148.
McHugh, M. C., & Hambaugh, J. (2010). She said, he said: Gender language and power. In J. C. Chrisler & D. R. McCreary (Eds.), *Handbook of gender research in psychology* (Vol. 1, pp. 379–410). New York, NY: Springer Science+Business Media.
McHugh, M. C., & Kasardo, A. E. (2012). Anti-fat prejudice: The role of psychology in explication, education and eradication. *Sex Roles, 66*(9-10), 617–627.
McHugh, P. R. (1995). Resolved: Multiple personality disorder is an individually and socially created artifact. *Journal of the American Academy of Child and Adolescent Psychiatry, 34*(7), 957–959.
McIntosh, D. N. (1996). Facial feedback hypotheses: Evidence, implications, and directions. *Motivation and Emotion, 20*(2), 121–147.
McIntosh, D. N., Zajonc, R. B., Vig, P. S., & Emerick, S. W. (1997). Facial movement, breathing, temperature, and affect: Implications of the vascular theory of emotional efference. *Cognition & Emotion, 11*(2), 171–196.
McKenna, J. J., & McDade, T. (2005). Why babies should never sleep alone: A review of the co-sleeping controversy in relation to SIDS, bedsharing and breast feeding. *Paediatric Respiratory Reviews, 6*(2), 134–152.
McKenna, P. J., McKay, A. P. & Laws, K. (2000). Memory in functional psychosis. In G. E. Berrios & J. R. Hodges (Eds.), *Memory disorders in psychiatric practice*. Cambridge, UK: Cambridge University Press.
McKenna, P., Ornstein, T., & Baddeley, A. D. (2002). Schizophrenia. In A. D. Baddeley, M. D. Kopelman, & B. A. Wilson (Eds.), *The handbook of memory disorders* (2nd ed., pp. 413–435). Chichester, UK: Wiley.
McKenzie, C. R. M. (2005). Reasoning. In K. Lamberts & R. L. Goldstone (Eds.), *Handbook of cognition* (pp. 321–338). London, UK: SAGE.
McKitrick, D. S., & Li, S. T. (2008). Multicultural treatment. In M. Hersen & A. M. Gross (Eds.), *Handbook of clinical psychology* (Vol. 1, pp. 724–751). Hoboken, NJ: Wiley.
McKnight-Eily, L. R., Eaton, D. K., Lowry, R., Croft, J. B., Presley-Cantrell, L., & Perry, G. S. (2011). Relationships between hours of sleep and health-risk behaviors in U.S. adolescent students. *Preventive Medicine, 53*(4), 271–273.
McLaughlin, S. A., & Malony, H. N. (1984). Near-death experiences and religion: A further investigation. *Journal of Religion and Health, 23*(2), 149–159.
McLean, R. (2003). *Recovered, not cured: A journey through schizophrenia*. Crows Nest, NSW, Australia: Allen & Unwin.
McLean, S. A., Paxton, S. J., Wertheim, E. H., & Masters, J. (2015). Photoshopping the selfie: Self photo editing and photo investment are associated with body dissatisfaction in adolescent girls. *International Journal of Eating Disorders. 48*(8), 1132–1140.
McLeod, K., & DiCola, P. (2011). *Creative license: The law and culture of digital sampling*. Durham, NC: Duke University Press.
McNally, R. J. (1987). Preparedness and phobias: A review. *Psychological Bulletin, 101*, 283–303.
McWhorter, J. H. (2014). *The language hoax: Why the world looks the same in any language*. New York, NY: Oxford University Press.
Means, M. K., & Edinger, J. D. (2006). Nonpharmacologic therapy of insomnia. In T. L. Lee-Chiong (Ed.), *Sleep: A comprehensive handbook* (pp. 133–136). Hoboken, NJ: Wiley-Liss.
Medin, D. L., Ross, N., Atran, S., Burnett, R. C., & Blok, S. V. (2002). Categorization and reasoning in relation to culture and expertise. *Psychology of Learning and Motivation, 41*, 1–41.
Medin, D. L., & Schaffer, M. M. (1978). Context theory of classification learning. *Psychological Review, 85*(3), 207–238.
Medin, D. L., Unsworth, S. J., & Hirschfeld, L. (2007). Culture, categorization, and reasoning. In S. Kitayama & D. Cohen (Eds.), *Handbook of cultural psychology* (pp. 615–644). New York, NY: Guilford Press.
Medina, J. (2014). *Brain rules: 12 principles for surviving and thriving at work, home and school*. (2nd ed.) Seattle, WA: Pear Press.
Mednick, S. C., Nakayama, K., Cantero, J. L., Atienza, M., Levin, A. A., Pathak, N., & Stickgold, R. (2002). The restorative effect of naps on perceptual deterioration. *Nature Neuroscience, 5*(7), 677–681.
Mednick, S., Nakayama, K., & Stickgold, R. (2003). Sleep-dependent learning: A nap is as good as a night. *Nature Neuroscience, 6*(7), 697–698.
Meece, J. L., & Holt, K. (1993). A pattern analysis of students' achievement goals. *Journal of Educational Psychology, 85*(4), 582–590.
Mehler, P. S., Birmingham, C. L., Crow, S. J., & Jahraus, J. P. (2010). Medical complications of eating disorders. In C. M. Grilo & J. E. Mitchell (Eds.), *The treatment of eating disorders: A clinical handbook* (pp. 66–80). New York, NY: Guilford Press.
Meier, E. P., & Gray, J. (2014). Facebook photo activity associated with body image disturbance in adolescent girls. *Cyberpsychology, Behavior, and Social Networking, 17*(4), 199–206.
Meintjes, E. M., Jacobson, J. L., Molteno, C. D., Gatenby, J. C., Warton, C., Cannistraci, . . . Jacobson, S. W. (2010), An fMRI study of number processing in children with fetal alcohol syndrome. *Alcoholism: Clinical and Experimental Research, 34*, 1450–1464.
Meinz, E. J., & Hambrick, D. Z. (2010). Deliberate practice is necessary but not sufficient to explain individual differences in piano sight-reading skill: The role of working memory capacity. *Psychological Science, 21*, 914–919.
Meixner, J. B. Jr. (2015). Applications of neuroscience in criminal law: Legal and methodological issues. *Current Neurology and Neuroscience Reports, 15*(2), 1–10.
Melchert, T. P. (2011). *Foundations of professional psychology: The end of theoretical orientations and the emergence of the biopsychosocial approach*. London: Elsevier.
Melnyk, L., Crossman, A. M., & Scullin, M. H. (2007). The suggestibility of children's memory. In M. P. Toglia, J. D. Read, D. F. Ross, & R. C. L. Lindsay (Eds.), *The handbook of eyewitness psychology: Memory for events* (Vol. I, pp. 401–427). East Sussex, UK: Psychology Press.
Meltzoff, A. N. (2011). Social cognition and the origins of imitation, empathy, and theory of mind. In U. Goswami (Ed.), *The Wiley-Blackwell handbook of childhood cognitive development* (2nd ed., pp. 49–75). Malden, MA: Wiley-Blackwell.

Meltzoff, J. (1998). *Critical thinking about research: Psychology and related fields*. Washington, DC: American Psychological Association.
Melzack, R., & Casey, K. L. (1968). Sensory, motivational, and central control determinants of pain. In D. R. Kenshalo (Ed.), *The skin senses* (pp. 423–439). Springfield, IL: Charles C. Thomas Publisher.
Melzack, R., & Wall, P. D. (1967). Pain mechanisms: A new theory. *Survey of Anesthesiology, 11*(2), 89–90.
Melzack, R., & Wall, P. D. (2008). *The challenge of pain* (2nd ed.). New York, NY: Penguin.
Menaker, M., Murphy, Z. C., & Sellix, M. T. (2013). Central control of peripheral circadian oscillators. *Current Opinion in Neurobiology, 23*(5), 741–746.
Mendell, L. M. (2014). Constructing and deconstructing the gate theory of pain. *Pain, 155*(2), 210–216.
Menon, U. (2003). Morality and context: A study of Hindu understandings. In J. Valsiner & K. Connolly (Eds.), *Handbook of developmental psychology* (pp. 431–449). Thousand Oaks, CA: SAGE.
Mental health: Does therapy help? (1995, November). *Consumer Reports*, 734–739.
Mercado, T., Alvarez, A., & Herranz, J. M. (2014). The fracking debate in the media: The role of citizen platforms as sources of information. *ESSACHESS – Journal for Communication Studies, 7*(1), 45–62.
Mesquita, B., & Karasawa, M. (2002). Different emotional lives. *Cognition & Emotion, 16*(1), 127–141.
Mesquita, B., & Leu, J. (2007). The cultural psychology of emotion. In S. Kitayama & D. Cohen (Eds.), *Handbook of cultural psychology* (pp. 734–759). New York, NY: Guilford Press.
Messer, S. B., & Wampold, B. E. (2002). Let's face facts: Common factors are more potent than specific therapy ingredients. *Clinical Psychology: Science and Practice, 9*(1), 21–25.
Messerly, J. G. (2009). Piaget's biology. In U. Müller, J. I. M. Carpendale, & L. Smith (Eds.), *The Cambridge companion to Piaget* (pp. 94–109). New York, NY: Cambridge University Press.
Meston, C. M., & Buss, D. M. (2007). Why humans have sex. *Archives of Sexual Behavior, 36*(4), 477–507.
Metzger, A. M. (1979). A Q-methodological study of the Kubler-Ross stage theory. *OMEGA—Journal of Death and Dying, 10*(4), 291–301.
Meyer, G. J. (2004). The reliability and validity of the Rorschach and Thematic Apperception Test (TAT) compared to other psychological and medical procedures: An analysis of systematically gathered evidence. In M. J. Hilsenroth & D. L. Segal (Eds.), *Comprehensive handbook of psychological assessment: Personality assessment* (Vol. 2, pp. 315–342). Hoboken, NJ: Wiley.
Meyer, I. H. (2003). Prejudice, social stress, and mental health in lesbian, gay, and bisexual populations: Conceptual issues and research evidence. *Psychological Bulletin, 129*(5), 674–697.
Meyer, O. L., & Takeuchi, D. T. (2014). Help seeking and service utilization. In F. T. L. Leong (Ed.), *APA handbook of multicultural psychology* (Vol. 2, pp. 529–541). Washington, DC: American Psychological Association.
Meyer, O. L., Zane, N., Cho, Y. I., & Takeuchi, D. T. (2009). Use of specialty mental health services by Asian Americans with psychiatric disorders. *Journal of Consulting and Clinical Psychology, 77*(5), 1000–1005.
Michel, J. S., Kotrba, L. M., Mitchelson, J. K., Clark, M. A., & Baltes, B. B. (2011). Antecedents of work–family conflict: A meta-analytic review. *Journal of Organizational Behavior, 32*(5), 689–725.
Micozzi, M. S. (2011). *Fundamentals of complementary and alternative medicine* (4th ed.) St. Louis, MO: Saunders/Elsevier.
Miczek, K. A., de Almeida, R. M., Kravitz, E. A., Rissman, E. F., de Boer, S. F., & Raine, A. (2007). Neurobiology of escalated aggression and violence. *The Journal of Neuroscience, 27*(44), 11803–11806.
Mihura, J. L., Meyer, G. J., Bombel, G., & Dumitrascu, N. (2015). Standards, accuracy, and questions of bias in Rorschach meta-analyses: Reply to Wood, Garb, Nezworski, Lilienfeld, and Duke (2015). *Psychological Bulletin, 141*, 250–260.
Mihura, J. L., Meyer, G. J., Dumitrascu, N., & Bombel, G. (2013). The validity of individual Rorschach variables: Systematic reviews and meta-analyses of the comprehensive system. *Psychological Bulletin, 139*, 548–605.
Mikami, A. Y. (2010). The importance of friendship for youth with attention-deficit/hyperactivity disorder. *Clinical Child and Family Psychology Review, 13*(2), 181–198.
Mikels, J. A., Reed, A. E., Hardy, L. N., & Löckenhoff, C. E. (2014). Positive emotions across the adult life span. In M. M. Tugade, M. N. Shiota, & L. D. Kirby (Eds.), *Handbook of positive emotions* (pp. 256–255). New York, NY: Guilford Press.
Miklowitz, D. J. (2009). Pharmacotherapy and psychosocial treatments for bipolar disorder. In I. H. Gotlib & C. L. Hammen (Eds.), *Handbook of depression* (2nd ed., pp. 604–623). New York, NY: Guilford Press.
Miklowitz, D. J., & Craighead, W. E. (2007). Psychosocial treatments for bipolar disorder. In P. E. Nathan & J. M. Gorman (Eds.), *A guide to treatments that work* (3rd ed., pp. 309–322). New York, NY: Oxford University Press.
Miklowitz, D. J., & Johnson, S. L. (2008). Bipolar disorder. In W. E. Craighead, D. J. Milkowitz, & L. W. Craighead (Eds.), *Psychopathology: History, diagnosis, and empirical foundations* (pp. 366–401). Hoboken, NJ: Wiley.
Miles, C., & Hardman, E. (1998). State-dependent memory produced by aerobic exercise. *Ergonomics, 41*(1), 20–28.
Miles, D. R., & Carey, G. (1997). Genetic and environmental architecture of human aggression. *Journal of Personality and Social Psychology, 72*(1), 207–217.
Miletich, R. S. (2009). Positron emission tomography for neurologists. *Neurologic Clinics, 27*(1): 61–88, viii.
Milgram, D. (2011). How to recruit women and girls to the science, technology, engineering, and math (STEM) classroom. *Technology and Engineering Teacher, 71*(3), 4–11.
Milgram, S. (1963). Behavioral study of obedience. *Journal of Abnormal and Social Psychology, 67*(4), 371–378.
Milgram, S. (1965). Some conditions of obedience and disobedience to authority. *Human Relations, 18*(1), 57–76.
Milgram, S. (1974). *Obedience to authority: An experimental view*. New York, NY: Harper and Row.
Miller, A., & Hom, H. L. (1990). Influence of extrinsic and ego incentive value on persistence after failure and continuing motivation. *Journal of Educational Psychology, 82*(3), 539–545.
Miller, A. R., & Igel, L. (2012, December 13). NFL's recent troubles: Are players "just following orders"? *Forbes*. Retrieved from http://www.forbes.com/sites/leeigel/2012/12/13/nfls-recent-troubles-are-players-just-following-orders/
Miller, D. J., & Thelen, M. H. (1986). Knowledge and beliefs about confidentiality in psychotherapy. *Professional Psychology Research and Practice, 17*(1), 15–19.
Miller, G. (2013, December 13). Did brain scans just save a convicted murderer from the death penalty? *Wired*. Retrieved from http://www.wired.com/2013/12/murder-law-brain/.
Miller, G. A. (1956). The magical number seven, plus or minus two: Some limits on our capacity for processing information. *Psychological Review, 63*(2), 81–97.
Miller, L., & Gur, M. (2002). Religiousness and sexual responsibility in adolescent girls. *Journal of Adolescent Health, 31*(5), 401–406.
Miller, N., & Pollock, V. E. (1996). Alcohol and aggression: A meta-analysis on the moderating effects of inhibitory cues, triggering events, and self-focused attention. *Psychological Bulletin, 120*(1), 60–62.
Miller, P. A., & Eisenberg, N. (1988). The relation of empathy to aggressive and externalizing/antisocial behavior. *Psychological Bulletin, 103*(3), 324–344.
Miller, P. H. (2011). Piaget's theory: Past, present, and future. In U. Goswami (Ed.), *The Wiley-Blackwell handbook of childhood cognitive development* (2nd ed., pp. 649–672). Malden, MA: Wiley-Blackwell.
Miller, R. (2011). *Vygotsky in perspective*. New York, NY: Cambridge University Press.
Miller, R. L. (2003). Ethical issues in psychological research with human participants. In S. F. Davis (Ed.), *Handbook of research methods in experimental psychology* (pp. 127–150). Malden, MA: Blackwell.
Miller, T. Q., Turner, C. W., Tindale, R. S., Posavac, E. J., & Dugoni, B. L. (1991). Reasons for the trend toward null findings in research on Type A behavior. *Psychological Bulletin, 110*(3), 469–485.
Miller, W. R., & Rollnick, S. (2013). *Motivational interviewing: Helping people change* (3rd ed.). New York, NY: Guilford Press.
Miller, W. R., & Rose, G. R. (2009). Toward a theory of motivational interviewing. *American Psychologist, 64*(6), 527–537.
Miller, W. R., & Rose, G. S. (2015). Motivational interviewing and decisional balance: Contrasting responses to client ambivalence. *Behavioural and Cognitive Psychotherapy, 43*(02), 129–141.
Millett, D. (2001). Hans Berger: From psychic energy to the EEG. *Perspectives in Biology and Medicine, 44*(4), 522–542.
Millon, T. (2004). *Personality disorders and modern life* (2nd ed.). Hoboken, NJ: Wiley.
Millon, T. (2009). Personality and its disorders: Structural models, mathematical methods, and theoretical conceptions. In P. H. Blaney & T. Millon (Eds.), *Oxford textbook of psychopathology* (2nd ed., 551–585). New York, NY: Oxford University Press.
Mills, J. A. (1998). *Control: A history of behavioral psychology*. New York, NY: New York University Press.
Milner, A. D., & Goodale, M. A. (2008). Two visual systems re-viewed. *Neuropsychologia, 46*(3), 774–785.
Milner, C. E., & Cote, K. A. (2009). Benefits of napping in healthy adults: Impact of nap length, time of day, age, and experience with napping. *Journal of Sleep Research, 18*(2), 272–281.
Mindell, J. A., Meltzer, L. J., Carskadon, M. A., & Chervin, R. D. (2009). Developmental aspects of sleep hygiene: Findings from the 2004 National Sleep Foundation Sleep in America Poll. *Sleep Medicine, 10*(7), 771–779.
Mindell, J. A., & Owens, J. A. (2015). *A clinical guide to pediatric sleep: Diagnosis and management of sleep problems* (3rd ed.). Philadelphia, PA: Wolters Kluwer.
Mineka, S., & Cook, M. (1993). Mechanisms involved in the observational conditioning of fear. *Journal of Experimental Psychology: General, 122*(1), 23–38.
Ming, G. L., & Song, H. (2011). Adult neurogenesis in the mammalian brain: Significant answers and significant questions. *Neuron, 70*(4), 687–702.
Minkov, M. (2013). *Cross-cultural analysis: The science and art of comparing the world's modern societies and their cultures*. Thousand Oaks, CA: SAGE.
Minkov, M., & Hofstede, G. (2010). Hofstede's fifth dimension: New evidence from the World Values Survey. *Journal of Cross-Cultural Psychology, 43*(1), 3–14.
Minkov, M., & Hofstede, G. (2011). The evolution of Hofstede's doctrine. *Cross Cultural Management: An International Journal, 18*(1), 10–20.
Minuchin, S. (1974). *Families and family therapy*. Cambridge, MA: Harvard University Press.
Minzenberg, M., Yoon, J. H., & Cameron, S. C. (2008). Schizophrenia. In R. E. Hales & S. Yudofsky (Eds.), *Textbook of clinical psychiatry* (pp. 407–456). Washington, DC: American Psychiatric Association Publishing.

Mio, J. S., Barker-Hackett, L., & Tumambing, J. S. (2009). *Multicultural psychology: Understanding our diverse communities* (2nd ed.). New York, NY: McGraw-Hill.

Mirsalimi, H. (2010). Perspectives of an Iranian psychologist practicing in America. *Psychotherapy: Theory, Research, Practice, Training, 47*(2), 151–161.

Misailidi, P. (2006). Young children's display rule knowledge: Understanding the distinction between apparent and real emotions and the motives underlying the use of display rules. *Social Behavior and Personality: An International Journal, 34*(10), 1285–1296.

Mischel, W. (1979). On the interface of cognition and personality: Beyond the person–situation debate. *American Psychologist, 34*(9), 740–754.

Mischel, W., & Shoda, Y. (1995). A cognitive-affective system theory of personality: Reconceptualizing situations, dispositions, dynamics, and invariance in personality structure. *Psychological Review, 102*(2), 246–268.

Missler, M., Stroebe, M., Geurtsen, L., Mastenbroek, M., Chmoun, S., & van der Houwen, K. (2011). Exploring death anxiety among elderly people: A literature review and empirical investigation. *OMEGA—Journal of Death and Dying, 64*(4), 357–379.

Mitamura, C., Leu, J., Campos, B., Boccagno, C., & Tugade, M. M. (2014). Traversing affective boundaries: Examining cultural norms for positive emotions. In M. M. Tugade, M. N. Shiota, & L. D. Kirby (Eds.), *Handbook of positive emotions* (pp. 229–240). New York, NY: Guilford Press.

Mitchell, B. A., & Gee, E. M. (1996). "Boomerang kids" and midlife parental marital satisfaction. *Family Relations, 45*(4), 442–448.

Mitchell, B. A., & Lovegreen, L. D. (2009). The empty nest syndrome in midlife families: A multimethod exploration of parental gender differences and cultural dynamics. *Journal of Family Issues, 30*(12), 1651–1670.

Mitchell, J. E., & Crow, S. J. (2010). Medical comorbidities or eating disorders. In W. S. Agras (Ed.), *The Oxford handbook of eating disorders* (pp. 259–268). New York, NY: Oxford University Press.

Mitchell, K. J., & Johnson, M. K. (2000). Source monitoring: Attributing mental experiences. In E. Tulving & F. I. M. Craik (Eds.), *The Oxford handbook of memory* (pp. 179–195). Oxford, UK: Oxford University Press.

Mitchell, S. A., & Black, M. J. (1995). *Freud and beyond: A history of modern psychoanalytic thought*. New York, NY: BasicBooks.

Mithen, S. (2012). Musicality and language. In M. Tallerman & K. R. Gibson (Eds.), *The Oxford handbook of language evolution* (pp. 296–298). Oxford, UK: Oxford University Press.

Mitler, M. M., Carskadon, M. A., Czeisler, C. A., Dement, W. C., Dinges, D. F., & Graeber, R. C. (1988). Catastrophes, sleep, and public policy: Consensus report. *Sleep, 11*(1), 100–109.

Miyamoto, Y., & Ryff, C. D. (2011). Cultural differences in the dialectical and non-dialectical emotional styles and their implications for health. *Cognition and Emotion, 25*(1), 22–39.

Miyamoto, Y., & Wilken, B. (2013). Cultural differences and their mechanisms. In D. Reisberg (Ed.), *The Oxford handbook of cognitive psychology* (pp. 970–987). Oxford, UK: Oxford University Press

Moayedi, M., & Davis, K. D. (2013). Theories of pain: From specificity to gate control. *Journal of Neurophysiology, 109*(1), 5–12.

Modinos, G., Ormel, J., & Aleman, A. (2010). Individual differences in dispositional mindfulness and brain activity involved in reappraisal of emotion. *Social Cognitive and Affective Neuroscience, 5*(4), 369–377.

Moe, A., & De Beni, R. (2004). Studying passages with the loci method: Are subject-generated more effective than experimenter-supplied loci pathways? *Journal of Mental Imagery, 28*, 75–86.

Moe, A., & De Beni, R. (2005). Stressing the efficacy of the loci method: Oral presentation and the subject-generation of the loci pathway with expository passages. *Applied Cognitive Psychology, 19*, 95–106.

Moen, P. (2003). Midcourse: Navigating retirement and a new life stage. In J. T. Mortimer & M. J. Shanahan (Eds.), *Handbook of the life course* (pp. 269–291). New York, NY: Springer Science+Business Media.

Moen, P., and Roehling, P. (2005). *The career mystique: Cracks in the American dream*. Boulder, CO: Rowman & Littlefield.

Moffitt, T. E., Caspi, A., Belsky, J., & Silva, P. A. (1992). Childhood experience and the onset of menarche: A test of a sociobiological model. *Child Development, 63*(1), 47–58.

Mohr, J. J., & Rochlen, A. B. (1999). Measuring attitudes regarding bisexuality in lesbian, gay male, and heterosexual populations. *Journal of Counseling Psychology, 46*(3), 353–369.

Moline, M. L., Broch, L., Zak, R., & Gross, V. (2003). Sleep in women across the life cycle from adulthood through menopause. *Sleep Medicine Reviews, 7*(2), 155–177.

Moller, H., & Pedersen, C. S. (2004). Hearing at low and infrasonic frequencies. *Noise and Health, 6*(23), 37–57.

Mollon, J. D., Pokorny, J., & Knoblauch, K. (Eds.). (2003). *Normal and defective colour vision*. New York, NY: Oxford University Press.

Mols, F., & Denollet, J. (2010). Type D personality among noncardiovascular patient populations: A systematic review. *General Hospital Psychiatry, 32*(1), 66–72.

Moltz, H. (1965). Contemporary instinct theory and the fixed action pattern. *Psychological Review, 72*(1), 27–47.

Monat, A., Lazarus, R. S., & Reevy, G. (2007). Introduction. In A. Monat, R. S Lazarus, & G. Reevy (Eds.), *The Praeger handbook on stress and coping* (pp. xxvii–xxxvi). Westport, CT: Praeger.

Mondimore, F. M. (2006). *Depression, the mood disease* (3rd ed.). Baltimore, MD: Johns Hopkins University Press.

Mondloch, C. J., Lewis, T. L., Budreau, D. R., Maurer, D., Dannemiller, J. L., Stephens, B. R., & Kleiner-Gathercoal, K. A. (1999). Face perception during early infancy. *Psychological Science, 10*(5), 419–422.

Monk, T. H. (2012). Sleep and human performance. In C. M. Morin & C. A. Espie (Eds.), *The Oxford handbook of sleep and sleep disorders* (pp. 95–109). Oxford, UK: Oxford University Press.

Monk, T. H., Petrie, S. R., Hayes, A. J., & Kupfer, D. J. (1994). Regularity of daily life in relation to personality, age, gender, sleep quality and circadian rhythms. *Journal of Sleep Research, 3*(4), 196–205.

Monroe, S. M., & Simons, A. D. (1991). Diathesis-stress theories in the context of life stress research: Implications for the depressive disorders. *Psychological Bulletin, 110*(3), 406–425.

Montgomery, G. H., DuHamel, K. N., & Redd, W. H. (2000). A meta-analysis of hypnotically induced analgesia: How effective is hypnosis? *International Journal of Clinical and Experimental Hypnosis, 48*(2), 138–153.

Montoya, R. M., & Horton, R. S. (2012). A meta-analytic investigation of the processes underlying the similarity-attraction effect. *Journal of Social and Personal Relationships. 30*(1), 64–94.

Montoya, R. M., Horton, R. S., & Kirchner, J. (2008). Is actual similarity necessary for attraction? A meta-analysis of actual and perceived similarity. *Journal of Social and Personal Relationships, 25*(6), 889–922.

Mook, D. (2004). *Classic experiments in psychology*. Westport, CT: Greenwood Press.

Moore, B. A. & Krakow, B. (2007). Imagery rehearsal therapy for acute posttraumatic nightmares among combat soldiers in Iraq. *The American Journal of Psychiatry, 164*, 683–684.

Moore, B. C. J. (2001a). Basic auditory processes. In E. B. Goldstein (Ed.), *Blackwell handbook of perception* (pp. 379–407). Oxford, UK: Blackwell.

Moore, B. C. J. (2001b). Loudness, pitch, and timbre. In E. B. Goldstein (Ed.), *Blackwell handbook of perception* (pp. 408–436). Oxford, UK: Blackwell.

Moore, B. C. J. (2010). Audition. In E. B. Goldstein (Ed.), *Encyclopedia of perception* (pp. 133–138). Thousand Oaks, CA: SAGE.

Moore, B. C. J. (2012). *An introduction to the psychology of hearing*. Bingley, UK: Emerald.

Moore, B. E., & Fine, B. D. (Eds). (1990). *Psychoanalytic terms & concepts*. New Haven, CT: American Psychoanalytic Association.

Moore, M., & Tasso, A. F. (2008). Clinical hypnosis: The empirical evidence. In M. R. Nash & A. J. Barnier (Eds.), *The Oxford handbook of hypnosis: Theory, research, and practice* (pp. 697–726). Oxford, UK: Oxford University Press.

Moore, P. S., March, J. S., Albano, A. M., & Thienemann, M. (2010). Anxiety disorders in children and adolescents. In D. J. Stein, E. Hollander, & B. O. Rothbaum (Eds.), *Textbook of anxiety disorders* (2nd ed., pp. 629–649). Washington, DC: American Psychiatric Association Publishing.

Moore, R. Y. (2006). Biological rhythms and sleep. In T. L. Lee-Chiong (Ed.), *Sleep: A comprehensive handbook* (pp. 25–30). Hoboken, NJ: Wiley-Liss.

Morabia A., Costanza M. C. (1998). World Health Organization collaborative study of neoplasia and steroid contraceptives. International variability in ages at menarche, first livebirth, and menopause. *American Journal of Epidemiology*, 148, 1195–205.

Moradi, B., & Huang, Y. P. (2008). Objectification theory and psychology of women: A decade of advances and future directions. *Psychology of Women Quarterly, 32*(4), 377–398.

Moran, R. T., Youngdahl, W. E., & Moran, S. V. (2009). Intercultural competence in business. In D. K. Deardorff (Ed.), *The SAGE handbook of intercultural competence* (pp. 287–303). Thousand Oaks, CA: SAGE.

Moreland, R. L., & Beach, S. R. (1992). Exposure effects in the classroom: The development of affinity among students. *Journal of Experimental Social Psychology, 28*(3), 255–276.

Morelli, G., Rogoff, B., & Angelillo, C. (2003). Cultural variation in young children's access to work or involvement in specialised child-focused activities. *International Journal of Behavioral Development, 27*(3), 264–274.

Moretti, R. J., & Rossini, E. D. (2004). The Thematic Apperception Test (TAT). In M. J. Hilsenroth & D. L. Segal (Eds.), *Comprehensive handbook of psychological assessment: Personality assessment* (Vol. 2, pp. 356–371). Hoboken, NJ: Wiley.

Morey, L. C., & Hopwood, C. J. (2008). Objective personality evaluation. In M. Hersen & A. M. Gross (Eds.), *Handbook of clinical psychology* (Vol. 1, pp. 451–474). Hoboken, NJ: Wiley.

Morgan, C. D., & Murray, H. A. (1935). A method for investigating fantasies: The Thematic Apperception Test. *Archives of Neurology and Psychiatry, 34*(2), 289–306.

Morgan, E. S., & Scheibe, S. (2014). Reconciling cognitive decline and increased well-being with age: The role of increased emotion regulation efficiency. In P. Verhaeghen & C. K. Hertzog (Eds.), *The Oxford handbook of emotion, social cognition, and problem solving in adulthood* (pp. 155–173). New York, NY: Oxford University Press.

Morgan, K. (2012). The epidemiology of sleep. In C. M. Morin & C. A. Espie (Eds.), *The Oxford handbook of sleep and sleep disorders* (pp. 303–323). Oxford, UK: Oxford University Press.

Morgan, L. P. K., & Roemer, L. (2015). Mindfulness/meditation. In R. L. Cautin & S. O. Lilienfeld (Eds.), *The encyclopedia of clinical psychology* (pp. 1830–1839). West Sussex, UK: Wiley-Blackwell.

Morgan, W. P., & Stegner, A. J. (2008). Hypnosis in sport: Cases, techniques and issues. In M. R. Nash & A. J. Barnier (Eds.), *The Oxford handbook of hypnosis: Theory, research, and practice* (pp. 681–695). Oxford, UK: Oxford University Press.

Morganstern, K. P. (1973). Implosive therapy and flooding procedures: A critical review. *Psychological Bulletin, 79*(5), 318.

Mori, D., Chaiken, S., & Pliner, P. (1987). "Eating lightly" and the self-presentation of femininity. *Journal of Personality and Social Psychology, 53*(4), 693–702.

Morland, K., Roux, A. V. D., & Wing, S. (2006). Supermarkets, other food stores, and obesity: The atherosclerosis risk in communities study. *American Journal of Preventive Medicine, 30*(4), 333–339.

Morland, K., Wing, S., & Roux, A. D. (2002a). The contextual effect of the local food environment on residents' diets: The atherosclerosis risk in communities study. *American Journal of Public Health, 92*(11), 1761–1768.

Morland, K., Wing, S., Roux, A. D., & Poole, C. (2002b). Neighborhood characteristics associated with the location of food stores and food service places. *American Journal of Preventive Medicine, 22*(1), 23–29.

Morling, B., & Kitayama, S. (2008). Culture and motivation. In J. Y. Shah & W. L. Gardner (Eds.), *Handbook of motivation science* (pp. 417–433). New York, NY: Guilford Press.

Morling, B., & Lamoreaux, M. (2008). Measuring culture outside the head: A meta-analysis of individualism-collectivism in cultural products. *Personality and Social Psychology Review, 12*(3), 199–221.

Morrell, C. H., Gordon-Salant, S., Pearson, J. D., Brant, L. J., & Fozard, J. L. (1996). Age- and gender-specific reference ranges for hearing level and longitudinal changes in hearing level. *The Journal of the Acoustical Society of America, 100*(4), 1949–1967.

Morrison, J. (2008). *The first interview* (3rd ed.). New York, NY: Guilford Press.

Morrison, S. J., & Demorest, S. M. (2009). Cultural restraints on music perception and cognition. In J. Y. Chaio (Ed.), *Cultural neuroscience: Cultural influences on brain function* (pp. 67–77). Amsterdam: Elsevier.

Morse, M., Castillo, P., Venecia, D., Milstein, J., & Tyler, D. C. (1986). Childhood near-death experiences. *American Journal of Diseases of Children, 140*(11), 1110–1114.

Mortensen, P. B., Pedersen, C. B., Westergaard, T., Wohlfahrt, J., Ewald, H., Mors, O., . . . Melbye, M. (1999). Effects of family history and place and season of birth on the risk of schizophrenia. *New England Journal of Medicine, 340*(8), 603–608.

Morton, J., & Johnson, M. H. (1991). CONSPEC and CONLERN: A two-process theory of infant face recognition. *Psychological Review, 98*(2), 164–181.

Mosak, H. H., & Maniacci, M. (1999). *A primer of Adlerian psychology: The analytic-behavioral-cognitive psychology of Alfred Adler*. Philadelphia, PA: Brunner/Mazel.

Moshman, D. (2003). Developmental change in adulthood. In J. Demick & C. Andreoletti (Eds.), *Handbook of adult development* (pp. 43–62). New York, NY: Springer Science+Business Media.

Moshman, D. (2009). Adolescence. In U. Müller, J. I. M. Carpendale, & L. Smith (Eds.), *The Cambridge companion to Piaget* (pp. 255–269). New York, NY: Cambridge University Press.

Moskovich, A., Hunger, J., & Mann, T. (2011). The psychology of obesity. In J. H. Cawley (Ed.), *The Oxford handbook of the social science of obesity* (pp. 87–104). New York, NY: Oxford University Press.

Moskowitz, J. T. (2011). Coping interventions and the regulation of positive affect. In S. Folkman (Ed.), *Oxford handbook of stress, health, and coping* (pp. 407–427). Oxford, UK: Oxford University Press.

Moskowitz, J. T., & Saslow, L. R. (2014). Health and psychology: The importance of positive affect. In M. M. Tugade, M. N. Shiota, & L. D. Kirby (Eds.), *Handbook of positive emotions* (pp. 413–431). New York, NY: Guilford Press.

Moss, C. F., & Surlykke, A. (2001). Auditory scene analysis by echolocation in bats. *The Journal of the Acoustical Society of America, 110*(4), 2207–2226.

Moynihan, R., & Cassels, A. (2005). *Selling sickness*. New York, NY: Nation Books.

Mozaffarian, D., Hao, T., Rimm, E. B., Willett, W. C., & Hu, F. B. (2011). Changes in diet and lifestyle and long-term weight gain in women and men. *New England Journal of Medicine, 364*(25), 2392–2404.

Mu, Q., Mishory, A., Johnson, K. A., Nahas, Z., Kozel, F. A., Yamanaka, K., . . . George, M. S. (2005). Decreased brain activation during a working memory task at rested baseline is associated with vulnerability to sleep deprivation. *Sleep, 28*(4), 433–446.

Mueser, K. T., & Duva, S. M. (2011). Schizophrenia. In D. H. Barlow (Ed.), *The Oxford handbook of clinical psychology* (pp. 469–503). New York. NY: Oxford University Press.

Mueser, K. T., Bolton, E., & McGurk, S. R. (2006). Schizophrenia. In M. Hersen & J. C. Thomas (Eds.), *Comprehensive handbook of personality and psychopathology* (Vol. 2, pp. 262–277). Hoboken, NJ: Wiley.

Mueser, K. T., Deavers, F., Penn, D. L., & Cassisi, J. E. (2013). Psychosocial treatments for schizophrenia. *Annual Review of Clinical Psychology, 9*, 465–497.

Mueser, K. T., & Jeste, D. V. (2008). Preface. In K. T. Mueser & D. V. Jeste (Eds.), *Clinical handbook of schizophrenia* (pp. xii–xvi). New York, NY: Guilford Press.

Mueser, K. T., & Roe, D. (2016). Schizophrenia disorders. In J. C. Norcross, G. R. VandenBox, & D. K. Freedheim (Eds.), *APA handbook of clinical psychology* (Vol. 4, pp. 225–251). Washington, DC: American Psychological Association.

Mullen, B., Brown, R., & Smith, C. (1992). Ingroup bias as a function of salience, relevance, and status: An integration. *European Journal of Social Psychology, 22*(2), 103–122.

Mullen, B., & Hu, L. T. (1989). Perceptions of ingroup and outgroup variability: A meta-analytic integration. *Basic and Applied Social Psychology, 10*(3), 233–252.

Mullen, M. K. (1994). Earliest recollections of childhood: A demographic analysis. *Cognition, 52*(1), 55–79.

Müller, M. J. (2013). Depressive attribution style and stressor uncontrollability increase perceived pain intensity after electric skin stimuli in healthy young men. *Pain Research & Management, 18*, 203–206.

Müller, U. (2009). Infancy. In U. Müller, J. I. M. Carpendale, & L. Smith (Eds.), *The Cambridge companion to Piaget* (pp. 200–228). New York, NY: Cambridge University Press.

Müller, U. & Racine, T. P. (2010). The development of representation and concepts. In W. F. Overton (Ed.), *Handbook of life-span development* (Vol. 1, pp. 346–390). Hoboken, NJ: Wiley.

Munger, S. D. (2010). Olfactory receptors and transduction. In E. B. Goldstein (Ed.), *Encyclopedia of perception* (pp. 699–703). Thousand Oaks, CA: SAGE.

Munoz, R. F., & Mendelson, T. (2005). Toward evidence-based interventions for diverse populations: The San Francisco General Hospital prevention and treatment manuals. *Journal of Consulting and Clinical Psychology, 73*(5), 790–799.

Murakami, J. L. (2006). Mental illness in the world of wizardry. In N. Mulholland (Ed.), *The psychology of Harry Potter* (pp. 175–188). Dallas, TX: BenBella Books.

Murayama, K., Elliot, A. J., & Friedman, R. (2012). Achievement goals. In R. M. Ryan (Ed.), *The Oxford handbook of human motivation* (pp. 191–207). New York, NY: Oxford University Press.

Murdock, B. B., Jr. (1962). The serial position effect of free recall. *Journal of Experimental Psychology, 64*(5), 482–488.

Murphey, R. J., Ruprecht, M. J., Baggio, P., & Nunes, D. L. (1979). The use of mild punishment in combination with reinforcement of alternate behaviors to reduce the self-injurious behavior of a profoundly retarded individual. *Research and Practice for Persons with Severe Disabilities, 4*(2), 187–195.

Murphy, G. L. (2002). *The big book of concepts*. Cambridge, MA: MIT press.

Murphy, G. L., & Hoffman, A. B. (2012). Concepts. In K. Frankish & W. M. Ramsey (Eds.), *The Cambridge handbook of cognitive science* (pp. 151–170). Cambridge, UK: Cambridge University Press.

Murray, C. J. L., & Lopez, A. D. (Eds.). (1996). *The global burden of disease: A comprehensive assessment of mortality and disability from diseases, injuries, and risk factors in 1990 and projected to 2020*. Cambridge, MA: Harvard University Press.

Murray, D. J. (1988). *A history of Western psychology* (2nd ed.). Englewood Cliffs, NJ: Prentice Hall.

Murray, H. A. (1943). *Thematic Apperception Test: Manual*. Cambridge, MA: Harvard University Press.

Murtagh, D. R., & Greenwood, K. M. (1995). Identifying effective psychological treatments for insomnia: A meta-analysis. *Journal of Consulting and Clinical Psychology, 63*(1), 79–89.

Musgrave, C. (1997). The near-death experience: A study of spiritual transformation. *Journal of Near-Death Studies, 15*, 187–202.

Must, A., & Evans, E. W. (2011). The epidemiology of obesity. In J. H. Cawley (Ed.), *The Oxford handbook of the social science of obesity* (pp. 9–34). New York, NY: Oxford University Press.

Must, A., Hollander, S. A., & Economos, C. D. (2006). Childhood obesity: A growing public health concern. *Expert Review of Endocrinology and Metabolism, 1*(2), 233–254.

Must, A., Spadano, J., Coakley, E. H., Field, A. E., Colditz, G., & Dietz, W. H. (1999). The disease burden associated with overweight and obesity. *JAMA, 282*(16), 1523–1529.

Muzina, D. J., & Calabrese, J. R. (2006). Guidelines for the treatment of bipolar disorder. In D. J. Stein, D. J. Kupfer, & A. F. Schatzberg (Eds.), *The American Psychiatric Publishing textbook of mood disorders* (pp. 463–483). Washington, DC: American Psychiatric Publishing.

Myers, D. G., & Bishop, G. D. (1970). Discussion effects on racial attitudes. *Science. 169*(3947), 778–779.

Myers, D. G., & Lamm, H. (1976). The group polarization phenomenon. *Psychological Bulletin, 83*(4), 602.

Myles, S., Lea, R. A., Ohashi, J., Chambers, G. K., Weiss, J. G., Hardouin, E., . . . Kimura, R. (2011). Testing the thrifty gene hypothesis: The Gly482Ser variant in PPARGC1A is associated with BMI in Tongans. *BMC Medical Genetics, 12*(1), 10.doi:10.1186/1471-2350-12-10

Nadal, K. L. (2013). *That's so gay!: Microaggressions and the lesbian, gay, bisexual, and transgender community*. Washington, D.C: American Psychological Association.

Nadal, K. L., Issa, M. A., Leon, J., Meterko, V., Wideman, M., & Wong, Y. (2011a). Sexual orientation microaggressions: "Death by a thousand cuts" for lesbian, gay, and bisexual youth. *Journal of LGBT Youth, 8*(3), 234–259.

Nadal, K. L., Wong, Y., Issa, M. A., Meterko, V., Leon, J., & Wideman, M. (2011b). Sexual orientation microaggressions: Processes and coping mechanisms for lesbian, gay, and bisexual individuals. *Journal of LGBT Issues in Counseling, 5*(1), 21–46.

Nadal, K. L., Wong, Y., Griffin, K., Sriken, J., Vargas, V., Wideman, M., & Kolawole, A. (2011c). Microaggressions and the multiracial experience. *International Journal of Humanities and Social Sciences, 1*(7), 36–44.

Nagata, D. K., & Trierweiler, S. J. (2006). Revising a research manuscript. In F. T. L. Leong & J. T. Austin, *The psychology research handbook: A guide for graduate students and research assistants* (pp. 370–380). Thousand Oaks. CA: SAGE.

Naglieri, J. A., & Bornstein, B. T. (2003). Intelligence and achievement: Just how correlated are they? *Journal of Psychoeducational Assessment, 21*(3), 244–260.

Naglieri, J. A., Drasgow, F., Schmit, M., Handler, L., Prifitera, A., Margolis, A., & Velasquez, R. (2004). Psychological testing on the Internet: New problems, old issues. *American Psychologist, 59*(3), 150–162.

Nagy, T. F. (2012). Competence. In S. J. Knapp (Ed.), *APA handbook of ethics in psychology* (Vol. 1, pp. 147–174). Washington, DC: American Psychological Association.

Nail, P. R., & Boniecki, K. A. (2011). Inconsistency in cognition: Cognitive dissonance. In D. Chadee (Ed.), *Theories in social psychology* (pp. 44–71). West Sussex, UK: Wiley-Blackwell.

Nairne, J. S., & Rescorla, R. A. (1981). Second-order conditioning with diffuse auditory reinforcers in the pigeon. *Learning and Motivation, 12*, 65–91.

Nakamura, A., Yamada, T., Goto, A., Kato, T., Ito, K., Abe, Y., . . . Kakigi, R. (1998). Somatosensory homunculus as drawn by MEG. *Neuroimage, 7*(4), 377–386.

Nakatani, E., Nakgawa, A., Ohara, Y., Goto, S., Uozumi, N., Iwakiri, M., . . . Yamagami, T. (2003). Effects of behavior therapy on regional cerebral blood flow in obsessive-compulsive disorder. *Psychiatry Research: Neuroimaging, 124*(2), 113–120.

Nakayama, K. (2001). Modularity in perception, its relation to cognition and knowledge. In E. B. Goldstein (Ed.), *Blackwell handbook of perception* (pp. 737–759). Oxford, UK: Blackwell.

Nash, M. R. (2008). Foundations of clinical hypnosis. In M. R. Nash & A. J. Barnier (Eds.), *The Oxford handbook of hypnosis: Theory, research, and practice* (pp. 487–502). Oxford, UK: Oxford University Press.

Nassar, S. A. (1998). *A beautiful mind: The life of mathematical genius and Nobel Laureate John Nash*. New York, NY: Touchstone Books.

Nathan, D. (2011). *Sybil exposed*. New York, NY: Free Press.

Nathan, P. E., & Gorman, J. M. (Eds.). (2007). *A guide to treatments that work* (3rd ed.). New York, NY: Oxford University Press.

Nathan, P. W. (1976). The gate-control theory of pain: A critical review. *Brain, 99*(1), 123–158.

National Center for Health Statistics (2009). *Health United States*. Atlanta, GA: Center for Disease Control and Prevention.

National Center for Transgender Equality (2014). Transgender terminology. Retrieved from http://www.transequality.org/sites/default/files/docs/resources/TransTerminology_2014.pdf.

National Institute on Drug Abuse (2014, December). DrugFacts: Prescription and Over-the-Counter Medications. Retrieved from http://www.drugabuse.gov/publications/drugfacts/prescription-over-counter-medications.

National Public Radio (2014, August 29). J Dilla's lost scrolls. Retrieved from http://www. npr.org/2014/08/29/344255548/j-dillas-lost-scrolls.

National Sleep Foundation (2011). 2011 Sleep in America Poll. Washington, DC: National Sleep Foundation.

National Vital Statistics. (2010). Births, marriages, divorces, deaths: Provisional data for November 2009. *National Vital Statistics Reports, 58*, 1–5.

Nave, C. S., Sherman, R. A., Funder, D. C., Hampson, S. E., & Goldberg, L. R. (2010). On the contextual independence of personality: Teachers' assessments predict directly observed behavior after four decades. *Social Psychological and Personality Science, 1*(4), 327–334.

Nave, C. S., Sherman, R. A., Funder, D.C., Hampson, S. E., & Goldberg, L. R. (2010). On the contextual independence of personality: Teachers' assessments predict directly observed behavior after four decades. *Social Psychological and Personality Science, 1*, 327–334.

Naveh-Benjamin, M., & Jonides, J. (1984). Maintenance rehearsal: A two-component analysis. *Journal of Experimental Psychology: Learning, Memory, and Cognition, 10*(3), 369–385.

Navon, D. (1977). Forest before trees: The precedence of global features in visual perception. *Cognitive Psychology, 9*(3), 353–383.

Nawrot, P., Jordan, S., Eastwood, J., Rotstein, J., Hugenholtz, A., & Feeley, M. (2003). Effects of caffeine on human health. *Food Additives & Contaminants, 20*(1), 1–30.

Neel, J. V. (1962). Diabetes mellitus: A "thrifty" genotype rendered detrimental by "progress"? *American Journal of Human Genetics, 14*(4), 353–362.

Neel, J. V. (1999). The "thrifty genotype" in 1998. *Nutrition Reviews, 57*(5), 2–9.

Neill, John (1990). Whatever became of the schizophrenogenic mother? *American Journal of Psychotherapy, 44*(4), 499–505.

Neimark, E. D. (1975). Longitudinal development of formal operations thought. *Genetic Psychology Monographs, 91*(2), 171–225.

Neimeyer, R. A., Currier, J. M., Coleman, R., Tomer, A., & Samuel, E. (2011). Confronting suffering and death at the end of life: The impact of religiosity, psychosocial factors, and life regret among hospice patients. *Death Studies, 35*(9), 777–800.

Neisser, U. (1987). From direct perception to conceptual structure. In U. Neisser (Ed.), *Concepts and conceptual development: Ecological and intellectual factors in categorization* (pp. 11–24). New York, NY: Cambridge University Press.

Neisser, U., & Libby, L. K. (2000). Remembering life experiences. In E. Tulving & F. I. M. Craik (Eds.), *The Oxford handbook of memory* (pp. 315–332). Oxford, UK: Oxford University Press.

Neisser, U., Boodoo, G., Bouchard T. J., Jr., Boykin, A. W., Brody, N., Ceci, S. J., & Urbina, S. (1996). Intelligence: Knowns and unknowns. *American Psychologist, 51*(2), 77–101.

Neisser, U., Winograd, E., Bergman, E. T., Schreiber, C. A., Palmer, S. E., & Weldon, M. S. (1996). Remembering the earthquake: Direct experience vs. hearing the news. *Memory, 4*, 337–357.

Nelson, C. A. III, Thomas, K. M., & De Haan, M. (2006). Neural bases of cognitive development. In D. Kuhn & R. Siegler (Vol. Eds.), *Handbook of child psychology* (6th ed., Vol. 2, pp. 3–57). Hoboken, NJ: Wiley.

Nelson, D. I., Nelson, R. Y., Concha-Barrientos, M., & Fingerhut, M. (2005). The global burden of occupational noise-induced hearing loss. *American Journal of Industrial Medicine, 48*(6), 446–458.

Nelson, E. A. S., Taylor, B. J., Jenik, A., Vance, J., Walmsley, K., Pollard, K., . . . ICCPS Study Group. (2001). International child care practices study: Infant sleeping environment. *Early Human Development, 62*(1), 43–55.

Nelson, E. L., & Bui, T. (2010). Rural telepsychology services for children and adolescents. *Journal of Clinical Psychology, 66*(5), 490–501. doi:10.1002/jclp.20682

Nelson, S. K., & Lyubomirsky, S. (2014). Finding happiness: Tailoring positive activities for optimal well-being benefits. In M. M. Tugade, M. N. Shiota, & L. D. Kirby (Eds.), *Handbook of positive emotions* (pp. 275–293). New York, NY: Guilford Press.

Nelson, T. O. (1985). Ebbinghaus's contribution to the measurement of retention: Savings during relearning. *Journal of Experimental Psychology: Learning, Memory, and Cognition, 11*(3), 472–479.

Nemeroff, C. B., & Schatzberg, A. F. (2007). Pharmacological treatments for unipolar depression. In P. E. Nathan & J. M. Gorman (Eds.), *A guide to treatments that work* (3rd ed., pp. 271–287). New York, NY: Oxford University Press.

Nemeth, C. J., Connell, J. B., Rogers, J. D., & Brown, K. S. (2001). Improving decision making by means of dissent. *Journal of Applied Social Psychology, 31*(1), 48–58.

Nemeth, C., & Rogers, J. (2011). Dissent and the search for information. *British Journal of Social Psychology, 35*(1), 67–76.

Nesse, R. M. (2005). Natural selection and the regulation of defenses: A signal detection analysis of the smoke detector principle. *Evolution and Human Behavior, 26*(1), 88–105.

Nettle, D. (2001). *Strong imagination: Madness, creativity and human nature*. Oxford, UK: Oxford University Press.

Nettle, D. (2007). *Personality: What makes you the way you are*. New York, NY: Oxford University Press.

Nettle, D. (2011). Evolutionary perspectives on the five-factor model of personality. In D. M. Buss & P. H. Hawley (Eds.), *The evolution of personality and individual differences* (pp. 5–28). New York, NY: Oxford University Press.

Nettle, D., & Clegg, H. (2006). Schizotypy, creativity and mating success in humans. *Proceedings of the Royal Society B: Biological Sciences, 273*(1586), 611–615.

Neubauer, A. C., & Freudenthaler, H. H. (2005). Models of emotional intelligence. In R. Schulze and R. D. Roberts (Eds.), *Emotional intelligence: An international handbook* (pp. 31–50). Cambridge, MA: Hogrefe & Huber.

Neuberg, S. L., & Cottrell, C. A. (2006). Evolutionary bases of prejudices. In M. Schaller, J. A. Simpson, & D. T. Kenrick (Eds.), *Evolution and social psychology* (pp. 163–187). New York, NY: Psychology Press.

Neuberg, S. L., Kenrick, D. T., & Schaller, M. (2010). Evolutionary social psychology. In S. T. Fiske, D. T. Gilbert, & G. Lindzey (Eds.), *Handbook of social psychology* (5th ed., Vol. 2, pp. 761–796). New York, NY: John Wiley & Sons.

Neuberg, S. L., Kenrick, D. T., & Schaller, M. (2010). Evolutionary social psychology. In S. T. Fiske, D. T. Gilbert, & G. Lindzey (Eds.), *Handbook of social psychology* (5th ed., Vol. 2, pp. 761–796). Hoboken, NJ: Wiley.

Neupert, S. D., Almeida, D. M., & Charles, S. T. (2007). Age differences in reactivity to daily stressors: The role of personal control. *The Journals of Gerontology Series B: Psychological Sciences and Social Sciences, 62*(4), P216–P225.

Neuschatz, J. S., Lampinen, J. M., Toglia, M. P., Payne, D. G., & Cisneros, E. P. (2007). False memory research: History, theory, and applied applications. In M. P. Toglia, J. D. Read, D. F. Ross, & R. C. L. Lindsay (Eds.), *The handbook of eyewitness psychology: Memory for events* (Vol. I, pp. 239–260). East Sussex, UK: Psychology Press.

Neville, H., & Sur, M. (2009). Introduction. In M. S. Gazzaniga (Ed.), The cognitive neurosciences (4th ed., pp. 89–90). Cambridge, MA: MIT Press.

New York Times, 4/22/2013. Retrieved June 2, 2015 from http://www.nytimes.com/interactive/2013/04/22/sports/boston-moment.html.

Newberg, A. B. (2010). The neurobiology of meditation. In D. A. Monti & B. D. Beitman (Eds.), *Integrative psychiatry* (pp. 339–358). New York, NY: Oxford University Press.

Newby-Clark, I. R. (2004). Getting ready for the bad times: Self-esteem and anticipatory coping. *European Journal of Social Psychology, 34*(3), 309–316.

Newey, C. A., & Hood, B. M. (2004). Determinants of shift-work adjustment for nursing staff: The critical experience of partners. *Journal of Professional Nursing, 20*(3), 187–195.

Newman, C. F. (2006). Bipolar disorder. In M. Hersen & J. C. Thomas (Eds.), *Comprehensive handbook of personality and psychopathology* (Vol. 2, pp. 244–261). Hoboken, NJ: Wiley.

Newman, K. S. (2012). *The accordion family: Boomerang kids, anxious parents, and the private toll of global competition*. Boston, MA: Beacon Press.

Newman, L. C., & Larsen, R. J. (Eds.) (2011). *Taking sides: Clashing views in personality psychology*. New York, NY: McGraw-Hill.

Newman, R. (2010). *Security and access control using biometric technologies*. Boston, MA: Course Technology.

Newport, F., & Gates, G. J. (2015). San Francisco Metro Area Ranks Highest in LGBT Percentage. Retrieved from http://www.gallup.com/poll/182051/san-francisco-metro-area-ranks-highest-lgbt-percentage.aspx?utm_source=Social%20Issues&utm_medium=newsfeed&utm_campaign=tiles.

Neyer, F. J., & Lang, F. R. (2003). Blood is thicker than water: Kinship orientation across adulthood. *Journal of Personality and Social Psychology, 84*(2), 310–321.

Nezu, A. M. (2010). Cultural influences on the process of conducting psychotherapy: Personal reflections of an ethnic minority psychologist. *Psychotherapy: Theory, Research, Practice, Training, 47*(2), 169–176.

Ng, K. Y., Van Dyne, L., & Ang, S., (2012). Cultural intelligence: A review, reflections, and recommendations for future research. In A. M. Ryan, F. T. L. Leong, & F. L. Oswald (Eds.), *Conducting multinational research: Applying organizational*

psychology in the workplace (pp. 29–58). Washington, DC, American Psychological Association.
Ng, T. W. H., Sorensen, K. L., and Eby, L. T. (2006). Locus of control at work: A meta-analysis. *Journal of Organizational Behavior, 27*(8), 1057–1087.
Nguyen, B. H., Pérusse, D., Paquet, J., Petit, D., Boivin, M., Tremblay, R. E., & Montplaisir, J. (2008). Sleep terrors in children: A prospective study of twins. *Pediatrics, 122*(6), e1164–e1167.
Nguyen, H. H. (2006). Acculturation in the United States. In D. L. Sam, & J. W. Berry (Eds.), *The Cambridge handbook of acculturation psychology* (pp. 311–330). New York, NY: Cambridge University Press.
Nicholls, R. E., Alarcon, J. M., Malleret, G., Carroll, R. C., Grody, M., Vronskaya, S., & Kandel, E. R. (2008). Transgenic mice lacking NMDAR-dependent LTD exhibit deficits in behavioral flexibility. *Neuron, 58*(1), 104–117.
Nicholson, N., Cole, S. G., & Rocklin, T. (1985). Conformity in the Asch situation: A comparison between contemporary British and U.S. university students. *British Journal of Social Psychology, 24*(1), 59–63.
Nicolaus, L. K., Hoffman, T. E., & Gustavson, C. R. (1982). Taste aversion conditioning in free-ranging raccoons (*Procyon lotor*). *Northwest Science, 56,* 165–169.
Nielsen, T. A. (1995). Describing and modeling hypnagogic imagery using a systematic self-observation procedure. *Dreaming, 5*(2), 75–94.
Nielsen, T. A. (2000). A review of mentation in REM and NREM sleep: "Covert" REM sleep as a possible reconciliation of two opposing models. *Behavioral and Brain Sciences, 23*(06), 851–866.
Nielsen, T. A. (2004). Chronobiological features of dream production. *Sleep Medicine Reviews, 8*(5), 403–424.
Niemeier, H. M., Raynor, H. A., Lloyd-Richardson, E. E., Rogers, M. L., & Wing, R. R. (2006). Fast food consumption and breakfast skipping: Predictors of weight gain from adolescence to adulthood in a nationally representative sample. *Journal of Adolescent Health, 39*(6), 842–849.
Niemiec, C. P., Ryan, R. M., & Deci, E. L. (2009). The path taken: Consequences of attaining intrinsic and extrinsic aspirations in post-college life. *Journal of Research in Personality, 43*(3), 291–306.
Nippold, M. A., & Duthie, J. K. (2003). Mental imagery and idiom comprehension: A comparison of school-age children and adults. *Journal of Speech, Language, and Hearing Research, 46*(4), 788–799.
Nisbett, R. (1995). Race, IQ, and scientism. In S. Fraser (Ed.), *The bell curve wars: Race, intelligence, and the future of America* (pp. 36–57). New York, NY: Basic Books.
Nisbett, R. (2003). *The geography of thought: How Asians and Westerners think differently ... and why*. New York, NY: Free Press.
Nisbett, R. E., & Masuda, T. (2003). Culture and point of view. *Proceedings of the National Academy of Sciences, 100*(19), 11163–11170.
Nisbett, R. E., & Miyamoto, Y. (2005). The influence of culture: Holistic versus analytic perception. *Trends in Cognitive Sciences, 9*(10), 467–473.
Nisbett, R. E., Aronson, J., Blair, C., Dickens, W., Flynn, J., Halpern, D. F., & Turkheimer, E. (2012). Intelligence: New findings and theoretical developments. *American Psychologist, 67*(2), 130–159.
Nisenson, L., Berenbaum, H., & Good, T. (2001). The development of interpersonal relationships in individuals with schizophrenia. *Psychiatry, 64*(2), 111–125.
Nishida, M., Pearsall, J., Buckner, R. L., & Walker, M. P. (2009). REM sleep, prefrontal theta, and the consolidation of human emotional memory. *Cerebral Cortex, 19*(5), 1158–1166.
Niu, W., & Brass, J. (2011). Intelligence in worldwide perspective. In R. J. Sternberg & S. B. Kaufman (Eds.), *The Cambridge handbook of intelligence* (pp. 623–646). Cambridge, UK: Cambridge University Press.
Niu, W., & Sternberg, R. J. (2001). Cultural influences on artistic creativity and its evaluation. *International Journal of Psychology, 36*(4), 225–241.
Noar, S. M., Benac, C. N., & Harris, M. S. (2007). Does tailoring matter? Meta-analytic review of tailored print health behavior change interventions. *Psychological Bulletin, 133*(4), 673–693.
Noble, J. & McConkey, K. M. (1995). Hypnotic sex change: Creating and challenging a delusion in the laboratory. *Journal of Abnormal Psychology, 104*(1), 69–74.
Nobler, M. S., & Sackeim, H. A. (2006). Electroconvulsive therapy and transcranial magnetic stimulation. In D. J. Stein, D. J. Kupfer, & A. F. Schatzberg (Eds.), *The American Psychiatric Publishing textbook of mood disorders* (pp. 317–336). Washington, DC: American Psychiatric Publishing.
Nolen-Hoeksema, S. (2000). The role of rumination in depressive disorders and mixed anxiety/depressive symptoms. *Journal of Abnormal Psychology, 109*(3), 504–511.
Nolen-Hoeksema, S., & Hilt, L. M. (2009). Gender differences in depression. In I. H. Gotlib & C. L. Hammen (Eds.), *Handbook of depression* (2nd ed., pp. 386–404). New York, NY: Guilford Press.
Nolen-Hoeksema, S., Stice, E., Wade, E., & Bohon, C. (2007). Reciprocal relations between rumination and bulimic, substance abuse, and depressive symptoms in female adolescents. *Journal of Abnormal Psychology, 116*(1), 198–207.
Noll, R. (2007). *The encyclopedia of schizophrenia and other psychotic disorders* (3rd ed.). New York, NY: Facts on File.
Nolte, J. (2008). *The human brain: An introduction to its functional anatomy* (6th ed.) St. Louis, MO: Mosby.
Norcross, J. C. (2000). Clinical versus counseling psychology: What's the diff? *Eye on Psi Chi, 5*(1), 20–22.
Norcross, J. C. (2005). A primer on psychotherapy integration. In J. C. Norcross & M. R. Goldfried (Eds.), *Handbook of psychotherapy integration* (2nd ed., pp. 3–24). New York, NY: Oxford University Press.
Norcross, J. C., & Karpiak, C. P. (2012). Clinical psychologists in the 2010s: 50 years of the APA Division of Clinical Psychology. *Clinical Psychology: Science and Practice, 19,* 1–12.
Norcross, J. C., & Lambert, M. J. (2011). Evidence-based therapy relationships. In J. C. Norcross (Ed.), *Psychotherapy relationships that work: Evidence-based responsiveness* (2nd ed., pp. 3–21). New York, NY: Oxford University Press.
Norcross, J. C., & Newman, C. F. (1992). Psychotherapy integration: Setting the context. In J. C. Norcross & M. R. Goldfried (Eds.), *Handbook of psychotherapy integration* (pp. 3–45). New York, NY: Basic Books.
Norcross, J. C., & Sayette, M. A. (2012). *Insider's guide to graduate programs in clinical and counseling psychology*. New York, NY: Guilford Press.
Norcross, J. C., & Wampold, B. E. (2011). Evidence-based therapy relationships: Research conclusions and clinical practices. In J. C. Norcross (Ed.), *Psychotherapy relationships that work: Evidence-based responsiveness* (2nd ed., pp. 423–430). New York, NY: Oxford University Press.
Norcross, J. C., Freedheim, D. K., & Vandenbos, G. R. (2011). Into the future: Retrospect and prospect in psychotherapy. In J. C. Norcross, G. R. Vandenbos, & D. K. Freedheim (Eds.), *History of psychotherapy: Continuity and change* (2nd ed., pp. 743–760). Washington, DC: American Psychological Association.
Norcross, J. C., Karpiak, C. P., & Santoro, S. O. (2005). Clinical psychologists across the years: The division of clinical psychology from 1960 to 2003. *Journal of Clinical Psychology, 61,* 1467–1483.
Norcross, J. C., Karpiak, C. P., & Santoro, S. O. (2005). Clinical psychologists across the years: The division of clinical psychology from 1960 to 2003. *Journal of Clinical Psychology, 61*(12), 1467–1483.
Norcross, J. C., Kohout, J. L., & Wicherski, M. (2005). Graduate study in psychology: 1971–2004. *American Psychologist, 60,* 959–975.
Nordby, V. J., & Hall, C. S. (1974). *A guide to psychologists and their concepts*. New York, NY: W. H. Freeman.
Norem, J. K. (2003). Pessimism: Accentuating the positive possibilities. In E. C. Chang & L. J. Sanna (Eds.), *Virtue, vice, and personality: The complexity of behavior* (pp. 91–104). Washington, DC: American Psychological Association.
Norem, J. K. (2008). Defensive pessimism, anxiety, and the complexity of evaluating self-regulation. *Social and Personality Psychology Compass, 2*(1), 121–134.
Norem, J. K. (2010). Resisting the hegemony of the five-factor model: There is plenty of personality outside the FFA. *Psychological Inquiry, 21*(1), 65–68.
Norem, J. K., & Cantor, N. (1986). Defensive pessimism: Harnessing anxiety as motivation. *Journal of Personality and Social Psychology, 51*(6), 1208–1217.
Norenzayan, A., Choi, I., & Peng, K. (2007). Perception and cognition. In S. Kitayama & D. Cohen (Eds.), *Handbook of cultural psychology* (pp. 569–594). New York, NY Guilford Press.
Nosofsky, R. M., & Johansen, M. K. (2000). Exemplar-based accounts of "multiple-system" phenomena in perceptual categorization. *Psychonomic Bulletin and Review, 7*(3), 375–402.
Nosofsky, R. M., Clark, S. E., & Shin, H. J. (1989). Rules and exemplars in categorization, identification, and recognition. *Journal of Experimental Psychology: Learning, Memory, and Cognition, 15*(2), 282–304.
Nowak, N. T., Murali, A., & Driscoll, I. (2015). Factors related to sex differences in navigating a computerized maze. *Journal of Environmental Psychology, 43,* 136–144.
Nucci, L. P. & Gingo, M. (2011). The development of moral reasoning. In U. Goswami (Ed.), *The Wiley-Blackwell handbook of childhood cognitive development* (2nd ed., pp. 420–445). Malden, MA: Wiley-Blackwell.
Nurminen, T. (1998). Shift work and reproductive health. *Scandinavian Journal of Work, Environment & Health,* 24(Suppl. 23), 28–34.
Nyklíček, I., & Kuijpers, K. F. (2008). Effects of mindfulness-based stress reduction intervention on psychological well-being and quality of life: Is increased mindfulness indeed the mechanism? *Annals of Behavioral Medicine, 35*(3), 331–340.
O'Brien, W. H., & Tabaczynski, T. (2007). Unstructured interviewing. In M. Hersen & J. C. Thomas (Eds.), *Handbook of clinical interviewing with children* (pp. 16–29). Thousand Oaks, CA: SAGE.
O'Connor, M. G., & Kaplan, E. F. (2003). Age-related changes in memory. In J. Demick & C. Andreoletti (Eds.), *Handbook of adult development* (pp. 121–130). New York, NY: Springer Science+Business Media.
O'Connor, M. J., Shah, B., Whaley, S., Cronin, P., Gunderson, B., & Graham, J. (2002). Psychiatric illness in a clinical sample of children with prenatal alcohol exposure. *The American Journal of Drug and Alcohol Abuse, 28*(4), 743–754.
O'Connor, M., & Verfaillie, M. (2002). The amnesic syndrome: Overview and subtypes. In A. D. Baddeley, M. D. Kopelman, & B. A. Wilson (Eds.), *The handbook of memory disorders* (2nd ed., pp. 145–166). Chichester, UK: Wiley.
O'Donohue, W. (2009). A brief history of cognitive behavior therapy: Are there troubles ahead? In W. T. O'Donohue & J. E. Fisher (Eds.), *General principles and empirically supported techniques of cognitive behavior therapy* (pp. 1–14). Hoboken, NJ: Wiley.
O'Donohue, W. (2009). A brief history of cognitive behavior therapy: Are there troubles ahead? In W. T. O'Donohue & J. E. Fisher (Eds.), *General principles and empirically supported techniques of cognitive behavior therapy* (pp. 1–14). Hoboken, NJ: Wiley.
O'Hara, R. E., Gibbons, F. X., Gerrard, M., Li, Z., & Sargent, J. D. (2012). Greater exposure to sexual content in popular movies predicts earlier sexual debut and increased sexual risk taking. *Psychological Science, 23*(9), 984–993.
O'Malley, D., Quigley, E. M., Dinan, T. G., & Cryan, J. F. (2011). Do interactions between stress and immune responses lead to symptom exacerbations in irritable bowel syndrome? *Brain, Behavior, and Immunity, 25*(7), 1333–1341.

O'Neal, J. M. (1984). First person account: Finding myself and loving it. *Schizophrenia Bulletin, 10*(1), 109–110.
O'Riordan, K. (2012). The life of the gay gene: From hypothetical genetic marker to social reality. *Journal of Sex Research, 49*(4), 362–368.
Oakley, D. A. (2008). Hypnosis, trance, and suggestion: Evidence from neuroimaging. In M. R. Nash & A. J. Barnier (Eds.), *The Oxford handbook of hypnosis: Theory, research, and practice* (pp. 365–392). Oxford, UK: Oxford University Press.
Oaksford, M., Chater, N., & Stewart, N. (2012). Reasoning and decision making. In K. Frankish & W. M. Ramsey (Eds.), *The Cambridge handbook of cognitive science* (pp. 131–150). Cambridge, UK: Cambridge University Press.
Oas, P. T. (2010). Current status on corporal punishment with children: What the literature says. *The American Journal of Family Therapy, 38*(5), 413–420.
O'Boyle, E. H., Humphrey, R. H., Pollack, J. M., Hawver, T. H., & Story, P. A. (2011). The relation between emotional intelligence and job performance: A meta-analysis. *Journal of Organizational Behavior, 32*(5), 788–818.
O'Brien, K. S., Latner, J. D., Ebneter, D., & Hunter, J. A. (2013). Obesity discrimination: The role of physical appearance, personal ideology, and anti-fat prejudice. *International Journal of Obesity, 37*(3), 455–460.
Ocampo-Garcés, A., Molina, E., Rodríguez, A., & Vivaldi, E. A. (2000). Homeostasis of REM sleep after total and selective sleep deprivation in the rat. *Journal of Neurophysiology, 84*(5), 2699–2702.
Ofen-Noy, N., Dudai, Y., & Karni, A. (2003). Skill learning in mirror reading: How repetition determines acquisition. *Cognitive Brain Research, 17*(2), 507–521.
Ogden, J. (2012, January 16). HM, the man with no memory. *Psychology Today*. Retrieved from https://www.psychologytoday.com/blog/trouble-in-mind/201201/hm-the-man-no-memory
Ogloff, J. R. P. (Ed.). (2002). *Taking psychology and law into the twenty-first century*. New York, NY: Kluwer Academic/Plenum Press.
Ohashi, M. M., & Yamaguchi, S. (2004). Super-ordinary bias in Japanese self-predictions of future life events. *Asian Journal of Social Psychology, 7*(2), 169–185.
Ohayon, M. M., & Guilleminault, C. (2006). Epidemiology of sleep disorders. In T. L. Lee-Chiong (Ed.), *Sleep: A comprehensive handbook* (pp. 73–82). Hoboken, NJ: Wiley-Liss.
Ohayon, M. M., Carskadon, M. A., Guilleminault, C., & Vitiello, M. V. (2004). Meta-analysis of quantitative sleep parameters from childhood to old age in healthy individuals: Developing normative sleep values across the human lifespan. *Sleep, 27*, 1255–1274.
Ohayon, M. M., Guilleminault, C., & Priest, R. G. (1999). Night terrors, sleepwalking, and confusional arousals in the general population: Their frequency and relationship to other sleep and mental disorders. *Journal of Clinical Psychiatry, 60*(4), 268–276.
Ohayon, M. M., Priest, R. G., Zulley, J., Smirne, S., & Paiva, T. (2002). Prevalence of narcolepsy symptomatology and diagnosis in the European general population. *Neurology, 58*(12), 1826–1833.
Öhman, A., & Mineka, S. (2001). Fears, phobias, and preparedness: Toward an evolved module of fear and fear learning. *Psychological Review, 108*(3), 483.
Oishi, S. (2002). The experiencing and remembering of well-being: A cross-cultural analysis. *Personality and Social Psychology Bulletin, 28*(10), 1398–1406.
Ojeda, L., Navarro, R. L., Meza, R. R., & Arbona, C. (2012). Too Latino and not Latino enough: The role of ethnicity-related stressors on Latino college students' life satisfaction. *Journal of Hispanic Higher Education, 11*(1), 14–28.
Okaichi, Y., & Okaichi, H. (2001). Music discrimination by rats. *Japanese Journal of Animal Psychology, 51*, 29–34.
Okami, P., Weisner, T., & Olmstead, R. (2002). Outcome correlates of parent-child bedsharing: An eighteen-year longitudinal study. *Journal of Developmental & Behavioral Pediatrics, 23*(4), 244–253.
O'Keeffe, G. S., & Clarke-Pearson, K. (2011). The impact of social media on children, adolescents, and families. *Pediatrics, 127*(4), 800–804.
Olatunji, B. O., & Feldman, G. (2008). Cognitive-behavioral therapy. In M. Hersen & A. M. Gross (Eds.), *Handbook of clinical psychology* (Vol. 1, pp. 551–584). Hoboken, NJ: Wiley.
Olejniczak, P. (2006). Neurophysiologic basis of EEG. *Journal of Clinical Neurophysiology, 23*(3), 186–189.
Olff, M., Langeland, W., Draijer, N., & Gersons, B. P. (2007). Gender differences in posttraumatic stress disorder. *Psychological Bulletin, 133*(2), 183–204.
Olfson, M., Marcus, S. C., Tedeschi, M., & Wan, G. J. (2006). Continuity of antidepressant treatment for adults with depression in the United States. *American Journal of Psychiatry, 163*(1), 101–108.
Oliver, B. R., & Plomin, R. (2007). Twins' Early Development Study (TEDS): A multivariate, longitudinal genetic investigation of language, cognition and behavior problems from childhood through adolescence. *Twin Research and Human Genetics, 10*(01), 96–105.
Oliver, G., & Wardle, J. (1999). Perceived effects of stress on food choice. *Physiology & Behavior, 66*(3), 511–515.
Oliver, M. B., & Hyde, J. S. (1993). Gender differences in sexuality: A meta-analysis. *Psychological Bulletin, 114*(1), 29–51.
Olkin, R., & Taliaferro, G. (2006). Evidence-based practices have ignored people with disabilities. In J. C. Norcross, L. E. Beutler, & R. F. Levant (Eds.), *Evidence-based practices in mental health: Debate and dialogue on the fundamental questions* (pp. 353–359). Washington, DC: American Psychological Association.
Ollendick, T. H., Alvarez, H. K., & Greene, R. W. (2004). Behavioral assessment: History of underlying concepts and methods. In S. N. Haynes & E. M. Heiby (Eds.), *Comprehensive handbook of psychological assessment* (Vol. 3, pp. 19–34). Hoboken, NJ: Wiley.
Ollendick, T. H., Weist, M. D., Borden, M. C., & Greene, R. W. (1992). Sociometric status and academic, behavioral, and psychological adjustment: A five-year longitudinal study. *Journal of Consulting and Clinical Psychology, 60*(1), 80–87.
Oller, D. K. (2000). *The emergence of the speech capacity*. Mahwah, NJ: Lawrence Erlbaum.
Olson, C. R., & Colby, C. L. (2013). The organization of cognition. In E. R. Kandel, J. H. Schwartz, T. M. Jessell, S. A. Siegelbaum, & A. J. Hudspeth (Eds.), *Principles of neural science* (5th ed., pp. 392–411). New York, NY: McGraw-Hill.
Olson, I. R., & Marshuetz, C. (2005). Facial attractiveness is appraised in a glance. *Emotion, 5*(4), 498–502.
Olson, M. A., & Fazio, R. H. (2009). Implicit and explicit measures of attitude: The perspective of the MODE model. In R. E. Petty, R. H. Fazio, & P. Brinol (Eds.), *Attitudes: Insights for the new implicit measures* (pp. 19–63). New York, NY: Psychology Press.
Oman, C. M. (1990). Motion sickness: A synthesis and evaluation of the sensory conflict theory. *Canadian Journal of Physiology and Pharmacology, 68*(2), 294–303.
Oman, D., Shapiro, S. L., Thoresen, C. E., Plante, T. G., & Flinders, T. (2008). Meditation lowers stress and supports forgiveness among college students: A randomized controlled trial. *Journal of American College Health, 56*(5), 569–578.
Ong, A. D., & Allaire, J. C. (2005). Cardiovascular intraindividual variability in later life: The influence of social connectedness and positive emotions. *Psychology and Aging, 20*(3), 476–485.
Ong, A. D., Burrow, A. L., Fuller-Rowell, T. E., Ja, N. M., & Sue, D. W. (2013). Racial microaggressions and daily well-being among Asian Americans. *Journal of Counseling Psychology, 60*(2), 188–199.
Opfer, J. E., & Gelman, S. A. (2011). Development of the animate-inanimate distinction. In U. Goswami (Ed.), *The Wiley-Blackwell handbook of childhood cognitive development* (2nd ed., pp. 213–238). Malden, MA: Wiley-Blackwell.
O'Regan, J. K., Rensink, R. A., & Clark, J. J. (1999). Change-blindness as a result of "mudsplashes." *Nature, 398*(6722), 34.
Orlick, T., Zhou, Q. Y., & Partington, J. (1990). Co-operation and conflict within Chinese and Canadian kindergarten settings. *Canadian Journal of Behavioural Science, 22*(1), 20–25.
Orlinsky, D. E., & Howard, K. I. (1995). Unity and diversity among psychotherapies: A comparative perspective. In B. Bongar & L. E. Beutler (Eds.), *Comprehensive textbook of psychotherapy: Theory and practice* (pp. 3–23). New York, NY: Oxford University Press.
Ormont, L. R. (1992). *The group therapy experience: From theory to practice*. New York, NY: St. Martin's Press.
Ornstein, R. M., Rosen, D. S., Mammel, K. A., Callahan, S. T., Forman, S., Jay, M. S., . . . Walsh, B. T. (2013). Distribution of eating disorders in children and adolescents using the proposed DSM-5 criteria for feeding and eating disorders. *Journal of Adolescent Health, 53*(2), 303–305.
Ortiz, S. O., & Dynda, A. M. (2005). Use of intelligence tests with culturally and linguistically diverse populations. In D. P. Flanagan & P. L. Harrison (Eds.), *Contemporary intellectual assessment: Theories, tests, and issues* (2nd ed., pp. 545–556). New York, NY: Guilford Press.
Osby, U., Brandt, L., Correia, N., Ekbom, A., & Sparen, P. (2001). Excess mortality in bipolar and unipolar disorder in Sweden. *Archives of General Psychiatry, 58*(9), 844–850.
Osipow, S. H. (2006). Dealing with journal editors and reviewers. In F. T. L. Leong & J. T. Austin (Eds.), *The psychology research handbook: A guide for graduate students and research assistants* (pp. 381–386). Thousand Oaks: SAGE Publications.
Ostir, G. V., Markides, K. S., Peek, M. K., & Goodwin, J. S. (2001). The association between emotional well-being and the incidence of stroke in older adults. *Psychosomatic Medicine, 63*(2), 210–215.
Otake, K., Shimai, S., Tanaka-Matsumi, J., Otsui, K., & Fredrickson, B. L. (2006). Happy people become happier through kindness: A counting kindnesses intervention. *Journal of Happiness Studies, 7*(3), 361–375.
Otto, M. W., & Applebaum, A. J. (2011). The nature and treatment of bipolar disorder and the bipolar spectrum. In D. H. Barlow (Ed.), *The Oxford handbook of clinical psychology* (pp. 294–310). New York, NY: Oxford University Press.
Otto, R. K., & Heilbrun, K. (2002). The practice of forensic psychology: A look toward the future in light of the past. *American Psychologist, 57*, 5–18.
Otto, R. K., Buffington-Vollum, J. K., & Edens, J. F. (2003). Child custody evaluation. In A. M. Goldstein (Ed.), *Handbook of psychology* (Vol. 11, pp. 179–208). Hoboken, NJ: Wiley.
Ouellette, S. C., & DiPlacido, J. (2001). Personality's role in the protection and enhancement of health: Where the research has been, where it is stuck, how it might move. In A. Baum, T. A. Revenson, & J. Singer (Eds.), *Handbook of health psychology* (pp. 175–193). Mahwah, NJ: Lawrence Erlbaum.
Overmier, J. B., & LoLordo, V. M. (1998). Learned helplessness. In W. O'Donohue (Ed.), *Learning and behavior therapy* (pp. 352–373). Boston, MA: Allyn and Bacon.
Overmier, J. B., & Seligman, M. E. P. (1967). Effects of inescapable shock on subsequent escape and avoidance responding. *Journal of Comparative and Physiological Psychology, 63*, 28–33.
Overton, W. F. (2006). Developmental psychology: Philosophy, concepts, methodology. In R. M. Lerner (Vol. Ed.), *Handbook of child psychology* (6th ed., Vol. 1, pp. 18–88). Hoboken, NJ: Wiley.
Overton, W. F. (2010). Life-span development: Concepts and issues. In W. F. Overton (Ed.), *Handbook of life-span development* (Vol. 1, pp. 1–29). Hoboken, NJ: Wiley.

Owen, J. J., Tao, K., Leach, M. M., & Rodolfa, E. (2011). Clients' perceptions of their psychotherapists' multicultural orientation. *Psychotherapy (Chic)*, *48*(3), 274–282.
Owen, J., & Fincham, F. D. (2011). Young adults' emotional reactions after hooking up encounters. *Archives of Sexual Behavior*, *40*(2), 321–330.
Owen, J., Tao, K. W., Imel, Z. E., Wampold, B. E., & Rodolfa, E. (2014). Addressing racial and ethnic microaggressions in therapy. *Professional Psychology: Research and Practice*, *45*(4), 283–290.
Owen, J., Tao, K., Leach, M., & Rodolfa, E. (2011). Clients' perceptions of their psychotherapists' multicultural orientation. *Psychotherapy*, *48*, 274 –282.
Owen, P. R. (2012). Portrayals of schizophrenia by entertainment media: A content analysis of contemporary movies. *Psychiatric Services*, *63*(7), 655–659.
Owens, E. B., Cardoos, S. L., & Hinshaw, S. P. (2015). Developmental progression and gender differences. In R. A. Barkley (Ed.). *Attention-deficit hyperactivity disorder: A handbook for diagnosis and treatment* (4th ed., pp. 223–255). New York, NY: Guilford Press.
Owens, J. A., Belon, K., & Moss, P. (2010). Impact of delaying school start time on adolescent sleep, mood, and behavior. *Archives of Pediatrics & Adolescent Medicine*, *164*(7), 608–614.
Owens, J., Cook, E. W., & Stevenson, I. (1990). Features of "near-death experience" in relation to whether or not patients were near death. *The Lancet*, *336*(8724), 1175–1177.
Owens, R. E. (2014). *Language development: An introduction* (8th ed.). Upper Saddle River, NJ: Pearson.
Oyserman, D., Coon, H. M., & Kemmelmeier, M. (2002). Rethinking individualism and collectivism: Evaluation of theoretical assumptions and meta-analyses. *Psychological Bulletin*, *128*(1), 3–72.
Ozer, D. J., & Benet-Martinez, V. (2006). Personality and the prediction of consequential outcomes. *Annual Review of Psychology*, *57*, 401–421.
Padgett, D. K., Patrick, C., Burns, B. J., & Schlesinger, H. J. (1994). Ethnicity and the use of outpatient mental health services in a national insured population. *American Journal of Public Health*, *84*(2), 222–226.
Padilla, A. M. & Olmedo, E. (2009). Synopsis of key persons, events, and associations in the history of Latino psychology. *Cultural Diversity and Ethnic Minority Psychology*, *15*(4), 363–373.
Padilla, A. M., & Borrero, N. E. (2006). Acculturative stress. In P. T. P. Wong and L. C. J. Wong (Eds.), *Handbook of multicultural perspectives on stress and coping* (pp. 299–318). New York, NY: Springer Science+Business Media.
Pagani, L., Tremblay, R. E., Nagin, D., Zoccolillo, M., Vitaro, F., & McDuff, P. (2009). Risk factor models for adolescent verbal and physical aggression toward fathers. *Journal of Family Violence*, *24*, 173–182.
Pagani, L., Tremblay, R., Nagin, D., Zoccolillo, M., Vitaro, F., & McDuff, P. (2004). Risk factor models for adolescent verbal and physical aggression toward mothers. *International Journal of Behavioral Development*, *28*(6), 528–537.
Page, L., & Page, K. (2010). Last shall be first: A field study of biases in sequential performance evaluation on the Idol series. *Journal of Economic Behavior & Organization*, *73*(2), 186–198.
Pager, D., & Shepherd, H. (2008). The sociology of discrimination: Racial discrimination in employment, housing, credit, and consumer markets. *Annual Review of Sociology*, *34*, 181–209.
Pagliano, P. J. (2012). *The multisensory handbook: A guide for children and adults with sensory learning disabilities*. New York, NY: Routledge.
Pagura, J., Cox, B. J., & Enns, M. W. (2009). Personality factors in the anxiety disorders. In M. M. Antony & M. B. Stein (Eds.), *Oxford handbook of anxiety and related disorders* (pp. 190–208). New York, NY: Oxford University Press.
Paine, S. J., Gander, P. H., Harris, R., & Reid, P. (2004). Who reports insomnia? Relationships with age, sex, ethnicity, and socioeconomic deprivation. *Sleep*, *27*(6), 1163–1169.
Pakenham, K. I. (2011). Benefit-finding and sense-making in chronic illness. In S. Folkman (Ed.), *Oxford handbook of stress, health, and coping* (pp. 242–268). Oxford, UK: Oxford University Press.
Pakkenberg, B., & Gundersen, H. J. G. (1997). Neocortical neuron number in humans: Effect of sex and age. *Journal of Comparative Neurology*, *384*(2), 312–320.
Panksepp, J., Siviy, S., & Normansell, L. A. (1985). Brain opioids and social emotion. In M. Reite & T. Field (Eds.), *The psychobiology of attachment and separation* (pp. 3–49). New York, NY: Academic Press.
Papafragou, A. (2007). Space and language-cognition interface. In P. Carruthers, S. Laurence, & S. Stich (Eds.), *The innate mind: Foundations and the future* (pp. 272–292). Oxford, UK: Oxford University Press.
Papagno, C. (1998). Transient retrograde amnesia associated with impaired naming of living categories. *Cortex*, *34*(1), 111–121.
Papp, L. A. (2010). Phenomenology of generalized anxiety disorder. In D. J. Stein, E. Hollander, & B. O. Rothbaum (Eds.), *Textbook of anxiety disorders* (2nd ed., pp. 159–171). Washington, DC: American Psychiatric Association Publishing.
Paquette, V., Lévesque, J., Mensour, B., Leroux, J. M., Beaudoin, G., Bourgouin, P., & Beauregard, M. (2003). "Change the mind and you change the brain": Effects of cognitive-behavioral therapy on the neural correlates of spider phobia. *Neuroimage*, *18*(2), 401–409.
Paradis, C. M., Cukor, D., & Friedman, S. (2006). Cognitive-behavioral therapy with Orthodox Jews. In P. A. Hays & G. Y. Iwamasa (Eds.), *Culturally responsive cognitive-behavioral therapy: Assessment, practice, and supervision* (pp. 161–175). Washington, DC: American Psychological Association.
Paranjpe, A. C. (2006). From tradition through colonialism to globalization: Reflections on the history of psychology in India. In A. C. Brock (Ed.), *Internationalizing the history of psychology* (pp. 56–74). New York, NY: New York University Press.
Pardo, J. V., Lee, J. T., Sheikh, S. A., Surerus-Johnson, C., Shah, H., Munch, K. R., . . . Dysken, M. W. (2007). Where the brain grows old: Decline in anterior cingulate and medial prefrontal function with normal aging. *Neuroimage*, *35*(3), 1231–1237.
Pargament, K. I. (2007). *Spiritually integrated psychotherapy: Understanding and addressing the sacred*. New York, NY: Guilford Press.
Pargament, K. I. (2011). Religion and coping: The current state of knowledge. In S. Folkman (Ed.), *Oxford handbook of stress, health, and coping* (pp. 269–288). Oxford, UK: Oxford University Press.
Paris, J. (2004). Gender differences in personality traits and disorders. *Current Psychiatry Reports*, *6*(5), 71–74.
Paris, J. (2007). The nature of borderline personality disorder: Multiple dimensions, multiple symptoms, but one category. *Journal of Personality Disorders*, *21*(5), 457–473.
Paris, J. (2009). Borderline personality disorder. In P. H. Blaney & T. Millon (Eds.), *Oxford textbook of psychopathology* (2nd ed., pp. 723–737). New York, NY: Oxford University Press.
Paris, J. (2013a). Preface. In J. Paris & J. Phillips (Eds.), *Making the DSM-5: Concepts and controversies* (pp. v–vi). New York, NY: Springer Science+Business Media.
Paris, J. (2013b). *The intelligent clinician's guide to DSM-5*. New York, NY: Oxford University Press.
Park, C. L. (2011). Meaning, coping, and health and well-being. In S. Folkman (Ed.), *Oxford handbook of stress, health, and coping* (pp. 227–241). Oxford, UK: Oxford University Press.
Park, D. C., Lautenschlager, G., Hedden, T., Davidson, N. S., Smith, A. D., & Smith, P. K. (2002). Models of visuospatial and verbal memory across the adult life span. *Psychology and Aging*, *17*(2), 299–320.
Park, H., & Reder, L. M. (2004). Moses illusion. In R. F. Pohl (Ed.), *Cognitive illusions: A handbook on fallacies and biases in thinking, judgement, and memory* (pp. 275–291). East Sussex, UK: Psychology Press.
Park, N., Lee, S., & Kim, J. H. (2012). Individuals' personal network characteristics and patterns of Facebook use: A social network approach. *Computers in Human Behavior*, *28*(5), 1700–1707.
Parker, J. G., & Asher, S. R. (1987). Peer relations and later personal adjustment: Are low-accepted children at risk? *Psychological Bulletin*, *102*(3), 357–389.
Parker, J. G., & Asher, S. R. (1993). Friendship and friendship quality in middle childhood: Links with peer group acceptance and feelings of loneliness and social dissatisfaction. *Developmental Psychology*, *29*, 611–621.
Pascalis, O., de Schonen, S., Morton, J., Deruelle, C., & Fabre-Grenet, M. (1995). Mother's face recognition by neonates: A replication and an extension. *Infant Behavior and Development*, *18*(1), 79–85.
Pascual-Leone, A., & Torres, F. (1993). Sensorimotor cortex representation of the reading finger in Braille readers: An example of activity-induced cerebral plasticity in humans. *Brain*, *116*(1), 39–52.
Pass, J. J. (2007). Industrial/organizational (I/O) psychology as a career: Improving workforce performance and retention. In R. J. Sternberg (Ed.), *Career paths in psychology: Where your degree can take you* (2nd ed., pp. 249–257). Washington, DC: American Psychological Association.
Pasterski, V., Golombok, S., & Hines, M. (2011). Sex differences in social behavior. In P. K. Smith & C. H. Hart (Eds.), *The Wiley-Blackwell handbook of childhood social development* (2nd ed., pp. 281–298). Malden, MA: Wiley-Blackwell.
Patel, K. C. (2012). Eastern traditions, consciousness, and spirituality. In L. J. Miller (Ed.), *The Oxford handbook of psychology and spirituality* (pp. 343– 359). New York, NY: Oxford University Press.
Patrick, C. J. (2007). Antisocial personality disorder and psychopathy. In W. O'Donohue, K. A. Fowler, & S. O. Lilienfeld (Eds.), *Personality disorders: Toward the DSM-V* (pp. 109–166). Thousand Oaks, CA: Sage.
Patrick, M. E., Maggs, J. L., & Abar, C. C. (2007). Reasons to have sex, personal goals, and sexual behavior during the transition to college. *Journal of Sex Research*, *44*(3), 240–249.
Pattie, F. A. (1994). *Mesmer and animal magnetism: A chapter in the history of medicine*. Hamilton, NY: Edmonston Publishing.
Paul, G. L. (2007). Psychotherapy outcome can be studied scientifically. In S. O. Lilienfeld & W. T. O'Donohue (Eds.), *The great ideas of clinical science: 17 principles that every mental health professional should understand* (pp. 119–147). New York, NY: Routledge.
Paulhus, D. L., Trapnell, P. D., & Chen, D. (1999). Birth order effects on personality and achievement within families. *Psychological Science*, *10*(6), 482–488.
Paunonen, S. V., & Jackson, D. N. (2000). What is beyond the big five? Plenty! *Journal of Personality*, *68*, 821–835.
Paus, T. (2009). Brain development. In R. M. Lerner & L. Steinberg (Eds.), *Handbook of adolescent psychology* (3rd ed., Vol. 1, pp. 95–115). Hoboken, NJ: Wiley.
Pause, B. M., Sojka, B., Krauel, K., Fehm-Wolfsdorf, G., & Ferstl, R. (1996). Olfactory information processing during the course of the menstrual cycle. *Biological Psychology*, *44*(1), 31–54.
Pavlov, I. P. (1927). *Conditioned reflexes: An investigation of the physiological activity of the cerebral cortex*. London, UK: Oxford University Press.
Pavlov, I. P. (1928). *Lectures on conditioned reflexes*. New York, NY: Liveright.
Pearce, L. J., & Field, A. P. (2016). The impact of "scary" TV and film on children's internalizing emotions: A meta-analysis. *Human Communication Research*, *42*(1), 98–121.
Pearson, J. D., Morrell, C. H., Gordon-Salant, S., Brant, L. J., Metter, E. J., Klein, L. L., & Fozard, J. L. (1995). Gender differences in a longitudinal study of

age-associated hearing loss. *The Journal of the Acoustical Society of America, 97*(2), 1196–1205.
Pearson, K. G., & Gordon, J. E. (2013). Spinal reflexes. In E. R. Kandel, J. H. Schwartz, T. M. Jessell, S. A. Siegelbaum, & A. J. Hudspeth (Eds.), *Principles of neural science* (5th ed., pp. 790–811). New York, NY: McGraw-Hill
Pearson, P. (2008). *A brief history of anxiety [yours and mine]*. New York, NY: Bloomsbury USA.
Pedersen, D. M., & Wheeler, J. (1983). The Müller-Lyer illusion among Navajos. *The Journal of Social Psychology, 121*(1), 3–6.
Pedersen, N. L., McClearn, G. E., Plomin, R., & Nesselroade, J. R., et al. (1991). The Swedish adoption/twin study of aging: An update. *Acta Geneticae Medicae et Gemellologiae: Twin Research, 40*(1), 7–20.
Pedersen, N. L., Plomin, R., McClearn, G. E., & Friberg, L. (1988). Neuroticism, extraversion, and related traits in adult twins reared apart and reared together. *Journal of Personality and Social Psychology, 55*(6), 950–957.
Pedersen, P. (1990). The multicultural perspective as a fourth force in counseling. *Journal of Mental Health Counseling, 12*(1), 93–95.
Pedersen, P. (1999). *Multiculturalism as a fourth force*. Philadelphia, PA: Brunner/Mazel.
Pedersen, P. B. (2008). Ethics, competence, and professional issues in cross-cultural counseling. In P. B. Pedersen, J. G. Draguns, W. J. Lonner, & J. E. Trimble (Eds.), *Counseling across cultures* (6th ed., pp. 5–20). Thousand Oaks, CA: SAGE.
Pedersen, S. S., & Denollet, J. (2003). Type D personality, cardiac events, and impaired quality of life: A review. *European Journal of Cardiovascular Prevention & Rehabilitation, 10*(4), 241–248.
Pedersen, S. S., & Denollet, J. (2006). Is Type D personality here to stay? Emerging evidence across cardiovascular disease patient groups. *Current Cardiology Reviews, 2*(3), 205–213.
Pederson, E., Danziger, E., Wilkins, D., Levinson, S., Kita, S., & Senft, G. (1998). Semantic typology and spatial conceptualization. *Language, 74*(3), 557–589.
Peigneux, P., Schmitz, R., & Urbain, C. (2010). Sleeping and forgetting. In S. Della Sala (Ed.), *Forgetting* (pp. 165–184). East Sussex, UK: Psychology Press.
Peigneux, P., Urbain, C., & Schmitz, R. (2012). Sleep and the brain. In C. M. Morin & C. A. Espie (Eds.), *The Oxford handbook of sleep and sleep disorders* (pp. 11–37). Oxford, UK: Oxford University Press.
Pelayo, R., & Lopes, M. C. (2006). Narcolepsy. In T. L. Lee-Chiong (Ed.), *Sleep: A comprehensive handbook* (pp. 145–150). Hoboken, NJ: Wiley-Liss.
Pellegrini, A. D., Long, J. D., Roseth, C. J., Bohn, C. M., & Van Ryzin, M. (2007). A short-term longitudinal study of preschoolers' (*Homo sapiens*) sex segregation: The role of physical activity, sex, and time. *Journal of Comparative Psychology, 121*(3), 282–289.
Penades, R., Boget, T., Lomena, F., Mateos, J. J., Catalan, R., Gasto, C., & Salamero, M. (2002). Could the hypofrontality pattern in schizophrenia be modified through neuropsychological rehabilitation? *Acta Psychiatrica Scandinavica, 105*(3), 202–208.
Pendick, D. (2002). Memory loss at the movies. *Memory Loss & the Brain: The Newsletter of the Memory Disorders Project at Rutgers University*. Retrieved from http://www.memorylossonline.com/spring2002/memlossatmovies.htm.
Penev, P. D. (2007). Sleep deprivation and energy metabolism: To sleep, perchance to eat? *Current Opinion in Endocrinology, Diabetes and Obesity, 14*(5), 374–381.
Penhollow, T., Young, M., & Bailey, W. (2007). Relationship between religiosity and "hooking up" behavior. *American Journal of Health Education, 38*(6), 338–345.
Penley, J. A., Tomaka, J., & Wiebe, J. S. (2002). The association of coping to physical and psychological health outcomes: A meta-analytic review. *Journal of Behavioral Medicine, 25*(6), 551–603.
Penny, H., & Haddock, G. (2007). Anti-fat prejudice among children: The "mere proximity" effect in 5–10 year olds. *Journal of Experimental Social Psychology, 43*(4), 678–683.
Peplau, L. A. (2003). Human sexuality: How do men and women differ? *Current Directions in Psychological Science, 12*(2), 37–40.
Peplau, L. A., & Fingerhut, A. W. (2007). The close relationships of lesbians and gay men. *Annual Review of Psychology, 58*, 405–424.
Peplau, L. A., & Garnets, L. D. (2000). A new paradigm for understanding women's sexuality and sexual orientation. *Journal of Social Issues, 56*(2), 330–350.
Pepperberg, I. M., Koepke, A., Livingston, P., Girard, M., Hartsfield, L. A. (2013) Reasoning by inference: Further studies on exclusion in grey parrots (*Psittacus erithacus*). *Journal of Comparative Psychology, 127*, 272–281.
Perez-Albeniz, A., & de Paul, J. (2003). Dispositional empathy in high- and low-risk parents for child physical abuse. *Child Abuse & Neglect, 27*(7), 769–780.
Pérez, J. C., Petrides, K. V., & Furnham, A. (2005). Measuring trait emotional intelligence. In R. Schulze & R. D. Roberts (Eds.), *Emotional intelligence: An international handbook* (pp. 181–201). Cambridge, MA: Hogrefe & Huber.
Perkins, D. V., & Saris, R. N. (2001). A "jigsaw classroom" technique for undergraduate statistics courses. *Teaching of Psychology, 28*(2), 111–113.
Perlis, M. L., Giles, D. E., Mendelson, W. B., Bootzin, R. R., & Wyatt, J. K. (1997). Psychophysiological insomnia: The behavioural model and a neurocognitive perspective. *Journal of Sleep Research, 6*(3), 179–188.
Pernanen, K. (1991). *Alcohol in human violence*. New York, NY: Guilford Press.
Perner, J. (1999). Theory of mind. In M. Bennett (Ed.), *Developmental psychology: Achievements and prospects* (pp. 205–230). Philadelphia, PA: Psychology Press.
Perner, J., Leekam, S. R., and Wimmer, H. (1987). Three-year-olds' difficulty with false belief: The case for a conceptual deficit. *British Journal of Developmental Psychology, 5*, 125–137.
Perri, M. G., and J. A. Corsica (2002). Improving the maintenance of weight lost in behavioral treatment of obesity. *Handbook of obesity treatment* (pp. 357–379). New York, NY: Guilford Press.
Perrin, J. S., Hervé, P. Y., Leonard, G., Perron, M., Pike, G. B., Pitiot, A., . . . Paus, T. (2008). Growth of white matter in the adolescent brain: Role of testosterone and androgen receptor. *The Journal of Neuroscience, 28*(38), 9519–9524.
Perry, B. L., Harp, K. L., & Oser, C. B. (2013). Racial and gender discrimination in the stress process: Implications for African American women's health and well-being. *Sociological Perspectives, 56*(1), 25–48.
Pervin, L. A. (1994). A critical analysis of current trait theory. *Psychological Inquiry, 5*(2), 103–113.
Pesta, B. J., Bertsch, S., McDaniel, M. A., Mahoney, C. B., & Poznanski, P. J. (2012). Differential epidemiology: IQ, neuroticism, and chronic disease by the 50 U.S. states. *Intelligence, 40*(2), 107–114
Peter, B. (2005). Gassner's exorcism—not Mesmer's magnetism—is the real predecessor of modern hypnosis. *International Journal of Clinical and Experimental Hypnosis, 53*(1), 1–12.
Peter, M., Vingerhoets, A. J., & Van Heck, G. L. (2001). Personality, gender, and crying. *European Journal of Personality, 15*(1), 19–28.
Peters, M., Reimers, S., & Manning, J. T. (2006). Hand preference for writing and associations with selected demographic and behavioral variables in 255,100 subjects: The BBC Internet study. *Brain and Cognition, 62*(2), 177–189.
Peters, R., & McGee, R. (1982). Cigarette smoking and state-dependent memory. *Psychopharmacology, 76*(3), 232–235.
Petersen, J., & Hyde, J. S. (2010a). Gender differences in sexuality. In J. C. Chrisler & D. R. McCreary (Eds.), *Handbook of gender research in psychology* (Vol. 1, pp. 471–491). New York, NY: Springer Science+Business Media.
Petersen, J. L., & Hyde, J. S. (2010b). A meta-analytic review of research on gender differences in sexuality, 1993–2007. *Psychological Bulletin, 136*(1), 21–38
Peterson, C. (2006). Writing rough drafts. In F. T. L. Leong & J. T. Austin, *The psychology research handbook: A guide for graduate students and research assistants* (pp. 360–370). Thousand Oaks, CA: SAGE Publications.
Peterson, L. R. (1966). Short-term verbal memory and learning. *Psychological Review, 73*(3), 193–207.
Peterson, L., & Peterson, M. J. (1959). Short-term retention of individual verbal items. *Journal of Experimental Psychology, 58*(3), 193–198
Peterson, M. A. (2001). Object perception. In E. B. Goldstein (Ed.), *Blackwell handbook of perception* (pp. 168–203). Oxford, UK: Blackwell.
Petit, D., Pennestri, M. H., Paquet, J., Desautels, A., Zadra, A., Vitaro, F., Montplaisir, J. (2015). Childhood sleepwalking and sleep terrors: A longitudinal study of prevalence and familial aggregation. *JAMA Pediatrics, 169*(7), 653–658.
Petrie, K. J., Cameron, L. D., Ellis, C. J., Buick, D., & Weinman, J. (2002). Changing illness perceptions after myocardial infarction: An early intervention randomized controlled trial. *Psychosomatic Medicine, 64*(4), 580–586.
Petrie, K., & Weinman, J. (2006). Why illness perceptions matter. *Clinical Medicine, 6*(6), 536–539.
Petry, N. M., Alessi, S. M., & Rash, C. J. (2013). Contingency management treatments decrease psychiatric symptoms. *Journal of Consulting and Clinical Psychology, 81*(5), 926–931.
Petscher, E. S., Rey, C., & Bailey, J. S. (2009). A review of empirical support for differential reinforcement of alternative behavior. *Research in Developmental Disabilities, 30*(3), 409–425.
Pettigrew, T. F. (1997). Generalized intergroup contact effects on prejudice. *Personality and Social Psychology Bulletin, 23*(2), 173–185.
Pettigrew, T. F., & Tropp, L. R. (2006). A meta-analytic test of intergroup contact theory. *Journal of Personality and Social Psychology, 90*(5), 751–783.
Petty, R. E., & Briñol, P. (2012). The elaboration likelihood model. In P. A. M. Van Lange, A. W. Kruglanski, & E. T. Higgins (Eds.), *Handbook of theories of social psychology* (Vol. 1, pp. 224–245). Thousand Oaks, CA: SAGE.
Petty, R. E., & Cacioppo, J. T. (1986). The elaboration likelihood model of persuasion. *Advances in Experimental Social Psychology, 19*(1), 123–205.
Petty, R. E., Fazio, R. H., & Brinol, P. (Eds.). (2009a). *Attitudes: Insights from the new implicit measures*. New York, NY: Psychology Press.
Petty, R. E., Fazio, R. H., & Brinol, P. (2009b). The new implicit measures. In R. E. Petty, R. H. Fazio, & P. Brinol (Eds.), *Attitudes: Insights from the new implicit measures* (pp. 3–18). New York, NY: Psychology Press.
Petty, R. E., Haugtvedt, C. P., & Smith, S. M. (1995). Elaboration as a determinant of attitude strength: Creating attitudes that are persistent, resistant, and predictive of behavior. In R. E. Petty & J. A. Krosnick (Eds.), *Attitude strength: Antecedents and consequences* (pp. 93–130). Mahwah, NJ: Erlbaum Associates.
Petty, R. E., Wegener, D. T., & Fabrigar, L. R. (1997). Attitudes and attitude change. *Annual Review of Psychology, 48*(1), 609–647.
Pew Research Center (2015, May 12). America's Changing Religious Landscape. Retrieved from http://www.pewforum.org/2015/05/12/americas-changing-religious-landscape/.
Pfiffner, L. J., & Haack, L. M. (2015). Nonpharmacologic treatments for childhood attention-deficit/hyperactivity disorder and their combination with medication. In P. E. Nathan & J. M. Gorman (Eds.), *A Guide to Treatments That Work* (4th ed., pp. 55–84). New York, NY: Oxford University Press.
Phan, K. L., Wager, T., Taylor, S. F., & Liberzon, I. (2002). Functional neuroanatomy of emotion: A meta-analysis of emotion activation studies in PET and fMRI. *Neuroimage, 16*(2), 331–348.

Phelps, E. A. (2006). Emotion and cognition: Insights from studies of the human amygdala. *Annual Review of Psychology, 57*, 27–53.

Phelps, E. A., & LeDoux, J. E. (2005). Contributions of the amygdala to emotion processing: From animal models to human behavior. *Neuron, 48*(2), 175–187.

Phelps, L., Johnston, L. S., Jimenez, D. P., Wilczenski, F. L., Andrea, R. K., & Healy, R. W. (1993). Figure preference, body dissatisfaction, and body distortion in adolescence. *Journal of Adolescent Research, 8*(3), 297–310.

Philip, R. C., Dauvermann, M. R., Whalley, H. C., Baynham, K., Lawrie, S. M., & Stanfield, A. C. (2012). A systematic review and meta-analysis of the fMRI investigation of autism spectrum disorders. *Neuroscience & Biobehavioral Reviews, 36*(2), 901–942.

Phillips, J. (2013). The conceptual status of DSM-5 diagnoses. In J. Paris & J. Phillips (Eds.), *Making the DSM-5: Concepts and controversies* (pp. 159–175). New York, NY: Springer Science+Business Media.

Phillips, K. (2009, July 23). "Blogtalk: Gates, Obama, Race and the Police." The *New York Times*. http://thecaucus.blogs.nytimes.com/2009/07/23/blogtalk-gates-obama-race-and-the-police/

Photos, V. I., Michel, B. D., & Nock, M. K. (2008). Single-case research. In M. Hersen & A. M. Gross (Eds.), *Handbook of clinical psychology* (Vol. 1, pp. 224–245). Hoboken, NJ: Wiley.

Piaget, J. (1924). *Judgment and reasoning in the child*. London, UK: Kegan Paul.

Piaget, J. (1926). *The language and thought of the child*. New York, NY: Harcourt, Brace.

Piaget, J. (1929). *The child's conception of the world*. London, UK: Routledge and Kegan Paul.

Piaget, J. (1936/1952). *The origins of intelligence in children*. New York, NY: International University Press.

Piaget, J. (1954). *The construction of reality in the child*. New York, NY: Basic Books.

Piaget, J. (1962). *Play, dreams and imitation in childhood*. New York, NY: Norton.

Piaget, J. (1983). Piaget's theory. In P. Mussen (Ed.), *Handbook of child psychology* (4th ed., Vol. 1, pp. 103–128). New York, NY: Wiley.

Piaget, J., & Inhelder, B. (1969). *The psychology of the child*. New York, NY: Basic Books.

Piccione, C., Hilgard, E. R., & Zimbardo, P. G. (1989). On the degree of stability of measured hypnotizability over a 25-year period. *Journal of Personality and Social Psychology, 56*(2), 289–295.

Picillo, M., De Rosa, A., Pellecchia, M. T., Criscuolo, C., Amboni, M., Erro, R., . . . Barone, P. (2015). Olfaction in homozygous and heterozygous SYNJ1 Arg258Gln mutation carriers. *Movement Disorders Clinical Practice, 2*(4), 413–416.

Pickles, J. O. (2013). *An introduction to the physiology of hearing*. (4th ed.). Leiden, Netherlands: Brill.

Pickrell, J. E., Bernstein, D. M., & Loftus, E. F. (2004). Misinformation effect. In R. F. Pohl (Ed.), *Cognitive illusions: Handbook on fallacies and biases in thinking, judgement*, and memory (pp. 345–361). East Sussex, UK: Psychology Press.

Pickren, W. E., & Degni, S. (2011). A history of the development of health psychology. In H. S. Friedman (Ed.), *The Oxford handbook of health psychology* (pp. 15–41). Oxford, UK: Oxford University Press.

Pickren, W. E., & Rutherford, A. (2010). *A history of modern psychology in context*. Hoboken, NJ: Wiley. Pitman, R. K., Altman, B., Greenwald, E., & Longpre, R. E. (1991). Psychiatric complications during flooding therapy for posttraumatic stress disorder. *Journal of Clinical Psychiatry*. *52*(1): 17–20.

Pierre, J. M. (2013). Overdiagnosis, underdiagnosis, synthesis: A dialectic for psychiatry and the DSM. In J. Paris & J. Phillips (Eds.), *Making the DSM-5: Concepts and controversies* (pp. 105–124). New York, NY: Springer Science+Business Media.

Piet, J., & Hougaard, E. (2011). The effect of mindfulness-based cognitive therapy for prevention of relapse in recurrent major depressive disorder: A systematic review and meta-analysis. *Clinical Psychology Review, 31*(6), 1032–1040.

Pilcher, J. J., & Walters, A. S. (1997). How sleep deprivation affects psychological variables related to college students' cognitive performance. *Journal of American College Health, 46*(3), 121–126.

Piliavin, I. M., Rodin, J., & Piliavin, J. A. (1969). Good samaritanism: An underground phenomenon? *Journal of Personality and Social Psychology, 13*(4), 289–299.

Pilkington, K., Kirkwood, G., Rampes, H., Cummings, M., & Richardson, J. (2007). Acupuncture for anxiety and anxiety disorders—a systematic literature review. *Acupuncture in Medicine, 25*(1–2), 1–10.

Pilkington, K., Kirkwood, G., Rampes, H., Fisher, P., & Richardson, J. (2006). Homeopathy for anxiety and anxiety disorders: A systematic review of the research. *Homeopathy, 95*(3), 151–162.

Pillemer, D. B. (2009). "Hearing the news" versus "being there": Comparing flashbulb memories and recall of first-hand experiences. In O. Luminet & A. Curci (Eds.), *Flashbulb memories: New issues and new perspectives* (pp. 125–140). East Sussex, UK: Psychology Press.

Pinel, J. P. J. (2011). *Biopsychology* (8th ed.). Boston, MA: Allyn & Bacon.

Pinel, J. P., Assanand, S., & Lehman, D. R. (2000). Hunger, eating, and ill health. *American Psychologist, 55*(10), 1105–1116.

Pingitore, R., Dugoni, B. L., Tindale, R. S., & Spring, B. (1994). Bias against overweight job applicants in a simulated employment interview. *Journal of Applied Psychology, 79*(6), 909–917.

Pinker, S. (1994) *The language instinct*. New York, NY: HarperCollins.

Pinker, S. (2007). The evolutionary social psychology of off-record indirect speech acts. *Intercultural Pragmatics, 4*(4), 437–461.

Pinker, S. (2011). Indirect speech, politeness, deniability, and relationship negotiation: Comment on Marina Terkourafi's "The Puzzle of Indirect Speech." *Journal of Pragmatics, 43*(11), 2866–2868.

Pinto, D. J., Brumberg, J. C., & Simons, D. J. (2000). Circuit dynamics and coding strategies in rodent somatosensory cortex. *Journal of Neurophysiology, 83*(3), 1158–1166.

Pinto, J. M., Schumm, L. P., Wroblewski, K. E., Kern, D. W., & McClintock, M. K. (2014). Racial disparities in olfactory loss among older adults in the United States. *The Journals of Gerontology, Series A: Biological Sciences and Medical Sciences, 69*(3), 323–329.

Pintrich, P. R., & De Groot, E. V. (1990). Motivational and self-regulated learning components of classroom academic performance. *Journal of Educational Psychology, 82*(1), 33–40.

Piskor, E. (2013). *Hip hop family tree* (Vol. 1). Seattle, WA: Fantagraphics.

Plante, T. G., & Aldridge, A. (2005). Psychological patterns among Roman Catholic clergy accused of sexual misconduct. *Pastoral Psychology, 54*(1), 73–80.

Plaud, J. J., & Martini, J. R. (1999). The respondent conditioning of male sexual arousal. *Behavior Modification, 23*(2), 254–268.

Plester, B., Wood, C., & Bell, V. (2008). Txt msg n school literacy: Does texting and knowledge of text abbreviations adversely affect children's literacy attainment? *Literacy, 42*(3), 137–144.

Plester, B., Wood, C., & Joshi, P. (2009). Exploring the relationship between children's knowledge of text message abbreviations and school literacy outcomes. *British Journal of Developmental Psychology, 27(1)*, 145–161.

Pliner, P., & Chaiken, S. (1990). Eating, social motives, and self-presentation in women and men. *Journal of Experimental Social Psychology, 26*(3), 240–254.

Pliszka, S. R. (2015). Comorbid psychiatric disorders in children with ADHD. In R. A. Barkley (Ed.), *Attention-deficit hyperactivity disorder: A handbook for diagnosis and treatment* (4th ed., pp. 140–168). New York, NY: Guilford Press.

Plomin, R. & Dale, P. S. (2000). Genetics and early language development: A UK study of twins. In D. V. M. Bishop & L. B. Leonard (Eds.), *Speech and language impairments in children: Causes, characteristics, intervention and outcome* (pp. 35–51). New York, NY: Psychology Press,

Plutchik, R. (2001). The nature of emotions. *American Scientist, 89*(4), 344–350.

Plutchik, R. (2003). *Emotions and life: Perspectives from psychology, biology, and evolution*. Washington, DC: American Psychological Association.

Pohl, R. F. (2004a). Effects of labeling. In R. F. Pohl (Ed.), *Cognitive illusions: A handbook on fallacies and biases in thinking, judgement, and memory* (pp. 327–344). East Sussex, UK: Psychology Press.

Pohl, R. F. (2004b). Hindsight bias. In R. F. Pohl (Ed.), *Cognitive illusions: A handbook on fallacies and biases in thinking*, judgement, and memory (pp. 363–378). East Sussex, UK: Psychology Press.

Polanczyk, G. V., Willcutt, E. G., Salum, G. A., Kieling, C., & Rohde, L. A. (2014). ADHD prevalence estimates across three decades: An updated systematic review and meta-regression analysis. *International Journal of Epidemiology, 43*(2), 434–442.

Polanczyk, G., de Lima, M. S., Horta, B. L., Biederman, J., & Rohde, L. A. (2007). The worldwide prevalence of ADHD: A systematic review and metaregression analysis. *American Journal of Psychiatry, 164*(6), 942–948.

Poling, A., Ehrhardt, K. E., & Ervin, R. A. (2002). Positive punishment. In M. Hersen & W. Sledge (Eds.), *Encyclopedia of psychotherapy* (Vol. 2, pp. 359–366). San Diego, CA: Academic Press.

Poling, A., Weetjens, B. J., Cox, C., Beyene, N. W., & Sully, A. (2011). Using giant African pouched rats (*Cricetomys gambianus*) to detect landmines. *The Psychological Record, 60*(4), 11.

Poling, A., Weetjens, B. J., Cox, C., Beyene, N., Bach, H., & Sully, A. (2010). Teaching giant African pouched rats to find landmines: Operant conditioning with real consequences. *Behavior Analysis in Practice, 3*(2), 19.

Polinko, N. K., & Popovich, P. M. (2001). Evil thoughts but angelic actions: Responses to overweight job applicants. *Journal of Applied Social Psychology, 31*(5), 905–924.

Polk, D. M. (2011). Evaluating fairness: Critical assessment of equity theory. In D. Chadee (Ed.), *Theories in social psychology* (pp. 163–190). West Sussex, UK: Wiley-Blackwell.

Pollack, M. H., & Simon, N. M. (2009). Pharmacotherapy for panic disorder and agoraphobia. In M. M. Antony & M. B. Stein (Eds.), *Oxford handbook of anxiety and related disorders* (pp. 295–307). New York, NY: Oxford University Press.

Pollack, M. H., Smoller, J. W., Otto, M. W., Hoge, E., & Simon, N. (2010). Phenomenology of panic disorder. In D. J. Stein, E. Hollander, & B. O. Rothbaum (Eds.), *Textbook of anxiety disorders* (2nd ed., pp. 367–379). Washington, DC: American Psychiatric Association Publishing.

Polman, J., Orobio de Castro, B., & Van Aken, M. (2008). Experimental study of the differential effects of playing versus watching violent video games on children's aggressive behavior. *Aggressive Behavior, 34*, 256–264.

Polman, J., Orobio de Castro, B., & Van Aken, M. (2008). Experimental study of the differential effects of playing versus watching violent video games on children's aggressive behavior. *Aggressive Behavior, 34*(3), 256–264.

Pomerantz, A. M. (2005). Increasingly informed consent: Discussing distinct aspects of psychotherapy at different points in time. *Ethics & Behavior, 15*(4), 351–360.

Pomerantz, A. M. (2012). Informed consent to psychotherapy (empowered collaboration). In S. J. Knapp (Ed.), *APA handbook of ethics in psychology* (Vol. 1., pp. 311–332). Washington, DC: American Psychological Association.

Pomerantz, A. M. (2015). Informed consent, psychotherapy. In R. L. Cautin & S. O. Lilienfeld (Eds.), *The encyclopedia of clinical psychology* (pp. 1467–1470). West Sussex, UK: Wiley-Blackwell.
Pomerantz, A. M., & Handelsman, M. M. (2004). Informed consent revisited: An updated written question format. *Professional Psychology: Research and Practice, 35*(2), 201–205.
Pomerantz, A. M., & Seely, E. A. (2000). Under what conditions is individual psychotherapy distressing to clients' romantic partners? An empirical analogue study. *Journal of Contemporary Psychotherapy, 30*, 255–260.
Pomerantz, J. R., & Portillo, M. C. (2010). Perceptual organization: Vision. In E. B. Goldstein (Ed.), *Encyclopedia of perception* (pp. 786–790). Thousand Oaks, CA: SAGE.
Pope, K. S. (1994). *Sexual involvement with therapists: Patient assessment, subsequent therapy, forensics.* Washington, DC: American Psychological Association.
Pope, K. S. (2011). Ethical issues in clinical psychology. In D. H. Barlow (Ed.), *The Oxford handbook of clinical psychology* (pp. 184–209). New York, NY: Oxford University Press.
Pope, K. S., & Vasquez, M. J. T. (2011). *Ethics in psychotherapy and counseling: A practical guide* (4th ed.). Hoboken, NJ: Wiley.
Popenoe, D. (2009). Cohabitation, marriage, and child wellbeing: A cross-national perspective. *Society, 46*(5), 429–436.
Popova, S., Patra, J., Mohapatra, S., Fischer, B., & Rehm, J. (2009). How many people in Canada use prescription opioids non-medically in general and street drug using populations? *Canadian Journal of Public Health/Revue Canadienne de Sante' Publique, 100*(2), 104–108.
Popple, A. (2010). Individual differences in perception. In E. B. Goldstein (Ed.), *Encyclopedia of perception* (pp. 492–495). Thousand Oaks, CA: SAGE.
Popplestone, J. A., & McPherson, M. W. (1998). *An illustrated history of American psychology* (2nd ed.). Akron, OH: University of Akron Press.
Poran, M. A. (2002). Denying diversity: Perceptions of beauty and social comparison processes among Latina, Black, and White women. *Sex Roles, 47*(1), 65–81.
Poropat, A. E. (2009). A meta-analysis of the five-factor model of personality and academic performance. *Psychological Bulletin, 135*(2), 322–338.
Portaluppi, F., Tiseo, R., Smolensky, M. H., Hermida, R. C., Ayala, D. E., & Fabbian, F. (2012). Circadian rhythms and cardiovascular health. *Sleep Medicine Reviews, 16*(2), 151–166.
Porter, J., Anand, T., Johnson, B., Khan, R. M., & Sobel, N. (2005). Brain mechanisms for extracting spatial information from smell. *Neuron, 47*(4), 581–592.
Porter, S., Yuille, J. C., & Lehman, D. R. (1999). The nature of real, implanted, and fabricated memories for emotional childhood events. *Law and Human Behavior, 23*(5), 517–537.
Posner, M. I., & Keele, S. W. (1970). Retention of abstract ideas. *Journal of Experimental Psychology, 83*(2), 304–308.
Post, R. M., & Weiss, S. R. (1997). Emergent properties of neural systems: How focal molecular neurobiological alterations can affect behavior. *Development and Psychopathology, 9*(4), 907–929.
Postman, L., & Phillips, L. W. (1965). Short-term temporal changes in free recall. *Quarterly Journal of Experimental Psychology, 17*(2), 132–138.
Potenza, M. N. (2006). Should addictive disorders include non-substance-related conditions? *Addiction, 101*(S1), 142–151.
Potter, W. Z., Padich, R. A., Rudorfer, M. V., & Krishnan, K. R. R. (2006). Tricyclics, tetracyclics, and monoamine oxidase inhibitors. In D. J. Stein, D. J. Kupfer, & A. F. Schatzberg (Eds.), *The American Psychiatric Publishing textbook of mood disorders* (pp. 251–262). Washington, DC: American Psychiatric Publishing.
Powell, D., & Dixon, M. (2011). Does SMS text messaging help or harm adults' knowledge of standard spelling? *Journal of Computer Assisted Learning, 27*(1), 58–66.
Powell, L. M., & Bao, Y. (2009). Food prices, access to food outlets and child weight. *Economics & Human Biology, 7*(1), 64–72.
Powell, L. M., & Chaloupka, F. J. (2009). Food prices and obesity: Evidence and policy implications for taxes and subsidies. *Milbank Quarterly, 87*(1), 229–257.
Powell, L. M., Auld, M. C., Chaloupka, F. J., O'Malley, P. M., & Johnston, L. D. (2007). Access to fast food and food prices: Relationship with fruit and vegetable consumption and overweight among adolescents. *Advances in Health Economics and Health Services Research, 17*, 23–48.
Power, M., & Brewin, C. R. (2011). From Freud to cognitive science: A contemporary account of the unconscious. *British Journal of Clinical Psychology, 30*(4), 289–310.
Prabhu, V., Sutton, C., & Sauser, W. (2008). Creativity and certain personality traits: Understanding the mediating effect of intrinsic motivation. *Creativity Research Journal, 20*(1), 53–66.
Prescott, J. (2010). Taste: Supertasters. In E. B. Goldstein (Ed.), *Encyclopedia of perception* (pp. 964–967). Thousand Oaks, CA: SAGE.
Prescott, J., Bell, G. A., Gillmore, R., Yoshida, M., O'Sullivan, M., Korac, S., Yamazaki, K. (1997). Cross-cultural comparisons of Japanese and Australian responses to manipulations of sweetness in foods. *Food Quality and Preference, 8*(1), 45–55.
Pressman, S. D., Cohen, S., Miller, G. E., Barkin, A., Rabin, B. S., & Treanor, J. J. (2005). Loneliness, social network size, and immune response to influenza vaccination in college freshmen. *Health Psychology, 24*(3), 297–306.
Pressman, S. D., Kraft, T. L., & Cross, M. P. (2015). It's good to do good and receive good: The impact of a "pay it forward" style kindness intervention on giver and receiver well-being. *The Journal of Positive Psychology, 10*(4), 293–302.
Pressnitzer, D., Patterson, R. D., & Krumbholz, K. (2001). The lower limit of melodic pitch. *The Journal of the Acoustical Society of America, 109*(5), 2074–2084.
Pretzer, J., & Beck, J. S. (2004). Cognitive therapy of personality disorders: Twenty years of progress. In R. L. Leahy (Ed.), *Contemporary cognitive therapy: Theory, research, and practice* (pp. 299–318). New York, NY: Guilford Press.
Preuss, T. M. (2009). The cognitive neuroscience of human uniqueness. In M. S. Gazzaniga (Ed.), *The cognitive neurosciences* (4th ed., pp. 49–66). Cambridge, MA: MIT Press.
Pribram, K. H. (1960). A review of theory in physiological psychology. *Annual Review of Psychology, 11*(1), 1–40.
Priess, H. A., & Hyde, J. S. (2010). Gender and academic abilities and preferences. In J. C. Chrisler & D. R. McCreary (Eds.), *Handbook of gender research in psychology* (Vol. 1, pp. 297–316). New York, NY: Springer Science+Business Media.
Prinstein, M. J., & La Greca, A. M. (2003). Peer crowd affiliation and internalizing distress in childhood and adolescence: A longitudinal follow-back study. *Journal of Research on Adolescence, 12*(3), 325–351.
Prinstein, M. J., Choukas-Bradley, S. C., & Guan, K. (2013). Deciding to apply and successfully gaining admission to graduate schools in psychology. In M. J. Prinstein (Ed.), *The portable mentor: Expert guide to a successful career in psychology (*pp. 13–44). New York, NY: Springer.
Prislin, R., & Crano, W. D. (2012). A history of social influence research. In A. W. Kruglanski & W. Stroebe (Eds.), *Handbook of the history of social psychology* (pp. 321–339). New York, NY: Psychology Press.
Privette, G. (1983). Peak experience, peak performance, and flow: A comparative analysis of positive human experiences. *Journal of Personality and Social Psychology, 45*(6), 1361–1368.
Prochaska, J. O., & Norcross, J. C. (2010). *Systems of psychotherapy: A transtheoretical analysis* (7th ed.). Belmont, CA: Brooks/Cole.
Prochaska, J. O., & Velicer, W. F. (1997). The transtheoretical model of health behavior change. *American Journal of Health Promotion, 12*(1), 38–48.
Prochaska, J. O., DiClemente, C. C., & Norcross, J. C. (1993). In search of how people change: Applications to addictive behaviors. *Journal of Addictions Nursing, 5*(1), 2–16.
Pryor, K. (2009). *Reaching the animal mind: Clicker training and what it teaches us about all animals*. New York, NY: Scribner.
Pryzgoda, J., & Chrisler, J. C. (2000). Definitions of gender and sex: The subtleties of meaning. *Sex Roles, 43*(78), 553–569.
Puhl, R., & Brownell, K. D. (2012). Bias, discrimination, and obesity. *Obesity Research, 9*(12), 788–805.
Qin, J., Mitchell, K. J., Johnson, M. K., Krystal, J. H., Southwick, S. M., Rasmusson, A. M., & Allen, E. S. (2003). Reactions to and memories for the September 11, 2001 terrorist attacks in adults with posttraumatic stress disorder. *Applied Cognitive Psychology, 17*(9), 1081–1097.
Quaglia, J. T., Brown, K. W., Lindsay, E. K., Creswell, J. D., & Goodman, R. J. (2015). From conceptualization to operationalization of mindfulness. In K. W. Brown, J. D. Creswell, & R. M. Ryan (Eds.), *Handbook of mindfulness: Theory, research, and practice* (pp. 151–170). New York, NY: Guilford Press.
Quattrone, G. A., & Tversky, A. (1988). Contrasting rational and psychological analyses of political choice. *American Political Science Review, 82*(3), 719–736.
Querido, J. G., Warner, T. D., & Eyberg, S. M. (2002). Parenting styles and child behavior in African American families of preschool children. *Journal of Clinical Child and Adolescent Psychology, 31*(2), 272–277.
Quesenberry, C. P., Caan, B., & Jacobson, A. (1998). Obesity, health services use, and health care costs among members of a health maintenance organization. *Archives of Internal Medicine, 158*(5), 466–472.
Quinn, P. C. (2011). Born to categorize. In U. Goswami (Ed.), *The Wiley-Blackwell handbook of childhood cognitive development* (2nd ed., pp. 129–152). Malden, MA: Wiley-Blackwell.
Quintana, S. M. (2011). Ethnicity, race, and children's social development. In P. K. Smith & C. H. Hart (Eds.), *The Wiley-Blackwell handbook of childhood social development* (2nd ed., pp. 299–316). Malden, MA: Wiley-Blackwell.
R. F. Belli (Ed.), *True and false recovered memories: Toward a reconciliation of the debate* (pp. 193–242). New York, NY: Springer Science+Business Media.
Rabin, B. S. (2005). Introduction to immunology and immune-endocrine interactions. In K. Vedhara & M. Irwin (Eds.), *Human psychoneuroimmunology* (pp. 1–24). New York, NY: Oxford University Press.
Rabkin, J. G., McElhiney, M., Moran, P., Acree, M., & Folkman, S. (2009). Depression, distress and positive mood in late-stage cancer: A longitudinal study. *Psycho-oncology, 18*(1), 79–86.
Racine, E., Bar-Ilan, O., & Illes, J. (2005). fMRI in the public eye. *Nature Reviews Neuroscience, 6*(2), 159–164.
Racine, E., Waldman, S., Rosenberg, J., & Illes, J. (2010). Contemporary neuroscience in the media. *Social Science & Medicine, 71*(4), 725–733.
Raffaelli, M. (2005). Adolescent dating experiences described by Latino college students. *Journal of Adolescence, 28*(4), 559–572.
Raffel, G. (1936). Two determinants of the effect of primacy. *The American Journal of Psychology, 48*(4), 654–657.
Raiford, S. E., Coalson, D. L., Saklofske, D. H., & Weiss, L. G. (2010). Practical issues in WAIS-IV administration and scoring. In L. G. Weiss, D. H. Saklofske, D. Coalson, & S. E. Raiford (Eds.), *WAIS-IV clinical use and interpretation: Scientist-practitioner perspectives* (pp. 25–60). London, UK: Elsevier.
Raine, A. (2013). *The anatomy of violence: The biological roots of crime*. New York, NY: Pantheon Books.
Raine, A., Buchsbaum, M., & LaCasse, L. (1997). Brain abnormalities in murderers indicated by positron emission tomography. *Biological Psychiatry, 42*(6), 495–508.

Raine, A., Reynolds, C., Venables, P. H., Mednick, S. A., & Farrington, D. P. (1998). Fearlessness, stimulation-seeking, and large body size at age 3 years as early predispositions to childhood aggression at age 11 years. *Archives of General Psychiatry, 55*(8), 745.

Rainville, P., & Price, D. D. (2003). Hypnosis phenomenology and the neurobiology of consciousness. *International Journal of Clinical and Experimental Hypnosis, 51*(2), 105–129.

Rakic, P., Arellano, J. L., & Breuing, J. (2009). Development of the primate cerebral cortex. In M. S. Gazzaniga (Ed.), *The cognitive neurosciences* (4th ed., pp. 7–28). Cambridge, MA: MIT Press.

Rakic, P., Eugenius, S., Ang, B. C., & Breuing, J. (2004). Setting the stage for cognition: Genesis of the primate cerebral cortex. In M. S. Gazzaniga (Ed.), *The new cognitive neurosciences III* (pp. 33–50). Cambridge, MA: MIT Press.

Rakison, D. H., & Poulin-Dubois, D. (2001). Developmental origin of the animate–inanimate distinction. *Psychological Bulletin, 127*(2), 209–228.

Rama, A. N., Cho, S. C., & Kushida, C. A. (2006). Normal human sleep. In T. L. Lee-Chiong (Ed.), *Sleep: A comprehensive handbook* (pp. 3–10). Hoboken, NJ: Wiley-Liss.

Ramachandran, V. S., & Hirstein, W. (1998). The perception of phantom limbs. The D. O. Hebb lecture. *Brain, 121*(9), 1603–1630.

Ramírez-Esparza, N., García-Sierra, A., and Kuhl, P. K. (2014). Look who's talking: Speech style and social context in language input to infants are linked to concurrent and future speech development. *Developmental Science, 17*, 880–891.

Ramos, K. D., & Youngclarke, D. M. (2006). Parenting advice books about child sleep: Cosleeping and crying it out. *Sleep, 29*(12), 1616.

Rand, R. (2004). *Dancing away an anxious mind: A memoir about overcoming panic disorder*. Madison, WI: University of Wisconsin Press.

Randall, W. L. (2007). From computer to compost: Rethinking our metaphors for memory. *Theory & Psychology, 17*(5), 611–633.

Ranganath, C., Libby, L. A., & Wong, L. (2012). Human learning and memory. In K. Frankish & W. M. Ramsey (Eds.), *The Cambridge handbook of cognitive science* (pp. 112–130). New York, NY: Cambridge University Press.

Rankin, D. M., Scotney, B. W., Morrow, P. J., & Pierscionek, B. K. (2012). Iris recognition failure over time: The effects of texture. *Pattern Recognition, 45*(1), 145–150.

Rao, M., Afshin, A., Singh, G., & Mozaffarian, D. (2013). Do healthier foods and diet patterns cost more than less healthy options? A systematic review and meta-analysis. *BMJ Open, 3*(12), e004277. doi.10.1136/bmjopen-2013-004277

Rapee, R. M. (1993). The utilisation of working memory by worry. *Behaviour Research and Therapy, 31*(6), 617–620.

Rapee, R. M., Kennedy, S., Ingram, M., Edwards, S., & Sweeney, L. (2005). Prevention and early intervention of anxiety disorders in inhibited preschool children. *Journal of Consulting and Clinical Psychology, 73*(3), 488–497.

Rapee, R. M., Schniering, C. A., & Hudson, J. L. (2009). Anxiety disorders during childhood and adolescence: Origins and treatment. *Annual Review of Clinical Psychology, 5*, 311–341.

Rash, J. A., Matsuba, M. K., & Prkachin, K. M. (2011). Gratitude and well-being: Who benefits the most from a gratitude intervention? *Applied Psychology: Health and Well-Being, 3*(3), 350–369.

Rattenborg, N. C. (2007). Response to commentary on evolution of slow-wave sleep and palliopallial connectivity in mammals and birds: A hypothesis. *Brain Research Bulletin, 72*(4), 187–193.

Rattenborg, N. C., Lima, S. L., & Amlaner, C. J. (1999). Facultative control of avian unihemispheric sleep under the risk of predation. *Behavioural Brain Research, 105*(2), 163–172.

Rattenborg, N. C., Martinez-Gonzalez, D., & Lesku, J. A. (2009). Avian sleep homeostasis: Convergent evolution of complex brains, cognition and sleep functions in mammals and birds. *Neuroscience & Biobehavioral Reviews, 33*(3), 253–270.

Raup, J. L., & Myers, J. E. (1989). The empty nest syndrome: Myth or reality? *Journal of Counseling & Development, 68*(2), 180–183.

Rayner, K. (1998). Eye movements in reading and information processing: 20 years of research. *Psychological Bulletin, 124*(3), 372–422.

Rayner, K., & Pollatsek, A. (2010). Eye movements and reading. In E. B. Goldstein (Ed.), *Encyclopedia of perception* (pp. 433–416). Thousand Oaks, CA: SAGE.

Rayner, K., Li, X., Williams, C. C., Cave, K. R., & Well, A. D. (2007). Eye movements during information processing tasks: Individual differences and cultural effects. *Vision Research, 47*(21), 2714–2726.

Redecker, C., Ala-Mutka, K., & Punie, Y. (2010). Learning 2.0: The impact of social media on learning in Europe. Policy brief. *JRC scientific and technical report. EUR JRC56958 EN.* Retrieved from: http://ipts.jrc.ec. europa.eu/publications/pub.cfm?id=3099

Redelmeier, D. A., Katz, J., & Kahneman, D. (2003). Memories of colonoscopy: A randomized trial. *Pain, 104*(1), 187–194.

Redmond, D. (2012, July 27). Derek Redmond: The day that changed my life. DailyMail.com. Retrieved from http://www.dailymail.co.uk/femail/article-2179361/Derek-Redmond-The-day-changed-life.html.

Reed, C. L. (2010). Body perception. In E. B. Goldstein (Ed.), *Encyclopedia of perception* (pp. 216–220). Thousand Oaks, CA: SAGE.

Reed, C. L., Stone, V. E., Bozova, S., & Tanaka, J. (2003). The body-inversion effect. *Psychological Science, 14*(4), 302–308.

Reed, C. L., Stone, V. E., Grubb, J. D., & McGoldrick, J. E. (2006). Turning configural processing upside down: Part and whole body postures. *Journal of Experimental Psychology: Human Perception and Performance, 32*(1), 73–87.

Reed, S. K. (1972). Pattern recognition and categorization. *Cognitive Psychology, 3*(3), 382–407.

Regan, B. C., Julliot, C., Simmen, B., Vienot, F., Charles-Dominique, P., & Mollon, J. D. (2001). Fruits, foliage and the evolution of primate colour vision. *Philosophical Transactions of the Royal Society of London B: Biological Sciences, 356*(1407), 229–283.

Reger, G. M., Holloway, K. M., Candy, C., Rothbaum, B. O., Difede, J., Rizzo, A. A., & Gahm, G. A. (2011). Effectiveness of virtual reality exposure therapy for active duty soldiers in a military mental health clinic. *Journal of Traumatic Stress, 24*(1), 93–96.

Reger, M. A., & Gahm, G. A. (2009). A meta-analysis of the effects of Internet- and computer-based cognitive-behavioral treatments for anxiety. *Journal of Clinical Psychology, 65*(1), 53–75.

Regier, D. A., Kuhl, E. A., & Kupfer, D. J. (2013). The DSM-5: Classification and criteria changes. *World Psychiatry, 12*(2), 92–98.

Regier, T., Kay, P., & Cook, R. S. (2005). Focal colors are universal after all. *Proceedings of the National Academy of Sciences of the United States of America, 102*(23), 8386–8391.

Reich, S. M., & Vandell, D. L. (2011). The interplay between parents and peers as socializing influences in children's development. In P. K. Smith & C. H. Hart (Eds.), *The Wiley-Blackwell handbook of childhood social development* (2nd ed., pp. 263–280). Malden, MA: Wiley-Blackwell.

Reichert, T., & Carpenter, C. (2004). An update on sex in magazine advertising: 1983 to 2003. *Journalism & Mass Communication Quarterly, 81*(4), 823–837.

Reid, A., Maldonado, C. C., & Baker, F. C. (2002). Sleep behavior of South African adolescents. *Sleep, 25*(4), 423–427.

Reid, K. J., & Zee, P. C. (2004). Circadian rhythm disorders. *Seminars in Neurology 24*(3), 315–325.

Reifman, A., Larrick, R., & Fein, S. (1991). Temper and temperature on the diamond: The heat-aggression relationship in major league baseball. *Personality and Social Psychology Bulletin, 17*(5), 580–585.

Reiger, T, Kay, P., Gilbert, A. L., & Ivry, R. B. (2010). Language and thought. Which side are you on anyway? In B. Malt & P. Wolff (Eds.), *Words and the mind: How words capture human experience* (pp. 165–182). Oxford, UK: Oxford University Press.

Reiner, R. (2008). Integrating a portable biofeedback device into clinical practice for patients with anxiety disorders: Results of a pilot study. *Applied Psychophysiology and Biofeedback, 33*(1), 55–61.

Reis, H. T., & Gosling, S. D. (2010). Social psychological methods outside the laboratory. In S. T. Fiske, D. T. Gilbert, & G. Lindzey (Eds.), *Handbook of social psychology* (5th ed., Vol. 1, pp. 82–114). Hoboken, NJ: Wiley.

Reis, S. M., & McCoach, D. B. (2000). The underachievement of gifted students: What do we know and where do we go? *Gifted Child Quarterly, 44*(3), 152–170.

Reis, S. M., & Renzulli, J. S. (2011). Intellectual giftedness. In R. J. Sternberg & S. B. Kaufman (Eds.), *The Cambridge handbook of intelligence* (pp. 235– 252) Cambridge, UK: Cambridge University Press.

Reisberg, D., & Heuer, F. (2004). Memory for emotional events. In D. Reisberg & P. Hertel (Eds.), *Memory and emotion*, 3–41. Oxford: Oxford University Press.

Reisberg, D., & Heuer, F. (2007). The influence of emotion on memory in forensic settings. In M. P. Toglia, J. D. Read, D. F. Ross, & R. C. L. Lindsay (Eds.), *The handbook of eyewitness psychology: Memory for events*, (Vol. I, pp. 81–116). East Sussex, UK: Psychology Press.

Reisenzein, R. (1983). The Schachter theory of emotion: Two decades later. *Psychological Bulletin, 94*(2), 239–264.

Reisman, J. M. (1991). *A history of clinical psychology* (2nd ed.). New York, NY: Hemisphere.

Renner, J., Stafford, D., Lawson, A., McKinnon, J., Friot, E., & Kellogg, D. (1976). *Research, teaching, and learning with the Piaget model*. Norman, OK: University of Oklahoma Press.

Renner, M. J., & Rosenzweig, M. R. (1987). *Enriched and impoverished environments effects on brain and behavior recent research in psychology*. New York: Springer-Verlag.

Renninger, K. A., & Hidi, S. (2011). Revisiting the conceptualization, measurement, and generation of interest. *Educational Psychologist, 46*(3), 168–184.

Renninger, K. A., & Su, S. (2012). Interest and its development. In R. M. Ryan (Ed.), *The Oxford handbook of human motivation* (pp. 167–190). New York, NY: Oxford University Press.

Renninger, K. A., Cai, M., Lewis, M. C., Adams, M. M., & Ernst, K. L. (2011). Motivation and learning in an online, unmoderated, mathematics workshop for teachers. *Educational Technology Research and Development, 59*(2), 229–247.

Rensink, R. A. (2000). Seeing, sensing, and scrutinizing. *Vision Research, 40*(10), 1469–1487.

Rensink, R. A. (2010). Change detection. In E. B. Goldstein (Ed.), *Encyclopedia of perception* (pp. 241–244). Thousand Oaks, CA: SAGE.

Rensink, R. A. (2013). Perception and attention. In D. Reisberg (Ed.), *Oxford handbook of cognitive psychology* (pp. 97–116). Oxford, UK: Oxford University Press.

Rentfrow, P. J. (2010). Statewide differences in personality: Toward a psychological geography of the United States. *American Psychologist, 65*(6), 548–558.

Rentfrow, P. J., Gosling, S. D., & Potter, J. (2008). A theory of the emergence, persistence, and expression of geographic variation in psychological characteristics. *Perspectives on Psychological Science, 3*(5), 339–369.

Renzulli, J. S., & Park, S. (2002). *Giftedness and high school dropouts: Personal, family, and school-related factors* (RM02168). Storrs, CT: University of Connecticut. National Research Center on the Gifted and Talented.

Rescorla, R. A. (1976). Second-order conditioning of Pavlovian conditioned inhibition. *Learning and Motivation, 7*, 161–172.

Rescorla, R. A. (1980). *Pavlovian second-order conditioning: Studies in associative learning*. Hillsdale, NJ: Lawrence Erlbaum.

Rescorla, R. A. (1988a). Behavioral studies of Pavlovian conditioning. *Annual Review of Neuroscience, 11*, 329–352.

Rescorla, R. A. (1988b). Pavlovian conditioning: It's not what you think. *American Psychologist, 43*, 151–160.

Rescorla, R. A. (1997). Spontaneous recovery after Pavlovian conditioning with multiple outcomes. *Animal Learning & Behavior, 25*, 99–107.

Resick, P. A., Monson, C. M., & Rizvi, S. L. (2008). Posttraumatic stress disorder. In D. H. Barlow (Ed.), *Clinical handbook of psychological disorders: A step-by-step treatment manual* (4th ed., pp. 65–122). New York, NY: Guilford Press.

Resnick, R. J. (2005). Attention deficit hyperactivity disorder in teens and adults: They don't all outgrow it. *Journal of Clinical Psychology, 61*(5), 529–533.

Resnick, R. J., & Norcross, J. C. (2002). Prescription privileges for psychologists: Scared to death? *Clinical Psychology: Science and Practice, 9*, 270–274.

Reuter, J., Raedler, T., Rose, M., Hand, I., Gläscher, J., & Büchel, C. (2005). Pathological gambling is linked to reduced activation of the mesolimbic reward system. *Nature Neuroscience, 8*(2), 147–148.

Rhee, E., Uleman, J. S., Lee, H. K., & Roman, R. J. (1995). Spontaneous self-descriptions and ethnic identities in individualistic and collectivistic cultures. *Journal of Personality and Social Psychology, 69*(1), 142–152.

Rhee, S. H., & Waldman, I. D. (2002). Genetic and environmental influences on antisocial behavior: A meta-analysis of twin and adoption studies. *Psychological Bulletin, 128*(3), 490–529.

Rhodes, G. (2006). The evolutionary psychology of facial beauty. *Annual Review of Psychology, 57*, 199–226.

Ricciardelli, L. A. (1992). Creativity and bilingualism. *The Journal of Creative Behavior, 26*(4), 242–254.

Richard, D. C. S., & Lauterbach, D. (2003). Computers in the training and practice of behavioral assessment. In S. N. Haynes & E. M. Heiby (Eds.), *Comprehensive handbook of psychological assessment* (Vol. 3, pp. 222–245). Hoboken, NJ: Wiley.

Richards, J. M., & Gross, J. J. (2000). Emotion regulation and memory: The cognitive costs of keeping one's cool. *Journal of Personality and Social Psychology, 79*(3), 410–424.

Richards, J. M., & Gross, J. J. (2006). Personality and emotional memory: How regulating emotion impairs memory for emotional events. *Journal of Research in Personality, 40*(5), 631–651.

Richardson, A., Field, T., Newton, R., & Bendell, D. (2012). Locus of control and prenatal depression. *Infant Behavior and Development, 35*(4), 662–668.

Richardson, G. S. (2006). Shift work sleep disorder. In T. L. Lee-Chiong (Ed.), *Sleep: A comprehensive handbook* (pp. 395–400). Hoboken, NJ: Wiley-Liss.

Richelle, M. N. (1993). *B. F. Skinner: A reappraisal*. East Sussex, UK: Psychology Press.

Richerson, G. B., Aston-Jones, G., & Saper, C. B. (2013). The modulatory functions of the brain stem. In E. R. Kandel, J. H. Schwartz, T. M. Jessell, S. A. Siegelbaum, & A. J. Hudspeth (Eds.), *Principles of neural science* (5th ed., pp. 1038–1055). New York, NY: McGraw-Hill.

Richman, L. S., & Leary, M. R. (2009). Reactions to discrimination, stigmatization, ostracism, and other forms of interpersonal rejection: A multimotive model. *Psychological Review, 116*(2), 365–383.

Richter, A. (2003). Sleeping time in early Chinese literature. In B. Steger & L. Brunt (Eds.), *Night-time and sleep in Asia and the West: Exploring the dark side of life* (pp. 24–44). Vienna, Austria: University of Vienna Press.

Rideout, V. J., Foehr, U. G., & Roberts, D. F. (2010). *Generation M^2: Media in the lives of 8- to 18-year-olds*. Menlo Park, CA: Henry J. Kaiser Family Foundation.

Rideout, V., & Hamel, E. (2006). *The media family: Electronic media in the lives of infants, toddlers, preschoolers and their parents*. Menlo Park, CA: Henry J. Kaiser Family Foundation.

Ridley, C. R., Tracy, M. L., Pruitt-Stephens, L., Wimsatt, M. K., & Beard, J. (2008). Multicultural assessment validity: The preeminent ethical issue in psychological assessment. In L. A. Suzuki & J. G. Ponterotto (Eds.), *Handbook of multicultural assessment: Clinical, psychological, and educational applications* (3rd ed., pp. 22–33). Hoboken, NJ: Wiley.

Riediger, M., & Freund, A. M. (2008). Me against myself: Motivational conflicts and emotional development in adulthood. *Psychology and Aging, 23*(3), 479–494.

Riediger, M., & Rauers, A. (2014). Do everyday affective experiences differ throughout childhood? A review of ambulatory-assessment evidence. In P. Verhaeghen & C. K. Hertzog (Eds.), *The Oxford handbook of emotion, social cognition, and problem solving in adulthood* (pp. 61–81). New York, NY: Oxford University Press.

Riediger, M., Schmiedek, F., Wagner, G. G., & Lindenberger, U. (2009). Seeking pleasure and seeking pain: Differences in prohedonic and contra-hedonic motivation from adolescence to old age. *Psychological Science, 20*(12), 1529–1535.

Rieger, G., Linsenmeier, J. A., Gygax, L., Garcia, S., & Bailey, J. M. (2010). Dissecting "gaydar": Accuracy and the role of masculinity–femininity. *Archives of Sexual Behavior, 39*(1), 124–140.

Riemann, D., & Nissen, C. (2012). Sleep and psychotropic drugs. In C. M. Morin & C. A. Espie (Eds.), *The Oxford handbook of sleep and sleep disorders* (pp. 190–222). Oxford, UK: Oxford University Press.

Riffin, C., Ong, A. D., & Bergeman, C. S. (2014). Positive emotions and health in adulthood and later life. In P. Verhaeghen & C. K. Hertzog (Eds.), *The Oxford handbook of emotion, social cognition, and problem solving in adulthood* (pp. 115–127). New York, NY: Oxford University Press.

Riley, E. P., & McGee, C. L. (2005). Fetal alcohol spectrum disorders: An overview with emphasis on changes in brain and behavior. *Experimental Biology and Medicine, 230*(6), 357–365.

Rilling, J. K. (2006). Human and nonhuman primate brains: Are they allometrically scaled versions of the same design? *Evolutionary Anthropology: Issues, News, and Reviews, 15*(2), 65–77.

Rimé, B., Mesquita, B., Boca, S., & Philippot, P. (1991). Beyond the emotional event: Six studies on the social sharing of emotion. *Cognition & Emotion, 5*(5-6), 435–465.

Rindermann, H., Flores-Mendoza, C., & Woodley, M. A. (2012). Political orientations, intelligence and education. *Intelligence, 40*(2), 217–225.

Ring, K. (1984). *Heading toward omega: In search of the meaning of the near-death experience*. New York, NY: William Morrow.

Ring, K. (1996). Near-death experiences: Implications for human evolution and planetary transformation. In L. W. Bailey & J. Yates (Eds.), *The near-death experience: A reader* (pp. 179–198). New York, NY: Routledge.

Rips, L. J., Smith, E. E., & Medin, D. L. (2012). Concepts and categories: Memory, meaning, and metaphysics. In K. J. Holyoak and R. G. Morrison (Eds.), *The Oxford handbook of thinking and reasoning* (pp. 177–209). Oxford, UK: Oxford University Press.

Rivera, L. M. (2008). Acculturation and multicultural assessment: Issues, trends, and practice. In L. A. Suzuki & J. G. Ponterotto (Eds.), *Handbook of multicultural assessment: Clinical, psychological, and educational applications* (3rd ed., pp. 73–91). Hoboken, NJ: Wiley.

Rivera, L. M. (2010). Acculturation. In J. G. Ponterotto, J. M. Casas, L. A. Suzuki, & C. M. Alexander (Eds.), *Handbook of multicultural counseling* (3rd ed., pp. 331–341). Thousand Oaks, CA: SAGE.

Rivkees, S. A. (2003). Developing circadian rhythmicity in infants. *Pediatrics, 112*(2), 373–381.

Rizzi, T. S., & Posthuma, D. (2013). Genes and intelligence. In D. Reisberg (Ed.), *The Oxford handbook of cognitive psychology* (pp. 823–841). Oxford, UK: Oxford University Press.

Rizzolatti, G., & Craighero, L. (2004). The mirror-neuron system. *Annual Review of Neuroscience, 27*, 169–192.

Rizzolatti, G., & Kalaska, J. F. (2013). Voluntary movement: The parietal and premotor cortex. In E. R. Kandel, J. H. Schwartz, T. M. Jessell, S. A. Siegelbaum, & A. J. Hudspeth (Eds.), *Principles of neural science* (5th ed., pp. 865–893). New York, NY: McGraw-Hill.

Rizzolatti, G., & Strick, P. L. (2013). Cognitive functions of the premotor systems. In E. R. Kandel, J. H. Schwartz, T. M. Jessell, S. A. Siegelbaum, & A. J. Hudspeth (Eds.), *Principles of neural science* (5th ed., pp. 412–425). New York, NY: McGraw-Hill.

Rizzolatti, G., Fabbri-Destro, M., & Cattaneo, L. (2009). Mirror neurons and their clinical relevance. *Nature Clinical Practice Neurology, 5*(1), 24–34.

Robbins, S. B., Lauver, K., Le, H., Davis, D., Langley, R., & Carlstrom, A. (2004). Do psychosocial and study skill factors predict college outcomes? A meta-analysis. *Psychological Bulletin, 130*(2), 261.

Roberson, D. (2005). Color categories are culturally diverse in cognition as well as in language. *Cross-Cultural Research, 39*(1), 56–71.

Roberson, D., & Hanley, J. R. (2010). An account of the relationship between language and thought in the color domain. In B. C. Malt & P. Wolff (Eds.), *Words and the mind: How words capture human experience* (pp. 183–198). New York, NY: Oxford University Press.

Roberson, D., Davidoff, J., Davies, I. R., & Shapiro, L. R. (2004). The development of color categories in two languages: A longitudinal study. *Journal of Experimental Psychology: General, 133*(4), 554–571.

Roberson, D., Davidoff, J., Davies, I. R., & Shapiro, L. R. (2005a). Color categories: Evidence for the cultural relativity hypothesis. *Cognitive Psychology, 50*(4), 378–411.

Roberson, D., Davies, I. R., Corbett, G. G., & Vandervyver, M. (2005b). Free-sorting of colors across cultures: Are there universal grounds for grouping? *Journal of Cognition and Culture, 5*(3), 349–386.

Roberson, D., Davies, I., & Davidoff, J. (2000). Color categories are not universal: Replications and new evidence from a stone-age culture. *Journal of Experimental Psychology: General, 129*(3), 369–398.

Robert, G., & Zadra, A. (2008). Measuring nightmare and bad dream frequency: Impact of retrospective and prospective instruments. *Journal of Sleep Research, 17*(2), 132–139.

Roberto, C. A., & Brownell, K. D. (2011). The imperative of changing public policy to address obesity. In J. H. Cawley (Ed.), *The Oxford handbook of the social science of obesity* (pp. 587–608). New York, NY: Oxford University Press.

Roberto, C. A., Swinburn, B., Hawkes, C., Huang, T. T. K., Costa, S. A., Ashe, M., . . . Brownell, K. D. (2015). Patchy progress on obesity prevention: Emerging examples, entrenched barriers, and new thinking. *The Lancet, 385*(9985), 2400–2409.

Roberts, A., Cash, T., Feingold, A., & Johnson, B. T. (2006). Are black-white differences in females' body dissatisfaction decreasing? A meta-analytic review. *Journal of Consulting and Clinical Psychology, 74*(6),1121–1131.

Roberts, B. W. (1997), Plaster or plasticity: Are adult work experiences associated with personality change in women? *Journal of Personality, 65*, 205–232. doi:10.1111/j.1467-6494.1997.tb00953.x

Roberts, B. W., Robins, R. W., Trzesniewski, K. H., & Caspi, A. (2003). Personality trait development in adulthood. In J. T. Mortimer & M. J. Shanahan (Eds.), *Handbook of the life course* (pp. 579–595). New York, NY: Kluwer.

Roberts, B. W., Walton, K. E., & Viechtbauer, W. (2006). Patterns of mean-level change in personality traits across the life course: A meta-analysis of longitudinal studies. *Psychological Bulletin, 132*(1), 1–25.

Roberts, B. W., Wood, D., & Caspi, A. (2008). The development of personality traits in adulthood. In O. P. John, R. W. Robins, & L. A. Pervin (Eds.) *Handbook of personality: Theory and research* (3rd ed.), 375–398). New York, NY: Guilford Press.

Roberts, D. F., Foehr, U. G., Rideout, V. J., & Brodie, M. (1999). *Kids and media @ the new millennium: A comprehensive national analysis of children's media use.* Menlo Park, CA: Henry J. Kaiser Family Foundation.

Roberts, D. F., Henriksen, L., & Foehr, U. G. (2009). Adolescence, adolescents, and media. In R. M. Lerner & L. Steinberg (Eds.), *Handbook of adolescent psychology* (3rd ed., Vol. 2, pp. 314–344). Hoboken, NJ: Wiley.

Roberts, R. E., Deleger, S., Strawbridge, W. J., & Kaplan, G. A. (2003). Prospective association between obesity and depression: Evidence from the Alameda County Study. *International Journal of Obesity, 27*(4), 514–521.

Roberts, S. (2004). *Who we are now: The changing face of America in the 21st century.* New York, NY: Times Books.

Roberts, W., Milich, R., & Barkley, R. A. (2015). Primary symptoms, diagnostic criteria, subtyping, and prevalence of ADHD. In R. A. Barkley (Ed.), *Attention-deficit hyperactivity disorder: A handbook for diagnosis and treatment* (4th ed., pp. 51–80). New York, NY: Guilford Press.

Robiner, W. N., Bearman, D. L., Berman, M., Grove, W. M., Colon, E., Armstrong, J., et al. (2002). Prescriptive authority for psychologists: A looming health hazard? *Clinical Psychology: Science and Practice, 9,* 231–248.

Robins, R. W., Caspi, A. and Moffitt, T. E. (2002). It's not just who you're with, it's who you are: Personality and relationship experiences across multiple relationships. *Journal of Personality, 70,* 925–964

Robins, R. W., & Pals, J. L. (2002). Implicit self-theories in the academic domain: Implications for goal orientation, attributions, affect, and self-esteem change. *Self and Identity, 1*(4), 313–336.

Robinson, D. N. (1997). Aristotle and psychology. In W. G. Bringmann, H. E. Lück, R. Miller, & C. E. Early (Eds.), *A pictorial history of psychology* (pp. 3–7). Carol Stream, IL: Quintessence Publishing.

Robinson, M. D., & Johnson, J. T. (1997). Is it emotion or is it stress? Gender stereotypes and the perception of subjective experience. *Sex Roles, 36*(3-4), 235–258.

Robinson-Wood, T. L. (2009). Extending cultural understanding beyond race and ethnicity. In C. C. Lee, D. A. Burnhill, A. L. Butler, C. P. Hipolito-Delgado, M. Humphrey, O. Munoz, & H. Shin (Eds.), *Elements of culture in counseling* (pp. 31–41). Upper Saddle River, NJ: Pearson.

Roche, S. M., & McConkey, K. M. (1990). Absorption: Nature, assessment, and correlates. *Journal of Personality and Social Psychology, 59*(1), 91–101.

Röcke, C., Li, S. C., & Smith, J. (2009). Intraindividual variability in positive and negative affect over 45 days: Do older adults fluctuate less than young adults? *Psychology and Aging, 24*(4), 863–878.

Rockstuhl, T., & Ng, K.-Y. (2008). The effects of cultural intelligence on interpersonal trust in multicultural teams. In S. Ang & L. Van Dyne (Eds.), *Handbook of cultural intelligence: Theory, measurement, and applications* (pp. 206–220). New York, NY: Sharpe.

Roediger, H. L. III. (2007). Teaching, research, and more: Psychologists in an academic career. In R. J. Sternberg (Ed.), *Career paths in psychology: Where your degree can take you* (2nd ed., pp. 9–33). Washington, DC: American Psychological Association.

Roediger, H. L., & Gallo, D. A. (2004). Associative memory illusions. In R. F. Pohl (Ed.), *Cognitive illusions: A handbook on fallacies and biases in thinking,* judgement, and memory (pp. 309–326). East Sussex, UK: Psychology Press.

Roediger, H. L., & Karpicke, J. D. (2011). Intricacies of spaced retrieval: A resolution. In A. S. Benjamin (Ed.), *Successful remembering and successful forgetting: A Festschrift in honor of Robert A. Bjork* (pp. 23–47). New York, NY: Psychology Press.

Roediger, H. L., & McDermott, K. B. (2000). Distortions of memory. In E. Tulving & F. I. M. Craik (Ed.), *The Oxford handbook of memory* (pp. 149–162). Oxford, UK: Oxford University Press.

Roediger, H. L., Weinstein, Y., & Agarwal, P. K. (2010). Forgetting: Preliminary considerations. In S. Della Sala (Ed.), *Forgetting* (pp. 1–22). East Sussex, UK: Psychology Press.

Roemer, L., & Orsillo, S. M. (2009). *Mindfulness- and acceptance-based behavioral therapies in practice.* New York, NY: Guilford Press.

Roemer, L., Molina, S., & Borkovec, T. D. (1997). An investigation of worry content among generally anxious individuals. *The Journal of Nervous & Mental Disease, 185*(5), 314–319.

Roenneberg, T., Kumar, C. J., & Merrow, M. (2007). The human circadian clock entrains to sun time. *Current Biology, 17*(2), R44–R45.

Roese, N. J., Pennington, G. L., Coleman, J., Janicki, M., Li, N. P., & Kenrick, D. T. (2006). Sex differences in regret: All for love or some for lust? *Personality and Social Psychology Bulletin, 32*(6), 770–780.

Roffman, J. L., Marci, C. D., Glick, D. M., Dougherty, D. D., & Rauch, S. L. (2005). Neuroimaging and the functional neuroanatomy of psychotherapy. *Psychological Medicine, 35*(10), 1385–1398.

Roger, P. R., & Stone, G. (2014). *Counseling vs. clinical.* Retrieved from http://www.div17.org/about/what-is-counseling-psychology/counseling-vs-clinical/.

Rogers, C. R. (1957). The necessary and sufficient conditions of therapeutic personality change. *Journal of Consulting Psychology, 21*(2), 95–103.

Rogers, C. R. (1959). Client-centered therapy. In S. Arieti (Ed.), *American handbook of psychiatry* (Vol. 3). New York, NY: Basic Books.

Rogers, C. R. (1961). *On becoming a person.* Boston, MA: Houghton-Mifflin.

Rogers, C. R. (1980). *A way of being.* Boston. MA: Houghton-Mifflin.

Rogers, C. R. (1986). Reflection of feelings and transference. *Person-Centered Review, 1,* 375–377.

Rogers, D. T. (2015). Further validation of the Learning Alliance Inventory: The roles of working alliance, rapport, and immediacy in student learning. *Teaching of Psychology, 42*(1), 19–25.

Rogoff, B. (2003). *The Cultural Nature of Human Development.* Oxford, UK: Oxford University Press.

Rohde, T. E., & Thompson, L. A. (2007). Predicting academic achievement with cognitive ability. *Intelligence, 35*(1), 83–92.

Rolland, J. S., & Walsh, F. (2009). Family systems theory and practice. In G. O. Gabbard (Ed.), *Textbook of psychotherapeutic treatments* (pp. 499–531). Washington, DC: American Psychiatric Publishing.

Rollman, G. B. (2010). Pain: Cognitive and contextual influences. In E. B. Goldstein (Ed.), *Encyclopedia of perception* (pp. 716–720). Thousand Oaks, CA: SAGE.

Romans, S. E., Martin, J. M., Gendall, K., & Herbison, G. P. (2003). Age of menarche: The role of some psychosocial factors. *Psychological Medicine, 33*(5), 933–939.

Ronningstam, E. (2009). Narcissistic personality disorder. In P. H. Blaney & T. Millon (Eds.), *Oxford textbook of psychopathology* (2nd ed., pp. 752–771). New York, NY: Oxford University Press.

Room, R., Babor, T., & Rehm, J. (2005). Alcohol and public health. *The Lancet, 365*(9458), 519–530.

Rosch, E. (1975). Cognitive representations of semantic categories. *Journal of Experimental Psychology: General, 104*(3), 192–233.

Rosch, E., & Mervis, C. B. (1975). Family resemblances: Studies in the internal structure of categories. *Cognitive Psychology, 7*(4), 573–605.

Rosch, E., Mervis, C. B., Gray, W. D., Johnson, D. M., & Boyes-Braem, P. (1976). Basic objects in natural categories. *Cognitive Psychology, 8*(3), 382–439.

Rose, A. J. (2002). Co-rumination in the friendships of girls and boys. *Child Development, 73*(6), 1830–1843.

Rose, A. J., Carlson, W., & Waller, E. M. (2007). Prospective associations of co-rumination with friendship and emotional adjustment: Considering the socioemotional trade-offs of co-rumination. *Developmental Psychology, 43*(4), 1019–1031.

Rose, L. T., & Fischer, K. W. (2009). Dynamic development: A neo-Piagetian approach. In U. Müller, J. I. M. Carpendale, & L. Smith (Eds.), *The Cambridge companion to Piaget* (pp. 400–421). New York, NY: Cambridge University Press.

Rose, N. S., & Abi-Rached, J. M. (2013). *Neuro: The new brain sciences and the management of the mind.* Princeton, NJ: Princeton University Press.

Rose, T., Kaser-Boyd, N., & Maloney, M. P. (2001). *Essentials of Rorschach assessment.* New York, NY: Wiley.

Rosen, L. D., Chang, J., Erwin, L., Carrier, L. M., & Cheever, N. A. (2010). The relationship between "textisms" and formal and informal writing among young adults. *Communication Research, 37*(3), 420–440.

Rosenberg, J., & Tunney, R. J. (2008). Human vocabulary use as display. *Evolutionary Psychology, 6*(3), 538–549.

Rosenfeld, G. W. (2009). *Beyond evidence-based psychotherapy: Fostering the eight sources of change in child and adolescent treatment.* New York, NY: Routledge.

Rosenman, R. H., Brand, R. J., Jenkins, C. D., Friedman, M., Straus, R., & Wurm, M. (1975). Coronary heart disease in the Western Collaborative Group Study: Final follow-up experience of 8 1/2 years. *JAMA, 233*(8), 872–877.

Rosenman, R. H., Friedman, M., Straus, R., Wurm, M., Kositchek, R., Hahn, W., & Werthessen, N. T. (1964). A predictive study of coronary heart disease: The Western Collaborative Group Study. JAMA, *189*(1), 15–22.

Rosenstock, J. (2003). Beyond a beautiful mind: Film choices for teaching schizophrenia. *Academic Psychiatry, 27*(2), 117–122.

Rosenthal, L. (2016). Incorporating intersectionality into psychology: An opportunity to promote social justice and equity. *American Psychologist, 71*(6), 474–485.

Rosenthal, L., & Lobel, M. (2011). Explaining racial disparities in adverse birth outcomes: Unique sources of stress for Black American women. *Social Science & Medicine, 72*(6), 977–983.

Rosenthal, L., Merlotti, L., Roehrs, T. A., & Roth, T. (1991). Enforced 24-hour recovery following sleep deprivation. *Sleep, 14*(5), 448–453.

Rosenzweig, M. R., Krech, D., Bennett, E. L., & Diamond, M. C. (1962). Effects of environmental complexity and training on brain chemistry and anatomy: A replication and extension. *Journal of Comparative and Physiological Psychology* 55, 429–437. doi:10.1037/h0041137

Rosenzweig, S. (1936). Some implicit common factors in diverse methods of psychotherapy. *American Journal of Orthopsychiatry, 6*(3), 422–425.

Rosete, D., & Ciarrochi, J. (2005). Emotional intelligence and its relationship to workplace performance outcomes of leadership effectiveness. *Leadership & Organization Development Journal, 26*(5), 388–399.

Rosner, R. I. (2015). Beck, Aaron T. In R. L. Cautin & S. O. Lilienfeld (Eds.), *The encyclopedia of clinical psychology* (pp. 293–296). West Sussex, UK: Wiley-Blackwell.

Rosnow, R. L., Rotheram-Borus, M. J., Ceci, S. J., Blanck, P. D., & Koocher, G. P. (1993). The Institutional Review Board as a mirror of scientific and ethical standards. *American Psychologist, 48,* 821–826.

Rosqvist, J., Thomas, J. C., & Truax, P. (2011). Effectiveness versus efficacy studies. In J. C. Thomas & M. Hersen (Eds.), *Understanding research in clinical and counseling psychology* (2nd ed., pp. 319–354). New York, NY: Taylor & Francis.

Ross, C. A. (1997). *Dissociative identity disorder: Diagnosis, clinical features, and treatment of multiple personality* (2nd ed.). New York, NY: Wiley.

Ross, L. (1977). The intuitive psychologist and his shortcomings: Distortions in the attribution process. *Advances in Experimental Social Psychology, 10,* 173–220.

Ross, L., & Nisbett, R. E. (1991). *The person and the situation.* New York, NY: McGraw-Hill.

Ross, L., Lepper, M., & Ward, A. (2010). History of social psychology: Insights, challenges, and contributions to theory and application. In S. T. Fiske, D. T. Gilbert, & G. Lindzey (Eds.), *Handbook of social psychology* (5th ed., Vol.1, pp. 3–50). Hoboken, NJ: Wiley.

Ross, M., & Wang, Q. (2010). Why we remember and what we remember: Culture and autobiographical memory. *Perspectives on Psychological Science, 5*(4), 401–409.

Ross, M., Xun, W. E., & Wilson, A. E. (2002). Language and the bicultural self. *Personality and Social Psychology Bulletin, 28*(8), 1040–1050.

Rostan, S. M. (1994). Problem finding, problem solving, and cognitive controls: An empirical investigation of critically acclaimed productivity. *Creativity Research Journal, 7*(2), 97–110.

Rostosky, S. S., Regnerus, M. D., & Wright, M. L. C. (2003). Coital debut: The role of religiosity and sex attitudes in the Add Health Survey. *Journal of Sex Research, 40*(4), 358–367.

Rotenberg, K. J., Betts, L. R., Eisner, M., & Ribeaud, D. (2012). Social antecedents of children's trustworthiness. *Infant and Child Development, 21,* 310–322.

Roth, A., & Fonagy, P. (2005). *What works for whom? A critical review of psychotherapy research* (2nd ed.). New York, NY: Guilford Press.

Roth, D. A., Eng, W., & Heimberg, R. G. (2002). Cognitive behavior therapy. In M. Hersen & W. Sledge (Eds.), *Encyclopedia of psychotherapy* (Vol. 1, pp. 451–458). San Diego, CA: Academic Press.

Rothbart, M. K. & Bates, J. E. (2006). Temperament. In N. Eisenberg (Vol. Ed.), *Handbook of child psychology* (6th ed., Vol. 3, pp. 99–166). Hoboken, NJ: Wiley.

Rothbart, M. K. (2007). Temperament, development, and personality. *Current Directions in Psychological Science, 16*(4), 207–212.

Rothbart, M. K., Ahadi, S. A., & Evans, D. E. (2000). Temperament and personality: Origins and outcomes. *Journal of Personality and Social Psychology, 78*(1), 122–135.

Rothbaum, F., Weisz, J. R., & Snyder, S. S. (1982). Changing the world and changing the self: A two-process model of perceived control. *Journal of Personality and Social Psychology, 42*(1), 5–37.

Rothman, J. (2011, September 14). American's new military culture. *Boston Globe.* Retrieved May 14, 2012, from http://articles.boston.com/2011-09-14/bostonglobe/30155869_1_military-values-american-military-culture-civil-society.

Rothstein, H. R. (2012). Accessing relevant literature. In H. Cooper (Ed.), *APA handbook of research methods in psychology* (Vol. 1, pp. 133–144). Washington, DC: American Psychological Association.

Rothstein, M. G., & Goffin, R. D. (2006). The use of personality measures in personnel selection: What does current research support? *Human Resource Management Review, 16*(2), 155–180.

Rotter, J. B. (1966). Generalized expectancies for internal versus external control of reinforcement. *Psychological Monographs, 80*(1), 1–28.

Rotter, J. B. (1975). Some problems and misconceptions related to the construct of internal versus external control of reinforcement. *Journal of Consulting and Clinical Psychology, 43*(1), 56–67.

Rotter, J. B. (1989). Internal versus external control of reinforcement: A case history of a variable. *American Psychologist, 45*(4), 489–493.

Routh, D. K. (1996). Lightner Witmer and the first 100 years of clinical psychology. *American Psychologist, 51*(3), 244–247.

Routh, D. K. (2011). A history of clinical psychology. In D. H. Barlow (Ed.), *The Oxford handbook of clinical psychology* (pp. 23–33). New York, NY: Oxford University Press.

Rubenzer, S. J., & Faschingbauer, T. R. (2004). *Personality, character, and leadership in the White House: Psychologists assess the presidents.* Washington, DC: Brassey's.

Rubin, D. C., & Kontis, T. C. (1983). A schema for common cents. *Memory & Cognition, 11*(4), 335–341.

Rubin, K. H., Bukowski, W. M., & Parker, J. G. (2006). Peer interactions, relationships, and groups. In N. Eisenberg (Vol. Ed.), *Handbook of child psychology* (6th ed., Vol. 3, pp. 571–645). Hoboken, NJ: Wiley.

Rubin, K. H., Coplan, R., Chen, X., Buskirk, A. A., & Wojslawowicz, J. C. (2005). Peer relationships in childhood. In M. H. Bornstein & M. E. Lamb (Eds.), *Developmental science: An advanced textbook* (5th ed., pp. 469–512). Mahwah, NJ: Lawrence Erlbaum.

Rubinstein, G., & Strul, S. (2007). The Five Factor Model (FFM) among four groups of male and female professionals. *Journal of Research in Personality, 41*(4), 931–937.

Ruble, D. N., & Martin, C. L. (1998). Gender development. In W. Damon & N. Eisenberg (Eds.), *Handbook of child psychology* (5th ed., Vol. 3, pp. 933–1016). New York, NY: Wiley.

Ruble, D. N., Martin, C. L., & Berenbaum, S. A. (2006). Gender development. In N. Eisenberg, W. Damon, & R. M. Lerner (Eds.), *Handbook of child psychology* (6th ed., Vol. 3, pp. 858–932). Hoboken, NJ: Wiley.

Ruch, W. (1995). Will the real relationship between facial expression and affective experience please stand up: The case of exhilaration. *Cognition & Emotion, 9*(1), 33–58.

Ruddy, N. B., Borresen, D. A., & Gunn, W. B., Jr. (2008). *The collaborative psychotherapist: Creating reciprocal relationships with medical professionals.* Washington, DC: American Psychological Association.

Rudmin, F. W. (2003). Critical history of the acculturation psychology of assimilation, separation, integration, and marginalization. *Review of General Psychology, 7*(1), 3–37.

Rudmin, F. W., & Ahmadzadeh, V. (2001). Psychometric critique of acculturation psychology: The case of Iranian migrants in Norway. *Scandinavian Journal of Psychology, 42*(1), 41–56.

Rudolph, C. W., Wells, C. L., Weller, M. D., & Baltes, B. B. (2009). A meta-analysis of empirical studies of weight-based bias in the workplace. *Journal of Vocational Behavior, 74*(1), 1–10.

Rudolph, U., Roesch, S., Greitemeyer, T., & Weiner, B. (2004). A meta-analytic review of help giving and aggression from an attributional perspective: Contributions to a general theory of motivation. *Cognition and Emotion, 18*(6), 815–848.

Rueger, S. Y., Malecki, C. K., & Demaray, M. K. (2010). Relationship between multiple sources of perceived social support and psychological and academic adjustment in early adolescence: Comparisons across gender. *Journal of Youth and Adolescence, 39*(1), 47–61.

Rule, N. O., Freeman, J. B., & Ambady, N. (2013). Culture in social neuroscience: A review. *Social Neuroscience, 8*(1), 3–10.

Rummell, C. M., & Joyce, N. R. (2010): "So wat do u want to wrk on 2day?": The ethical implications of online counseling. *Ethics & Behavior, 20*(6), 482–496

Russac, R. J., Gatliff, C., Reece, M., & Spottswood, D. (2007). Death anxiety across the adult years: An examination of age and gender effects. *Death Studies, 31*(6), 549–561.

Russell, G. F. M. (1979). Bulimia nervosa: An ominous variant of anorexia nervosa. *Psychological Medicine, 9*(3), 429–448.

Russell, J. A. (1994). Is there universal recognition of emotion from facial expressions? A review of the cross-cultural studies. *Psychological Bulletin, 115*(1), 102–141.

Russell, S. T., & Consolacion, T. B. (2003). Adolescent romance and emotional health in the United States: Beyond binaries. *Journal of Clinical Child and Adolescent Psychology, 32*(4), 499–508.

Russell, S. T., & Fish, J. N. (2016). Mental health in lesbian, gay, bisexual, and transgender (LGBT) youth. *Annual Review of Clinical Psychology, 12,* 465–487.

Russell, S. T., Muraco, A., Subramaniam, A., & Laub, C. (2009). Youth empowerment and high school gay-straight alliances. *Journal of Youth and Adolescence, 38*(7), 891–903.

Rusting, C. L., & DeHart, T. (2000). Retrieving positive memories to regulate negative mood: Consequences for mood-congruent memory. *Journal of Personality and Social Psychology, 78*(4), 737.

Rutherford, A. (2009). *Beyond the box: B. F. Skinner's technology of behavior from laboratory to life, 1950s–1970s.* Toronto, Canada: University of Toronto Press.

Rutledge, T., Reis, S. E., Olson, M., Owens, J., Kelsey, S. F., Pepine, C. J., . . . Matthews, K. A. (2004). Social networks are associated with lower mortality rates among women with suspected coronary disease: The National Heart, Lung, and Blood Institute-sponsored Women's Ischemia Syndrome Evaluation study. *Psychosomatic Medicine, 66*(6), 882–888.

Rutter, M. (2000). Psychosocial influences: Critiques, findings, and research needs. *Development and Psychopathology, 12*(3), 375–405.

Rutter, M. (2006). *Genes and behavior: Nature–nurture interplay explained.* Oxford, UK: Blackwell.

Rutter, M. (2011). Biological and experiential influences on psychological development. In D. P. Keating (Ed.), *Nature and nurture in early child development* (pp. 7–44). New York, NY: Cambridge University Press.

Ryan, L., Hoscheidt, S., & Nadel, L. (2008). Perspectives on episodic and semantic memory retrieval. In E. Dere, A. Easton, L. Nadel, & J. P. Huston (Eds.), *Handbook of episodic memory* (pp. 5–18). Amsterdam, Netherlands: Elsevier Science.

Ryan, R. M. (2012). Motivation and the organization of human behavior: Three reasons for the reemergence of a field. In R. M. Ryan (Ed.), *The Oxford handbook of human motivation* (pp. 2–12). New York, NY: Oxford University Press.

Ryan, R. M., & Deci, E. L. (2000a). Self-determination theory and the facilitation of intrinsic motivation, social development, and well-being. *American Psychologist, 55*(1), 68–78.

Ryan, R. M., & Deci, E. L. (2000b). Intrinsic and extrinsic motivations: Classic definitions and new directions. *Contemporary Educational Psychology, 25*(1), 54–67.

Ryan, R. M., & Deci, E. L. (2003). On assimilating identities to the self: A self-determination theory perspective on internalization and integrity within cultures. In M. R. Leary & J. P. Tangney (Eds.), *Handbook of self and identity* (pp. 254–274). New York, NY: Guilford.

Ryan, R. M., Connell, J. P., & Plant, R. W. (1990). Emotions in nondirected text learning. *Learning and Individual Differences, 2*(1), 1–17.

Ryan, T., & Xenos, S. (2011). Who uses Facebook? An investigation into the relationship between the Big Five, shyness, narcissism, loneliness, and Facebook usage. *Computers in Human Behavior, 27*(5), 1658–1664.

Rychtarik, R. G., Silverman, W. K., Van Landingham, W. P., & Prue, D. M. (1984). Treatment of an incest victim with implosive therapy: A case study. *Behavior Therapy, 15*(4), 410–420.

Rycroft, C. (1968). *A critical dictionary of psychoanalysis.* London, UK: Nelson.

Ryder, A. G., Alden, L. E., & Paulhus, D. L. (2000). Is acculturation unidimensional or bidimensional? A head-to-head comparison in the prediction of personality, self-identity, and adjustment. *Journal of Personality and Social Psychology, 79*(1), 49–65.

Rygh, J. L., & Sanderson, W. C. (2004). *Treating generalized anxiety disorder: Evidence-based strategies, tools, and techniques.* New York, NY: Guilford Press.

Saarenpaa-Heikkila, O. A., Rintahaka, P. J., Laippala, P. J., & Koivikko, M. J. (1995). Sleep habits and disorders in Finnish schoolchildren. *Journal of Sleep Research, 4*(3), 173–182.

Sachs, G. S. (2004). Strategies for improving treatment of bipolar disorder: Integration of measurement and management. *Acta Psychiatrica Scandinavica. Supplementum, 110*(422), 7–17.

Sackett, P. R. (2012). Faking in personality assessments: Where do we stand? In M. Ziegler, C. MacCann, & R. D. Roberts (Eds.), *New perspectives on faking in personality assessment* (pp. 330–344). New York, NY: Oxford University Press.

Sadeh, A. V. I., Mindell, J. A., Luedtke, K., & Wiegand, B. (2009). Sleep and sleep ecology in the first 3 years: A web-based study. *Journal of Sleep Research, 18*(1), 60–73.

Sadler, P. M., Sonnert, G., Hazari, Z., & Tai, R. (2012). Stability and volatility of STEM career interest in high school: A gender study. *Science Education, 96*(3), 411–427.

Sadri, G., and Robertson, I. T. (1993), Self-efficacy and work-related behaviour: A review and meta-analysis. *Applied Psychology: An International Review, 42*(2), 139–152.

Safdar, S., Friedlmeier, W., Matsumoto, D., Yoo, S. H., Kwantes, C. T., Kakai, H., & Shigemasu, E. (2009). Variations of emotional display rules within and across cultures: A comparison between Canada, USA, and Japan. *Canadian Journal of Behavioural Science, 41*(1), 1–10.

Saffran, J. R., & Thiessen, E. D. (2003). Pattern induction by infant language learners. *Developmental Psychology, 39*(3), 484.

Safran, J. D., Abreu, I., Ogilvie, J., and DeMaria, A. (2011), Does psychotherapy research influence the clinical practice of researcher–clinicians? *Clinical Psychology: Science and Practice, 18*(4), 357–371.

Sagarin, B. J., Vaughn Becker, D., Guadagno, R. E., Nicastle, L. D., & Millevoi, A. (2003). Sex differences (and similarities) in jealousy: The moderating influence of infidelity experience and sexual orientation of the infidelity. *Evolution and Human Behavior, 24*(1), 17–23.

Saha, S, Chant, D, Welham, J., & McGrath, J. (2005). The systematic review of the prevalence of schizophrenia. *PLoS Med*, 2(5): e141.

Sajatovic, M., Madhusoodanan, S., & Fuller, M. A. (2008). Clozapine. In K. T. Mueser & D. V. Jeste (Eds.), *Clinical handbook of schizophrenia* (pp. 178–185). New York, NY: Guilford Press.

Sakai, Y., Kumano, H., Nishikawa, M., Sakano, Y., Kaiya, H., Imabayashi, E., . . . Kuboki, T. (2006). Changes in cerebral glucose utilization in patients with panic disorder treated with cognitive-behavioral therapy. *Neuroimage, 33*(1), 218–226.

Saks, E. R. (2007). *The center cannot hold: My journey through madness*. New York, NY: Hyperion Books.

Sallis, J. F., Adams, M. A., & Ding, D. (2011). Physical activity and the built environment. In J. H. Cawley (Ed.), *The Oxford handbook of the social science of obesity* (pp. 433–451). New York, NY: Oxford University Press.

Salmon, P. (2001). Effects of physical exercise on anxiety, depression, and sensitivity to stress: A unifying theory. *Clinical Psychology Review, 21*(1), 33–61.

Salovey, P. (2005). Foreword. In R. Schulze and R. D. Roberts (Eds.), *Emotional intelligence: An international handbook* (pp. v–x). Cambridge, MA: Hogrefe & Huber Publishers.

Salovey, P., & Mayer, J. D. (1989). Emotional intelligence. *Imagination, Cognition, and Personality, 9*(3), 185–211.

Salter, D. S., & Salter, B. R. (2012). Competence with diverse populations. In S. J. Knapp (Ed.), *APA handbook of ethics in psychology* (Vol. 1, pp. 217–240). Washington, DC: American Psychological Association.

Salthouse, T. A. (2009). When does age-related cognitive decline begin? *Neurobiology of Aging, 30*(4), 507–514.

Salthouse, T. A., & Babcock, R. L. (1991). Decomposing adult age differences in working memory. *Developmental Psychology, 27*(5), 763–776.

Salvy, S. J., Jarrin, D., Paluch, R., Irfan, N., & Pliner, P. (2007). Effects of social influence on eating in couples, friends and strangers. *Appetite, 49*(1), 92–99.

Sam, D. L. (2006). Acculturation: Conceptual background and core components. In D. L. Sam, & J. W. Berry (Eds.), *The Cambridge handbook of acculturation psychology* (pp. 11–26). New York, NY: Cambridge University Press.

Sam, D. L., & Berry, J. W. (2006). Introduction. In D. L. Sam, & J. W. Berry (Eds.), *The Cambridge handbook of acculturation psychology* (pp. 1–10). New York, NY: Cambridge University Press.

Samaras, K. (2008). Twin studies and genetics of obesity. In K. Keller (Ed.), *Encyclopedia of obesity* (Vol. 2, pp. 759–760). Los Angeles, CA: SAGE.

Sammons, M. T. (2011). Treatment modalities: Pharmacotherapy. In J. C. Norcross, G. R. Vandenbos, & D. K. Freedheim (Eds.), *History of psychotherapy: Continuity and change* (2nd ed., pp. 516–532). Washington, DC: American Psychological Association.

Samuels, N., Gropp, C., Singer, S. R., & Oberbaum, M. (2008). Acupuncture for psychiatric illness: A literature review. *Behavioral Medicine, 34*(2), 55–64.

Sánchez, F. J., & Vilain, E. (2013). Transgender identities: Research and controversies. In C. J. Patterson & A. R. D'Augelli (Eds.), *Handbook of psychology and sexual orientation* (pp. 42–54). New York, NY: Oxford University Press.

Sanders, A. R., Martin, E. R., Beecham, G. W., Guo, S., Dawood, K., Rieger, G., . . . Bailey, J. M. (2015). Genome-wide scan demonstrates significant linkage for male sexual orientation. *Psychological Medicine, 45*(7), 1379–1388.

Sanders, K. A., & Bruce, N. W. (1997). A prospective study of psychosocial stress and fertility in women. *Human Reproduction, 12*(10), 2324–2329.

Sanders, M. H. & Givelber, R. J. (2006). Overview of obstructive sleep apnea in adults. In T. L. Lee-Chiong (Ed.), *Sleep: A comprehensive handbook* (pp. 231–240). Hoboken, NJ: Wiley-Liss.

Sandler, J., & Freud, A. (1985). *The analysis of defense: The ego and the mechanisms of defense revisited*. New York, NY: International Universities Press.

Sandstrom, M. J., Cillessen, A. H., & Eisenhower, A. (2003). Children's appraisal of peer rejection experiences: Impact on social and emotional adjustment. *Social Development, 12*(4), 530–550.

Sandy, C. J., Gosling, S. D., & Durant, J. (2013). Predicting consumer behavior and media preferences: The comparative validity of personality traits and demographic variables. *Psychology & Marketing, 30*(11), 937–949.

Sanes, J. N., & Donoghue, J. P. (2000). Plasticity and primary motor cortex. *Annual Review of Neuroscience, 23*(1), 393–415.

Sanes, J. N., Suner, S., & Donoghue, J. P. (1990). Dynamic organization of primary motor cortex output to target muscles in adult rats. I. Long-term patterns of reorganization following motor or mixed peripheral nerve lesions. *Experimental Brain Research, 79*(3), 479–491.

Sanes, J. N., Wang, J., & Donoghue, J. P. (1992). Immediate and delayed changes of rat motor cortical output representation with new forelimb configurations. *Cerebral Cortex, 2*(2), 141–152.

Sanes, J. R. & Jessell, T. M. (2013d). Repairing the damaged brain. In E. R. Kandel, J. H. Schwartz, T. M. Jessell, S. A. Siegelbaum, & A. J. Hudspeth (Eds.), *Principles of neural science* (5th ed., pp. 1284–1305). New York, NY: McGraw-Hill.

Sanes, J. R., & Jessell, T. M. (2013a). The growth and guidance of axons. In E. R. Kandel, J. H. Schwartz, T. M. Jessell, S. A. Siegelbaum, & A. J. Hudspeth (Eds.), *Principles of neural science* (5th ed., pp. 1209–1232). New York, NY: McGraw-Hill.

Sanes, J. R., & Jessell, T. M. (2013b). Formation and elimination of synapses. In E. R. Kandel, J. H. Schwartz, T. M. Jessell, S. A. Siegelbaum, & A. J. Hudspeth (Eds.), *Principles of neural science* (5th ed., pp. 1233–1258). New York, NY: McGraw-Hill.

Sanes, J. R., & Jessell, T. M. (2013c). Experience and the refinement of synaptic connections. In E. R. Kandel, J. H. Schwartz, T. M. Jessell, S. A. Siegelbaum, & A. J. Hudspeth (Eds.), *Principles of neural science* (5th ed., pp. 1259–1283). New York, NY: McGraw-Hill.

Sanson, A., Hemphill, S. A., Yarmurlu, B., & McClowry, S. (2011). Temperament and social development. In P. K. Smith & C. H. Hart (Eds.), *The Wiley-Blackwell handbook of childhood social development* (2nd ed., pp. 227–245). Malden, MA: Wiley-Blackwell.

Saper, C. B., Lumsden, A. G. S., & Richerson, G. B. (2013). The sensory, motor, and reflex functions of the brain stem. In E. R. Kandel, J. H. Schwartz, T. M. Jessell, S. A. Siegelbaum, & A. J. Hudspeth (Eds.), *Principles of neural science* (5th ed., pp. 1019–1037). New York, NY: McGraw-Hill.

Saper, C. B., Scammell, T. E., & Lu, J. (2005). Hypothalamic regulation of sleep and circadian rhythms. *Nature, 437*(7063), 1257-1263.

Satel, S. L., & Lilienfeld, S. O. (2013). *Brainwashed: The seductive appeal of mindless neuroscience*. New York, NY: Basic Books.

Saucier, D. M., Green, S. M., Leason, J., MacFadden, A., Bell, S., & Elias, L. J. (2002). Are sex differences in navigation caused by sexually dimorphic strategies or by differences in the ability to use the strategies? *Behavioral Neuroscience, 116*(3), 403–410.

Saucier, D., & Ehresman, C. (2010). The physiology of sex differences. In J. C. Chrisler & D. R. McCreary (Eds.), *Handbook of gender research in psychology* (Vol. 1, pp. 215–233). New York, NY: Springer Science+Business Media.

Saunders, H. (2012, May 2). See photos of J Dilla's Recently Discovered Record Collection. *Paste Magazine*. Retrieved from http://www.pastemagazine.com/blogs/awesome_of_the_day/2012/05/record-store-owner-finds-j-dillas-record-collection-home-tapes. html.

Saxton, M. (2010). *Child language: Acquisition and development*. London, UK: SAGE.

Scalera, G., & Bavieri, M. (2008). Role of conditioned taste aversion on the side effects of chemotherapy in cancer patients. In S. Reilly & T. R. Schachtman (Eds.), *Conditioned taste aversion: Neural and behavioral processes* (pp. 513–542), New York, NY: Oxford University Press.

Scarborough, E., & Furumoto, L. (1987). *Untold lives: The first generation of American women psychologists*. New York, NY: Columbia University Press.

Schachter, S., & Singer, J. (1962). Cognitive, social, and physiological determinants of emotional state. *Psychological Review, 69*(5), 379–399.

Schachtman, T. R., Walker, J., & Fowler, S. (2011). Effects of conditioning in advertising. In T. R. Schachtman & S. S. Reilly (Eds.), *Associative learning and conditioning theory: Human and non-human applications* (pp. 481–506). New York, NY: Oxford University Press.

Schacter, D. L. (2001). *The seven sins of memory: How the mind forgets and remembers*. Boston, MA: Houghton Mifflin.

Schacter, D. L., & Wagner, A. D. (2013). Learning and memory. In E. R. Kandel, J. H. Schwartz, T. M. Jessell, S. A. Siegelbaum, & A. J. Hudspeth (Eds.), *Principles of neural science* (5th ed., pp. 1441–1460). New York, NY: McGraw-Hill.

Schacter, D. L., Wagner, A. D., & Buckner, R. L. (2000). Memory systems of 1999. In E. Tulving & F. I. M. Craik (Eds.), *The Oxford handbook of memory* (pp. 627–643). Oxford, UK: Oxford University Press.

Schafe, G. F., & LeDoux, J. E. (2004). The neural basis of fear. In M. S. Gazzaniga (Ed.), *The new cognitive neurosciences III* (pp. 987–1004). Cambridge, MA: MIT Press.

Schaffer, M., Clark, S., & Jeglic, E. L. (2009). The role of empathy and parenting style in the development of antisocial behaviors. *Crime & Delinquency, 55*(4), 586–599.

Schaie, K. W. (2012). *Developmental influences on adult intelligence: The Seattle longitudinal study*. New York, NY: Oxford University Press.

Schaller, M., & Cialdini, R. B. (1988). The economics of empathic helping: Support for a mood management motive. *Journal of Experimental Social Psychology, 24*(2), 163-181.

Schank, J. A., Helbok, C. M., Haldeman, D. C., & Gallardo, M. E. (2010). Challenges and benefits of ethical small-community practice. *Professional Psychology: Research and Practice, 41*(6), 502–510.

Schank, J., Slater, R., Banerjee-Stevens, D., & Skovholt, T. M. (2003). Ethics of multiple and overlapping relationships. In W. O'Donohue & K. Ferguson (Eds.), *Handbook of professional ethics for psychologists: Issues, questions, and controversies* (pp. 181–193). Thousand Oaks, CA: SAGE.

Scheier, M. F., & Carver, C. S. (1985). Optimism, coping, and health: Assessment and implications of generalized outcome expectancies. *Health Psychology, 4*(3), 219–247.

Schenck, C. H., & Mahowald, M. W. (1994). Review of nocturnal sleep-related eating disorders. *International Journal of Eating Disorders, 15*(4), 343–356.

Schenck, C. H., Arnulf, I., & Mahowald, M. W. (2007). Sleep and sex: What can go wrong? A review of the literature on sleep related disorders and abnormal sexual behaviors and experiences. *Sleep, 30*(6), 683–702.

Schenck, C. H., Hurwitz, T. D., O'Connor, K. A., & Mahowald, M. W. (1993). Additional categories of sleep-related eating disorders and the current status of treatment. *Sleep, 16*(5), 457–466.

Scher, C. D., Steidtmann, D., Luxton, D., & Ingram, R. E. (2006). Specific phobia: A common problem, rarely treated. In T. G. Plante (Ed.), *Mental disorders of the new millennium* (pp. 245–263). Westport, CT: Praeger.

Schindler, R. M. (1992). The real lesson of New Coke: The value of focus groups for predicting the effects of social influence. *Marketing Research, 4*(4), 22–27.

Schirillo, J. A. (2010). Gestalt approach. In E. B. Goldstein (Ed.), *Encyclopedia of perception* (pp. 469–472). Thousand Oaks, CA: SAGE.

Schlegel, A. (2009). Cross-cultural issues in the study of adolescent development. In R. M. Lerner & L. Steinberg (Eds.), *Handbook of adolescent psychology* (3rd ed., Vol. 2, pp. 570–589). Hoboken, NJ: Wiley.

Schlesinger, J. (2009). Creative mythconceptions: A closer look at the evidence for the "mad genius" hypothesis. *Psychology of Aesthetics, Creativity, and the Arts, 3*(2), 62–72.

Schloss, J. G. (2004). *Making beats: The art of sample-based hip-hop*. Middletown, CT: Wesleyan University Press.

Schmader, T., & Johns, M. (2003). Converging evidence that stereotype threat reduces working memory capacity. *Journal of Personality and Social Psychology, 85*(3), 440–452.

Schmader, T., Johns, M., & Forbes, C. (2008). An integrated process model of stereotype threat effects on performance. *Psychological Review, 115*(2), 336–356.

Schmidt, F. L., & Hunter, J. (2004). General mental ability in the world of work: Occupational attainment and job performance. *Journal of Personality and Social Psychology, 86*(1), 162–173.

Schmidt, M. H. (2014). The energy allocation function of sleep: A unifying theory of sleep, torpor, and continuous wakefulness. *Neuroscience & Biobehavioral Reviews, 47*, 122–153.

Schmidt, P. J., Murphy, J. H., Haq, N., Rubinow, D. R., & Danaceau, M. A. (2004). Stressful life events, personal losses, and perimenopause-related depression. *Archives of Women's Mental Health, 7*(1), 19–26.

Schmidt, S. R. (2007). Unscrambling the effects of emotion and distinctiveness on memory. In H. L. Roediger & J. S. Nairne (Eds.), *The foundation of remembering* (pp. 141–158). New York, NY: Psychology Press.

Schmitt, D. P., Allik, J., McCrae, R. R., & Benet-Martínez, V. (2007). The geographic distribution of Big Five personality traits patterns and profiles of human self-description across 56 nations. *Journal of Cross-Cultural Psychology, 38*(2), 173–212.

Schmitz, S. (1997). Gender-related strategies in environmental development: Effects of anxiety on wayfinding in and representation of a three-dimensional maze. *Journal of Environmental Psychology, 17*(3), 215–228.

Schneider, B. H., Atkinson, L., & Tardif, C. (2001). Child–parent attachment and children's peer relations: A quantitative review. *Developmental Psychology, 37*(1), 86–100.

Schneider, B. H., Benenson, J., Fülöp, M., Berkics, M., & Sándor, M. (2011). Cooperation and competition. In P. K. Smith & C. H. Hart (Eds.), *The Wiley-Blackwell handbook of childhood social development* (2nd ed., pp. 472–490). Malden, MA: Wiley-Blackwell.

Schneider, G. E. (2014). *Brain structure and its origins: In development and in evolution of behavior and the mind*. Cambridge, MA: MIT Press.

Schneider, W. (2011). Memory development in childhood. In U. Goswami (Ed.), *The Wiley-Blackwell handbook of childhood cognitive development* (2nd ed., pp. 347–376). Malden, MA: Wiley-Blackwell.

Schnupp, J., Nelken, I., & King, A. (2012). *Auditory neuroscience: Making sense of sound*. Cambridge, MA: MIT Press.

Schoenemann, P. T. (2006). Evolution of the size and functional areas of the human brain. *Annual Review of Anthropology, 35*, 379–406.

Schoenemann, P. T., Sheehan, M. J., & Glotzer, L. D. (2005). Prefrontal white matter volume is disproportionately larger in humans than in other primates. *Nature Neuroscience, 8*(2), 242–252.

Scholer, A. A., & Higgins, E. T. (2012). Too much of a good thing? Trade-offs in promotion and prevention focus. In R. M. Ryan (Ed.), *The Oxford handbook of human motivation* (pp. 65–84). New York, NY: Oxford University Press.

Schooler, J. W., & Eich, E. (2000). Memory for emotional events. In E. Tulving & F. I. M. Craik (Eds.), *The Oxford handbook of memory* (pp. 379–392). Oxford, UK: Oxford University Press.

Schore, A. N. (2001). Effects of a secure attachment relationship on right brain development, affect regulation, and infant mental health. *Infant Mental Health Journal, 22*(1–2), 7–66.

Schreer, G. E., Smith, S., and Thomas, K. (2009), "Shopping while Black": Examining racial discrimination in a retail setting. *Journal of Applied Social Psychology, 39*(6), 1432–1444.

Schreiber, F. R. (1973). *Sybil*. New York, NY: Warner Books.

Schubert, C. R., Cruickshanks, K. J., Nondahl, D. M., Klein, B. E., Klein, R., & Fischer, M. E. (2013). Association of exercise with lower long-term risk of olfactory impairment in older adults. *JAMA Otolaryngology–Head & Neck Surgery, 139*(10), 1061–1066.

Schultheis, H., & Carlson, L. A. (2013). Spatial reasoning. In D. Reisberg (Ed.), *The Oxford handbook of cognitive psychology* (pp. 719–732). Oxford, UK: Oxford University Press.

Schultheiss, O. C., & Pang, J. S. (2007). Measuring implicit motives. In R. W. Robins, R. C. Fraley, & R. F. Krueger (Eds.), *Handbook of research methods in personality psychology* (pp. 322–344). New York, NY: Guilford Press.

Schultz, R. T. (2005). Developmental deficits in social perception in autism: The role of the amygdala and fusiform face area. *International Journal of Developmental Neuroscience, 23*(2), 125–141.

Schulz, R., & Beach, S. R. (1999). Caregiving as a risk factor for mortality: The Caregiver Health Effects Study. *The Journal of the American Medical Association, 282*(23), 2215–2219.

Schulze, R., Roberts, R. D., Zeidner, M., & Matthews, G. (2005). Theory, measurement, and applications of emotional intelligence: Frames of reference. In R. Schulze and R. D. Roberts (Eds.), *Emotional Intelligence: An international handbook* (pp. 3–30). Cambridge, MA: Hogrefe & Huber.

Schutte, N. S., Malouff, J. M., Post-Gorden, J. C., & Rodasta, A. L. (1988). Effects of playing videogames on children's aggressive and other behaviors. *Journal of Applied Social Psychology*, 18, 454–460.

Schutte, N. S., Malouff, J. M., Thorsteinsson, E. B., Bhullar, N., & Rooke, S. E. (2007). A meta-analytic investigation of the relationship between emotional intelligence and health. *Personality and Individual Differences, 42*(6), 921–933.

Schwartz, B. G., McDonald, S. A., & Kloner, R. A. (2013). Super Bowl outcome's association with cardiovascular death. *Clinical Research in Cardiology, 102*(11), 807–811.

Schwartz, B., & Sommers, R. (2013). Affective forecasting and well-being. In D. Reisberg (Ed.), *The Oxford handbook of cognitive psychology* (pp. 704–718). Oxford, UK: Oxford University Press.

Schwartz, J. H., Barres, B. A., & Goldman, J. E. (2013). The cells of the nervous system. In E. R. Kandel, J. H. Schwartz, T. M. Jessell, S. A. Siegelbaum, & A. J. Hudspeth (Eds.), *Principles of neural science* (5th ed., pp. 71–99). New York, NY: McGraw-Hill.

Schwartz, J. H., & Javitch, J. A. (2013). Neurotransmitters. In E. R. Kandel, J. H. Schwartz, T. M. Jessell, S. A. Siegelbaum, & A. J. Hudspeth (Eds.), *Principles of neural science* (5th ed., pp. 289–306). New York, NY: McGraw-Hill.

Schwartz, M. S., & Andrasik, F. (2005). *Biofeedback: A practitioner's guide* (3rd ed.). New York, NY: Guilford Press.

Schwartz, M. W., & Porte, D. (2005). Diabetes, obesity, and the brain. *Science, 307*(5708), 375–379.

Schwarz, A. (2016). *ADHD nation: Children, doctors, big pharma, and the making of an American epidemic*. New York, NY: Scribner.

Schwarzer, R. (2011). Health behavior change. In H. S. Friedman (Ed.), *The Oxford handbook of health psychology* (pp. 591–611). Oxford, UK: Oxford University Press.

Schwarzer, R., & Leppin, A. (1991). Social support and health: A theoretical and empirical overview. *Journal of Social and Personal Relationships, 8*(1), 99–127.

Schweickert, R., & Boruff, B. (1986). Short-term memory capacity: Magic number or magic spell? *Journal of Experimental Psychology: Learning, Memory, and Cognition, 12*(3), 419–425.

Scott, K. M., Bruffaerts, R., Simon, G. E., Alonso, J., Angermeyer, M., de Girolamo, G., . . . Kessler, R. C. (2008). Obesity and mental disorders in the general population: Results from the world mental health surveys. *International Journal of Obesity, 32*(1), 192–200.

Scott, L., & O'Hara, M. W. (1993). Self-discrepancies in clinically anxious and depressed university students. *Journal of Abnormal Psychology, 102*(2), 282–287.

Scoville, W. B., & Milner, B. (1957). Loss of recent memory after bilateral hippocampal lesions. *Journal of Neurology, Neurosurgery, and Psychiatry, 20*(1), 11–21.

Sedgwick, H. A. (2001). Visual space perception. In E. B. Goldstein (Ed.), *Blackwell handbook of perception* (pp. 128–167). Oxford, UK: Blackwell.

Sedlmeier, P., Eberth, J., Schwarz, M., Zimmermann, D., Haarig, F., Jaeger, S., & Kunze, S. (2012). The psychological effects of meditation: A meta-analysis. *Psychological Bulletin, 138*(6), 1139–1171.

Seeman, M. V. (2009). The changing role of mother of the mentally ill: From schizophrenogenic mother to multigenerational caregiver. *Psychiatry: Interpersonal and Biological Processes, 72*(3), 284–294.

Seeman, T. E. (1996). Social ties and health: The benefits of social integration. *Annals of Epidemiology, 6*(5), 442–451.

Segal, N. L. (2011). Twin, adoption, and family methods as approaches to the evolution of individual differences. In D. M. Buss & P. H. Hawley (Eds.), *The evolution of personality and individual differences* (pp. 303–337). New York, NY: Oxford University Press.

Segal, Z. V., Williams, J. M. G., & Teasdale, J. D. (2012). *Mindfulness-based cognitive therapy for depression: A new approach for preventing relapse* (2nd ed.). New York, NY: Guilford Press.

Segerstrom, S. C., & Miller, G. E. (2004). Psychological stress and the human immune system: A meta-analytic study of 30 years of inquiry. *Psychological Bulletin, 130*(4), 601–630.

Segerstrom, S. C., Taylor, S. E., Kemeny, M. E., & Fahey, J. L. (1998). Optimism is associated with mood, coping, and immune change in response to stress. *Journal of Personality and Social Psychology, 74*(6), 1646–1655.

Seligman, M. E. (2004). *Authentic happiness: Using the new positive psychology to realize your potential for lasting fulfillment*. New York, NY: Simon and Schuster.

Seligman, M. E. P. (1970). On the generality of the laws of learning. *Psychological Review, 77*, 406–418.

Seligman, M. E. P. (1971). Phobias and preparedness. *Behavior Therapy, 2*, 307–320.

Seligman, M. E. P. (1975). *Helplessness: On depression, development, and death*. San Francisco, CA: Freeman.

Seligman, M. E. P. (1991). *Learned optimism*. New York, NY: Knopf.

Seligman, M. E. P. (1995). The effectiveness of psychotherapy: The *Consumer Reports* survey. *American Psychologist, 50*(12), 965–974.

Seligman, M. E. P. (2011). *Flourish: A visionary new understanding of happiness and well-being*. New York, NY: Free Press.

Seligman, M. E. P., & Czikszentmihalyi, M. (2000). Positive psychology: An introduction. *American Psychologist, 55*(1), 5–14.

Seligman, M. E. P., & Hager, J. L. (1972). Sauce-béarnaise syndrome. *Psychology Today, 6*, 59.

Seligman, M. E. P., & Maier, S. F. (1967). Failure to escape traumatic shock. *Journal of Experimental Psychology, 74*, 1–9.

Seligman, M. E., Rashid, T., & Parks, A. C. (2006). Positive psychotherapy. *American Psychologist, 61*(8), 774–788.

Seligman, M. E., Steen, T. A., Park, N., & Peterson, C. (2005). Positive psychology progress: Empirical validation of interventions. *American Psychologist, 60*(5), 410–421.

Sell, C. S. (2014). *Chemistry and the sense of smell*. Hoboken, NJ: Wiley.

Sellbom, M., Fischler, G. L., & Ben-Porath, Y. S. (2007). Identifying MMPI-2 predictors of police officer integrity and misconduct. *Criminal Justice and Behavior, 34*(8), 985–1004.

Selye, H. (1936). A syndrome produced by diverse noxious agents. *Nature, 138*(32), 659–661.

Selye, H. (1952). *The story of the adaptation syndrome: Told in the form of informal, illustrated lectures*. Montreal: Acta.

Selye, H. (1956). *The stress of life*. New York, NY: McGraw-Hill.

Semendeferi, K., Armstrong, E., Schleicher, A., Zilles, K., & Van Hoesen, G. W. (2001). Prefrontal cortex in humans and apes: A comparative study of area 10. *American Journal of Physical Anthropology, 114*(3), 224–241.

Senghas, A., Kita, S., and Özyürek, Asli. 2004. Children creating core properties of language: Evidence from an emerging sign language in Nicaragua. *Science 305*(5691), 1779–1782.

Senko, C., Durik, A. M., & Harackiewicz, J. M. (2008). Historical perspectives and new directions in achievement goal theory: Understanding the effects of mastery and performance-approach goals. In J. Y. Shah & W. L. Gardner (Eds.), *Handbook of motivation science* (pp. 100–113). New York, NY: Guilford Press.

Serdula, M. K., Coates, R. J., Byers, T., Simoes, E., Mokdad, A. H., & Subar, A. F. (1995). Fruit and vegetable intake among adults in 16 states: Results of a brief telephone survey. *American Journal of Public Health, 85*(2), 236–239.

Sergeant, M. J., Dickins, T. E., Davies, M. N., & Griffiths, M. D. (2006). Aggression, empathy and sexual orientation in males. *Personality and Individual Differences, 40*(3), 475–486.

Serido, J., Almeida, D. M., & Wethington, E. (2004). Chronic stressors and daily hassles: Unique and interactive relationships with psychological distress. *Journal of Health and Social Behavior, 45*(1), 17–33.

Serskovits, M. J. (1966). The influence of culture on visual perception. In H. Toch & C. Smith (Eds.), *Social perception* (pp. 1–5). New York, NY: Bobbs-Merrill.

Servick, K. (2014). New support for "gay gene." *Science, 346*(6212), 902.

Sewell, H. (2009). *Working with ethnicity, race, and culture in mental health: A handbook for practitioners*. London, UK: Jessica Kingsley.

Shackelford, T. K., Schmitt, D. P., & Buss, D. M. (2005). Universal dimensions of human mate preferences. *Personality and Individual Differences, 39*(2), 447–458.

Shah, M., Khan, M., & Doty, R. L. (2010). Olfactory central processing. In E. B. Goldstein (Ed.), *Encyclopedia of perception* (pp. 685–690). Thousand Oaks, CA: SAGE.

Shahin, I., & Einarson, A. (2011). Knowledge transfer and translation: Examining how teratogen information is disseminated. *Birth Defects Research. Part A, Clinical and Molecular Teratology, 91*(11), 956–961.

Shams, L. (2010). Multimodal interactions: Visual–auditory. In E. B. Goldstein (Ed.), *Encyclopedia of perception* (pp. 593–599). Thousand Oaks, CA: SAGE Publications.

Shan, Z. Y., Liu, J. Z., Sahgal, V., Wang, B., & Yue, G. H. (2005). Selective atrophy of left hemisphere and frontal lobe of the brain in old men. *The Journals of Gerontology. Series A, Biological Sciences and Medical Sciences, 60*(2), 165–174.

Shane, S. (1993). Cultural influences on national rates of innovation. *Journal of Business Venturing, 8*(1), 59–73.

Shane, S. A. (1992). Why do some societies invent more than others? *Journal of Business Venturing, 7*(1), 29–46.

Shang, A., Huwiler-Müntener, K., Nartey, L., Jüni, P., Dörig, S., Sterne, J. A., . . . Egger, M. (2005). Are the clinical effects of homoeopathy placebo effects? Comparative study of placebo-controlled trials of homoeopathy and allopathy. *The Lancet, 366*(9487), 726–732.

Shannon, L. M., & Begley, T. M. (2008). Antecedents of the four-factor model of cultural intelligence. In S. Ang & L. Van Dyne (Eds.), *Handbook of cultural intelligence: Theory, measurement, and applications* (pp. 41–55). New York, NY: Sharpe.

Shapiro, C. M., Trajanovic, N. N., & Fedoroff, J. P. (2003). Sexsomnia—a new parasomnia? *Canadian Journal of Psychiatry, 48*(5), 311–317.

Shapiro, D. A., & Shapiro, D. (1982). Meta-analysis of comparative therapy outcome studies: A replication and refinement. *Psychological Bulletin, 92*(3), 581–604.

Shapiro, E. (1999). Cotherapy. In J. R. Price, D. R. Hescheles, & A. R. Price (Eds.), *A guide to starting psychotherapy groups* (pp. 53–61). San Diego, CA: Academic Press.

Shapiro, M. (2000). *J. K. Rowling: The wizard behind Harry Potter*. New York, NY: St. Martin's Griffin.

Shapiro, S. L. (2009). The integration of mindfulness and psychology. *Journal of Clinical Psychology, 65*(6), 555–560.

Shapiro, S. L. (2009a). Mediation and positive psychology. In S. J. Lopez & C. R. Snyder (Eds.), *Oxford handbook of positive psychology* (pp. 601–610). Oxford, UK: Oxford University Press.

Shapiro, S. L. (2009b). The integration of mindfulness and psychology. *Journal of Clinical Psychology, 65*, 555–560.

Shapiro, S. L., & Jazaieri, H. (2015). Mindfulness-based stress reduction for healthy stressed adults. In K. W. Brown, J. D. Creswell, & R. M. Ryan, *Handbook of mindfulness: Theory, research, and practice* (pp. 269–282). New York, NY: Guilford Press.

Shapiro, S. L., & Walsh, R. (2003). An analysis of recent meditation research and suggestions for future directions. *The Humanistic Psychologist, 31*(2–3), 86–114.

Sharif, Z., Bradford, D., Stroup, S., & Lieberman, J. (2007). Pharmacological treatment of schizophrenia. In P. E. Nathan & J. M. Gorman (Eds.), *A guide to treatments that work* (3rd ed., pp. 203–241). New York, NY: Oxford University Press.

Shaw, J. (2014, March–April). The price of healthy eating. *Harvard Magazine*. Retrieved from http://harvardmagazine.com/2014/03/the-price-of-healthy-eating.

Shedler, J., & Westen, D. (2004). Dimensions of personality pathology: An alternative to the five-factor model. *American Journal of Psychiatry, 161*(10), 1743–1754.

Sheldon, K. M., Boehm, J. K., & Lyubomirsky, S. (2012). Variety is the spice of happiness: The hedonic adaptation prevention (HAP) model. In Boniwell, I. & David, S. (Eds.), *Oxford handbook of happiness* (pp. 901–914). Oxford, UK: Oxford University Press.

Sheldon, K. M., Ryan, R. M., Deci, E. L., & Kasser, T. (2004). The independent effects of goal contents and motives on well-being: It's both what you pursue and why you pursue it. *Personality and Social Psychology Bulletin, 30*(4), 475–486.

Sheldon, P. (2013). Examining gender differences in self-disclosure on Facebook versus face-to-face. *The Journal of Social Media in Society, 2*(1), 88–105.

Shelton, R. C., & Lester, N. (2006). Selective serotonin reuptake inhibitors and newer antidepressants. In D. J. Stein, D. J. Kupfer, & A. F. Schatzberg (Eds.), *The American Psychiatric Publishing textbook of mood disorders* (pp. 263–280). Washington, DC: American Psychiatric Publishing.

Shenger-Krestovnikova, N. R. (1921). Contributions to the physiology of differentiation of visual stimuli, and determination of limit of differentiation by the visual analyzer of the dog. *Bulletin of Institute of Lesgaft (iii).*

Sher, A. E. (2006). Upper airway surgery for obstructive sleep apnea. In T. L. Lee-Chiong (Ed.), *Sleep: A comprehensive handbook* (pp. 365–372). Hoboken, NJ: Wiley-Liss.

Shergill, S. S., Brammer, M. J., Williams, S. C., Murray, R. M., & McGuire, P. K. (2000). Mapping auditory hallucinations in schizophrenia using functional magnetic resonance imaging. *Archives of General Psychiatry, 57*(11), 1033.

Sherif, M. (1936). *The psychology of social norms.* Oxford, UK: Harper.

Shiffrin, R. M., & Nosofsky, R. M. (1994). Seven plus or minus two: A commentary on capacity limitations. *Psychological Review, 101*(2), 357–360.

Shikatani, B., Fracalanza, K., & Antony, M. M. (2015). Behavior therapies. In R. L. Cautin & S. O. Lilienfeld (Eds.), *The encyclopedia of clinical psychology* (pp. 354–365). West Sussex, UK: Wiley-Blackwell.

Shim, J. W., & Paul, B. (2007). Effects of personality types on the use of television genre. *Journal of Broadcasting & Electronic Media, 51*(2), 287–304.

Shiota, M. N. (2014). The evolutionary perspective in positive emotion research. In M. M. Tugade, M. N. Shiota, & L. D. Kirby (Eds.), *Handbook of positive emotions* (pp. 44–59). New York, NY: Guilford Press.

Shiraev, E. (2011). *A history of psychology: A global perspective*. Thousand Oaks, CA: SAGE.

Shizgal, P. B., & Hyman, S. E. (2013). Homeostasis, motivation, and addictive states. In E. R. Kandel, J. H. Schwartz, T. M. Jessell, S. A. Siegelbaum, & A. J. Hudspeth (Eds.), *Principles of neural science* (5th ed., pp. 1095–1115). New York, NY: McGraw-Hill.

Shlomo, S. B., Taubman-Ben-Ari, O., Findler, L., Sivan, E., & Dolizki, M. (2010). Becoming a grandmother: Maternal grandmothers' mental health, perceived costs, and personal growth. *Social Work Research, 34*(1), 45–57.

Shweder, R. A., Goodnow, J. J., Hatano, G., LeVine, R. A., Markus, H. R., & Miller, P. J. (2006). The cultural psychology of development: One mind, many mentalities. In R. M. Lerner (Ed.), *Handbook of child psychology* (6th ed., Vol. 1, pp. 716–792). Hoboken, NJ: Wiley.

Shochat, T., Flint-Bretler, O., & Tzischinsky, O. (2010). Sleep patterns, electronic media exposure and daytime sleep-related behaviours among Israeli adolescents. *Acta Paediatrica, 99*(9), 1396–1400.

Shonkoff, J. P., Boyce, W. T., & McEwen, B. S. (2009). Neuroscience, molecular biology, and the childhood roots of health disparities: Building a new framework for health promotion and disease prevention. *The Journal of the American Medical Association, 301*(21), 2252–2259.

Shorter, E. (1997). *A history of psychiatry: From the era of the asylum to the age of Prozac*. New York, NY: Wiley.

Shorter, E., & Healy, D. (2007). *Shock therapy: A history of electroconvulsive treatment in mental illness*. New Brunswick, NJ: Rutgers University Press.

Shrager, Y., & Squire, L. R. (2009). Medial temporal lobe function and human memory. In M. S. Gazzaniga (Ed.), *The cognitive neurosciences* (4th ed., pp. 675–690). Cambridge, MA: MIT Press.

Shu, L. L., Gino, F., & Bazerman, M. H. (2011). Dishonest deed, clear conscience: When cheating leads to moral disengagement and motivated forgetting. *Personality and Social Psychology Bulletin, 37*(3), 330–349.

Shulman, R. G. (2013). *Brain imaging: What it can (and cannot) tell us about consciousness*. Oxford, UK: Oxford University Press.

Shweder, R. A., & Bourne, E. J. (1982). Does the concept of the person vary cross-culturally? In A. Marsella & G. White (Eds.), *Cultural conceptions of mental health and therapy* (pp. 97–137). Dordrecht, Netherlands: Reidel.

Shweder, R. A., Goodnow, J. J., Hatano, G., LeVine, R. A., Markus, H. R., & Miller, P. J. (2006). The cultural psychology of development: One mind, many mentalities. In R. M. Lerner (Ed.), *Handbook of child psychology* (6th ed., Vol. 1, pp. 716–792). Hoboken, NJ: Wile

Shweder, R. A., Jensen, L. A. and Goldstein, W. M. (1995). Who sleeps by whom revisited: A method for extracting the moral goods implicit in practice. *New Directions for Child and Adolescent Development, 67,* 21–39.

Sibley, C. G., & Duckitt, J. (2008). Personality and prejudice: A meta-analysis and theoretical review. *Personality and Social Psychology Review, 12*(3), 248–279.

Siegel, J. M. (2005). Clues to the functions of mammalian sleep. *Nature, 437*(7063), 1264–1271.

Siegel, J. M. (2009). Sleep viewed as a state of adaptive inactivity. *Nature Reviews Neuroscience, 10*(10), 747–753.

Siegelbaum, S. A., & Kandel, E. R. (2013a). Overview of synaptic transmission. In E. R. Kandel, J. H. Schwartz, T. M. Jessell, S. A. Siegelbaum, & A. J. Hudspeth (Eds.), *Principles of neural science* (5th ed., pp. 177–188). New York, NY: McGraw-Hill.

Siegelbaum, S. A., & Kandel, E. R. (2013b). Prefrontal cortex, hippocampus, and the biology of explicit memory storage. In E. R. Kandel, J. H. Schwartz, T. M. Jessell, S. A. Siegelbaum, & A. J. Hudspeth (Eds.), *Principles of neural science* (5th ed., pp. 1487–1522). New York, NY: McGraw-Hill.

Siegelbaum, S. A., Kandel, E. R., & Sudhof, T. C. (2013a). Neurotransmitter release. In E. R. Kandel, J. H. Schwartz, T. M. Jessell, S. A. Siegelbaum, & A. J. Hudspeth (Eds.), *Principles of neural science* (5th ed., pp. 260–288). New York, NY: McGraw-Hill.

Siegelbaum, S. A., Kandel, E. R., & Yuste, R. (2013b). Synaptic integration in the central nervous system. In E. R. Kandel, J. H. Schwartz, T. M. Jessell, S. A. Siegelbaum, & A. J. Hudspeth (Eds.), *Principles of neural science* (5th ed., pp. 210–235). New York, NY: McGraw-Hill.

Siev, J., & Chambless, D. L. (2007). Specificity of treatment effects: Cognitive therapy and relaxation for generalized anxiety and panic disorders. *Journal of Consulting and Clinical Psychology, 75*(4), 513–522.

Signorielli, N. (2012). Television's gender-role images and contribution to stereotyping. In D. G. Singer & J. L. Singer (Eds.), *Handbook of children and the media* (2nd ed., pp. 321–339). Los Angeles, CA: SAGE.

Silber, M. H., Ancoli-Israel, S., Bonnet, M. H., Chokroverty, S., Grigg-Damberger, M. M., Hirshkowitz, M., Iber, C. (2007). The visual scoring of sleep in adults. *Journal of Clinical Sleep Medicine, 3*(2), 121–131.

Silbersweig, D. A., Stern, E., Frith, C., Cahill, C., Holmes, A., Grootoonk, S., . . . Frackowiak, R. S. J. (1995). A functional neuroanatomy of hallucinations in schizophrenia. Nature *378*, 176–179.

Silke, A. (2003). Deindividuation, anonymity, and violence: Findings from Northern Ireland. *The Journal of Social Psychology, 143*(4), 493–499.

Silva, E. J. & Duffy, J. F. (2008). Sleep inertia varies with circadian phase and sleep stage in older adults. *Behavioral Neuroscience, 122*(4), 928–935.

Silverstein, S. (1964). *The giving tree*. New York, NY: Harper Collins.

Silvia, P. J. (2008). Interest—The curious emotion. *Current Directions in Psychological Science, 17*(1), 57–60.

Silvia, P. J. (2012). Curiosity and motivation. In R. M. Ryan (Ed.), *The Oxford handbook of human motivation* (pp. 157–166). New York, NY: Oxford University Press.

Silvia, P. J., Martin, C., & Nusbaum, E. C. (2009). A snapshot of creativity: Evaluating a quick and simple method for assessing divergent thinking. *Thinking Skills and Creativity, 4*(2), 79–85.

Simmons, B. L., & Nelson, D. L. (2007). Eustress at work: Extending the holistic stress model. In B. L. Simmons & D. L. Nelson (Eds.), *Positive organizational behaviour* (pp. 40–53). London, UK: SAGE.

Simon, B., & Mummendey, A. (2012). Perceptions of relative group size and group homogeneity: We are the majority and they are all the same. *European Journal of Social Psychology, 20*(4), 351–356.

Simon, D. A., & Bjork, R. A. (2001). Metacognition in motor learning. *Journal of Experimental Psychology: Learning, Memory, and Cognition, 27*(4), 907.

Simon, G. E., Von Korff, M., Saunders, K., Miglioretti, D. L., Crane, P. K., Van Belle, G., & Kessler, R. C. (2006). Association between obesity and psychiatric disorders in the U.S. adult population. *Archives of General Psychiatry, 63*(7), 824–830.

Simon, L. (1998). *Genuine reality: A life of William James*. New York, NY: Harcourt Brace.

Simon-Rusinowitz, L., Krach, C. A., Marks, L. N., Piktialis, D., & Wilson, L. B. (1996). Grandparents in the workplace: The effects of economic and labor trends. *Generations—Journal of the American Society on Aging, 20*(1), 41–44.

Simons, D. J., & Ambinder, M. S. (2005). Change blindness theory and consequences. *Current Directions in Psychological Science, 14*(1), 44–48.

Simons, D. J., & Chabris, C. F. (1999). Gorillas in our midst: Sustained inattentional blindness for dynamic events. *Perception-London, 28*(9), 1059–1074.

Simons, D. J., & Levin, D. T. (1997). Change blindness. *Trends in Cognitive Sciences, 1*(7), 261–267.

Simons, D. J., & Rensink, R. A. (2005). Change blindness: Past, present, and future. *Trends in Cognitive Sciences, 9*(1), 16–20.

Simonsen, E. (2010). The integration of categorical and dimensional approaches to psychopathology. In T. Millon, R. F. Krueger, & E. Simonsen (Eds.), *Contemporary directions in psychopathology: Scientific foundations of the DSM-V and ICD-11* (pp. 350–361). New York, NY: Guilford Press.

Simonton, D. K. (2000). Creativity: Cognitive, personal, developmental, and social aspects. *American Psychologist, 55*(1), 151–158.

Simonton, D. K. (2008). Bilingualism and creativity. In J. Altarriba & R. R. Heredia (Eds.) *An introduction to bilingualism: Principles and processes* (pp. 147–166). Mahwah, NJ: Lawrence Erlbaum.

Simonton, D. K., & Damian, R. I. (2013). Creativity. In D. Reisberg (Ed.), *The Oxford handbook of cognitive psychology* (pp. 795–809). Oxford, UK: Oxford University Press.

Simpkins, C. A., & Simpkins, A. M. (2009). *Meditation for therapists and their clients*. New York, NY: W. W. Norton.

Sin, N. L., & Lyubomirsky, S. (2009). Enhancing well-being and alleviating depressive symptoms with positive psychology interventions: A practice-friendly meta-analysis. *Journal of Clinical Psychology, 65*(5), 467–487.

Sinclair, R. C., Hoffman, C., Mark, M. M., Martin, L. L., & Pickering, T. L. (1994). Construct accessibility and the misattribution of arousal: Schachter and Singer revisited. *Psychological Science, 5*(1), 15–19.

Singer, D. G. & Singer, J. L. (2012). Introduction: Why a handbook on children and the media? In D. G. Singer & J. L. Singer (Eds.), *Handbook of children and the media* (2nd ed., pp. 1–6). Los Angeles, CA: SAGE.

Singer, D. G., & Revenson, T. A. (1996). *A Piaget primer* (Rev. ed.). New York, NY: Plume.

Sinha, P., Ostrovsky, Y., & Russell, R. (2010). Face perception. In E. B. Goldstein (Ed.), *Encyclopedia of perception* (pp. 445–449). Thousand Oaks, CA: SAGE.

Sivertsen, B., Omvik, S., Pallesen, S., Bjorvatn, B., Havik, O. E., Kvale, G., Nordhus, I. H. (2006). Cognitive behavioral therapy vs zopiclone for treatment of chronic primary insomnia in older adults: A randomized controlled trial. *Journal of the American Medical Association, 295*(24), 2851–2858.

Skelton, R. M. (Ed.). (2006). *The Edinburgh international encyclopaedia of psychoanalysis*. Edinburgh, UK: Edinburgh University Press.Skinner, B. F. (1938). *The behavior of organisms: An experimental analysis*. New York, NY: Appleton-Century.

Skelton, R. M. (Ed.). (2006). *The Edinburgh international encyclopaedia of psychoanalysis*. Edinburgh, UK: Edinburgh University Press.

Skibbe, L. E., Justice, L. M., Zucker, T. A., & McGinty, A. S. (2008). Relations among maternal literacy beliefs, home literacy practices, and the emergent literacy skills of preschoolers with specific language impairment. *Early Education and Development, 19*(1), 68–88.

Skinner, B. F. (1938). *The behavior of organisms: An experimental analysis*. New York, NY: Appleton-Century.

Skinner, B. F. (1961). Teaching machines. *Scientific American, 205*(5), 91–102.

Skinner, B. F. (1971). *Beyond freedom and dignity*. New York, NY: Bantam/Vintage.

Skinner, B. F. (1974). *About behaviorism*. New York, NY: Random House.

Skinner, B. F. (1976). *Walden two (Reissued)*. New York, NY: Macmillan.

Slater, A., & Johnson, S. P. (1998). Visual sensory and perceptual abilities of the newborn: Beyond the blooming, buzzing confusion. In F. Simion & G. Butterworth (Eds.), *The development of sensory, motor and cognitive capacities in early infancy* (pp. 121–141). Hove, UK: Psychology Press.

Slavin, L. A., Rainer, K. L., McCreary, M. L., & Gowda, K. K. (1991). Toward a multicultural model of the stress process. *Journal of Counseling & Development, 70*(1), 156–163.

Sleiman, M., Gundel, L. A., Pankow, J. F., Jacob, P., Singer, B. C., & Destaillats, H. (2010). Formation of carcinogens indoors by surface-mediated reactions of nicotine with nitrous acid, leading to potential thirdhand smoke hazards. *Proceedings of the National Academy of Sciences, 107*(15), 6576–6581.

Sloman, S. A. (1996). The empirical case for two systems of reasoning. *Psychological Bulletin, 119*(1), 3–22.

Slovic, P. (1975). Choice between equally valued alternatives. *Journal of Experimental psychology: Human Perception and Performance, 1*(3), 280–287.

Small, S. A., & Heeger, D. J. (2013). Functional imaging of cognition. In E. R. Kandel, J. H. Schwartz, T. M. Jessell, S. A. Siegelbaum, & A. J. Hudspeth (Eds.), *Principles of neural science* (5th ed.), pp. 426–441). New York, NY: McGraw-Hill.

Smetana, J. G., & Villalobos, M. (2009). Social cognitive development in adolescence. In R. M. Lerner & L. Steinberg (Eds.), *Handbook of adolescent psychology* (3rd ed., Vol. 1, pp. 187–228). Hoboken, NJ: Wiley.

Smith, A. R., Hames, J. L., & Joiner, T. E. (2013). Status update: Maladaptive Facebook usage predicts increases in body dissatisfaction and bulimic symptoms. *Journal of Affective Disorders, 149*(1), 235–240.

Smith, D., & Cummins, S. (2011). Food desserts. In J. H. Cawley (Ed.), *The Oxford handbook of the social science of obesity* (pp. 452–462). New York, NY: Oxford University Press.

Smith, E. E., & Medin, D. L. (1981). *Categories and concepts* (pp. 51–83). Cambridge, MA: Harvard University Press.

Smith, J. D., & Minda, J. P. (1998). Prototypes in the mist: The early epochs of category learning. *Journal of Experimental Psychology: Learning, Memory, and Cognition, 24*(6), 1411–1436.

Smith, J. D., & Minda, J. P. (2000). Thirty categorization results in search of a model. *Journal of Experimental Psychology: Learning, Memory, and Cognition, 26*(1), 3–27.

Smith, K. (2012). Against homeopathy–A utilitarian perspective. *Bioethics, 26*(8), 398–409.

Smith, K. D., Keating, J. P., & Stotland, E. (1989). Altruism reconsidered: The effect of denying feedback on a victim's status to empathic witnesses. *Journal of Personality and Social Psychology, 57*(4), 641.

Smith, L. (2009). Introduction II. Jean Piaget: From boy to man. In U. Müller, J. I. M. Carpendale, & L. Smith (Eds.), *The Cambridge companion to Piaget* (pp. 18–27). New York, NY: Cambridge University Press.

Smith, L. D. (1996). Conclusion: Situating B. F. Skinner and behaviorism in American culture. In L. D. Smith & W. R. Woodward (Eds.), *B. F. Skinner and behaviorism in American culture* (pp. 294–315). Bethlehem, PA: Lehigh University Press.

Smith, M. L., & Glass, G. V. (1977). Meta-analysis of psychotherapy outcome studies. *American psychologist, 32*(9), 752–760.

Smith, M. L., Glass, G. V., & Miller, T. I. (1980). *The benefits of psychotherapy*. Baltimore, MD: Johns Hopkins University Press.

Smith, M. T., Perlis, M. L., Park, A., Smith, M. S., Pennington, J., Giles, D. E., & Buysse, D. J. (2002). Comparative meta-analysis of pharmacotherapy and behavior therapy for persistent insomnia. *American Journal of Psychiatry, 159*(1), 5–11.

Smith, N., Young, A., & Lee, C. (2004). Optimism, health-related hardiness and well-being among older Australian women. *Journal of Health Psychology, 9*(6), 741–752.

Smith, P. J., Blumenthal, J. A., Hoffman, B. M., Cooper, H., Strauman, T. A., Welsh-Bohmer, K., . . . Sherwood, A. (2010). Aerobic exercise and neurocognitive performance: A meta-analytic review of randomized controlled trials. *Psychosomatic Medicine, 72*(3), 239–252.

Smith, R. A., & Davis, S. F. (2003). The changing face of research methods. In S. F. Davis (Ed.), *Handbook of research methods in experimental psychology* (pp. 106–126). Malden, MA: Blackwell.

Smith, R. S., Guilleminault, C., & Efron, B. (1997). Sports, sleep, and circadian rhythms: Circadian rhythms and enhanced athletic performance in the National Football League. *Sleep, 20*(5), 362–365.

Smith, S. M. (2011). Blocking out blocks: Adaptive forgetting of fixation in memory, problem solving, and creative ideation. In A. S. Benjamin (Ed.), *Successful remembering and successful forgetting: A Festschrift in honor of Robert A. Bjork* (pp. 153–174). New York, NY: Psychology Press.

Smith, S. M., & Vela, E. (2001). Environmental context-dependent memory: A review and meta-analysis. *Psychonomic Bulletin & Review, 8*(2), 203–220.

Smith, S. M., & Ward T. B. (2012). Cognition and the creation of ideas. In K. J. Holyoak and R. G. Morrison (Eds.), *The Oxford handbook of thinking and reasoning* (pp. 456–474). Oxford, UK: Oxford University Press.

Smith, S. R., & Archer, R. P. (2008). Introducing personality assessment. In R. P. Archer & S. R. Smith (Eds.), *Personality assessment* (pp. 1–35). New York, NY: Routledge.

Smith, T. W., & MacKenzie, J. (2006). Personality and risk of physical illness. *Annual Review of Clinical Psychology, 2*, 435–467.

Smits, J. A. J., O'Cleirigh, C. M., & Otto, M. W. (2006). Panic and agoraphobia. In M. Hersen & J. C. Thomas (Eds.), *Comprehensive handbook of personality and psychopathology* (Vol. 2, pp. 121–137). Hoboken, NJ: Wiley.

Smoller, J. W., Gardner-Schuster, E., & Misiaszek, M. (2008). Genetics of anxiety: Would the genome recognize the DSM? *Depression and Anxiety, 25*(4), 368–377.

Snarey, J. R. (2012). Lawrence Kohlberg: Moral biography, moral psychology, and moral pedagogy. In W. E. Pickren, D. A. Dewsbury, & M. Wertheimer (Eds.), *Portraits of pioneers in developmental psychology* (pp. 277–296). New York: Psychology Press.

Snowden, L. R. (2007). Explaining mental health treatment disparities: Ethnic and cultural differences in family involvement. *Culture, Medicine and Psychiatry, 31*(3), 389–402.

Snowden, L. R. (2012). Health and mental health policies' role in better understanding and closing African American–White American disparities in treatment access and quality of care. *American Psychologist, 67*(7), 524–531.

Snowden, L. R., & Yamada, A. M. (2005). Cultural differences in access to care. *Annual Review of Clinical Psychology, 1*, 143–166.

Snowden, L. R., Masland, M. C., Peng, C. J., Lou, C. W. M., & Wallace, N. T. (2011). Limited English proficient Asian Americans: Threshold language policy and access to mental health treatment. *Social Science & Medicine, 72*(2), 230–237.

Snowden, L. R., Masland, M., & Guerrero, R. (2007). Federal civil rights policy and mental health treatment access for persons with limited English proficiency. *American Psychologist, 62*(2), 109–117.

Snowling, M. J., & Hulme, C. (Eds.). (2008). *The science of reading: A handbook* (Vol. 9). Malden, MA: Wiley.

Snyder, C. R., Lopez, S. J., & Pedrotti, J. T. (2011). *Positive psychology: The scientific and practical explorations of human strengths* (2nd ed.). Los Angeles, CA: SAGE.

Snyder, M., & Deaux, K. (2012). Personality and social psychology: Crossing boundaries and integrating perspectives. In K. Deaux & M. Snyder (Eds.), *The Oxford handbook of personality and social psychology* (pp. 3–9). New York, NY: Oxford University Press.

Sobkowicz, P., Thelwall, M., Buckley, K., Paltoglou, G., & Sobkowicz, A. (2013). Lognormal distributions of user post lengths in Internet discussions—A consequence of the Weber-Fechner law? *EPJ Data Science, 2*(1), 1–20.

Society for Community Research and Action. (2016). What we do. Retrieved from http://www.scra27.org/what-we-do/.

Sokal, M. M. (2002). Origins and early years of the American psychological association, 1890–1906. In W. E. Pickren & D. A. Dewsbury (Eds.), *Evolving perspectives on the history of psychology* (pp. 141–168). Washington, DC: American Psychological Association.

Soldz, S., & Vaillant, G. E. (1999). The Big Five personality traits and the life course: A 45-year longitudinal study. *Journal of Research in Personality, 33*(2), 208–232.

Solomon, R. C. (2008). The philosophy of emotions. In M. Lewis, J. M. Haviland-Jones, & L. F. Barrett (Eds.), *Handbook of emotions*, (3rd. ed., pp. 3–16). New York, NY: Guilford Press.

Somary, K., & Strieker, G. (1998). Becoming a grandparent: A longitudinal study of expectations and early experiences as a function of sex and lineage. *The Gerontologist, 38*(1), 53–61.

Sommers-Flanagan, J., & Sommers-Flanagan, R. (2009). *Clinical interviewing* (4th ed.). Hoboken, NJ: Wiley.

Sommers-Flanagan, R. (2012). Boundaries, multiple roles, and the professional relationship. In S. J. Knapp (Ed.), *APA handbook of ethics in psychology* (Vol. 1, pp. 241–277). Washington, DC: American Psychological Association.

Somerville, L. H. (2013). The teenage brain sensitivity to social evaluation. *Current Directions in Psychological Science, 22*(2), 121–127.

Son, L. K. (2004). Spacing one's study: Evidence for a metacognitive control strategy. *Journal of Experimental Psychology: Learning, Memory, and Cognition, 30*(3), 601.

Son, L. K. (2005). Metacognitive control: Children's short-term versus long-term study strategies. *The Journal of General Psychology, 132*(4), 347–364.

Son, L. K., & Kornell, N. (2008). Research on the allocation of study time: Key studies from 1890 to the present (and beyond). In J. Dunlosky & R. A. Bjork (Eds.), *Handbook of metamemory and memory* (pp. 333–351). New York, NY: Psychological Press.

Song, H., Kempermann, G., Wadiche, L. O., Zhao, C., Schinder, A. F., & Bischofberger, J. (2005). New neurons in the adult mammalian brain: Synaptogenesis and functional integration. *The Journal of Neuroscience, 25*(45), 10366–10368.

Sonnby-Borgström, M. (2002). Automatic mimicry reactions as related to differences in emotional empathy. *Scandinavian Journal of Psychology, 43*(5), 433–443.

Sonne, J. L. (2012). Sexualized relationships. In S. J. Knapp (Ed.), *APA handbook of ethics in psychology* (Vol. 1, pp. 295–310). Washington, DC: American Psychological Association.

Soraci, S. A., Carlin, M. T., Read, J. D., Pogoda, T. K., Wakeford, Y., Cavanagh, S., & Shin, L. (2007). Psychological impairment, eyewitness testimony, and false memories: Individual differences. In M. P. Toglia, J. D. Read, D. F. Ross, & R. C. L. Lindsay (Eds.), *The handbook of eyewitness psychology: Memory for events* (Vol I, pp. 261–297). East Sussex, UK: Psychology Press.

Sorce, J. F., Emde, R. N., Campos, J. J., & Klinnert, M. D. (1985). Maternal emotional signaling: Its effect on the visual cliff behavior of 1-year-olds. *Developmental Psychology, 21*(1), 195–200.

Sorkin, D., Rook, K. S., & Lu, J. L. (2002). Loneliness, lack of emotional support, lack of companionship, and the likelihood of having a heart condition in an elderly sample. *Annals of Behavioral Medicine, 24*(4), 290–298.

Sorkin, J. D., Muller, D. C., & Andres, R. (1999). Longitudinal change in height of men and women: Implications for interpretation of the body mass index: The Baltimore longitudinal study of aging. *American Journal of Epidemiology, 150*(9), 969–977.

Soto-Faraco, S., & Alsius, A. (2009). Deconstructing the McGurk–MacDonald illusion. *Journal of Experimental Psychology: Human Perception and Performance, 35*(2), 580–587.

Sourander, A. (2001). Emotional and behavioural problems in a sample of Finnish three-year-olds. *European Child & Adolescent Psychiatry, 10*(2), 98–104.

Soussignan, R. (2002). Duchenne smile, emotional experience, and autonomic reactivity: A test of the facial feedback hypothesis. *Emotion, 2*(1), 52–74.

South, S. C., Oltmanns, T. F., & Krueger, R. F. (2011). The spectrum of personality disorders. In D. H. Barlow (Ed.), *The Oxford handbook of clinical psychology* (pp. 530–550). New York, NY: Oxford University Press.

Sparr, L. F., & Pitman, R. K. (2007). PTSD and the law. In M. J. Friedman, T. M. Keane, & P. A. Resick (Eds.), *Handbook of PTSD: Science and practice* (pp. 449–468). New York, NY: Guilford Press.

Sparrenberger, F., Cichelero, F. T., Ascoli, A. M., Fonseca, F. P., Weiss, G., Berwanger, O., . . . Fuchs, F. D. (2009). Does psychosocial stress cause hypertension?: A systematic review of observational studies. *Journal of Human Hypertension, 23*(1), 12–19.

Speakman, J. R., Levitsky, D. A., Allison, D. B., Bray, M. S., de Castro, J. M., Clegg, D. J., . . . Hebebrand, J. (2011). Set points, settling points and some alternative models: Theoretical options to understand how genes and environments combine to regulate body adiposity. *Disease Models & Mechanisms, 4*(6), 733–745.

Spear, N. E. (2007). Retrieval: Properties and effects. In H. L. Roediger, Y. Dudai, & S. M. Fitzpatrick (Eds.), *Science of memory: Concepts* (pp. 215–219). Oxford, UK: Oxford University Press.

Spearman, C. (1904). "General intelligence," objectively determined and measured. *The American Journal of Psychology, 15*(2), 201–292.
Spearman, C. (1923). *The nature of "intelligence" and the principles of cognition*. London, UK: Macmillan.
Speekenbring, M., & Shanks, D. R. (2013). Decision making. In D. Reisberg (Ed.), *The Oxford handbook of cognitive psychology* (pp. 682–703). Oxford, UK: Oxford University Press.
Spence, S. H., Donovan, C. L., March, S., Gamble, A., Anderson, R. E., Prosser, S., & Kenardy, J. (2011). A randomized controlled trial of online versus clinic-based CBT for adolescent anxiety. *Journal of Consulting and Clinical Psychology, 79*(5), 629–642.
Spencer, A. (2001). Morphology. In M. Aronoff & J. Rees-Miller (Eds.), *The handbook of linguistics* (pp. 213–237). Malden, MA: Blackwell.
Spencer, S. J., Steele, C. M., & Quinn, D. M. (1999). Stereotype threat and women's math performance. *Journal of Experimental Social Psychology, 35*(1), 4–28.
Sperling, G. (1960). The information available in brief visual presentations. *Psychological Monographs: General and Applied, 74*(11), 1–29.
Sperry, L. (2016). *Handbook of diagnosis and treatment of the DSM-5 personality disorders* (3rd ed.). New York, NY: Taylor & Francis.
Spiegel, D. (2003). Negative and positive visual hypnotic hallucinations: Attending inside and out. *International Journal of Clinical and Experimental Hypnosis, 51*(2), 130–146.
Spiegler, M. D., & Guevremont, D. C. (2010). *Contemporary behavior therapy* (5th ed.). Belmont, CA: Wadsworth.
Spielman, A. J., Saskin, P., & Thorpy, M. J. (1987). Treatment of chronic insomnia by restriction of time in bed. *Sleep, 10*(1), 45–56.
Spokas, M. E., Rodebaugh, T. L., & Heimburg, R. G. (2008). Treatment research. In M. Hersen & A. M. Gross (Eds.), *Handbook of clinical psychology* (Vol. 1, pp. 300–338). Hoboken, NJ: Wiley.
Spoormaker, V. I., & Lancee, J. (2012). Lucid dreaming therapy for nightmares. In D. Barrett & P. McNamara (Eds.), *Encyclopedia of sleep and dreams: The Evolution, Function, Nature, and Mysteries of Slumber* (Vol. 1, pp. 401–403). Santa Barbara, CA: Greenwood.
Sprecher, S. (1987). The effects of self-disclosure given and received on affection for an intimate partner and stability of the relationship. *Journal of Social and Personal Relationships, 4*(2), 115–127.
Sprecher, S., & Regan, P. C. (2007). Passionate and companionate love in courting and young married couples. *Sociological Inquiry, 68*(2), 163–185.
Spring, B., & Neville, K. (2011). Evidence-based practice in clinical psychology. In D. H. Barlow (Ed.), *The Oxford handbook of clinical psychology* (pp. 128–149). New York, NY: Oxford University Press.
Squire, L. R. (1992). Memory and the hippocampus: A synthesis from findings with rats, monkeys, and humans. *Psychological Review, 99*(2), 195–231.
Squire, L. R. (2004). Memory systems of the brain: A brief history and current perspective. *Neurobiology of Learning and Memory, 82*(3), 171–177.
Squire, L. R., & Zola, S. M. (1996). Structure and function of declarative and nondeclarative memory systems. *Proceedings of the National Academy of Sciences, 93*(24), 13515–13522.
Srivastava, S., John, O. P., Gosling, S. D., & Potter, J. (2003). Development of personality in early and middle adulthood: Set like plaster or persistent change? *Journal of Personality and Social Psychology, 84*, 1041–1053.
Srivastava, S., Tamir, M., McGonigal, K. M., John, O. P., & Gross, J. J. (2009). The social costs of emotional suppression: A prospective study of the transition to college. *Journal of Personality and Social Psychology, 96*(4), 883–897.
Sroufe, L. A. (2005). Attachment and development: A prospective, longitudinal study from birth to adulthood. *Attachment & Human Development, 7*(4), 349–367.
Sroufe, L. A., Egeland, B., Carlson, E. A., & Collins, W. A. (2005). *The development of the person: The Minnesota study of risk and adaptation from birth to adulthood*. New York, NY: Guilford Press.
Srull, T. K., & Wyer, R. S. (1979). The role of category accessibility in the interpretation of information about persons: Some determinants and implications. *Journal of Personality and Social Psychology, 37*(10), 1660–1672.
Stadler, M. A. & Frensch, P. A. (Eds.). (1998). *Handbook of implicit learning*. Thousand Oaks, CA: SAGE.
Stagner, R. (1988). *A history of psychological theories*. New York, NY: Macmillan.
Stake, J. E., & Eisele, H. (2010). Gender and personality. In J. C. Chrisler & D. R. McCreary (Eds.), *Handbook of gender research in psychology* (Vol. 1, pp. 19–40). New York, NY: Springer Science+Business Media.
Stalder, D. R. (2005). Learning and motivational benefits of acronym use in introductory psychology. *Teaching of Psychology, 32*, 222–228.
Stam, K. R., & Stanton, J. M. (2010). Events, emotions, and technology: Examining acceptance of workplace technology changes. *Information Technology & People, 23*(1), 23–53.
Stangor, C., & McMillan, D. (1992). Memory for expectancy-congruent and expectancy-incongruent information: A review of the social and social developmental literatures. *Psychological Bulletin, 111*(1), 42–61.
Stankiewicz, J. M., & Rosselli, F. (2008). Women as sex objects and victims in print advertisements. *Sex Roles, 58*(7-8), 579–589.
Stanovich, K. (2011). *Rationality and the reflective mind*. Oxford, UK: Oxford University Press.
Stanovich, K. E. (2013). *How to think straight about psychology* (10th ed.). Boston, MA: Pearson.
Stathopoulou, G., Powers, M. B., Berry, A. C., Smits, J. A., & Otto, M. W. (2006). Exercise interventions for mental health: A quantitative and qualitative review. *Clinical Psychology: Science and Practice, 13*(2), 179–193.
Stattin, H., & Klackenberg, G. (1992). Discordant family relations in intact families: Developmental tendencies over 18 years. *Journal of Marriage and the Family, 54* (4), 940–956.
Stavro, K., Pelletier, J., & Potvin, S. (2013). Widespread and sustained cognitive deficits in alcoholism: A meta-analysis. *Addiction Biology, 18*(2), 203–213.
Steele, C. M. (1997). A threat in the air: How stereotypes shape intellectual identity and performance. *American Psychologist, 52*(6), 613–629.
Steele, C. M. (2010). *Whistling Vivaldi: And other clues to how stereotypes affect us*. New York, NY: W. W. Norton.
Steele, C. M., & Aronson, J. A. (2004). Stereotype threat does not live by Steele and Aronson alone. *American Psychologist*, 59(1), 47–48.
Steenari, M. R., Vuontela, V., Paavonen, E. J., Carlson, S., Fjällberg, M., & Aronen, E. T. (2003). Working memory and sleep in 6- to 13-year-old schoolchildren. *Journal of the American Academy of Child & Adolescent Psychiatry, 42*(1), 85–92.
Steere, J., & Cooper, P. J. (1993). The effects on eating of dietary restraint, anxiety, and hunger. *International Journal of Eating Disorders, 13*(2), 211–219.
Steger, B. (2003). Negotiating sleep patterns in Japan. In B. Steger & L. Brunt (Eds.), *Night-time and sleep in Asia and the West: Exploring the dark side of life* (pp. 65–86). Vienna, Austria: University of Vienna Press.
Steger, B., & Brunt, L. (2003). Introduction: Into the night and the world of sleep. In B. Steger & L. Brunt (Eds.), *Night-time and sleep in Asia and the West: Exploring the dark side of life* (pp. 1–23). Vienna, Austria: University of Vienna Press.
Steiger, H., & Bruce, K. R. (2009). Eating disorders. In P. H. Blaney & T. Millon (Eds.), *Oxford textbook of psychopathology* (2nd ed., pp. 431–451). New York, NY: Oxford University Press.
Stein, D. J., & Williams, D. (2010). Cultural and social aspects of anxiety disorders. In D. J. Stein, E. Hollander, & B. O. Rothbaum (Eds.), *Textbook of anxiety disorders* (2nd ed., pp. 717–729). Washington, DC: American Psychiatric Association.
Stein, S. (2008). Genetics. In K. Keller (Ed.), *Encyclopedia of obesity* (Vol. 2, pp. 321–325). Los Angeles, CA: SAGE.
Steinberg, L. (1981). Transformations in family relations at puberty. *Developmental Psychology, 17*(6), 833–840.
Steinberg, L. (1990). Interdependence in the family: Autonomy, conflict, and harmony in the parent–adolescent relationships. In S. S. Feldman & G. Elliott (Eds.), *At the threshold: The developing adolescent* (pp. 255–276). Cambridge, MA: Harvard University Press.
Steinberg, L., Elmen, J. D., & Mounts, N. S. (1989). Authoritative parenting, psychosocial maturity, and academic success among adolescents. *Child Development, 60*(6), 1424–1436.
Steinberg, L., Lamborn, S. D., Dornbusch, S. M. and Darling, N. (1992). Impact of parenting practices on adolescent achievement: Authoritative parenting, school involvement, and encouragement to succeed. *Child Development, 63*(5), 1266–1281.
Steinberg, L., Mounts, N. S., Lamborn, S. D., & Dornbusch, S. M. (1991). Authoritative parenting and adolescent adjustment across varied ecological niches. *Journal of Research on Adolescence, 1*(1), 19–36.
Steinberg, L., & Silk, J. S. (2002). Parenting adolescents. In M. H. Bornstein (Ed.), *Handbook of parenting* (Vol. 1, pp. 103–133). Mahwah, NJ: Lawrence Erlbaum.
Steiner, J. E. (1977). Facial expressions of the neonate infant indicating the hedonics of food-related chemical stimuli. In J. M. Weiffenbach (Ed.), *Taste and development: The genesis of sweet preference* (pp. 173–188). Bethesda, MD: Department of Health, Education, and Welfare.
Stephan, W. G., & Stephan, C. W. (2000). An integrated threat theory of prejudice. In S. Oskamp (Ed.), *Reducing prejudice and discrimination* (pp. 23–45). Mahwah, NJ: Lawrence Erlbaum.
Stepper, S., & Strack, F. (1993). Proprioceptive determinants of emotional and nonemotional feelings. *Journal of Personality and Social Psychology, 64*(2), 211–220.
Steptoe, A., Leigh, E. S., & Kumari, M. (2011). Positive affect and distressed affect over the day in older people. *Psychology and Aging, 26*(4), 956–965.
Steptoe, A., Lipsey, Z., & Wardle, J. (1998). Stress, hassles and variations in alcohol consumption, food choice and physical exercise: A diary study. *British Journal of Health Psychology, 3*(1), 51–63.
Sternberg, R. J. (1986). A triangular theory of love. *Psychological Review, 93*(2), 119–135.
Sternberg, R. J. (1999). The theory of successful intelligence. *Review of General Psychology, 3*(4), 292–316.
Sternberg, R. J. (2000). The concept of intelligence. In R. J. Sternberg (Ed.), *Handbook of intelligence* (pp. 3–15). Cambridge, UK: Cambridge University Press.
Sternberg, R. J. (2006). The nature of creativity. *Creativity Research Journal, 18*(1), 87–99.
Sternberg, R. J. (2007). Triangulating love. In T. Oord (Ed,), *The altruism reader: Selections from writings on love, religion, and science* (pp. 331–337). West Conshohocken, PA: Templeton Press.
Sternberg, R. J. (2011). Individual differences in cognitive development. In U. Goswami (Ed.), *The Wiley-Blackwell handbook of childhood cognitive development* (2nd ed., pp. 749–774). Malden, MA: Wiley-Blackwell.
Sternberg, R. J., & Barnes, M. L. (1989). *The psychology of love*. Princeton, NJ: Yale University Press.
Sternberg, R. J., & Lubart, T. I. (1991). An investment theory of creativity and its development. *Human Development, 34*(1), 1–31.

Sternberg, R. J., & Sternberg, K. (2010). *The psychologist's companion: A guide to writing scientific papers for students and researchers* (5th ed.). New York, NY: Cambridge University Press.
Sternberg, R. J. & Sternberg, K. (2012). *Cognitive psychology*. Belmont, CA: Wadsworth Cengage Learning.
Sterns, H. L., & Huyck, M. H. (2001). The role of work in midlife. In M. E. Lachman (Ed.), *Handbook of midlife development* (pp. 447–486). Hoboken, NJ: Wiley.
Sternthal, M. J., Jun, H. J., Earls, F., & Wright, R. J. (2010). Community violence and urban childhood asthma: A multilevel analysis. *European Respiratory Journal, 36*(6), 1400–1409.
Stevens, G., Owens, D., & Schaefer, E. C. (1990). Education and attractiveness in marriage choices. *Social Psychology Quarterly, 53*(1), 62–70.
Stewart, J. W., Quitkin, F. M., & Davies, C. (2006). Atypical depression, dysthymia, and cyclothymia. In D. J. Stein, D. J. Kupfer, & A. F. Schatzberg (Eds.), *The American Psychiatric Publishing textbook of mood disorders* (pp. 547–560). Washington, DC: American Psychiatric Association.
Stewart, W. (2008). *A biographical dictionary of psychologists, psychiatrists and psychotherapists*. Jefferson, N.C: McFarland.
Stewart, W. F., Ricci, J. A., Chee, E., Hahn, S. R., & Morganstein, D. (2003). Cost of lost productive work time among U.S. workers with depression. *Journal of the American Medical Association, 289*(23), 3135–3144.
Stice, E. (2002). Risk and maintenance factors for eating pathology: A meta-analytic review. *Psychological Bulletin, 128*(5), 825–848.
Stice, E., Marti, C. N., & Rohde, P. (2013). Prevalence, incidence, impairment, and course of the proposed DSM-5 eating disorder diagnoses in an 8-year prospective community study of young women. *Journal of Abnormal Psychology, 122*(2), 445–457.
Stice, E., Ragan, J., & Randall, P. (2004). Prospective relations between social support and depression: Differential direction of effects for parent and peer support? *Journal of Abnormal Psychology, 113*(1), 155–159.
Stockman, A. (2010). Color mixing. In E. B. Goldstein (Ed.), *Encyclopedia of perception* (pp. 262–264). Thousand Oaks, CA: SAGE.
Stoffregen, T. A., & Riccio, G. E. (1991). An ecological critique of the sensory conflict theory of motion sickness. *Ecological Psychology, 3*(3), 159–194.
Stoller, M. K. (1994). Economic effects of insomnia. *Clinical Therapeutics, 16*(5), 873–897.
Stone, A. A., & Brownell, K. D. (1994). The stress-eating paradox: Multiple daily measurements in adult males and females. *Psychology and Health, 9*(6), 425–436.
Stone, J., & Fernandez, N. C. (2008). To practice what we preach: The use of hypocrisy and cognitive dissonance to motivate behavior change. *Social and Personality Psychology Compass, 2*(2), 1024–1051.
Stone, M. H. (1997). *Healing the mind: A history of psychiatry from antiquity to the present*. New York, NY: W. W. Norton.
Storbeck, J., & Clore, G. L. (2005). With sadness comes accuracy; with happiness, false memory: Mood and the false memory effect. *Psychological Science, 16*(10), 785–791.
Strack, F., & Mussweiler, T. (1997). Explaining the enigmatic anchoring effect: Mechanisms of selective accessibility. *Journal of Personality and Social Psychology, 73*(3), 437–446.
Straker, G. 2013. Continuous traumatic stress: Personal reflections 25 years on. *Peace and Conflict: Journal of Peace Psychology, 19*(2), 209–217.
Straker, G., Moosa, F., & Team, S. C. (1988). Post-traumatic stress disorder: A reaction to state-supported child abuse and neglect. *Child Abuse & Neglect, 12*(3), 383–395.
Strakowski, S. M., & Shelton, R. C. (2006). Antipsychotic medications. In D. J. Stein, D. J. Kupfer, & A. F. Schatzberg (Eds.), *The American Psychiatric Publishing textbook of mood disorders* (pp. 291–304). Washington, DC: American Psychiatric Publishing.
Straube, T., Glauer, M., Dilger, S., Mentzel, H. J., & Miltner, W. H. (2006). Effects of cognitive-behavioral therapy on brain activation in specific phobia. *Neuroimage, 29*(1), 125–135.
Strauman, T. J. (1989). Self-discrepancies in clinical depression and social phobia: Cognitive structures that underlie emotional disorders? *Journal of Abnormal Psychology, 98*(1), 14–22.
Strauman, T. J. (2002). Self-regulation and depression. *Self and Identity, 1*(2), 151–157.
Straus, M. A., & Stewart, J. H. (1999). Corporal punishment by American parents: National data on prevalence, chronicity, severity, and duration, in relation to child and family characteristics. *Clinical Child and Family Psychology Review, 2*(2), 55–70.
Strenze, T. (2007). Intelligence and socioeconomic success: A meta-analytic review of longitudinal research. *Intelligence, 35*(5), 401–426.
Striano, J. (1988). *Can psychotherapists hurt you?* Santa Barbara, CA: Professional Press.
Stricker, G. (2010). *Psychotherapy integration*. Washington, DC: American Psychological Association.
Stringaris, A. (2013). Editorial: The new DSM is coming – it needs tough love. . . . *Journal of Child Psychology and Psychiatry, 54*(5), 501–502.
Strohmetz, D. B., Rind, B., Fisher, R., & Lynn, M. (2006). Sweetening the till: The use of candy to increase restaurant tipping. *Journal of Applied Social Psychology, 32*(2), 300–309.
Stronge, S., Greaves, L. M., Milojev, P., West-Newman, T., Barlow, F. K., & Sibley, C. G. (2015). Facebook is linked to body dissatisfaction: Comparing users and non-users. *Sex Roles, 73*(5-6), 200–213.
Stroud, L. R., Salovey, P., & Epel, E. S. (2002). Sex differences in stress responses: Social rejection versus achievement stress. *Biological Psychiatry, 52*(4), 318–327.
Stroup, T. S., Kraus, J. E., & Marder, S. R. (2006). Pharmacotherapies. In J. A. Lieberman, T. S. Stroup, & D. O. Perkins (Eds.), *The American Psychiatric Publishing textbook of schizophrenia* (pp. 303–325). Washington, DC: American Psychiatric Publishing.
Strube, M. J., Miles, M. E., & Finch, W. H. (1981). The social facilitation of a simple task: Field tests of alternative explanations. *Personality and Social Psychology Bulletin, 7*(4), 701–707.
Strupp, H. H. (1996). The tripartite model and the Consumer Reports study. *American Psychologist, 51*(10), 1017–1024.
Strupp, H. H., & Hadley, S. W. (1977). A tripartite model of mental health and therapeutic outcomes: With special reference to negative effects in psychotherapy. *American Psychologist, 32*(3), 187–196.
Stryker, S., & Statham, A. (1986). Symbolic interaction and role theory. In G. Lindzey & E. Aronson (Eds.), *The handbook of social psychology* (3rd ed., Vol.1, pp. 311–378). New York, NY: Random House.
Stubbe, M., & Holmes, J. (1995). You know, eh and other "exasperating expressions": An analysis of social and stylistic variation in the use of pragmatic devices in a sample of New Zealand English. *Language & Communication, 15*(1), 63–88.
Stunkard, A. J., Foch, T. T., & Hrubec, Z. (1986a). A twin study of human obesity. *JAMA, 256*(1), 51–54.
Stunkard, A. J., Sørensen, T. I., Hanis, C., Teasdale, T. W., Chakraborty, R., Schull, W. J., & Schulsinger, F. (1986b). An adoption study of human obesity. *New England Journal of Medicine, 314*(4), 193–198.
Sturm, R. & Datar, A. (2005). Body mass index in elementary school children, metropolitan area food prices and food outlet density. *Public Health, 119*(12), 1059–1068.
Sturm, R. (2002). The effects of obesity, smoking, and drinking on medical problems and costs. *Health Affairs, 21*(2), 245–253.
Sturmey, P., Ward-Horner, J., Marroquin, M., & Doran, E. (2007). Operant and respondent behavior. In P. Sturmey (Ed.), *Functional analysis in clinical treatment* (pp. 23–50). Burlington, MA: Elsevier.
Stuve, P., & Salinas, J. A. (2002). Token economy. In M. Hersen & W. Sledge (Eds.), *Encyclopedia of psychotherapy* (Vol. 2, pp. 821–827). San Diego, CA: Academic Press.
Suarez, L. M., Bennett, S. M., Goldstein, C. R., & Barlow, D. H. (2009). Understanding anxiety disorders from a "triple vulnerability" framework. In M. M. Antony & M. B. Stein (Eds.), *Oxford handbook of anxiety and related disorders* (pp. 153–172). New York, NY: Oxford University Press.
Subrahmanyam, K., & Greenfield, P. (2012). Digital media and youth: Games, Internet, and development. In D. G. Singer & J. L. Singer (Eds.), *Handbook of children and the media* (2nd ed., pp. 75–96). Los Angeles, CA: SAGE.
Sue, D. W. (2010a). *Microaggressions and marginality: Manifestation, dynamics, and impact*. Hoboken, NJ: Wiley.
Sue, D. W. (2010b). *Microaggressions in everyday life: Race, gender, and sexual orientation*. Hoboken, NJ: Wiley.
Sue, D. W., & Sue, D. (2013). *Counseling the culturally diverse: Theory and practice* (6th ed.). Hoboken, NJ: Wiley.
Sue, D. W., Capodilupo, C. M., Torino, G. C., Bucceri, J. M., Holder, A., Nadal, K. L., & Esquilin, M. (2007). Racial microaggressions in everyday life: Implications for clinical practice. *American Psychologist, 62*(4), 271–286.
Sue, D. W., Ivey, A. E., & Pedersen, P. B. (1996). *A theory of multicultural counseling and therapy*. Pacific Grove, CA: Brooks/Cole.
Sue, S. (1998). In search of cultural competence in psychotherapy and counseling. *American Psychologist, 53*(4), 440–448.
Sue, S. (2006). Cultural competency: From philosophy to research and practice. *Journal of Community Psychology, 34*(2), 237–245.
Sue, S. (2009). Ethnic minority psychology: Struggles and triumphs. *Cultural Diversity and Ethnic Minority Psychology, 15*(4), 409–415.
Sue, S., & Consolacion, T. B. (2003). Clinical psychology issues among Asian/Pacific Islander Americans. In J. S. Mio & G. Y. Iwamasa (Eds.), *Culturally diverse mental health: The challenges of research and resistance* (pp. 173–189). New York, NY: Brunner-Routledge.
Sue, S., & Sue, D. (2008). *Counseling the culturally diverse* (5th ed.). New York, NY: Wiley.
Sue, S., & Sue, D. (2012). *Counselling the culturally diverse* (6th ed.). New York, NY: Wiley.
Sue, S., & Zane, N. (2006). Ethnic minority populations have been neglected by evidence-based practices. In J. C. Norcross, L. E. Beutler, & R. F. Levant (Eds.), *Evidence-based practices in mental health: Debate and dialogue on the fundamental questions* (pp. 329–337). Washington, DC: American Psychological Association.
Suh, E., Diener, E., Oishi, S., & Triandis, H. C. (1998). The shifting basis of life satisfaction judgments across cultures. *Journal of Personality and Social Psychology, 74*(2), 482–493.
Sulaiman, A. H., Husain, R., & Seluakumaran, K. (2014). Evaluation of early hearing damage in personal listening device users using extended high-frequency audiometry and otoacoustic emissions. *European Archives of Oto-Rhino-Laryngology, 271*(6), 1463–1470.
Sulaiman, A. H., Seluakumaran, K., & Husain, R. (2013). Hearing risk associated with the usage of personal listening devices among urban high school students in Malaysia. *Public Health, 127*(8), 710–715.

Sullivan, B. F. & Pomerantz, A. M. (2014). Forensic psychology. In A. M. Pomerantz, *Clinical psychology: Science, practice, and culture* (3rd ed., DSM-5 Update), pp. 479–504. Los Angeles: SAGE.

Sullivan, E. V., & Marsh, L. (2003). Hippocampal volume deficits in alcoholic Korsakoff's syndrome. *Neurology, 61*(12), 1716–1719.

Sullivan, P. F., Daly, M. J., & O'Donovan, M. (2012). Genetic architectures of psychiatric disorders: The emerging picture and its implications. *Nature Reviews Genetics, 13*(8), 537–551.

Sullivan, S. A., & Birch, L. L. (1990). Pass the sugar, pass the salt: Experience dictates preference. *Developmental Psychology, 26*(4), 546–551.

Sulloway, F. J. (1996). *Born to rebel: Birth order, family dynamics, and creative lives*. New York, NY: Pantheon.

Sulloway, F. J. (2001). Birth order, sibling competition, and human behavior. In H. R. Holcomb III (Ed.), *Conceptual challenges in evolutionary psychology: Innovative research strategies* (pp. 39–83). Boston, MA: Kluwer Academic Publishers.

Sulloway, F. J. (2009). Sources of scientific innovation: A meta-analytic approach. *Perspectives on Psychological Science, 4*(5), 455–459.

Sulloway, F. J. (2011). Why siblings are like Darwin's finches: Birth order, sibling competition, and adaptive divergence within the family. In D. M. Buss & P. H. Hawley (Eds.), *The evolution of personality and individual differences* (pp. 86–120). New York, NY: Oxford University Press.

Sulloway, F. J., & Zweigenhaft, R. L. (2010). Birth order and risk taking in athletics: A meta-analysis and study of major league baseball. *Personality and Social Psychology Review, 14*(4), 402–416.

Suls, J., & Wheeler, L. (2012). Social comparison theory. In P. A. M. Van Lange, A. W. Kruglanski, & E. T. Higgins (Eds.), *Handbook of theories of social psychology* (Vol.1, pp. 460–482). Thousand Oaks, CA: SAGE.

Summerfield, Q. (1992). Lipreading and audio-visual speech perception. *Philosophical Transactions of the Royal Society of London. Series B: Biological Sciences, 335*(1273), 71–78.

Sundberg, M. L., Michael, J., Partington, J. W., & Sundberg, C. A. (1996). The role of automatic reinforcement in early language acquisition. *The Analysis of Verbal Behavior, 13*, 21–37.

Super, C. M. & Harkness, S. (2013). Culture and children's sleep. In A. R. Wolfson & H. Montgomery-Downs, *The Oxford handbook of infant, child, and adolescent sleep and behavior* (pp. 81–98). New York, NY: Oxford University Press.

Surawski, M. K., & Ossoff, E. P. (2006). The effects of physical and vocal attractiveness on impression formation of politicians. *Current Psychology, 25*(1), 15–27.

Susman, E. J., & Dorn, L. D. (2009). Puberty: Its role in development. In R. M. Lerner & L. Steinberg (Eds.), *Handbook of adolescent psychology* (3rd ed., Vol. 1, pp. 116–151). Hoboken, NJ: Wiley.

Susser, E., & Opler, M. (2006). Prenatal events that influence schizophrenia. In T. Sharma & P. D. Harvey (Eds.), *The early course of schizophrenia* (pp. 3–18). Oxford, UK: Oxford University Press.

Sutherland, C. (1990). Changes in religious beliefs, attitudes, and practices following near-death experiences: An Australian study. *Journal of Near-Death Studies, 9*, 21–31.

Sutherland, P. A. (1992). *Cognitive development today: Piaget and his critics*. Thousand Oaks, CA: SAGE.

Suzuki, L. A. & Ponterotto, J. G. (Eds.) (2008). *Handbook of multicultural assessment: Clinical, psychological, and educational applications* (3rd ed.). San Francisco, CA: Jossey-Bass.

Suzuki, L. A., Short, E. L., & Lee, C. S. (2011). Racial and ethnic group differences in intelligence in the United States. In R. J. Sternberg & S. B. Kaufman (Eds.), *The Cambridge handbook of intelligence* (pp. 273– 292). Cambridge, UK: Cambridge University Press.

Suzuki, W. A. (2009). Comparative analysis of the cortical afferents, intrinsic projections, and interconnections of the parahippocampal region in monkeys and rats. In M. S. Gazzaniga (Ed.), *The cognitive neurosciences* (4th ed., pp. 659–674). Cambridge, MA: MIT Press.

Swaab, D. F., & Hofman, M. A. (1990). An enlarged suprachiasmatic nucleus in homosexual men. *Brain Research, 537*(1), 141–148.

Swain, J., Hancock, K., Hainsworth, C., & Bowman, J. (2013). Acceptance and commitment therapy in the treatment of anxiety: A systematic review. *Clinical Psychology Review, 33*(8), 965–978.

Swanson, H. L., & Berninger, V. W. (1996). Individual differences in children's working memory and writing skill. *Journal of Experimental Child Psychology, 63*(2), 358–385.

Swartz, H. A., & Markowitz, J. C. (2009). Techniques of individual interpersonal psychotherapy. In G. O. Gabbard (Ed.), *Textbook of psychotherapeutic treatments* (pp. 309–338). Washington, DC: American Psychiatric Publishing.

Swartz, K. L. (2007). *Depression and anxiety: Your personal guide to prevention, diagnosis, and treatment (The Johns Hopkins white papers)*. Baltimore, MD: Johns Hopkins Medicine.

Sweeney, T. J. (1998). *Adlerian counseling and psychotherapy: A practitioner's approach* (5th ed.). New York, NY: Routledge.

Symms, M., Jäger, H. R., Schmierer, K., & Yousry, T. A. (2004). A review of structural magnetic resonance neuroimaging. *Journal of Neurology, Neurosurgery & Psychiatry, 75*(9), 1235–1244.

Sysko, R., & Wilson, G. T. (2011). Eating disorders. In D. H. Barlow (Ed.), *The Oxford handbook of clinical psychology* (pp. 387–404). New York, NY: Oxford University Press.

Taber, K. H., Wen, C., Khan, A., & Hurley, R. A. (2004). The limbic thalamus. *Journal of Neuropsychiatry and Clinical Neurosciences, 16*(2), 127–132.

Tafarodi, R. W., & Smith, A. J. (2001). Individualism–collectivism and depressive sensitivity to life events: The case of Malaysian sojourners. *International Journal of Intercultural Relations, 25*(1), 73–88.

Taiana, C. (2006). Transatlantic migration of the disciplines of the mind: Examination of the reception of Wundt's and Freud's theories in Argentina. In A. C. Brock (Ed.), *Internationalizing the history of psychology* (pp. 34–55). New York, NY: New York University Press.

Tait, D. M., & Carroll, J. (2010). Color deficiency. In E. B. Goldstein (Ed.), *Encyclopedia of perception* (pp. 257–262). Thousand Oaks, CA: SAGE.

Takahashi, M., & Kaida, K. (2006). Napping. In T. L. Lee-Chiong (Ed.), *Sleep: A comprehensive handbook* (pp. 197–202). Hoboken, N.J: Wiley-Liss.

Takeuchi, D. T., Chun, C. A., Gong, F., & Shen, H. (2002). Cultural expressions of distress. *Health, 6*(2), 221–236.

Talarico, J. M., & Rubin, D. C. (2009). Flashbulb memories result from ordinary memory processes and extraordinary event characteristics. In O. Luminet & A. Curci (Eds.), *Flashbulb memories: New Issues and New Perspectives* (pp. 79–97). East Sussex, UK: Psychology Press.

Tallis, F. (1998). *Changing minds: The history of psychotherapy as an answer to human suffering*. London, UK: Cassell.

Tallis, F. (2004). *Love sick: Love as a mental illness*. New York, NY: Thunder's Mouth Press.

Tallis, R. C. (1996). Burying Freud. *The Lancet, 347*(9902), 669–671.

Tamres, L. K., Janicki, D., & Helgeson, V. S. (2002). Sex differences in coping behavior: A meta-analytic review and an examination of relative coping. *Personality and Social Psychology Review, 6*(1), 2–30.

Tan, L. H., Spinks, J. A., Gao, J. H., Liu, H. L., Perfetti, C. A., Xiong, J., & Fox, P. T. (2000). Brain activation in the processing of Chinese characters and words: A functional MRI study. *Human Brain Mapping, 10*(1), 16–27.

Tanaka, J. W., & Taylor, M. (1991). Object categories and expertise: Is the basic level in the eye of the beholder? *Cognitive Psychology, 23*(3), 457–482.

Tang, C. S. K., Lai, F. D. M., & Chung, T. K. (1997). Assessment of sexual functioning for Chinese college students. *Archives of Sexual Behavior, 26*(1), 79–90.

Tang, N., Bensman, L., & Hatfield, E. (2012). The impact of culture and gender on sexual motives: Differences between Chinese and North Americans. *International Journal of Intercultural Relations, 36*(2), 286–294.

Tang, Y. Y., & Liu, Y. (2009). Numbers in the cultural brain. *Progress in Brain Research, 178*, 151–157.

Tanimoto, H., Heisenberg, M., & Gerber, B. (2004). Experimental psychology: Event timing turns punishment to reward. *Nature, 430*(7003), 983–983.

Tannock, R. (2013). Rethinking ADHD and LD in DSM-5 proposed changes in diagnostic criteria. *Journal of Learning Disabilities, 46*(1), 5–25.

Taras, H., and Potts-Datema, W. (2005). Sleep and student performance at school. *Journal of School Health, 75*, 248–254.

Tardif, T., Fletcher, P., Liang, W., Zhang, Z., Kaciroti, N., & Marchman, V. A. (2008). Baby's first 10 words. *Developmental Psychology, 44*(4), 929–938.

Tarique, I., & Takeuchi, R. (2008). Developing cultural intelligence: The roles of international nonwork experiences. In S. Ang & L. Van Dyne (Eds.), *Handbook of cultural intelligence: Theory, measurement, and applications* (pp. 56–70). New York, NY: Sharpe.

Tate, R. L. (2002). Emotional and social consequences of memory disorders. In A. D. Baddeley, M. D. Kopelman, & B. A. Wilson (Eds.), *The handbook of memory disorders* (2nd ed., pp. 785–808). Chichester, UK: Wiley.

Taylor, B. E. S. (2007). *ADHD & me: What I learned from lighting fires at the dinner table*. Oakland, CA: New Harbinger Publications.

Taylor, D. M. (2006). *Schizophrenia in focus*. London, UK: Pharmaceutical Press.

Taylor, S. (2002). Exposure. In M. Hersen & W. Sledge (Eds.), *Encyclopedia of psychotherapy* (Vol. 1, pp. 755–759). San Diego, CA: Academic Press.

Taylor, S. E. (2002). *The trending instinct: How nurturing is essential to who we are and how we live*. New York, NY: Holt.

Taylor, S. E. (2011a). Affiliation and stress. In S. Folkman, *Oxford handbook of stress, health, and coping* (pp. 86–100). Oxford, UK: Oxford University Press.

Taylor, S. E. (2011b). Social support: A review. In H. S. Friedman (Ed.), *The Oxford handbook of health psychology* (pp. 189–214). Oxford, UK: Oxford University Press.

Taylor, S. E., Kemeny, M. E., Reed, G. M., Bower, J. E., & Gruenewald, T. L. (2000a). Psychological resources, positive illusions, and health. *American Psychologist, 55*(1), 99–109.

Taylor, S. E., Klein, L. C., Lewis, B. P., Gruenewald, T. L., Gurung, R. A., & Updegraff, J. A. (2000b). Biobehavioral responses to stress in females: Tend-and-befriend, not fight-or-flight. *Psychological Review, 107*(3), 411.

Taylor, S. E., Sherman, D. K., Kim, H. S., Jarcho, J., Takagi, K., & Dunagan, M. S. (2004). Culture and social support: Who seeks it and why? *Journal of Personality and Social Psychology, 87*(3), 354–367.

Taylor, S., Cox, B. J., & Asmundson, G. J. G. (2009). Anxiety disorders: Panic and phobias. In P. H. Blaney & Theodore Millon (Eds.), *Oxford textbook of psychopathology* (2nd ed., pp. 119–145). New York, NY: Oxford University Press.

Taylor, V. J., & Walton, G. M. (2011). Stereotype threat undermines academic learning. *Personality and Social Psychology Bulletin, 37*(8), 1055–1067.

Teachman, J., Tedrow, L., & Kim, G. (2013). The demography of families. In G. W. Peterson & K. R. Bush (Eds.), *Handbook of marriage and the family* (3rd ed. pp. 39–63). New York, NY: Springer Science+Business Media.

Teglasi, H. (2010). *Essentials of TAT and other storytelling assessments* (2nd ed.). Hoboken, NJ: Wiley.

Teigen, K. H. (1994). Yerkes-Dodson: A law for all seasons. *Theory & Psychology, 4*(4), 525–547.

Teitcher, A. (2011). Weaving functional brain imaging into the tapestry of evidence: A case for functional neuroimaging in federal criminal courts. *Fordham Law Review, 80*(1), 355–401.

Tellegen, A., Lykken, D. T., Bouchard, T. J., Wilcox, K. J., Segal, N. L., & Rich, S. (1988). Personality similarity in twins reared apart and together. *Journal of Personality and Social Psychology, 54*(6), 1031–1039.

Temoshok, L. (1986). Personality, coping style, emotion and cancer: Towards an integrative model. *Cancer Surveys, 6*(3), 545–567.

Temoshok, L., Heller, B. W., Sagebiel, R. W., Blois, M. S., Sweet, D. M., DiClemente, R. J., & Gold, M. L. (1985). The relationship of psychosocial factors to prognostic indicators in cutaneous malignant melanoma. *Journal of Psychosomatic Research, 29*(2), 139–153.

Templer, K. J., Tay, C., & Chandrasekar, N. A. (2006). Motivational cultural intelligence, realistic job preview, realistic living conditions preview, and cross-cultural adjustment. *Group & Organization Management, 31*, 154–173.

Tennen, H., Affleck, G., & Zautra, A. (2006). Depression history and coping with chronic pain: A daily process analysis. *Health Psychology, 25*(3), 370–379.

Tennen, H., Affleck, G., Armeli, S., & Carney, M. A. (2000). A daily process approach to coping: Linking theory, research, and practice. *American Psychologist, 55*(6), 626–636.

Terkourafi, M. (2011). The puzzle of indirect speech. *Journal of Pragmatics, 43*(11), 2861–2865.

Terman, D. M. (2012). Self psychology. In G. O. Gabbard, B. E. Litowitz, & P. Williams (Eds.), *Textbook of psychoanalysis* (2nd ed., pp. 199–210). Washington, DC: American Psychiatric Publishing.

Tesser, A., & Martin, L. (2005). Reviewing empirical submissions to journals. In R. J. Sternberg (Ed.), *Reviewing scientific works in psychology* (pp. 3–29). Washington, DC: American Psychological Association.

Teti, D. M., & Teti, L. O. (1996). Infant-parent relationships. In N. Vanzetti & S. Duck (Eds.). *A lifetime of relationships* (pp. 77–104). Belmont, CA: Brooks/Cole.

Tett, R. P., Freund, K. A., Christiansen, N. D., Fox, K. E., & Coaster, J. (2012). Faking on self-report emotional intelligence and personality tests: Effects of faking opportunity, cognitive ability, and job type. *Personality and Individual Differences, 52*(2), 195–201.

Teufel, M., Stephan, K., Kowalski, A., Käsberger, S., Enck, P., Zipfel, S., & Giel, K. E. (2013). Impact of biofeedback on self-efficacy and stress reduction in obesity: A randomized controlled pilot study. *Applied Psychophysiology and Biofeedback, 38*(3), 177–184.

Thaler, N. S., Thames, A. D., Cagigas, X. E., & Norman, M. A. (2015). IQ testing and the African American client. In L. T. Benuto & B. D. Leany (Eds.), *Guide to psychological assessment with African American clients* (pp. 63–77). New York, NY: Springer.

Thapar, A., Cooper, M., Eyre, O., & Langley, K. (2013). Practitioner review: What have we learnt about the causes of ADHD? *Journal of Child Psychology and Psychiatry, 54*(1), 3–16.

Thase, M. E. (2006). Major depressive disorder. In M. Hersen & J. C. Thomas (Eds.), *Comprehensive handbook of personality and psychopathology* (Vol. 2, pp. 207–230). Hoboken, NJ: Wiley.

The White House (2010). Remarks by the First Lady at a Grocery Manufacturers Association Conference. Retrieved from https://www.whitehouse.gov/the-press-office/remarks-first-lady-a-grocery-manufacturers-association-conference.

Theokas, C., & Bloch, M. (2006). Out-of-school time is critical for children: Who participates in programs? Research-to-Results Fact Sheet. Publication #2006-20. Washington, DC: Child Trends.

Theriault, M., De Beaumont, L., Tremblay, S., Lassonde, M., & Jolicoeur, P. (2011). Cumulative effects of concussions in athletes revealed by electrophysiological abnormalities on visual working memory. *Journal of Clinical and Experimental Neuropsychology, 33*(1), 30–41.

Thiedke, C. C. (2001). Sleep disorders and sleep problems in childhood. *American Family Physician, 63*(2), 277–284.

Thomas, A. & Chess, S. (1977). *Temperament and development*. New York, NY: Brunner/Mazel.

Thomas, A., Chess, S., & Birch, H. G. (1970). The origin of personality. *Scientific American, 223*(2), 102–109.

Thomas, M. L. (2011). Detection of female mating status using chemical signals and cues. *Biological Reviews, 86*(1), 1–13.

Thomas, M. S., & Johnson, M. H. (2008). New advances in understanding sensitive periods in brain development. *Current Directions in Psychological Science, 17*(1), 1–5.

Thompson, B. (2013). Overview of traditional/classical statistical approaches. In T. D. Little (Ed.), *The Oxford handbook of quantitative methods, Vol. 2: Statistical analysis,* (pp. 7–25). New York, NY: Oxford University Press.

Thompson, D., Brown, J. B., Nichols, G. A., Elmer, P. J., & Oster, G. (2001). Body mass index and future healthcare costs: A retrospective cohort study. *Obesity Research, 9*(3), 210–218.

Thompson, E. M., & Morgan, E. M. (2008). "Mostly straight" young women: Variations in sexual behavior and identity development. *Developmental Psychology, 44*(1), 15–21.

Thompson, K. (2009, July 21). "Harvard Professor Arrested At Home." *The Washington Post*. http://www.washingtonpost.com/wp-dyn/content/article/2009/07/20/AR2009072001358.html

Thompson, P. (1980). Margaret Thatcher: A new illusion. *Perception, 9*, 483–484.

Thompson, R. A. (1998). Early sociopersonality development. In W. Damon & N. Eisenberg (Eds.), *Handbook of child psychology* (5th ed., Vol. 3, pp. 25–104). New York, NY: Wiley.

Thompson, R. A. (2006). The development of the person: Social understanding, relationships, conscience, self. In N. Eisenberg (Vol. Ed.), *Handbook of child psychology* (6th ed., Vol. 3, pp. 24–98). Hoboken, NJ: Wiley.

Thompson, T. (2013). *Fracking*. Detroit, MI: Greenhaven Press.

Thomson, D. M., & Tulving, E. (1970). Associative encoding and retrieval: Weak and strong cues. *Journal of Experimental Psychology, 86*(2), 255–262.

Thorleifsdottir, B., Björnsson, J. K., Benediktsdottir, B., Gislason, T. H., & Kristbjarnarson, H. (2002). Sleep and sleep habits from childhood to young adulthood over a 10-year period. *Journal of Psychosomatic Research, 53*(1), 529–537.

Thorndike, E. (1898). Animal intelligence: An experimental study of the associative processes in animals. *Psychological Review Monograph Supplement, 2*, 1–109.

Thorndike, E. (1900). The associative processes in animals. *Biological lectures from the Marine Biological Laboratory of Woods Hole 1899* (pp. 61–91). Boston, MA: Ginn & Company.

Thorndike, E. (1911). *Animal intelligence.* New York, NY: Macmillan Company.

Thorndike, E. (1927). The law of effect. *The American Journal of Psychology, 39*, 212–222.

Thornhill, R., & Gangestad, S. W. (1999). Facial attractiveness. *Trends in Cognitive Sciences, 3*(12), 452–460.

Thornton, M. A., & Conway, A. R. (2013). Working memory for social information: Chunking or domain-specific buffer? *NeuroImage, 70*, 233–239.

Thorpy, M. J. (2010). History of sleep and man. In C. P. Pollak, M. J. Thorpy, & J. Yager (Eds.), *The encyclopedia of sleep and sleep disorders* (3rd ed., pp. xvii–xxxviii). New York, NY: Infobase Publishing.

Thurstone, L. L. (1938). *Primary mental abilities*. Chicago, IL: University of Chicago Press.

Tietzel, A. J., & Lack, L. C. (2002). The recuperative value of brief and ultra-brief naps on alertness and cognitive performance. *Journal of Sleep Research, 11*(3), 213–218.

Tiggemann, M., & Kuring, J. K. (2004). The role of body objectification in disordered eating and depressed mood. *British Journal of Clinical Psychology, 43*(3), 299–311.

Tiggemann, M., & Slater, A. (2013). NetGirls: The Internet, Facebook, and body image concern in adolescent girls. *International Journal of Eating Disorders, 46*(6), 630–633.

Tigue, C. C., Borak, D. J., O'Connor, J. J., Schandl, C., & Feinberg, D. R. (2012). Voice pitch influences voting behavior. *Evolution and Human Behavior, 33*(3), 210–216.

Till, B. D., & Priluck, R. L. (2000). Stimulus generalization in classical conditioning: An initial investigation and extension. *Psychology & Marketing, 17*, 55–72.

Tiller, J. M., Sloane, G., Schmidt, U., Troop, N., Power, M., & Treasure, J. L. (1997). Social support in patients with anorexia nervosa and bulimia nervosa. *International Journal of Eating Disorders, 21*(1), 31–38.

Timmers, M., Fischer, A. H., & Manstead, A. S. (1998). Gender differences in motives for regulating emotions. *Personality and Social Psychology Bulletin, 24*(9), 974–985.

Timmers, M., Fischer, A., & Manstead, A. (2003). Ability versus vulnerability: Beliefs about men's and women's emotional behaviour. *Cognition & Emotion, 17*(1), 41–63.

Timney, B. (2010). Animal depth perception. In E. B. Goldstein (Ed.), *Encyclopedia of perception* (pp. 50–52). Thousand Oaks, CA: SAGE.

Timney, B., & Keil, K. (1999). Local and global stereopsis in the horse. *Vision Research, 39*(10), 1861–1867.

Tindale, C. W. (2007). *Fallacies and argument appraisal*. Cambridge, UK: Cambridge University Press.

Tinterow, M. M. (1970). *Foundations of hypnosis: From Mesmer to Freud*. Springfield, IL: Charles C. Thomas.

Tirodkar, M. A., & Jain, A. (2003). Food messages on African American television shows. *American Journal of Public Health, 93*(3), 439–441.

Toates, F. (2009). *Burrhus F. Skinner: Shaper of behaviour*. Hampshire, UK: Palgrave Macmillan.

Toepfer, S. M., Cichy, K., & Peters, P. (2012). Letters of gratitude: Further evidence for author benefits. *Journal of Happiness Studies, 13*(1), 187–201.

Tokumoto, J. (2009). Human immunodeficiency virus. In B. P. Jacobs & K. Gundling (Eds.), *The ACP evidence-based guide to complementary and alternative medicine* (pp. 201–222). Philadelphia, PA: American College of Physicians.

Tolin, D. F., & Foa, E. B. (2006). Sex differences in trauma and posttraumatic stress disorder: A quantitative review of 25 years of research. *Psychological Bulletin, 132*(6), 959–992.

Tolin, D. F., Gilliam, C. M., & Dufresne, D. (2010). The economic and social burden of anxiety disorders. In D. J. Stein, E. Hollander, & B. O. Rothbaum (Eds.), *Textbook of anxiety disorders* (2nd ed., pp. 731–746). Washington, DC: American Psychiatric Association.

Tolman, E. C. (1923). The nature of instinct. *Psychological Bulletin, 20*(4), 200–218.

Tolman, E. C. (1932). *Purposive behavior in animals and man*. New York, NY: Century.

Tolman, E. C. (1948). Cognitive maps in rats and men. *Psychological Review, 55*, 189–208.

Tolman, E. C., & Honzik, C. H. (1930). Introduction and removal of reward, and maze performance in rats. *University of California Publications in Psychology, 4*, 257–275.

Tomaka, J., & Blascovich, J. (1994). Effects of justice beliefs on cognitive appraisal of and subjective physiological, and behavioral responses to potential stress. *Journal of Personality and Social Psychology, 67*(4), 732–740.

Tomasello, M. (2004). Syntax or semantics? Response to Lidz et al. *Cognition, 93*(2), 139–140.

Tomasello, M., Carpenter, M., Call, J., Behne, T., & Moll, H. (2005). Understanding and sharing intentions: The origins of cultural cognition. *Behavioral and Brain Sciences, 28*(5), 675–690.

Toomey, R. B., Ryan, C., Diaz, R. M., & Russell, S. T. (2011). High school gay–straight alliances (GSAs) and young adult well-being: An examination of GSA presence, participation, and perceived effectiveness. *Applied Developmental Science, 15*(4), 175–185.

Topolinski, S., & Reber, R. (2010). Gaining insight into the "Aha" experience. *Current Directions in Psychological Science, 19*(6), 402–405.

Toppari, J., & Juul, A. (2010). Trends in puberty timing in humans and environmental modifiers. *Molecular and Cellular Endocrinology, 324*(1), 39–44.

Torres, A., Vidal, A., Puig, O., Boget, T., & Salamero, M. (2006). Gender differences in cognitive functions and influence of sex hormones. *Actas Españolas Psiquiatría, 34*(6), 408–415.

Torres, L., Driscoll, M. W., & Burrow, A. L. (2010). Racial microaggressions and psychological functioning among highly achieving African-Americans: A mixed-methods approach. *Journal of Social and Clinical Psychology, 29*(10), 1074–1099.

Torrey, E. F. (1986). *Witchdoctors and psychiatrists: The common roots of psychotherapy and its future*. New York, NY: Perennial Library.

Torrey, E. F. (2008). *The insanity offense: How America's failure to treat the seriously mentally ill endangers its citizens*. New York, NY: W. W. Norton.

Torrey, E. F., Miller, J., Rawlings, R., & Yolken, R. H. (1997). Seasonality of births in schizophrenia and bipolar disorder: A review of the literature. *Schizophrenia Research, 28*(1), 1–38.

Toubiana, L., Hanslik, T., & Letrilliart, L. (2001). French cardiovascular mortality did not increase during 1996 European football championship. *BMJ: British Medical Journal, 322*(7297), 1306.

Tov, W., & Diener, E. (2007). Culture and subjective well-being. In S. Kitayama & D. Cohen (Eds.), *Handbook of cultural psychology* (pp. 691–713). New York, NY: Guilford Press.

Townsend, J. M., & Wasserman, T. H. (2011). Sexual hookups among college students: Sex differences in emotional reactions. *Archives of Sexual Behavior, 40*(6), 1173–1181.

Traig, J. (2004). *Devil in the details: Scenes from an obsessive girlhood*. New York, NY: Little, Brown.

Tramer, M. (1929). Uber die biologische, bedeutung des geburtsmonates, insbesondere fur die psychoseerkrankung. *Archive fur Neurologie und Psychiatrie, 24*, 17–24.

Treffert, D. A., & Christensen, D. D. (2009, December 23). Inside the mind of a savant. *Scientific American*. Retrieved September 1, 2013, from http://www.scientificamerican.com/article.cfm?id=inside-the-mind-repost.

Tremblay, R. E. (2011). Origins, development, and prevention of aggressive behavior. In D. P. Keating (Ed.), *Nature and nurture in early child development* (pp. 169–187). New York, NY: Cambridge University Press.

Tremblay, R. E., & Nagin, D. S. (2005). The developmental origins of physical aggression in humans. In R. E. Tremblay, W. W. Hartuup, & J. Archer (Eds.), *Developmental origins of aggression* (pp. 83–106). New York, NY: Guilford Press.

Triandis, H. C. (2007). Culture and psychology: A history of the study of their relationship. In S. Kitayama & D. Cohen (Eds.), *Handbook of cultural psychology* (pp. 59–76). New York. NY: Guilford Press.

Triandis, H. C., Bontempo, R., Villareal, M. J., Asai, M., & Lucca, N. (1988). Individualism and collectivism: Cross-cultural perspectives on self-ingroup relationships. *Journal of Personality and Social Psychology, 54*(2), 323–338.

Tribbensee, N. E., & Claiborn, C. D. (2003). Confidentiality in psychotherapy and related contexts. In W. O'Donohue & K. Ferguson (Eds.), *Handbook of professional ethics for psychologists: Issues, questions, and controversies* (pp. 287–300). Thousand Oaks, CA: SAGE.

Trimble, J. E., & Clearing-Sky, M. (2009). An historical profile of American Indians and Alaska natives in psychology. *Cultural Diversity and Ethnic Minority Psychology*, 15(4), 338–351.

Trinidad, D. R., & Johnson, C. A. (2002). The association between emotional intelligence and early adolescent tobacco and alcohol use. *Personality and Individual Differences, 32*(1), 95–105.

Trockel, M. T., Barnes, M. D., & Egget, D. L. (2000). Health-related variables and academic performance among first-year college students: Implications for sleep and other behaviors. *Journal of American College Health, 49*(3), 125–131.

Tropp, L. R., & Molina, L. E. (2012). Intergroup processes: From prejudice to positive relations between groups. In K. Deaux & M. Snyder (Eds.), *The Oxford handbook of personality and social psychology* (pp. 545–570). New York, NY: Oxford University Press.

Truax, P. (2002). Behavioral case conceptualization for adults. In M. Hersen (Ed.), *Clinical behavior therapy: Adults and children* (pp. 3–36). New York, NY: Wiley.

Truax, P., & Thomas, J. C. (2003). Effectiveness versus efficacy studies: Issues, designs, and methodologies. In J. C. Thomas & M. Hersen (Eds.), *Understanding research in clinical and counseling psychology* (pp. 342–378). Mahwah, NJ: Lawrence Erlbaum.

Truscott, D. (2010). *Becoming an effective psychotherapist: Adopting a theory of psychotherapy that's right for you and your client*. Washington, DC: American Psychological Association.

Tryon, W. W. (2008). History and theoretical foundations. In M. Hersen & A. M. Gross (Eds.), *Handbook of clinical psychology* (Vol. 1, pp. 3–37). Hoboken, NJ: Wiley.

Tsai, J. L., Louie, J. Y., Chen, E. E., & Uchida, Y. (2007). Learning what feelings to desire: Socialization of ideal affect through children's storybooks. *Personality and Social Psychology Bulletin, 33*(1), 17–30.

Tskhay, K. O., & Rule, N. O. (2013). Accuracy in categorizing perceptually ambiguous groups: A review and meta-analysis. *Personality and Social Psychology Review, 17*(1), 72–86.

Tu, H.-W, & Hampton, R. R. (2013). One-trial memory and habit contribute independently to matching-to-sample performance in rhesus monkeys (*Macaca mulatta*). *Journal of Comparative Psychology, 127*(3), 319–328.

Tuber, S. (2012). *Understanding personality through projective testing*. Lanham, MD: Jason Aronson.

Tudor, K., & Worrall, M. (2006). *Person-centered therapy: A clinical philosophy*. New York, NY: Routledge.

Tugade, M. M. (2011). Positive emotions and coping: Examining dual-process models of resilience. In S. Folkman (Ed.), *Oxford handbook of stress, health, and coping* (pp. 186–199). Oxford, UK: Oxford University Press.

Tugade, M. M., & Fredrickson, B. L. (2004). Resilient individuals use positive emotions to bounce back from negative emotional experiences. *Journal of Personality and Social Psychology, 86*(2), 320–333.

Tulving, E. (1972). Episodic and semantic memory. In E. Tulving & W. Donaldson (Eds.), *Organization of memory* (pp. 381–403). New York, NY: Academic Press.

Tulving, E. (1976). Ecphoric processes in recall and recognition. In J. Brown (Ed.), *Recall and recognition* (pp. 37–73). London, UK: Wiley.

Tulving, E. (1983). *Elements of episodic memory*. Oxford, UK: Clarendon Press.

Tulving, E. (1998). Neurocognitive processes of human memory. In C. von Euler, I. Lundberg, & R. Llinas (Eds.), *Basic mechanisms in cognition and language* (pp. 261–281). Amsterdam, Netherlands: Elsevier.

Tulving, E. (2007). Are there 256 different kinds of memory? In H. L. Roediger & J. S. Nairne (Eds.), *The foundation of remembering* (pp. 39–52). New York, NY: Psychology Press.

Tulving, E., & Osler, S. (1968). Effectiveness of retrieval cues in memory for words. *Journal of Experimental Psychology, 77*(4), 593–601.

Tulving, E., & Thomson, D. M. (1973). Encoding specificity and retrieval processes in episodic memory. *Psychological Review, 80*(5), 352–373.

Tuma, R. S. (2010). Thirdhand smoke: Studies multiply, catchy name raises awareness. *Journal of the National Cancer Institute, 102*(14), 1004–1005.

Tuorila, H. (2010). Taste and food preferences. In E. B. Goldstein (Ed.), *Encyclopedia of perception* (pp. 969–973). Thousand Oaks, CA: SAGE.

Turiel, E. (2002). *The culture of morality: Social development, context, and conflict*. Cambridge, UK: Cambridge University Press.

Turiel, E. (2006). The development of morality. In N. Eisenberg (Vol. Ed.), *Handbook of child psychology* (6th ed., Vol. 3, pp. 789–857). Hoboken, NJ: Wiley.

Turiel, E. (2008). The development of children's orientations toward moral, social, and personal orders: More than a sequence in development. *Human Development, 51*(1), 21–39.

Turiel, E. (2010). The development of morality: Reasoning, emotions, and resistance. In W. F. Overton (Ed.), *Handbook of life-span development* (Vol. 1, pp. 554–583). Hoboken, NJ: Wiley.

Turk, D. C., & Melzack, R. (2011). The measurement of pain and the assessment of people experiencing pain. In D. C. Turk & R. Melzack (Eds.), *Handbook of pain assessment* (3rd ed., pp. 3–16). New York, NY: Guilford.

Turkington, C., & Harris, J. R. (2001). *The encyclopedia of memory and memory disorders* (2nd ed.). New York, NY: Facts on File.

Turner, C. W., Layton, J. F., & Simons, L. S. (1975). Naturalistic studies of aggressive behavior: Aggressive stimuli, victim visibility, and horn honking. *Journal of Personality and Social Psychology, 31*(6), 1098–1107.

Turner, R. J., & Avison, W. R. (1989). Gender and depression: Assessing exposure and vulnerability to life events in a chronically strained population. *The Journal of Nervous and Mental Disease, 177*(8), 443–455.

Turow, J. (2012). Nurses and doctors in prime time series: The dynamics of depicting professional power. *Nursing Outlook, 60*(5), S4–S11.

Tversky, A., & Kahneman, D. (1971). Belief in the law of small numbers. *Psychological Bulletin, 76*(2), 105–110.

Tversky, A., & Kahneman, D. (1973). Availability: A heuristic for judging frequency and probability. *Cognitive Psychology, 5*(2), 207–232.

Tversky, A., & Kahneman, D. (1974). Judgment under uncertainty: Heuristics and biases. *Science, 185*(4157), 1124–1131.

Tversky, A., & Kahneman, D. (1981). The framing of decisions and the psychology of choice. *Science, 211*(4481), 453–458.

Tversky, A., & Kahneman, D. (1982). Judgments of and by representativeness. In D. Kahneman, P. Slovic, & A. Tversky (Eds.), *Judgment under uncertainty: Heuristics and biases* (pp. 84–98). Cambridge, UK: Cambridge University Press.

Tversky, A., & Kahneman, D. (1986). Rational choice and the framing of decisions. *Journal of Business, 59*(4), S251–S278.

Tweed, R. G., & Conway III, L. G. (2006). Coping strategies and culturally influenced beliefs about the world. In P. T. P. Wong and L. C. J. Wong (Eds.), *Handbook of multicultural perspectives on stress and coping* (pp. 133–154). New York, NY: Springer Science+Business Media.

Tweed, R. G., White, K., & Lehman, D. R. (2004). Culture, stress, and coping internally- and externally-targeted control strategies of European Canadians, East Asian Canadians, and Japanese. *Journal of Cross-Cultural Psychology, 35*(6), 652–668.

Tweney, R. D. (1997). Edward Bradford Titchener. In W. G. Bringmann, H. E. Lück, R. Miller, & C. E. Early (Eds.), *A pictorial history of psychology* (pp. 153–161). Carol Stream, IL: Quintessence Publishing

Twenge, J. M., & Campbell, S. M. (2008). Generational differences in psychological traits and their impact on the workplace. *Journal of Managerial Psychology, 23*(8), 862–877.

Twenge, J. M., Gentile, B., DeWall, C. N., Ma, D., Lacefield, K., & Schurtz, D. R. (2010). Birth cohort increases in psychopathology among young Americans, 1938–2007: A cross-temporal meta-analysis of the MMPI. *Clinical Psychology Review, 30*(2), 145–154.

Twenge, J. M., Zhang, L., & Im, C. (2004). It's beyond my control: A cross-temporal meta-analysis of increasing externality in locus of control, 1960–2002. *Personality and Social Psychology Review, 8*(3), 308–319.

Twomey, J., LaGasse, L., Derauf, C., Newman, E., Shah, R., Smith, L., . . . Lester, B. (2013). Prenatal methamphetamine exposure, home environment, and primary caregiver risk factors predict child behavioral problems at 5 years. *American Journal of Orthopsychiatry, 83*, 64–72. doi:10.1111/ajop.12007

Tzeng, O. J. (1973). Positive recency effect in a delayed free recall. *Journal of Verbal Learning and Verbal Behavior, 12*(4), 436–439.

U.S. Census Bureau (2006). *Statistical abstracts of the United States*. Washington, DC: U.S. Government Printing Office.

U. S. Census Bureau (2008). *Marriage*. Washington, DC: U.S. Government Printing Office.

U.S. Census Bureau. (2008). *Percent of the projected population by race and Hispanic origin for the United States: 2010 to 2050* (NP2008–T6). Retrieved from www.census.gov/ipc/www/ usinterimproj/

Uchida, M., Spencer, T. J., Faraone, S. V., & Biederman, J. (2015). Adult outcome of ADHD: An overview of results from the MGH Longitudinal Family Studies of Pediatrically and Psychiatrically Referred Youth With and Without ADHD of Both Sexes. *Journal of Attention Disorders*. doi:10.1177/1087054715604360

Uchida, Y. & Kitayama, S. (2009). Happiness and unhappiness in east and west: Themes and variations. *Emotion, 9*(4), 441–456.

Uchida, Y., Norasakkunkit, V., & Kitayama, S. (2004). Cultural constructions of happiness: Theory and empirical evidence. *Journal of Happiness Studies, 5*(3), 223–239.

Uchino, B. N. (2006). Social support and health: A review of physiological processes potentially underlying links to disease outcomes. *Journal of Behavioral Medicine, 29*(4), 377–387.

Ucros, C. G. (1989). Mood state-dependent memory: A meta-analysis. *Cognition and Emotion, 3*(2), 139–169.

Udry, J. R., & Chantala, K. (2006). Masculinity–femininity predicts sexual orientation in men but not in women. *Journal of Biosocial Science, 38*(6), 797–809.

Uleman, J. S., & Saribay, S. A. (2012). Initial impressions of others. In K. Deaux & M. Snyder (Eds.), *The Oxford handbook of personality and social psychology* (pp. 337–366). New York, NY: Oxford University Press.

Umberson, D., Pudrovska, T., & Reczek, C. (2010). Parenthood, childlessness, and well-being: A life course perspective. *Journal of Marriage and Family, 72*(3), 612–629.

Underwood, B. J. (1957). Interference and forgetting. *Psychological Review, 64*(1), 49–60.

United Nations Office on Drugs and Crime (UNODC) (2012). UNODC Homicide Statistics. http://www.unodc.org/unodc/en/data-and-analysis/homicide.html

United States Department of Agriculture, 2014. Food Expenditures: Table 13. Accessed on October 13, 2015 at http://www.ers.usda.gov/data-products/food-expenditures.aspx.

Urbina, S. (2011). Tests of intelligence. In R. J. Sternberg & S. B. Kaufman (Eds.), *The Cambridge handbook of intelligence* (pp. 20–38). Cambridge, UK: Cambridge University Press.

Ursin, R., Bjorvatn, B., & Holsten, F. (2005). Sleep duration, subjective sleep need, and sleep habits of 40- to 45-year-olds in the Hordaland Health Study. *Sleep, 28*(10), 1260–1269.

USCB [United States Census Bureau] (2011). Statistical abstract of the United States. Section 1: Population. Retrieved from http://www.census.gov/prod/2011pubs/11statab/pop.pdf.

Ustun, T. B., & Sartorius, N. (Eds.) (1995). *Mental illness in general health care: An international study*. Chichester, UK: Wiley.

Vadeboncoeur, C., Townsend, N., & Foster, C. (2015). A meta-analysis of weight gain in first year university students: Is freshman 15 a myth? *BMC Obesity, 2*(1), 22. doi.10.1186/s40608-015-0051-7

Vagi, K. J., Rothman, E. F., Latzman, N. E., Tharp, A. T., Hall, D. M., & Breiding, M. J. (2013). Beyond correlates: A review of risk and protective factors for adolescent dating violence perpetration. *Journal of Youth and Adolescence, 42*(4), 633–649.

Vago, D. R. & Silbersweig, D. A. (2012). Self-awareness, self-regulation, and self-transcendence (S-ART): A framework for understanding the neurobiological mechanisms of mindfulness. *Frontiers in Human Neuroscience, 6*, 296.

Vahia, I. V., & Cohen, C. I. (2008). Psychopathology. In K. T. Meuser & D. V. Jeste (Eds.), *Clinical handbook of schizophrenia* (pp. 82–90). New York, NY: Guilford Press.

Valencia, M. J. (2015, March 5). In gripping testimony, carnage in Marathon attacks is recalled: Seven witnesses tell of moments before and after blasts. *Boston Globe*. Retrieved from http://www.bostonglobe.com/metro/2015/03/05/more-bombing-survivors-expected-testify-tsarnaev-trial/t06u2dvauhQDHyMwuPpCAN/story.html

Valenza, E., Simion, F., Cassia, V. M., & Umiltà, C. (1996). Face preference at birth. *Journal of Experimental Psychology: Human Perception and Performance, 22*(4), 892–903

Vallières, A. & Bastille-Denis, E. (2012). Circadian rhythm disorders II: Jet lag. In C. M. Morin & C. A. Espie (Eds.), *The Oxford handbook of sleep and sleep disorders* (pp. 648–665). Oxford, UK: Oxford University Press.

Van Ameringen, M., Mancini, C., & Patterson, B. (2009). Pharmacotherapy for social anxiety disorder and specific phobia. In M. M. Antony & M. B. Stein (Eds.), *Oxford handbook of anxiety and related disorders* (pp. 321–333). New York, NY: Oxford University Press.

van de Vijver, F. J. R., & Matsumoto, D. (2011). Introduction to the methodological issues associated with cross-cultural research. In D. Matsumoto & F. J. R. van de Vijver (Eds.), *Cross-cultural research methods in psychology* (pp. 1–14). New York, NY: Cambridge University Press.

van den Berg, P., Paxton, S. J., Keery, H., Wall, M., Guo, J., & Neumark-Sztainer, D. (2007). Body dissatisfaction and body comparison with media images in males and females. *Body Image, 4*(3), 257–268.

Van den Bulck, J. (2004). Television viewing, computer game playing, and Internet use and self-reported time to bed and time out of bed in secondary-school children. *Sleep, 27*(1), 101–104.

van der Hart, O., & Nijenhuis, E. R. S. (2009). Dissociative disorders. In P. H. Blaney & Theodore Millon (Eds.), *Oxford textbook of psychopathology* (2nd ed., 452–481). New York, NY: Oxford University Press.

van der Linden, D., Scholte, R. H., Cillessen, A. H., Nijenhuis, J. T., & Segers, E. (2010). Classroom ratings of likeability and popularity are related to the Big Five and the general factor of personality. *Journal of Research in Personality, 44*(5), 669–672.

van der Veer, R., & Valsiner, J. (1994) (Eds.). *The Vygotsky Reader*. Malden, MA: Blackwell.

Van Dongen, H. P., Maislin, G., Mullington, J. M., & Dinges, D. F. (2003). The cumulative cost of additional wakefulness: Dose-response effects on neurobehavioral functions and sleep physiology from chronic sleep restriction and total sleep deprivation. *Sleep, 26*(2), 117–126.

Van Horn, J. D. (2004). Cognitive neuroimaging: History, developments, and directions. In M. S. Gazzaniga (Ed.), *The new cognitive neurosciences III* (pp. 1281–1294). Cambridge, MA: MIT Press.

van Lommel, P. (2010). *Consciousness beyond life: The science of the near-death experience*. New York, NY: HarperOne.

Van Os, J., Hanseen, M., & Bak, M., et al. (2003). Do urbanicity and familial liability co-participate in causing psychosis? *American Journal of Psychiatry, 160*(3), 477–482.

Van Os, J., Hanseen, M., Bijl, R. v., Vollebergh, W. (2001). Prevalence of psychotic disorder and community level of psychotic symptoms. *Archives of General Psychiatry, 58*(7), 663–668.

van Oudenhoven, J. P. (2006). Immigrants. In D. L. Sam & J. W. Berry (Eds.), *Cambridge handbook of acculturation psychology*, pp. 163–180. Cambridge, UK: Cambridge University Press.

van Praag, H., Christie, B. R., Sejnowski, T. J., & Gage, F. H. (1999). Running enhances neurogenesis, learning, and long-term potentiation in mice. *Proceedings of the National Academy of Sciences, 96*(23), 13427–13431.

van Praag, H., Kempermann, G., & Gage, F. H. (2000). Neural consequences of environmental enrichment. *Nature Reviews Neuroscience, 1*(3), 191–198.

van Praag, H., Schinder, A. F., Christie, B. R., Toni, N., Palmer, T. D., & Gage, F. H. (2002). Functional neurogenesis in the adult hippocampus. *Nature, 415*(6875), 1030–1034

Van Rooy, D. L., & Viswesvaran, C. (2004). Emotional intelligence: A meta-analytic investigation of predictive validity and nomological net. *Journal of Vocational Behavior, 65*(1), 71–95.

Van Solinge, H., & Henkens, K. (2005). Couples' adjustment to retirement: A multi-actor panel study. *The Journals of Gerontology. Series B, Psychological Sciences and Social Sciences, 60*(1), S11–S20.

Van Solinge, H., & Henkens, K. (2007). Involuntary retirement: The role of restrictive circumstances, timing, and social embeddedness. *The Journals of Gerontology: Series B: Psychological Sciences and Social Sciences, 62*(5), S295–S303.

van Veen, V., Krug, M. K., Schooler, J. W., & Carter, C. S. (2009). Neural activity predicts attitude change in cognitive dissonance. *Nature Neuroscience, 12*, 1469–1474. doi:10.1038/nn.2413

van Vugt, M. K. (2015). Cognitive benefits of mindfulness meditation. In K. W. Brown, J. D. Creswell, & R. M. Ryan (Eds.), *Handbook of mindfulness: Theory, research, and practice* (pp. 190–207). New York, NY: Guilford Press.

Van Vugt, M., & Van Lange, P. A. M. (2006). The altruism puzzle: Psychological adaptations for prosocial behavior. In M. Schaller, J. A. Simpson, & D. T. Kenrick (Eds.), *Evolution and social psychology* (pp. 237–261). New York, NY: Psychology Press.

VanderLaan, D. P., Blanchard, R., Wood, H., Garzon, L. C., & Zucker, K. J. (2015). Birth weight and two possible types of maternal effects on male sexual orientation: A clinical study of children and adolescents referred to a Gender Identity Service. *Developmental Psychobiology, 57*(1), 25–34.

Vandewater, E. A., & Wartella, E. A. (2011). Food marketing, television, and video games. In J. H. Cawley (Ed.), *The Oxford handbook of the social science of obesity* (pp. 350–366). New York, NY: Oxford University Press.

Vargha-Khadem, F., Gadian, D. G., Watkins, K. E., Connelly, A., Van Paesschen, W., & Mishkin, M. (1997). Differential effects of early hippocampal pathology on episodic and semantic memory. *Science, 277*(5324), 376–380.

Vartanian, L. R., Herman, C. P., & Polivy, J. (2007). Consumption stereotypes and impression management: How you are what you eat. *Appetite, 48*(3), 265–277.

Vasquez, M. (2015). Ethics code, APA. (2015). In R. L. Cautin & S. O. Lilienfeld (Eds.), *The encyclopedia of clinical psychology* (pp. 1124–1126). West Sussex, UK: Wiley-Blackwell.

Vasquez, M. J. T. (2010). Ethics in multicultural counseling practice. In J. G. Ponterotto, J. M. Casas, L. A. Suzuki, & C. M. Alexander (Eds.), *Handbook of multicultural counseling* (3rd ed., pp. 127–145). Thousand Oaks, CA: SAGE.

Vaux, B. (2003). American dialects. Retrieved from http://www.choicesmagazine.org/magazine/pdf/article_115.pdf

Vazire, S., & Carlson, E. N. (2010). Self-knowledge of personality: Do people know themselves? *Social and Personality Psychology Compass, 4*(8), 605–620.

Vecera, S. P., & Lee, H. (2010). Vision: Cognitive influences. In E. B. Goldstein (Ed.), *Encyclopedia of perception* (pp. 1048–1053). Thousand Oaks, CA: SAGE.

Vedhara, K., & Irwin, M. (2005). *Human Psychoneuroimmunology*. Oxford, UK: Oxford University Press.

Veenhoven, R. (2012a). Average happiness in 149 nations 2000–2009: How much people enjoy their life as-a-whole on scale 0 to 10. World database of happiness. Erasmus University Rotterdam, Netherlands. http://worlddatabaseofhappiness.eur.nl/hap_nat/findingreports/RankReport_AverageHappiness.php

Veenhoven, R. (2012b). Cross-national differences in happiness: Cultural measurement bias or effect of culture? *International Journal of Wellbeing, 2*(4), 333–353.

Veerman, J. L., Van Beeck, E. F., Barendregt, J. J., & Mackenbach, J. P. (2009). By how much would limiting TV food advertising reduce childhood obesity? *The European Journal of Public Health, 19*(4), 365–369.

Velayudhan, L., Pritchard, M., Powell, J. F., Proitsi, P., & Lovestone, S. (2013). Smell identification function as a severity and progression marker in Alzheimer's disease. *International Psychogeriatrics, 25*(7), 1157–1166.

Vella-Zarb, R. A. & Elgar, F. J. (2009). The "freshman 5" A meta-analysis of weight gain in the freshman year of college. *Journal of American College Health, 58*(2), 161–166.

Velmans, M. (2009). How to define consciousness: And how not to define consciousness. *Journal of Consciousness Studies, 16*(5), 139–156.

Verhaeghen, P., & Salthouse, T. A. (1997). Meta-analyses of age–cognition relations in adulthood: Estimates of linear and nonlinear age effects and structural models. *Psychological Bulletin, 122*(3), 231–249.

Verwoerd, J., & Wessel, I. (2010). Unwanted traumatic intrusions: The role of pre-trauma individual differences in executive control. In J. H. Mace (Ed.), *The act of remembering: Toward an understanding of how we recall the past* (pp. 337–360). Chichester, UK: Wiley-Blackwell.

Veselka, L., Schermer, J. A., & Vernon, P. A. (2011). Beyond the Big Five: The Dark Triad and the supernumerary personality inventory. *Twin Research and Human Genetics, 14*(2), 158–168.

Vessey, J. T., & Howard, K. I. (1993). Who seeks psychotherapy? *Psychotherapy: Theory, Research, Practice, Training, 30*(4), 546–553.

Viamontes, G. I., & Beitman, B. D. (2009). Brain processes informing psychotherapy. In G. O. Gabbard (Ed.), *Textbook of psychotherapeutic treatments* (pp. 781–808). Washington, DC: American Psychiatric Publishing.

Villa, M., & Reitman, D. (2007). Overview of interviewing strategies with children, parents, and teachers. In M. Hersen & J. C. Thomas (Eds.), *Handbook of clinical interviewing with children* (pp. 2–15). Thousand Oaks, CA: SAGE.

Villamar, A. J., Donohue, B. C., & Allen, D. N. (2008). Applied behavior analysis. In M. Hersen & A. M. Gross (Eds.), *Handbook of clinical psychology* (Vol. 1, pp. 161–170). Hoboken, NJ: Wiley.

Villamarin-Salomon, R. M., & Brustoloni, J. C. (2010). Using reinforcement to strengthen users' secure behaviors. *Proceedings of the 28th international conference on human factors in computing systems* (pp. 363–372).

Vimal, R. (2009). Meanings attributed to the term "consciousness": An overview. *Journal of Consciousness Studies, 16*(5), 9–27.

Vingerhoets, A. J., & Scheirs, J. (2000). Sex differences in crying: Empirical findings and possible explanations. *Gender and Emotion: Social Psychological Perspectives, 2*, 143–165.

Vingerhoets, A. J., Cornelius, R. R., Van Heck, G. L., & Becht, M. C. (2000). Adult crying: A model and review of the literature. *Review of General Psychology, 4*(4), 354–377.

Virnig, B., Huang, Z., Lurie, N., Musgrave, D., McBean, A. M., & Dowd, B. (2004). Does Medicare managed care provide equal treatment for mental illness across races? *Archives of General Psychiatry, 61*(2), 201–205.

Visser, S. N., Danielson, M. L., Bitsko, R. H., Holbrook, J. R., Kogan, M. D., Ghandour, R. M.,. . . Blumberg, S. J. (2014). Trends in the parent-report of health care provider-diagnosed and medicated attention-deficit/hyperactivity disorder: United States, 2003–2011. *Journal of the American Academy of Child & Adolescent Psychiatry, 53*(1), 34–46.

Visu-Petra, L., Cheie, L., Benga, O., & Alloway, T. P. (2011). Effects of anxiety on memory storage and updating in young children. *International Journal of Behavioral Development, 35*(1), 38–47.

Visu-Petra, L., Miclea, M., & Visu-Petra, G. (2013). Individual differences in anxiety and executive functioning: A multidimensional view. *International Journal of Psychology, 48*(4), 649–659.

Viswesvaran, C., & Ones, D. S. (1999). Meta-analyses of fakability estimates: Implications for personality measurement. *Educational and Psychological Measurement, 59*(2), 197–210.

Vits, S., Cesko, E., Enck, P., Hillen, U., Schadendorf, D., & Schedlowski, M. (2011). Behavioural conditioning as the mediator of placebo responses in the immune system. *Philosophical Transactions of the Royal Society B: Biological Sciences, 366*(1572), 1799–1807.

Vogel, G. W. (1991). Sleep-onset mentation. In S. J. Ellman & J. Antrobus (Eds.), *The mind in sleep* (pp. 125–136). New York, NY: Wiley.

Vogele, C., & Gibson, E. L. (2010). Mood, emotions, and eating disorders. In W. S. Agras (Ed.), *The Oxford handbook of eating disorders* (pp. 180–205). New York, NY: Oxford University Press.

Vogler, G. P., Sørensen, T. I., Stunkard, A. J., Srinivasan, M. R., & Rao, D. C. (1995). Influences of genes and shared family environment on adult body mass index assessed in an adoption study by a comprehensive path model. *International Journal of Obesity and Related Metabolic Disorders, 19*(1), 40–45.

Vøllestad, J., Nielsen, M. B., & Nielsen, G. H. (2012). Mindfulness- and acceptance-based interventions for anxiety disorders: A systematic review and meta-analysis. *British Journal of Clinical Psychology, 51*(3), 239–260.

von Hofsten, C. (2003). On the development of perception and action. In J. Valsiner & K. Connolly (Eds.), *Handbook of developmental psychology* (pp. 114–140). Thousand Oaks, CA: SAGE.

Vonofakou, C., Hewstone, M., & Voci, A. (2007). Contact with out-group friends as a predictor of meta-attitudinal strength and accessibility of attitudes toward gay men. *Journal of Personality and Social Psychology, 92*(5), 804–820.

Voracek, M., Manning, J. T., & Ponocny, I. (2005). Digit ratio (2D: 4D) in homosexual and heterosexual men from Austria. *Archives of Sexual Behavior, 34*(3), 335–340.

Vorona, R. D., Szklo-Coxe, M., Wu, A., Dubik, M., Zhao, Y., & Ware, J. C. (2011). Dissimilar teen crash rates in two neighboring southeastern Virginia cities with different high school start times. *Journal of Clinical Sleep Medicine, 7*(2), 145–151.

Voss, J. L. (2009). Long-term associative memory capacity in man. *Psychonomic Bulletin & Review, 16*(6), 1076–1081.

Voss, M. W., Nagamatsu, L. S., Liu-Ambrose, T., & Kramer, A. F. (2011). Exercise, brain, and cognition across the life span. *Journal of Applied Physiology, 111*(5), 1505–1513.

Voss, M. W., Prakash, R. S., Erickson, K. I., Basak, C., Chaddock, L., Kim, J. S., . . . Kramer, A. F. (2010). Plasticity of brain networks in a randomized intervention trial of exercise training in older adults. *Frontiers in Aging Neuroscience, 2*, 32.

Vouloumanos, A., & Werker, J. F. (2004). Tuned to the signal: The privileged status of speech for young infants. *Developmental Science, 7*(3), 270–276.

Vouloumanos, A., & Werker, J. F. (2007). Listening to language at birth: Evidence for a bias for speech in neonates. *Developmental Science, 10*(2), 159–164.

Vouloumanos, A., Hauser, M. D., Werker, J. F. and Martin, A. (2010), The tuning of human neonates' preference for speech. *Child Development, 81*, 517–527.

Vouloumanos, A., Kiehl, K. A., Werker, J. F., & Liddle, P. F. (2001). Detection of sounds in the auditory stream: Event-related fMRI evidence for differential activation to speech and nonspeech. *Journal of Cognitive Neuroscience, 13*(7), 994–1005.

Vrangalova, Z., & Savin-Williams, R. C. (2012). Mostly heterosexual and mostly gay/lesbian: Evidence for new sexual orientation identities. *Archives of Sexual Behavior, 41*(1), 85–101.

Vroom, V. H. (2007). Teaching the managers of tomorrow: Psychologists in business schools. In R. J. Sternberg, *Career paths in psychology: Where your degree can take you* (2nd ed., pp. 51–67). Washington, DC: American Psychological Association.

Vul, E., Harris, C., Winkielman, P., & Pashler, H. (2009). Puzzlingly high correlations in fMRI studies of emotion, personality, and social cognition. *Perspectives on Psychological Science, 4*(3), 274–290.

Vyas, M. V., Garg, A. X., Iansavichus, A. V., Costella, J., Donner, A., Laugsand, L. E., Hackam, D. G. (2012). Shift work and vascular events: Systematic review and meta-analysis. *BMJ, 345*, doi:10.1136/bmj.e4800.

Vygotsky, L. (1986). *Thought and language* (Rev. ed., A. Kozulin, Trans.) Cambridge, MA: MIT Press.

Vygotsky, L. S. (1978). In M. Cole, S. Scribner, & E. Souberman, Eds., *Mind in society: The development of higher psychological processes* (Rev. ed.) Cambridge, MA: Harvard University Press.

Wachtel, P. L. (1977). *Psychoanalysis and behavior therapy: Toward an integration*. New York, NY: Basic Books.

Wacker, D. P., Harding, J., Berg, W., Cooper-Brown, L. J., & Barretto, A. (2009). Punishment. In W. T. O'Donohue & J. E. Fisher (Eds.), *General principles and empirically supported techniques of cognitive behavior therapy* (pp. 506–512). Hoboken, NJ: Wiley.

Wadden, T. A. (1995). Characteristics of successful weight loss maintainers. In D. B. Allison and F. X. Pi-Sunyer (Eds.), *Obesity treatment: Establishing goals, improving outcomes, and reviewing the research agenda* (pp. 103–111). New York, NY: Plenum Press.

Wadden, T. A., Butryn, M. L., & Wilson, C. (2007). Lifestyle modification for the management of obesity. *Gastroenterology, 132*(6), 2226–2238.

Wade, K. A., Garry, M., Read, J. D., & Lindsay, D. S. (2002). A picture is worth a thousand lies: Using false photographs to create false childhood memories. *Psychonomic Bulletin & Review, 9*(3), 597–603.

Wade, T. D. (2010). Genetic influences on eating and the eating disorders. In W. S. Agras (Ed.), *The Oxford handbook of eating disorders* (pp. 103–122). New York, NY: Oxford University Press.

Wagner, B. C., & Petty, R. E. (2011). The elaboration likelihood model of persuasion: Thoughtful and non-thoughtful social influence. In D. Chadee (Ed.), *Theories in social psychology* (pp. 96–116). West Sussex, UK: Wiley-Blackwell.
Wagner, P. S., & Spiro, C. S. (2005). *Divided minds: Twin sisters and their journey through schizophrenia*. New York, NY: St. Martin's Press.
Wagner, R. K. (2011). Practical intelligence. In R. J. Sternberg & S. B. Kaufman (Eds.), *The Cambridge handbook of intelligence* (pp. 550–563). Cambridge, UK: Cambridge University Press.
Wagner, R. K., & Sternberg, R. J. (1985). Practical intelligence in real-world pursuits: The role of tacit knowledge. *Journal of Personality and Social Psychology, 49*(2), 436–458.
Wagner, U., Gais, S., & Born, J. (2001). Emotional memory formation is enhanced across sleep intervals with high amounts of rapid eye movement sleep. *Learning & Memory, 8*(2), 112–119.
Wahlstrom, K. (2002). Changing times: Findings from the first longitudinal study of later high school start times. *NASSP Bulletin, 86*(633), 3–21.
Wahlstrom, K. L. (2002a). Accommodating the sleep patterns of adolescents within current educational structures: An uncharted path. *Adolescent sleep patterns: Biological, social, and psychological influences* (pp. 172–197). Cambridge, UK: Cambridge University Press.
Wahlstrom, K. (2002b). Changing times: Findings from the first longitudinal study of later high school start times. *NASSP Bulletin, 86*(633), 3–21.
Wakefield, J. C. (2013). DSM-5: An overview of changes and controversies. *Clinical Social Work Journal*, 41(2), 139–154.
Walburn, J., Vedhara, K., Hankins, M., Rixon, L., & Weinman, J. (2009). Psychological stress and wound healing in humans: A systematic review and meta-analysis. *Journal of Psychosomatic Research, 67*(3), 253–271.
Walker, E., & Lewine, R. J. (1990). Prediction of adult-onset schizophrenia from childhood home movies of the patients. *American Journal of Psychiatry, 147*(8), 1052–1056.
Walker, I., & Crogan, M. (1998). Academic performance, prejudice, and the jigsaw classroom: New pieces to the puzzle. *Journal of Community & Applied Social Psychology, 8*(6), 381–393.
Walker, J. (2012, December. 5). Advocates push for tougher texting while driving law. *The Virginian-Pilot*. Retrieved from http://hamptonroads.com/2012/12/advocates-push-tougher-texting-while-driving-law
Walker, L. J. (2006). Gender and morality. In M. Killen & J. G. Smetana (Eds.), *Handbook of moral development* (pp. 93–115). Mahwah, NJ: Lawrence Erlbaum.
Walker, M. P. (2012). The role of sleep in neurocognitive function. In C. M. Morin & C. A. Espie (Eds.), *The Oxford handbook of sleep and sleep disorders* (pp. 110–130). Oxford, UK: Oxford University Press.
Wallace, D. S., Paulson, R. M., Lord, C. G., & Bond, C. F., Jr. (2005). Which behaviors do attitudes predict? Meta-analyzing the effects of social pressure and perceived difficulty. *Review of General Psychology, 9*(3), 214–227.
Wallace, M. N. (2010). Auditory system: Structure. In E. B. Goldstein (Ed.), *Encyclopedia of perception* (pp. 194–196). Thousand Oaks, CA: SAGE.
Wallace, P. M., & Gotlib, I. H. (1990). Marital adjustment during the transition to parenthood: Stability and predictors of change. *Journal of Marriage and Family, 52*(1), 21–29.
Waller, D., Loomis, J. M., & Haun, D. B. (2004). Body-based senses enhance knowledge of directions in large-scale environments. *Psychonomic Bulletin & Review, 11*(1), 157–163.
Walls, N. E., Kane, S. B., & Wisneski, H. (2010). Gay-straight alliances and school experiences of sexual minority youth. *Youth & Society, 41*(3), 307–332.
Walsh, J. K., & Engelhardt, C. L. (1999). The direct economic costs of insomnia in the United States for 1995. *Sleep, 22*, S386–S393.
Walsh, R., & Shapiro, S. L. (2006). The meeting of meditative disciplines and Western psychology: A mutually enriching dialogue. *American Psychologist, 61*(3), 227–239.
Walters, R. H., & Demkow, L. (1963). Timing of punishment as a determinant of response inhibition. *Child Development, 34*, 207–214.
Walvoord, E. C. (2010). The timing of puberty: Is it changing? Does it matter? *Journal of Adolescent Health, 47*(5), 433–439.
Wampold, B. E. (2001). *The great psychotherapy debate: Models, methods, and findings*. Mahwah, NJ: Lawrence Erlbaum.
Wampold, B. E. (2006). Designing a research study. In F. T. L. Leong & J. T. Austin (Eds.), *The psychology research handbook: A guide for graduate students and research assistants* (pp. 93–103). Thousand Oaks,CA: SAGE.
Wampold, B. E. (2010a). *The basics of psychotherapy: An introduction to theory and practice*. Washington, DC: American Psychological Association.
Wampold, B. E. (2010b). The research evidence for the common factors model: A historically situated perspective. In B. L. Duncan, S. D. Miller, B. E. Wampold, & M. A. Hubble (Eds.), *The heart & soul of change: Delivering what works in therapy* (2nd ed., pp. 49–81). Washington, DC: American Psychological Association.
Wang, A. Y., & Thomas, M. H. (2000). Looking for long-term effects on serial recall: The legacy of Simonides. *American Journal of Psychology, 113*, 331–340.
Wang, F. (2008). Motivation and English achievement: An exploratory and confirmatory factor analysis of a new measure for Chinese students of English learning. *North American Journal of Psychology, 10*(3), 633–646.
Wang, H., Qi, H., Wang, B. S., Cui, Y. Y., Zhu, L., Rong, Z. X., & Chen, H. Z. (2008). Is acupuncture beneficial in depression: A meta-analysis of 8 randomized controlled trials? *Journal of Affective Disorders, 111*(2), 125–134.
Wang, J. (2007). Mental health treatment dropout and its correlates in a general population sample. *Medical Care, 45*(3), 224–229.
Wang, J., Leu, J., & Shoda, Y. (2011). When the seemingly innocuous "stings": Racial microaggressions and their emotional consequences. *Personality and Social Psychology Bulletin, 37*(12), 1666–1678.
Wang, P. S., & Kessler, R. C. (2006). Global burden of mood disorders. In D. J. Stein, D. J. Kupfer, & A. F. Schatzberg (Eds.), *The American Psychiatric Publishing textbook of mood disorders* (pp. 55–68). Washington, DC: American Psychiatric Association Publishing.
Wang, Q. (2004). The emergence of cultural self-constructs: Autobiographical memory and self-description in European American and Chinese children. *Developmental Psychology, 40*(1), 3–15.
Wang, Q. (2006). Earliest recollections of self and others in European American and Taiwanese young adults. *Psychological Science, 17*(8), 708–714.
Wang, Q. (2008). Being American, being Asian: The bicultural self and autobiographical memory in Asian Americans. *Cognition, 107*(2), 743–751.
Wang, Q. (2013). *The autobiographical self in time and culture*. New York, NY: Oxford University Press.
Wang, Q., & Aydin, C. (2009). Cultural issues in flashbulb memory. In O. Luminet & A. Curci (Eds.), *Flashbulb memories: New issues and new perspectives* (pp. 247–268). New York, NY: Psychology Press.
Wang, Q., & Conway, M. A. (2004). The stories we keep: Autobiographical memory in American and Chinese middle-aged adults. *Journal of Personality, 72*(5), 911–938.
Wang, Q., & Ross, M. (2005). What we remember and what we tell: The effects of culture and self-priming on memory representations and narratives. *Memory, 13*(6), 594–606.
Wang, Q., Conway, M. A., & Hou, Y. (2004). Infantile amnesia: A cross-cultural investigation. *Cognitive Sciences, 1*(1), 123–135.
Wang, Q., Leichtman, M. D., & Davies, K. I. (2000). Sharing memories and telling stories: American and Chinese mothers and their 3-year-olds. *Memory, 8*(3), 159–177.
Wansink, B. (2006). *Mindless eating: Why we eat more than we think*. New York, NY: Bantam Books.
Wansink, B. (2011). Mindless eating: Environmental contributors to obesity. In J. H. Cawley (Ed.), *The Oxford handbook of the social science of obesity* (pp. 385–414). New York, NY: Oxford University Press.
Wansink, B., & Cheney, M. M. (2005). Super bowls: Serving bowl size and food consumption. *JAMA, 293*(14), 1723–1728.
Wansink, B., & Kim, J. (2005). Bad popcorn in big buckets: Portion size can influence intake as much as taste. *Journal of Nutrition Education and Behavior, 37*(5), 242–245.
Wansink, B., & Park, S. (2001). At the movies: How external cues and perceived taste impact consumption volume. *Food Quality and Preference, 12*(1), 69–74.
Wansink, B., & Van Ittersum, K. (2003). Bottoms up! The influence of elongation on pouring and consumption volume. *Journal of Consumer Research, 30*(3), 455–463.
Wapner, S. & Demick, J. (2003). Adult development: The holistic, developmental, and systems-oriented perspective. In J. Demick & C. Andreoletti (Eds.), *Handbook of adult development* (pp. 63–84). New York, NY: Springer Science+Business Media.
Warburton, W. A., Williams, K. D., & Cairns, D. R. (2006). When ostracism leads to aggression: The moderating effects of control deprivation. *Journal of Experimental Social Psychology, 42*(2), 213–220.
Ward, C., Leong, C. H., & Low, M. (2004). Personality and sojourner adjustment: An exploration of the big five and the cultural fit proposition. *Journal of Cross-Cultural Psychology, 35*(2), 137–151.
Ward, L. M., Epstein, M., Caruthers, A., & Merriwether, A. (2011). Men's media use, sexual cognitions, and sexual risk behavior: Testing a mediational model. *Developmental Psychology, 47*(2), 592–602.
Ward, L. M., & Friedman, K. (2006). Using TV as a guide: Associations between television viewing and adolescents' sexual attitudes and behavior. *Journal of Research on Adolescence, 16*(1), 133–156.
Ward, L. M., Reed, L., Trinh, S. L., & Foust, M. (2014). Sexuality and entertainment media. In D. L. Tolman & L. M. Diamond (Eds.), *APA handbook of sexuality and psychology* (Vol. 2, pp. 373–423). Washington, DC: American Psychological Association.
Ward, N. S., Oakley, D. A., Frackowiak, R. S. J., & Halligan, P. W. (2003). Differential brain activations during intentionally simulated and subjectively experienced paralysis. *Cognitive Neuropsychiatry, 8*(4), 295–312.
Wardle, J., & Cooke, L. (2005). The impact of obesity on psychological well-being. *Best Practice & Research Clinical Endocrinology & Metabolism, 19*(3), 421–440.
Wardle, J., Haase, A. M., Steptoe, A., Nillapun, M., Jonwutiwes, K., & Bellisie, F. (2004). Gender differences in food choice: The contribution of health beliefs and dieting. *Annals of Behavioral Medicine, 27*(2), 107–116.
Wardle, J., Herrera, M. L., Cooke, L., & Gibson, E. L. (2003). Modifying children's food preferences: The effects of exposure and reward on acceptance of an unfamiliar vegetable. *European Journal of Clinical Nutrition, 57*(2), 341–348.
Warner, R. (2004). *Recovery from schizophrenia* (3rd ed.). New York, NY: Brunner-Routledge.
Wartella, E., & Robb, M. (2007). Young children, new media. *Journal of Children and Media, 1*(1), 35–44.
Warwick-Evans, L. A., Symons, N., Fitch, T., & Burrows, L. (1998). Evaluating sensory conflict and postural instability. Theories of motion sickness. *Brain Research Bulletin, 47*(5), 465–469.
Wason, P. C., & Johnson-Laird, P. N. (1972). *Psychology of reasoning: Structure and content*. Cambridge, MA: Harvard University Press.

Wasow, T. (2001). Generative grammar. In M. Aronoff & J. Rees-Miller (Eds.), *The handbook of linguistics* (pp. 295–318). Malden, MA: Blackwell.

Wasserman, J. D., & Tulsky, D. S. (2005). A history of intelligence assessment. In D. P. Flanagan & P. L. Harrison (Eds.), *Contemporary intellectual assessment: Theories, tests, and issues* (2nd ed., pp. 3–22). New York, NY: Guilford Press.

Watkins, A. J., & Makin, S. J. (2007). Perceptual compensation for reverberation in speech identification: Effects of single-band, multiple-band and wideband noise contexts. *Acta Acustica united with Acustica, 93*(3), 403–410.

Watkins, A. J., Raimond, A. P., & Makin, S. J. (2011). Temporal-envelope constancy of speech in rooms and the perceptual weighting of frequency bands. *The Journal of the Acoustical Society of America, 130*(5), 2777–2788.

Watkins, C. E., Campbell, V. L., Nieberding, R., & Hallmark, R. (1995). Contemporary practice of psychological assessment by clinical psychologists. *Professional Psychology: Research and Practice, 26,* 54–60.

Watkins, P. C., Grimm, D. L., & Kolts, R. (2004). Counting your blessings: Positive memories among grateful persons. *Current Psychology, 23*(1), 52–67.

Watkins, P. C., Vache, K., Verney, S. P., Muller, S., & Mathews, A. (1996). Unconscious mood-congruent memory bias in depression. *Journal of Abnormal Psychology, 105,* 34–41.

Watkins, P. C., Mathews, A., Williamson, D. A., & Fuller, R. D. (1992). Mood-congruent memory in depression: Emotional priming or elaboration? *Journal of Abnormal Psychology, 101,* 581–586.

Watson, D., & Casillas, A. (2003). Neuroticism: Adaptive and maladaptive features. In E. C. Chang & L. J. Sanna (Eds.), *Virtue, vice, and personality: The complexity of behavior* (pp. 145–161). Washington, DC: American Psychological Association.

Watson, J. B. (1913). Psychology as the behaviorist views it. *Psychological Review, 20,* 158–177.

Watson, J. B. (1914). *Behavior: An introduction to comparative psychology*. New York, NY: Henry Holt.

Watson, J. B. (1924). *Behaviorism*. Chicago, IL: People's Institute.

Watson, J. C., & Bohart, A. (2015). Humanistic/existential/phenomenological psychotherapy. In R. L. Cautin & S. O. Lilienfeld (Eds.), *The encyclopedia of clinical psychology* (pp. 1416–1425). West Sussex, UK: Wiley-Blackwell.

Watson, R. I. (1973). Investigation into deindividuation using a cross-cultural survey technique. *Journal of Personality and Social Psychology, 25*(3), 342–345.

Watson, R. I., Sr., & Evans, R. B. (1991). *The great psychologists*. New York, NY: HarperCollins.

Watt, H. M. G. (2010). Gender and occupational choice. In J. C. Chrisler & D. R. McCreary (Eds.), *Handbook of gender research in psychology* (pp. 379–400). New York, NY: Springer Science+Business Media.

Watters, E. (2010). *Crazy like us: The globalization of the American psyche*. New York, NY: Free Press.

Waxman, S. R., & Leddon, E. M. (2011). Early word-learning and conceptual development: Everything had a name, and each name gave birth to a new thought. In U. Goswami (Ed.), *The Wiley-Blackwell handbook of childhood cognitive development* (2nd ed., pp. 180–208). Malden, MA: Wiley-Blackwell.

Way, N. (2006). The cultural practice of close friendships among urban adolescents in the United States. In X. Chen, D. French, & B. Schneider (Eds.), *Peer relationships in cultural context* (pp. 403–425). New York, NY: Cambridge University Press.

Wear, D., Aultman, J. M., Varley, J. D., & Zarconi, J. (2006). Making fun of patients: Medical students' perceptions and use of derogatory and cynical humor in clinical settings. *Academic Medicine, 81*(5), 454–462.

Wearing, D. (2005). *Forever today: A memoir of love and amnesia*. London, UK: Doubleday.

Weaver, J. B. (2003). Individual differences in television viewing motives. *Personality and Individual Differences, 35*(6), 1427–1437.

Weaver, T. E., & Ye, L. (2012). Sleep-related breathing disorders. In C. M. Morin & C. A. Espie (Eds.), *The Oxford handbook of sleep and sleep disorders* (pp. 666–689). Oxford, UK: Oxford University Press.

Webb, T. L., Miles, E., & Sheeran, P. (2012). Dealing with feeling: A meta-analysis of the effectiveness of strategies derived from the process model of emotion regulation. *Psychological Bulletin, 138*(4), 775–808.

Webb, W. B., & Agnew, H. W., Jr. (1974). Regularity in the control of the free-running sleep-wakefulness rhythm. *Aerospace Medicine, 45*(7), 701–704.

Weber, B. (2009, December 26). Kim Peek, inspiration for "Rain Man," dies at 58. *New York Times*. Retrieved September 1, 2013 from http://www.nytimes.com/2009/12/27/us/27peek.html?_r=2&.

Webster, M. (2010). Color perception. In E. B. Goldstein, *Encyclopedia of perception* (pp. 266–270). Thousand Oaks, CA: SAGE.

Wedding, D., Boyd, M. A., & Niemiec, R. M. (2010). *Movies and mental illness: Using films to understand psychopathology*. Cambridge, MA: Hogrefe.

Weems, C. F., Scott, B. G., Banks, D. M., & Graham, R. A. (2012). Is TV traumatic for all youths? The role of preexisting posttraumatic-stress symptoms in the link between disaster coverage and stress. *Psychological Science, 23*(11), 1293–1297.

Wegenek, A. R., Buskist, W., & American Psychological Association. (2010). *The insider's guide to the psychology major: Everything you need to know about the degree and profession*. Washington, DC: American Psychological Association.

Wegner, R., Abbey, A., Pierce, J., Pegram, S. E., & Woerner, J. (2015). Sexual assault perpetrators' justifications for their actions: Relationships to rape supportive attitudes, incident characteristics, and future perpetration. *Violence Against Women, 21,* 1018–1037.

Weimer, S. M., Dise, T. L., Evers, P. B., Ortiz, M. A., Welidaregay, W., & Steinmann, W. C. (2002). Prevalence, predictors, and attitudes toward cosleeping in an urban pediatric center. *Clinical Pediatrics, 41*(6), 433–438.

Weinberg, R. (2004). 94: Derek and dad finish Olympic 400 together. Retrieved from http://espn.go.com/espn/espn25/story?page=moments/94./

Weiner, B. (1993). On sin versus sickness: A theory of perceived responsibility and social motivation. *American Psychologist, 48*(9), 957–965.

Weiner, B., Perry, R. P., & Magnusson, J. (1988). An attributional analysis of reactions to stigmas. *Journal of Personality and Social Psychology, 55*(5), 738–748.

Weiner, D. B. (1994). "Le geste de Pinel": The history of a psychiatric myth. In M. S. Micale & R. Porter (Eds.), *Discovering the history of psychiatry* (pp. 232–247). New York, NY: Oxford University Press.

Weiner, I. B. (2004). Rorschach inkblot method. In M. W. Maruish (Ed.), *The use of psychological testing for treatment planning and outcomes assessment* (3rd ed., Vol. 3, pp. 553–587). Mahwah, NJ: Lawrence Erlbaum.

Weingarten, C. P., & Strauman, T. J. (2015). Neuroimaging for psychotherapy research: Current trends. *Psychotherapy Research, 25*(2), 185–213.

Weinstein, N., & Ryan, R. M. (2010). When helping helps: Autonomous motivation for prosocial behavior and its influence on well-being for the helper and recipient. *Journal of Personality and Social Psychology, 98*(2), 222–244.

Weisberg, D. S., Keil, F. C., Goodstein, J., Rawson, E., & Gray, J. R. (2008). The seductive allure of neuroscience explanations. *Journal of Cognitive Neuroscience, 20*(3), 470–477.

Weisenberger, J. M. (2001). Cutaneous perception. In E. B. Goldstein (Ed.), *Blackwell handbook of perception* (pp. 535–566). Oxford, UK: Blackwell.

Weiss, L. G., Saklofske, D. H., Coalson, D. L., & Raiford, S. E. (2010). Theoretical, empirical, and clinical foundations of the WAIS-IV index scores. In L. G. Weiss, D. H. Saklofske, D. Coalson, & S. E. Raiford (Eds.), *WAIS-IV clinical use and interpretation: Scientist-practitioner perspectives* (pp. 61–94). London, UK: Elsevier.

Weissman, M. M. (1995). *Mastering depression: A patient's guide to interpersonal psychotherapy*. Albany, NY: Graywind.

Weissmark, M. S., & Giacomo, D. A. (1998). *Doing psychotherapy effectively*. Chicago, IL: University of Chicago Press.

Weisz, J. R., Rothbaum, F. M., & Blackburn, T. C. (1984). Standing out and standing in: The psychology of control in America and Japan. *American Psychologist, 39*(9), 955–969.

Welchman, K. (2000). *Erik Erikson: His life, work and significance*. Philadelphia, PA: Open University Press.

Welfel, E. R., Werth, J. L., Jr., & Benjamin, G. A. H. (2012). Treating clients who threaten others or themselves. In S. J. Knapp (Ed.), *APA handbook of ethics in psychology* (Vol. 1, pp. 377–400). Washington, DC: American Psychological Association.

Wellman, H. M. (2011). Developing a theory of mind. In U. Goswami (Ed.), *The Wiley-Blackwell handbook of childhood cognitive development* (2nd ed., pp. 258–284). Malden, MA: Wiley-Blackwell.

Wellman, H. M., Cross, D., & Watson, J. (2003). Meta-analysis of theory-of-mind development: The truth about false belief. *Child Development, 72*(3), 655–684.

Wells, W. R. (1923). The anti-instinct fallacy. *Psychological Review, 30*(3), 228–234.

Wentzel, K. R. (2003). Sociometric status and adjustment in middle school: A longitudinal study. *The Journal of Early Adolescence, 23*(1), 5–28.

Wentzel, K. R., Barry, C. M., & Caldwell, K. A. (2004). Friendships in middle school: Influences on motivation and school adjustment. *Journal of Educational Psychology, 96*(2), 195–203.

Wenzlaff, R. M., Meier, J. S., & Salas, D. M. (2002). Thought suppression and memory biases during and after depressive moods. *Cognition & Emotion, 16,* 403–422.

Wermter, A. K., Laucht, M., Schimmelmann, B. G., Banaschweski, T., Sonuga-Barke, E. J., Rietschel, M., & Becker, K. (2010). From nature versus nurture, via nature and nurture, to gene × environment interaction in mental disorders. *European Child & Adolescent Psychiatry, 19*(3), 199–210.

Werner, S., & Thies, B. (2000). Is "change blindness" attenuated by domain-specific expertise? An expert–novices comparison of change detection in football images. *Visual Cognition, 7*(1–3), 163–173.

Werth, J. L., Hastings, S. L., & Riding-Malon, R. (2010). Ethical challenges of practicing in rural areas. *Journal of Clinical Psychology, 66*(5), 537–548.

Werth, R. (2006). Visual functions without the occipital lobe or after cerebral hemispherectomy in infancy. *European Journal of Neuroscience, 24*(10), 2932–2944.

Wertheimer, M. (2012). *A brief history of psychology* (5th ed.). New York: Psychology Press.

Wertsch, J. V., & Tulviste, P. (1992). L. S. Vygotsky and contemporary developmental psychology. *Developmental Psychology, 28*(4), 548–557.

Wertz, A. T., Ronda, J. M., Czeisler, C. A., & Wright, K. P. (2006). Effects of sleep inertia on cognition. *JAMA, 295*(2), 159–164.

Wessely, S. (2008). How shyness became social phobia. *The Lancet, 371*(9618), 1063–1064.

West, C., & Zimmerman, D. H. (1983). Small insults: A study of interruptions in cross-sex conversations between unacquainted persons. In B. Thorne, C. Kramarae, & N. Henley (Eds.), *Language, gender and society* (pp. 102–117). Rowley, MA: Newbury House.

West, M. A. (1987). Traditional and psychological perspectives on meditation. In M. A. West (Ed.), *The psychology of meditation* (pp. 5–22). New York, NY: Oxford University Press.

Westbrook, G. L. (2013). Seizures and epilepsy. In E. R. Kandel, J. H. Schwartz, T. M. Jessell, S. A. Siegelbaum, & A. J. Hudspeth (Eds.), *Principles of neural science* (5th ed., pp. 1116–1139). New York, NY: McGraw-Hill.

Westen, D., Gabbard, G. O., & Ortigo, K. M. (2008). Psychoanalytic approaches to personality. In O. P. John, R. W. Robins, & L. A. Pervin (Eds.), *Handbook of personality: Theory and research* (3rd ed., pp. 61–113). New York, NY: Guilford Press.

Wever, R. A. (1984). Sex differences in human circadian rhythms: Intrinsic periods and sleep fractions. *Experientia, 40*(11), 1226–1234.

Wheeler, L., Reis, H., & Nezlek, J. B. (1983). Loneliness, social interaction, and sex roles. *Journal of Personality and Social Psychology, 45*(4), 943–953.

Wheeler, M. A. (2000). Episodic memory and autonoetic awareness. In E. Tulving & F. I. M. Craik (Eds.), *The Oxford handbook of memory* (pp. 597–608). Oxford, UK: Oxford University Press.

White, B. P., Becker-Blease, K. A., & Grace-Bishop, K. (2006). Stimulant medication use, misuse, and abuse in an undergraduate and graduate student sample. *Journal of American College Health, 54*(5), 261–268.

Whitehurst, G. J., Falco, F. L., Lonigan, C. J., Fischel, J. E., DeBaryshe, B. D., Valdez-Menchaca, M. C., & Caulfield, M. (1988). Accelerating language development through picture book reading. *Developmental Psychology, 24*(4), 552–559.

Whiteman, S. D., McHale, S. M. and Crouter, A. C. (2003), What parents learn from experience: The first child as a first draft? *Journal of Marriage and Family, 65*, 608–621.

Whiting, B. B., & Edwards, C. P. (1988). *Children of different worlds: The formation of social behavior*. Cambridge, MA: Harvard University Press.

Whitmer, R. A., Gunderson, E. P., Barrett-Connor, E., Quesenberry, C. P., Jr., & Yaffe, K. (2005). Obesity in middle age and future risk of dementia: A 27 year longitudinal population based study. *BMJ: British Medical Journal, 330*(7504), 1360–1362.

Whitney, P., & Rosen, P. J. (2013). Sleep deprivation and performance: The role of working memory. In T. P. Alloway & R. G. Alloway (Eds.), *Working memory: The connected intelligence* (pp. 175–186). New York, NY: Psychology Press.

Whooley, O., & Horwitz, A. V. (2013). The paradox of professional success: Grand ambition, furious resistance, and the derailment of the DSM-5 revision process. In J. Paris & J. Phillips (Eds.), *Making the DSM-5: Concepts and controversies* (pp. 75–92). New York, NY: Springer Science+Business Media.

Whorf, B. L. (1956). *Language, thought, and reality* (J. Carroll, Ed.). Cambridge, MA: MIT Press.

Widiger, T. A. (2005). Classification and diagnosis: Historical development and contemporary issues. In J. E. Maddux & B. A. Winstead (Eds.), *Psychopathology* (pp. 63–83). Mahwah, NJ: Lawrence Erlbaum.

Widiger, T. A., & Costa, P. T. (2012). *Personality disorders and the five-factor model of personality* (3rd ed.). Washington, DC: American Psychological Association.

Widiger, T. A., & Edmundson, M. (2011). Diagnoses, dimensions, and DSM-5. In D. H. Barlow (Ed.), *The Oxford handbook of clinical psychology* (pp. 254–278). New York, NY: Oxford University Press.

Widiger, T. A., & Lowe, J. R. (2010). Personality disorders. In M. M. Antony & D. H. Barlow (Eds.), *Handbook of assessment and treatment planning for psychological disorders* (2nd ed., pp. 571–605). New York, NY: Guilford Press.

Widiger, T. A., & Mullins-Sweatt, S. (2008). Personality disorders. In A. Tasman, J. Kay, J. A. Lieberman, M. B. First, & M. Maj (Eds.), *Psychiatry* (3rd ed., Vol. 2, pp. 1718–1753). Chichester, UK: Wiley.

Widiger, T. A., & Trull, T. J. (2007). Plate tectonics in the classification of personality disorder: Shifting to a dimensional model. *American Psychologist, 62*(2), 71–83.

Wierson, M., Long, P. J., & Forehand, R. L. (1993). Toward a new understanding of early menarche: The role of environmental stress in pubertal timing. *Adolescence, 28,* 913–924.

Wilbert-Lampen, U., Leistner, D., Greven, S., Pohl, T., Sper, S., Völker, C., . . . Steinbeck, G. (2008). Cardiovascular events during World Cup soccer. *New England Journal of Medicine, 358*(5), 475–483.

Wilcox, L. M., & Allison, R. S. (2010). Binocular vision and stereopsis. In E. B. Goldstein (Ed.), *Encyclopedia of perception* (pp. 208–212). Thousand Oaks, CA: SAGE.

Wilcutt, E. G. (2012). The prevalence of DSM-IV attention-deficit/hyperactivity disorder: A meta-analytic review. *Neurotherapeutics, 9*(3), 490–499.

Wild, E. (2005). Deja vu in neurology. *Journal of Neurology, 252*(1), 1–7.

Wild, S. H., Roglic, G., Green, A., Sicree, R., & King, H. (2004). Global prevalence of diabetes: Estimates for the year 2000 and projections for 2030. *Diabetes Care, 27*(5), 1047–1053.

Wiley, R. E., and Berman, S. L. (2013), Adolescent identity development and distress in a clinical sample. *Journal of Clinical Psychology. 69*(12), 1299–1304. doi:10. 1002/jclp.22004

Wilgus, J., & Wilgus, B. (2009). Face to face with Phineas Gage. *Journal of the History of the Neurosciences, 18*(3), 340–345.

Willcutt, E. G., & Pennington, B. F. (2000). Psychiatric comorbidity in children and adolescents with reading disability. *Journal of Child Psychology and Psychiatry, 41*(08), 1039–1048.

Williams, A. A., & Marquez, B. A. (2015). The lonely selfie king: Selfies and the conspicuous prosumption of gender and race. *International Journal of Communication, 9*, 1775–1787.

Williams, A. D., & Moulds, M. L. (2010). The content, nature, and persistence of intrusive memories in depression. In J. H. Mace (Ed.), *The act of remembering: Toward an understanding of how we recall the past* (pp. 361–383). Malden, MA: Wiley-Blackwell.

Williams, C. L., & Butcher, J. N. (2011). *A beginner's guide to the MMPI-A*. Washington, DC: American Psychological Association.

Williams, G. C., Cox, E. M., Hedberg, V. A., & Deci, E. L. (2000). Extrinsic life goals and health-risk behaviors in adolescents. *Journal of Applied Social Psychology, 30*(8), 1756–1771.

Williams, G. C., Freedman, Z. R., & Deci, E. L. (1998). Supporting autonomy to motivate patients with diabetes for glucose control. *Diabetes Care, 21*(10), 1644–1651.

Williams, G. C., Grow, V. M., Freedman, Z. R., Ryan, R. M., & Deci, E. L. (1996). Motivational predictors of weight loss and weight-loss maintenance. *Journal of Personality and Social Psychology, 70*(1), 115–126.

Williams, G. C., McGregor, H., Sharp, D., Kouides, R. W., Lévesque, C. S., Ryan, R. M., & Deci, E. L. (2006a). A self-determination multiple risk intervention trial to improve smokers' health. *Journal of General Internal Medicine, 21*(12), 1288–1294.

Williams, G. C., McGregor, H. A., Sharp, D., Lévesque, C., Kouides, R. W., Ryan, R. M., & Deci, E. L. (2006b). Testing a self-determination theory intervention for motivating tobacco cessation: Supporting autonomy and competence in a clinical trial. *Health Psychology, 25*(1), 91–101.

Williams, K. A., Kolar, M. M., Reger, B. E., & Pearson, J. C. (2001). Evaluation of a wellness-based mindfulness stress reduction intervention: A controlled trial. *American Journal of Health Promotion, 15*(6), 422–432.

Williams, K., Harkins, S. G., & Latané, B. (1981). Identifiability as a deterrent to social loafing: Two cheering experiments. *Journal of Personality and Social Psychology, 40*(2), 303–311.

Williams, M., Davids, K., Burwitz, L., & Williams, J. (1993). Cognitive knowledge and soccer performance. *Perceptual and Motor Skills, 76*(2), 579–593.

Williams, R. L. (1972). *The BITCH Test:(Black Intelligence Test of Cultural Homogeneity)*. St. Louis, MO: Williams and Associates.

Williams, T. J., Pepitone, M. E., Christensen, S. E., Cooke, B. M., Huberman, A. D., Breedlove, N. J., . . . Breedlove, S. M. (2000). Finger-length ratios and sexual orientation. *Nature, 404*(6777), 455–456.

Williams, T., Connolly, J., Pepler, D., & Craig, W. (2003). Questioning and sexual minority adolescents: High school experiences of bullying, sexual harassment and physical abuse. *Canadian Journal of Community Mental Health, 22*(2), 47–58.

Willinger, M., Ko, C. W., Hoffman, H. J., Kessler, R. C., & Corwin, M. J. (2003). Trends in infant bed sharing in the United States, 1993–2000: The National Infant Sleep Position study. *Archives of Pediatrics & Adolescent Medicine, 157*(1), 43–49.

Willis, J. O., Dumont, R., & Kaufman, A. S. (2011). Factor-analytic models of intelligence. In R. J. Sternberg & S. B. Kaufman (Eds.), *The Cambridge handbook of intelligence* (pp. 39–57). Cambridge, UK: Cambridge University Press.

Willis, M. S., Esqueda, C. W., & Schacht, R. N. (2008). Social perceptions of individuals missing upper front teeth. *Perceptual and Motor Skills, 106*(2), 423–435.

Willis, R. W., & Edwards, J. A. (1969). A study of the comparative effectiveness of systematic desensitization and implosive therapy. *Behaviour Research and Therapy, 7*(4), 387–395.

Wills, G. I. (1984). A personality study of musicians working in the popular field. *Personality and Individual Differences, 5*(3), 359–360.

Wills, G. I. (2003). Forty lives in the bebop business: Mental health in a group of eminent jazz musicians. *The British Journal of Psychiatry, 183*(3), 255–259.

Wilson, R. S., de Leon, C. F. M., Bienias, J. L., Evans, D. A., & Bennett, D. A. (2004). Personality and mortality in old age. *The Journals of Gerontology Series B: Psychological Sciences and Social Sciences, 59*(3), P110–P116.

Wilson, T. D., Aronson, E., & Carlsmith, K. (2010). The art of laboratory experimentation. In S. T. Fiske, D. T. Gilbert, & G. Lindzey (Eds.), *Handbook of social psychology* (5th ed., Vol.1, pp. 51–82). Hoboken, NJ: Wiley.

Wilson, T. D., Wheatley, T., Meyers, J. M., Gilbert, D. T., & Axsom, D. (2000). Focalism: A source of durability bias in affective forecasting. *Journal of Personality and Social Psychology, 78*(5), 821–836.

Wimmer, H., & Perner, J. (1983). Beliefs about beliefs: Representation and constraining function of wrong beliefs in young children's understanding of deception. *Cognition, 13*(1), 103–128.

Winawer, J., Witthoft, N., Frank, M. C., Wu, L., Wade, A. R., & Boroditsky, L. (2007). Russian blues reveal effects of language on color discrimination. *Proceedings of the National Academy of Sciences, 104*(19), 7780–7785.

Windholz, G. (1997). Ivan P. Pavlov: An overview of his life and psychological work. *American Psychologist. 52*, 941–946.

Wingate, L. (2011). Black Intelligence Test of Cultural Homogeneity. In S. Goldstein & J. A. Naglieri (Eds.), *Encyclopedia of child behavior and development* (pp. 261–262). New York, NY: Springer.

Winickoff, J. P., Friebely, J., Tanski, S. E., Sherrod, C., Matt, G. E., Hovell, M. F., & McMillen, R. C. (2009). Beliefs about the health effects of "thirdhand" smoke and home smoking bans. *Pediatrics, 123*(1), e74–e79.

Winkelman, J. W. (1998). Clinical and polysomnographic features of sleep-related eating disorder. *The Journal of Clinical Psychiatry, 59*(1), 14–19.

Winocur, G., McDonald, R. M., & Moscovitch, M. (2001). Anterograde and retrograde amnesia in rats with large hippocampal lesions. *Hippocampus, 11*(1), 18–26.

Winston, J. S., Gottfried, J. A., Kilner, J. M., & Dolan, R. J. (2005). Integrated neural representations of odor intensity and affective valence in human amygdala. *The Journal of Neuroscience, 25*(39), 8903–8907.

Winter, W. C., Hammond, W. R., Green, N. H., Zhang, Z., & Bliwise, D. L. (2009). Measuring circadian advantage in Major League Baseball: A 10-year retrospective study. *International Journal of Sports Physiology and Performance, 4*(3), 394–401.

Winton, W. M. (1987). Do introductory textbooks present the Yerkes-Dodson Law correctly? *American Psychologist, 42*(2), 202–203.

Wirtz, D., Kruger, J., Scollon, C. N., & Diener, E. (2003). What to do on spring break? The role of predicted, on-line, and remembered experience in future choice. *Psychological Science, 14*(5), 520–524.

Witt, P. L., Wheeless, L. R., & Allen, M. (2004). A meta-analytical review of the relationship between teacher immediacy and student learning. *Communication Monographs, 71*(2), 184–207.

Witte, D. R., Bots, M. L., Hoes, A. W., & Grobbee, D. E. (2000). Cardiovascular mortality in Dutch men during 1996 European football championship: Longitudinal population study. *BMJ: British Medical Journal, 321*(7276), 1552–1554.

Wittgenstein, L. (1968). *Philosophical investigations* (G. E. M. Anscombe, Trans.) New York, NY: MacMillan.

Wixted, J. (2010). The role of retroactive interference and consolidation in everyday forgetting. In S. Della Sala (Ed.), *Forgetting* (pp. 285–312). East Sussex, UK: Psychology Press.

Wolf, A. W., Lozoff, B., Latz, S., & Paludetto, R. (1996). Parental theories in the management of young children's sleep in Japan, Italy, and the United States. In S. Harkness & C. M. Super (Eds.), *Parent's cultural belief systems: Their origins, expressions, and consequences* (pp. 364–384). New York, NY: Guilford Press.

Wolf-Meyer, M. (2013). Where have all our naps gone? Or Nathaniel Kleitman, the consolidation of sleep, and the historiography of emergence. *Anthropology of Consciousness, 24*(2), 96–116.

Wolfson, A. R. & Carskadon, M. A. (2005). A survey of factors influencing high school start times. *NASSP Bulletin, 89*(642), 47–66.

Wolfson, A. R., & Carskadon, M. A. (2003). Understanding adolescents' sleep patterns and school performance: A critical appraisal. *Sleep Medicine Reviews, 7*(6), 491–506.

Wolfson, A. R., & O'Malley, E. B. (2012). Sleep-related problems in adolescence and emerging adulthood. In C. M. Morin & C. A. Espie (Eds.), *The Oxford handbook of sleep and sleep disorders* (pp. 746–768). Oxford, UK: Oxford University Press.

Wolfson, A. R., & Richards, M. (2011). Young adolescents: Struggles with insufficient sleep. In M. El-Sheikh (Ed.), *Sleep and development: Familial and socio-cultural considerations* (pp. 265–299). New York, NY: Oxford University Press.

Wolfson, A. R., Spaulding, N. L., Dandrow, C., & Baroni, E. M. (2007). Middle school start times: The importance of a good night's sleep for young adolescents. *Behavioral Sleep Medicine, 5*(3), 194–209.

Wolf-Wendel, L., Ward, K., & Kinzie, J. (2009). A tangled web of terms: The overlap and unique contribution of involvement, engagement, and integration to understanding college student success. *Journal of College Student Development, 50*(4), 407–428.

Wolman, D. (2012). The split brain: A tale of two halves. *Nature, 483*(7389), 260–263.

Wolpe, J. (1958). *Psychotherapy by reciprocal inhibition*. Stanford, CA: Stanford University Press.

Wolpe, J. (1969). *The practice of behavior therapy*. New York, NY: Pergamon Press.

Wolpert, D. M., Pearson, K. G., & Ghez, C. P. J. (2013). The organization and planning of movement. In E. R. Kandel, J. H. Schwartz, T. M. Jessell, S. A. Siegelbaum, & A. J. Hudspeth (Eds.), *Principles of neural science* (5th ed., pp. 743–767). New York, NY: McGraw-Hill.

Wolters, C. A. (2004). Advancing achievement goal theory: Using goal structures and goal orientations to predict students' motivation, cognition, and achievement. *Journal of Educational Psychology, 96*(2), 236–250.

Wong, G., Derthick, A. O., David, E. J. R., Saw, A., & Okazaki, S. (2014). The what, the why, and the how: A review of racial microaggressions research in psychology. *Race and Social Problems, 6*(2), 181–200.

Wood, A. M., Froh, J. J., & Geraghty, A. W. (2010). Gratitude and well-being: A review and theoretical integration. *Clinical Psychology Review, 30*(7), 890–905.

Wood, C., Jackson, E., Hart, L., Plester, B., & Wilde, L. (2011). The effect of text messaging on 9- and 10-year-old children's reading, spelling and phonological processing skills. *Journal of Computer Assisted Learning, 27*(1), 28–36.

Wood, J. M., Garb, H. N., & Nezworski, M. T. (2007). Psychometrics: Better measurement makes better clinicians. In S. O. Lilienfeld & W. T. O'Donohue (Eds.), *The great ideas of clinical science: 17 principles that every mental health professional should understand* (pp. 77–92). New York, NY: Routledge.

Wood, J. M., Lilienfeld, S. O., Nezworski, M. T., Garb, H. N., Allen, K. H., & Wildermuth, J. L. (2010). Validity of Rorschach inkblot scores for discriminating psychopaths from non-psychopaths in forensic populations: A meta-analysis. *Psychological Assessment, 22*(2), 336–349.

Wood, J. M., Nezworski, M. T., Lilienfeld, S. O., & Garb, H. N. (2003). *What's wrong with the Rorschach?* San Francisco: Jossey-Bass.

Wood, N., & Cowan, N. (1995). The cocktail party phenomenon revisited: How frequent are attention shifts to one's name in an irrelevant auditory channel? *Journal of Experimental Psychology: Learning, Memory, and Cognition, 21*(1), 255–260.

Wood, W., & Eagly, A. H. (2010). Gender. In S. T. Fiske, D. T. Gilbert, & G. Lindzey (Eds.), *Handbook of social psychology* (5th ed., Vol.1, pp. 629–667). Hoboken, NJ: Wiley.

Woodbury, D., & Black, I. B. (2004). Stem cell plasticity: Overview and perspective. In M. S. Gazzaniga (Ed.), *The cognitive neurosciences III* (pp. 161–170). Cambridge, MA: MIT Press.

Woody, S. R., & Nosen, E. (2009) Psychological models of phobic disorders and panic. In M. M. Antony & M. B. Stein (Eds.), *Oxford handbook of anxiety and related disorders* (pp. 209–224). New York, NY: Oxford University Press.

Wool, Z. H. (2013). War sick: Meaningful illness and military victimhood. *Focaal: Journal of Global and Historical Anthropology, 66*, 139–147.

World Health Organization. (2003). Joint WHO/FAO Expert Consultation on Diet, Nutrition, and the Prevention of Chronic Disease. Geneva, Switzerland: World Health Organization.

Worringham, C. J., & Messick, D. M. (1983). Social facilitation of running: An unobtrusive study. *The Journal of Social Psychology, 121*(1), 23–29.

Worthen, J. B., & Hunt, R. R. (2011). *Mnemonology: Mnemonics for the 21st century*. New York, NY: Psychology Press.

Worthman, C. M. (2011). Developmental cultural ecology of sleep. In M. El-Sheikh (Ed.), *Sleep and development: Familial and socio-cultural considerations* (pp. 167–194). New York, NY: Oxford University Press.

Wozenilek, A. C., Pomerantz, A. M., Pettibone, J. C., & Segrist, D. J. (2012). When clients no-show: An empirical analogue study of psychologists' response strategies. *Journal of Contemporary Psychotherapy, 42*, 87–92.

Wozniak, R. H. (1997). Behaviorism. In W. G. Bringmann, H. E. Lück, R. Miller, & C. E. Early (Eds.), *A pictorial history of psychology* (pp. 198—205). Carol Stream, IL: Quintessence Publishing

Wray, A. (1998). Protolanguage as a holistic system for social interaction. *Language & Communication, 18*(1), 47–67.

Wray, A. (2000). Holistic utterances in protolanguage: The link from primates to humans. In C. Knight, M. Studdert-Kennedy, & J. R. Hurford (Eds.), *The evolutionary emergence of language: Social function and the origins of linguistic form* (pp. 285–302). Cambridge, UK: Cambridge University Press.

Wren, A. M., Seal, L. J., Cohen, M. A., Brynes, A. E., Frost, G. S., Murphy, K. G., . . . Bloom, S. R. (2001). Ghrelin enhances appetite and increases food intake in humans. *Journal of Clinical Endocrinology and Metabolism, 86*(12), 5992–5995.

Wright, K. P., McHill, A. W., Birks, B. R., Griffin, B. R., Rusterholz, T., & Chinoy, E. D. (2013). Entrainment of the human circadian clock to the natural light-dark cycle. *Current Biology, 23*(16), 1554–1558.

Wright, P., Albarracin, D., Brown, R. D., Li, H., He, G., & Liu, Y. (2008). Dissociated responses in the amygdala and orbitofrontal cortex to bottom-up and top-down components of emotional evaluation. *Neuroimage, 39*(2), 894–902.

Wright, R. J., Mitchell, H., Visness, C. M., Cohen, S., Stout, J., Evans, R., & Gold, D. R. (2004). Community violence and asthma morbidity: The inner-city asthma study. *American Journal of Public Health, 94*(4), 625–632.

Wright, S. C., Aron, A., McLaughlin-Volpe, T., & Ropp, S. A. (1997). The extended contact effect: Knowledge of cross-group friendships and prejudice. *Journal of Personality and Social Psychology, 73*(1), 73–90.

Wu, G. (2002). Evaluation of the effectiveness of Tai Chi for improving balance and preventing falls in the older population—A review. *Journal of the American Geriatrics Society, 50*(4), 746–754.

Wu, G., & Gonzalez, R. (1996). Curvature of the probability weighting function. *Management Science, 42*(12), 1676–1690.

Wyart, C., Webster, W. W., Chen, J. H., Wilson, S. R., McClary, A., Khan, R. M., & Sobel, N. (2007). Smelling a single component of male sweat alters levels of cortisol in women. *The Journal of Neuroscience, 27*(6), 1261–1265.

Wykes, T., Brammer, M., Mellers, J., Bray, P., Reeder, C., Williams, C., & Corner, J. (2002). Effects on the brain of a psychological treatment: Cognitive remediation therapy: Functional magnetic resonance imaging in schizophrenia. *British Journal of Psychiatry, 181*(2), 144–152.

Wymbs, B., Molina, B., Pelham, W., Cheong, J., Gnagy, E., Belendiuk, K., . . . Waschbusch, D. (2012). Risk of intimate partner violence among young adult males with childhood ADHD. *Journal of Attention Disorders, 16*(5), 373–383.

Wynn, K. (1992). Addition and subtraction by human infants. *Nature, 358*(6389), 749–750.

Wyrwicka, W. (2000). *Conditioning: Situation versus intermittent stimulus*. New Brunswick, NJ: Transaction Publishers.

Yager, J. (2010). The sociology of sleep. In C. P. Pollak, M. J. Thorpy, & J. Yager, *The encyclopedia of sleep and sleep disorders* (3rd ed., pp. xxxix–xliii). New York, NY: Infobase Publishing.

Yalom, I. D. (1983). *Inpatient group psychotherapy*. New York, NY: Basic Books.

Yalom, I. D. (2005). *The theory and practice of group psychotherapy* (5th ed.). New York, NY: Basic Books.

Yang, C. K., Kim, J. K., Patel, S. R., & Lee, J. H. (2005). Age-related changes in sleep/wake patterns among Korean teenagers. *Pediatrics, 115*(Suppl. 1), 250–256.

Yang, Y., & Raine, A. (2009). Prefrontal structural and functional brain imaging findings in antisocial, violent, and psychopathic individuals: A meta-analysis. *Psychiatry Research: Neuroimaging, 174*(2), 81–88.

Yapko, M. D. (2008). Hypnotic approaches to treating depression. In M. R. Nash & A. J. Barnier (Eds.), *The Oxford handbook of hypnosis: Theory, research, and practice* (pp. 549–568). Oxford, UK: Oxford University Press.

Yardley, L. (1992). Motion sickness and perception: A reappraisal of the sensory conflict approach. *British Journal of Psychology, 83*(4), 449–471.

Yarkoni, T. (2009). Big correlations in little studies: Inflated fMRI correlations reflect low statistical power—Commentary on Vul et al. (2009). *Perspectives on Psychological Science, 4*(3), 294–298.

Yarkoni, T. (2010). Personality in 100,000 words: A large-scale analysis of personality and word use among bloggers. *Journal of Research in Personality, 44*(3), 363–373.

Yasnitsky, A. (2012). Lev Vygotsky: Philologist and defectologist, a sociointellectual biography. In W. E. Pickren, D. A. Dewsbury, & M. Wertheimer (Eds.), *Portraits of pioneers in developmental psychology* (pp. 109–133). New York, NY: Psychology Press.

Yeh, C. J., Arora, A. K., & Wu, K. A. (2006). A new theoretical model of collectivistic coping. In P. T. P. Wong and L. C. J. Wong (Eds.), *Handbook of multicultural perspectives on stress and coping* (pp. 55–72). New York: Springer Science+Business Media.

Yeh, C., & Inose, M. (2002). Difficulties and coping strategies of Chinese, Japanese and Korean immigrant students. *Adolescence, 37*, 69–82.

Yerkes, R. M., & Dodson, J. D. (1908). The relation of strength of stimulus to rapidity of habit-formation. *Journal of Comparative Neurological Psychology, 18*, 459–482.

Yeshurun, Y., Lapid, H., Haddad, R., Gelstein, S., Arzi, A., Sela, L., . . . Sobel, N. (2009). Olfaction: From percept to molecule. In M. S. Gazzaniga (Ed.), *The cognitive neurosciences* (4th ed., pp. 321–342). Cambridge, MA: MIT Press.

Yoon, J. A., Han, D. H., Noh, J. Y., Kim, M. H., Son, G. H., Kim, K., . . . Cho, S. (2012). Meal time shift disturbs circadian rhythmicity along with metabolic and behavioral alterations in mice. *PLoS ONE, 7*(8), e44053.

Yost, W. A. (2001). Auditory, localization, and scene perception. In E. B. Goldstein (Ed.), *Blackwell handbook of perception* (pp. 437–468). Oxford, UK: Blackwell.

Yost, W. A. (2010). Audition: Pitch perception. In E. B. Goldstein (Ed.), *Encyclopedia of perception* (pp. 151–154). Thousand Oaks, CA: SAGE.

Young, L. R. & Nestle, M. (2007). Portion sizes and obesity: Responses of fast-food companies. *Journal of Public Health Policy, 28*(2), 238–248.

Young, L. R., & Nestle, M. (2002). The contribution of expanding portion sizes to the US obesity epidemic. *American Journal of Public Health, 92*(2), 246–249.

Young, S. D. (2012). *Psychology at the movies*. West Sussex, UK: Wiley-Blackwell.

Young, T. (1802). The Bakerian lecture: On the theory of light and colours. *Philosophical Transactions of the Royal Society of London, 92*(1802), 12–48.

Young, T., & Peppard, P. E. (2005). Clinical presentation of OSAS: Gender does matter. *Sleep, 28*(3), 293–295.

Young, T., Hutton, R., Finn, L., Badr, S., & Palta, M. (1996). The gender bias in sleep apnea diagnosis: Are women missed because they have different symptoms? *Archives of Internal Medicine, 156*(21), 2445–2451.

Young, T., Palta, M., Dempsey, J., Skatrud, J., Weber, S., & Badr, S. (1993). The occurrence of sleep-disordered breathing among middle-aged adults. *New England Journal of Medicine, 328*(17), 1230–1235.

Young, T., Skatrud, J., & Peppard, P. E. (2004). Risk factors for obstructive sleep apnea in adults. *JAMA, 291*(16), 2013–2016.

Yzerbyt, V., & Demoulin, S. (2010). Intergroup relations. In S. T. Fiske, D. T. Gilbert, & G. Lindzey (Eds.), *Handbook of social psychology* (5th ed., Vol. 2, pp. 1024–1083). Hoboken, NJ: Wiley.

Zachar, P., & Kendler, K. S. (2010). Philosophical issues in the classification of psychopathology. In T. Millon, R. F. Krueger, & E. Simonsen (Eds.), *Contemporary directions in psychopathology: Scientific foundations of the DSM-V and ICD-11* (pp. 127–148). New York, NY: Guilford Press.

Zacks, R. T., & Hasher, L. (2002). Frequency processing: A twenty-five year perspective. In P. Sedlmeier & T. Betsch (Eds.), *Etc.: Frequency processing and cognition* (pp. 21–36). New York, NY: Oxford.

Zacks, R. T., Hasher, L., & Sanft, H. (1982). Automatic encoding of event frequency: Further findings. *Journal of Experimental Psychology: Learning, Memory, and Cognition, 8*(2), 106.

Zadra, A. & Pilon, M. (2012). Parasomnias II: Sleep terrors and somnambulism. In C. M. Morin & C. A. Espie (Eds.), *The Oxford handbook of sleep and sleep disorders* (pp. 577–596). Oxford, UK: Oxford University Press.

Zagorsky, J. L. (2007). Do you have to be smart to be rich? The impact of IQ on wealth, income and financial distress. *Intelligence, 35*(5), 489–501.

Zajonc, R. B. (1968). Attitudinal effects of mere exposure. *Journal of Personality and Social Psychology, 9*, 1–27.

Zajonc, R. B. (1980). Feeling and thinking: Preferences need no inferences. *American Psychologist, 35*(2), 151–175.

Zajonc, R. B. (1984). On the primacy of affect. *American Psychologist, 39*(2), 117–123.

Zajonc, R. B., Murphy, S. T., & Inglehart, M. (1989). Feeling and facial efference: Implications of the vascular theory of emotion. *Psychological Review, 96*(3), 395–416.

Zald, D. H. (2003). The human amygdala and the emotional evaluation of sensory stimuli. *Brain Research Reviews, 41*(1), 88–123.

Zanker, J. M. (2010). *Sensation, perception and action: An evolutionary perspective*. Basingstoke, UK: Palgrave Macmillan.

Zapata Sola, A., Kreuch, T., Landers, R. N., Hoyt, T., & Butcher, J. N. (2009). Personality assessment in personnel selection using the MMPI-2: A cross-cultural comparison. *International Journal of Clinical and Health Psychology, 9*(2), 287–298.

Zautra, A. J., & Reich, J. W. (2011). Resilience: The meanings, methods, and measures of a fundamental characteristic of human adaptation. In S. Folkman (Ed.), *Oxford handbook of stress, health, and coping* (pp. 173–185). Oxford, UK: Oxford University Press.

Zea, M. C., & Nakamura, N. (2014). Sexual orientation. In F. T. L. Leong (Ed.), *APA handbook of multicultural psychology* (Vol. 1, pp. 395–410). Washington, DC: American Psychological Association.

Zeidan, F. (2015). The neurobiology of mindfulness meditation. In K. W. Brown, J. D. Creswell, & R. M. Ryan (Eds.), *Handbook of mindfulness: Theory, research, and practice* (pp. 171–189). New York, NY: Guilford Press.

Zeidan, F., Martucci, K. T., Kraft, R. A., Gordon, N. S., McHaffie, J. G., & Coghill, R. C. (2011). Brain mechanisms supporting the modulation of pain by mindfulness meditation. *Journal of Neuroscience, 31*(14), 5540–5548.

Zeidan, F., Martucci, K. T., Kraft, R. A., McHaffie, J. G., & Coghill, R. C. (2013). Neural correlates of mindfulness meditation-related anxiety relief. *Social Cognitive and Affective Neuroscience*, 9(6), 751–759.

Zelazo, P. D. & Lee, W. S. C. (2010). Brain development: An overview. In W. F. Overton (Ed.), *Handbook of life-span development* (Vol. 1, pp. 89–114). Hoboken, NJ: Wiley.

Zellner, D. A. (2010). Multimodal interactions: Color-chemical. In E. B. Goldstein (Ed.), *Encyclopedia of perception* (pp. 584–585). Thousand Oaks, CA: SAGE.

Zellner, D. A. (2013). Color–odor interactions: A review and model. *Chemosensory Perception, 6*(4), 155–169.

Zellner, D. A., Bartoli, A. M., & Eckard, R. (1991). Influence of color on odor identification and liking ratings. *The American Journal of Psychology, 104*(4), 547–561.

Zellner, D. A., Loaiza, S., Gonzalez, Z., Pita, J., Morales, J., Pecora, D., & Wolf, A. (2006). Food selection changes under stress. *Physiology & Behavior, 87*(4), 789–793.

Zeman, J., & Garber, J. (1996). Display rules for anger, sadness, and pain: It depends on who is watching. *Child Development, 67*(3), 957–973.

Zhang, Z. J., Chen, H. Y., Yip, K. C., Ng, R., & Wong, V. T. (2010). The effectiveness and safety of acupuncture therapy in depressive disorders: Systematic review and meta-analysis. *Journal of Affective Disorders, 124*(1), 9–21.

Zhao, L. R. (2015). Neural stem cells in response to microenvironment changes inside and outside of the brain. In L. Zhao & J. H. Zhang (Eds.), *Cellular therapy for stroke and CNS injuries* (pp. 17–32). New York, NY: Springer.

Zhao, Y., Qiu, W., & Xie, N. (2012). Social networking, social gaming, texting. In D. G. Singer & J. L. Singer (Eds.), *Handbook of children and the media* (2nd ed., pp. 97–112). Los Angeles, CA: SAGE.

Zhou, W., Yang, X., Chen, K., Cai, P., He, S., & Jiang, Y. (2014). Chemosensory communication of gender through two human steroids in a sexually dimorphic manner. *Current Biology, 24*(10), 1091–1095.

Ziegler, M., MacCann, C., & Roberts, R. D. (2012). Faking: Knowns, unknowns, and points of contention. In M. Ziegler, C. MacCann, & R. D. Roberts (Eds.), *New perspectives on faking in personality assessment* (pp. 3–16). New York, NY: Oxford University Press.

Zilboorg, G., & Henry, G. W. (1941). *A history of medical psychology*. New York, NY: W. W. Norton.

Zimbardo, P. G. (1972). Pathology of imprisonment. *Society, 9*, 4–8.

Zimbardo, P. G., Haney, C., Banks, W. C., & Jaffe, D. (1973, April 8). The mind is a formidable jailer: A Pirandellian prison. *New York Times Magazine*. Retrieved from http://www.nytimes.com/1973/04/08/archives/a-pirandellian-prison-the-mind-is-a-formidable-jailer.html?_r=0

Zimman, L. (2013). Hegemonic masculinity and the variability of gay-sounding speech: The perceived sexuality of transgender men. *Journal of Language and Sexuality, 2*(1), 1–39.

Zinbarg, R. E., Uliaszek, A. A., & Lewis, A. R. (2009). Anxiety. In R. E. Ingram (Ed.), *The international encyclopedia of depression* (pp. 27–30). New York, NY: Springer.

Zoellner, L. A., Abramowitz, J. S., Moore, S. A., & Slagle, D. M. (2008). Flooding. In W. T. O'Donohue & J. E. Fisher (Eds.), *Cognitive behavior therapy: Applying empirically supported techniques in your practice* (2nd ed., pp. 202–210). Hoboken, NJ: Wiley.

Zohar, D., Tzischinsky, O., Epstein, R., & Lavie, P. (2005). The effects of sleep loss on medical residents' emotional reactions to work events: A cognitive-energy model. *Sleep, 28*(1), 47–54.

Zosuls, K. M., Miller, C. F., Ruble, D. N., Martin, C. L., & Fabes, R. A. (2011). Gender development research in sex roles: Historical trends and future directions. *Sex Roles, 64*(11-12), 826–842.

Zuckerman, M. (1999). *Vulnerability to psychopathology: A biosocial model*. Washington, DC: American Psychological Association.

Zuckerman, M., Oltean, M., Monashkin, I. (1958.) The parental attitudes of mothers of schizophrenics. *Journal of Consulting Psychology, 22*(4), 307–310.

Zur, O. (2007). *Boundaries in psychotherapy: Ethical and clinical explorations*. Washington, DC: American Psychological Association.

Zur, O. (2009). Therapeutic boundaries and effective therapy: Exploring the relationships. In W. O'Donohue & S. R. Graybar (Eds.), *Handbook of contemporary psychotherapy: Toward an improved understanding of effective psychotherapy* (pp. 341–357). Thousand Oaks, CA: SAGE.

Zuroff, D. C., Kelly, A. C., Leybman, M. J., Blatt, S. J., & Wampold, B. E. (2010). Between-therapist and within-therapist differences in the quality of the therapeutic relationship: Effects on maladjustment and self-critical perfectionism. *Journal of Clinical Psychology, 66*(7), 681–697.

Name Index

NOTE: Page numbers preceded by A indicate the Appendix.

Subject Index

NOTE: Page numbers followed by f indicate figures; those followed by t indicate tables; and those preceded by A indicate the Appendix.